The North Carolina Century is a comprehensive look at the people whose life's work shaped the state during the most dynamic period since colonial times. The changes that transformed North Carolina between 1900 and 2000 are richly chronicled in individual stories against the backdrop of an overview by the state's official historian, Dr. Jeffrey Crow, deputy secretary of the Office of Archives and History.

More than 160 persons — whites, African Americans and Native Americans — are the subjects of narrative biographical profiles in this collection. An equal number of persons are mentioned in the introductions to various categories — arranged to make these stories accessible to students, journalists and the general public. These categories include agriculture, engineering and architecture, arts and literature, business, education, law, media, religion, public service, popular culture, religion, social movements, and sports.

Many of the persons in these pages are well known. For instance, the names of Aycock, Hodges, Jordan, Graham, Cannon, Alexander, Sanford, Green, and Helms are associated with very visible accomplishments in public life. But still others whose contributions may have been obscured by the passage of time are also here; their legacy undiminished. Within the limits of one volume, this collection provides as balanced and complete a picture as possible.

The subjects of the full profiles in this collection were chosen during months of consideration by a panel of distinguished historians and other expert observers, led by former University of North Carolina President William Friday. The panel solicited nominations from all across the state as well as seeking public comment. Celebrity or notoriety alone was insufficient for inclusion. Authors of the profiles were carefully chosen for their experience, expertise, knowledge of the subject, and their writing and research ability. To enable readers to easily identify and locate additional resources, a photograph and a bibliography accompanies each of the major entries.

THE NORTH CAROLINA CENTURY

Howard E. Covington Jr. and Marion A. Ellis, Coeditors

THE NORTH CAROLINA CENTURY

Tar Heels Who Made a Difference, 1900–2000

Levine
Museum of the New South

Charlotte, North Carolina

© 2002 Levine Museum of the New South

Published by Levine Museum of the New South
200 E. Seventh Street
Charlotte, North Carolina 28202

Distributed by the University of North Carolina Press
Post Office Box 2288
Chapel Hill, North Carolina 27515-2288
1-800-848-6224

Printed in the United States of America
Design and production by Julie Allred, B. Williams & Associates

The paper in this book meets the guidelines for permanence
and durability of the Committee on Production Guidelines
for Book Longevity of the Council on Library Resources.

Library of Congress Cataloging-in-Publication Data
The North Carolina century : Tar Heels who made a difference,
1900–2000 / Howard E. Covington Jr. and Marion A. Ellis, coeditors.
        p. cm.
Includes bibliographical references and index.
ISBN 0-8078-2757-6 (cloth : alk. paper)
1. North Carolina—Biography. 2. Biography—20th century.
I. Covington, Howard E. II. Ellis, Marion A.
CT252.N67 2002
920.0756'09'04—dc21
[B]   2002073098

06   05   04   03   02   5   4   3   2   1

CONTENTS

PREFACE

The twentieth century was North Carolina's century. That is the story that unfolds in Dr. Jeffrey Crow's introduction to this collection. And against that backdrop, North Carolina was transformed by thousands of remarkable people whose work, energy, and interests invigorated the state with their ambitions, their ideas, their vision, and their creativity.

The persons included in this collection raised North Carolina to a position of prominence, and excellence, in industry, the arts, education, and political leadership of the South and the nation. Some of those persons who created that record left deep and lasting impressions, and their names remain familiar. Others performed their life's work quietly, without fanfare, often overshadowed by the rush of events and the passage of time. All of their stories are important if one is to understand the North Carolina Century now, or fifty years from now.

This collection was created to recognize those persons and add to the body of literature about a remarkable state during a dynamic period. This is not a collection of superlatives such as the best farmer, or the most successful businessman, or most prolific artist. Indeed, there are subjects included in this collection whose contributions were vain, mean-spirited, and even dangerous. They are in this collection because they too shaped life between 1900 and 2000. This collection was designed to be broad and inclusive and provide as complete a picture as possible of a land undergoing growth and expansion, as well as trial and struggle.

Most of those selected for narrative profiles are native Tar Heels. That was an important distinction in the selection process, but it was not exclusionary. Also included are persons who were born outside of the state but whose careers or contributions to the shape of history are closely associated with the state. Likewise, readers should not expect to find persons who were born here, but whose names became more closely associated with places beyond the place of their birth. These movie stars, musicians, and others of fame were not overlooked. Many are mentioned in the section introductions as a matter of record.

The profiles also include persons who were still living in 2000. If a subject could only qualify by being dead, then many of those who were involved in the last quarter of the century would be absent. Whenever possible, the writers conducted tape-recorded interviews with the living subjects. These recordings are now part of the archive of the Levine Museum of the New South and will be available to researchers and others who wish to learn more about their subjects.

Identifying the men and women who are part of the 160 narrative profiles was no easy task. In fact, the initial list of those proposed for this collection—by historians, journalists, citizens and by the editors—numbered more than 400. Altogether, more than 160 persons are included because of the nature of history. In some cases, entries record the lives of more than one person because the group collectively created a particular institution. In other cases, the narrative includes the contributions of more than one generation of a family. To focus on just one family member, or officer in a business enterprise, would have created an incomplete and inaccurate picture.

The editors relied upon the advice of scholars, journalists, historians, and private citizens to compile the list. The editors tried to throw a wide net in gathering nominations. Names were offered by an advisory committee of scholars and they were solicited from more than 300 persons from all across the state. Unsolicited nominations, many of which arrived following news reports of the project, also were welcomed. All became part of a list that was clearly too great for the physical and fiscal limitations of this project. Choices had to be made.

The final selections were made by the editors and an advisory committee of scholars, which also established the criteria for selection. This committee was led by Dr. David Goldfield of the University of North Carolina at Charlotte and included William Friday, former president of the University of North Carolina; William S. Powell, retired professor of history and former curator of the North Carolina Collection at the University of North Carolina at Chapel Hill; Dr. Margaret Barrett, professor of history at North Carolina A & T State University; Dr. Sydney Nathans, professor of history at Duke University; Dr. Harry Watson, professor of history at UNC-Chapel Hill; Dr. William Link, chair of the history department at the University of North Carolina at Greensboro; Dr. Percy Murray, professor of history at North Carolina Central University, Dr. Linda Oxendine of the University of North Carolina at Pembroke; Dr. Gail O'Brien of North Carolina State University; and Dr. Jeffrey Crow, deputy secretary of the Office of Archives and History, N.C. Department of Cultural Resources.

The editors encouraged a range of voices in the writing of the narratives. Contributors were chosen for their knowledge of the subject and their ability to present their subject in an interesting, readable, and credible fashion. Among the writers are historians, current and former journalists, freelance writers, published authors as well as scholars preparing for careers in the classroom.

This volume is the product of the North Carolina Biography Project, which received an early endorsement from former Bank of America executive Joe Martin of Charlotte, who recommended it to the Levine Museum of the New South. Financial support came from individuals and foundations with an interest in North Carolina history. Grants were received from the North Carolina Humanities Council, the Knight Foundation, the William R. Kenan, Jr. Charitable Trust, the A. J. Fletcher Foundation, the Kenan Family Foundation, the Broyhill Family Foundation, the James G. Hanes Memorial Fund, Wachovia Foundation, the Ralph W. Ketner Family Donor Advised Fund, the Hurley-Trammell Foundation, the Josephus Daniels Charitable Fund, the Mary Duke Biddle Foundation, the Belk Foundation, the Cannon Foundation, CP&L, a Progress Energy Company, the James J. and Angelia M. Harris Foundation, the Z. Smith Reynolds Foundation, the Blanche and Julian Robertson Foundation, Joseph M. Bryan Jr., Sally and Russell Robinson, Erskine Bowles, and Mrs. Betty Kenan.

The editors are indebted to the Levine Museum of the New South, which adopted this project as part of its program, and especially the support of Sally Robinson, a founder of the Museum, whose advice, insight, and encouragement led to the successful completion of this work. The editors also relied heavily on the support of the museum staff, including Director Emily Zimmern, Historian Dr. Thomas Hanchett, and Judy Mitchell, who saw that all the writers were paid promptly. In addition, curators and archivists at libraries across the state were helpful in gathering the photographs that appear with the entries. The editors are especially indebted to Thomas F. Harkins at Duke University Archives; Steve Massengill of the North Carolina Office of Archives and History; Janie C. Morris at the Special Collections Library at Duke University; Hermann J. Trojanowski of the North Carolina State University Archives; the Tufts Archives of Givens Memorial Library in Pinehurst; the Forsyth County Library; the Robinson-Spangler Carolina Room of the Public Library of Charlotte-Mecklenburg County; Davie Hinshaw, photo editor of the *Charlotte Observer*; and Hugh Morton of Grandfather Mountain, whose camera captured much of the life and times of the second half of the century.

—Howard E. Covington Jr. and Marion A. Ellis, coeditors

INTRODUCTION

The North Carolina Century: Two Paths to the Future

by Dr. Jeffrey J. Crow

A<small>T THE DAWN</small> of the twentieth century, North Carolina enjoyed a reputation as the brawny industrial leader of the New South. The emerging textile and tobacco industries had catapulted North Carolina to the front ranks of southern states attempting to diversify their economies beyond staple-crop production. Yet North Carolina remained a land defined by the rhythms of agriculture, with only five towns boasting a population of ten thousand or more. Wilmington claimed the distinction of being the largest urban center in the state. Out of a population of 1.9 million in 1900, only 9.8 percent of North Carolinians lived in urban areas.

A century later the state stood transformed. With a population exceeding eight million, North Carolina, declared Governor James G. Martin in 1987, was the most industrialized state in the nation. Governor Martin based that assertion on a statistical curiosity. With 830,000 manufacturing workers, North Carolina had "the largest per-capita manufacturing work force in the country." Various surveys proclaimed North Carolina either the "best" state in which to start a business or the "best" place to live. Tourism vied with manufacturing and agriculture to become the largest industry in the state. Agriculture remained an important sector of the state's economy, but whereas in 1947 forty of every one hundred North Carolina jobs related to farming, by 1992 that number had declined to two of a hundred jobs. In 1939 only 19 percent of farms had electricity. By 1971 electricity powered 99 percent of the state's farms.

In 2000 Charlotte was the largest city and had been since 1910. More than half the state's citizens lived in urban areas, chiefly along the Piedmont Crescent. That crescent paralleled the route of the North Carolina Railroad. Built during the mid-nineteenth century, the North Carolina Railroad heralded North Carolina's modern economy. Stretching from the Raleigh-Durham-Chapel Hill Triangle to the Piedmont Triad of Greensboro, Winston-Salem, and High Point and on to Metrolina, represented by Charlotte and Mecklenburg County, the Piedmont Crescent powered the state's economy. Business, industry, education, medicine, banking, research, and government services emanating from the Piedmont Crescent extended to all corners of the state.

North Carolina always has been a land of contrasts. Beginning at the Outer Banks on the coast, the state covers a vast territory—from the wetlands, sandy loam, and loblolly pines of the coastal plain, to the red clay and hardwoods of the piedmont, to the verdant ranges of the Blue Ridge and Great Smoky Mountains more than five hundred miles west of the Atlantic Ocean. During the course of the twentieth century, boosters and social scientists variously described North Carolina as the "Good Roads State," a "Progressive Plutocracy," a "Dixie Dynamo," and a "Progressive Myth." While North Carolina enjoyed a reputation as a progressive southern state that measured its progress by national standards, it also harbored a stubborn resistance to government interference, higher taxes, expanded social and political rights for women and African Americans, and costly federal programs. Indeed, at the height of the Great Depression, Governor Clyde R. Hoey proudly announced that North Carolina had received fewer funds per capita from New Deal programs than any other state.

Two paths to the future lay before North Carolina at the start of the twentieth century. One fork charted new routes to solve social, economic, and political problems with the support of government. The other fork clung to familiar paths and byways in which government played a limited role. By the end of the century North Carolina was a state that could elect to statewide office a conservative United States senator, Jesse Helms, and a progressive governor, James B. Hunt Jr. With so many contrasts and paradoxes, how did the twentieth century become the North Carolina century?

North Carolina entered the twentieth century at the climax of a political and social resettlement that would persist for more than another six decades. During the last third of the nineteenth century, the Republican Party competed vigorously with the Democratic Party for domination of the state. As much as 80 percent of Republican strength depended upon African American votes. When dissident farmers bolted the Democratic Party in the 1890s to join the newly formed Populist Party, Republican strategists saw a way to return to power twenty years after Reconstruction's end. Combining tickets in 1894 and 1896 in an alliance known as "fusion," Republicans and Populists swept all state offices and won control of the General Assembly.

Stunned, the Democrats, led by Furnifold M. Simmons and Charles B. Aycock, launched furious white supremacy campaigns in 1898 and 1900 to recapture the state. The Democratic victory effected political and social changes that would last for generations. Democrats disfranchised African American and poor white voters in 1900 with a suffrage amendment that imposed poll taxes and literacy tests. Formal segregation also began with laws mandating the separation of races in public places. The Democrats' stranglehold on politics continued until 1972 and the election of Republicans James E. Holshouser Jr. to the governorship and Jesse Helms to the United States Senate. African Americans did not vote in sizeable numbers again until passage of the federal Voting Rights Act in 1965. Likewise, it took the civil rights movement of the 1960s to tear down the walls of segregation.

Irony marked the so-called Progressive Era of the early twentieth century. First, progressivism was "for whites only," in the words of North Carolina-trained historian C. Vann Woodward. Second, in order to reform the political system, certain voters no longer could vote. Third, despite a reluctance to pay higher taxes for government services, North Carolina embarked on an ambitious program to modernize the state.

Charles B. Aycock, elected governor in 1900, became known as the "education governor." With the highest illiteracy rates in the nation (one in five whites and one of two blacks), North Carolina built three thousand new schools between 1901 and 1920. Aycock campaigned for public education across the state during his administration. The General Assembly doubled its annual appropriation, and local governments nearly doubled tax support for schools. The principle of separate but equal facilities in public schools for blacks and whites never existed. Black schools, educational opportunities, and literacy rates lagged behind those of whites.

In other areas Progressives also made significant gains. In 1908 North Carolinians voted by referendum to authorize statewide prohibition. North Carolina anticipated the Eighteenth Amendment to the U.S. Constitution by a dozen years. The state also moved to abolish child labor. In 1900 about one of every four textile workers in North Carolina was a child between the ages of ten and sixteen. Working as many as seventy-five hours a week for very low wages, those children could not attend school and faced a future of drudgery in the mills. A series of child labor laws proved unenforceable until 1919, when the General Assembly raised the minimum age for child laborers to fourteen and established a child welfare commission to enforce it.

Efforts to extend voting rights to women proved less successful. Led by Gertrude Weil of Goldsboro, the North Carolina Equal Suffrage League fought hard to make North Carolina the thirty-sixth state to ratify the Nineteenth Amendment to the United States Constitution in 1920. The General Assembly rejected the amendment because of the opposition of U.S. Senators Furnifold Simmons and Lee S. Overman. Although women voted for the first time in 1920 (Tennessee became the thirty-sixth ratifying state a day after North Carolina declined the honor), North Carolina did not approve the Nineteenth Amendment until 1971.

In many ways the Progressive movement culminated in the 1920s. North Carolina epitomized the decade's "business progressivism." State services helped support the growth and economic vitality of basic industries and agriculture. Public schools provided an educated workforce. Good roads connected the state's towns, farms, and industries. Before 1921 counties built and maintained all roads. Governor Cameron Morrison—prodded by Frank Page Jr., chairman of the Highway Commission, and Harriet M. Berry, a leader of the N.C. Good Roads Association—embraced a system of statewide roads maintained by the state. The state borrowed $50 million in bonds to undertake the ambitious program. Taxes on vehicle licenses and gasoline repaid the loan. North Carolina received accolades as the "Good Roads State" because it had the best roads in the South. Governor Angus McLean, a seasoned businessman and banker, continued Morrison's road-building campaign and poured more money into rural schools to equalize them with urban schools. McLean's emphasis on efficiency provided a $2.5 million surplus when he left office. That cushion proved critical to his successor when the Great Depression descended on the state and nation.

Another banker, John Sprunt Hill of Durham, championed rural credit associations. To meet the needs of farmers for credit, marketing, and cooperation, Hill carried his message across the state and helped create the strongest rural credit union movement in the nation.

The Progressive Era also established a pattern of political leadership in the state that lasted throughout the twentieth century—the so-called "Progressive Plutocracy." With a few notable exceptions, the state's governors came from a class of moderately conservative lawyers and businessmen, friendly to business and willing to assist it with the powers of the state. Government was relatively scandal free. While racial politics never disappeared entirely, especially during seasons of social tension and change, North Carolina escaped the raw racial demagoguery that stained other southern states.

Three major industries dominated North Carolina's business community before Charlotte emerged as one of the nation's leading banking centers in the late twentieth century. Each of the industries had its roots in the nineteenth century. The R.J. Reynolds Company grew up around the small town of Winston, while the American Tobacco Company, led by James B. Duke, centered its operations in Durham and Reidsville. Cigarettes, manufactured in North Carolina and shrewdly marketed nationally and internationally, became commonplace, part of the everyday life of America. Trade names such as Camel, Lucky Strike, Winston, and Salem dominated the cigarette business. Duke's American Tobacco Company became so ascendant that the United States Supreme Court broke up the trust in 1911.

The textile industry grew just as spectacularly. One mill owner termed it "not a business but a social enterprise." Jobs in textile mills became the salvation of displaced farmers and their families who had lost their homes and farms to economic hardship and low prices for crops. Wages were low and hours long. Whereas African Americans made up two thirds of the workforce in the tobacco industry, white women and children comprised the majority of the workers in textiles, at least before 1920. Mill villages—compared to "industrial plantations" —sprang up around textile mills. There workers and their families lived, shopped, studied, played, and worshiped. Charles A. Cannon gave towels and sheets a national brand name and presided over Kannapolis, at one time the largest unincorporated "city" in the world. Likewise the Cone family of Greensboro operated denim mills that once were the largest in the world.

The furniture industry was North Carolina's third major industrial enterprise. High Point became the center of the state's furniture industry. The North Carolina Railroad and later a network of roads and interstate highways served as the industry's spine. They offered easy transportation of both raw materials and finished goods. Durham anchored the industry in the east as Asheville did in the west. Town names such as Thomasville, Lexington, Statesville, Morganton, Hickory, Mount Airy, and Lenoir became synonymous with the furniture industry, as did James E. Broyhill, who founded a furniture empire. Until its closure in 1993, the White Furniture Company of Mebane had operated continuously since 1881.

With limited access to educational facilities and scant political power, the

African American community turned inward and strived to build its own economic and social institutions. Durham became the "Capital of the Black Middle Class." Established in 1898, the North Carolina Mutual Life Insurance Company began with three employees—John Merrick, Dr. Aaron McDuffie Moore, and Charles Clinton Spaulding. A half century later it was the largest black-owned business in the United States. The success of North Carolina Mutual bred other middle-class enterprises. In 1908 Richard Burton Fitzgerald and William Gaston Pearson started Mechanics and Farmers Bank. James E. Shepard founded a religious training school in 1910 that by the 1920s had become the North Carolina College for Negroes (now North Carolina Central University).

For all its industrial and business strength, North Carolina remained an important agricultural state. Its two great staple crops were cotton and tobacco. After a surge in prices during World War I, prices dropped precipitously during the 1920s. Overproduction caused low farm prices. Complicating the agricultural economy further was the increasing concentration of land in fewer and fewer hands. Independent farmers—black and white—found themselves unable to compete and fell into tenancy and sharecropping.

The coming of the Great Depression in 1929 hit North Carolina hard. By 1932 farm income had fallen to less than half of 1929 levels. Landowners evicted thousands of tenant farmers. In the textile and furniture industries sales also dropped by one half. Some industries cut production but remained profitable. Tobacco seemed to be Depression-proof for manufacturers. Tobacco farmers too shared in the prosperity as production limits, introduced by the federal government during the 1930s, assured them a steady, reliable income for the next half century. Industrial laborers, however, struggled with low pay and oppressive working conditions. At the depths of the Depression in 1932, more than 144,000 of the state's wage earners were unemployed.

North Carolina's governors during the Great Depression—O. Max Gardner, J. C. B. Ehringhaus, and Clyde R. Hoey—could not undertake a "Little New Deal" because of a state constitutional requirement to balance the budget. Temperamentally and philosophically, none of them were likely to support funding for recovery or relief, relying instead on the private sector and philanthropy. Gardner slashed spending deeply and centralized authority for administration of schools, roads, and government spending in Raleigh. Ehringhaus continued those policies. The enactment of a three-cent sales tax, excluding only a few food products, ensured that state government would continue to deliver critical services. Ehringhaus courageously rejected what he termed "disastrous and destructive policies . . . urged by hysterical thinking" to keep North Carolina "solvent, saving, sane and sanguine."

Ehringhaus and Hoey accepted federal funds generated by the New Deal in Washington to relieve suffering and to put the unemployed to work on public projects. Rural electrification, construction of the Blue Ridge Parkway, and the creation of the Social Security system mitigated the worst effects of the Depression. The Civilian Conservation Corps (CCC) proved extremely popular with North Carolinians. It put thousands of young men to work on soil conservation and forestry projects and promoted a value that North Carolinians fully endorsed—the work ethic. The route selected for the Blue Ridge Parkway, constructed by the CCC, passed remarkably close to the farm of Robert Doughton, chair of the House Ways and Means Committee.

Despite the suffering brought on by the Great Depression, North Carolina remained hostile territory for organized labor. Governor Gardner—himself a mill owner—called out the National Guard to crush the Loray Mill strike of 1929 in Gastonia. The National Textile Workers' Union, a communist-led group, tried to organize striking workers protesting the "stretch-out" system. Under that system weavers were assigned additional looms to operate. The strike ended in violence and bloodshed. The Gastonia chief of police died in a raid on union headquarters. Ella May Wiggins, a mill worker who composed a song in support of the union, died in an attack on strikers. Several strikers were convicted in the killing of the police chief. Wiggins's killers went unpunished.

Sporadic strikes and anti-union sentiment marked North Carolina's labor history throughout the twentieth century. When sixty-five thousand textile mill workers joined the General Strike of September 1934 spreading across the South, Governor Ehringhaus summoned the National Guard. In 1939 only 4 percent of North Carolina's industrial workers belonged to unions. During the twentieth century the percentage of unionized workers in North Carolina ranked near or at the bottom nationally.

When Governor Gardner instituted sweeping organizational changes in state government, one of his most controversial reforms was the consolidation of the University of North Carolina (Chapel Hill), North Carolina State College (Raleigh), and the North Carolina College for Women (Greensboro) in 1931. While the consolidation proved unpopular with many alumni, it presaged the sixteen-campus University of North Carolina system that emerged in the 1970s as part of yet another government reorganization under Governor Robert W. Scott.

The first president of the consolidated university—Frank Porter Graham—though short in stature, cast a long shadow across the North Carolina century. Even before Graham's presidency, the University of North Carolina had earned a reputation as a bastion of liberalism in the South, especially under the administration of Harry Woodburn Chase. Faculty unflinchingly studied the South's social and economic problems and helped establish regionalism as a legitimate field of study. The University of North Carolina Press, under the daring leadership of William Terry Couch, gave voice to the leading writers and social thinkers in the South. Graham's presidency during the 1930s and 1940s created an atmosphere for such critical thinking. One of Graham's protégé's, William C. Friday, took the university to even higher levels of accomplishment during his distinguished thirty-year presidency. With the organization of Duke University around Trinity College in 1924 by James B. Duke's $40 million bequest, a friendly rivalry spurred both Duke and the University of North Carolina to greater achievements in the classroom, in the laboratory, and on the athletic fields.

North Carolina became known for its many fine institutions of higher learning. Yet before the 1950s, the schools remained segregated. Efforts to integrate both undergraduate and graduate schools at the University of North Carolina during the 1930s failed. African Americans could attend one of five publicly supported institutions of higher learning, not to mention many smaller, denomination-affiliated colleges. With the largest Native American population east of the Mississippi River, as early as 1887 North Carolina established a teachers' college for Indians at Pembroke—now the University of North Carolina at Pembroke. At the end of the twentieth century the University of North Carolina system ranked among the top echelon of public universities nationally.

In many respects World War II was a watershed in southern history. Demographic changes, increasing industrialization and urbanization, an infusion of federal moneys for military installations and accompanying housing, and mechanization of agriculture transformed the South. Approximately one fourth of the region's farm population left the land. Workers went into defense plants or the armed services. The Great Migration of African Americans out of the South, which began during World War I (1914–1918), accelerated during World War II.

Out-migration of blacks from North Carolina had begun as early as 1880. The black population steadily decreased during the first half of the twentieth century, including a whopping 14.8 percent during the 1940s. Through the antebellum era of the nineteenth century, the black population hovered around one third of the state's total population. By the late twentieth century, the black population had stabilized at 22 percent of the total population. Interestingly, after 1980 in-migration of blacks to North Carolina exceeded out-migration from the state.

The contours of the modern South took shape during World War II, and North Carolina reflected those changes. About 362,000 North Carolinians served in the military, about 7,000 of whom died. North Carolina hosted numerous military training bases. Having grown to 100,000 troops by 1945, Fort Bragg was the largest artillery post in the world. Marines, including the first black marines in the history of that branch of the service, trained at Camp Lejeune. Other military encampments included Camps Battle, Butner, Sutton, and Davis. Aviators received training at air bases at Cherry Point, Goldsboro, Fayetteville, and Elizabeth City, among other places. Shipbuilding for the navy thrived in the coastal towns of Wilmington, New Bern, and Elizabeth City. This strong military presence in North Carolina would continue for the rest of the twentieth century.

Domestically, North Carolina contributed to the war effort in other ways. Textile mills produced tents, uniforms, blankets, towels, socks, and other commodities. Farmers grew more of every crop. By 1944 the value of crops had doubled that of 1929. In all, the federal government spent $2 billion producing war supplies in North Carolina, a huge fillip to the state's economy.

As late as 1950 North Carolina remained more than two-thirds rural out of a total population of just over four million. By 1980 those populations had nearly reversed, with 63 percent of North Carolinians classified as urban out of a total population of 5.8 million. In the last two decades of the twentieth century North Carolina grew an astonishing 40 percent, surpassing 8 million in population, of whom 5.4 million (nearly 68 percent) were urban.

That growing urbanization paralleled the industrial boom that followed the Second World War. Throughout the South business-oriented political moderates showed a willingness to support public education and address social and economic problems. Essentially urban in outlook, they applied sound business practices to government. They wanted to create a good atmosphere for industrial development. The advocates of economic growth practiced racial segregation, but they understood that inflexible race relations could have a damaging effect on the region's economy. Governor Luther H. Hodges epitomized the businessman-politician. He stated the purpose of his administration simply: "Industrialization, . . . with all its advantages to the people and to the state, became the number one goal of my administration."

Hodges's greatest accomplishment was the creation of the Research Triangle Park with three nationally distinguished centers of higher learning—the University of North Carolina at Chapel Hill, North Carolina State University, and Duke University—at its corners. Textiles, furniture, and tobacco traditionally had been low-wage industries. Hodges sought technological and research-driven businesses. The idea for a research center originated with Howard W. Odum, the distinguished sociologist at the University of North Carolina. Romeo Guest, a commercial builder in Greensboro, packaged the idea and gave it a name, Research Triangle Park (RTP). By 1959 the Research Triangle was a reality. Twenty years later it had become the South's most successful locus for high technology—a blend of corporate and government laboratories. By the end of the century the RTP hosted the world's leading technology companies, including SAS of Cary, the largest privately held software company in the world. SAS grew out of an effort to find a better way to measure agricultural production.

If Hodges epitomized the businessman-politician, then Charlotte symbolized North Carolina's economic transformation in the twentieth century. During the antebellum period the presence of a branch of the U.S. Mint, established in 1837 because of the nearby gold mines, set Charlotte on a course toward business dominance. The arrival of railroads and the rise of the textile industry made Charlotte a regional urban and economic power by the early twentieth century. In 1905 Charlotte stood at the center of a textile universe. Within a one-hundred-mile radius of Charlotte, more than half the looms in the South produced fabric. It was at precisely that moment that banking emerged as the most vibrant enterprise in the Queen City. The establishment of North Carolina National Bank—forerunner of the Bank of America—and First Union National Bank during the first decade of the twentieth century presaged Charlotte's most important economic activity over the next one hundred years. In 1927 the location of a branch of the Federal Reserve Bank in Charlotte solidified the city's growing strength as a financial center. Because of the dynamic leadership of such businessmen as Bank of America's Hugh McColl, by the end of the century only New York surpassed Charlotte as a banking nexus.

The absence of labor unions in many respects accounted for North Carolina's appeal to businesses and industries. After Congress passed the Taft-Hartley Act in 1947, North Carolina became a so-called "right to work" state and prohibited labor contracts allowing union-only or "closed shops." At the end of the 1950s only 9 percent of the state's industrial workers belonged to unions.

During the decades immediately after World War II, North Carolina's two paths to the future converged in ways that sullied the state's progressive reputation. The serious violence that accompanied the Harriet-Henderson Mills strike of 1958–59 showed that, just as in the 1920s and 1930s, state government would intervene to suppress labor unrest and the threat of unionization. Blasts of dynamite and Molotov cocktails, rock throwing, and acts of industrial sabotage damaged property and injured a number of people, but no fatalities occurred. Just like earlier governors, Luther Hodges called out the National Guard and the State Highway Patrol to protect strikebreakers. Hodges tried to mediate the dispute but concluded in exasperation that "just about everyone was at fault."

Boyd Payton, southern regional director of the Textile Workers Union of America, and seven other union members were convicted of conspiracy to blow up a power station and two mill buildings. The sole evidence against Payton came from a telephone call by a paid informant of the State Bureau of Investigation. Sentenced to serve six to ten years in prison, Payton was released after nine months when Governor Terry Sanford reduced the sentences of all eight. In 1964 Sanford pardoned Payton.

North Carolina's image of enlightenment and progressivism suffered a further blow when race-tinged politics and the civil rights movement challenged the state's complacency—or what historian William H. Chafe called "civility" —toward its African American citizens. In 1949 political scientist V. O. Key Jr. famously asserted: "The state has a reputation for fair dealings with its Negro citizens. . . . Nowhere has co-operation between white and Negro leadership been more effective."

Key's analysis, however, belied whites' traditional, conservative attitudes toward African Americans. The 1950 Democratic senatorial primary between Frank Porter Graham and Willis Smith introduced racial politics in a way that North Carolina had not experienced for a half century. In 1949 Governor W. Kerr Scott had surprised the political establishment by naming Graham, president of the University of North Carolina, to the U.S. Senate seat left vacant by the death of J. Melville Broughton. Smith, a Raleigh attorney, represented the conservative wing of the Democratic Party. His supporters portrayed Graham as a liberal who coddled communists and radicals at the university, supported racial equality with blacks, and generally held views repugnant to North Carolinians. The unapologetic racism of the Smith campaign defeated Graham and set a dark precedent for North Carolina politics in the years to come. It unmasked North Carolina's reputation for progressive race relations.

Conservative whites triumphed in the Smith-Graham contest, but they soon faced new challenges from the U.S. Supreme Court. The Court's 1954 *Brown v. Board of Education* decision dismayed the southern states. Unlike several of her sister states, North Carolina avoided wholesale violence and the closing of public schools, but it moved slowly to integrate its public schools. Indeed, the state edged to the brink of shutting down its schools under the so-called Pearsall Plan of 1956. That plan involved a series of constitutional amendments that allowed local school districts to close in order to avoid desegregation and to provide tuition aid to white students in order to attend private schools.

Five years after the implementation of the Pearsall Plan only eighty-nine black students had integrated previously all-white schools. No whites had integrated traditionally all-black schools. In 1966 only 6 percent of the state's black children attended integrated schools. It was not until *Swann v. Charlotte-Mecklenburg Board of Education* (1971) that integration of North Carolina's schools occurred. That Supreme Court decision, upholding an earlier decision by federal district judge James B. McMillan of Charlotte, ordered busing to achieve integration of the schools.

African American leaders during the twentieth century walked a narrow line. If they worked in publicly supported institutions, such as schools and universities, they had to appease white administrators and politicians. If they were employed in the private sector, they faced economic retaliation or worse. Thus, the Greensboro sit-ins that began on February 1, 1960, challenged both white and black leaders. Four black students from North Carolina Agricultural and Technical College took seats at the lunch counter of a Woolworth's store and were refused service. They returned in subsequent days to protest the segregated facilities, accompanied by swelling crowds of black and white supporters. Within days sit-ins spread to fifty-four cities in nine states. That same spring the Student Nonviolent Coordinating Committee was organized at Shaw University in Raleigh. The civil rights movement had found a strategy, an army of volunteers among students, and specific reforms that would culminate in what C. Vann Woodward termed the Second Reconstruction.

By the end of the twentieth century African American political power had never been greater. The federal Voting Rights Act of 1965 and a series of subsequent court decisions assured African Americans a voice in the political process. In 1947 only 15 percent of voting-age blacks were registered to vote. In 1966 the number of registered black voters surpassed 50 percent for the first time since the turn of the twentieth century. By 1998 that number had grown to 65.5 percent. Hundreds of African Americans held positions of authority and influence throughout the state, from mayors, to councilmen, to sheriffs, to superintendents of education. Henry Frye, the first African American elected to the General Assembly in the twentieth century (1968), later served almost two decades on the North Carolina Supreme Court. In 1969 Howard Lee became the first black in the South to be elected mayor of a majority white community—Chapel Hill. Floyd McKissick of Durham became one of the first blacks to break the color barrier at the University of North Carolina when he entered the law school in 1951. In 1966 he rose to the national directorship of the Congress of Racial Equality (CORE) and later tried to establish Soul City in Warren County. Dan Blue, a legislator from Raleigh, became speaker of the state House of Representatives, 1991–94. Former Charlotte mayor Harvey Gantt challenged Jesse Helms for the latter's United States Senate seat in 1990 and 1996. Perhaps most symbolically, Eva Clayton and Mel Watt won election to Congress in 1992 and in the four succeeding elections. They were the first African Americans to represent North Carolina in Congress since George H. White left the House of Representatives in 1901.

During the final decades of the twentieth century, North Carolina's two paths to the future propelled its respective defenders and advocates to national attention and stature. At the state level, several progressive-minded, activist governors, beginning with Terry Sanford, extended state services, promoted public education, created a healthy business climate, and built roads to speed tourists to vacation destinations and agricultural and manufacturing products to distant markets. Opportunities for women and minorities also expanded. Judge Susie Sharp became the first woman to serve as a superior court judge in 1949. Appointed to the state supreme court by Governor Sanford in 1962, she was elected chief justice in 1974. At the national level North Carolina often sounded a conservative note in the halls of Congress. Senator Sam Ervin opposed the Civil Rights Act of 1964 and the Equal Rights Amendment for women. Yet he became a national folk hero during the televised Watergate hearings with his astute handling of the investigation of the Nixon White House. Although educated in the law at Harvard after attending the University of North Carolina, Ervin described himself as "just a country lawyer." The nation discovered otherwise.

Terry Sanford's administration came at a critical point in the state's racial history. In the 1960 Democratic gubernatorial primary he faced a serious challenge from an arch segregationist. Sanford prevailed, endorsed John F. Kennedy's presidential aspirations at an early stage when other southerners supported Lyndon B. Johnson, and in a period of civil rights demonstrations showed that not every southern state would follow repressive and violent policies. A steadfast advocate of education, Sanford also introduced programs to identify and address social and economic problems throughout the state. The North Carolina Fund, which he established in 1963, set precedents for such federal programs as the War on Poverty and the Peace Corps.

Such activist government would not go unchallenged for long. Two political figures dominated the political landscape of North Carolina during the last three decades of the twentieth century. The first was Jesse Helms, arguably the most powerful North Carolinian ever to serve in Congress. The second was James B. Hunt Jr., arguably the most powerful governor in the state's history.

Helms and Hunt personified North Carolina's dualistic character. Helms represented conservative, traditional values, found on the farms, in the mills, and along the main streets of small towns in North Carolina. Helms and his followers opposed an activist government that promoted civil rights, spending on welfare programs, and what they perceived as threats to religious orthodoxy and patriotism. Helms also invoked the race issue openly in his campaigns when seriously challenged, especially in 1984 against Jim Hunt and in 1990 against Harvey Gantt. The Christian Right became a significant part of the Helms coalition. Yet, for all the talk of reducing unbridled government spending, Helms staunchly supported increased military appropriations and federal price supports for tobacco.

Jim Hunt represented a different tradition in North Carolina. His political heroes were progressive governors such as W. Kerr Scott and Terry Sanford. After serving one term as lieutenant governor, Hunt won election to the governorship in 1976. During his first term he pushed through a constitutional amendment allowing a governor to serve two successive terms. He promptly won reelection in 1980. His attempt to unseat Helms in the 1984 senatorial election —an epic contest pitting the two most powerful politicians in the state against each other—failed. After eight years in the private sector practicing corporate law, Hunt returned to the capitol by winning two more terms as governor in 1992 and 1996. During his second tenure as governor, Hunt, with the help of a Republican majority in the state House of Representatives, squeezed through a constitutional amendment giving the governor a veto. Never in the state's long history since the Fourth Provincial Congress promulgated the constitution of 1776 had a North Carolina governor had that power.

How could North Carolinians elect Jesse Helms and Jim Hunt at the same time? Interestingly, North Carolinians seemed to favor the conservative views of Helms in Washington and of Republican candidates in presidential elections. The only Democratic presidential candidate to carry North Carolina after 1964 was the Georgian Jimmy Carter in 1976. At home, North Carolinians preferred the services of a state government that could provide good roads, improved schools, competitive jobs, and economic opportunity. Even Republican Governors Holshouser and Martin, while preaching economy in government, pursued essentially moderate policies unlike those espoused by the Helms wing of the Republican Party.

In a way, the two paths pursued by Helms and Hunt captured the essence of the North Carolina century. North Carolinians never drifted far from the values of home, work, and family. They worked hard in the fields and factories and supported their communities, churches, and schools. Self-reliant, North Carolinians did not expect government to support them, but they did expect government to remove impediments to improvement of their own lives and especially those of their children.

Not just social, economic, and political trends defined the North Carolina century, however. At the end of the twentieth century North Carolina boasted a state symphony, a state zoo, and congeries of museums, aquariums, and historic sites more comprehensive than those of most other states. College basketball along Tobacco Road feverishly gripped the state each winter and early spring. The University of North Carolina at Chapel Hill, North Carolina State University, and Duke University each won multiple NCAA basketball championships. Michael Jordan, an alumnus of the University of North Carolina at Chapel Hill, became the greatest professional basketball player in the history of the NBA. The first NASCAR-sanctioned stock car race took place in Charlotte in 1949. In the following years, North Carolina produced renowned drivers on the NASCAR circuit, including Junior Johnson, Richard Petty, and Dale Earnhardt.

Beginning with Thomas Wolfe's *Look Homeward, Angel* in 1929 at the height of the Southern Literary Renaissance, North Carolina spawned many distinguished writers of fiction and nonfiction. Pulitzer Prize-winning playwright Paul Green created the outdoor drama with the debut of *The Lost Colony* in 1937 at Manteo. Edward R. Murrow, Gerald Johnson, Jonathan Daniels, David Brinkley, and Charles Kuralt reached national audiences in journalism. In the post-World War II era, writers such as Reynolds Price, Doris Betts, John Ehle, Lee Smith, Kaye Gibbons, Fred Chappell, Randall Kenan, and Charles Frazier won national acclaim and awards for their works of fiction.

North Carolina writers exhibited a strong sense of place in their works. Thomas Wolfe wrote lyrically of Asheville and Chapel Hill, although his portrayal of certain people and places, only thinly disguised, offended local sensibilities. Paul Green forthrightly confronted the race issue and injustice in the South and in his native state. Reynolds Price used Warrenton and Macon for scenes of much of his fiction; Doris Betts set her works in Statesville; and Fred Chappell and John Ehle placed their writings in familiar mountain hollows and ridges. In his award-winning novel *Cold Mountain,* Charles Frazier offered a virtual odyssey of North Carolina from Raleigh to the Great Smoky Mountains during the Civil War.

In the arts North Carolina provided a rainbow of artists, capturing many different traditions. Art styles ranged from Romare Bearden, an African American visual artist from Charlotte who specialized in collages, to the potters of Seagrove in Randolph and surrounding counties who lifted an everyday craft to a high art form. In music North Carolina's contributions reflected its diversity as well. Thelonious Monk's piano and John Coltrane's saxophone introduced highly original idioms to jazz. Arthur Smith's early radio and television programs in Charlotte helped bring the sound of country music—notably "Dueling Banjos" —to the nation. The folk traditions of Charlie Poole and Doc Watson exported "old-time" music to the rest of the nation.

Entering the twenty-first century, North Carolina faced many challenges. Because of the North American Free Trade Act (NAFTA), many jobs, especially in textiles, were being lost to overseas manufacturers. Likewise, tobacco was no longer the backbone of the agricultural economy. Health considerations, international competition, and reduced production quotas had all but eliminated the family farm that depended on the tobacco crop for a livelihood. The mass production of poultry and hogs and even Christmas trees had become increasingly important to the rural economy.

Despite the shiny skyscrapers of Charlotte, the booming technology of the Research Triangle, and a thriving tourist industry, not all of North Carolina shared equally in the prosperity and progress. In the mountains air and water pollution threatened to destroy the region's natural beauty. Acid rain, a byproduct of a century of progress, left Mount Mitchell, the highest peak east of the Mississippi River, barren of fir trees. Intensive hog and poultry farming greatly imperiled the quality of water and land in eastern North Carolina. After many decades of poverty, the Eastern Band of Cherokee turned to gambling casinos in the 1990s to bring a modicum of prosperity to its corner of the mountains. North Carolina ranked thirty-second nationally in personal per capita income ($27,194), but twenty-third in household per capita income ($50,200), reflecting the large number of working mothers. Despite slashing welfare rolls by more than 60 percent since 1995, the state made little headway in reducing poverty. In 2000 nearly 13 percent of North Carolinians still lived in poverty, about the same percentage as in 1990. In literacy rates North Carolina ranked forty-first nationally in 1997. In the wake of the state's push to improve education, however, high school graduation rates ranked twelfth in 2000.

Eastern North Carolina, for centuries the state's agricultural breadbasket, lagged behind the piedmont and western North Carolina in many economic indicators. Poverty rates exceeded 20 percent in eleven of the forty-one eastern counties. With the lowest per capita income in the state, the region suffered the highest unemployment rates, the lowest levels of adult literacy, and the highest levels of school dropout rates. Eastern North Carolina trailed the rest of the state in availability of water and sewer service, highways, housing, and availability of natural gas. Hurricane Floyd (1999), the most devastating natural disaster in the state's history, exacerbated those problems. For the twenty-first century, much remained unfinished on North Carolina's agenda.

If one were to ask someone outside North Carolina to identify the state's most recognizable native, one of two names likely would be offered—Billy Graham or Andy Griffith. For a half century evangelist Billy Graham proselytized millions of people throughout the world with his message of hope and redemption. Andy Griffith, however, advanced his own homespun homily. His television program *The Andy Griffith Show* proved a durable success during the 1960s. When Griffith left the program, it still remained among the highest-rated shows on television. Griffith enjoyed other successes, but none approached his original show, which still aired in syndication more than thirty years later.

Why the enduring appeal? Griffith's show celebrated small-town values of honesty, decency, community, personal responsibility, respect for teachers, parents, and figures of authority, and simple pleasures in the company of friends and family. Perhaps neither North Carolina nor any other place ever precisely reached such rarefied standards of conduct and character. But Griffith's fictional Mayberry made people feel that once they had enjoyed a long-lost innocence that probably always was elusive.

Griffith on one occasion explained what made him so proud to be a North Carolinian. "As I grew up in North Carolina," he recalled, "every time I needed help, and every time it looked like I wasn't going to make it, some person or some group or sometimes an entire area in this wonderful state looked my way and gave me a hand." That sense of community runs deep in North Carolina. The state's diversity and contrasts have made it strong. Despite class tensions, racial differences, and vast social and economic changes, North Carolina surmounted those challenges during the twentieth century to create a commonwealth both more democratic and more representative of all the people. Through it all North Carolina maintained its "down-home" character, preserving the state's best attributes while exploring new possibilities. Efforts to extend the state's bounty and opportunities to all its citizens remained unrealized, but a century of change had shown that North Carolina had the will, the determination, and the leadership to prevail in the face of adversity. Perhaps a third path, a "road not taken," awaited North Carolina in the twenty-first century.

Jeffrey J. Crow is the deputy secretary of the Office of Archives and History, N.C. Department of Cultural Resources. In that capacity, he is state historian, state historic preservation officer, and state historical records coordinator. He received his Ph.D. from Duke University, where he was elected to Phi Beta Kappa. His publications range from the colonial-Revolutionary period to the New South era, with a special emphasis on African-American history. From 1982 to 1995 he served as editor in chief of the North Carolina Historical Review.

AGRICULTURE

DURING THE TWENTIETH CENTURY, North Carolina agriculture evolved from mules to machinery and from hit-or-miss methods to scientific approaches to growing crops and livestock. The state's money crops of tobacco and cotton were supplemented by soybeans, peanuts, sweet potatoes, and a variety of others. Hog farming, raising and processing poultry, and even cultivating Christmas trees, moved into prominence.

At the beginning of the century, small farms dominated the state's economy; cotton and tobacco were indeed kings. North Carolina was eighth among cotton-producing states and second in tobacco only to Kentucky. But the state ranked near the bottom in livestock production and small farmers were burdened by crop liens and tenancy.

The conditions of Tar Heel farmers inspired a number of leaders whose creativity and energy helped shape agriculture at home and throughout the nation. In 1908, Wilmington businessman and town builder Hugh MacRae opened farm colonies for European immigrants in Pender, Columbus, and New Hanover counties. The best known of these communities were St. Helena (Italian), Castle Hayne and Van Eden (Dutch), and New Berlin (German).

MacRae's innovative ideas were applauded by boosters of the cause of small farmers and agricultural diversification like Clarence Poe, editor of the Raleigh-based *Progressive Farmer*, which grew to become the South's largest circulation publication for agriculture. Poe constantly urged farmers to adopt new methods and supported the emerging home demonstration program for farm families that was spearheaded by Jane S. McKimmon.

MacRae's resettlement ideas were revived during the Depression at Penderlea near Wilmington at about the same time that the nation began to grasp the vision of another North Carolinian, Hugh Hammond Bennett, who had waged war for two decades for better care of the land. Known as the father of soil conservation, Bennett had been promoting the cause since 1903 in the U.S. Department of Agriculture, but with little success. Finally, when soil devastation was clearly demonstrated by the Dust Bowl, the national Soil Conservation Service was created in 1935, and the husky, genial Bennett became its first director. He introduced such methods as crop rotation; planting grasses; cultivating woodlands; contour plowing; terracing; building ponds and drainage systems; and planting soybeans, kudzu, and lespedeza to prevent and control erosion. By the end of 1946, 26.7 million acres had been treated for erosion in the South. New cash crops of soybeans, sorghum, and conifers (source of turpentine, timber, and pulpwood) also were introduced.

After World War II, emphasis again began to shift to more modern methods of raising crops and livestock, and North Carolina State College in Raleigh (later North Carolina State University), which had been founded in 1889, began serious research into finding substitute uses for vast amounts of land formerly used for cotton farming. Through its increasingly important research efforts, N.C. State began experimenting with the use of Kentucky 31, or fescue grass, and artificial insemination to increase livestock production.

When Dr. Dean W. Colvard took over as dean of agriculture at N.C. State in 1953, he adopted the agribusiness concept and urged farmers to use the most up-to-date concepts and run their farms as efficient businesses. (Colvard later became president of Mississippi State University and then the first chancellor of the University of North Carolina at Charlotte in 1966.) During Colvard's tenure in Raleigh, North Carolina began its move to become one of the nation's top poultry-producing states, largely as a result of the efforts of researchers at N.C. State's agriculture department.

There was no better-known farm advocate in the second half of the century than Commissioner of Agriculture James A. Graham, who dedicated nearly four decades in office to diversifying and promoting the state's agricultural fortunes. By the time Graham left office, North Carolina had become one of the nation's top poultry and hog production states.

Wendell Holmes Murphy saved $3,000 from his salary as a vocational agriculture teacher and in 1962 borrowed $1,300 from his tobacco-farmer father to begin building Murphy Family Farms of Rose Hill into the number one hog producer in the nation. By the end of the century, Murphy was listed by *Forbes* magazine as one of America's wealthiest people.

Chicken and turkey processing also flourished, with the leading firm being Holly Farms, established by the Lovett family in North Wilkesboro. Holly Farms was the nation's third largest poultry processor in 1989 when it was sold to the number one poultry producer, Tyson Foods of Springdale, Ark., for $1.5 billion.

Cotton was on the rebound in North Carolina fields by 2000, but the once-familiar sound of the tobacco auctioneer was heard less and less. By the end of the century most tobacco farmers had either given up the crop or become contract growers for large tobacco companies. The change in agricultural life was no more evident than in Raleigh, where incumbent Jim Graham was succeeded by Meg Scott Phipps, whose professional training was in the law. Her roots in agriculture ran deep, however. She was the granddaughter of a former commissioner of agriculture and governor—Kerr Scott—who had given Graham his first job and whose own father had been a farm leader a century before.

HUGH HAMMOND BENNETT

By Jonathan Phillips

IN 1950, an *Atlanta Constitution* columnist wrote that Hugh Hammond Bennett should be one of the ten people kept safe in the event of nuclear war because he would be needed to "confront the tortured earth" resulting from an atomic blast. By the early 1950s, Hugh Bennett, then chief of the U.S. Soil Conservation Service, had devoted fifty years of his life to transforming tortured and exhausted cropland into fertile and highly productive soil.

Bennett, or "Big Hugh" as he was called, made the nation "erosion-conscious" in the 1930s with his unflagging advocacy of soil preservation and rejuvenation, along with his artful manipulation of politicians in a time of desperate economic conditions and the environmental disaster of the Dust Bowl. His efforts resulted in the first sustained federal action to promote conservation practices, for both soil and water, on private farmland. Paul Sears, a noted American conservationist, once observed that "most great movements of history have their fiery apostles, their practical leaders, and their chroniclers. Seldom are these functions combined in one individual as [with] Hugh Bennett. . . ."

The legacy of soil conservation is decidedly mixed, as anyone who has had to battle kudzu undoubtedly knows, and Bennett occasionally exaggerated the impact of soil erosion, arguing, for example, that soil problems could lead to widespread starvation in the United States. Nonetheless, his intentions were noble and, in his impact on American agriculture, he had few equals. In the spring of 2000, *Progressive Farmer* magazine ranked Bennett among the top ten people who had the greatest impact on American agriculture in the twentieth century, along with Franklin Roosevelt, Henry Wallace, Rachel Carson, and Henry Ford.

Born on April 15, 1881, into a cotton-farming family near Wadesboro in Anson County, Bennett saw the deleterious effect of soil erosion firsthand on his father's 1,200-acre plantation. Throughout his life, Bennett told listeners that his father, William Osborne Bennett, had inspired in him a deep "reverence for and love of dirt." He remembered well the springtime ritual of marking off terrace lines in order to "keep the land from washing away," in the words of his father. Born in 1833, the senior Bennett had lived through rapidly changing times. In the years between the births of father and son, the acreage of cul-

Hugh Hammond Bennett (Courtesy of Southern Historical Collection)

tivated land in the United States had more than doubled. Farmers no longer had the option of buying additional fertile land once existing acreage became unproductive. Farmers had to make do with what they had, and in the Pee Dee River basin, the location of the Bennett plantation, soils proved to be particularly susceptible to overuse. By the time Hugh Bennett came of age, much of his native Anson County was gullied and useless as farmland.

Bennett studied at the University of North Carolina in 1897; spent two years (1899–1901) working in Wadesboro in order to fund the remainder of his college education; and eventually graduated in 1903. He turned down an offer of employment abroad after deciding to pursue a position as chemist in the Bureau of Soils of the Department of Agriculture. Successful in his quest, Bennett began his long and distinguished public service career in 1903. He spent the next few years traveling throughout much of the South and Southwest, upstate New York, and even Cuba, conducting soil surveys.

Bennett witnessed the destructive power of sheet erosion in Louisa County, Virginia, just east of Charlottesville, in 1905. Forested and grass-covered land was protected from this form of erosion, but overcultivated farmland lost topsoil in thin "sheets" with every rain. Eventually, the topsoil disappeared entirely. And, unlike the more obvious gullied erosion, sheet erosion was far less noticeable to the farmer until it was too late.

In 1909, in Fairfield County, South Carolina, Bennett examined more than 136,000 acres of farmland once considered high-quality but rendered unusable due to overproduction and erosion. Ironically, in the same year, the Bureau of Soils published *Bulletin 55*, entitled *Soils of the United States,* which stated that "soil is the one indestructible, immutable asset that the nation possesses. It is the one resource that cannot be exhausted; that cannot be used up." Bennett later remarked, "I didn't know that so much costly misinformation could be put into a single brief sentence." He spent the next forty years of his government service refuting the assumptions of *Bulletin 55*. Along with professional frustration, Bennett experienced personal tragedy. In 1909, his wife, Sarah Edna Bennett, died. They had been married only two years.

Not only did *Bulletin 55* run counter to Bennett's field observations, but the pamphlet also contradicted what many conservationists of the era had already concluded. Turn-of-the-century conservationists compared farming techniques to the wasteful operations of loggers. The Progressive Era conservation efforts spearheaded by Theodore Roosevelt and his forester, Gifford Pinchot, addressed farmland erosion. In 1909, the year of *Bulletin 55*'s release, Roosevelt's National Conservation Commission reported on the "connection between population, soil exhaustion, and supply of agricultural land." Other Progressive Era groups reinforced the claims of conservationists. The Country Life movement, for example, blended the conservation ethic with a concern for the quality of rural life. In 1908, the Commission on Country Life issued a report in which it recognized that soil deterioration could result in a deterioration of rural society. Bennett often commented that "soil erosion led to social erosion."

Bennett spent the next two decades trying and failing to make his cause a national issue. One editor told him, quite simply, that no one was interested in the "mechanics of farming." Regardless, Bennett and several of his colleagues at the bureau kept toiling away, writing reports, and conducting surveys. Bennett published countless technical papers on the subject and found his audience small but growing by the 1920s. Finally, in 1928, the Department of Agriculture approved publication of *Circular 33, Soil Erosion: A National Menace.* Soon thereafter, Bennett was invited to speak before a congressional appropriations committee.

He did not disappoint. As Jonathan Daniels, editor of the *News and Observer,* once said of "Big Hugh's" style, "Bennett broke every rule of elocution he knew, but he never failed to get his point across." Perhaps most important, Bennett could speak persuasively to anyone, from the president of the United States to the most poorly educated farmer.

The committee authorized Bennett to develop and administer several soil erosion research sites around the country. Bennett selected sites with severe but correctable erosion problems. As his biographer Wellington Brink noted, "He stretched funds and selected locations where erosion conditions and farming practices promised large returns." This was just the beginning of Bennett's demonstration projects. By the late 1940s, millions of Americans had attended hundreds of events in which entire farms were transformed in a single day to Bennett's standards.

In 1933, Secretary of the Interior Harold Ickes, with the support of Assistant Secretary Rexford Tugwell, appointed Bennett to direct a new agency, the Soil Erosion Service, or SES. As with many New Deal-inspired agencies, the SES grew rapidly in the first few years of its creation. In 1934, the SES had demonstration projects covering four million acres in thirty-one states and by 1935, it had 6,622 employees, not including the countless Civilian Conservation Corps workers. The SES employed "engineers, agronomists, nurserymen, biologists, foresters, soil surveyors, economists, accountants, clerks, stenographers," among other specialties—and all with one common goal: the practical application of scientific principles to prevent soil erosion. Eventually, a new profession would emerge—the soil conservationist —complete with Civil Service Commission authorization, with the backing of a professional organization, the Soil Conservation Society of America, and with the support of college agricultural extension services.

Although known in government circles by the mid-1930s, Bennett's star rose noticeably in 1935, one of the worst years of the Dust Bowl. Congress passed legislation creating a permanent agency, the Soil Conservation Service, as part of the Department of Agriculture (the SES had been part of the Interior Department), and Bennett became a household name in much of the country.

Unfortunately, New Deal land conservation programs often worked at cross-purposes and the battle to defeat the Dust Bowl clearly demonstrated the lack of unity among federal programs. The Soil Conservation Service, along with agronomists in county extension programs, provided expertise to farmers so that they could prevent soil erosion and thus produce more. As Bennett noted in 1943, "By increasing per acre, per-farm, and per-nation supply of food and fiber, conservation technology can provide a basis for an improved standard of living and simultaneously reduce the hunger and discontent among people which so frequently leads to discord, dictatorships, and war." Bennett always believed that the solution to the plight of the American farmer was to increase production.

Thanks to the Dust Bowl, Bennett now had the nation's attention but he knew that demonstration projects could only help so much. He needed a national plan of action. Though sensitive to concerns regarding overarching federal power, Bennett argued repeatedly for the national government to initiate "conservancy" districts based upon regional watersheds. Federal action was required because erosion control was simply too large and complex a problem for local governments and, in addition, watersheds crossed political boundaries. In this effort, Bennett garnered considerable support from the New Deal land-use planners. Tugwell and his colleagues supported Bennett's plan because it kept power out of the hands of existing local governments, known derisively as "courthouse" gangs. In addition, many New Deal land-use programs already used watershed boundaries. Bennett also pushed strongly for federal involvement in the control of private land. Eventually, he conceded to voluntary participation and a "vigorous campaign of farmer education as a first step."

By 1937, soil conservation districts were established under the auspices of state governments based upon boilerplate language prepared by the Soil Conservation Service. The first district to fulfill all federal requirements, the Brown Creek Soil Conservation District, started in 1937 in Anson County, Bennett's birthplace. A decade later, soil conservation districts had been established in all forty-eight states and by 1948, eight states and two U.S. territories had been fully incorporated into districts. The federal government provided guidance and funding, but each district's projects were initiated and over-seen by a committee of local farmers. Bennett was quick to remind his employees that "they were soil conservation districts, not Soil Conservation Service Districts."

Bennett masterfully kept soil erosion in the news throughout the war years. He worked hard, and successfully, to demonstrate how soil and agricultural production impacted geopolitics. In a 1943 article, "Acres Are Acres," he again gained the attention of Congress when he compared the arable land available to the Axis and Allied powers. Although Bennett's article was certainly opportunistic, he had long been interested in the global effects of soil erosion. During his life, he traveled to over eight nations, working with officials to improve soil conditions and increase agricultural production. One congressman, who made a world tour in the 1950s to study agricultural problems, noted that wherever he went—Europe, South America, the Middle East, East Asia—he heard Bennett's name.

Bennett never lost touch with his family in Anson County. He had remarried in 1921 to the former Betty Virginia Brown. They had one son, Hugh Hammond Jr. The Bennetts lived in Arlington, Va., and Hugh never stopped farming. Friends and colleagues noticed that he became a noticeably smaller "Big Hugh" during the growing season, the result of many hours of manual labor in the hot sun. In his later years, he provided substantial support to his siblings and visited Wadesboro and environs when he could.

In 1946, Anson County celebrated Hugh Bennett Conservation Day. As Jonathan Daniels noted in his address that day, "It is perhaps the greatest mark of the genius of Hugh Bennett that we honor him because he has indicted us as a nation of destroyers—careless, greedy, in a hurry—and has still kept this nation's respect and its affection, too."

During his career, Bennett published countless scholarly articles, government reports, and popular pieces. For many years *Soil Conservation* (1939) was considered the definitive work in the field. His popular articles, such as those published in *Hammond's Magazine of the South*, demonstrated that Bennett, although certainly not an environmentalist by today's standards, had a strong admiration and respect for natural ecosystems. Bennett understood that agriculture must be adjusted to adapt to the physical environment, and not the reverse.

Known by his critics as an "alarmist" and by his supporters as the "Messiah of Soil" or the "Father of Soil Conservation," all could agree that "Big Hugh" made an impression on those who met him. He certainly made an impact on the Tar Heel State. Even for the least observant citizen, it is hard to miss the Soil Conservation District signs placed throughout the state and even harder to miss the kudzu, introduced in many parts of the South by the Soil Conservation Service as an anti-erosion plant.

The Natural Resources Conservation Service (formerly the Soil Conservation Service) of the U.S. Department of Agriculture oversees the nation's three thousand soil conservation districts and follows the guidelines established by Bennett in the 1930s. The service has even promoted "Big Hugh" to greater status. He is now the "father of soil and *water* conservation."

Bennett died on July 7, 1960, at the age of seventy-nine, in Burlington. He was buried in Arlington National Cemetery. The *Washington Post* noted upon his death that "Hugh Bennett had the good fortune to be acknowledged as a prophet in his own country and in his own time."

Jonathan Phillips's doctoral dissertation in history at the University of North Carolina at Chapel Hill examined the economic and cultural impact of the military presence in the Fayetteville and Sandhills region of North Carolina. In 2000–2001 he was a fellow at the Center of Military History.

For more information, see:
Bennett, Hugh Hammond. Papers. Southern Historical Collection, University of North Carolina at Chapel Hill.

"The Amazing Story of Kudzu." University of Alabama Center for Public Television and Radio. www.cptr.ua.edu/kudzu.
Bennett, Hugh Hammond. *Soil Conservation*. McGraw-Hill, 1939.
Brink, Wellington. *Big Hugh: The Father of Soil Conservation*. Macmillan, 1951.
Natural Resources Conservation Service. Web site. www.nc.nrcs.usda.gov/history/bennett.htm.
Simms, D. Harper. *The Soil Conservation Service*. Praeger, 1970.
Worster, Donald. *Dust Bowl: The Southern Plains in the 1930s*. Oxford University Press, 1979.

JAMES A. GRAHAM

By Ned Cline

THERE WERE MORE TALES told about Commissioner of Agriculture Jim Graham than there were golden leaves in a field of his beloved cash crop of tobacco. Some were true. Others had been stretched, like fish tales, over time with each telling. It didn't really matter to Graham, because every story likely contained at least an element of truth. He loved them all, just as he loved his job as the nation's longest-running elected agricultural administrator and everything else touched by people of the soil.

For nearly forty years in the last half of the twentieth century, from his appointment to fill a vacancy in July 1964 until he stepped down in December 2000, Graham outlasted every political opponent, seven governors, the boll weevil, and dozens of federal bureaucrats destined to destroy tobacco, the crop that had done so much for the state's economy. The death of his wife after a decade of debilitating disease, his own declining health, and disenchantment with the high cost of campaigning convinced him not to seek another four-year term. "It is time," Graham said at the time, "to give someone else a chance."

No opponent had much of a chance against Graham. He beat all comers with relative ease; a close call was a margin of 166,000 votes. There were two reasons for his victories. First, he was credited with being one of the state's best-ever candidates and was certainly one of the best-known during his four decades in office. Second, he worked day and night to protect agricultural interests and improve the quality of products as well as the livelihood of farmers. He genuinely cared about the people and the responsibilities of monitoring the state's food chain and improving the rural economy.

It was said of Graham that he always used his left hand to pass the collection plate when he ushered at church so he could keep his right arm free for shaking hands with voters across the aisle. That's not literally true, Graham said, but he conceded he had whispered a little politics a time or two as the plate made its way back to the altar.

"Every day is an election time," Graham said. "When it comes to your political opponents you just have to out work, out think and out son-of-a-bitch them all the time." Actually, he didn't have to do much of the latter because he was so astute at the other two. Graham was the epitome of a politician who had

neither the need nor the desire to degrade his opponents. He simply campaigned on what he had done and could do to help people and then proceeded to prove he could keep his word. When voters looked at Graham, what they saw was what they got. There was never a shred of sham about him.

A man of the soil himself who maintained a family farm in the western piedmont of North Carolina throughout his years in office, Graham knew virtually every nook and cranny of the state and arguably knew more voters by name than anyone. Graham began honing his talent for remembering names as a freshman at N.C. State College in the late 1930s. It paid off by the time he was a senior when he was elected president of the graduating class and could call the name of every classmate. He was president of the Class of 1942, following in the steps of Class of 1941 President William Friday, who would later serve as president of the University of North Carolina system almost as long as Graham was agriculture commissioner.

Politicians liked to lament that North Carolina is a l-o-n-g state when they campaigned from Manteo to Murphy, but such talk was not specific enough for Graham. "Manteo to Murphy ain't quite right," he would say. "It is from Hanging Dog to Hatteras and from Otto to Ocracoke." Graham had been in all four communities and virtually every one in between.

His allegiance to the Democratic Party was as legendary as his faith in and devotion to agriculture and farmers because, he said, Democrats were more willing to help people with real needs. He never once wavered from solid support for his party even when it hurt because he didn't share some of the philosophy of national candidates. Who else would perform a donkey bray on national television for presidential candidate Jimmy Carter as Graham did in 1976? He learned to imitate the real thing as a teenager on his daddy's farm while listening to the sound of a donkey in heat about to mate with a mare.

Who else would promise to kiss the ass of a donkey —the Democratic Party's symbolic mascot since 1828 when North Carolina native and Democrat Andrew Jackson was labeled a "jackass" by his opponents because of his populist views—if Wilkes County went Democratic in 1976? Graham had made the pledge as a joke because Wilkes had been a rock-ribbed Republican territory for one hundred years and when the im-

James A. Graham (Courtesy of Salisbury Post)

lege and study for the ministry. But being a man of the cloth didn't have the lure of being a man of the land and Graham never seriously considered the pulpit over politics or pig production.

Graham's heroes growing up were his father and his high school agriculture teacher P. H. Satterwhite. Both men taught him the value of hard work, honesty, perseverance, and loyalty. "In the days of my youth, a strong agriculture teacher, next to your daddy, was your best friend," Graham said in an interview late in his career. "After my parents who taught me virtues, Mr. Satterwhite was the most influential person in my life."

Following his earned degree in agriculture from N.C. State, Graham moved through a series of jobs, all dealing with the land. He taught high school agriculture in Iredell County, was superintendent of the Agricultural Research Station in northwest North Carolina, was manager of the Winston-Salem Fair, served as secretary of the N.C. Hereford Association, and was general manager of the Raleigh Farmers Market. He had been rejected for military service because he was blind in one eye, the result of a firecracker exploding near his face when he was a teen.

Graham initially wasn't keen on starting the western research station job because he didn't know much about the mountain folks, but he was politically astute enough to know that the region might be fertile ground in future political campaigns. Furthermore, it was Governor Kerr Scott, a family friend, who asked him to take the job. "He just told me to go up there, do the job, learn the people and keep my mouth shut," Graham recalled. Graham followed orders except for the closed mouth. He endeared himself to the mountain people through talk and action and they voted for him for more than thirty years.

Graham was devoted to Scott for his interest in farmers and the "little people" and had special affection for a Scott protégé named Terry Sanford. While it was Scott who began grooming Graham for the agriculture commissioner's job with the mountain research post, it was Sanford who initially appointed Graham to the job in July 1964, following the death of Commissioner L. Y. "Stag" Ballentine, who had succeeded Scott in the job.

Graham won a full term that November and never looked back. He spent $10,000 on his first campaign and never spent more than $100,000 on any reelection. Graham talked frequently through the years about seeking the governor's office, but he was never serious.

As custodian of the state's farming and food interests for thirty-six years, Graham witnessed and advocated the diversity of products and a change of atti-

probable came true, he puckered up as promised. A pre-kiss shot of Wilkes-produced corn liquor and tissue between his lips and the donkey's skin helped Graham fulfill the pledge.

He was born James Allen Graham on April 17, 1921, in the western Rowan County community of Cleveland, hard by Third Creek and Barber Junction. His Scotch-Irish ancestors settled on that land in 1744 and a Graham family member has farmed the soil ever since. As a teenager, Graham made a trip to Raleigh with his father, James Turner Graham, and met then Agriculture Commissioner William A. Graham (no kin). On the way home, he told his daddy he wanted to be commissioner of agriculture when he grew up.

That choice of a career and a decision to enroll at North Carolina State College (later North Carolina State University) suited the elder Graham just fine, but not his mother, Laura Allen Graham, a devoted Presbyterian. She wanted her son to attend Davidson Col-

tudes. While he never shrank from his loyalty to tobacco's importance in the state's history and economy, he became a reluctant believer that tobacco could be harmful to good health.

"Too much of anything is hurtful," he said near the end of his term. "Tobacco can and has caused health problems. But look what the industry has meant to this state, to institutions like Duke and N.C. State. It's still a legal product and I won't abandon it. I just wish through research there could be some good use found for the crop. You would think with so many smart people out there, someone would come up with a beneficial use that could be used to help with illnesses. I still hope that will happen." Graham bristled when he talked of the perception that he had not led efforts to wean the state's farmers from tobacco production. That's an unfair and inaccurate claim, he said.

At the end of the twentieth century, North Carolina was still the top producer of flue-cured tobacco, ahead of Tennessee and Kentucky. But during Graham's terms in office, tobacco had dropped from producing almost half the state's farm income to less than 15 percent. During the same years, livestock and poultry receipts climbed from less than 30 percent to almost 60 percent and greenhouse and nursery production rose from less than 2 percent to 12 percent. As tobacco declined, North Carolina had moved to first in the nation in turkey and sweet potato production and was in the top three states in production of hogs, Christmas trees, cucumbers, and trout. By the time Graham left office, North Carolina was the third most diversified agricultural state.

"I'm proud of that and the changes we've been able to make," Graham said. "I'm proud that we've been able to do what we have toward diversity, improving food quality, improving the health and safety of our people through careful monitoring of what we do and how we do it with crop production. I would hope my legacy would be that I opened up markets for more people, helped put money in the little man's pockets and that I was part of building up agriculture rather than bringing on its demise."

It was Graham's push for diversity of crop production without abandoning the traditional roles of basic crops that earned him the deserved nickname of the "Sodfather," a title he embraced with pride. Graham also was the steward of the constantly expanding role of his office as it moved from a primary focus on growing crops to sensitive environmental issues, particularly pollution and pesticides. He chafed at the suggestion that farming was the primary source of waterway contamination, insisting that commercial development, "over fertilizing" lawns, and malfunctioning city sewage systems ought to share the blame.

As Graham prepared to leave office, he presided over a state Department of Agriculture that had more than seventeen divisions and fifteen hundred employees with responsibilities stretching far beyond the farm. The department workers' duties ranged from inspecting grocery stores to monitoring gasoline pumps. There were few agriculture titles or honors that Graham hadn't won, been associated with, or created as a way of promoting the importance of farming and food. He had also created a scholarship endowment at N.C. State to help lead others into the field of agriculture.

During the last decade of his term in office, Graham combined his job with faithfully caring for his ailing wife, Helen Ida Kirk, a victim of Alzheimer's disease. She suffered from the disease for a decade and was confined to bed for the last eight years of her life before her death in December 1999. The Grahams had two daughters, Alice Graham Underhill of New Bern, who was elected to the North Carolina House of Representatives in 2000; and Connie Graham Brooks of Nashville, Tennessee; and seven grandchildren.

People joked about it being hard to fill Graham's shoes. That wasn't likely to literally happen: he wore a size fifteen boot. Boot size aside, Graham's earned imprint on efforts to improve the state's farming industry will remain, longer perhaps than his service in office. For him, there could be no finer tribute.

During Ned Cline's career as a journalist he worked as a reporter and editor with The Charlotte Observer *and the Greensboro* News and Record. *He is a graduate of Catawba College and was a Neiman Fellow at Harvard University, where he studied southern politics. He is the author of* Adding Value: The Joseph M. Bryan Story: From Poverty to Philanthropy.

For more information, see:
Graham, James A. Interview by author, May 30, 2000. Levine Museum of the New South, Charlotte.

———. Interview by Howard E. Covington Jr. and Marion A. Ellis, February 22, 1995. Duke University Archives, Durham.

———. *The Sodfather: Memoirs of Jim Graham.* N.C. State Graham Scholarship Endowment, 1998.

HUGH MACRAE

By Ralph Grizzle

IN 1945, a reporter was talking with Hugh Morton, owner of Grandfather Mountain and grandson of Hugh MacRae, the Wilmington industrialist, agriculturalist, and resort developer. Though the eighty-year-old MacRae's list of entrepreneurial achievements was legendary, not to mention broadly varied, his grandson knew what made his grandfather's heart race most. "His passion in life is agriculture," Morton said at the time. "Some men think that the most beautiful thing in the world is a good-looking woman. Others put a thoroughbred horse or a trim yacht at the head of the list. I believe the most beautiful thing in the world to Grandfather is a herd of cows grazing in a nice pasture."

During his eight-and-a-half decades in North Carolina, MacRae took on a variety of projects. A graduate of the Massachusetts Institute of Technology, he worked mica, feldspar, and kaolin deposits as a mining engineer near Spruce Pine. He later acquired sixteen thousand acres encompassing Grandfather Mountain and formed the Linville Improvement Company, which developed the town of Linville, which later became an exclusive resort community at the base of Grandfather Mountain. To provide access to his town, MacRae constructed the Yonahlossee (Cherokee for "trail of the black bear") Road between Linville and Blowing Rock. All of this (with more to come), and it was grazing cows that MacRae loved best.

MacRae believed that for farmers to sustain themselves, they had to keep their fields green in winter. Commenting on the economic decline in the South, MacRae said in 1934, "I feel sure that we have got to rebuild our economic structure beginning at the base, which means a reshaping of rural life."

MacRae, a short, stocky man with boundless energy, invested much of his life in an effort to overhaul southern agriculture. He argued that by raising only tobacco, corn, and cotton, southern farmers were depleting their land. On his 1,400-acre farm in Pender County, which he called Invershiel in recognition of his family's Scottish heritage, he spent three decades developing a grazing program that would support his dairy herd year-round. He cultivated fifty fields, encompassing some 750 acres, to experiment with feed crops. In some fields, MacRae used hay, corn, and commercial dairy feed. In others, he released his herd into spreads of vetch, clovers, and hearty grasses. Through trials, he eventually found five crops, consisting of clovers and grasses, which were ideal for year-round grazing.

He had proved, at least to his own satisfaction, that the South could be made the nation's leading beef and dairy cattle region because of its fertile land and longer growing season. With the promise of prosperity, he then tried to persuade Midwestern farmers to relocate to North Carolina's "green winters."

Even before his Carolina Trucking Company printed brochures and hired agents to scout for potential families to settle the communities he had developed to carry on his experiments, he had extended his offer across the Atlantic. Europeans responded favorably, and between 1905 and 1909 MacRae colonized six rural communities in three southeastern counties. The immigrants paid $240 for a three-bedroom house and $300 for a ten-acre tract of farmland. To ensure that the denizens would be prosperous and continue to reproduce, MacRae gave brides five-dollar gold pieces and ten dollars in gold to each child born in the settlements. He loaned money for fertilizer, seeds, and equipment to make the land itself prosperous.

At first, the communities were kept nationally distinct—with Hollanders comprising Van Eden and Castle Hayne; Germans and Hungarians populating New Berlin (later renamed Delco due to anti-German sentiment); Greeks making their homes in Marathon; Poles in Artesia; and Italians at St. Helena. Their farms became prosperous, with the *State* magazine reporting in 1945 that New Hanover County ranked second in per farm income in the South.

The immigrant population's prosperity was equally demonstrated by the fact that they were able to repay their notes, for houses and land, at a time when the country was only recently emerging from the throes of the Great Depression. "During a period when emergency calls for farm relief were being made from every section of the country," reported the *State* in 1934, "the farmers who had settled in these colonies . . . were paying off not only notes that were due but notes that would not be due until one and two years hence. While the cancerous depression was eating the core out of farming financially . . . these colonies were teeming with prosperity in comparison."

The communities thrived despite such setbacks as the state legislature's prohibition law that put an end

Hugh MacRae (Courtesy of Hugh Morton)

War. But when Federal occupation of the port city ended, the MacRaes returned home. Hugh was two years old. He attended school in Wilmington, and later in Mebane, at Bingham's School. At age sixteen he entered MIT and graduated at age twenty in 1885. The next year, the young college graduate began work as a mining engineer at Bailey Mountain, near Spruce Pine.

A friend of his father had become impressed with the scenic possibilities in the area that would become Linville, so Donald MacRae asked his son to go look at the valley. The sturdy young man made his way on horseback into Avery County. Overwhelmed by the beauty he found there, he wrote to his father for funds to purchase nearly sixteen thousand acres, mostly owned by Walter Waightstill Lenoir, grandson of General William Lenoir, for whom the town of Lenoir is named.

In 1889, the MacRaes formed the Linville Improvement Company, purchased the land, and began building a town. To make Linville accessible by carriage from Blowing Rock, MacRae's company built the Yonahlossee Road on the southern slope of Grandfather Mountain along a route that later became part of U.S. 221. "The state simply came along and paved it," said Hugh Morton, boasting of his grandfather's engineering prowess. "Not a single curve has been straightened since 1892."

MacRae's dream was for a fully functional village, but legal entanglements stalled land sales and new settlers were slow to arrive. Meanwhile, temporary residents in the form of summer tourists flocked to Linville's hotel, the Eseeola. By the turn of the century it had become a popular mountain retreat featuring cool mountain air, fine trout fishing, and golf on what was one of the first courses in the state. (Historians list the first course as one at Cape Fear Country Club, where MacRae was a member, which opened in 1896. The previous winter MacRae told club members that Eseeola guests had been playing the season before.)

By 1913, tourists had fully discovered this rich region of western North Carolina and summer homes covered with chestnut bark harvested from the company's sawmills began filling the valley. Linville became a stop on the Eastern Tennessee and Western North Carolina Railroad, known as Tweetsie because of the shrill whistle of its narrow-gauge steam engines. A horseback trail that led to the Grandfather Mountain overlook known as Cliffside was widened into a one-lane road for automobiles, whose drivers paid a toll to travel up the mountain to a wooden viewing platform.

to the manufacture of wine, pinching off the livelihood of Italian grape growers in St. Helena. The resilient Italians switched to dairy farming, producing impressive amounts of milk and other dairy products. The communities were situated along the Atlantic Coast Line Railroad and MacRae promoted export of their produce to markets in Baltimore and New York. From Castle Hayne, farms annually shipped 250 carloads of fresh vegetables to northern markets. Dutch settlers shipped ten thousand cartons of flowers and bulbs abroad each season.

Born March 30, 1865, Hugh MacRae was the son of Julia Norton and Donald MacRae, a merchant, manufacturer, and farmer who served as British vice-consul in Wilmington prior to the Civil War. Scottish blood coursed through the infant's veins. His great-great-grandfather set a course from Scotland to land in Wilmington in 1770. Entrepreneurial blood was also part of his heritage. His grandfather was president of the Wilmington and Weldon Railroad.

Hugh was born in Carbonton, the MacRae's summer place. Donald MacRae considered Wilmington to be unsafe for his expectant wife as the fight for strategic Fort Fisher raged on at the end of the Civil

MacRae loved the mountains but his heart was not in resort building. Despite Linville's success, he remained mostly in Wilmington, where he was president of Wilmington Cotton Mills Company and the head of Wilmington Gas Light Company, which later merged with the Wilmington Street Railway and the Seacoast Railway to become the Consolidated Railways, Light and Power Company. This entity eventually became the Tide Water Power Company, which MacRae sold in 1929, but not before using it to improve the quality of life in New Hanover County.

In *Chronicles of the Cape Fear River,* James Sprunt wrote of the Tide Water Power Company in 1916, "All the electric railway, electric light, electric power and gas systems not only in the city of Wilmington but in all New Hanover County are owned and operated by this company, and its success is due chiefly to the enterprise and excellent management of Hugh MacRae."

Along the tracks that Wilmington Street Railway operated to Wrightsville Beach, MacRae developed the Wilmington suburban areas of Winter Park, Oleander, and Audubon. He extended the line to Carolina Place, Sunset Park, and Carolina Heights to hasten development in these outlying areas. In 1905 and 1906, he erected the legendary pavilion Lumina at the beach. But even with all of this to occupy him, MacRae was already at work on what would become the chief interest in his life—agriculture, land development, promotion, and more settlements.

In the years following his experiments at Castle Hayne and the other rural communities, MacRae's agricultural successes caught the eye of the Roosevelt administration, which called upon the Wilmingtonian to head up a Depression-era subsistence homestead project in Pender County for the Department of the Interior. President and manager of the resettlement project at Penderlea, MacRae told the *State* in 1934 that he considered the 4,500-acre tract to be "the best planned rural community in the world." A model farm community, Penderlea was developed to demonstrate the "transformation that can be effected in rural life, particularly in the Southern states, at the same time offering a better chance to families brought together in a group than they would have under isolated conditions. . . . "

One hundred families were to arrive shortly. "Community gardens will have been planted and 40,000 cans of food put up so that no family will be in want while waiting the products of their own garden, which will be already cleared, drained, prepared and in readiness for the planting of winter crops." The fertile soils of Penderlea and the attractive government subsidies represented hope to homesteaders who were down on their luck or who had farmed out their own soils. Unfortunately, Penderlea was not to last. World War II enabled Americans to find jobs, and when the war ended, the new developing prosperity in the rapidly industrializing South allowed more people to abandon subsistence farming.

MacRae died October 20, 1951, at age eighty-six in Wilmington's James Walker Memorial Hospital, the birthplace of his grandson Hugh Morton, who carried on his grandfather's legacy at Grandfather Mountain. MacRae's widow, Rena, remained the grand dame of Linville for years. In 1952, her grandson's mile-high swinging bridge on the mountain let her reach Linville Peak one more time. For his exceptional achievement in southern agriculture and industry, MacRae was awarded an honorary degree by the University of North Carolina in the years before his death.

Ralph Grizzle of Asheville is a contributing editor of Our State *magazine and the author of* Remembering Charles Kuralt.

For more information, see:

MacRae, Hugh. Papers. Special Collections, Perkins Library, Duke University, Durham.

Covington Jr., Howard. *Linville: A Mountain Home for 100 Years*. Linville Resorts, 1992.
Riley, Jack. *Carolina Power and Light Company, 1908–1958*. Edwards & Broughton, 1958.
Sprunt, James. *Chronicles of the Cape Fear River, 1660–1916*. 1916.

JANE S. MCKIMMON

By Jane Veronica Charles

BORN DURING RECONSTRUCTION, Jane Simpson McKimmon saw the raw poverty that claimed most of North Carolina during those days and she determined to try to improve the plight of the state's rural farm women. "Miss Jenny," as she was affectionately known, started a series of "tomato clubs" for her target audience and eventually was named the state's first official home demonstration agent.

The oldest of eight children, McKimmon was born on November 13, 1867, in Raleigh to William and Anne Cannon Shank Simpson, who shared a Scottish ancestry (both sets of grandparents emigrated from Scotland) and strong religious beliefs. They had married in 1860 and raised Jane in an environment rooted in strong Christian ideals.

William Simpson worked as a retail druggist for thirty-eight years. Active in his profession, he not only lectured at the School of Pharmacy at Shaw University, but also became president of the National Pharmaceutical Association in 1894. Simpson's drive and capacity as one of the leaders of a state and national movement profoundly influenced Jane's desire and ability to take civic action. Jane's relationship with her blind uncle, Dr. John A. Simpson, who taught music at the North Carolina School for the Blind in Raleigh for fifty-seven years, also cultivated her interest in public welfare. During her youth, she frequently read to him, which fostered her ambition to both learn and help people with special needs.

Jane attended Raleigh's Peace Institute, later known as Peace College, for five years after spending four years in public schools, and, at age sixteen, she became the youngest student to graduate from Peace. Three years later in 1886 she married forty-year-old Charles McKimmon, a Raleigh merchant. Together the couple raised four children: Charles, Anne, William, and Hugh. They settled on Blount Street in the heart of Raleigh, a city still imbued with a rural way of living, where one could observe government workers going about their business alongside farmers selling their wares. This budding mixture of city and country life later opened the door for Jane to extend her ability as a homemaker of twenty-two years by reaching out to farm women in need of direction.

The McKimmons' neighbor was I. O. Schaub, a native North Carolinian who had worked as a professor of soils at Iowa State College before returning to

Jane S. McKimmon (Courtesy of University Archives, N.C. State University)

his home state in 1909 to eventually direct the North Carolina Agricultural Extension Service. One afternoon while they worked in their gardens, Schaub told Jane about the Boys Corn Club, a group that provided each boy with the opportunity to raise and sell an acre of corn. He also told her about the success of boys and girls clubs in neighboring states, where farm children learned to grow, harvest, preserve, and even sell various crops, and along the way learned the value of fellowship and support. These innovative clubs intrigued Jane. Realizing that he had piqued her interest, Schaub asked Jane to start a tomato-canning club in North Carolina. She immediately accepted.

In 1908 McKimmon lectured for the women's division of the Farmer's Institute, and two years later became the director of the division. McKimmon subsequently traveled throughout the state recruiting girls to join tomato clubs. Her arduous, tireless work paid off: what started out as a small group of girls interested in cultivating tomatoes burgeoned into a multitude of mothers and daughters who wanted to hone other useful skills, such as sewing. In order to obtain the resources needed to help these women, Jane encouraged them to beseech their local commissioners to create the salary-paying position of home agent. The commissioners complied. In 1911 "Miss Jenny," as farm women called her, became the first home demonstration agent in North Carolina, thereby officially launching the state's home demonstration movement.

A sense of camaraderie permeated the early get-togethers, as McKimmon likened the first club meetings to church gatherings. The women often met in churches, as well as homes, markets, schools, courthouses, and yards, where the early demonstrations concentrated on gardening, canning, food preparation, and marketing. Yet these demonstrations gave farm women the knowledge and skill to turn surplus butter, eggs, poultry, cream, and vegetables produced on the farm into additional family income. This money wasn't mere "pin money"—it was used for essentials such as school clothing. In fact, by 1915 over one hundred young women subsidized their college tuition by selling their wares to college dining halls. Upon graduation, with home economics degrees in hand, many of the women became home demonstration agents.

McKimmon relied on many techniques to ease the demonstration process. During meetings she employed simple rather than technical language when demonstrating how to carry out certain tasks. She also supplied informative bulletins, lesson sheets, and guidebooks. Later on, demonstrations expanded to extensive farm and home tours, where both men and women could observe scientific cropping systems and note gardening and home management techniques.

During the first year in her new position McKimmon effectively organized tomato clubs in fourteen counties, assigning one home agent to each county. Initially the fourteen agents worked only two months out of the year. After one year, however, the booming movement required the agents, highly educated women with much experience in homemaking and rural life, to work full time with commensurate pay. By the middle of the second decade of the century, McKimmon had expanded the grassroots home demonstration activities into an organized movement spearheaded by trained specialists and supervisors.

In 1914 Congress appropriated money for the Farmers Cooperative Demonstration Work, founded to diversify and improve farming methods in the South, with the passage of the Smith-Lever Act. What made this law a milestone was the fact that members of Congress designed the bill to specifically benefit farm women, to "lessen her heavy burdens."

The program quickly broadened to include the instruction of nutrition, clothing, child care, home furnishings, laborsaving devices, landscaping, home management, family relationships, and leisure activities, such as reading and music appreciation. The expansion of the projects provided people with more food, better clothing, and improved overall health. Farmers built community clubhouses where their families and neighbors convened to support one another and develop friendships, which helped to sustain unity in farming communities during tough times.

According to McKimmon, "The best work a home demonstration agent and her community leaders are doing is the fine contact established with the farm women in her home; the inspiration they have given to the hopeless; and the results obtained in raising the standards of living."

This work paid off, for in 1912 only 374 farm girls participated, but only twenty-five years later, almost 60,000 women, young and old and black and white, reaped the benefits of McKimmon's groundbreaking work. Moreover, by 1945 nearly 100,000 women had benefited from home demonstration work in all one hundred North Carolina counties.

McKimmon's home demonstration program emphasized the importance of education and leadership. McKimmon and other agents traveled miles on foot, by bus, via horse and buggy, by train, and by car to the homes of white and African American families throughout the state. Wake County hired the first black demonstration agent in 1925; the first club for African-American women was established the following year. Although African American home demonstration agents made less money than their white counterparts and clubs remained separate for a number of years, white and black demonstration agents often worked and traveled together when Jim Crow reigned in the South.

McKimmon was an articulate and persuasive orator, an effective administrator, and eventually a revered leader. She educated people about her work by speaking at various club meetings, conferences, and universities throughout the nation. She regularly contributed to leading newspapers and agricultural magazines and gave advice about homemaking on the radio. She also endeavored to secure appropriations to improve facilities and supply books to people in rural North Carolina.

Governor Thomas W. Bickett recognized McKimmon's leadership in the movement in 1917 when he appointed her director of home economics with the task of aiding in the administration of the Food Conservation Program, established during World War I. This effort continued throughout the deadly 1918 influenza epidemic, the Depression, and World War II. During these tumultuous times McKimmon and her fellow agents increased their efforts by caring for the sick and even taking on nursing duties. Governor J. C. B. Ehringhaus took notice of her role in these efforts, and in 1935 named her to the Rural Electrification Authority, where she was vice-chair.

Governors Clyde R. Hoey and J. Melville Broughton recognized her diligence by appointing her to the State Council for National Defense during World War II. These North Carolina governors also selected her to serve on the board of directors of the Farmers Cooperative Exchange. In addition, she served on the Committee on Hospital and Medical Care for Rural People during Broughton's administration.

After McKimmon accepted the position of assistant director of extension in 1924, she decided to further her own education. In 1927 she received a bachelor of science degree from North Carolina State College and at age fifty-nine was the first woman to graduate from that school. Two years later she received a master of science degree. The University of North Carolina awarded her an honorary doctor of laws degree in 1934.

In 1927 North Carolina home demonstration agents established the Jane S. McKimmon Loan Fund in honor of her outstanding achievement in leadership and adult education. That same year the National Honor Society of Phi Kappa Phi inducted her into the organization, and the National Honorary Society of the Agricultural Extension Service, Epsilon Sigma Phi, presented her with the Distinguished Service Ruby in 1936 (she was the first woman to receive this honor). Additional honors included the North Carolina Grange's "Distinguished Service to Agriculture" award in 1940; *Progressive Farmer*'s Woman of the Year in Agriculture award that same year; and the Southern Agricultural Conference's bronze medallion in 1942.

Throughout her career, McKimmon remained active in her community through a number of service organizations. She helped found the National Home Economics Association and served as the organization's president. She was also a member of both the North Carolina and the National Granges. McKimmon belonged to several nonagricultural organizations as well, including the North Carolina Literary and Historical Associations, the Fortnightly Book Club, and the Raleigh Woman's Club. She served as soloist in the choir of Christ Episcopal Church of Raleigh. She attended a number of political conventions and vigorously supported the Democratic Party.

After McKimmon resigned from her position as state home demonstration agent in 1937, she wrote *When We're Green We Grow*, a book that chronicles the history of her work, published in 1945. In 1946, nearing eighty years of age, McKimmon entered full retirement. She died at age ninety on December 1, 1957, in the Wake Forest Rest Home, and was buried in Oakwood Cemetery in Raleigh.

In 1966 McKimmon was the first woman elected to the Agricultural Hall of Fame. In 1976 the Jane S. McKimmon Center for Extension and Continuing Education was completed at North Carolina State University, in honor of a woman who dedicated much of her adult life to improving the lot of North Carolina farm women through education and direct action.

Jane Veronica Charles received her master's degree in history from N.C. State University and is a project archivist for the historical collection/labor archives unit of the special collections department at Pennsylvania State University. She is the author of several entries in The Mythical West: An Encyclopedia of Legend, Lore, and Popular Culture.

For more information, see:

McKimmon, Jane Simpson. Papers. North Carolina Office of Archives and History, Raleigh.

Christensen, Janice R., ed. *And That's the Way It Was: 1920–1980; The 60-Year History of Extension Home Economics Work in North Carolina*. North Carolina Extension Homemakers Association, 1980.

College of Agricultural and Life Sciences Extension. Papers. North Carolina State University Archives, Raleigh.

McKimmon, Jane Simpson. *When We're Green We Grow*. University of North Carolina Press, 1945.

Smith, Margaret Supplee, and Emily Herring Wilson. *North Carolina Women: Making History*. University of North Carolina Press, 1999.

WENDELL H. MURPHY

By Marion A. Ellis

WENDELL HOLMES MURPHY never forsook the soil while transforming agribusiness in North Carolina through the introduction of contract hog farms that made his company the largest pork producer in the nation and left Murphy with a fortune that *Forbes* magazine estimated at more than $1 billion.

Four decades before he became a billionaire, Murphy was teaching school when he and another teacher, Billy Register, passed a small feed mill near the town of Warsaw in eastern North Carolina one afternoon. "You know, I believe one of those little feed mills would go good in our community," Register said. "It was just like lightning," Murphy recalled. "I mean it just came to me all at once—that's exactly what I wanted to do."

A year later, in 1962, the twenty-four-year-old Murphy took $3,000 he saved from teaching vocational agriculture, borrowed $1,300 from his tobacco-farmer father, and bought a small feed mill in rural eastern North Carolina. But building such a mill would cost at least $13,000, so Murphy convinced his father to co-sign a bank loan after he agreed to keep his teaching job until the debt was repaid. "The hardest sell I ever had to make was trying to convince Daddy to co-sign that $10,000 note," Murphy once told the *News and Observer*. "He didn't loan me the money because he didn't have the money. Our little farm had never had a mortgage on it, so I didn't dare ask him to mortgage the farm. I just asked him to sign with me."

For the next three years, Murphy held two full-time jobs, teaching during the day and running the mill at night. "Sometimes Wendell would have to stay all night at the grain mill, sleeping in his car and looking after the milling process," said Terrence Coffey, a former North Carolina State University professor who became head of operations for Murphy Family Farms. "He would take his kids to school in the morning and then go to work teaching school."

When the loan was repaid, Murphy quit teaching and devoted himself to his business. He saw a potential profit in the corn husks and cobs that other millers were throwing away, and he began grinding them into feed. "We have always done what others would consider inconvenient," Murphy said. "On Saturday nights, we would be still shelling corn at mid-

Wendell H. Murphy (Courtesy of Murphy Family Farms)

night, and the neighboring businesses had closed up at noon. That same principle we have applied throughout our entire business: to look around and see what we can do that other people chose not to."

In the late 1960s, when new combine machines threatened to make traditional feed mills obsolete, Murphy moved into the hog business. He began by buying feeder pigs on sale, raising them on dirt lots on his farm, and feeding them with corn from his mill. Before long, he was making more profit feeding his own animals than he was selling feed to others.

In 1973, when widespread hog cholera threatened his livestock, Murphy borrowed an idea from the poultry business and began contracting with neighboring farmers to raise his pigs. "We furnished the wire and the fence posts; they furnished the labor," he said. Murphy paid his first growers a dollar per pig to raise his animals on dirt lots. Later, he switched to climate-controlled confinement barns and automated feeding equipment.

Hundreds of North Carolina farmers were drawn

to Murphy's contract growing as a way to earn money while protecting themselves from fluctuations in the market for other crops they raised. By the mid-1980s, Murphy was ready to export his methods to Iowa and Missouri, where feed costs were cheaper and packing plants more accessible. By 1987, Murphy Farms was the biggest hog producer in the nation, and contract hog production was on its way to becoming an industry standard.

"For better or worse, Murphy changed the entire business," Al Tank, chief executive officer of the National Pork Producers Council, told the *News and Observer*. "Everyone else followed his model."

But Murphy's influence extended over far more than hogs. He served five terms in the state legislature and emerged in 1982 as one of the state's most powerful political figures. He was a member of the state Advisory Budget Commission, which controlled spending and helped set the governor's spending priorities. He also served on the boards of two banks, a half-dozen college foundations, the North Carolina State University board of trustees, and the Research Triangle World Trade Corporation. He flew former presidents and governors in his company aircraft and provided financial backing for numerous Democratic candidates.

On one occasion, he used his airplane to rescue the North Carolina Museum of History from disaster on its opening day of April 22, 1994. Just hours before the ceremony where all five of the state's surviving governors were to participate, there was a snag: former Governor Jim Martin, a Republican, was returning from a trip abroad and was stranded in Atlanta. Murphy, a staunch Democrat, sent his corporate jet to pick up Martin and deliver him to the ceremony on time. He neither asked for nor received any compensation.

Murphy gave more than a half million dollars to his alma mater, North Carolina State University, which he called the "finest institution in the world." Along with his father, the university was "the reason for everything that I am—all the good, none of the bad," Murphy said. In addition to money, he used his influence to secure state funding for the university's Centennial Campus and its new basketball arena.

"I'm just a country boy who grew up on a small farm with tobacco and a few pigs in the back yard," Murphy once told the *News and Observer*. "Frankly, I don't know much about raising hogs, but fortunately we have some people that do."

Murphy's influence also made him an invaluable asset to the swine industry and to other agribusiness interests, and an irresistible target to groups who opposed the unbridled growth of hog farms, although

Murphy argued that the farms were environmentally responsible.

Murphy considered himself a realist when it came to business and politics. "Our trademark—our hallmark if you will—has been our willingness to recognize that change is inevitable, that we cannot continue to do in the future what we've done in the past. In almost any business, it's that way. Politics is that way. People who resist change are just going to get left behind."

As a realist, Murphy considered entering the pork processing business as well as his hog farming, but eventually he decided to sell to a competitor, Smithfield Foods, the world's largest hog producer and pork processor. The deal was driven by a rapidly consolidating pork industry and a run of brutally low hog prices. "We have known for a long time we needed to be in the pork-processing business," Murphy said at the time of the sale. "This was the right deal at the right time for everyone involved." The sale took place in September 1999 for $459.7 million worth of stock and assumed debt.

Experts said the sale to Smithfield represented a marriage of necessity for Murphy Family Farms, which had been hammered by low prices for more than a year. "Smithfield controls the entire pork production process, literally from a pig's birth all the way to the dinner plate," said National Pork Producers' spokesman Al Tank. "Murphy raised hogs better and cheaper than almost anyone else, but that was all they did."

Tank said Murphy was hit particularly hard in 1998 when the bottom dropped out of the U.S. hog market. In contrast, vertically integrated companies such as Smithfield were able to cover big losses from their hog-raising operations with higher profits from their pork-processing facilities.

In fact, big pork producers such as Murphy were so successful that the market became overwhelmed. With much more money invested in their infrastructure than the smaller growers who could sell their animals and wait for prices to improve, the big producers' only option was to maintain their production levels and keep paying their growers the higher prices negotiated before the market crashed. The ensuing glut eventually forced prices down to historic lows the year before Murphy sold. Hogs that cost forty to fifty dollars to produce were selling for twenty dollars. As a result, Murphy Farms was losing considerably more than $1 million per week.

Tank said the financial turmoil divided the pork business into two distinct groups. "The vertically integrated companies like Smithfield are now the haves, and the unintegrated companies like Murphy are now the have-nots," he said. "Murphy had become the biggest of the have-nots, so the company had to do something."

Before the sale, Murphy Farms and Smithfield had been partners in developing the world's largest hog farm on fifty thousand acres in southwest Utah. Murphy eventually pulled out of that arrangement.

After the sale to Smithfield, Murphy said he expected the one thousand or so farmers who grew hogs under contract with Murphy Farms to embrace the deal. "Given a choice, we would have preferred to keep things going on our own, but that wouldn't have been fair to our employees and our growers," Murphy said. "This deal will give the growers more financial stability in the long run."

As a former state senator, Murphy quietly led the effort to soften environmental laws, according to the *News and Observer*. "He was able to push through exemptions from zoning laws for intensive livestock operations," the newspaper said. Critics blamed Murphy Farms and other big hog companies for widespread pollution problems that plagued eastern North Carolina in the final decade of the twentieth century. But Murphy had just as many supporters who credited him with revitalizing the region's economy.

Environmentalists protested the large pools of waste that accompanied the factory-style farms that Murphy pioneered, but some gave him credit for being among the most innovative leaders in North Carolina agriculture. The Sierra Club printed a scathing article about Murphy's operation in the May 1996 issue of *Sierra*. "Like its liquefied manure, the hog industry flows downhill, to wherever it finds the fewest regulations and the lowest wages," the magazine said. "'One reason for the explosive growth in North Carolina is that there's been no control,' says Bill Holman, Sierra Club lobbyist there. His state's hog production has almost tripled in this decade, from 5 million in 1990 to 14 million by 1995."

The article continued, "The biggest player in North Carolina is Murphy Family Farms, whose down-home name belies its $200 million in hog sales last year and over $150,000 in campaign donations to North Carolina legislators in the past five years. The company's founder, Wendell Murphy, was a state legislator for ten years. By the time he left office in 1992, he had voted for seven laws that release the hog industry from various taxes and regulations. North Carolinians sardonically refer to the two he sponsored as 'Murphy's Laws.' One of these actually prevents counties from subjecting hog facilities to local zoning rules on the dubious grounds that these factories are 'bona fide farms,' and thus exempt."

Rural folks praised him for bringing badly needed economic development to eastern North Carolina as the fortunes of tobacco declined, but many also held him responsible for the virtual extermination of small, independent hog farms.

Marion A. Ellis is a Charlotte writer specializing in corporate histories and biographies. He is the coauthor with Howard E. Covington Jr. of Sages of Their Craft: The First Fifty Years of the American College of Trial Lawyers; Terry Sanford: Politics, Progress, and Outrageous Ambition; *and* The Story of NationsBank: Changing the Face of American Banking.

For more information, see:
Murphy, Wendell. File. North Carolina Office of
    Archives and History, Raleigh.

News and Observer electronic library.
    www.newsobserver.com.

CLARENCE H. POE

By Jonathan Phillips

JUST A MONTH before his death, Clarence Hamilton Poe, longtime editor and owner of the *Progressive Farmer,* wrote a column for the September 1964 issue advocating increased congressional representation for the nation's urban areas. For a man who devoted his entire life to helping and nurturing the small farmer, it was ironic that his final column considered the plight of city dwellers, a group that Poe had so often held in contempt, especially in his earlier years.

According to his only biographer, Joseph Cote, Poe believed that "rural residents were morally superior to urban dwellers and that citizen farmers could best safeguard the nation's heritage." But the rural population in the South had been declining for decades by the 1960s, and many farmers had moved with their families to the nation's cities, thus contributing to the need for congressional realignment.

During his sixty-year tenure, Poe took the *Progressive Farmer,* a struggling farm journal with populist inclinations and a meager circulation of five thousand in the late 1890s, and transformed it into the leading agrarian publication in the South by the 1930s. Poe served as senior editor while still a teenager and, by his early twenties, owned a controlling percentage of the journal. Although he had little formal education, he proved to be an adept journalist and a perceptive businessman. By the 1950s, the *Progressive Farmer* printed several regional editions and had a circulation approaching two million.

Throughout his career, business took second place to Poe's primary mission to restore and propagate the yeoman farmer's way of life. He hoped that southern farm families might avoid life in the industrial squalor of American cities. He participated in a variety of liberal, sometimes radical causes in the South. But in every case, his goal was the re-creation of the mythical agrarian land he had learned about as a small boy in piedmont North Carolina—not the fictional plantation world, but the Jeffersonian ideal of the prosperous and fiercely independent small landowner.

During his lifetime, Poe lent his name to a variety of progressive causes—education from primary grades through college, public health, transportation, penal reform, child labor reform, and Prohibition. He held positions on countless committees and boards. And like so many progressives of his time, especially those

with populist inclinations, he was inspired to act by fears of the ever-growing power of big business and sought to limit this power by using the authority of the federal government to improve the lives of ordinary people.

Poe's agenda fit well with the efforts of the more typical southern progressive in another more unfortunate way. In regard to race relations, Poe was certainly "a man of his time and place," as he once said of Josephus Daniels of the *News and Observer.* He regretted and opposed the violence inflicted upon black southerners, but at no time in his life did he conceive of African Americans as his intellectual equal. In his autobiography, *My First Eighty Years,* he failed to address his role in reinforcing geographic segregation in North Carolina and, as his biographer noted, letters concerning his leadership role in this effort are absent from his papers. Poe's vision of the progressive agrarian South was "for whites only," although his actions later in life suggested a slight moderation of his views.

With the exception of race relations, Poe was hardly provincial or narrow-minded. In his speeches and especially through his columns in the *Progressive Farmer,* he supported many causes and called for political action on a variety of issues quite out-of-step with the agenda of many politically active southerners. Poe opposed the Red Scare paranoia of Joseph McCarthy and the aggression of General Douglas MacArthur during the Korean War. He supported recognition of Franco's government in Spain and that of the Communist Chinese under Mao. In the early cold war years, he recommended giving the Soviets the secret of the atomic bomb in the interest of world peace. Earlier, when northerners volunteered to fund public health programs in the South, Poe graciously accepted the assistance—unlike many southerners who feared northern support would lead to northern domination.

Poe never experienced the good times of southern rural life he so fervently hoped would return. He was born in Oakland Township, Chatham County, on January 10, 1881, into a large farming family. In the early nineteenth century, this eastern piedmont land nestled between the Haw and Deep rivers looked to be one of the Tar Heel state's most active and burgeoning trade regions. Expectations never materialized. By the 1880s, most residents eked out a living on worn-out,

Clarence H. Poe (Courtesy of Southern Historical Collection)

a recently proposed tax increase in support of North Carolina's schools. Poe wrote a persuasive essay in favor of the tax and won the contest. Within a month, the *Progressive Farmer* hired the ambitious sixteen-year-old and he moved to Raleigh.

Six months later, Poe had been promoted to associate editor and had primary responsibility for running the journal. By 1898, Poe added more columns and writers and began reprinting stories from the state's more prominent newspapers. In addition, he placed greater emphasis on improving southern agriculture, following in the footsteps of the *Farmer's* founder. In 1899, Poe agonized over whether or not to attend Wake Forest College, but chose to stay with the *Progressive Farmer* when he was given the title of editor in chief. By this time, Poe had already developed a close friendship with Josiah Bailey, the future United States senator, who edited the *Biblical Recorder* and whose offices were next door to those of the *Farmer.*

Poe purchased the journal in 1903 with the financial assistance of four friends, including Bailey. In the next fifteen years, the journal increased its circulation from 5,000 to almost 200,000—mostly through the acquisition of other southern farm papers. Like most agrarians of his day, Poe vehemently opposed monopolization resulting from industrial mergers, but he used the same tactics to expand his own business. Although the *Progressive Farmer* would have good years and bad, and certainly struggled through the Depression years of the 1930s, it eventually served millions of readers throughout the South.

While continuing to expand the influence of the *Progressive Farmer* throughout North Carolina and the rest of the South, Poe embarked on the first of his campaigns to transform agriculture. In the 1890s, the People's Party had proposed a cooperative program called the sub-treasury plan. Although this plan failed, the idea of cooperatives continued to be looked upon favorably by many agrarians as the solution to the unjust economic system in the South. Poe hoped to help farmers to organize themselves with the support of local firms. Farmers would own all aspects of the business from elevators to telephones, livestock companies, and perhaps most important, credit organizations. Poe traveled widely in search of successful examples of cooperative efforts.

In North Carolina, the *Progressive Farmer* served as the official voice of the state's chapter of the Farmer's Educational and Cooperative Union. The cooperative program waxed and waned in popularity. When crop prices dropped, farmers became more interested in cooperative efforts. The cooperative move-

eroded land. Such was the plight of the Poe family. But while the Poes suffered from poor crop prices, low production, and inadequate credit, they did own the land on which they lived.

The Poes grew wheat, corn, tobacco, and cotton, in varying amounts. William Poe, Clarence's father, subscribed to agricultural journals and embraced any scientific improvement that he thought might increase the farm's profitability. A combination of factors led to bankruptcy in 1890. As a result, the family moved briefly to Greensboro but then returned to the farm. The financial problems of the 1890s drew William into the Farmer's Alliance and into the People's Party, of which Leonidas L. Polk, owner and editor of the *Progressive Farmer,* was a leading figure.

During his formative years, Clarence Poe's interest in the agrarian movement, coupled with the influence of religion in his life, did much to create within him the calling of an "agrarian crusader." Poe devoted the next seventy years to "spreading the word" of the benefits of agrarian life. Of course, he needed a vehicle, and that was his writing, which developed early in his life despite little formal education. In 1895, Poe submitted articles to various publications, including the *Progressive Farmer,* then edited by John Ramsey following the death of Polk in 1892. In 1897, the journal conducted a writing competition concerning

ment never achieved the success Poe had hoped but it did produce one of the most progressive credit union laws in the nation (1915) and established cooperative marketing and supply organizations, such as the farmers' exchanges that began to dot the South in the 1920s and 1930s. Some local co-ops even provided insurance coverage for members.

In the 1930s, Poe hoped that New Deal farm measures would provide the needed structural changes to rebuild rural communities. The farm proposals of the Roosevelt administration—production controls, loans, credits, tariff adjustments—were welcomed by the nation's farmers and provided some relief. And, although some North Carolinians such as Poe's old friend Josiah Bailey, now North Carolina's senior senator, argued against the ever-growing federal role in farm production, Poe recognized that national programs were the small farmer's only hope. Generally, however, New Deal farm policies, such as quotas, ended up helping large farmers at the expense of small landowners.

Poe continued to believe in the societal benefits and lifestyle of the family farm, but he knew that it was a world rapidly disappearing. As Joseph Cote noted in his biography of Poe, in the first sixty years of the century, the size of farms doubled while the total number of farms decreased from 5.7 million to 3.7 million. Farmers were moving with their families to the cities, or settling in mill villages. Poe could no longer speak so poorly of urban residents; many were former farmers.

Although a realist in his view of international affairs, Poe supported efforts to limit violence and end conflict around the globe. He advocated a policy of active involvement in world affairs and ardently supported such international bodies as the League of Nations, the World Court, and the United Nations. In the mold of most southerners, he opposed a substantial military buildup of U.S. forces prior to World War II and hoped that the United States could stay out of the conflict. After the bombing of Pearl Harbor, Poe supported the U.S. war effort and condemned those who inhibited the nation's ability to win quickly. He did not support the "unconditional surrender" doctrine, believing that it would only prolong the war and the suffering.

Though certainly not a supporter of communism, Poe looked more favorably upon the Soviet Union than did most Americans. Always fearful of capitalism run amok, he did see how the Soviet economic system could appeal to America's poor. As the cold war solidified in the late 1940s, Poe's favorable view darkened noticeably—especially after the Berlin block-

ade in 1948. Throughout the remainder of his life, Poe continued to believe that differing economic and political systems could coexist internationally.

In 1912, Poe had married Alice Aycock, daughter of North Carolina's influential turn-of-the-century governor, Charles B. Aycock. They had three children. William, Poe's second son, followed in his father's footsteps as an agricultural journalist. The elder Poe expected William to take over the reins of the journal. Unfortunately, William died in 1958 at the age of only forty-two.

During the 1950s, Poe relinquished some of his control of the *Progressive Farmer*. He remained senior editor and chairman of the board, but was no longer president. He continued to write a monthly column, but devoted more time to his children and grandchildren and to other interests such as maintaining the large family home in north Raleigh. He stayed active politically and supported various cultural preservation causes. One setback occurred in 1955 when the General Assembly did not reelect him to the board of trustees of the University of North Carolina. Conservative members of the legislature feared that Poe's progressive reputation might lead him to support integration of the state's university campuses. Poe had previously backed a plan to allow black county agricultural agents to sit with white agents in refresher courses at North Carolina State College. To many, it seemed a slap in the face to a man who had encouraged the creation of the consolidated university system in 1931. It also demonstrated a growing openmindedness on Poe's part in regard to race relations.

In 1963, Poe's autobiography, *My First Eighty Years*, was published by the University of North Carolina Press. Poe published several other works on various subjects such as cotton cultivation, travels in Europe, and the Civil War, and on his father-in-law, Governor Aycock. He had two works in progress at the time of his death.

On October 1, 1964, Poe suffered a stroke and died the next week at the age of eighty-three. Until the end, he continued his campaign on behalf of the farm family. For Poe, his quest was always about the preservation of rural southern culture and not specifically about economic progress. Yet he knew that for rural culture to survive, small farm families had to earn a living wage. By the 1960s, it was clear that many farmers had followed Poe, not in words, but in action, and had moved to urban areas. But at least Poe had prepared the farmer for urbanization.

His journal always addressed far more than just farm news. The *Progressive Farmer* helped rural southerners become better informed on national and international issues. His efforts made them healthier and better educated. And through it all, he gave them hope and made them feel good about being farmers and southerners—and this, perhaps, was his greatest contribution. At the time of his death, the foundation was already set for the creation of a new publication to be called *Southern Living*, which by the turn-of-the-century was the largest circulation magazine in the South and read widely by suburbanites from Washington to New Orleans.

Jonathan Phillips's doctoral dissertation in history at the University of North Carolina at Chapel Hill examined the economic and cultural impact of the military presence in the Fayetteville and Sandhills region of North Carolina. In 2000–2001 he was a fellow at the Center of Military History.

For more information, see:

Poe, Clarence Hamilton. Papers. Southern Historical Collection, University of North Carolina at Chapel Hill.

Cote, Joseph. "Clarence Hamilton Poe: Crusading Editor, 1881–1964." Ph.D. diss., University of Georgia, 1977.
———. "Clarence Hamilton Poe: The Formative Years, 1899–1917." M.A. thesis, East Carolina University, 1969.
Poe, Clarence Hamilton. *My First Eighty Years*. University of North Carolina Press, 1963.
Progressive Farmer. Microfilm. North Carolina Collection, University of North Carolina at Chapel Hill.

ARCHITECTURE, ENGINEERING, AND SCIENCE

ENGINEERS, ARCHITECTS, AND BUILDERS twice transformed North Carolina's destiny in the twentieth century, first as the state became the leader in the southern textile industry, and later as technology and research brought future Nobel Prize laureates to laboratories in the Research Triangle Park, the state's crown jewel of twenty-first-century enterprise.

D. A. Tompkins of Charlotte was a visionary who saw the potential in the natural and human energy of the region even before the twentieth century arrived. Trained as an engineer and builder, Tompkins corralled the enthusiasm of the post-Reconstruction era to entice the nation's textile mills away from their traditional home in New England. Tompkins personally organized, designed, financed, or equipped more than 350 cotton mills in the Carolinas and Georgia. He was also responsible for organizing schools of textiles at what later became North Carolina State University, Clemson University, Mississippi State University, and Texas A and M.

Long before Americans considered it possible to artificially cool their homes in the summer, a Tompkins protégé and mill owner, Stuart Cramer, had done just that in his textile mills with something he called "air-conditioning." The ability to control humidity and temperature accelerated the expansion of the textile industry in the South, where new mills were beginning to draw their energy from an abundant supply of electricity.

The new power came from the enterprise of the state's richest man, James B. Duke. Years before the U.S. Supreme Court broke up Duke's American Tobacco Company empire, Duke had hired a creative engineer named William States Lee to help him convert the power of the Catawba River. Lee-designed hydroelectric plants produced enough electricity to invigorate an entire region, from Durham to the upper reaches of South Carolina.

David Marshall Williams was far from the humming mills of piedmont North Carolina in the late 1920s as an inmate in the state's Caledonia prison. Williams had been convicted in a fatal shooting of a revenue agent during a liquor raid, but the warden allowed him to tinker with a new high-powered rifle. Williams subsequently was pardoned for his role in the shooting and freed from prison in 1929. His design of a lightweight .30-caliber carbine was later adopted and produced by the millions for the U.S. military. General Douglas MacArthur called it "one of the strongest contributing factors to our victory in the Pacific."

The war also gave Charlotte's J. A. Jones the boost he needed to create a construction company that by the 1960s was undertaking massive projects in all corners of the world.

For the most part, North Carolina industry in the 1950s looked much the same as it had for two, three, or even four decades before. Tobacco, textiles, and furniture dominated the state's economy. A Greensboro builder named

Romeo Guest had erected many industrial buildings and saw the opportunity for more when he proposed to Governor Luther Hodges that the state support a new idea, a research park for American industry. The result was the Research Triangle Park, which was transformed from Guest's early vision as a for-profit venture and began to expand and flourish in the late 1960s. At the close of the century, 43,000 people worked for 136 research-oriented companies in the 6,800-acre Park.

The Park harnessed the intellectual power of the university campuses in Durham, Raleigh, and Chapel Hill and became the very symbol of innovation and a model for the future. Charlotte architect A. G. Odell produced his attention-getting design for the Blue Cross Blue Shield headquarters, a raised, glass-clad, rhomboid-shaped building located between Durham and Chapel Hill. Odell was one of the first southerners to serve as president of the American Institute of Architects and his firm was a valued assignment for young architects graduating from the School of Design at North Carolina State University. One of the school's early deans was Henry Kamphoefner, whose parabolic design for Raleigh's Dorton Arena expressed new ideas for handling open space.

Scientists and researchers from around the world became familiar with the name of the Research Triangle Park in 1988 when Dr. Gertrude Elion and Dr. George Hitchings, two researchers at a company then called Burroughs Wellcome, were awarded the Nobel Prize in medicine for their groundbreaking invention of new compounds to treat malaria, leukemia, gout, organ-transplant rejection, and bacterial infections.

Ironically, it was the grandson of the man who had designed Duke's hydroelectric power grid at the dawn of the twentieth century who helped fashion a harness for nuclear power two generations later. William States Lee III was an early advocate for the use of nuclear energy for domestic power and he became one of the world's leading authorities in its usage. After the Chernobyl nuclear disaster in April 1986 in the Ukraine, Lee served as a consultant to the Soviet Union and later helped organize the World Association of Nuclear Operators, an organization he headed for two years.

STUART W. CRAMER

By Mark McGrath

TEN MILES east of Gastonia, Cramer Mountain rises abruptly from the red clay of the North Carolina piedmont. Looming like an aerie at the top is Maymont, a thirty-eight-room mansion that was once the summer home of Stuart W. Cramer, renowned mill engineer and textile industrialist. The quaint cottages of Cramerton, a mill village founded by and named after Cramer, are scattered at the foot of the mountain. To the workers who labored in the mills that were owned by one of the most innovative and successful textile barons of the early twentieth century, Maymont's Olympian perch could not help but symbolize the hierarchical social order of their world.

Cramer was born in Thomasville on March 31, 1868, the son of John Thomas Cramer and Mary Jane Cramer. His maternal grandfather was "Squire" John Warwick Thomas (1800–1871), a prominent landowner and the founder of Thomasville. Thomas owned Cedar Lodge plantation, where he operated a sawmill, furniture factory, shoe factory, and a small textile mill. Thomas also established a school for women, operated a gold mine, served as a state legislator, and was instrumental in organizing the North Carolina Railroad.

Following an unremarkable childhood and adolescence, Cramer began a postsecondary course of study at the United States Naval Academy. He graduated in June 1888, and took a postgraduate curriculum at the Columbia University School of Mines in 1888 and 1889. His father's failing health, attributable in part to injuries suffered in the Civil War, hastened Cramer's return to North Carolina in the summer of 1889. He was appointed chief assayer of the United States Assay office in Charlotte on July 1, 1889, a post that he held until 1893.

On June 24, 1889, Cramer married Bertha Hobart Berry, the daughter of Stephen and Sarah Berry of Portland, Maine. The couple had two children, Katherine Hobart, born June 21, 1890 (who later married Dr. James R. Angell, president of Yale University), and Stuart Warren Jr., born January 28, 1892. The younger Cramer would graduate from the United States Military Academy at West Point, N.Y., and serve with distinction in the Mexico border conflicts and World War I.

Bertha Cramer died on June 26, 1895. On September 8, 1896, Cramer married Kate Stanwood Berry, Bertha's sister, in accordance with Bertha's deathbed request that he do so. Tragically, Kate Cramer died only a few months later. On January 28, 1902, Cramer married his third wife, Rebecca Warren Tinkham, the daughter of Mr. and Mrs. George H. Tinkham of Boston, and the sister of Congressman George Holden Tinkham, also of Boston. Stuart and Rebecca had a son, George Bennett, who was born on July 15, 1903.

While Cramer was beginning a family in Charlotte, he was also embarking upon a career that would distinguish him as one of the foremost industrial leaders of the New South. From 1893 to 1895, Cramer served as chief engineer and manager of D. A. Tompkins Company in Charlotte. Founded by Daniel Augustus Tompkins, an industrialist and New South visionary, the company specialized in the manufacture and distribution of textile equipment. The firm also designed and outfitted textile mills throughout the South, and most of Cramer's activities involved mill architecture, design, and engineering.

When he left the Tompkins Company in 1895, Cramer opened an office in Charlotte and established what soon became a thriving independent mill design and contracting business. Due to the rapid growth of the textile industry in the central piedmont of North Carolina between 1880 and 1915, many northern textile machine firms opened regional offices in Charlotte. The hue and cry of the New South movement was "Bring the Mills to the Cotton," and Cramer was instrumental in making this slogan a reality. Cramer served as the local agent for several manufacturers of textile mill equipment and machinery, including the Whitin Machine Works, the American Moistening Company, Kitson Machine Company, Woonsocket Machine & Press Company, Parsons & Curtis, Corliss, and Westinghouse.

Even more significant, however, were Cramer's activities in the fields of mill architecture and design. In these areas, his contributions to the textile industry, and to the economy of the New South, are without parallel. Indeed, it is generally accepted that, between 1895 and 1915, Cramer planned or equipped nearly one-third of all the cotton mills in the South. In 1903, Cramer designed the state-of-the-art Highland Park Number 3 mill in North Charlotte, a facility that he and other mill engineers used as a prototype for textile mill design and construction.

Stuart W. Cramer (Courtesy of Forsyth County Public Library)

Cramer is also credited with numerous other technical innovations that revolutionized textile production in the South, especially in the field of workplace humidification. Proper humidity was a critical element in the proper handling of certain fabrics and fibers. Unfortunately, the South lacked the kind of natural humidity that benefited the mills in coastal New England, and this posed a considerable obstacle to the manufacture of fine yarns in North Carolina. After many years of research and development, Cramer devised a system that automatically regulated humidity and temperature inside the mills. Although the invention of air conditioning was widely credited to Willis Carrier, it was Cramer who coined the term "air conditioning" in 1906 to describe his textile mill humidification system.

Cramer was credited with other critical innovations in textile production as well. For many years, most textile mill machinery was run by a central power plant and connecting belts and shafts. Cramer believed, and ultimately proved, that the use of independent electric machines could increase production and efficiency. Cramer designed and patented many such devices, and in so doing dramatically transformed the manufacture of textiles.

Cramer was an early and enthusiastic proponent of electrical power and the creation of a power grid network. He collaborated with James B. Duke in establishing Duke Power Company and became a director of that company. Cramer was also a prolific author of books and articles on the textile industry, especially in the area of industrial engineering, mill design, and industrial welfare. Cramer published the highly influential four-volume treatise, *Useful Information for Cotton Manufacturers,* in 1906. This work was used by a generation of textile industrialists as a veritable how-to guide in the design, construction, outfitting, and operation of textile mills.

Cramer's ingenuity and industry were rewarded with considerable wealth. He actively invested in various textile mills and sometimes accepted shares in fledgling textile firms as partial payment for his goods and services. In the first decade of the century he became heavily involved with the Mays Mills in Gaston County. The mills were founded by J. H. Mays and L. A. Dodsworth, who constructed a spinning mill on the banks of the South Fork River in 1906. Cramer was an original director and founder of the firm, but did not become actively involved in the management of the mill until he became president of the company in 1910. In 1915, Cramer acquired a controlling interest in the corporation. Cramer changed the name of the company to the Cramerton Mills in 1922. Cramer was president and treasurer of this company until 1938 and was chairman of the board until his death in 1940. During this time frame, the mill underwent rapid and continuous expansion; its production increased from 5,000 spindles to 58,500 spindles.

Cramer designed and built a mill village to house workers in his mills. Since the opening of the original mills in 1907, the town had gone through a series of names, including Maysworth, Maysville, Mays' Worth, and Mayville. Cramer renamed the village Cramerton around 1915, a name that it has borne ever since. Designed by a professional landscaper, the village had paved streets, schools, churches, recreation centers, and even a golf course, and it was considered the model mill village of its time. Cramerton's streets were lined with neat cottages that featured indoor plumbing, kerosene-fueled water heaters, vegetable gardens, and flower beds. In 1911, Cramerton had a modest population of five hundred, but the town swelled to 4,325 by 1940. The mill owned all the houses and charged the workers a nominal twenty-five cents per room for electricity, water, and sewer service.

From its lofty perch atop Cramer Mountain, Maymont dominated the landscape. Cramer built the residence in 1917, at an estimated cost of fifty thousand dollars. Its design was inspired by manor homes that the Cramers had observed and admired during trips to England. In addition to its thirty-eight rooms, Maymont boasted eight stone fireplaces and a mammoth swimming pool that also served as a reserve water supply for the Cramerton fire department. The Cramers decorated the home with Oriental carpets and antiques collected on their frequent and extravagant vacations. Tiffany and Company of New York performed much of the interior decorating work in lavish art nouveau.

To help provision his village, Cramer established a farm in Cramerton called Mayfarm, which produced apples, pears, peaches, plums, nectarines, cherries, figs, grapes, pecans, and filberts. He also raised Leghorn hens, Hereford beef cattle, prize-winning Holstein dairy cattle, and other livestock at Mayfarm. Milk, fruits, and other goods grown or produced at Mayfarm were sold at bargain prices in Cramerton stores and, for many years, Cramer furnished families of five or more with free milk.

In some academic circles, it was unfashionable to bestow even an ounce of credit to the textile barons who established mill towns like Cramerton. For decades, their activities and accomplishments were decried as acts of blatant paternalism, motivated not by altruism, but a misguided sense of noblesse oblige. Clearly, there was an undeniable strain of paternalism in Cramer's business philosophy. But Cramer did much more than other mill owners of his era to ease the difficult lives of his workers. In addition to housing workers in attractive, well-maintained homes at nominal cost, Cramer also was known for paying the highest wages in the business. During the Depression, Cramer implemented what he called a "share the work" program. Instead of laying off workers, Cramer divided the work evenly among his existing operatives to ensure that each family had enough income to survive. It has been widely noted that no family in Cramerton was forced to accept government relief during the Depression. During the flu epidemic of 1918, Cramer personally paid for workers' prescriptions and used Mayfarm chickens to make large batches of chicken soup for those who had fallen ill.

Cramer resigned as president of the Cramerton Mills in 1938. Control of the corporation passed to his son, Major Stuart W. Cramer Jr. Cramer suffered a severe heart attack in October 1939 and never regained his health. He died on July 2, 1940, at his family's winter residence on East Morehead Street in Charlotte.

The mills did not outlive their founder for long; Burlington Industries purchased Cramerton Mills in 1946. In an open letter to the people of Cramerton dated July 1, 1946, Stuart W. Cramer Jr. thanked the people of the town for their years of loyalty and service, and then wistfully bid them farewell. With the stroke of a pen, the Cramer dynasty passed into history.

Stuart Cramer lived a full life. In addition to his professional activities, Cramer was deeply involved with the leading textile trade associations of his day. He was vice president of the Textile Institute; organized the American Cotton Manufacturers Association and served as its president from 1917 to 1918; and from 1920 to 1927 served as treasurer and director of the Textile Foundation. He was named a medalist for the National Association of Cotton Manufacturers in 1913.

Cramer also dedicated a significant portion of his time and energy to membership in government and civic bodies. During World War I, Cramer served as a member of the Production Engineering Committee of the Council of National Defense, the War Service Committee of the American Textile Industry, and the Advisory Tax Board of the Treasury Department. He was a member of the Cotton Textile Authority under the National Recovery Association, the Conference on Home Building and Home Ownership, the Committee on Continuity of Business and Employment, and the advisory committee to President Roosevelt's Organization on Unemployment Relief.

For many years, Cramer was one of the leading members of the North Carolina Republican Party. He was a presidential elector from North Carolina, a delegate to the Republican National Conventions in 1928 and 1932, and served on the convention committee that notified Herbert Hoover of his nomination for the presidency. More than sixty years after his death, some Cramerton residents still referred to him as "Mr. Cramer." Some even claimed an old man resembling him was seen occasionally at night walking near the old Southern Railway underpass, or along the banks of the South Fork River.

There was no denying Cramer's continuing influence over the town. In 1969, the village of Cramerton constructed a stone monument at the corner of Eighth Avenue and Center Street in the center of town. It bears the following inscription: "Erected in honor of Stuart W. Cramer, whose wisdom and generosity contributed greatly to the lives of the people who lived in Cramerton from 1920 to 1969." For all that Stuart Cramer accomplished in material terms, wisdom and generosity provide, perhaps, his most fitting epitaph.

Mark McGrath is a Durham attorney and freelance writer. A graduate of the University of Rochester, he received his

*master's degree at UNC-Chapel Hill where he studied under
historians William Leuchtenberg and John Kasson. After
graduating from the UNC School of Law in 1991, he practiced law in New York and then moved to North Carolina.*

For more information, see:

Andrews, Mildred Gwin. *The Men and the Mills: A
History of the Southern Textile Industry.* Mercer University Press, 1987.

Cramerton, North Carolina. Cramerton Mills, 1925.

Gaston Chamber Community Publications, 1994.

Gaston County Historical Society. "Cramerton Featured at May, 1974 Meeting."

Glass, Brent D. *The Textile Industry in North Carolina:
A History.* North Carolina Office of Archives and
History, 1992.

Hobbs, S. H., Jr. *Gaston County: Economic and Social.*
Edwards & Broughton, 1920.

Separk, James H., ed. *Gastonia and Gaston County:
Past, Present, and Future.* Gastonia Commercial
Club, 1936.

Van Pelt, Autrey. *Cramerton, North Carolina: The Best
Place I Ever Did Live.* Custom Marketing and
Printing, 1997.

Young, Marjorie W., ed. *Textile Leaders of the New
South.* R. L. Bryan Company, 1963.

ROMEO GUEST

By Jim Schlosser

EARING BIGGER NAMES might overshadow his own, Romeo Guest devoted his final years to staking his claim in North Carolina's history. The architectural engineer from Greensboro, who died in 1987 at age eighty-one, interviewed and wrote old colleagues to jog their memories about events of thirty to forty years earlier, and dug through old files and storage rooms for his own letters and daily diaries to document his role in conceiving and even naming perhaps North Carolina's greatest economic twentieth-century success story, the Research Triangle Park.

At the close of the century, 43,000 people worked for 136 research-oriented companies in the park, which covered 6,800 acres between Chapel Hill, Durham, and Raleigh. The park kindled the economic and population growth of a region that assumed the name of "The Triangle" and became known worldwide.

Guest was as diligent in backtracking his activities during the 1950s as he had been during that period pursuing the concept of establishing a corporate park dedicated to research, where researchers in private, for-profit companies would work with their academic counterparts at nearby Duke University, North Carolina State College in Raleigh, and the University of North Carolina at Chapel Hill. He believed the result would be new products, which would thereby create a need for new manufacturing plants. In turn, this would mean new business for his contracting company, which was erecting manufacturing and research buildings throughout the South. A similar idea of combining the talent of the region had been advanced earlier by Howard W. Odum, the UNC sociologist.

Guest's contribution to the park's beginnings received ample attention in a booklet written in 1967 by Louis Round Wilson, the venerated historian at UNC. But as Guest grew older and saw others receiving credit for the park's success, he worried his role might be reduced to a footnote when a definitive history was written.

After helping to buy most of the land for the park, Guest had reluctantly resigned from the Research Triangle Foundation's board in October 1959. According to Walter Harper, a state economic development official during that period and later president of Guest's industrial contracting company in Greens-

Romeo Guest (Courtesy of Charlotte Observer)

boro, Guest was frozen out because of the concern that he and his company would profit from what by then had become a not-for-profit operation.

Several fellow board members said Guest could not continue to serve on the foundation's board because he would be exposed to confidential information about companies considering a possible location in the park. That would give Guest an unfair advantage over competitors, they said. The move rankled his friends. "They showed him no respect," Harper said some years later. "They treated him awful."

Harper said that at one meeting, UNC official Billy Carmichael cracked up the room when he said, "Let me see, Romeo, if I really know what it is we are talking about here. You want the professors here and all of us to be the prostitutes and you're going to be the pimp." Guest laughed, but afterward told Harper he was unsure of Carmichael's meaning. Harper says Guest failed to understand academic people, even though he had studied among the best as a student in the 1920s at the Massachusetts Institute of Technology.

But Harper believed that Guest, after devoting nearly ten years to establishing the park, had become motivated by the long-range benefits to the state rather than to his company. "I would be hard pressed to say he didn't want business, but the park became a religion with him," said Harper, who worked for the state Department of Conservation and Development and was on the staff of N.C. State during the years the Park was being organized.

Harper and others who knew Guest could understand why his motives were questioned. The dapper, urbane contractor was obsessed with promoting Romeo Guest and Associates, the construction company his father had founded as C. M. Guest Company in 1893 in Anderson, S.C. In the 1940s and 1950s, Guest often appeared in Raleigh to chat with state officials who were pursuing new industry for the state. Guest hoped to learn about companies that might soon need his services.

Guest's idea for a research park dated to the 1920s when he was studying architectural engineering at MIT. He noticed companies locating research operations along Route 128 around Boston that wanted to be near MIT, Harvard, and other research institutions in the area. Guest's interest in teaming academic researchers with those in the private sector increased in 1939, when his company built a research plant for pharmaceutical maker Merck and Company in Elkton, Va., because the company wanted to be near the University of Virginia. Guest saw the obvious potential for the area between North Carolina's three major universities. He drew lines on a map, connecting Chapel Hill, Durham, and Raleigh. The result was a triangle.

Although one historian found people who said Guest used the phrase Research Triangle as early as 1952, Guest himself established the official date as October 10, 1953, when he wrote the name on his office calendar next to a planned meeting with executives at Celanese Corporation. Guest hoped to persuade Celanese to build between Raleigh, Durham, and Chapel Hill. Celanese wound up picking Charlotte.

Guest used the phrase often after that in letters and meetings with business leaders, such as Robert Hanes, president of Wachovia Bank and Trust Company, and state Treasurer Brandon Hodges, who urged Guest to take the concept to Governor Luther Hodges. Guest did just that on December 31, 1954, according to the governor's appointment calendar.

The day before he met with Hodges, Guest sent a letter to William Saunders, the director of the state Board of Conservation and Development, explaining why he felt so strongly that the land be set aside for research facilities. He saw the park as an incubator for creating badly needed new industry that would reduce North Carolina's dependence on tobacco and textiles. "The reason it is necessary to hatch our own industries at home is that the pace of migration of industries from other areas to the South has greatly slowed down and is about complete," he wrote to Saunders. "We should like you to join with us in the future development of the project." William Newell, then a textile research expert at N.C. State and a friend of Guest, is believed to have added the word "park" to Research Triangle.

In 1954, Guest employed Bennett Advertising Company in High Point to prepare the first brochure for the Research Triangle Park. In it and other promotional items, Guest asked interested parties to write or call his company in Greensboro. Such promotion of his services made academics and politicians suspicious of Guest's motives. As it turned out, Guest never erected a single building in the park.

Many of North Carolina's big contractors during the 1950s, such as H. L. Coble of Greensboro—who built the giant Lorillard Tobacco complex in Greensboro—and Nello Teer of Durham, started as common construction laborers. But Guest, who was born on August 4, 1887, had a company waiting for him in Anderson, after his parents sent him to the exclusive Phillips Exeter Academy in New Hampshire and to MIT, where he graduated in 1929.

Many boys would have been mortified if their parents had christened them "Romeo." Guest's mother was said to have favored the name because she thought it romantic. Guest seemed to embrace the name. Once he became owner of C. M. Guest and Sons, he kept his father in the title for a while, but subsequently changed the name to Romeo Guest and Associates. Guest opened a branch of his father's company in Greensboro in the mid-1930s.

Guest was a short, studious-looking man who favored tailored suits and spoke with an accent that sounded almost English. He would greet folks with a vigorous, "Hello! I'm RO-me-O Guest," stressing the first and last syllables. Those who were close to him say he was a man with expensive tastes and believed image was good for business. He rented space in Greensboro's most exclusive location of that time, the seventeen-story Jefferson Standard Life Insurance Company Building, which had been the tallest structure in the South for awhile after opening in 1923.

Guest soon built a spacious two-story, colonial-style home in Greensboro's best neighborhood, Irving Park, across from the seventh green of the Greensboro Country Club. The house faced Nottingham Drive, a lovely street, but one not quite as prestigious as Sunset Drive, which ran beside the house and was the future address of insurance executive Joseph Bryan and members of the Richardson family, creator of Vick's cough drops. Guest always drove a black Cadillac, keeping a car for years but maintaining it so it gleamed like new. To outfit his home and office, he picked Otto Zenke, a Greensboro interior designer with studios in Palm Beach and London.

Guest pioneered a business concept best described as one-stop shopping for clients who wanted new buildings and were undecided about where to build them. Guest and his colleagues would gather demographics and data about potential locations. They determined average income, quality of schools and recreation, tax rates, wage scale, labor supply, and union activity. If the findings suited a client, Guest would find land, buy it, build the plant, and even install equipment and furniture.

Guest insisted on negotiating contracts for his services rather than submitting bids for work. He believed bids were a waste of time and money, particularly if his bid was not successful. Even if he won a bid, problems might arise after work began, sending costs higher than anticipated. His method apparently worked. Romeo Guest and Associates stayed busy and ranged far, living up to its motto, "Construction in the South."

"He worked all the time at business," said Phyllis S. Case, who was Guest's executive secretary from 1947 to 1964. "He didn't like the social life. He liked the business life."

Guest had a calm demeanor. When business disagreements arose or when he felt insulted, as when he had to leave the park foundation's board, he reacted, but not with a show of anger. "If someone did him wrong, he acted like they were dead," Harper said. "He never spoke of him again." After banker Archie Davis of Winston-Salem, a leading figure in development of the park and head of Wachovia Bank, informed Guest that his services were no longer needed, Guest responded by closing his company and personal accounts at Davis's bank and never mentioning his name again.

Harper describes Guest as a man of many paradoxes. He watched company expenses closely and was slow to invest in new equipment, but he was quick to grab the check at fancy restaurants and spent company money lavishly on himself. Harper, who became

president of Romeo Guest and Associates in 1967, with Guest moving up to chairman, said he became upset when Guest hired Zenke to decorate the offices and when he continued to bill private club expenses to the business. As a former state employee, Harper had never had fancy office furnishings or perks such as a club membership, and didn't think either was essential for business.

In 1973, after forty-four years in the construction business, Guest approached brothers Dillard and Nello Teer Jr. to ask that Nello Teer and Company take over his business. He still had plenty of work, but Dillard Teer said Guest had ventured from what he knew best: constructing buildings for a negotiated price. He had won a bid for a sewage treatment plant for a city and the job was out of Guest's range of expertise. All that Guest feared about bid work came true. Problems drove costs out of sight; Teer said it nearly broke Guest's company.

Attracted by the value of Guest's well-known name and the value of his relatively new office and warehouse on booming Battleground Avenue, as well as one hundred acres of land owned by Guest in Moore County, the Teer brothers assumed the debts of Guest and Associates and took ownership of the Greensboro and Moore County property. They paid Guest a consultant's salary for a period of years, although Guest was not required to work.

In retirement, Guest set out to make sure historians knew of his role in the park's early days. In later years, Hodges had emerged as the reputed father of the park but Guest and others knew that Hodges hadn't initially embraced the idea when it was first presented in 1954, although he soon warmed to it. Guest never denied that Hodges's support was essential to success. One historian quoted Guest as saying, "I fail to understand why the midwife [Hodges] takes all the credit for this project and the daddy [Guest] is still alive." Hodges himself acknowledged Guest's role in a letter dated December 6, 1956, in which he wrote: "I just want to say that I have seen a new bulletin out on the Research Triangle, and we have not forgotten that it was your idea. We do appreciate all the work you put into it."

"Romeo was the captain," the governor wrote. "The park was his idea."

But Harper said others deserved credit for fleshing out the concept and making sure the right people bought into the idea. He mentioned state Treasurer Brandon Hodges, Sandy Campbell, a dean at N.C. State, and textile researcher William A. Newell. William Saunders also was vital.

After Nello Teer Company moved Romeo Guest

and Associates to Durham in 1984, Guest's company was sold twice and was nearly broke when long-time employee Jim Robbins bought it in 1990 and restored the name to its original out of respect to Romeo Guest. (The previous owner had shortened the name to Guest and Associates.) Under Robbins the company regained its position in business and returned to Romeo Guest's guiding principles of negotiated work and quality construction done in a timely manner.

In 1983, his research completed at last, Guest gathered the twenty cubic feet of records and hauled them to Durham and donated his papers to Duke University. At the turn of the century, plans were under way to erect a Wall of Fame in a small setting within Research Triangle Park to honor those who contributed to the park's founding and success. Guest's name was slated to be included on the wall. In fact, his name was

there during construction. The contractor's sign out front said: "Romeo Guest and Associates."

Jim Schlosser is a senior reporter for the News and Record *in Greensboro.*

For more information, see:

Guest, Romeo. Papers. Special Collections, Perkins Library, Duke University, Durham.

Hodges, Luther. *Businessman in the State House*. University of North Carolina Press, 1962.
Ivey, A. G. *Luther H. Hodges: Practical Idealist*. T. S. Denison and Company, 1968.
Link, Albert N. *A Generosity of Spirit: The Early History of the Research Triangle Park*. Research Triangle Foundation of North Carolina, 1995.

THE LEE FAMILY

By Alex Coffin

WILLIAM STATES "BILL" LEE III was used to reaching the top of things, whether it was climbing the Matterhorn as a nineteen-year-old, or as head of Duke Power Company in the 1980s. And there were other heights along the way—such as helping pull the nation back from what was feared to be a nuclear abyss after the first domestic nuclear disaster. Lee came from a family of leaders, but the highly energetic, stocky engineer with bushy eyebrows was clearly the highest achiever.

"Friendly fierce" is how he described himself. He had little pretense—or patience. He was insatiably curious and had charismatic enthusiasm, a lively sense of humor, and a puckish smile. He disliked wordiness and false pride. He was as comfortable talking with Duke Power linemen as he was conferring with Russian nuclear experts. Once when he was escorting some Russian scientists through the Charlotte airport, he was asked by one how he prayed, and he stopped to demonstrate. On another occasion, a Russian guest remarked, "I sure like the way you talk to God," after Lee had said the blessing over a meal.

He was a warrior for better race relations and once threatened to resign from the Charlotte and Quail Hollow country clubs if their memberships were not opened to minorities.

Few knew that he once crewed on Princeton scholar Albert Einstein's sailboat on Lake Carnegie, met T. S. Eliot while attending a weekly tutorial at a professor's home at Princeton, and took a physics class there from Robert Oppenheimer. During the summer of 1949, his Princeton rowing crew won the national title for 150-pounders and was invited to compete for the Henly Cup in Oxford, England. They won again. It was on a side trip that he climbed the Matterhorn.

In 1905, his grandfather, William States Lee, an engineer with experience in dam construction in South Carolina and Georgia, and Dr. W. Gill Wylie, a strong advocate of the future of electric power, combined their operational talents with James B. Duke in founding the Southern Power Company, which nineteen years later became Duke Power. Flush with his millions from the American Tobacco Company, Duke supplied the cash. Duke had sought out Lee and had previously met Wylie, who had treated him for a sore foot. Duke was familiar with hydroelectric power,

William States Lee III (Courtesy of Charlotte Observer)

having developed some hydro generation in the eastern part of the state.

Lee was educated at the South Carolina Military Academy, later The Citadel, in Charleston in 1893–94. He was so combative that he was once reduced in rank from captain to private after he and a rival captain got into a fistfight in the quadrangle. His class standing was twelfth, but his conduct grade was 5.65 out of a possible 21.25.

He graduated with a degree in civil engineering in the spring of 1894. After graduation, Lee did engineering work for the U.S. government at a project near Anderson, S.C. He was working on hydro projects for the Columbus Power Company in Georgia when Wylie hired him in 1903 to complete a Catawba River project, eighteen miles south of Charlotte.

In 1904, Wylie began discussions with Duke on financing an expansion of Wylie's Catawba Power Company to include several interconnected power plants.

Duke bought into the idea on the basis of Lee's engineering, and the Southern Power Company was formed, with Wylie as president and Lee as vice president and chief engineer. Duke was a director and took over as president when Wylie retired in 1910.

Hydroelectric power and the textile industry were a dream match. Duke's purpose had been to move textile manufacturing from Massachusetts to the South. By 1911, Southern Power was serving three-fourths of the South's cotton mills, and by 1928, the piedmont Carolinas led the nation in textile manufacturing.

In 1900, forty-five textile mills operated in Gaston and Mecklenburg counties. None used electricity. In 1920, ninety-two mills were in operation in these counties and all but seven were using electricity.

Between 1906 and 1928, Southern-Duke's electricity sales increased from 25 million kilowatt hours to 1.8 billion, and operating capacity increased from 6,600 kilowatts to 645,000 kilowatts.

Later, as chief engineer at Duke Power, Lee went on to design and build thirty-two hydroelectric stations and seven steam stations for the company. He was credited with being the first engineer to demonstrate the feasibility of transmitting power over wire for long distances.

This stimulated the growth and spread of factories and fueled the rapid industrialization of the state. Factories could be built anywhere at a distance from the stream banks rather than having to be tied close to the water. The source of much of the power was the Catawba River, which Lee's engineering transformed into a series of stair-step hydroelectric plants 238 miles long. Along with the dams came eleven lakes, which were used for recreation and flood control. The acres of shoreline along the lakes would provide recreation for another generation and flood control for the present. Lee believed that people could control the river, if it was done properly.

He became the first southerner elected president of the American Institute of Electrical Engineers.

Lee Sr., who died in 1934, and his wife, Mary Martin of Columbus, Ga., left three children and five grandchildren—including the man who would follow him with distinction at Duke Power.

The grandson who took over at Duke Power in 1978, William States III, was born on June 23, 1929, in Charlotte, where the Lee family was already prominent. In addition to his successful grandfather, his father was a Princeton-educated engineer who worked for a family engineering and construction company.

The third generation William States Lee attended Woodberry Forest preparatory school in Virginia, where his nickname became "BB Eyes," and then Princeton. He graduated in 1951 magna cum laude in civil engineering as a member of Phi Beta Kappa.

After graduation, Lee took a job with Bethlehem Steel in Pennsylvania, where he married Jan Rumberger (they had two daughters and a son), and subsequently volunteered in the navy's Civil Engineer Corps, better known as the Seabees. As part of his assignments, he was responsible for designing and building recruiting stations in sixty cities in the western United States.

Lee decided to return to Charlotte in 1955 because he wanted to work under the supervision of Duke Vice President David Nabow, one of the nation's top engineers. Lee had no plans to make a career at Duke when he arrived, but his talent was soon recognized and he moved from head of design engineering to head of design and construction and eventually became president in 1978 and chairman in 1982.

Lee took command at Duke at a time when the company was under intense public scrutiny and under criticism from many quarters as it embarked on an aggressive nuclear building program. He often said he didn't care what the company used to make electricity—water, coal, uranium, or buffalo chips—the "fuel of choice" only had to be available, affordable, and environmentally sound. In his mind, nuclear was better than other alternatives. He understood the technology and knew it would work.

Lee supported and encouraged the development of nuclear energy because he believed that without the use of nuclear fuels, the nation and the world would be unable to meet the energy needs of a growing population. But he never lost the context, often saying (if quietly) that if experience raised questions about the use of nuclear fuels, then he would rethink that commitment. He built a waterside retreat close to Duke Power's McGuire Nuclear Station on Lake Norman near Charlotte. He stayed there often and used the house to make a statement that if McGuire were the scene of an accident, he would be among those affected.

With Lee setting the tone and pace, Duke's nuclear program became one of the nation's most successful, which led to Duke taking a leadership role in the industry. Under Lee's leadership, the company built and operated seven nuclear units at three sites (Oconee, three units, built in 1973 and 1974; McGuire, two units, built in 1981 and 1983; and Catawba, two units, built in 1985 and 1986). In part because of that leadership, and in part because of the similarities in reactor design at Duke's Oconee units, Lee and Duke Power were called on to assist with the recovery efforts after the 1979 Three Mile Island accident in Pennsylvania.

It was then Lee's initiative that led to the formation of the Institute of Nuclear Power Operators.

Partly as a result of the 1973–81 "energy crisis," the yearly growth in the use of electricity slowed to 2 to 3 percent from highs of 7 to 10 percent through the 1960s and early 1970s. As a result of the slower growth, Duke Power cancelled two other nuclear stations (Perkins and Cherokee) in the early 1980s.

Lee was extremely likable and represented Duke with a different personality from that of his predecessors. Even longtime antinuclear-power activist Jesse Riley in Charlotte noted Lee's easy manner. Lee often greeted Riley by saying, "Hello, worthy opponent."

Lee was a master communicator. Once while trying to explain to a reporter what it was like to work in a Duke Power coal mine, Lee asked the reporter to crawl under the table with him to make the point that the workers had to stay in an uncomfortable crouch for long periods of time.

Lee received the nation's Outstanding Engineer Award from the National Society of Professional Engineers in 1980 for "outstanding contributions to public welfare and to the advancement of the profession." Specifically, in the aftermath of the Three Mile Island accident, Lee headed the cleanup operations and subsequently served on the Three Mile Island Oversight Committee.

After the Chernobyl nuclear power plant disaster in the Ukraine in 1986, Lee was called in as a consultant to the Soviet Union. He then helped organize the World Association of Nuclear Operators and headed the organization from 1989 to 1991.

Investments Decisions magazine credited Lee's leadership when it selected Duke Power as the nation's "best-managed" electric utility in 1985. *Financial World* magazine named him Utility Chief Executive Officer in 1989.

"It was obvious that the Three Mile Island accident occurred because of the performance of the people," Lee recalled. "So we had to address that head-on and we realized we couldn't simply sit back and let the government do it because you can't create a positive impact on the performance of people through punitive measures."

Despite his busy schedule, Lee still found time to tutor elementary students in the Charlotte-Mecklenburg schools for many years. He also was a leader in establishing more day-care facilities for the children of workers in uptown Charlotte, and he led the drive to raise $22 million to build the Blumenthal North Carolina Performing Arts Center in uptown Charlotte.

During his six-year stint as chairman of the Queens College board of trustees in Charlotte, Lee stopped by President Billy Wireman's office most Mondays to discuss any upcoming issues. Wireman recalled that at their first meeting he had a long agenda, but after he spent twenty minutes on the first item, Lee smiled, put his hand on Wireman's shoulder, and said, "I have a staff meeting in eight minutes. Get better organized and I'll see you next Monday."

Yet he could be a good listener and had great insight. "When I was young, I designed a bridge," he once said. "You don't have to design bridges. You can go into another line of work. But if that's what you do, you don't want it to be your bridge that falls. So you do the very best job that human beings with good materials and good management systems know how to do to make it safe. Then you accept responsibility for what you have done."

When Lee retired in 1994, he said he would like to be remembered as "a person who helped others achieve more than they could have without me." In retirement, he was suggested as a Republican candidate for governor, but never came close to running.

At the time of his death on July 10, 1996, accolades were plentiful. Governor James B. Hunt said, "I never met a man with more zest and energy than Bill Lee. He was one of the true giants of North Carolina. He lived his life to the fullest—whether it was building his company, building his community or building his state's economy."

Alex Coffin worked at newspapers in Charlotte, Atlanta, and Vancouver, British Columbia. He was a staff member for U.S. Representative Charles R. Jonas in Washington, D.C., and for Duke Power Company in Charlotte, before opening his own public relations firm in Charlotte in 1985.

For more information, see:

Chapman, Dan. "Bill Lee, Duke Power's Visionary Leader, Gets Ready to Say Farewell." *Charlotte Observer*, April 24, 1994.

Gaillard, Frye, and Dot Jackson. *The Catawba River*. Gardner-Webb Press, 1983.

Lefler, Hugh Talmage, and Albert Ray Newsome. *North Carolina: The History of a Southern State*. University of North Carolina Press, 1973.

Maynor, Joe. *Duke Power: The First 75 Years*. Delmar Publishing, 1979.

Perlmutt, David, and Pamela L. Moore. "Bill Lee, His Vision Guided a City, an Industry." *Charlotte Observer*, July 11, 1996.

Wildman, John. "Life Has Held More Peaks Than Valleys for Bill Lee." *Charlotte Observer*, April 9, 1982.

JAMES ADDISON JONES

By Ken Sanford

THE JOURNEY TO THE TOP of the Petronas Towers, the world's tallest buildings, in Kuala Lumpur, Malaysia, began in 1886 with the footsteps of a poor and meagerly educated seventeen-year-old North Carolina farm boy, James Addison Jones. The story about the young man walking more than seventy miles from near Asheboro to Charlotte to take a job in construction has taken on some aspects of legend, but there is no doubt that he left home at an early age to find employment as a construction worker in the burgeoning Carolina textile industry.

That teenager quickly became a skilled brick mason who worked his way up to found a construction company that operated in three centuries and built some of the world's largest and most complex buildings around the globe, including some of the Manhattan Project's Oak Ridge complex in Tennessee, which produced atomic bombs that led to the end of World War II. Following the war, the company prospered, became one of the nation's largest, and went on to complete in 1996 those twin buildings across the world in Malaysia.

Jones was born August 20, 1869, in Farmer, just outside Asheboro, to parents trying to recover from the impact of the Civil War. According to his son, Edwin L. Jones Sr., his father's education was "a few short years in a one-room schoolhouse. Yet, in later years, his detailed estimates of involved construction projects were models of accuracy, completeness and brevity. He was surely self educated to the nth degree."

Recruited to help build early textile mills in Charlotte for wages of twenty-five cents a day, plus room and board in construction camps, Jones initially helped make the brick that, along with the lumber, was produced on the building site. Within two years he was known as the most skilled and fastest mason on the site. He was promoted to foreman and then superintendent; with confidence gained on the job, he started contracting for the masonry work, setting an example for his men with his own hard work.

He became a general contractor about 1890, the year in which his company later marked its origin. That same year, Jones married Mary Jane (Minnie) Hooper, who bore twelve children before her death in 1914.

An early contract was almost the end of the business. Jones had won a bid to build an addition to the Southern Railway Station and the project was almost

James Addison Jones (Courtesy of Charlotte Observer)

complete when a cloudburst undermined the foundation and the walls. Jones went to work himself with his four-man crew to repair the damage. His reputation for reliability thus gained was an asset as he garnered other contracts, at first with Southern Railroad and then on his own again. Working from an office in a curtained area of his home in Fourth Ward, Jones began to win contracts for Charlotte's major buildings of the day.

But times were tough, and the future was uncertain. Jones was out of work when he bid on building Alexander Graham Junior High and he prayed fervently that he would get the school bid so that he could remain in business. When he received word that he had won, he cried tears of gratitude.

Jones's son Edwin was his father's first full-time employee. He was hired in January of 1913 at fifty dollars per month to do bookkeeping, estimating, and some job supervision. In 1916, Raymond, the next son, completed his studies in engineering at Georgia Tech and became assistant superintendent of the company. After completing business courses, a third son, Johnnie, took over accounting and detailed office work, freeing Edwin for finance, estimating, selling, and purchasing.

The firm was first incorporated in 1920 as J.A. Jones Construction Company with three stockholders: J. A. Jones, president and principal stockholder; Raymond A. Jones, vice president; and Edwin L. Jones Sr., secretary-treasurer. The company's capital was fifty thousand dollars. Edwin said the sons had to borrow to purchase their shares.

Charlotte enjoyed a resurgence after World War I and the Jones firm built the Cole Manufacturing Company plant, the first reinforced concrete structure in the area. The company also erected the Carolinas' first skyscraper, the twelve-story Independence Building. Other major projects in Charlotte included the Hoskins textile mill, the Selwyn Hotel, Efird's, Belk and Ivey's department stores, the YMCA, and First Presbyterian Church. In the area, the company was responsible for building First National Bank of Thomasville, the conversion of the Carnegie Library into Hill Hall on the campus of the University of North Carolina at Chapel Hill, and the Winthrop College Training School in Rock Hill, S.C.

Edwin Jones said that his father "founded a growing business rooted in honest dealing and integrity of word and deed. Many early contracts, he said, were verbal, a handshake, or a one-page letter."

In the early days of the Depression, Jones's firm was saved by government work. The company landed a contract to build an entire new military air base at the Canal Zone—Albrook Field. Edwin went to Panama for three years to supervise the work. This project allowed the company to increase its capital and gave it valuable training in offshore mobilization and operations in unfamiliar surroundings. It also required the company to build a large, loyal, hard-hitting, trained supervisory staff.

When President Franklin D. Roosevelt set in motion his programs to get the economy moving again, the Jones firm was in a good position to handle the building of housing, post offices, military bases, and other projects. The firm was awarded the contract for the first large-scale public housing project—Techwood in Atlanta—followed by others in Virginia, North and South Carolina, Florida, Alabama, Louisiana, Tennessee, and Kentucky.

It is no exaggeration to say that J. A. Jones and the company he founded helped win World War II. Aside from the Oak Ridge facilities, the company expanded military camps at Fort Jackson in South Carolina and Fort Rucker in Alabama, as well as at a dozen other base hospitals, supply depots, and air bases. One of the most significant contributions was building and operating shipyards at Panama City, Florida, and Brunswick, Georgia. The Panama City facility was up and operating first, and a friendly but fierce competition developed between the two shipyards. Their chief production was Liberty Ships.

Lieutenant General Leslie R. Groves, the head of the secret Manhattan Project, which was commissioned to build an atomic bomb, had observed the Jones firm's work at military bases and, according to Edwin Jones, "personally selected us because, as he said at the time, he had confidence in our ability and integrity." Oak Ridge became a half-billion dollar project and, at that time, was the largest construction project in the history of the world. One of the buildings was almost a mile long, six stories high, and filled with hundreds of miles of specialized wiring and piping, along with thousands of high-speed motors.

A historian in the development of the atomic bomb wrote, "Edwin L. Jones, a tall, erect man of fifty-two, had never touched liquor in his life, never smoked and never missed a Sunday service at the Methodist Church in Charlotte. There was an air of great sobriety about him—in his disciplined way of speaking, in his conservative dark suit, in the friendly but serious eyes behind the rimless glasses. . . . He firmly believed in hard work, temperance and living according to Holy Writ." Obviously he was a good fit for such a critical job.

A restructuring of the firm took place in 1943 when J. A. Jones became chairman of the board; Edwin L. Jones became president; Raymond Jones became executive vice president; J. P. Caldwell, E. J. Kratt, and H. V. Appen were made vice presidents; and John S. Stafford became treasurer. Later two younger brothers were given positions: Paul as secretary and Robert as vice president in charge of purchasing.

The company ventured into two new areas of work in 1946—heavy construction and highway work with projects such as the Cumberland River Dam in Kentucky and the Pan American Highway in Ecuador.

After World War II, the company continued to be an important player in defense contracts, building missile bases, the rocket-launching facilities at Cape Canaveral, missile-tracking stations, distant early-warning systems, and atomic energy plants. In 1954, Jones purchased Rea Construction Company of Charlotte, which specialized in complex road and highway construction projects. Another large acquisition was that of Charles H. Tompkins Company. The company built all kinds of projects, ranging from textile and tobacco plants to chemical, paper and pulp, woodworking, food processing, and electronics facilities.

Edwin Jones described the decade after the end of World War II as the greatest period of growth but also a period of great loss. His father died after sixty years of continuous business, civic, and church activities on May 25, 1950, just two weeks after the death of his son, Raymond. J. A. Jones was eighty years of age and had come to work every day until his death, assigning himself in his final years the task of opening the company mail.

The giant West German construction company, Philipp Holzmann AG, bought J. A. Jones Construction Company in 1978 but left it as a free-standing subsidiary. When Holzmann fell upon hard financial times in the late 1990s, the spirit of J. A. Jones was still apparent in the company he founded, as it remained a financially sound component of the global conglomerate.

Jones's company remained under family direction —by his sons and grandsons—for 103 years until May 1993, when Charles Davidson, a twenty-nine-year veteran of the firm, was named president and chief executive officer. During the intervening years, the presidency had been passed from J. A. Jones to Edwin L. Jones, to Edwin L. Jones Jr., then to Johnnie Jones, a first cousin of Edwin Jones Jr. In addition to those in top leadership, a number of other Jones family members played key roles in the firm over the years.

In 1990, the company's one-hundredth anniversary, it had surpassed the $1 billion mark in revenue and continued to build major projects in exotic places around the world, such as a radio relay station in Breich, Morocco; a U.S. embassy building in El Salvador; and the 450-foot-high Der bendi Dam on the Diyala River in Iraq.

Ken Sanford is a native North Carolinian who graduated from the University of North Carolina at Chapel Hill and worked on newspapers in the state before becoming the University of North Carolina at Charlotte's first director of public information. He is the author of Charlotte and UNC Charlotte: Growing Up Together, *published in 1996.*

For more information, see:

"J. A. Jones Company Annual Report 2000." J. A. Jones Company.

"J. A. Jones Company History—Milestones." http://www.jajones.com/History/ Milestones.htm.

Jones, Edwin L., Sr. "J. A. Jones Construction Company: 75 Years of Growth in Construction." Address to the Newcomen Society, March 30, 1965.

Smith, Beth Laney. *Jones Construction Centennial: Looking Back, Moving Forward.* Laney-Smith, 1989.

A. G. ODELL JR.

By Ken Sanford

GREAT ARCHITECTS leave behind their own monuments in the buildings they design. Called great by many of his peers, North Carolina architect Arthur Gould "Gouldie" Odell Jr. cut a wide swath across the urban landscape of his native region, although his boldness and outspoken nature drew critics' barbs as well. Odell railed against the architectural ugliness that pervaded the region and challenged planners and civic leaders to demand the highest quality that could be afforded. He was quoted as saying, "Our cities are an aesthetic outrage. . . . on our most valuable property in Charlotte 50 per cent of the buildings are trash. This is what makes cities die."

After Odell's death, longtime Charlotte journalist Jack Claiborne wrote, "He not only changed the face of Charlotte, Raleigh and other North Carolina cities, but he also raised expectations of what a city ought to be." In Odell's obituary, he was called "the man who changed the face of downtown North Carolina."

Odell was born on November 22, 1913, to a textile family in Concord where his father, grandfather, and great-grandfather had been textile industrialists and educators. He graduated from Staunton Military Academy and began a civil engineering course at Duke University, where his grandfather, William, was a trustee. Odell studied architecture at Cornell University and graduated in 1934. Then he studied for a year at L'Ecole des Beaux Arts in Paris. Upon his return to the United States, he apprenticed for Harrison & Fouilhoux, architects of the Rockefeller Center. There he helped produce two futuristic buildings that became the Trylon and Perisphere for the 1939 World's Fair. Odell rounded out his early career working in New York for the architect Wallace K. Harrison and for industrial designer Raymond Loewy, known for such products as the Studebaker automobile and the Sears Coldspot refrigerator.

Following his grandfather's death, Odell returned to Concord, opened an office, and became the first licensed architect in Cabarrus County. However, he soon moved to Charlotte and began attracting attention for his creative designs. In a 1987 tribute to Odell, architect Benjamin T. Rook said the significance of Odell's contribution to southern architecture was creativity, rather than the imitation being practiced by other regional architects. Odell quickly won commissions for a grammar school in Concord, a building

A. G. Odell Jr. (Courtesy of Charlotte Observer)

for WBT radio in Charlotte, a gymnasium for Second Ward School in Charlotte, and Charlotte's Temple Beth El.

Odell was not a one-dimensional architect. He once said, "Architecture is 90 per cent business and 10 per cent art." He added that he preferred the art but understood the importance of the business side. In her book *Charlotte 23,* Mary Snead Boger wrote, "From his guardian angel Odell may have gotten his talent, but his textile industrialist forebears gifted him with business acumen."

William Hartsell, chairman of the board and chief financial officer of the architectural firm of Freeman White, recounted how Odell used his shrewd business skills to limit his competition's maneuvering room. Freeman White previously had borne the name of Walter Hook, a pioneer architect and son of Charles Hook, North Carolina's first architect. The company successfully used the cachet of the Hook name for marketing purposes.

But Odell urged the state architectural organization to adopt a new rule that a firm couldn't continue to use the name of a deceased principal. "When we had to change the name in 1968, my bosses were really upset," Hartsell said. He added that it was perhaps fortuitous that the requirement had been dropped by the time Odell died, thus allowing his company to continue to capitalize on his well-known name. "However," Hartsell said, "it is extremely difficult for a firm established by such a talented leader as Odell to maintain its image and to continue to benefit from that well-known name. It speaks well of him that his firm continues to prosper." Hartsell gave credit to the training Odell provided for his young practitioners. "And then if you look across the Carolinas I couldn't tell you how many firms are now headed by architects who trained under Odell," Hartsell said.

Rook took note of Odell's training program. "In the greater Charlotte area in the 1960s, where more than one-third of the architects of the state of North Carolina were located, 30 percent of the firms were spawned by Odell Associates, and 30 percent of the members of the Charlotte section of the American Institute of Architects were present or former employees of Odell Associates."

Hartsell described Odell as an aggressive marketer and a great advocate for those issues in which he believed, which didn't always make him popular. Hartsell said that even when he was a student in design school at North Carolina State College in 1959, he was advised by a contractor to get a summer job with Odell, because he was already recognized as a leader in the profession. That job didn't work out, but Hartsell remembered the Odell name and watched it continue to rise into national prominence as he continued his studies and then began to practice. "Until some other high-profile architects, like Harry Wolfe and the principals at Clark Tribble Harris and Lee came to town, Odell's name stood alone in the region," Hartsell said.

A breakthrough event for Odell came in 1950 when he received the commission to design a coliseum-auditorium for Charlotte. After crafting an innovative design, he sold his plans as a "one of a kind Coliseum, the world's largest structural steel dome, with a 338-foot cover as big as a city block in diameter." That design gained attention for Odell far beyond the borders of the Carolinas, including a feature in *Look* magazine.

Several Odell projects won national awards, including Double Oaks School in Charlotte, the first North Carolina school and the first African American school to receive such recognition. Later his design for Wilson Junior High in Charlotte received two major awards.

Odell's work covered a wide spectrum of enterprises. His Concordia Evangelical Lutheran Church in Conover won a national citation. The architect even designed private residences, including a Charlotte home for James G. Cannon that featured a magnolia tree rising through the middle of the house.

Another design that drew the attention of his colleagues was the Charlottetown Mall, the first enclosed, air-conditioned shopping mall in the Southeast. In a 1962 *News and Observer* poll, North Carolina architects selected five Odell designs as among their top eight favorite architectural works, including the Charlotte Public Library, the Charlotte Coliseum and Auditorium, and the St. Andrews Presbyterian College campus in Laurinburg.

Odell set in motion a continuing effort to renew and reshape Charlotte's center city with his 1966 Master Plan. It was criticized as being too ambitious, yet much of it came to pass—a new civic center, an office tower and hotel, pedestrian walkways, parking garages, other office towers, and uptown housing. Moreover, it laid the groundwork for later master plans that would dramatically change the face of the city.

The architect also prepared the original master plan for the University of North Carolina at Charlotte campus and left his imprint on its core, although the state of North Carolina was stingy with capital appropriations to the new university, leading to quite Spartan designs for the early buildings. Other architects would contribute to and refine the original campus plan, blending their new buildings with Odell's original complex.

Money, of course, was always a consideration. When he created the Hampton Roads Coliseum in Virginia with a roof that suggested the sails of boats on the nearby water, Odell was quoted as saying, "It's better looking than Charlotte's, but they had more money to spend."

Among other attention-getting Odell designs were the Blue Cross and Blue Shield headquarters in Chapel Hill, the R.J. Reynolds Whitaker Park manufacturing facility in Winston-Salem, the Burlington Industries headquarters in Greensboro, the Raleigh Civic Center, the Baltimore Civic Center, and the Virginia Beach, Va., Pavilion.

As the award-winning buildings took shape, so did Odell's reputation within North Carolina and the nation. He served as president of the North Carolina Chapter of the American Institute of Architects, and was elected a fellow in 1958. In 1964, he became the first southerner to be elected president of the American Institute of Architects, the top position in his field. He issued a challenge to his country, saying, "We can wipe out ugliness. America doesn't have to be the ugliest place in the world."

In presenting Odell to the Newcomen Society, Thomas I. Storrs, then chairman of NCNB Corporation, which was to become Bank of America, said, "I have known relatively few certifiable, real-life geniuses. There were only a handful of those few that I really wanted to know better. Gouldie Odell stands tall in both groups." He added, "Odell Associates has been a postgraduate school for talented young architects and engineers over nearly fifty years." Storrs, as did others, recalled Odell's flair and panache. "One of my earliest memories of him was in an open sports car of 1930s vintage as he rolled down Fourth Street, a scarf flying from a buttoned-up trench coat. Even a new arrival to Charlotte could tell that here was a man who enjoyed living."

As his professional office holding grew, so did Odell's collection of awards. They included Grand Official of Orden del Sol del Peru; honorary member of the College of Architects of Peru and Chile; the Societies of Architects of Colombia, Venezuela, Mexico, and the Philippines; the Institute of Architects of Brazil; and the Royal Architectural Institute of Canada. Odell also received his home state's highest award, the North Carolina Award, established by the General Assembly to be presented to North Carolinians of great distinction. His citation read in part, "His buildings speak to us of a cherished past. This native of Concord looms increasingly larger on the national and international scene."

The more prominent Odell became, the more often he was called upon for public service roles. He was named chairman of a task force on making the Potomac a model of scenic and recreational values for the whole country. For his work on that project, which was widely acclaimed, Mrs. Lyndon B. Johnson presented him with a special citation from the American Institute of Architects.

Understanding the importance of public service at home, Odell served as president of the Charlotte Mint Museum and the Charlotte Community Concert series, director of the Charlotte Chamber of Commerce, and chairman of the state Building Code Council. He also served on the board of the Central Charlotte Association and as a member of the Charlotte-Mecklenburg Planning Board. In the July 1982 issue of *Building Design and Construction*, Odell Associates was cited as a giant architectural and engineering firm nationally.

Odell retired as chairman of his firm in August 1982 and became chairman emeritus. After his retirement, his firm continued to thrive, and its work could be found up and down the East Coast from Florida to Vermont, west to St. Louis, and overseas to Germany. He died April 21, 1988.

Ken Sanford is a native North Carolinian who graduated from the University of North Carolina at Chapel Hill and worked on newspapers in the state before becoming the University of North Carolina at Charlotte's first director of public information. He is the author of Charlotte and UNC-Charlotte: Growing Up Together, *published in 1996.*

For more information, see:

Boger, Mary Snead. *Charlotte 23.* Bassett Printing Corporation, 1972.

Rook, Benjamin T. "The Legacy of Architecture." Address to the Newcomen Society, June 24, 1987.

D. A. TOMPKINS

By Jack Claiborne

In the first ten years of the twentieth century, Daniel Augustus Tompkins was one of the most influential men in North Carolina and the South. Though a son of the agrarian Old South, he was for thirty years one of the region's most effective promoters of an entrepreneurial New South, organizing, designing, financing, or equipping more than 350 cotton mills in the Carolinas and Georgia. Much of North Carolina's reputation as a progressive, industrial state can be attributed to the economic foundations he helped to build.

Broad-shouldered, thick-chested, and curly-haired, Tompkins was a restless, energetic man of many talents. Though widely known as "a mill man," he was also a machinist and engineer, a newspaper writer and publisher, a spirited public speaker, and a tireless advocate of education and technical training. He was an early spokesman for road building, a promoter of savings and thrift institutions, a civic planner and builder of public parks, a backer of libraries and literacy movements, a prodigious producer of how-to-do-it pamphlets, a supporter of YMCAs and YWCAs, a prolific letter writer, and a promoter of diversified agriculture, including dairying, cattle raising, and truck farming.

Even so, his views on many turn-of-the-century social issues were often out of step with those of other progressives of the period. Though he blamed slavery for much of the South's economic ills and befriended many African Americans on a personal basis, he remained an outspoken racist and avowed segregationist. He was a social Darwinist who built schools but opposed laws requiring school attendance or regulating child labor. He opposed labor unions and most government efforts to regulate industry. Though he disdained organized politics and declined all offers to run for elective office, he was an effective molder of political opinion throughout his life.

Tompkins was a lifelong bachelor who lived most of his working years in boarding houses, hotel suites, and Pullman cars. The only home he ever owned was a mountain cottage he built in Montreat in the twilight of his life. He died there in October 1914. As a college student he had fallen in love with a young woman with whom he corresponded for ten years. But she fell ill with paralysis and died before they could afford to marry. He lived the rest of his life alone.

D. A. Tompkins (Courtesy of Charlotte Observer)

Tompkins was born in 1851 at Edgefield, on the western border of South Carolina, near Augusta. His father, DeWitt Clinton Tompkins, was a wealthy physician, cotton planter, and slave owner. His mother, Hannah Smyly Tompkins, was a cousin of John C. Calhoun and bore a strong facial resemblance to Calhoun. As a boy, Daniel Tompkins was a favorite of both of his parents and took full advantage of plantation life. Though he enjoyed hunting, fishing, swimming, and boating, he was also a willing worker, especially in the blacksmith's shop, where he learned to work with metals and developed a fascination for machinery. As a teenager he supervised various aspects of plantation operations. Though he had lost an eye in a childhood accident, he was a voracious reader and excelled in school.

During the Civil War, he watched the South's hopes gradually collapse and sensed the ruin that would result. Two years after Robert E. Lee's surrender at Appomattox, he entered the University of South Carolina, where he paid much of his expenses with money he had earned as a boy building bridges in the Edgefield area. In his studies, he was pleased to learn that the South once had been the nation's industrial pioneer, but turned its back on technology when it embraced the slave economy. That led him to believe that with the proper leadership and its abundant natural resources, the South could regain its previous leadership. He was disappointed that most of his classmates were not interested in such matters. They were preoccupied by rhetoric, oratory, and politics, activities that Tompkins felt had contributed to the South's downfall. He wanted to study engineering and technology, subjects he saw as essential to rebuilding the South, harnessing its resources, and restoring its competitive position.

One of his mentors at the university was General Edward Porter Alexander, an artillery man who had been Lee's chief engineer in the Confederate army. He advised Tompkins to go north for his technical training and recommended Rensselaer Polytechnic Institute in Troy, N.Y., just across the Hudson River from the capital at Albany. Tompkins enrolled there in the summer of 1869 and found it a place that honored not politicians, but scientists, engineers, and builders.

Tompkins proved to be a good student. During the summers he worked as a draftsman in the Troy Steel Works and there struck up a friendship with Augustus L. Holley, a brilliant young engineer then introducing the United States to the Bessemer process for making steel. After graduating in 1873 with a degree in civil engineering, Tompkins went to New York City to take a job with Holley as a designer and private secretary. A year later, Holley introduced him to John Fritz, America's foremost iron master, who hired Tompkins as a machinist in the Bethlehem Iron Works in Pennsylvania. At the end of five years, Fritz sent Tompkins to Westphalia, Germany, to oversee the installation of machinery for making barrel hoops. The experience exposed Tompkins to European technology, which he found exciting, and to European work ethics, which he found lax and inefficient.

During his training and travels, he stored up observations and information to take back to the South. On his return from Germany he visited his father's plantation in Edgefield and was appalled to find it in ruins, like much of the South. He returned to Bethlehem Iron Works and worked two more years as a draftsman, then spent two years as a master machinist at the Crystal Plate Glass Company in Crystal City, Mo., learning about the emerging plate glass industry that soon would transform urban retailing and office design.

In March 1883, having completed what he considered his apprenticeship, he was ready to return home. He carefully surveyed the region for the most promising place to settle and chose Charlotte. He thought railroad service there was good, water power was plentiful, industry was sprouting, and he liked the welcoming entrepreneurial spirit he found there. He rented an office and hung out a sign that read, "D. A. Tompkins, Engineer, Machinist, and Contractor." He also was a sales representative for the Westinghouse Company, which specialized in steam engines.

A year earlier, people in Charlotte had thrilled to the hum of the city's first cotton mill, and were looking for a wealthy investor who would come and build another. Tompkins began showing them that by saving their money regularly and buying shares of building and loan, they could build their own cotton mills on the installment plan. By 1889, they had accumulated enough capital to build three additional mills—the Ada, the Alpha, and the Victor—that Tompkins helped to design and build. He was soon producing pamphlets and books, advising investors across the South how to do the same thing. In time Tompkins built and equipped three mills of his own.

Tompkins led a similar drive to increase the number of cottonseed oil mills in the region. For years Southern planters and cotton processors had disposed of cotton seeds as useless waste. Huge piles of them could be seen rotting beside cotton gins. When it was demonstrated that the seeds were a source of valuable oil and animal feed, cottonseed oil mills began sprouting under the control of a northern trust.

After he had an opportunity to install steam engines in two cottonseed oil mills, Tompkins discovered that the mills controlled by the trust were inefficient, and that new mills could reclaim a large and highly profitable share of that business. He wrote stories to that effect in the *Manufacturer's Record* and helped form a company that created a chain of new mills across the South.

Between the spring and fall of 1886 he personally designed, equipped, staffed, and started operations at eight mills between North Carolina and Texas. For the next twenty years he was a pamphleteering and public-speaking missionary for the cottonseed oil industry that generated new wealth across North Carolina and the South.

In 1910, he began to turn over day-to-day operation of his businesses to others. In 1912, he built a mountain home in Montreat and entered retirement. As a pastime, he took up cooking, and wrote one friend that looking back on his life, he perhaps should have become a chef and worked his way into the ownership of a great hotel. Even when it came to household chores, Tompkins didn't think small. He died October 18, 1914, and was buried at Elmwood Cemetery in Charlotte.

The building that housed the School of Textiles at North Carolina State University was named for him. So was the public library at Edgefield, S.C.

For thirty-five years Jack Claiborne was a reporter, editor, and editorialist for the Charlotte Observer. *He was vice president and assistant to the chairman of Park Communications in Ithaca, New York, before becoming associate vice chancellor for university relations at UNC-Charlotte. He is the author of five books, including a centennial history of the* Charlotte Observer, *and coeditor of an anthology entitled* Discovering North Carolina: A Tar Heel Reader.

For more information, see:

Claiborne, Jack. *The Charlotte Observer: Its Time and Place, 1869–1986.* University of North Carolina Press, 1986.

Davidson, Elizabeth Huey. "Child Labor Reforms in North Carolina." *North Carolina Historical Review,* April 1937.

Hanchett, Thomas W. *Sorting Out the New South City: Race, Class, and Urban Development in Charlotte, 1875–1975.* University of North Carolina Press, 1998.

Steelman, Joseph F. "Jonathan Edward Cox and North Carolina's Gubernatorial Campaign of 1908." *North Carolina Historical Review,* 1964.

Winston, George T. *A Builder of the New South.* Doubleday Page, 1920.

ARTS AND LITERATURE

THE CULTURAL ARTS of North Carolina are a lot like a creation from one of
Penland School founder Lucy Morgan's looms: the colors are rich and vibrant, and the texture full enough to satisfy the varied interests and regions of a
state that produced writers, dancers, artists, potters, and thinkers. And the product of their hands and feet and minds was a generous and unforgettable contribution to the American scene.

North Carolina writers drew upon the sounds and scenes of the state to produce works that won acclaim throughout the world. Thomas Wolfe ushered in
the early quarter of the century with tales of life drawn from his mountain home
in Asheville—so-called folk tales first produced by Frederick Koch's Playmakers
at Chapel Hill—that also inspired other mountain-born writers like John Ehle
and Fred Chappell at mid-century and later. Reynolds Price and playwright
Paul Green found in eastern North Carolina the people, places, and style that
filled their works. Likewise, William Sydney Porter, who wrote under the name
of O. Henry, delighted first New Yorkers and then readers nationwide with tales
drawn from his days behind the counter at a pharmacy in Greensboro. Poet Sam
Ragan drew upon a career in the newspaper business to fashion words, and he
encouraged the creative side of the state as North Carolina's first secretary of
cultural affairs.

Historical novelists Inglis Fletcher, Burke Davis, and Legette Blythe found
in the history of the state, and the South, the stuff of storytelling. So did Thomas
Dixon of Shelby, whose novel *The Clansman* turned the myth of Reconstruction
into the stuff of racist legend when re-created as *The Birth of a Nation* by early-
twentieth-century moviemaker D. W. Griffith. Late in the century, Patricia Cornwell, whose early work was as a police reporter at the *Charlotte Observer*, and former newspaper columnist Jerry Bledsoe turned crime stories into popular
fiction (Cornwell) and nonfiction (Bledsoe).

Writers who reflected the life of North Carolina and the South found a welcome reception from publishers W. T. Couch and Louis Rubin Jr. Couch was
the sometimes irascible director of the University of North Carolina Press,
which was a fledgling operation when he came aboard in the early 1920s. By
the time he left for the University of Chicago more than fifteen years later, the
press had become one of the nation's leading university presses, producing informed commentaries on the region and the nation. Fifty years later, Rubin
gave regional writers such as Lee Smith, Clyde Edgerton, Kaye Gibbons, and
Jill McCorkle a door to a national readership with his Algonquin Books of
Chapel Hill.

Lucy Morgan founded the Penland School near Spruce Pine in the late 1920s
on the belief that native arts and crafts should not die and pass with the times.
Over the years, it became a mecca for weavers, potters, glassblowers, metal

sculptors, furniture makers, and others. Likewise, the visions of a once-slower pace were captured in the work of Bob Timberlake, whose artistry first began on canvas and then spread to all manner of commercial activity, including furniture stylings. Painter Ernie Barnes began life in Durham, the son of a domestic worker in the home of the city's wealthiest man, John Sprunt Hill, who invited the young black boy into his library to explore his collection of art books. Barnes later perfected his own style and in his book *From Pads to Palettes* told the story of his transition from professional football to art. Romare Bearden took a piece of Charlotte with him when his family moved to New York City; he then returned a generation later to standing exhibits of his work at the Mint Museum of Art. Statesville's Ben Long trained in Italy as a fresco artist and completed frescoes in Charlotte and Glendale Springs. Gastonia's John Biggers also achieved wide acclaim.

Potters of early North Carolina created vessels and utilitarian pieces that were also the staple of potters in the Seagrove community in central North Carolina. Ben Owen took that basic style and created a new center of art among potters whose glazes and shapes produced pieces that could hold pickles, or even hard liquor, but found their place on studio and museum shelves as collectors' items.

The arts flourished in the twentieth century in North Carolina, the first state to fund a public art collection or a state symphony orchestra. Under director Benjamin Swalin, the symphony traveled to the farthest reaches of the state to perform before amazed youngsters in public schools. The nation's first local arts council was organized in Winston-Salem in 1949; twenty years later the city celebrated the opening of the North Carolina School of the Arts, the nation's first state-supported residential school for the performing arts.

The School of the Arts was led in its early years by composer Robert Ward who, though not a native North Carolinian, eventually made his home here. The school flourished in the final quarter of the century and became the home of another uniquely North Carolina creation, the National Opera Company, which like the state symphony brought the world of opera to classrooms and local audiences throughout the state and the nation.

ROMARE BEARDEN

By Jane Grau

I N 1978, the artist Romare Bearden wrote a letter to Clarence, a ten-year-old schoolboy in Charlotte. He was warmed, he said, by the knowledge that someone from his hometown was doing well. He told Clarence that in 1911, when he was born there, Charlotte was "sleepy." Lest anyone believe that cliché, one look at Bearden's Mecklenburg County collages will tell them it was anything but sleepy. Bearden drew the Mecklenburg series from memory, as he only made summertime visits to Charlotte after moving away at age four. But his early experiences in and around his grandfather's store on Graham Street must have been vivid, for they nourished a lifetime of creativity.

Overriding images of constancy and security, solemn celebration, and unspoken communication in Bearden's collages is a shimmering declaration of love. He is unabashed in his affection for the people who populate his memory and in his appreciation for what he calls "the prevalence of ritual" that marked their day-to-day existence.

Even after his art had been hung in great museums next to the great masters, and he himself had been awarded the Presidential Medal of the Arts, he remained fascinated by the people around him. From his home on New York's Canal Street, he went to his fifth-floor Long Island City studio every day dressed in blue coveralls. (He also spent half the year at his island home in St. Martin, where his wife, Nanette, was born.) There, he fed the pigeons on his windowsill and searched his material—and his memory—for just the right scrap of cloth, photo of a train, or note of music that would inspire vivid scenarios of life on the street and in the home. Said his biographer, Myron Schwartzman: "On the whole, Bearden is at his most eloquent when his subject matter is most human."

The Presidential Medal came in 1987, after the artist had spent most of his life perfecting a medium that closely resembles reality. Because collage is composed of the tactile evidence of life already lived—tattered remnants of newspapers, packaging, photos, and clothing—it elicits an immediate, often visceral, response in viewers.

Art historians call Bearden's idiosyncratic style and emphasis on the ceremonial a reinvention of the "papier colle" traditions of Matisse, Picasso, and Braque. The combination of telling details from his own past in Mecklenburg County, Harlem, Pittsburgh, and Paris, with classic elements from art, literature, music, and philosophy, created a rich visual language easily understood by all. His favorite subjects were the rituals, both mundane and mannerly, that celebrated and cemented relationships. No matter the time or the place, no human activity was for him without import, no human emotion without color.

In Bearden's collages, said playwright and devotee August Wilson, life was "presented on its own terms, on a grand and epic scale, with all its richness and fullness, in a language that was vibrant and which, made attendant to everyday life, ennobled it, affirmed its value, and exalted its presence. It was the art of a large and generous spirit that defined not only the character of black American life but also its conscience."

It was for his conscience, influenced early by community-minded family members and intimate exposure to the luminaries of the Harlem Renaissance, as well as his art, that Bearden was revered in private and public circles.

Born in 1911, blonde, blue-eyed Fred Howard Romare Bearden was named after a childless family friend from Missouri and called "Romy" by four generations of what Schwartzman describes as "religious, concerned, middle-class" doctors, ministers, and the like. They, along with his parents, Howard and Bessye Bearden, instilled a strong sense of commitment and ambition in their offspring. The Beardens joined the family enclave in Charlotte after their marriage in Atlantic City.

Bucolic though it may have been at the beginning of the twentieth century, Charlotte was nevertheless full of opportunity for a free black man like H. B. Kennedy, Bearden's great-grandfather. In 1915, Kennedy, by then a Charlotte landowner and businessman, was listed among the city's most prominent citizens. His only daughter, Cattie Bearden, was the mother of Romare's father.

As they say in the South, Romy came by his own proclivities honestly. H. B.'s own painting of Custer's last stand enlivened the interior of his grocery store, while Cattie's body of work included a portrait of Abraham Lincoln. Cousin Charles Alston, whose early sculptures were made of North Carolina clay, was a cartoonist for the Office of War Information. Various relatives sang and played the organ, piano, and pianola professionally. Duke Ellington was a distant

Romare Bearden (Courtesy of Charlotte Observer)

cousin who often stopped by the Bearden's Harlem apartment to play the piano.

However, prospects were not as good for an educated black couple in the twentieth century—Howard had attended college in Greensboro and Bessye was a graduate of Virginia Normal and Industrial Institute —as they were for their predecessors during Reconstruction. Women had not yet been awarded suffrage and Jim Crow was rapidly becoming institutionalized. Moving north, when Romy was about four, meant a chance for advancement in a tolerant atmosphere.

The Beardens settled in Harlem in 1920, whereupon his mother set out on a long career in public life. She crusaded against bigotry as the New York editor of the *Chicago Defender,* founded the Negro Women's Democratic Association, and served as the first woman on the school board. She was national treasurer of the Council of Negro Women, a member of the executive board of the New York Urban League, and managed several political campaigns. She was a peer of Mary McLeod Bethune and other activists. As a young man, Romy escorted Eleanor Roosevelt on the subway to a girls' school where she was to speak.

In Harlem, Romy's mostly Irish, Jewish, and Italian schoolmates contributed to his ecumenical view of the world. It was at home where his famous con-

science was honed listening to the conversations of people such as Langston Hughes, Ralph Ellison, Fats Waller, Paul Robeson, and George Schuyler, as they sat around the Bearden dinner table.

Considering the decades and the places where Bearden lived, it's no surprise that social realism was the artist's first focus. His early manhood was marked by the constant questioning and exploring of life and art. Acting on his belief that knowledge of world history and culture was essential to the proper development of the individual as well as to civilization, he studied the classics as well as immersing himself in modern currents of thought.

Case in point: he attended three colleges and pitched against Satchel Paige in the Negro baseball leagues, turning down an offer to play for the majors if he were willing to pass for white. His lifelong affinity for mathematics (he earned a degree from New York University) and introduction to the great draftsmen Ingres, Holbein, and Dürer by George Grosz at the Art Students League established a foundation for his art which, along with its emotional content, gave it an enduring power.

His departure from abstract painting began in the early 1960s when he almost inadvertently created his first photomontages at a civil rights meeting. A friend suggested enlarging them to as much as eight feet. The results were powerful enough to put in a show. Projections were exhibited in New York and Washington in 1964–65. "They constitute a sort of re-living and re-telling of his memories as a Negro," said Arne Ekstrom, whose gallery handled Bearden for nearly thirty years. "The subjects range from burials to jam sessions, Harlem streets, Conjur women, etc. In these days of civil rights strife they are, on the sociological side, a unique statement of pride in tradition, dramatic in many instances but never a form of protest or agitation."

Even though he drew inspiration from the African American experience and used traditional motifs such as masks, his aim was not "to paint the Negro in terms of propaganda" but as "passionately and dispassionately as Breughel painted the life of his day."

"I have not created protest images," Bearden said at the time, "because the world within the collage, if it is authentic, retains the right to speak for itself."

The success of these riveting works enabled Bearden to devote his entire life to making art. His subjects fell primarily into three categories: variations on classic themes such as odalisques and mythology; the jazzy temper of city life; and the country life of his youth. By the end of the 1960s, he was regularly exhibiting in prestigious venues throughout the country. *Time* and *Fortune* magazines put works by Bearden on their covers. In 1970, his *Patchwork Quilt* was acquired by the Museum of Modern Art.

In the ensuing decade, the artist explored the psychological environs of Pittsburgh, where he lived briefly in his youth, Harlem, and Mecklenburg County. Though the time he spent in North Carolina was relatively short, the artist said that "in my mind and heart, I never left."

Nevertheless, he felt a profound sense of displacement when he returned to Charlotte in 1976. After an almost fifty-year absence, nothing was the same. Thereafter, he claimed that the memory from which he worked was, like life and art, a synthesis of experiences consisting of "putting something over something else" (also the title of an important 1977 profile in the *New Yorker* magazine). What was important, he said, was "going back to where you started to gain insights" because "things that aren't essential have been stripped away and the meaning of other things becomes clear."

A recurrent image of trains, for instance, links him directly to his southern childhood, when all through the day and even in his sleep, Bearden would have heard them whistle. The Southern Railway station, where New York, New Orleans, and Atlanta Specials arrived every morning, was within walking distance of the Kennedy home on Graham Street. While the comings and goings of the mighty engines were great entertainment for the whole community, the arrivals and departures of loved ones were registered forever on the emotional chart of this sensitive child.

The regularity of the trains echoed other customs that gave meaning and continuity to life. Bearden's visual vocabulary was made up of the material details, physical gestures, and emotional interplay of picnics, piano lessons, and psalm singing—images authentic not just to African Americans but to all segments of society. He believed that myths and rituals, "however different in their particulars, are universal to human experience."

The general public of North Carolina was largely unaware of his notoriety, however, until Jerald Melberg, then the curator of Charlotte's Mint Museum of Art, arranged a retrospective in 1980. Two years in the making, it was considered a landmark exhibition —for the opening, the artist shed his coveralls for a Brooks Brothers suit—with a catalog including essays by notables in the art world and the most thorough listing of Bearden's works yet published.

Subsequent showings in museums across the country confirmed what many already knew: Romare Bearden had defined an American identity that rendered race irrelevant. "He is usually referred to as one of America's best black artists," said one critic of the collection. "One of America's best artists is closer to the mark."

Following the Mint retrospective, Mecklenburg County seemed to have a gravitational pull on the artist. He completed a suite of atmosphere, time, and season-specific collages that included his first pure landscapes in collage. By then, he was working in a larger scale, roughly thirty inches by forty inches, and in a more painterly style that bordered on abstract. The term "Patchwork Cubism" was used to explain their disjointed figures, luminous color, and unique compositions that combined free play and structure.

In the early 1980s, when the artist was embarking on his eighth decade, three murals were installed in Baltimore, Manhattan, and Pittsburgh. In 1985, Jerald Melberg, who by then had established his own Charlotte gallery, displayed sixteen collages with the Mecklenburg theme. *Before Dawn,* a glass-tile mosaic mural depicting a typical rural North Carolina scene, was later installed in Charlotte-Mecklenburg's Public Library. He celebrated his presidential citation in 1987 with fellow recipient Ella Fitzgerald by stealing away from the White House to eat fried chicken.

Bearden died in 1988 at age seventy-seven. The generosity and humility that marked him as a man and that shone so clearly in his paintings was expressed in his 1978 letter to Clarence. "One of the things about being an artist, Clarence, is that you don't have to deal with words, our pictures explain the way we feel. . . . This talent you have has been given to you, entrusted to you, to have people see, and feel, and understand the world as you do. You have the insight which others of us who are not blessed with your talent do not have. However, when you share your talent with others they too have the benefit of your blessing." This bit of wisdom was followed by a revealing admonition: "Remember always, you will only be as good an artist as you are a good human being."

Jane Grau of Charlotte studied art at Skidmore College and has covered the arts for the Arts Journal, Carolina Arts, *the* Charlotte Observer, Creative Loafing, *and* Today's Charlotte Woman.

For more information, see:
Jerald Melberg Gallery, Charlotte, www. jeraldmelberg.com.
Schwartzman, Myron. *Romare Bearden: His Life and His Art.* Harry N. Abrams, 1990.
Studio Museum of Harlem, New York, N.Y. www.studiomuseuminharlem.org.

DORIS BETTS

By Laura McAuliffe

D ORIS BETTS was an award-winning writer of
short stories and novels who shared her farm
home with her husband and up to twenty-one Ara-
bian horses. This highly regarded writing teacher who
kept dog biscuits on hand for the campus pets was
recognized not only at home, where a distinguished
professorship was created in her honor, but also internationally as her books were published around the
world.

Betts considered her most rewarding recognition
to be the 1989 Medal of Merit for the Short Story
from the American Academy and Institute of Arts and
Letters. Yet the Doris Betts Professorship in Creative
Writing, the first professorship in the creative writing
department at the University of North Carolina at
Chapel Hill, was founded in the spring of 1998 to attract a nationally acclaimed writer. The $1 million en-
dowed professorship was announced on the same
night that Betts received the North Caroliniana Society Award for her contribution to the state's literary
and cultural heritage. In response, Betts said, "In case
I should have the lovely and unexpected beneficence
of having my name attached to anything so wonderful, it would have to be creative writing. I love the
whole university, of course, but my blood and bone
marrow have been spent there, and those students
and writers are our legacy."

First and foremost she was a writer. "I think of
work, so have always liked 'writer,' an honest term,"
she said. "Conveys nothing about how good the writing is, but describes the activity. 'Wife' and 'mother'
are lifelong. I like teaching, but feel it grew out of
writing."

Doris June Waugh Betts was born June 4, 1932, in
Iredell County, the only child of William Elmore and
Mary Ellen (Freeze) Waugh. She grew up in Statesville during the Depression and World War II in a
community of deep religious faith and patriotism. Her
parents encouraged an early interest in books, and her
mother used the Statesville Public Library as a baby-
sitter. For her fifth birthday, her parents gave her
a copy of Jesse Lyman Hurlbut's *Story of the Bible for
Young and Old*.

Betts's first published work was a column called
"Hitting the High Spots," which reported on daily
high school activities in the *Statesville Daily Record*. At
the age of seventeen, Betts recalled that she felt driven

Doris Betts (Courtesy of Southern Historical Collection)

to show her hometown that "you could come from
the wrong side of the tracks and still achieve." She was
voted "most talented" by her Statesville High School
graduating class of 1950, and hoped to study journalism at Woman's College of the University of North
Carolina (later the University of North Carolina at
Greensboro). Since there was no school of journalism
at Woman's College, she channeled her energy into
creative writing.

At the end of her sophomore year in 1952, she
married Lowry Matthews Betts, a law student whom
she met at a denominational summer camp. She completed half of her junior year, left college, and became a secretary to help support her husband as he
completed law school. "By the time he graduated we
already had two children," she said, "so there wasn't a
chance for me to finish my education."

By age twenty-one, Betts was a wife, mother, and
award-winning writer. In 1953, shortly after the birth
of a daughter, Doris LewEllyn, and a move to Chapel
Hill, she won the *Mademoiselle* college fiction contest
for "Mr. Shawn and Father Scott," which was included in *Best Short Stories of 1953*. The following year
her first book, *The Gentle Insurrection and Other Stories*,

won the UNC Putnam Booklength Manuscript Prize. That same year, a son, David Lowry, was born.

Betts worked as a newspaper reporter and editor throughout much of the 1950s. She was a stringer for United Press International and wrote for several North Carolina newspapers. When her first novel, *Tall Houses in Winter,* was published in 1957, Betts was a full-time office manager in Chapel Hill for the Simplified Farm Record Book Company, and a mother of two young children. The following year she won the Sir Walter Raleigh Award for the best book of fiction by a North Carolinian—a prize she would win again in 1965 and 1973—and a Guggenheim Fellowship in Creative Writing.

Betts continued to work as a journalist and a mother (a son, Erskine Moore, was born in 1960) until 1966, when she became a lecturer in the English department at the University of North Carolina at Chapel Hill. She rose from lecturer at UNC-Chapel Hill to alumni distinguished professor of English in 1980, the first woman to do so. In addition, she was the first woman to receive a full professorship at Chapel Hill's English department, to be named chair of the faculty, and to receive the Katherine Carmichael Teaching Award. While at Chapel Hill, Betts directed the freshman-sophomore English program, the honors program, and the fellows program. She delighted in teaching, because it "keeps the arteries from hardening."

As biographer Evans noted, "Some UNC colleagues quip that Betts is not an individual but an entire department—no one person could take on so many tasks, be assigned to so many committees, be elected to so many posts."

Her reputation as a writer continued to build during her teaching career. In 1964, she had published *The Scarlet Thread,* followed by *The Astronomer and Other Stories* in 1965. Later, *The River to Pickle Beach* was published in 1972 to be followed by *Beasts of the Southern Wild and Other Stories* in 1973, *Heading West* in 1981, *Souls Raised from the Dead* in 1994, and *The Sharp Teeth of Love* in 1997.

Beasts of the Southern Wild was named one of the twenty best books of the year by the *New York Times* in 1973; the following year it was nominated for the National Book Award. Twenty years later, *Souls Raised from the Dead* was also named by the *New York Times* as one of the best books of the year, and it won the Southern Book Award in 1995.

Her short story, "The Ugliest Pilgrim," was the inspiration for the Academy Award-winning short film, *Violet,* as well as the stage musical of the same name that won eight major theatrical prizes in New York in 1998, and has since been produced around the country from Boston to San Jose, California.

Her fiction was set for the most part in North Carolina, and she has been compared to Flannery O'Connor and Walker Percy. As one biographer noted, she chose to "depict blue collar workers and middle-class people who demonstrate perseverance, cheerfulness, and a refusal to be victimized." Anne Tyler said that "no one writes about love better than Doris Betts." She objected to restrictions implied by titles such as "southern writer" or "woman writer" and preferred the term "regional writer," suggesting one who used the immediate place she or he knows to comment upon the larger world.

Betts's writing and her religious beliefs were intertwined. Her work was infused with the strong biblical influence of her upbringing in the Associate Reformed Presbyterian Church. In later years, she labeled herself a "recovering Calvinist," and "the only French existentialist housewife in Sanford, North Carolina." Betts revealed that, "Sometimes it troubles me that writers whose orientation is entirely secular assume that religious faith is a dreadful constriction, [that it] imposes a steel template upon experience [and] actually distorts reality. In the sense that we all bring to experience our own interpretations, perhaps we all distort reality, the atheist no less than the fundamentalist."

Elizabeth Evans, Betts's biographer and author of several critical articles about Betts and her work, said that the Hurlbut *Bible Stories* and the King James Bible were never absent from her fiction. "Biblical allusion comes as easily—and almost as frequently—to Betts as breathing," Evans wrote. Betts herself wrote: "I am a storyteller whose themes are informed by faith, but I do not preach it. . . . Like mothers and kindergarten teachers, I find that whispering is also sometimes effective, and even with the volume turned down I hope my theology can be heard in my stories."

The church was an important part of Betts's life. She served as an elder and Sunday school teacher at a small mainstream Presbyterian Church near her home in Pittsboro. "I serve on several committees," she said, "and I'm an organist, but I play poorly. In a small church everybody has to pitch in." Betts clearly had strong feelings about the importance of the church. "As I say to students, 'Who else are you going to get to marry you, to name your child, and to bury you?' The church is indeed often a failure, but we don't have anything any better. It isn't fair just to walk away from it." Betts said that she "fled [her] religious heritage for quite a long time, rebelled hard. . . . I would also say that faith is not so much something I have, as something that continues under laborious construction."

The Bible was but one of many influences on Betts's writing. One critic noted, "Betts may not be familiar with Blondie, but without a doubt she is deeply familiar with the Bible, Flannery O'Connor and William Faulkner, Freud, Darwin, Konrad Lorenz, Navajo mythology, and the doctrine of Manifest Destiny." Another reviewer said, "Betts does seem to know everything." As Evans pointed out, "In every novel, Betts recounts interesting information from how to carve in stone (*The Scarlet Thread*), to the behavior of retarded adults (*The River to Pickle Beach*), to the majesty of the Grand Canyon (*Heading West*), to the suffering caused by anorexia and depression (*The Sharp Teeth of Love*)."

Betts considered herself not a novelist but a short story writer who wrote with a "mental jury" in mind. She wrote for people "whose opinions I respect. Many of them are fellow writers, but not all. Most of my family is not bookish. So if they are pleased and proud, it has to do with their affection for me. That's not to be sneezed at, but it's not the same thing. They're not critics. They think that if you get anything printed, it must be good. Would that it were true."

Evans believed that a lack of or difficulty in communication formed the dominant theme of Betts's fiction. Betts herself said, "A writer's duty is to put into words what it is like to be a human being in this world, even for the inarticulate."

Her writing, however, was not limited to short stories, novels, and newspaper articles. In 1988, the Florida Department of Agriculture consulted with her to prepare a thirty-page booklet about the future of forestry in Florida, entitled *Turning Over a New Leaf*. Two years later she was asked by the North Carolina governor's office to write a one-thousand-word article about the statewide problem of functional illiteracy.

She retired from teaching at Chapel Hill in spring 2001, where she was known for her devotion to her students. She described them as her "other children" but said the best part of her involvement with UNC was "to be with wonderful, book-loving people and to have that vantage point for seeing my state, my neighbors and the younger generation, all of which feed optimism."

In 1987 the UNC-Chapel Hill department of English created the Doris Betts Award to be given annually to a graduate student for excellence in teaching. Betts was also honored with an award for literature from the North Carolina legislature in 1975 and she received the R. Hunt Parker Award from the North

Carolina Literary and Historical Association in 1989. In 1992, Betts was named the recipient of the John Tyler Caldwell Award from the North Carolina Humanities Council for her "contribution to the literary life of the nation, expressed in material that was definitely southern in subject but universal in appeal."

Writing prizes established in her honor included the Doris Betts Fiction prize, awarded annually to a North Carolina writer by the North Carolina Writers Network. She also received six honorary degrees, including one from UNC-Greensboro.

At the beginning of the new century, Betts and her husband, a retired judge, owned an eighty-acre farm near Pittsboro in Chatham County. "Horses were to be my husband's retirement interest and writing mine," said Betts. "It turns out that writing is a solo interest and horse care involves more hands than two!"

Laura L. McAuliffe earned a B.F.A. in dramatic writing from New York University's Tisch School of the Arts, Institute of Film and Television, and an M.A. in history from the University of North Carolina at Charlotte. She is a contributor to Exploring Charlotte: A Pocket Guide to the Queen City *and has written for the* Charlotte Observer *and* Today's Charlotte Woman.

For more information, see:

Betts, Doris. Papers. Special Collections, Mugar Memorial Library, Boston University. Southern Historical Collection, University of North Carolina at Chapel Hill.

Alderson, Laura. "An Interview with Doris Betts." *Poets and Writers* 20, no. 1 (1992).

Brown, W. Dale. "Interview with Doris Betts." *Southern Quarterly* 34, no. 2 (1996).

Cockshutt, Rod. "Q & A with Doris Betts." *Tar Heel: A Magazine of North Carolina,* December 1981.

Evans, Elizabeth. "Conversations with Doris Betts." *South Carolina Review* 28, no. 2 (1996).

Harmon, A. G. "A Conversation with Doris Betts." *Image: A Journal of the Arts and Religion* 11 (1995).

Howard, Jennifer. "Doris Betts." *Publishers Weekly,* April 25,1994.

"Interview with Doris Betts." *Story Quarterly* 1 (1975).

Ketchin, Susan. "Doris Betts: Resting on the Bedrock of Original Sin." In *The Christ-Haunted Landscape: Faith and Doubt in Southern Literature.* University Press of Mississippi, 1994.

Powell, Dannye Romine. *Parting the Curtains: Interviews with Southern Writers.* John F. Blair, 1994.

Walsh, William J. *Speak So I Shall Know Thee: Interviews with Southern Writers.* Down Home Press, 1993.

FRED CHAPPELL

By Susannah Link

AT THE TURN OF THE CENTURY, North Carolina's poet laureate was Fred Chappell, an internationally renowned and gifted creator of poetry, novels, short stories, and literary criticism. His body of work—which celebrated and preserved the Appalachian mountain culture of his childhood—included fifty publications, several of which had been translated into other languages. He had received numerous literary awards and was the Burlington Industries Professor of English at the University of North Carolina at Greensboro, where he taught creative writing since 1964.

Born in Canton in the mountains of western North Carolina on May 28, 1936, Chappell graduated from Canton High School in 1954. As a child growing up in Appalachia, he was an acute observer of the hard mountain life of poverty. The son of two teachers, James Taylor and Ann Maye Davis Chappell, he said his parents were the only reason he learned to read and write when so many of his contemporaries did not.

Chappell started writing as a teenager. He was fascinated by science fiction, partly because it was the most readily available genre of fiction. He noted that his head was always full of memories of faces, sayings, gestures, and bits of music. Everything he saw and heard reminded him of something else he had seen and heard. As a boy, Chappell taught himself to listen to how people talked. Every experience and every activity, from childhood through adulthood, became "grist for the mill," as he observed in an interview.

In a 1997 interview that coincided with the publication of his novel, *Farewell, I'm Bound to Leave You,* Chappell said his novels set in Appalachia were designed to portray the essence of Appalachian life between 1900 and 1950, before changes from the outside world had taken their toll on the mountain culture. Legends and folktales abounded in the lives of the people, and time was twisted around in the book to show that people invent the past as much as they remember the past. He compared these novels to Marc Chagall's paintings of village life. Chappell was attracted to mountain people as subjects for his writing because of their independence of spirit, their ear for language, their skepticism, their strength in the face of hardship, and their ability to make do with what they had.

Fred Chappell (Courtesy UNCG University Relations)

Chappell noted that mountain stories were the history of his family, his mountains, and the human race, and that his work was an attempt to preserve the unique mountain culture. Female characters were central in these novels, because Chappell believed that women were the bearers and nurturers of tradition. They kept families together through hardship, they kept reading alive, and they told stories about their families.

A superb stylist, Chappell was conscious of creating a pattern and following particular themes in his writing, a lesson he learned from his writing instructor at Duke, the legendary William Blackburn. Blackburn taught other notable writers such as Mac Hyman, Reynolds Price, William Styron, and Anne Tyler, but in the foreword to his collection of Chappell's essays he told George Garrett that Chappell was the most gifted. "No question about it," Blackburn said, "though whether he will ever 'succeed' as a writer the way they have, I don't know." Chappell was equally complimentary about Blackburn, who taught him "absolute integrity of purpose. That is, whatever you're doing, you always give it your whole shot: you give it everything you got and you don't hold back, and you don't complain, you just go ahead and do it. . . . [The] respect that he brought to [writing] I try to bring to it every day of my life."

Chappell received his B.A. from Duke University in 1961 and his M.A. from Duke in 1964. Before graduating, he married Susan Nicholls, with whom he had attended high school. A son, Heath, was born in 1961.

Although Chappell considered himself primarily a poet at the start of his career, he wrote his first novel in five weeks while still in graduate school in order to support his family during the summer. *It Is Time, Lord* was published in 1963. His first collection of poetry, *The World Between the Eyes,* appeared in 1971 and won the Roanoke-Chowan Poetry Cup. His most ambitious project spanned three decades and included his first four novels, followed by a collection of four of his previously published collections of poetry, and concluding with a series of four more novels.

Chappell came to believe that prose and poetry were two very different genres. In a 1997 interview, he said that writing prose was like riding a bicycle—all the details whizzed by in a blur. Poetry, on the other hand, was like walking—a poet looked at everything in detail.

The first four novels, beginning with *It Is Time, Lord,* focused on darker themes and experimental styles. One important theme in his work, according to David Paul Ragan, was "the nature of time, how it is altered by human perceptions. . . . The inability of a character to cope with his position in time becomes emblematic of his incapacity to function within the context of human society." Like his first novel, Chappell's second, *The Inkling* (1965), introduced moral dilemmas that Chappell continued to explore in his third, *Dagon* (1968), for which he won a prize from the French Academy in 1971. His fourth novel, *The Gaudy Place* (1973), won the Sir Walter Raleigh Award and was set in Gimlet Street, the fictionalized version of Lexington Avenue in Asheville. This novel introduced a more comic tone than the first three and foreshadowed the quartet of novels that followed in the next two decades. David Paul Ragan, in his biographical entry about Chappell for the *Dictionary of Literary Biography,* wrote that Gimlet Street is "a microcosm of the universe. . . . Just as Gimlet Street is connected with all the other streets in the world, so are the people who inhabit it part of a larger social picture." According to Ragan, the main characters in Chappell's first four novels "have been displaced by a new society which has usurped an older, more stable culture. Chappell's books unfold during the period in which the traditional mountain culture is disintegrating."

After *The Gaudy Place* appeared, Chappell combined four previously published volumes of poetry into a four-part poem entitled *Midquest,* published in 1981. This work became the central piece in the thirty-year project that began with his first four novels and ended with his latest four. The collections of poetry that made up *Midquest* were *River* (1975), *Bloodfire* (1978), *Wind Mountain* (1979), and *Earthsleep* (1980). *Midquest* created a bridge from the more experimental and darker early novels and the Jess Kirkman Quartet, as the next four novels came to be known in reference to the main character. The four-part poem was set in Appalachia, and in addition to recording the mountain community, it created, according to John Lang, "a striking sense of literary community." Various elements in the book "reflect Chappell's commitment to literature and life as communal activities." *Midquest* received positive critical recognition and brought more attention to Chappell's work. Several journals devoted issues to Chappell's work, including *Abatis One, Mississippi Quarterly,* and *Iron Mountain Review.*

In the series of four novels published after *Midquest,* Chappell emphasized his Appalachian roots and focused on the life of Jess Kirkman. The first novel in the quartet, *I Am One of You Forever* (1985), received glowing praise and comparisons to such notables as Mark Twain, William Faulkner, and Eudora Welty. The second and third novels of the quartet, *Brighten the Corner Where You Are* (1989) and *Farewell, I'm Bound to Leave You* (1996), took place when the protagonist was a young man. The fourth, *Look Back All the Green Valley* (1999), was set thirty years later when Jess was a professor living in Greensboro and teaching at a university. This series of novels clearly had autobiographical elements that stemmed from Chappell's observations of the changes occurring in Appalachia.

Chappell told George Hovis that "the mountains are beginning to open up to economic opportunities that were never really appreciated before, to all kinds of cultural influx, and also to an awareness and understanding of the indigenous culture that was subdued before. But you can see the dangers just by driving around and looking at all the developments, all the golf courses, and so forth. It's easy enough to look into the future and see the older Appalachian way of life as an endangered species. The more development you get, the more you push the animals into smaller and tighter spaces, and that would be true of the Appalachians, too. But, like the animals, they will survive. They'll just spill out, and you'll have a good old-fashioned beer joint right next to a posh golf course."

Alex Albright wrote a survey of the Chappell collection at Duke and found evidence of Chappell's political concerns. After the infamous Speaker Ban Law was passed in the North Carolina General Assembly in 1963 when Chappell was still in graduate school, the stultifying effects of the law gradually seeped into the academic institutions in the state. The law stated that any institution of higher education receiving state funds could not bring speakers to campus who had ties to the Communist Party, had advocated the overthrow of the government, or had pleaded the Fifth Amendment when questioned about communist affiliations. New to the faculty at the Woman's College of the University of North Carolina (later the University of North Carolina at Greensboro), Chappell was among 175 university system faculty members who signed a statement saying they would leave their positions unless the law was repealed.

In a letter to the *Greensboro Daily News,* Chappell said that "to stay, to teach in the university, would be to give tacit approval to a law which is probably unconstitutional and certainly the product of bigotry. This I will not do. . . . Usually those persons who don't understand ideas try to close the mouths which voice them, just as persons who can't read books burn them, and those who can't love fight."

Chappell liked teaching and devoted the main part of his workday to it. In order to give his attention fully to his students, he arose early in the morning to write for several hours before classes began at 9 A.M. He taught his students to respect the craft of writing, to learn to be good observers of the world around them, and to read constantly to learn how words look and sound on paper. By keeping up his own reading, Chappell renewed his enthusiasm for teaching.

Chappell taught students to read poetry with an open mind and to listen to what the poet was saying. With his writing students, he tried to find the unique set of rules that governed their writing and then worked with them to revise their piece to fit that particular set of rules. His own high level of intellectual curiosity inspired intellectual curiosity in his students and helped to contribute to the vibrant atmosphere in the creative writing program at UNC-Greensboro.

His writing won him the Bollingen Prize in Poetry from Yale University Library in 1985, which he shared with John Ashbery. Among his other awards were the Prix de Meilleur des Lettres Etrangères from the French Academy (in 1971) and six Roanoke-Chowan Poetry Cups from the North Carolina Literary and

Historical Society. In addition, he won the Sir Walter Raleigh Award for the best fiction book by a North Carolina writer in 1973 and the T. S. Eliot Award from the Ingersoll Foundation in 1993. He won the Aiken Taylor Prize for poetry, the North Carolina Medal in Literature, and the Award in Literature from the National Institute of Arts and Letters. His fellowships included a Woodrow Wilson fellowship, a National Defense Act fellowship, and a Rockefeller Foundation grant in 1966, which paid for nine months in Florence, Italy, in 1967 and allowed him to read proofs of his third novel, *Dagon,* and finish drafts of his first collection of poems, *The World Between the Eyes,* and his fourth novel, *The Gaudy Place.* In 1986, he received the O. Max Gardner Award, the highest honor that the University of North Carolina can bestow on a faculty member. This award is given for service to humanity.

George Garrett summed up Chappell's contributions to the literary world by complimenting his talents as a poet, novelist, short story writer, and literary critic. "A true artist leaves his mark on all he touches. Fred Chappell as teacher has exercised an enormous and benign influence on contemporary letters."

Susannah J. Link graduated from Stanford University and continued her studies in American history at the University of Virginia. She has taught at the University of North Carolina at Greensboro and has worked as assistant editor for the Papers of James Madison *and a consulting editor for the* Papers of Woodrow Wilson. *She is the author of* Harriet Elliott: A Brief Appreciation.

For more information, see:
Chappell, Fred. Papers. Perkins Library, Duke University, Durham.
———. Works. University Archives, Jackson Library, University of North Carolina at Greensboro.

Bizzaro, Patrick, ed. *Dream Garden: The Poetic Vision of Fred Chappell.* Louisiana State University Press, 1997.
"The Fiction of Fred Chappell." *North Carolina Literary Review* 7 (1998): 96–155.
Gingher, Robert, ed. *The Rough Road Home: Stories by North Carolina Writers.* University of North Carolina Press, 1992.
The Greensboro Group, eds. *A Turn in Time: Piedmont Writers at the Millennium.* Trans Verse Press, 1999.
Hovis, George. "An Interview with Fred Chappell." *The Carolina Quarterly* 52, no. 1 (Fall/Winter 1999): 67–69.
Powell, Dannye Romine. *Parting the Curtains: Interviews with Southern Writers.* John F. Blair, 1994.

W. T. COUCH

By Karin Lisa Posser

ORIGINAL THINKING, writing, and publishing
are as necessary to the development of a society as air, water, and food for the life of an individual," the director of the University of North Carolina
Press, William Terry Couch, declared in 1946. "Institutions engaged in higher learning must do more than
conserve and transmit knowledge inherited from the
past . . . they also must stimulate invention, creation,
discovery."

That was Couch's credo throughout his twenty
years as director. And his steadfastness in this belief
was what made the press the single most influential
institution in launching modernist thought in the
American South during the 1920s and 1930s.

Indeed, the first director of the press, Dr. Louis
Round Wilson, along with the four other founders—
sociologist Howard W. Odum, University of North
Carolina President Henry Chase, biologist W. C.
Coker, and literary scholar Edwin Greenlaw—had
grandiose visions of creating a press that would be unlike any other in the region. They envisioned a publishing center that would be devoted to educating
laymen as well as scholars in an effort to "gain wide
influence on the thought of the entire South Atlantic
section." They established the institution with visions
of making it a major publishing center for the region,
one that would act as an arena for modernism and
critical thinking about the South.

Yet the founders' subsequent actions hardly kept
pace with their intentions. The choice of books the
press published during its initial stages, for instance,
were all highly scholarly and controversial subjects
were carefully avoided.

In May 1927, however, all of that changed. During
an emergency session of the press's board of governors—Chase; Wilson; Odum; Coker; James Finch
Royster, dean of the graduate school; historian J. G.
de Roulhac Hamilton; and R. H. Wettach of the law
school—gathered to decide the fate of a book entitled *Congaree Sketches*. This collection of tales told by
black raconteurs living along the Congaree River in
South Carolina had been solicited in an effort to collect and publish black folklore for Odum's Institute
for Research in Social Sciences. The stories themselves
contained nothing controversial. The problem was in
an emotional introduction written by one of the bold-

W. T. Couch (Courtesy of Southern Historical Collection)

est members of the university's philosophy department, Paul Green.

In his introduction, Green observed that, having
lived together in America for two hundred years,
"black and white are inextricably mingled in blood
and bone and intention." Yet the black man "stood in
the ditch doing the dirty digging" while the white man
stood above and gave orders. It was the white man's
obligation to society, in Green's eyes, to extend a helping hand and enable his black brother to climb out of
the ditch. He surely did not intend for the introduction to be an assault on the "separate but equal" doctrine. Rather, his essay was clearly written to urge a
more humane treatment of blacks in the South and
to laud the achievements of the Harlem Renaissance.

Nonetheless, these were strong sentiments which the timid university press felt reluctant to publish.

Committee members cast their votes and the foreseeable decision seemed unanimous in favor of excluding Green's introduction when a young man, barely twenty-five, suddenly spoke up. As assistant director, William Terry Couch had been running the day-to-day operations of the press for almost two years following the illness of Louis Wilson.

Couch proceeded to inform the board that more than one hundred advance copies of *Congaree Sketches* with Green's introduction had already been distributed. The *New York Times* had a copy as did the *New York Herald-Tribune*. Additionally, a number of other reviewers, leading literary figures, and major bookstores throughout the country had also received copies of the book. If the press stopped publication now, Couch suggested, would not some of these people begin to suspect foul play? Perhaps the best action to take in this matter was none at all. After his comments, another vote was taken and this time each member agreed to proceed with publication as written.

Significantly, following the publication, the press's fears of retaliation did not transpire and it did not receive one letter of protest. In short, by publishing *Congaree Sketches*, UNC Press lost no ground at home, while it garnered prestige elsewhere. And as a result, Couch was able to consolidate his control over the press, and few would attempt to challenge him again over what he could publish.

Couch was born December 4, 1901, in Pamplin, Va., a small town approximately thirty miles from Lynchburg, but he had deep roots in the Chapel Hill community. He was the son of John Henry Couch, a country Baptist preacher, and Sallie Love Terry, a school teacher. His mother's family had been fairly well-to-do planters in the Prince Edward County area prior to the Civil War. However, the war wiped out the family's fortune. Couch would later recall wading in Confederate currency up to his knees during his childhood visits to his grandmother's attic.

Couch's parents had to constantly scramble to make ends meet. In 1918, Couch's father finally decided to abandon the ministry and return to farming in the New Hope Creek area near Chapel Hill, where he was raised. John Couch believed that the move would not only provide his family with some stability, but would also provide his children with the opportunity to attend the nearby university.

William soon assisted his father in what proved to be a vain effort to revive the farm. During the following year, he worked at a generating station of the Southern Power Company, often on a twelve-hour, seven-day-per-week basis. The need to support himself and his family continued after he entered the University of North Carolina in 1922, and at one point he dropped out and enlisted in the army in hope of earning an appointment to West Point, which he failed to win because of medical problems.

Other modernist thinkers of the period between the world wars might have looked upon the lower classes with condescension, or, in contrast, attempted to sentimentalize them. But for Couch, neither was possible. His observation of existence at the bottom of southern society was grounded in extensive personal experience. Given this perspective, Couch refused to pity or romanticize the white southern masses.

Couch's social outlook and frankness was first displayed in 1924 when he became editor of *Carolina Magazine*, a fairly obscure student publication that soon became a prime topic of conversation on campus and statewide. Along with his own articles attacking Southern conservatism, Couch began printing letters from fundamentalists condemning the teaching of evolution, making the authors appear ridiculous. Couch's performance as editor of *Carolina Magazine* was enough to catch the eye of Louis Wilson, who in May 1925 was seeking an assistant to run the press while he was away on a medical leave of absence. Wilson hoped that Couch would enliven the press just as he had the small student publication. In that respect, he was not disappointed.

On June 15, 1925, Couch was named assistant director for half-time and he immediately began to bristle at the conservative attitudes he found at the press. Upon hiring Couch, Wilson told him that the press could never publish anything that dealt in substance with race, religion, or economics. Couch was in no mood for this advice. To him, those standards, based on the old gentility, constituted the enemy. It soon became apparent that Couch represented something new in the South—someone who invited contention rather than avoided it.

To Couch, conflict was positive; it was not a threat to scholarship, but rather its lifeblood. Without conflict, cultural life would rapidly degenerate into sterility, as it had in the nineteenth-century South. Not unlike the notorious assailant of "Southern Kultur," social and literary critic H. L. Mencken of Baltimore, Couch counseled his authors to break with politeness and become more critical of the South. And also like Mencken, who believed in "stirring up the animals" to encourage intellectual activity, Couch insisted that "nothing was more important than to bother people, to wake them up and get them activated. If that required stepping on some toes, so much the better."

A glance at the publishing schedule during Couch's tenure gives a good indication of how successful he was in using the institution to stimulate the region's intellectual life. In that time, the press issued over 450 titles, of which 170 dealt chiefly with southern topics. This included many volumes on southern history, the contemporary South, literary criticism, collections of white and black folklore, as well as books by non-southern writers. At the time, this was an unusual fare for a university press, not to mention a southern one.

In particular, two books published in the 1930s helped to illustrate Couch's method of action. In 1934, Couch edited one of the most influential books of the 1930s, which assessed and surveyed southern writing. A collaborative effort, *Culture in the South* contained work from over thirty writers and scholars and examined every conceivable aspect of southern life, character, and culture. In this work, Couch attempted to capture the normally unnoticed "patterns" of southern existence, especially those unspoken values and attitudes that often controlled behavior. The quality that Couch insisted upon most in the articles was candor. The result was an examination of southern culture that won nearly unanimous praise from reviewers.

These Are Our Lives evolved from an urgent plea to Couch by Henry G. Alsberg, director of the Federal Writers' Project, to rescue the stagnant program in the South. Couch responded in April 1938 with a proposal for collecting life histories from all the major social and occupational groups in the region, with special emphasis on the farm population. As he explained in his preface, the goal was to feel his way toward a new kind of social research that would reveal the "real workings of institutions, customs, habits" by taking into account the "whole life experience" of the individual. A series of sixteen volumes was planned to follow, each devoted to a different occupational group in the South. Couch did not get the chance to test this scheme. By the time *These Are Our Lives* appeared, congressional conservatives succeeded in forcing Alsberg out of the Writers' Project and otherwise gutting the program.

Whether or not Couch could have turned the sixteen-volume series of life histories into a success is unknown. One cannot question, however, his overall accomplishments as director of the press. Couch helped make the press through a willingness to participate in political activism. During a time when intellectuals viewed politics as a source of contamination, unfit for the gentleman scholar, scholars especially regarded political involvement as a breach of objectivity. For if a faculty member held strong views on a partisan issue, he was expected to keep those views to himself. Couch did not take long to challenge this policy. In April 1927, just prior to the board meeting regarding *Congaree Sketches,* Couch made his presence known on the editorial page of the *Durham Morning Herald,* where he penned a fierce attack against Southern conservatism.

Couch's actions undoubtedly caused controversy in Chapel Hill, and his methods of stimulating intellectual activity were often criticized in the university community and elsewhere. Although Couch's job was jeopardized due to his unorthodox beliefs, they did not lead to his termination. In 1945 he left Chapel Hill to accept a position as director of the University of Chicago Press. In 1950, Couch's controversial nature led to his dismissal. Two years later, he became editor in chief of *Collier's Encyclopedia* and *Yearbooks,* a position he held until 1959. In that year, Couch began to work as editor of the *American Oxford Encyclopedia.* Four years later, he moved to California and served for one year as codirector of the Center for American Studies in Burlingame, Calif.

Couch retired to Chapel Hill in 1968, and died on December 10, 1988, in Charlottesville, Va.

Karin Lisa Posser received her M.A. from the University of North Carolina at Greensboro where her primary areas of interest included early-twentieth-century American history, the South, intellectual history, and interdisciplinary studies of American civilization.

For more information, see:
Couch, William Terry. Interview by Louis Round Wilson, October 15, 1970. Oral History Memoir. Southern Historical Collection, University of North Carolina at Chapel Hill.
———. Papers. Southern Historical Collection, University of North Carolina at Chapel Hill.

Singal, Daniel. *The War Within: From Victorian to Modernist Thought in the South, 1919–1945.* University of North Carolina Press, 1982.
University of North Carolina Press. Papers. Southern Historical Collection, University of North Carolina at Chapel Hill.
Wilson, Louis R. *The University of North Carolina, 1900–1930: The Making of a Modern University.* University of North Carolina Press, 1957.

CHUCK DAVIS

By Alisa Ann Johnson

Dancer, historian, choreographer, and self-proclaimed "Goodwill Ambassador to the World," Chuck Davis met a daunting schedule. In the midst of his touring with the renowned African American Dance Ensemble (AADE), he filled speaking and teaching engagements, while serving on and chairing a variety of arts and dance panels. And, as the founder of Cultural Arts Safari, an educational organization, he led groups in annual pilgrimages to Africa for study and research.

However, despite all of the notoriety and prestige his skill as a dancer and choreographer brought him, he considered his reputation as a community builder his highest honor. With his characteristic West African chants of agoo and amee, Davis called thousands of people together and used dance to bind them to him in his love for and celebration of the human community. "When you're dancing, you don't have time to hate," he proclaimed. Six feet six inches tall, and weighing 280 pounds, Davis had a distinctive face with high cheekbones, intense brown eyes, and an enormous and dazzling smile.

The African proverb that it takes a whole village to rear a child was more than mere folk wisdom for Charles Rudolph Davis. Born in Raleigh on January 1, 1937, he was reared not only by his parents, Tony and Ethel Watkins Davis, but by his teachers, minister, and neighbors. Growing up in a poor, black, segregated neighborhood, Davis was very aware of the brutal inequities in society. But he was equally aware of the gifts that flowed naturally from being a part of a close-knit and vital community—a community in which the welfare of children played a central role.

"Growing up in a poor neighborhood steeped in 'old world' values was a blessing," Davis said in 2000. "I was fortunate to come up in a time when kids listened to their elders, when they had to learn in school, and when the doors of the church were never closed. Even the criminals respected the churches."

Of the many factors that would shape and mold Davis's career, few matched the happy childhood spent in the bosom of his Raleigh community. When Davis spoke of those times, the pride and pleasure in his voice was unmistakable. From the childhood turf battles he fought with neighboring kids, to the secrets he and his young friends discovered by spying on couples at the local lovers' lane, Davis explored

Chuck Davis (Photo by Kevin Keister)

the boundaries of his world, secure in the gently monitoring gaze of concerned and involved adults.

Davis reveled in the attention he received from the adults around him, which helped him control his own behavior. A self-described "roly-poly child with an angel's face," Davis had a penchant for mischief that could easily have gotten out of hand. As Davis recalled, "I loved the fact that I went to an all-black high school, wherein I had teachers who were concerned about my welfare, and who took the time to visit my house and sit down and talk with my parents. As a result, I thought twice before acting up in school because I knew that those teachers, my teachers, would be coming around the corner, and the last thing I wanted them to do was to talk to my daddy—who was a construction worker with *big* hands."

It was from his community that Davis learned the importance of education. Many parents who had been denied the chance to go to school were just as eager to receive an education as to provide one for their children. Davis recalled, "Before I went to school, I used to listen to Professor King [who] would go around to the different houses to the parents who had not had a chance to go to school and he would tutor them. My own mom knew that I would be going to school, and because of that she wanted to be able to sign her name."

At Ligon High School Davis discovered his second great love—theater. Educated in an all-black high school where the focus was on academics, Davis's exposure to the arts was limited. Attracted to performing at an early age, Davis was first encouraged to study music and won awards for his beautiful soprano (at the time) voice. Impressed by his natural poise and astounding presence on stage, his teachers suggested he study drama, which he embraced with a passion.

Enrolled in a special navy-sponsored program in his junior year, Davis took special classes with the understanding that he would join the navy immediately after graduation. Ironically, it was while serving in the navy that Davis was introduced to the art form that would later define his life—dance. As Davis recalled, "While in boot camp I met people from all over, and there was a fellow there who had studied dance. When we had USO, he would always perform, and I used to be really envious. Now I realize that it was just my spirit becoming restless. . . . Even though I was enjoying life, it wasn't real enjoyment, because there was no fulfillment."

Fulfillment would only come, Davis soon realized, with the study of art, which so intrigued him. Stationed on the outskirts of Washington, D.C., after boot camp, Davis became a regular at the Dunbar Hotel, which was then the primary entertainment spot for the city's African American and Latino residents. The club featured Roland Kave and his Latin American All-Stars, a band composed completely of African American musicians who performed only Latin American music. At the Dunbar, Davis experienced firsthand the intimate connection between Latin American and African rhythms, a connection he was to explore throughout his career.

After serving two years in the navy, Davis enrolled at Howard University. Although he had originally intended a career in nursing, Davis was reintroduced to theater, and slowly came to understand the importance of performance in his life. Surrounded by talented and gifted writers, actors, and directors, Davis absorbed their love of performance, which fueled his own. While at Howard, Davis took his first formal dance class. One of only two males in the dance department, the young and inexperienced Davis received plenty of practice. "When you're one of the only males [in the department] you have to be in every piece come recital time," he recalled cheerfully. "In the first two pieces we looked like little snow bumpkins because we were overdressed—we had to wear the costumes for all of the other pieces. That was why I was so skinny then!"

In addition to his dance classes, Davis perfected his skills on the dance floors of D.C. clubs. By the time Roland Kave relocated his band to the Casbah, Davis had made his way from the outskirts of the crowds to the throbbing center of the dance floor, where he regularly dazzled onlookers with his blend of traditional Latin styles and contemporary African American moves. Encouraged by the crowd reaction, Davis decided to form his first dance company—La Dalemo Trio (the first two letters of the last names of each of the three members with La added for flair.) With little formal training but an obvious passion for dance, Davis's trio soon developed a reputation.

As the requests for performances increased, Davis had his first taste of success. However, it was marred by his first serious encounter with racism. During a performance that involved using a machete as a prop, Davis was forced off stage by a white policeman and arrested for carrying a "concealed weapon." He saw the incident in a humorous vein later, but there was nothing funny about it at the time. Although born and reared in the South, the arrest was one of the first times he was confronted blatantly with racial prejudice. As Davis recalls, "He was white, and I was a black—and the fact that I was on stage did not matter. I had a knife—that was enough. He took me to jail while I was still in my costume."

Davis spent the night in jail before he met bail. Yet even with half of the club's patrons willing to appear in court as witnesses, Davis approached his court date with fear and uncertainty. Ultimately Davis's fears proved unfounded: a disbelieving judge dryly asked Davis, "Where did you hide it (the machete)?" The case was dismissed and the arresting officer reprimanded. Despite the outcome, the experience had a profound effect on him. Davis was unsettled by the reckless way he had been so dehumanized, and with this discomfort came another stirring—the need to find a way to bridge the chasm between people caused by prejudice and bigotry.

A surprising outcome of Davis's encounter with the police was increased notoriety. In 1963 he was asked to perform at a musical event that was offered in connection with the historic civil rights march on Washington. While dancing, Davis was spotted by the well-known African musician and performer Babatunde Olatunji, who invited Davis to join his group in New York.

Once there, Davis began his study of African dance in earnest. While retaining his Latin American style, he began to examine the various styles and movements of African dance with Olatunji. Wanting the broadest possible background, he explored a variety of dance styles, but realized with growing certainty that his passion was African dance. Rather than giving up his interest in other forms, however, Davis sought to synthesize them by seeking to uncover the African influences that existed within.

Davis performed a number of years with Olatunji, who guided his study of traditional African movement. Not content to know only the movement, Davis immersed himself in the study of various African cultures, particularly those of West Africa. He eventually left the company to study with noted choreographers Eleo Pomare and Lester Horton, and later performed with the Bernice Johnson Dance Company. But Davis's intensive study of the intricacies of traditional African dance led him to become more and more skeptical of the way dance and many other African art forms were being portrayed in the media. Davis came to believe that the western media reduced all African dance to "hip-swing orgiastic movement" designed to titillate. His study had revealed exactly the opposite, and had cultivated within him in a deep respect for the complexity of each movement in traditional African dance.

In 1968, frustrated by what he saw as the willful misrepresentation of African dance, Davis formed the Chuck Davis Dance Company. His goal was to counterbalance negative images of African dance with ones that showcased its precision and vitality. Recruiting talented young dancers, Davis committed himself to sharing the finest traditions of African dance and music. In addition, Davis took his crusade to present authentic African dance to other venues. He was instrumental in starting the Dance Africa Festival, a celebration of African culture. At the Brooklyn Academy of Music, Dance Africa became a premier showcase for African dance companies and a leader in the movement to preserve African dance.

Davis was also instrumental in introducing African dance to the American Dance Festival's (ADF) artistic lineup. His reputation as one of the foremost choreographers and teachers in traditional techniques of African dance led ADF founders Charles and Stephanie Rhinehart to recruit him both as an artist-in-residence and as head of ADF's outreach program. Davis joined the ADF faculty in 1974 and served until 1995. Through ADF's outreach program Davis introduced African dance to a generation of young dancers from all over the world, fulfilling his desire to use his art as a bridge to tolerance and understanding.

In 1980, Davis returned to North Carolina and the people and community he loved so well. He moved to Durham, and founded his second African dance company, the African American Dance Ensemble. Composed of dancers he had cultivated and trained in ADF's outreach program, the African American Dance Ensemble was the culmination of Davis's artistic vision. Founded to preserve and share the best traditions of African and African American dance, AADE became one of the premier American dance companies.

Over the span of his career, Davis's unquestionable skills and talents yielded a number of honors on the state and national levels. He won the North Carolina Dance Alliance Award, the North Carolina Artist Award, the President's Award (given by the North Carolina Association of Arts Council Directors), and the North Carolina Order of the Long Leaf Pine. Davis also received the North Carolina Award in Fine Arts, one of the state's highest honors. In addition, he received a congressional citation, the New York Bessie Award, and the Brooklyn Academy of Music's Award for Distinguished Service to the Arts World. In 1998, Davis received an honorary Doctorate of Fine Arts from Medgar Evers College in New York.

And yet, Chuck Davis measured his success not by his honors, but by the fact that audiences around the country remembered his dance moves and the motto he ended every performance with: peace, love, and respect—for everybody.

Dr. Alisha Ann Johnson is assistant professor of African American literature at Meredith College in Raleigh. A native North Carolinian, Johnson received her undergraduate degree at Guilford College and advanced degrees at the University of North Carolina at Chapel Hill. She is married to Lavender Burris, an original member of the African American Dance Ensemble.

For more information, see:
"Chuck Davis: Peace, Love, and Respect for Everybody." *Dance Teacher Now* (January 1998): 6–13.

JOHN M. EHLE JR.

by Leslie Banner

JOHN EHLE once admitted to a child that he was a very unhappy fourth grade student because the public school he attended "was not a school so much as a place of vengeance. . . . I would be an F person today if I had to stay in that place."

Although popularly recognized as the spellbinding novelist who told the story of North Carolina's mountain people to millions of readers both here and abroad, Ehle is less widely known for his public service as the education "idea man" of Governor Terry Sanford's administration. By extending his creative genius from the writing of books to the creation of schools, antipoverty programs, and philanthropies, Ehle helped thousands of children escape the alternative fate he imagined for himself.

Among his most visible—though not his only— legacies to the state were the Governor's School of North Carolina, the first state-supported summer residential program for gifted students; the North Carolina School of the Arts, the first state-supported residential high school and college for the performing arts; and the North Carolina School of Science and Mathematics, the first state-supported residential high school for students with special talent in science and math.

Ehle was born on December 13, 1925, in Asheville. His father, John Marsden Ehle of Morgantown, W.Va., was the son of immigrants John Francis Ihli (German) and Nancy Marsden (English). Ehle's mother, Gladys Starnes, traced her roots to early settlers of the Hudson River Valley, whose descendants populated western North Carolina following the Revolutionary War. Ehle was particularly close to his mother's family while growing up, and in later years this proximity to native Appalachian people and to the bustling tourist town and trading center of Asheville strongly influenced his imagination, leading him to set eight of his eleven novels in his hometown and surrounding areas of the Great Smoky, Unaka, Black, and other North Carolina mountain ranges.

Ehle was educated in the public schools of Asheville and briefly attended Asheville-Biltmore College (later the University of North Carolina at Asheville) before joining the war effort with the U.S. Army infantry in 1942. After mustering out in 1946, he completed the two-year degree then offered by Asheville-Biltmore, before continuing his education at the Uni-

John M. Ehle Jr. (Photo by Peter Julian)

versity of North Carolina at Chapel Hill, where he earned a B.A. in 1949 in radio, television, and motion pictures, and an M.A. in drama in 1953.

Hired as an instructor and a writer at the university's Communications Center before he had completed his bachelor's degree, Ehle soon affirmed his true vocation. From 1954 to 1956, he wrote and co-produced the award-winning "American Adventure" series, twenty-six radio plays broadcast on NBC, Radio Free Europe, the Voice of America, the Armed Forces Network, and the Network of the National Association of Educational Broadcasters.

In 1957 he published his first novel, *Move Over, Mountain,* about a black family's struggles in the North Carolina piedmont, and in 1959 he wrote about the state's coastal region in his second novel, *Kingstree Island.* With his third novel, *Lion on the Hearth* (1961), he found the subject that would drive his fiction for the rest of his life: the mountains and the mountain people of western North Carolina. While each of his eight mountain novels can be read independently, they are all set in and around Asheville, and are concerned with the Wright and King families. Together, they plot the history of the region from post-Revolutionary War settlement through the Civil War, the Great Depression, and on into the present day. Carefully researched, with special attention to the details of work, mores, and the economic impact of the region's terrain and history, these novels have been praised for Ehle's sensitive and accurate portrayal of an almost vanished culture. Critics noted the author's narrative power, his ear for authentic speech patterns, his poetic use of language, and the seeming ease with which he spins the gold of myth out of the everyday lives of ordinary people.

Ehle's nonfiction, while not as extensive, was well received and in several instances also made noteworthy contributions to the history of North Carolina. *The Free Men* (1965) is an account of the 1963 civil rights struggle in Chapel Hill from the point of view of a young professor (Ehle) who knew the students and townspeople involved. *Trail of Tears* (1988) is a careful but engrossing reading of the primary material surrounding the removal of the Cherokee Indians from western North Carolina. *Dr. Frank* (1993) is an affectionate portrait of Frank Porter Graham, the legendary president of the University of North Carolina.

In 1961 Ehle had earned promotion to associate professor on the UNC faculty, but he was restless and dissatisfied. In May of that year he published an article in the *News and Observer* that caused some consternation within the university community, especially the administration. "What's the Matter with Chapel Hill?" criticized the university for its lack of interest in the education and support of artists, and went on to extend that criticism to a general lack of creativity in its attitudes toward the humanities and even its land use policies. The article demonstrated to Governor Terry Sanford that here was a man with iconoclastic ideas about education and the energy to express them. Sanford needed that energy on his staff, for at that time the state constitution did not allow the governor to seek a second term.

In the spring of 1962, Ehle was poised to begin a sabbatical during which he planned to write another novel. Instead, he accepted Sanford's invitation to work as a special assistant, with the task of coming up with new ideas about education or anything else that might help the people of North Carolina, provided Ehle could find outside funding for his ideas. Two years later the national recognition the "New South" governor had achieved was exemplified by a *Newsweek* magazine profile in June 1964 that summed up Ehle's contributions as Sanford's aide. Calling Ehle the "creative spark for what will probably be considered one of the most successful administrations in North Carolina history," the magazine credited Ehle with instigating the North Carolina Film Board, Shakespeare in the Schools, the North Carolina School of the Arts, the Governor's School, the North Carolina Advancement School (to provide guidance and tutoring for underachieving eighth graders), the Learning Institute of North Carolina (to evaluate and assist in improving public education), and the North Carolina Fund. An attempt to break the cycle of poverty for poor children, the fund became a national model and the pattern for the community action plan in Lyndon Johnson's Anti-Poverty Program.

To finance these and other projects, Ehle sought some support from the federal government, but most of the financial support came from private foundations in North Carolina and, surprisingly, New York. Ehle had proven to be extraordinarily adept with foundation officials at Ford and Carnegie, and had persuaded them to meet with Sanford and even to tour the state, tactics which were almost unheard of at the time.

As is usually the case with politics and government, not everything that Ehle envisioned was created, nor did everything he create survive. Despite their success, many of the Ehle/Sanford antipoverty, educational research, and cultural programs were replaced or superseded by others as the times and the governors changed. Notable among the survivors, however, were the Institute of Outdoor Drama, the national leadership organization for the outdoor historical drama movement; some of the programs established by the North Carolina Fund (itself chartered for only five years), including most of the community action agencies and the Manpower Development Corporation (MDC); and two of the schools—the Governor's School and the North Carolina School of the Arts. The North Carolina School of Science and Mathematics was waiting in the wings; it was established during Governor James B. Hunt Jr.'s first term.

The genesis of these three schools can be traced to one of the earliest entries in Ehle's journal of the Sanford years. On April 24, 1962, he noted in his diary, "I mentioned to Terry my model high school, which was to be in the arts, and sciences and math, and languages and the humanities, social studies—but each with its own campus, contiguous to one another." Within days Ehle had met with officials at Carnegie to seek funding for both an arts school and a residential high school for the academically gifted. Carnegie agreed to provide half the support needed for three years to a summer school for rising juniors and seniors who showed exceptional talent in academics or art. With additional private funding from donors in Winston-Salem, the first of the schools born of Ehle's ideas and energy and Sanford's political courage, the Governor's School, opened on the campus of Salem College in the summer of 1963. So successful was the new school that it quickly became part of the educational fabric of North Carolina and other states as well. Funded since 1966 by the legislature, expanded in 1978 to a second campus at St. Andrews Presbyterian College in Laurinburg, and moved to Meredith College in Raleigh in 2000, the Governor's School was emulated so often that in 1988 the National Conference of Governors' Schools was incorporated to support communication and research among its constituent institutions

Establishing the Governor's School was a relatively straightforward and uncomplicated process compared to the furor that attended the birth of the North Carolina School of the Arts (NCSA). Still seeking funding for an arts initiative as well as for the antipoverty efforts that would result in the formation of the groundbreaking North Carolina Fund, Ehle secured the interest of key Ford Foundation officials as Governor Sanford was appointing a committee to consider whether the state should sponsor a music conservatory. Ehle persuaded Sanford to expand that idea to include professional training in all of the performing arts and accepted membership on and de facto leadership of the committee. While Sanford attended to the political rough-and-tumble of convincing the General Assembly to support legislation ridiculed across the state as the "toe-dancing bill," Ehle and the conservatory committee faced down strong opposition from educators and deans of music and drama in North Carolina's colleges and universities, and criticism in the Greensboro and Chapel Hill press (countered by strong support, however, in the Raleigh and Charlotte papers).

Through it all, Ehle juggled delicate negotiations with Ford and wrote the enabling legislation that was passed on June 21, 1963, thanks to Sanford lobbyists Hugh Cannon and Sam Ragan, and to the governor's director of secondary roads, Ben Roney, who traded asphalt for votes. He guided the work of the conservatory committee as they contacted artists for advice, held public hearings, and coordinated the search for a site. He became, in fact, a one-man clearinghouse for the project, but he often despaired as mean-spirited attacks, political uncertainty, lack of adequate funding, and the need for a ready-made campus in a supportive host city combined at times into a chorus of impossible dreams. But with the unflagging determination of a pragmatist and the "burning anger" of an idealist, he persevered.

In the autumn of 1965, the new school opened its doors on the campus of an abandoned high school in Winston-Salem. Unique in the nation, dedicated to training musicians, actors, dancers, theatrical designers, production managers, and craftspeople, and, since 1993, filmmakers, NCSA accepts students (approximately 50 percent from North Carolina) on the basis of talent alone and offers high school, college, and postgraduate diplomas. It would become one of the foremost conservatories in the world.

At the end of May 1964, Ehle left Sanford's staff to return to his life as an author, but his life of public service continued, both officially and unofficially, as he served on foundation and school boards, national commissions, and as an informal advisor to the state's leaders. Nor did he forget his model high school in science. For years his idea "attracted occasional bolts of lightning," he has noted, as those both in and out of power in Raleigh "prodded, shoved or kicked at it, but its awakening to detectable breathing came in the autumn of 1976" when Governor-elect Hunt accepted Ehle's proposal and committed his administration to creating a new residential high school for gifted students, the North Carolina School of Science and Mathematics (NCSSM).

The pattern for developing NCSSM was much the same as Ehle had followed for NCSA. The governor signed letters requesting advice from prominent scientists and named Ehle to a special commission. At subsequent public hearings, however, as Ehle predicted, the state Department of Public Instruction and administrators from the public schools opposed funding the new school, arguing that their own schools and programs needed the money. Opposition appeared in the state's press with charges of elitism and concern that NCSSM would siphon the best students from high schools all over North Carolina. Occasionally despondent but never defeated, once again Ehle poured enormous energy into the drive for a new school, chairing the site committee and finding in Hunt a committed, resourceful partner.

NCSSM opened in September 1980 on the campus of what was once Durham's Watts Hospital and School of Nursing. It thrived as yet another North Carolina model for the nation engendered by a man who identifies himself as a writer—primarily a novelist—not as an educator, lobbyist, or politician.

Ehle once told Hunt that the "work and wailing that go into starting a school can never be analyzed. . . . " Perhaps not, but analyzing the man who does the starting is even more daunting, although he answers the question of why him? quite simply: "A novelist is as likely as any other craftsman to be interested in any new idea, and he isn't terrified by the fact that that's all he has."

At the end of the century Ehle made his home in several places: in Winston-Salem, where he quietly administered two private foundations to identify and fund educational opportunities for talented minority students; in Penland, where he had befriended the Penland School of Crafts; and New York City and London, cities where he enjoyed the work of his Tony Award-winning wife and daughter, Rosemary Harris and Jennifer Ehle.

Dr. Leslie Banner is the author of A Passionate Preference: The Story of the North Carolina School of the Arts, *and coauthor of* Keeping an Open Door *with Dr. H. Keith H. Brodie, with whom she has collaborated as a writer and editor at Duke University since 1985.*

For more information, see:

Ehle, John. Papers. Southern Historical Collection, University of North Carolina at Chapel Hill.

Banner, Leslie. "John [Marsden] Ehle, Jr." In *Contemporary Fiction Writers of the South: A Bio-Bibliographical Sourcebook.* Ed. Joseph M. Flora and Robert Bain. Greenwood Press, 1993.

————. *A Passionate Preference: The Story of the North Carolina School of the Arts.* Down Home Press, 1991.

Mace, F. Borden. "Fanning the Spark of Exceptional Creativity." *The Journal for Secondary Gifted Education* (Winter 1997/1998): 51–56.

Mashburn, Rick. "Making Education Happen: North Carolina's One-Man Think Tank." *Carolina Alumni Review* (Winter 1984).

"One-Man Rand." *Newsweek,* June 1, 1964.

Pappas, Peter George. "A State Quest for Latter Day Redemption: The Origins of the North Carolina Fund." Honors thesis, University of North Carolina at Chapel Hill, 1978.

Sanford, Terry. *But What about the People?* Harper and Row, 1966.

PAUL GREEN

By Karin Lisa Posser

PAUL GREEN'S LIFE is a striking example of moral vision in action. As a dramatist, author, and teacher, the Harnett County native effectively incorporated his concern for human rights and steady advocacy for educational and social reform into his life and writing. Although he was best known as the author of the historical outdoor "symphonic drama" *The Lost Colony,* still performed annually in North Carolina, Green was part of that remarkable generation of writers who first brought Southern writing to the attention of the world. Through his life and work, Green contributed in fundamental ways to the emerging New South during the first half of the twentieth century.

The son of William Archibald and Betty Lorine Byrd, Green was born in Harnett County on March 17, 1894. He grew up on his father's farm and spent his first twenty-one years in a rural community along the Cape Fear River in the southeastern part of the state. Not unlike most post-Civil War southern families, the Green family was quite poor. Religion seemed to pass for culture in the household, where it provided not only moral direction, but social guidance as well. During Green's childhood, storytelling was part of an everyday routine and Green would later reflect on family evenings on the porch reciting stories. It was in this environment where Paul, named by his mother after her favorite saint, quickly acquired a love for storytelling. In fact, echoes of the cadences and devices of that oral tradition are present throughout his writing.

His mother, whom he loved dearly, died suddenly of a massive cerebral hemorrhage when Green was twelve. Already considered "different" from other children, he soon withdrew into a world of his own creation. Green read books as he plowed, and taught himself to play the violin. For a time he even played professional baseball for a team in nearby Lillington and his remarkable skill as a pitcher, due to his ambidexterity, was widely acclaimed.

Yet it was clear that writing was his true passion. After graduating from nearby Buies Creek Academy in 1914, he earned enough money to enter the University of North Carolina in 1916 "to learn to be a poet." In Chapel Hill, he wrote poems that were published in the *Carolina Magazine,* and, to help with his expenses at the university, Green worked as an instructor in

Paul Green (Courtesy Paul Green Foundation)

a freshman English course. But World War I interrupted his teaching and his educational pursuits.

In April 1917, before finishing his first year at Chapel Hill, Green enlisted in the army. Because he was not certain that he would return to pursue a literary career, he published at his own expense a thin volume of poems, *Trifles of Thought by P. E. G.,* before leaving for France. While in the service, Green rose rapidly through the ranks, from private, to corporal, to sergeant, and to sergeant-major with the 105th Engineer Battalion of the 30th Division. He was then commissioned a second lieutenant with the chief of engineers in Paris. Although he was reluctant to speak of the experience, he also participated in several months of heavy combat in the trenches during a year's service at the front in Belgium and France.

Green returned to the university in 1919 and graduated in 1921 with a major in philosophy. He remained for a year of graduate work in philosophy. While there, Green studied under Professor Frederick Koch, a newly arrived member of the faculty who had organized the Carolina Playmakers Group in 1918. He encouraged Green and other budding playwrights such as Thomas Wolfe to write "folk plays" based on local subjects and personal experiences. It was here that Green found not only his vocation, but his wife Elizabeth Lay as well. Also one of Koch's students, Lay was one of seven children of an Episcopalian minister. Tall, with blue-green eyes and a mass of copper hair, Lay soon became Green's spiritual companion. She, like Green, had grown up in a world of books and understood, as no one else could, his hunger for and love of literature. The two were married by Lay's father in 1922.

After performing graduate work in philosophy for a year under Professor Horace Williams at Chapel Hill, Green and his wife moved to upstate New York where Green completed a second year of graduate study in philosophy at Cornell University. In the summer of 1923 the couple returned to North Carolina and Green accepted a position as assistant professor of philosophy at UNC. He remained a faculty member in the philosophy department for sixteen years. In 1939, Green moved to UNC's department of drama and became a professor in dramatic art. Five years later, in 1944, Green decided to devote more time to writing and resigned from teaching.

Green was involved in a number of endeavors during his twenty-one years at UNC. He and his wife collaborated with others for many years in the production of "The Literary Lantern," a newspaper column of book reviews and book news. Green also served as editor of the literary journal the *Reviewer* and contributed to a number of newspapers, including the *News and Observer*. He was quite prolific while part of the UNC faculty, writing plays as well as short stories, novels, and poetry. The Carolina Playmakers produced most of his plays, but some of his works were also produced in New York, Washington, D.C., and elsewhere.

His stories depicted a wide variety of human experiences in the small-town, rural South of the early part of the twentieth century. Green's many stories often featured wandering bands of gypsies and the Lumbee Indians of the southeastern North Carolina region. African Americans were also important characters in a number of his works. Green's political views, particularly regarding race, permeated his writings. In the 1920s, Green began writing "Negro plays" and stories, which were among the first attempts in southern literature to seriously consider the experiences of black women, men, and children. Significantly, a defining trait in Green's black characters was how each responded to the dehumanizing pressures of a segregated society. In the preface to an early collection of one-act plays, *Lonesome Road: Six Plays for the Negro Theatre,* Green discussed the history of black people in the South. The black experience, Green explained, consisted of continuous exploitation and defiance of exploitation from the early days of slavery on into the years of segregation. A brief rationale for the book concluded his preface: "In the following pages a first effort is made to say something of what these people . . . have suffered and thought and done. For it seems apparent now that such things are worthy of record."

A number of pieces in this anthology featured black characters. But unlike the other works included in the collection, Green's play *In Abraham's Bosom* had a black focal character. This particular play gained great public acclaim in 1926–27 when it was produced at the Garrick Theater on Broadway and earned Green the Pulitzer Prize in drama that season. (His other Broadway plays included *The House of Connelly, Roll Sweet Chariot, Johnny Johnson,* and *Native Son.*) Set around the turn of the century, *In Abraham's Bosom* focused on an African American man with a Moses-like vision of leading his people out of the bondage of poverty and ignorance through education.

In 1928, Green received a Guggenheim Fellowship, which gave him the opportunity to study theater in Europe. He, Elizabeth, and their two children—they would eventually have four children—spent sixteen months in Europe, first in Berlin, then in London. While there, Green and his family lived simply among the people, and the writer studied German drama. It was here that he became convinced that the history, folktales, and music of the people could—and should —be incorporated into playwriting.

On his return, Green welcomed the opportunity to spend the years from 1932 to 1936 in Hollywood writing under contract for Warner Brothers. While there, he wrote scripts for such stars as Will Rogers, Bette Davis, Clark Gable, and Lionel Barrymore. Yet, although well-paid for his efforts, Green was often unsatisfied with the final artistic quality of the products produced on the big screen. Finally, in 1964, he ended his association with the motion picture industry and moved back to the Tar Heel State.

While in California, Green had become increasingly interested in a new form of drama. Partially inspired by the plays he saw while in Germany, he decided to use the theme of the "Lost Colony" of Roanoke Island in a dramatic production. In 1937, *The Lost Colony* became a reality. The first of Green's outdoor historical plays, *The Lost Colony* gained historical significance as the work largely responsible for reshaping a genre.

In Europe historical pageantry has a rich tradition going back to the Middle Ages. In America, the late nineteenth and early twentieth centuries brought a number of large and spectacular staged events that ministered to civic pride in one way or another. These pageants were not plays, but chronicles, with events following one another according to historical chronology, not dramatic necessity. They had no characters in a dramatic sense, but only representations of prominent figures who were likely to step forward one at a time and give speeches.

Although it makes direct use of historical material, *The Lost Colony* is unmistakably a play. It is a well-constructed dramatic work with points of interest appropriate to a drama. Its success has encouraged a movement over the last half century in which hundreds of historical plays have been produced all over the country. This first "symphonic drama," as Green termed this new type of play, employed the spoken word, song, music, dance, and pantomime, and was first produced in 1937 in an outdoor theater on the site of the 1587 settlement on Roanoke Island.

Green consistently demonstrated sympathy and compassion for blacks, the poor, and others whom he saw around him in his rural community. In Chapel Hill during the 1920s, he was one of the first individuals to speak out for the rights of African Americans. During the 1930s he devoted a significant amount of time to social causes, such as aid to workers in southern textile mills, prison reform, and the abolition of capital punishment. Later, he was an influential supporter of school desegregation, following the 1954 Supreme Court ruling in *Brown v. Board of Education*.

Civil rights, fighting poverty, and political oppression were all causes of concern to Green, and he lent support for them in person, in print, and financially. He spoke out against and wrote plays dealing with war, prejudice, and lynching. In the 1960s, Green was an early and outspoken opponent of the U.S. involvement in the Vietnam War. In the 1970s, he also frequently took on fellow North Carolinian Senator Jesse Helms with his vigorous arguments for disarmament and against the arms race between the nuclear superpowers.

Although his beliefs were often unpopular ones in the American South, it was also understood that Green was "haunted by the ideal of perfection" and believed "in the uniqueness of man as responsible to his neighbor and to God." Green died on May 4, 1981, at the age of eighty-seven.

Karin Lisa Posser received her M.A. from the University of North Carolina at Greensboro where her primary areas of interest included early-twentieth-century American history, the South, intellectual history, and interdisciplinary studies of American civilization. Her major graduate research focused on social and literary critic H.L. Mencken and his influence on the Southern Literary Renaissance of the early twentieth century.

For more information, see:

Green, Paul. Papers. Southern Historical Collection, University of North Carolina at Chapel Hill.

Avery, Laurence G., ed. *A Paul Green Reader.* University of North Carolina Press, 1998.
———. *A Southern Life: Letters of Paul Green, 1916–1981.* University of North Carolina Press, 1994.
Paul Green's Wordbook: An Alphabet of Reminiscence. Paul Green Foundation with Appalachian Consortium Press, 1990.
Roper, John Herbert, ed. *Paul Green's War Songs: A Southern Poet's History of the Great War, 1917–1920.* North Carolina Wesleyan College Press, 1993.

RANDALL JARRELL

By Susannah Link

I N THE LIFE and work of Randall Jarrell, North Carolina can lay claim to one of the best-known poets of the Middle Generation, that group of modernist writers who followed W. H. Auden and T. S. Eliot. By helping to identify North Carolina with a literary tradition, Jarrell also contributed to the reputation of the Woman's College of the University of North Carolina (later the University of North Carolina at Greensboro) as a center of literary culture. Through his prodigious body of work as a writer of both poetry and prose and as a literary critic, he influenced a generation of writers and students in North Carolina and the nation.

Among the outstanding features of Jarrell's career was the National Book Award for *The Woman at the Washington Zoo* in 1962, Guggenheim Fellowships in 1946 and 1963, and the University of North Carolina's O. Max Gardner Award in 1962. He received numerous other literary awards and poetry prizes between 1936 and 1965. Jarrell published nine books of poetry between 1940 and 1965, three books of essays, one book of fiction, four children's books, four translations, and six anthologies.

Jarrell was born on May 6, 1914, in Nashville, Tenn., to Owen and Anna Campbell Jarrell. In the 1920s, he moved with his parents to Long Beach, Calif., where his father worked as a portrait photographer. After his parents separated, he lived with his paternal grandparents and his great-grandmother in Hollywood for a year. That year was a highlight in his childhood, and he was bitterly disappointed when he had to return to live with his mother in Nashville. Some of the most prominent themes of Jarrell's subsequent work —change, loneliness, insecurity—grew out of this emotional experience.

He never spoke with or wrote to his grandparents again, although memories of that part of his childhood inspired many of the poems in *The Lost World,* published in 1965. In 1962, his mother had returned to him the letters that he had written to her during his year in Hollywood, and in rereading those, Jarrell was moved to confront that part of his past. Jarrell's childhood was probably not as unhappy as he made it seem, most likely depicted that way for dramatic effect. These letters suggest a child in a warm relationship with his mother who was happily involved in youthful pursuits. William Pritchard, one of Jarrell's

Randall Jarrell, left, with Peter Taylor (Courtesy of UNCG University Relations)

biographers, observes that "Jarrell strove to pay tribute to the mixed nature of life, good and evil growing together in its branches and issuances."

Jarrell was an insatiable reader, as he himself admitted. "I went to school, played, did what the grown-ups made me do," he recalled, "but no matter how little time I had left, there were never books enough to fill it—I lived on the ragged edge of having nothing to read." Jarrell's extensive knowledge of myths and legends charmed the two sculptors of Nashville's replica of the Parthenon. As a boy, Jarrell was chosen to pose for the sculpture of Ganymede, cupbearer of the gods, and as the sculptors worked, Jarrell entertained them with stories. During his high school years, Jarrell became an intense tennis player, and he continued to enjoy the game for the rest of his life.

After Jarrell graduated from high school, his mother's brother, Howell Campbell, a businessman in Nashville, sent him to a commercial school in Nashville. Jarrell's business studies were brief, however, and he convinced his uncle to send him to Vanderbilt University.

In the fall of 1932, he entered Vanderbilt as a freshman. His reputation as a brilliant, widely read scholar was established early in his college career, as was his reputation as a biting critic. During his first trimester, he took Advanced Composition with John Crowe Ransom. During the winter trimester, he enrolled in Robert Penn Warren's general survey of literature. Warren, in his late twenties at the time, was disturbed by Jarrell's condescending attitude toward the other freshmen. Jarrell made his disgust with the intellectually immature students obvious by grimacing and shaking his head at their questions and responses. Ransom said Jarrell was an "insistent and almost overbearing talker," an "*enfant terrible*." On the other hand, judging from Jarrell's writing, Ransom realized that the young man "had to become one of the important people in the literature of our time."

Rather than majoring in English, Jarrell became fascinated by psychology and chose that subject as his major, with a minor in philosophy. He graduated in three years, in December of 1935, and was ranked seventh out of 137 students in his class. He was also elected to Phi Beta Kappa. After graduation, Jarrell began graduate studies in psychology, but soon found the scientific aspects of the subject unappealing. He switched to English and received his M.A. degree in 1939. His former teachers, Ransom and Warren, continued to be influential mentors after he left Vanderbilt. Warren went on to teach at Louisiana State University and became an editor at the *Southern Review,* where he published some of Jarrell's poems and reviews. Jarrell won the *Southern Review* poetry contest prize in 1936.

In 1937, when Ransom left Vanderbilt to teach at Kenyon College in Ohio, Jarrell went with him as a part-time instructor and coach. There he met and became lifelong friends with Peter Taylor, a writer who also spent, off and on, twenty years of his career teaching at the Woman's College of the University of North Carolina in Greensboro during the years that Jarrell was there. Jarrell also became friends with the poet Robert Lowell, who was an undergraduate at Kenyon, having transferred from Harvard to work with Ransom.

Jarrell left Kenyon in 1939 to teach at the University of Texas at Austin, where he met Mackie Langham, who had just received her M.A. from Texas and who would become his first wife in June 1940. During this period, Jarrell's career both as a poet and as a literary critic began in earnest. His first collection of poems appeared in *Five Young American Poets* in 1940 and, in 1942, a collection of Jarrell's poems alone, *Blood for a Stranger,* was published.

Some of Jarrell's strongest and most dramatic poetry came out of his military experiences. These war poems were published in 1945 in *Little Friend, Little Friend*. Jarrell joined the army air corps in 1942 and started his training in aviation, but did not succeed as a pilot. Instead, he spent his service at Chanute Field in Illinois as an aviation and celestial-navigation instructor. His war poems dealt with the subject of loss —of humanity, of life, of innocence. In addition to these wartime losses, Jarrell's poems also addressed everyday losses that humans face, even in peacetime.

In 1946, when Jarrell finished his military service, he received a Guggenheim Fellowship. He spent the next year filling in for Margaret Marshall as editor of the *Nation* in New York while she was on sabbatical. During this same period, he taught classes at Sarah Lawrence College in Bronxville, N.Y. His novel *Pictures from an Institution,* published in 1954, was based on his experiences at Sarah Lawrence. By 1947, Jarrell was ready to move on. He and Mackie followed Peter Taylor and his wife, poet Eleanor Ross Taylor, to North Carolina, where he took a position as associate professor of English at the Woman's College of the University of North Carolina. Mackie took a position as an instructor. The Taylors and the Jarrells bought a duplex together at 1924 Spring Garden Street.

To his friends from New York, the move to Greensboro seemed like a move to obscurity. Lowell tried to explain the move by emphasizing Jarrell's love of teaching. He quoted Jarrell saying that "if I were a rich man, I would pay money for the privilege of being able to teach." Lowell added by way of explanation that "probably there was no better teacher of literature in the country, and yet he was curiously unworldly about it, and welcomed teaching for almost twenty years in the shade or heat of his little-known southern university for girls in Greensboro. There his own community gave him a compact, tangible, personal reverence that was incomparably more substantial and poignant than the empty, numerical long-distance blaze of national publicity."

Most of Jarrell's poetry was published in four books within a ten-year timespan. During the 1950s, Jarrell devoted his time less to poetry and more to writing the essays and reviews which were collected in *Poetry and the Age* (1953), and to writing his novel, *Pictures from an Institution* (1954). During this period, he also taught at the Woman's College, held visiting positions (at Salzburg, Princeton, and the Indiana School of Letters), and was poetry consultant to the Library of Congress from 1956 to 1958. This dry period for poetry lasted until 1963, when he had a burst of creativity and wrote the poems that comprised his last book.

In July 1951, Jarrell accepted a position at the Rocky Mountain Writers' Conference in Boulder, Colo., where he met and fell in love with Mary von Schrader. Three years earlier, at the Salzburg Seminar in American Civilization, Jarrell had become romantically involved with Elizabeth Eisler, but had decided against leaving Mackie for Elizabeth. His romance with Mary was different. During his year in Princeton, Jarrell continued to write intimate letters to Mary, and Mackie spent the year back in Texas pursuing a Ph.D. (and caring for Jarrell's beloved black cat, Kitten).

During the years from 1950 to 1952, Jarrell produced his most significant literary criticisms of several major poets, reviewing the works of e. e. cummings and Wallace Stevens, as well as Robert Lowell, Richard Wilbur, and William Carlos Williams. He rediscovered Walt Whitman in a critical essay in which he argued that Whitman was a poet "of the greatest and oddest delicacy and originality and sensitivity, so far as words are concerned." According to Jarrell's biographer, William Pritchard, "nobody could have read the Whitman essay—or can read it still, for that matter—without marveling at how little of this poet one really *knows,* and how good is much or most of what Jarrell quotes." Many of the famous lines by which we know Whitman were made famous by Jarrell's essay. The crowning achievement of Jarrell's reviews during this period was an important essay on Robert Frost titled "To the Laodiceans."

During his two years in Washington as poetry consultant, Jarrell made numerous public appearances. He gave poetry readings at several state universities in California, as well as readings and lectures at ten other schools around the country. He also translated some of Rainer Maria Rilke's poems and several fairy tales of the Brothers Grimm. His poetry production decreased during this period, and few recent poems appeared in his collection titled *The Woman at the Washington Zoo,* which was published in 1960 and for which he won the National Book Award in 1961.

Between 1960 and his death in October 1965, Jarrell wrote several important pieces of children's literature, turning professionally to a subject which had always interested him less formally. Various children

in his life knew him as a great storyteller, from those he babysat as a young man in Nashville to Mary's two daughters, Alleyne and Beatrice. He had charmed the Nashville Parthenon sculptors with his recounting of myths and legends. In the early 1960s, at the suggestion of Michael di Capua, a children's book editor at Macmillan, Jarrell wrote the first of four children's books, *The Gingerbread Rabbit.* A second book, *The Bat-Poet,* was published in 1964. It was the most popular of his children's books and was illustrated by Maurice Sendak, who also illustrated his other two books, *The Animal Family* and *Fly by Night.*

In the midst of his work on the children's books, Jarrell was invited to give one of the speeches at the first National Poetry Festival in Washington in the fall of 1962. For his speech, he wrote a long retrospective piece titled "Fifty Years of American Poetry." Many of the evaluations included in this speech are still valuable. His immersion in the world of poetry and his lack of interest in the politics of the day were illustrated at the close of the festival. The Cuban missile crisis coincided with the conference, and a sherry party hosted by First Lady Jacqueline Kennedy was canceled. Several poets left early, but Jarrell was too wrapped up with the poetry events to give much thought to the Cubans and Russians.

The assassination of President John F. Kennedy in November 1963, however, had a profoundly depressing effect on Jarrell. He was fatigued and ill, partly as a result of a bout of hepatitis. He was downcast about turning fifty in May 1964. A psychiatrist in Cincinnati prescribed Elavil for his depression, and by late 1964, Jarrell was feeling better and was doing more writing. His manner became almost manic—he started more projects than he could finish, his lectures ran overtime, and he began to ramble in his conversations. He had trouble getting along with his best friends, particularly Peter Taylor and Mary. He slept only a few hours at night, tipped a waitress in Nashville with a $1,500 check, and flew to Nashville to visit his sick mother three times in two weeks, charging his tickets with abandon on his credit card. According to Jarrell, he and Mary separated briefly.

Mary had him admitted for psychiatric treatment to the hospital in Chapel Hill. The doctors replaced the Elavil with Thorazine, which left him depressed, even after it was discontinued. Near the end of April 1965, while he was back at home in Greensboro, he slashed his left wrist in a suicide attempt. The incident lifted his depression. After several stints at the hospital, he was home for good by July. He went back to teaching in the fall, but his wrist was not healing properly, so he went to a hand clinic in the medical school at Chapel Hill. He took work with him, had plans for future writing and speaking engagements, and seemed upbeat.

On the evening of October 14, while walking along a road near Chapel Hill, he was struck by a car and killed. Whether or not he purposely stepped into the path of the car has been a subject of debate. Robert Lowell and Peter Taylor believed that he had committed suicide, but Mary felt that the evidence pointed to an accident. Either way, Jarrell was finally released from his obsession with "the passage of time" and his "desire to escape from the real world to a place where time does not exist."

Susannah J. Link graduated from Stanford University and continued her studies in American history at the University of Virginia. She has taught at the University of North Carolina at Greensboro and has worked as assistant editor for the Papers of James Madison *and a consulting editor for the* Papers of Woodrow Wilson. *She is the author of* Harriet Elliott: A Brief Appreciation.

For more information, see:
The most complete collection of primary sources on Jarrell is in Special Collections, Jackson Library, University of North Carolina at Greensboro. The Berg Collection at the New York Public Library also contains letters and manuscripts.

Bawer, Bruce. *The Middle Generation: The Lives and Poetry of Delmore Schwartz, Randall Jarrell, John Berryman, and Robert Lowell*. Archon Books, 1986.

Ferguson, Suzanne. *The Poetry of Randall Jarrell*. Louisiana State University Press, 1971.

Hungerford, Edward B., ed. *Poets in Progress*. Northwestern University Press, 1962.

Jarrell, Mary von Schrader, ed. *Randall Jarrell's Letters*. Houghton Mifflin Co., 1985.

———. *Remembering Randall*. Harper Collins, 1999.

Lowell, Robert, Peter Taylor, and Robert Penn Warren, eds. *Randall Jarrell, 1914–1965*. Farrar, Straus, & Giroux, 1967.

Pritchard, William H. *Randall Jarrell: A Literary Life*. Farrar, Straus, & Giroux, 1990.

Quinn, Sister Bernetta, O.S.F. *Randall Jarrell*. G. K. Hall & Co., 1981.

Rosenthal, M. L. *Randall Jarrell*. University of Minnesota Press, 1972.

Shapiro, Karl. *Randall Jarrell*. Published for the Library of Congress by Gertrude Clarke Whittall Poetry and Literature Fund, 1967.

LUCY MORGAN

By Laura McAuliffe

Lucy C. Morgan, standing, with a Penland weaver (Courtesy of North Carolina Collection)

Lucy Morgan, founder of the Penland School of Crafts, once said that her school "began by chance and survived on luck." Described as a "diminutive dynamo of action," Morgan aggressively pursued her dream. "There were two things I hoped to do in the mountains," she said. "I wanted to bring about a revival of handweaving, which had become an all-out dead art in the United States, and I wanted to provide our neighbor mothers with a means of adding to their meager incomes."

Morgan would go on to accomplish both, and much more, establishing from humble beginnings one of the country's most highly touted schools of crafts. As author Philis Alvic said, "She was an expert at seizing possibilities and expanding her vision to encompass them. Any story of Penland and its weavers is the story of Lucy Morgan."

Lucy Calista Morgan was born September 20, 1889, in a log cabin in the Cartoogechaye community of Macon County, the daughter of Alfred and Fannie Eugenia (Siler) Morgan. She was the sixth of nine children, and although she lived in a home without plumbing or electricity, she would later write, "I never think of it as having been a difficult way of living." Her father had a printing office and her mother helped to raise money to build an Episcopal church. Morgan's mother died when she was fourteen and her father remarried Ada Warner, whom Morgan described as "just about the age of our eldest sister." Morgan received her earliest education at a private school operated by her aunt in Hickory, and by then had already been raised on a diet of Charles Dickens. She went on to the Central Michigan Normal School in Mount Pleasant, Mich., and earned a life certificate.

She then entered one of the few professions open to women in 1915, teaching.

From 1915 until 1920, Morgan taught in Farwell and Traverse City, Mich.; Berwyn, Ill.; and Havre, Mont. During the summers of 1916 and 1917, she studied at the University of Chicago, and for a year afterward worked for the Children's Bureau of Chicago.

In 1920, Morgan was called back to her home state. Traveling by train, she arrived in Penland, a small community on the Toe River, on June 1, 1920. She moved to Mitchell County to help her brother Rufus, an Episcopal minister, run the Appalachian School, a boarding school for elementary-age children who lacked care because of death or family trauma; it also allowed local children within walking distance to attend. Morgan soon took on the role of both teacher and principal. "In casting my lot with Penland, I had elected to stay in my kind of country with my kind of folk. . . . I've never been away from the mountains for any great length of time, and I never expect to be," she said.

During the winter holiday of January 1923, Morgan accompanied Bonnie Willis to Berea College in Kentucky at the request of Willis's parents, in order to keep an eye on her. Morgan asserted that Willis didn't need watching, so she spent her nine weeks there learning handweaving from Anna Ernberg, a Swedish woman who served as director of the school's Fireside Industries. Morgan knew that handweaving and vegetable dyeing had once been prevalent activities in the mountains but had fallen out of practice. At the end of the holiday, she returned from Berea and established her own version of Fireside. Initially, it was planned that the weaving would be taught to the older girls at the Appalachian School. However, Morgan had seen at Berea how weaving had provided women in the community with the opportunity to supplement their family incomes by money they made from working with their hands. She later wrote: "I would say if I had to put my finger on the time and place, that the idea of establishing an institution such as the Penland School of Handicrafts was born then and there [at Berea]." She decided it would be beneficial to institute a community weaving program for Penland, so she brought counterbalance looms back with her from Berea College.

Without taking any salary the first year and using her own savings to institute and continue the community weaving program, Morgan traveled extensively on foot throughout the surrounding mountains, as there was no other way to reach many of the families. A friend, Bishop Horner, would later furnish Morgan with a Model T Ford complete with a truck bed, but Morgan never learned how to use the truck's reverse gear. Bonnie Willis's mother, Martha Adele Willis, who had sent Morgan to Berea, became the first Penland community weaver.

Morgan provided looms, materials, and instruction in weaving, and then bought the handicrafts for resale. The program grew, and Morgan quickly saw the fruits of her labor. "I saw innumerable women in modest mountain homes, happily engrossed in weaving beautiful homespuns in delightful old designs, their worries vanishing, their hopes brightening their children's futures." In January 1924, less than a year after Morgan herself learned to weave, her Fireside Industries offered more than twenty items for sale. Despite all Morgan's talents, she despised bookkeeping, accounting, and making speeches. However, she was determined to make her community weaving program a success, even if it meant taking on the ledger books.

Morgan's Fireside Industries was renamed the "Penland Weavers and Potters" in 1928, a year in which Edward F. Worst of Chicago, an expert on handweaving, arrived in Penland. Although Morgan remained single, Worst played a crucial role in Morgan's life and his book on handweaving became Morgan's Bible. Worst visited Penland in August 1928, and so loved the place that he vowed to return to teach, which he did each summer until his death.

In 1929, Penland began to accept students from outside the immediate area, and the Penland School was founded on a thirty-acre tract of land owned by Morgan, which she later gave to the school. For the first five years of its existence, the school was known as the Weaving Institute and only offered courses in weaving. By the summer of 1930, Penland's Institute had sixteen students, doubling the number from the previous year, which it continued to do as long as space permitted. From 1929 until 1953, Morgan's only steady income came from vocational education work she did for the government. Without this money, Morgan said, "I'm sure we could never have weathered the Depression."

During the Depression Morgan took one of the greatest risks of her career. Although the state of North Carolina did not have a booth at the 1933 Chicago World's Fair, Mitchell County, and thus Penland, did. Morgan traveled with Howard "Toni" Ford (who married Bonnie Willis) to Chicago and set up a booth featuring the wares of Penland. This wasn't the first time Morgan had done something like this. She had a history of traveling to cities as far away as New Orleans and setting up a table at a convention to sell Penland's handicrafts. The Chicago World's Fair experiment proved to be an enormous success, even beyond what Morgan had hoped to achieve.

Morgan watched Penland grow in size and stature throughout the 1930s. In 1935, just twelve years after she first sat at a loom, Morgan was appointed to represent the Southern Mountain Handicraft Guild as a consulting delegate to the International Exhibition of Folk Arts held in Berne, Switzerland. But with Penland's increasing status came an even greater benefit to the impoverished people who lived in the mountain homes: money. In a brochure Bonnie Willis Ford authored in the late 1930s, she wrote, "We would find that one woman had bought herself some new false teeth, another a range stove, another a Victrola, and so on all down the line of necessities and comforts." The weaving program allowed them to enjoy a better quality of life based upon their own efforts.

Learning to weave was not only appreciated by women in the community program. As one student wrote in 1945, "I've never known a place where one experiences such a feeling of liberation, of a taking for granted that mistakes are a normal part of the learning process, of tolerant acceptance of people as they are, yet faith in their desire and ability to grow." When the war ended, occupational therapy was added to the focus of the school so that veterans could receive formal instruction during the year.

Throughout the fifties, the rest of the world began to take notice of Morgan and her school. In 1949, she established an annual craft study tour to Scandinavian countries and a system of student exchange between Finland and Penland. She made her second trip to Europe on a craft tour in 1953, traveling to Holland, Denmark, Germany, Sweden, Finland, Norway, Switzerland, and France.

When she was home, she was busy receiving honors. Her alma mater, Central Michigan Normal School (later Central Michigan University), awarded her an honorary doctorate of humanities in 1951. She received a second honorary degree, in humane letters, from the Woman's College of the University of North Carolina (later the University of North Carolina at Greensboro) in 1955, and in 1958 the Epsilon Beta Chapter of Chi Omega Fraternity awarded her the North Carolina Distinguished Service Award for Women. She also received the North Carolina Folklore Society's Brown Hudson Award for her contributions to state culture.

In addition to her position at the helm of Penland, Morgan remained active in many other organizations. She was a member of the Democratic Party, the Episcopal Church, Alpha Sigma Tau, Delta Kappa Gamma, the Business and Professional Women's Club, and the Southern Highlands Handicraft Guild, for which she was a trustee. She once listed her hobbies as handicrafts and collecting seashells, although she never mentioned going to the beach.

As late as 1961, the year before her retirement, prospective students wrote directly to Lucy C. Morgan to receive further information and a Penland catalog. The school was obviously her child, and she played the role of the proud mother. It became a tradition for the Penland students to gather around Morgan during teatime and listen to her tell the story of the beginning of the school. Although she never married, Morgan initiated a policy to pay for the wedding reception of any couple who had met at Penland. She not only fed 125 people at the LaFrance/Conley wedding luncheon, but also arranged for the couple to honeymoon in the North Carolina mountain cabin near Franklin where she was born. Morgan wrote in her memoir, "Although I have never entered the state I do thoroughly believe in marriage and I always have to discipline myself to keep from pushing a little when I see romance going slowly. . . . It's poor business consigning anybody up here to the permanent status of old maid and perennial bachelor."

Morgan retired from the helm of the school on September 1, 1962, saying that she wanted to turn over the school to its new director, Bob Brown, "while I was still young enough to show good judgement." Brown admired that good judgment. He later said that he didn't "believe in five-year plans. I just take Miss Lucy's advice and try to keep it open just one more day."

When Morgan arrived at Penland in June 1920, she had to "trudge up a twisting trail to the school." When she departed forty-three years later, she drove a car "over a road paved all the way to Penland Station." But Morgan did more for Penland than make it a place worth paving. Even more than establishing one of the most highly regarded crafts schools in the country, Morgan gave a gift to the women of the surrounding community. Greater than the financial gains they made through their handiwork, Morgan gave them an ability, a talent, and the accompanying self-esteem. No story of Morgan's accomplishments would be complete without recounting an episode in her memoir in which Ruby Burkheimer told Morgan about traveling to Seattle to visit her family. "But oh, it was wonderful!" recalled Burkheimer. "You know, I had never been anybody to my own family before, except just mother. I never had an identity of my own, and I wasn't expected to have. . . . But now I'm somebody. I am a celebrity. I can really do something. When they saw all the things I had made, they were stunned out of their normal way of thinking about me. 'Why Mother,' they raved, 'did you make all these? Did you actually make these beautiful things yourself?'"

Morgan recognized the power she had, although she always gave credit to the school. "Our greatest achievements at Penland have not been the beautiful and useful things we have made there," she wrote. "I am quite convinced that we cannot hold in our hands, we cannot run sensitive fingers over, we cannot study with discriminating eyes the textures or forms or colorings of our most beautiful and useful Penland productions. I say these are the Penland intangibles, the wondrous handicrafts of the spirit, things impossible to feel in your fingers or examine under a magnifying glass but real, nevertheless, and tremendously important and of value inestimable."

Morgan died at her home in Webster on July 3, 1981. She was buried in a small cemetery near Franklin, adjacent to St. John's, a church her brother Rufus rebuilt that had been a family place of worship.

"Providence seems to look with special kindness upon orphans, widows and old maids running mountain schools," she wrote. Well past her death, Penland offered courses in a broad range of artistic disciplines: making books and paper; pottery; drawing; glass blowing; working with iron and metals; photography; printmaking; making textiles; woodworking; and movement; and it featured studios in daily use by students ranging in age from nineteen to ninety.

Laura L. McAuliffe earned a B.F.A. in dramatic writing from New York University's Tisch School of the Arts, Institute of Film and Television, and an M.A. in history from the University of North Carolina at Charlotte. She is a contributor to Exploring Charlotte: A Pocket Guide to the Queen City *and has written for the* Charlotte Observer *and* Today's Charlotte Woman.

For more information, see:

The papers of Legette Blythe, who cowrote Morgan's *Gift from the Hills,* are in the Manuscripts Department of the Wilson Library at the University of North Carolina at Chapel Hill. The Blythe papers include correspondence with Lucy Morgan and a manuscript fragment from *Gift from the Hills.*

The Penland School of Crafts records and the Howard C. and Bonnie Willis Ford papers relating to the Penland School of Crafts are housed at the Archives of American Art at the Smithsonian Institution in Washington, D.C.

Alvic, Philis. *Weavers of the Southern Highlands: Penland.* P. Alvic, 1992.

Coyne, John. "Keeping Old Crafts Alive and Well." *Smithsonian,* November 1975.

Ennis, Lynn. *Penland and the Revival of Craft Traditions: A Study of the Making of American Identities.* Ph.D. diss. (A copy is housed at the Penland School of Crafts.)

Ford, Bonnie Willis. *The Story of the Penland Weavers.* Penland School of Crafts, 1945.

Morgan, Lucy, with LeGette Blythe. *Gift from the Hills: Miss Lucy Morgan's Story of Her Unique Penland School.* University of North Carolina Press, 1971.

Smith, Margaret Supplee, and Emily Herring. *North Carolina Women: Making History.* University of North Carolina Press, 1999.

"The Dream of Miss Lucy Morgan." *American Craft* 41 (Oct–Nov 1981).

OWEN FAMILY POTTERS

By Steve Bouser

Ben Owen III's earliest memories were of wet clay and spinning kick-wheels and fiery furnaces —and of a grandfather with magic in his hands. "I would ask, 'Why are we eating off dinnerware Grand-dad made?,'" he recalled. "So I got interested very early in how you could make this stuff from mud." Owen built a life around "this stuff"—the high-quality, hand-fashioned vases and bowls and cups and jugs that attract more and more visitors every year to the creative little corner of northern Moore and southern Randolph counties known as "pottery country."

As this cottage industry flourished, the Owen clan —whose members threw pots in these parts for seven generations—faced more and more competition. Sometimes it seemed like you couldn't look down any rutted lane for miles around without seeing another little shed that someone had transformed into a studio/kiln/gallery. But Ben Owen III, who pushed the family business to new levels of commercial and artistic success, was the undisputed crown prince of this quaint and out-of-the-way realm.

"One of the most important things my grandfather taught me was to keep it simple," Owen, then thirty with a child of his own, said one day in 2000, as he threw a blob of light-gray clay onto his wheel. "He used to say that it's so easy to make things in life complicated. The hard thing is to keep it simple."

Owen worked in a modern studio next to the old log building in which Ben the Elder plied his craft. By the natural light streaming into the airy workspace from a large window, the shapeless clay took life under Owen's husky hands. It writhed and rippled at first, as if resisting his plans. But soon it submitted to his persuasive touch and rose gracefully into an egg-shaped vase. He added delicate diagonal grooving with a wooden tool called a "rib" and then cut the vase away from the wheel with a string and placed it on a drying shelf alongside a dozen other vases-in-progress, all displaying subtle variations in size and shape. After about a week, they would go into a kiln for a first firing.

The history of pottery in North Carolina has many chapters, dating to the arrival of Moravians in the piedmont in the 1750s. They and other European set-tlers brought their pottery-making traditions with them, modifying them over the years to meet local

needs. They were at first attracted to the Seagrove area by its abundance of orange-red clay, though their de-scendants used clays from all over the Southeast.

For the first century and a half, Tar Heel potters engaged in a strictly utilitarian industry, producing the basic, rugged items that the farmers in the grow-ing region needed for everyday living: churns for mak-ing butter, dinnerware for the table, pitchers for mo-lasses, crocks for pickling, jugs for liquor—whether legal or illegal. Even after the craft had largely faded away elsewhere, it hung on into the early twentieth century in rural and tradition-bound North Carolina.

But the advent of cheap, mass-produced glass and china, along with the prohibition of alcoholic bever-ages, took a heavy toll. By the 1920s, the pottery re-gion of Moore County had become a depressed area in which a handful of old men—described as carry-ing on "a more or less Elizabethan existence"—still produced a few dishes and pickle jars for the use of their backwoods neighbors. It was an endangered craft under imminent threat of extinction.

Then came the memorable day when prominent Raleigh artist Juliana Busbee, who was looking for some tin plates in which to display apples at a county fair in Lexington, sent an assistant to the nearest hardware store. The helper came back instead with a dozen plates fired from native clay in a brilliant or-ange glaze. Intrigued, she tracked down their maker, who happened to be Rufus Owen, great-grandfather of Ben III.

Busbee and her historian husband, Jacques, soon become obsessed with reviving and helping market this vanishing native work, some examples of which they began selling in a shop they owned in New York's Greenwich Village. The modern denizens of pottery country still speak with reverence of the Busbees as the patron saints behind their renaissance and tireless champions who first saw the potential in elevating North Carolina pottery from a moribund craft by-passed by progress into a fresh and vibrant art form.

"Jacques and Juliana Busbee created Jugtown pot-tery," Owen said. "It is still run by my cousin, Ver-non Owen, and his wife, Pam, who come from a branch of the family that added an s to their name. The Busbees decided that this does not need to be a dying art. It could be a living, ongoing tradition. They actively sought out new shapes and forms, and

Ben Owen and Ben Owen III (Courtesy of Ben Owen III)

Ben Owen III (Courtesy of Ben Owen III)

they wanted somebody younger to help develop them. That's where my grandfather, Ben Owen, came in. He was young and eager to work and try new things."

The first Ben was only eighteen when the Busbees hired him to work at Jugtown. They opened his eyes to a wider world, taking him to museums in New York and Washington. They introduced him to Oriental styles that were to prove a lasting influence on his work and later on that of his grandson. Through the patronage of the Busbees (with whom he lived for years until marrying Lucille Harris), Ben soon achieved wide recognition in the field of art pottery, with exhibits in galleries and stores across the nation. His own version of "Chinese blue" became a trademark.

"Under Jacques' guidance, Ben incorporated this new material into his traditional vocabulary and as a result, Oriental translations emerged from the Moore County clay," wrote James C. Jordan III, the curator of decorative arts at Charlotte's Mint Museum of Art. "His achievement, while still utilitarian in nature, was now more recognized for its artistic merit. Mentor and craftsman had formed a new ceramic tradition in North Carolina."

Owen took special pride in the title "Master Potter," which was bestowed on him at the Chapel Hill Dogwood Festival in 1934. He used it on his personal stamp when he opened Old Plank Pottery in 1959, on property at the rural intersection where the family business stood more than forty years later.

Ben III was born September 13, 1968, in nearby Asheboro, where his parents were living temporarily. His grandfather had already retired when, in the 1970s,

the youth began to feel the first stirrings of the family tradition in his blood. His mother, Shirley Owen, encouraged him. "I remember sitting on the front porch, hearing my grandfather talk about history and about his life," Ben III recalled. "When I was about eight, he started bringing me out here, to the place where his wheel was. We started on centering the ball of clay in the wheel, which is the hardest thing to do, getting it absolutely true. Then on opening or shaping the clay, just a lot of the fundamental skills that needed to be learned in the early stages."

As the boy grew and learned the day-to-day activities of the pottery business, it became clear to other family members that the grandson had inherited the genius of the grandfather, who said: "Ben really has the touch and the patience." (Benjamin Wade Owen II, the father, known as Wade, had taken more of an interest in the glazing and firing process than in the shaping of pots. Though he still became involved in the business on occasion at the end of the twentieth century, he made his living as a cattle farmer.)

There is a rhythm to old-fashioned pottery-making that young Ben found irresistible. The relatively unhurried weeks of turning and glazing pots climax with the intensity of a major firing, when temperatures get as high as 2,500 degrees inside the wood-stoked kiln that sits under a tin-roofed shelter just outside the studio. Then, after the long cooling period, comes the drama of the opening, when the potter learns how well his glazes worked and how many of his pots—often a significant percentage—emerge cracked or flawed and have to be discarded.

"When I was a kid," Ben said, "I had the opportunities of making a pot and making money at it, too. It was a good responsibility for me. It helped me develop a lot of learning skills."

Ben Owen died in 1983, leaving his grandson feeling "kind of lost" for a time. After high school, he studied business at Pfeiffer University and taught pottery under an assistantship. Two years later, he transferred to East Carolina University where research into various aspects of form and color fed his interest and influenced his developing style. He graduated with a bachelor of fine arts in ceramics in 1993, winning outstanding senior awards.

Though the assumption was that he would go back into the family business, he had to make his own decision on his own terms. "I did have interest in other careers, such as mechanical engineering," he said. "Early on, people would ask, 'Do you really want to pursue this (pottery), or is it something your family is pressuring you to do?' But over time, I began to realize how important it was and how things could evolve in the future for me, if I could show to the public that it was not just because I had come from a traditional family that my pottery has a particular presence, but also because I have put my own hard work and effort into it and made the transition into my own character and style. It took me going to school away from here to realize how important a part of my life this all was. It's my responsibility to preserve and enrich and continue this heritage."

Ben III became the proprietor of his grandfather's Ben Owen Pottery, which his father had reopened in 1981. He was a member of the board of directors of the North Carolina Pottery Center in nearby Seagrove. His wares sold internationally, and he had a long line of faithful clients who eagerly awaited every opening. Magazines such as *Our State* and *Smithsonian* wrote major articles on him. He taught workshops at Penland School of Arts and Crafts in Penland, the Hambidge Center in Rabun Gap, Ga., and Arrowmont School of Arts and Crafts in Gatlinburg, Tenn.

The Owen enterprise became part of another renaissance, fired by a hankering for handmade objects in a high-tech age, that saw the number of potteries in the neighborhood multiply. "It's a friendly competition," Owen said. "People come here and see almost a hundred potteries. It used to be seasonal. Now it's the year around."

A turning point in Ben's artistic development came in 1995, when he traveled to Japan to participate in a ceramics workshop in Tokoname. There he experienced firsthand the culture that had so influenced his grandfather, who had never been able to go there himself. "It was a way for me to travel down the roots of the tree that my grandfather had planted," he said. "I understood why these forms were made in a particular way, like the simple flaring of the bowls and the vases. In Japan, they keep a corner in every home for a place of beauty, but they keep it very, very simple. It was interesting to see how they value simplicity, just as my grandfather valued simplicity."

Steve Bouser has been editor of the Pilot *of Southern Pines since August 1997. Before that he was editor of the* Salisbury Post *for eleven years and worked with the U.S. aid programs of assistance to independent media in the former Soviet Union, living in Russia and Washington and traveling extensively in Russia and Eastern Europe.*

For more information, see:
Crawford, Jean. *Jugtown Pottery: History and Design.* John F. Blair, 1964.
DeNatale, Douglas, Jane Przybysz, and Jill R. Stevens, eds. *New Ways for Old Jugs: Tradition and Innovation at the Jugtown Pottery.* University of South Carolina Press, 1994.
Kay, Kathy L., ed. *Built Upon Honor: The Ceramic Art of Ben Owen and Ben Owen III.* The Hambidge Center and Mint Museum of Art, 1995.
Lock, Robert C., et al. *The Traditional Potters of Seagrove, N.C., and Surrounding Areas from the 1800s to the Present.* Antiques & Collectibles Press, 1994.
Sweezy, Nancy. *Raised in Clay: The Southern Pottery Tradition.* Smithsonian Institution Press, 1984.
Zug, Charles G. III. *Turners and Burners: The Folk Potters of North Carolina.* University of North Carolina Press, 1984.

REYNOLDS PRICE

By Rosemary Roberts

EYNOLDS PRICE'S FATHER sold appliances door-to-door in the 1930s and 1940s and the family's home address changed thirteen times in fourteen years as his father, William, who had conquered a drinking problem, sought more fertile territory, or when his mother found a more suitable apartment on the other side of town. "She had a gypsy soul," Price said with a laugh. "She'd say, 'Get a box and put your toys in it. We're moving over on Park Street.'"

This peripatetic childhood left no emotional scars on Price, one of America's most gifted writers. If anything it enriched him. He was a watchful child, a close observer of people, their quirks, their turns of speech. Years later he based composite characters on the people he'd known in Macon, Asheboro, and Warrenton, the small North Carolina towns where he spent his childhood.

"But, I don't write autobiographical fiction," he insisted while sitting in his wheelchair at his home in a wooded neighborhood of Durham. The walls were lined with paintings and drawings, including some works of his own. As a teenager, he considered pursuing his budding talent as an artist, but a teacher persuaded him that words were his future. Classical music, another of his passions, played softly in the background as Price talked about his life.

Price was confined to a wheelchair in 1984 when cancer of the spine paralyzed him from the waist down. Far from impeding his work, the paralysis led to the most productive period of his literary career. A man of prodigious talent, Price wrote novels, short stories, essays, poetry, and plays. He won many awards, beginning in 1962 when he received the William Faulkner Award for a notable first novel. The book, *A Long and Happy Life,* was never out of print. In 1986, he received the coveted National Book Critics Circle Award for his memorable novel, *Kate Vaiden.* He was a member of the American Academy of Arts and Letters. For more than four decades, Price also taught English literature and creative writing at Duke University where students vied for seats in his popular classes. Former students included Pulitzer Prize-winner Anne Tyler and Josephine Humphreys.

Price, a gregarious bachelor, was reared on the southern tradition of storytelling. He preserved the custom by sprinkling his own conversation with witty anecdotes and family lore, all spoken in his rich bari-

Reynolds Price (Courtesy of Les Todd, Duke University Photography)

tone voice. Listeners to National Public Radio's *All Things Considered* began hearing that voice in 1995 when Price started broadcasting regular commentaries. *Feasting the Heart* became a published collection of fifty-two of these essays.

Price was born February 1, 1933, in Macon, a sleepy village near the Virginia border in eastern North Carolina. He was the son of William Solomon and Elizabeth Rodwell Price and a cherished only child for eight years before a brother was born. His early years were formative. In his memoir *Clear Pictures,* he recalled sitting in a porch swing on summer evenings listening to his family tell stories. Variations of these tales later found their way into his fiction, as did the colloquialisms and speech of eastern North Carolina.

It was an idyllic Southern childhood spent in a small and isolated world. "You didn't know any Yankees," Price recalled. "And I can truthfully say I think I was nineteen or twenty before I actually met a divorced person."

The limits of his world did not inhibit a curious

mind. He was a precocious boy with an insatiable taste for books, art, and music. "My parents were not readers, and there was no theater or music except at church. My mother's parents read the *News and Observer* and the *Upper Room* (a Methodist booklet of daily devotionals) and that was it. But my parents never thought of me as an odd child. If I wanted a book, they bought it for me."

Price's world expanded in the mid-1940s when his family moved to Raleigh. He was fourteen. "In those days there was a healthy concert circuit in America and for $3.50 in Raleigh you could go hear Kirsten Flagstad, Ezio Penza, Marian Anderson, and Arthur Rubinstein. They all came to Raleigh." Not only did Price hear Marian Anderson, he met her. Discovering that Anderson was in town after a concert, Price's father took his son to meet the famous black contralto. Charmed by a teenager who loved music, Anderson invited him to return the following day to talk some more. "She was the first big piece of the outside world I encountered," he recalled.

There was also a "magical" English teacher, Phyllis Peacock, at Raleigh's Broughton High School who had a profound influence. She praised his work and reconfirmed his ambition to become a writer. By the time he entered Duke University in 1951, Price thought of himself as a writer. He studied with William Blackburn, the legendary creative writing teacher of William Styron and Fred Chappell. When Eudora Welty came to campus and read one of Price's short stories, she was so impressed that she sent it to her publisher.

After graduation from Duke, Price was awarded a Rhodes Scholarship to study at Merton College, Oxford University. He remembered England of the mid-1950s as "depressing and still recovering from World War II—cold rooms, horrible food, bad plumbing." But his three years at Oxford were fruitful. His professors were England's foremost men of letters: W. H. Auden, Stephen Spender, and David Cecil. Spender, who became a lifelong friend, was coeditor of *Encounter*. It was the first professional magazine to publish Price's work. Amid the ancient spires of Oxford, Price began working on his first novel. *A Long and Happy Life* is the story of a country girl and boy in North Carolina whose lives are removed from stately Oxford.

In 1958, his last year at Oxford, a letter arrived from Duke inviting him to teach freshman English for $4,800 a year. "I never felt, oh God, here I go back to the benighted Old South. I had started writing short stories before I left Duke. All those stories were set in this part of the South and I wanted to come back and get that sound back in my ear." Financial responsibilities tugged on him as well. His father had died while Price was at Duke, and his mother had taken a job as a sales clerk, the first job of her life. She had a younger son to support and a mortgage to pay. By returning to Duke, Price could be near his family and help with the bills. He never left North Carolina, or Duke. And while many writers of his generation hopped on the first bus out of Dixie and headed for New York, he never had the urge to leave. "I just found I was happy to go on living here," he said.

The decision paid off. His body of work—thirty-three books at the end of the century—drew praise for its strong sense of place (usually North Carolina) and vividly drawn characters. "People read for characters, not about plot," Price explained. "They want to watch other people have their lives."

Though his fiction was not autobiographical, the central figure in his prize-winning *Kate Vaiden* was derived from his mother. The rural characters in *A Long and Happy Life* were "country friends" of his childhood. They came from "the lower-middle-class tobacco-farming rural world outside a small county seat like Warren County where I was born. Their lives had already become the lives they were going to live forever, working on a farm, graduating at age eighteen, and marrying the sweetheart down the road. So that's where a lot of the early stuff came from." In later novels, Price wrote about the solid middle class of his own family.

Price did not anguish over his books once they were published. "I don't feel like the person who wrote them because I've gone so far in time beyond them." He said there are none he wished he'd never written, but he called *Blue Calhoun* his favorite, or "pet book."

Price was devastated in 1984 when he became crippled after a cancerous tumor was discovered on his spinal cord. He described the trauma in *A Whole New Life,* an inspiring memoir about the illness, his operations, and the aftermath. Following his surgery, he suffered months of depression before resuming work on *Kate Vaiden,* the story of a southern woman who lived through the Depression and World War II. "The very fact that I could go in there every day and be somebody else, be a woman all day long, a kind of feisty, brave but very skittish woman, was a big help."

A deeply spiritual man, Price had stopped attending church when he was in his twenties. "The Protestant church in the South and everywhere else has missed the boat on everything—race, women, now homosexuals. You name it. They've missed the boat." But Price described himself as a "convinced Christian" and his theological essays, as well as *Three Gospels,* translations of the Gospels of Mark and John with a modern apocryphal gospel by Price, drew wide acclaim. In *A Whole New Life,* Price wrote about a vision in which Jesus appears at the Sea of Galilee. Jesus led him into cool water and poured handfuls over his head, telling him his sins were forgiven. "Am I also cured?" Price asked. "That too," Jesus replied.

During his sixteen years in a wheelchair, Price wrote far more than before his illness. He was often asked if this flurry of productivity stemmed from a race against death. Not at all, he would reply. He said he was more prolific because he didn't spend time on errands to the grocery store, the bank, or the dry cleaners that used to gobble up his time. Instead, he wrote.

It helped that he was disciplined. "Writing was a struggle for me through the first four or five books. I was learning how to do it. Nobody ever said, until I worked it out for myself, that writing is a job. You need to do it every day, you need to turn up at the typewriter or keyboard or legal pad and sit there and do it until it's done." Price worked six days a week while an assistant handled the errands.

The assistants, usually Duke graduates, lived at his house and helped with his care. "The job lasts twelve months and nobody thinks they're trapped. If they walk in the door and can't boil water, I say, 'Here's the *Joy of Cooking* and we're having Hungarian goulash tonight.' I've taught sixteen guys how to cook."

Witty, resilient, and with no bitterness over his fate, Price said, "If you or God said to me, 'Give me one word to describe the last sixteen years (in a wheelchair), I'd say, 'Interesting.' And if you said, 'Would you reverse what's happened in the last sixteen years,' the answer is no because I do think it has enriched my work, and I think it's made me a better human being."

Rosemary Roberts first met Price in New York shortly after publication of his first novel. A columnist for Greensboro's News and Record, *she also worked for the* Charlotte Observer *and the* New York Times. *She is a graduate of the University of North Carolina at Chapel Hill and earned a master's degree in history from the University of North Carolina at Greensboro. She also was a Knight Fellow at Stanford University.*

For more information, see:
Interview, January 2001. North Carolina Biography
    Project. Levine Museum of the New South.

Price, Reynolds. *Clear Pictures: First Loves, First
    Guides.* Atheneum, 1989.
———. *Clear Pictures: Reynolds Price.* Guggenheim
    Productions, 1995. Videocassette.
———. *Learning a Trade: A Craftsman's Notebooks,
    1955–1997.* Duke University Press, 1998.
"Talk about Writing: Reynolds Price." N.C. State
    University Humanities Extension's Portrait of
    North Carolina Writers, 1991.
———. *A Whole New Life: An Illness and Healing.*
    Antheneum, 1994.

LOUIS D. RUBIN JR.

By Ralph Grizzle

BORN NOVEMBER 19, 1923, Louis Decimus Rubin Jr. grew up in Charleston, S.C. He took more than four decades to land permanently in North Carolina—doing so in 1967—but the Old North State was quick to embrace him as one of its prized citizens.

Never mind that Rubin was a prolific author and editor whose name was attached to more than fifty books, half of which he either edited or compiled, the other half of which he wrote himself. But this lofty accomplishment was not what earned Rubin the permanent embrace of the state. It was his charity, and not the monetary kind, that won over a generation of North Carolinians who have had the good fortune to meet him.

Simply, Rubin gave of himself to launch the careers of many aspiring North Carolina writers, including Kaye Gibbons, Jill McCorkle, John Barth, and Annie Dillard, to name a few. All were Rubin's students at the University of North Carolina at Chapel Hill and at Roanoke's Hollins College. "I wouldn't be a writer today if it weren't for Louis," says Hillsborough-based writer Lee Smith. "If a young writer runs into Louis at the right time, like I and so many others did, it's a fortunate thing. He is tireless in the interest he shows toward his students and his writers. He took us all on for life."

Of course, Rubin shunned any credit due to him. Of his role in his former students' success, he said: "All I tried to do was encourage them and make them think that what they were doing was worthwhile and dignified and a very powerful thing to do. I think a great deal of teaching involves that kind of encouragement."

But truth is, Rubin did more than teach and encourage. He cofounded and gave much of his life to a publishing company—Algonquin Books of Chapel Hill. And he did so to level the playing field for those writers who could not break into the New York publishing houses. Though Rubin relished the role of editor and publisher, it came with a heavy price. He spent sleepless nights worrying about how Algonquin was going to pay its bills—print runs and book promotion being capital-intensive. But he worried willingly, all so that his writers could claim their places in American literature.

Rubin's career as a writer began when he was a child in Charleston. As a boy, he often dawdled along

Louis D. Rubin Jr. (Courtesy of Charlotte Observer)

the port city's bustling waterfront, casting his eyes on the choppy harbor. He remembered watching shrimp trawlers chug their way to the dock, where they disgorged their bountiful harvests. He watched cargo launches push away from the piers. The ships were starting their long, mysterious journeys to exotic lands. The comings and goings of these boats and ships fueled the young boy's imagination, and it was there on the wondrous waterfront that he fell in love with the smell of salt air and images of ships and sea.

Those images later resided in Rubin's Chapel Hill residence, where the walls and tabletops were decorated with paintings of ships and freighters, all illustrated by Rubin himself. Eight decades later, Rubin still engaged in the same interest that he did as a boy on the Charleston waterfront. Rubin's enduring passions were the source of his creativity.

Only a handful of years before, Rubin and an old college friend began researching a book about southern seaports. They traveled from Hampton Roads to Corpus Christi, Texas, photographing ports and writing about them. When *Seaports of the South: A Journey* was published in 1998, it was Rubin's forty-eighth book.

In his teen years Rubin matriculated at the College

of Charleston, where he spent two years before serving in the army from 1943 to 1946. He then went to the University of Richmond in Virginia where he majored in history and took a job as a newspaper reporter at the *Bergen* (New Jersey) *Evening Record*. In his spare time he photographed trains, another passion. And so in the fall of 2000, Rubin published his fiftieth book, a look back at his love affair with the diesel locomotives, which was followed by one on baseball, another passion.

Rubin shared his Chapel Hill home with his wife, Eva Redfield Rubin, professor emeritus of political science at North Carolina State University. Their home occupied a narrow plot of ground within walking distance of the university where Rubin spent more than two decades helping young writers get their start. Seated in a leather chair in his study, cigar perched between his lips, Rubin conjured the type of romantic writerly image of Hemingway or Fitzgerald. An Underwood #5 typewriter sat atop a desk. Did he sit there pecking out his books, working until the wee hours of the morning, as did Carl Sandburg, who also smoked cigars while he worked?

"Oh no," Rubin responded, pointing to a translucent Apple iMac on a desk around the corner. "I use that. I only use the typewriter to address envelopes. You know, computers don't do that very well."

On a corkboard above the typewriter were snapshots of writers whom Rubin helped start on their careers. They stayed in touch with him, sending pictures of their children and notes wishing him well. "He is loyal and good to his writers and the people he mentors," said writer Clyde Edgerton. "He stands in for physically or emotionally departed fathers in ways he would be reluctant to admit and probably even recognize."

Rubin himself was the father of two sons, but perhaps the strongest illustration of his paternal instinct was wrapped in his founding of Algonquin Books. Rubin was still newspapering in 1948 when he decided to apply to graduate school at Johns Hopkins. While serving as editor of the *Hopkins Review* from 1950 until 1954, he earned a Ph.D. in aesthetics of literature. There, in 1953, Rubin coedited his first book, *Southern Renascence,* a work that established him as a major figure in southern literature. In 1955, he published *Thomas Wolfe: The Weather of His Youth.*

He taught writing at Johns Hopkins and later at the University of Pennsylvania, before taking a job as an associate editor at the *News-Leader* in Richmond, Virginia. Rubin credited his work as a newspaper journalist for providing him with the ability to produce so rapidly. "On a newspaper, you do the best you can and get it out," he said. "You don't hold it forever. It's a matter of discipline, and I have found it to be very valuable."

In 1957, he settled in Roanoke, Va., and worked his way up from associate professor to professor and, finally, chairman of the English department at Hollins College. There, he founded a creative writing program that he headed for a decade.

He transferred to the University of North Carolina at Chapel Hill in 1967 as a professor of American literature. In 1981, something happened that caused him to rethink what he was doing. That year, Rubin traveled to New York to attend a panel meeting sponsored by the Modern Language Association. The panel discussed the plight of young writers. "The more we talked, the gloomier I got," Rubin said. "I realized it was almost impossible for young writers from the provinces to get a book looked at by New York agents or publishers. It was pretty depressing the more we talked about it. And here I had been encouraging young writers for many years, encouraging them to do something that was becoming harder and harder to do anything with."

He returned to Chapel Hill with the resolve to do something about that. In 1982, with plenty of optimism but with little working capital, he launched Algonquin, so that regional writers "would not have to run the New York gauntlet." He wrote his former Hollins College student, Shannon Ravenel, to ask if she would join him. She would. The two raised capital among a small group of friends and financial backers. Rubin and Ravenel worked without pay. They did so because money was always a problem.

Algonquin was not able to dole out large advances or pay tremendous royalties. "Some of our advances were embarrassingly low," Rubin said, noting that many advances did not even reach four figures. "But we started the company in order to help young writers get launched. We wanted to do the best possible thing for the writers. We never lost an author on an advance."

At times, however, Algonguin's meager capitalization frustrated writers. Jill McCorkle had written a book, *The Cheerleader,* but Rubin told her she would have to wait until the company could afford to publish it. "We restricted ourselves with fiction, because we thought nonfiction would sell best," he said, noting that Algonquin chose to publish only one fiction title per catalog. "Of course, that proved to be wrong."

In the meantime, McCorkle wrote another book, *July 7th.* Rubin and Ravenel wanted to publish both of McCorkle's books, but money was thin. Nonetheless, they took a chance. The two editors thought it not only feasible to market both books but also plausible that marketing both would be a good publicity hook. It worked.

Reviews of McCorkle's books were published in newspapers nationwide. Unfortunately, Algonquin did not have the funds for proper follow-up, such as sending the author on tour or taking out ads in major publications. Sales lagged, despite the positive critical response. Algonquin sold only three thousand copies of each of McCorkle's two books.

With Clyde Edgerton's *Raney*, fledgling Algonquin found itself too strapped for cash to afford large press runs. The company sold nineteen thousand copies during the first season—but in five separate printings. Grossly inefficient, the five printings offered no economies of scale to reduce the cost of printing. "We couldn't take the chance of printing a large number of books and getting a low per unit cost," Rubin said. "We couldn't afford to get stuck with them. We simply did not have the capital to take the chances."

Money became increasingly more of an issue. Rubin began to lose sleep. "I was waking up at three in the morning wondering how we were going to pay the bills," Rubin said. "It put a tremendous strain on us."

In 1989, the company was forced to sell to New York-based Workman Publishing, a publisher of children's books, cookbooks, and calendars. Workman provided the financial support and marketing strength to give Algonquin a national presence. "It's easy to find good editors but difficult to find good marketing people," Rubin says. "That's what Workman provided."

That same year, Rubin retired from teaching and soon left Algonquin too. While the company continued to operate fairly autonomously, "it wasn't the same," Rubin lamented. "We could no longer call our own shots. If we wanted to take a chance on a writer, we had to clear it with New York." That meant that regional writers would once again have to run the New York gauntlet. Disheartened, Rubin decided to call it a day in 1992.

Algonquin prospered with Workman, and though glad for that, Rubin enjoyed an ambivalent sense of satisfaction for his role. "I guess we proved a point but failed in setting up a small southern independent publishing house that would publish regional authors

nationally," he said. "When I look back, though, we made very few mistakes."

He said that given the chance to do it all over again, he would chart the same course. But he would tell his writers that after they had made a certain amount of money, they would need to find another publisher. "Literary publishing houses have to stay small to profitably survive," he said, noting that big authors require big promotional budgets that small publishing houses just don't have.

But the Algonquin story is only part of Louis Rubin's life story. Given the perspective of almost eight decades, the retired publisher and professor relished his role as teacher most of all. And while he was proud of Algonquin, its success was not the thing he was most proud of in his professional career. That distinction belongs to his students. And not just the ones who went on to become famous—all of them, he said.

A journalism graduate of the University of North Carolina at Chapel Hill, Ralph Grizzle of Asheville is a contributing editor to Our State *magazine and author of* Remembering Charles Kuralt.

For more information, see:
Rubin's novels include *The Golden Weather* (1961), *Surfaces of a Diamond* (1981), and *The Heat of the Sun* (1995). In academic circles, he is well known for his literary criticism. His works include *Thomas Wolfe: The Weather of His Youth* (1955), *The Mockingbird in the Gum Tree: A Literary Gallimaufry* (1991), and *The Edge of the Swamp: A Study of Literature and Society of the Old South* (1989). Rubin also wrote books on building boats, baseball, and Virginia's bicentennial history.

Rubin, Louis. Papers. Wilson Library, University of North Carolina at Chapel Hill.

Rubin, Louis. *Babe Ruth's Ghost: And Other Historical and Literary Speculations*. University of Washington Press, 1996.
———. *Thomas Wolfe: The Weather of His Youth*. Louisiana State University Press, 1955.
———. *The Wary Fugitives: Four Poets and the South*. Louisiana State University Press, 1978.
———. *A Writer's Companion*. Louisiana State University Press, 1995.

LEE SMITH

By Amy Rogers

RUNDY, VA., the little coal-mining town where novelist Lee Smith grew up, provided plenty of inspiration for a young writer. Not only were Grundy's residents noted for their storytelling ability, the town itself was the setting of the many daily dramas, as well as the occasional catastrophic events, from which writers often draw that inspiration. "I started telling stories as soon as I could talk—true stories, and made-up stories, too. It has always been hard for me to tell the difference between them," Smith wrote in 1997.

Born November 1, 1944, to Ernest and Virginia Smith, young Lee was gifted with an active imagination. Her father ran the local dime store, and she put herself in charge of taking care of the dolls. She named them and gave each of them an elaborate life story. In an act of child's play that no one could have foreseen leading to a career in literature, she began to watch through her father's office window the goings-on in the store. "I witnessed not only shoplifting, but fights and embraces as well," she reflected in 2000. "Thus I learned the position of omniscient narrator, who sees and records everything, yet is never visible. It was the perfect education for an early fiction writer."

Another part of that education was the story-telling tradition of the Appalachian Mountains. "My mother could make a story out of anything; she'd go to the grocery store and come home with a story." Local lore sometimes became legend: Smith relates a tale of a mountain so steep that a cow fell off it, crashed through the roof of a nearby house, and landed in the kitchen.

As a child, Smith's favorite place to read and write was a tool shack on the riverbank. Although the shack washed away in 1957 during one of Grundy's devastating floods, it was rebuilt. The budding author wrote her first "novel" when she was eight: The story featured film star Jane Russell and presidential candidate Adlai Stevenson falling in love and going west in a covered wagon. "Even at that age," Smith wrote many years later, "I was fixed upon glamour and flight, two themes I returned to again and again as I wrote my way throughout high school and college."

As a student at Hollins College she began work on a senior thesis project, which eventually became her first published novel, *The Last Day the Dogbushes Bloomed*. After her graduation in 1967, she embarked on a career in journalism and worked at the *Richmond*

Lee Smith (Photo by Susan Woodley Raines)

News Leader and the *Tuscaloosa News*. A reporter's job might not seem a natural choice for an evolving novelist, but Smith found that the experience enhanced her storytelling ability. "Journalism is helpful for a fiction writer. You can go into other people's lives," she explained, then emphasized, "Fiction is made of real stuff."

Her other early novels, *Something in the Wind* and *Fancy Strut*, helped establish her reputation as an emerging southern talent, although it wouldn't be until her later books were published that the broadest audience of readers would find in those works the characters that engaged them most. Smith became known for heroines who were often flawed but feisty members of lovingly drawn, dysfunctional families that resonated especially with female readers.

Smith's marriage to poet James Seay produced two sons; the couple later divorced. It was after Smith relocated to Chapel Hill in 1974 that she began to publish collections of her short stories. With an engaging and exuberant personality, she enjoyed a long career as a teacher, in high schools from 1973 to 1981, and as a professor of English at North Carolina State University from 1989 to 2000. Her favorite books to discuss in the classroom included Virginia Woolf's *To the Lighthouse,* Ellen Glasgow's *The Sheltered Life,* and William Faulkner's *Absalom, Absalom!* "I love to teach literature, read with a bright, bright group, and argue about it," Smith said. "[Students] don't know what they think until you challenge them on it."

Eudora Welty, a matriarch of southern literature, wrote in *One Writer's Beginnings* about the importance of "listening," "learning to see," and "finding a voice." Smith believed such awareness can lead even further, to what she called "finding a language for the self."

Like many writers, it was only after moving away from her hometown that Smith came to view Grundy and its inhabitants as essential sources of literary richness. One event in particular stood out as a turning point. Smith was in the midst of reviewing the proofs for one of her own books while teaching in Abingdon, Va. She gave her class an assignment. "I'll never forget it," she remembered, more than twenty years later. "I asked them to bring in the first paragraph of something they were working on." Lou Crabtree, then an unpublished writer, had written about a woman who suffered thirteen miscarriages and "named every one of them." The power of those images and Crabtree's use of language so astonished Smith that two things happened. First, she told Crabtree, "Keep going." Then, Smith began to incorporate into her own work the voices, characters, and settings from Appalachia that so closely tied her to the time and place where she grew up. In her earlier work, Smith recalled, "I'd used a teeny bit of Appalachian material. But I'd been taking notes; I had a closetful of folklore."

It was in response to her novels *Black Mountain Breakdown, Oral History, Family Linen,* and *Fair and Tender Ladies* that critics began to use terms such as "deft and assured," "effortless," and "masterly," and to commend Smith's work for its lyricism.

In *Oral History,* Smith began to explore multiple points of view within a single story; in *Family Linen* she introduced elements of comic mystery. *Fair and Tender Ladies* may have had the most unusual genesis: a packet of cast-off letters found at a garage sale and purchased for seventy-five cents. The book's heroine, Ivy Rowe, begins her story with a letter to a pen-pal. "I am a girl 12 years old very pretty I have very long hair and eight brothers and sisters and my Mother and my Father, he is ill. We live on a farm on the Sugar Fork of Home Creek on Blue Star Mountain the closest town is Majestic, Virginia. It is so pretty up here but right now it is so cold. I want to be a fa-

mous writer when I grow up, I will write of Love," Ivy promises. By employing vernacular language to describe the harshness of Ivy's farm life, and by setting the story against the stark beauty of a changing Appalachia, Smith created one of her most memorable books.

The Devil's Dream is the sprawling, multi-generational story of country music star Katie Cocker, who is warned that "the fiddle is a instrument of the Devil," while the holiday novella *The Christmas Letters* unfolds entirely through letters and recipes handed down by war bride Birdie Pickett to her daughter and granddaughter.

In *Saving Grace,* Smith incorporated into her story the religious phenomenon of serpent handling, an activity that had fascinated her when she was growing up. The book's central character is no-nonsense Florida Grace Shepherd, and as in Smith's other novels, this narrator has her own distinct voice: "My name is Florida Grace Shepherd, Florida for the state I was born in, Grace for the grace of God. I am the eleventh child of the Reverend Virgil Shepherd, born to him and his third wife, Fannie Flowers. They say I take after her, and I am proud of this, for she was as lovely as the day is long, in spirit as well as flesh. It isn't true, however. I am and always have been contentious and ornery, full of fear and doubt in a family of believers."

A longtime pillar of North Carolina's literary community, Smith didn't consider herself a "writerly writer," but wanted readers to hear in her work the voice of what she termed "a real person speaking." Rather than the spare and fast-moving prose some contemporary novelists favor, Smith instead reveled in her characters' eccentricities, and in the sound of conversations that unfolded with all the languor of a summer day.

As for Grundy, Smith's hometown, metamorphosis was inevitable. To escape the Levisa River's floodwaters that nearly destroyed the town time and time again, Grundy adopted a plan to move to higher ground, and to abandon and ultimately demolish the old Grundy where Smith played as a child in her father's dime store.

Knowing that a certain number of residents would move away once the town relocated, Smith returned to Grundy beforehand to work with high school students as they gathered oral histories, "to create a family album of the town." She edited the resulting book, *Sitting on the Courthouse Bench: An Oral History of Grundy, Virginia.* "Grundy exemplifies the plight of a lot of small towns where the economy dwindles and dries up," she said in 2001. "I asked, 'How many of you expect to be living here in ten years?' and not one hand went up." Like her encounter with Lou Crabtree some twenty years earlier, the experience affected Smith profoundly. "As I would edit, I would remember things I'd forgotten. It was like getting a big part of my own past back," she said.

Smith retired from teaching in 2000, but not from the art and craft of writing. Gathering the details that bring a work of fiction to life can be an exhausting, unseen process. "Before I write anything, I make a map and put it on the wall," Smith said. To research *The Last Girls,* in which a group of college friends reunite for a river rafting trip, Smith traveled the Mississippi River from Memphis to New Orleans. Doing so allowed her "to pay a closer kind of attention." She continued to write, in longhand, at the Hillsborough home she shared with her husband, fellow writer Hal Crowther, whom she married in 1985. On occasion, she traveled to a rural North Carolina cabin for her work. It's a place that helped "activate the imagination."

Often compared to Flannery O'Connor and Eudora Welty, Smith's work distinguished her not only as a favorite southern author, but one who could translate to the printed page what is memorable and heartfelt about human nature. Her narrative authenticity and finely wrought observations about the everyday lives of everyday people combined to create unapologetic portraits of real southerners. "Writing is very exciting to me and remains so," she said in a 2001 interview. "It's a chance to have another life."

Smith was honored with the 1999 Academy Award in Fiction from the American Academy of Arts and Letters, the 1995–97 Lila Wallace-Reader's Digest Fund Writers' Award, the 1991 Robert Penn Warren Prize for Fiction, the 1984 North Carolina Award for Literature, the Sir Walter Raleigh Award for *Oral History* (1983) and *Fair and Tender Ladies* (1989), and the 1979 and 1981 O. Henry Award.

Amy Rogers is a freelance writer and editor who has profiled many notable North Carolinians. She lives in Charlotte.

For more information, see:
Smith, Lee. *Cakewalk.* G. P. Putnam's Sons, 1981.
———. *Me and My Baby View the Eclipse.* G. P. Putnam's Sons, 1990.
———. *News of the Spirit.* G. P. Putnam's Sons, 1997.

BENJAMIN F. SWALIN

By Steve Bouser

HE LITTLE COUNTRY GIRL stood watching as musicians piled out of a bus onto the gravel parking lot of a motel, unloading tubas, kettledrums, and oboes. The North Carolina Symphony had arrived for yet another in the thousands of concerts it had given over the years in every remote corner of the state.

"Honey, do you live around here?" one of the musicians asked.

"Yes, sir," the child replied earnestly, pointing to a house in the distance. "Right over yonder, 'side the hard-circus road."

Benjamin Swalin, the orchestra's musical director and conductor from 1939 to 1972, never saw that little girl again. But her phrase (for "hard-surface road") so endeared itself to him that he used it as the title of his 1987 book about a career spent bringing culture to the masses: *Hard-Circus Road: The Odyssey of the North Carolina Symphony.*

There have always been elements of a traveling circus in the peregrinations of North Carolina's uniquely mobile state orchestra, whose members have been described as "a gypsy crowd." And the roads have indeed been hard, as Swalin wrote—"miles upon hundreds of miles, asphalt and concrete, unyielding, frigidly cold, steaming hot, straight, curving, twisting, ascending steeply, falling away fast to the flatlands, unrolling for us changing panoramas of sights and sounds and places and people."

The North Carolina Symphony was organized by Lamar Stringfield in 1932 as a federal make-work project for down-at-the-heels musicians. But Swalin, through a bulldozer-like force of will that won him many friends and some enemies over the years, was the one who almost single-handedly brought the orchestra into existence in its present form and won it recognition as one of the nation's great symphonies. He had grown up in Minnesota, never setting foot in North Carolina until he was well into his thirties, and he spoke his immaculate English with a noticeable Scandinavian accent to the end. But traveling all those highways for all those years made him more familiar with North Carolina and its people—and he more familiar to them—than most born-and-bred Tar Heels. Untold thousands of adults all across the state still treasure childhood memories of the day the distinguished-looking Swalin and his petite wife, Max-

Benjamin F. Swalin (Courtesy of North Carolina Collection)

ine, showed up in the school gym with their entourage of players to delight and enlighten them.

"At a time and in a place where others despaired that great music had no place," said Voit Gilmore of Southern Pines, former president of the Symphony Society and Swalin's longtime friend, "he stuck to the battle and converted even a tough rural legislature. He helped North Carolina grow and enjoy one of the dimensions that other Southern states just didn't have. He was a very independent and heroic character who well earned the title of one of North Carolina's all-time greats."

Benjamin Franklin Swalin was born at the turn of the century in Minneapolis. Showing an early proclivity for music, and especially the violin, he auditioned with the Minneapolis Symphony Orchestra (later the Minnesota Symphony) after graduating from high school in 1919. He was accepted as the orchestra's youngest member. The Minneapolis Symphony spent a lot of time on the road, a factor that may have proved greatly influential in a later time and in a distant place.

"During my two years with the orchestra," Swalin wrote, "I learned a great deal from its experienced musicians; while on tour in Winnipeg, Canada, I bought a handsome Panormo violin, still one of my treasured possessions. And I developed a desire for a university education, inspired by the numerous stops made by our touring orchestra at colleges and universities."

But first, Swalin felt a need for more violin training. So he headed to New York in the spring of 1921 to study with renowned violinist Franz Kneisel. After two years of private lessons under Kneisel, he studied further under him at the Institute of Musical Art, which later became the Juilliard School of Music.

"In New York—and in Blue Hill, Maine, during the summers of 1921–23—" he wrote, "I learned not only from my lessons with the great master but also from hearing some of the eminent violinists who were his friends and colleagues."

After Kneisel's death in 1926, Swalin studied with Professor Leopold Auer. To keep body and soul together, he took up a number of musical jobs in New York, playing first violin with the Capitol Theater Orchestra, giving private violin lessons to the daughter of novelist John Erskine, working in the WOR Radio Orchestra, and playing in more than three hundred performances of a radio show called *Up She Goes*. At the same time, he earned undergraduate and graduate degrees in English literature at Columbia University.

In 1930, one of his Columbia professors, Carl Van Doren, persuaded him to accept an international fellowship to study in Vienna. He arrived at the Musikhochschule with only a few sentences of German in his vocabulary, but eventually earned a Ph.D. from the University of Vienna after studying violin, composition, and conducting.

"I then set out in January 1933 to visit various sections of Europe in which I had a special interest," he wrote. "In my travels—to Pisek, Czechoslovakia; to Berlin; to Sweden, the land of my parents; to Copenhagen; and to Cambridge—I sought out the scholars and musicians whose work I had admired, and I was fortunate to meet them. . . . Enriched, I returned to New York and the Depression, fearing that work would be hard to find for someone with no secretarial skills."

But typing proved unnecessary, because he had soon landed a job as professor of violin and theory at DePauw University in Indiana. In 1926, while studying at the Institute of Musical Art, he met and fell in love with a fellow student, a vivacious Iowa girl with the alliterative name Martha Maxine McMahon. They spent as much time together as possible in New York, but soon their academic paths took them in different directions. The years passed and she returned to Iowa to teach, enduring his various wanderings with increasing impatience. The last straw before the DePauw move was Ben's sojourn in Bolshevik Russia, from which he returned with a Trotskyite-looking goatee that horrified her conservative parents.

In 1935, while listening to a sermon entitled "Time for Decision," Maxine experienced a moment of truth that she described in her own book, *An Ear to Myself,* privately published in Chapel Hill in 1996. Overwhelmed by a longing for marriage and tired of waiting, she ran out of the church and into the manse next door, where she called Ben long-distance. When he expressed alarm at her breathless sobs, she explained that she had just heard a sermon.

"About decision."

"You mean . . . now?"

"Yes. I do."

Then, reverting to the exaggerated Swedish accent that was a family joke, he asked: "Maxine, vil you mar-ry me?"

When the northern newlyweds arrived in the alien territory of Chapel Hill in June 1935, it was supposed to be just a temporary stay while Swalin taught in the summer session at the University of North Carolina. But the move became permanent when he so impressed Music Department Chairman Glen Hayden and University President Frank Porter Graham that they invited him to join the teaching staff. The Swalins settled into the comfortable and stimulating existence enjoyed by Chapel Hill faculty members and spouses, and there they might have stayed for life.

But various factors converged to pull—and push —Ben Swalin in an unexpected direction. After several years, he began to weary of faculty politics and to worry about his future with the university. His violin classes were full and his book on the violin concerto was selling, but his expected promotion to associate professor and raise in pay were slow in coming. Meanwhile, the university orchestra he had inherited was of poor quality, with too few trained musicians. His efforts to encourage an increase in string classes in the state's high schools, and thereby assure a steadier flow of new talent, came to naught.

Then came a pivotal day, early in World War II, when Swalin was asked to get some musicians together for a "Bundles for Britain" concert in Greensboro. He had a nucleus of players from Chapel Hill, Greensboro, and High Point, but he needed more. He found them in some former members of the old

North Carolina Symphony, which had faded from existence in the mid-thirties. Their hastily organized performance of Schumann's Piano Concerto was a hit.

"That night," Mrs. Swalin wrote, "leading citizens asked why this group could not stay together and become a new North Carolina Symphony."

And that, despite initial opposition to the idea from Chairman Hayden, is exactly what happened. The old North Carolina Symphony Society was reorganized, with Colonel Joseph Hyde Pratt of Chapel Hill as its president. Support began to solidify.

"Of course there was no money, rehearsal hall, office, secretarial help, publicity chairman, personnel or business manager," Mrs. Swalin recalled of those bleak but bracing early months. "There was no music available. Two great friends and enthusiastic supporters, Johnsie Burnham and author Paul Green, accompanied Ben to the Bank of Chapel Hill to borrow $200 for tympani. . . . Musicians pooled their wartime gasoline to rehearsals and concerts. Salaries were never spoken of, only 'honorariums' from a shared pool."

After the orchestra played at Raleigh's Sesquicentennial Celebration in 1942, Swalin managed to get an appointment with Governor J. Melville Broughton. Making the most of this audience, he poured out his hopes for the new orchestra: that it be an educational institution with broad popular appeal, that it go on the road to bring great music to North Carolinians from every walk of life in towns and schools from Murphy to Manteo, and that it receive regular financial support from the General Assembly.

The governor was taken with the idea. His wife lobbied for it with legislators. And on March 8, 1943, in the depths of war, the legislators approved Senate Bill 248—which became known far and wide as the "Horn-Tootin' Bill." It declared the symphony a quasi-state agency under the "patronage and control of the state." The North Carolina Symphony had become the first in the nation to enjoy support, however minimal, from a continuing state appropriation. Swalin was granted a leave of absence from his teaching duties. Less than a decade after he and Maxine had taken one leap of faith by coming to Chapel Hill, they took another one in separating from the university and hitting the road in pursuit of his dream. He was forty-five. She was forty-three.

"The Horn-Tootin' Bill was laughed at and ridiculed at first by many a rural legislator, who thought that was the last thing anyone needed," recalls Gilmore. "But Ben would load the symphony into one or two buses and take them to legislators' home districts. And when they saw little kids just stomping and whistling and being taught not only Tchaikovsky but also American melodies, he began to get under their skin and into their hearts. He toughed it out and built up a network of supporters like me that finally got him entrenched all across the state. He was stubborn enough to make the damn thing work where fainter hearts would have given up long before. He did it through determination—and also through the strong support of Maxine, his second heartbeat in anything, who was a charming but equally dedicated lady who gave incredible amounts of time."

With Swalin's leadership, state funding, Maxine's energy, and the support of symphony societies springing up in dozens of counties, the N.C. Symphony grew steadily in size and reputation over the years— becoming, in the words of the *Durham Sun,* "one of the most acclaimed and esteemed institutions of the state, and a model for similar organizations elsewhere in the United States." Articles about this beacon of enlightenment in a still-segregated South appeared in *Time, Life,* and *Newsweek,* and NBC broadcast its concerts coast-to-coast in May 1948 and April 1958.

In the early years, a trade arrangement developed. If supporters in a given locale raised enough money to bring the orchestra to town for an evening concert, the symphony would play a free afternoon concert for any group of schoolchildren designated locally. In Southern Pines, Gilmore recalled a condition attached to the deal by Katharine Boyd, publisher of the *Pilot* and widow of novelist James Boyd: "I will contribute enough to justify your playing at least two children's concerts. And I want one of them to be for the black children." Swalin was more than happy to comply.

In the weeks before an appearance, books written by the symphony's education director, Adeline McCall, were distributed to the students. Local music teachers attended workshops ahead of time and brought recordings back to class to acquaint the children with the music to come. In stop after stop, Maxine Swalin spoke to the rapt children before a show and introduced them to the sounds of the various instruments. She took pride in the fact that many student musicians who had the opportunity to perform as soloists with the visiting symphony went on to professional careers. Since she and Ben were childless, their relationships with dozens of young musicians around the state often took the place of family.

As the symphony achieved national stature, Swalin received recognition for making it what it had become. He won the Morrison Award for Achievement in the Performing Arts, the Doctor of Fine Arts degree from the University of North Carolina, the North Carolina Award for Achievement in the Fine Arts, and a citation and life membership from the National Federation of Music Clubs.

Governor Terry Sanford, former Duke University president and U.S. senator, was one of Swalin's most ardent admirers and defenders. Though he recognized that Swalin could be difficult to deal with, he also knew that that very cussedness was what had brought the symphony into existence when few others believed in it. He loved the democratic spirit that Swalin's symphony represented.

"Determined that the job of good music should be brought not just to black-tie audiences in acoustically attuned concert halls but to all the people," Sanford wrote in the foreword to *Hard-Circus Road,* "the orchestra traveled by bus and played in factories, schoolhouses and churches across the hundreds of miles. This is truly a human story of two people. But for Ben Swalin, the North Carolina Symphony would not be. But for Maxine, Ben would not have prevailed. Bravo!"

The symphony, homeless for years, eventually came more and more to make its home in Raleigh. A major turning point came in 1966, when the orchestra received a grant of $1 million from the Ford Foundation. This helped relieve some of the financial strictures, but other tensions grew, both externally and internally. Swalin, though still a beloved public figure, found himself sometimes at odds with his younger players and longed for a slower pace. He retired in 1972 and suffered a fatal stroke in 1989. His body was returned to his native Minneapolis, where he was buried in Lakeside Cemetery.

His beloved Maxine, born in 1903, lived into the twenty-first century, still going strong and still championing artistic and musical causes, but still regretting that she and her husband had had no children. "Ben would have been a radiant father," she wrote, "eager to guide, to teach, probably expecting too much too fast."

When aging members recalled the North Carolina Symphony's first three decades, they shared fond sto-
ries of being snowed in in the Appalachians, stranded by a storm on Ocracoke Island, getting lost, enduring fleabag hotels and endless cocktail receptions, getting interrupted in the middle of a piece by barking dogs, losing instruments, and getting locked in dressing rooms or out of hotel rooms. And in the middle of it all they remember the dapper Ben Swalin, usually gracious, sometimes imperiously demanding, always committed to bringing quality music to the people and getting them to like it in spite of themselves.

"Through the years," he wrote, "our programs were based upon what we regarded as good music. It was the kind of music we hoped our listeners would experience, for we believed that the symphony must lead the way . . . chart the direction of the public taste."

In the matter of elevating the public taste of North Carolinians, Swalin probably did as much as anyone in the twentieth century. "Rarely will you find a man with so vast a knowledge of music and a passion for making it heard," the *Charlotte Observer* wrote at the time of his retirement. "He nursed the North Carolina Symphony to health and gave it vigorous direction. He planted the seeds for enjoying music among the state's youngest audiences. He has served us well."

Steve Bouser has been editor of the Pilot *of Southern Pines since August 1997. Before that he was editor of the* Salisbury Post *for eleven years and worked with the U.S. aid programs of assistance to independent media in the former Soviet Union, living in Russia and Washington and traveling extensively in Russia and Eastern Europe.*

For more information, see:
"He Founded Our Symphony." *Our State,* November 1991.
Swalin, Benjamin. *Hard-Circus Road: The Odyssey of the North Carolina Symphony.* North Carolina Symphony Society, 1987.
————. *The Violin Concerto.* Reprint, Da Capo Press, 1973.
Swalin, Maxine. *An Ear to Myself.* 1996.

ROBERT E. WARD

By Timothy Lindeman

IN MANY WAYS Robert Eugene Ward's life was a typical American success story. Given his modest upbringing and lack of great family-derived talent (neither of his parents were professional musicians), his artistic success could not have been predicted. Rather, his remarkable career as a composer, conductor, teacher, publisher, and early leader of the North Carolina School of the Arts was of his own making. To be sure, he was helped along the way by many mentors, composers, and friends, but his success was a story of love for his art, hard work, and making the best of whatever circumstances in which he found himself.

At the turn of the century, Ward, at age eighty-three, was an affable man working on his autobiography. Undoubtedly his memory of the sequence of important events of his life had been sharpened by this work. Nonetheless, one sensed that he could easily recall his early days as a high school student with a budding passion for music, as a student under Howard Hanson at the Eastman School of Music, his studies at the Juilliard School in New York, and his years as a composer without the aid of the work on his memoirs.

Ward was born in Cleveland, Ohio, on September 13, 1917, the youngest of five children. His father was in the moving and storage business. His mother could play the piano and organ, but Ward remembered her talents as being in the "folk arts," such as sewing, and making things for the home. Music was a constant presence in the Ward home, as all of Robert's siblings were involved in music. His two sisters played piano, one of his brothers studied the violin, and the other one played jazz by ear. As a youngster, Robert would sneak down the stairs late at night to listen to everyone gathered around the piano singing the popular songs of the day at the end of a party.

Robert possessed a good boy soprano voice, and he sang in school and in the Presbyterian church choir. He began studying piano at the age of ten, but was forced to give up lessons because of the Depression. Later, when he was in high school, and he decided to "make music my life," he began to study again. He studied with Ben Burtt, the pianist for the Cleveland Orchestra, who was also a songwriter. Robert paid for his lessons by copying his teacher's songs. Robert later recalled fondly that he had become proficient

Robert E. Ward (Courtesy of Charlotte Observer)

enough on the keyboard to accompany his brother, who was then taking voice lessons.

Because of the financial hardship caused by the Depression, Robert's plans to attend the Eastman School of Music were delayed for a year. During that year he worked odd jobs, but also sang as part of the Cleveland Orchestra, which brought him into contact with some of the world's great choral masterpieces. He continued to study harmony and composition with his high school music teacher, John Elliot, and was fascinated with the examples of contemporary music he found in his textbook. His first conducting experiences consisted of waving his arms and leading the orchestra that emanated from the phonograph in his living room at home.

At Eastman, he had the opportunity to write for the Rochester Philharmonic Orchestra under the direction of Howard Hanson, which gave him a secure understanding of orchestration. Although Hanson's name is better known, it was Bernard Rogers to whom Ward gave the most credit for help in composing. Ward eagerly embraced the new composers of the time: Bartók, Stravinsky, Sibelius, and Prokofiev. He also learned the music of Debussy and Ravel. One especially memorable occasion was a trip with friends to Cleveland to hear a performance of the brand new opera by Shostakovich, *Lady Macbeth of Mtsensk*.

During Ward's Eastman year he had his first meeting with Aaron Copland. At that time, Copland was living in New York and had already begun to take his place as one of the American music giants. He welcomed young composers into his studio, and when Ward dropped by, the two discussed music. The younger composer would later hear Copland play his Piano Sonata, a personal performance that remained a vivid memory.

After graduation from Eastman, he continued his composition studies at Juilliard with Frederick Jacobi, who had him analyze the works of Haydn, Mozart, Schubert, and Stravinsky in order to come to a deeper understanding of musical structure. Ward also studied conducting there, preparing himself for a performing career. His First Symphony, written in 1941, won the Juilliard Publication Award the next year. During these years, he also began teaching at Queens College, but military service temporarily interrupted his career.

In 1942, Ward joined the army, where he was able to continue his work as a musician. His military service brought him into contact with the popular styles of the day such as jazz and swing, which he gleefully absorbed and incorporated into his own compositions. His first theater work also came from this period, when Ward and other musicians toured army camps performing *The Life of Riley*. He had the opportunity to hone his conducting skills with concert, military, and swing bands. He wrote several compositions during the war years, including his *Adagio and Allegro* and *Jubilation—An Overture*. Ward also met his wife during the service; they had five children.

After the war, Ward returned to civilian life with several important compositions under his belt, some of which were receiving frequent performances. In fact, *Jubilation—An Overture* was so popular that most of the compositions that Ward wrote from then on were for commission. He dove into the musical scene in New York with youthful exuberance. He returned to Juilliard, concluded his postgraduate studies, and began to teach conducting there and at Columbia University in 1946. He took on conducting duties for

the Third Street Music School Settlement and the Doctors Orchestral Society of New York, both of which were filled by refugees from the war. These ensembles allowed Ward to learn new scores that he never had a chance to study; the scores came from the New York Public Library's Work Projects Administration collection.

It was at this time that Ward made the conscious decision to focus his career path somewhat. He was a rising conductor of several ensembles, he was involved in composing theater music for the CBS orchestra with the potential of becoming a Hollywood composer, he was a teacher, and he was a composer of "serious" music. He was somewhat leery of the commercial music route because of the lack of control over the artistic output and the secondary nature that music played in the theater. Thus he made the hard and potentially less financially lucrative choice to direct his energies toward composition and teaching, and away from conducting.

In 1956, after ten years of teaching, Ward left Juilliard to become executive vice president and managing editor of Galaxy Music Corporation and Highgate Press, which was the primary publisher of his music. Although the composer had no previous experience in the music publishing industry, he felt the opportunity to become involved in publishing was too inviting to pass up. As in all his previous endeavors, he devoted himself to the task with energy and enthusiasm. He made it a point to learn all aspects of the publishing industry from the ground up and visited music stores to understand sales and marketing. He remained with Galaxy until 1967.

Ward's years in New York were extremely productive in terms of composition. He wrote three symphonies (numbers 2–4), as well as his first opera, *He Who Gets Slapped (Pantaloon),* with a libretto by Bernard Stambler. The librettist, who held degrees from Cornell in English literature and musicology, was a colleague of Ward's at Juilliard. The work was first performed by the New York City Opera in 1956. It received rave reviews from the critics, leading the composer to search for a good subject for another opera. That opera turned out to be his most famous work.

The Crucible came into being when the composer saw an off-Broadway production of the Arthur Miller play of the same title and was overwhelmed by its power. Eventually Ward and Miller met to discuss the opera; when Miller declined to write the libretto, Ward recruited Stambler again. The premiere took place at the New York City Opera in 1961, garnering even more glowing praise than his previous opera. *The Crucible* won both the Pulitzer Prize and the New

York Music Critics' Circle Award in 1962, and with these awards, Ward moved into the front ranks of American composers. Other compositions written during these years encompass a number of choral works, cantatas, and chamber music, as well as the two operas. Many of the works received several performances after their premiere.

In 1967 Ward left New York to take on a new task, the presidency of the North Carolina School of the Arts, taking the place of the first president, Vittorio Giannini. Giannini, who opened the school two years earlier, had secured most of the faculty and had begun to build the school's reputation. Under Ward's leadership, the school flourished. The school's design and production program, separate from the school of drama, was created, as was a high school visual arts program. The size of the student body grew as well.

When Ward went to the School of the Arts, he had told the board of trustees that he would accept the post for only five years, as he knew it was extremely difficult to be an administrator and composer at the same time. He remained as president, however, until 1975, and then he joined the school's composition faculty, where he taught for five years. Many of the works that he wrote while at the School of the Arts either were designed for or would later be performed in North Carolina. For example, the *Fifth Symphony: Canticles of America,* written in 1972, was commissioned by the Charlotte Oratorio Singers and first performed in Charlotte. The opera *Claudia Legare* (1977) premiered in Minneapolis, but was subsequently performed at Duke University.

Ward then served as Mary Duke Biddle Professor of Music at Duke University from 1979 until his retirement in 1987. His Sixth Symphony, the Concerto for Violin, and *Appalachian Ditties and Dances* for violin and piano were written during these years. These compositions too were designed to be heard by North Carolina audiences. After his retirement from Duke, Ward made his home in Durham, where he spent his time attending concerts of his own works or new music and working on his autobiography.

Ward called himself a "melodist," a trait he credited to his early years as a singer, and his composi-tional style has its roots in melody. According to the composer, this melody comes with an inherent harmonic and rhythmic structure, which needs to be worked out. While the melody came in a key, Ward freely moved that key to suit the instrumentation for which he was writing. In addition, he chose the formal structure, depending on the genre in which he was working.

Much has been made of Ward's "American" sound, a trait that he did not deny. Although he occasionally incorporated folk material in his compositions, in general his music often conjured up a certain expansiveness and optimism that, like Copland's work, seemed to embody the American spirit. Not that Ward sounded like Copland. His music was distinctively his own: tonal, accessible, forthright, solidly structured, with plenty of drama.

At the end of the twentieth century, classical music had begun to return to a more accessible and tonal language; many contemporary composers designed their scores with the express purpose of communicating with large audiences. Robert Ward's music fit this bill perfectly and awaited rediscovery.

Timothy Lindeman of Greensboro is chair of the music department at Guilford College and earned his Ph.D. in music theory from Indiana University. He is a reviewer for Triad Style *and the* News and Record *in Greensboro. In 1993, Dr. Lindeman was one of twelve scholars accepted to a Harvard University seminar on the Beethoven string quartets.*

For more information, see:
Robert Ward's manuscripts and notes are in the Manuscripts Department, Perkins Library, Duke University, Durham.

Huband, Daniel J. "Robert Ward's Instrumental Music." *American Music* 13 (1995): 333.
Jackson, Richard. "Ward, Robert (Eugene)." In *The New Grove Dictionary of Music and Musicians,* ed. Stanley Sadie, 20: 212. 20 vols. Macmillan, 1980.
Kreitner, Kenneth. *Robert Ward: A Bio-Bibliography.* Greenwood Press, 1988.

THOMAS WOLFE

By Ted Mitchell

THOMAS WOLFE left an indelible mark on American letters. Perhaps the most overtly autobiographical of the nation's major novelists, his youth in his mother's boardinghouse in Asheville colored his work and influenced the rest of his life. His reminiscences were so frank and realistic that his epic first novel, *Look Homeward, Angel,* was banned from his hometown public library for more than ten years. Today, Wolfe is celebrated as one of Asheville's most famous citizens, and all of his novels are still in print —more than half a century after his death.

Thomas Clayton Wolfe was born October 3, 1900, at 92 Woodfin Street in Asheville. He was the last of W. O. and Julia Wolfe's eight children. His father descended from hardy Pennsylvania German-Dutch-English farmers; his mother was a third-generation North Carolinian of Scotch-Irish-English stock. All of which led Wolfe to claim that "one half of me is great fields and mighty barns, and one half of me is the great hills of North Carolina."

By the time W. O. Wolf married Julia in 1885, he had already established a successful tombstone shop on the edge of Asheville's great square. Thomas admired the fact that his father was largely a self-educated man. Along with the broad rhetoric he affected, W. O. could recite soliloquies from Shakespeare, as well as the poetry of Gray and Poe. He also passed on the importance of hard work to his son: "writing is a business just the same as any other occupation," Wolfe told an interviewer in 1938. "You have to use what you've got; you can't use what you haven't got. My father got calluses on his hands from his occupation of stone cutting and I get calluses on my hand from writing with a pencil." But it should also be noted that Thomas Wolfe inherited a good share of his talent and prodigious memory from his mother, an inveterate storyteller.

Julia Wolfe was an enterprising and resourceful woman who worked hard to improve her family's economic position. She accepted boarders at the Woodfin Street house and speculated in the real estate market of the growing resort town. Her marriage was plagued by her husband's violence and alcoholism, and when the eighteen-room, Victorian boarding house called "Old Kentucky Home" went up for sale in 1906, she purchased it, taking only six-year-old

Thomas Wolfe (Courtesy Pack Memorial Public Library, Asheville)

Tom with her. The other children remained with their father.

The house (called "Dixieland" in *Look Homeward, Angel*) would rarely be a happy home for Wolfe. Deprived of privacy and security, the move began a bewildering new era of his life. "Thus, before he was eight, Eugene gained another roof and lost forever the tumultuous, unhappy, warm centre of his home," Wolfe wrote in *Look Homeward, Angel.* The disintegration of his family's unity and his move had a lasting effect. Wolfe developed deep insecurities that would plague him throughout his life.

Wolfe experienced a release from his dismal existence when at the age of eleven he met his new teacher, Margaret Roberts, who along with her husband operated a college preparatory school, the North State Fitting School in Asheville. A major influence upon Wolfe's life, Mrs. Roberts nurtured his talent as a writer and awakened in him a love for fine literature. She soon became the invincible mentor he called the "mother of my spirit."

After graduating from the Roberts' school in the summer of 1916, Wolfe engaged in a heated debate with his family over where he was to go to college—despite the fact that he was still only fifteen. W. O. believed the University of North Carolina at Chapel Hill would prove valuable for connections that would be important for the career in law or politics that he saw for his son. Despite Wolfe's preference for Princeton or the University of Virginia, his father told him that he would have to go to the state university or get a job. Wolfe grudgingly accepted his father's dictum and despite his initial disappointment admitted, "Carolina is a good school, and perhaps everything is for the best."

Wolfe escaped his family by train and his love for trains and traveling to new places never abated. He was three weeks short of his sixteenth birthday and already six feet, three inches tall—three inches short of his adult height—when he arrived in Chapel Hill on September 12, 1916, the first day of registration. Almost from the start he knew he had found "the magical campus."

"We belong, perhaps, to an older and simpler race of men: we belong with the Mythmakers," Wolfe brashly proclaimed of Eugene Gant in *Look Homeward, Angel*. "For him, the sun was a lordly lamp to light him on his grand adventuring. . . . He exulted in his youth, and he believed that he could never die." Although his first year was also filled with loneliness and pain, he quickly moved into the mainstream of campus activity. Despite his literary portrait of an introverted Gant, Thomas Wolfe was quite gregarious on campus.

In 1917, Wolfe began to publish. He wrote stories and poems for the college magazine and in 1918 joined the newly organized Carolina Playmakers, Frederick H. Koch's course in playwriting. Koch emphasized the importance of writing "folk plays," and Wolfe was an eager participant. He returned to his mountain roots and his first play, *The Return of Buck Gavin,* was written in just three hours at one sitting. It was one of the first productions of the Playmakers and Wolfe portrayed the tall mountain outlaw of the title.

Wolfe graduated with a bachelor of arts degree in 1919 and set his sights on graduate study at Harvard. Urged to attend Harvard by Frederick Koch, who had studied playwriting under George Pierce Baker in his renowned 47 Workshop, Wolfe was convinced his dream of becoming a dramatist would be realized at Harvard. He entered the graduate school of arts and sciences in September 1920, and for three years enrolled in the same course with Baker. Away from home and family, Wolfe turned to his writing with a fierce tenacity. More than 140 plays, drafts, and fragments of plays are cataloged in Harvard's Wolfe collection.

His first play written at Harvard was a folk play about North Carolina, *The Mountains,* and was staged by the 47 Workshop in 1921. Although he received his master's degree in June 1922, Wolfe returned to work with Baker for another year. The 47 Workshop staged Wolfe's play *Welcome to the City* in 1923; the curtain went up at 8 P.M. and did not go down until midnight. In a letter to Baker, Wolfe stated his lofty theatrical ambitions: "Some day I'm going to write a play with fifty, eighty, a hundred people—a whole town, a whole race, a whole epoch—for my soul's ease and comfort." By late 1923, he had served his apprenticeship under Baker, and while waiting for a professional production on Broadway, Wolfe realized that he would have to support himself. He was hired to teach at the Washington Square branch of New York University, Washington Square College, and began teaching in January 1924.

Although a dedicated instructor, Wolfe accomplished little creative work while teaching, finding it impossible to teach and write at the same time. Convinced that traveling in Europe and absorbing its culture was necessary for his training as a writer, he initially planned to take a leave of absence from New York University and write while traveling through Europe for two months. On October 25, 1924, he sailed for England. He maintained his resolve to write fifteen hundred words a day while abroad, but he did not return to his teaching post until the following year. Sailing home aboard the *Olympic* in August 1925, he met and fell in love with Aline Bernstein, a renowned New York stage and costume designer. Nineteen years older than Wolfe and married, Mrs. Bernstein became the great love of his life, and supplied Wolfe with not only the emotional support and belief in his talent that allowed him to write *Look Homeward, Angel,* but financial assistance as well.

In June 1926 Wolfe once again sailed for Europe and began writing notes and phrases for the novel about his life that became *Look Homeward, Angel.* He wrote in large accounting ledgers, believing his hands too big and unwieldy for a typewriter. For the next two years he divided his time between Europe and New York, working feverishly to complete his massive manuscript he initially called, *O Lost.* Completing the novel in spring 1928, the manuscript began making the rounds of publishers while Wolfe continued his travels abroad.

In the fall of 1928, while in Vienna, Wolfe received a letter from Maxwell E. Perkins, the legendary editor at Charles Scribner's Sons, asking him to meet him in New York to discuss *O Lost*. Wolfe returned to New York and on January 9, 1929, the manuscript was formally accepted for publication by Scribner's. The original manuscript totaled 1,114 pages and contained 330,000 words. Over the next four months, Wolfe worked closely with Perkins, editing the manuscript to a more comfortable length of 240,000 words. That spring Wolfe gave the novel a more provocative title — *Look Homeward, Angel.*

The novel was published on October 18, 1929, and created an uproar in Asheville. It was condemned from street corner to pulpit and banned from the public library. There are more than two hundred characters in the novel, all easily identifiable citizens of Asheville. Wolfe received death threats and it was not until 1937 that he felt safe to return to his hometown. Surprisingly, the novel elicited praise from the Asheville newspapers and received rave reviews nearly everywhere else.

Look Homeward, Angel proved a critical and commercial success, and Maxwell Perkins was eager for Wolfe to produce a new novel as soon as possible. However, it was not until spring 1935 that a second was published. Wolfe found he was having "second book trouble" and recorded in one of his notebooks: "I am all broken up in fragments myself at present and all that I can write is fragments. The man is his work; if the work is whole, the man must be whole." Also, along with chronic depression, he fought a tendency to alcoholism which increased toward the end of his life.

In 1931 Wolfe moved to Brooklyn and settled down to work steadily on a variety of material. He worked standing up, usually with the top of the refrigerator as his desk. Over the following years he wrote dozens of short stories as well as the massive manuscript for his second novel, *Of Time and the River.*

In September 1934, without Wolfe's knowledge, Perkins sent the *Of Time and the River* manuscript to the printers. When informed that proof was coming in, the horrified Wolfe told Perkins that he needed six more months to work on it. Perkins answered that if he were to allow that, then Wolfe would just demand six months more, and the book likely would never be finished to his satisfaction. By the time the novel was published on March 8, 1935, Wolfe had already sailed for Europe, not wanting to face the reviewers. He was sure the book was an unfinished product. Much to his surprise the novel proved an even greater success than *Look Homeward, Angel,* and his literary reputation was secure.

By spring 1937 Wolfe decided to set out on his long-anticipated return to Asheville. On his way home he told a newspaper reporter in Virginia, "One has to go away, before he learns how deeply he is attached to his own people and his own country." As soon as he arrived, a crowd of friends and autograph seekers formed around him on the street corner. He was photographed with his mother on the porch of the shabby, desolate boardinghouse he had immortalized in his book, and for four days the telephone rang constantly as well-wishers and friends called to welcome him home.

Wolfe's self-imposed exile had ended in triumph, although many of the victims of his work would be slow to forget and forgive what Wolfe had written about them and their families. Even in 1938, many in Asheville were still not quite ready to bury the hatchet when they buried Thomas Wolfe.

Hoping for seclusion, Wolfe rented a cabin in nearby Oteen, planning to write all summer there. But he accomplished little work. Friends, family, and curiosity-seekers flocked to the cabin and he later complained to a correspondent, "my stay here this summer has really resembled a three-ring circus." Wolfe returned to New York, disturbed by several confrontations with his family as well as the toll the Depression had taken on Asheville. By the end of the year he was already contemplating a book to be called *You Can't Go Home Again.*

Wolfe had broken with Perkins and Scribner's in 1937 following accusations that he could not publish a novel without the editorial assistance of Perkins. Wolfe negotiated with various publishers, finally settling on Harper and Brothers. His new novel would render his growing social concerns and span 145 years of his family's history, from 1793 to 1938. The manuscript that Wolfe left with his editor at Harper's, Edward Aswell, totaled more than four thousand typewritten pages and contained over 1.2 million words. Shortly after delivering the rough draft in May 1938, Wolfe became ill with pneumonia during a vacation in Seattle. The pneumonia reopened an old tubercular lesion in his right lung and tubercular cells suffused his bloodstream, infecting his brain. Taken to Johns Hopkins Hospital in Baltimore for treatment, Wolfe died of brain tuberculosis on September 15, 1938.

Because Wolfe's final manuscript was ten times the

size of the average novel, Aswell realized there would be a small reading public for anything of such proportions. The manuscript was published as two novels: *The Web and The Rock* appeared in 1939 and *You Can't Go Home Again* in 1940. A collection of stories and fragments, *The Hills Beyond,* appeared in 1941.

Wolfe was buried in Asheville's Riverside Cemetery, near the grave of another North Carolina literary luminary, O. Henry. Carved on Wolfe's gravestone are two quotes from his novels: "The last voyage, the longest, the best" from *Look Homeward, Angel,* and "Death bent to touch his chosen son with mercy, love and pity, and put the seal of honor on him when he died," from *The Web and The Rock.*

Ted Mitchell is the author of twenty-four works on Wolfe, including a biography, Thomas Wolfe: A Writer's Life. *Other articles have appeared in* Our State, Blue Ridge Digest, *the* Thomas Wolfe Review, *the* North Carolina Review, *and the* Asheville Citizen-Times.

For more information, see:

Donald, David Herbert. *Look Homeward: A Life of Thomas Wolfe.* Little, Brown, 1987.

Kennedy, Richard S. *The Window of Memory: The Literary Career of Thomas Wolfe.* University of North Carolina Press, 1962.

Magi, Aldo P., and Richard Walser, eds. *Thomas Wolfe Interviewed, 1929–1938.* Louisiana State University Press, 1985.

Mitchell, Ted. *Thomas Wolfe: A Writer's Life.* North Carolina Division of Archives and History, Historical Publications, 1999.

Watkins, Floyd C. *Thomas Wolfe's Characters: Portraits from Life.* University of Oklahoma Press, 1957.

BUSINESS

Tobacco, textiles, and furniture brought North Carolina workers from the farm to the factory in the first half of the twentieth century, but driving the Tar Heel economy was a mix of businesses built on entrepreneurial skill as businessmen met the demands of a surging market at home and across the nation.

The big names in the major industries—the textile companies of Cannon, Cone, Love, Hanes, and the Stowe and Lineberger families in the textile center of Gaston County; the Reynolds tobacco dynasty; and Broyhill in furniture—all built manufacturing plants that employed hundreds of thousands in communities, spawning demands that proved to be incubators of extraordinary dimensions. In Winston-Salem, for example, trucking executive Malcolm McLean figured out how to convert the road trailers he used to carry Reynolds cigarettes to customers into containerized shipping, and his new company, Sea-Land, revolutionized international trade. In Salisbury, Thomas and Fred J. Stanback found a market for their headache powders—"Snap Back with Stanback"—among the local textile mill workers just as Thad Lewallen did for his Goody's Headache Powders, sold first to tobacco workers of Durham.

There were no retailers more creative in their organization and their strategy than men like William Henry Belk of Charlotte, who opened more than four hundred stores on Main Streets across the Southeast. His sons later reorganized the company to meet modern challenges in retailing for upscale shoppers in suburban shopping malls. Other Charlotte entrepreneurs achieved retail success as well. Leon Levine opened his first Family Dollar self-service discount store in 1959 when he was only twenty-one; by 2002, Levine had built a network of 4,200 stores in thirty-nine states with annual sales of $3 billion. Wayland H. Cato founded the Cato Corporation in 1946 in Charlotte with his sons, Wayland Jr. and Edgar. In 2001, the Cato Corporation had sales of $640 million from more than 800 stores in twenty-three states. Salisbury's Ralph Ketner's ambition to succeed in the highly competitive grocery business led to the creation of Food Lion, which became one of the nation's largest food retailers.

The home improvement giant that became Lowe's was born in the mountain foothills in North Wilkesboro. Carl Buchan started the company, but Robert Stickland, who died in his forties of a heart attack, is generally credited with expanding the company into its current marketing approach.

Durham became known as the "capital of the black middle class" by virtue of a unique combination of talent and circumstance. The city was home to the North Carolina Mutual Insurance Company that by 1924 had spawned a commercial bank, a savings and loan, a fire insurance company, and a cotton mill.

But it was a law passed long before the textile mills and furniture and tobacco factories created cities that pushed North Carolina into the forefront of the modern economy. The state was young when the General Assembly approved legislation to allow a Wilmington bank to open a branch office in Fayetteville, a hundred miles away. Banking remained a regional affair well into the twentieth century. The Holding family's First Citizens Bank was a leader in the eastern part of the state while Edwin Duncan, the creator of Northwestern Bank, brought needed capital and investment to western North Carolina from his base in the tiny mountain town of Sparta. Meanwhile, Winston-Salem's Wachovia Bank and Trust Company dominated as the premier institution of the Southeast. Wachovia executives Robert M. Hanes, the first southerner to head the American Bankers Association, and Archie Davis, were bankers' bankers.

That all changed in twenty years during a thundering period of mergers and acquisitions. North Carolina bankers used their experience in multicity operations to break the prohibitions against interstate banking, and two of the nation's largest, First Union and Bank of America (which began as North Carolina National Bank), had their headquarters in Charlotte by the end of the century.

At the same time, North Carolina became part of the global market, which upset the old standards. Burlington Industries, at one time the world's largest textile concern under founder J. Spencer Love, was sold off in parts in the 1980s. Even the mighty tobacco concerns were humbled by the end of the century. R.J. Reynolds was owned by a company whose name was most closely associated with cookies, and during a period of transition in the late 1990s not a single cigarette was made in Durham, the town where prerolled smokes had been given their start under the Dukes.

Companies came and went. A stop at Frank Sherrill's S & W cafeteria was once a staple in a family's night out. Thomas H. Davis of Winston-Salem took a childhood love of flying and turned it into Piedmont Airlines, a carrier that became the first link that medium-sized markets of the region had ever known. It was merged into US Airways. Grier Beam of Cherryville began hauling vegetables in the early years of the Depression and created a trucking company whose rigs later carried the red Carolina name from Maine to Miami before it was sold and marginalized. Burlington Industries survived a takeover attempt in the 1980s that only preceded the decline of the state's textile industry. By 2000, plants were sold and production had moved out of the country. Mighty Burlington eventually filed for bankruptcy.

Tourism and travel emerged as an important part of the new economy. Pinehurst, the patch of scrub pines and sand that James W. Tufts had bought in the Sandhills to create a mid-South resort, became synonymous with world-class golf. William A. V. Cecil, the grandson of the builder of Biltmore, turned what once looked like the largest privately owned residence in the nation into a tourist attraction of international fame. Vineyards and a winery supplanted the once-familiar dairy herd.

Diversity replaced the conforming restrictions of the old age. At the end of the century, the state's wealthiest man was James Goodnight, whose SAS Institute in Cary (a barely noticed crossroads a generation earlier) produced computer software that made sense out of the dazzling heaps of data collected by other computers. And one of the nation's most successful initial public stock offerings of 2000 was Krispy Kreme, a Winston-Salem company that made doughnuts.

C. GRIER BEAM

By Ken Sanford

C GRIER BEAM'S involvement in providing health care, education, and employment opportunities to his community and region secured his legacy, despite the fact that the big trucks with the red lettered "Carolina" on their white trailers disappeared from America's highways after the company was sold and dissolved after his death. Yet his story was dramatic enough for him to be remembered for his rise from a farm-boy entrepreneur in the Depression to chief executive of what became the nation's sixth-largest trucking company.

Born on January 15, 1906, in Lincoln County, Beam was one of ten children to farmer, carpenter, and businessman Charles Beam and his wife, Nancy Carpenter Beam. Grier learned about hard work from an early age on his family's farm and in businesses—cotton gin, sawmill, and wheat threshing—and his own poultry enterprise that he started with a dozen chicks. He didn't plan on going to college, although his older siblings had done so, but the grueling, hard work in his father's enterprises taught him that he could do better in life with an education.

Beam worked his way through Weaver Junior College (later Brevard College) by sweeping the halls and cleaning bathrooms. At first his studies were a struggle, but he persisted and transferred to North Carolina State College where he majored in animal husbandry and poultry science. The poultry business was a logical career choice, but he finished college in 1931 in the depths of the Depression. He left for a job with a poultry producer in Florida, with the intention of going into business for himself, only to find that when the price of eggs plunged to ten cents a dozen, his employer had to let him go.

He had no choice but to return to work for his father, where he happened upon a used truck—a 1931 Chevrolet—on a lot in Lincolnton. With his father's help, Beam borrowed $500 and bought the truck. To make some money, he hauled anything that needed transportation, and with the help of part-time drivers, particularly the Homesley brothers, he began hauling coal for fuel to Lincoln County schools. His business began to take the shape of a true trucking company when he began hauling sweet potatoes to Florida and returning with tomatoes and fruit, which were sold to wholesalers and distributors and peddled from the back of the truck.

C. Grier Beam (Courtesy of Charlotte Observer)

The trucking business was so tenuous that Beam took a government job in Lincolnton, handing out public aid to others on hard times. This work allowed James Homesley to use the truck to make whatever money he could. When the government job ended, Beam took back the truck, which by now had been traded up to a new Ford.

In a short time, Beam married Lena Sue Brawley of Mooresville, a schoolteacher at North Brook High School. "When we got married," she later said, "we didn't have much, just a bedroom suite. We had a house with six rooms and two of them furnished." Beam's new bride became part of the enterprise, helping with the bookkeeping and learning to accept his long hours at work.

Beam's big break came when Cross Cotton Mills in Marion not only contracted with him to haul cotton yarn to New England, but also agreed to help him purchase trucks. Beam opened an office in his brother's Shell service station in Cherryville that became the first home of Beam Trucking Company, later known as Carolina Freight Carriers.

Bad roads, bad tires, bad credit, and tough competition made the trucking business hazardous in the 1930s. In fact, Beam had to join forces with some other small trucking companies to survive. One competitor, Mauney Transfer, had filed an ambitious plan under the new Motor Carrier Act to haul goods over much of the East Coast. The company's reach was too great, however, and it became vulnerable to purchase. Beam and his partner, Cone Beam (who was not related), took in additional partners and investors and purchased Mauney. The Depression was still on and, after a short time, the other investors sold their interests to Beam.

Still in need of investors, Beam turned to his brother Dewey, a banker. Dewey Beam soon joined the company full time, and the brothers and their wives bought out the other investors to become the sole stockholders. They bought their first property on N.C. 150 in Cherryville in 1938 and began to build modestly what later became a major warehouse and office complex with twenty-seven employees, gross revenues of $135,818, a fleet of fifty-three vehicles, and —best of all—a profit.

After World War II broke out, Grier Beam and Carolina Freight waged war of their own on two fronts. The company was engaged in a long-term court battle against a restrictive Interstate Commerce Commission (ICC) ruling that limited the company to hauling to one direction. Essentially, the ICC had ruled that the rights of Mauney Transfer did not pass on to Carolina Freight at the time of purchase. A legal battle ensued. The Beams hired attorney and future governor R. Gregg Cherry and, in 1942, the U.S. Supreme Court ruled in favor of Carolina Freight Carriers.

The other battle was to meet the demands of the government and its armed forces in delivering the goods required to win the war. The company expanded to meet the business and built terminals as close as Charlotte and as far away as Providence, Rhode Island. Expansion continued after the war but with expansion came change. Carolina Freight's drivers organized a Teamsters' Union local, the first in North Carolina. And John L. "Buck" Fraley, who as a kid had sold produce on the streets with Grier Beam, joined the company in 1949 with the assignment of gaining new commitments from textile mills on the

southern end of the trucking runs and from garment businesses on the northern end.

By the end of the 1940s, the company's gross receipts had reached $3 million, and the service area expanded to cover the area from the Florida Keys to New England. In the 1960s, the company expanded its service area into Chicago, Cincinnati, and other midwestern cities. By 1970, revenue had reached $60.4 million.

The Beams retained control of the company until 1962, when stock was sold to employees. In 1963, stock was offered to the public. New terminals were opened in New York and Connecticut and the company won awards from the American Trucking Association for loss and damage prevention, while company drivers won numerous driving awards.

A milestone in the company's history occurred in 1969 when Dewey Beam retired as secretary-treasurer, selling his stock to his brother, Grier. A new team began moving into key positions: Fraley as president, Ken Mayhew Jr. as treasurer, and Palmer Huffstetler as secretary. In 1971, the company's stock was listed on the New York Stock Exchange. In 1974 Carolina Freight acquired Leonard's Express of Greenburg, Pa., and in 1975 company revenue exceeded $100 million for the first time.

Grier Beam celebrated the company's fiftieth anniversary by opening the C. Grier Beam Truck Museum in Cherryville with a replica of his first truck —that 1931 Chevrolet. Advances in the anniversary year included the beginning of service to California and Texas and even to Europe. Another major acquisition in 1984 brought in Red Arrow Freight Lines, and by 1987, employment exceeded ten thousand.

At Grier Beam's death on March 20, 1992, the company he had started with one truck had grown to one with more than 16,000 trucks, some 11,000 employees, and yearly revenue of $600 million. Service had been expanded to more than a hundred countries, and the company had offices in Europe, Mexico, Canada, and Puerto Rico.

Grier Beam was sometimes described as gruff and intimidating but with a tender heart, particularly for those less fortunate. As chairman of the Gaston County Board of Commissioners from 1960 to 1976, he was an activist leader who participated in the county's major decision-making process in a pivotal period in its history—a time of transition away from the old textile-mill-based economy. He supported consolidation of the county's public schools, even though it meant that Cherryville surrendered its independence.

When voters didn't share his vision for the future

of his county, Beam found ways to convince them. After voters turned down a $7.9 million bond issue to pay for buildings at Gaston College, Beam donated a tract of his own land to be sold to benefit the college, and he helped persuade his brother Dewey and his wife, Prue, to make major gifts. He raised money from other Gaston County donors and won credit from the North Carolina Community College System, which reported in 1981, "More than anything else, Gaston College's successful development efforts can be traced to one individual, C. Grier Beam, and his ability to put his hands on the money."

Lena Sue Beam attributed her husband's interest in Gaston College to his love of education and his interest in the young people of the region. The college responded by naming the main approach to the campus for Beam. Other buildings bear his name and that of his wife, Lena Sue.

Ken Sanford is a native North Carolinian who graduated from UNC-Chapel Hill and worked on newspapers in the state before becoming UNC-Charlotte's first director of public information. After his retirement, he wrote Charlotte and UNC Charlotte: Growing Up Together, *which was published in 1996.*

For more information, see:
Atkins, Garland. *Carolina Freight Corporation: A History, 1932–1985.* Carolina Freight Corporation, 1985.
Sanford, Ken. *Building a Future from the Past: The History of Gaston College, 1964–1999.* Gaston College, 1999.

THE BELK FAMILY

By Alex Coffin

WILLIAM HENRY BELK opened his leased 22-by-70-foot brick store at the corner of Main and Morgan streets in Monroe on May 29, 1888, launching one family's contributions to North Carolina's business, civic, social, religious, and political life. More than a hundred years later, the family-run enterprise had more than two hundred fashion department stores in thirteen states and was one of the largest privately owned retail firms in the nation.

A case could be made that few other families made such an impact on business as the Belks. The times were uncertain as the South struggled to recover from the devastation of the Civil War and Reconstruction. William Henry Belk was born June 2, 1862, the son of Abel Nelson Washington Belk, who was drowned by Union troops in 1865, and Sarah Walkup Belk, who was then left to raise three young sons. After the war, in 1873, she married Colonel John R. Simpson and the family moved across the state line from Lancaster, S.C., to Monroe in Union County.

Henry, as William Henry became known, was educated at home and decided against accepting a scholarship to the University of North Carolina in order to stay in Monroe and achieve his dream of becoming a merchant. He went to work for dry goods merchant B. D. Heath at the age of fourteen for five dollars a month, and his "education" at Heath's store lasted twelve years until he opened his own store, one he called the New York Racket.

Belk's first store was simple, with goods displayed on rough boards and packing crates. But he introduced a relatively new concept in merchandising—one he had found in the North. Most merchants in the South negotiated prices and then sold on credit. Belk challenged both concepts: he marked his goods with one price and sold for cash only, usually for less than his competitors, since he wasn't carrying the cost of credit. His emphasis on cash sales was a gamble, but it allowed him to close his first year in business debt free and with a profit of $3,300. Cash sales would remain a hallmark of the Belk business until the middle of the twentieth century, when the company finally introduced an in-store credit card long after other companies had allowed charge accounts.

The business was so successful that Henry's brother, Dr. John Montgomery Belk, abandoned his own medical practice to become a partner, and they changed the name of the stores to W. H. Belk and Bro. The brothers opened their first branch store in 1893 across the South Carolina border in Chester. A year later, Union, S.C., had a Belk store, and in 1895 they opened at 11 East Trade Street in Charlotte, then the state's second most populous city at fifteen thousand behind Wilmington. Henry moved to Charlotte to manage the new store that offered the same value-priced basic merchandise the brothers promoted in smaller towns, and left the more fashion-oriented ready-to-wear business to competitor Ivey's.

By the turn of the century, the Belk brothers were expanding steadily out of Charlotte using a system of partnerships they created with owner-store managers, all of whom were trained personally by the brothers. The young men considered themselves "Mr. Henry's boys," and often came right off the farm. They were given menial chores at first and if they showed industry and ambition, they were promoted and eventually began accompanying Belk and his buyers on business trips. In time, they were dispatched to cities and towns around the Carolinas to open stores under their own name and that of the Belks. For example, D. R. Harry of Charlotte took a one-third interest in a store in Greensboro, and Harry-Belk Brothers opened there in March 1899. Brothers Sam and Arthur Harry opened the Belk-Harry store in 1902 in Salisbury. The Matthews family developed business in Gastonia and the Hudson brothers opened their doors in Raleigh.

The concept proved marvelously successful. By the end of the 1930s, Belk stores could be found in county seats from the shores of Albemarle Sound in eastern North Carolina, across South Carolina to the hill towns of northern Georgia. Except for the Depression era, the volume of sales increased yearly. William Henry Belk and his partners did more than $30 million in sales in 1939 and the Charlotte store—enlarged and remodeled many times over—was one of the grandest in the South. Admirers of the Belk system called it a "merchant democracy," as all the owner-managers had started from the same point and built their own personal success stories.

Belk was as devoted to the Presbyterian Church as he was to his business even though he did not join the church until he was twenty-one. "I just didn't think I was good enough," he later said. As Belk's wealth grew, he enjoyed his benefactions to Presbyterian in-

Left to right: William Henry Belk, John M. Belk, Tom and John Belk
(Courtesy of Belk Inc.)

stitutions, particularly colleges and hospitals. On Monday mornings, his office in Charlotte—where he greeted visitors from his chair beside a large rolltop desk—was usually visited by a Presbyterian preacher or two, who reported at the direction of his flock to seek help for a struggling new church. Belk usually responded by offering to pay for the brick for a new building if the congregation would raise the additional money to erect it.

Before John's death in 1928, the Belks established a large hospital in Tai-Chow, China, and named it in honor of their mother. They also supported missionaries sent to establish churches in the area. Altogether, the John M. Belk Memorial Fund established after John's death helped build 335 Presbyterian churches and manses, and Belk philanthropies supported the Montreat retreat center, Charlotte's Presbyterian Hospital, Queens College in Charlotte, St. Andrews College in Laurinburg, and Davidson College.

Presbyterian Hospital had the longest association with the Belks. Belk had helped purchase the hospital site on Hawthorne Lane on land where he later built a grand mansion. He married late in life and raised his family there

Belk was fifty-three in 1915 when he married Mary Irwin, who was the daughter of a Charlotte surgeon. Together, they raised a family of five sons and a daughter. The eldest son, William Henry Jr., joined the business in the late 1930s and was followed by his brothers and sisters after World War II, although their father remained active right until his death on February 21, 1952, at the age of eighty-nine. After the death of his wife in 1968, the family property became part of the hospital and headquarters to the Presbyterian Hospital Foundation.

Henry Jr. succeeded his father, but a family dispute led to his departure in the mid-1950s when his brothers, John and Tom, became the leaders of the next generation of merchants. Brothers Irwin and Henderson also took a hand in the business, along with their sister, Sarah Belk Gambrell, who for many years ran the women's apparel division in New York City. But it was Tom as the merchandiser and John as the leader who propelled the Belk organization to relocate the business from downtown to shopping centers and transform the stores from bargain to fashion merchandise.

In 1956, the Belks completed the acquisition of the rival Efird department store chain, thereby gaining an even greater grasp in the Carolinas and Virginia. John led the company into new markets in shopping centers, including the establishment of the company's flagship store at SouthPark in Charlotte that eventually replaced the family's huge store on North Tryon Street.

The Belk partnership arrangement that William Henry Belk created served the company well in the early days, although it required the skill of a corporate lawyer and the attention of a genealogist to understand a half century later. Belk and his partners had opened stores in each town under separate companies, and annually the partner-owners had reported to Charlotte for stockholder meetings that were held around the rolltop desk of William Henry Belk, who owned the controlling interest. Belk usually took his annual vacation in Florida in February, where he would recuperate from days of hundreds of fifteen-minute stockholder meetings where partners reported annual sales.

This same arrangement remained in place at the

height of the company's expansion in the 1960s, when the Belk name could be found on more than four hundred stores in cities and towns in eighteen states and Puerto Rico. The retail market was changing, however. Shopping centers were drawing customers away from the familiar downtown locations where nearly all Belk stores could be found. Discount operations also were cutting into the budget sales that had been a mainstay of the Belk line.

Beginning in the late 1960s and continuing through the mid-1980s, John and Tom led the company through a period of change. Old stores on Main Street were replaced with large anchor stores in modern regional malls. The merchandise mix was upgraded to appeal to a fashion-conscious suburban customer, while work clothes and bargains eventually disappeared. Slowly, as the second and third generations of the families of the original partners moved further from the business, minority stockholders in closely held corporations were bought out and ownership became more consolidated. In 1998, the remaining 112 corporations were merged into one company, Belk Inc. The Belk family retained a controlling interest but for the first time, the company's financial records became public.

John was credited with the diplomacy and skill that eliminated the balkanized and complicated empire started by his father. At the same time he was building an impressive record as a political and civic leader in Charlotte. He served as mayor of Charlotte from 1969 to 1977—longer than anyone else in its history—and considered a campaign for the Democratic nomination for governor. At one point, he was so busy that his secretary kept three calendars for him—one for the mayor's office, one for Belk business, and one for his duties as president of the National Retail Merchants Association. Both he and his brother, Tom, were among some of the best fund-raisers in the region, and led campaigns to benefit the Boy Scouts (John received the elite Silver Beaver, Silver Antelope, and Silver Buffalo awards), Presbyterian Hospital, St. Andrews College, and UNC-Charlotte, where the Belk Tower illuminated the nighttime sky. John Belk also created the John Belk Scholars at Davidson College, which, when fully funded, provided full scholarships for forty Davidson students.

John was often complimented for his unabashed love of his hometown, and responded to occasional public gaffes with a self-deprecating sense of humor. He once said, "I couldn't lead a silent prayer" and on another occasion declared, "You don't have to confuse me because I don't know enough to be confused."

But he always had the last laugh at the ballot box and in the business world.

For a time, Irwin Belk managed the Belk companies' financial affairs, but he took a greater interest in politics. In the 1960s he was elected to the state legislature, where he was instrumental in the creation of the University of North Carolina at Charlotte. Henderson Belk served on the Charlotte school board before he sold his share in the business to his bothers, John and Tom. Sarah Belk Gambrell worked in the company's New York buying office for many years. In 1996, John and Tom also bought Irwin's interest in the many Belk corporations.

Tom was a quiet, intense man who could be as private as John was public. He reshaped the company's image as Belk moved away from competition with discounters into higher-priced merchandise of designer fashions. To do so, he overcame the company's reputation as the retailer to farmers and mill workers in the rural South, and positioned it as a fashion leader in the newer upscale markets growing around the region's rapidly expanding cities. It took more than twenty years before Belk stores in some tiny county-seat markets were closed, but by the 1990s the high-end Belk stores carried the names of virtually all the world's fashion leaders.

Tom died unexpectedly January 25, 1997. In a subsequent reorganization, his three sons—Tim, McKay, and John R.—assumed equal roles as presidents of major divisions. Henry Jr., who had little to do with the business after 1970, died in 2001.

Alex Coffin worked at newspapers in Charlotte, Atlanta and Vancouver, British Columbia, in addition to being a staff member for U.S. Representative Charles R. Jonas in Washington, D.C., and for Duke Power Company in Charlotte, before opening his own public relations firm in Charlotte in 1985.

For more information, see:
Belk, Henderson. *Early Belk Partners*. The Belk Press, 1994.
Blythe, LeGette. *William Henry Belk: Merchant of the South*. University of North Carolina Press, 1958.
Coffin, Alex. *Brookshire and Belk: Businessmen in City Hall*. University of North Carolina at Charlotte, 1994.
Covington, Howard E., Jr. *Belk: A Century of Retail Leadership*. University of North Carolina Press, 1988.

THE BROYHILL FAMILY

By Kathryn Staley

James Broyhill, J. Edgar Broyhill, and Paul Broyhill (Courtesy of Broyhill family)

For more than eighty years the Broyhill family changed life in western North Carolina and the state's emerging furniture industry. With the early collaboration of his older brother Thomas, James Edgar Broyhill founded Broyhill Furniture Industries, which he and his sons developed into an international company. Throughout western North Carolina, and especially in Caldwell, Wilkes, and Watauga counties, the Broyhill name was recognized as a major figure in furniture production, philanthropy, and public service.

In 1892, James Edgar Broyhill was born the seventh of nine children to Isaac and Margaret Parsons Broyhill in Boomer, a small Wilkes County community. Isaac was a farmer who also worked in a sawmill and as a blacksmith. He and his wife encouraged his children to work hard, ensured that all the children

got at least a grade school education in public schools, and instilled an entrepreneurial spirit in their offspring.

In 1900, Thomas, the Broyhills' oldest child, left the farm for nearby Lenoir to explore the furniture business, which was beginning to show promise as a thriving enterprise in the state. Born in 1877, Thomas had already worked on the farm and in the sawmill before his youngest brother, Ed, was born. He used his sawmill experience to tap the local forests and by 1912 had established what became known as the Lenoir Furniture Corporation.

Young Ed knew that farm life was not for him, but he was unsure about his future plans. He finished all available local schooling—the equivalent of a fourth-grade education—and then enrolled in Boone at Appalachian Training School for Teachers (later Appalachian State University), where he met his future wife, Satie Hunt, who was studying music and education. Before he could earn a degree, Ed was drafted into the army in World War I. After his discharge, he went to work for his brother in Lenoir.

At first he worked for nothing but at the end of 1919, his brother gave him $1,800 for past work and put him on the payroll. The young Broyhill showed a talent for selling and by 1923 he was in charge of design, pricing, and sales. The company had been making odd pieces when he arrived and by the mid-1920s, Ed had introduced suites of furniture, including the heart of the line, a seven-piece bedroom suite consisting of a dresser, vanity, nightstand, bench, poster bed, chair or rocker, and a glass-door chifforobe. Together, the brothers bought several failing furniture plants and transformed them into thriving factories. In 1926, Ed ventured out on his own and founded the Lenoir Chair Company, which, though independent, remained associated with Tom's company.

Heart problems forced Tom's retirement in 1937 and all responsibilities of the company then passed to Ed, although Tom continued to provide advice and support. In the ensuing years, Ed continued to purchase failing factories and eventually managed six operations at diverse locations. Finally, in 1945 he established a central selling agency named Broyhill Furniture Factories to oversee his growing number of plants. The company name was subsequently changed to Broyhill Furniture Industries.

In addition to managing the business, Ed Broyhill, or "Mr. J. E." as he became known, undertook the expansion of North Carolina's entire furniture industry. During the early years of his career, High Point's twice-a-year Southern Furniture Market was largely a regional affair, but by 1927, the industry was part of North Carolina's big three—tobacco, textiles, and furniture. Ed Broyhill had begun traveling to national furniture markets such as the American Furniture Mart in Chicago in 1924, and he started developing a similar annual market for North Carolina.

In 1943, the Southern Furniture Manufacturers' Association elected Ed president and then reelected him president for another three terms. The board of governors of the American Furniture Mart named him "Furniture Man of the Year." By the 1950s, the number of furniture showrooms had grown to the point that the major companies organized the Furniture Factories Marketing Association of the South to systematize the annual markets. In 1952, Ed bought Blowing Rock's Green Park Hotel to encourage attendance at the Southern Market. Later, his service to the furniture industry was recognized with the Southern Furniture Manufacturers Association's James T. Ryan Award.

During this time, Ed and Satie Broyhill were raising a family in Lenoir and became active in civic life. A daughter, Allene, was born in 1922, Paul in 1924, James in 1927, and Bettie in 1929. The children were educated in Caldwell County public schools and North Carolina public universities. Throughout their childhood, the boys regularly visited the plants to help their father, and the elder Broyhill dreamed they would succeed him. As for his daughters, both attended college, married, and raised families. Allene's first husband, William Stevens, also worked for the company.

Ed Broyhill's influence extended beyond his family and business. Politics, hobbies, and philanthropy also occupied his time. An avid Republican, he was a delegate to the national convention in 1944 and North Carolina's national committeeman for twenty-eight years.

An enthusiastic golfer, Ed helped create many golf courses in western North Carolina, including ones in Lenoir, Blowing Rock, Boone, and the Cedar Rock Country Club. He was also involved with the Shriners and in 1966 celebrated his fiftieth year as a Mason.

Ed's civic work was shared by Satie as well. She was instrumental in the founding of Broyhill Hall at the Southeastern Baptist Theological Seminary in Wake Forest, the Broyhill Chapel at Wake Forest University, the J. E. Broyhill Park in Blowing Rock, and the Broyhill lecture services, which circulated among several North Carolina colleges. Satie also served on the board of trustees at Appalachian State from 1957 to 1965. In 1983, the university dedicated the Satie Hunt Broyhill Music Center in her honor. In 1992, she was named the first recipient of the university's Appalachian Medallion for service to Appalachian State.

The Broyhill Family Foundation was incorporated in 1945 to offer scholarships, give assistance to child development and community service, and encourage free enterprise. The foundation's work carried on after Ed's death in 1988 at age ninety-six, and Satie's in 1997 at ninety-eight.

The Broyhills' eldest son, Paul, followed his father into the furniture business after serving in the army during World War II and graduating from the University of North Carolina at Chapel Hill. He joined the company in 1948 and continued in various capacities, including design, merchandising, and sales. After his uncle, Tom, died in 1955, he became general manager. In 1956, he married Faye Arnold and they had three children, Claire, Caron, and Hunt.

After becoming president in 1960, Paul led Broyhill Furniture Industries through even more growth than his father and uncle. One major improvement was the opening of contemporary-style offices and a showroom building in Lenoir in 1966. Beginning in the 1960s, Paul also acted as president of the foundation until his son took over, and then Paul became chairman. After his father became chair emeritus of the company board in 1976, Paul became chairman.

In 1980, many changes occurred in the company. In addition to Paul's retirement, St. Louis-based Interco bought the business for $151.5 million. Paul became one of Interco's vice presidents and a member of the board. Paul also served as a trustee at Meredith College in Raleigh. The sale produced wealth throughout the region as over the years the Broyhills had extended stock ownership to their employees.

Paul's younger brother, James, chose a career in politics. After graduating from the University of North Carolina at Chapel Hill, James went to work with his father, but left the company in 1964 after he was elected to Congress from North Carolina's Ninth District. His fiscal conservatism and diligence led him to be reelected eleven subsequent two-year terms. He was a member of the Energy and Commerce Committee and Oversight and Investigations Subcommittee. In July 1986, he was appointed to fill the unexpired term of U.S. Senator John East, but later lost a bid to a full term to Democrat Terry Sanford.

After leaving the senate, James Broyhill was appointed chairman of the North Carolina Economic Development Board and he served as state secretary of commerce from 1980 to 1991. After his retirement from public office that year, he remained busy with many civic activities. In 1993, he was named to the Appalachian State University board of trustees, which he chaired.

Kathryn Staley is the W. L. Eury Appalachian Collection archivist at Appalachian State University. She is a graduate of Appalachian State University's Appalachian Studies Master's Program.

For more information, see:

Broyhill, J. Edgar, and James Thomas Broyhill. Papers. W. L. Eury Appalachian Collection, Carol G. Belk Library, Appalachian State University, Boone.

Broyhill, Paul. Interview. American Furniture Hall of Fame Member Oral Interviews. The Center for the Study of the American South, University of North Carolina at Chapel Hill.

Broyhill, Satie. Interview. Appalachian State University Oral History Project. University Archives, Appalachian State University, Boone.

Caldwell County Heritage Book. Volume I. Hunter Publishing Company, 1983.

Stevens, William. *Anvil of Adversity: Biography of a Furniture Pioneer.* Kingsport Press, 1968.

CHARLES A. CANNON

By Benjamin A. Jolly

WHEN JAMES WILLIAM CANNON began building a textile empire before the arrival of the twentieth century, he hoped his company would become a household word. More than a hundred years after Cannon opened his first textile mill, his surname continued to be synonymous with the state's textile industry which transformed the state's industrial life and moved countless North Carolinians from farm to factory.

Born in Mecklenburg County on April 25, 1852, James William Cannon was the fourth of six children of Joseph Allison and Eliza Long Cannon. Following the conclusion of the Civil War, Cannon worked as a clerk in a Charlotte general store co-owned by his brother, David. Three years later, James purchased an interest in the store and became the lead partner of the business at age nineteen. Even though he did not have much formal education, James was an adept salesman with a keen business sense.

During the next fifteen years, James Cannon developed his company into one of Cabarrus County's leading businesses. Despite his stature as a successful businessman, Cannon aspired to be in the textile industry. In 1887 he invested virtually all of his savings in the purchase of forty acres along Franklin Avenue in Concord. He built Cannon Manufacturing Company's first mill, as well as homes for workers and the superintendent, and a railroad siding that connected the Richmond and Danville railroads to the mill.

Using steam-generated power and four thousand spindles, Cannon Manufacturing Company produced yarn for the first time on April 1, 1888. Unlike most southern textile mills, which made yarn and sold it to New England factories, Cannon Manufacturing Company spun the yarn, wove it into fabric, and marketed the product as "Cannon Cloth." At the end of its first year in operation, Cannon Manufacturing Company turned a profit of $1,255.25.

Even though Cannon Cloth did well, sales were limited, and Cannon realized that he would need to diversify in order to ensure future growth. More people were starting to use cotton towels, and Cannon became the first manufacturer in the South to manufacture them. Eventually, Cannon Manufacturing Company made towels exclusively, a decision that ultimately produced the largest towel mill in the world.

Sales boomed and Cannon opened new mills in

Charles A. Cannon (Courtesy of Charlotte Observer)

Salisbury, Albemarle, Mt. Pleasant, and China Grove, and later in various towns in South Carolina, Georgia, and Alabama. To maintain an effective marketing network, Cannon opened a sales office in New York City, becoming the first textile manufacturer to do so. Two years later, he opened a second sales office in Philadelphia. Cannon's goal was to develop a method that would label the Cannon name on every towel created. This goal would not be achieved by Cannon, but by his son, Charles.

When James Cannon died in 1921, he was succeeded by his youngest son, Charles, who was born on November 29, 1892. He was one of ten children born to James and his wife, Mary Ella Bost of Concord. Charles had attended schools in Concord as well as the Fishburne Military Academy before enrolling at Davidson College. After a brief stint at Davidson, he left college to work for his father at Cannon Manufacturing. He was nineteen when he began his career as an office clerk and started learning the business. At first, he worked at the mill during the day and used his nights to master the various phases of the textile field. A voracious reader, he became conversant in politics, engineering, publishing, international events, arts, banking, architecture, and human affairs.

After several months in various factory jobs, Charles Cannon became the manager of the Barringer Manufacturing Company, a small spinning operation in Rockwell. In that same year, 1912, he married Ruth Louise Coltrane, daughter of D. B. Coltrane, a prominent Methodist layman and a four-year Confederate veteran. Charles and Ruth had four children: William C., Ruth, Mariam, and Charles A. Jr. In 1913, Charles Cannon was named secretary-treasurer of the Barringer mill.

By the time he was thirty-two, Cannon, always a savvy marketer, had designed the famous Cannon trademark—a cannon flanked by a stack of cannon balls—which was attached to every towel produced. In 1926, Cannon was named president of Cabarrus Bank and Trust Company in Concord. He was also appointed as a director of the Federal Reserve Bank in Charlotte and began serving on the National Council of the YMCA. During the same year, he was elected president of Efird Manufacturing Company in Albemarle and turned down the Republican Party's nomination for the United States Senate. In 1928, Cannon consolidated the company's eleven plants, and the company was reorganized as Cannon Mills Company with Cannon as president.

Despite his lack of a college degree, Cannon demonstrated a lifelong commitment to education, particularly on the college level. In 1928, he was elected a trustee of Davidson College, as well as of the University of North Carolina and Duke University.

In addition to his service and benevolence to these institutions, Cannon also contributed his time and money to other institutions, including Wingate and Pfeiffer universities. His personal papers are archived at Wingate, where several buildings are named for him and his wife. Cannon was also awarded numerous honorary degrees during his lifetime.

Cannon lived in Concord, but his textile empire was headquartered in Kannapolis, which would grow into the state's largest unincorporated town with a population exceeding 30,000. It was home to the Cannon headquarters, thousands of simple clapboard houses rented to workers, a YMCA with the largest membership in the South, and a complete downtown shopping district with buildings designed in the Williamsburg style, a favorite of Mrs. Cannon. Cannon built churches and schools and controlled the local newspaper, the *Kannapolis Independent*. Urban functions usually handled by a municipal government were taken care of in Raleigh or by county officials. In later years, the company subsidized the Cabarrus County sheriff's office, which provided local police service. "City" streets were actually state roads. When the mill decided local ordinances were necessary—to control farm animals in the residential neighborhoods, for instance—Cannon sent word to the state legislature to pass a new law. The town was finally incorporated in the mid-1980s, some years after the company had left Cannon family control.

Because so many details in local affairs were dependent on the state, Cannon took a keen interest in affairs in Raleigh. Democratic Governor O. Max Gardner appointed him to the North Carolina State Highway Commission. He also served on the State Parks Commission and represented North Carolina as a delegate to the National Conference of State Parks. Always an admirer of North Carolina's natural resources, he was instrumental in the establishment of the Blue Ridge Parkway and the Great Smoky Mountains National Park.

The state also needed Cannon. In 1931, the state was close to default on its bonds when Cannon and John W. Hanes of Winston-Salem persuaded New York bankers to renew North Carolina's short-term obligations. Because of his efforts, Cannon received a citation from Governor Gardner, which became one of his most prized possessions.

Taking care of his community's physical health was always a priority during Charles A. Cannon's life. In 1917, he had urged his father to employ a nurse to help care for the health needs of the company employees and their families. This service eventually grew into home nurse visitation programs and regular inoculation clinics. Around the time that Cannon began leading the company, he began his longtime involvement in the detection and prevention of tuberculosis. In 1955, Cabarrus County citizens were among the first in the nation to receive polio vaccinations, thanks to Charles Cannon's generosity, which funded the program.

During the Depression, the Cannon family was instrumental in the establishment of Cabarrus Memorial Hospital, which later became Northeast Medical Center. Cannon secured legislative authorization for a local bond referendum to provide funds to build the hospital. After voters approved the bonds his mother donated over five acres on which the hospital was built. Charles Cannon was elected chairman of its board of trustees in 1935 and served in that capacity until 1967. During that time, he contributed over $11 million to the hospital.

Cannon was also a member of the Hospital Advisory Council of the North Carolina Medical Care Commission and the North Carolina Sanatorium Commission. For his outstanding contributions to health care, Cannon was selected as an honorary member of the American Hospital Association in 1948. In 1956, he received an Award of Merit from the National Foundation of Infantile Paralysis. Four years later, Cannon encouraged and helped finance the construction of a hundred-bed hospital in Banner Elk, which was named in honor of his son, Charles A. Cannon Jr., who died in World War II.

Even after Cannon stepped down as president of Cannon Mills Company in 1962, he continued as chairman of the board and maintained regular office hours until his death on April 2, 1971. By the end of his life, Cannon had introduced pastel colors for towels as well as matching towel sets, making Cannon Mills one of the largest textile companies in the country. During Cannon's fifty years as president, the company created over 20,000 new jobs. During the Depression, Cannon kept employees working, even though company warehouses were overstocked with inventory.

Cannon's wife, Ruth Louise Coltrane Cannon, made significant contributions to the cultural, educational, and religious life of Cabarrus County and the state. She was primarily responsible for the publication of *A History of Cabarrus County in the Wars*. A lover of history, Mrs. Cannon was recognized as an authority on local history and was very active in the restoration and preservation of some of the state's important landmarks. She helped create the Elizabethan Gardens in Manteo and assisted in the restoration of Tryon Palace in New Bern. For over twenty years, she served on the Tryon Palace Commission, of which she was an original member. Mrs. Cannon also collected data for a book, *Old Homes and Gardens of North Carolina*, which was published under her direction as chairman of the restoration committee of the North Carolina Garden Club.

Like her husband, Ruth Cannon was active in many phases of civic life. She organized the women's auxiliary at Northeast Medical Center and served on the Concord Board of Education. She was also instrumental in the addition of a women's department at the Kannapolis YMCA. One of her most notable accomplishments was the restoration of downtown Kannapolis, which was modeled after Colonial Williamsburg architecture. Ruth Cannon died on December 22, 1965, at her home in Concord.

The sale of Cannon Mills in 1982 to California financier David Murdoch was followed by a merger with Fieldcrest Mills in 1985, making Cannon a world leader in household textiles. In 1997, Fieldcrest Cannon was purchased by Pillowtex Corporation but retained the Fieldcrest Cannon name.

Charles A. Cannon established the Cannon Foundation in 1943 to support health, educational, and religious organizations throughout North Carolina. Cannon's daughter, Mariam Cannon Hayes, became president of the foundation. His grandson, Robin Hayes, who was elected to Congress in 1998, also served on the foundation board. Other descendants of James W. and Charles A. Cannon continued to make their marks in business, education, and public service. A large number of educational and health care buildings, dormitories, parks, and schools in North Carolina bear the Cannon name. The family legacy will endure for many years.

Benjamin A. Jolly has written for the Montgomery Herald, the Stanly News and Press, the Norwood Times, and the Norwood News. He also wrote biographical sketches for The Dictionary of North Carolina Biography. Since 1995, Jolly has been a freelance writer and business and community relations manager at Stanly Memorial Hospital in his hometown of Albemarle.

For more information, see:
Hayes, Mariam Cannon. Interview by author.
    Levine Museum of the New South.

Kearns, Paul R., M.D. *Weavers of Dreams*. Mullein Press, 1995.
Young, Marjorie W. *Textile Leaders of The South*. R. L. Bryan Company, 1963.

WILLIAM A. V. CECIL

By Ralph Grizzle

IN THE LATE 1950s, William Amherst Vanderbilt Cecil boarded an airplane in Charlotte for a flight that would change his life. A junior officer at Chase National Bank (later Chase Manhattan), Cecil had traveled from New York to Asheville to visit his family's eight-thousand-acre dairy farm and country estate. Biltmore House in those days was not the attraction that it was by the turn of the century. Opened for tourism at the city and county's request in 1930, the 250-room French Renaissance chateau was losing $250,000 a year and, by 1960, was a serious financial drain subsidized by the profitable dairy farm.

Inside, the house was in disrepair; there were no funds to preserve and restore the home that was completed in 1895. The business itself, bleeding red ink, appeared to be coming to collapse. The young Cecil had returned simply to "see what could be done about the old family homestead." He left Asheville ambivalent about whether he should give up his job to commit to such a project. His ambivalence diminished, however, once he boarded that airplane in Charlotte. On the flight to New York, Cecil ran into a friend and senior officer at Chase Manhattan Bank, David Rockefeller, who had been in Charlotte to open a new shopping center.

"What are you going to do with that white elephant at Biltmore?" Rockefeller asked.

"I'm going to turn it into a black elephant," Cecil replied.

"Can't be done," Rockefeller insisted. "I've tried it at Williamsburg" [Virginia, where Rockefeller served on the board of trustees].

Rockefeller's defiance strengthened Cecil's resolve. He would return to his birthplace in western North Carolina and pump new blood into the old family homestead. In doing so, his own life story would become intertwined with that of Biltmore.

Had it not been for the floodwaters of Asheville's Swannanoa River, Bill Cecil would have been born in a delivery room. But as the river was spilling over its banks, prohibiting travel across it to the hospital, Cecil was born in 1928 in his mother's bed on the country estate that had belonged to his maternal grandfather, George Washington Vanderbilt. On his father's side, the infant descended from William Cecil, Lord Burghley, the lord high treasurer to Queen Elizabeth I. Lord Burghley's lineage joined with the Vanderbilts in 1924, when his heir, John Francis Amherst Cecil, married the only child of George Washington Vanderbilt and Edith Stuyvesant Dresser, Cornelia, born in 1900.

As a toddler, young Bill and his brother George, who was three years older, played inside the towering house, sliding down the banisters and romping about the rooms. The young boys thought nothing unusual about their house until 1930. That year, the Cecils opened Biltmore House to the public at the request of Asheville and Buncombe County officials eager to boost local employment through tourism. The family lived in a suite of rooms at the north end of the house. With only about a thousand visitors a year, the boys and their parents hardly noticed the tourists. "The tours were self-guided," Cecil says. "The guards stationed at the various points would answer questions —if they were awake." In the evening the family would move to the sitting parlor, later the Billiard Room. Before retiring for the night, they had to spruce up the room for visitors the next day.

When he turned four, Bill's parents divorced. The estate eventually was put into a trust for Bill and his brother, who both attended school in England. After a few years in England, the boys traveled by train to Switzerland to attend school there. The year was 1936. World War II was beginning to brew.

In 1943, Bill and his brother left Switzerland by way of France and Spain, and eventually reached Portugal. In Lisbon, they were to board a plane for London but were bumped for a VIP. "The rumor was that it was Churchill," Cecil said. Later that night, German warships shot down the plane. The passenger on board was not Churchill but actor Leslie Howard (who played Ashley Wilkes in *Gone With The Wind*). "That was his end, which was unfortunate," said Cecil, acutely aware of his own good fortune in having missed that plane.

The two boys boarded a seaplane destined for London. To avoid being targeted by German warships, their plane made a wide arc beyond the coast of Europe. "It seems that we went nearly to the coast of America, well out of reach of the Germans, and ended up in England," Cecil said. In England, Cecil finished his schooling, and at age seventeen, he joined the British navy as a signalman just a few days before the end of World War II. He left England in 1949 and

William A. V. Cecil (Courtesy of Charlotte Observer)

returned to America to matriculate at Harvard, graduating a year ahead of his class in 1952.

The young Harvard graduate joined Chase National Bank in New York, rising up the ranks to become an officer in the foreign department. When a vacancy opened at the bank's Washington branch, Cecil and his wife, whom he had married in 1957, moved with their baby boy to the nation's capital for the next three years. "It was an interesting period of time, but not my cup of tea," Cecil said in his English accent. "There was too much partying and not enough banking. It was more of a diplomatic show-the-flag sort of thing." He moved back to New York.

Being eager and in his early thirties, Cecil wanted the challenge of hard work. Biltmore presented that challenge. The estate's president, who had been hand-picked by Cecil's grandmother, George Vanderbilt's widow, was getting on in years and was being forced into retirement. "I thought it would be interesting to be at Biltmore," Cecil said. "So I came down to look at what could be done. I left figuring that I could do something with it." With Rockefeller's "it can't be done" still fresh in his mind, Cecil moved his family to Asheville to begin the process of resurrecting his home.

At first, he wore all caps—manager, promoter, even ticket salesman. "The work was so diverse," he said. "If I tired of doing one thing, I could go do another." He demonstrated a keen instinct for publicizing Biltmore. When the publisher of the *Asheville Citizen* refused to buy staff photographers special lenses to capture an eclipse, Cecil took pictures with his camera and gave them to the paper free of charge. "Of course, I had the silhouette of Biltmore right underneath the eclipse," Cecil said with a laugh.

Newspapers were so important to Biltmore's success that Cecil had a rule that employees had to do all they could to look after reporters. One Thanksgiving, an employee skipped lunch to accompany a reporter who had brought along his wife and baby. The story ended up being just about that, hospitality, Biltmore-style. "Our goal was to cement relationships with the press, because you never knew when or where they would be useful," Cecil said. "The rule was that you never lost touch with them. If they moved, you got a forwarding address."

When a regional reporter relocated to Oregon, Cecil remained in contact and never missed an opportunity to remind his old friend about Biltmore. During one blistery heat wave on the West Coast, Cecil sent the reporter a photo of Biltmore in the snow. "He had a chuckle and ran it on the front page," Cecil said.

Newspapers not only raised awareness of the country's largest privately owned house but helped Biltmore raise its reputation in other areas. While trying to land a contract for restoring the capitol building in Harrisburg, Pennsylvania, Cecil and crew were proving to be no match for regional interests who had much more political clout. Cecil got on the phone to the reporter who had been graciously entertained, along with his wife and baby, during that Thanksgiving dinner. The reporter was then an editor at a paper in Philadelphia. "I told him it was doubtful we would get the work because all the good old boys wanted it," Cecil recalls. "Next afternoon, he ran a front-page story about Biltmore and all the restoration work we had done. They couldn't (and did not) turn us down after that."

Cecil also used newspapers as direct marketing vehicles. An eight-page insert in eight southern metropolitan papers generated a better-than-average response. The catch: an offer to obtain a free recipe of a dish served at Biltmore in 1901. "It became so popular that we later decided we would sell the recipes for a quarter each," Cecil said. People from all over sent in a quarter and a self-addressed-stamped envelope in exchange for a turn-of-the-century recipe.

Revenue of any sort was all-important. Cecil experimented with raising mushrooms and salad tomatoes. "We did anything that we could," he said. "Even landscaping for outsiders. We couldn't afford a full-time landscaping crew, so we tried to fill in their time doing work off the estate."

Increasingly, however, Cecil began to focus his efforts on tourism. It took eight years before the house realized a meager profit: $16.34. The year was 1968, and Bill Cecil had proved Rockefeller wrong. And while $16.34 might not have been much to boast about, Cecil was elated: "It made my day," he said. "It certainly was better than losing half-a-million dollars." Biltmore House was able to sustain itself without needing subsidies from the dairy farm. In 1979, the brothers Bill and George split their inheritance — George took the farm and some land; Bill held on to the house and grounds.

The two brothers were fulfilling their grandfather's vision of a self-sustaining estate. Ironically, however, had George Vanderbilt not died prematurely, the estate may never have fulfilled his ambition. Shortly before his death, at age 54, Vanderbilt was lobbying the U.S. Department of Agriculture to take control of the house. Simply, he had spent most of his inheritance building the house, and the country's new income and inheritance taxes meant that he could no longer afford the upkeep.

Vanderbilt developed appendicitis, and after a successful appendectomy, he died of a heart attack. Biltmore House passed to Vanderbilt's widow, who deeded away all but 11,000 of 125,000 acres to stay solvent. Much of that land now flanks Asheville's southwestern edge as national forest and rises to and beyond distant Mount Pisgah.

The expanse of land that the Vanderbilts once owned boggles the mind. How could one family have acquired so much? The Vanderbilt fortune had its beginning in George Vanderbilt's grandfather, "Commodore" Cornelius Vanderbilt, who earned his money in shipping. During the War of 1812, the government commissioned the Commodore to deliver supplies upriver to Fort Hudson. The young man was paving the way for his son, William, who expanded the family business to encompass international shipping and railroads. When passed down to George Vanderbilt, the entire estate would have dwarfed even that of Bill Gates, according to *Forbes* magazine.

But the grandson George Vanderbilt was no entrepreneur. A studious young man, he spoke six languages and read eight. He traveled to Europe, and on his trips, he accumulated enough paintings and books so that he returned home to New York in need of a place to put all that he acquired. Not particularly fond of the New York social life, Vanderbilt traveled south and purchased land in Asheville with the intention of building a country home. "He wanted a very solemn mansion, with columns and a place to sit out on the front porch," Cecil said. But architect Richard Morris Hunt persuaded Vanderbilt to build a mansion instead. "Biltmore was, in reality, Hunt's glory piece, and my grandfather was happy to let him build it," Cecil says.

Occupying four acres of floor space, the house boasted unheard-of amenities in those days — central heating, electric lights, its own power plant, two elevators, a heated indoor pool, and a sophisticated paging system. Each bedroom had its own bath. Sophisticates like Edith Wharton enjoyed their visits and wrote of the pleasantries of life in the Appalachian retreat. Others, such as Henry James who visited while suffering from gout, were appalled by the "vast sequestered remoteness . . . the showy colossal heartbreaking home and the desolation and the discomfort of the whole thing."

On his visit, Gifford Pinchot remarked that "as a feudal castle, [Biltmore] would have been beyond criticism. But in the U.S. of the nineteenth century and among the one-room cabins of the Appalachian mountaineers, it did not belong. . . . "

By the turn of the century, Biltmore was one of the great marvels of the western North Carolina mountains — thanks to Bill Cecil. For three-and-a-half decades, he relentlessly poured his energy into the "old family homestead," putting Biltmore on the map for tourists worldwide. Nearly one million visitors passed through the gates in the year 2000, compared with 361,000 visitors in 1979. 1998 revenues, the last year for which figures were available, exceeded $53 million, compared to 1979 revenues of $3 million. In spring of 2001, when a 213-room deluxe inn opened on the property, Biltmore had a payroll of more than 1,200 employees, compared with 129 in 1979.

Admission to Biltmore, $2.50 in the early 60s, approached $35 at the end of the millennium. Later visitors, however, had much more to see. "When it was $2.50, you got to see the ground floor, the gardens, the greenhouse and the dairy barn, and that was about it," Cecil said. Later, nearly all but the servants' rooms were open to the public, and for an additional fee, guests could even tour those rooms on a behind-the-scenes tour.

One of Cecil's proudest accomplishments was the winery. Built in 1985, the winery completed Vanderbilt's vision of the self-sustaining estate. "We looked around and asked what was missing," Cecil said. "There was the house, the river down below. There were the fields and everything else, so why not a vineyard? A proper French chateau has a vineyard." Moreover, annual sales of 90,000 cases of wine uncorked additional profitability.

But infusing Biltmore with additional revenue sources was not motivated only by a desire for profit. Driven by aspirations to maintain the family home, Cecil talked of the European sense of home, of how families in the Old Country held onto their homes, while Americans tended to give up their homes when better jobs or better lifestyles presented themselves. Thus, Cecil's efforts to preserve Biltmore worked the other way around: the desire to make more money was prompted by the desire to preserve.

Cecil retired from Biltmore in 1995, during the centennial year of the house's opening. He left the business in the care of his son, Bill Jr., who became CEO and president. It took the elder Cecil ten years to prepare his successor. Cecil's daughter, Diana "Dini" Pickering, served as chair of the board of directors.

Ralph Grizzle is a freelance writer who lives in Asheville. He is a contributing editor of Our State *magazine and author of* Remembering Charles Kuralt.

For more information, see:
Cecil Family. Papers. Biltmore Estate, Asheville.

"Backstage at Biltmore." *Historic Preservation,* November/December 1995.
"Estate Planning." Raleigh *News and Observer,* August 16, 1992.
"Here's the House That Lots and Lots of Jack Built." *Smithsonian,* September 1992.
"Opening His Door to 700,000 Visitors." *New York Times,* December 13, 1992.
"Paying Guests." Special Issue, America's 400 Richest People. *Forbes,* 1998.

THE CONE FAMILY

By Alex Coffin

THE CONES of Greensboro were indeed pioneers of the southern textile industry, building what at one time was the largest denim plant in the world. But they also used their success to build schools and hospitals and help establish the North Carolina Institute of Government, among other institutions.

The Cone family was settled in Jonesboro, Tenn., until 1870, when Herman Cone moved to Baltimore with his family to establish a wholesale grocery business. Moses and Ceasar—the oldest of Herman's ten children—traveled the South as salesmen for their father's company. As the brothers moved throughout a sales territory that extended from Maryland to Alabama, they noticed that few cotton mills existed in the South and that southern farmers were shipping their cotton to England or to the northeastern United States, where the raw material was turned into cloth and yarn.

After the grocery business was dissolved in 1890, the two brothers used their many contacts from around the South to form the Cone Export and Commission Company, which marketed the products coming from the new mills that had begun to open across the region. They also invested with partners in new businesses before erecting two large mills of their own—the Proximity and Revolution mills—in Greensboro, a town of about three thousand that was centrally located between the farms of the South and the markets of the North. Their product was denim, the tough cloth of indigo blue that was the work uniform of American workers. When their largest plant, called White Oak, opened in 1905, it was the largest cotton mill in the South and the largest denim plant in the world.

While Moses, who was called "Brother Moses" within the family, and Ceasar were the founders of the textile empire that became Cone Mills Corporation in 1948, they were joined by their brothers Julius, Clarence, and Bernard, who was an attorney. Moses was company president, Ceasar was vice president, and Julius was secretary-treasurer.

"Handsome and brilliant were these two Baltimore characters," one magazine writer said of Moses and Ceasar, "compassionate and possessed of unquestionable integrity. They did not build an empire on the backs of their employees and customers, but on the good will which they earned along with their fortune."

The company provided more than work for about four thousand employees. On the thousands of acres surrounding the Cones' mills, located just off Greensboro's northeast corner, the company built houses in a mill village that featured graded streets, trees and shrubs, and sanitation features not often found in such communities. The company awarded prizes to employees for upkeep of their homes and hired trained nurses to care for the sick. A model dairy farm was maintained to provide fresh milk, and schools were built for workers' children. At a time when the state required only four months of schooling, Cone classrooms were open nine months of the year. Although the Cones were Jewish, they established churches for other faiths. The domed Proximity United Methodist Church in Greensboro was the last remaining church established with company assistance and is still in its original building.

The brothers' interest in welfare and cultural stewardship came naturally. Claribel, their sister, earned a medical degree and taught pathology and conducted research at Johns Hopkins University in Baltimore. She traveled extensively in Europe, where she became acquainted with author Gertrude Stein, who caricatured Claribel and her sister, Etta, as early patrons of the artists Matisse and Picasso in *Two Women*. Claribel's purchase of Matisse's *Blue Nude* in 1926 was probably the sisters' most outstanding acquisition.

A brother, Sidney, became a Baltimore surgeon who also collected art over the years. The Baltimore Museum of Art later displayed his collection of art, textiles, and jewelry in a special Cone wing. Sixty-seven duplicate lithographs and six small Matisse bronzes—a portion of the collections of Sidney Cone and other family members—were later given to the Weatherspoon Art Gallery at the University of North Carolina at Greensboro.

Before his death in 1908, Moses built a mansion in the heart of a 3,500-acre estate in the mountains south of Boone, where he had taken an interest in the conversion of the Watauga Academy into Appalachian Training School, the founding institution for Appalachian State University. He attempted in vain to have the institution located in Blowing Rock, rather than Boone. In 1907, Greensboro Mayor L. J. Brandt called Moses Cone "the largest single factor in the development of Greensboro from a hamlet to the Gate City

Ceasar Cone and Moses H. Cone (Courtesy of Cone Mills)

of the Carolinas. . . . Your hand has touched on every phase of our life, always to build, never to tear down."

Moses had no children and his widow, Bertha, remained in mourning for the thirty-nine years she lived after his death, usually wearing black. Even her personal stationery had black borders.

Ceasar succeeded his brother. The *New York Herald* credited Ceasar with establishing "spotless towns" around his mills and the newspaper even said Ceasar, who died in 1917, had solved the nation's labor problems with the company's attention to the care of its workers.

Julius followed Ceasar as president. Until 1938, he not only ran the company, but also served on the Greensboro city council under six mayors. Ceasar's son, Herman II, followed his uncle, Julius, as president during a period when the Cone schools became part of the Greensboro public school system. After his aunt, Bertha Cone, died in 1947, her estate was left to build Moses Cone Memorial Hospital, which the family offered to the University of North Carolina as an incentive to locate its newly authorized four-year medical school in Greensboro. The school remained in Chapel Hill, but Cone Hospital later be-

came an integral part of doctor training as one of the state's Area Health Education Centers.

Benjamin, Ceasar's second son, was a Greensboro city council member, mayor of Greensboro—when the city adopted one-way streets—and served in the state legislature in the 1930s. In 1932, he had a visit from Albert Coates, a former classmate at the University of North Carolina who after his graduation from Harvard Law School had returned to teach in Chapel Hill. Coates told Cone of his vision of an institute where local officials—sheriffs, police officers, council members, and others—could come for short courses on state law to help them do their jobs better. When Coates's Institute of Government "drew its first breath" in 1932, it was a result of gifts from Benjamin Cone, who along with his younger brother, Ceasar II, provided financial support for Coates throughout the Depression.

Benjamin was chairman of the board of the family business from 1956 to 1965 and president of Moses H. Cone Memorial Hospital for nearly two decades. He said his personal philosophy was based on the advice his grandfather Herman had received in 1846 in a letter from his brother-in-law, Joseph Rosengart: "Place all your full trust and confidence in God who will send his angels to guard you. . . . So do not be discouraged, and do not be afraid. . . . but consider your fate a good fortune, designed for you by God. . . . 'Do right, trust in God and fear no man.' "

Ceasar II attended Oak Ridge Military School, the University of North Carolina at Chapel Hill, and received a master's degree in business from Harvard University. At Chapel Hill, he was business manager of the yearbook and played on the tennis team. After his death, his widow donated funds to build an indoor tennis facility at the university. He worked out of the Cone Mills' New York and Chicago offices in the late 1930s and moved to Greensboro in 1938 when he was named treasurer. At his brother Herman's death, he became president of Cone Mills and served as chairman from 1965 until 1973.

Ceasar II was noted for his "inexhaustible charitableness" and for being "a hard-driving and self-assured leader." He was instrumental in providing the first building and swimming pool for the segregated Hayes-Taylor YMCA, which was named in honor of two household servants. He was also referred to as "Mr. Airport" because of his leadership culminating with the building of Guilford County's airport.

Western Pacific Industries attempted to gain control of Cone Mills in 1983, but the effort was rebuffed when the firm's executives responded with a leveraged buyout. After that no Cone family member was active in the company.

Moses Cone's mansion in the mountains was often suggested as a mountain retreat for North Carolina's governors. It subsequently became part of the Blue Ridge Parkway and is maintained as a historic site.

Alex Coffin worked at newspapers in Charlotte, Atlanta and Vancouver, British Columbia, in addition to being a staff member for U.S. Representative Charles R. Jonas in Washington, D.C., and for Duke Power Company in Charlotte, before opening his own public relations firm in Charlotte in 1985.

For more information, see:

Coates, Albert. *What the University of North Carolina Meant to Me.* William Byrd Press, 1969.

Cone, Ed. "Shirtsleeves to Matisse." *Forbes,* October 11, 1999.

Jones, Abe, Jr. *Greensboro 27.* Bassett Printing Company, 1976.

Lefler, Hugh Talmadge. *History of North Carolina.* Vol. 4: *Family and Personal History.* Lewis Historical Publishing Company, 1956.

Noblitt, Philip T. *A Mansion in the Mountains.* Parkway Publishers, 1996.

ARCHIBALD K. "ARCHIE" DAVIS

By Frank Tursi

ARCHIE DAVIS was mortally embarrassed by it all. Stories about your life, accompanied by big photographs that take up half a page in the Sunday newspaper, seemed so gauche, so blatantly self-promoting, so ungentlemanly. Davis had declined previous requests for a profile in his hometown *Winston-Salem Journal,* and his acceptance, finally, was less than enthusiastic. His attitude hadn't softened at the interview weeks later.

"Is there any way I can talk you out of this?" he said as he sat down on the couch in his office that overlooked the Square in Old Salem.

It had to be done, Davis was told. He meant too much to the city and state.

Davis sighed. The doleful portraits of Jackson and Lee on the far wall seemed to sigh with him.

He understood. The reporter had a job to do, and characteristically Davis felt it was his duty to help out.

"This is rather embarrassing," Davis said then, "because it's sort of egotistical when you get to talking. I'm serious about it."

No doubt, he would have the same uneasy feeling nine years later, in 1998, when the same newspaper ran his obituary stripped along the top of its front page. It was full of glowing comments from friends and expressions of gratitude from governors and senators about all Davis had done for his city and state. Whatever he accomplished in life, Davis would have modestly countered, could never repay the debts he owed Winston-Salem and North Carolina. Though he would have strenuously disagreed, the bill was repaid with interest well before Archibald Kimbrough Davis died on that March 13 at age eighty-seven.

Davis was probably best known as a banker. He was *the* banker in Winston-Salem for more than thirty years. As senior vice president and then chairman of Wachovia Bank and Trust Company, Davis was the man anyone needing serious money made a point to see. The sum of his life's ledger, though, totaled more than that. Some of the added accomplishments rose in the form of the glinting steel and shiny glass of Research Triangle Park, which wouldn't be what it was without Davis's vision and fund-raising talents. Neither would the National Humanities Center, Old Salem Inc., Salem Academy and College, his beloved University of North Carolina, and the many other or-

Archibald K. "Archie" Davis (Courtesy of Charlotte Observer)

ganizations across the state that benefited from Davis's touch.

"I would call him one of the truly great citizens of North Carolina in this century," said Terry Sanford, who outlived his old friend by just a few weeks. "When you start looking at people who made a tremendous mark, you don't come up with many. Archie was one of those people."

Gravely courteous and tactful in a very southern sort of way, Davis always tried to deflect such praise. He would explain that all he ever tried to do was give back to the city and state that made him what he was. "If you don't want me to do anything for the state, don't ask," Davis said during that painful interview in 1989. "It's that simple, it really is."

Despite the hurried world that he inhabited late in life, Davis clung to such quaintly old-fashioned notions. But, then, this was also a deeply rooted man who was devoted to his wife, Mary Louise, and their four children, and to the Moravian Church. He was the sort of man who had an abiding interest in history, particularly in the Civil War. After retiring from Wachovia, Davis returned to the University of North Carolina at Chapel Hill as a sixty-three-year-old graduate student, and he turned his flawless dissertation on a Confederate colonel into a book. His home in the Buena Vista section of Winston-Salem was a virtual museum of old books, paintings, historical furniture, and memorabilia.

"What an exemplary man he was," said William C. Friday, the retired president of the university whose friendship with Davis spanned almost fifty years. "Grace is a word that fitted him. Not many people in this world understand that word anymore. He lived it. I never once heard him be profane or denigrate anyone or put people down. To the contrary, the value of his life was the role he played as a teacher and as a successful public servant. It was a privilege to be his friend."

While growing up on West End Boulevard in Winston-Salem, Davis listened to the stories his mother, Frances, told of her Moravian roots. She was a Conrad whose people had come down the Great Wagon Road from Pennsylvania in the eighteenth century to help build the village of Salem. Davis became so enamored of his hometown that he would never seriously consider living elsewhere.

He carried on another long love affair with the University of North Carolina. After attending public grammar school and Woodberry Forest, a private prep school in Virginia, Davis entered the university in 1929. He graduated three years later with a degree in history, a Phi Beta Kappa key, and an enduring fondness for UNC. He later served as a trustee and gave freely of his time and money to university projects. He would return often to Chapel Hill, sometimes just to stroll through the old parts of campus.

Davis's father, Thomas, was a doctor who had instilled confidence in his four sons by advising them to do what they wanted in life. Davis, after graduating from UNC, had intended to follow the advice and enter law school at Princeton University. Then the phone rang. It was the personnel director at Wachovia Bank who offered Davis a job. Davis had never considered being a banker, but decided that a job during the depths of the Depression was, after all, a job.

At Wachovia, Davis fell under the tutelage of Robert M. Hanes, the bank's president. As a clerk in the loan division, Davis often traveled with Hanes to smaller banks in the region to lend money to people those banks couldn't afford to serve. Hanes lectured his young employee about the responsibility bankers had to their communities.

"I remember riding with Bob Hanes, and he'd say that the bank's primary responsibility is public service. We owe a debt to the people. They make it possible for the bank to survive," Davis said in 1989. "If there's any one man to whom I give tremendous credit for any inspirational effort I've had in respect to the state, it's Bob Hanes. He was just a remarkable man."

After graduating from Stonier Graduate School of Banking at Rutgers University in 1940, Davis was promoted to assistant vice president of Wachovia and then to senior vice president in charge of the Winston-Salem operations. He was elected chairman of the board in 1955. When Davis retired nineteen years later, Wachovia was one of the largest banks in the Southeast. Its assets under his watch increased from $552 million to $3.3 billion, and its branches from 37 to 181.

Those are just numbers. Davis's influence on Wachovia extended far beyond the balance sheet, noted John G. Medlin, the chairman of Wachovia. Davis was the bank's link to its past, the man who best embodied the principles laid down by Hanes and the bank's founders, Medlin said. "Archie was one of my most revered and respected mentors," he said. "He was one of the reasons why I came to Wachovia, seeing a man of such substance—he was one of the torchbearers of Wachovia's fame, and he taught us that each person had the duty and privilege of carrying out that tradition."

That the American Bankers Association, with its 18,000 member banks, chose Davis as its president in 1965 says something about the esteem other bankers had for him. Businessmen in general thought highly of Davis because he was the only person to head both the bankers association and the U.S. Chamber of Commerce, which had five million members when he was elected its president in 1971.

Traveling the country for each of the groups, Davis became an influential spokesman for the rising postwar South. He abhorred big government because it tended to ignore the wishes of those being governed. The genius of the American system, he said often in his speeches, rested with state and local governments. Progress, he stressed, began at home.

It was that philosophy that guided Davis through two terms in the state senate. First elected in 1958, Davis distinguished himself as a no-nonsense fiscal conservative. He advocated holding the line on government spending and was one of six senators to vote against raising the minimum wage to seventy-five cents an hour. He also opposed a multimillion-dollar education package proposed by Governor Terry Sanford because Sanford wanted to pay for it by taxing food and drugs. Davis thought that unfair and he had the courage to stand before PTAs and teachers and say so.

Davis was respected in Raleigh, even by liberals. Though only a freshman senator, he was made vice chairman of the powerful Appropriations Committee and was chosen for the committee that planned the new Legislative Building. There was talk at the time of greater things in Davis's political future, but he decided not to seek a third term after his wife became ill.

The idea of a research park anchored by universities in Durham, Chapel Hill, and Raleigh dated back to 1949, but it wasn't until the mid-1950s when various interests, led by Governor Luther H. Hodges, came together. They formed a private corporation that bought some tired piney woods near the schools, but the project failed to generate much financial support. Hodges and Bob Hanes asked Davis to head an effort to sell stock in the venture. Davis studied the proposal and came to an important conclusion in September 1958: The park could only succeed if a nonprofit group took control and appealed to business and government. The people of the state, through the universities, must be the ultimate beneficiaries, Davis concluded.

His argument was persuasive, and in 1959 Davis accepted the presidency of the Research Triangle Foundation. He spearheaded an effort to raise $1.4 million in sixty days, and the concept of a nonprofit research park took shape. During the twenty-eight years that Davis was the Research Triangle's guiding light, fifty-four blue-chip corporations invested $3 billion in research labs and industrial plants that employed 30,000 people.

Davis's fund-raising talents were called on again in 1975 when the American Academy of Arts and Sciences was looking for a place for its National Humanities Center. Along with Friday, Davis started a campaign to bring the center, which was being courted by fifteen states, to the Research Triangle. He stunned the members of the academy's site-selection committee at a meeting in Boston when he pulled a tattered envelope from his pocket and read the names of forty people, corporations, or foundations that had pledged $1.5 million for the center in North Carolina.

The committee, of course, chose the Research Triangle, and Davis personally tapped corporations and foundations for millions more to put the center on sound financial footing. Appropriately, the striking modern building, a classroom for visiting scholars, was named for Davis in 1979.

H. G. Jones didn't quite know how to react on that day in 1973 when Davis walked into his office at the state Office of Archives and History, closed the door, and pulled his chair close to Jones's desk. Davis wanted some advice. He said he was getting ready to retire from Wachovia and was thinking about returning to Chapel Hill to get his master's degree in history. "My first reaction was that he'd probably never do it, but he ought to be encouraged," said Jones, the division's director at the time. "But I didn't tell him that."

Instead, Jones said that he thought it was a smashing good idea. Little did he know that two years later he would retire from his state job, teach history at UNC-Chapel Hill, and become one of Davis's faculty advisers.

Davis's fascination with the Civil War stemmed from his trip to Raleigh as a teenager to visit his grandfather, Tom Davis, who had been a captain in the Confederate army. His interest in the war grew, but it had nothing to do with battle flags or, as Davis once termed it, "the North-South business." Davis simply was interested in the sacrifices North Carolinians made during the war.

"There are so many people who can't understand that a person can have the love for the Confederacy without having some of the connotations we have today," Jones explained. "I never saw a mean streak in him. He had as much respect for the Union as he did for the Confederacy. One of the significant things, I think, is that he is the only North Carolinian who was elected to the Massachusetts Historical Society."

Davis chose Henry K. Burgwyn, one of the Confederacy's youngest colonels, as the topic of his master's thesis. He excelled in his classes and received his degree in 1975. Not satisfied, Davis continued his research. He didn't have the time to bother with the bureaucratic technicalities for a formal Ph.D., but he produced a 1,313-page dissertation on Burgwyn that his faculty advisers described as flawless. "We put him through the mill over his dissertation," Jones remembered, "and he came out with shining colors." A shortened version of the work, *Boy Colonel of the Confederacy,* was published three years later by the University of North Carolina Press.

While working on the thesis and dissertation, Davis often chuckled at the form letters he received each fall from banks. They were addressed to incoming college freshmen and offered a small loan and advice on how to handle their money. Though he never attended another class at UNC after finishing the thesis, Davis continued to enroll each fall. "When I die, I hope my obituary will say that I was still a student at the University of North Carolina," Davis said.

When he died, Davis was still a student in good standing.

Frank Tursi is a former staff writer for the Winston-Salem Journal, *which he joined in 1978 after working for various newspapers, including the* Miami Herald. *He has written* Winston-Salem: A History, *and a history of the* Winston-Salem Journal. *Tursi has won numerous national and state writing awards, including the History*

Book Award from the N.C. Society of Professional Historians.

For more information, see:

Most of the information was derived through twenty years of interviews and informal sessions with Archie Davis. The clip files at the *Winston-Salem Journal* contain four thick envelopes spanning more than sixty years.

Link, Albert N. *A Generosity of Spirit: The Early History of the Research Triangle Park*. Research Triangle Foundation of North Carolina, 1995.

THOMAS H. DAVIS

By Walter R. Turner

Thomas H. Davis, right, with Piedmont CEO William G. McGee (Courtesy of Hugh Morton)

TOM DAVIS, the founder and longtime president of Winston-Salem-based Piedmont Airlines, left a legacy of an airline known for safety, incomparable customer service, and a family-like atmosphere among its workers. Even years after Davis was gone and Piedmont was a part of US Airways, the refrain "I miss Piedmont" was still heard in airports across the region.

Thomas Henry Davis was born in Winston-Salem on March 15, 1918, the youngest of Egbert and Annie Shore Davis's four children. He developed an early fondness for airplanes and aviation, and in 1927, when Charles Lindbergh flew the *Spirit of St. Louis* nonstop from New York to Paris, the nine-year-old Davis followed the dramatic story by radio. That fall, when Lindbergh spoke in Winston-Salem, Davis was there to see his hero in person. It was a highlight of his childhood.

"Tom and I built a wooden model of the *Spirit of*

St. Louis with a three-foot wing span," recalled his brother Egbert. "Using rubber bands, we flew it from the driveway to a soft landing in a pea patch behind the house."

At sixteen, Davis soloed in a Taylor Cub (a two-seat, thirty-seven horsepower plane) and received his pilot's license—a remarkable accomplishment for one so young. During summer vacations, his supportive family traveled by car or train as far as Seattle, stopping at airports along the way so that Tom could see a variety of aircraft and occasionally rent a small plane for a flight.

A lifelong asthmatic condition that sapped his strength and limited his physical activity led Davis to the University of Arizona and a drier climate in the fall of 1935. His dreams took him more and more into the skies, and he qualified for a commercial pilot's license with a flight instructor's rating. This success, however, disrupted his academic pursuits. On the verge of completing a premed degree, he came home to Winston-Salem for the summer of 1939, ending what might have been a career in medicine.

Blue skies took over. Davis accepted a summer job selling airplanes for Camel City Flying Service, a small company that sold and serviced Piper Cub (two-seater) and Stinson Reliant (five-seater) airplanes. The company also flew charters, provided flying lessons, and organized air shows. The gangly youth with a friendly nature and love of airplanes was a persuasive salesman. He was having fun. Things were not so bright, however, for the owners of Camel City Flying Service. Financial difficulties led them to seek a new owner the next year.

Davis discussed the opportunity with his father, Egbert Davis Sr. The elder Davis was an entrepreneur who had started a company to sell plumbing, heating, and industrial supplies, then bought a small insurance company and built it into Security Life and Trust Company (later the giant Integon Corporation). With his father's support, Tom assumed Camel City's mortgage of $14,487 and became its major stockholder in 1940. Although headquarters remained at Winston-Salem's airport, Davis changed the company's name to Piedmont Aviation, which he felt better reflected the region it served.

By the end of 1943, Piedmont Aviation was making a profit. With sixty-five full-time employees and contracts with the Civil Aeronautics Administration, the company had trained nearly a thousand students to be pilots and flight instructors for World War II. But when changes in military training priorities caused the War Department to suddenly suspend all civilian pilot training programs, Davis had to inform most of the staff that their jobs were being eliminated.

How could Piedmont find new business and retain those jobs? The solution, he concluded, was to start a passenger airline. Davis had earned loyalty from his workers. Although he conveyed the impression of modesty, he was always proud of what he and the "Piedmont family" were creating. Bill Barber, a retired Piedmont vice president who worked in the parts department during that period, said, "If you went to him with a problem, it was solved right there."

With his wonderful memory for names, Davis organized socials for the workers and their families and listened to concerns and suggestions. "He could relax with the guys over a scotch and soda," Barber remembered. "He loved his people and they loved him."

Finally, in 1947, the Civil Aeronautics Board (CAB) announced that Piedmont would receive a "certificate of public convenience and necessity" for passengers, mail, and freight on a route linking the Carolinas

and Virginia with the Ohio Valley. To raise the needed funds to begin passenger service and augment a loan from Wachovia Bank, Davis and Piedmont's board of directors made Piedmont a publicly traded company. The airline offered a total of 675,000 shares, each costing one dollar. Tar Heels responded, and every available share of stock was sold.

During 1948, Piedmont started three routes. The first one covered Wilmington, Fayetteville, Pinehurst-Southern Pines, Charlotte, Asheville, and on to Cincinnati. The second connected Morehead City (during the summers), New Bern, Goldsboro, Raleigh-Durham, Greensboro-High Point, Winston-Salem, and eventually Louisville. The third route was Norfolk to Cincinnati. Crew bases were established in Winston-Salem, Wilmington, and Norfolk. Within ten years, Piedmont also served Hickory, Jacksonville, Rocky Mount, and Elizabeth City.

Though Davis and Piedmont gradually acquired new routes, none was lucrative. In 1961, to replace the aging DC-3s, Piedmont purchased used forty-four-passenger Martin 404 planes from TWA, which proved to be reliable. The next year, Piedmont was granted route extensions to Atlanta and other points, increasing the airline's flight mileage by 50 percent. The key advantage of the expansion was the ability to offer connecting flights to the Delta and Eastern airline hubs in Atlanta. A North Carolinian could fly Piedmont to Atlanta and catch a convenient connecting flight to the Caribbean, New Orleans, Texas, or the West Coast.

In 1966, Piedmont began flying to New York's La-Guardia Airport, where passengers could transfer by helicopter to international flights from John F. Kennedy Airport. A modest advertising budget was used to full advantage. Piedmont's eye-catching slogan in New York was, "Piedmont puts New York City on the map."

Piedmont acquired a fleet of Boeing 737 jets that seated ninety passengers, establishing a close business relationship with Boeing Aircraft Corporation. These aircraft, along with the subsequent larger versions, became the workhorses of the airline.

Passengers and profits escalated during the decade. Under Davis's careful management, profits increased to more than $1 million in 1965 and nearly $2 million by 1967. Stockholders benefited from several stock and cash dividends. As Piedmont Airlines entered the jet age, it became established as one of the country's strongest regional airlines. A new headquarters building was opened at Smith Reynolds Airport in Winston-Salem in 1968. More than three times the size of the 1956 headquarters it replaced, the sprawling complex included administrative offices and hangars for six jets. In 1974 Piedmont started an in-flight magazine, *Pace*. Many passengers enjoyed reading their favorite columnists while flying, turning to Davis for an update on the airline, Ernest Fitzgerald for inspiration, or Bruce Baldwin for tips on business management.

Davis knew how to cultivate loyalty among his employees, passengers, business associates, and stockholders. Zeke Saunders, the retired senior vice president for operations and maintenance, recalled, "His main quality was his ability to get along with and motivate people." Throughout his career and retirement, Davis answered every letter he received with a type-written response.

Congress passed the Airline Deregulation Act in 1978, giving airlines a great deal of leeway in setting fares and routes. In the same year, the New York Stock Exchange began trading Piedmont stock.

When Davis retired in 1983, airline employees demonstrated their affection by organizing a huge retirement party in Winston-Salem, giving him a Mercedes-Benz, which he drove the rest of his life, and establishing scholarships in his name at Wake Forest University. Davis remained an active member of Piedmont's Board of Directors, serving as chairman of the executive committee. Bill Howard, a former vice president with Eastern Airlines who had been with Piedmont for five years, became Piedmont's president and CEO.

Piedmont experienced explosive growth during its final years under Howard's leadership. The addition of a second parallel runway and a new terminal building at Charlotte-Douglas International Airport made it possible to create a Piedmont hub there in the early 1980s. This growth meant increased services for Piedmont passengers as Charlotte gained nonstop services to the West Coast and London.

Shortly before Davis's wife, Nancy, died of cancer in 1985, he and Piedmont named a new 737 jet the *Nancy Davis Pacemaker*. Three of their five children worked for Piedmont. Largely because of Davis's ability to be a "father figure" and stay in touch with the airline's employees, the airline kept its family spirit in the midst of rapid growth.

Davis participated in key merger talks that led to USAir (later US Airways) buying Piedmont for $1.6 billion in the late 1980s. But he, like all Piedmont workers, was sad to see Piedmont Airlines no longer operate. His devotion to aviation continued during his retirement years. Despite a series of asthma-related illnesses, Davis enjoyed flying his restored Taylor Cub airplane on short trips (the same airplane he had learned to fly as a teenager), attending meetings of aviation enthusiasts, and going to his office regularly at the Smith Reynolds Airport.

In 1999, Davis died in Winston-Salem at age eighty-one. Following a funeral attended by several hundred former Piedmont workers at Wake Forest Baptist Church on the Wake Forest University campus, he was buried in Salem Cemetery in the Old Salem area of the city.

Overcoming great odds, Davis established Piedmont Airlines and helped it grow into a company that brought economic strength, vitality, and prestige to North Carolina. During his lifetime, he received a number of civic and aviation awards. However, one of his most cherished honors was the prestigious Tony Jannus Award, presented to airline founders, industry leaders, and inventors who contributed to the advancement of scheduled air service.

Robert Sterling, prominent aviation historian, summarized, "Tom Davis was a class act."

Walter R. Turner is historian at the North Carolina Transportation Museum in Spencer. A fifth-generation North Carolinian, he holds degrees from Fayetteville's Methodist College and the University of North Carolina at Chapel Hill. His articles on transportation topics have appeared in Our State, Business North Carolina, *and the* American Aviation Historical Society Journal.

For more information, see:
Tom Davis Collection (Private). Piedmont Aviation Historical Society, Smith Reynolds Airport, Winston-Salem.

Dunn, J. A. C. "A History of Piedmont Airlines." *Pace,* December 1988.
Piedmont Aviation Collection. Carolinas Aviation Museum/Commission, Charlotte-Douglas International Airport.
Piedmont Aviation Collection. North Carolina Transportation Museum, Spencer.

JAMES GOODNIGHT

By David Mildenberg

EVEN IN A PRO-BUSINESS STATE filled with remarkable entrepreneurial success stories, the magnitude of James Goodnight's accomplishments were notable. The cofounder of SAS Institute in Cary built the world's largest privately owned software company in a methodical style befitting its statistician-owner.

He started literally from scratch as a sophomore at North Carolina State University in Raleigh, where he enrolled in the only computer science course offered, and built a business based on more than ten million lines of software code. At the turn of the century, customers paying $50,000 or more annually for licenses to SAS products included most of the nation's largest companies, along with many federal agencies and research universities. Revenues topped $1 billion in 1999 after double-digit growth for twenty-four consecutive years.

Goodnight did it all in a unique manner that drew almost unparalleled praise from academics, Wall Street analysts, and management consultants. Unlike most software firms, virtually all of SAS revenues came from licensing fees, rather than from selling products. Because more than 90 percent of users resubscribed every year, SAS enjoyed a much more predictable stream of revenue than many of its rivals.

The personal payoff was huge: By the 1990s, Goodnight ranked as the Tar Heel State's wealthiest person in *Forbes* magazine's annual listing. When stock market conditions warranted a much-anticipated initial public offering, Goodnight's two-thirds ownership of SAS was expected to be valued at more than $10 billion, industry analysts speculated.

Born in Salisbury in 1943, Goodnight spent much of his youth in Greensboro and later Wilmington, where his father owned a hardware store. After graduating from N.C. State with a master's degree, he and his wife, Anne, moved to Florida where he worked as a programmer for a General Electric subsidiary that produced communications equipment used in the Apollo space capsules. Working in a cramped cubicle in the midst of a noisy environment profoundly affected Goodnight, who soon returned to N.C. State to complete his Ph.D. in statistics.

In Raleigh he teamed with N.C. State colleague Jim Barr, a former IBM programmer, to create the initial 300,000 lines of code of what they would call SAS—Statistical Analysis System. Their goal was to create a program capable of interpreting the mountains of agricultural data streaming into N.C. State from various sources. Other users, including schools of agriculture and pharmaceutical and insurance companies, started leasing the system, which became a pioneer in what became known as data mining, or in layman's terms, discovering patterns and meaning after sifting through massive amounts of information. The federal government, for example, used SAS to determine the Consumer Price Index.

Interest from corporate clients came in handy when, after Goodnight earned his degree in 1971, N.C. State offered him a faculty post on the condition that he raise grant money to pay his salary. In 1976, Goodnight and Barr were amazed at the interest shown by prospective customers during the first SAS user conference. So they opened an office for their new company across the street from N.C. State with four employees. (John Sall and Jane Helwig were the other two employees; Barr and Helwig left SAS after several years.) At the time, the university ceded rights to the program in perpetuity in exchange for free upgrades, marking one of the most expensive financial decisions ever made by N.C. State.

SAS was profitable in its first year. It typically sought a 17 percent profit margin, while investing nearly a third of its revenues every year into research and development. Employment boomed from 1,900 in 1994, to 5,400 in 1998, and to 7,500 in late 2000.

How all that growth occurred directly correlated with Goodnight's unusual vision of how to treat employees. In 1980 he moved SAS to a sprawling tract of farmland in Cary, which was becoming a large bedroom community sandwiched between Raleigh and Research Triangle Park. The campus eventually included twenty buildings. Goodnight saved forty-seven acres for his own estate, where he lived in a 7,500-square-foot brick home next to a fourteen-acre lake.

The campus's corporate culture became the stuff of legend, and a routine part of many M.B.A. schools' studies of organizational behavior. Years before such perks become popular, SAS offered on-site child-care centers, well-equipped athletic facilities, and an upscale cafeteria featuring a pianist playing soothing music. The company even laundered workout clothes for employees, eliminating an excuse for not getting to the gym. Most famous of all, perhaps, was Good-

James Goodnight (Courtesy of SAS)

night's command that free M&Ms be distributed on Wednesdays to every floor of every building. Complimentary coffee and soft drinks were always available, a direct response to Goodnight's early career experience in which he had to pay for his own. In contrast to the frantic, 24-7 work approach of many technology companies, Goodnight pushed to have SAS workers out of their offices by 5 P.M. and the campus gates locked at 6 P.M.

As a result, the company had an annual average turnover rate of 4 percent, a fifth of the industry average, even though no stock options were available and SAS salaries were often slightly below prevailing rates. "It's better to be happy than to have a little more money," software tester Larnell Lennon told *Fast Company* magazine in 1999, explaining why he took a 10 percent pay cut in 1991 to leave Nortel and join SAS. Stanford University management professor Jeffrey Pfeffer estimated the low turnover saved SAS $70 million annually because of the high expense of replacing workers. That came to more than $10,000

per year per employee that SAS could spend on various benefits, the *Fast Company* article noted.

Such benevolence didn't mean Goodnight was a softy. He was known, in and out of SAS, for a terse, cut-to-the-quick style. Nothing happened at his company without his imprint, company insiders said. From his computer the boss could examine detailed sales and performance information for virtually every employee. He largely avoided public settings, rarely showing any interest in ceremonial or civic projects at which many corporate executives often shine. At a users conference in mid-2000 attended by a *Triangle Business Journal* reporter and 100-some SAS clients, Goodnight spent more of his thirty-minute presentation showing how he played blackjack and other card games over the Internet than he did promoting software.

Despite its unparalleled success, until the late 1990s SAS had not played a key role in promoting the Triangle's tech community. It had shown little interest in the region's highly touted Council for Entrepreneurial Development. Still, Goodnight's visibility—along with SAS's marketing efforts—increased markedly after 1998, when he first started making rumblings about a potential initial public offering (IPO). The company undertook a major national advertising campaign, utilizing mainstream business publications rather than just computer industry trade journals. In mid-2000 SAS hired former Oracle executive and venture capitalist Andre Boisvert to oversee the company's strategic direction and acquisition plans. Several purchases of small technology companies with products somewhat related to SAS quickly followed.

Goodnight's penchant for privacy belied the huge impact he had on the Triangle region. As the principal financial backer of the 1,400-acre Preston neighborhood, along with several other planned communities in Cary, no one else played as important a role in the town's explosive growth, which went from 44,000 people in 1990 to nearly 100,000 a decade later. At its peak, Preston was creating annual revenues of $20 million, Goodnight told the Raleigh *News and Observer* in 1997.

Goodnight's influence on the region, though usually hidden from public view, was obvious. In a famous incident in the late 1980s, he showed up for a public hearing in which a landowner was seeking the Cary Town Council's permission to build a convenience store near the SAS campus. Goodnight, who opposed the change, met with the owner during a break in the meeting and bought the property. He then told the council members they didn't need to discuss the matter any further. In 1997, after the town declined to take part in a major hotel project, SAS sold land for one dollar to a Missouri developer, who then built a 272-room Embassy Suites hotel across from its campus. A year later, Goodnight and his longtime partner John Sall stepped in to buy control of struggling Midway Airlines, investing about $22 million. They recouped much of their money after installing a new CEO and taking the company public. "I just felt it would be a blow to our area to lose its major airline," Goodnight told Raleigh's *Business Leader* magazine in 1999.

Meanwhile, Goodnight's influence was also being felt in secondary education because of his investment of more than $10 million in Cary Academy, a private school that opened in August 1997 near the SAS campus. Upset with their son's experience in a Wake County public school, Goodnight and his wife, along with Sall and SAS employee John Boling, spent two years studying how to develop computer-based courses for middle- and high-school students. SAS then created a division for developing curricula. Cary Academy, which had facilities superior to many small colleges, became their first proving ground in what school officials expected to become a national model.

Goodnight's biggest business challenge became helping SAS make the transition to the Internet age. "Today computing is all about, and business is all about, one thing: 'e'" (referring to electronic commerce), he wrote in the company's 1999 annual report. "SAS is in the best position to help our customers not only succeed in the e-arena, but thrive there."

Goodnight was bullish about SAS's ability to make that transition, projecting that the company's annual revenues would double to $2 billion in 2003 and reach $5 billion by 2005. To do so, SAS revenues would have to grow at a rate of about 20 percent, up from the 16–17 percent pace in the late 1990s.

That seemed entirely possible to Goodnight, who had intentionally built his firm for the long haul, eschewing efforts to grow too fast. "We plan to grow at 20 percent a year," he told the *Upside Today* Web site in September 2000. "But we can grow much more than 20 percent a year."

David Mildenberg is the associate editor of bizjournals.com, the Internet division of American City Business Journals. He previously was editor of the Business Journal *in Raleigh and worked for* Business North Carolina, *the* News and Record *of Greensboro, the* Charlotte Observer, *and the* Charlotte News. *A Minnesota native, he earned a B.S. in journalism from Northwestern University and a M.B.A. from the University of North Carolina at Charlotte.*

For more information, see:

"Business Leader of the Decade." *Business Leader,* November 1999.

Eisenstadt, Steven. "Citizen Goodnight: He Calls the Shots at SAS—and Sometimes in Cary." *News and Observer,* July 21, 1996.

Fishman, Charles. "Sanity Inc." *Fast Company,* January 1999.

"SAS Steps into Success Spotlight." *Info World,* July 13, 1998.

L. GORDON GRAY

By Frank Tursi

AMID THE HUNDREDS of photographs of Gordon Gray saved at the University of North Carolina, there is one that says more about him than any other. The black-and-white picture, taken in April 1942, shows the young Gray boarding a bus in Winston-Salem that would take him off to war. Wearing a suit and tie, he was dressed pretty much like the other young men on the bus and probably would have slipped aboard unnoticed, a Gray trait, if not for the newspaper photographer trailing in his wake.

Though just thirty-three, Gray was a state senator and publisher of the local newspaper. As a member of one of Winston-Salem's most prominent families, he was a man of money, power, and connections and could have left town in a limousine with a captain's commission in his pocket. That was not the Gray way. A man succeeded on his own merits, the stern Bowman Gray Sr. had told his younger son, Gordon, who grew to believe it. To prove his point, the father, then the vice president of R.J. Reynolds Tobacco Company, put his ten-year-old boy to work at the lowliest job in the factory, pushing hogsheads of tobacco across the floors. In later summers, Gordon would advance to machine operator, but he was expected to report promptly at 7:20 each morning like everyone else and to work the normal fifty-five hours a week. Gray learned the lesson well. After graduating at the top of his class at the University of North Carolina, he turned down the Harvard Law School because it was willing to accept him immediately—a sign that it might not be taxing enough. Yale's law school, on the other hand, required an entrance exam. Gray chose Yale.

The same went for the army. The easy way would have been to accept the captain's commission and angle for some cushy duty defending San Francisco. Instead, Gray waited in line with other men at the local army recruiting office, signed up as a buck private, and boarded a bus for Fort Bragg with the other volunteers. The army soon learned what Gray's family and friends already knew: he was brilliant and determined to achieve. His score on the IQ test given to all recruits was one of the highest anyone at Fort Bragg had ever seen. Within seven years this red-haired buck private with the mild manners and aloof bearing would soar through the ranks to Secretary of the Army.

L. Gordon Gray (Courtesy of Charlotte Observer)

In the service of his government, Gordon Gray excelled. He was many things in life: lawyer, newspaper publisher, politician, university president, businessman. Nothing excited him more, though, than high officialdom. He stood at the pinnacle of power, where miscalculation could mean disaster half a world away. The global complexities of the problems he faced every day challenged Gray's mind, while working unseen by the public in the shadows of government suited his shy, quiet temperament. "Gordon Gray was not a publisher, he was not a lawyer," his son, Gordon Jr., said. "Gordon Gray was a public servant in the mid-nineteenth-century British style: stiff upper lip, you go to the ministry and put in seven days. He made better judgments than most people did. He was extremely bright and could turn out a good thought. He could turn out material better than anyone."

He was an "idea man" who knew a great deal could be accomplished if he didn't care who got the public credit for his ideas. Such men go far. Presidents put Gray's incisive mind to work disentangling their thorniest problems. Harry Truman put him in charge of the army and then had him devise a plan to fight communism. Needing a cool head to look into the loyalty of America's top nuclear scientist, Dwight Eisenhower reached into Chapel Hill and borrowed Gray, who was president of the state university system at the time. Later, Gray appeared at Ike's elbow as his national security adviser, and he helped shape the country's cold war policy. Even in retirement, he advised presidents as different as John Kennedy and Gerald Ford on foreign policy and national security.

Reserved and cautious by nature, Gray spent a lifetime guarding his private life while cultivating the image of the dedicated public servant. He wrote thousands of letters during his various careers, many of which have been preserved, but few offer any glimpse into the soul of the writer. Reflecting Gray's personality, they are direct and businesslike, rarely exceeding a page in length. Even his letters to his children at camp read as if they had been dictated to a secretary. Generals sang his praises when Secretary Gray left the army, but on close questioning none could reveal any details about their former boss. Employees on the newspapers that Gray owned for thirty-two years felt the same way. He spent fewer than seven of those years as an active publisher of the *Journal* and the afternoon *Twin City Sentinel,* leaving Winston-Salem for Washington in September 1947 and returning maybe once or twice a year for stockholders' meetings. By 1953, *Sentinel* reporter Frances Griffin could write in the company newsletter that "the newsroom now sees him so seldom that many sitting at typewriters there have never seen him. . . ."

In the void, the myth of Gordon Gray developed. He took the form of a rich, benevolent uncle who held an important but rather hazy job in Washington. Some even whispered that he was a spy.

Gordon Gray realized early in life that he had a weighty family name to uphold. His great-grandfather Robert Gray had moved from his native Randolph County to the new county of Forsyth in 1849 and bought the first lot in the yet-unnamed county. He became one of early Winston's leading merchants. His son, James, helped found Wachovia National Bank, and his grandchildren—Gordon's father and uncle—worked diligently to turn the town's leading employer, R.J. Reynolds Tobacco Company, into the world's largest tobacco manufacturer.

The Gray boys attended West End Graded School, Winston's first public school, and the private Reynolda School before moving on to Woodberry Forest, an exclusive prep school in Virginia. Gordon entered the University of North Carolina in 1926 and finished at the top of his class, serving as president of the Phi Beta Kappa chapter.

With a degree in psychology, Gray thought he would like to teach, but again his father interceded. At Yale, Gray was again an honor student and was appointed to the editorial board of the *Yale Law Journal* in January 1932 in recognition of his high ranking in his class.

After graduating the next year, Gray joined Carter, Ledyard and Milburn, a law firm in New York. The death of his father on July 7, 1935, brought Gray home to settle the estate. He remained and worked briefly for Hendren, Carlyle, and Womble, Winston-Salem's most prestigious law firm, before embarking on a new career.

James A. Gray Jr., who succeeded his brother Bowman as Reynolds's president, asked his nephew Gordon in 1936 to head an effort by Winston-Salem's most powerful businessmen to wrest control of Winston-Salem's two newspapers from Owen Moon. Gray convinced Moon to sell the newspapers in 1937 and was rewarded for his effort by being named publisher. He did not really want the job and, in fact, hoped to return to his law career after shoring up the newspapers' crumbling financial foundations. Though he stayed on, the job just never excited him as his high-level positions in Washington later did.

Still a bachelor when he took over the newspapers, Gray arrived at the office early and stayed late into the evening, often bringing his lunch in a paper bag and eating at his desk. He was partial to egg sandwiches.

Gray, a staunch Democrat like everyone else who mattered in North Carolina at the time, announced his candidacy for the state senate on April 2, 1938, after the incumbent in the Twenty-second District said he would not seek reelection. He had no opposition in the Democratic primary and handily beat his Republican opponent in November.

It was a family man who left for Raleigh the following January. Gray married Jane Boyden Craige, a childhood friend, on June 11, 1938, in an elaborate ceremony at St. Paul's Episcopal Church in Winston-Salem. The newlyweds, Gray reported to a friend, received more than nine hundred presents.

Gray would serve three terms in the state senate—two before World War II and one after—and became known for his liberalism by supporting higher teacher salaries, tax relief, and better health care.

After the Japanese bombed Pearl Harbor, Gray decided not to run for reelection in 1942. Instead, he spent the summer at Fort Bragg, where he completed basic training and was promoted to corporal. He graduated from Officer Candidate School in 1943 as a second lieutenant and next found himself at Counter Intelligence School in Chicago. Gray was outranked by 90 percent of his classmates but finished at the top of the class. Promoted to first lieutenant and then captain, Gray was eventually shipped to Europe, where he spent the end of the war as an intelligence officer on the staff of General Omar Bradley and the 12th Army Group. He was back home by March 1945.

Kenneth Royall, the secretary of the army, needed an assistant two years later. A native of Goldsboro, Royall recommended a fellow North Carolinian for the job. President Truman announced on September 24, 1947, that Gray, a newspaper publisher in Winston-Salem, would be the new assistant secretary of the army. Gray left for Washington, which would be his home for most of the next thirty-five years. He put Bill Hoyt in charge of his newspapers.

Truman appointed Gray secretary to replace Royall in June 1949. The first buck private to ever rise to secretary commanded more than 658,000 men and controlled a budget of $1 billion. His schedule left little time for his wife, Jane, and their four boys: Gordon Jr., Burton, Boyden, and Bernard.

As secretary, Gray took the first tentative steps toward integrating the army. The era of black civil rights would soon dawn, and like many southerners of his generation, Gray was caught unprepared. His innate conservatism, though, told him to go slow. At his newspapers, with the army, and later in Chapel Hill, he would support policies that provided for gradual integration. In October 1949, Gray ordered commanders to give black troops equal treatment and opportunities. The army was still segregated on the company level, but black and white companies could serve side by side in battalions. By early 1950, "qualified" blacks were allowed into formerly all-white units.

By then, Gray was heading elsewhere. Surprising many of his friends and officials in the Truman administration, he resigned as army secretary in the spring of 1950 to accept the job as president of the consolidated University of North Carolina. "I don't

think that he wanted to come back to North Carolina to be president of UNC," Gordon Gray Jr., said. "It was a diversion, but I think he could not say no."

Gray sold the *Journal* and the *Sentinel* in 1969 to Media General, a newspaper holding company owned by his friend, D. Tennant Bryan of Richmond, Va. He remained chairman of Triangle Broadcasting Company, which included WSJS radio and television. He sold the television station in 1975 and formed Summit Communications in Winston-Salem, which owned and operated WSJS Radio and a number of television stations and cable television franchises.

Gray died at his home in Georgetown in 1982 after a long bout with throat cancer. He was seventy-three. William Friday, then president of UNC, said that his predecessor took seriously the biblical injunction "to whom much is given, of him much is expected."

Frank Tursi is a former staff writer for the Winston-Salem Journal, *which he joined in 1978 after working various newspapers, including the* Miami Herald. *He has written* Winston-Salem: A History, *and a history of the* Winston-Salem Journal. *Tursi has won numerous national and state writing awards, including the History Book Award given by the N.C. Society of Professional Historians.*

For more information, see:

Gray, Gordon. Papers. Southern Historical Collection, University of North Carolina at Chapel Hill.

Gray, James A., III. "Gordon Gray: Patriot, Public Servant, and Preservationist." Speech to the Conference of Historic Preservation, Fredericksburg, Va., May 30, 1986. (In the author's possession.)

Linn, Jo White. *The Gray Family and Allied Lines.* Privately published, 1976.

Martin, John Sanford. Papers. Letters, memoranda, and other personal papers, Special Collections Library, Duke University, Durham.

Snider, William D. *Light on the Hill: A History of the University of North Carolina.* University of North Carolina Press, 1992.

Tursi, Frank V. *The Winston-Salem Journal, Magnolia Trees, and Pulitzer Prizes.* John F. Blair, 1997.

THE HANES FAMILY

By Stan Brennan

THE FORTUNE of Winston-Salem's Hanes family was born during the formative years of the state's tobacco industry but expanded into textiles in the twentieth century when the Hanes name on hosiery became more popular than the Reynolds name on cigarettes. At the same time, the children and grandchildren of Alexander and Jane Hanes produced a legacy that included the development of Wachovia Bank and Trust Company as the leading bank in the Southeast by mid-century, the founding of the North Carolina School of the Arts, restoration of Old Salem, and years of service in local and state offices.

One grandson, Robert M. Hanes, became the first North Carolinian to head the American Bankers Association and was considered one of the founding fathers of the Research Triangle Park. Meanwhile, his brother, J. Gordon, used his influence as a Winston-Salem councilman, mayor, and community leader to put his city in the forefront of school desegregation in the 1950s. His son, Gordon Jr., became a benefactor of the North Carolina Museum of Art, while Gordon Jr.'s cousin, Phillip, helped ensure that Winston-Salem became the site of the North Carolina School of the Arts.

The family's fortune began with the four sons of Alexander and Jane Hanes: Pleasant Henderson, John Wesley, Philip, and Ben Franklin—who in the years after the Civil War started the P. H. Hanes and B. F. Hanes tobacco businesses, which were merged after the death of B. F. in 1885.

They were contemporaries of R. J. Reynolds and in 1900 sold out to R. J. Reynolds, who was part of the emerging tobacco trust, for cash and stock worth about $1 million, a tidy sum in pre-tax America. With their profits and an interest in pursuing a business that was more uplifting to humankind, the brothers moved into the burgeoning textile business; Pleasant started the P. H. Hanes Knitting Company, while John W. opened Shamrock Hosiery Mills in 1902.

John W. Hanes died in 1903, the same year as his brother Phillip, but he left eight children whose careers would help shape the state. His son, J. Gordon, graduated from the University of North Carolina in 1909 and returned home to take over the family's Shamrock Hosiery Mills, which one observer said was "a $60,000 operation with a $70,000 debt." Less than a decade later, he had improved the company's posi-

tion considerably and was named president of the company, which had been renamed the Hanes Hosiery Mills Company.

J. Gordon Hanes immersed himself in the community as well as the business, as did his siblings. After the neighboring towns of Winston and Salem were merged in 1913, Gordon served on the city's board of aldermen, was elected mayor in 1921, reelected to a second term, and then served as a county commissioner for thirty-two years. During his tenure as mayor, the city built five new schools, three fire stations, and four major public buildings, including City Hall, Reynolds Auditorium, and a large addition to City Memorial Hospital. He was elected board chairman of Hanes Hosiery Mills in 1938 and by the time of his retirement to emeritus status in 1954, the Hanes company had become the world's largest producer of women's seamless nylon hosiery.

James G. Hanes worked quietly in the name of racial peace in the community. He was a longtime participant in the National Urban League and the Human Betterment League of North Carolina. In 1957, when the Supreme Court's *Brown* decision was three years old and the local schools were still rigidly segregated, he urged a pragmatic course to fellow community leaders. Though he personally "deplored" school integration, he told them the law would be enforced. Further resistance would bring lawsuits and would jeopardize the city's reputation for good race relations. He asked them to put their leadership behind any effort to integrate the schools.

He shared his work in textiles with his brother, R. Phillip, who was working in a New York bank—where his brother Alex later became an investment banker—when his brothers insisted he return to Winston-Salem. They established Phillip in the pocketing material business, which he detested, referring to it as a "glorified laundry business" and himself as a "pants pocket dryer." Hanes founded the Hanes Dye and Finishing Company, but his real interests were in architecture and interior design. In time, he became a primary leader in developing such community projects as the restoration of Old Salem (Hanes was chairman of the restoration committee), the North Carolina School of the Arts, and a broad spectrum of other cultural programs in Winston-Salem, including the public library system, the Little Theater, the Winston-

Left to right: Robert M. Hanes (courtesy of Hugh Morton), J. Gordon Hanes Jr. (courtesy of Charlotte Observer), Phillip Hanes Jr. (courtesy of Forsyth County Library)

Salem Symphony, and the Civic Ballet as well as the Civic Music Association. The library system to a large extent owes its existence to Hanes. He made it his personal responsibility to see that the necessary funds were raised to build the new facility.

Another brother, Dr. Frederic M. Hanes, studied medicine and became a doctor and was chairman of the department of medicine at Duke University. In the early years of the century he all but embarrassed the board of directors at R.J. Reynolds Tobacco Company into creating a medical department at the company. When he spoke to the Reynolds board about the need to keep employees in good condition, just as they did their machinery, he began his talk by complimenting the members for their forward thinking in creating a medical department, which had not been approved. John Wesley Hanes Jr. became president of the Ecusta Paper Company, which manufactured cigarette papers for Reynolds, and later served as an undersecretary of the treasury. Meanwhile, John's sister, Lucy, married Thurmond Chatham of Elkin, who served as congressman from North Carolina's fifth district until 1956, when he was defeated for reelection after he refused to sign the so-called Southern Manifesto, the segregationists' call to oppose the Supreme Court's desegregation decision. Another sister, Daisy, became the wife of Robert Lassiter, a prominent businessman in Charlotte and chairman of the Richmond Federal Reserve Bank.

Before brother Robert Hanes joined Wachovia Bank and Trust Company in 1919 and became a model for bankers around the nation, he had worked for the Crystal Ice Company in Winston-Salem, a job he could never shake. ("They say I am still cold from that job," he would later joke.) He had graduated from the University of North Carolina and studied at the Harvard business school before he entered the army in 1917, where he saw service as a captain in the field artillery in France. When he returned as a major in 1919, he went to work for Wachovia Bank and Trust Company. Throughout the 1920s he worked as a loan officer until he was elected administrative vice president under Wachovia founder Colonel Francis H. Fries. In 1931, Hanes was named president after Fries's death.

Hanes's reach extended beyond Winston-Salem. He represented Forsyth County in the state house in 1929 and 1931 and in the state senate in 1933. While in the legislature, he became a leader in the fight for adoption of a state sales tax and appealed for the state to be operated on a balanced budget. He pushed for a tax system that was fair to all of North Carolina and would be encouraging, although not unfairly encouraging, to the movement of industry into the state.

His fellow bankers elected him president of the North Carolina Bankers Association in 1931, and in the early years of the Depression he led the development of the National Credit Association, a forerunner of the Reconstruction Finance Corporation, aimed at rebuilding failing banks. In 1939, he was elected president of the American Bankers Association, which was a signal achievement for a southern banker, and in 1945 was elected president of the Association of Reserve City Bankers, an equally prestigious honor. The Chase National Bank of New York —then the nation's largest—offered Hanes its top job, but he turned it down.

In 1954, when Hanes was chosen Citizen of the Year by the North Carolina Citizens Association, he was nearing the end of his career. Wachovia was the dominant bank by far in North Carolina and on its way to its peak in 1970 as the largest bank in the Southeast. He died in 1959, but not before he put his name and reputation behind Governor Luther Hodges's efforts to develop the Research Triangle Park, which was considered a risky venture by some. The first building that opened in the park as the first home of the Research Triangle Institute was named in his honor.

A third generation of Haneses made an equally significant impact on the arts community of the state. In 1947, North Carolina had commissioned a state art museum, the first in the nation, and one of its leading promoters was James Gordon Hanes Jr., who had become president and chairman of the board of the Hanes Corporation. Hanes believed that those with money had a responsibility to give something back to their communities. He once told a convention of business executives, "We must take the lead. A management that isn't civic-minded will discourage employees from giving time to public service during working hours. If the top people work hard, then the people down the line will do the same."

Hanes had become fascinated with African masks after seeing some at the home of a friend. Moved by their beauty, Hanes began to form a collection of African art that would intrigue other North Carolinians, especially those schoolchildren whose ancestors created it. "I went immediately to New York the next week to begin collecting African art for the North Carolina Museum of Art, and I've been collecting it ever since," he said. Hanes became a leading patron of the museum, donating more than 130 works of art. He was a member of the museum's board for eighteen years and shaped the development of the museum's collection, mission, and even the facilities.

In 1963, Hanes had just begun the first of his two terms as a member of the state senate when Governor Terry Sanford proposed a state conservatory of music. The project immediately captured the attention of Winston-Salem, which considered itself the home of cultural arts in the state. Phillip Hanes Jr., the president and chief executive officer of the Hanes Dye and Finishing Company, was particularly intrigued. In 1949, Winston-Salem had organized the first local arts council in the nation and Hanes, a recent graduate of Yale, was among the first board members because, he later said, they wanted some businessmen involved.

In Leslie Banner's history of the N.C. School of the Arts, Hanes recalled ". . . the more I got involved in the thing, the more people thought that was sort of strange. And that made me madder and madder . . . and the madder I got, the more involved I got." The son of the man who wanted to be an architect, Phillip Hanes later recalled telling his friends in the arts how wonderful it was that we were going to have this marvelous conservatory for the performing arts. "And there was just no response at all." They finally wished him luck but added: "You can't do that. Do you realize that every conservatory of any consequence backs right up to a major symphony or major opera or major dance company, where people just walk across the street and give classes? Hell, you're four or five hundred miles from the nearest possible place to get these master teachers. . . . You can't do it. It's impossible." Hanes's response: "Well, we'll do it."

Hanes wrote John Ehle, the author who was working as Sanford's cultural aide: "I think we could round up enough funds and interest to get it [the North Carolina School of the Arts] going here in Winston-Salem. . . . We not only have the oldest Arts Council in America but are considered to have the finest arts management in this country. . . . Winston-Salem . . . has the largest cultural program by far of any city in the state. . . . Winston-Salem . . . can provide larger audiences for amateur performances than any other city in our state. . . . " Hanes sent Governor Sanford a *Twin City Sentinel* editorial urging Winston-Salem to decide immediately whether it wanted the school and urging the establishment of a steering committee.

Winston-Salem Mayor M. C. Benton appointed a committee to corral the arts school for Winston-Salem, with Hanes as chairman. In addition to Winston-Salem, other cities mentioned as possible sites for the school were Charlotte, Greensboro, Raleigh, and Hillsborough.

Sanford appointed an advisory board of artists to visit the sites. Agnes de Mille, one of the invited artists, said she "was impressed that the entire [Winston-Salem] community—and by that I really mean to include the Hanes, the Reynolds, and the other very rich people in the entire community—they were all absolutely behind it, and fervently and intelligently enthusiastic." De Mille added: "That these rich, rich people, who obviously dealt in making money in one way or another, were interested now in people's souls, struck me as novel. . . . "

Hanes and others began a campaign to secure major financial support for the school. The results were staggering. Within a two-day telephone campaign, Hanes and others raised $1 million to locate the proposed school in Winston-Salem. In 1964, Governor Sanford named the school's first board of trustees, which included Phillip Hanes. The School of the Arts graduated its first class in 1968.

The P. H. Hanes Knitting Company and the Hanes Hosiery Mill Company were merged to form the Hanes Corporation. In 1979, Hanes stockholders overwhelmingly approved the merger of their company with Consolidated Foods Corporation of Chicago. Hanes, a major producer of hosiery and women's foundation garments, had 1977 sales of $414 million. Consolidated's purchase of Hanes was for approximately $250 million.

Stan Brennan is a retired journalist. He was a reporter and an editor at the Charlotte Observer *for thirty-two years. Previously he worked for newspapers in Birmingham, Ala.; Richmond, Va.; Greensboro; and Durham. He has bachelor's and master's of arts degrees from the University of North Carolina at Chapel Hill.*

For more information, see:
Hanes Family. Files. Forsyth County Public Library System.

Banner, Leslie. *A Passionate Preference: The Story of the North Carolina School of the Arts*. North Carolina School of the Arts Foundation, 1987.
Fries, Adelaide, Stuart Thurman Wright, and J. Edwin Hendricks. *Forsyth: The History of a County on the March*. University of North Carolina Press, 1976.
Linn, Jo White. *People Named Hanes*. Privately published, 1980.
Whitaker, John C. Address to the Newcomen Society, April 13, 1956.

RALPH W. KETNER

By Mark Wineka

ON A NOVEMBER MORNING in 1967, Ralph W. Ketner arrived at the Manger Motel in Charlotte with five big cardboard boxes, a card table, and an adding machine. The boxes contained six months of invoices for Food Town, a small chain of seven grocery stores headquartered in nearby Salisbury. Ketner, the company's president, planned to take the numbers from those invoices and install a new, low-pricing formula that, if it failed, would undoubtedly wreck the company. But he was willing to take the risk because he was tired of seeing Food Town stumble along, barely making a profit each year while disappointing its hometown investors.

Over three feverish days, Ketner reduced every price in the Food Town stores and littered the motel room floor with wads of paper calculations. He cut ten categories of food to cost or below, including cereals, coffee, shortening, rice, grits, and detergent. He figured that roughly one-sixth of everything in his warehouse could be sold at cost or less and decided to sell the rest of his groceries between 6 and 10 percent cheaper than his competitors. Ketner hoped the lower prices on everything would create a new kind of customer excitement, leading to a dramatic increase in the volume of sales—a volume big enough to compensate for the lost margins.

"I'd rather make five fast pennies than one slow nickel," he explained years later. "It separates the men from the boys. We'd rather sell five cans of beans at two cents profit and make a dime, where our competitors would rather sell two cans at a nickel profit each and make the same dime."

After all the price-cutting, Ketner determined he had sliced into his company's gross profit by 60 percent. He then had to figure out how much increased sales volume would be necessary to offset that loss. When he emerged from the motel room and headed for home, Ketner had his answer. Food Town could break even with this across-the-board cost cutting if sales increased at least 50 percent. Always a gambler, Ketner was ready to bet the company on what he came to call "The Big Change."

As Ketner said, "Advertisement is whatever causes the customer to trade with you. Low price is the best advertisement in the world."

Ketner's low-pricing concept caught on and propelled the sleepy grocery chain and its stock to in-

Ralph W. Ketner (Courtesy of Ketner Family)

credible growth and national prominence. Within two decades, Food Town, which changed its name to Food Lion in 1983, became North Carolina's largest publicly held retailer. By 1982, *Forbes* magazine had dubbed the company America's fastest growing grocery chain. By 1990, Food Lion was among the top ten grocery chains in the United States.

By 2000, Food Lion had become part of Delhaize America, which included nearly 1,400 stores throughout the eastern United States with about $11 billion in annual sales. The company employed more than 95,000 people. Ketner remained a shareholder but had distanced himself from the company's operations, which he micromanaged for more than thirty years. Instead, he had become a great philanthropist, donating millions of dollars to local, state, and national causes. From one Salisbury store in 1957, Food Lion grew phenomenally to make millionaires of Ketner and scores of the original investors. Salisbury and Rowan County especially benefited from the company's success and from generous stockholders such as Ketner.

Ketner's low-pricing concept hit a nerve with the public. He promised to save his customers money, and they believed him after shopping at Food Town. The more successful his formula was, the more he lowered prices. It became his obsession, and Food Lion employees became equally impassioned to keep costs, and prices, as low as possible.

Ketner developed a company culture, a Food Lion personality for which recruiters actually tested. He led by example. As chief executive officer and chairman, Ketner worked long hours, poring over every sales report, deliberating on every price, examining each store lease, and doggedly getting after his staff to find him answers. Employees knew to take a notebook and pen with them into Ketner's office because he usually gave them a list of things to research. "With me, 98 is failing," Ketner said once. "If you're going to make 2 percent errors in business, you can't make it."

No one was better with numbers, a better buyer, or a better negotiator than Ketner. Or more demanding. He once told his office staff members that they must memorize the multiplication tables—the twelfth table up to fifty—so they wouldn't have to waste time on adding machines. He periodically tested them with flash cards.

Ketner and the other executives always worked on Saturdays. He discouraged any hobbies, memberships, or outside interests that robbed time from the company. With his dedicated lieutenants, Ketner also installed a system of forward and centralized buying, merchandising, store location, distribution, cost cutting, training, and employee incentives that complemented the chain's pricing concept. The love of work and the love of winning at work seemed to drive Ketner, who came to symbolize a lean, mean, growing machine.

"I know my dad never worked to get rich," said daughter Linda Ketner, who headed Food Town's first training department in the mid-1970s. "I mean, when I was growing up, I never heard him talk about money, wanting things. Dad's the most unmaterialistic person I've ever been around. It wasn't his motivation. His motivation was he loved to work. He loved to achieve."

Born September 20, 1920, in the Rimertown community near the Rowan-Cabarrus County line, Ralph Wright Ketner was one of five boys and two girls of George Robert "Bob" Ketner and Effie Yost Ketner. The fourth son, Harry, was born in 1919, but lived only six days. Bob Ketner farmed and butchered, taking beef, veal, and pork to Salisbury and Concord markets. Exasperation over what he had to pay retail for meat led Ketner to buy Taylor's Meat Market in Salisbury in 1923 and move his family to the bunga-

low behind the store. Ketner eventually added groceries and went to a cash-only operation. He operated six Ketner's Cash and Carry stores by 1931, including a store in Kannapolis. The father was a flamboyant promoter and always invited customers to compare his prices with other stores.

Ralph Ketner learned to kill and dress chickens in the backyard of the family's house in Salisbury, receiving a penny for each plucked chicken. He disliked school so much that in the first grade he ran home and hid under the house. Except for subjects dealing with numbers, Ketner maintained his dislike for school for much of his childhood.

A flu epidemic claimed his mother's life on March 10, 1926, when she was only thirty-three. Ketner, who was five at the time, almost died, too. As part of his treatment, doctors had to put a tube in his side to drain fluid from his lungs. Bob Ketner later married Allene Glover Lyerly, who played a big role in raising Ralph and his two younger sisters, Mary and Dorothy. Late on a February night in 1932, a doctor wrongly diagnosed Bob Ketner's appendicitis as constipation. His appendix burst and peritonitis developed and killed him after several days. Ralph was eleven.

The father died without a will and had never incorporated his businesses. The stores had to be auctioned off to settle his estate. Ralph's oldest brother, Glenn, only twenty-one, was able to buy the Kannapolis store with the help of his wife's family. He soon assumed the role of family patriarch.

As a youngster, Ralph became a crackerjack bowler in the duckpin lanes of Salisbury. His other major pastime revolved around earning personal spending money. He worked in his family's stores and peddled ice cream and newspapers. Because of his proficiency with numbers, his family sometimes pulled him out of school when a Ketner's Cash and Carry needed an extra clerk. As a high school student, Ralph often hitchhiked the sixteen miles from Salisbury to Kannapolis to work in one of Glenn's stores, usually catching a ride back to Salisbury with someone from the 11 P.M. shift change at Cannon Mills.

Ketner took his share of money from the settlement of his father's estate and attended Tri-State College in Angola, Ind., in 1937. He liked Tri-State because it allowed him to start courses in his accounting major from the beginning and offered forty-eight weeks of school each year. He completed his accounting courses and advanced auditing, but failed public speaking, even though he took it five times.

Ketner suffered from severe stage fright: "Every time it was my turn to talk, I would drop the course," he said. He eventually ran out of money and returned home, six months from graduation. By this time, however, Ketner was a stubborn, independent, restless young man who would spend the next several years bouncing from one job to the next, serving in the military for forty-five months, getting married, and finally looking to settle down when his wife, the former Ruth Jones, became pregnant with their son, Robert.

In the army, Ketner shipped out with his unit to assemble auto parts in Casablanca. He became the unit's head auditor. Stateside, his many jobs included stints with his brother Glenn's grocery operations, Cannon Mills, Central Motor Lines, the Army Exchange, a Philadelphia appraisal company, the Internal Revenue Service, the state Department of Revenue, and others. He stayed in the grocery business for good when he took a position in brother Glenn's warehouse.

Ralph Ketner, brother Brown Ketner, and friend Wilson Smith played important roles in Glenn Ketner's grocery stores, which became self-service markets and ushered in prepackaged produce and meats in North Carolina. In early 1956, Glenn Ketner merged his eight stores with fifteen smaller Piggly Wiggly stores in eastern North Carolina, thinking he could some day fill in the space between Raleigh and Salisbury along the new Interstate 85.

But weeks later, Glenn Ketner agreed to sell to Winn-Dixie in exchange for important North Carolina jobs in the bigger grocery chain for himself, his brothers, and Smith. The former Salisbury grocers and many of the people who used to work for Glenn Ketner soon soured on their Winn-Dixie responsibilities and began talking about starting their own grocery company. Glenn Ketner had signed a no-compete agreement, leaving him to focus on his many properties. But Ralph Ketner, Brown Ketner, and Wilson Smith believed they had a strong nucleus among themselves to start a new store to compete with the likes of Winn-Dixie, Colonial, and A&P.

From their own funds, the trio could put up only half of the $125,000 they needed. To raise the rest, they paged through the Salisbury telephone book, writing down names of people they knew to approach about investing in their venture. Ralph Ketner was thirty-seven at the time. Ketner and his cohorts successfully raised the additional $62,500 from all walks of life: teachers, railroaders, bankers, doctors, salesmen, housewives, attorneys, druggists, mill workers, merchants, and mailmen. Some people paid as little as $50 for five shares, or as much as $1,000 for one hundred shares of Food Town stock. While certain investors who initially agreed to buy stock backed out, the others who stuck with the Ketners and Smith did so out of friendship and on faith from the men's experience with Glenn Ketner's operation.

On December 12, 1957, a bitterly cold day, the men opened the first fifteen-thousand-square-foot Food Town store in a new shopping center on the west end of Salisbury. Their landlord: Glenn Ketner. Surviving an early price war with other Salisbury stores that almost put them out of business, the Food Town founders opened a second Salisbury location within a year. But after ten years of what Ralph Ketner came to call "research and development," Food Town had opened sixteen stores and closed or sold nine of them. Annual sales were only $5.8 million, and earnings totaled less than $37,000.

"We didn't deserve to succeed," Ketner said once, looking back, "because all we were was a 'me, too.' You make a car as good as somebody else, you haven't offered anything to the public they didn't already have."

As the low-pricing concept caught on, the company's rallying cry became LFPINC—Lowest Food Prices in North Carolina. In 1968, Food Town sales went from $5.8 million to $8.95 million—a 54 percent increase that Ketner figured was more like 80 percent, based on projections for the year after the first two weeks in January without "The Big Change." The company took off, finding a niche with low prices, while being efficient, convenient, and neighborly.

As Food Town grew, Ketner hired a former bag boy, Tom Smith, as a buyer for his warehouse in 1970. He promised Smith that some day he could be president, if he stuck with the company. He also gave Smith the first company stock option and fulfilled his promise by making Smith president in 1981. In 1974, looking for an infusion of cash to spur his company's growth and finally give original investors some cash value for their stock, Ketner negotiated a deal allowing the Delhaize company of Belgium to acquire 34 percent of Food Town. By 1976, Delhaize acquired 51 percent of the company but remained in the background, allowing Ketner to run things.

The name change to Food Lion came out of necessity, to allow the company's expansion westward into Tennessee, where stores named Food Town already existed. Ketner saved the company $500,000 in sign costs by suggesting the "Lion" name, because it meant that only an L and an I would have to be purchased for the block letters outside every store.

Ketner relinquished the chief executive officer title to Tom Smith in 1986 and remained chairman of the board. He officially retired in May 1991, took the title of chairman emeritus, and moved his office to Ralph W. Ketner Hall at Catawba College. Ketner and his second wife, Anne, had given $3 million to the college to help establish the Ketner School of Business. The college considered him an "executive-in-residence." By 1991, at his retirement, a person who had invested $1,000 with Food Town in 1957 would have had stock worth about $23 million.

In retirement, Ketner became a sharp critic of Tom Smith and Food Lion, especially in their handling of a 1992 national television report questioning Food Lion's meat-handling practices. He shocked many people by divorcing himself from the company and not seeking reelection to the board in 1993. But he did not stop questioning many of the company's business decisions and its ever-changing corporate structure.

Otherwise, Ketner enjoyed occasional public speaking events, lecturing business students, and giving advice to entrepreneurs. He used his personal wealth to travel the world with his wife and to help others, from the homeless to first-time homeowners. "I believe it's true that you make a living with what you get, but you make a life with what you give," he said.

Mark Wineka is a staff writer at the Salisbury Post *and the author of* A Family Affair, *a book about the Hurley family's ownership of the* Post, *and the coauthor of* Lion's Share, *which told of the Food Lion grocery chain's rise and dramatic impact on its small-town investors. He won the N.C. Associated Press News Council's O. Henry Award for writing in 1998.*

For more information, see:

Ketner, Ralph W. *Five Fast Pennies*. Salisbury Printing Company, 1994.

Wineka, Mark, and Jason Lesley. *Lion's Share*. Down Home Press, 1991.

J. Spencer Love

By Marion A. Ellis

THE FOUNDER OF BURLINGTON INDUSTRIES, J. Spencer Love, was a risk taker who knew no match. In 1923, he launched his new company, Burlington Mills, with two hundred workers and at the same time decided to gamble on a new product— rayon. Then, in the middle of the Depression, he continued to expand and introduce new products. Eventually the business became Burlington Industries, at one time the largest textile-manufacturing concern in the world.

At the same time, Love was very active in a wide range of business, political, community, and philanthropic activities. He was the director of the Textile, Clothing, and Leather Board of the War Production Board during World War II. He served on the governing boards of industrial councils and associations from New York and Washington, D.C., to Raleigh, including the Economic Club of New York and the North Carolina Symphony Society. He was president of the National Rayon Weavers Association, chairman of the Davidson College Development Commission, and state chairman of the Christmas Seal sale. He received several honorary degrees, including ones from the University of North Carolina at Chapel Hill and N.C. A & T College (later N.C. A & T State University).

Yet, he often took a different road from his contemporaries. While he was known for his opposition to labor unions, he persistently supported the federal minimum wage and even sought clemency for one of the men convicted of conspiracy in connection with a rancorous textile strike in Henderson. When most in the industry stood solidly with Republicans, Love surprised his subordinates when he announced his support for Democratic presidential candidate John Kennedy in 1960.

James Spencer Love was born July 6, 1896, in Cambridge, Mass., where his father, James Lee Love, was a mathematics professor at Harvard College. His father was originally from Gaston County, where Spencer's great-grandfather, Andrew Love, was a wealthy slaveholder. Robert Calvin Grier Love, Spencer's grandfather—who married the eldest daughter of Moses H. Rhyne, a pioneer of the Carolina textile industry—survived the Civil War with his plantation intact, and then broadened his interests to include cotton manufacturing and eventually built four mills

J. Spencer Love (Courtesy of Charlotte Observer)

in Gaston County, including Loray Mills. Spencer's maternal grandmother, Cornelia Phillips Spencer, was a pioneer in women's education and rang the bell to reopen the University of North Carolina after the Civil War.

Love grew up in Cambridge and attended the Cambridge Latin School. From there he went to Harvard College, earning a business degree in just three years. He then spent a year at the Harvard School of Business. "When I was a student, I didn't know what I wanted to do," Love once said. "My mother wanted me to go to the Harvard Law School, but I leaned toward business and when I graduated I went to business school. I hadn't thought of textiles particularly."

He went into the army as a lieutenant in World War I and was sent to France, where he rose quickly to major and served as divisional adjutant, excelling in administration. He was discharged in 1919 and returned to the Boston area, but soon decided to take a job as paymaster at a textile mill in Gastonia owned by his uncle. By the end of the summer in 1919, Spencer and his father bought the mill and Spencer became manager. He was twenty-three years old.

In 1923, he and his father sold the plant for $200,000 and moved the machinery to Burlington, a small town east of Greensboro known for its railroad shops, where he opened another mill, employing about two hundred persons. Love decided to move to the Burlington location for two reasons—the town's abundance of skilled labor and the fact that Burlington citizens subscribed $200,000 worth of stock in the new company. Love chose to manufacture products from rayon, a new synthetic fiber that had arrived in the South in 1925. He was one of the region's first mill owners to start producing rayon products and his gamble paid off a few years later during the Depression when consumers switched from silk to rayon because it was cheaper.

In 1926, Love formed another new company in Burlington and started manufacturing bedspreads. That same year he built another mill nearby, which began making upholstered goods, draperies, and spreads. In 1928, he built two more plants to manufacture rayon dress goods. Love was more than just a manager. In 1929, he broke with custom and engaged his own selling agent in New York, establishing direct contact between Burlington and its customers.

By 1930 the demand for rayon dress goods was more than Love's existing mills could handle, so he took advantage of the Depression to expand. But instead of building in Burlington, he began buying closed or failing textile concerns across the North Carolina piedmont, mainly for their buildings, where he replaced old machinery with new Jacquard looms for weaving rayon.

One industry observer at the time remarked of his methods: "It requires freedom from hampering tradition and considerable courage to scrap machinery that is still capable of doing its work, and the leaders in the weaving industry today are those who have met these requirements." But selling the machinery for scrap also prevented the competition from using it to make lower-quality, cheaper fabrics.

At the end of 1936, only twelve years from the day the first yarn was spun under Burlington's name, the company had twenty-two plants operating in nine communities. The next year Love consolidated his units into the Burlington Mills Corporation and listed its stock on the New York Stock Exchange.

Love's goals were flexible, but not even he anticipated the rapid expansion that occurred during the 1930s. He thought the company was "near the satura-tion point of what we can handle" in 1931, and he likened the growth of the previous few years to the rise of other giant corporations: "If we continued to expand in the future with the same rapidity as we have in the past year or two we would be as big as the Standard Oil Company before a great many years." The thought spurred him on, and when opportunities for expansion arose, he seized them.

Love was a thoughtful mill owner as well as a successful one. In 1929 he responded to a query from the editor of the *Southern Textile Bulletin* on what was wrong with the cotton-manufacturing industry by not only identifying the problems but proposing solutions as well. He argued that exorbitant profits made by the mills during the war had lulled their owners into failing to modernize. Until such mills were eliminated, he foresaw very close margins in the industry. He pointed to the need for new methods of cost accounting to adjust for the obsolescence of machinery and for the mixing of rayon and other fibers with cotton, which made manufacturing more complex. And he identified the need to pay closer attention to selling and distribution policies.

Love was innovative in personnel management. Over the years he became one of the first textile men to turn shop floor supervision into a professional specialty. Love did not believe that overseers had to be "steeped in technology with a textile engineering degree" or to have worked their way up through the ranks in order to be good managers. If they knew business, they could pick up textiles, much as he had. One observer summed up Love's policy concerning supervisors: "He recruited . . . from the graduate business schools, tossed them more responsibility than most could handle soon after they arrived, culled out those who faltered, and rapidly promoted the rest."

Attention to current fashion, professional management, and a dedication to modern equipment fueled Burlington's growth. By 1934, the company was the largest weaver of rayon in the nation and Love was called a hero.

In his quest for profits, Love insisted on having a free hand with labor. Like most textile executives, he was adamantly opposed to unions. But the tactics he employed to defeat them were in some ways as rationalized as his other management policies. He tried to keep his wage scale just above the competition, simultaneously providing an incentive for workers to choose Burlington and defeating one motive for unionizing. He also carefully screened potential employees. He had men in the mills who kept their ears open for gossip and complaints in order to anticipate and head off trouble. He issued photo identification cards, which workers had to show to security guards in order to enter the plant. He also scattered his plants throughout the piedmont where labor was plentiful, and this tactic made it more difficult for union organizers to operate.

Soon after the end of World War II, Love began buying more plants and moved into cotton and nylon hosiery. Eventually he expanded into carpet and started joint ventures with firms in France, Germany, England, Mexico, Canada, Colombia, South Africa, and eleven other countries.

A lanky, brown-haired man of average height and weight with gray-green eyes, Love spoke with a southern drawl, despite his New England upbringing. He was an avid tennis player, but he worked virtually every waking hour. Constantly on the move, often traveling an average of two thousand miles per week, he commuted by company airplanes to homes and offices in Greensboro, New York, Palm Beach, and Linville in the North Carolina mountains. He also kept a three-room suite at the Berkshire Hotel in New York City, where he usually spent Mondays and Tuesdays tending to business at his sales offices. He spent Wednesdays, Thursdays, and Fridays in Greensboro, where Burlington Industries was headquartered. On weekends, he usually could be found at his home in Linville. Vacations were taken at his oceanfront estate in Palm Beach.

In February 1961, President John F. Kennedy appointed Love to the national advisory committee on labor-management policy that Kennedy had created in an attempt to stave off disputes between labor and management. Love told the *Greensboro Daily News:* "It's been quite an experience sitting at the same table with Walter Reuther [a top labor representative] and Henry Ford and seeing them go at it."

In 1961, *Fortune* magazine listed Burlington Industries as the forty-eighth largest corporation in the United States, with sales of $913 million. The company employed 62,000 people in eighteen states and seven foreign countries.

Love was a member of Greensboro's First Presbyterian Church. He also was on the visiting committee at Harvard Business School and a trustee at Davidson College and UNC-Chapel Hill. Before he died on January 20, 1962, at the age of sixty-five, an interviewer asked what had motivated him and Love replied, "The challenge of competition, the desire to keep your organization on top, the personal satisfaction of accomplishment, the desire to improve yourself."

Marion A. Ellis is a Charlotte-based writer specializing in corporate histories and biographies. He is the coauthor with Howard E. Covington Jr. of Greensboro of Sages of Their Craft: The First Fifty Years of the American College of Trial Lawyers; Terry Sanford: Politics, Progress, and Outrageous Ambitions; *and* The Story of NationsBank: Changing the Face of American Banking.

For more information, see:

Love, Spencer. File. Robinson-Spangler Room, Public Library of Charlotte-Mecklenburg County.
———. Papers. Southern Historical Collection, University of North Carolina at Chapel Hill.

Hall, Jacquelyn Dowd, James Leloudis, Robert Korstad, Mary Murphy, Lu Ann Jones, and Christopher B. Daly. *Like A Family: The Making of a Southern Cotton Mill World*. University of North Carolina Press, 1987.

Carl McCraw, C. C. Cameron, and Edward E. Crutchfield (First Union Corporation)

By Marion A. Ellis

Forty-two years after he quit his job at an oil company to launch a small financial firm with borrowed money, Charles Clifford Cameron finally cut his ties to the company he helped build—First Union Corporation of Charlotte. That was in 1991, when Cameron was seventy-one years old and the bank had $41 billion in assets. He had announced his retirement as a director in 1990 after twenty-six years on the board. He had retired in 1984 as chief executive officer and as chairman in 1985, but had continued on the executive committee until 1990. By the end of the twentieth century, First Union had grown to become the nation's sixth largest bank with seventy thousand employees and assets of $253 billion.

First Union had its genesis in 1908 when H. M. Victor founded the company by selling one hundred shares at a thousand dollars each. It started growing in 1958 under its president, Carl McCraw Sr., but it really wasn't until Cameron came on board as executive vice president in 1964 that the bank began its meteoric assent.

Coming back from combat in World War II in early 1946, Cameron decided not to return to his native Mississippi, where he was born January 4, 1920, but to use his chemical engineering degree and join an oil company in Louisiana. But in 1949 he moved to Raleigh to start a mortgage banking business. He chose the North Carolina capital because an army buddy, James Poyner, had started a law practice there and he told Cameron it was a good place to start a business.

"I thought I was crazy at first," Cameron told the *Charlotte Observer* at the time of his retirement. "I didn't know anything about mortgage banking, and he [Poyner] didn't either, but we figured we were intelligent and could learn." They had little capital, but one of their investors, Raymond Bryan, a wealthy building contractor in Goldsboro, agreed to personally endorse notes at Wachovia Bank and Trust Company.

"I'd go down to Goldsboro," Cameron recalled, "and he'd endorse a whole sheath of notices, and I'd take 'em back and put them in a lock box at Wachovia. Then, whenever I needed money, I'd add my signature—which wasn't worth anything—and they'd lend us money." The initial loans were in the $25,000 to $50,000 range, but there were a lot of people wanting to build homes. "We handled hundreds of homes at $6,000 apiece with 100 percent financing," Cameron said. The Wachovia loans grew and grew—up to a "few hundred thousand"—before the firm became strong enough to use more standard measures, Cameron said.

After six years, Cameron merged his company with a similar one in Greensboro, Brown-Hamel, to form Cameron-Brown Company. By 1964, it was servicing $400 million in mortgages. At that size, the company attracted merger offers from the state's big banks. Cameron eventually chose First Union over Wachovia and NCNB because First Union was smaller and "I felt I wouldn't get as lost as I would in a larger institution," according to Cameron. The owners of Cameron-Brown received about $4 million in First Union stock, he said.

Cameron didn't have to worry about getting lost. He was initially an executive vice president of the bank, as well as Cameron-Brown's chief executive. But within two years, he became chairman, president, and chief executive officer of the bank and the one-bank holding company that had been formed with the acquisition of Cameron-Brown.

Cameron supervised twenty-five in-state acquisitions for First Union from 1966 to his retirement as chairman and CEO nearly twenty years later. "If you can get the guy to like and respect you and have a good relationship where you know enough about him that you aren't afraid to 'get in bed' with him then you can almost let him write his own ticket, as long as it's not unreasonable," Cameron said. "That's the way you consummate deals. You get to know people—the CEOs, the board members—and get them sold on what you can do together. It's a very time-consuming business." First Union reached $1 billion in 1968, doubled in size in six years, and had reached the $7 billion mark when Cameron retired.

After he left First Union, he devoted his life to public service, heading the state's budget office for

Left to right: Carl McCraw, C. C. Cameron, Edward E. Crutchfield (Courtesy of Charlotte Observer)

six years without pay, and serving in a variety of other high-level civic and charitable offices, including chairman of the UNC-Charlotte Foundation and the University Research Park board. His personal resumé listed more than a hundred businesses and civic activities, ranging from heading Meredith College's board of trustees to longtime service on the board of the University of North Carolina system.

Cameron had picked out his successor long before he retired. He was a hard-charging former Davidson College football star named Edward E. Crutchfield, who became chief executive officer in 1984 and chairman in 1985. Crutchfield had joined the bank in 1965 after receiving his M.B.A. from Wharton School of Finance at the University of Pennsylvania in Philadelphia. After handling several tough assignments for Cameron, he was named president in 1973 at the age of thirty-two.

Crutchfield was born July 14, 1941, and grew up in Albemarle, just northeast of Charlotte. His father was a lawyer who became a state Superior Court judge and his mother was a teacher. At six-foot-two, Crutchfield played tackle for the Albemarle High Bulldogs, which ranked number one in the state among schools of that size in 1957, his junior year. Quick for his size and a team leader, Crutchfield won a scholarship to Davidson, where he majored in economics and persevered through four seasons on mediocre teams. His grades were good enough to get him into Wharton, where he excelled. After graduation there, he chose First Union, which was small, but offered opportunity for an ambitious young man. He started by establishing the bank's municipal bond department.

Cameron started moving Crutchfield around the bank. "As tough jobs came up, I called on Ed," Cameron said. He would turn things around, line up his successor, and be back in Cameron's office looking for another assignment. "I reviewed him every year, and I'd say, 'Ed, what's your ambition here?' and he'd say, 'To get your job.' I'll never forget that."

As the bank grew, Crutchfield became adept at acquisitions, first acquiring Greensboro-based Northwestern Bank in 1985, the year after he became CEO of the corporation. It cemented First Union's position as a dominant player in North Carolina. Northwestern's CEO was Ben Craig, who had played football at Davidson eight years ahead of Crutchfield, and was a good friend. Craig became president of First Union's holding company, a job he held until his death in 1988 at age fifty-five.

When barriers to regional interstate banking fell in 1985, Crutchfield wasted no time. By the end of that year, First Union had announced six acquisitions, including Florida's Atlantic Bancorp, and completed three. Assets jumped from $7.3 billion to $16.6 billion. By 1987, First Union had nearly doubled in size, to $27.6 billion, posting strong profits. The stock price took off. For the five years ending March 31, 1990, First Union's 24.7 percent compound annual return to stockholders ranked it number one among the nation's twenty-five largest banks.

Crutchfield and his top lieutenants were always on the lookout for good buys in the banking business. When First Union was pursuing the Bank of Pasco County in Florida in 1985, Crutchfield and President John Georgius dropped by the headquarters in Dade

City unannounced and literally dressed to kill. "They were heading on a hunting trip and just stopped in to see how things were going," former Pasco CEO Hjalma Johnson said.

Ten years after the Bank of Pasco County deal, Crutchfield engineered what was at the time the biggest banking deal in U.S. history when he announced that First Union was buying the New Jersey-based First Fidelity Bancorporation for $5.4 billion. Crutchfield eventually put together more than fifty-seven deals for First Union. His down-home personality seemed suited for the role. "Growing up in a town of 15,000, you have to become self-aware because everybody knows everything," he told *Charlotte* magazine in a 1996 interview.

Crutchfield stepped down as CEO and announced his retirement as chairman in March 2000, to be effective December 31, 2001, saying he wanted to devote his energy to treatment for lymphoma, a curable form of cancer. He later moved his retirement date up to March 2001. He was succeeded by G. Kennedy Thompson, a former Morehead Scholar at the University of North Carolina at Chapel Hill who had joined First Union in 1976 after earning his M.B.A. at Wake Forest University.

At the end of the twentieth century, Crutchfield had helped build First Union into a national power with $253 billion in assets, sixteen million customers, and offices in twelve states and the District of Columbia. The company also had registered investment brokers in 265 offices in forty-three states.

Truly national banks began to emerge after the mid-1980s when a new federal law allowed bank mergers and acquisitions across state lines. In the summer of 1985, the U.S. Supreme Court gave its assent to interstate banking and the merger mania began in earnest. Crutchfield's secretary brought him the news of the court decision, a tear sheet ripped from the Dow business wire, and Crutchfield immediately picked up the phone. He called Billy Walker, the CEO of Atlantic BankCorp, one of the prominent financial institutions in Florida. They met the next day at a beach resort outside Jacksonville and hammered out a deal. The stakes were daunting in this game of buying banks. In Crutchfield's mind, it was grow or die, and it was clear by 1995 that First Union was to be one of the survivors.

A former First Union executive, C. C. Hope Jr., had a hand in one of the biggest deals of the era. Ironically, it involved a former competitor, not First Union. Hope was one of the three directors of the Federal Deposit Insurance Corporation (FDIC) in 1986, a post he had accepted after ending a long career at First Union, retiring as vice chairman, and after having served as president of the American Bankers Association. FDIC Chairman William Seidman was unimpressed when NCNB first approached him about buying FirstRepublic Bank, a troubled Texas bank, but Hope convinced him that the Charlotte bank could handle the transaction of buying the Dallas-based company.

Earlier in his career Hope had worked with Carl McCraw Sr., president of Union National Bank of Charlotte, when it merged with First National Bank of Asheville in 1958 to create First Union National Bank. McCraw had targeted the Asheville bank as a likely partner for his Charlotte bank because it had branches in the mountain communities in and around Asheville. With Hope driving the car, McCraw worked out the analysis during a 120-mile trip over mountain roads. The acquisition set the bank in an entirely new direction, followed by the all-important purchase of Cameron-Brown Company in 1964.

McCraw was the first in the long line of aggressive managers at the company. "In 1958, Union National's management, led by President Carl McCraw, Sr., saw that the future of banking lay in a strong branching network," First Union's official history states. They were driven by the same competitive spirit that would later exist at NCNB—to outdistance the leading North Carolina bank, Wachovia Bank and Trust Company, which had not grown as fast as either of its competitors.

In 2001, First Union achieved a milestone in North Carolina banking when it merged with Wachovia, following a bidding war with an out-of-state bank. The resulting combination, which made First Union the fourth largest bank in the nation, assumed the Wachovia name.

Marion A. Ellis is a Charlotte-based writer specializing in corporate histories and biographies. He is the co-author with Howard E. Covington Jr. of Greensboro of Sages of Their Craft: The First Fifty Years of the American College of Trial Lawyers; Terry Sanford: Politics, Progress, and Outrageous Ambitions; *and* The Story of NationsBank: Changing the Face of American Banking.

For more information, see:

Cameron, C. C. File. Robinson-Spangler Room, Public Library of Charlotte-Mecklenburg County.

Covington, Howard E., Jr., and Marion A. Ellis. *The Story of NationsBank: Changing the Face of American Banking*. University of North Carolina Press, 1993.

John Merrick, Aaron Moore, and C. C. Spaulding (North Carolina Mutual Life Insurance Company)

By Leslie Brown

John Merrick, Aaron Moore, and C. C. Spaulding (Courtesy of Duke University Special Collections Library)

ONCE THE LARGEST black business in the world, North Carolina Mutual Life Insurance Company of Durham remained at the beginning of the twenty-first century the largest and oldest African American insurance company in the United States. With assets nearing $10 billion, and over a billion dollars of insurance in force, the company ranked among the top 10 percent of all insurance companies in America.

Historically, North Carolina Mutual served as a symbol of race pride and progress, of self-sufficiency and self-help, and of racial solidarity for African Americans. Its story was central to the history of race in North Carolina. The Mutual and the range of busi-

nesses and institutions that grew as a result of its success engendered Durham's reputation as the "Capital of the Black Middle Class," and Parrish Street, where two of its offices were located, earned a designation as a "Black Wall Street of America."

John Merrick, Aaron M. Moore, and Charles C. Spaulding emerged as the central historical figures associated with the company, known as the "Greatest Negro Life Insurance Company in the World." Described by Merrick's biographer as a Triumvirate, a triangle that "kindly fate brought together and cast into one frame," they complemented each other's talents and personalities, leaving a collective mark on the Mutual and the South. The modern Mutual became the extension of the twenty years the Triumvirate worked together.

Merrick was considered the connecting link, not only among the coterie of black entrepreneurs, but also between a past of slavery and a future in freedom, among African Americans of different classes, and between blacks and whites during an explosive historical period. Charming and graceful, impeccably dressed, and exceptionally handsome, Merrick struck an effective balance between pride and respectability for African Americans on the one hand, and a pleasing countenance toward whites on the other. Admired by blacks and whites alike, and known occasionally to tip his hat to a white man while calling him a son of a bitch under his breath, he kept his distaste for most whites behind a mask and absorbed news, information, and white perspectives for the benefit of his community.

One might not have known that Merrick was born a slave and reared in abject poverty except that Merrick insisted that such humble beginnings should never be forgotten; he publicly identified with "the working classes like myself." Merrick was born in 1859 in Sampson County. His mother was a slave; her master was Merrick's father. Freed at the end of the war, the family sought work off the plantation and moved to Chapel Hill, where his mother worked as a domestic. At age twelve Merrick went to work as a brickyard laborer. Upon moving to Raleigh, he worked as a hodcarrier and later as a brick mason, building the Shaw University campus. He learned the trade of barbering while working as a bootblack and porter during a lull in the construction industry. Upon hearing of booming Durham, Merrick and his friend John Wright struck out for new opportunities in 1880, setting up a barbershop in a mostly uncultured town. They counted among their customers the most prominent white businessmen around: the Dukes, the Carrs, and the Blackwells. With their skills in high demand, Merrick and Wright soon opened several shops, three for whites and three for blacks.

Merrick possessed the heart of an entrepreneur, but the soul of an organizer. As his barbering business grew he moved into real estate, buying small plots of land, salvaging lumber, and building houses for rent to the expanding black population, as well as experimenting with a preparation for dandruff. But Merrick's most crucial talents were revealed when he coordinated diverse people to engage in enterprise. He brought eight men together in 1898 to form the North Carolina Mutual and Provident Association, of which he was president. Merrick also became head of Mechanics and Farmer's Bank, a business born of the same ideology that had brought about the Mutual upon the death of the bank's first president. When Merrick died in 1919, he had witnessed African Americans' transition from slaves to soldiers in World War I and become poised to bring the struggle for freedom to the southern home front.

Aaron M. Moore was born in 1863. After a short stint as a teacher, he enrolled in Shaw University in 1885, graduated from Leonard Medical School at Shaw, and having placed second in the medical board exam, moved to Durham in 1888 as the town's first black doctor. As much missionary as businessman, Moore was influential as a force of black philanthropy. He pushed for the building of Lincoln Hospital (one of the few black hospitals in the nation), established the Colored Library, and garnered a Rosenwald grant for a rural school building. The scholar of the group, Moore connected the Mutual to a philosophic base of benevolence and leadership as a means of public service in the pursuit of social justice. He served as president of the Mutual upon Merrick's death, and simultaneously as the superintendent of Lincoln Hospital. He died in 1923, having worked himself to death in the hospital he had established and where he found his soulful home.

If Merrick had the entrepreneurial spirit, and Moore the philosophical grounding, Charles C. Spaulding provided the energy and drive to turn ideas into reality. In the early years, Spaulding opened the offices, swept and mopped in the morning, put on his jacket to sell insurance, and then rolled up his sleeves to do the books in the evening. Aaron Moore's nephew, he was born among the post-Emancipation generation in 1874 in Columbus County. Restless and dissatisfied with rural life on his father's farm, Spaulding left in the early 1890s. He worked several jobs, finished his education in Durham's public schools, and then took charge of a cooperative grocery store. Merrick and Moore recognized his talents, and Spaulding joined the Mutual in 1900. His story, thereafter, had the makings of the great American success story.

After Booker T. Washington's death, Spaulding presided over Washington's favored project, the National Negro Business League. Spaulding complemented the Triumvirate, but after the deaths of Merrick and Moore, he emerged as Mr. Negro Businessman himself, a national leader among African Americans of the urban black elite, imbued with the gospel of work and wealth, to lead the Mutual into the era of modern capitalism.

The company created by the three men was praised not only in the second decade of the twentieth century by Booker T. Washington and W. E. B.

Du Bois, but also by the black intelligentsia and political leaders of the 1920s. Under Spaulding, Durham became renowned as the Capital of the Black Middle Class, the corporate counterpart of the Harlem Renaissance, and under his guidance the Mutual survived the Depression. Spaulding stepped into the role of southern New Dealer in the 1930s; and he took an early leadership role in interracial organizing through the Commission on Interracial Cooperation and the Southern Regional Council. When he died in 1952, black political allegiance had moved from the Republican Party of Lincoln to the Democratic Party of Roosevelt, in the South as well as the North, and the race men of Durham had reinserted themselves into the political discourse of the next half century.

The history of the Mutual reflects the irony of racism: the Mutual was created because of racial segregation, as blacks were refused service by whites, but segregation also created a captive customer base that ensured the company's success. Paradoxically, the Mutual's success was due to capabilities among its leaders and employees that some whites assumed blacks did not have and could not achieve: integrity, determination, resourcefulness, and hard work.

"We have great faith in luck," Moore once told a meeting of the National Negro Business League, "but infinitely more in pluck." To create a company like the Mutual required more than a financial investment; it required courage and daring, moral fiber, and spirit.

The company arose at the center of the black business movement in the urban New South. Originally founded as North Carolina Mutual and Provident Association in October 1888, it began as an outgrowth of the Royal Knights of King David, a traditional African American mutual aid society. In 1883, Merrick bought out the Royal Knights and then convinced colleagues and friends to invest, reshape the mutual aid concept, and sell insurance to the general public rather than solely to a membership. The original investors included Merrick; Moore; William G. Pearson, a teacher and business associate of Merrick; Pinkney Dawkins, also a teacher; James E. Shepard, a politician and pharmacist (later founder and president of North Carolina College for Negroes); and Edward A. Johnson, dean of the law school at Shaw University. Dock Watson, a local craftsman and another investor, was the company's only full-time employee, selling insurance on commission.

Each man pledged fifty dollars toward the venture, and Johnson drew up the charter. Spaulding was hired to manage the business. For all except Watson, who also recruited salespeople, selling insurance was a sideline, and the company struggled. The first

month brought little more than a dollar in collections after commission, and most of the policies sold were the unprofitable nickel-a-week variety that paid $1.60 in sick benefits and a twenty-dollar death benefit. According to legend, the first death claim broke the bank, and all but Moore and Merrick rescinded their financial interests. Spaulding stayed on as manager.

All of the original founders were notable in some way. Many were among the black Republican leadership of North Carolina in the late nineteenth century. Indeed, historians have argued that the Mutual's founding represented an inward turn away from partisan politics in the face of the hardening color line. As racial hostility and violence escalated, culminating with the Wilmington Riot in 1898 and black disfranchisement at the turn of the century, it could be said that out of fear, the Mutual founders refocused their energies. They built upon the themes of progress, thrift, and uplift as a way of countering racial fears and anxieties rather than evading them. Indeed, because black prosperity incurred racial reprisals, the founding of the Mutual was itself an intrepid execution of racial aspirations.

If anything, the Mutual formulated a shrewd race politic. It publicly aligned itself with Booker T. Washington, crediting him with inspiring the idea. Thus ingratiating themselves to the Tuskegee machine, the Mutual founders earned political capital by intrinsic association with Washington's moderate position on race relations. Furthermore, the founders made no public effort to refute the improbable story that tobacco magnate Washington Duke advised Merrick to invest in an insurance company.

Yet the Mutual founders also viewed themselves as exemplars of W. E. B. Du Bois's "talented tenth," the echelon of African Americans who should guide the black masses. In fact, the Mutual provided professional employment for hundreds of college-educated African American women and men who were otherwise denied. To work for the Mutual was to be a paragon of respectability and achievement, but also a model of community responsibility and awareness. Finally, despite the barriers against black voting, after 1920 (and women's suffrage), Spaulding, then president, took new employees to the Durham County courthouse to register to vote, repeatedly returning with those who were rebuffed or whose reading abilities were deemed inadequate by the white registrar.

From the beginning the Mutual embraced philanthropic intents. In addition to providing for widows, orphans, the sick, those injured by accident, and for the burial of the dead, its charter also specified that "a certain percent per annum . . . shall be turned over to the Colored Asylum at Oxford, North Carolina," as the orphanage for black children was known. With its motto, "the Company with a Soul and a Service," the Mutual offered itself as a resource in community development. The Mutual and its founders were instrumental in establishing the John Avery Boys (and Girls) Club, the (Harriet Tubman) YWCA, the National Training School (later North Carolina Central University), Hillside High School, the Durham Committee of Negro Affairs (the Durham Committee on the Affairs of Black People), Lincoln Hospital (Lincoln Community Health Center), and Colored Library (the Stanford L. Warren Library/Stanford L. Warren Branch of the Durham Public Library).

Virtually any initiative that Durham's African Americans undertook during the age of segregation proceeded with the Mutual's knowledge, if not always its sanction. The Mutual supported newspapers; the National Association for the Advancement of Colored People and other national black organizations; the Old North State Medical Association and other professional alliances; countless schools, colleges, and churches; and myriad local neighborhoods, institutions, and individuals.

In addition, the company laid the foundation upon which black Durham could build the astonishing array of successful businesses for which it was known: Merrick-Moore-Spaulding Real Estate Company, Mechanics and Farmers Bank, the Bull City Drug Company, the Durham Textile Mill, the Mutual Community Savings Bank, Bankers Fire Insurance Company, the National Negro Finance Corporation, and North Carolina Mutual Capital. Through the "Double Duty Dollar," money invested in a policy with the Mutual was reinvested in the black community through jobs, loans, and economic growth. With that growth, the Mutual founders believed, would come political strength, as Merrick once laid out the central fact of politics: "having something to represent." By advancing the accumulation of capital, the Mutual founders resolved to restore African American citizenship rights.

At its core, however, the Mutual responded to basic concerns of the urban working class: the eventuality of sickness, accident, and death. More important than seeing themselves as part of a movement, Merrick, Moore, and Spaulding recognized that communities were based on individuals held together by common needs and dreams. From their home base they witnessed the precarious nature of black urban life: high mortality, frequent outbreaks of disease, and unstable income presented impenetrable barriers

to race progress. Aware that the work of a lifetime could be confounded by these everyday factors, the Mutual might have profited more by allowing policies to lapse, rather than by pressing customers to keep up payments. Instead, the Mutual fought disease and death by hiring local doctors and nurses, setting up health clinics, participating in health education programs, and supporting health initiatives in service to communities. The Mutual advertisements presented buying insurance as a family responsibility. Insurance was not a luxury, the Mutual preached, it was a necessity: "Death is pursuing you at this moment," one ad read.

The Mutual believed it would do better by maintaining a communal perspective rather than simply a cost-effective one. Still, the company was, most importantly, a business that capitalized on the need for insurance in a world where African Americans faced a staggering death rate.

Early trial and error led its executives to develop business acumen. Because they felt that the failure of any black insurance company reflected poorly on their credibility, the Mutual's executives preferred to purchase and reorganize failing businesses rather than letting them go under. Thus, one of its first expansions was to buy out People's Insurance Company in Charlotte. By 1904 the company had expanded beyond its Durham home base and into South Carolina. Within the next twenty years the Mutual had established offices in Georgia, Virginia, Washington, Maryland, Tennessee, and Alabama. Offices of North Carolina Mutual and Provident Association, renamed North Carolina Mutual Life Insurance Company in 1919, could be found at the turn of the twentieth century in twenty-two states.

It was C. C. Spaulding's nephew, Asa T. Spaulding, who carried the Mutual into the era of modern business. Graduating from the University of Michigan with an advanced degree, A. T. Spaulding returned during the difficult 1930s to the business where he had worked as a college student. One of the first African American actuaries in the United States, he brought to the Mutual the science of accounting and risk taking. Among the few highly technically trained employees, he was known for his sharp intellect and aptitude for numbers. He solidified the company as a business, enhanced its reputation as a secure investment for its customers, and ironically made it competitive in an increasingly competitive market by encouraging the shift away from the social philosophy that had grounded the Mutual's early success.

Asa T. Spaulding followed William J. Kennedy Jr.,

the Mutual's historian, to become president of the company in 1959. During the turbulent 1960s, Spaulding became a leading black voice in race relations at the local, state, and national levels. Frequently criticized for his conservative or moderate stance, Spaulding, as perhaps the most prominent black businessman in the United States, pierced seemingly impenetrable racial barriers. Like the founders before him, he employed the shrewd and intricate racial politics of the appearance of black tolerance.

Even going into the postmodern era of business and politics, when African Americans crossed the racial lines that had created the Mutual, the company continued the tradition of serving as a symbol of black historical achievement. Indeed, the figure of the North Carolina Mutual agent remained a familiar enough figure in black culture to appear at the opening of Toni Morrison's novel *Song of Solomon*. Shining in the skyline of Durham, Mutual Life Insurance Company remains grounded in the visions, insights, and aspirations of its early founders, and most certainly in the convictions of John Merrick, Aaron M. Moore, and Charles C. Spaulding.

Leslie Brown in an assistant professor of history and African and Afro-American studies at Washington University in St. Louis. She earned her B.A. from Tufts University, and her M.A. and Ph.D. in history from Duke University. Her research interests focus on African American urban communities in the twentieth century.

For more information, see:

Anderson, Jean Bradley. *Durham County: A History of Durham County, North Carolina.* Duke University Press, 1990.

Andrews, R. McCants. *John Merrick: A Biographical Sketch.* Press of the Seeman Printery, 1920.

Brown, Leslie. "Common Spaces, Separate Lives: Gender and Racial Conflict in the 'Capital of the Black Middle Class.'" Ph.D. diss., Duke University, 1997.

Frazier, E. Franklin. "Durham: The Capital of the Black Middle Class." In *The New Negro: An Interpretation,* ed. Alain Locke, 3310–341. Albert and Charles Boni, 1925. Reprint, Atheneum/Macmillan Publishing, 1992.

Weare, Walter B. *Black Business in the New South: A Social History of the North Carolina Mutual Life Insurance Company.* University of Illinois Press, 1973. Reprint, Duke University Press, 1993.

———. "Charles Clinton Spaulding: Middle Class Leadership in the Age of Segregation." In *Black Leaders of the Twentieth Century,* ed. John Hope Franklin and August Meier, 167–190. University of Illinois Press, 1982.

JULIAN PRICE

By M. S. Van Hecke

AT AGE THIRTY-EIGHT, Julian Price had achieved only one notable mark in business: He had sold a small-town merchant an entire freight-car load of snuff. "I'll bet he still has some," a chuckling Price told a friend years later. A doctor friend, however, thought the personable Virginian was capable of better things than peddling snuff for the American Tobacco Company. He suggested that Price try the fledgling business of selling life insurance.

If ever there was a man well suited to his work, it was Julian Price. He didn't just succeed, he catapulted into statewide and national prominence and became one of North Carolina's most admired public citizens as president of Jefferson Standard Life Insurance Company. He was frequently mentioned as a possible candidate for governor or U.S. senator but preferred building the South's largest insurance company. Among the mourners at his 1946 funeral were the governors of North Carolina and South Carolina, congressmen, the president of the Southern Railway System, and insurance leaders from across the nation.

Born two and a half years after General Robert E. Lee's surrender to General Ulysses Grant at Appomattox in 1865, Price spent his childhood on the family farm and behind the counter at the family country store, where early on he showed a capacity for hard work. Even as a lad he disliked idleness. In later life he exclaimed to a friend: "A lazy man! A crook, now, has energy. He does things, and sometimes you can get the best out of him. Occasionally you can reform a crook, and a reformed crook is a good worker. But a lazy man—every day you keep him you are throwing your money away. I try to keep one from being hired anywhere in our organization."

The farm boy demonstrated an early talent for pleasing customers. He cut and sold wood to the nearby railroad company for its wood-burning locomotives, and he hung around the station until he learned Morse code and could fill in as a billing clerk and ticket agent. At age eighteen, the railroad hired him as a dollar-a-day telegraph operator and dispatcher in small towns along its lines in Virginia, then transferred him to Richmond at a lordly $60 a month. But the ambitious youngster, yearning for more adventure than was available in the recovering South, set his sights on romantic Alaska. Learning later, to his chagrin, that there were no railroads in Alaska, Price

Julian Price (Courtesy of Jefferson-Pilot Corporation)

settled down on a New Mexico cattle ranch, riding with the cowboys.

The Southern Railway superintendent, however, knew a good thing and summoned Price back to Richmond. He had been there only a few weeks when the dispatcher's office was moved to Durham, so in 1895, Price became a Tar Heel. The railroad moved him again, this time to Greensboro, but Price could not leave behind a nurse he had met in Durham named Ethel Clay. They were married three years before the close of the nineteenth century.

"When we had little, I was happy," Price once recalled, "just as happy as when we have lots. That's mainly because I've got a good wife, one who feels about things the same as I do. She was happy, and I was happy when we had nothing, and she was nursing the children and doing the cooking." The Prices had two children, Ralph and Kathleen.

Price stuck with the railroad as its chief dispatcher

for another six years until his growing family forced him to seek more lucrative work. He joined American Tobacco in sales, even though he did not use either snuff or cigarettes. He did like cigars, but he finally quit altogether on his doctor's advice. After three years covering the Carolinas, Price decided to take the plunge into life insurance and invested his savings of $250 and a borrowed $1,000 in a new firm called Greensboro Life Insurance Company.

Profiler Lou Rogers described the novice agent: "He spent his days soliciting business and his nights in mastering the details of the insurance business. That was back in the days when insurance was not appreciated as it is today. Price did not have an article for sale that people wanted to buy. He had to convince them first of its value, but he had faith in what he was selling and knew he was going to succeed."

His own account of those early days was in a lighter vein. He said one of his first prospects seemed worried about the strength of the new company. "How many policies does your company have, Julian?" the prospect asked. "Damned if I know," Price said he responded, "but when we get your application they'll sure as hell have one." He made the sale.

Price was an immediate success. He soon became general agent for the company, and in 1909 was made secretary and agency manager. In 1912, Greensboro Life merged with two other young firms, Security Life Annuity of Greensboro and Jefferson Standard Life of Raleigh. The new company kept the Jefferson name and the headquarters was established in Greensboro. Assets totaled $4 million, with $38 million of life insurance in force.

Price's steady rise continued. He became a vice president in 1914, but once tried to return to the sales field. The Jefferson board rejected his request and in 1919 elevated him to president. When he took over, assets totaled $9.7 million with life insurance in force of $81.6 million.

The company adopted a slogan, "Giant of the South," prompting a magazine to waggishly report, "Some of the officers began smoking 10-cent cigars instead of the 5-cent variety." But more seriously, Price's elevation set the stage for undreamed of growth.

Price reportedly had an artist prepare a promotion showing a cow being fed in the South and milked in the North. "Why send your life insurance premiums to New York, Massachusetts, Connecticut and other Northeastern cities," the caption read, "when they could be kept at home and invested locally."

Price persuaded the board of directors to authorize an almost unlimited expansion into states beyond the Carolinas and Virginia, with high standards set for each new agent and office. The *Greensboro Daily News* described the company's rapid expansion, saying, "These men are selected for excellence in education, high standing in their respective communities, appearance, knowledge of insurance and salesmanship. . . . They strive to give insurance services, not to load up their clients with more insurance than they can carry."

Price pushed for additional company benefits: group life insurance for employees, a rarity in its day; purchase of a farm outside Greensboro for an employee country club, and a splendid new office building in downtown Greensboro. The seventeen-story, $2.5 million building, completed in 1923, was unusual in a city of 19,000, and drew some sly jabs from residents of neighboring cities. If a person identified himself as being from Greensboro, folks from Winston-Salem would teasingly ask, "Which floor?"

Price's cow picture accurately described the problem facing southern businessmen: having to approach credit markets in the North to ask for loans, often unsuccessfully. Price determined to use his company's income to help finance southern industry.

How well he accomplished this was widely recognized. The *Spartanburg Herald* in South Carolina said: "He knew that insurance builds up capital that the South needed so badly to develop and prosper." Clarisa Adams, executive vice president of the American Life Convention, said: "He had great faith in the South and was willing to bet on it. . . . He was one of the shrewdest traders you could find. He loaned on everything from churches and graveyards to mortuaries, textile mills and newspaper plants."

James E. Dunn wrote in the *Insurance Index:* "He did more in practical and constructive ways for North Carolina and other Southern states than any man in his time. . . . The South could hardly finance its own enterprises. Price reversed tradition. He not only proved himself a great benefactor to the South but also showed the world that in a comparatively sparsely settled community you could build a great insurance institution."

In the 1920s, Price bought an interest in the *Greensboro Record* and sold it several years later at a healthy profit. This led him into a number of newspaper loans and investments in such cities as Tulsa, Indianapolis, and Philadelphia.

The company continued to grow even during the Depression. In a 1934 interview with the *State* magazine, Price said, "The amount of insurance in our company as of June 30 was shown to be more than $310 million, which constitutes a material gain over the total as of Jan. 1. . . . Our assets increased approximately $1 million during the first half of 1934, the total now being $56.4 million."

The *State* also quoted an unidentified "magazine of national circulation" with this appraisal of Price: "Here is the most unusual individual we have ever met. Not because he built the largest ordinary writing life insurance company in the South; not because his first thought has been the development of the South; not because the 'Old No'th state' has honored him time and again—but because of his human traits. What a storehouse that marvelous mind of his must be to be weighted down with the activities of the other fellow and still permit him to push the Jefferson Standard ahead as he does."

A Greensboro newspaper, The *Democrat,* once ran page after page of anecdotes about Price—the paper called them Juliana—which showed the executive's human side.

Among the anecdotes was one about a seedily dressed man who somehow made his way through the company's executive suite into Price's office and complained that his shoes were worn out. Learning they both wore the same size, Price took off his own shoes and gave them to the visitor, then made his way in his socks to the first-floor Van Story haberdashery and bought a new pair.

On another occasion, Price was admonishing a subordinate, when the man said, "Well, I guess this means I'm fired." Price replied, "Hell, no, if I had any intention of firing you, I wouldn't be standing here cussing you out."

Price habitually wore his fedora in the office. When asked why, he would give one of several explanations, always with a straight face. One story was that he had acquired the habit while working as a railroad station manager when he might have to run out into bad weather at a moment's notice.

Price also was a joiner. Among a long list, he was a Rotarian; an Elk, a 33rd Degree Mason; a past potentate of the Oasis Shrine Temple; a member of the Sedgefield, Greensboro, and Congressional country clubs; and the Southern Society in New York. He also served as president of the Atlantic and Yadkin Railroad, as chairman of the state Salary and Wage Commission, and for eight years as a Greensboro city council member.

On October 24, 1946, Price was en route to the North Carolina mountains to visit a 3,500-acre tract he had bought for the company outside Blowing Rock. Rounding a slight curve near North Wilkesboro, his chauffeur lost control of the car and it ran off the road, killing Price. He was seventy-eight. The accident fell on the event of the third anniversary of the death of his beloved wife. When his will was probated, it showed Price had cash, stock, and property worth $3.7 million. How much insurance he carried on himself was never divulged.

Just prior to Price's death, Jefferson Standard had acquired Pilot Life. The two firms were merged in 1987 to form Jefferson-Pilot Corporation. Its 1999 annual report listed assets of $26 billion and life insurance in force of $214 billion.

The mountain property near Blowing Rock was donated to the Blue Ridge Parkway. The Julian Price Memorial Park abuts the Moses Cone Memorial Park. The two properties, honoring the longtime Greensboro friends, constitute one of the parkway's largest recreational areas.

One of Jefferson's last acquisitions under Price's leadership was the 1945 purchase of WBT radio station in Charlotte from CBS for $1.5 million. With the subsequent addition of WBTV, the state's first television station, and other outlets the Jefferson-Pilot communications subsidiary has become a major media company. One report credits it with generating 10 percent of the parent company's annual revenue.

M. S. Van Hecke is a former editor-writer for the Charlotte Observer *now living in Waxhaw. He wrote and produced* A Free and Independent People, *a video history of Charlotte and Mecklenburg County narrated by Charles Kuralt.*

For more information, see:
Democrat (Greensboro), November 26, 1942.
Greensboro Daily News, November 19, 1933; October 26, 1946; February 2, 1947.
Insurance Index, November 1946.
Jeffersonian (Jefferson Life Insurance Company), November 1946.
Spartanburg Herald, October 28, 1946.
State, August 11, 1934; August 6, 1936.

Addison H. Reese, Thomas I. Storrs, and Hugh L. McColl Jr. (Bank of America)

By Marion A. Ellis

A RELATIVELY SMALL Charlotte bank in what most considered a financial backwater outsmarted and outmuscled all of its competitors to become the largest in the United States by the end of the twentieth century. A principal architect of that meteoric ascent was an unlikely one—a mediocre student from a small South Carolina town who had been turned down when he first applied for a job at the bank. Eventually Hugh Leon McColl Jr. overcame all barriers to lead the gigantic Bank of America, which had $656 billion in assets in 2000.

That was a long way from North Carolina National Bank's (NCNB) $500 million dollars in assets when it was formed on July 1, 1960. But McColl himself was the first to acknowledge that although he had been at the helm for much of the explosive growth, in reality he was following a legacy of his predecessors as chairman—Thomas Storrs and Addison Reese. He often explained: "The fundamental strengths of our corporate culture have survived . . . with Addison Reese's vision, his meritocracy of fairness and equity, his intensely competitive nature, and with Tom Storrs's cool-headed leadership, his demand for perfection with the numbers, his intellect and foresight."

Addison Hardcastle Reese, a native of Baltimore, Md., was forty-two years old when he moved to Charlotte in 1951 to take over as president of American Trust Company, the bank that eventually merged first with another Charlotte bank and later a Greensboro bank to become NCNB in 1960. Reese was tall and distinguished-looking, with a taste for art and summers on Nantucket. He also was a fierce competitor and encouraged young executives like McColl to help him build a bank to equal Wachovia Bank and Trust Company in Winston-Salem, then the state's leading financial institution.

The sixties were a period of frantic merger activity as Reese and his competitors at First Union and Wachovia took advantage of North Carolina's liberal branch banking laws to expand operations across the state. Unlike most states, North Carolina allowed intrastate banking under a law that had been on the books since the early part of the nineteenth century,

when a Wilmington bank appealed to the state legislature to open an office in Fayetteville, ninety miles away. Before Reese stepped down in 1974, he had managed the growth of the bank through mergers and acquisitions to one with $3.6 billion in assets.

Thomas Irvin Storrs, a Virginian, had joined NCNB in October 1960, moving to the new bank from the Charlotte office of the Federal Reserve. On January 1, 1974, when Storrs officially succeeded Reese, NCNB was the nation's twenty-sixth largest bank. Storrs provided a steady hand during the turbulent economic downturn of the mid-1970s, and then began expanding the bank throughout the state. He also eagerly eyed expansion to other states.

At the time, interstate banking was considered impossible under existing laws, and bankers were not eager to invite competitors into their home states. This was especially true in Florida, which Storrs considered one of the most tempting markets in the Southeast. Storrs talked quietly with other bankers who held his view of the future, but most agreed it was not possible without a major change in state and federal banking policy.

Undeterred, Storrs urged NCNB's lawyers to aggressively pursue opportunities to expand. They finally found a way in 1982, when Storrs used an Orlando, Fla., trust company that NCNB had purchased ten years before to buy a small bank in Lake City, Fla., thus giving them an important toehold. Florida banks, and other competitors outside the state, opposed the move, but bank regulators approved the purchase. The door had been opened and NCNB stole a march on all its competitors.

Storrs pushed NCNB's expansion in Florida until he retired in August 1983 and was succeeded by McColl. In July 1985, McColl signed an agreement to buy Bankers Trust of South Carolina, which gave NCNB the distinction of being the first regional banking company to establish connections in three states in the Southeast. By the end of that same month in 1985, McColl had moved NCNB into Georgia. In 1986, he engineered purchases in Maryland and a year later in Virginia.

Left to right: Addison H. Reese, Thomas I. Storrs, Hugh L. McColl Jr. (Courtesy of Charlotte Observer)

McColl was at the helm in 1988 when the bank pulled off its coup in Texas, doubling its size to $65 billion with the acquisition of First RepublicBank of Dallas. It was called the deal of the century and brought NCNB into the ranks of national players. Receiving FDIC approval to buy First Republic allowed NCNB to take over the Texas bank's forty operating banks with their 178 offices across the state.

"This marks a new era, in our judgment, for regional expansion," Goldman, Sachs and Company announced. "Among the largest regionals, NCNB is arguably at the forefront of true, broad national expansion with its Texas move."

"The deal set several precedents, especially with its provision for FDIC ownership of a bank," according to *The Story of NationsBank,* published in 1993. "The decision to award the First Republic deal to NCNB marked the first time ever that the agency had entered into a partnership with an outside party. It also was the first time the FDIC had guaranteed the risk on the loan portfolio and other real estate retained on the balance sheet of the restructured company. The agency liked the way NCNB proposed handling the bad loans because, by having NCNB care for the pool of assets, the costs involved were below the FDIC's internal costs."

McColl continued his acquiring ways in 1991 by merging his bank with C&S/Sovran to create Nations-Bank, the nation's third largest bank, with assets of $119 billion, 59,000 employees, and 2,000 branches. "What we are seeing is enterprises that took a hundred years to build up being taken out in one fell swoop,"

McColl said at the time. "There is going to be a radical change in banking."

NationsBank continued to expand, buying the $41-billion Boatmen's Bank of St. Louis in 1996, and adding seven new states: Missouri, Kansas, Arkansas, Oklahoma, New Mexico, Iowa, and Illinois. The two banks overlapped only in Tennessee and Texas. Geographically, no other bank even came close to the combined territories. In 1997, NationsBank bought Barnett Bank of Florida.

In 1998, NationsBank merged again, this time to create the new $633-billion Bank of America, keeping headquarters in Charlotte, not San Francisco. In mid-2000, the company had 155,000 employees and served thirty million households, as well as two million businesses in the United States and thirty-seven other countries.

The man behind such phenomenal expansion was McColl, who was born June 18, 1935, in the small South Carolina town of Bennettsville, just south of the North Carolina line. His father, grandfather, and great-grandfather had been bankers. In high school, he lettered in four sports, was the quarterback of the football team, and president of his class. His father had closed the Bank of Marlboro in Bennettsville during the Depression and opened a cotton gin. When young Hugh was old enough, he was enlisted to keep the books. His father was such a stickler for accuracy that he caused his son to stay home one weekend to look for a missing penny, knocking him out of a beach trip with his friends.

Rugged and fit at just under five-feet seven-inches

tall, McColl was the ultimate competitor—at banking, sailing, or tennis. He even competed against himself, working large, monochromatic jigsaw puzzles by the hour. He had been told all his life not to settle for second best; he had been expected to be the winner, the leader. A significant childhood memory was the story *The Little Engine That Could,* which his mother read to him.

After graduating from the University of North Carolina at Chapel Hill, McColl spent two years as a Marine Corps officer, and then applied for a job at American Commercial Bank in Charlotte, whose chief executive officer was Addison Reese. He was turned down, but taken on board after his father, who had done business with the bank, asked key officers to reconsider.

Once hired, McColl worked his way up through the ranks, excelling in international business to become president in 1974 at the age of thirty-eight. Known for his aggressive style and military metaphors, McColl was the opposite of a staid, conservative banker and was widely quoted. "I don't like my competitors," he said. "I don't eat with them, don't do anything with them except try to waste them. To me it's a zero-sum game. When I lose business, it's like taking bread off my children's table."

Fortune magazine tried to capture his style in an August 21, 1995, article. "Add a monumental ego to those skin-you-alive dealmaking skills, and you have a man who's going to make other big bankers sweat," the magazine said. "Of course, that's not the image McColl wants to project. Equal parts Southern gentleman and in-your-face ex-Marine, he likes to flash a toothy grin, which makes him appear disarming in a mischievous sort of way. Don't be fooled. Says a pal who's played cards with him for 30 years: 'Hugh is driven by competitiveness. The most important thing to him is winning.'"

In addition to his banking prowess, McColl was a leader in bringing the Olympics to Atlanta in 1996, giving its organizing committee a $40-million line of credit. He also was instrumental in the creation of the Carolinas' first National Football League franchise, the Carolina Panthers of Charlotte, and paving the way for the construction of the team's new stadium in central Charlotte. He led the way in his huge bank's sponsorship of the arts, not only in Charlotte, but also in other cities where his bank operated.

After his bank had opened its first office in London in 1972, McColl came back with yet another vision he thought he would like to accomplish someday. Why couldn't Charlotte be more like London? he asked himself. London's center was vibrant, bustling with peo-

ple and activity. Charlotte's was dull and listless, with hardly anybody on the streets. It had no close-in housing except rundown boarding houses and government-subsidized apartments.

McColl became an early leader in the revitalization of Charlotte's center city. In 1978, he led the establishment of the NCNB Community Development Corporation, a nonprofit company that would undertake general real estate development in the public interest. In 1981, the bank established a partnership with the Committee to Restore and Preserve Third Ward. There were many other projects in Charlotte's center city during the eighties that McColl and his bank sponsored. The bank began assembling land for later development of the $350-million Gateway Center on West Trade Street. Construction of the 306,000-square-foot building began in January 1988. The bank also agreed to be the anchor tenant of the new Independence Center at the northwest corner of Trade and Tryon. And the bank began construction of its Child Development Center in Fourth Ward at West Sixth and Poplar Street.

But the construction of the $300-million sixty-story corporate center on the northeast corner of Trade and Tryon was the crowning achievement. Subsequently, this complex was extended to include Founders Hall and the North Carolina Blumenthal Performing Arts Center. McColl's leadership also earned him plaudits for encouraging Bank of America employees to volunteer in schools on company time. *Working Mother* magazine honored him and the bank for the company's work-and-family programs.

McColl retired in April 2001, one year later than he had planned, after the board of directors asked him to remain. His successor was Ken Lewis, another veteran of the NCNB organization.

Marion A. Ellis is a Charlotte-based writer specializing in corporate histories and biographies. He is the coauthor with Howard E. Covington, Jr. of Greensboro of Sages of Their Craft: The First Fifty Years of the American College of Trial Lawyers; Terry Sanford: Politics, Progress, and Outrageous Ambitions; *and* The Story of NationsBank: Changing the Face of American Banking.

For more information, see:
Covington, Howard E., Jr., and Marion A. Ellis. *The Story of NationsBank.* University of North Carolina Press, 1993.
Yockey, Ross. *McColl: The Man With America's Money.* Longstreet Press, 1999.

R. J. REYNOLDS

By Frank Tursi

RICHARD JOSHUA REYNOLDS rode into Winston on horseback in 1874, took off his hat, and scanned the dusty little town—as the statue of him on Main Street attests. Presumably, he was looking for a place to build his tobacco factory. The company he started the following year on a lot about the size of a tennis court would one day sprawl over one hundred acres of downtown and dominate Winston-Salem's psyche as well as its real estate.

Reynolds came to Winston merely to take advantage of the little town's rail connection, but his tobacco company ended up defining the city. The two grew up together, and their histories are so intertwined that it is impossible for most people to think of one without the other. People who know nothing about Winston-Salem know that it is the home of R.J. Reynolds Tobacco Company.

The company's leaders would come to dominate the city's politics and social structure, and its founder set the pattern. R. J. Reynolds was so influential that it was forty-one years after his death in 1918 before company officials summoned the nerve to hang the portraits of other chief executives next to his in the boardroom. By the time he was forty years old, Reynolds was Winston's leading citizen. He was called on to lend his support or his money to numerous projects. Reynolds helped start a savings and loan, served on the town board, championed public schools, and fought J. P. Morgan's railroad monopoly. His money helped build a school for black persons, an opera house, and a YMCA.

Josephus Daniels, the publisher of the *News and Observer* in Raleigh, described his friend this way: "He was a strange man, Dick Reynolds was, a bold, daring and audacious man with little education and little polish. . . . North Carolina has not produced another merchant of such vigor and success."

Born in 1850, Reynolds grew up in comfortable surroundings on a plantation in what is now Critz in southwestern Virginia. His father, Hardin, had amassed a small fortune based on a prosperous empire of making chewing tobacco and running a store. He was one of the largest planters in Virginia when the Civil War started and one of the few not bankrupted by the war. When he died in 1882, Hardin owned more than eight thousand acres in Virginia and three thousand in Stokes County in North Carolina.

R. J. Reynolds (Courtesy of N.C. Office of Archives and History)

R. J. Reynolds, then, had opportunities that other children of the time and place didn't. He attended a private school, but didn't care much for books. An eye defect that apparently prevented him from visualizing words probably had a lot to do with it. He was bright and quick-witted, though. In an often-told story from his Civil War-era boyhood, a teacher asked Reynolds what covered the mountains. "Rocks and deserters," he replied.

Emory and Henry College didn't interest Reynolds. He left after two years because he didn't do well in any subject except math. A business college in Baltimore was good for about six months.

Books may have eluded Reynolds, but he knew tobacco and people. Riding a wagon through the mountains of Virginia, Tennessee, and Kentucky, he peddled his father's chewing tobacco. He found times tough, money scarce, and the tobacco almost impossible to sell. So he traded it for anything of value—

animal hides, beeswax, tallow, yarn, old furniture, and jewelry. He then auctioned off the items, often selling them for more than what the tobacco was worth.

Selling tobacco that way was, at best, uncertain, and at times unprofitable. To succeed at this business, Reynolds decided he needed access to a railroad. Since there was not one in Critz, Reynolds packed up and rode the sixty miles to Winston, where the Northwest North Carolina Railroad—later Southern Railway—had completed a spur line to Greensboro in 1873. He went, Reynolds said later, "for the benefit of the railroad facilities, and on account of this town being located in the center of the belt in which the finest tobacco in the world is grown."

Reynolds was only twenty-three when he arrived in the hardscrabble little town that was just a year older than he was. He immediately bought a lot next to the railroad tracks from the Moravian Church, built a two-story wooden factory, hired a dozen seasonal black workers, and was in business.

It wasn't much of a business at first. Reynolds sold about 150,000 pounds of chewing tobacco his first year—minuscule by later standards. By 1879, business was good enough that Reynolds added to the factory and bolstered the workforce to seventy-five employees. From then on, he built additions or new factories or bought out competitors every two years. At the time of his death, his company owned 121 buildings in the merged Winston-Salem. His brother, Harbour, was so impressed when he visited in 1884 that he wrote their mother that "Dick is the biggest blood in Winston."

He would only get bigger. Reynolds once said that he would retire when he made $100,000. But in 1892, when his net worth more than doubled that figure, Reynolds embarked on the most aggressive part of his career. He replaced the original factory that year with a six-story plant that was the largest building in Winston. It had steam power, electric lights, and a smokestack that cost more than the first factory.

The factory was one of thirty-nine tobacco factories in Winston in 1897. Twelve remained two years later. Fierce competition in a crowded industry and the cutthroat tactics of James B. Duke's American Tobacco Company broke their backs.

Formed in 1890, American was one of the biggest monopolies in the country. It was despised by wholesalers, who were forced to do business with it; by farmers, who blamed it for low leaf prices; by warehousemen, who saw it as a threat because it was large enough to buy leaf directly from farmers; and by the public, who thought it was keeping prices high. By undercutting independents and pressuring retailers, American drove competitors to bankruptcy or forced them to sell out. With its subsidiary, the Continental Tobacco Company, American cornered the plug tobacco market by the late 1890s.

Though he publicly railed against Duke, Reynolds willingly joined the trust in 1899. An astonished Josephus Daniels, an avowed enemy of the Duke trust, asked Reynolds why he sold to Duke. "Sometimes," Reynolds replied, "you have to join hands with a fellow to keep him from ruining you and to get the under hold yourself. . . . I don't intend to be swallowed. Buck Duke will find out he has met his equal, but I am fighting him now from the inside. . . . If you will keep your eyes open, you will find that if any swallowing is done, Dick Reynolds will do the swallowing. . . ."

There was also the matter of money. Reynolds was perpetually short of the cash that he needed to expand his factories. Using American's money, Reynolds went on a buying spree. Along with buying out most of the other tobacco companies in Winston and in Martinsville, Va., he built fourteen major factories himself. When the U.S. Supreme Court dissolved the so-called Tobacco Trust in 1911, Reynolds assumed control of his company again. He had done well under Duke's benign dictatorship. His company emerged from the trust as the largest in North Carolina. Its sales exceeded $12 million, a fourfold increase since Reynolds joined with Duke. RJR was the undisputed king of chewing tobacco, and its Prince Albert, which was introduced in 1908, was the most popular pipe tobacco in the country and had given the company its first national product. Reynolds planned to continue his assault on the tobacco industry and his old rival Buck Duke. "Watch me and see if I don't give Buck Duke hell," he said.

Winston's businessmen could be forgiven for thumping their chests and boasting of their economic prowess in 1906. The city's rise from a sleepy hamlet where goats and pigs wandered through the courthouse square to an energetic city at the forefront of the state's industrial revolution was indeed headspinning. The numbers tell the story: Winston's factories led the state by turning out $11.3 million in products, a 132 percent increase in just six years. The town's capitalists had more money invested in manufacturing than six other cities in the state combined. "We are in a class by ourselves," the Winston Board of Trade, the forerunner of the chamber of commerce, boasted in a pamphlet.

So was R.J. Reynolds Tobacco Company. Because of the astuteness of its founder, the company entered the twentieth century as the biggest business in town and one of the leading manufacturers in the South. Its president, who stood six-feet-two and had dark hair and eyes, was the most eligible bachelor in the state before marrying Katharine Smith in 1905. He often was chosen to lead parades and emcee balls and other social events.

Less than five months after Winston and neighboring Salem were joined by a hyphen, an event occurred that would ensure the continued success and growth of the new city. Camels arrived. R.J. Reynolds Tobacco Company introduced its Camel cigarettes on October 19, 1913. The brand's immense popularity made Reynolds the leading tobacco company in the world and Winston-Salem the leading producer of tobacco products. That meant jobs and prosperity for the company and the town.

Reynolds had been reluctant to enter the cigarette market. He had made his fortune on chewing tobacco and Prince Albert. Unlike cigarettes, neither required sophisticated machinery or skilled workers. A savvy businessman, Reynolds couldn't ignore the trends, though. Most people, he knew, still rolled their own cigarettes and disliked the manufactured brands, but cigarette smoking was becoming more popular and would one day overtake chewing.

Never one to risk everything on one roll of the dice, Reynolds decided to make four brands of cigarettes, each using a different blend of tobacco. Only Camels survived. They were a mixture of domestic burley and bright tobacco, with Turkish leaf added for taste and aroma, along with a generous amount of sweetener. Most cigarette brands were made of straight Turkish tobacco, and Camels are credited with being the first truly American cigarette.

To appeal to American smokers' taste for Turkish tobacco, Reynolds wanted a simple name that evoked the Middle East. He also knew that many of the brand's customers would be illiterate and he wanted a name that could easily be depicted by a picture on the pack. Company legend has it that he settled on a camel because it was his favorite animal while growing up. The camel of Reynolds's boyhood memories, however, was nothing like the pathetic figure that appeared on the first pack. It had one hump, a drooping neck and an unkempt shaggy coat. All in all, it was a rather lackluster creature that suggested the same was true of the cigarettes inside.

As luck would have it, and as company legend insists, the Barnum & Bailey Circus was in town, and Reynolds sent his secretary, Roy Haberkern, to the circus in search of a zippier camel. Haberkern found

two to his liking, but the animal boss—a disagreeable fellow named Patterson—refused to allow his camels to be photographed, citing the animals' notorious temperament. Patterson found out something that late September day that many Reynolds employees would learn during the forty-two years that Haberkern was with the company: He could be just as ill-tempered as any beast of burden or its handler. He reminded Patterson that Mr. Reynolds closed his factories for a day to allow employees to attend the circus. That could change, Haberkern noted ominously.

Such a threat coming from a lowly secretary didn't carry much weight with Patterson, who insisted that it come from Reynolds himself. Haberkern rushed back to the office, which had already closed for the day. He climbed through a window, wrote it all down on company stationery and signed his boss's name.

The forgery fooled Patterson, who trotted out a two-humped camel and a one-humped dromedary that Haberkern had chosen. The camel behaved for the picture-taking, but Old Joe, the dromedary, snorted, kicked, and generally refused to cooperate. Patterson gave the animal a stout whack on the nose. An astonished Old Joe threw back his head, closed his eyes and raised his tail. The ungainly pose was captured by the photographer and faithfully copied by the illustrator.

That was the Old Joe that found its way onto the front panel of the Camel pack. He was surrounded by a desert and flanked by two pyramids and three palm trees. The obligatory mosques and oasis covered the back. Everything was bathed in a soothing reddish-brown tint. The package pleased Reynolds, who committed $250,000 to Camel's initial advertising. Preceding the brand's release, a series of teaser ads began appearing in selected newspapers across the country. The first pictured Old Joe and simply read, "Camels." It was followed a few days later with one that noted, "The Camels Are Coming." The final ad promised that "Tomorrow there'll be more Camels in this town than in all Asia and Africa combined."

They came and they conquered. About 1.1 million were made that first year. More than eighteen billion were produced in 1921, when half the cigarettes smoked in the United States were Camels. A few years later, the company turned out thirty billion Camels a year. The cigarettes were so successful that competitors spread rumors that workers in Reynolds's cigarette room had leprosy or syphilis.

Part of the brand's success stemmed from aggressive and imaginative advertising. The idea for one of the most famous advertising slogans in history came in 1918, when a foursome of golfers ran out of cigarettes. One said to Martin Reddington, who handled outdoor ads for Reynolds, "I'd walk a mile for a Camel." The slogan first appeared on a billboard in June 1921.

Katharine Smith was twenty-five, almost thirty years younger than Reynolds, when she married him in 1905. She had known her husband since she was a child. Reynolds and her father, Zachary Taylor Smith, were cousins who had grown up together in Virginia. Reynolds often visited Smith at his home in Mount Airy and teased the young Katharine that he would one day marry her. After graduating from college with a degree in English literature, Miss Smith took a job as Reynolds's secretary and won a thousand dollar prize in a company-sponsored contest. Reynolds said later that he married her to get his money back.

He got his money's worth. Katharine Reynolds urged her husband, whom she always called "Mr. Reynolds," to shorten his employees' work week and to improve the conditions in his factories by providing lunchrooms, a medical department, and a day nursery. Reynolds, a good man who gave freely of his time and money to worthwhile community projects, didn't need much prodding. He granted each of his wife's wishes.

Reynolds, Katharine, and their four children— Richard Jr., Mary, Nancy, and Zachary Smith—lived in a rambling Victorian house on West Fifth Street, Winston-Salem's first Millionaire's Row. Their neighbors included most of the city's prosperous families who had built its tobacco and textile industries—the Grays, the Haneses, and Reynolds's brother and partner, William Neal, who was known as "Uncle Will" to all the children on the street. Enticed by the affluence they enjoyed after the merger of Winston and Salem, the city's wealthy abandoned their mansions on West Fifth for secluded enclaves west of town.

The Reynolds family set the tone. Katharine was in charge of the family's new house. She started buying the thousand acres for the estate in 1909. She hired the architect, the famed Charles Barton Keen of Philadelphia, and made most of the decisions. "She could read a blueprint like an engineer," an employee said. The name of the estate, Reynolda, purported to be a feminine form of Reynolds, told who was boss. Katharine had a higher purpose than merely building a house for a rich family.

It was a model farm where she taught local farmers the most current methods of scientific, diversified farming. Employees lived in a village on the estate and had their own schools and churches. During the eight years of construction, Mrs. Reynolds offered evening classes to workers who wanted to learn to read and write.

The family moved in just before Christmas in 1917, but Reynolds had little time to enjoy the sixty-room house that his wife modestly called a bungalow. Stricken by pancreatic cancer, Reynolds died on July 29 the following year, at age sixty-eight. Not everyone who worked for him mourned his passing. The old man could squeeze a dollar and was something of a slave driver. Nearly everyone, though, admired what he had accomplished. As Camel had shown, he wasn't afraid to take risks and relished competing against the other, stronger tobacco companies. In the process, he had devised a simple, yet successful, formula: Keep costs low, production centralized, and concentrate on a few good brands. "I have written the book," a dying Reynolds told worried underlings. "All you have to do is follow it."

Richard Joshua Reynolds—described by the epitaph on his tombstone in Salem Cemetery as a "workman of the world"—left an estate of $100 million, or about $1.2 billion in year 2000 dollars.

Reynolds's influence didn't end with his death. The company that he founded was, for much of the twentieth century, Winston-Salem's largest employer and greatest benefactor. As the largest tobacco company in the world in the late 1950s, R.J. Reynolds Tobacco Company employed almost one in five workers in Winston-Salem. Hundreds of civic projects, from charity drives to new museums, were made possible by the donations from the company or its executives.

Wake Forest College would never have decided in 1946 to move from Wake County to Winston-Salem had it not been for the Reynolds family's largesse. RJR's children donated a sizable portion of the family estate at Reynolda for the new campus, and the Z. Smith Reynolds Foundation committed its yearly income to an endowment for the school.

Reynolds's three remaining children started the foundation in 1936 as a memorial to their youngest brother, Zachary Smith Reynolds, who had been found shot at the Reynolda mansion four years earlier. His death was initially ruled a suicide, but a coroner's inquest later determined that Reynolds had been murdered. The ruling and the subsequent indictment of Reynolds's beautiful showgirl wife and best friend attracted reporters from around the country. Soon, stories began to appear about drunken orgies at Reynolda, Reynolds's impotence, and his wife's alleged affair with his best friend. Faced with such negative publicity, William N. Reynolds, RJR's brother and the family patriarch, wrote the district attorney that the family would be "relieved" if the charges were dropped. They were, and no trial was ever held.

Something positive, though, came from the tragedy. After a protracted lawsuit over Smith's estate, his siblings used their share, about $7.5 million, to start the foundation, which was directed by its charter to do good works for the people of North Carolina. No other general-purpose foundation as large as the Z. Smith Reynolds—which had grown to $520 million in assets by the end of the century—had a mandate to make grants in a single state.

The foundation was a force for good throughout North Carolina. Its grants, which totaled about $20 million in 2000, were used by nonprofit groups to protect the environment, aid economic development, and better the lives of minorities and women.

Mary Reynolds Babcock, another of RJR's children, created a foundation with a $12 million bequest in 1953. Since then, the foundation that bears her name has given away nearly $100 million in the Southeast to assist a wide variety of charitable, educational, recreational, literary, religious, and scientific projects.

Smith Bagley, R. J. Reynolds's grandson, presided over the board of the Z. Smith Reynolds Foundation. During his years in Winston-Salem, Bagley was a businessman and active in civic affairs. A Democrat, he ran unsuccessfully for Congress in 1966 and 1968. He subsequently moved to Washington, where he became a major donor and fund-raiser for the Democratic Party. His wife, Elizabeth, was a former ambassador to Portugal.

Frank Tursi joined the Winston-Salem Journal *as a staff writer in 1978 after working for various newspapers, including the* Miami Herald. *He wrote* Winston-Salem: A History, *and a history of the* Winston-Salem Journal. *Tursi has won numerous national and state writing awards, including the History Book Award given by the N.C. Society of Professional Historians.*

For more information, see:

Eaton, Clement. "Winston-Salem in the First Quarter of the 20th Century: A Recollection." Southern Historical Collection, University of North Carolina at Chapel Hill, 1976.

Fries, Adelaide L. *Forsyth: A County on the March.* University of North Carolina Press, 1949.

Tilley, Nannie. *The R.J. Reynolds Tobacco Story.* University of North Carolina Press, 1985.

Tise, Larry E., et al. *Winston-Salem in History.* 13 vols. Historic Winston-Salem, 1976.

Tursi, Frank V. *Winston-Salem: A History.* John F. Blair, 1994.

JULIAN H. ROBERTSON JR.

By Mark Wineka

JULIAN H. ROBERTSON JR.'s mid-life crisis came in 1979 as he was in the midst of a quiet, distinguished career on Wall Street. Over two decades, Robertson had risen through the ranks of Kidder, Peabody and Company to head its money management subsidiary and become a director and vice president. He was, in his own words, "an honest slob they could count on."

But Robertson wanted something more, and he abruptly moved his young family to Auckland, New Zealand, where he intended to write a novel about a southern boy who made it big in New York. The move and his writing efforts proved less than satisfying. Within thirteen months, he returned to New York with thoughts of tackling the financial world on his own terms. Robertson and Thorpe McKenzie, a younger man who had been handling his customers during his absence, raised $8.8 million to start the Tiger Fund in May 1980. From there, Robertson lived out the story line of his ill-fated novel: the southern boy did make it big in New York.

A Salisbury native, Robertson came to captain the operations of one of the world's biggest and most successful hedge funds ever. Tiger prospered from the beginning. Until 1998, it lost money in only one year, when the market crashed in 1987. During several years, its returns exceeded 40 percent. Even counting the toughest years of 1998 and 1999, Tiger registered a 27 percent average annual gain over twenty years. Financial observers heaped praise on Robertson and routinely sought his insights. *Assets,* a *Business Week* publication, called him the world's best money manager in 1990.

Financial World magazine described him as the maestro of the financial world. He also picked up the title "Wizard of Wall Street." By 1997, billionaire Robertson ranked number 165 on the *Forbes* list of the 400 richest Americans. By 1998, Tiger's six different hedge funds had $23 billion under their management for elite investors.

Robertson tackled his craft and life with a rare combination of southern charm and Yankee impatience. He also became a great benefactor, using his wealth to make the biggest individual gift ever to the Lincoln Center for the Performing Arts. He established a multi-million-dollar foundation in his North Carolina hometown that gave out hundreds of thou-

Julian H. Robertson Jr. (Courtesy of Tiger Management)

sands of dollars in grants each year to worthy causes. His Tiger Foundation, funded and managed by Robertson's employees, helped disadvantaged children and their families in New York. In 1999, *Worth* magazine listed him thirty-fourth among the one hundred most generous Americans.

But every novel has an ending, and Robertson's came by April 2000. His legendary Wall Street hedge fund firm fell victim to rapidly changing world financial markets that led to huge investment losses and big withdrawals. The combination left Tiger with just $5.2 billion in assets, not enough to generate the incentive fees needed to cover operating expenses in his offices around the world. Robertson liquidated Tiger Management, and most of its remaining assets were returned to investors. "We are in a market where reason does not prevail," Robertson wrote in one of his last letters to shareholders in early 2000.

Born June 25, 1932, Julian Hart Robertson Jr. grew up the son of a textile executive, who proved to be a shrewd investor himself. Julian H. Robertson Sr. continued to invest in stocks even after the 1929 crash. The senior Robertson eventually did quite well with his selections when the market began rebounding in the late 1930s and early 1940s.

"When he and his sisters were kids," the father told *Business North Carolina* magazine in 1990, "we'd all sit out on the living room floor and compare statements from Esso and Texaco to see who got the most sales per dollar of investment."

A tenth-generation descendant of Pocahontas and a native of Wilmington, Julian Sr. starred in tennis and basketball at what became Clemson University. He ran the Erlanger textile enterprises over a forty-seven-year career. He served as president or chairman of companies that included N.C. Finishing in Spencer, Erlanger Mills in Lexington, and its parent company, Erlanger Enterprises Corporation in New York. The senior Robertson also became a director of American Trust Company of Charlotte in 1953 and was instrumental in its evolution into North Carolina National Bank, which became NationsBank and later Bank of America. Robertson served on the NCNB board until 1969.

Julian Jr. was the oldest of three children, including sisters Blanche and Wyndham. Friends credit his mother, also named Blanche, for giving her son the sensitive side of his personality that often allowed him to become generous to charities. Blanche Robertson also left with her children a deep affection for nature, especially gardening. Julian Jr. was fond of saying in later years that he met a lot of people in the New York financial world who were smarter than he was, but none knew more about flowers.

The Robertson family made its home near the Salisbury Country Club. Robertson said Fred Stanback, of Stanback headache powder fame, taught him to play Monopoly when they were children. Another friend was Jimmy Hurley, whose family owned the *Salisbury Post* newspaper.

A grassy lot next to the Robertson's served as both baseball diamond and football field to a generation of Salisbury boys and their pickup games. "The home run lanes were a little short, so baseball had to be given up at around the age of 11," Robertson wrote in the *Salisbury Post* in 1997, "but we played football into the early teens."

Hurley recalled later that Robertson spent more time announcing the games than playing them. "He made us feel like we were playing in the Rose Bowl or World Series," Hurley said. "His play-by-plays were as serious and as exciting as Bill Stern or Red Barber. None of us dreamed he would take Wall Street by storm. I thought he'd scratch out a living as a sportscaster. He'd have been a good one, too."

Robertson attended public schools in Salisbury until his junior year in high school, when he left for Episcopal School in Alexandria, Va., from which he graduated. He then earned a business degree from the University of North Carolina at Chapel Hill in 1955. He entered the navy as an ensign, serving much of his time on a munitions ship. When his navy commitment was finished, Robertson followed his father's advice and went to New York. "I told him that was where the money was, and he has a damn sight better nose for where the money was than I did," the senior Robertson said in 1990.

Robertson always maintained a strong affection for Salisbury, where his parents lived until their deaths in the 1990s. In the office at his Long Island home, he hung a picture of the Salisbury house he had grown up in and routinely visited as an adult. He believed his small-town upbringing allowed him to meet all kinds of people and never permitted him to become too elitist, despite coming from a wealthy family.

"There's something about a small town like Salisbury," Robertson told the *Post* in 1998. "It's sort of sad that all young people can't be exposed to it, in terms of morals and the way the community gets involved and makes things right." Robertson became a robust, strapping six-footer. He found that his southern drawl and courtly manners helped him in New York, often disarming people. "He's so nice and humble," Salisbury Mayor Susan Kluttz said after meeting Robertson in New York in 1998. "You get the feeling when you talk to him that he's still a Salisburian."

As a money manager, Robertson was known as demanding, quick-tempered, and impatient for answers. He built a reputation for commanding competent, if not brilliant, young researchers and analysts in the hunt for bargains. His legacy was quite evident on Wall Street by 2000, when thirteen hedge funds, known as Tiger Cubs, were being run by Tiger alumni.

Friends and colleagues often said that money didn't motivate Robertson as much as his love for winning. He was extremely competitive, stubborn, curious, and intuitive, with contacts everywhere. He relentlessly interrogated those contacts on the telephone. Josephine, his wife, told a reporter once that she believed the cellular telephone was invented for her husband.

Robertson waited to marry until he was forty years old. He and the former Josephine Vance Tucker of San Antonio had three boys: Spencer, Jay, and Alexander. It was in his wife's honor in 1998 that Robertson gave $25 million to New York's Lincoln Center. In return, the plaza outside the Lincoln Center now bears her name. Robertson, ever the sentimentalist, said it's one of New York's most beautiful spots and it's lucky to have her name.

When he was little, Robertson's oldest son, Spencer, suggested the name "Tiger" for his father's new company. Robertson had a habit of calling people he liked "Tiger," though he admitted to an interviewer years later that he actually didn't like cats, because they killed birds. Still, a whole family of cat investment funds followed under the Tiger umbrella, including Jaguar, Puma, Lion, and two Ocelot funds. The names suggested an ability to strike fast.

A colleague once said Robertson "goes after ideas the way a large-mouth bass strikes a lure." His strategy somehow seemed to blend daring and caution. A *Forbes* article in 1985 quoted Eliot Fried, then chief of Shearson Lehman Brothers: "Julian is not a gunslinger like the other hedge fund guys," Fried said. "Tiger doesn't invest and then investigate."

With his "value investing" approach, Robertson bought underpriced stocks and shorted overpriced ones—what a true hedge fund does. He made massive leveraged bets on companies with strong fundamentals that might be temporarily out of favor with the market, such as Citicorp in the early 1990s. Robertson also was shrewd in currency trading. He told the *Bloomberg News* in 1997 that managing a completely hedged portfolio "is the ideal thing because company selection is where we are good. I have no belief in ours, or anyone else's, ability to pick markets."

Robertson knew all along that the markets he played for so long and so well could be fickle. Sometimes, he said, he was right for the wrong reason and wrong for the right reason. When he was bearish on brokerage stocks in August 1981, he shorted Dean Witter at $29 a share. Sears soon announced it was taking over Dean Witter, and he was forced to cover the stock at $48, losing $250,000 in the process.

"I once went long on Babcock and Wilcox because I was bullish on nuclear power," Robertson told an interviewer. "Along came McDermont to acquire B&W, and I made a bundle. Eventually, I was right about Witter and wrong on B&W, but I made money where I was wrong and lost money where I was right. You have to have a sense of humor in this business."

After one particularly good day in the fall of 1997, during a highly volatile market, Robertson retired to bed early with a Popsicle. "I think the best thing to do when you have one of these days," Robertson told the *Salisbury Post* between bites, "is just go to bed.

Not even go to work, because everything you do is always wrong."

Things quickly caved in on Tiger. Robertson found himself on the wrong side of a series of big investment bets. He lost $600 million in the autumn of 1998 when Russia defaulted on its debt. A billion-dollar loss on the Japanese yen came a year later, forcing Robertson to refocus on beaten-down U.S. stocks in the "old" economy. Tiger invested heavily in U.S. Airways Group, Bowater Incorporated, and Sealed Air Corporation, but they were disappointing and lagged far behind the booming technology sector.

Analysts said that by insisting on getting bargains, Robertson was often pessimistic about high-tech stocks, believing that they were outrageously overpriced. He found that old rules for stocks did not apply in the 2000 bull market. Robertson's funds were down 19 percent in 1999 and 13 percent early in 2000 before the end came. *Business Week* described it as the biggest hedge fund collapse in history.

Back in Salisbury, as word filtered through the business media that Robertson's hedge fund company was on the brink of closing, friends worried more about Robertson than the financial condition of the local foundation he had endowed in 1997. "You run out of adjectives to describe the level of generosity of Mr. Robertson to this community," said David Setzer, executive director of the Blanche and Julian Robertson Foundation.

With additional contributions from his sisters, Robertson had established the foundation in his parents' honor with close to an $18 million gift. He added an additional $5 million in February 2000, but he had always left decisions about grants to an eleven-member board, of which son Spencer Robertson was a member. "I wanted to keep out of it and have kept out of it," Robertson said in 1998, "and I think they're doing a great job. I know the money there is going to be very well spent."

By the spring of 2000, the foundation had awarded 109 grants, totaling more than $4.3 million. Robertson also made key contributions to Salisbury's Catawba College and for a park near the city's train station. The park bears his family's name, too.

He and his wife, Josie, created and funded the Robertson Scholars Program, a unique scholarship opportunity designed to be in the same league with the University of North Carolina's famous Morehead Scholars. The first thirty undergraduate Robertson Scholars were chosen in the spring of 2001. Half would enroll at UNC-Chapel Hill and half at Duke University and attend classes on both campuses. They would receive full tuition, room, and living stipends at UNC or full tuition at Duke, along with summer enrichment opportunities and travel in the United States and abroad.

James Hurley, a member of the foundation board and an investor with Robertson, said his old boyhood friend did something for him in 1996 that he would never forget. Hurley suffered a brain aneurysm while he was in Naples, Fla., for his brother Haden's funeral. The last thing Hurley remembered was being rushed to the hospital in an ambulance before waking up eight days later after a major operation. Hurley opened his eyes and looked around the hospital room. There was Robertson, sitting in a chair beside the bed. "What in the world are you doing here?" Hurley asked. "I heard you were sick," Robertson answered, "so I thought I'd fly in to see if you were faking."

Hurley claimed the visit perked him up and made him realize he would survive. "Later I read in *Forbes* magazine where he was one of the country's 400 richest men," Hurley said. "Julian may be a billionaire I said to myself, but he hasn't forgotten the people he grew up with."

Mark Wineka is a staff writer at the Salisbury Post *and the author of* A Family Affair, *a book about the Hurley family's ownership of the Post, and the coauthor of* Lion's Share, *which told of the Food Lion grocery chain's rise and dramatic impact on its small-town investors. He won the N.C. Associated Press News Council's O. Henry Award for writing in 1998.*

For more information, see:

Donsky, Martin. "When a Tiger Is King of the Jungle." *Business North Carolina,* August 1990.

Longman, Phillip J. "The Bull That Ate Tiger." *U.S. News & World Report,* April 10, 2000.

Post, Rose. "Honor Thy Mother." *Salisbury Post,* December 6, 1992.

———. "Lessons from My Mother." *Salisbury Post,* November 28, 1997.

Rowe, Frederick E., Jr. "The Best Instincts in the Jungle." *Forbes,* September 16, 1991.

Wineka, Mark. "Robertson Never Forgets Home." *Salisbury Post,* January 1, 1997.

VERNON C. RUDOLPH

By J. Howell Smith

VERNON CARVER RUDOLPH was the epitome of the twentieth-century American entrepreneur. With only a recipe and borrowed flour, he built a national corporation based on fresh, hot Krispy Kremes —doughnuts first made in Winston-Salem and eventually appreciated from New York to Los Angeles.

Rudolph was born on July 30, 1915, in rural Marshall County, Ky., near the community of Haiti. He was the eldest son of Plume Harrison and Retie Imo Rudolph. He finished elementary school in Haiti and high school in Aurora, six miles away. Rudolph's father operated a general store that sold and bartered the store goods needed by his farming clientele. It was good training for young Vernon.

When later analysts tried to explain Rudolph's management skills, some recalled an episode in his early days when he had no money. Spying a woman's sagging clothesline, he solved the problem with a stack of unused poles he had seen. Finding a nail, he hammered it in slantwise near the top of a pole, and sold the pole to her as a clothesline prop. With that money he bought more nails and sold the rest of the poles.

Rudolph entered the doughnut business in 1933. According to tradition, the Krispy Kreme doughnut was first created by a French river barge cook named Joseph G. LeBoeuf, who traveled from New Orleans to Paducah, Ky., and became known for the wonderful flapjacks, coconut cakes, and doughnuts he made for the barge crews. Ishmael Armstrong, Vernon's uncle, admired the doughnuts and asked for the recipe. LeBoeuf was flattered and readily gave it to him. The recipe called for the softest flour a dough would allow, fluffed egg whites, mashed potatoes, sugar, shortening, skimmed milk, a deep fat fryer, and a sugar glaze. By legend the recipe would remain a family secret kept in company vaults. Unofficial lore says the secret recipe involved mixing a starter cream that included potato flour and a combination of soft and hard wheat flours. Ironically, when LeBoeuf died in 1998, he loved Krispy Kreme doughnuts, but had no idea that they were the offspring of his own recipe.

Armstrong put his nephew to work making and selling the doughnut treats door-to-door. A 1934 picture showed Rudolph in standard white uniform with a flour-dusted shoe propped on the running board of his car.

Because of the depressed economy of the Paducah

Vernon C. Rudolph (Courtesy of Krispy Kreme Corporation)

area, Armstrong moved his doughnut business to Nashville, Tenn. Vernon's father, who had closed his store, moved to Nashville to join the business. The father, Vernon, and brother Lewis bought the business from Armstrong in 1935 and began a pattern of expansion. In 1936, P. H. Rudolph and Vernon opened a shop in Charleston, W. Va., and in 1937, the father and a jobber opened a shop in Atlanta.

Fried dough pastries had been in the culture earlier, perhaps since pre-Columbian times, but had not met the mass market. In nineteenth-century New England, a ship captain's mother, Elizabeth Gregor, put nuts in the center of her fried dough cakes and called them "doughnuts." Her son, Hanson, claimed credit for using a tin pepperbox to cut out "the first doughnut hole ever seen by mortal eyes." But it was not until World War I, when female volunteers delivered millions of doughnuts to the troops overseas as a touch of home, that a mass-market appetite developed. In New York City, Adolph Levitt mechanized the process by inventing a machine that dropped perfectly shaped rings of dough into the cooking oil, right before the eyes of the hungry customers. In the Depression years doughnuts would be a cheap but tasty treat.

At age twenty-two Vernon Rudolph wanted to establish his own business. Rudolph was ready to take his Krispy Kremes to new areas where there would be new customers with more money. He and two friends set out with two hundred dollars, a 1936 green four-door Pontiac, a set of cooking equipment, and the recipe. In 1937 Rudolph fulfilled his plan by moving his entrepreneurship to Winston-Salem. By legend he was in Peoria, Ill., unsuccessfully looking for a fertile field for the doughnut business when he pulled out a pack of Camel cigarettes. The label caught his eye and he noted that the cigarettes were made in Winston-Salem. "Why not Winston?" the story goes. "A town with a company producing a nationally advertised product has to be a good bet."

Considering that he was a shrewd young businessman, and that Winston-Salem, with its dominating Reynolds Tobacco Company and thriving Hanes Knitwear and Hanes Hosiery plants, was ranked as one of the most promising territories in the South and perhaps in the nation, it was doubtful that the choice was controlled by the luck of the cigarette pack.

He arrived in Winston-Salem with twenty-five dollars, the recipe, and doughnut-making equipment that included a gas burner, iron kettle, rolling pin, galvanized wash tub, and cutters. The money went for a down payment on rent for two adjacent buildings on Main Street in Salem, near the tobacco shop. Rudolph and his friends persuaded a grocer to let them have the necessary potatoes, sugar, and milk on credit. They built delivery racks in the Pontiac and on the hot summer day of July 13, 1937, began cooking and delivering Krispy Kremes.

The market was ready for the young entrepreneurs. To attract attention, they cut the doughnuts in the front window of the shop. The appeal of the fresh, hot Krispy Kremes brought customers to the kitchen, so Rudolph put a hole in a wall and began selling the "hot Krispy Kremes" through the window while customers watched them cook. The doughnuts sold two for a nickel or a dozen for twenty-five cents. A good doughnut cutter could make 120 doughnuts an hour.

Within a year the business was a success, and it was time to expand. With another uncle, Rudolph opened a Krispy Kreme Doughnut Shop in Charlotte. Expansion in another direction came with the purchase of a fried pie recipe and a separate production line from the Ole Timey Pie Company, later known as the Flaky Fruit Pie Company, and then Krispy Kreme Pies, but the main line was always doughnuts.

While the 1930s meant hard times for many businesses, it was a time of expansion and acquisition for Rudolph and his family. His father sold the Atlanta business and bought the Krispy Kreme Do-Nut Company in Knoxville. Brother Lewis, at age twenty, leased the Nashville shop from his father. Vernon Rudolph opened a new shop in Raleigh. He enlarged his facilities in Winston-Salem, and in 1941 bought out his uncle in Charleston, W.Va. He now owned three shops and shared ownership of the Charlotte shop. When a Columbia, S.C., restaurant owner wanted to make Krispy Kreme doughnuts, Rudolph agreed, with the stipulation that the recipe be protected and the quality standards be monitored and maintained. It would be the first of what would later be called associate-operated shops.

World War II brought responsibilities and disruption to Rudolph. In 1939 the successful young bachelor married Ruth Ayers from Orangeburg, S.C. Soon a daughter, Patsy, joined the family. The disruption was the war. Vernon Rudolph had learned to fly in 1940. When war was declared, he leased his two planes to the government and flew coastal patrols as a member of the Civil Air Patrol. He also applied for a commission in the Office of Flying Safety. After a brief interlude as a draftee at Fort Bragg, he received an appointment in the Army Air Corps as a second lieutenant in the Office of Flying Safety. Stationed in Atlanta, he served as an investigator of air crashes.

Personnel he had hired managed the company, with the stipulation that when ingredients were not available to produce quality doughnuts, then the doughnuts would not be made. In 1941 his youngest brother, Ernest, entered the business, working with brother Lewis in Nashville. In 1944 the well-managed life was disrupted when Ruth Ayers Rudolph died in an automobile accident. After eighteen months in the service, Vernon Rudolph returned to Winston-Salem and focused his attention on his business.

The year 1946 was a time of recovery from personal loss and from the war years. His personal life was re-energized with his marriage to Lorraine Flynt of Winston-Salem. They raised a daughter, Beverly Britton Rudolph, and three sons—Vernon Carver Rudolph Jr., Sanford Harrison Rudolph, and Curtis Flynt Rudolph. His professional life was invigorated by the fact that his doughnut business had emerged from the war with great vitality. With a thriving business in hand, Vernon Rudolph as personal entrepreneur and family company leader was ready to move with Krispy Kreme. He understood the necessity of upgrading the business organization of the enterprise, and the importance of responding to the growing mass market by selling it a reliable product sold with a recognizable standard trademark.

In 1946, he patented the trademark "Krispy Kreme." Company legend credited Vernon Rudolph's father with the original depiction of the name in slanted script with banners across the top and bottom. In the mid-1950s the red and green colors of the name became standard, and the smaller image of two crowned K's crowned with doughnuts was added to accompany the slogan "King of America's Doughnuts."

In the same year Rudolph talked with his family and the Atlanta proprietor about unifying their businesses. On October 1, 1946, the owners of the consenting proprietorships and partnerships formed a corporation, Krispy Kreme Doughnut Company. On October 5 the corporation acquired the assets and assumed the liabilities of all proprietorships except the Atlanta shop.

On June 3, 1947, Rudolph led the stockholders of Krispy Kreme Doughnut Company in organizing a new corporation called Krispy Kreme Corporation, whose business would be the manufacture and sale of standardized dry mixes for making doughnuts in all of the Krispy Kreme shops. It would also deal in development of doughnut production equipment and supplies. Significantly, the new corporation was authorized to use the Krispy Kreme trademark in a franchising program.

Both the company and the corporation operated from offices in the First National Bank Building in Winston-Salem. Although the two corporate organizations had separate charters, Vernon Rudolph was chairman of the board and president of both, and Lewis Rudolph was vice-president and a member of the boards.

Using its authorization to create a franchising plan, the corporation in 1947 began licensing independent operators to make doughnuts from the company mixes using company methods and to sell them under the Krispy Kreme trademark. The Associates' Agreements, as they were called, required that the standards of the original company be met. By the end of 1948 Rudolph's corporation was licensing doughnut makers in ten states.

The strongest sign of the shift to standardization and uniform quality was the building of the Ivy Avenue mixing plant in Winston-Salem. Lewis Randolph moved from Nashville to Winston-Salem to supervise the production of dough mixes that could be shipped in bags to the shops. He and an accountant developed the dry mix that would replace the original wet mix that had been the basic ingredient in the secret recipe. With flour, sugar, and shortening stored in bins and mixed by increasingly sophisticated automation before being bagged and shipped to the outlets, Rudolph's Krispy Kreme created an industry. The small shops selling hot Krispy Kremes across the region had become extensions of the doughnut factory.

In 1951 the local newspaper reported that the city, already a tobacco and textile center, was making a strong bid for the title "World Doughnut Capital." "Responsible for this new distinction is a young man named Vernon Rudolph and the bustling, mushrooming corporation he has built in 14 years from a scrap of paper with his . . . recipe scribbled on it," the paper reported.

The plant also provided a place for Rudolph to bring inventors and technicians to build the newest and most innovative equipment for making the company's doughnuts and other baked goods. He had the vision to say, "Don't look at the cost, look at the end result." In 1960, when the company was moving toward bulk mixing production, Rudolph declared that the next ten years would be the most productive period Krispy Kreme had ever known. He envisioned a time when a sack of mix would be poured into one end of a machine, which would then provide continuous mixing, fermentation, forming, proofing, frying, glazing, cooling, and packaging. But the quality would never be sacrificed to the machine.

In the era of expansion, Rudolph maintained excellence, but also added other products and services. The Krispy Kreme Corporation produced cake doughnuts, fruit pies, honey buns, baking and frying equipment, and dough mixes formulated to the needs of independent bakers. Rudolph's success was recognized by awards such as the superior rating from the American Institute of Baking and the Outstanding Achievement Award from the Quality Bakers of America.

In 1996 the Smithsonian Institution put the company's records in its archives, preserving the remarkable files of a "privately held twentieth-century company whose history was documented from day one." The museum also obtained the Ring King Junior mechanized doughnut-maker that had been used to make Krispy Kremes in the factory and in demonstrations around the globe. Spencer Crew, director of the National Museum of American History, described Rudolph's Krispy Kreme story as a portrayal of "entrepreneurship and invention, of the introduction of mass production and the marketing of prepared foods, and the connections between regional culture and commercial culture."

Given Rudolph's leadership, it was no surprise that

the company's records were meticulously kept. When he died on August 16, 1973, at age fifty-eight, contemporaries remembered the man and the management style of "a perfectionist with a photographic memory and an eye that detected details, which would elude most people." He also was a leader who took pride in introducing good people to the company as employees and franchisers.

Three years after Rudolph's death, his company was sold to Beatrice Foods, which operated it for half a decade. Then several of the franchisers whom Rudolph had encouraged into the business bought the company back and, using the qualities he had affirmed, expanded the company with a flourish of national success. The company's initial stock offering in 2000 was considered the most successful in the market.

J. Howell Smith has been a professor of history at Wake Forest University since 1965. He has published Industry and Commerce, 1896–1975 *in the* Winston-Salem in History *series and is a student of industrial development of the city.*

For more information, see:
Krispy Kreme. Corporate records and artifacts. Smithsonian Institution, Washington, D.C.
Krispy Kreme. Files. North Carolina Room, Forsyth County Public Library.

Joyner, Louise Skillman. *Krispy Kreme: A Man and an Enterprise*. Krispy Kreme Doughnut Corporation, 1977.
Taylor, David. A. "Ring King." *Smithsonian* 28, no. 12 (March 1998), 20–24.

C. D. "Dick" Spangler Jr.

By Marion A. Ellis

For eleven years, Clemmie Dixon "Dick" Spangler Jr. took on one of the toughest jobs in North Carolina, worked for free, and enjoyed every minute of it. As president of the University of North Carolina sixteen-campus system from 1986 to 1997, he returned more than his $190,000 yearly salary to the state, used his own private plane for business trips, and drove a state-owned 1985 white Ford LTD until his retirement. But then he had been a shrewd investor who routinely made *Forbes* magazine's list of the most wealthy and had a personal fortune estimated in 2000 at $1.6 billion.

Spangler was born April 5, 1932, in Charlotte and attended public schools before going to Woodberry Forest preparatory school in Virginia. He lettered in basketball and football and the 1950 Woodberry Forest yearbook described him as a sharp dresser who was "on the ball, both on hardwood and with femmes." Spangler graduated from the University of North Carolina in 1954 and then earned a graduate degree from the Harvard Business School, which had turned him down on his first attempt at admission. While he was at Harvard, his father completed the Advanced Management Program at the same time.

After finishing at Harvard in 1956, he served in the army for two years and in 1958 he became president of his father's business, C. D. Spangler Construction Company in Charlotte. He held that job for twenty-eight years as the firm built apartments, warehouses, and motels. Spangler said he had always "assumed I was going in the construction business," although he had no specific plan in mind.

In 1973, when one of his father's investments, the Bank of North Carolina, got into financial trouble, he reluctantly became chairman of the bank. His father had been one of the founders after World War II when he was building a portion of Camp Lejeune in eastern North Carolina and found bank financing slow and hard to obtain. The younger Spangler was handed a business in trouble, but he used his Harvard business training to turn the bank around and by 1982 it had $425 million in assets and seventy branches located primarily in eastern North Carolina. The bank's recovery became a case study at Harvard Business School and Spangler himself made the presentation to the students upon the insistence of one of his former professors.

C. D. "Dick" Spangler Jr. (Courtesy of Charlotte Observer)

Spangler had talked with North Carolina National Bank (NCNB) of Charlotte about a merger, but regulatory attorneys in Washington had advised NCNB that there was too much overlap with their own existing offices, and they feared bank regulators would disallow such a move. In January 1982, the regulatory climate shifted and the result was the largest bank merger in the state at that time. NCNB exchanged just more than 2.1 million shares worth about $32.2 million for the Bank of North Carolina.

After joining the NCNB board, Spangler was elected to other major boards, including Jefferson-Pilot Corporation and Bell South. He refused to relinquish many of his private posts when he became president of the UNC system in 1986 and ignored criticism from some who claimed it created a potential for conflicts of interest. "I don't know how being friends with people who are influential—how that can lead to compromising the university's strengths or me," Spangler said.

Spangler was still president of the university system in 1991 when he filed a report with the Securities and Exchange Commission revealing that he had bought $100 million worth of NCNB stock in recent weeks. His wife, Meredith, had taken his place on the bank's board. According to *The Story of NationsBank,* "The stock was tremendously depressed—he bought some shares at $19—but he believed in the bank's primary market and had confidence that (Chairman and CEO Hugh) McColl and NCNB's management would work out of the depressed situation."

The purchases left Spangler as the largest single shareholder in the corporation, with eight million shares, or 7.78 percent of the total number of outstanding shares. The stock purchase proved to be a tremendous investment and helped cement his friendly relations with McColl.

Spangler never flaunted his wealth. He wore off-the-rack suits and kept personal cars for years. His favorite after-work activity was repairing antique clocks. He and his wife, who was a Wellesley College graduate and attended the London School of Economics, liked to frequent Chinese and Mexican restaurants in Chapel Hill, and each year made a trip to view new plays in London's West End theater district.

Before he was chosen as president of the university, Spangler had been involved in public education as a member of the Charlotte-Mecklenburg Board of Education and as chairman of the state board of education. Because his father and mother placed importance on education, but had never had the chance to pursue their dreams, Spangler said his interest "was clearly connected to my mother and dad's awe of education."

He decided to run for the Charlotte-Mecklenburg Board of Education in 1972 primarily because he felt the public education system needed support following court-ordered busing. "We ought to be more concerned about school at the end of the bus ride, rather than the length of the bus ride," Spangler told voters in that campaign.

He served four years and left feeling the local schools "were in pretty good shape." But he was remembered by many as the school board member who made the motion at a televised meeting to fire then-Superintendent Rolland Jones. "It carried, and Spangler was roundly criticized for the way he did it—in public, without giving Jones prior warning," the *Charlotte Observer* reported. "But most school officials agreed it was necessary to restore confidence to the system."

Spangler said that public education was as central to the nation as democracy itself. "You cannot live in our country and have an elitist society," he said. "You're always going to have discrepancies in the net worth of these people, our citizens, but you cannot have discrepancies in their ability to think, reason and read."

In 1982, Governor Jim Hunt asked him to become chairman of the state board of education and Spangler accepted "simply to broaden my knowledge." He enjoyed traveling the state to study the public schools and worked hard to try to get more money for public education. Spangler had been in office for only a few days when University of North Carolina President Bill Friday asked him, "Why do you want to do this?" Spangler said he told Friday: "Partly, it was my public education, partly because my mother and father couldn't go to college, and partly because my grandfather couldn't read or write."

Spangler had left the state board and returned to the family business in 1985 when a friend in Charlotte nominated him to become president of the university to succeed Friday, who was about to retire. "I was surprised and more than a little shocked," Spangler said. At first, he turned down the offer and then reconsidered after his wife pointed out that the university had plenty of academic leaders but needed an administrator, which was his strong suit. "I liked the university from the very start," Spangler said. "I liked our team."

His choice as president was unexpected. During Friday's thirty-year tenure the university system had expanded from three campuses to sixteen, with 125,500 students, 28,200 employees, and an annual operating budget of more than $1 billion. But Spangler said he was not intimidated by the Friday legend. "I would rather follow Bill Friday than any other president I could imagine," he told the *Charlotte Observer* shortly after his selection. Spangler always kept a large portrait of Friday on a wall in his office to remind himself and his visitors of Friday's influence on the university system.

Although some on campus considered him aloof, Spangler was not a man of pretense. He often answered his own telephone and kept two Kennedy rockers in his office so he could leave his desk to sit closer to a visitor.

Spangler said his business background helped him link the academic community with business and industry. One of his goals as president of the university system was to increase the amount of scientific and medical research, especially in biotechnology and microelectronics, conducted within the university system. "North Carolina is an emerging state, from the standpoint of economic opportunities," he told the *Charlotte Observer*. "It really is North Carolina's time at bat, and I think the university is one of the prime places where thinking about the future can take place."

Spangler was a tireless promoter of the campuses and used his business connections to push for reforms. He organized a statewide effort in 1993 supporting a $310 million UNC bond issue to build new buildings. After publicly noting that the system needed more female leaders, he named women chancellors at the University of North Carolina at Asheville and the University of North Carolina at Greensboro. During his tenure, he oversaw the selection of new chancellors at all sixteen campuses, as leaders either retired or were replaced.

Spangler took a very personal approach to his job as president. After the chancellor of a campus in eastern North Carolina suspended classes because a broken water main left buildings without water, Spangler complained that the chancellor should have called him in advance to find another solution. "We could have bused in water," he said. He then called the town's mayor and forcefully urged him to have a water tower built that would prevent a repeat of the mishap. "I went down there about six months later and saw the biggest water tower I have ever seen," Spangler said.

He never stopped being a capitalist even while managing the university. In 1988 he tried unsuccessfully to buy RJR Nabisco, then the nation's nineteenth-largest corporation, after former RJR President Ross Johnson proposed moving the company's headquarters from Winston-Salem to Atlanta. Spangler proposed a leveraged buyout to Equitable Life Assurance Society Chairman Richard Jenrette, an old friend from UNC and Harvard Business School. "I wasn't particularly pleased about their moving to Atlanta," Spangler said, adding that he thought if he could buy the company, he would keep its headquarters in Winston-Salem.

Spangler's nose for deals continued with the $1.2 billion takeover of National Gypsum Company in 1995 through his investment firm, Delcor, Inc. Spangler began investing in Charlotte-based National Gypsum in 1993 after the nation's second largest wallboardmaker emerged from bankruptcy court reorganization. National Gypsum was founded in 1925 in Buffalo, N.Y. Its main business, Gold Bond Building Products, moved to Charlotte in 1978 and its corporate headquarters moved there in 1993. It employed about 2,600 people, with 250 in Charlotte.

Spangler remained proud of his university service to the end. "I am now well into my tenth year as president of the university," he wrote to the board of trustees in 1995. "With each day I am more impressed by its strengths and by the varied source of those strengths." He pledged to keep tuition low for in-state students, saying, "One of the university's historical and unique characteristics is its low tuition, rooted in the state constitution and protected for two centuries. The concept that the cost of higher education should be borne by all taxpayers, all of whom benefit, rather than by students and their families, is fundamental to this university's success."

Eventually Spangler and his wife endowed professorships at each of the sixteen UNC campuses, each in the name of a person who had played a significant role in the development of that particular campus. After leaving UNC, the Spanglers moved back to Charlotte, but they bought a home in Chapel Hill, where they continued to spend much of their time because they loved the ambience of the university town.

Over the years, the Spangler Foundation, started by Spangler's father, contributed to nearly three dozen colleges and charitable organizations, including an $8 million gift to Myers Park Baptist Church in Charlotte to build a family life and education center. The family had been among the charter members of the church when it was formed in 1943, and Spangler spent a lot of time there as a youth. Spangler recalled that as a teenager, his weekly church schedule began with Sunday school and continued with church and fellowship on Sunday, choir on Tuesday night, Boy Scouts on Wednesday night and family dinners on Thursday night. "We spent a lot of time at the church and it was all enjoyable," Spangler said.

In January 2001, Spangler was a guest of honor at the dedication of the Spangler Center at Harvard Business School. The 121,050-square-foot building, which Spangler gave to the university, serves as the campus center for the business school. One of Spangler's daughters, Anna Spangler Nelson, received her M.B.A. from Harvard in 1988 after graduating from Wellesley College. Anna's husband, Thomas C. Nelson, also graduated from Harvard Business School in 1988. Another daughter, Abigail, also a Wellesley graduate, received her Ph.D. in political science from Columbia University.

Spangler received the Harvard Business School's Alumni Achievement Award in 1988. He cochaired his class's thirtieth and fortieth reunion gift campaigns, and, along with his wife, has served on the business school's Board of Directors of the Associates, one of the school's principal advisory bodies. Spangler became a member of Harvard University's Board of

Overseers in 1998 and in 2000 was made chairperson of the business school's visiting committee.

"Dick and Meredith have been wonderfully generous in their support of HBS over the years," Dean Kim B. Clark said. "They live the values and principles the school holds dear. It is an honor to have their names linked to the Harvard Business School in perpetuity through the building that will bear their name."

At a Class Day gathering in June 2000, Spangler explained why he gave the university the new campus center by quoting a passage from Samuel Beckett's play *Waiting for Godot:* " 'Let us do something while we have the chance. It is not every day that we are needed.' "

Marion A. Ellis is a Charlotte-based writer specializing in corporate histories and biographies. He is the coauthor with Howard E. Covington Jr. of Greensboro of Sages of Their Craft: The First Fifty Years of the American College of Trial Lawyers; Terry Sanford: Politics, Progress, and Outrageous Ambitions; *and* The Story of NationsBank: Changing the Face of American Banking.

For more information, see:
Spangler, C. D., Jr. File. Robinson-Spangler Carolina Room, Public Library of Charlotte-Mecklenburg County.
———. Interview by author. Levine Museum of the New South, 2001.

Covington, Howard E., Jr., and Marion A. Ellis. *The Story of NationsBank: Changing the Face of American Banking.* University of North Carolina Press, 1993.
Ellis, Marion A. *By a Dream Possessed: Myers Park Baptist Church.* Myers Park Baptist Church, Charlotte, 1997.

LOUIS V. SUTTON

By Charles A. Clay

"Low Voltage" and high-powered? They seem a contradiction in terms. In a way, though, they both applied to L. V. Sutton, the man who built the foundation that enabled Carolina Power and Light Company to become a Fortune 500 company. In a barb aimed at CP&L's opposition to Rural Electrification Administration (REA) electric cooperatives during the early 1950s, Governor W. Kerr Scott christened Sutton "Low Voltage" Sutton, although his name really was Louis Valvelle.

Sutton had registered his opposition to what he called the "creeping socialism" of the federally financed REA program. He was acknowledged as a national leader and spokesman for private power companies and as a genius in the financial structuring and organization of such firms.

In March 1951, when the *News and Observer* featured him as a "Tar Heel of the Week," Sutton said he felt he had lived and worked long enough in the state to be considered a native. He had moved from Virginia to North Carolina in 1912 at the age of twenty-three. Sutton was born in Richmond in 1889, just three years after Thomas A. Edison had invented the light bulb at Menlo Park, N.J. Sutton's father, a tobacco manufacturer, encouraged his son's fascination with electricity by building him an electrical workshop in their backyard, instead of requiring him to work in the family business.

Sutton graduated from Virginia Polytechnic Institute in Blacksburg in 1910 with a degree in electrical engineering. While there he met Cantey McDowell Venable, a daughter of University of North Carolina President Francis P. Venable, and they were married in 1912, the same year Sutton went to work for CP&L. Dr. Venable, who was president of the university from 1900 to 1914, also was a renowned chemist. His daughter was a vivacious young actress and painter who became a leader in the arts and cultural affairs of North Carolina. Thus, Sutton arrived in the state with good connections.

CP&L was founded in 1908 when the harnessing of electricity from the state's rivers was in its infancy, and electric lights were still found only in the cities and towns. The company had about 1,150 customers in Raleigh and a few other smaller towns and annual revenues of about $145,000. After signing on with CP&L, Sutton spent the next twelve years learning the

Louis V. Sutton (Courtesy of Carolina Power & Light Co.)

business under the tutelage of P. A. Tillery, whom he later succeeded as president and general manager. On the way up the corporate ladder, Sutton served as statistician, assistant engineer, division manager, commercial manager, and assistant to the vice president.

Years later, in a 1958 address to the Newcomen Society in New York, Sutton spoke of an important lesson Tillery taught him as a young executive: "In 1926, he summed up his compelling interest in industrial development thus: 'There may have been room for argument as to which came first, the hen or the egg, but today there is no uncertainty as to which must come first, power supply or industrial development. Industry cannot and does not come first and power development second. . . . The modern power company must and does build new plants in anticipation of future demand and need of the communities it serves. . . . "

On the occasion of the 1958 speech, North Carolina Governor Luther H. Hodges introduced Sutton.

The CP&L president returned the favor by telling his audience that Hodges had courageously pushed a corporate income tax reduction through the 1957 General Assembly. It "immediately brought announcement of millions of dollars in new industry and prompted our sister state to the south to seek the same revision of its own tax structure," Sutton said.

Evidently in recognition of his organizational genius among other private power company leaders in the South, Sutton was lured to Arkansas in 1924, and then to Mississippi in 1927, before returning to CP&L in 1933. Sutton was assistant general manager of the Arkansas Power Company, which had been created by the merger of several small ones. He went to Mississippi Power and Light Company as vice president, general manager, and a director. During the six years he was there, Sutton helped bring about the merger of several smaller firms with the company.

It was during his work in the early years that Sutton recalled attending meetings where Edison lectured on such wondrous things to come as television, air conditioning, talking movies, and all-electric homes. At the same time, Sutton drew a philosophical difference between himself and the electrical wizard of Menlo Park. Also in his 1958 Newcomen speech, Sutton said that Edison, who had died in 1931, "was a humanitarian who turned his inventive genius to the 'service of mankind,' as he put it. He once said: 'The poor man with a family is the man who has my sympathy, and he's the man I'm working for.'"

Sutton added that the private power industry "has continued in the dedication to the 'service to mankind' but it has worked equally for all men, the rich and the poor alike. . . . All industry, including electric utilities, should be afforded the opportunity to continue its 'service to mankind' within the framework of a free enterprise concept of the economy, in which the hope of the highest reward remains the incentive for the greatest effort."

As far back as 1914, Sutton began encouraging the greater use of timesaving electrical devices in the home. "The men who make the most of electricity in their factories and on their farms should afford their wives the same advantages at home," he said. In this matter, Sutton led by example and installed one of the first electric ranges in the home economics department of Meredith College, a school for women in Raleigh. He arranged for the home economics teacher there to test the stove. "It does cook," she reported. "I just baked a fine batch of biscuits." So Sutton put a range in his home where he and his wife tested and developed recipes that went into an "electric cook book" he wrote and published. Slowly, elec-

tric range sales inched upward, along with requests for the cookbook.

These activities were a source of amusement for many of Sutton's power company colleagues, who were dubious about his insistence upon the home market's potential for increasing electricity sales. But this same financial strategy helped Sutton save CP&L during the Depression when Tillery died and Sutton succeeded him as president and general manager on March 23, 1933.

As the Depression worsened, CP&L found trouble on all sides. In response to a general hue and cry for electric rate cuts, state regulators in the Carolinas applied political pressure. Hard-hit consumers were using less and less electricity despite an abundant supply. They called for lower rates that would have reduced earnings further. Also, CP&L's holding company was urging more earnings and reduced operating expenses. Amid the financial peril, CP&L cut the salaries of most of its employees by 10 percent and for those in the upper brackets by 15 percent. Then the order came down for another 10 percent reduction. But Sutton, relying on more revenues once again from the home market, managed to stave off the second salary reduction.

The Depression came in the face of what Sutton called "a great surplus of hydroelectric capacity" and his company reduced rates as demand fell. In 1934, Sutton also introduced an "inducement rate," which cut costs for residential customers who agreed to use more electricity. A question arose over whether rates that differentiated between residential customers would pass regulatory muster. CP&L's parent company, Electric Share and Bond Company of New York, warned against the so-called inducement rate on that basis.

The rate not only went uncontested, it increased home use by CP&L customers by 50 percent in its first two years. And it was put into effect in Tide Water Power Company territory when Sutton personally negotiated CP&L's acquisition of that firm in 1952, adding about eight thousand square miles and sixty thousand new customers to CP&L territory. Between 1932, the year of the Depression's worst impact on the company, and 1958, the year of Sutton's New York talk and CP&L's fiftieth anniversary, the firm's total operating revenues grew from about $9 million to about $70 million. Another high point in Sutton's leadership came in 1948 when CP&L severed its ties to its parent company and became a fully independent, investor-owned utility regulated by the state.

Sutton, who raised about $300 million for CP&L's ongoing construction program during his tenure, relinquished the presidency in 1963 to Shearon Harris, but remained as chief executive officer and chairman of the board. He retired from full-time duty in 1968, but remained as chairman of the board.

Sutton died in Raleigh's Rex Hospital on January 5, 1970, at the age of eighty, too soon to witness the marriage of his grandson (and namesake) to a grand-daughter of Governor Scott, the man who had once dubbed him "Low Voltage." Louis V. Sutton III and Susan Scott, daughter of former Governor Robert Scott, met while they were students at the University of North Carolina at Chapel Hill and were married on May 17, 1980.

Sutton was a leader in numerous organizations concerned with the electrical industry. But he said his election in 1950 to the presidency of the Edison Electric Institute was his greatest achievement. The institute is one of the oldest, largest, and most respected of its kind. Sutton was the first southerner to be elected to its presidency, attesting to the national leadership role he played.

Perhaps the best testimony to the kind of man Sutton was came from the longtime liberal editor of the

News and Observer, Jonathan Daniels. Sutton's death, Daniels wrote, "marked the end of a great American generation" that brought remarkable change to the world. The editorial added: "It was easy to disagree with Louis Sutton; it was never possible to dislike him. He had a firm jaw, but a wide grin. Intensely serious in his business, he enjoyed life more than most men around him. He was both a good builder and good company. He will be missed for both his good works and his high spirits."

Writer Charles A. Clay of Raleigh writer was editor of the Fayetteville Observer *from 1965 to 1978. Prior to that he was a journalist in Durham and Raleigh. He was a member of the North Carolina Industrial Commission from 1980 to 1986 and is the author of a biographical novel,* The Alien Corn.

For more information, see:

"Louis V. Sutton." Tar Heel of the Week. Raleigh *News and Observer,* March 25, 1951.
Riley, Jack. *Carolina Power and Light—A Corporate Biography.* Edwards and Broughton, 1958.

THE TUFTS FAMILY

By M. S. Van Hecke

JAMES W. TUFTS must have been startled. He had spent a small fortune in 1895 and 1896 to develop a charming little winter resort village for sickly middle-class folks. Now, some of his guests were out there in the middle of a pasture playing some fool game. Golf had come to Pinehurst.

In the following century, the name Pinehurst became synonymous with golf. Dozens of amateur and professional tournaments were held on the Pinehurst courses, and the U.S. Golf Association's Hall of Fame was established in the shade of the longleaf pines. In 1999, the U.S. Open, one of golf's four major tournaments, was played on the Pinehurst courses.

James Tufts could not have known that. As a matter of fact, he never played golf, which had been introduced in the United States only a few years earlier. Tufts had no plans to include golf in his fledgling resort, designed as a replica of a New England village. But as Richard Tufts told it, golf came to his grandfather.

"Some hardy enthusiast brought a set of clubs to Pinehurst and by the fall of 1897 it was reported that people were disturbing the cows in their dairy field by chasing a little white ball around," Richard Tufts said in his book, *The Scottish Invasion*. James Tufts surrendered, grudgingly. He ultimately built a six-hole course to satisfy golf-crazed visitors from the North, where the game had been popularized.

It was not much by Pinehurst's later standards—where the No. 2 course came to be regarded as one of the world's greatest. "The early holes consisted of no more than built up tees and a few feet of rolling ground around the hole, but at least it was a start," Tufts recalled.

It took three generations of Tufts to create Pinehurst, considered by many to be the mecca of modern American golf. After its founding by James W., his son Leonard then took it over and made golf there an institution. Leonard was succeeded by his son, Richard, who came to be respected worldwide as an authority on the game.

The Tufts' saga began in the 1860s in Somerville, Mass., where James operated an apothecary shop. The evidence is unclear whether he adapted and improved an idea of a nearby druggist or invented the soda fountain himself, but Tufts became its leading developer and manufacturer.

Until then apothecaries simply sold medications. However, a soda fountain—a marble structure with fizz water and gleaming metal covers over canisters of chocolate, cherry syrup, and other delectables—changed things. Instead of simply a place that dispensed drugs, a shop with a soda fountain became a neighborhood sweetshop and gathering place.

Tufts was modestly successful at making and selling a variety of the marble soda fountains, but he had higher goals. At a high risk, he paid an incredible $50,000 for the right to exhibit his fountains at the 1876 Centennial Exposition in Philadelphia. He did not conduct $50,000 worth of business there, but exhibition visitors from across the country went home to tell about the newfangled invention. Sales of what became the American Soda Fountain Company flourished. Every town had to have at least one. By century's end, one of every two soda fountains in the nation was made by Tufts's firm.

Tufts became a rich man but he was not so fortunate in his personal health. He took frequent vacations and in the winter he headed south, away from the frigid northern weather. In these visits, he conceived the idea of an idyllic retreat where ordinary people in frail health could visit to find comfort.

Tufts's vision led him to an unusual geological formation in North Carolina known as the Sandhills. The region's sandy soil was the remnant of an ancient ocean floor. The land Tufts found had been cleared of timber and was considered unsuitable for cultivation by the locals. However, a Boston friend who had visited the area suggested that Tufts take a look.

Tufts agreed to pay $1 (some say $1.25) an acre to the Page family of the nearby town of Aberdeen to purchase 5,890 acres. Walter Hines Page, a prominent North Carolinian who later became ambassador to Great Britain, wrote a friend: "An old chap in Boston had a wild scheme to make a resort here in the barrens and wastes but is likely to change his mind and forfeit the down payment of $500 when he returns home and thinks it over." Tufts did not change his mind. Encouraged by an author-minister friend, Dr. Edward Everett Hale, he set about creating a new self-sufficient community dedicated to health restoration for people of modest means.

Finding ample labor available at rates of one dollar a day for whites and fifty cents for blacks, Tufts moved

Richard Tufts (Courtesy of Charlotte Observer) and James W. Tufts (Courtesy of Tufts Archives)

quickly. He hired famed landscape architect Frederick Law Olmstead, the designer of New York's Central Park, to plan the village. Construction took a remarkably short seven months. In addition to cutting the winding streets with all utilities, the 450-man workforce in 1895–96 built the forty-five-room Holly Inn, two apartment houses, four boarding houses, and fourteen cottages. The Casino, a community center, also had rooms for boarders. The general store included space for a post office and library. A power plant was erected and a trolley line laid to a nearby train station. A fence surrounded the village to keep out deer and, more importantly, the wild boars that roamed the area. More than 200,000 seedlings and shrubs were planted.

The new community initially was called Tuftsville, but the founder spotted a name he liked better on a list for a development on Martha's Vineyard, where he had a summer home. The name was Pinehurst, which Tufts decided was appropriate since pine trees were abundant in the Sandhills and "hurst" meant a wooded hill in Old English. He obtained permission to use the name. By December 31, 1895, the Holly Inn opened with a few guests, but by April of 1896 the inn was host to one hundred patrons. Room and board were available for twelve to twenty dollars per week.

Writing in the *New England Journal,* James J. Moss described the three-story Holly Inn: "The architecture, simple 'colonial,' had no 'gingerbread cornices or frills,' according to an 1896 promotional piece. The exterior was dominated by broad verandas where visitors could sit and drink in the atmosphere. . . . The walls were 'hand-frescoed;' the furniture was 'the best that money can procure' and each floor boasted 'bath and toilet rooms, one for men and one for women, with hot and cold water. . . . The chef was described as 'a genius in the invention of new dishes,' and guests were served by 'pretty table girls of the white persuasion,' carefully selected by the manager for their 'female charms and feminine grace.'"

Tufts sent letters to medical friends in the North suggesting Pinehurst for patients with weak lungs, a practice he quickly discontinued when he learned that tuberculosis had been found to be contagious. On January 1, 1901, Tufts opened the Carolina Hotel, the centerpiece of the village. With its handsome white columns and wide verandas, the hotel was to become the symbol of Pinehurst and ultimately the name was changed to the Pinehurst Hotel. Although Tufts continued to push development, probably his wisest decision was to overcome his impression that golf was a passing fad and hire a young Scotsman named Donald Ross to teach the sport and direct course construction.

Death came to James Tufts in February 1902 in his quarters at the Carolina Hotel. The *Pinehurst Outlook* reported, "Pinehurst mourns. The founder sleeps. James W. Tufts is dead. He was good. He was great. He was a man among men."

Left to direct the affairs of the American Soda Fountain Company when his father had departed for Pinehurst, Leonard Tufts looked askance at the heavy expenses piling up in the new resort. "In 1904, the resort was losing so much money," the *State* magazine later reported, "he was impelled to come down and liquidate this whimsical white elephant. He came, saw and was conquered." The operating company owed more than a million dollars, according to one report, and there were naysayers who predicted Pinehurst would become "a ghost village." They did not know Leonard. "He stayed with it, sweated out the lean days and started building anew," the *State* reported.

Although his father was a sharp businessman, Leonard was quicker to realize the economic power of golf. He teamed with course builder Donald Ross to develop golf as the attraction that made Pinehurst famous. The partial course started by James Tufts was expanded to become No. 1. Pinehurst's premier course, No. 2, was completed in 1907. No. 3 was added in 1910, with No. 4 followed in 1919.

The clientele, meanwhile, was changing. No longer was Pinehurst promoted as a resort for the infirm middle-aged. Golf at that time was a rich man's game, and the rich fled the snowy North to play winter golf on Pinehurst's famed sand greens. For the first three decades of the twentieth century, Pinehurst was one of the elite places to be. Tufts ensured that the visitors had a good time. In addition to golf, he added bird hunts, horse races, fox hunts, archery, and even polo. He also ordered the construction of a newer, closer train station, with direct service to New York City, so a visitor could board at night and be in Pinehurst for a 9 A.M. tee time.

After the famous sharpshooter Annie Oakley was injured in a train accident, she was invited to Pinehurst to recover. She stayed for years, giving exhibitions and teaching easterners how to shoot.

The wealthy northerners were not the only ones to play at Pinehurst. Tournament after tournament was staged for leading amateur and professional golfers. The 1936 Professional Golf Association (PGA) Championship, the North-South Open, North-South Amateur, and the 1951 Ryder Cup (which the U.S. won) were all played there.

Ben Hogan, who had not had a win after eight years on the tour, beat Sam Snead to win the 1940 North-South Open, while the legendary Bobby Jones watched from the gallery. Snead won the next year. The University of North Carolina's Harvey Ward won the 1948 North-South Amateur, defeating Wake Forest's Arnold Palmer in the semifinals. Morganton's colorful amateur, Billy Jo Patton, won three tournaments at Pinehurst.

Leonard Tufts retired in 1928 and lived until 1945. He turned Pinehurst over to his son, Harvard-educated Richard, who had joined management of the resort in 1919 after serving in the navy during World War I. A fine amateur golfer in his own right, Richard became a leading writer about the sport and wrote *The Principles of the Rules of Golf*. He was a member of the Royal and Ancient Golf Club of St. Andrews, Scotland, and served as president of the U.S. Golf Association.

Richard had the sand greens replaced with grass ones in 1935, had No. 4 course rebuilt, and added No. 5 in 1961. He served as captain of the 1963 U.S. Walker Cup team of amateurs, rallying his players after they had fallen behind. He described the 12-to-8 victory as "far and away the greatest thrill I've had in golf."

Pinehurst's golden era ended with the stock market crash of 1929 and the Depression. Things got even worse with World War II. The Mid-Pines resort, a Tufts venture designed to attract Pinehurst regulars to an exclusive club, went into default and was sold to John Sprunt Hill of Durham. There were other things to think about besides golf. Despite the turn of events, many of the great families of American business and finance still maintained winter homes at Pinehurst and it continued to be the capital of golf in the South. General George Marshall retired there after serving as U.S. secretary of state.

But economics continued to work against the luxury resort. In 1970, Pinehurst was sold to the Diamondhead Corporation, a New York real estate company, for $9 million. As real estate developers were wont to do, Diamondhead began to vastly increase the size of the resort, adding courses No. 6, 7, and 8, building condominiums by the dozens, and selling newly developed lots. It did not work out well. After successive annual losses of $3 million, $8 million, and $11 million, lenders foreclosed in 1980. That same year, a saddened Richard Tufts died.

Club Corporation of America soon took over, moderated many of Diamondhead's changes, and began to restore much of the luster. As a tribute to Pinehurst's place in golf, the prestigious U.S. Open was held there in 1999. Millions watched on television as the popular golfer Payne Stewart rolled in a fifteen-foot birdie putt on the 18th green to dramatically seize the championship. It was played, of course, on Pinehurst No. 2.

M. S. Van Hecke is a former editor-writer for the Charlotte Observer *now living in Waxhaw. He wrote and produced* A Free and Independent People, *a video history of Charlotte and Mecklenburg County narrated by Charles Kuralt.*

For more information, see:

Capps, Gil. "How Golf Arrived in Pinehurst." N.C. Citizens for Business and Industry, March 1999.

"Constructing Eden." *New England Quarterly,* September 1999.

Leighton, Jeff. *Pinehurst.* Pinehurst, Inc., 1997. Videocassette.

North, Raymond. *The Barren Land: The Pinehurst Story.* Resorts of Pinehurst, 1985.

"Pinehurst and the Village Chapel." Pinehurst Religious Association, 1957.

Stewart, Payne. "A Golfers Scrapbook." PGA-TOUR.com.

JOHN H. WHEELER

By Alice Eley Jones

DURHAM BANKER John H. Wheeler stood out among that city's elite African American businessmen in his steadfast support for civil rights reform, relying on a favorite creed: "The Battle for Freedom Begins Every Morning." At the same time, he used the Mechanics and Farmers Bank to build black businesses and develop the potential of young African Americans, from tennis professional Arthur Ashe to the Urban League's Vernon Jordan.

Fresh from graduation at Atlanta's Morehouse College, Wheeler joined the black-owned Mechanics and Farmers Bank in Durham in 1929 and rose through the ranks to become its president twenty-three years later. During civil rights demonstrations in the sixties, Wheeler opened the bank doors as a refuge for marchers in the cold, wintry days and helped pay for food and drink for demonstrators out of his own pocket. He pushed Governor Terry Sanford to move faster and go further, often advocating a modern equivalent of the Emancipation Proclamation. Then, he helped Sanford found the North Carolina Fund, the state's most ambitious antipoverty project of the era.

Born January 1, 1908, on the campus of Kittrell College in Vance County, John Hervey Wheeler was the second child and only son of John Leonidas and Margaret Hervey Wheeler. His father was president of Kittrell College, a four-year college that had been founded by the African Methodist Episcopal Church in 1885. Young John grew up in a home filled with Christian values, intellectual stimulation, music, art, and the belief in being of service to your fellow man, as the Wheelers prepared their children to be useful citizens and responsible adults.

The year of John's birth was one of transition for the Wheeler family. John L. Wheeler left Kittrell College to work for North Carolina Mutual Life Insurance Company in Durham. Even though the company preached Booker T. Washington's philosophy of industrial training for the black masses, Mutual employees came from the "talented tenth," the intellectual education philosophy of W. E. B. Du Bois. Of the twenty full-time staff members in 1912, eleven were women, the majority of whom had college experience. Three-fourths of the employees came from North Carolina and about half from Durham. Most of the men had been "professors."

John H. Wheeler (Courtesy of Charlotte Observer)

Wheeler managed the Raleigh district before moving to Atlanta in 1912 to become the state agent and supervisor for Alabama, Georgia, South Carolina, and Tennessee. Young John attended public school as far as the seventh grade, which was the limit of public education for black children, and then finished at Atlanta's Morehouse College, which taught grades eight through college.

Wheeler's family was part of Atlanta's substantial middle class that included men and women whose names would become known across the land. Among them were Walter White, who later became head of the National Association for the Advancement of Colored People (NAACP); the Reverend Martin Luther King Sr.; Mattiwilda Dobbs, who later performed with the Metropolitan Opera in New York; Bishop Wesley J. Gaines of the A.M.E. Church, who was the founder of Atlanta's Morris Brown College and the guiding force behind the building of Big Bethel A.M.E. Church in Atlanta (the Wheelers' church); and Dr. John Hope, the president of Morehouse. Alonzo P. Herndon, the city's wealthiest black and founder of Atlanta Mutual Life Insurance Company in 1905, also was a contemporary.

John majored in accounting and finance and worked as an assistant in the Auburn Avenue branch of the Atlanta Public Library system. In the 1927–28 school year, he was chosen to direct operations of the Morehouse College Library while the librarian was away. His talent as a violinist made him a local celebrity.

The most ambitious self-help agency in Atlanta was the Neighborhood Union, a pioneer effort in community organization begun in 1908 by Mrs. Lugenia Hope, the wife of the Morehouse president. Starting with a house-by-house survey to determine the needs and grievances of black residents of Atlanta's West End, the organization quickly established a health clinic, which also served as a community center, combining educational, social, and political activities. The union was child-oriented, providing vocational classes for children and a boys' and girls' club.

Union leaders were active lobbyists who frequently appeared before the city council to denounce inadequate or nonexistent public facilities in black areas. The group also went to the school board to request more schools and higher pay for teachers. By 1911 the Neighborhood Union covered five black sections, and four years later expanded its services to the entire city. Years later the legacy of Atlanta's Neighborhood Union would inspire Wheeler's work as chairman of the Durham Committee on the Affairs of Black People.

Wheeler was interested in working in Durham and while he was a senior at Morehouse, he talked to people at both Mechanics and Farmers Bank and North Carolina Mutual. The bank had been founded in 1908 by a group of African American businessmen, most of whom were affiliated with the insurance company. Just before graduating with honors in 1929, he received a wire from Mechanics and Farmers offering him a job at $60 a month, and he accepted. He later learned that North Carolina Mutual had agreed to offer him a job as auditor at $110 a month. However, Wheeler believed his chances of advancement were better at the bank and never regretted the decision. Wheeler started as an assistant cashier and within two years he was promoted to vice president and cashier.

Mechanics and Farmers Bank was located on Durham's West Parrish Street and shared office space with North Carolina Mutual. The combined assets of the bank and insurance company—which was the largest African American business in the world—elicited the claim that West Parrish Street was America's "Black Wall Street."

Mechanics and Farmers Bank struggled during the Depression but it never closed its doors. "After the bank holiday in 1933, a quantity of banks were not allowed to re-open, but we opened our doors the first day of business. The criteria for allowing banks to re-open included strength of management and soundness of assets," Wheeler later said.

On December 25, 1935, Wheeler married Selena Warren, the only child of Dr. Stanford L. Warren, a prominent physician who had helped found Durham's Lincoln Hospital. Dr. Warren's wife was a Howard University graduate who had come to Durham to teach but in 1919 opened Durham's first beauty salon to serve both black and white patrons. John Wheeler and Selena Warren courted for three years while John established himself at the bank, and Selena finished her studies at Howard University and Hampton Institute, where she earned degrees in library science. They married, and their first child, Julia, was born in 1937. She later succeeded her father as president and CEO of Mechanics and Farmers Bank before her retirement in 2000. A second child, Warren Hervey, who became a pilot and owner of his own commuter airline, was born in 1943.

In 1936, Selena Wheeler became director of the Stanford L. Warren Library, one of only a handful of private African American libraries in the country. The library, which had opened in 1913 in the basement of White Rock Baptist Church, was named in honor of her father. Under Selena Wheeler's administration, various educational, cultural, social, and recreational activities were implemented, similar to those of Atlanta's Neighborhood Union. She served on the board of trustees of the library, which was incorporated into the public library system in 1946, until 1966. She served as a member of the Durham County Library Board from 1978 until 1985. On April 8, 1990, the Negro Collection was named the Selena Warren Wheeler Collection to honor her and her staff.

During the war years of the 1940s, John Wheeler enrolled as a law student at North Carolina College for Negroes (later North Carolina Central University). Due to a shortage of students during the war, the college scheduled its classes at night, which allowed Wheeler to continue working full-time at the bank during the day. He became one of the first to graduate in 1947 and was admitted to the North Carolina Bar that same year. Admitted to the bar with him were Conrad O. Pearson and Floyd McKissick, who became Durham's leading civil rights attorneys during the coming decade. Wheeler was sworn in as a practicing member of the Supreme Court bar.

After he was named president of Mechanics and Farmers in 1952, Wheeler led the bank to a position as one of the nation's leading African American financial institutions. He was a longtime member of the NAACP and assisted in the litigation that brought about the desegregation of the Durham city schools. In recognition for his service, the NAACP awarded him the Page One Award.

Wheeler's influence was most evident through his leadership of the Durham Committee on Negro Affairs (DCNA). The committee, one of the nation's most effective political organizations, became a powerful force in the politics of Durham and North Carolina. Founded in 1935 at the Algonquin Tennis Club, a private black club where Arthur Ashe and Althea Gibson once played, the committee was organized around smaller committees and dealt with issues of housing, health, politics, education, economic development, and business, much like the Neighborhood Union of Atlanta. The committee organized black voters and endorsed candidates, thereby influencing the outcome of Democratic Party primary elections, as well as votes on local bond issues.

Wheeler's bank became the headquarters of the DCNA, which was later renamed the Durham Committee on the Affairs of Black People. The Mutual and its leaders functioned as the catalysts in the conversion from the old politics of abstinence to the New South politics of re-enfranchisement. At a practical level, the Mutual supplied the men and the means to organize the electorate and to keep it organized. As dean of this talented group, Wheeler served as its ablest tactician and toughest negotiator.

Wheeler's strength lay in his access to the white political establishment and his ability to remain untouched by the pressure brought to bear on black businessmen who depended on the white economy. Wheeler lobbied steadily for change. When black students in Durham launched sit-ins and picketed segregated establishments in 1960, Wheeler was pressured by leading white interests in the city to stop the demonstrations. In response, he drafted a statement of support and joined the picketers himself to make his position unmistakable. He also arranged for black businesses to furnish bail assistance for young people arrested in demonstrations.

Wheeler was instrumental in securing Ford Foundation grants for the North Carolina Fund, which was created by Governor Terry Sanford in 1963. The grants supported the fund's five years of work in improving education, housing, and care for impoverished whites and blacks. Ford Foundation President Henry Heald's visit to Wheeler's office in Durham was the first such call paid by a member of the foundation's senior management.

Wheeler became the leading figure of West Parrish Street. Well-dressed, self-assured, friendly, quiet spoken, a critical thinker, and a man of compassion who felt at ease with factory workers and presidents, he supported community causes and believed in the dignity of every man. His office was open to any who sought his help, including Benjamin Ruffin, a student at North Carolina Central and a leader in the demonstrations in the early 1960s who would later chair the University of North Carolina's Board of Governors. He visited Wheeler's office and their talks profoundly affected his life.

Wheeler gave his support to other African Americans seeking careers in banking. He instituted a training and internship program at the bank that provided leadership skills and expertise not generally open to prospective black bankers in the nation and state. He singled out young people whom he thought had potential and helped them with counsel and encouragement. Among those he helped were Wimbledon champions Arthur Ashe and Althea Gibson (Wheeler was a talented tennis player), Howard Lee, who became state Secretary of Natural Resources and Community Development, and Vernon Jordan, later the executive director of the National Urban League.

Wheeler was instrumental in shaping health care in the city. He served on a commission that established Durham County Hospital and later secured federal funds to convert the old Lincoln Hospital, established by his father-in-law, into the Lincoln Community Health Center.

Wheeler was the first African American elected president of the Southern Regional Council, an honor of which he was particularly proud. He was a member of the Commission on Race and Housing, the President's Committee on Equal Employment Opportunity, the President's Committee on Urban Housing, and the Governor's Council for Economic Development.

In 1964, President Lyndon Johnson appointed Wheeler to a team of Americans visiting the Republic of Germany to review its progress under the Marshall Plan. He was a consultant and lecturer for the State Department in Egypt and Syria, and was chairman of a White House Conference Work Session entitled "To Fulfill These Rights."

Wheeler was chairman of the board of Atlanta

University and was the youngest member ever (at age twenty-nine) to be appointed to the board of trustees of Morehouse College. John H. Wheeler Hall on the Morehouse campus, which houses the business administration and social sciences departments, was dedicated in his honor in 1975. He received honorary degrees from Duke University, Morehouse, Shaw University, Johnson C. Smith University, and North Carolina Central University.

Wheeler suffered a stroke on June 20, 1978, and died on July 6. Following the example of community service established by her family, Wheeler's daughter donated the former Mechanics and Farmers Bank building at 615 Old Fayetteville Street to the St. Joseph Historic Foundation for use as a museum dedicated to the history of Durham's African American community. In 1997 the bank also donated land at Fayetteville and Pilot streets to the North Carolina Central University Foundation.

Wheeler maintained a vision for his people in the New South. He embodied qualities that African Americans will need to follow through, qualities that were summed up in his own personal credo: "Hard work, thorough training and tenacity, a genuine interest in other people, and intense self-discipline."

Alice Eley Jones of Durham is a history consultant and owner of Historically Speaking. She is a graduate and former history instructor at North Carolina Central University and has served as an adjunct professor at Duke University. Her research and curricula are centered on African American history and culture in North Carolina.

For more information, see:

Anderson, Jean Bradley. *Durham County: A History of Durham County, North Carolina.* Duke University Press, 1990.

"Banker with a Mission." *Business Week,* May 16, 1964.

"Decision Led to Banking." *Durham Morning Herald,* August 2, 1953.

Little, Lloyd. "Wheeler: His Commitments Go Far Beyond His Bank." *Carolina Financial Times,* February 9, 1976.

Weare, Walter B. *Black Business in the New South: A Social History of the North Carolina Mutual Life Insurance Company.* University of Illinois Press, 1973.

EDUCATION

O<small>N THE EVE</small> of the twentieth century, Walter Hines Page, a journalist, ambassador, and one of the state's loving critics, lamented the lack of libraries in the state. " . . . nor do the people yet read," Page went on, "nor have the publishing houses yet reckoned them as patrons, except the publishers of school books." The reason was simple: Nearly three out of four white North Carolinians were illiterate, and the number of illiterate African Americans was even higher. While textbooks did exist, they were used less than a month out of the year, with the few public schools operating on sporadic schedules interrupted by lack of funding and the harvest cycle. Education was an afterthought amidst the economic wreckage of the late nineteenth century, despite the state constitution's bold declaration to the contrary.

Considering the situation, it is surprising that North Carolina produced any leaders in education at all, or at the very least so many early in the century. But it was perhaps because conditions were so deplorable that determined and dedicated men and women overcame considerable odds to raise institutions that would later provide the state with a reputation for enlightened and creative leadership.

No one person improved the level of public education more than J. Y. Joyner, an easterner who as state superintendent of public instruction in the century's first twenty years not only implemented the education program wrought by Governor Charles B. Aycock, but carried it well beyond. Joyner created the modern school for the state and pursued legislation to see that children were in classrooms with a teacher rather than inside a textile mill.

It took another champion, Dallas Herring, also an easterner, to shape a vision for the future of public education out of the turmoil of the era of desegregation. He spearheaded the leap forward in state funding for education in the early 1960s and the creation of the modern community college system, which extended post–high school education to virtually every corner of the state.

From the start, education in the state's rural reaches was almost a secondary consideration among those who worked the land and saw little use for schooling. Sheer grit and determination steeled Blanford B. Dougherty and his brother, Dauphin D., to continue their Watauga Academy, a simple private school in Boone that offered critical supplemental education following the state's ten weeks of "free school." B. B. Dougherty was unrelenting in pressuring the General Assembly to train more teachers. His work led to the founding of Appalachian Training School, the forerunner of what later became Appalachian State University. Likewise, President Leo Jenkins, the persistent champion of East Carolina University, used political persuasion and regional ambition to expand his school from a regional teachers' college into a research university with a four-year medical school and teaching hospital.

The odds against success were even greater for Durham's James Shepard, who opened a training school for African American ministers and teachers that in 1925 became North Carolina Central University and the first liberal arts college for African Americans in the nation. Other black educators like Charlotte Hawkins Brown also struggled against discrimination in funding that usually left black students and teachers with worn-out textbooks and rickety school buildings. Brown's privately funded Palmer Institute near Greensboro flourished for more than fifty years as the parents of African American children across the South sought an alternative to the separate and unequal standards that were finally overturned by the Supreme Court's 1954 decision. Equally steadfast in upholding the dignity of education was Willa B. Player of Greensboro, the president of Bennett College, a Methodist school in Greensboro. Her students were known for their white-glove manners and social graces, but President Player stood with them when they freely accepted jail over the humiliation of being turned away at a downtown Greensboro lunch counter.

No leader of a private college was more ambitious than William P. Few, whose Trinity College in Durham shared the support of the state's Methodist Church. With James B. Duke's money, Few transformed Trinity College into a modern university named for Duke's father, Washington Duke. With Duke's money Trinity surged past the other major denominational campuses at Davidson College (Presbyterian) and Wake Forest College (Baptist), whose courageous president, William L. Poteat, defended academic freedom in North Carolina with his opposition to antievolution legislation in the 1920s.

The private and public campuses were home to world-renowned scholars like Chapel Hill's Archibald Henderson, a mathematician and biographer of George Bernard Shaw, and historian John Hope Franklin, the state's only Medal of Freedom honoree, who began his teaching career at Raleigh's St. Augustine's College and ended it with emeritus status at Duke.

Throughout most of the century, the University of North Carolina at Chapel Hill was considered the brightest light in the public education firmament. A parsimonious legislature hobbled growth in the early years until the vision of one inspired president—Edward Kidder Graham—produced money for a campus built by yet another—Harry Chase. Their eventual successor, William Friday, maintained standards established by these men and other UNC leaders, such as Presidents Frank Porter Graham and Gordon Gray, business manager W. D. Carmichael Jr., and librarian Louis Round Wilson. Friday's term lasted an unprecedented span of nearly thirty years as he directed the growth of higher education that saw the inclusion of the new campus at Charlotte, whose University of North Carolina at Charlotte grew from a postwar GI program managed by Bonnie Cone to one of the largest student bodies in the state. Added to the system, too, were the campus at Pembroke, the first institution of higher learning created for Native Americans, and Shepard's North Carolina College.

CHARLOTTE HAWKINS BROWN

By Lydia Hoffman

Charlotte Hawkins Brown (middle) (Courtesy of N.C. Office of Archives and History)

CHARLOTTE HAWKINS BROWN'S brand of racial uplift earned her the name "the first lady of social graces" from former First Lady Eleanor Roosevelt, and this daughter of North Carolina used her well-honed skills in rhetoric and social engagement to confront and challenge the system of Jim Crow, not only in her home state, but nationally. Her tireless efforts as an advocate for interracial cooperation and women's rights secured her place as a noted political activist during the nadir of post-emancipation African American history. Through the school she founded at age eighteen and led for over fifty years, Brown helped to educate a generation of young black men and women who would become leaders in the struggle for political equality in the United States.

Lottie Hawkins, as she was known as a child, spent her early years in the farming community of Henderson, where she was born in 1883. With her mother

Caroline (Carrie) Frances Hawkins and her brother Mingo, she lived in a small cottage that sat not far from where her grandparents once worked as slaves. She believed that her father, Edmund H. Hight, once lived on the adjacent plantation, but the specifics remain unknown. He did not stay with the family after her birth.

The Hawkins's home was one were children thrived and were "well brought up." No one dared to smoke, drink, or gamble in Carrie Hawkins's presence. Although strict, Hawkins created an environment where her children would become self-confident, well educated, and aspire to live beyond the constraints of discrimination. Instruction in what she believed to be proper conduct and culture would help them to challenge the regulated second-class position of African Americans in the post–Civil War South.

She taught her children to read and to appreciate

oration, art, and music. The family regularly held poetry readings and five-year-old Lottie participated by reciting a short psalm or two. The piano that stood in the front parlor, which no one in the house could play, imparted to the young Hawkinses that they and other African Americans belonged in a house with cultural amenities, and that the color of one's skin did not dictate how one should live.

Although the Hawkins family fared better than many other African Americans in turn-of-the-century North Carolina, the omnipresence of white supremacy relegated them to the margins of society. To escape the suffocating effects of Jim Crow laws and segregation, Carrie and others in her extended family moved to Cambridge, Mass., in 1889.

Soon after they migrated, Lottie's mother married Nelson Willis, a native North Carolinian, and the four moved into a large house near Harvard College. Lottie's mother ran a laundry in the basement and boarded African American students who could not find housing in the restricted dormitories nearby. Her daughter helped by ironing handkerchiefs and sewing buttons onto shirts. Lottie Hawkins attended public schools in Cambridge and, at her mother's insistence, she began piano and voice lessons. The most profound change from the segregated South was the makeup of the neighborhood: white and black children, from middle-class homes led by educated parents, attended school together.

During her senior year at the prestigious English High School, Lottie Hawkins changed her name to Charlotte Eugenia, which she considered to be more dignified. By this time she had also lost any trace of her North Carolina accent and her words rang out like a native New Englander.

Her years in Cambridge earned Charlotte a reputation as a determined and intelligent student and community leader. She organized the kindergarten at her church, coordinated the Cambridge High School Association's events, and received praise from both faculty and fellow students for her high marks, oral presentations, and beautifully crafted watercolors. A chance meeting and Charlotte's accomplishments brought her to the attention of Alice Freeman Palmer, the president of Wellesley College, who sponsored Charlotte's entrance into Salem's State Normal School, where she studied to become a teacher.

As the story was told, Palmer noticed a "colored girl" reading Virgil while pushing the pram of a neighbor's child she was baby-sitting. After a short chat regarding Charlotte's knowledge of the classics, the college president made inquiries at the high school about the young scholar's academic performance and future aspirations. She was impressed and maintained tabs on the young woman's progress. When it was time for Charlotte to apply to college, Palmer, a member of Salem's board of trustees, provided a strong letter of recommendation.

Charlotte had been attending Salem Normal School for two years when she met a field secretary for the American Missionary Association on her commute home to Cambridge. The AMA representative explained that she was looking for a person to teach at a small rural school in Sedalia, approximately ten miles east of Greensboro. Charlotte had one more year before she earned her degree, but believed that she could complete her course work over the summer. By the end of their conversation, the woman offered Hawkins the position.

Returning to North Carolina and running a school with little, if any, assistance did not deter eighteen-year-old Charlotte Hawkins. She wanted to teach. She was not unaware that in going south she would have to interact with those who were opposed to the idea of African Americans obtaining instruction in the liberal arts. During this era, industrial education was favored as a means to prepare blacks to become more productive laborers. It was argued that in learning a skill an African American would become an economic asset instead of a burden to the white South. In her first years in Sedalia, Brown accommodated this position, although she believed it was limiting to her students' potential. She wanted to imbue them with the ability to look beyond the kitchen and the workbench and to see themselves as equal participants in American society.

In 1901, the American Missionary Association revoked its funding and Sedalia's school closed for lack of financial support. Although this gave the novice teacher the opportunity to implement her own educational vision of a liberal arts curriculum, free from the tether of a conservative organization, it also meant that she no longer had the AMA to legitimize the school and help bring in funds. As the ruling white establishment in North Carolina was parsimonious in supporting African American schools, what were the chances of a lone black woman procuring funds to improve a ragged, underfunded school of ill-prepared students?

Charlotte had an arduous task before her, but she was not completely alone. Sedalia's Bethany Congregational Church donated an old blacksmith building and a fifteen-acre plot on which to establish a school. The town rallied behind the young teacher and donated time and materials to improve the structure and maintain the grounds, but the school still needed funds for books, desks, writing tablets, and other essentials.

Hawkins turned to the white women she had met during her years in Cambridge for funds to help her realize her vision. In speech after speech at New England summer resorts and Boston churches, she described her plan to build a school in the South "for the betterment of her race." She successfully solicited money from philanthropists, and with two hundred dollars in hand, she returned to Sedalia to open what would become the Alice Freeman Palmer Memorial Institute, named after her benefactress.

After the school's opening in 1902, Hawkins's fundraising efforts to keep the one-room institution open became a full-time job. She hired four women to take over most of the teaching duties. Charlotte lived on the second floor with her colleagues and the girls whose homes were too far away to make the daily trek to campus. Palmer boys lived in rented rooms in the surrounding community or in a donated cabin down the road. With each subsequent year, the number of students arriving from all over Guilford County to attend the only colored school in the county's eastern region grew steadily. They brought with them pigs, goats, sacks of flour, corn, and potatoes—anything that would help sustain the burgeoning program and cover tuition.

Hawkins reached out to local educators for help. With letters of introduction in hand, she called upon Charles McIver, the first president of the State Normal and Industrial School for Girls in Greensboro (later the University of North Carolina at Greensboro), not long after her arrival in Sedalia. Her mission was to procure his endorsement, as president of the Southern Education Association, for Palmer. The president was not available and his wife received the young woman. Their meeting proved to be fortuitous, as Charlotte captured her hostess's interest as she mapped out her plan for building a living and learning academy. Upon her husband's return, Mrs. McIver sang Hawkins's praises to her husband. Sight unseen, McIver wrote a letter in support of Palmer's program. Hawkins used this technique often, currying favor with women connected to men of power or finance to help her access political, academic, and banking institutions.

The town of Sedalia also benefited from her presence. In 1907 she established the Sedalia Home Ownership Association to assist local African American farmers in the purchase of land, thereby helping to create a predominantly black township free from the yoke of sharecropping and tenant farming. Hawkins sponsored parenting and health classes to instruct young mothers and fathers in modern housecleaning methods, basic economics, and the preparation of nutritionally balanced meals, while farmers could attend seminars in agricultural techniques to improve their crop production.

While most of her time was spent in the service of others during Palmer's early years, she did take some time out for herself. She met Edward S. Brown in 1909, during a trip to visit her parents in Cambridge. Brown had been a teacher at Gilbert Academy in New Orleans and rented a room in the Willis's home while taking classes at Harvard. After a summer courtship, Hawkins returned to Sedalia engaged, despite warnings from friends that it might be difficult to balance a marital commitment with the stresses of developing an educational institution.

Edward and Charlotte were married on June 14, 1911, in Cambridge. They did not honeymoon; rather, the new Mrs. Brown spent the summer fund-raising in the Boston area. In the fall, the couple moved to Sedalia. Edward's days were consumed with teaching and serving in the capacity of Palmer's assistant principal. However, he felt more like a competitor than a partner. Students, at times, referred to him as "Mr. Hawkins" instead of "Mr. Brown," adding to his frustration. The two did not have a private residence, and Edward slept with the male students and teachers in the boys' dormitory. Charlotte returned to her room in the girls' dorm. Sadly, Charlotte's friends were correct, and the strained relationship dissolved in 1912, with Edward moving to Tennessee. Their divorce was final in 1916.

During her separation from Edward, Charlotte penned the first of two books. In 1914, she published *Mammy: An Appeal to the Heart of the South* as a general letter of introduction to potential southern allies. The thin volume was intended to disarm her neighbors by appealing to their image of their best selves. She used literature as a means of communicating that she was a respectable lady of letters and worthy of attention. The book told the story of a nonthreatening black woman whose survival depended upon her relationship with whites. Brown's story subtly highlighted the failure of the white majority to address the "Negro problem" of an unemployed and undereducated population of black citizens. Based on an incident that occurred on a farm near Sedalia, *Mammy* told the story of "a faithful colored servant," Granny Polly, who "was but one of many who [were] left destitute in old age by those she ha[d] been faithful to unto death."

Brown brought the same political savvy to her associations with organizations such as the YWCA and

North Carolina Federation of Negro Women's Clubs. She became president of the North Carolina Federation in 1912, went on to hold that post for two decades, and was named as the African American representative on the national board of the YWCA in 1916. She also worked at strengthening networks between herself and other African American educators such as Nannie Helen Burroughs, the founder of the National Training School for Women and Girls in Washington, D.C., and Mary McLeod Bethune, the founder of Daytona Educational and Industrial Institute and later a member of President Franklin Roosevelt's "black cabinet." Brown, Burroughs, and Bethune, the "Three Bs of Education," developed educational programs for African Americans that coupled instruction in academic fundamentals with character development to combat the misconceptions about black life and capability.

Over the years, various institutions and organizations invited Brown to speak on topics of interracial relations, women's issues, and education. In 1927, she became the first African American lecturer on education at Wellesley College. Her affiliation with the National Association of Colored Women, the Southern Interracial Commission, the Interracial Committee of the Federal Council of Churches, the National Urban League, and the Executive Board of the National Association of Teachers of Colored Schools earned her respect as an expert on racial affairs. However, her reputation did not free her from the constraints of her skin color.

During a trip to Memphis, where she was scheduled to speak before the Woman's Missionary Convention (a white women's club organization), train employees physically removed her from the Pullman car for which she held a ticket. As she was marched to the car designated for African Americans, she recognized some of the white women en route to the same meeting. Not one stood or spoke out in her defense. Angered by this experience, Brown inserted the episode into her speech, challenging her audience to resist racist traditions and act in support of African Americans, like herself, who were denied access to that which was their right as citizens. She later filed suit against the Pullman Company for her mistreatment.

Brown's reputation for exceedingly polished manners earned her the attention of Eleanor Roosevelt, and more importantly, became a major factor in the decision of middle-class African American families all over the country to send their children to Palmer during and after World War II. On March 10, 1940, Brown delivered an address on the "Negro and the Social Graces" to a national audience via the CBS morning radio program *Wings Over Jordan*. Not long after the broadcast, Brown began working on her second and final book that focused on this topic. *The Correct Thing to Do, to Say, and to Wear* codified Brown's advice on black folks' behavior. "By social graces I do not mean an attitude of cheap servility assumed for the purpose of currying favor," she wrote. "I mean simply doing the courteous thing. . . . After all, the success of the American Negro depends upon his contacts with other races, [who] through the years have had greater advantages of learning the proper approach to life and its problems. . . ."

Brown was adamant in defining etiquette as a nonracial system available to all classes. She argued that good manners existed as a neutral body of rules and codes of behavior which "white folks have just had more practice in applying." After years of utilizing her good manners and reputation to build networks for the procurement of funds and political influence, Brown's expertise in the rules of behavior became the center of Palmer's curriculum.

In 1961, she succumbed to diabetes in a small hospital in Greensboro at the age of seventy-seven. Funeral services were held Sunday, January 15, in the Alice Freeman Palmer Building on the campus of the same name. Howard University President Mordecai Johnson delivered the eulogy for the school founder and lauded her as a "pioneer in education and race relations for more than fifty years."

The campus Brown created in Sedalia began to lose its appeal with the advent of the changes wrought by the integration of public schools and the rise of the Black Power movement. But the respected and admired educator did not live to see its complete disintegration. The school did not close with her death, as she had feared, although its dependence on her personal efforts and example made it vulnerable. Three presidents followed, but they did not have the powerful personality, dedication, and reputation of their predecessor. In 1971, after a fire had destroyed the central campus building, the Palmer Memorial Institute closed forever. In 1987, the grounds were reopened when the state established the Charlotte Hawkins Brown Memorial.

Lydia Charles Hoffman is a former director of the Charlotte Hawkins Brown Historic Site. She received her B.A. in history from the University of California at Berkeley and her M.A. in history from the University of North Carolina at Chapel Hill. While completing doctoral work in cultural studies at George Mason University, she worked in the Smithsonian Institution's National Museum of American History Affiliations Program Department.

For more information, see:

Brown, Charlotte Hawkins. Papers. Schlesinger Library, Radcliffe College, Cambridge, Mass.

Brown, Charlotte Hawkins. *The Correct Thing to Do, to Say, and to Wear.* Christopher Publishing House, 1941. Charlotte Hawkins Brown Historical Foundation, Inc., 1990.

———. *Mammy: An Appeal to the Heart of the South.* 1914. Reprinted in *African American Women Writers 1910–1940*, general ed. Henry Louis Gates Jr. G. K. Hall, 1995.

Hoffman, Lydia Charles. "The Minding and Marketing of Manners in the Jim Crow South: Charlotte Hawkins Brown and the Palmer Memorial Institute." Master's thesis, University of North Carolina at Chapel Hill, 1997.

Hunter, Tera. "The Correct Thing: Charlotte H. Brown and the Palmer Institute." *Southern Exposure* 11 (September/October 1983): 37–43.

Smith, Sandra N., and Earle H. West. "Charlotte Hawkins Brown." *Journal of Negro Education* 51 (Summer 1982): 191–206.

The Charlotte Hawkins Brown Historic Site is located on the grounds of the Palmer Institute off Interstate 85/40 near Sedalia at Exit 135. For information, call (336) 449-4846.

OLIVE DAME CAMPBELL

By David Whisnant

OLIVE DAME CAMPBELL founded the John C. Campbell Folk School in 1925 at Brasstown and was a tireless and effective worker on behalf of culturally and economically marginalized people in the southern Appalachian region for nearly a half century.

She was born in 1882 in Medford, Mass., and grew up in a genteel environment. Her school principal father stressed education and travel, and the family summered on Nantucket. After graduating from Tufts College in 1903, she taught school for several years. On a trip to the British Isles with her mother and sister, she met and fell in love with John C. Campbell, whose wife had died several years earlier, and who was fifteen years her senior. The two were married the following spring.

After a nine-month honeymoon to Europe, the couple returned to the mountains of north Georgia so that John could resume his work as president of Piedmont College at Demorest. He resigned soon thereafter, however, with the idea of working more broadly in the southern mountains. Nearly ten years of educational work in the Alabama, Georgia, and Tennessee mountains had made him keenly aware of the social and economic needs of the area. After obtaining a small grant from the newly created Russell Sage Foundation to conduct a survey of social conditions in the southern mountains, he and his wife moved to Asheville, where he opened the foundation's Southern Highlands Division.

In 1909, the Campbells set off on a 1,500-mile tour of the mountains, traveling by horseback, wagon, and on foot, and visiting scores of schools and hundreds of homes. John Campbell compiled meticulous data on population, natural resources, working conditions, education, religion, and health and sanitation, while Olive paid particular attention to culture, to children and families, and to class differences. At that time public images of and discourse about mountaineers cast them alternately as either backward and degenerate social misfits or picturesque and uncorrupted full-blooded WASP Americans of the oldest stock. The Campbells, however, approached their work with balance, sophistication, and a deep respect for mountain people, as well as uncommon awareness of the social, economic, and cultural variations in the mountains, and how structural economic and

Olive Dame Campbell (Courtesy of Southern Historical Collection)

social factors impinged upon individual and family life.

Back in their home in Asheville, the Campbells devoted most of their attention to his work on the social survey and to beginning their own family. Two daughters were born to them (Jane in 1912 and Barbara in 1915), but the first died at three months, and the second died when she was two years old. The difficulties of this period in their lives were increased by John's deteriorating health, but they remained optimistic, engaged in their work in the mountains, and remarkably productive.

They were instrumental in founding the Southern Mountain Workers Conference, later the Council of the Southern Mountains, in 1913, which drew together scores of workers in the many church and independent schools and agencies. In 1917, 150 people attended the annual conference, which John Campbell called "one of the best things—if not the best—that I have brought to pass." He died in 1919 at the age of 51, but his wife continued to work in the conference for another decade, helping to guide it through its early years, when denominational and other factional tensions threatened to terminate its work.

During the years of personal anguish and grief surrounding the deaths of her children and husband, Campbell's interest in and work with culture in the mountains expanded and deepened. She was powerfully drawn to the music she heard in people's homes and churches, the quilts and coverlets on their beds, and the baskets and tools they made and used, and she took reams of notes on what she saw and heard. It was cultural work of a pioneering sort, undertaken in unfamiliar territory by a young New England woman who had almost no formal training for the job, but who was bright, observant, and deeply respectful of mountain people.

She had begun her cultural work with ballad singers, some of whom she first heard at eastern Kentucky's Hindman Settlement School in 1908, only months after her arrival in the region. During the months that followed, she collected ballads and songs more widely in eastern Kentucky, north Georgia, and east Tennessee. The scholarly and public interest in ballads that was growing on both sides of the Atlantic soon brought her into a working alliance with British collector Cecil Sharp, and she encouraged him to extend his collecting into the southern mountains. The disruptions of World War I delayed their collaboration, but Sharp returned to collect in 1916, and with Campbell published *English Folk Songs of the Southern Appalachians* the following year. Although it excluded some categories of music known to be present in the area (fiddle tunes, sacred music, and popular songs, for example), it was the first major, carefully documented collection of mountain folk music that was presented in a dignified way, with the integrity of text and tune preserved.

Following the death of her husband, Campbell paused to complete the book he had left unfinished, *The Southern Highlander and His Homeland,* and then turned her full attention to a plan they had discussed together for nearly a decade: to establish in the southern mountains a school modeled on the Danish folk high schools. They had first heard of such schools from U.S. Commissioner of Education Philander P. Claxton at an early meeting of the Conference of Southern Mountain Workers. The schools—which developed out of the ideas of Bishop Nikolai Grundtvig in the 1840s—were designed to educate and "enliven" Danish farmers and rural people. By the turn of the century, folk schools—widely valued for raising the intellectual level of rural people, heightening their political sophistication, and cultivating patriotism—had spread to neighboring countries. Campbell believed that such schools could offer a valuable, culturally based program for the southern mountains that the scores of "church and independent" and industrial schools already there could not offer.

In late 1922, Campbell embarked upon a fourteen-month study tour of Scandinavian folk schools—a trip first planned with her husband nearly a decade earlier, but postponed when World War I broke out in Europe. She visited dozens of schools throughout Scandinavia, ranging from politically and culturally conservative rural ones to politically radical ones that served industrial workers in urban areas. She found herself generally drawn to the simple, gracious daily rituals of folk school life and to the sense of order that underlay them, but she clearly preferred the reassuring rural schools that placed traditional culture at the center of their programs and stressed the personal development of individuals, rather than the urban ones that foregrounded radical political ideology and envisioned major social change.

Campbell returned home convinced of "the soundness of several basic principles of the Danish folk schools," and of their applicability to the southern mountains, despite the failure of efforts by predecessors to establish them among Danish immigrants in the upper Midwest. She chose a site for her experiment at Brasstown, in western North Carolina, near Murphy, and in the spring of 1925 the John C. Campbell Folk School came into being. With volunteer and hired labor from the community, buildings were built on donated land, and the first small classes (in history, geography, agriculture, and Danish gymnastics) were held in late 1927. The school quickly added more buildings, acquired two hundred acres of land for a model farm, and built a dam for its own water supply.

A demonstration farm got off to an auspicious start with a registered Jersey herd, registered breeding stock, a variety of efforts toward scientific farming, and a teaching program for young local farmers. Danish-derived winter folk school courses, handicrafts instruction, short courses on specialized topics, and cooperatives rounded out the program. Campbell's optimistic projections for the agricultural program appeared to be justified. The school was situated on the border of two small, relatively unproductive agricultural counties (Clay and Cherokee), which were far from urban-industrial centers. The region had a substantial and growing number of both farms and farmers, and with some assistance some of the farmers could remain on the land and make decent lives for themselves, rather than emigrate to piedmont textile mills or to low-paying jobs in the city.

The school's work to establish cooperatives was bold and effective in the short term. The cooperative Brasstown Savings and Loan Association was established in early 1926; four years later there were 150 members and depositors. The Brasstown Farmers' Association (a cooperative purchasing association and hatchery) followed in 1928, and by 1934 the Mountain Valley Cooperative creamery was producing over 100,000 pounds of butter annually. Money from private donors provided low-interest loans and leases to young men who wanted to start their own farms.

It was a bold beginning, but not an auspicious time. Just as the school's agricultural programs were becoming fully operational, the Depression drove down farm prices. The advent of the Tennessee Valley Authority in 1933 inflated land prices in the two counties and enticed young men off the farms with the promise of construction work at high wages. World War II drew even more away. By about 1943 it was clear that the conditions that had given birth to the school and facilitated its substantial growth for fifteen years were changing dramatically. Campbell retired as head of the school in 1946 and returned to Massachusetts and to summers on Nantucket, although she continued to offer counsel and advice thereafter. By 1952 the farm and herds were run down, the creamery had been leased to a private operator, and only a few students remained.

Campbell was succeeded as head of the school by Dr. D. F. Folger, who endeavored to retrench and accommodate its program to the postwar needs of returning veterans and the development needs of small communities undergoing rapid social and economic change. Folger's survey of former agricultural students cast doubt on the school's agricultural program: only five of sixty former students were full-time farmers; the majority had settled in cities throughout fourteen states. Disturbed by Folger's analysis and ideas, the board asked for his resignation. The ideas of radical southern churchman Howard Kester, who succeeded Folger, were even less congenial to the school's conservative board; he remained as head only eighteen months.

And yet the school survived, mainly through its cultural—rather than agricultural—programs. From her earliest days in the mountains, Campbell had believed that local culture might offer a possible base for social reconstruction. She toured and studied craft revival and other cultural preservation efforts through-

out the mountains, and came to see the Danish folk schools as models in their incorporation of local culture into all aspects of their programs. When it came to designing cultural programs for the John C. Campbell Folk School, however, it was not merely Danish theory, but also Danish culture itself, that dominated. Early photos attest to the presence of local fiddlers, guitar pickers, and banjo players at cooperative meetings and other school functions, but Danish songs and dances were prominent, with local young people taught by immigrant Danish teachers to execute unfamiliar dances and dance steps such as the "double Tyrolean" and the "Anders hop."

Weaving and woodcarving were especially important in the school's program. A craft guild organized in 1929 grew rapidly; by 1934 it had fifty members, one student was supporting himself and his family by carving, and two former students had opened a woodworking shop. By the early 1940s, ninety local craftspeople were involved, a sawmill and kiln had been installed, and the shop was turning out furniture and church pews.

Connections between the crafts enterprise and local traditions and aesthetics were tenuous at best, however. Instead of adopting the designs of an old furniture maker who lived and worked in Murphy, Campbell asked her family in Massachusetts to send pictures of more elegant New England pieces that folk school students might use as models. Regardless of the models, however, the craft objects made at the school were rendered increasingly anachronistic within the broad process of modernization that was changing local lifeways in Cherokee and Clay counties —bringing in radios and refrigerators, movies and motor cars.

Concurrently with her cultural work in the folk school, Campbell became a founding member of the Southern Highlands Handicraft Guild in 1929. It was a coordinating organization that grew out of the crafts revival "producing centers" that dotted the mountains in the 1920s and 1930s. Emerging initially from informal discussions at meetings of the Conference of Southern Mountain Workers, the guild quickly became the most powerful arbiter of the entire organized crafts enterprise in the mountains. Its committee on standards could in effect certify or discredit any mountain craftsperson. Its prestigious logo was reserved for craft items made by its members, and no other producers were allowed to place items in its crafts exhibitions. In the name of preserving tradition, the guild in effect became a major change agent, shaping design and production standards to respond to the perceived preferences of the middle-class, urban consumers who constituted the bulk of the crafts market.

The John C. Campbell Folk School and its staff played a major role in the guild's development. Campbell took an active part in the meetings that led to its founding, and hers was a respected voice in its protracted discussions of the desirability of commercializing traditional crafts, the relative merit of traditional designs compared with those preferred by studio-trained craftspeople, and the potential of crafts work, however organized, to provide mountain people with significant income. The folk school's crafts director, Louise Pitman, joined the guild's board in the early 1940s, and in 1943 Campbell chaired a committee to chart the organization's future prior to its formal incorporation two years later. She withdrew from active involvement when she retired from the folk school in the mid-1940s, but Pitman became head of the guild soon thereafter.

Olive Dame Campbell was one of the brightest and most sensitive and effective of the many highly motivated young New England women who came to work in the southern mountains between the 1890s and the 1930s. She had a grasp of the relationship between culture and underlying economic and social structures shared by few of her contemporaries. Her nearly forty years of working in the mountains ended in 1946, but her ideas were seminal ones, and her influence has persisted in many forms.

David Whisnant, a native of western North Carolina, is the author of many books and articles on the Appalachian region, vernacular culture, and the politics of culture. He is retired from the faculty of the University of North Carolina and lives in Chapel Hill with his wife, Anne, and two sons, Evan and Derek.

For more information, see:

Papers of John C. and Olive Dame Campbell are archived in the Southern Historical Collection at the University of North Carolina at Chapel Hill.

Becker, Jane S. *Selling Tradition: Appalachia and the Construction of an American Folk, 1930–1940.* University of North Carolina Press, 1998.

Campbell, John C. *The Southern Highlander and His Homeland.* Russell Sage Foundation, 1921.

Whisnant, David E. *All That Is Native and Fine: The Politics of Culture in an American Region.* University of North Carolina Press, 1983.

WILLIAM D. CARMICHAEL JR.

By Kenneth Joel Zogry

CREDIT FOR THE TREMENDOUS GROWTH of the University of North Carolina during the twentieth century, both conceptually and physically, is rightly given to two of its presidents: Frank Porter Graham and William Friday. What is less well known, however, is that the system's success is also due in large measure to the behind-the-scenes work of William D. "Billy" Carmichael Jr. For two critical decades Carmichael served as a liaison, lobbyist, and buffer between the generally politically liberal educators and administrators of the university and the more conservative state legislators, alumni, and large corporate donors.

Carmichael was born July 28, 1900, in Durham, one of four sons of William Donald and Margaret McCaull Carmichael. The family was Catholic, something of a rarity in North Carolina at the time, and he remained close to his faith throughout his life. His father was a former Durham school superintendent who later became an executive with the Liggett & Myers Tobacco Company. Young Carmichael entered the university at Chapel Hill in 1917 on an academic scholarship, but took a year off to serve as a private in the army during World War I.

He returned to the campus in 1919, graduating with a degree in commerce in 1921. Active in campus life, Carmichael was a star basketball player and was a member of the squad his senior year when the team won the Southern Intercollegiate Athletic Association Championship. In 1922 Carmichael moved to New York City and began what became a very successful career in advertising and securities trading. His first position in advertising was with the Newell Emmett Agency, which he left in 1931 to become an associate with Campbell Starling, an investment brokerage. In 1936 he became a partner with Carmichael and Carson and took a seat on the New York Stock Exchange.

In 1940, Carmichael was visited in New York City by Frank Porter Graham, who was the first president of the new consolidated university system that had been created in 1931. Graham was a visionary, an idealist, and an inspired educator. He was not, however, always the most practical administrator and frequently upset the conservative power structure in North Carolina. Aware of his own shortcomings, Graham persuaded Carmichael to give up his lucrative career and

William D. Carmichael Jr. (Courtesy of North Carolina Collection)

return to North Carolina to serve as the university's controller. Graham believed that Carmichael's financial and advertising skills, in conjunction with his political and social connections, wit, and tireless work habits would insure the growth of the university, with its campuses in Chapel Hill, Raleigh, and Greensboro. Graham's powers of persuasion were formidable, and Carmichael could not resist the opportunity to help his alma mater.

Upon his return to Chapel Hill, Carmichael set about making changes to the financial and administrative operations of the university system, along with strengthening ties to the institution's traditional constituency in the state. He freely used school facilities on the Chapel Hill campus such as the Monogram Club, the Carolina Inn, and the box at Kenan Stadium as public relations tools to win the favor of wealthy alums and captains of state industries. He was particularly adept in dealing with legislators, who had the power to make or break the university's budget. Partly in response to the university's dependence on the generosity of legislators, as well as to the haphazard system of fund-raising that existed at the time, Carmichael consolidated, professionalized, and centralized financial giving. This led to several of the largest donations UNC ever received, including the gift by John Motley Morehead of the planetarium on the Chapel Hill campus that bears his name. Though later standard practice, Carmichael was the first administrator to realize the potential of private and corporate partnerships with the public UNC system.

During 1949 and 1950 Carmichael faced the greatest challenges of his career with the university. In March of 1949, Governor W. Kerr Scott appointed Graham to the United States Senate to complete the term of the recently deceased J. Melville Broughton. Though Graham was well-liked and even respected by conservatives as a university president, his liberal social beliefs and organizational affiliations caused widespread concern, especially against the backdrop of the proceedings of the infamous House Un-American Activities Committee. Graham left for Washington immediately, and Carmichael was named acting president. No sooner had he taken over the reins than the University of North Carolina at Chapel Hill was accused of harboring a communist agitator named Hans Friestadt, an Austrian-born graduate student and instructor who was in the United States on a federal scholarship.

The story hit the press, and although Friestadt signed a loyalty oath stating he was not a communist, Carmichael realized the potential damage this could cause the university in the highly charged political atmosphere of the time. To stave off a major public relations fiasco, he called upon his considerable marketing and advertising talents to produce a slick brochure entitled "If We Would Keep The University Free, Then We Must Keep It Free From Those Who Would Destroy It," which was presented to the university's board of trustees in May of 1949. The trustees unanimously approved the document, which stated that the university "in all three of its institutions stands united—unequivocally opposed to Communism . . . because the Communists would destroy the free universities like the University of North Carolina." In an effort to enhance the UNC reputation, Carmichael blanketed the nation with these brochures and was widely praised for the strong stand.

The Freistadt controversy gave Carmichael good reason to believe that the university was under attack for its perceived liberalism, and the North Carolina

senatorial primary of 1950 only increased his anxiety. Graham, with barely a year in office, ran in the spring of 1950 to be the Democratic candidate in the fall and serve the remaining four years of the term. The election was one of the most bitter contests in the state during the twentieth century, and supporters of Graham's opponent, Willis Smith, took aim at Graham with a double-barreled attack accusing him of supporting racial integration and having communist sympathies. To critics of the nascent civil rights movement the connection with communist agitators seemed natural, and Graham's previous political affiliations made him suspect on both fronts.

In the political climate of the cold war South, the combination was lethal: Graham was defeated in a second primary and retired from politics. In the aftermath of the election, Carmichael, who some in the state believed had always tempered Graham's liberalism, faced serious attacks on the university. If Graham supported racial equality and was soft on communism, the prevailing thinking rationalized, then those ideals must be festering at the university he ran for two decades. The future growth and ultimate stability of the university was publicly called into question.

Carmichael saw the change in the political climate and worked tirelessly to maintain a delicate balance between academic freedom and the appeasement of the university's traditional constituency, who controlled the flow of public and private funds into the system. Part of this appeasement included supporting racial segregation, an issue which was ultimately settled when the university was integrated by court order in 1955. Knowing that integration had little support among alumni and powerful state leaders, Carmichael sought to maintain at least the appearance of traditional racial roles on the Chapel Hill campus even after the first African Americans became students.

Carmichael was so successful at steering the university through the treacherous political waters of 1949–1950 as acting president that a number of trustees encouraged him to throw his hat in the ring to fill the position permanently. Carmichael refused, citing his lack of an advanced academic degree and his Catholicism (which he feared might be problematic). Gordon Gray was named president in 1950, and he was succeeded in 1956 by William Friday. Both Gray and Friday relied heavily on Carmichael, particularly in dealings with legislators and trustees. Though his title changed several times, throughout the 1950s Carmichael continued to work his particular brand of magic to help the system move forward, and to maintain peace, particularly between the educators and the legislators. He was well known for being able to diffuse a situation with humor, and for being involved in every aspect of a project (including minute details such as overseeing the design and writing the text for the menus for the Carolina Inn).

Carmichael's projects at all three of the campuses were many and varied. At Chapel Hill, along with projects like the Monogram Club and Morehead Planetarium, he was heavily involved in the postwar Good Health Campaign that led to the development of Chapel Hill's health programs, including the creation of a four-year teaching hospital. At North Carolina State College in Raleigh, he was the driving force behind the construction of the first nuclear laboratory; Reynolds Coliseum; and the completion of the long-neglected memorial bell tower. At the University of North Carolina at Greensboro he was responsible for a large new library and a soda shop. At all three campuses he was instrumental in developing educational television (later UNC Public Television).

Carmichael's health was always precarious and he succumbed to heart failure at the age of 60 in 1961. He was widely mourned by the university community, and in tribute new buildings at each of the three campuses were named in his honor. Three decades after his death, Friday remembered how Carmichael's skills and abilities were keenly missed, especially in such university crises of the 1960s as the cancellation of the Dixie Classic Basketball Tournament in 1961, the Speaker Ban controversy of 1963 and the Food Workers' Strike in 1969.

Kenneth Joel Zogry is executive director of the Pope House Museum Foundation in Raleigh and a doctoral candidate in American history at the University of North Carolina at Chapel Hill. He is the author of The University's Living Room: A History of the Carolina Inn *and* The Best the Country Affords: Vermont Furniture, 1765–1850, *which won the Charles F. Montgomery Award.*

For more information, see:

No archive contains a collection of Carmichael's papers, but a few pieces of correspondence can be found in the papers of Frank Porter Graham, James Spencer Love, Louis Round Wilson, and Gordon Gray at the Southern Historical Collection at the University of North Carolina at Chapel Hill. Papers relating to his tenure with the University of North Carolina may be found in the Records for the Vice President for Finance, University Archives, Wilson Library, University of North Carolina at Chapel Hill.

Board of Trustees, University of North Carolina. "William D. Carmichael Jr.: 1900–1961." Printed resolution. North Carolina Collection, University of North Carolina at Chapel Hill.

Link, William A. *William Friday: Power, Purpose, and American Higher Education.* University of North Carolina Press, 1995.

Zogry, Kenneth Joel. *The University's Living Room: A History of the Carolina Inn.* University of North Carolina at Chapel Hill, 1999.

BONNIE E. CONE

By Laura McAuliffe

BONNIE ETHEL CONE is responsible for nothing less than creating and building a university. In addition, Cone touched so many lives during her lifetime that it seems everyone who came in contact with her (even many who had not) had nothing but wonderful things to say about her. One newspaper reporter described her as "not much taller than her classroom pointer" (she stood five-feet-two) but for such a small woman, she had a huge impact.

Shortly after a profile of Cone appeared in *Time* magazine in 1965, Nigerian Moses F. Ekpo wrote to her saying, "Ain't you the happiest woman in the states? Ain't you in the lucky group of people who live to see their dreams coming off?" Cone is certainly in that lucky group, for she hoped to establish a university that existed previously only in her dreams.

Cone was born June 22, 1907, the fourth child of Charles Jefferson and Addie Lavinia Harter Cone. She grew up in Lodge, S.C., a community of about two hundred residents near Walterboro in the low country. Her father was the mayor of Lodge, as well as a farmer who ran an automobile dealership. Cone knew she wanted to be a teacher before she started the first grade. Her penchant for teaching the chickens in her yard at feeding time became part of her myth. By the time she was seventeen, however, her parents thought she was too timid to attend the school of her choice, Winthrop College, and felt she was too young to attend college right out of high school. Instead she repeated a course in geometry with a different teacher. "It was an enlightening experience," she would later recall. "Under the second teacher, it occurred to me that it wasn't the subject that made the difference, but the teacher."

She entered Coker College, a small institution where the "timid" Bonnie went on to become a student leader, serving as president of the math club and the YWCA, and participating in student government, the science club, basketball, swimming, hockey, and canoeing. She costumed the drama club and was in May Day programs. After graduating magna cum laude in 1928, she began her career as a teacher in South Carolina high schools, where she worked for twelve years under somewhat Spartan conditions. Her starting salary was sixty dollars a month for an eight-month year, and her contract stipulated no card playing, dancing, or riding in cars after dark.

Bonnie E. Cone (Courtesy of Charlotte Observer)

Cone's employment at Central High School in Charlotte, where she began teaching in 1940, set her on the path to building a new university. As Mary Snead Boger wrote in 1972, "Bonnie Cone was 33 when she came to Charlotte—a good teacher, a friendly person, but hardly one to set the educational world aflame. The beauty in her story lies in the continual growth. Each phase of life readied her for the next step."

Cone taught at Central High School on the condition that she would be allowed to teach more than one subject so she would not become bored. She became a roving math instructor, teaching algebra, plane geometry, trigonometry, solid geometry, and calculus. "I had to take my ruler and protractor and carry it from room to room," she said, "but that didn't bother me."

After three years of teaching mathematics, Cone

moved on to Duke University in Durham, where she spent two years as the only woman instructor in the navy's V-12 officer training program. In her free time, she completed her master's degree. Cone wanted to pursue a doctorate, but never found the time. Her parents' only unmarried child, she felt an obligation to be near them. "I didn't want to be away doing doctoral work when I felt I needed to be close to them," she said in 1986.

In 1945, she was called to Washington for a position with the Statistical Division of the Naval Ordnance Laboratory, where she worked in the department that used actuation data to detect mines. During the war, she was considered for the WAVES, a branch of the navy established for women, but was rejected because she wasn't "perfect" (she was missing a molar). At war's end, she resigned and returned to Charlotte and teaching.

In 1946, the University of North Carolina set up twelve extension centers to handle the influx of returning veterans seeking education under the GI Bill. The Charlotte Center, one of the extension offices, operated out of Central High School. In addition to her regular workload, Cone spent seven hours a week teaching forty students engineering math in the evenings. She also took sole responsibility for the testing program, which helped young veterans find their direction.

When the directorship of the Charlotte Center became available in 1947, Superintendent Elmer Garinger named his first choice for the position: Bonnie Cone. She initially turned down the offer because she was sure the job would not last. "I'll just have to keep it going long enough for them to get somebody else and surely they will go out and work to find someone else," she said in 1972.

No one replaced "Miss Bonnie," who found herself running the largest extension program in the state from the former lost-and-found office in the high school. She had a handmade desk and a two-drawer filing cabinet and was given one month to secure the teachers and books she needed to start the second year at the center. She did it. Between administration and teaching, she worked eighteen-hour days, seven days a week. "They were long, hard days, but you had the feeling that you were doing something that was really important," she said. She would not get her own secretary until 1957, ten years later.

Cone tackled her position with gusto, serving as director of the Charlotte Center from 1947 to 1949. When the extension centers began closing in 1949 after the emergency had passed, Cone fought diligently to keep the Charlotte Center open, contending that there was no state college in the Charlotte area that could accommodate students who wanted to continue their education. "There was such a need for a college here," she told *Charlotte* magazine in 1969. "Even after the University at Chapel Hill could take care of the veterans, we still had plenty who needed to attend school here in Charlotte."

Such was the genesis of Charlotte College, which was established as a two-year institution in 1949, with the help of Cone, her friends, and Charlotte city officials. Cone was named director of the college as well as director of the Charlotte Community College System, a position she held until 1961, when she became president of Charlotte College.

Though her responsibilities had expanded well beyond the classroom, she continued to teach until 1959, although she devoted considerable time to lobbying trips to Raleigh. "Teaching was my relaxation," she said. "Basically I'm a teacher, and teaching took some of the frustrations out of administration." The year she stopped teaching was the year the college purchased 270 acres north of the city for a campus of its own rather than old public school buildings. By 1961, when Charlotte College relocated to its northeast Charlotte location, the campus had expanded to nine hundred acres.

Cone's exhaustive lobbying of the legislature paid off. Two years after becoming president of Charlotte College, the General Assembly expanded Charlotte College to a four-year state institution and made it a campus of the University of North Carolina, the first such change since 1931. The expansion of Charlotte College allowed students to commute to the University of North Carolina at Charlotte while they held full-time or part-time jobs, rather than leave their homes and work to enroll at the other state universities in Greensboro, Raleigh, and Chapel Hill.

Cone worked tirelessly to see that the students as well as the college succeeded. She was hardly an impersonal administrator. "I like working with students," she said in 1963, "helping them with their problems —what to study, how to finance their educations, what to do about a personal situation. . . . I just love working with people."

Many of Cone's former students have said they were headed for a mediocre future until Cone got her hands on them and turned their lives around. Jim Matthews, a former biology department chair, recalled Cone's response to students who telephoned the school during a freezing rain to find out if the evening's classes were cancelled. She would "take the headset from the switchboard operator and ask where the student lived, then say, 'If you can't make it, I will come get you.'"

Former Charlotte Mayor Ken Harris said of Cone: "She's the reason I went to college. . . . she's my second Mom. . . . she's a second mom to thousands of kids in this area." Reece A. Overcash Jr., a World War II veteran who enrolled at the Charlotte Center in 1946 and later became head of American Credit Company in Charlotte, said, "She's just the most incredible person I've ever known."

It was Cone's talent for working with people that served her so well. The diminutive woman with bright blue eyes was said to practice "a sweet, subtle witchcraft, which turns strong, single-minded businessmen into sentimental philanthropists." It was this talent for dealing with people that allowed Cone to convince important and powerful men and women to contribute to her dream of a university. One civic leader said, "When Bonnie Cone gets you on the phone, you might as well just say, O.K., we'll do it, and then enjoy a pleasant conversation with her."

Coker College, her alma mater, referred to this ability in its alumni magazine as being bitten by the "Bonnie bug." Ed Williams, editor of the *Charlotte Observer's* editorial page, wrote in his column celebrating Cone's ninetieth birthday, "From the start, Bonnie Cone had three strengths as an advocate: she was uncommonly smart, persistent, and gifted in sensing how to put people in a position in which they wanted to say yes."

On July 1, 1965, Cone saw her long-held dream come true. She rang the campus bell with Governor Dan K. Moore, officially marking the transition of Charlotte College to the University of North Carolina at Charlotte. At the time of the elevation from college to university, a chancellor had still not been selected, and Cone was asked to serve as acting chancellor.

There was some speculation at the time as to why Cone was not asked to be chancellor of the university she was responsible for building. Some felt it was because she was a woman, others because she did not hold an earned doctorate. Supporters began working to find her a college presidency or government position, but Cone felt she could not abandon the school she helped to create. Instead, she accepted the position of vice chancellor for student and community relations in 1966 and held that position until her retirement in 1973. It was the perfect position for Cone, allowing her to utilize her tremendous strength of working with people. As Cone herself said about the students she worked with, "If we got them to a certain point, we weren't going to let them stop and not achieve their goals if we could do anything about it."

This attitude earned Cone many accolades and the respect of the community and former students. When the *Time* article appeared in 1965, she received congratulatory letters from former students, members of Congress, famous writers, bank presidents, businessmen, college presidents and deans, and even strangers from as far away as Nigeria, Vietnam, and the Philippines.

Cone's existence was predicated on her ability to go above and beyond the call of duty. She convinced her own dentist to put in two front teeth for a student free of charge. She also unknowingly pioneered integration in Charlotte. "I admitted black girls to the nursing school at Charlotte College," Cone admitted. "It never occurred to me that I couldn't. They didn't have a nursing school."

Some may argue that Cone's devotion to the creation of a university was at the expense of a personal life. She has enjoyed many hobbies—needlepoint, the piano, an uncanny ability to grow exquisite roses —but she never married. Her response to questions regarding romance were typical of her spunk. Asked at the age of seventy-eight if she ever realized she was going to be single for all of her life, Cone said: "Well, I'm not sure I'm going to be a single woman for all of my life." She said she "didn't deliberately set out to be a single woman," but her ultimate decision to remain so also allowed her to devote the passion of a zealot to creating a home for all of her thousands of children at the University of North Carolina at Charlotte.

Following her retirement in 1973, Cone served as liaison officer for the UNC Charlotte Foundation until 1977, continuing to work for the school she so loved. The Bonnie E. Cone University Center, Bonnie E. Cone Scholarship, and the Bonnie E. Cone Distinguished Professorships for Teaching at UNC-Charlotte were established to honor her remarkable commitment. In the midst of all of her work on behalf of the university, Cone also served on countless professional organizations; governing boards; and school, business, and service organizations. She earned a list of awards several pages long, received ten honorary doctorates, and also had an orchid named after her.

By 2000, the school "Miss Bonnie built" from the lost-and-found office at Central High School had grown to become the fourth largest of the sixteen institutions in the University of North Carolina system, and one of the top twenty southern universities. Enrollment exceeded 17,000 students, including about

2,700 graduate students. And, from the one-year Charlotte Extension Center started in 1946, UNC Charlotte in 2000 offered programs within its six colleges leading to bachelor's, master's, and doctoral degrees. As former Governor James Holshouser said, "She never meant to build a monument, but didn't she build a grand one?"

Laura L. McAuliffe earned a B.F.A. in dramatic writing from New York University's Tisch School of the Arts Institute of Film and Television and an M.A. in history from the University of North Carolina at Charlotte. She is a contributor to Exploring Charlotte: A Pocket Guide to the Queen City *and has written for the* Charlotte Observer *and* Today's Charlotte Woman.

For more information, see:

Boger, Mary Snead. *Charlotte 23*. Bassett Printing Corporation, 1972.

"Bonnie Cone: The Gentle Persuader." *Coker College Alumnae Magazine,* Winter 1966.

"College Creator." *Southern Living*, December 1967.

McCorkle, Joe. *Rogues 'n' Rascals*. UNC Charlotte, 1973. Yearbook.

Powell, William S. *North Carolina Lives: The Tar Heel Who's Who*. Historical Record Association, 1962.

Sanford, J. Kenneth. *Charlotte and UNC Charlotte: Growing Up Together*. University of North Carolina at Charlotte, 1996.

"The School Miss Bonnie Built." *Time,* July 16, 1965.

B. B. AND D. D. DOUGHERTY

by Karl E. Campbell

IT COULD BE SAID that Blanford Barnard (B. B.) Dougherty did not go far in life. He was born in Boone, grew up in the surrounding mountains, left home for only a few years to get an education, returned to Boone to start a school in 1899, and worked as the head of that same institution for the next half of a century.

What Dougherty accomplished in his mountain valley, however, was truly impressive. Under his leadership, the little two-room academy grew into a four-year college and graduate school that became Appalachian State University. To help his isolated school, Dougherty lobbied for roads and railroads to connect Boone to the rest of the state, which stimulated the economic renaissance of northwestern North Carolina in the twentieth century. As his school grew, Dougherty became increasingly involved in statewide education policy, helping to shape reforms such as extending the length of the school term, standardizing teacher certification, and pushing for the revolutionary equalization fund. *Time* magazine called Dougherty "a history-maker in education, worthy to rank with Massachusetts' Horace Mann." Not bad for a mountain boy who never strayed far from home.

When Dougherty was born on October 21, 1870, Boone was only a handful of buildings clustered in the valley under the shadow of Howard's Knob. Locals referred to it as Council's Store Community in honor of the proprietor of the first trading store in the area. Dougherty's father, Daniel Baker Dougherty, had recently purchased a large tract of farmland in the valley and converted the old store building into a home for his growing family. Blanford's older brother, Dauphin Disco (D. D.) Dougherty, had been born the year before. In 1875, five years after Blanford's birth, his mother gave birth to a sister, Lura Etta Mae. Sadly, the young mother's tragic death sixteen months later forced Daniel to give his infant daughter to nearby relatives to raise as their own.

Blanford, or "Blan" as his friends called him, later described his early life as one of "hard work and frugality." He grew up helping his father and older brother run the family farm, gristmill, and blacksmith shop. One of his earliest memories was watching his father striking an anvil to fashion tools out of the red-hot metal. Farming was a precarious enterprise in the isolated northwest mountains before the turn of the century. To deliver crops to the nearest railroad depots at North Wilkesboro or Lenoir, Blanford had to drive a horse-drawn wagon over rough mountain roads for two full days.

Such an isolated location offered few educational opportunities for the Dougherty brothers. Blanford received little formal schooling during his boyhood, attending a few months of classes every so often in various one- and two-room schoolhouses around the Boone area. He was twenty years old and attending the Globe Academy in Caldwell County when he applied for a teaching license and began teaching school in several local communities.

Sensing the need for additional training, Blanford followed his older brother to Wake Forest in 1892. The president of the college advised him to enter the sub-freshman class. Instead, Blanford took courses with the regular freshmen without registering. By the year's end he had not only earned a place but led the class in mathematics and Latin. His spelling, however, remained poor. On one test he missed sixteen of twenty-five words. In characteristic stubbornness, Dougherty not only improved his ability to spell but later wrote a textbook for teaching spelling.

B. B. Dougherty left Wake Forest after passing his freshman exams and spent the next several years alternating between teaching school back home and pursuing his education. He attended classes at Holly Springs College in Tennessee and later at Carson-Newman, where he earned a bachelor of science degree in 1896. Three years later he received permission to enroll in the senior class at the University of North Carolina. After meeting with individual professors in Chapel Hill to determine his credits, Dougherty presented the university president with enough credits to qualify for a degree without further study. The president observed: "Mr. Dougherty, a young man of your experience and turn of mind is likely to get more credit from the professors than he is entitled to." Dougherty replied, "Don't you think anyone who can do that is entitled to those credits?" The meeting ended with Dougherty required to take six quarter hours of electives, although he actually took eighteen hours before receiving a bachelor of philosophy degree in 1899.

At their father's urging, Blanford and his brother returned to Boone to found the Watauga Academy in

B. B. Dougherty and D. D. Dougherty (Courtesy of University Archives, Appalachian State University)

1899. That same year the Watauga County Board of Directors named Blanford as the superintendent of the county schools, or "free school" as it was called at that time, a position he held for the next sixteen years. The public school ran for ten weeks, after which the students could continue their education for a fee in the private Watauga Academy. The little school boasted a broad curriculum for all ages, but an advertisement in the local newspaper noted: "Special attention will be given to public school teachers." The academy was an immediate success, boasting more than 150 students within the year.

The Dougherty brothers quickly discovered that tuition alone would not sustain their little school, so Blanford went to Raleigh in 1903 to ask the state for financial support. Dougherty presented a new plan and a new name for the school. The state-supported Appalachian Training School would expand its mission to offer a complete program of teacher training to help address the critical shortage of qualified teachers in the mountains.

Dougherty made his proposal during Governor Charles Aycock's crusade to improve the public schools. Three years earlier North Carolina had passed, at Aycock's urging, constitutional amendments to reduce African American participation in state politics, including a new literacy requirement for voting. Aycock lobbied for the amendments by promising the white citizens better schools to prepare their children to pass the literacy tests. Dougherty cleverly exploited these political trends and, against significant odds, managed to convince the governor and the legislature to appropriate the funds.

From 1903 until his retirement in 1955, Dougherty never missed a legislative session, earning a reputation as one of the most successful and persistent lobbyists in Raleigh. On one occasion during the lean years of World War II, Dougherty concluded his request to a legislative committee for library resources by telling the story of a mountain pastor serving in Unionist eastern Tennessee during the Civil War. The pastor was uneasy about being reelected by the congregation of his church, so he told his parishioners: "The time has come to elect a pastor and if there are no objections, and I see none, I will take the vote. All of you that want me for pastor; all of you that believe in the New Testament; and all of you that are standing solidly behind the Union, stand up." Everyone jumped to their feet and the pastor announced his unanimous election.

Dougherty then told the committee: "If there are no objections, and I see none, I will take the vote on my funding request. All of you that are in favor of appropriating $5,000 to the library at Appalachian College, all of you that believe North Carolina is the finest state in the Southland, all of you that want to whip Old Hitler in this war, keep your seats for a moment and look wise." The committee members laughed, kept their seats, and Dougherty's library got its money.

When asked why he never married, Dougherty would smile and say: "Ask the other party." But more than one of his friends suggested he had no time for a family because he was married to the school. He and his brother served as coprincipals of the Appalachian Training School from 1903 until 1921, when Blanford became superintendent. In 1925 he was named president of the new Appalachian State Normal School and in 1929 of Appalachian State Teachers College (later Appalachian State University). Dauphin died in 1929. B. B. Dougherty remained head of the school until his retirement in 1955, when, at age eighty-four, he was believed to be the oldest college president in the country. His life story is the history of the school, which for years was simply referred to as "Dougherty's college."

Dougherty's life was so intertwined with Appalachian State, however, that on one occasion neighbors suspected foul play. During the Depression the college employed local farmers to help with hauling and dirt moving on the campus. Among the teams of horses was one from the Dougherty farm. When funds became scarce, Dougherty let the other teams go, but kept his on the job, leading to speculation that he was using his position to make a few extra dollars. What suspicious locals did not know was that the Dougherty team was working without pay.

At a public meeting called to clear the air, one of the farmers who had been laid off was asked: "Do you think Dr. Dougherty would steal?" "Well sir, I'd say yes," the farmer responded. The shocked questioner stuttered: "Do you mean to sit there and tell me Blan Dougherty would steal?" "I said yes," the farmer explained, "I think he would steal from himself for this college."

Dougherty also worked diligently toward the development of Boone and the surrounding area. He served as president of the Northwestern Bank of Boone from 1947 to 1957 and led efforts to establish a regional hospital and power company. But the biggest problem Dougherty's college and the surrounding community faced was geographic isolation. Few areas of North Carolina were as cut off from the rest of the state as were the "Lost Provinces" of Watauga, Avery, Ashe, and Mitchell counties and sections of

Wilkes and Caldwell counties on the western side of the Blue Ridge.

Dougherty realized that for his school to prosper he had to improve transportation into the mountains. He passionately lobbied for state funding for a railroad from Wilkesboro to Boone, but the project died when floods in 1916 and 1918 washed away the track. Dougherty was more successful in getting the narrow-gauge railroad from Johnson City extended all the way up to Boone in 1918 — the famous Tweetsie Railroad. Regretfully, the rails ran the wrong way, toward Tennessee, and did little to connect the college with the rest of North Carolina.

It was the automobile that eventually opened the northwestern counties. Dougherty threw himself into the campaign for better roads in the early 1920s and helped lobby for completion of the Boone Trail Highway, which ran east from Blowing Rock, and a paved road connecting Boone to North Wilkesboro and Winston-Salem.

Each of these projects required local support, which was not always forthcoming from mountain people suspicious of change and outsiders. The road to North Wilkesboro had to run through Deep Gap, where farmers let it be known that they saw little reason to pay a tax so other people could drive automobiles over their farmland on the way to Boone. Dougherty faced down his opponents at a contentious meeting in the Deep Gap schoolhouse. He argued that the road would enable the farmers to get their crops to better-paying markets and allow them to return to their own beds that same night. He also suggested, prophetically, that the road would bring tourists and their money to the mountains. On election day the citizens of Deep Gap voted for the road, which became the primary route bringing both commerce and college students into North Carolina's Lost Provinces.

From the beginning of his career, Dougherty had been interested in improving public education. He served as a member of the State Textbook Commission in 1916, the State Board of Equalization (1927–33), the State School Commission (1933–41), and the State Board of Education (1941–43, 1944–57). In 1962 he was inducted posthumously into the North Carolina Educational Hall of Fame. Dougherty helped push several important reforms through the legislature, including the expansion of public school terms to six and then eight months, rural consolidation, the Hancock Bill of 1929, and creation of a statewide system of teacher certification. In the 1950s, Dougherty supported paying African American teachers the same as their white counterparts, although the state's tardy action in this area came only when the Supreme Court appeared ready to strike down separate but equal facilities, as it did soon thereafter in the *Brown v. Board of Education* ruling of 1954.

By far the most significant of Dougherty's education reforms was the creation and expansion of the equalization fund. Coming from a poor county, Dougherty understood the discrepancies in the quality of public education across the state. Because each county had to pay for its own public school system, wealthy counties such as Forsyth could afford to spend $10,000 for each child's education, while what Dougherty called "the pauper counties" could only manage $1,500. In 1912, twenty-one years before the state assumed financial responsibility for operating all of the schools, Dougherty wrote a letter to the *Charlotte Observer* calling for such a system.

"North Carolina is a unit," Dougherty argued. "County lines should not interfere with the education of our children. No State can be great when even a part of her children are neglected." The state eventually came around to Dougherty's way of thinking. It created a partial equalization fund in 1927, expanded it in 1931, and became the first state in the nation to take over complete financial responsibility for all its public schools in 1933. According to one source, Dougherty deserved to be called "the father of the present state-wide system."

A story told about Blanford Dougherty early in his career when he was teaching in the Globe Academy near Blowing Rock concerned a visit he made to town one day. He met a fellow mountaineer who called out: "Blan, do you know what I said about you when I saw you coming down the street? I told these people here I would rather be a knot on a fence rail than to be a little one-horse schoolteacher." "Oh, sure," Dougherty shot back. "You are so much better prepared for a position of that kind."

More than half a century later, he was still teaching in a mountain school and still known for not suffering fools gladly. By the time of his retirement, Dougherty's college had grown into a major educational institution with a campus valued at over seven million dollars and a student population of more than two thousand. The expanding school was the economic engine of Boone, which had become the nexus of a reinvigorated regional economy. In addition, Dougherty's contemporaries credited him with having exerted more influence on the state's public school system than any other man of their time. Satisfied with his accomplishments, Dougherty stepped down in 1955. He died two years later. B. B. Dougherty's vision, however, continued in the tradition of educational reform he championed, the regional development he pursued, and the institution he led for fifty-six years.

Karl E. Campbell is an assistant professor of history at Appalachian State University, where he specializes in North Carolina history. He is a graduate of Warren Wilson College and earned his master's and Ph.D. degrees from the University of North Carolina at Chapel Hill.

For more information, see:
Dougherty, Blanford Barnard. Papers. University Archives, Appalachian State University, Boone.

Lanier, Ruby J. *Blanford Barnard Dougherty: Mountain Educator*. Duke University Press, 1974.

The Dougherty House and Appalachian Heritage Museum is located at 175 Mystery Hill Lane, Blowing Rock.

WILLIAM P. FEW

By William E. King

I N 1927 a newspaper headline in Durham read "Largest Building Permit in the History of the South Issued Today." Even acknowledging the evident boosterism, the announcement of a $21-million construction project as the nation was slipping into economic depression merited attention. The article was touting the construction of two new campuses for Trinity College as part of its transformation into Duke University.

The original campus, dating from the relocation of the college to Durham in 1892, was redesigned and rebuilt in a Georgian-style red brick campus as a coordinate college for women, and nearby a dramatic new Gothic-style campus of native stone was built for the undergraduate men and professional schools. Even more demanding than bricks and mortar was the expansion of a liberal arts college into a modern research university. Overseeing this transformation was William Preston Few, president of Trinity from 1910 to 1924 and of Duke University from 1924 to 1940.

A native of South Carolina, Few had ancestral ties to the Durham region. His great-great-grandfather, William, left Maryland to settle near Hillsborough in a log cabin later added to and now preserved as the Piper-Dickson House in the Eno River State Park. His great-grandfather James participated in the Regulator Movement against British tyranny and paid with his life when he was captured by the forces of Royal Governor William Tryon and hanged on May 17, 1771. His grandfather William then settled in the back country of South Carolina. His father, Benjamin Franklin Few, married Rachel Kendrick and after serving as a surgeon in the Confederate Army, settled in Sandy Flat, S.C., where William Preston Few was born on December 29, 1867.

Raised in a family that valued education, William initially was tutored at home because of a "sickly childhood." After graduating from high school in nearby Greer he entered Wofford College, a Methodist institution in Spartanburg, S.C., graduating in 1889. He was a teacher for three years and then enrolled at Harvard University, earning M.A. and Ph.D. degrees in modern languages in 1893 and 1896.

William Preston Few's forty-four-year career at Trinity and Duke began in 1896 when President John C. Kilgo, who knew him at Wofford, asked him to come to Trinity for a year to fill in for a professor on

William P. Few (Courtesy of Duke University Archives)

leave. Few was such a success that Kilgo appealed to Benjamin N. Duke to pay Few's salary so he could continue.

A popular classroom teacher, Few was also a mentor. An admiring student described him as being "a model of prudence." "To Dr. Few," he wrote, "I owe about all the balance I may have in my make-up." Though far from being athletic, a baseball player noted that Few took the time to umpire practice games, marking balls and strikes in the dirt with his cane. Few became so well-liked by students and faculty that Kilgo appointed him the first dean of Trinity College in 1902.

In 1903, Few played an important but behind-the-scenes role in the so-called Bassett Affair, an event that figured prominently at Trinity as well as in the history of the development of academic freedom in American higher education. Professor John Spencer

Bassett, founder of the scholarly journal the *South Atlantic Quarterly,* wrote a series of articles on the racial climate in the South. He deplored the successful disfranchisement campaign against African Americans then sweeping the region, predicted a continued struggle for equality, and described Booker T. Washington, the renowned African American educator, "as the greatest man, save General Lee, born in the South in a hundred years." Democratic leaders, some of whom who were on the Trinity board of trustees, sought to bolster the party's role as defender of the status quo by demanding Bassett's resignation. Partisan local newspapers across the state followed the lead of the party organ, the *News and Observer* in Raleigh, and took up the cry for Bassett's dismissal, even viciously spelling the historian's name as "bASSett." In a dramatic late-night vote after a spirited debate at their meeting in December 1903, the trustees voted eighteen to seven not to request Bassett's resignation. The trustees also approved a stirring report in support of academic freedom that was prepared by Few. Trinity received widespread acclaim and even national attention when President Theodore Roosevelt extolled its stand for academic freedom while speaking in Durham on his widely publicized tour of the South in 1904.

As dean, Few supported Kilgo's leadership in establishing standards of accreditation in colleges and universities in the South, and he implemented the college's developing practice of favoring quality over numbers in the admission of students and hiring of faculty. When Kilgo was elected a bishop in the Methodist Church in 1910, Few succeeded him as president. The students were so elated at his appointment that the editor of the campus newspaper wrote that it would not be long before Few would "make Trinity College the Harvard of the South."

One has to probe deeply in assessing the reasons for Few's successful tenure as president. He easily could be underestimated at first impression. A typical reaction was recorded by a visiting official from Olmsted Associates, the renowned landscaping firm, when the new Gothic campus was being planned. His report to the home office praised several university officials but of Few he wrote, "He had little to say and seemed not a very forceful man."

Few led by the force of his commitment and by seizing opportunity and building upon success, not by dynamic personality. He was a complex man who was difficult to describe. In the phraseology of his biographer, Robert H. Woody, Few was slight of build, with a certain gauntness. To some he had an almost "Lincolnesque" appeal. He had large, luminous brown eyes, capable of a kindly twinkle, yet they were not without sharpness on occasion. Modest, timid, and even diffident at times, he possessed a quiet charm most effective in small gatherings. He had to do a great deal of public speaking, but his clear emphasis was on a thoughtful expression of ideas, not on dramatic presentation.

To Woody, "Few, in short, looked like what he was, a college president, shy, earnest, devoted to the causes of education and the church, and anxious to do great good and little harm. He was a scholar, yet, all in all, a man of sound judgment. . . . He was a student by preference, a scholar by training, and an administrator only by force of circumstances."

The average citizen of the state probably knew more about Frank P. Graham at the University of North Carolina and even William L. Poteat at Wake Forest College than Few, because of their outspoken stands and visibility on public issues. Few worked quietly, yet persistently, and often behind-the-scenes, on behalf of higher education, especially private education, which was hardly a consistent concern of the public in his day.

A large measure of Few's success was in articulating a vision and enlisting businessmen, academicians, students, and alumni in the quest. He saw Trinity College as a model not only for the region but for the nation as well. He well knew the special educational needs of the South. But he also believed it was possible, even desirable, to unite strong undergraduate instruction with the emerging modern research university. And he also believed a private institution could and should include a religious, but not narrowly sectarian, emphasis, along with an obligation of service to mankind as an integral part of its mission. He firmly believed, and won many over to his belief, that historical circumstances presented a special role for Trinity College.

Foremost among his converts was James Buchanan Duke, one of the region's and nation's most successful entrepreneurs in the manufacture and sale of tobacco products and the production, transmission, and sale of electric power. Since 1889, Duke's father, Washington, his older brother, Benjamin, and sister, Mary, had been primary financial supporters of Trinity, an institution founded by Methodists, the church of their faith. Few persuaded James B. Duke to spectacularly increase the family's support of the college. In December 1924, Duke made the institution one of the primary ongoing beneficiaries of his philanthropic foundation, the Duke Endowment, which he created to support higher education, hospitals, and orphanages in North and South Carolina;

and the Methodist Church in North Carolina. In addition, Duke gave money for the construction and equipping of two modern campuses for a new university in Durham.

Consequently, President Few proposed renaming Trinity College Duke University. Duke declined, preferring continued relative anonymity, but Few persisted, saying the new university needed a new name because there were a dozen institutions named Trinity throughout the world. Duke finally agreed to the new name if it were understood that Duke University was named after his father and family, a fact often overlooked in the ensuing publicity.

Few's dream for Trinity was fulfilled by the Duke Endowment and gifts for construction of a greatly expanded campus. The liberal arts college with an engineering curriculum and a law school became a university with undergraduate colleges for men, women, engineers, and nurses; an expanded law school; and new schools of religion, medicine, forestry, and graduate education.

This growth of a small regional college into a nationally known university perhaps represented the greatest transformation in the shortest period of time of an educational institution in the South, and maybe the nation. The accomplishment was recognized in 1938 when the new university was admitted to membership in the prestigious Association of American Universities. At Few's inauguration in 1910, President Abbott Lawrence Lowell of Harvard University commented that much had been said congratulating Few, but, in truth, the college should be congratulated for selecting Few as president. Events of the ensuing three decades proved Lowell's perceptivity.

In 1911, Few married Mary Reamey Thomas of Martinsville, Va., who was a graduate of Trinity and one of his former students. They had five sons: William, Lynne Starling, Kendrick Sheffield, Randolph Reamey, and Yancy Preston. The family was an inte-gral part of campus life and one measure of Few's success is that he genuinely enjoyed his work and family. Late in life he wrote that one of his great privileges had been living intimately with students since he was sixteen. As heavy as were his presidential responsibilities, he frequently was seen about campus. One student guessed that Few probably knew 40 percent of the students on the Gothic West Campus and reported that he unfailingly greeted you by name with a polite "good morning" and tip of the hat.

There was genuine sadness on campus when Few died in Duke hospital on October 16, 1940, after a brief illness. He was buried in the crypt of Duke Chapel, the building he took pride in as the symbol of the university.

William E. King, a native of Salisbury, earned his Ph.D. in history from Duke University, where he was the first archivist of the university. His publications include If Gargoyles Could Talk: Sketches of Duke University. *He narrated a portion of* Far Fetched and Dear Bought, *a documentary on four architects who changed North Carolina.*

For more information, see:
Records of the President. William P. Few, 1910–1940. Duke University Archives, Durham.

Durden, Robert F. *The Dukes of Durham, 1865–1929.* Duke University Press, 1975.
———. *Lasting Legacy to the Carolinas: The Duke Endowment, 1924–1994.* Duke University Press, 1998.
———. *The Launching of Duke University, 1924–1949.* Duke University Press, 1993.
King, William E. *If Gargoyles Could Talk: Sketches of Duke University.* Duke University Press, 1997.
Porter, Earl W. *Trinity and Duke, 1892–1924.* Duke University Press, 1964.
Woody, Robert H., ed. *Papers and Addresses of William Preston Few.* Duke University Press, 1951.

JOHN HOPE FRANKLIN

By Marsha Cook Vick

FOR THREE-YEAR-OLD John Hope Franklin, "child's play" meant sitting quietly and drawing pictures where his mother could watch him in the back of her elementary classroom. No one suspected until two years later, when his mother found that he was writing words, composing sentences, and reading the newspaper, that he also had been paying attention to the academic lessons that were meant for her school-age pupils. "From that point on," he later explained, "I would endeavor to write, and through the written word, to communicate my thoughts to others." His love of education, engendered by his mother's teaching and his father's custom of reading and writing every evening, and his superior intellectual ability became recognizable traits throughout his career as a historian, educator, and prolific author.

Franklin was born on January 2, 1915, in Rentiesville, Okla., the fourth and youngest child of Buck Colbert Franklin and Mollie Parker Franklin. His parents named him after John Hope, the African American educator they had encountered during their college years and who later served as the first president of Atlanta University. John Hope Franklin's paternal grandfather was a former slave who had served in the Union army and settled in Oklahoma (then called the Indian Territory). Franklin's father and mother were both college graduates; his father was one of the first African Americans to pass the bar in Oklahoma.

Seeking asylum from racial discrimination, which had been the cause of his expulsion from a courtroom in Louisiana where he was representing a client, Buck Franklin moved his family to the small frontier community of Rentiesville, an all-black town of fewer than two hundred people. He farmed, edited the local newspaper, served as postmaster and justice of the peace, and was the town's only lawyer. John Hope Franklin later explained that "living apart provided neither protection nor privilege; it was not the answer to race and ethnicity," a view he has held all his life.

Unable to make a sufficient living in Rentiesville, Buck Franklin moved in 1921 to Tulsa, about sixty miles away, with plans to save money and send for his family. The Tulsa race riot in the summer of 1921 changed his plans, however, when angry whites burned his law office and all of his belongings, along with most of the other black-owned businesses and homes in

John Hope Franklin (Courtesy of Duke University Archives)

town. He reopened his law practice in a tent, but family members, who had their hearts set on moving to the large city, had to wait until 1925 to join him.

At the age of sixteen, John Hope Franklin graduated as valedictorian of his class at Booker T. Washington High School and won a scholarship to Fisk University, where he enrolled in 1931. In his first few weeks there he met Aurelia Whittington, a fellow student who became his sweetheart and later his wife. His ambition was to study law and become a partner with his father, but in his sophomore year, Theodore S. Currier, a white professor of history, lured him into a love of history that changed the direction of his professional life. Under Currier, who was a superior teacher and also a friend and mentor, Franklin decided to make the study and teaching of history his life's work. He received his B.A. degree and graduated magna cum laude in 1935.

Denied admission to the all-white graduate school at the University of Oklahoma, Franklin went to Harvard University instead. With $500 that Currier borrowed and lent to him, Franklin enrolled as a graduate student in history and finished his M.A. degree in 1936. While still a doctoral student, he accepted a teaching position at St. Augustine's College in Raleigh in 1939. His research for his dissertation focused on free African Americans in antebellum North Carolina. The first African American to seek access to the North Carolina state archives, Franklin found that the state's policy denied African Americans the right to sit in the same room with white researchers. With the help of a fair-minded official at the archives, Franklin was admitted to a separate area to do his research. He received his Ph.D. degree from Harvard in 1941.

In 1943 Franklin and Aurelia, whom he married in 1940, left St. Augustine's for Durham so that Franklin could teach at North Carolina College for Negroes (NCC, later North Carolina Central University). That same year, his revised dissertation was published by the University of North Carolina Press as *The Free Negro in North Carolina, 1790–1860*. In this book Franklin counteracted the image of African Americans in the popular consciousness, proving that not all persons of color were slaves—that, indeed, before the Civil War there were a quarter of a million free African Americans in the slave states alone.

Publisher Alfred Knopf approached him about writing a history of African Americans, an offer that he accepted in 1945. With a $500 advance from Knopf and financial support from Aurelia, who was a librarian at NCC, Franklin was able to spend a year conducting his research at the Library of Congress in Washington, D.C., and writing *From Slavery to Freedom: A History of Negro Americans,* the groundbreaking work published in 1947 that made him famous early in his career. Printed in multiple editions and co-authored with Alfred A. Moss Jr. from the fifth edition on, the title was one of the country's oldest textbooks in continuous use. It was translated into Japanese, German, French, Portuguese, and Chinese, and there were more than three million copies in print. The book detailed African American history, from life in Africa to slavery to the civil rights movement in the twentieth century.

In 1947 Franklin began a nine-year tenure as professor of history at Howard University. Two years later, the prominent historian C. Vann Woodward invited him to read a paper at a meeting of the influential Southern Historical Association, the first time an African American had had such an opportunity. Franklin accepted in order to advance the opportunities for African Americans in the profession. The success of his action was obvious not only in the subsequent acceptance of African Americans as members, but also in his election as president of the organization twenty years later.

Shortly after the Franklins' son was born in 1952, Franklin accepted Thurgood Marshall's invitation to become a member of the research team that Marshall assembled to prepare the legal case against segregated public schools. Franklin's historical research on the adverse economic and social factors affecting African Americans was a significant contribution to Marshall's success with the 1954 Supreme Court decision in *Brown v. Board of Education.*

News of Franklin's selection as the first African American chair of the history department at Brooklyn College appeared on the front page of the *New York Times* in 1956. His fifty-two white colleagues in the department admired and accepted his leadership, but he was not so warmly received in the racially segregated community at large. It took him a year to find a home and a lending institution that would accept his application for a mortgage. In 1961 he published his revisionist historical study, *Reconstruction After the Civil War.* In this book, he successfully discredited earlier interpretations of the origins of the presidential Reconstruction era in the South after the Civil War, changing the understanding of this historical period forever.

In 1964 Franklin accepted a professorship at the University of Chicago, a position that attracted him because of the opportunity to teach graduate students. He taught undergraduate and graduate students and continued to pursue and publish his own research. He also served for three years as chairman of the history department and was appointed the John Matthews Manly Distinguished Service Professor. He enhanced the opportunities and experiences of his graduate students through such innovations as developing fieldwork based in North Carolina for the purpose of using primary sources for research on southern history. As he had hoped to do, Franklin trained a number of graduate students who entered academia and published books on subjects vital to his field of southern history. He instilled in his students the same high standards of scholarship and integrity that characterized his own work.

In 1980 Franklin took a leave of absence to study and write at the National Humanities Center at the Research Triangle Park in North Carolina. In 1982 he retired from the University of Chicago but retained his named professorship, with emeritus status. His first retirement ended the same year it began when he joined the faculty at Duke University as the James B. Duke Professor of History.

Among the books he published while at Duke were *George Washington Williams: A Biography* (1985), which took four decades to complete because of the difficulty of locating the details of Williams's life, and *Race and History: Selected Essays, 1938–88* (1989), a collection of essays that span a half century of his career and provide not only his insights on history but also a record of his extraordinary life.

A second retirement began in 1985 when he took emeritus status in Duke's history department, but it ended immediately when he became professor of legal history at the Duke Law School, a position he held until 1992. During January 1995, the month of his eightieth birthday, Duke held a university-wide celebration of his life and his contributions to the field of history and to the social progress of the nation. In honor of its eminent historian, Duke also established in Perkins Library the John Hope Franklin Research Center for African and African American Documentation, a collection with Franklin's writings and scholarly papers as its cornerstone.

Through his professional accomplishments, Franklin not only revolutionized the way southern history was viewed but also made history himself. He was the only person to hold the office of national president of the five major organizations of scholars: the American Studies Association, the Southern Historical Association, the United Chapters of Phi Beta Kappa, the Organization of American Historians, and the American Historical Association.

As of mid-year 2000, he had received 126 honorary doctoral degrees from colleges and universities in America and abroad. He was the author of 12 books and 115 scholarly articles, editor of 8 books, and co-author of 4. His latest work in progress was an autobiography entitled *The Vintage Years*. His professional accomplishments were recognized with numerous honors and awards, including the Jefferson Medal of the Council for the Advancement and Support of Education (1984), the Encyclopedia Britannica's Gold Medal for the Dissemination of Knowledge (1990), induction into the North Carolina Literary Hall of Fame (1998), and the Lincoln Prize for Excellence in Civil War studies (2000).

His life was witness to an ability to meaningfully combine broad educational and social concerns with a central interest in southern history. Even though his encyclopedic knowledge of American history provided a powerful motivation for personal activism, his experiences involving racial slights were probably the greater influence.

Beginning as early as his seventh year, when he,

his mother, and his sister were put off a train miles from Rentiesville for mistakenly entering the white coach and then refusing to change cars on the moving train, Franklin learned the hurtful dimensions of racism but also the dignity exemplified in his mother's handling of the insult. He never fully avoided racial prejudice, having had to overcome barriers to public archives, professional organizations, and hotels accommodating academic conferences. In an incident late in life Franklin was standing at a hotel registration desk when he was approached by a guest who asked him to take his bags to his room. Franklin replied with his characteristic wit, "I'm retired."

During his career, Franklin was careful to keep his scholarship separate from his activities relating to public policy. His insistence upon impartial rules of research and evidence prevented the intrusion of personal frustration into his scholarly objectivity. The integrity of his work, nevertheless, led to frequent opportunities for him to influence history by serving as an important force behind much constructive social change in America and greater cooperation in the international intellectual community. He testified before congressional committees and championed civil rights, affirmative action, and the importance of individual initiative. In 1965 he joined more than thirty of his colleagues—historians from all over the country—in Martin Luther King Jr.'s march for racial equality in Alabama.

Among his numerous honors and awards for significant contributions to society were Turner Broadcasting's Trumpet Award for contributions to humanity (1994), the NAACP's Spingarn Medal for distinguished merit and achievement by an African American (1995), and the Presidential Medal of Freedom (1995), the nation's highest civilian honor. In 1997, President Bill Clinton appointed Franklin to lead his advisory board for "One America in the 21st Century: The President's Initiative on Race." Franklin demonstrated remarkable capacities for reason and compassion in the challenges he faced in leading the fifteen-month national dialogue on race in America.

Age did not diminish Franklin's regal demeanor, his quiet dignity, his disarming honesty, his wit, or his mental acuity. It did, however, leave him lonely after Aurelia's death in 1999. At age eighty-five, he remained a trustee of the Duke Endowment, the first African American elected to that board, and was active in professional and education organizations, speaking at numerous events. He continued to write, exercise, fish, and, of course, tend his beloved orchids—in excess of three hundred plants—in the greenhouse at his Durham home. Having an officially registered variety of the orchid named for him—*Phalaenopsis John Hope Franklin*—was one more honor.

Pernell Canaday, the cab driver who regularly ferried John Hope Franklin to and from Raleigh-Durham International Airport, added one more important accolade to the hundreds that this remarkable man had received from nearly every segment of American society: "He's down to earth. He likes to do a lot of fishing. He talks about his greenhouse. He's just an average Joe."

Marsha Cook Vick is the author of Black Subjectivity in Performance: A Century of African American Drama on Broadway. *Other publications include an article on the ideology of race in* Moby-Dick *in the* CLA Journal *(1992) and several biographical essays in the reference volumes* Notable Black American Women *(1992),* Epic Lives: One Hundred Black Women Who Made a Difference *(1993), and* The Oxford Companion to African American Literature *(1997). She was a speechwriter and research assistant for U.S. Senator Terry Sanford and taught in the Afro-American Studies Curriculum at UNC-Chapel Hill.*

For more information, see:

Anderson, Eric, and Alfred A. Moss, Jr., eds. *The Facts of Reconstruction: Essays in Honor of John Hope Franklin*. Louisiana State University Press, 1991.

Clabby, Catherine. "Historian John Hope Franklin, Reaping Honors at 80, Not Done Yet." Raleigh *News and Observer,* January 17, 1995.

Edgers, Geoff, and Laurie Willis. "John Hope Franklin: Tar Heel of the Year." Raleigh *News and Observer,* December 27, 1998.

Franklin, John Hope. *Race and History: Selected Essays, 1938–1988*. Louisiana State University Press, 1989.

Hill, Lemuel L. "A Biographical Presentation of Dr. John Hope Franklin, Historian." Thesis, San Jose State University, 1983.

Smith, Jessie Carney, ed. *Black Heroes of the Twentieth Century*. Invisible Ink Press, 1998.

Stocking, Ben. "A New Campaign in a Long War." Raleigh *News and Observer,* July 19, 1997.

Young, Dick. *First Person Singular: John Hope Franklin*. PBS. Dick Young Productions, 1997.

WILLIAM C. FRIDAY

By William Link

WILLIAM CLYDE FRIDAY, university president, educational statesman, and philanthropic leader, occupied the University of North Carolina presidency for thirty years, during a period of unparalleled growth, change, and turmoil in American higher education.

Born July 13, 1920, in Rapine, Va., Friday was the son of David Nathan and Mary Elizabeth Friday. He grew up in Dallas, in Gaston County, in the southwestern corner of the piedmont. Attending public schools in Dallas, Friday came of age during the Depression, which profoundly affected Gaston County, a major cotton textile manufacturing center. A participant in high school debating and in athletics, especially baseball, Friday attended Wake Forest College for one year (1937–38) and then transferred to North Carolina State College in Raleigh, where he earned a degree in textile engineering. On his graduation in June 1941, Friday worked with Dumont Corporation textile manufacturing plant in Waynesboro, Va. Remaining in that position only briefly, he returned to Raleigh in September 1941 to work as State College's chief dormitory assistant.

During his senior year at State College, Friday met Ida Howell, then an undergraduate at Meredith College. After his graduation, they courted and then were married on May 13, 1942.

Like many of his contemporaries, World War II consumed Friday's early adulthood, and he was commissioned as an ensign in the navy in 1942. Following training at Notre Dame University, Friday was stationed as an ordnance officer at the Naval Gun Factory in Washington, D.C., where he received specialized training in weaponry. He was then transferred to the Naval Ammunition Depot (NAD) at St. Julien's Creek, then a part of the massive World War II–era buildup in the Norfolk, Va., area. Beginning as a plant operations manager, Friday rose to the rank of full lieutenant by the end of the war, when he refused a permanent commission in the navy. Friday became ill with catarrhal fever and spent late 1945 stationed on the admiral's staff of the commandant of the naval district in Charleston, South Carolina. He was mustered out on February 1, 1946, and he and Ida moved to Chapel Hill, where he enrolled in the University of North Carolina School of Law.

Friday found Chapel Hill in the 1940s a bustling,

William C. Friday (Courtesy of Hugh Morton)

energetic place overflowing with returning war veterans, many of whom would become future compatriots in higher education and politics. Finishing his law degree in 1948, Friday had little interest in practicing the law and, because Ida had received a fellowship obligating her to remain in North Carolina for two years, he took a job as assistant dean of students at UNC. He would never leave Chapel Hill.

In his assignment with UNC Dean of Students Fred H. Weaver, Friday was introduced to a remarkable group of university leaders: William "Billy" Carmichael Jr., UNC's financial and operational leader; UNC Chancellor Robert Burton House; and UNC President Frank Porter Graham. Known nationally for his espousal of liberal causes in labor and race relations, Graham played a role in the University of North Carolina's emergence during the 1930s as the South's leading public university. Attracting able faculty and steady support from the state's leadership, Graham inspired an entire generation of North Carolina leaders, including Bill Friday, who became one of many

Graham protégés. Departing the UNC presidency for the United States Senate to fill the unexpired term of deceased Senator J. Melville Broughton, Graham was sworn in as senator on March 29, 1949. Friday, meanwhile, remained in Chapel Hill to work with Graham's successor, Gordon Gray.

Friday's ascent in the UNC hierarchy continued under Gray. Unlike Graham, Gray, who was inaugurated president on February 6, 1950, was of aristocratic bearing. His father, Bowman Gray, was president of R.J. Reynolds Tobacco Company and Gordon grew up in Winston-Salem's Graylyn, the state's second largest private home. Where Graham was personable and charismatic, Gray was an introvert and distant. Friday became his right-hand man. On April 16, 1951, he was named Gray's assistant. Four years later, in February 1955, Friday was appointed secretary of the university, a position that gave him greater access and influence with UNC's one-hundred-member board of trustees. When Gray resigned on June 10, 1955, to become President Dwight D. Eisenhower's assistant secretary of defense for international security affairs, the board chose the thirty-five-year-old Friday as acting president. Performing well in that capacity, Friday was appointed president on October 18, 1956, and inaugurated at William Neal Reynolds Coliseum at State College on May 8, 1957.

Almost immediately Friday confronted two troublesome issues: intercollegiate athletics and anticommunism. During the late 1950s the expanding basketball empires of N.C. State Coach Everett Case and Frank McGuire, the coach at Chapel Hill, were threatened by a consistent pattern of recruiting violations at State and a hint of point shaving (in which athletes were bribed to increase or reduce the margin of victory). Then, in May 1961, Friday learned of an even greater scandal, when three State players admitted shaving points during the Dixie Classic, a large and popular holiday basketball tournament held annually in Raleigh. Determined to reform the basketball programs that were careening out of control, Friday acted decisively. On May 22, 1961, he informed the UNC trustees that the Dixie Classic would end, athletic scholarships would be severely limited, and State and Carolina would play a limited schedule of only fourteen (rather than twenty-five) games. Though Friday's decision was unpopular, it helped to turn around a deteriorating situation at North Carolina's leading public university campuses.

Friday faced an even more serious challenge on June 25, 1963, when the General Assembly hastily passed legislation barring any "known" communist or person who had invoked the Fifth Amendment from speaking at any of the state's public colleges or universities. The enactment of the "Speaker Ban" was directed not so much at communists—few of whom visited UNC campuses—as it was at the supposed "threat" of civil rights activists, who were leading a statewide revolt against segregation during the summer of 1963. Angry at civil rights activists—who were demonstrating at the legislature's doorstep in Raleigh—legislators became convinced that white UNC liberals were behind the mostly African American uprising. The Speaker Ban law placed Friday in a difficult position: As an employee of the state, he was required to enforce the law, yet the Speaker Ban compromised free speech and damaged UNC's national reputation. Over the next two years, Friday worked hard to revise and, ultimately, repeal the law. After a visiting accreditation team from the Southern Association of Colleges and Schools declared that the Speaker Ban threatened accreditation, a special session of the General Assembly met in November 1965 and awarded greater discretion in enforcing the law to campus administrators.

But student radicals then challenged this law in the spring of 1966 by inviting outside speakers Herbert Aptheker, a Communist Party member, and Frank Wilkinson, an activist who had taken the Fifth Amendment. The political compromise disintegrated. Only after student leaders—some of whom Friday secretly sponsored—mounted a challenge in court was UNC finally rid of this odious free-speech restriction. On February 19, 1968, a three-judge federal district court in Greensboro declared the Speaker Ban an unconstitutional restriction of the First Amendment's protection over free speech.

The student activism that emerged in the Speaker Ban continued during the late 1960s, with opposition to the war in Vietnam and, in particular, with the cafeteria workers' strike in 1969. UNC cafeteria workers, all of whom were African American, joined with black student leaders in challenging the status quo at Chapel Hill, and during the spring of 1969 students occupied several buildings on campus. Reacting sharply to this, Governor Robert Scott dispatched units of the State Highway Patrol to evict the protesting students on March 7, 1969.

While facing disruptive campus conditions, Friday also led the University of North Carolina during a period of growth, reorganization, and restructuring. In 1962, Governor Terry Sanford appointed a commission headed by Winston-Salem attorney Irving E. Carlyle to examine the challenges facing educational institutions beyond high school with the anticipated arrival of thousands of "baby boom" students. The so-called Carlyle Commission recommended major changes in the UNC system. Its most important recommendation was that the UNC system rationalize itself with the three campuses becoming UNC-Chapel Hill, UNC-Greensboro, and UNC-Raleigh. All campuses—including the single-sex Woman's College at Greensboro—would become coeducational. Although a nasty legislative fight mounted by N.C. State supporters prevented a name change, the Woman's College at Greensboro became the University of North Carolina at Greensboro in 1963. Meanwhile, the UNC system during the 1960s expanded from a three-campus to a six-campus system with the addition of new campuses at Charlotte in 1965 and Wilmington and Asheville in 1969.

Higher education underwent further change during the late 1960s and early 1970s, culminating in a wholesale restructuring. Much of the pressure came from an alliance of the former state teachers' colleges that fashioned an effective political alliance. In 1967, the legislature granted university status to four former teachers' colleges. Two years later, in 1969, all the remaining five public colleges were made into universities. In the same year, moreover, the legislators awarded regional universities the ability to establish doctoral programs. At the same time, East Carolina University began a long and eventually successful campaign to establish a state-supported medical school in Greenville. All these changes were vigorously opposed in the General Assembly by Friday and the UNC trustees, but legislative logrolling prevailed.

In response, Governor Scott began an effort to reorganize the entire system. In late 1970, he organized a committee headed by Goldsboro attorney and state senator Lindsay Warren to study North Carolina higher education and suggest ways to improve it. The report of the Warren Committee appeared in March 1971, and it recommended wholesale changes, including the incorporation of the UNC system into a larger, statewide structure. With UNC trustees firmly opposed to the changes, a fight erupted in the legislature and the result, determined in a special session in October 1971, was a compromise—the creation of a revamped sixteen-campus system, but the continuing influence of UNC administrators and trustees over the new system.

After the expanded UNC system came into existence in July 1972, perhaps the greatest challenge confronting Friday was how to deal with the heritage of racial segregation in higher education. Until the 1950s, the UNC campuses excluded African Americans, and this all-white system coexisted with pub-

licly supported, all-black institutions at Greensboro, Durham, Fayetteville, Winston-Salem, and Elizabeth City, along with a historically Native American, publicly supported college at Pembroke. When the 1971 restructuring occurred, almost immediately Friday and UNC administrators confronted the dilemma of integration. At the same time, the UNC system faced direct pressure from officials of the federal government, especially the Department of Health, Education, and Welfare, and, after 1980, the Department of Education. Those officials, between 1973 and 1981, launched an on-again, off-again campaign to desegregate North Carolina public higher education.

Where Friday's and federal officials' opinions diverged was less about whether desegregation should occur but about how it should occur. While federal officials favored applying the same model used in elementary and secondary education—primarily pupil assignment and other compulsory measures—Friday and UNC officials favored an aggressive program of incentives to encourage students to attend minority institutions. This disagreement, which led to a lawsuit filed by UNC in federal court in 1979, resulted in a consent decree in 1981 affirming UNC's approach.

Throughout his tenure at the university, Friday was a proponent of public television. He helped establish the state's public network, UNC-TV, under the auspices of the university and got it on the air in the 1950s. Through the years he nurtured its growth and development. In 1971 he began hosting a popular weekly interview show, *North Carolina People,* which was still being produced in 2000. In its thirty years on the air, Friday and his producers created the largest video archive of state personalities in business, politics, the arts, and civic affairs.

Friday retired from the UNC presidency in 1986 to become executive director of the William R. Kenan Jr. Charitable Trust, along with other Kenan philanthropies. For more than a decade, he helped lead those philanthropies toward major initiatives in the arts, literacy, and education. He became an outspoken advocate of the state's poor, and helped to found a new Rural Economic Development Center in 1986. Friday played a leading role in the creation of a national commission, the Knight Commission, which examined all aspects of intercollegiate sports and eventually offered a wide-ranging set of recommendations for reform. In 1999, Friday retired from the Kenan Trust, but, as he neared age eighty, continued an active life in Chapel Hill, working from an office in the refurbished Graham Memorial building on the UNC campus.

William A. Link is Lucy Spinks Keker Excellence Professor and Head, Department of History, University of North Carolina at Greensboro, where he joined the faculty in 1981. A scholar of the American South, Link is the author of three major books: A Hard Country and a Lonely Place: Schooling, Society, and Reform in Rural Virginia, 1870–1920; The Paradox of Southern Progressivism, 1880–1930, *and* William Friday: Power, Purpose, and American Higher Education, *all published by the University of North Carolina Press.*

For more information, see:

The primary source for the life of William Friday exists in University Archives, UNC-Chapel Hill, which contain the records of his UNC presidency, as well as those of Frank Porter Graham, Gordon Gray, and the UNC chancellors. In the Southern Historical Collection (SHC), private manuscript collections include the Frank Porter Graham Papers and the Gordon Gray Papers, among others; important recollections of Friday and his contemporaries can be found in the Southern Oral History Program, SHC. Also consult the university archives at North Carolina State University in Raleigh and the University of North Carolina at Greensboro.

Ashby, Warren. *Frank Porter Graham: A Southern Liberal.* John Blair, 1980.

Link, William A. *William Friday: Power, Purpose, and American Higher Education.* University of North Carolina Press, 1995.

King, Arnold K. *The Multicampus University of North Carolina Comes of Age, 1956–1986.* University of North Carolina, 1986.

Wilson, Louis Round. *The University of North Carolina, 1900–1930: The Making of a Modern University.* University of North Carolina Press, 1957.

———. *The University of North Carolina under Consolidation, 1931–1963.* University of North Carolina Press, 1964.

FRANK PORTER GRAHAM

By D. G. Martin

As president of the University of North Carolina from 1930 until 1949 and U.S. senator from 1949 until 1950, Frank Porter Graham was a tenacious defender of free expression and a powerful influence on generations of North Carolina leaders. In his only political campaign—a losing one to retain the senate seat to which he had been appointed—Graham set out a political vision that provided the basis on which progressive North Carolina political candidates built their campaigns in the second half of the twentieth century.

Born on October 14, 1886, in Fayetteville, Graham was the sixth of nine children of Alexander and Katherine Sloan Graham. His father, a Confederate veteran, had been appointed superintendent of schools in Fayetteville on the recommendation of Frank Porter, a lawyer and a University of North Carolina classmate for whom Frank's parents named him. When Frank was four years old, his family moved to Charlotte, where his father became superintendent of the city's two schools—one for whites and one for African Americans.

Frank's parents had Scottish forebears and were loyal Presbyterians, and their intensity and sense of morality were a part of his upbringing. So too was his father's commitment to public education. At a time when many people viewed public education as radical or even socialistic, Frank's father mustered support for the idea. Frank often witnessed his father's persistent advocacy, as well as his father's patience and respect for those who differed with him. Some years later, Charlotte honored Alexander Graham by naming a junior high school in his honor.

Frank was small for his age and plagued with health problems throughout his life. Nonetheless, he became an excellent baseball player. When poor eyesight and illness delayed his entry into the University of North Carolina, his father sent him for a year's training and physical conditioning at his uncle John Graham's academy in Warrenton. When he arrived at the university in 1905 at age eighteen, he stood five-feet four-inches tall and weighed just ninety pounds.

He was active from the start: serving as class president, president of the honor council, and editor of the *Daily Tar Heel,* as well as playing baseball and cheerleading. The campus YMCA was a center for service work and conferences and Graham became its presi-

Frank Porter Graham (Courtesy of Southern Historical Collection)

dent. He was a student and great admirer of his cousin, Edward Kidder Graham, who a few years later would be chosen as university president. Graham was the model student. One of his biographers, Warren Ashby, noted that the young man held to a vow not to smoke or drink and throughout his life he remained idealistic and a bit naive. He became a "custodian of the morals of men. The moral skepticism and relativism so typical of the young in every age and the normal gnawing religious doubts never touched him."

The university never knew a more devoted disciple. Graham's senior-class-day speech urging greater state support for the university so impressed the university president that he had it printed and distributed throughout the state. In the fall of 1909 Graham entered law school at Chapel Hill and remained active in campus life. Law school did not excite Graham. He took a two-year break to teach and coach at a high school in Raleigh before returning to Chapel Hill. After a second year in law school he was admitted to the bar in 1913. He remained uncertain about a career in law and immediately accepted the position of secretary of the university YMCA.

In 1914 he taught an American history course where students said he made history come alive. He seldom lectured, but emphasized discussion, debate, and class reenactments of critical events. His colleagues worried that his students did not always learn the critical facts, but Graham thought the clash of ideas was the core of the learning experience. Graham was invigorated by the classroom, but he believed that he could not make teaching a career without further preparation. In 1915 he entered Columbia University, where he earned a master's degree in June 1916 before recurring eye problems forced him to discontinue his studies. Seeking treatment and rest, he went to Minnesota where his brother, Archie, was an eye specialist.

In 1917, as the United States entered World War I, Graham was still in Minnesota. He tried to enlist but was turned down because of his weight and his poor eyesight. Later, the marines, with encouragement from Secretary of the Navy Josephus Daniels, a North Carolinian, accepted Graham, but he failed in his efforts to be sent overseas.

After the war, Graham returned to Chapel Hill as dean of students. The following year he welcomed the chance to return to the classroom to teach history. Graham was teaching four courses when he ignited a public campaign to increase state appropriations for the university. He became a leader in a successful campaign that produced the first major expansion of university facilities in more than a quarter century. Graham's energetic and inspirational leadership put him in contact with government leaders and university alumni and supporters throughout the state, who saw in him a man who could inspire public support for the university.

But he wanted to teach, and renewed his postgraduate education that had been interrupted by the war. In the fall of 1921 he entered the University of Chicago and from there went on to further graduate work at the Brookings Institution in Washington in 1923 and then on to the London School of Economics in 1924. In the fall of 1925 he once again was in a classroom in Chapel Hill, where he found the new buildings he had campaigned for four years earlier. He was thirty-eight years old, unmarried, without a

Ph.D., and had only two years of full-time teaching experience under his belt. Yet his studies and times of reflection had solidified his commitment to a lifetime of teaching and work to improve the conditions of people in North Carolina.

He became an active speaker and a promoter of causes, such as community libraries throughout the state, workers' compensation, and a bill of rights for labor. He seemed to be virtually everywhere in the state, although he never troubled himself to learn to drive a car. His support of labor rights during a time of violent strikes made some business leaders suspicious. When UNC President Harry Chase resigned in 1930, Graham refused to be considered as a successor, saying, "The job would never be offered me because of my recent battles. But even if it were, I wouldn't accept it."

But there also was widespread support for his election among the university trustees, including Governor O. Max Gardner, and Graham was elected over his strongly stated plea that he be allowed to continue as a teacher. He accepted, saying only, "Well, with your help and with the help of God" in what may have been one of the shortest acceptance speeches ever heard.

The new president immediately faced several serious challenges. First in his mind was an angry reaction from many North Carolinians to the visits to the university of socialist Bertrand Russell, black writer Langston Hughes, and other so-called radicals of the day. Graham was uncompromising in his defense of the university as a place of free expression. In his inaugural address in 1931, he had said that freedom of the university meant not only "the freedom of the scholar to report the truth honestly without interference by the university, the state, or any interests whatever," but also "the free voice not only for the unvoiced millions but also for the unpopular and even hated minorities."

The problems of the Great Depression pushed upon him immediately. The state's depleted treasury forced drastic budget cuts, and personal financial hardships threatened to keep many students away from campus. Graham hit the road to build support for the university and for the students for whom he raised scholarship funds, and he became a popular speaker. Despite his efforts, the university budget was cut substantially, but he averted complete disaster, sometimes calling on wealthy individuals for contributions to the university. His efforts kept the faculty morale high and the university's reputation as a leading center of learning and a resource for the entire state grew, even in hard times.

Graham's most severe test came with the implementation of a reorganization of the state's program of higher education, an economy move based on the recommendation of a Brookings Institute study. Governor Gardner enthusiastically pushed for the consolidation of the University at Chapel Hill, North Carolina State College in Raleigh, and the Woman's College at Greensboro into a single entity. Graham ultimately became president of the reorganized university and the leader of its three campuses, although he drew the undying enmity of some trustees who vehemently opposed changes such as the relocation of the engineering program at Chapel Hill to the campus in Raleigh.

On July 21, 1932, the forty-five-year-old Graham married Marian Drane, the daughter of an Episcopal clergyman from Edenton. Some wondered if the wedding would ever take place. Their small ceremony had to be postponed three times when threatened budget cuts to the university required Graham's attention. Finally, Governor Gardner promised Graham that there would be no further university budget cuts, at least "not until you are back from your wedding trip."

Graham was an inspirational leader and advocate for the university. But often the administrative details were like his desk—a mess. At the same time, he knew the name of virtually every student on the campus and often could tell a youngster's family history. Ironically, he was criticized for becoming involved in so many non-university projects. Chief among the competitors for his time were organizations that pushed for better working and living conditions for poor southerners. President Franklin Roosevelt also drew Graham away from the campus by placing him on many national boards and commissions. During World War II, Graham spent most of the time in Washington serving on the War Labor Board. He handled much university business by telephone and on the weekends, although by this time the trustees had hired W. D. Carmichael Jr., a Chapel Hill graduate who left a successful New York business career to handle the administrative details of the university.

In 1947, Secretary of State George Marshall called Graham to serve on a United Nations committee to negotiate a dispute between the colonial Dutch powers and the Indonesian forces that were establishing an independent republic. Graham's persistence and his ability to develop good working relations with both sides helped lead to a truce agreement in early 1948, and he again returned to Chapel Hill, where he plunged into university matters and controversial progressive causes.

Graham had served since 1946 as chairman of the board of the Oak Ridge Institute of Nuclear Studies. Critics suggested that he was a security risk because a number of the organizations that he had joined were "communist fronts." By early 1949, Fulton Lewis Jr., a national radio commentator, charged that Graham was not safe with atomic secrets.

The question of Graham's associations and beliefs became a topic for discussion in both houses of Congress in early 1949. On February 3, a Louisiana congressman said it was "disgraceful that a man in so great a position should so conduct himself" and that he had no right to remain head of the University of North Carolina. On March 3, Senator Spessard Holland of Florida said that Graham was "regarded as an ultra-liberal, as on the 'pinkish' side." Against this backdrop of criticism of his commitment to liberalism and his association with groups tagged as communist fronts, it was difficult to believe what next happened to Graham.

On March 22, 1949, Governor W. Kerr Scott announced that he intended to appoint Graham to the senate to fill a vacancy caused by the death of U.S. Senator Melville Broughton on March 6. Just how and why the politically savvy governor of a conservative southern state decided to appoint an unapologetic liberal under attack for association with communists was a question pondered for years, until the consensus of all the stories settled on one version. The governor was persuaded by his wife, who when hearing a list of the candidates under consideration said, "You can stop right there. So far as I'm concerned, that's it."

Jonathan Daniels, the editor of the News and Observer and one of the most influential Democrats in Raleigh, also urged Scott to name Graham, even though Graham strenuously resisted. He eventually agreed to leave the university one more time. On March 29, less than a month after he had been criticized on the senate floor, he was himself sworn in as a member.

Graham had less than a year before he would face election for the balance of Broughton's term. At first it appeared he would have only token opposition, but in February before the May Democratic Party primary, conservative Democrats recruited Willis Smith, a distinguished Raleigh attorney and former president of the American Bar Association, to oppose him.

Both men enjoyed wide respect throughout the state—even from those who disagreed with them. Graham was perhaps the best known in the field of four that also included former senator Robert "Our Bob" Reynolds from western North Carolina and Olla Ray Boyd, an eastern North Carolina pig farmer.

Smith raised some sensitive issues, particularly Graham's association with liberal organizations, but Graham ran strong and collected 48.9 percent of the vote. If Reynolds and Boyd had not been in the race, the campaign would have ended there.

But state law allowed Smith, who had placed second, to call for a runoff, which he did just hours before the deadline. Political folklore grew out of an evening rally on the lawn of Smith's Raleigh home, where supporters urged Smith to stay in the race. Most had been drawn there by radio ads placed by a young Raleigh radio newsman named Jesse Helms.

Smith faced an enormous challenge in the runoff—how to persuade large numbers of working-class Democrats to vote for a conservative business-oriented lawyer. In 1950, race and communism were two things that could persuade a lot of North Carolina whites to vote against their economic interests and Graham was vulnerable on both issues. Smith's supporters exploited both issues. Although Smith distanced himself from what turned into a race-baiting campaign, handbills with doctored photographs, newspaper ads, and the mail were all used to arouse racial emotions. Graham soon was overwhelmed by allegations that he supported mixing the races in the workplace and virtually everywhere else. To a lesser degree, Smith's followers played up Graham's membership in organizations that were supposedly communist fronts.

Graham refused to respond in kind. His supporters attempted, with little success, to arouse voters against Smith's "big business" leanings. Among his clients were some of the largest corporations in the state. Smith came from well behind and easily defeated Graham.

The Graham-Smith contest was a proving ground for competitors to come. Helms, who subsequently went to Washington with Smith, was later elected to the Senate as a Republican in 1972. Among Graham's supporters were Terry Sanford, later governor, senator, and president of Duke University, and William Friday, who became president of the UNC system.

Typically, Graham put aside all bitterness after the primary and even campaigned for Smith in the fall election. But the loss had hurt him deeply. Biographer William Ashby summed it up: "For the first time in his life he, who had been lavished with love, was publicly rejected, apparently hated—and in North Carolina. The hurt was greatest of all because he was rejected by the very people—the textile workers, the farmers and the sharecroppers, the small businessmen —for whom he had lived and fought. And it had happened because he was misunderstood."

Graham left the Senate in 1950 at the age of sixty-four with no plans. In January 1951, at the request of President Truman, he chaired a labor management conference, which developed a pathway to settle labor disputes during the Korean War without labor stoppages. In 1951 he agreed to serve on a United Nations commission seeking a solution to the dispute between India and Pakistan over Kashmir. His qualities of persistence and patience were no match for this problem—one that remained unresolved half a century later. But Graham would not give it up. He remained at the United Nations until 1967 when Marian's death and a heart attack prompted a move back to North Carolina.

From 1967 until his death on February 16, 1972, he lived with his sister in Chapel Hill. He and Marian were buried in the cemetery adjoining the campus. A stone marking their grave reads: "They had faith in youth and youth responded with their best."

D. G. Martin is a newspaper columnist and hosts UNC-TV's North Carolina *Bookwatch, a program that features interviews with North Carolina authors. He is a lawyer and former vice president of public affairs for the University of North Carolina.*

For more information, see:

Graham, Frank Porter. Papers. Southern Historical Collection, University of North Carolina at Chapel Hill.

Ashby, Warren. *Frank Porter Graham: A Southern Liberal.* John F. Blair, 1980.
Dr. Frank: The Life and Times of Frank Porter Graham. John Wilson Productions, 1994.
Ehle, John. *Dr. Frank: Life with Frank Porter Graham.* Franklin Street Books, 1993.
Pleasants, Julian, and Augustus M. Burns III. *Frank Porter Graham and the 1950 Senate Race in North Carolina.* University of North Carolina Press, 1990.
Snider, William D. *Light on the Hill: A History of the University of North Carolina at Chapel Hill.* University of North Carolina Press, 1992.

W. DALLAS HERRING

By Jonathan Phillips

AT AN EARLY AGE, William Dallas Herring knew that North Carolina's education system must be improved. He learned this as a student in the schools of rural Duplin County in the 1920s and 1930s. The failings of the state's public school system were further reinforced after he entered Davidson College and found he was woefully unprepared for the rigors of college academics after only eleven years in a state-supported classroom.

For some, the answer was simple: send your children to private schools. But this was not Herring's solution. He saw much that was good in the concept of public schooling and would devote most of his life to improving the quality of and increasing the accessibility to public education in the Tar Heel State. Most notably, he played a prominent role in two of North Carolina's greatest challenges since World War II—school integration and industrial training.

North Carolina's official reaction to the 1954 Supreme Court's *Brown v. Board of Education* decision prohibiting segregation was in large part the state leadership's response to the proposals of Dallas Herring. Herring served on the Pearsall Committee, the group Governor William Umstead asked to formulate a response to the Court's decision. Although Herring found the Court's ruling unfortunate, at no time did he waver from his position that the law of the land should not be broken. Most importantly, Herring pressed for a compromise solution that kept the public schools open at a time when massive resistance held broad currency.

Herring also pursued an expansive program of postsecondary vocational training. He embraced the philosophy of "total education," his term for educational opportunity for everyone. North Carolina hoped to lure industry to the Tar Heel state, but without a well-trained workforce, the state simply could not provide workers with the appropriate skills. Herring convinced Governor Luther Hodges of the need for industrial education centers. By the 1970s, Herring's training centers had evolved into the state's community college system.

Herring was born in Rose Hill on March 15, 1916, the second son of six children, to Dallas Burke and Lula Southernland Herring. He spent his boyhood years in the flat, hot coastal plain that by the turn of the century would be dominated by large-scale poul-

W. Dallas Herring (Courtesy of News and Observer)

try and hog farms. Although his father's illness and the resulting family commitments interrupted his college studies, he received his bachelor's degree, cum laude, in 1938 from Davidson College. He returned to Rose Hill to run the family business, the Atlantic Coffin and Casket Company, and assumed the presidency later that year. In 1939, at the age of twenty-three, he was elected mayor of Rose Hill, and, according to the League of Municipalities, became the youngest mayor in the nation. During his eleven-year tenure, Rose Hill constructed a town hall and public works system, and organized a fire department. In addition, the town's streets were paved and sidewalks were built. During the 1930s and 1940s, many small towns had such infrastructure improvements in mind, especially after World War II, but few municipalities actually accomplished so much.

Beginning in 1951, he served a term as chairman of the Duplin County Board of Education. He became known within the state's education circles for successfully consolidating the county's numerous small one-room schools into seven high schools. Consolidation not only improved the cost of education, but also allowed greater opportunity for children with special needs—those who required the most challenging courses and those who needed remedial training.

Unlike many white southerners, Herring also favored policies that emphasized the equal in the "separate but equal" clause of the 1896 *Plessy v. Ferguson* decision that led to institutionalized segregation throughout the South. During his tenure on the school board, the budget was allocated equally between black and white schools based upon a per student amount and Duplin County successfully upgraded school buildings for students of both races. The effort for equality was especially surprising in eastern North Carolina, where black students typically suffered from appallingly unequal conditions.

During the 1930s and 1940s, North Carolina's leadership had placed greater emphasis on the "equal" part of the separate-but-equal doctrine, but fell well short. If the state's education system demonstrated a veneer of racial equality, it was because white schools were well below the national average, as Herring knew all too well, and not that the quality of nonwhite schools was improving. The 1954 Court decision forced white North Carolinians to face up to racial equality in education and the possibility of integrated schools. The great majority of whites supported segregated schools. However, they were sharply divided on how to respond to the Supreme Court decision. Some advocated defiance of the Court order, as was seen elsewhere in the South. If the federal government insisted on integration, then North Carolina should either ignore the order or close the public schools.

Other North Carolinians, such as Herring, looked for ways to continue segregated schooling without violating the decision. As southern legal experts quickly determined, the ruling did not mandate integration, but instead merely stated that segregation must end. The 1957 clarification of the decision required states to end segregation "with all deliberate speed." This bought time for southern moderates.

But how could the state continue segregation lawfully? As a member of the Pearsall Committee, Herring worked diligently to answer this question. Most importantly, he wanted to keep the schools open. Eventually, Herring submitted a proposal to the committee entitled "Save Our Schools," which advocated a pupil assignment plan based upon aptitude test scores. North Carolina's schools would be segregated based upon ability and not upon race. In a separate and unequal school system, even a bad one, white students had better schools and materials, and easily surpassed nonwhites on standardized aptitude tests. At the time, no thought was given to cultural bias in testing or to the environmental disadvantages of minority students.

Many found Herring's strategy troubling. Some nonwhite students scored very high on the tests and would therefore have the opportunity to attend the schools designed for high achievement. At the same time, a small number of white students scored very poorly on the tests. Under Herring's plan, these white students would be assigned to attend the largely nonwhite schools.

Herring did not know how segregation based upon test scores would change over time. Would nonwhite students eventually reach parity with white students and gradually integrate the schools? Herring admitted at the time that he did not know the answer. According to one scholar of North Carolina education, Herring did not hold that nonwhites were inherently intellectually inferior to white students. However, Herring's research into the question probably led him to think otherwise at the time. As he noted in 1955, "I ought to say plainly that my understanding of Christianity and of democracy has not led me to the conclusion that segregation is wrong." And even in the northeastern states where some school districts had been fully integrated for years, blacks scored much lower on achievement tests, according to Herring's research.

In addition, differences existed between the races on tests given in the first grade in Duplin County. But Herring did not lose sight of his ultimate goal—to keep school doors open in the face of a Supreme Court decision that was ardently opposed by the great majority of whites. In the context of the time, Herring did not consider full integration as politically possible. And on this assumption, the white leadership concurred, hard-liners and moderates alike.

The problem of what to do with low-scoring whites proved to be the death knell to Herring's proposal. Although Herring feared a violent backlash from poor whites, his greatest concern was that middle- and upper-class whites would transfer their children to private or parochial schools. The Pearsall Committee eventually recommended that integration should not be attempted; that the possibility of closing the state's public schools should be considered; and that the General Assembly should enact legislation giving ". . . complete authority over enrollment and assignment of children in public schools and school buses . . ." to local school boards. In essence, the state placed the responsibility on local school boards, thus discouraging a single lawsuit to integrate the entire system at once. Herring reluctantly agreed to the plan, under intense pressure from Governor Luther Hodges, but only after Hodges assured him that he did not intend to close any schools.

Based on Hodges's pledge, Herring publicly supported the Pearsall Committee's report, which has led some historians to place him with the hard-line segregationists. Although this conclusion can be drawn from his actions in the months following the release of the report, it is a serious misreading of Herring's efforts and overlooks his earlier efforts in Duplin County. Herring supported the report because, at the time, he sincerely believed it to be the best of what were all bad options, at least from his perspective. In the context of the turmoil of the 1950s, the Pearsall report, if applied, was the least likely to commit the state to wholesale school closure. As Herring stated at the time, "I am opposed to integration, but I am also opposed to lawlessness."

Although Herring disagreed with Hodges on the state's response, the governor appointed Herring to the state Board of Education in 1955. Initially frustrated by the board's lack of initiative, Herring continued to serve and by 1957 was elected chairman—a position he held until 1977. In 1956, Hodges also appointed Herring to the state Board of Higher Education, where Herring devoted his energy to expanding educational opportunities for all North Carolinians. However, his greatest contribution came in the realm of adult education, or re-education—as it was initially conceived.

At the time, Hodges was vigorously engaged in the "selling of North Carolina," to borrow a phrase of one historian of the South, in an effort to recruit new businesses to the state. He was well known in New York business circles for his aggressive campaign to lure business southward, where land and labor were cheap and the climate far superior to the Northeast. However, as Hodges learned, the single greatest impediment to his program was a lack of skilled labor.

After Herring told Hodges in 1957 that it was unrealistic to expect farmers with no previous training to begin working in industrial plants, the governor asked Herring to prepare a proposal for industrial education. Although his initial plan was voted down in 1957, he succeeded in 1958 with a less ambitious program of industrial education centers, the first of which opened in Burlington in 1959. The state provided funding for equipment and buildings while federal programs covered the cost of administration and instruction. In time, these industrial education centers became the community colleges of another generation.

Creating a substantive community college system in North Carolina was no easy task. In 1953, the Community College Act had been defeated in the state legislature. Primary opposition came from the supporters of higher education, who wanted to develop liberal arts junior colleges, and in 1957 the supporters of this plan succeeded. The state established a junior college system, which was called the community college system. Unlike junior colleges, community colleges, by definition, included a substantial vocational component. Before a college could be included in the system, according to the 1957 legislation, it must first divorce itself from all vocational training—or find a way to pay for nonacademic training without using state monies. In addition, the community college system established in 1957 was segregated, while the industrial education centers were integrated from the very beginning. Such was the division of labor, however, that Hodges refused to support the establishment of libraries in the industrial centers until Herring explained that even industrial students needed to refer to technical manuals.

Some Tar Heel educators, especially those involved with higher education, suspected incorrectly that Herring was only interested in vocational training. Herring understood that "the community college system had to be built as events would allow." He always intended for these centers to expand their course offerings to include academic courses. "We may gradually introduce . . . some basic academic courses . . . ," Herring stated in 1958. "Following this, it will only be a step to introduce college-level academic programs of a junior college character." In 1963, Herring got his wish when the legislature passed the Community College Act at the urging of Governor Terry Sanford, who adopted Herring's plan to expand educational opportunities beyond high school. The act permanently established a comprehensive community, and not junior, college system in the state. By 1973, over 400,000 students attended the state's fifty junior colleges.

Herring found a willing ally in Sanford. The young governor admired Herring's work on the state board and his leadership in a statewide citizen's committee called the United Forces for Education (UFE). Sanford understood the need for curriculum reform, teacher certification, tougher standards, and perhaps most importantly, increased funding for primary and secondary education. During his campaign for governor, Sanford fully endorsed the UFE program and in 1961 won legislative approval to extend the state sales tax to cover food in order to raise the money to pay for the UFE program. It was a risky political decision, and one that dogged Sanford for the rest of his political life.

Throughout his career, Herring received numerous accolades and awards. Sanford called him "North Carolina's greatest spokesman for education in the twentieth century." Governor James B. Hunt called him an "educational giant." He was North Carolina's "Education's Man of the Year" in 1954 and received the state's highest award for citizenship in 1972. In 1980, he accepted the Hugh McEniry award from the North Carolina Association of Colleges and Universities for his outstanding service on behalf of higher education. In 1979, the Duplin County Board of Commissioners established May 6–12 as Dallas Herring Week, and later that year North Carolina State University began its fund-raising campaign for the Dallas Herring Professorship in Community College Education. In 1985, a scholarship was established in his name at James Sprunt Technical College, where he served on the board of trustees. He also was awarded three honorary doctorates.

Herring devoted the later years of his life to the history of Duplin County. A lifelong bachelor, his home in Rose Hill was the virtual and literal home of the library of the Duplin County Historical Society. He also enjoyed painting and sketching. In 1992, he published *What Has Happened to the Golden Door?*, a collection of his writings concerning education in North Carolina. In his later years, Herring became increasingly concerned about the limits to education created by the rising cost of tuition. He also lamented the loss of citizen involvement in the decision-making process in education.

Herring spent his life opening doors to learning. That was his quest in the 1950s and he practiced it at home. Hardly a day went by when he didn't have at least one historical researcher in his house. As he said in 1979, "If I could have one plea, it is that we close no doors, that we stand in the way of no individual's desire to learn."

Jonathan Phillips's doctoral dissertation in history at the University of North Carolina at Chapel Hill examined the economic and cultural impact of the military presence in the Fayetteville and Sandhills region of North Carolina. In 2000–2001 he was a fellow at the Center of Military History.

For more information, see:

Herring, William Dallas. Interview by Jay Jenkins, February and May 1987. Southern Oral History Project. Southern Historical Collection, University of North Carolina at Chapel Hill.

———. Interview by William A. Link, February 1990. Southern Oral History Project. Southern Historical Collection, University of North Carolina at Chapel Hill.

———. Papers. N.C. State Archives, Raleigh.

Batchelor, John Ellsworth. "Rule of Law: North Carolina School Desegregation, 1954–1974." Ed.D. diss., North Carolina State University, 1992.

Herring, William Dallas. *What Has Happened to the Golden Door?* Bedwyr Historical Press, 1992.

Hodges, Luther. *Businessman in the Statehouse: Six Years as Governor of North Carolina.* University of North Carolina Press, 1962.

Link, William A. *William Friday, Power, Purpose, and American Higher Education.* University of North Carolina Press, 1995.

Mayberry, Lena Pearl Dula. "William Dallas Herring: Leader in Five Issues in Education in North Carolina 1955–1965." Ph.D. diss., North Carolina State University, 1972.

LEO W. JENKINS

By Kathryn Schwille

AFTER LEO JENKINS had retired as chancellor of East Carolina University, a reporter asked if his fight to bring a medical school to eastern North Carolina had been worth it. Jenkins answered with a story about his visit to ECU's Neonatal Intensive Care Unit, where six critically ill babies were expected to recover. He asked a doctor what would have happened to the infants before the school was built. The doctor replied that two would be dead, two would be severely retarded, and two would be borderline. "Does that answer the question, 'Was it worthwhile?'" Jenkins said.

Twenty-five years after its creation, critics still said building a state-supported medical school in Greenville was an unnecessary expense. Few would argue, though, that ECU's medical school is a testament to the long-standing power of eastern North Carolina politicians and Jenkins's relentless ambition. During his eighteen years as president, from 1960 to 1978, Jenkins's name became synonymous with the school, an institution that embodied the aspirations of a region some outsiders called backward and hopelessly insular. Over the course of his tenure, Jenkins was accused of playing politics, empire building, and expanding the university to satisfy his ego. Jenkins maintained that all he wanted was a university that could be a cultural, educational, and athletic center for a region that had, in his words, been "put down and taken for granted."

Born in New Jersey in 1913, Leo Warren Jenkins was an unlikely candidate to become such a ferocious promoter for a slice of the rural South. His father worked for Standard Oil and he grew up in Elizabeth, an industrial port city south of Newark. His neighborhood was full of European immigrants struggling to adapt to America in the face of hard times and dismissive cultural assumptions. Jenkins would later tell audiences that his was the only native-born family on the block, but that from his neighbors he learned to respect how much people can yearn to improve their lives.

After graduating in 1931 from Jefferson High School for Boys, where he was president of the senior class, Jenkins enrolled at Rutgers University. He majored in political science and took enough education courses to qualify for a teaching certificate. In 1935 he began

Leo W. Jenkins (Courtesy of Charlotte Observer)

teaching high school near Atlantic City. Assigned to teach English to fifty mostly disinterested boys, Jenkins devised a plan to spark their enthusiasm for reading. When *Ivanhoe* failed to captivate them, he tried using *Esquire* magazine for a text. Within a year many of the boys had become avid readers and their vocabularies had expanded. He would later describe his youthful approach as "brazen," but he was proud of the results.

In 1936 Jenkins made his first trip south for a summer fellowship at Duke University. For the next several years, while teaching high school, he spent weekends and summers in graduate studies. He earned a master's degree from Columbia University and in 1941 was awarded a doctorate in education from New York University. The following year he married another schoolteacher, Lillian Jacobsen of Lavallette, N.J. Shortly after their wedding he enlisted in the U.S. Marine Corps, which prompted his second trip to the South—boot camp at Parris Island, S.C.

The military offered Jenkins another opportunity for educational experiments. Upon completion of Officers' Candidate School, Jenkins was sent to Guadalcanal. There, and later in Guam, he launched an off-duty volunteer school for marines who wanted to pursue high school or college studies. By the end of World War II, eight thousand soldiers had been enrolled in the schools he initiated. For his battlefield efforts in Guam and Iwo Jima, Jenkins was awarded a Bronze Star.

After his discharge, Jenkins became a political science instructor at New Jersey State Teachers College in Montclair. The next year he landed a post as assistant to the New Jersey commissioner of higher education and dreamed of being the commissioner. After his boss suggested he needed more experience on a college campus, Jenkins took that advice and in 1947, at age thirty-four, became dean at East Carolina Teachers College. The school of 1,600 mostly female students had been founded in 1907 on a cotton field east of Greenville. He expected to stay a year or so before returning to New Jersey. He remained for thirty-one years, and lived in North Carolina for the rest of his life.

A popular dean, Jenkins was later named vice president of the school. The father of six children, he was a fixture at public school gatherings, civic functions, and St. James United Methodist Church. When John Messick resigned as college president in 1959, the forty-six-year-old Jenkins was the obvious choice to succeed him.

Jenkins was inaugurated on May 13, 1960. The keynote speaker was William C. Friday, president of the Consolidated University of North Carolina, which was then composed of the state's three campuses at Chapel Hill, Greensboro, and Raleigh. In his remarks, Friday noted the dramatic growth of East Carolina and its significant impact on life in eastern North Carolina. What Friday didn't know was that Jenkins would become a college chief executive like none the state had ever known, a man whose big ideas and populist ways would be a thorn in the side of the education establishment Friday represented and steadfastly defended.

Jenkins started his campaign for expansion with his inaugural address. Governor Luther Hodges, who had a short list of other people he favored for president, told the crowd the school should concentrate on what it did best—educating teachers. Jenkins challenged the governor's opinion. "If the citizens of North Carolina will define any new duties that they wish East Carolina College to fulfill," Jenkins said in

his speech, "and if they will support the college with money, confidence, and more important, faith, this great college will assume them and justify this faith and support in the future as it has in the past." It was a philosophy he would come back to time and again as he rallied public sentiment for the school's development. The state Board of Higher Education had already rejected his first proposal—to start a master's program in business administration. He had only begun to fight.

Jenkins's first years as president were marked by phenomenal growth at the school. Between 1960 and 1967, enrollment doubled, from 4,500 to 9,000, making it the largest "college" in the South. Jenkins encouraged organization along university lines—the education department became the School of Education, for instance. Graduate programs were established, though not without protracted struggles with the state Board of Higher Education.

As an administrator Jenkins focused on long-range planning, leaving the day-to-day operations to his dean. A tireless public speaker, he dictated ideas into a pocket tape recorder as he drove from county to county on the small-town banquet circuit, drumming up support. He wanted a powerhouse football team and a new stadium. An amateur painter, he set his sights on having a prestigious arts program and tried to lure poet Carl Sandburg out of the mountains to become writer-in-residence. When Jenkins learned the Tar River was going to be dredged, he persuaded two Ivy League schools to donate used racing shells in hopes of starting a crew team. The Tar proved unsuitable, but the team was established on the Pamlico River.

Jenkins loved sports and was fond of giving pregame pep talks to the football team. When it was time to build a new stadium, he picked Greenville insurance executive W. M. Scales Jr. to lead the fundraising. Scales and five well-heeled friends prowled Greenville together in a big car and put the touch on business owners, raising $215,000 in a week. The new sixteen-thousand-seat stadium opened in the fall of 1963. The East Carolina Pirates went 9–1 for the season and were invited to their first bowl game.

Though eastern North Carolina was growing, it still had the highest infant mortality rate in the country. In 1964, the counties east of Interstate 95 had fewer than 50 physicians per 100,000 residents, while the state's average was 75 and the national average was 125.

The only state-supported medical school was at Chapel Hill, but graduates rarely chose to practice in the rural east. Jenkins seized on the statistics when he began to pursue the idea of a medical school on his campus. He also turned to his strongest ally in the legislature—state senator Robert B. Morgan, who was chair of East Carolina's board of trustees and president pro tem of the senate. When Morgan proposed funding the medical school to the 1965 General Assembly, he met stiff resistance. The three other medical schools in the state—UNC, Duke, and Wake Forest—feared competition for federal and state funds. Other officials thought if the state were going to build a second medical school it should be in a more urban area, namely Charlotte. East Carolina was deemed academically ill-equipped to support such a venture.

But the idea had tremendous support back home. When the joint appropriations committee took up the proposal, two hundred people appeared to support it. The General Assembly appropriated $250,000 to build a new science hall and begin planning for a two-year medical program, over the objections of Governor Dan K. Moore and the state Board of Higher Education. It would be nine more years before a four-year medical school would be funded.

In 1967 the legislature approved a system of regional universities that gave East Carolina the university title it coveted. The press for a medical school continued. "In a state where so distressingly few of its students go to college," Jenkins told a meeting of professors in Chapel Hill, "it constitutes a gall beyond all accounting for any individual, agency, board or commission to dare to say that North Carolina needs only this or that particular number of trained educated young men and women."

Jenkins liked to say the state's big daily newspapers collaborated with his opponents in the medical school fight. But Jenkins relished being well known and loved to see his name in print or his face on television. He might have been fired, he said years later, but his opponents "didn't know who would come to my rescue."

William Friday, still in charge of the UNC system, was alarmed by the threat of unregulated expansion for politically powerful regional schools such as Western Carolina, Appalachian State, and especially East Carolina. Friday thought educators, not politicians, should control higher education. Jenkins and ECU assumed the role of a David taking on the Goliath of Chapel Hill's influence. The underdog status delighted him and he played it to the hilt. ECU appealed to the legislature in 1969 and again in 1971 for money to establish the medical school, but each time the General Assembly backed off. Governor Bob Scott,

who supported a second medical school at ECU, predicted the "blue bloods" of UNC would not prevail.

When the state's universities were restructured in 1971, ECU became part of the system of sixteen campuses controlled by a new board of governors. Jenkins worried that the ECU medical program, which was still only a one-year preparation that fed students to other medical schools, would never be more than a "satellite" to the four-year school at Chapel Hill. He asked the board of governors for permission to develop a two-year program as a first step to a full-fledged medical school. The board responded by proposing increased enrollment at Chapel Hill's medical school, and, at Friday's urging, appointed a "blue ribbon panel" of outside experts to examine the ECU medical school issue.

ECU officials called the panel a smoke screen for Chapel Hill interests. Jenkins was confident the General Assembly was on his side, no matter what the panel reported, but he could no longer appeal directly to legislators. Under the restructuring he had become chancellor of ECU and now reported to Friday, who didn't allow his chancellors to lobby the legislature without permission. But ECU had vocal support on the board of governors. After the outside experts reported that a medical school at ECU was premature, the board voted to limit the ECU program to one year. Eight dissenting members sent the legislature a minority report calling for the four-year school.

The question of expanding ECU's program dominated a session of the General Assembly in 1974. The possibility of such a big appropriation hung over every other money issue that came up. Democratic Lieutenant Governor Jim Hunt, an ECU supporter, warned if the state Board of Higher Education didn't establish the school, the legislature would. Friday saw the handwriting on the wall. Though he still opposed it, he would say years later that "there was no point in fighting it any longer." He recommended to the board of governors that a four-year school be established at ECU. In 1975 the General Assembly appropriated $43 million to build it. The first students graduated from Brody Medical School in 1981.

The Jenkins era at ECU was marked by other issues that occupied campuses in the 1960s and 1970s, including student protests. Jenkins tolerated most protests as long as there was no great disturbance. When students gathered to lower the campus flag after the Kent State shootings, he met them at the flagpole and turned away their plans to occupy the administration building. But when about a thousand students, some of them unruly, protested at his off-campus home over the issue of dorm visitation, he called police and thirty-four students were arrested.

Jenkins often made gifts of the landscapes he painted and proudly signed. In honor of his love of art and his efforts on behalf of the arts school, a new fine arts building was named for him while he was still chancellor. Once or twice during his tenure he flirted with the idea of running for governor. It was more of a tactical maneuver to gain attention for the school. He never formally announced his candidacy. He retired from ECU in 1978 and moved to a condominium near Morehead City, where he died of cancer in January 1989. Later that year the medical school's cancer center was named in his honor.

Kathryn Schwille is a journalist and fiction writer. Her nonfiction has appeared in Charlotte Magazine *and in the* Atlanta Journal-Constitution, *the* St. Paul Pioneer-Press, *and other newspapers. She has an MFA from the Program for Writers at Warren Wilson College, and is a former political editor at the* Charlotte Observer. *Her fiction has been published in* Sycamore Review, Sou'wester, *and* No Hiding Place, *an anthology of Charlotte writers.*

For more information, see:

Bratton, Mary Jo Jackson. *East Carolina University: The Formative Years, 1907–1982*. East Carolina University Alumni Association, 1986.

"Dr. Leo Jenkins, the Man Who Asked 'Why Not.'" *ECU Medical Review* 8, no. 3 (December 1985).

Jenkins, Leo W. "Struggle to Serve." Address to the American Association of University Professors, March 16, 1967. University of North Carolina at Chapel Hill.

Link, William A. *William Friday, Power, Purpose, and American Higher Education*. University of North Carolina Press, 1995.

Savage, Stuart. "Decade of Furthering East's Progress." *Greenville Daily Reflector,* January 25, 1970.

Taylor, Mike. "Jenkins Champions Eastern Causes." *Downeaster,* August 6, 1975.

J. Y. JOYNER

By Kathryn Schwille

WHEN JAMES JOYNER took a cut in pay and left a job he loved to become state superintendent of public instruction in 1902, he thought the posting would be a short one. His old college friend, Charles B. Aycock, had been elected governor and was leaning on him to take the appointment. Joyner accepted reluctantly, finally conceding that since Aycock had declared education his top priority, he should have the man he wanted for school superintendent.

Joyner expected he would have the position only as long as Aycock was governor. But he stayed seventeen years, long after Aycock had died. By the time Joyner left, he had helped bring such modern notions as compulsory attendance, longer school terms, and local tax support for schools to a state that had one of the highest illiteracy rates in the country. His legacy as one of the architects of the public school movement would help make North Carolina a leader in the education crusade spreading across the South, and would complicate the issue of race and schools as never before. Created against the prevailing politics of white supremacy, the drive would bring new schools and better teachers to white children, but leave black children further behind than when it started.

James Yadkin Joyner was born August 7, 1862, in the Davidson County community of Yadkin College. It was not his family's home, but a temporary refuge where his father, John Joyner, had fled with his pregnant wife and six children after Federal troops moved in to New Bern, not far from the family's Lenoir County plantation.

Joyner was not to know much of a permanent home in his youth. His mother, Sarah, died when he was six months old and his father, already in poor health, died before Joyner turned two. He was put in the care of his maternal grandfather, Council Wooten, a prominent planter and Democratic politician in Lenoir County.

Though Joyner would later credit his grandfather with exerting a great influence on his character, his grandfather died when he was only ten and the boy moved again, this time to the home of his twenty-six-year-old uncle, Shadrack Wooten. Wooten had few resources and a new family of his own, but he was determined that Joyner would make good. The boy's inheritance provided enough money for private schooling at nearby LaGrange Academy.

J. Y. Joyner (Courtesy of N.C. Office of Archives and History)

At sixteen, Joyner left LaGrange for the University of North Carolina, where he found, in 1878, an institution eager to be the intellectual incubator for a generation of young men who had come of age in the postwar South. Among Joyner's classmates were Edwin A. Alderman and Charles D. McIver—men whose families, like Joyner's, were so affected by the war that they could offer few prospects to their sons. Arriving at the university in search of a new life, the three young men and others like them filled their evenings with exuberant talk of how to make the world a better place. Joyner and his colleagues spent at least one summer vacation attending classes and taking part in debates. Years later, their friend and fellow reformer Marcus Noble would single out that experience as the starting point of what he called "their life and devotion and labor in behalf of public education."

Joyner and his idealistic companions came to see how education could be a tool to shape social and economic forces in the state, and they wanted to be part of it. By the 1890s, Alderman, McIver, and Joyner would emerge as the core of a group of nearly thirty university men who found not just vocations in education, but, as Alderman put it, "a cause to which a man might nobly attach himself."

After graduating in 1881 with a bachelor of philosophy degree, Joyner returned to LaGrange Academy to teach Latin. While principal there in 1882, he was appointed school superintendent for Lenoir County, the youngest man ever to hold that post. In 1884, he joined McIver as a teacher at a school in Winston, but at the same time began studying law as a hedge against uncertainty. Schools were financially unstable and offered no guarantee of steady income. McIver, who also was contemplating law, noted the "dividends of gratitude and homage" did not come to those who taught children.

Joyner must have felt the same frustrations, for in 1886 he left the classroom. He opened a law practice in Goldsboro, where he could be near his future wife, Effie E. Rouse, a graduate of Peace Institute and a teacher. Yet Joyner maintained his interest in education. For two years he chaired the Wayne County Board of Education, and in the summer of 1889, he joined Alderman and McIver in conducting institutes that offered many teachers across the state their first professional training. Though a successful lawyer, Joyner quit after three years to return to his calling as superintendent of the Goldsboro Graded Schools. The chairman of the Goldsboro Board of Education was his old friend, Charles Aycock.

Meanwhile, McIver had stuck with teaching and his career flourished. He had been named president of the State Normal and Industrial School at Greensboro (later the University of North Carolina at Greensboro), and in 1893, he persuaded Joyner to become head of the English department and dean of faculty there.

When Joyner assumed responsibility for the teacher training programs, the college was the first state institution to train women for the classroom. With such a variety of duties, Joyner happily combined his love of reading and poetry with his interest in teaching. He liked Greensboro and was popular there. He was elected to the city council and served on the board of trustees of the new Agricultural and Technical College for African Americans. He became president of the state Teachers Assembly, and spoke out on educational issues, particularly state support of higher education.

Though there was much talk about education reform in North Carolina, politicians in the late 1890s were far more mindful of a less lofty issue. The Democratic Party had lost its grip on the legislature in 1894, defeated by a coalition of African Americans,

Republicans, and farmers. To restore their position, the Democrats launched a campaign of racial fear. Newspapers harangued blacks as an "inferior race" and asserted the God-given right of white men to lead civilization. In 1900, voters approved a constitutional amendment that effectively disenfranchised African Americans, thus breaking the back of the Republican Party in the state. Aycock, a Democrat who claimed education as his priority, steadfastly defended white supremacy and won the governorship.

When the legislature met in 1901, a spirited education lobby set up headquarters at a Raleigh hotel. Joyner was named chief strategist in the effort to convince the legislators to amend the constitution and require four-month school terms, even though only about one-fourth of the state's schools were in session that long. The General Assembly approved the amendment, but provided no funds, a pattern it followed with most of the educational initiatives that came along over the next fifteen years.

McIver was at the center of an educational reform movement spurred by northern philanthropists. Collaborating with Aycock and Superintendent of Public Instruction Thomas F. Toon, he put together a conference in Raleigh of about forty educators and civic-minded men. Out of the meeting came a document outlining the state's vast educational shortcomings. During the planning for the conference, Toon had contracted pneumonia, and he died of a heart attack a few days after the Raleigh conference convened on February 25, 1902. Aycock appointed the thirty-nine-year-old Joyner to replace him.

When Joyner took office, only about half of the state's school-age children were enrolled, compared with the national average of nearly 70 percent. There were more than five thousand white rural school districts in the state. The typical schoolhouse had a dirt ramp, instead of steps, into a room with six windows and a dilapidated wood stove that was no match for the cold winds that blew through cracks in the walls. Students sat on homemade benches and faced a teacher who had a chair but no desk, and was paid between eighteen and thirty dollars a month. The average value of a white rural schoolhouse was $206. That was less, Joyner complained, "than the value of almost the poorest house in any city or town." He was deeply troubled by the conditions of the schools. "A respectable school house," he said, "is not only necessary for conducting successfully the business of public education but is absolutely essential for commanding the respect of the community for that business."

Following the Raleigh meeting, North Carolina

launched its public school movement. The first push involved raising money in urban areas to use in persuading rural voters to approve local school taxes. Joyner, McIver, and campaign coordinator Eugene C. Brooks prepared a 176-page document outlining the state's educational troubles, and ten thousand copies were printed and distributed. Joined by other reform-minded educators, they put their case to the people in a series of rallies, hoping to impress upon voters the idea that tax-supported, free public schools were a community responsibility. The first rally, in Rockingham on June 19, 1902, drew fifteen-hundred people, including every teacher in the county. In rural areas, though, reception to the idea was much colder. "The thing for us to do," said Alderman, "is to hammer on until the desire for better schools and all that belongs to better schools, becomes a contagion with the people." Brooks planned another campaign the next year, drawing on orators from every section of the state.

Sentiment for publicly funded education grew, but many whites insisted that all local taxes should be used to support white schools, and legislation was prepared to prevent black schools from being financed by taxes paid by whites. In his first biennial report, Joyner explained his opposition to such a move: "We have made many grievous mistakes in the education of the negro. We have too often flung him the part of the money that the Constitution required us to give and then left him without direction to waste it at his will." In admonishing proponents of the separate tax, Joyner said, "If part of the taxes actually paid by individual white men ever reaches [blacks] for school purposes, the amount is so small that the man that would begrudge it or complain about it ought to be ashamed of himself."

Joyner warned that to deny education to black children would only hasten trouble. "Who can estimate the danger that lurks in such a mass of ignorance, if these Negroes be left uneducated?" He saw only one alternative to the race war that whites feared, or certain failure if African Americans were not educated. "With the Negro," he argued, "it must be elevation through proper education or extermination." To Joyner, the governor, and most of their colleagues, the concept of universal education meant free public schools for all, but those schools must train blacks to serve, not to lead.

Joyner took over McIver's job of directing the public schools campaigns when McIver died in 1906. The rallies for local taxation continued relentlessly, with some success. Total revenues for public schools increased by almost five times between 1900 and 1915,

about twice the increase of wealth in the same period. Local tax funds, which were negligible in 1900, amounted in 1915 to more than the total of the school funds fifteen years earlier. The average length of the school term almost doubled, as did average attendance. This was growth that no other state could match. Yet black schoolchildren, who made up one-third of the population, received in 1900 about 28 percent of the meager school funds itemized by race. By 1915, that number had fallen to 13 percent.

In 1913 Joyner rallied public support for a mandatory school attendance law. The 1910 census had placed North Carolina at the top of the list for white illiteracy and at the bottom for state expenditures per child. The resulting law required children between the ages of eight and fourteen to attend school four months out of the year. A complementary measure prohibited the employment of children under fourteen —a law vigorously opposed by cotton and textile interests in the state. When the twin laws went into effect in 1914, the result was 75,919 more children attending school. Joyner concluded that this was the largest enrollment increase for any one year in the history of the state, or perhaps any state.

During his tenure as superintendent, two goals held special claim for Joyner. He wanted to increase the number of public high schools, and he wanted to see teachers better trained. He called for the development of high schools that would prepare not only college-bound students, but also farmers and homemakers. For the first time, in 1907, the state appropriated money for the support of secondary education, though no black high schools were built. Joyner also urged a uniform system of teacher certification and more money for schools to train black teachers. At Joyner's urging, legislation was passed that established a teacher-training school in Boone, which became Appalachian State University, and another in Greenville, which became East Carolina University.

In November 1918, Joyner triumphed when voters approved a constitutional amendment extending the minimum school term from four to six months. A month later, at fifty-six, he announced his retirement. He returned to LaGrange and a new career in the farming and promotion of tobacco and cotton. He became president of the North Carolina Tobacco Growers Association in 1922. From 1926 to 1932 he sold insurance for Prudential Life. In 1933 he was influential in getting the largest farm organization in the state to endorse eight-month school terms.

Joyner lived to be ninety-one. Throughout his life he remained interested in education and farming. He was dubbed the "grand old man" of education in

North Carolina. The University of North Carolina awarded him an honorary LL.D. He had been a trustee at UNC, East Carolina Teacher's College, and Meredith College, where he was a trustee for fifty-four years. The library at East Carolina, built in 1954, is named for him. An elementary school in Greensboro bears his name. He died on January 24, 1954, and is buried beside his wife in Oakwood Cemetery in Raleigh.

Kathryn Schwille is a journalist and fiction writer. Her non-fiction has appeared in Charlotte Magazine *and in the At-lanta Journal-Constitution, the* St. Paul Pioneer-Press, *and other newspapers. She has an MFA from the Program for Writers at Warren Wilson College, and is a former political editor at the* Charlotte Observer. *Her fiction has been pub-lished in* Sycamore Review, Sou'wester, *and* No Hiding Place, *an anthology of Charlotte writers.*

For more information, see:
Joyner, James Yadkin. Papers. Superintendent of Public Instruction Papers, State Archives, Raleigh.

Arnett, Ethel Stephens. *For Whom Our Public Schools Are Named*. Piedmont Press, 1973.
Hanchett, Thomas W. *Sorting Out the New South City*. University of North Carolina Press, 1998.
Harlan, Louis R. *Separate and Unequal: Public School Campaigns and Racism in the Southern Seaboard States, 1901–1915*. University of North Carolina Press, 1958.
Johnson, Elmer D. "James Yadkin Joyner, Educa-tional Statesman." *North Carolina Historical Review 33* (July 1956).
Leloudis, James L. *Schooling the New South: Pedagogy, Self, and Society in North Carolina: 1880–1920*. Univer-sity of North Carolina Press, 1996.
Moses, Maryem Iy Ilu. *Universal Education for African Americans in North Carolina: A Historical Survey of the Beginning Years through 1927*. North Carolina State University, 1989.
Prather, H. Leon, Sr. *Resurgent Politics and Educational Progressivism in the New South*. Associated University Presses, 1979.

W. L. Moore and English Jones

By Becky L. Goins

Every institution has a history that makes it unique and within that history is a group of people who worked to make it a success. There are times, however, when the efforts and sacrifices of a few become the foundation from which everything else rises. Within the history of the University of North Carolina at Pembroke, the Reverend W. L. Moore and Dr. English E. Jones prepared and strengthened the foundation.

The years following Reconstruction were especially hard for the Indians of Robeson County. Though the 1868 state constitution provided for some measure of racial equality, it did little to improve the state of affairs for Indians. Years of discrimination and treatment as inferior citizens had taken their toll. Illiteracy rates within the Indian community were extremely high. The Indian people of Robeson County began to realize that the only hope they had of improving their status was to establish a school of their own.

In 1885 state representative Hamilton McMillan sponsored legislation to recognize the Indians of Robeson County, give them a legal identity, and establish separate schools for Indian people that they would run themselves. Though they now had legislation granting them their own schools, no schools were immediately established. The community realized that something more needed to be done. They needed a leader, and they found the Reverend Moore.

William Luther Moore was born on October 12, 1857, in Columbus County. As one of the thirteen children of James and Carolina Spaulding Moore, W. L. was raised with a deep appreciation for religion and education. At the age of seventeen and after completing a four-year theological course in Columbus County, he began teaching in the Columbus County schools. Five years later he moved to Robeson County to teach. It was there that he met and in 1879 married Mary Catherine Oxendine, who would later become the first Indian woman to teach in public schools. They settled in the Prospect community, where they raised a family of five children. In 1885 W. L. was ordained at Prospect Methodist Church, which he would go on to pastor for forty-four years.

In February 1887 Moore and seventy-two others petitioned the General Assembly as "Croatan Indians of Robeson County," asking for a "Normal School in Robeson County for our race." Legislators responded and in March created the school, giving the control of the institution to a board of seven trustees that included Moore. The school was given five hundred dollars to pay teachers while the community was required to provide a suitable facility and provide the supplies needed to maintain the school.

Because of the unstable political climate of the area, many Indian people were skeptical of the legislation and were reluctant to contribute to the funding efforts. Moore, however, saw the potential of the school for the community and immediately dedicated himself to raising the necessary funds. He headed a subscription drive to which he personally donated two hundred dollars—a considerable sum at the time. Because of his efforts and dedication, the community began to come together and donated the supplies and labor to build a one-room school. The Croatan Indian Normal School opened its doors in the fall of 1887 with an enrollment of fifteen students. Moore was the first principal and only teacher of the school for the first three years at a salary of $62.50 per month.

By 1889 factionalism within the religious community began to affect the school's progress. The Methodist community was divided between those wishing to maintain their affiliation with national Methodism and those wishing to form an all-Indian conference. Moore led those wishing to remain with the national organization. A campaign was mounted to discredit Moore and the division resulted in a loss of faith in the school. To minimize any damage to the school or its progress, Representative McMillan recommended that Moore be replaced as head of the school. Moore left in 1889, turning the school over to Ezra Bauder, although Moore remained associated in an unofficial capacity. A year later, Moore petitioned Congress and the federal Bureau of Indian Affairs to appropriate additional funding for the school, but his petition was denied.

By 1905 Moore had initiated training sessions for teachers with the help of D. F. Lowry, the first graduate of the Normal School. Teachers were required to attend a one-week session during the school term and a two-week session during the summer. The sessions included classes on the importance of libraries in public schools, the importance of reading, and how to identify the teaching of arithmetic within life.

W. L. Moore and English Jones (Courtesy of University of North Carolina at Pembroke)

As a result of the sessions the Lumbee teachers formed a professional association. (In 1953, the tribal name was officially changed to Lumbee to more appropriately identify the Indians of Robeson County. The names "Croatan" and "Cherokee" were given to the Indians by non-Indian legislators, but Lumbee is the name the Indians of Robeson County used to describe themselves.)

Moore was a leader in the community both in education and religion. He helped to start or rebuild six churches and ministered for over fifty years. He served as president of the Methodist Protestant Churches in the Robeson County area. He died December 22, 1930, and in 1951, Moore Hall was dedicated in recognition of his many contributions to the school. Moore was memorialized as a man "devoted to making the world a better place to live in."

His grandson, Adolph Dial, described him by saying, "Truly he left footprints on the sands of time that will forever guide mankind." In the history of the institution he is remembered as "Founder, Erector, Teacher."

Over the years the school went through many changes. In 1911 the word Croatan was dropped from the school's name and in 1913 the name was changed to the Cherokee Indian Normal School under the mistaken belief that there was a tribal connection between the Cherokee Indians of western North Carolina and the Indians of Robeson County. In 1941 the name was again changed to Pembroke State College for Indians and its doors were opened for Indians other than Lumbees to attend.

In the same way that Moore was primarily responsible for ensuring the establishment of the school, Dr. English E. Jones was mainly responsible for insuring the continued success and growth of the institution. Jones's contributions shaped the future of the university and laid a solid foundation for the educational growth of the school. His success was the result of years of hard work, determination, and perseverance.

Jones was born October 22, 1921, in Robeson County. When he was four his family moved to South Carolina, where he was raised on a farm near Dillon. He did not attend school until he was ten. When classes began in 1931, the local principal, James K. Brayboy, realized English was not in class. He approached the boy's father, James, and asked if he would allow English to attend school. His father consented, and English began attending Leland Grove Elementary School near Dillon.

After completing the seventh grade, the highest offered at Leland Grove, English had to make a decision about his education. He could attend a school near Dillon or he could attend Pembroke High School in Pembroke, some twenty-five miles away, where most of the Indian students were enrolled. It was a long commute and Jones stayed over during the week and worked as a janitor for money to support himself. When it was time to return home, many times he would set out on foot, walking the twenty-five miles.

During his freshman year his mother, Elizabeth, died. His father could not afford to support his education and offered him two choices: he could return home and go to work on the family farm or he could find a way to put himself through school on his own. English decided to find a way to continue his education. At the age of fifteen, English was on his own. He lived in what would later be considered foster homes, where families allowed him to stay through the winter, and in exchange, he worked on their farms in the summer. His summers in the fields helped fuel his desire to finish his education.

"When I was out in those fields, I realized that education was the key to having a better life. It seemed everything was based on one's educational level. I was determined to obtain one to improve my status in life," Jones later said.

He refused to allow his financial hardships to interfere with his performance or participation in school. He served four years as president of Future Farmers of America, was class president in his freshman, junior, and senior years, and was vice president and president of the student body. When he was a senior he captained the varsity basketball, baseball, and football teams. In 1942 he graduated with honors, intending to go to college after high school, but upon graduation he was drafted.

His aptitude tests qualified him for mechanics school in the Army Air Corps. On his first furlough home during his training he married Margaret Sheppard, his childhood sweetheart. Six weeks later he was promoted to corporal and put in charge of a troop train headed for California. He was subsequently promoted to sergeant and placed in command of a platoon.

Jones was deployed to Europe, where he would remain until the end of the war. As a mechanics engineer Jones was responsible for keeping the planes flying but he also flew on sixty-one combat missions over Germany. Six days after D Day he landed in France and was later stationed in Germany, where he would remain until the end of the war.

By the time of his discharge in 1946, Jones had obtained the rank of first sergeant and had 1,028 men under his command. His military career left him with many interesting memories. While stationed in California, he played baseball (as catcher) against Joe DiMaggio and other major leaguers in the service. He met General Dwight D. Eisenhower and served in the honor guard for the funeral of General George Patton in France. While stationed in England, he went one-on-one with heavyweight boxing champion Joe Louis—in a game of table tennis.

After returning home, Jones used the GI Bill to study at Western Kentucky University, where, in 1948, he received a bachelor of science degree in agriculture. He immediately began making plans to return to Pembroke, where his former principal, Elmer Lowry, agreed to give him a job teaching agriculture at Pembroke High. He remained with the school for four years, during which time he organized and educated many of the county's farmers. More than 170 farmers attended classes one night each week for four years to learn about improved farm practices.

In 1952 the position of Indian county agent—discontinued during the war—was reestablished under the state extension service at North Carolina State College. Jones resigned his position at the high school and became the assistant Robeson County agricultural agent. He organized fourteen 4-H clubs that involved more than a thousand boys and girls. He also established an Adult Leader Core made up of more than two hundred men and women.

In 1956 Jones became an associate professor at Pembroke State College (PSC) and immediately began working toward earning his master's degree in agriculture, which he received in 1957 from North Carolina State University. He then began a long and successful career in university administration.

In 1957 Jones became the dean of men and three years later was promoted to dean of student affairs and administrative assistant to the president, Walter J. Gale. After Gale had left the institution, Jones was appointed interim president in 1961 until he was named president a year later. With his appointment he became the first Indian to serve as president of a four-year college in the United States and the first Lumbee to serve as president of the university.

Under his leadership Pembroke State became one of the most integrated institutions of higher learning in the state. In 1969 the school became a regional university and the name changed to Pembroke State University. Jones established a university graduate council to begin preparing proposals to incorporate graduate programs into the university curriculum, and the first graduate courses were offered in 1972.

With the reorganization of the state system of higher education in 1971, Pembroke became part of the Consolidated University of North Carolina and the name changed again, this time to University of North Carolina at Pembroke. Jones remained as chancellor.

Under Jones's administration the school experienced tremendous growth on almost all levels. Enrollment increased from 570 to 2,158. The number of graduates in a year went from 98 to 410. Financial aid increased from $30,000 to $977,000. The number of dormitory beds went from 134 to 834. Faculty was increased from 35 to 135. The number of faculty members with doctorates rose from 22 to 173. The number of buildings went from nine to twenty-five with a plant value that increased from $1,448,239 to $13,466,000. Total university acreage increased from thirty-five acres to ninety-five acres. The university's operating budget rose from $453,000 to $6.1 million.

In 1979 Dr. Jones announced his retirement, saying he had done what he came to do. "During my tenure here I wanted to build a university, both facility-wise and academically, that would be a credit to the University of North Carolina. I feel satisfied that we have accomplished these things. In view of that fact, I believe this is the appropriate time for me to step aside and give someone else—with new ideas and new energies—an opportunity to step in, grab the reins and really go with the university." Governor Jim Hunt proclaimed April 20, 1979, as Dr. English E. Jones Day across the state. A parade, banquet, and other festivities were held to pay tribute to a man who had given so much in service to both the university and the community.

Throughout his career Jones was the recipient of many honors and awards and was appointed to numerous boards and committees. Before becoming president of PSC, Jones was appointed by President Dwight D. Eisenhower to the White House Conference on Children and Youth. In 1965 he became the first vice president of the State Baptist Convention. That same year he was awarded an honorary doctorate of laws degree from Wake Forest University. In 1981 he was awarded an honorary doctorate of humanities degree from Pembroke State University. He was the recipient of the Henry Berry Lowry Memorial Award for his contributions and service to Indian people. The English E. Jones Health and Fitness Complex at PSU was named in his honor.

Jones died May 18, 1981, after a lengthy illness. In remembering Jones, William Friday, president of the University of North Carolina, characterized him as one who "served the university with uncommon devotion, great energy and with total personal commitment. . . . He was always inspiring, always helpful and he shared his friendship with thousands of us."

Becky L. Goins, a graduate of the University of North Carolina at Pembroke, is public information assistant in the Native American Resource Center. She is co-director of the Miss Indian North Carolina scholarship program and adult advisor for the North Carolina Native American Youth Organization and the North Carolina Native American Council on Higher Education.

For more information, see:

Dial, Adolph L. *The Lumbee.* Chelsea House, 1993.

———, and David Eliades. *The Only Land I Know: A History of the Lumbee Indians.* Syracuse University Press, 1996.

Eliades, David, and Linda Ellen Oxendine. *Pembroke State University: A Centennial History.* Brentwood University Press, 1996.

Smith, Joseph Michael. *The Lumbee Methodists: Getting to Know Them.* Commission of Archives and History. North Carolina Methodist Conference, 1990.

WILLIAM L. POTEAT

By Randal L. Hall

WILLIAM LOUIS POTEAT served his home state of North Carolina in many capacities during a long life of eighty-one years. He tirelessly performed his many duties as a professor of biology and then president of Wake Forest College, as a leading liberal member of the Baptist State Convention, as a dedicated progressive social reformer, and as a prominent voice opposing antievolution legislation during the 1920s. In each role, Poteat helped to broaden the intellectual options available to North Carolinians.

Poteat was born on October 20, 1856, in Caswell County to James and Julia McNeill Poteat, who owned a tobacco plantation and a mansion called Forest Home. With southern slaveholding society at its peak, William had a child slave approximately his own age. Following the war, he and his family moved to the nearby county seat of Yanceyville and operated a hotel for the remainder of Poteat's adolescence while cultivation of the plantation lands fell to tenants.

Education became the vocation not only of William, but also of his younger brother, Edwin, and younger sister, Ida. Their own education began under governesses at home, and William continued his studies at a local private academy where he began to acquire the knowledge of classical languages, an integral element of higher education in the nineteenth century. In 1872, at age fifteen, he enrolled in Wake Forest College, a Baptist institution comfortably situated in the town of Wake Forest, just north of Raleigh. He made his way easily through the classical curriculum. Poteat also took full advantage of the Euzelian literary society, where he polished the skills of oration, writing, and debate that would make him a persuasive leader and activist later in life.

He graduated in 1877 but never left. For just under sixty full years, Poteat worked at Wake Forest as a teacher and administrator, always helping the state's young Baptist men, who often had quite poor educational backgrounds, to begin to discover the joy of learning. After graduation he returned to Yanceyville for a year before Wake Forest brought him back as a tutor, teaching beginning language skills. After two years at that task, the trustees of the college named him an assistant professor of natural science. In 1883, he took over more specific subject matter as professor of natural history, a post that was renamed professor of biology in 1892. Until called to the job of president

William L. Poteat (Courtesy of Wake Forest University Archives)

in 1905, he concentrated on his work as a member of the small faculty. In 1881, he married Emma J. Purefoy, and they had a son, Hubert, and two daughters, Louise and Helen.

Poteat closely followed the latest intellectual findings of the Victorian world. He did so in small ways such as by reading newspapers and periodicals from London and New York and by attending major fairs or expositions in New Orleans and Chicago. He devoured lovingly the work of British poets of the time, as well as social critics such as Matthew Arnold and John Ruskin. At various times, his brother Edwin guided churches in Philadelphia and Connecticut, and William was an occasional visitor. He periodically traveled outside of the South to religious meetings. Most substantially, however, his profession as teacher of science brought Poteat into contact with the cutting edge of thought for his time.

Though never a great researcher himself, Poteat made important contributions to the development of science. When he took up his teaching duties, the laboratory was a foreign place and he knew virtually nothing of science. By reading voraciously he not only developed competence as a teacher, he began to perform basic scientific research, published a few minor papers, and even presented his work at a conference of the American Association for the Advancement of Science. He took part in the pioneering Elisha Mitchell Scientific Society at the University of North Carolina, created a Wake Forest Scientific Society that was active for a time in the 1890s, and was a charter member and first president of the North Carolina Academy of Science in 1902.

He reached this level of accomplishment by following the current of scientific ideas flowing through more cosmopolitan parts of the world. He attended a summer training session for teachers on Martha's Vineyard in 1883 and while in the North toured facilities at Brown, Yale, and Harvard. In 1887 he visited the laboratories of Johns Hopkins University, a leader in promoting research in America. In 1888 he made his way to Germany to study for part of a summer at the University of Berlin, and in 1893 he took part in classes at the Marine Biological Laboratory at Woods Hole, Mass. These quests enabled Poteat to introduce his students to such methods as creating a college science museum, gathering specimens for laboratory analysis, and using a microscope—a hands-on style of studying science that was still rare in the South. As a result of his work, Wake Forest awarded him a master's degree in 1889.

After testing the intellectual waters of his time, Poteat adopted two crucial new intellectual stances: acceptance of the theory of evolution and a sympathetic view of the systematic critical study of the Bible. Both beliefs were at odds with the majority of the people in the South, and Poteat faced some criticism from within the Baptist denomination. He encountered the theory of evolution almost immediately when he began studying science in 1880, and after some resistance he gradually accepted the doctrine over the course of the decade. Opposition to him was somewhat blunted because theistic evolution was the version he expounded throughout his life. He believed that the Christian God was the driving force behind evolutionary changes. This view forced him to eschew literal interpretations of biblical stories, and he enthusiastically adopted critical study of the Bible, enjoying the new scholarship that was revealing more about the authors of the Bible, their cultures, and the literary and symbolic merits of the canonical writings.

Poteat began to assume leadership roles at Wake Forest and in various denominational groups in the 1890s. He also became a well-known speaker, always ready to take the podium to discuss literature, science, religion, or education, and as a writer in the Baptists' newspaper, the *Biblical Recorder*. Despite views that some found too liberal, Poteat found wide acceptance among the Baptist leadership. As a result, he was the natural choice to replace Charles E. Taylor as president of Wake Forest in 1905. Poteat guided Wake Forest for twenty-two years. By the time he stepped down in 1927, the college had refined Taylor's modernization of the curriculum, endured the difficult times of World War I, built many new buildings, added significantly to the endowment, and more than doubled its enrollment.

Though he left to his successor many challenging needs for better facilities and additional endowment, Poteat led the college during a crucial time in its development. His philosophy for the college, one shared by other denominational educators, contrasted sharply with the guiding principles of educators at emerging southern state research universities. The New South boosters at such schools as the University of North Carolina and the University of Virginia sought to create useful knowledge and equip students with the practical intellectual tools needed for a developing region. Poteat, on the other hand, believed denominational colleges should immerse students in liberal culture and prepare them in a more general way to be cultivated, righteous leaders. Vocational skills in law, medicine, education, or other pursuits could come later.

Never one to remain within the quiet confines of the campus, Poteat sought to put his beliefs in action by taking leadership roles. Once he moved beyond literal interpretations of the Bible, Poteat decried elaborate theological systems; nevertheless, he had a strong belief in the duty of Christians to work for social betterment in pursuit of the Kingdom of God on earth. In this respect he was relatively rare among Baptists in the South.

He advocated Prohibition, better public primary and secondary education, international peace, interracial cooperation within the practice of segregation, changes in marriage laws, and eugenics. He promoted his beliefs in such organizations as the Southern Baptist Convention's Commission on Social Service and a similar body within the state Baptist Convention; the North Carolina Peace Society; the North Carolina Teachers' Assembly; the Southern Baptist Education Association; the Anti-Saloon League; the United Dry Forces of North Carolina; the Commission on Interracial Cooperation; the Southern Sociological Congress; the North Carolina Mental Hygiene Society; and the North Carolina Conference for Social Service. Beneath Poteat's seemingly varied reform objectives ran a consistent current of desire to maintain a stable, moral society led by educated, benevolent Christians.

In the early 1920s many of Poteat's most cherished roles and values came under fire from conservative Baptists. Though throughout his career he openly supported evolution and a somewhat liberal understanding of theology, not until then did his opponents come together in an organized way to try to oust him as head of Wake Forest. In the context of conservative and fundamentalist efforts around the nation to remove religious liberals from positions of influence and to secure antievolution policies in public education, certain Baptists began attacking Poteat in 1920, urging that he be removed.

Thomas T. Martin, a Tennessee evangelist, began the barrage with a series of articles in the *Louisville Western Recorder* that criticized not only Poteat's theological understanding of the atonement but also his support of evolution. Poteat responded by publicly affirming his Christian faith, without in any way diluting his stances on theology and science, and the controversy faded for a time. Opposition emerged with renewed vigor in 1922 when Poteat published articles on evolution in the denominational paper, and condemnation of his leadership poured from Baptist associations across the state.

The crisis reached a climax in November 1922 at the gathering of the Baptist State Convention. Poteat skillfully defused the situation and avoided a showdown with a well-known speech entitled "Christianity and Enlightenment," which sidestepped the topic of evolution while passionately calling for faith in Jesus and cooperation among Christians.

The importance of the issue of evolution did not diminish for several years. In May 1925 Poteat delivered the McNair lectures at the University of North Carolina, a forum expressly devoted to discussion of the relationship between science and religion, and condemned those who stood in the way of young Christians by erecting false barriers to their attempts to combine intellectual striving and religious faith.

The University of North Carolina Press published the talks as *Can a Man Be a Christian Today?,* and the book spread Poteat's thoughts throughout the state. The lectures came soon after the North Carolina legislature had defeated a bill that would have barred the teaching of evolution in public institutions, and they roused the ire of conservative Baptists once again. Forced to rally his supporters, Poteat found once again the backing of a sufficient number of Wake Forest alumni and trustees and well-educated denominational leaders to avoid ouster at the Baptist State Convention in November 1925, but the group did take steps to control more actively the appointment of trustees for Wake Forest. As a result of his determined refusal to back down from his beliefs, even to please members of the body that controlled the college he led, Poteat was able in 1927 to retire from the presidency and to specify carefully that he did so from age alone, not from a surrender to his critics. He returned to full-time teaching of biology until a few months before his death on March 12, 1938.

Poteat's legacy is justifiably one of struggling for freedom of thought. Though he was in many ways limited by traditional thought, he did accept the findings of modern scientific and biblical scholarship well before many residents of North Carolina. Much of his importance rested in his indefatigable zeal to share his belief in the compatibility of science and religion.

By being such a visible representative of the more liberal residents of the state and surviving explicit attacks on his ideas, Poteat became an emblem of intellectual progress. Within the Baptist denomination, he also left a dissenting tradition of strong concern for bringing the Kingdom of God on earth through a commitment by Christians to social change.

Randal L. Hall is the author of William Louis Poteat: A Leader of the Progressive-Era South. *He is assistant director of the merit-based scholarships program at Wake Forest University in Winston-Salem.*

For more information see:
Poteat, William Louis. Papers. Special Collections, Z. Smith Reynolds Library, Wake Forest University, Winston-Salem.

Bryan, George McLeod. "The Educational, Religious, and Social Thought of William Louis Poteat. . . . " Master's thesis, Wake Forest College, 1944.
Hall, Randal L. *William Louis Poteat: A Leader of the Progressive-Era South.* University Press of Kentucky, 2000.
Linder, Suzanne Cameron. *William Louis Poteat: Prophet of Progress,* University of North Carolina Press, 1966.
Poteat, William Louis. *Can a Man Be a Christian To-day?* University of North Carolina Press, 1925.
———. *Laboratory and Pulpit: The Relation of Biology to the Preacher and His Message.* Philadelphia, 1901.

JAMES E. SHEPARD

By Stan Brennan

I T BEGAN with a man's dream and about twenty-five acres of what many considered to be worthless land cut by deep ravines and ugly gullies and overgrown by tall reedlike grass in Hayti, the center of African American life in Durham. The man was James E. Shepard. As early as 1908 he envisioned creating a religious training school for members of his race, a school where African American ministers could come for six-week periods, or longer, and receive instruction and inspiration. The cost had to be nominal because of the financial plight of the student body. It took many years before Shepard's dream was fully realized, but the final result was North Carolina Central University, the first state-supported liberal arts college for blacks in the nation.

James Edward Shepard was born in Raleigh on November 3, 1875, the oldest of twelve children born to Augustus and Hattie Whitted Shepard. He received his early education in public schools and then attended Shaw University in Raleigh, graduating in 1894 with a degree in pharmacy. He opened a pharmacy in Durham but was not satisfied and moved on to Washington, D.C., in 1898, where he was employed as a comparer of deeds in the recorder's office. The following year he returned to North Carolina and from 1899 to 1905 worked as deputy collector of internal revenue for the federal government. He was a field superintendent of the International Sunday School Board for work among African Americans.

Shepard's hard work kept the dream alive over those years. The result was the founding on July 5, 1910, of the National Religious Training School and Chautauqua. Shepard was president and the land for the school was given by the citizens of Durham. Despite a shortage of money during the first years, ten buildings had been erected on the campus by 1912. During this early period, support came from student fees and private donations, but times were lean. Room rent was only $7 per month; monthly tuition was a dollar. Faculty members were paid between $500 and $1,000 per year, depending upon their degrees and experience, yet the school began with a staff of twenty-one and an enrollment of 109. Initial plans included establishing the school as a four-year college but this was found impractical. In addition to the training school for ministers, Shepard also wanted to include a commercial school and a home economics school.

James E. Shepard (Courtesy of N.C. Office of Archives and History)

Perhaps a clue as to why Shepard chose Durham for the school can be found in the comments of two men. Booker T. Washington, a practical idealist who believed that existing conditions were a sound basis for progress, wrote: "Of all the southern cities I have visited I found here the sanest attitude of the white people toward the black . . . I never saw in a city of this size so many prosperous carpenters, brickmasons, blacksmiths, wheelwrights, cotton mill operatives, and tobacco factory workers among the Negroes." He added that he found in Durham fewer signs of poverty among his race than elsewhere. And W. E. B. DuBois, an outspoken advocate for an absolute alteration in race relationship, said: "There is in this small city a group of five thousand or more colored people, whose social and economic development is perhaps more striking than that of any similar group in the nation."

Durham's African American entrepreneurs had shown a strength not found elsewhere in the South and had successfully cultivated support from the white business establishment. For example, Julian S. Carr, a prominent Democrat and banker-businessman, loaned money to John Merrick to start his business career; white bankers aided in the organization of the first African American bank; and a printing press was given for the publication of the community's first newspaper. Both Benjamin and James B. Duke provided support for black institutions from their American Tobacco Company fortune.

Shepard traveled widely seeking financial support for the school, but the ongoing shortage of funds forced him to sell the school's land and buildings in 1915 to satisfy creditors. It reopened after Mrs. Russell Sage of New York provided a personal donation that enabled Shepard to repurchase its property and reorganize as the National Training School. Shepard and the school's board of advisers shifted the emphasis from training ministers to preparing black teachers.

World War I brought more financial problems. Two plans were considered to solve the recurring shortage of funds—allow a religious denomination to assume control or deed the property to the state and have it administered as a public institution. The latter plan was adopted and the school's name was changed to the Durham State Normal School.

In 1925 Shepard and his supporters concluded a successful legislative campaign to make the school the first state-supported liberal arts college for blacks in the nation. As a result, the name was changed to the North Carolina College for Negroes. New funds, including $42,000 from Ben Duke, $8,000 from citizens of Durham, and $100,000 from the state, enabled the school to substantially expand its physical facilities.

Shepard took note of the school's progress but like others found times hard during the Depression. In an October 15, 1934, memo to teachers and employees, he wrote: "After a month of work, I think I can say that I see signs of progress and increasing interest on the part of the teachers and the whole student body. For this I am very appreciative." He continued: "This is a very hard year for all institutions, and especially for this one since we are carrying a large number of students at reduced rates. In order to break even, we have got to make and practice every economy possible, and in this we are expecting your hearty cooperation."

Shepard provided insight into his thinking of the role of a college and university in a November 26, 1943, memo to administrative officers and teachers. In part, it raised these questions: "Since the Ameri-can college is being severely criticized at the present by its failure to correct so many evils and misunderstandings in the world, what is your college doing to bring about a simpler way of life and to convey to students the fact that mere book knowledge will not be sufficient for the world of tomorrow?

"What is your institution doing to stress character, with the prime emphasis on genuine efficiency, loyalty, and dependability?

"How far does your institution project itself into the community of state life, and how do you judge this?

"What do you hold up before the young men and women as the chief stabilizing force in their lives?

"In stressing character which embraces punctuality and dependability, do they have living examples set before them?

"Point out those upon your faculty or administrative staff who exert an up-lifting and broadening influence upon the student body as a whole, or upon the individual students, or community life. Be perfectly frank to name the persons and give your reasons for selection of same.

"Apart from the mere teaching of any subject, what practical example or accomplishments in the subject taught, or in life has been brought to your attention by any instructor or professor on your staff?"

Shepard was often compared to Booker T. Washington in that he rejected legislation and confrontation to better race relations. Instead, he favored conciliation at the conference table. He argued that "we cannot legislate hate out of the world or love into it." He presented his views on racial issues in a series of statewide radio broadcasts in the 1930s and 1940s and in speeches and writings for national audiences in which he supported and defended the progress of North Carolina.

In the August 1944 issue of *Negro Digest,* Shepard wrote that "in spite of the many hardships and struggles that I have experienced in my efforts to establish a worthwhile educational institution for Negroes, I am sure that I would undertake the same task again. For to me it appears that nowhere in the history of the world has the transforming effect of education upon the life of a people been more clearly demonstrated that in the case of the American Negro."

Shepard set forth his views on the South and its relationship to blacks in an article for the September 1945 issue of *Negro Digest.* "My personal attitude, which can be discovered in all of my writings and public utterances, is not to defend the status quo in the South and say here let us rest; my efforts have been to champion and stimulate the progress that is being made in better race relations and in the improvement of the status of the Negro by the realistic approach of cooperation between sensible men and women of good will in both races. . . . This attitude, or approach, more often than is generally admitted, finds its counterpart in the North, and its good results there, as well as in the South, are evidence of its effectiveness."

He continued: "In considering the trend of the southern attitude it is important to recall the comparative history of the two sections, the pertinent facts of which the limits of this article prevent my setting forth, except to remind ourselves that the immediate aftermath of slavery was in many instances more cruel in its oppression of the Negro than slavery itself was.

"Nevertheless, throughout the darkest periods of the South's history there have been intelligent and liberal-minded white people who have regretted the conditions and burdens imposed upon the Negro by the existing situation, and they have worked for a change. The good results of their efforts cannot be denied. Many will admit that in gainful occupations, the Negro has many opportunities in the South which are denied him in the North."

Shepard was a Republican in national politics but supported Democrats locally. Despite the critics, Shepard successfully presented his college's case to the overwhelmingly Democratic state legislature. One political commentator observed that many legislators regarded Shepard as "the best politician ever to come before them. He probably got a larger percentage of his requests than anyone did and he generally aimed high."

The legislature praised Shepard posthumously in 1948, saying, "this native-born North Carolinian labored . . . with wisdom and foresight for the lasting betterment of his race and his state, not through agitation or ill-conceived demands, but through the advocacy of a practical, well considered and constant program of racial progress." But some blacks found his approach "disgusting Uncle-Tomism." In fact, one black critic said that Shepard "speaks not for the New Negro but for his little band of bandana wearers and them alone."

In 1945 the *High Point Enterprise* called him one of the state's ten most valuable citizens. He received honorary degrees from Muskingham College (1912), Selma University (1913), Howard University (1925), and Shaw University (1945). He was a grand master of Prince Hall Masons in North Carolina, grand patron of the Eastern Star, secretary of finance for the Knights of Pythias, and director of the Mechanics and Farmers Bank. He was president of the North Carolina Colored Teachers Association, the International Sunday School Convention, and the State Industrial Association of North Carolina; a trustee of Lincoln Hospital and Oxford Colored Orphanage; and a member of the North Carolina Agricultural Society. He was the only black speaker at the World Sunday School Convention held in Rome in 1910.

Just months before Shepard's death of a cerebral hemorrhage at his home in Durham on October 6, 1947, the General Assembly renamed the school North Carolina College at Durham. At his death, the institution was one of only four Negro colleges in the nation to be fully accredited by the Association of American Universities. Its faculty had grown to over 70 and its student body to 1,500. The library at the college was named for him in 1951 and his statue stands on the campus. As part of the reorganization of the state's higher education system in the late 1960s, the school was given university status and renamed North Carolina Central University in 1969.

Donations from citizens and organizations across the state helped create the James E. Shepard Memorial Foundation, which was established in tribute and to provide scholarships for worthy black students.

Upon his death, *The Campus Echo,* student newspaper of the college, said: "The magnanimity of the man cannot be measured by mere words or facts . . . we doubt if we will live to see the complete effects that Dr. Shepard has wrought on this city, this state and country. The fruits of his labor will outlive us."

Stan Brennan is a retired journalist. He was a reporter and an editor at the Charlotte Observer *for thirty-four years. Previously he worked for newspapers in Birmingham, Ala., Richmond, Va., Greensboro, and Durham. He has bachelor's and master's of arts degrees from the University of North Carolina at Chapel Hill.*

For more information, see:

Shepard, James E. Papers. Shepard Library, North Carolina Central University, Durham.

Crittenden, Christopher, William S. Powell, and Robert H. Woody, eds. *100 Years 100 Men, 1871–1971.* Edwards and Broughton, 1971.

Huff, James, and Ernestine Huff. *Paths Toward Freedom: A Biographical History of Blacks and Indians in North Carolina.* Center for Urban Affairs, North Carolina State University at Raleigh, 1976.

Negro Digest. August 1944 and September 1945.

Seay, Elizabeth Irene. "A History of the North Carolina College for Negroes." Master's thesis, Duke University, 1941.

NORMAN A. WIGGINS

By J. Barlow Herget

IN DECEMBER 1966, Campbell College, a two-year junior college located in tiny Buies Creek, North Carolina, had just received its accreditation as a four-year institution when a search was launched for a new president to succeed longtime president Leslie H. Campbell, the son of the school's founder. When the committee met with Norman Adrian Wiggins a few months later, the Wake Forest University law professor didn't hesitate to tell the committee that he saw the small Baptist college in Buies Creek as a university with graduate school programs.

The ex-marine's forceful personality convinced the committee that he was not a wistful, academic dreamer but a man of strong faith—faith in his God and faith in his own ability to achieve his goals. He received a unanimous recommendation and on June 6, 1967, he assumed the duties of Campbell's presidency, to becoming only the third chief executive since the school was founded as a private academy in 1887.

Over the next thirty-four years, Wiggins's vision became reality as he set a record unmatched by any other North Carolina college or university president during the final quarter of the twentieth century. By 2001, Campbell University had a thriving and respected four-year undergraduate liberal arts program, as well as five graduate schools in law, business, education, pharmacy, and divinity. Its Norman Adrian Wiggins School of Law and School of Pharmacy graduates regularly made news for their high scores and overall success rates on state bar and pharmacy exams.

Wiggins was born February 6, 1924, a member of what television broadcaster Tom Brokaw would later call America's "Greatest Generation." Like many of his contemporaries, he was a child of the Great Depression. His father and mother, Walter James and Margaret Ann Wiggins, operated a small, neighborhood grocery store attached to their house in Burlington, a textile town in North Carolina's rolling piedmont. "They lived on the 'southside,' the mill area where a lot of mill families lived," remembered Don Bolden, executive editor and fifty-two-year employee of the *Burlington Daily Times*. The couple had five children, three boys and two girls. A Campbell University historian described them as "God-fearing, hard-working, caring, patriotic, Christ-centered, church oriented people."

Norman A. Wiggins (Courtesy of Campbell University)

H. H. "Skinny" Brown, who went on to fame as a professional baseball player for the Boston Red Sox, Baltimore Orioles, and New York Yankees, was Wiggins's first cousin. Brown lived in nearby Greensboro and was himself one of eight children. About the same age as Wiggins, Brown recalled his summertime "vacations" at his cousin's home. "I would get on the train in Greensboro, sometimes by myself. Adrian was closest to me in age but a little bit older. His home was like my home. There were two or three of us sleeping in each bedroom. Most of the time, we were up at the schoolyard or playing ball. Our mothers were Chasons and both were strict, 'hard-shell' Baptists. Church was something we all did; it was our social life."

Work also was something they all did. Brown said children were expected to help with the family income. When he left for college, Brown was bringing home more money from his newspaper route than his father earned at the textile mill. Wiggins was similarly employed. He worked in the family store, carried newspapers, helped in the school cafeteria, and held part-time jobs at one of the textile mills, and at the post office at Christmas. Like Brown, he was a good athlete and lettered in basketball, baseball, and football at Burlington High School.

He began college in 1942, selecting Campbell College, then a two-year institution with close ties to the Southern Baptist Church. The school's location, in rural Harnett County in the village of Buies Creek near the Cape Fear River, placed it about seventy miles from Wiggins's home, and its Baptist heritage fit his family's conservative faith. In 1943, he joined the marines and fought in the Pacific, returning to Campbell four years later in 1947. He made extra money firing the school's boilers, tending the tennis courts, and grading papers. He graduated with an associate of arts degree and married fellow student Mildred Harmon of nearby Coats on April 14, 1948.

The newlyweds moved to Wake Forest, a small town about fifteen miles north of Raleigh, and then home to Wake Forest College. The school already was destined to move to Winston-Salem, a transition that ten years later would affect Campbell and later, Wiggins's own hopes for Campbell. He earned his bachelor of arts in 1950 and entered Wake Forest School of Law the same year. When he graduated in 1952, he specialized in estate, trust, and banking laws. He would later publish books on the topics.

"Skinny" Brown told the following story about Wiggins's brief banking career. Brown was warming up in the pitcher's bullpen at Yankee Stadium in New York City in late summer 1953 when Wiggins and his wife paid him a surprise visit. When Brown asked Wiggins what he was doing in New York, his cousin replied that he had entered Columbia University School of Law. Wiggins had been working as a trust officer for Planters National Bank and Trust in Rocky Mount in eastern North Carolina, the state's principal agriculture region. "There had been a bad drought in the [previous] summer," said Brown, "and Adrian had to foreclose on a lot of farmers. He told me that being a good Baptist, he just couldn't foreclose on all those people." Wiggins graduated from Columbia, where he was a Harlan Fiske Stone Fellow, with the LL.M. degree in 1956, and in 1964 he received a J. D. At the same time, Mildred Wiggins received a master's degree in social work from Columbia.

Wiggins returned to Wake Forest School of Law, which had moved to Winston-Salem. He joined his mentor Dean Carroll Weathers on the faculty and established a reputation as a demanding teacher and good administrator. He was named general counsel for the university in 1961. When he received the telephone call from Campbell's search committee, Wiggins was considered by many to be the person who would succeed his friend Weathers as dean of Wake Forest's law school. Instead, he accepted Campbell's invitation to interview for the presidency. On April 21, 1967, the committee recommended his name to the board of trustees.

Wiggins was forty-three when he arrived at Campbell in the summer of 1967. He knew that the school's founder and namesake, J. A. Campbell, had actually owned the college at one time and had been succeeded by his son, Leslie H. Campbell, who had served as teacher and then president for a total of fifty-two years. That the new president was not a Campbell did not hamper the transition in leadership. He now commanded a school that had an enrollment of about 2,200 students, facilities valued at $7 million, and an operating budget of $2.7 million. The campus totaled 570 acres and twenty-seven buildings.

He recognized that for Campbell to attract new and larger benefactors, the campus needed to be attractive. He soon persuaded the trustees to hire a landscape architect to provide oversight on campus development, and in 1969, he hired a Chicago consulting firm to examine the college's various operations and to recommend changes. Ideas began to circulate for new buildings—a religion center, student center, fine arts center, and physical education facilities—and expansions of the library and science facilities.

While Wiggins represented a definite change in leadership, he strongly supported his predecessors' mission to provide students a college education in a religious atmosphere. He had told the search committee that he believed that North Carolina Baptists, especially those in the east, should have another four-year college. It was a view that had gained currency when Wake Forest College moved to the city of Winston-Salem in 1956. Someone at the *Goldsboro News-Argus* had written that year: "Removal of Wake Forest 150 miles farther west will reduce the number of eastern Carolinians, percentage-wise, in its student body. Its removal will leave the great eastern half of the state without a four-year, co-educational, liberal arts college." Campbell had begun to fill that void by 1967, but equally important to Wiggins was the religious vacuum in higher education left by Wake Forest's departure.

Campbell's trustees believed that as Wake Forest College settled into its urban setting, the school would cast a wider net for students and gradually would disengage from the thinking of the Baptist State Convention. Wiggins wanted Campbell to maintain its strong Baptist connection and saw it as part of Campbell's identity. After a few months on the job, Wiggins told a school chapel congregation, "To the extent permitted by our resources, we are choosing as our goal distinctive Christian Education of an optimum quality for all students."

He was more direct when he spoke at a fall faculty meeting several years later: "We have a number of faculty members who have not been with us before. We welcome you. . . . You have doubtless heard that Campbell College is affiliated with the Baptist State Convention of North Carolina. That is not true; we are not affiliated with the Baptist State Convention of North Carolina. The Baptist State Convention of North Carolina owns Campbell College. And we are glad to have it so; we feel fortunate in having it so." Other marks of Wiggins's Baptist devotion was his prohibition of Sunday sporting events for Campbell's athletic teams and spurning fees for televised basketball games.

Wiggins's loyalty to the Baptist church was matched by his expectation of loyalty to his administration. His own stature—he stood six-feet two-inches—and coal-black hair seemed to underscore Wiggins's devotion to the Marine Corps motto "Semper Fidelis." "There is the assumption that you will do it like Dr. Wiggins wants it," said Gene Puckett, a friend, part-time faculty member, and editor of the influential *Biblical Recorder* between 1982 and 1998. Thus, in 1971 during the Vietnam War, when many college and university presidents distanced themselves from the military Reserve Officer Training Corps (ROTC), Wiggins established an ROTC program at Campbell. No faculty or students objected.

There was a precision to Wiggins's management style, too. Said Puckett, "He runs a very tight ship. The top level management team often meets at 7 A.M., and you don't arrive at 7:05." The meetings with trustees were similarly efficient. "He had an administrative style that had a stamp on it," said Randall Lolley, a trustee between 1963 and 1971. "Trustee meetings started on time, they stayed on agenda, and they got out on time."

Wiggins worked hard at his new job. In the words of J. Earl Danieley, president of Elon College from 1957 to 1973, he had "limitless energy." If Wiggins wanted to relax, said Danieley, "he just went back to work." His dedication to the school and his strong feelings about the Baptist church brought new benefactors to Campbell's mission. He exploited his knowledge of trust and estate law to attract bankers, establishing an academic major in the subject in the school's business curriculum. The board of trustees was enlarged and a new "Presidential Board of Advisors" was formed in 1968. Contributions from these two groups accounted for $174,192 in 1973 and 1974. He obtained the school's first $1 million gift from Garner resident E. P. Sauls several years later.

He also sought public money. In 1969, he helped start the state's Association of Independent Colleges and Universities and led the group in its effort to win public tuition grants for their North Carolina students. "He was a leader in whatever group he was in," said Danieley, who worked with Wiggins when the 1971 General Assembly first approved a twenty-five-dollar per student grant to be paid per student to the state's private colleges and universities for each North Carolina resident enrolled. Danieley and Wiggins were told not to worry about the amount the first time as long as the appropriation was placed in the main budget. Thereafter, the debate in subsequent legislatures would be over only the size of the grants. In 2001, the tuition grant for each qualifying student was $2,900.

Wiggins's most notable legacies were the graduate schools that earned the one-time private academy the status of university in June 1979, twelve years to the day after he began work as president. In 1973, he laid the groundwork among trustees and supporters first for the law school, as well as graduate programs in business and education. At the time, there were three law schools in the state at the University of North Carolina, Duke University, and Wake Forest University. Opposition was swiftly voiced, but Wiggins won the support of state representative Hartwell Campbell, grandson of the founder, and Wiggins himself was widely respected among the Baptist faithful. After two years of study and debate, the Baptist State Convention's General Board approved Wiggins's plans in July 1975. The law school, later named the Norman A. Wiggins School of Law, opened in 1976.

With the Baptist State Convention's approval in hand, Wiggins had his mandate to pursue the next two graduate programs. Wiggins found a family of wealthy, conservative admirers in nearby Clinton: Burrows and Mabel Lundy and their daughter and son-in-law, Lewis and Annabelle Lundy Fetterman, owners of one of the region's largest meatpacking companies. Presbyterians and staunch believers in free enterprise and "traditional" values, the Lundys first endowed a teaching chair in business in 1975. The Fettermans followed that with a gift to "underwrite" the Lundy-Fetterman School of Business in 1980. The school opened its doors in 1982 for over one hundred M.B.A. candidates.

Wiggins continued his march for graduate schools. In 1985, Campbell, now an accredited university, established a School of Education. The early success of the law and business schools paved the way for Wiggins when he announced in 1985 that Campbell would establish a School of Pharmacy. He had quietly raised money for the school and won the trustees' unanimous approval before seeking the Baptist State Convention's blessing. It was the state's second pharmacy school and the first new one in the country in thirty-seven years. The charter class began in 1986.

While viewed as a conservative among Baptists, Wiggins held fast to the denomination's populist tradition of autonomous congregations. He was elected president of the Baptist State Convention in 1984, and in 1986, during his tenure, the convention adopted a resolution that affirmed the right of local churches to ordain women. Such positions sometimes put him at odds with the new fundamentalist leaders in the church, especially when they threatened the funding for Baptist schools. The fundamentalists took command in 1987 of the Southeastern Seminary located on the old Wake Forest College campus, and the schism between mainstream and fundamentalist Baptists grew wider. Wiggins, said one friend, was a very conservative person, but he didn't approve of the methods of fundamentalism. He wanted a religious school that reflected the church's traditional values, and in 1996, Campbell University established its graduate Divinity School.

Wiggins was seventy-six when Campbell University began the twenty-first century. He continued his busy schedule, but he took a medical leave after he was diagnosed with cancer in 2001. As one of his fellow college presidents noted, "Until his illness, no one ever told Adrian how old he was or that he would not continue on forever." He was hailed by admirers and critics as one of the state's true leaders of his time in higher education, especially among religious colleges and universities. Said others: "an icon," "you sense that he wants to be in charge," "dynamic," "a statesman in the church," "conservative in the best sense of the word," "a solid rock." And in the words of his cousin "Skinny" Brown, "If he tells you something, you can take it to the bank."

Wiggins built a university that reached far beyond little Buies Creek. There were cooperative programs in Malaysia, and Campbell courses were taught at Ft. Bragg in Fayetteville, Seymour-Johnson Air Force Base in Goldsboro, Peace College in Raleigh, and North Carolina Wesleyan College in Rocky Mount. There was an extension program in Cardiff, Wales. The campus included 145 buildings and the assets were valued at $140 million in the year 2000. Enrollment at the main campus was 3,482; total enrollment in the system was 9,220.

Never a father, Wiggins made Campbell University his family, his child.

J. Barlow Herget is a Raleigh writer who coauthored The Insiders' Guide to the Triangle *and served two terms on the Raleigh City Council. He received his master's degree in history from the University of Virginia and was a Neiman Fellow at Harvard University in 1970. He is a former editorial writer for the* News and Observer.

For more information, see:
Pearce, J. Winston. *Campbell College*. Broadmoor Press, 1976.

LAW

As swirls of change buffeted the legal profession, North Carolina provided more than its share of leading and controversial figures whose involvement in the law reshaped life during the twentieth century. The careers of some, such as U.S. District Court Judge James B. McMillan of Charlotte, who authored a controversial decision to use busing to end segregated schools, held implications that were felt all across the land.

North Carolina lawyers participated in the leadership of the legal profession across the nation. Willis Smith of Raleigh, who was elected to the U.S. Senate in 1950, was a president of the American Bar Association, as was Charles Rhyne of Charlotte, who during his term claimed credit for creating Law Day in the United States. A. P. Carlton Jr. of Raleigh was elected to head the ABA in 2002–2003. Charlotte lawyer E. Osborne Ayscue Jr. was the first North Carolinian to be elected president of the prestigious American College of Trial Lawyers.

Many of those who practiced law in the first half of the century hung out their shingles and accepted clients who arrived at the door. When Ayscue graduated from the University of North Carolina Law School in 1960, he was the seventh lawyer to join a Charlotte firm, but by 2000 the firm had grown to nearly two hundred lawyers. Likewise, Winston-Salem's Irving Carlyle, who contributed to the restructuring of North Carolina higher public education in mid-century, would hardly have recognized his law firm in 2000, which had grown to more than four hundred lawyers with offices in eight cities.

In the early part of the century Walter McKenzie Clark, a native of Halifax County, led the N.C. Supreme Court, where his opinions became a lightning rod for controversy, largely due to his advocacy of progressive ideas. During his thirty-five years on the court—including nearly two dozen as chief justice—he wrote more than three thousand opinions.

John J. Parker of Charlotte was something of an anomaly, a Republican who found great respect and support from Democrats all over the state. Parker's reputation as a brilliant, analytical lawyer led President Calvin Coolidge to appoint him in 1925 at age forty to the Court of Appeals for the Fourth Circuit. Five years later, President Herbert Hoover nominated Parker for a seat on the U.S. Supreme Court. Labor unions and the nascent National Association for the Advancement of Colored People (NAACP) opposed Parker's nomination—largely based on Parker's statements on race and union activity made during his unsuccessful campaign for governor in 1920—and it was defeated by a vote of forty-one to thirty-nine. He served on the Court of Appeals until 1958 and was chief judge for the last twenty-one years of his term.

While women outnumbered men in law schools by the end of the century, Susie Sharp of Rocky Mount was the object of ridicule when she attended UNC Law School in the 1920s. She was the only female in her class and only the fourth female in the history of the institution. Before graduating in 1929, she was an editor of the *North Carolina Law Review*.

After having served as a Superior Court judge, Sharp was named to the state Supreme Court in 1962 by Governor Terry Sanford. She won election in 1962 to serve the remaining four years of an unexpired term and in 1966 she was elected to a full eight-year term. In 1974, her election marked the first time a woman was elected chief justice in the nation.

One of Sharp's contemporaries was Albert Coates, a son of Johnson County who received his legal training at Harvard before returning to Chapel Hill to teach at the UNC Law School. Coates moved the law from the classroom into the political and governmental life of the state with the creation of the Institute of Government, which became a training ground for all manner of public and local officials.

Julius Chambers of Mount Gilead helped break the color barrier at the UNC Law School, where he was the first African American to edit the *North Carolina Law Review*. Chambers used his Charlotte law practice to challenge racial segregation—which more than once put his life in danger—and subsequently rose to prominence for his brilliant argument before the U.S. Supreme Court in the *Swann v. Charlotte-Mecklenburg Board of Education* case. In 1984, he was named director-counsel of the NAACP's Legal Defense and Education Fund in New York. Later, he returned to his native state as chancellor of North Carolina Central University at Durham.

Henry E. Frye of Ellerbe provided another first for the state when he became the first African American to become chief justice of the state Supreme Court. In 1963, Frye was appointed an assistant U.S. attorney for the middle district of North Carolina, the first African American federal prosecutor in North Carolina. In 1967, he resumed his private practice in Greensboro and in 1968 was elected to the North Carolina house, where he was the first African American state legislator in the twentieth century.

In 1983, Frye was appointed to fill a vacancy on the seven-member Supreme Court, where he became the first of his race to hold a seat. A year later, in 1984, Frye was elected to a full eight-year term to become the first African American elected to statewide office. In 1992, he was reelected to a second eight-year term. In 1999 Governor Hunt named Frye chief justice to fill a vacancy. His tenure as chief justice ended in 2000 when he was defeated for election to a full eight-year term.

IRVING E. CARLYLE

By Charles A. Clay

IRVING EDWARD CARLYLE was a bona fide liberal and a leader in North Carolina's political and educational establishment who died at his desk while worrying about the future of the University of North Carolina at Chapel Hill. This may seem an odd generalization to make in recalling his life, but the facts clearly and dramatically bear it out.

Carlyle was born to his Southern Baptist heritage on September 20, 1896, in Wake Forest when it was a small Baptist college town in Wake County near Raleigh. His father was John B. Carlyle, a native of Robeson County and a Latin professor, and his mother was the former Dora Dunn, described as a "liberal Baptist from Tennessee" who liked to dance.

Carlyle and the late I. Beverly Lake, who twice ran as a segregationist candidate for governor of North Carolina in the 1960s, grew up near each other in the early years of the century at Wake Forest College. The two became friends, but later Carlyle would help defeat Lake in the political arena.

Carlyle graduated summa cum laude from Wake Forest in 1917 and taught French, German, and American government in schools in Rocky Mount and Davidson County before enlisting in the army in World War I. He returned to Wake Forest after the war and coached the college's baseball and basketball teams before deciding to take a six-week course in the law school there.

After completing his legal education at the University of Virginia, Carlyle moved to Winston-Salem in 1922 and opened a one-man law office. He was soon asked to join the firm of Manley, Hendren and Womble, which evolved over the years into one of the most prestigious law firms in the state. Also in his early years in Winston-Salem, Carlyle married the former Mary Belo Moore of New Bern in 1928 and they had two daughters.

From his vantage point in the law firm, Carlyle played a key role in the movement of Wake Forest College to Winston-Salem, a complex, expensive, and challenging undertaking that began in 1935. That year, Bowman Gray, father of Gordon Gray and president of R.J. Reynolds Tobacco Company, gave the college $750,000 with the condition that it establish a medical school in Winston-Salem.

Wake Forest's Bowman Gray School of Medicine opened in 1941, paving the way for the eventual move

Irving E. Carlyle (Courtesy of Charlotte Observer)

of the entire college. Carlyle, who was president of the college board of trustees at the time, worked with Gray to move the institution. Subsequently, Carlyle, who had become city attorney for Winston-Salem, headed the Forsyth County campaign to raise money for the move, which was completed in the mid-1950s.

A dramatic test of Carlyle's political conscience as a rare and courageous liberal came in 1954 after he had backed William B. Umstead of Durham in his successful race for governor in 1952. Weeks before the state Democratic convention, scheduled for May 20, 1954, Umstead had picked Carlyle to deliver the convention's keynote speech. Then, three days before the convention opened, on May 17, 1954, the U.S. Supreme Court handed down its decision in the *Brown* case, declaring racially segregated public schools unequal and unconstitutional. Umstead publicly joined the southern political chorus of bitter disappointment at the Court's ruling, but Carlyle said, "I faced my conscience and I knew I had to say something meaningful to that convention."

He told the convention goers: "The Supreme Court of the United States has spoken. As good citizens we have no choice but to obey the law as laid down by the Court. To do otherwise would cost us our respect for law and order, and if we lost that in these critical times, we will have lost that quality which is the source of our strength as a state and as a nation." The speech drew loud applause but it was a reflection of the moment rather than the issue. Southerners were enraged at the Court's opinion.

Speaking some time later, Carlyle said, "I didn't talk about it with Governor Umstead. I knew he wouldn't like what I was going to say, and I didn't want to argue about it." However, when Umstead finally delivered a lengthy statement, he too opposed massive resistance but argued that the Court had overstepped its bounds.

The speech probably cost Carlyle a seat in the U.S. Senate. He was on the short list of candidates to replace Senator Clyde Hoey, who died within a few weeks of the Court's decision; Carlyle was widely considered the likely successor. Umstead, however, chose Wilmington lawyer Alton Lennon.

Carlyle continued to argue with the state's efforts to circumvent the Court's ruling. Later in 1954, Umstead died and was succeeded by Luther Hodges, who appointed a committee that came up with a proposal for the state to give tuition grants to public school pupils who were against attending desegregated schools. Another such proposal, by Beverly Lake, would have stripped North Carolina's Constitution of its requirement for a public school system.

Carlyle vigorously and vocally opposed any and all efforts to get around the law and called for beginning school integration in the early grades first. In an obviously heartfelt speech to the North Carolina State Bar in 1956, Carlyle urged lawyers to make the case for obeying the law as rendered in the *Brown* case. "The superior knowledge of the lawyer about the law gives to him a unique and privileged role, to be played fearlessly for the public good," he said. "His silence at a time like this is a betrayal of his trust. . . . "

In the elections of 1960, the first in which Lake ran for governor, Carlyle backed Terry Sanford. In the crucial runoff election between Lake and Sanford in June 1960, in a time when winning the Democratic nomination was tantamount to election, Carlyle appeared with Sanford and his campaign manager, Bert Bennett of Winston-Salem, in their election-eve television appeal for votes.

Sanford won handily and appointed Carlyle to head the Governor's Commission on Education Beyond the High School, providing Carlyle the opportunity to make one of his most important contributions to the state. The Carlyle commission's report to the governor and people in August 1962 was considered the most intensive and comprehensive study ever made of the state's higher educational system. Out of the commission came the highly successful statewide community college system, which Sanford considered the greatest single achievement of his 1961–65 administration.

Sanford had appointed the commission at the urging of the leadership of the Consolidated University of North Carolina, the embodiment of the state's one-university concept in higher education. "We have no real blueprint for the future," Sanford said at the time, although the 1955 General Assembly had created the State Board of Higher Education for planning purposes.

The 1963 Higher Education Act, passed in response to the Carlyle commission's report, not only created the community college system but also kept the Consolidated University intact, with its campuses in Chapel Hill, Raleigh, and Greensboro. It meant that UNC's branches would continue to be the only public institutions with authority to offer doctoral degree programs and would remain primarily responsible for scientific research and extension programs.

The act did not, however, as Carlyle had passionately hoped, assure the continuance of the one-university concept in North Carolina, and succeeding legislative sessions enacted major structural changes in the system. The 1963 act itself made community colleges in Asheville, Charlotte, and Wilmington into public senior colleges, and succeeding sessions added these institutions to the Consolidated University. In the 1967 and 1969 sessions, all nine of the state's independent four-year colleges were renamed regional universities with authority to offer doctoral programs, subject to the approval of the Board of Higher Education, although no money was appropriated for that purpose.

Throughout this period, Carlyle warned strongly against the destruction of the Consolidated University. The turmoil in public higher education at the time led Governor Robert Scott to name another study commission in 1970. In 1971, it came with a "regency" plan of governance which would have replaced the six-campus Consolidated University, its board of trustees, and its president with a strengthened version of the largely ineffective state Board of Higher Education. The regency proposal, which failed to win approval in the regular session of the 1971 General Assembly, was scheduled to be taken up again in October of that year.

Meanwhile, in early June, Carlyle, who had suffered a serious heart attack two-and-a-half years earlier, worked on a speech opposing the regency plan at his home in Winston-Salem. He was to give it to a legislative committee the next week. He read a rough draft to his family and as he readied for bed on Friday, June 5, he told his wife, "I'll get up early and work on it."

The next morning, Carlyle was found slumped in his chair at his desk, dead of a heart attack. His pen had fallen to the floor and his speech lay on the desk in front of him. Among many things, it read: "To dismantle . . . the Consolidated University would be a tragic mistake. One of the great universities of America will have disappeared for good, never to be resurrected. . . . A board of regents . . . will level all institutions down and push none up; will replace unique individuality and academic independence . . . with dull uniformity and dispel quality education . . . in exchange for mediocrity. . . . "

At a special session in October 1971, the General Assembly brought all of the sixteen degree-granting public institutions of higher learning under a new University of North Carolina administrative umbrella. It created a thirty-two-member board of governors to replace the Board of Higher Education and the Consolidated University's board of trustees, and gave the new board authority over all the institutions. Sixteen of the new board's original members were trustees of the Consolidated University.

John Sanders, who headed the staff on the Carlyle commission, said he thought the restructuring act of 1971, which redefined the university, responded to most of Carlyle's objections. His worst fears had not been realized, Sanders indicated. In an article in the fall 1993 issue of *Popular Government,* the publication of the Institute of Government in Chapel Hill, Sanders wrote that the UNC board and its president were given "almost complete management authority" over the institutions, including the power to determine degree programs and other major activities, such as budgets and the appointment of chancellors. The article concluded that the "present structure of the multi-campus university has proved more durable and successful than many in 1971 thought it would be."

Throughout his career as a liberal corporation lawyer, Carlyle remained an outspoken leader in Baptist affairs, most notably where his beloved Wake Forest University was concerned. He served almost two decades on the board of trustees, including five one-year terms as president of the board, and helped win the Baptist State Convention's permission for non-Baptist trustees to serve on the board.

In the decade of the 1940s, Carlyle represented Forsyth County in both the state house and senate. On at least one occasion, he riled his Baptist brethren across the state when he was chairman of a committee that killed an anti-liquor bill being pushed by the Baptists.

Throughout his life, Carlyle remained true to his liberal principles. He spoke out strongly but vainly against the death sentence before the General Assembly in April 1971, not long before his death. "Only the poor and uneducated blacks and occasionally a poor white are ever put to death by the state," he said, and the main purpose of the penalty is "to keep the blacks in check." Carlyle also came to be an opponent of the war in Vietnam and was cochairman of the North Carolina Committee to End the War in Indochina at his death.

In 2000, Sanders said Carlyle was a "very pleasant person to work with. There was nothing pompous or self-righteous about him. He was really on top of whatever he was dealing with. He typified a kind of person that is passing from the scene now, a person who was very successful in his personal business but also very interested in public service. They did a great deal for North Carolina."

Charles A. Clay of Raleigh was editor of the Fayetteville Observer *from 1965 to 1978. Prior to that he was a journalist in Durham and Raleigh. He served on the North Carolina Industrial Commission from 1980 to 1986. He also is the author of a biographical novel,* The Alien Corn.

For more information, see:

"Irving E. Carlyle, Tar Heel of the Week." Raleigh *News and Observer,* October 15, 1961.

Report of the Governor's Commission on Education Beyond the High School. North Carolina Institute of Government, University of North Carolina at Chapel Hill, 1962.

Tursi, Frank V. *The Winston-Salem Journal, Magnolia Trees, and Pulitzer Prizes.* John F. Blair, 1996.

JULIUS L. CHAMBERS

By Marsha Cook Vick

I N THE COURSE of his remarkable career as a civil
rights attorney, Julius Chambers was always in the
forefront of the struggle for social justice and for
change in federal civil rights law. He rose to national
prominence in the 1970s for his brilliant argument
before the U.S. Supreme Court in *Swann v. Charlotte-
Mecklenburg Board of Education,* the landmark case that
established busing as an appropriate means to integrate
the nation's public schools. Chambers's far-reaching
efforts to secure constitutional rights for citizens had
a major impact in the South and across the land, but
were countered with threats to his life and with the
firebombing of his home, his office, his car, and his
father's business. In the face of this fierce racial bigotry, Julius Chambers stood with rocklike firmness,
having never lost the tough and pugnacious quality
that he developed as a child in North Carolina.

Chambers's attraction to the law began when he
was twelve years old and realized that his father's need
for a lawyer to help him collect a bill from a customer
was a matter far more important than an ordinary
business dispute. "My father was an automobile mechanic and owned a garage," Chambers recalled. "He
had fixed a truck for a white citizen who refused to pay
him. No lawyer would represent my father. It wasn't
right. I decided then to pursue a career that would
change it." As a freshman in college, Chambers got a
further perspective on racial discrimination when a
driver forced him off an interstate bus for refusing to
move to the back and give his seat to a white person.
Such experiences shaped Chambers's approach to his
legal career, but his exceptional intellect and caring
heart for the disadvantaged were also qualities that
made him one of America's leading civil rights attorneys and most enlightened and steadfast educational
leaders.

Julius Levonne Chambers was born in Mt. Gilead
on October 6, 1936, the third of four children born to
Matilda Chambers and William Chambers. Though
the family lived in the segregated South, with all the
attending disparities in facilities and opportunities,
his parents consistently encouraged their children to
go to college. When Julius was fourteen years old, he
joined a mail-order book club that helped enrich his
mind and overcome the disadvantage of having a limited school library and no access to the town's public
library. He traveled twelve miles to Troy to attend Pea-

Julius L. Chambers (Courtesy of Charlotte Observer)

body High School, where he played football and baseball and was president of the student government association during his junior and senior years. He graduated in 1954 and entered North Carolina College
(renamed North Carolina Central University in 1969)
with excitement and anticipation. To him, the larger
city of Durham seemed comparable to New York City.

As a college student, Chambers excelled in his academic work while also participating in the extracurricular life of the school. He was vice president of his
class, president of the history club, president of the
Alpha Phi Alpha fraternity, and president of the student body in his junior and senior years. He also
played quarterback on the football team for two years.
With his characteristic sense of humor, he commented
on this experience: "I weighed 115 pounds, and after
being thrown across the field by a long-time friend
of mine, John Baker of Raleigh, I decided that was
enough!" (Baker later became a professional football player.) In 1958, Chambers graduated summa cum

laude with a B.A. degree in history. He won a scholarship to the University of Michigan and earned an M.A. degree in history in 1959.

While working in Washington, D.C., in the summer of 1959, to earn money for a legal education, he met Vivian Giles, the sister of a college friend. He entered the University of North Carolina Law School in the fall of 1959, and he and Vivian married the following year. In his second year of law school, Chambers was voted editor in chief of the *North Carolina Law Review* and became the first African American to hold this position at any historically white law school in the South. He was inducted into the Order of the Coif, the national legal honor society, and into the Order of the Golden Fleece, the University of North Carolina's highest honor society for student leaders. In 1962 Chambers received his J.D. degree, ranking first academically in his class of one hundred students. He spent the next year studying and teaching at the Columbia University School of Law, where he received an L.L.M. degree in 1963.

U.S. Supreme Court Justice Thurgood Marshall, then a prominent civil rights attorney and counsel for the Legal Defense and Education Fund, an affiliate of the National Association for the Advancement of Colored People (NAACP), selected Julius Chambers as the first legal intern for the Legal Defense Fund. Chambers worked for a year as a litigator in civil rights cases, including several involving Dr. Martin Luther King Jr., in Virginia, North Carolina, Georgia, and Alabama. "That experience," he remembered, "exposed me to the real practice of law. . . . I hadn't had anything like that in law school—that is, how one might develop legal theories to deal with unexpected and unusual situations." The contrast in Chambers's modest and soft-spoken manner and his aggressive litigation in the courtroom puzzled some observers. "I don't believe in yelling and screaming," he explained. "I believe in reasoning with people." Chambers's wholehearted dedication to the causes for which he worked rather than to personal celebrity also helped to account for his uncommon style.

After being urged by several black leaders in Charlotte to practice law in their city, Chambers established a law firm there in 1964 and continued to work with the lawyers at the Legal Defense Fund, litigating cases throughout North Carolina. "I took two summer interns, Adam Stein and James Ferguson," he recalled. "After they got out of law school, they joined the firm and we were the first integrated law firm in the state."

In 1965 Chambers filed the *Swann v. Charlotte-Mecklenburg Board of Education* suit on behalf of ten

black families whose children had been denied admission to all-white schools. The case was named for James Swann, the first of these students who attempted to enroll in a white school. As the case began its path of appeals in the courts, Chambers's car was dynamited on a public street in New Bern as he met with African Americans in a nearby church. Later that year, Chambers represented forty-one black plaintiffs in a suit to integrate the Shrine Bowl football game, a high school all-star event played annually in Charlotte's Memorial Stadium. Ten days after he filed this suit in federal court, the Chambers's home in Charlotte was firebombed. "I don't know how we escaped bodily harm," he said, "except for the grace of God." In the next few years, their two children were born, Derrick Levonne in 1966 and Judy LaVern in 1970.

After the U.S. Supreme Court unanimously upheld the previous rulings in the *Swann* case in 1971, Chambers's law office was burned. Undeterred, he continued to litigate civil rights cases involving the constitutionality of discrimination in housing, employment, and other private rights of citizens. In the early 1970s Chambers also emerged as a leader in higher education. He taught in the law schools at Harvard, Columbia, Virginia, and Pennsylvania, educating law students not only in the specifics of constitutional and civil rights law, but also in the need for legal advocacy of equal access to opportunities for all people. A member of the board of trustees of North Carolina Central University, he began serving in 1972 as their representative on the board of the Consolidated University of North Carolina, the board responsible for overseeing the recently reorganized UNC system. During his five-year tenure on the Board of Governors, Chambers continually pointed out the inequitable state funding of the historically black colleges and universities, which, he argued, were prevented from playing an equal role with the white institutions in providing higher education. In 1977, two years before his term ended, Chambers resigned, frustrated with the futility of efforts to encourage voluntary state commitment to bring the black institutions up to par and with the board's delays in further integrating the universities and improving the opportunities for black students.

When he accepted the position of director-counsel of the NAACP's Legal Defense and Education Fund in 1984, Chambers moved to New York City, the once distant place that he had imagined with such excitement as a youth. Trying to prevent what he saw as the indifference of the U.S. Supreme Court and the U.S. Justice Department to the victims of discrimination in the country during the 1980s, Chambers supervised the litigation of cases that benefited racial minorities, women, and the disabled in the areas of voting rights, employment, school desegregation, capital punishment, and housing. He argued cases, directed twenty-four staff attorneys and several hundred cooperating attorneys across the nation, and organized an educational campaign to heighten awareness of the erosion of civil rights protections by the courts and the federal government.

In 1992, C. D. Spangler Jr., president of the University of North Carolina system, visited Chambers in New York to discuss the search for a chancellor for North Carolina Central University. When Spangler casually listed the first qualification as "someone who finished first in his class at the University of North Carolina Law School," Chambers was shocked, because he fit the description. While he had not considered becoming an educational administrator, Chambers began to see the chancellorship as an opportunity to improve and repay the institution whose professors had helped to shape his leadership skills. The first alumnus of the institution to serve as its chief administrator, Chambers became chancellor of North Carolina Central University on January 1, 1993.

Speculation about the possibility of his being appointed a federal judge began during the administration of President Jimmy Carter and continued through the early years of Chambers's tenure as chancellor. When Justice Harry Blackmun announced his resignation from the U.S. Supreme Court in 1994, a number of legal, educational, and political leaders urged President Bill Clinton to consider Chambers as his replacement. Chambers later acknowledged having talked to representatives of both Presidents Carter and Clinton, but he withdrew his name from consideration in every instance, he said, because he was not willing to contend with the partisan politics within North Carolina's U.S. Senate delegation, whose support would have been required for confirmation.

Instead, Chambers reduced his participation in the practice of law and focused on reestablishing North Carolina Central University as one of the best historically black universities in the state and nation. His love for students and their potential for leadership in society led to fast and significant change. As chancellor, he improved academic programs and performance by raising admission standards, establishing an honors curriculum, creating endowed chairs, encouraging faculty and departments to reach a higher degree of academic competitiveness, and engendering pride and spirit on the campus.

Even though he encountered opposition in the university community, Chambers promoted a more ra-

cially diverse student body. He actively recruited and enrolled white students, believing that students of all races have to learn to live together and respect each other. The reality that more black students were going to historically white institutions and thus causing a dwindling pool of candidates also influenced Chambers to make this bold push. "We all are better off because of it," he said. "I think all of us have learned in the process."

His insistence on better academic credentials from applicants caused even more vocal concern when enrollment dropped and triggered the loss of faculty and a portion of the university's state funding. Unwilling to settle for second best, Chambers weathered the controversy without apology while enrollment gradually increased and the university recovered from the losses. "We are showing people," he said, "that we have produced as good a student as can be found in any institution. We are having an impact around the country with the contributions that we have made, and we are all very proud of what we've been able to do with the limited resources we have."

He also worked to transform the university from an underfinanced undergraduate college into a major research institution. The Julius L. Chambers Biomedical Biotechnology Research Institute building and the School of Education's new building were testaments to both his farsightedness in advancing the university's involvement in important academic research and training, and his effectiveness in obtaining increased state funding and major gifts for campus expansion. Chambers also extended the reach of the university beyond its campus with his initiatives on health and economic enterprise in Durham and his insistence on making community service a graduation requirement for all undergraduate students. Assessing where his alma mater stood at the end of his tenure as chancellor, he said, "We still have the problem with resources. We still have to address the inequities, and the State has to decide what our mission, the mission of the historically black colleges and universities, is going to be."

Unafraid to hold and express his independently achieved beliefs and positions in his several careers, Chambers exhibited that same self-direction in his participation in a broad range of humanitarian causes —from Native American, community, and children's groups to corporate boards and research institutes. His articles in respected law reviews and books contributed notably to the professional application of constitutional and civil rights law. He received many honors, including numerous honorary degrees, Distinguished Alumni Awards from the Columbia University School of Law and the University of North Carolina at Chapel Hill, and a rarely given Courageous Advocacy Award from the American College of Trial Lawyers. Also, he received the Kelly M. Alexander Sr. Humanitarian Award, the Aetna Voice of Conscience Award, the Congressional Black Caucus Foundation's Adam Clayton Powell Award for Legislative and Legal Perfection, and the Josephine D. Clement Award for Exemplary Community Leadership for Public Education in Durham.

Chambers retired as chancellor of North Carolina Central University in June 2001. Vivian Chambers believed that her husband probably would never fully retire, even though he put golfing and fishing on his agenda. Chambers said that he hoped to implement his vision of a cooperative program among the law schools at North Carolina Central University, Duke University, and the University of North Carolina, and perhaps teach in that program. He also planned to return to the practice of law in Charlotte. One of his main objectives, he said, would be to work for poor people's access to legal representation and to the courts. "The Constitution guarantees equal protection, but there is still a great deal of discrimination in this country. We still have work to do in education, employment, housing, health care, voting rights, and the administration of criminal justice."

Marsha Cook Vick is the author of Black Subjectivity in Performance: A Century of African American Drama on Broadway. *Dr. Vick was a speechwriter and research assistant for U.S. Senator Terry Sanford and taught in the Afro-American Studies Curriculum at the University of North Carolina at Chapel Hill.*

For more information, see:

Chambers, Julius. "Ethnicity and Education." Interview by Wayne Pond, February 20, 1994. Sound Recording. National Humanities Center, Research Triangle Park.

———. Interview, June 18, 1990. Southern Oral History Collection. Southern Historical Collection, University of North Carolina at Chapel Hill.

———. Interview by Marsha Cook Vick, February 1, 2001. Levine Museum of the New South, Charlotte.

Armstrong, Robin. "Julius Chambers." In *Contemporary Black Biography,* ed. Barbara Carlisle Bigelow, 3:31–33. Gale Research, 1993.

Chambers, Julius L. "Black Americans and the Courts: Has the Clock Been Turned Back Permanently?" In *The State of Black America 1990,* 9–24. The National Urban League, 1990.

———. *"Brown v. Board of Education."* In *Race in America: The Struggle for Equality,* ed. Herbert Hill and James E. Jones Jr., 182–194. University of Wisconsin Press, 1993.

———. "Race and Equality: The Still Unfinished Business of the Warren Court." In *The Warren Court: A Retrospective,* ed. Bernard Schwartz, 21–67. Oxford University Press, 1996.

Elliot, Jeffrey M. "Julius LeVonne Chambers: Correcting Political Inequities." In *Black Voices in American Politics,* 201–215. Harcourt Brace Jovanovich, 1986.

Evans, Gaynelle. "Julius Chambers: Moving Forward by Taking a Step Back." *Black Issues in Higher Education* 9, no. 21 (December 17, 1992): 12–13.

WALTER M. CLARK

By Michael T. Smith

FOR MOST OF THE FIRST quarter of the century, North Carolina's Supreme Court was presided over by a jurist who championed organized labor, opposed the growing conglomeration of railroad and tobacco companies, and supported the right of women to vote. Walter McKenzie Clark led a remarkable life that included command of a company of men in the Civil War at the age of fourteen before attending the university in Chapel Hill in wartime to earn his degree and study law.

Clark's personal and legal career drew attention all across the land. His life spanned eighty-one years, extraordinary in an era when life expectancy was half what it was a century later. During his thirty-five years on the court—including nearly two dozen as chief justice—he wrote more than three thousand opinions.

He was born in Halifax County on August 19, 1846. His father, David Clark II, was one of the wealthiest planters and largest slave owners in the state, who later served as a brigadier general of North Carolina troops during the Civil War. His mother, Anna Maria Thorne, also belonged to a prosperous family from the same region, although she received part of her education in New York. Clark grew up on the family plantation, Ventosa, located on the Roanoke River. Walter displayed precocious intellectual abilities at an early age and received a solid classical education at several local schools during the antebellum years. When the Civil War began in 1861, Clark was fourteen and a student at a military academy in Hillsborough. He took a commission as a second lieutenant and became drill master in the 22nd North Carolina Regiment, commanded by Colonel James Johnston Pettigrew.

Despite his youth, Clark, a staunch believer in Southern rights and supporter of the Confederacy, was promoted to first lieutenant in the 35th North Carolina Regiment in August 1862, and served as adjutant to regimental commander Matt W. Ransom, who was later general and served as a U.S. Senator from North Carolina. "Little Clark," as he was known in the army, participated in several grueling and bloody campaigns, including Second Manassas in 1862, the capture of Harper's Ferry, and the Battle of Antietam, where he received a slight wound to his hand. He resigned his commission the following February in order to continue his studies at the Uni-

Walter M. Clark (Courtesy of Southern Historical Collection)

versity of North Carolina and graduated in June of 1863. Clark also began studying law in Chapel Hill under the direction of William H. Battle, a lawyer and former judge.

Upon his graduation Clark reentered the army on garrison duty, having been elected major of the 17th North Carolina Regiment, before joining General Joseph E. Johnston's command in early 1865 and participating in the Battle of Bentonville. At the end of the war, his former slave, Neverson, an 1859 gift from his father, was still at his side.

Following the war Clark assumed the management of his family's extensive property, as his father's health had been seriously impaired by the rigors of wartime service. Despite great difficulty in raising capital and finding workers, Clark managed through careful supervision and hard work to transform his family's farmland into a profitable enterprise once again. He also resumed the study of law for several months in 1866 at Washington's Columbian Law School (later George Washington University). He began practicing law at the age of twenty in Halifax County, and soon earned a reputation as an effective trial lawyer. Clark received an M.A. from the University of North Carolina in 1867, and moved to Raleigh in 1873, in part to court Susan Washington Graham, the daughter of former governor and senator William A. Graham. They were married in 1875 and had seven children.

Clark purchased a part interest in the *Raleigh News* and took an active role in managing the newspaper, notwithstanding his busy schedule as a lawyer and as a director and general counsel for several railroad companies. Clark wrote many editorials and letters for the paper, including most notably the so-called mudcut letters, exposing the wastefulness and mismanagement accompanying the state's extension of the Western North Carolina Railroad across the Blue Ridge Mountains. To some extent in response to Clark's arguments, a special session of the General Assembly met and voted to sell the uncompleted road to a private company.

Clark also devoted himself during this time to completing his *Code of Civil Procedure of North Carolina,* popularly known as *Clark's Code,* which went into several subsequent editions and became a standard reference book for the state's lawyers. This work reflected his intense, lifelong interest in promoting judicial efficiency. He also played a leading role in organization of the Methodist Church, attending church conferences around the world, including one in London in 1881, and wrote many articles about the denomination's history.

In April 1885 Governor Alfred M. Scales, recognizing Clark's reputation as a lawyer and growing stature in the Democratic Party, appointed him to the state superior court. Clark had declined a nomination as attorney general, preferring to enter into a career as a jurist, to which he would devote the remainder of his life. As a judge, Clark traveled throughout the state hearing criminal cases. Traveling from one remote county seat to another, often by buggy, made this position a demanding and tiresome one, but Clark was more than equal to his responsibilities. He distinguished himself by his even-tempered firmness, deep knowledge, and unusually well-developed work habits. He declined the first of several tendered gubernatorial nominations in 1888, and received an appointment to the state Supreme Court the following year.

Although most of the opinions Clark wrote were for the majority, he particularly won renown for his more than three hundred dissents. He usually accompanied these with extensive government and scientific reports and other factual data and they frequently served the purpose of persuading the public, the legislature, or his fellow justices to adopt his views. In ad-

dition to writing over one hundred decisions per year, Clark published many well-received articles in legal, historical, and government journals and magazines. S. D. Thompson, editor of the *American Law Review,* informed Clark in 1892 that he "would welcome anything from your pen."

U.S. Senator Robert M. LaFollette, editor of *LaFollette's,* similarly informed him twenty-one years later that "anything from your pen on any subject would have distinct value and peculiar interest for our readers." Clark edited sixteen volumes of the *State Records of North Carolina* (1866–97) and the five-volume *Histories of the Several Regiments and Battalions from North Carolina, in the Great War 1861–1865* (1901), among many other literary and historical endeavors. The latter work, which included essays by North Carolina veterans of every rank from private to lieutenant general, was at the time the most thoroughly documented study of any southern state's role in the Civil War.

From his earliest years on the state Supreme Court, Clark became a lightning rod for controversy. This was largely due to his advocacy of progressive ideals and condemnations of corruption and injustice, which offended many of the state's most powerful interests. Clark criticized railroad companies for forming monopolies and using unfair tactics to take over smaller, independent lines and raise prices. He was especially outraged by the illegal but widespread practice of distributing free railroad passes to legislators in exchange for their political support.

Clark increasingly believed that big business, as exemplified by the railroads, threatened both government integrity and individual rights, and had to be checked and regulated. He also opposed the formation and practices of James B. Duke's American Tobacco Company, which he felt cheated small farmers by setting unfairly low prices for tobacco in the pursuit of huge corporate profits.

Clark, a longtime member of Trinity College's board of trustees, clashed with President John Kilgo in 1897 over the issue of the school's growing alliance with the Dukes, beginning with James B. Duke's father, Washington, who gave substantial sums to the college before the turn of the century. Clark's criticisms of Kilgo's controversial stance led to his ouster from the board the following year, after a bitterly divisive hearing in which Clark was not allowed to make a full statement of his position. Nevertheless, in 1902 Clark won a decisive victory at the Democratic state convention and was chosen to become chief justice, reflecting his status as one of North Carolina's leading progressives. His nomination was opposed by the railroad companies, the American Tobacco Company, and the majority of the state's newspapers, with the exception of Raleigh's *News and Observer,* edited by his friend and ally Josephus Daniels.

As chief justice, Clark continued to fight for a variety of reforms in keeping with his often-stated belief that "the public welfare is the supreme law." He advocated the direct election of senators, abolition of life tenure for federal judges, a more humane prison system, and a crackdown on lynching, noting that "the failure of the Courts to punish murders is anarchy." He favored federal supervision of telegraph and telephone communications by the post office, which he felt should be managed with a view toward the public interest, and not making a profit.

Clark worked hard to improve the legal status of married women in North Carolina, who were virtually without rights. After marriage, women could not own property or make contracts, and could legally be beaten with a switch no wider than her husband's thumb. Clark insisted that the state's 1868 Constitution reversed this practice, but that judges had failed to implement these provisions. Clark's 1911 *Rea vs. Rea* decision put his opinion into law, and was hailed as signifying the emancipation of married women.

Clark supported the right of women to hold public office, publicly noting that many of the world's greatest leaders, including Great Britain's two most distinguished monarchs (Elizabeth and Victoria), had been women, and that English common law offered no justification for denying this right to females. His support of women's suffrage in advance of any other major male political figure in the South particularly distinguished him as a courageous and egalitarian leader.

Clark served as legal advisor to the state League of Women Voters, and corresponded with Carrie Chapman Catt, the organization's national leader. Clark advised suffragist leaders on political tactics and legal means of bringing about changes to both the federal and state constitutions. His deep emotional commitment to this cause was reflected by the fact that he once openly wept while watching Catt address the North Carolina General Assembly.

Clark was a leading judicial advocate of the labor movement. He argued that late-nineteenth-century economic changes and the growth of business and industry threatened the nation's future by excluding the majority of its population, the workers, from the benefits of the new prosperity. This wealth had to be more equitably divided, Clark believed. He argued in favor of eliminating child labor, making business and factory owners legally responsible for injuries suffered by their workers, and establishing a minimum wage and an eight-hour workday.

Union leader Samuel Gompers, president of the American Federation of Labor, regarded Clark as "one of [labor's] ablest and best friends," and encouraged him to publicize his views as well as run for higher office. Clark did in fact seek a seat in the United States Senate in 1912, running against conservative incumbent Furnifold M. Simmons and Governor William W. Kitchin. Aided by overwhelming financial support from business interests, Simmons won easily, and Clark remained on the bench.

President Woodrow Wilson considered Clark for a nomination to the U.S. Supreme Court in 1914, despite the urgings of North Carolina's congressional delegation, Secretary of State William Jennings Bryan, and others, but Wilson did name Clark an umpire for the National War Labor Board three years later. Clark wrote an important ruling in favor of the creation of an eight-hour workday, arguing that it would increase both productivity and the health of workers. He continued to maintain a busy speaking and writing schedule until the end of his life, including correspondence with such prominent progressive figures as Anna Howard Shaw, Gifford Pinchot, Theodore Roosevelt, Louis Brandeis, and Upton Sinclair. He also led the effort to adopt "Esse Quam Videri" (to be rather than to seem) as North Carolina's state motto.

Clark died in Raleigh on May 19, 1924, and was buried in that city's historic Oakwood Cemetery. At his request, his grave featured only a simple marker in respect of his wish that he be remembered solely for his work on behalf of North Carolina's citizens. "This is the only monument I care for," he informed his son a year prior to his death.

Michael Thomas Smith has published articles in the North Carolina Historical Review *and the* Maryland Historical Magazine *and is pursuing his Ph.D. in American history at Pennsylvania State University.*

For more information, see:
Clark, Walter. Papers. N.C. Office of Archives and History, Raleigh.

Brooks, Aubrey Lee. *Walter Clark: Fighting Judge.* University of North Carolina Press, 1944.
———, and Hugh T. Lefler, eds. *The Papers of Walter Clark.* 2 vols. University of North Carolina Press, 1948–50.
Whichard, Willis P. "A Place for Walter Clark in the American Judicial Tradition." *North Carolina Law Review* (1985).

ALBERT COATES

By Milton S. Heath Jr.

A BIOGRAPHICAL SKETCH of Albert Coates could be deceptively short and simple because of the intense and single-minded focus of the man. His place in history arises from his creation and nurturing of an extraordinary vehicle for the improvement of local and state government through education, the Institute of Government of the University of North Carolina at Chapel Hill—the extension arm of the university to the public service. In the words of John L. Sanders, Coates's successor as director of the Institute, Coates was the Institute's "founder, and for thirty years its identity and his fused in ways that defied distinction."

Albert Coates was born in Johnston County on August 25, 1896. He was the fourth of nine children, a country-bred boy, like so many of North Carolina's leaders during the years of the early and mid-twentieth century, which were, as Sanders wrote, those "hopeful years of the progressive era of American politics, when the conviction was widely shared that the public institutions of the nation were perfectible, and that perfecting them was worthy of the best efforts of the best citizens."

The Coates family not only grew farm products but also grew children with a yen for "the lifting power of education," in the words of Charles B. Aycock, North Carolina's education governor of the turn of the century. Two of Albert's siblings, Dora and Kenneth, would have long and distinguished careers as university professors. His other siblings each either taught school at one time or married educators. Albert enrolled at the University of North Carolina in the fall of 1914 and completed his undergraduate degree just in time to enter military service in 1918. He was commissioned a second lieutenant in the army, but armistice intervened before he was called into combat.

During his bright college years Coates was exposed to the beliefs of UNC President Edward Kidder Graham that the university should serve not only its on-campus student body but also the people of the whole state. Coates also was a protégé of E. C. Branson, the chair of the Department of Rural Economics and Sociology, who encouraged students to organize county clubs for the study of the economic and social life of North Carolina's one hundred counties. In his senior year, Coates assisted Branson in a detailed study of county government, which would

Albert Coates (Courtesy of Institute of Government)

provide the underpinnings for later examination of county government under the umbrella of the Institute of Government.

Coates entered Harvard Law School in 1920, graduating with an LL.B. in 1923. A talented pair of Tar Heel roommates shared his time at Harvard: Thomas Wolfe of *Look Homeward, Angel,* and William Polk, later attorney and editorialist with the *Greensboro Daily News.* Another Tar Heel, Sam Ervin, also spent Cambridge time with Coates as a law student and the two became lifelong friends.

Coates moved directly from law school to an assistant professorship at UNC Law School in 1923, an associate professorship in 1925, and a full professorship in 1927. Criminal law was his first love as a teacher, competing for his attention with municipal law, legislation, and family law. These four courses became, in time, the enduring nucleus of the Institute of Government. The Institute would develop a unique legislative service and would undertake intensive training, research, and consulting with city and county officials, with social service personnel, and with court and criminal justice officials. Much later it would build from these subjects to its current involvement with all of state and local government in North Carolina.

Early on, Coates began experimenting with bringing the real world into his teaching. He asked law enforcement, court, and correctional officials into his classrooms, rode with police officers on their beats, followed them into the criminal courts, and followed convicted persons into the prisons. He lobbied Dean Maurice T. Van Hecke of the UNC Law School to accept the Coatesian notion that the "law in books" should mirror the "law in action," and to broaden the mission of the law school to encompass the public service. The dean and the law faculty were not tempted by this invitation offered in the face of budget and salary cuts brought on by the Depression. In the long run this may have been a blessing in disguise, one that enabled Coates to develop an independent organizational setting to pursue his ideas.

While continuing to teach his law school courses with the reluctant acquiescence of the law faculty, Coates launched the Institute as a private venture. In 1931 he began with a series of conferences for law enforcement officers held throughout the state. By the fall of 1932 an Institute of Government had been formally created, the first issue of its magazine *Popular Government* was published, and its first statewide conference had been held with Dean Roscoe Pound of the Harvard Law School as its principal speaker. But it had no staff, no organizational or physical home, and no reliable funding—conditions that would dog Albert Coates all too often for the next decade.

During the lean years of the Depression, there would be other high spots. One was the hiring of the first of a series of outstanding professional staff members. (The first three were Henry Brandis, later dean of the UNC Law School; Buck Grice, later deputy state auditor; and Dillard Gardner, later marshal and librarian of the North Carolina Supreme Court.) Another encouraging note was a trail of gifts from generous donors whose names comprised a who's who of North Carolina business leadership—the Cones, the Haneses, the Grays, the Hills, Clay Williams, Ashley Penn, A. H. Bahnson, Ed Millis, and Spencer Love. The special beneficence of Julian Price and the brothers Gordon and Bowman Gray made possible the completion of the Institute's first home in 1939 on downtown Franklin Street.

But for all the highs, there would be years of frustrating lows. Albert and his wife, Gladys, exhausted their own meager financial resources, borrowed on insurance, and moved into a rented cottage. When operating funds ran out, the original staff had to be let go, and later some of their replacements. Only Coates's extraordinary tenacity, endurance, and salesmanship would carry the skeleton of the Institute through its hard times, coinciding with the depth of the Depression.

Coates the promoter finally captured the fancy of a key ally in 1940, recently installed University Controller W. D. Carmichael Jr., a financier of unusual vision. Together they prevailed upon Spencer Love to keep the Institute afloat through 1942, and upon Governor J. Melville Broughton to recommend a $15,000 state appropriation by the 1943 General Assembly. These resources and these compelling personalities persuaded the UNC Board of Trustees to formally accept the Institute as a part of the university in 1942. It would be another fifteen years before the university in 1957 would give Institute staff members full faculty status as assistant professors, associate professors, and professors.

Coates was a master recruiter who rarely took "no" for an answer. Over the years he persuaded some of North Carolina's brightest and best to cast their lots with the Institute—the likes of Terry Sanford, Bill Cochrane, Dickson Phillips, Robert Byrd, Malcolm Seawall, Paul Johnston, Edward Scheidt, Alex McMahon, Mary Oliver, George Esser, Clyde Ball, Philip Green, Donald Hayman, Lee Bounds, Jack Elam, Roddey Ligon, Beta McCarthy, Ruth Mace, Basil Sherrill, Hugh Cannon, Clifford Pace, John Fries Blair, Fannie Memory Farmer, Richard Myren, John Scarlett, Jake Wicker, John Sanders, and Henry Lewis. In time these ex-Institute faculty would number a governor, a U.S. senator, state legislators and judges, a state attorney general, law school deans, major corporate presidents, a publisher, state cabinet officers, city and county managers and attorneys, city and regional planners, the head of the North Carolina Fund, and later Institute directors.

A lifelong workaholic, Coates expected no less of his staff. These expectations first and foremost generated rich dividends for the citizens of North Carolina in terms of productive work for the public good. Their flip side is another story. "Meet me at the Carolina Inn for breakfast" meant starting the workday an hour early and being prepared perhaps to pick up the tab—the latter probably a holdover from the desperate threadbare days of the 1930s.

In 1956, the Institute moved into its home on South

Road at the entrance to the UNC campus, the Joseph Palmer Knapp Building. It was financed by a $500,000 grant from the Joseph Palmer Knapp Foundation and a matching appropriation of $500,000 by the 1953 General Assembly.

The dedication of the Knapp Building would leave Coates only five years until mandatory retirement as administrative director of the Institute in 1962. Its annual operating budget was $400,316—state appropriations accounting for $254,154 and publication sales, fees for services, and dues from counties and cities amounting for most of the balance. (Coates had early persuaded counties and cities to pay voluntary membership "dues.") The Institute published its own guidebooks, texts, bulletins, and magazine for public officials. Its faculty also wrote extensively in national journals and taught a number of courses in the graduate and professional schools of the university. These combined resources reached thousands of local and state officials every year through training, consulting, and research.

After retirement Coates taught in the law school for another six years. He also turned to some unfinished business in support of civics and government teachers in the public schools. With the backing of Governor Terry Sanford, Coates created an Institute of Civic Education in the University's Extension Division. Well into his seventies he held workshops for civics teachers and taught civics to Raleigh high school students. In 1980 the State Board of Education approved the Albert Coates Citizenship Education Program as part of the public schools curriculum.

Coates wrote a dozen law review articles between 1936 and 1968, mainly on criminal law, constitutional law, and local government law topics. In the same period he served as editor of the Institute's magazine and turned out a steady stream of articles. He also authored or coauthored a half dozen major Institute publications in the form of guidebooks, constitutional commentaries, and reports to the governor or General Assembly.

The extraordinary history of Coates's long and desperate struggle to build the Institute is best captured in two publications—*The Story of the Institute of Government* (1944) and *What The University of North Carolina Meant to Me* (1969).

Late in his eighth decade Coates wrote two remarkable full-length books that plumbed the depths of his feelings for family and loved ones. Inspired by his long and happy marriage to Gladys, one was an epic "saga of women in North Carolina," *By Her Own Bootstraps,* warmly dedicated to his beloved Gladys. The second of these deeply personal accounts was a full-scale biography of his brother, Professor Kenneth Coates, who devoted a forty-one-year career of teaching at Wofford College and of shared community concerns with his friends and neighbors in Spartanburg.

Gladys Hall had just completed her junior year at Randolph Macon College in the summer of 1923 when she met Albert. They were engaged in 1925 and married in 1928. Their long, rewarding, and eventful life together in the Chapel Hill neighborhood where they began married life would go on for sixty-one years until his death in 1989. No child was born to this union, nor ever needed to compete for attention with the offspring of Albert's creative mind, the Institute. By the time Gladys and Albert settled into married life, he was well into sketching his dream of the Institute to come. In the new century that Albert never saw, Gladys Coates still lived in the home they built on Hooper Lane, which became their lasting home in the early 1960s.

Coates accumulated more visible monuments, awards, and honors in a lifetime than most humans could imagine. A distinguished professorship at the University of North Carolina bears his name, endowed by Paul and Margaret Johnston. Two buildings also bear his name: the Coates Local Government Center in Raleigh (home of the North Carolina League of Municipalities and Association of County Commissioners) and the Albert and Gladys Coates Building in Chapel Hill (the original Institute of Government building on Franklin Street). Decorating the foyer of the Coates Building in Raleigh is a bust that faithfully records the craggy Coatesian visage in bronze.

The university reflected its respect and indebtedness to Coates by awarding him three of its most cherished honors: the O. Max Gardner Award in 1952, as the faculty member who has contributed the most to the welfare of the human race; the William Richardson Davis Award in 1984; and the Di Phi Award in 1951. Three universities awarded Coates honorary LL.D. degrees: Wake Forest in 1960, Duke University in 1971, and the University of North Carolina at Chapel Hill in 1974.

He was given the John J. Parker Award of the North Carolina Bar Association in 1964, and a certificate of appreciation by the North Carolina State Bar in 1977. He was inducted into the State Bureau of Investigation Hall of Fame in 1987. Coates was given the North Carolina Award in 1967 and the North Caroliniana Society Award in 1979. The North Carolina Citizens Association awarded Coates its citation for Distinguished Public Service in 1978.

Two markers were lasting monuments to Gladys:

the original Institute building on Franklin Street—now called the Albert and Gladys Coates Building—and a distinguished professorship at the Institute endowed in name by Paul and Margaret Johnston, the Gladys Hall Coates Professorship. She was the first recipient of the university's Bell Award in 1993, the UNC General Alumni Association Distinguished Service Medal in 1992, and the Randolph-Macon Woman's College Alumnae Achievement Award in 1990.

At the east end of the Old Chapel Hill Cemetery on South Road, across from the current home of the Institute of Government, are a dozen or more rows of tombstones that resonate with the history of Chapel Hill and the university since the 1930s. The roll call makes the ears ring with familiar sounds: Graham, Odum, House, Branson, Kyser, Koch, Green, Lefler, Wettach, McCall, Hobbs, Couch, Cobb, Johnston (Paul and Margaret), Carroll, Bason—and on they go.

One more stone, along the last paved path, carries a message that will echo as long as anyone remembers Gladys and Albert Coates: "Married June 23, 1928, and lived happily ever after." The long, productive, dynamic life of public service that was Albert Coates ended at his Chapel Hill home in 1989.

Milton S. Heath Jr. is a longtime faculty member of the University of North Carolina Institute of Government, and an adjunct professor in the UNC School of Public Health and Duke's Nicholas School of the Environment. He grew up as a faculty child in the Chapel Hill of the 1930s, the son of family friends and neighbors of Albert and Gladys Coates. His first encounter with the Institute of Government came in 1940 when he was sent to the library of the new Institute building to complete a sixth-grade civics assignment. He is a product of the Chapel Hill public schools, Phillips Exeter, Harvard College, and Columbia Law School. Albert Coates appointed him to the Institute in 1957. He served under Coates for five years and under each of Coates's successors as directors of the Institute.

For more information, see:

Coates, Albert. *Bridging the Gap Between Government in Books and Government in Action.* N.p., 1974.

———. *By Her Own Bootstraps: A Saga of Women in North Carolina.* N.p., 1975.

———. *Edward Kidder Graham, Harry Woodburn Chase, Frank Porter Graham: Three Men in the Transition of the University of North Carolina at Chapel Hill from a Small College to a Great University.* A. Coates, 1988.

———. *Presidents and the People with Whom I Have Lived and Worked from 1914 to 1969.* William Byrd Press, 1969.

———. *The Story of the Institute of Government, the University of North Carolina, Chapel Hill.* National University Extension Association, 1944.

———. *Talks on the Rule of Law and the Role of Government in the Cities, the Counties, and the State of North Carolina.* Professor Emeritus Fund, 1971.

———. *Talks to Students and Teachers: The Structure and Workings of Government in the Cities and the Counties, and the State of North Carolina.* Creative Printers, 1972.

———. *The University of North Carolina at Chapel Hill: A Magic Gulf Stream in the Life of North Carolina.* N.p., 1978.

———, and James C. N. Paul. *A Report to the Governor of North Carolina on the Decision of the Supreme Court of the United States on the 17th of May 1954.* Institute of Government, 1954.

Green, Philip P., and John L. Sanders. "Albert Coates." *Popular Government* 54 (Spring 1989): 2–6.

Olivier, Warner. "The Ugly Duckling at Chapel Hill." *Saturday Evening Post,* February 24, 1945, 14–15, 72, 74.

Sanders, John L. "Albert Coates: Institution Builder." *Popular Government* 54 (Spring 1989): 7.

HENRY E. FRYE

By David Scanzoni

Ⅰ T WAS a humid August morning in 1956. Inside the tiny town hall of Ellerbe, population 750, the voter registrar, an older white man, peered at the twenty-four-year-old black man who had come to register to vote. He told the man that he first would have to pass a "literacy" test. In reality, it was a lengthy trivia quiz on American history. Virtually no one could pass it.

Name five signers of the Declaration of Independence. Name the twelfth president (Zachary Taylor). And so on. The test's underlying purpose was to keep blacks from voting. All blacks who wanted to vote had to take the test. All whites—including those who were illiterate —were exempt.

The black man in the registrar's office that day— Henry E. Frye—told the registrar that he didn't know the answers and didn't need to know them. The registrar replied that he therefore failed the test and could not register. The registrar had no idea that the man he had just failed would one day become chief justice of the North Carolina Supreme Court.

"I was shocked, surprised and disheartened," Frye recalled forty-four years later during an interview in the court's chambers in Raleigh. At the time of the incident, Frye was a college graduate and had recently completed two years of service as an air force officer that included sixteen months overseas. He had been accepted into law school and was about to begin his studies in a few weeks. None of that impressed the registrar. As an African American seeking to register to vote in North Carolina in 1956, Frye was simply an unwelcome rarity.

"I was one of the few (blacks in Ellerbe who tried to register)," he said. His parents were not registered, and neither were most of his African American friends.

He eventually was allowed to register a few days later, thanks to intervention by the apologetic chairman of the Richmond County Board of Elections. The chairman, a white man, "expressed regret and said if I went back, I wouldn't have any difficulty," Frye said. Still, the incident left a lasting impression. "After that happened, I decided that one day, things would change, and that I would work to see that they changed." During his lifetime, Frye would change many things, charting significant new ground for African Americans and others across North Carolina. His story is one of firsts.

Henry E. Frye (Courtesy of N.C. Supreme Court)

To understand Frye's childhood is to understand the drive and determination that would propel his adult accomplishments. He was born August 1, 1932, in Ellerbe, a farming community in northern Richmond County about ten miles north of Rockingham. He was the eighth of twelve children (six girls, six boys) raised by Walter and Pearl Frye, who were second-generation descendants of slaves. They had limited schooling, but hard work, innate intelligence, and an entrepreneurial spirit offset their lack of formal education. Though their house was small, their possessions few, and their income limited, Walter and Pearl were able to provide the basics for their large family. This, despite the calamity of the Depression that struck all Americans with intensity, and most black Americans with severity. "We were not destitute. We didn't go hungry," Frye recalled. "But we were not middle class."

In the late 1920s, his father borrowed money from a local bank to buy a forty-six-acre tobacco and cotton farm, making him one of the few blacks who owned farms in Ellerbe at that time. Later, during Henry's early teenage years, his father bought a small sawmill from its white owner. His father's determination to overcome racial barriers and build social bridges served as a blueprint for Henry's later life. His mother also played a significant role in shaping his future. "She was very encouraging," he said.

At Ellerbe Colored School, the official name of the all-black public school that Frye attended from first through twelfth grade, he found African American adult mentors. "My principal and his wife, my eighth-grade teacher and basketball coach and Boy Scout leader, they all talked about the fact that we could succeed and do things, and change things, and make things better," Frye said. "They believed in us. They encouraged us to do well and criticized us when we didn't."

"I didn't like it (racially segregated schools)," Frye recalled. I thought it was unnecessary. But, unlike some people, I never got bitter about it. I took it in stride and said, 'One day, it will change.'"

Frye graduated from high school in 1949 as valedictorian of his twenty-four-member senior class. Later that year, he enrolled at North Carolina A & T College in Greensboro (later North Carolina A & T State University), which was then the largest state college for blacks. He joined the Reserve Officers Training Corps, military cadet program, and graduated with highest honors in 1953 with a bachelor's degree in biology.

After college, he entered the air force as a second lieutenant and served as an ammunition officer in Japan and Korea during the Korean War. In 1955, at the end of his two years of active duty, he was a first lieutenant and returned home to marry Edith Shirley Taylor, an A & T classmate, who had earned a bachelor's degree in education. A month after their 1956 wedding, he was a member of one of the first classes that included blacks at the University of North Carolina Law School. He graduated with honors in 1959.

Frye chose Greensboro to begin a law practice. At first, he handled a variety of cases, but he considered his representation of the powerless, mostly low-income African Americans in Greensboro his most important work. Then, in 1963, at age thirty-one, Frye took a leave from private practice when he was appointed assistant U.S. attorney for the middle district of North Carolina. He was the first African American federal prosecutor in North Carolina and one of only a handful in the nation at the time. Frye left the justice department in 1965 to become a law professor at North Carolina College (later North Carolina Central University) in Durham and in 1967 he resumed his private practice in Greensboro.

In 1968, Greensboro voters elected Frye to the North Carolina House, where he became the first African American legislator in North Carolina in modern times. Taking office in early 1969 as a newly elected member, Frye made abolishment of the literacy test that he had encountered twenty years earlier his top priority. Both houses of the legislature approved his proposed constitutional amendment to repeal the test, but North Carolina voters rejected the amendment in 1970. Federal action, however, made the issue moot. In 1965, Congress had passed the Voting Rights Act, banning literacy tests in states with a history of racial discrimination. In 1970, Congress extended the ban nationwide. North Carolina's literacy test—though long invalid—remained in the state's constitution at the turn of the century.

While he was in the legislature he continued to practice law and also helped found Greensboro National Bank, the city's first African American-owned bank. (It later became Mutual Community Savings Bank.) The bank made loans to low- and moderate-income customers who faced roadblocks when trying to borrow from mainline banks. "It was a need that I saw, so I pulled some people together to organize it, even though I didn't know anything about banking and didn't have any money," said Frye, who served as the bank's president.

Frye served twelve years in the state house and had just finished his first term in the state senate when Governor Jim Hunt appointed him to fill a vacancy on the seven-member North Carolina Supreme Court, where he became the first of his race to sit on the state's highest court. A year later, in 1984, Frye was elected to a full eight-year term. By winning that election, Frye became the first African American elected to statewide office. In 1992, he was reelected to a second eight-year term.

On the court, as in the legislature, Frye brought alternative views and a fresh perspective to a previously all-white institution. He added depth and dimension to the court's deliberations, particularly in cases involving the economically or politically powerless. Frye said he gave his fellow justices a greater "understanding of discrimination based on race from my own personal background" and from a historical perspective. "If you understand black history, you understand the deprivation through which blacks developed," he said.

In 1999 Governor Hunt named Frye chief justice to fill a vacancy. As chief justice, Frye was not only responsible for the direction of the Supreme Court, but of the entire state court system. He set policy and supervised judges, magistrates, clerks, and other staff in more than three hundred courts in every district, superior, and appellate court statewide. In all, he directed more than five thousand employees and managed a $360 million annual budget. During his term, Frye helped launch a five-year plan to upgrade the court system's outdated computers. He advocated mediation and arbitration as alternatives to lawsuits. He supported new approaches to domestic disputes, including an experimental family court. He also worked to make court information more accessible to the news media. Frye's tenure as chief justice ended in 2000 when he was defeated for election to a full eight-year term by Republican I. Beverly Lake Jr., an associate justice on the court.

Though sixty-eight at the time of his loss, Frye said he was far from retirement. "I could not retire, in the sense of going home and sitting in a rocking chair," he told the *News and Observer*. "I'm a very active person, and I plan to stay that way." He said he would not accept a future reappointment to the supreme court and returned to Greensboro, where his son was a superior court judge, to resume the private practice of law.

David Scanzoni is a Charlotte-based freelance writer and communications consultant.

For more information, see:

Frye, Henry E. Interview by author, October 23, 2000. Levine Museum of the New South, Charlotte.

"Henry Frye, Chief Justice—An Interview." *Legends of North Carolina*. North Carolina Museum of History, Spring 2000.

Jones, Abe D., Jr. *Greensboro 27*. Bassett Printing, 1976.

JAMES B. MCMILLAN

By E. Osborne Ayscue Jr.

U.S. DISTRICT COURT JUDGE James B. McMillan's most visible case was *Swann v. Charlotte-Mecklenburg Board of Education.* A six-year marathon that was as much a modern morality play as a legal proceeding, it changed the face of education as school districts all across the nation began to use busing to balance the racial makeup of classes. McMillan was an unlikely actor in that play because he had grown up in one of the most racially segregated communities in the state. A product of his time and place, he had accepted racial segregation as a fact of life.

Admittedly skeptical about the merits of the case at first, McMillan gradually changed his mind as the evidence of discrimination piled up. Ultimately he arrived at the conclusion that housing, zoning, city planning, and school location policies had coincided over time to create geographic racial segregation that was neither innocent nor de facto. He decided that geographic segregation made desegregation of the public schools impossible without significantly departing from the neighborhood school concept.

His first ruling, that the existing pupil assignment plan violated the U.S. Constitution, was never seriously challenged. A sharply divided Charlotte-Mecklenburg Board of Education, reflecting a sharply divided community, failed to act. Ultimately he ordered the board to utilize all available means, including busing, to achieve the desegregation of the public schools. His ruling in *Swann* was ultimately affirmed by a unanimous Supreme Court in an opinion published over the signature of its most conservative member, Warren Burger, and busing became a widespread means of achieving racial balance.

The Charlotte community responded and McMillan had the wisdom to back off, to order the board of education to do the same, and to allow a group of citizens, drawn from all segments of the community, to propose its own pupil assignment plan. The result was a plan which he, the board, and the community embraced and which served the community well for over a decade.

At the height of the turmoil over *Swann,* McMillan was hanged in effigy. He also received repeated telephone death threats and suffered demonstrators in his front yard and destruction to his property. For a time he and his wife, Margie, literally had to take refuge in the home of their minister. Escorted in public by fed-

James B. McMillan (Courtesy of Charlotte Observer)

eral law enforcement officers, he was provided with and taught to use a handgun for self-defense, although he never had to use it. More painful perhaps than the venom of strangers were the coldness and occasional outright hostility that he suffered from people who had once been his friends. He bore all of these things with remarkable dignity and calmness and never lost his sense of humor. Throughout that entire time he never had an unlisted telephone number.

Swann had many of the characteristics of a Greek play. Each player was destined by who he was and where he came from to do exactly as he did, to take the positions that he took. The one person who clearly understood all this at the time was McMillan.

Swann accomplished something more for Charlotte-Mecklenburg than the desegregation of its schools. It pricked the conscience of the community, which ultimately responded to the challenge with a spirit and a quality of leadership that for years thereafter set it apart. The genesis of the transformation of Charlotte from those dark and uncertain days to the thriving city it became, confident of what it could accomplish, can be traced to the community's response to the challenge of *Swann.* The catalyst for that change was one man who, confronted with the ugly truth of a segregated society, had the moral courage to use the powers of his office to force his neighbors to confront and deal with it.

Time magazine, commenting on the role of federal district judges, particularly southern judges, in the task of desegregation, observed, "A solid majority of Southern federal judges have in fact carried out their responsibilities, whatever their initial personal feelings. Judge McMillan is in the best of that tradition." In his book *Southern Voices,* Frye Gaillard said, "Before their appointments to the federal bench, these men were often pillars of their communities, widely respected, popular enough to be picked from the crowd. Almost none were boat-rockers by nature, but almost invariably that became their role. A few may have flinched, but most of them handled it with uncommon courage. One of the last of these judicial heroes was Judge James B. McMillan."

James Bryan McMillan was born on December 19, 1916, in Goldsboro, the son of Robert Hunter McMillan and Louise Outlaw McMillan. In 1930 when her husband died, Louise McMillan took her four children back to the family farm near the town of McDonalds in Robeson County to raise them.

Graduating from Lumberton High School in 1932 at the age of fifteen, McMillan worked his way through Presbyterian Junior College (later St. Andrews College), finishing second in his class. A year later, he entered the University of North Carolina, graduating in 1937. At the age of twenty he entered the Harvard Law School and graduated, in the top quarter of his class, three years later.

Shortly after the Japanese attack on Pearl Harbor he volunteered for the navy and became a bomb disposal and communications officer. He also took part in the North African campaign and the invasion of Sicily, then had tours of duty in the Pacific Theater and finally in Washington, D.C.

In 1944 he married Margaret "Margie" Blair Miles of Marion, Md., whom he had met while working in Washington. In March 1946 he came to work in the Charlotte law firm of Helms and Mulliss. He practiced in that firm, which was to become Helms Mulliss McMillan and Johnston, for the next twenty-two years.

He quickly became one of the ablest and most effective civil trial lawyers in the state. His hallmark as a lawyer was meticulous attention to facts. He had a natural curiosity about how things worked. A traditionalist in the use of the English language, he had a direct manner of speaking. His writing was simple, clear, and understandable. He did not dwell on technicalities. He believed that there were no complicated lawsuits, only ones that lawyers made complicated. He

was a tenacious advocate for his clients, but there was an overarching sense of fairness in everything he did.

At his death the *Charlotte Observer* commented that he was one of an extraordinary generation of North Carolina leaders who grew up in small cities, towns, and rural areas; learned to value reverence, education, and hard work; and came home from World War II with a compelling conviction that it was their duty to make the world a better place.

That sense of duty manifested itself early in Jim McMillan. He was president of the Mecklenburg Bar Association at the age of forty-one and of the N.C. Bar Association at forty-three. He was one of a group of young lawyers who made a floundering court reform movement a bar project, nursed it through the General Assembly, and sold it to the electorate, creating one of the most progressive statewide court systems in the nation. In 1963 he was appointed to the N.C. Courts Commission, created by the General Assembly to implement those reforms.

In 1968, when a seat on the federal bench in the western district of North Carolina became vacant, U.S. Senator Sam J. Ervin Jr. asked the Mecklenburg bar to get behind one nominee. Emerging from a bar-sponsored referendum as that nominee, McMillan had the unique distinction of being selected for the federal bench by his own bar. A lifelong Democrat, he was appointed by President Lyndon Johnson and in June 1968 was sworn in. On the bench he became known as a judge who tried cases, rather than managing dockets. The court on which he sat ranked consistently near the top among all the federal district courts in the country in cases tried.

McMillan came to the federal bench at the beginning of an era when the courts were becoming vehicles for the reexamination of fundamental premises long taken for granted. Endowed with an inquiring and open mind and a willingness to reexamine his own long-held beliefs and biases, coupled with absolutely impeccable integrity, he became a magnet for significant cause-oriented cases. Those cases and the publicity that attended them shaped his public persona. He became, in the words of one distinguished law professor, a national folk hero.

One of his law clerks noted that what made him an outstanding jurist was his curiosity, his intellect, his open-mindedness, and his sense of the law, combined with a profound sense of compassion and of social justice and an ability to understand the problems confronting disempowered people. His beliefs were not theoretical abstractions; they were grounded in his intense involvement in his work and sprang from an unusual degree of reflection on and understanding of the often turbulent and troubling events around him.

Active for over forty years in the First Presbyterian Church, of which he was an elder, he also served as vice chairman of the Permanent Judicial Commission of the Presbyterian Church in the United States. He sang tenor in the church choir. His own brand of Scotch Presbyterian faith shaped his entire life, formed his conscience, and gave birth to his understanding of the human condition.

McMillan believed in the jury system with an almost religious fervor, going to great lengths to see that a jury understood the importance of its role and that it understood the case before it. By his own count he found it necessary to overturn fewer than a half-dozen jury verdicts in all his years on the bench. As a judge, he never lost the affection for lawyers, even the most difficult among them, that his early experience as a practicing lawyer engendered.

His sense of humor was legendary. On at least one occasion when faced with the necessity of following a precedent of the United States Supreme Court with which he did not agree, he noted that he was acceding "to the authority, but not the wisdom" of that Court. His opinions were laced with statements such as, "Constitutional rights will not be denied here simply because they may be denied elsewhere. There is no 'Dow Jones Average' for such rights." And, rejecting an argument based on probability offered in support of the constitutionality of a statute, "The court is not a bookie."

His sense of duty motivated him to give the same attention to an *in forma pauperis* petition that he gave to cases involving great principles or millions of dollars, to begin a pressing preliminary injunction hearing the day after the funeral of his younger brother, and to continue to do justice to his caseload despite the illness and death of his first wife, Margie, of cancer in 1985.

Many of his decisions, particularly those in the turbulent seventies, first articulated principles of law, controversial at the time, that became an accepted part of federal jurisprudence. Many of them dealt with the tension between the rights of a private citizen and the prerogatives of his government: that a prisoner must be credited on his sentence for time spent in jail awaiting trial; that schoolchildren have a right to due process before suspension or discharge from school; that discharge of a schoolteacher because he gave honest answers to questions about Darwin's theories of evolution was unlawful; that the state could not warehouse mentally retarded people who were not mentally ill in state psychiatric hospitals; and that Social Security disability payments could not be arbitrarily denied without due process. These rulings understandably often provoked the ire of elected officials, law enforcement officers, and legislators. He was also called on to implement the civil rights legislation of the time, presiding over the dismantling of various forms of discrimination in many private businesses. These decisions did not always endear him to the business community.

McMillan continued on the bench for many years after *Swann*. One of his law clerks later recalled, "Some of my most vivid memories are of jurors who approached Judge McMillan after a trial to state that his unshakable fairness on the bench had dissolved all of their worst prejudgments about the man who had ordered busing in their community."

In 1987 he married Holly Smith Neaves of Elkin, an alumna of the University of North Carolina at Chapel Hill and the widow of a lawyer. He took senior status in 1989, then retired from the bench when poor health overtook him.

Judge McMillan was publicly honored in many ways: the Algernon Sidney Sullivan Award from Presbyterian Junior College (now St. Andrews); an honorary membership in Omicron Delta Kappa from Davidson College; the Order of the Golden Fleece at the University of North Carolina at Chapel Hill; an honorary membership in the Order of the Coif from the University of North Carolina Law School. The North Carolina Bar Association bestowed on him its highest award, the John Johnston Parker Award, and the American Civil Liberties Union gave him its Frank Porter Graham Award. He was the recipient of numerous honorary degrees: from Belmont Abbey College, Davidson College, St. Andrews College, North Carolina Central University (posthumously), and UNC-Chapel Hill, the latter for his "prophetic understanding of the law." The Mecklenburg Bar Foundation established the James Bryan McMillan Scholarship Fund to endow public service internships for law students, to honor his selfless example, and to encourage them to emulate it.

Of slight physical stature, with a gentle, almost shy demeanor, he hardly looked the part of a federal judge. If he harbored any lasting ill will toward those who had pilloried him for his decisions, it was not apparent to those around him. He never took himself too seriously. He had no taste for the trappings of status or power. The federal judgeship he assumed paid barely half what he had earned in private practice. The modest brick house in which he died was the only home he ever owned. His only extravagance was membership in a private country club, attracted principally by its golf course.

He seemed genuinely embarrassed at the suggestion that someone might regard him as a hero. He once suggested to a reporter that the real heroes of the *Swann* case were all of those people who had to go to the wrong school, every person who held his tongue instead of saying what he thought at the moment, everyone who accepted things he did not like because they were being required as a matter of law.

McMillan died on March 4, 1995, after a three-year battle with cancer. His portrait hangs in the federal courthouse in Charlotte.

E. Osborne Ayscue Jr. is a Charlotte lawyer who has practiced with Judge McMillan's former law firm, Helms Mulliss & Wicker, for more than forty years. A past president of the North Carolina Bar Association, the Mecklenburg County Bar Association, and the American College of Trial Lawyers, Ayscue is the author of numerous articles on legal matters.

For more information, see:
McMillan, James B. Papers. Southern Historical Collection, University of North Carolina at Chapel Hill.

Gaillard, Frye. *The Dream Long Deferred*. University of North Carolina Press, 1988.

Note: The proceedings that attended McMillan's portrait presentation are reported in vol. 808 of West's *Federal Supplement*.

JOHN J. PARKER

By Jonathan E. Buchan Jr.

JUDGE JOHN JOHNSTON PARKER sprang from the bull-tallow clay soil of Union County on November 20, 1885 to become one of the most distinguished lawyers and judges in North Carolina's history. From the time he began his studies at the University of North Carolina at Chapel Hill in 1903 until his death at age seventy-three in 1958, Parker garnered virtually every available award for scholarship, character, and leadership. He counted among his friends some of the most outstanding lawyers, judges, and political figures of this century. Although he served as a judge on the U.S. District Court of Appeals for the Fourth Circuit from 1925 until 1958—the last twenty-one years as chief judge—his place in history will revolve around the Senate's narrow defeat of his 1930 U.S. Supreme Court nomination by President Herbert Hoover.

Parker graduated from the University of North Carolina in 1907 with a string of honors. He was president of the Phi Beta Kappa Society, won the W. J. Bryan Prize in Economics, was president of the student body and president of his senior class, won the Mangum Medal for Oratory, and was appointed a Fellow in Greek. A year later he graduated from the University of North Carolina School of Law, where he received the Henry R. Bryan Law Prize.

After practicing law briefly in Greensboro, Parker returned to Monroe, where he practiced law with A. M. Stack. In 1922, Parker moved to Charlotte, forming the firm Parker, Stewart, McCrae and Bobbit, where he became recognized as a skilled, effective trial lawyer who handled both controversial criminal and complicated civil cases.

From the beginning of his career, Parker was interested in politics. He was nominated by the Republican Party in 1910 as a candidate for Congress, in 1916 for attorney general of North Carolina, and in 1920 for governor. Although the dominance of the Democratic Party in North Carolina politics in those years prevented any hope of victory, Parker's reputation as a brilliant, analytical lawyer led President Calvin Coolidge to appoint him in 1925 at age forty to the United States Court of Appeals for the Fourth Circuit, which heard appeals from the federal trial courts in Maryland, Virginia, West Virginia, and the Carolinas.

Five years later, Hoover nominated this rising young judicial star to the Supreme Court. (If con-

John J. Parker (Courtesy of Parker Family)

firmed, he would have been the first North Carolinian to join the Court since Parker's mother's ancestor James Iredell was appointed in 1791.) He was not, however, destined to sit on the nation's highest court. An unlikely combination of organized labor, southern Democrats, and the nascent National Association for the Advancement of Colored People (NAACP) orchestrated his narrow defeat in the Senate.

Parker's political career had coincided with the attempt by the Republican Party to match the Democratic Party's successful efforts in the South to marginalize black participation in the electoral process. The Republican Party in North Carolina, as in other parts of the South, worked to disown its previous association with black voters and to become "lily-white."

Parker's 1920 campaign for governor evidenced his New South progressivism: he supported women's suffrage, increased funding for public education, industrial development, safeguards for workers, estate and income taxes, and better public roads. On the issue of race, however, he denied he had black support and openly accepted the lily-white movement within the Republican Party, which advocated the exclusion of blacks. Ten years later, Parker's quotes from his gubernatorial campaign—asserting that neither blacks nor whites desired the participation by blacks in the North Carolina political process—became the focus of the NAACP's effective lobbying campaign against his confirmation.

The opposition to Parker's nomination by organized labor stemmed from an opinion he had written in which the court of appeals upheld a district court injunction preventing the United Mine Workers union from urging West Virginia coal miners to join the union, despite contracts signed by the miners with their employers not to join a union. Such contracts were referred to disparagingly by organized labor as "yellow dog" contracts. Although Parker's supporters correctly noted that he had simply relied upon existing Supreme Court decisions forbidding even peaceful union interference with such contracts, Parker was portrayed by opponents to his confirmation as actively anti-union.

The combined, sustained opposition of organized labor and the NAACP gathered strength as the confirmation hearings proceeded. Ironically, many southern Democrats, fearful of the potential political appeal of a successful "lily-white" Republican Party in the South, also opposed Parker's confirmation. Finally, many senators from more liberal states were already concerned that the Court was too conservative on issues involving progressive legislation and feared Parker's prior positions indicated strong conservative views. Parker's nomination failed in the Senate by a vote of 41–39, with sixteen senators voting neither for nor against. A one-vote swing would have caused a tie vote, which would have been broken in Parker's favor by Republican Vice President Charles Curtis.

Parker was perceived by most observers as a southern moderate on racial desegregation. In *Austin v. School Board of the City of Norfolk,* Parker wrote the opinion which reversed a federal court decision that had upheld unequal salaries for black and white teachers in Virginia. Parker's opinion held that such unequal treatment violated the United States Constitution. In *Rice v. Elmore,* Parker wrote the opinion affirming South Carolina District Court Judge Waties Waring's ruling that found the South Carolina Democratic Party's all-white primary elections to be unconstitutional. Parker did not, however, establish any new legal precedent in those cases. He instead applied principles of constitutional legal protection established by other courts.

In 1951, Parker played a key role in *Briggs v. Elliott,* the case challenging the South Carolina state law requiring segregated—but theoretically equal—public schools. *Briggs* was one of the five cases consolidated and decided in the United States Supreme Court's landmark decision in *Brown v. Board of Education,* which found segregated public schools to violate the constitutionally protected equal rights of black students.

Thurgood Marshall, the architect of the NAACP's nationwide litigation strategy on desegregation, was reluctant to bring such a frontal assault on segregated public schools in a locale as bleak as Clarendon County, S.C., where the population was 70 percent black and the white community was determined to maintain segregation. Marshall knew that the three-judge panel assigned to hear the case would consist of Waring, a Charleston district judge known as an outspoken opponent of segregation; George Bell Timmerman, a staunch supporter of segregation; and Parker, the chief judge of the fourth circuit, who would be the swing vote on the panel. Parker's history as a moderate on desegregation issues was sufficiently troublesome to segregation proponents that former South Carolina Governor Strom Thurmond urged Clarendon County's legal counsel to consider conceding the case so any court ruling would affect only Clarendon County, thereby avoiding a precedent that might affect the entire state.

At the outset of the brief trial in May 1951, the county conceded—in a surprise move designed to avoid the plaintiffs' factual presentation on the significant disparities in the funding of the county's white and black schools—that its black schools were woefully inferior to the schools attended by whites, and it promised to spend the funds to make them equal. Parker, in an opinion concurred in by Timmerman, ruled that the United States Supreme Court's 1896 decision in *Plessey v. Ferguson*—which held that "separate but equal" facilities on railroads were constitutional—applied to public school facilities. He declined, over Waring's dissent, to find that segregated schools were inherently unequal. In 1954, the U.S. Supreme Court reversed *Briggs v. Elliott.*

In many ways Parker was a lawyer's lawyer and a judge's judge. He was renowned throughout his thirty-three-year tenure as a judge for his tireless efforts and committee work on behalf of the improvement of the administration of justice in the United States, both in the federal and state courts. He was one of the key leaders in the push for the adoption of the Federal Rules of Civil Procedure. He was active in the American Law Institute, the American Judicature Society, the American Society of International Law, the American Academy of Political Science, and the American Bar Association.

In 1945, by appointment of President Harry Truman, Parker served as an alternate member of the International Military Tribunal, which, in Nuremberg, Germany, tried high Nazi officials on charges of war crimes. Two years earlier, he had received the American Bar Association Medal, the association's highest award, for his efforts in improving the administration of justice. In giving him the medal, Arthur T. Vanderbilt praised Parker's judicial skills and temperament. "No lawyer who has ever appeared in his court will forget the experience—a court in which all three judges have read the briefs in advance and so know what the issues are; a court which gives counsel a fair chance to state his case and then by straight-forward but firm questions seeks to prove the soundness of his position; a court which never fails to extend the time for argument if the argument merits it; a court where the judges, once the argument is over, step down from the bench to shake hands with counsel and to chat for a minute or two, before going on with the next case; a most delightful court in which to argue, if counsel is well-prepared, and especially so, if he is on the right side."

Parker, the son of Monroe merchant John Daniel Parker and Frances Johnston Parker (daughter of Dr. Samuel Iredell Johnston of Edenton), was the oldest of four children. In 1910 he married Maria Burgwin Maffit of Wilmington, who became his lifelong companion. One of his sons, Francis Iredell Parker, a partner in the Charlotte law firm of Parker, Poe, Adams and Bernstein, served briefly on the North Carolina Supreme Court in 1986.

Parker was a key member of the University of North Carolina Board of Trustees for many years. Many credit Parker and *News and Observer* publisher Josephus Daniels with preventing the conservative opponents of University President Frank Porter Graham from forcing Graham prematurely from office. He also blocked repeated attempts by legislative leaders to hike tuition at the university. He saw the historically low tuition as an opportunity for the children of the poor as well as the privileged to achieve a college education.

Parker, an active Episcopalian, held broad views of faith. Shortly before his death, Parker accepted the National Brotherhood Award of the National Conference of Christians and Jews and noted: "This doctrine of brotherhood is not a mere sentimental matter, as some vainly imagine, but a profound philosophy of human relationships, taught by Protestants and Catholics alike and going far back into the teachings of the Jewish people long before there were any Protestants or Catholics. It is based upon the concept that there is one God, the loving Father of all mankind, and that we are all his children and of equal value in His sight. Democracy is but the recognition of this great truth; for democracy, my friends, is not a mere form of government. It is a philosophy of life—a philosophy based upon the worth and importance of the individual man—a philosophy which believes that institutions exist for men, not men for institutions, and that the happiness of the poor and the humble is of as much importance as the happiness of the great and the proud."

Parker's focused intellect, joined to his highly disciplined work ethic, made him a prodigiously busy man. He was, nonetheless, devoted to his family and to his friends. Francis Parker remembered his father as a "serious-minded fellow but not stuffy about it." "He had great respect for authority and for people who held positions of authority. I remember when I was about twenty-one and about to be commissioned in the Navy, I made a derogatory remark about President Franklin Roosevelt. My father, even though he was a Republican, took me greatly to task. He said that was no way to speak about the president of the United States."

"We used to go to St. Martin's Episcopal Church on Seventh Street in Charlotte," his son recalled. "In those days, there was no air conditioning. You would just sit there in the heat in the summertime and the only relief was the cardboard fans provided by the local funeral directors. I remember once the minister announced that it was so hot, it would be appropriate for the gentlemen to remove their suit jackets. Most of them did. My father did not.

"After church, as the folks gathered outside to gab a little bit as they used to do, someone asked my father why he had not removed his jacket. He said, 'If anyone came into my courtroom and took off his coat, I would have him held in contempt of court. Certainly the Lord God Almighty is entitled to at least the same respect.'"

Charlotte lawyer Tom Lockhart, whose father died when Lockhart was an infant, knew Parker almost as a surrogate father. "He was so generous with his time with me, and I was so unaware of the demands on his time. I went to his office many a time as a young person when something was upsetting me for whatever reason, and he'd be writing an opinion or something, and his wonderful secretary would tell him I was there. I'd go in there, and he knew I had something, and I needed somebody to talk to. And he'd put aside his opinion writing, and he'd talk with me for a couple of hours."

A month after Parker's death, Chief Justice Earl Warren of the U.S. Supreme Court joined the judges of the Fourth Circuit Court of Appeals and other distinguished judges and guests in the courtroom in Richmond for a memorial service. Parker's former law partner and then Associate Justice of the North Carolina Supreme Court William H. Bobbit remembered his friend by saying: "John J. Parker was a big man in every sense, physically, intellectually, morally and spiritually. . . . Few men equaled and none excelled him in courage and in love of his country; and none worked with greater industry and zeal to contribute to the well-being of our society and nation. His devotion to his family, his concern and affection for his friends, and his unwavering purpose to do justly, love mercy, and walk humbly with his God are essentials of a complete personality which expressed itself not only in notable public service, but in sympathy, courtesy and consideration to his fellow man, whether in humble circumstances or in high position."

Jonathan E. Buchan Jr. is a partner with Helms Mulliss & Wicker in Charlotte, where he concentrates his practice on media law, intellectual property, and commercial litigation. He is a graduate of Princeton University with a degree in American history and a graduate of Duke University Law School.

For more information, see:

Goings, Kenneth. *The NAACP Comes of Age: The Defeat of Judge John J. Parker.* Indiana University Press, 1990.

In Memoriam: Honorable John Johnston Parker, 253 F.2d 1 (1958).

Kluger, Richard. *Simple Justice.* Alfred A. Knopf, 1976.

McCarter, G. W. C. *"Confirmation Denied: The Senate Rejects John J. Parker."* Senior thesis, Firestone Library, Princeton University, 1971.

SUSIE M. SHARP

By Michael T. Smith

Susie Marshall Sharp, the first woman to sit on North Carolina's highest trial and appellate courts, was a soft-spoken and diminutive daughter of a school-teacher who became a lawyer after several failed attempts at business.

James Merritt Sharp was the director of the Sharp Institute, a boarding school for boys and girls that enjoyed a wide reputation before his daughter was born on July 7, 1907. He subsequently failed at business before settling on a career as a lawyer and moving to Reidsville in 1914, where he began a practice that lasted nearly four decades. An active Democrat, Sharp served two terms in the state senate during the 1920s.

Susie's mother, Annie Britt Blackwell of Vance County, met her husband through her sister, who was a teacher at his school. After a whirlwind courtship, they married and left on a honeymoon on which Annie wore black, because her father had recently died. After James Sharp died in August 1952, Annie survived to see her daughter become the first woman to sit on the state supreme court.

As the oldest of the children, Susie carried significant responsibility for the care and nurturing of her siblings, but she did not neglect her studies. She attended Reidsville public schools, where she distinguished herself on the high school debating team, which she joined after being cut from the basketball squad. The debate coach had defeated her father in a sharply contested election for a seat on the state superior court, but Sharp recalled that he expressed admiration for her performance: "He praised me to the skies, and I worked like a dog." Her debating skills convinced many of her teachers that she should consider a legal career. She graduated second in her high school class in 1924, and entered the North Carolina Woman's College in Greensboro (later the University of North Carolina at Greensboro).

The Sharps could not afford to pay college tuition for more than one child at a time, so with her next-youngest sibling just five years behind, Susie set out to finish as quickly as possible. After two years in Greensboro, she transferred directly to the University of North Carolina Law School, where she was the only female in her class and only the fourth female in the history of the law school. Some of her classmates were downright hostile and left offensive notes at her desk, but Susie excelled academically. She was an ed-

Susie M. Sharp (Courtesy of Southern Historical Collection)

itor of the *North Carolina Law Review* and graduated with honors in 1929, meeting her deadline.

Sharp passed the bar exam in 1928 even before completing her formal studies and returned to Reidsville to go into practice with her father, who remained her law partner for the next twenty years. Since she was the first woman to practice law in Rockingham County, many locals regarded her as something of a curiosity. On one occasion, an elderly man entered her office and inquired whether she was "that lady lawyer." When she said she was and asked what legal assistance he required, the man told her that he was not interested in hiring an lawyer, but "just wanted to see what you looked like."

Some of her clients suggested that she charge less than her male counterparts, but "I disabused them of that notion." Her family name attracted clients at first but she soon had a growing caseload based on her considerable skill, no-nonsense manner, and tireless work ethic. In 1939 she became Reidsville city attorney, the first woman to hold such a job in the state.

Sharp and her father helped elect W. Kerr Scott governor in 1948 by managing his Rockingham County campaign. A year later, Scott returned the favor and appointed her to the state superior court bench, where she was the first woman to hold such a high judicial office. She had her doubts about accepting Scott's offer, but her father urged her to take the seat that had earlier eluded him. Some critics complained that the delicate nature of women made them unfit to preside over gruesome or lurid criminal cases, and Sharp once had a witness in a murder trial refuse to take the stand in her courtroom, because, the woman said, "It just ain't fittin' fer a woman to be a judge."

Sharp's firm manner and competence silenced narrow-minded doubters even though she later confessed there were aspects of crime and the law exhibited in her courtroom that were outside her experience. She told an interviewer that she "thought that after twenty years as a practicing attorney I was fairly sophisticated," but "there were times when I felt like a babe in the woods." Eventually, she came to regard this position as "the most interesting job to be had anywhere."

In 1962, Governor Terry Sanford went his former political mentor Kerr Scott one better and named Sharp to the state Supreme Court despite objections from the chief justice that it was "a man's court." Upon arriving in Raleigh, Sharp moved into the Sir Walter Hotel, telling the clerk, "I would like a room here for a short time until I can find an apartment, and I'll start looking for one as soon as I find the time." She lived at the hotel for thirteen years before finally moving to the Raleigh Town Apartments in 1975.

Sharp won election in 1962 to serve the remaining four years of an unexpired term, and in 1966 she was elected to a full eight-year term. In 1974, following the retirement of Chief Justice William H. Bobbitt, custom dictated that Sharp as the senior member of the court run for election as successor. Assured of the support of all of her colleagues, she handily won the Democratic nomination but for the first time in fifty years a Republican filed as a candidate for the job as well. Her opponent, James Newcomb, a former fire extinguisher salesman, lacked any legal training or experience, a fact that she made much of during the campaign.

She won in a landslide, receiving more votes than any statewide candidate. Her election marked the first time a woman was elected chief justice in the nation. Nevertheless, she regarded the campaign as a "demoralizing experience," and noted, "I doubt that I would ever voluntarily go through anything like that again. An incumbent judge cannot campaign for office . . . and satisfactorily perform the duties of his office." She later successfully advocated an amendment to the state constitution requiring that all judges be lawyers.

During her seventeen years on the court, Sharp wrote over six hundred decisions, most of them for the majority, which proved a testament to her influence with her colleagues, as well as her conservatism. She became a leading advocate of prison reform, insisting that "we cannot fight crime by breeding it." North Carolina's tradition of rigid governmental economy and punitive rather than humane treatment of prisoners had led to serious abuses and sometimes unbearable living conditions. Her speeches and rulings on this issue significantly contributed to the passage of laws that greatly reduced the often barbaric treatment of inmates in the state penal system. She approved the adoption of a revised motto for the court in 1975: "Suum Cuique Tribuere" (to give to everyone his due).

Reflecting her basically conservative approach, Sharp emerged as a formidable opponent of the Equal Rights Amendment (ERA). In 1970 she wrote a letter to her political friend U.S. Senator Sam J. Ervin, which he read on the floor of the Senate as part of his argument that the ERA would not really benefit women. "If this amendment would do what its proponents believe it would, I would certainly be for it," she wrote Ervin. She believed that women already enjoyed essentially full legal equality and that the proposed amendment would actually deprive women of needed protections, such as exemption from the draft.

Having never married or given birth, Sharp differed with advocates who argued that women could successfully balance career and family. She insisted that "I could not have had the career I have had and done justice to a husband and children. . . . Few women can attain fulfillment. Women have to make choices and compromises."

Her position enraged many, including those who had seen her service on the court as an advancement for women's causes. A college professor angrily wrote that although she had been delighted with Sharp's election to lead the Supreme Court, "your action on ERA has . . . negated any happiness I may have felt." Stung by such criticism, Sharp subsequently attempted to keep her distance from the issue, belatedly claiming that the separation of powers in state government prevented her from expressing any opinion on matters pertaining to the legislature.

She was "greatly distressed" in 1975 by a news report "which seems to have blanketed the country" recalling her earlier public statement regarding the ERA. She did place a call to the senator representing her district in 1977, and asked him to vote against the amendment. He reversed his earlier position, voted as she asked, and contributed to the bill's narrow defeat.

During Sharp's years on the court, North Carolina political leaders recommended her nomination for a seat on the United States Supreme Court. In 1967 the General Assembly passed a joint resolution requesting President Lyndon B. Johnson to appoint her, an idea endorsed by the governor and both of the state's senators. In response to another such movement eight years later, Sharp expressed her appreciation for the compliment, but stated that "it is my sincere belief that the time for me to go to Washington has passed."

Upon reaching the mandatory retirement age of seventy-two in 1979, she stepped down. On May 9, her last day on the court, Associate Justice Joseph Branch gave a glowing tribute to her service. "It is only we who have had the privilege to serve with her who are fully aware of the long hours, far beyond the call of duty, that she has given to her state," he admiringly noted. "Only we know that never has she been too busy to share her superior intellect with any one of us when we become entangled in the maze of legal problems. Only we know that her understanding and keen sense of humor have made days of drudgery and days of trial more bearable."

Tragedy darkened Sharp's later years. She never fully recovered after being struck by a car while taking her morning walk in 1986. A year earlier she had been devastated by the death of her niece and namesake, Susie Sharp Newsom, who died along with her two young sons in a car explosion during a police chase in Greensboro. The young woman was later implicated in several murders, including that of her own mother, Susie Sharp's younger sister. Haunted by this tragedy, Justice Sharp later said, "I don't know that I'll ever have any more peace on this earth."

The 1992 death of her close friend William H. Bobbitt, a widower, was another severe blow. Their relationship had long been the source of considerable Capitol Square gossip. The *News and Observer* noted in 1971, for example, in a profile of Bobbitt that "he often walks and dines with Justice Susie Sharp." Sharp and Bobbitt always addressed one another in public as "Judge," and she answered persistent rumors that they would marry by gently insisting that they were "just friends, but very dear friends."

Justice Sharp died on March 1, 1996, after several years of declining health.

Michael Thomas Smith has published articles in the North Carolina Historical Review *and the* Maryland Historical Magazine *and is a Ph.D. candidate in American history at Pennsylvania State University.*

For more information, see:
Sharp, Susie M. Collection. North Carolina Supreme Court Historical Society.
————. Papers. Southern Historical Collection, University of North Carolina at Chapel Hill.

Bledsoe, Jerry. *Bitter Blood: A True Story of Southern Family Pride, Madness, and Multiple Murder.* E. P. Dutton, 1988.

MEDIA

Josephus Daniels claimed the title of "Tar Heel Editor" for himself in his multivolume autobiography published at the close of his career as a newspaperman, presidential advisor, and diplomat. Indeed, the Daniels family and its century-long ownership of the *News and Observer* in Raleigh was synonymous with North Carolina journalism. Yet, it was the newspapers in towns and cities all across the state—the number was once as high as 229—that produced reporters and editors who made their mark in both print and broadcast journalism in the twentieth century.

In fact, the first Pulitzer Prizes awarded to Tar Heel papers went to the *Tabor City Tribune* (in 1952) and the Whiteville *News Reporter* (in 1953). And it was a feisty, even outrageous country editor named William Oscar Saunders at the Elizabeth City *Independent* whose words stung the self-righteous and helped turn back state-imposed teaching of creationism.

Before the last quarter of the century, when broadcasting eclipsed newspapers as the primary source of news for North Carolinians, the state boasted daily newspapers, both afternoon and evening, in Wilmington, Raleigh, Durham, Greensboro, Winston-Salem, Charlotte, and Asheville. From these newsrooms came men and women who later became known around the world for their professional skill. David Brinkley, who pioneered nightly thirty-minute newscasts for NBC, began his career in Wilmington. Charles Kuralt of CBS edited the *Daily Tar Heel* when he was a student at Chapel Hill and later was a writer for the *Charlotte News*. Eugene Roberts started his career in Goldsboro, where one of his daily jobs was reading the paper to Henry Belk, the blind editor of the *News-Argus*. He later was an editor at the *New York Times* and led the *Philadelphia Inquirer* to multiple Pulitzers.

Other familiar Tar Heel names at the *New York Times* included reporter and columnist Tom Wicker from Hamlet, whose writing included a novel replete with political characters and incidents he gathered while covering North Carolina politics, and Marjorie Hunter, who was one of the *Winston-Salem Journal*'s outstanding reporters. Clifton Daniels, President Harry Truman's son-in-law and senior editor at the *New York Times,* began life in Zebulon, a small town north of Raleigh, while the icon of broadcast journalism, Edward R. Murrow, is claimed by Greensboro as a native son.

Gerald W. Johnson grew up in Thomasville and became one of the South's best-known liberal voices in the first half of the century, first at Greensboro's *Daily News* and later as a columnist and editorial writer at Baltimore's Sunpapers. Adlai Stevenson once called him "the conscience of America" but he had thoroughly dissected the South before he took on the nation. Vermont Royster led the *Wall Street Journal* to its position of prominence in American journalism. P. B. Young of Littleton learned the trade of printing at Raleigh's St. Augustine's College and went on to found the Norfolk *Journal and Guide,* one of the most influential black-owned papers in the nation during the first half of the century.

The strength of the North Carolina media was a host of quality weeklies and daily newspapers, such as the *Salisbury Post,* where the Hurley family provided a training ground for journalists. The *Post* was one of the last of the locally owned newspapers of note to relinquish ownership to a newspaper chain in a wave of sales that swept the state in the 1980s. Most newspapers held close to the Democratic Party. (There was a time that the *News and Observer* published a giant red rooster—once the party symbol—on the front page when Democrats won in November.) Such partisanship held sway without competition until the 1960s when a new voice was heard. Raleigh lawyer and businessman A. J. Fletcher won the Federal Communication Commission's grant of Channel 5 for Raleigh and turned WRAL-TV into a conservative alternative to the Daniels' *News and Observer* when he put commentator and later U.S. Senator Jesse Helms on the air in 1960.

WRAL-TV was a relative latecomer to the development of broadcasting in the state. By the time it went on the air in 1957, Charlotte's WBTV had been broadcasting for nearly a decade. Its radio signal was already one of the strongest in the South, as the station owned by the Jefferson Standard Life Insurance Company began a southern broadcast anchor for the CBS network.

Beginning in the mid-1930s, Durham's *Carolina Times* became a steady voice for African Americans. It joined the *Wilmington Journal,* established in 1927, and was followed in 1940 by Raleigh's *Carolinian,* both of which were owned by the Jervay family. And the religious press, from the Methodists' *Christian Advocate* to the Baptists' *Biblical Recorder,* flourished. One early editor of the *Recorder* was Josiah Bailey, who later won election to the United States Senate.

One of the most successful publishing enterprises in the South was born in the state. Under editor and publisher Clarence Poe, the *Progressive Farmer* was a voice for advanced farm practices, better farm credit, rural electrification, and conservation. In later years, one of its satellite publications, *Southern Living,* became the largest circulation monthly in the region before it was melded into one of the world's largest media groups, AOL-Time Warner Corporation.

Alternative publishers like Harry Golden, the publisher of the *Carolina Israelite,* and Bob Hall have found audiences in the state. Hall's *Southern Exposure,* a journal of social issues and problems published from Chapel Hill, was the first publication to raise the issue of occupational health problems among textile workers, a subject that was later investigated by the *Charlotte Observer,* which was awarded the Pulitzer Public Service award for its coverage in 1981. The *Observer* received another Pulitzer in 1988 for its coverage of the television ministry of Jim Bakker. The *News and Observer* was recognized in 1996 for its investigation of problems in the hog farms of eastern North Carolina, as was the *Winston-Salem Journal* in 1971, for its coverage of environmental issues. Pulitzer Prizes also went to the *Charlotte Observer*'s editorial cartoonists Eugene Payne (in 1968) and Doug Marlette (in 1988), and to the *News and Observer*'s Claude Sitton (in 1993) for commentary and Michael Skube (in 1989) for book reviews.

W. J. CASH

By Jerry Shinn

BEGINNING SOMETIME IN 1932 and continuing until the summer of 1940, a young man named Wilbur Joseph Cash worked in his parents' home, the back room of the Boiling Springs Post Office, and a rented room in Charlotte to produce an extraordinary book—a long, eloquent, brooding, brilliant, caustically honest, and grudgingly loving meditation on the American South.

Titled *The Mind of the South,* it was the single, splendid, monumental achievement of a life that otherwise was often unproductive, generally unhappy, sometimes miserable, and eventually tragic. Its publication in February of 1941 appeared to launch its forty-year-old author on a promising literary career. Less than five months later he had killed himself.

In his book, Cash challenged the popular image of the antebellum South as a sort of Camelot in the cotton fields. He said that was largely a myth, created and sustained by romantic novelists and poets. He also challenged the assumption that the Old South was "gone with the wind"—destroyed by the Civil War and Reconstruction and replaced by a different kind of society. In the new industrial South, he wrote, the paternalistic mill village was itself "a plantation, essentially indistinguishable in organization from the familiar plantation of the cotton fields."

Cash asserted that the quintessential southern white man was neither the aristocratic cavalier of Old South plantation romances, nor the "poor white trash" of New South realism. He was instead a pioneer farmer and his descendants, shaped by the frontier, were unspoiled by the privileges of aristocracy and unencumbered by its obligations. He was not subject to the limitations of class imposed by older, structured societies, and he knew little about life and culture beyond his immediate horizons. Thus he was individualistic, self-reliant, provincial, loyal to his neighbors, but wary of everyone else.

That description probably fit Cash's ancestors, and his understanding of the culture and social structure of the southern mill village was based on personal experience and observation from his earliest years. He was born Joseph Wilbur Cash on May 2, 1900, in Gaffney, S.C., where Cash's father, John William Cash, was clerk at the company store of the cotton mill managed by John's older brother, Ed. His mother was Nannie Mae Lutitia Hamrick Cash, a music teacher

W. J. Cash (Courtesy of Charlotte Observer)

and church organist. At some point Joseph Wilbur reversed the order of his first and middle names. Either way, to his family he was, boy and man, Wilbur. His childhood nickname was "Sleepy," because of his tendency to squint behind the eyeglasses he wore from an early age. As an adult, to his friends and colleagues at the *Charlotte News,* he was Jack.

Although of modest means, the Cash family ranked a cut above the mill workers who lived nearby and who—men, women, and children—worked twelve-hour shifts six days a week in the lint-clouded factory. By comparison, Wilbur had a privileged childhood. His mother helped him learn to read when he was five, and he read voraciously for the rest of his life. He read the Bible and would keep one nearby for the rest of his life, but Sundays at the Cherokee Avenue Baptist Church did not instill in him the docile faith of his parents, but a lasting aversion to religious intolerance and intimidation.

Years later he recalled both those childhood impressions in a letter to the iconoclastic journalist H. L. Mencken: "The keening of the five-o'clock whistles in the morning drilled me in sorrow," he wrote. "And for years, under the influence of the Baptist preacher's too-graphic account of the Second Coming, I watched the West take fire from the sunset with a sort of ecstatic dread." Other scarring memories from those early years were of the lynchings, cross burnings, and other forms of violence against black people, reported in sensationally graphic language in the local newspaper.

In 1913 the Cash family moved a few miles north across the state line to Boiling Springs in Cleveland County, where John Cash accepted an offer from his father-in-law to run a general store there. At Boiling Springs High School, Wilbur developed a healthy adolescent appreciation for the opposite sex, but he remained an introvert, more interested in reading and his own solitary musings than in sports or socializing. His mother recognized and tried to nurture his intelligence and sensitivity. His father wished the boy were more athletic and competitive. But both were loving, supportive parents through his boyhood and, indeed, for all of his life.

Wilbur and the class of 1917 graduated two weeks after the United States declared war on Germany. After being turned down by the navy because of poor eyesight, he joined the Students' Army Training Corps and worked at shipyards and training camps before enrolling in the fall of 1918 at Wofford College in Spartanburg, S.C., not far from home.

After an unhappy year there and an even shorter stay at Valparaiso University in Indiana, in 1920 Cash settled in at Wake Forest College in the village of the same name just north of Raleigh. It was a Baptist school and many of its five hundred or so students were training for the ministry, but it tolerated considerable intellectual freedom. Its president, William Louis Poteat, was a Christian who understood and believed in Darwin's theory of evolution, and he had attracted a talented faculty.

Cash chewed tobacco, smoked cigarettes, drank liquor, and enjoyed arguing about philosophy, literature, and politics with other bright young men under the influence of stimulating teachers. He published a few poems and stories in the campus literary magazine, but his primary extracurricular activity was the student newspaper. In his senior year, he wrote editorials defending Poteat against his fundamentalist critics and chiding the state's Baptist journal, the *Biblical Recorder,* for its moralistic hand-wringing over dancing in the White House.

When the student newspaper's editorials touched on the subject of race, they reflected a humane paternalism but never questioned segregation. At that point, Cash probably was certain that black people should be treated as human beings, but not so sure white people should treat them as equals. Even that put him a considerable moral and intellectual distance from his turn-of-the-century Carolina roots. Cash graduated in 1922 and, at his father's urging, spent the next year at Wake Forest Law School. But he didn't want to be a lawyer, he told his father, because "you have to lie too much."

He worked the summer of 1923 as a reporter at the *Charlotte Observer,* where he helped cover a strike at the Highland Park Mill in north Charlotte. His family background had given him little regard or respect for organized labor, but watching the owners of the mill break the strike, he was offended by their arrogance and power.

That fall he taught English at Georgetown College in Kentucky. While there he fell in love for the first time, but the affair ended badly, leaving him brokenhearted and afraid that he was impotent. He returned to North Carolina in the summer of 1926 and took a job with the *Charlotte News.*

By early 1927 he was back home in Boiling Springs too sick to work. A Charlotte urologist diagnosed a recurring hyperthyroidism and advised Cash to get some rest. Cash persuaded his parents to help him pay for a trip to Europe. He walked and bicycled across the continent, experiencing its great cities in classic bohemian style.

He returned to the *News* in late 1927, this time as an editorial writer and book reviewer. The following spring he launched a weekly column of literate musings on a wide range of topics. But a few weeks later he was again too depressed to work and his doctor prescribed thiamin, fresh air, and exercise. Cash again went home to recuperate. That fall a local printer and businessman, C. J. Mabry, decided to start a biweekly newspaper in nearby Shelby and offered Cash the job as editor. Cash liked the idea because he could live at home, work at a relatively leisurely pace, and provide an editorial alternative to Shelby's conservative *Star.*

Cash's *Cleveland Press* appeared in September 1928, in the midst of bitter controversy over the Democratic Party's nomination of Al Smith for president. North Carolina was part of the Democrats' "solid South." But Smith was Catholic and anti-Prohibition, or "wet," and probably liberal on issues involving race. Prominent Protestant clergy such as Methodist Bishop Edwin Mouzon and powerful political leaders such as longtime U.S. Senator Furnifold Simmons were urging North Carolina Democrats to support Republican Herbert Hoover.

Cash immediately began to editorialize against the anti-Catholic bigotry. He skewered Mouzon and Simmons and other local religious and political leaders. A lot of people in Cleveland County must have wondered what had gotten into John and Nannie's boy. In fact, it took a great deal of courage for Cash, and after the election, in which Hoover carried North Carolina and the nation, Cash found himself again depressed and debilitated, and the *Press* soon went out of business.

By the following spring he was feeling better. He wrote an article for Mencken's *American Mercury* in the July 1929 issue, and Mencken asked for more. Cash responded with one called "The Mind of the South," introducing themes he would explore at greater length in his book. That article appeared in the October issue and in March 1930 Mencken published a third piece by Cash, "The War in the South," about the violent 1929 Gastonia textile strike.

Mencken provided Cash with access to Alfred and Blanche Knopf of the prestigious Alfred A. Knopf publishing house. In March 1930, he shared some of his ideas for a book with Blanche Knopf in a letter: "My thesis is that the Southern mind represents a very definite culture, or attitude towards life, a heritage, from the Old South, but greatly modified and extended by conscious and unconscious efforts over the last hundred years to protect itself from the encroachments of three hostile factors: the Yankee Mind, the Modern Mind, and the Negro."

But before he could make a serious start on his project, he again became ill. He spent two months in a Charlotte hospital, but his doctor, who had treated him before, could find nothing physically wrong except the hyperthyroid condition. Cash was sent home with orders to rest and avoid any writing, studying, or even reading.

Cash finally started writing again in 1931, produced more pieces for Mencken, and began working on his book. In 1935, he was again writing editorials for the *News*. Early the next year, he mailed 306 manuscript pages to the Knopfs and assured them more would come soon. They paid him an advance of $250, and he signed a contract promising to finish by July 15. But it was three more years before he would. In November 1937 he moved to Charlotte and became associate editor of the *News*.

In the spring of 1938, Cash was introduced to Mary Bagley Ross Northrop, a divorcée who had won a local short story contest and wrote occasionally for the paper's book page. A Charlotte native from a solid Episcopalian family, she liked to smoke and drink and had a vivacious personality. Cash by then was mostly bald, had a potbelly, was indifferently groomed, and still squinted. But the attraction was immediate and mutual. Even as love blossomed, events in Europe exacerbated his depression. He became obsessed with Hitler and would scream tirades against him in the newsroom when a new report would arrive from Europe. Cash and Mary Northrop drove to York, S.C., where they were married on Christmas Day by a justice of the peace.

Meanwhile, the Knopfs were demanding a complete manuscript. On July 27, 1940, Cash mailed the last of it, bringing the total to some eight hundred pages. The book was scheduled for publication in February. When it appeared, it impressed most critics, but earned the author only a few hundred dollars. The main result was that no one ever again would be able to write credibly about the American South without some reference to it.

Cash applied for a Guggenheim Fellowship, which provided $2,000 for a year to work on another book, this time a novel. In early June he and Mary went to Mexico City, where they hoped lower living costs would help them stretch the grant money. Cash tried to work, but his behavior became bizarre.

One evening he told Mary he could hear Nazi agents outside their apartment planning to kill him and her. On July 1, Mary located an American psychiatrist, who gave Cash an injection of B1. But back at the apartment he continued to insist that Nazi agents were lurking outside. A frightened Mary went looking for a friend to help calm her husband, but by the time he returned Cash was gone. He was found dead that night in a nearby hotel, hanging by his necktie in the bathroom doorway. There was no evidence that his death was anything but suicide.

Jerry Shinn is a Phi Beta Kappa graduate of the University of North Carolina at Chapel Hill. He worked in advertising, public relations, and broadcasting, but most of his career was spent at the Charlotte Observer, *where he was a columnist, reporter, and associate editor at the time of his retirement in 1998.*

For more information, see:

Cash, W. J. *The Mind of the South*. Vintage Books, 1941.

Clayton, Bruce. *W. J. Cash: A Life*. Louisiana State University Press, 1991.

Morrison, Joseph L. *W. J. Cash: Southern Prophet*. Alfred A. Knopf, 1967.

Josephus, Jonathan, and Frank Daniels

By Kenneth Joel Zogry

There was no more influential publishing dynasty in North Carolina during the twentieth century than the Daniels family of Raleigh, whose ownership and operation of the *News and Observer* coincided chronologically with the century and reflected and influenced North Carolina's changing political climate. For 101 years, from 1894 to 1995, the Daniels name was synonymous with the *N and O*, and with the evolving ideology of the Democratic Party on race and other issues on both a state and national level.

Not content to merely sit on the sidelines and editorialize, various family members also served in public office, most notably the patriarch, Josephus, and his eldest son, Jonathan. Father and son were both official and unofficial advisors to every Democratic president of their era, between them spanning administrations from Grover Cleveland to Lyndon Johnson.

Josephus Daniels was born in Washington, N.C., on May 18, 1862, to Josephus and Mary Cleaves Seabrook Daniels. His father, of Irish ancestry, was a ship carpenter who worked in the Confederate shipyards in Wilmington. The Civil War cost him his life; he was killed in January of 1865 when the steamboat on which he was riding was accidentally fired upon by Confederate troops.

Mary Daniels was left to raise three children in the midst of the uncertainty of the last months of the Civil War. She moved the family to Wilson, where she became postmistress and later enrolled Josephus in the Wilson Collegiate Institute. From Mary he learned a strong work ethic and a strong Methodist faith (including abstinence from tobacco and alcohol), which he practiced for the rest of his life. His newspaper career began in Wilson, as he became editor of the *Wilson Advance* in 1880 and then purchased it in 1882. Within the next few years he became part owner of both the *Kinston Free Press* and the *Rocky Mount Reporter,* and in 1885 he was elected president of the North Carolina Press Association. Daniels's formal college education also began and ended in 1885, when he decided to enroll in the law school of the University of North Carolina at Chapel Hill. He became a loyal alumnus, trustee, and staunch supporter of the school, a family tradition of involvement that would last for generations.

Soon after passing the state bar, Daniels moved to Raleigh, his home for the rest of his life, to take control of a new weekly newspaper, the *Daily State Chronicle,* recently created from the consolidation of two failing papers. The twenty-three-year-old Daniels was clearly out to make his mark, and set about both to create an even bigger name for himself in publishing and to establish himself among the social elite. He achieved the former by becoming a principal spokesman for the Democratic Party, which increased the circulation of his paper and helped his legislative appointment as state printer for four years between 1887 and 1893. His strong political partisanship also won notice on a national level, and in 1893 President Grover Cleveland named him to a post in the Department of the Interior.

During this period Daniels fell in love with Addie Worth Bagley, whom he married in 1888. His new wife was the granddaughter of Governor Jonathan Worth, who served in the years immediately following the Civil War, and though the family did not possess great wealth, they were members of the capital's highest social circles. Soon after the wedding, the couple moved in with the bride's mother in the Bagley family home in southeast Raleigh, an arrangement that would continue for fifteen years.

Daniels joined the newly formed Watauga Club, which counted among its members future leaders of the New South such as fellow editor Walter Hines Page and educator Charles McIver. The basic philosophy of the New South creed was rooted in the belief that the region needed to move away from its antebellum rural economy toward one based on modern farming techniques and a strong industrial base. A key element of this philosophy was education, and graded schools that promoted progressive learning soon replaced one-room schoolhouses across the state.

At the university, supporters fought for increased state funding and pushed for the establishment of an agricultural and mechanical college in 1887 that later became North Carolina State University. Though these concepts were certainly progressive, debates raged about how equitable and accessible this new education should be across racial lines. The debate ranged from the concept that "education spoiled a good

Left to right: Josephus Daniels (courtesy of N.C. Office of Archives and History), Frank Daniels Jr. (courtesy of Hugh Morton), Jonathan Daniels (courtesy of N.C. Office of Archives and History)

field hand" to the idea that the South would never progress economically with a permanent underclass.

In 1894, with the financial backing of investors, Daniels acquired operating control of the *News and Observer* in Raleigh and returned from Washington to run the paper. From the beginning, the intention was for the paper to be faithful to the principles of the Democratic Party, whose control of the state was being seriously challenged by a "fusion" of the Republican and Populist parties. From 1895 to 1900 Daniels, the *News and Observer,* and the Democrats waged a so-called white supremacy campaign to break the political fusion of the two rival parties by luring white voters back to the Democratic cause through merciless race-baiting.

Daniels's beliefs on race were in line with his white intellectual contemporaries; he held the paternalistic notion that the South's former slaves were childlike and needed to be governed by benevolent whites. He believed that people of color had no place in government, and that the progressive agenda needed to move the state forward could not be implemented until blacks were subjugated to white rule. One of Daniels's favorite political targets was fellow Raleigh newspaper publisher James H. Young, a man of African American ancestry who had been appointed to the board of the North Carolina School for the Blind by Republican Governor Daniel Russell and who was one of three men of color elected to the state legislature in 1896.

In his own newspaper, the *Raleigh Gazette,* Young attempted to fight back by calling the *N and O* the "Police Gazette," charging that it and other "negro howling sheets . . . [are run by] blatant foul mouths. . . . [who appeal to] Democratic pie suckers." In 1896 Daniels was sent by state party chairman Furnifold Simmons on a fact-finding mission to Louisiana to learn how the Democrats in that state had effectively disfranchised African American men, thus permanently ending the threat of future political fusion. He brought back a plan to add an ironically titled "suffrage amendment" to the state constitution, which consisted of a literacy test for voting. With heavy promotion by the *N and O,* the amendment passed in 1900, and Democratic rule was assured for nearly three-quarters of a century.

Daniels was an early and ardent supporter of Democrat William Jennings Bryan, and worked tirelessly for him in his unsuccessful bid for president in 1896. The two became friends, and Bryan was entertained on occasion in the Daniels home. Daniels's political abilities impressed the party bosses, and he was appointed to the Democratic national committee that year, a post he held until 1916. An unexpected event also drew the Daniels family into the Spanish-American War on a very personal level. On May 11, 1898, Ensign Worth Bagley, Addie Bagley Daniels's beloved younger brother and recent graduate of the Naval Academy, became the first American officer killed in that conflict.

The dawn of the twentieth century saw Daniels's personal and political fortunes on the rise. The *News and Observer* became so successful that Daniels bought out many of his financial backers in 1905, and became sole owner as well as editor and publisher in 1928. By this time, the Danielses also had four sons: Josephus Jr., Worth Bagley, Jonathan Worth, and Frank Arthur (two daughters died in infancy). Though he remained loyal to Bryan, Daniels was eager to see any Democrat retake the White House after sixteen years, and strongly supported the candidacy of Woodrow Wilson in 1912. Daniels's support was rewarded with the plum cabinet position of secretary of the navy. Again the family moved to Washington, where Daniels enjoyed two full terms on the Wilson cabinet and a close personal relationship with the president. Though some thought his plain, methodical Southern style inappropriate for a cabinet official, Daniels proved to be an effective secretary who deftly steered the department through the stormy waters of World War I. One of those most critical of Daniels in the early days was his under secretary, an urbane, inexperienced, young New Yorker by the name of Franklin Delano Roosevelt. Over time Roosevelt came to admire Daniels, and a strong bond developed that lasted for the remainder of their lives.

In 1921, at the end of the Wilson administration, the Daniels family returned to Raleigh and a grand stone mansion built on the outskirts of town in one of the most fashionable new suburbs. The move was necessitated by historical irony clearer from the vantage point of time; Daniels's promotion of separation of the races led to the first residential segregation in Raleigh, and the venerable Bagley family home stood in what had become a predominately African American neighborhood. The new house, called "Wakestone" (it was built of stone quarried in the county), became the center of life for the extended family. Within a few years three of the four sons had built homes which adjoined Wakestone's grounds, thus forming a family compound (one son, Worth Bagley, remained in Washington where he was a practicing physician). Always the loyal Democrat, Daniels heartily supported his old assistant, Franklin D. Roosevelt, when he ran for president in 1932.

On matters of race the two men disagreed, but they still enjoyed warm relations and the new president appointed his former boss as ambassador to Mexico in 1933. Daniels and Addie loved living and working in Mexico, and their son, Jonathan, later noted that it was the perfect position for him in the twilight of his career. In 1941, due to Addie's poor health, he returned to Raleigh. During this period of retirement

he completed his massive autobiography, which ran to five volumes and was published between 1939 and 1947. With the advantage of time, Daniels was able to reflect on his part in the white supremacy campaign that disfranchised African Americans, led to segregation, and so altered the course of the state in the twentieth century. Though he continued to believe that what was done was right for the times, he did express regret over the personal and vicious tone of the attacks.

Josephus Daniels died at his home in Raleigh in January of 1948 at the age of eighty-five. Though in his will he stated that he did "not believe the dead hand should attempt to control the living spirit," he made certain provisions for the continued success of the family newspaper. Chief among these provisions was the division of the stock among his heirs in such a way "to avoid any one of the grandchildren holding shares in the company substantially in excess of any other." For the next two decades the four sons maintained ownership in relative harmony, as each fell into a specific role. Jonathan became editor and Frank became business manager, between them assuming most of the responsibility for the daily operations. Worth, who continued to practice medicine in Washington, became the arbiter and final decision maker; and Josephus Jr., whose interests were in other directions, remained largely on the sidelines.

Jonathan Daniels was not his father, and the editorial direction of the *News and Observer* changed under his administration. Born in the family home in southeast Raleigh in 1902, the third of four sons, his early experience with race was markedly different from most southern children of his class. The house stood immediately across the street from Shaw University, the African American school established soon after the Civil War. Thus, along with the expected black household servants and local black children, Jonathan was exposed at an early age to the concept that African Americans were also intelligent enough to attain a college education.

Jonathan attended private schools in Raleigh and Washington, D.C., and then enrolled at the University of North Carolina, where he served as editor of the *Daily Tar Heel*. After graduation in 1921 he continued on to receive a graduate degree in English and then attended Columbia University Law School. Though he flunked out of Columbia, he did pass the North Carolina bar examination.

In 1923, Daniels joined the family business, working as a reporter, sports editor, and Washington correspondent. By 1930 he was establishing a national reputation as a writer, rather than in politics as his father had done. In that year he moved to New York and began to write for *Fortune* magazine as his first novel, *Clash of Angels,* was published to great acclaim. The novel led to a Guggenheim Fellowship in creative writing, which provided him a year of travel and writing in Europe. He returned to the *N and O* as associate editor in 1932, and remained in that position until the outbreak of World War II.

In 1942 Jonathan went to Washington to serve in various departments during the war, which eventually led to his appointment as Roosevelt's last press secretary in 1945. Daniels stayed on after Roosevelt's death to help Harry Truman for a few months, but then returned to Raleigh and became editor upon his father's death in 1948. He remained on good terms with Truman, whose biography he wrote in 1950.

As editor from the late 1940s to the late 1960s, Jonathan continued to be a strong supporter of the Democratic party, and a red rooster, the old symbol of the white supremacy years, was boldly printed on the front page on the occasion of Democratic victories. At the same time, Daniels struggled with questions of race and the evolving civil rights movement. Historian Charles Eagles explained that within Daniels "various mixtures of economic realism, paternalism, and democratic idealism combined to form his basic attitudes toward Negroes and their role in the South." He was certainly more enlightened on the matter than his father, and was seen at the time as such. He was decidedly opposed to discrimination and unfair treatment of African Americans, which won him many friends on the political left and angered many traditional southern whites. On the other hand, he was also opposed to any restructuring of the established social order—including forced school desegregation—and this position was criticized by some (including Martin Luther King Jr.) as being too moderate.

Daniels also wrote magazine articles, novels, biography, and history. As he focused more and more on his books in the mid-1960s (including *The Time Between the Wars* in 1966, which told for the first time of FDR's affair with Lucy Mercer), he little by little gave up editorial control of the *N and O*. Meanwhile, his brother Frank kept the business on an even keel and handled most of the daily operations. In 1968 the first nonfamily member, Claude Sitton, was named editor, and Jonathan retired to his home on Hilton Head Island, where he died in 1981.

Frank Jr., succeeded his father as president and publisher of the paper in 1971. During the 1980s the *N and O* purchased several smaller papers in North and South Carolina, and a small group of heirs consolidated its holdings by buying shares held by other family members. The paper remained staunchly Democratic, though in 1988 tradition was broken when for the first time in history the *N and O* supported a Republican—for county register of deeds.

By the mid-1990s it was clear that the next generation of Danielses was not interested in running the paper, and the decision was made to sell. The Triangle area and indeed all of North Carolina had grown dramatically since World War II, and the *News and Observer* was a desirable property. A deal was struck between the family and the McClatchy Group in May of 1995, and the paper was sold for $373 million dollars —a tidy return on the $10,000 Josephus Daniels had bought it for in 1894.

Kenneth Joel Zogry is executive director of the Pope House Museum Foundation in Raleigh and a doctoral candidate in American history at the University of North Carolina at Chapel Hill. He has published numerous journal and magazine articles, and two books, including The University's Living Room: A History of the Carolina Inn *(1999).*

For more information, see:

Daniels, Frank A., Jr. Interview with author, May 16, 2000. Levine Museum of the New South, Charlotte.

Daniels, Jonathan Worth. Papers. Southern Historical Collection, University of North Carolina at Chapel Hill.

Daniels, Josephus. Papers. Library of Congress, Washington, D.C.

Daniels, Josephus. *Editor in Politics*. University of North Carolina Press, 1941.

———. *Tarheel Editor*. University of North Carolina Press, 1939.

Eagles, Charles W. *Jonathan Daniels and Race Relations: The Evolution of a Southern Liberal*. University of Tennessee Press, 1982.

Morrison, Joseph L. *Josephus Daniels: The Small-d Democrat*. University of North Carolina Press, 1966.

A. J. FLETCHER

By Howard E. Covington Jr.

W HEN Alfred Ira Johnson Fletcher was born in 1887, the village of Jefferson in the heart of mountainous Ashe County in North Carolina's northwest corner, fast by the borders of Tennessee and Virginia, was one of the most isolated corners of the state. Most called the region "The Lost Provinces." The only link to the outside was a mountain road that was closed during heavy snowfalls.

Times weren't just hard; they were downright cruel for the Fletcher family. Called by the Lord when he was a teenager, Fletcher's father was a missionary Baptist preacher who ministered to tiny congregations in churches in a circuit of up to fifty miles that he covered on foot. But "God said go," Fletcher later wrote, and his father set out each day with little more than his faith and a breakfast of cold cornbread and water.

A. J. Fletcher would never forget the hard times of his early years, the faith and independence of his father, and the teachings of his mother. Throughout his career as a lawyer, businessman, and finally, as a broadcaster, he often set an independent course against considerable odds. By the time of his death in 1979, Fletcher had shaped the course of North Carolina politics at the same time he brought the rare sound of opera to more than a million school children. Among his legacies were the National Opera Company and the Fletcher School of Opera at the North Carolina School of the Arts and a political protégé named Jesse Helms.

First and foremost, Fletcher considered himself a lawyer. His older brother, Arthur (a historian, one-time state labor commissioner, and political opposite to his brother), had helped him win admission to Wake Forest College despite a spotty educational record in rural public schools, and on graduation helped guide him into the editorship of a weekly newspaper in rural Wake County. A. J.—then known as Fred— took a wife and built a bank account sufficient to support a return to Wake Forest for law school. He studied long enough to satisfy requirements to pass the bar when he headed back to the northwest mountains, where he opened his one-man practice in Sparta.

Sparta and Alleghany County were home to the Doughton brothers. Rufus had served as lieutenant governor and in 1914, his brother, Robert, was elected to Congress. He asked Fletcher to come with him to

A. J. Fletcher (Courtesy of A. J. Fletcher Foundation)

Washington. Doughton remained for forty years, but Fletcher only stayed for one term before he headed back to North Carolina to begin a law practice in Fuquay Springs, another rural Wake County town where he also started a weekly newspaper. Three years later, Fletcher, his wife, and three sons moved to Raleigh, which would be his home for the next sixty years. A daughter was born after the move to Raleigh.

The law was always Fletcher's first love and professional pursuit, but he had an eye for financial opportunities. At the peak of the good times in the 1920s he formed an insurance company he called Dixie Life Insurance Company. His timing was poor, however, and four years later, as the Depression bore down on North Carolina, he merged his company with the Southern Life and Accident Company of Greensboro to form the Southern-Dixie Life Insurance Company. In another venture, he and J. Melville Broughton, a Wake Forest classmate who later became governor and a United States senator, opened a new cemetery they called Montlawn in Raleigh. They also started a commercial laundry.

The synergy of business fascinated Fletcher. His interest in the cemetery grew from the claims paid by his insurance company. Likewise, when he began the work on Montlawn, he organized a nursery company to provide the trees and shrubbery for a landscape design he personally created.

Raleigh was beginning to pull out of the Depression when Fletcher began to indulge in the two passions for which he would be most remembered—music and broadcasting. Music had always been a part of Fletcher's life. The furnishings of his family's mountain cabin in Ashe County had included little beyond necessities, but there was an organ. He had sung with a well-tuned college quartet and he had been active in vocal groups in Apex, Fuquay, and Raleigh. His rich baritone was a familiar sound at Raleigh's Hayes-Barton Baptist Church, where Fletcher and his wife, Elizabeth, were charter members.

In the late 1930s, a friend asked Fletcher to consider filling in for a missing singer in the Raleigh Little Theater's production of *Bohemian Girl,* and he took the role of Devilshoof, the chief of the gypsies in William Balfe's opera. The chance request was the fulfillment of a lifelong dream. Fletcher had heard his first opera as a teenager when he chanced upon a recording while working at a North Wilkesboro hotel. It captured his imagination immediately. He followed *Bohemian Girl* with roles in other performances and by the late 1940s had organized the Raleigh Music Opera Group, a troupe of amateurs who offered performances to music clubs and civic groups around the state. This led to the formation of the Grass Roots Opera Company and Fletcher's support of the Carolina Opera School, a temporary arrangement with the University of North Carolina extension program.

By the late 1950s, Fletcher was personally underwriting what was then called the National Opera Company (the name was changed in an effort to gain more stature). It had been expanded from its original composition of amateur singers to become a training ground for aspiring professionals, and their performances were being heard around the South. An integral part of the program was a series of performances at public schools all across North Carolina. By the late 1960s, Fletcher's opera program had introduced more than a million school children to the fantasy and pleasure of opera.

For Fletcher, who sang in performances during the early years, opera was a moving and profoundly personal experience. "I've had it shock me into tears," he would later write. "There are phrases in various numbers of opera that thrill me beyond compare. I hear something which startles me into the recognition that here is something that is a work of great art." His contribution to spreading the gospel of opera would bring him national recognition in the music world and give rise to the careers of some of opera's finest performers, including Samuel Ramey, a celebrated performer around the world, and Arlene Saunders, who won acclaim on European stages.

Fletcher's interest in the performing arts blended well with his other interest in broadcasting. In 1939, at the urging of his son Frank, who was a Washington, D.C., lawyer with considerable experience at the Federal Communications Commission (FCC), A. J. Fletcher applied for and received a license for radio station WRAL. It was a low-power operation and no match for Raleigh's leading station, WPTF, whose voice was heard throughout eastern North Carolina.

Fletcher turned the station over to his eldest son, Fred, who had a flair for creativity and promotion. By the close of World War II, WRAL had survived its initial years and was a spunky alternative for Raleigh listeners. Its signal barely penetrated the city limits, but Fred Fletcher used gimmicks, games, and his own talents to build a following. It was during one of his segments as the "Fairy Tale Man," where he read stories for children, that one of the first broadcasts of "Rudolph, the Red-Nosed Reindeer" was heard.

Politics became a mainstay of the station's news coverage and in January 1948, Fletcher hired a Raleigh newspaperman named Jesse Helms as WRAL's news department. Helms and his heavy wire recorder became a familiar figure around the legislature and the governor's office as he single-handedly produced news reports for WRAL. In 1950, Helms became part of the news when he paid for the station to broadcast public appeals to Willis Smith to remain in the race for the U.S. Senate nomination against Frank Porter Graham. A year after Smith arrived in Washington, he convinced Helms to leave the station and join his staff.

Television was still new in 1953 when Fletcher beat the FCC's filing deadline by thirty minutes to apply for the new VHF signal allocated to Raleigh. His competition was WPTF, the well-financed, well-tuned, financially successful, and supremely confident broadcasting voice downtown. It was not until FCC hearings opened in 1954 that WPTF officers realized they faced trouble from this tiny upstart. The FCC's resulting decision to give Fletcher's untested operation the prize caught the company completely off guard.

WRAL-TV went on the air in 1957. The company's

station house was not even built and early programming originated from the National Opera Company's home, a turn-of-the-century mansion on Hillsborough Street. Fred Fletcher handled programming, but it was his father's vision of the power of broadcasting that would make it more than another profit center.

The FCC had agreed with Fletcher's argument that eastern North Carolina needed an independent voice when it gave the new Channel 5 to Fletcher's Capitol Broadcasting Company. Fletcher had long been rankled by the editorial dictums of the leading newspaper in the region, Raleigh's *News and Observer,* and he saw WRAL-TV as an opportunity to present an opposing point of view. In 1960, within a few weeks of the election of John F. Kennedy to the White House and Terry Sanford as governor, Jesse Helms returned to the air with one of the first regular broadcast editorials in the nation. His *Viewpoint* aired as part of the evening newscast and reflected Fletcher's own political philosophy of self-reliance, limited government, and fierce opposition to communism.

Fletcher had succeeded in one of his ambitions for his station. "I didn't start this thing for the money or for any other reasons," he said late in life. "I felt there was a compelling need to establish a means of presenting another side to the liberal positions presented and advocated by many of the state's newspapers — principally the *News and Observer.* I wanted the strongest voice I could get to present the other side and I went out and got the strongest one I could find."

For twelve years Helms's editorials promoted his own and Fletcher's profession of free enterprise and self-determination as the salvation of the nation. Helms skewered Democrats from the state house to the White House and he was particularly scornful of civil rights leaders and the movement for racial equality then sweeping the nation. Fletcher and Helms plowed on with relentless enthusiasm in a campaign that eventually led to Helms's recruitment by Republicans as a candidate for the U.S. Senate in 1972. He won handily to begin one of the longest Senate careers of any North Carolinian.

Fletcher remained hearty well into his eighties with daily rounds of golf on a course he owned on the edge of Raleigh. Physical fitness had always been a priority. In his early years he was a competitive tennis player. He had never smoked nor indulged in liquor, although his heavy-laden luncheon table was legendary. He died April 1, 1979, not really aware of what he had created. Much of his wealth passed to a foundation whose resources mushroomed within a few years of his death. In 1986, the foundation's assets nearly doubled to more than $45 million after the sale of Southern Life Insurance Company. His Capitol Broadcasting Company was on its way to becoming one of the most valuable and innovative properties in the nation under the direction of Fletcher's grandson, James Goodmon of Raleigh.

A primary beneficiary of the foundation was — as it had always been — the National Opera Company, which in 2000 became part of the North Carolina School of the Arts after the foundation endowed the program and presented the school with a $10 million commitment. Under the direction of Thomas McGuire, the foundation also had begun to reach into a variety of areas beyond the arts, such as human services, youth programs, and historic preservation, including the restoration of Raleigh's Briggs Building, where the foundation established its offices.

Before the United States entered World War I, A. J. Fletcher had become intrigued with a new company with a high-sounding name. It was Radio Corporation of America and had just completed its first cross-Atlantic transmission. Fletcher, then a struggling lawyer, thought it was worth his attention. "I thought it was awfully hard to believe that this thing could be developed and have commercial appeal. But I thought that if it was possible, there would be an unbounded use for it." He approached life much the same way, even suggesting to the disbelief of his friends and neighbors that schoolchildren could appreciate opera. He followed both dreams to change life in North Carolina.

Howard E. Covington Jr.'s history of the National Opera Company and biography of A. J. Fletcher, Uncommon Giving, *was published in 1999. Other histories and biographies by Covington include* The Story of NationsBank, Changing the Face of American Banking; *and* Terry Sanford: Politics, Progress, and Outrageous Ambitions *(with Marion A. Ellis);* Linville: A Mountain Home for 100 Years; *and* Belk: A Century of Retail Leadership.

For more information, see:
Fletcher, A. J. "Incidents in the Life of A. J. Fletcher." Unpublished manuscript. Fletcher Archives. A. J. Fletcher Foundation, Raleigh.

Covington, Howard E., Jr. *Uncommon Giving: A. J. Fletcher and A North Carolina Legacy.* A. J. Fletcher Foundation, 1999.
Fletcher, A. J. *The Story of a Mountain Missionary.* A. J. Fletcher Foundation, 1966.

CARL GOERCH

By Amy Jo Wood

I MET A MAN in Asheville last Wednesday by the name of Pants. That's a fact—Frederick L. Pants of Richmond, Va. And I would have to ask him if he was any relation to Albert Coates of Chapel Hill. He didn't seem to appreciate the question, either."—Carl Goerch, *The State* magazine, April 7, 1934

In 1933 Carl Goerch, publisher, author, and broadcaster, embarked on three endeavors that not only would shape his career and subsequently contribute to North Carolina, but would alter the manner in which the citizens of the state thought about the tales they shared with one another. Through humorous anecdotes, he made back-porch stories front-page news when, at age forty-two, he started a series of Sunday-night broadcasts entitled *Carolina Chats* on radio station WPTF in Raleigh. It was, Goerch later said, a show about big and small happenings about the state, and "full of good humor," and it ran until September 10, 1961. On the same station, he broadcast a program called *Doings of the Legislature*. His long-term position as reading clerk for the state House of Representatives made him particularly qualified for the job, and the show ran through fourteen regular and three extra sessions of the General Assembly for a total of twenty-eight years.

But Goerch's most lasting legacy from his busy year in 1933 rose from the magazine that he created and named, *The State: A Weekly Survey of North Carolina*. The prolific publisher wrote many of the stories, sold the advertising, and hawked subscriptions for a publication that he said would "make North Carolinians better acquainted with their state and appreciate what we have here" by promoting North Carolina industry, tourist attractions, and natural resources. Still in publication at the turn of the century as a monthly under the name *Our State: Down Home in North Carolina,* the magazine continued to celebrate Goerch's passion for the travel, history, and folklore of the state.

Ironically, the man who was designated "Mr. North Carolina" in 1971 by the General Assembly hailed from Tarrytown, N.Y. Born June 10, 1891, to Augusta Boetcher and Herman Goerch, both natives of Poland, he received his formal education at the public schools of Tarrytown, graduated from Washington Irving High School, and worked on the staff of his hometown paper. Goerch's account of what happened next typi-

Carl Goerch (Courtesy of Goerch Family)

fies his conversational writing style and respect for serendipitous events from his own life that he often wrote about in his magazine, either as publisher from 1933 to 1951, or as a contributing writer until his death on September 16, 1974.

In a piece entitled "There Ain't Nobody Had Any More Fun," in the April 15, 1970, issue, Goerch wrote, "I was doing newspaper work up in Tarrytown and decided I'd like to see some of the country. So I put an ad on one of our trade journals: 'Wanted a job as a reporter.' I got two answers—one from Orange, Texas, and the other from Washington, North Carolina.

"Jim Mayo was publisher of the *Washington Daily News* at the time. He picked up the paper that contained my ad, glanced at it, and threw it into the wastepaper basket. That same afternoon, the press at the

Daily News office broke down and caused a delay of half an hour or so. Jim went back to his desk, looked around for something to read, reached into the wastebasket, picked up this same paper, and this time he saw my ad. We corresponded and he offered me the position."

Initially, Goerch accepted the newspaper job in Orange, because as he wrote, "Texas sounded rather romantic," but only stayed for six months before asking Mayo if the *Daily News* offer was still stood. Goerch spent enough time in Texas to meet his future wife, Sibyl Wallace. He wrote that they corresponded every day for a year after he moved to North Carolina and then he went to Texas to marry her. Goerch's story about his arrival in the state included a slightly philosophical slant that characterized much of his writing in the *State*. "And another thing about coming to North Carolina," he wrote. "It's surprising how often some trivial, inconsequential little thing will have a marked effect on our future career. Like the press breaking down in the *Daily News* office. If this hadn't occurred on that particular afternoon, the chances are I never would have come to this part of the country, and I shudder to think what I would have missed." What many North Carolinians would have missed was an individualist with an insatiable hunger for experiences that created community, a conservative with a booming voice, and a realist with an unbridled love for practical jokes—a man who managed to infuse his unique style of enthusiasm into all his endeavors.

During his early years in North Carolina, Goerch worked as editor of the *Washington Daily News* (1916–20); editor of the *New Bern Sun-Journal* (1920–22); publisher and editor of the *Wilson Mirror* (1922–25); and editor of the *Progress* in Washington (1925–33).

Undoubtedly, due to Goerch's journalistic experience, much of the *State*'s early editorial content came from newspaper articles. One of the regular features in the 1930s, "What The State Papers Are Saying," comprised snippets from newspapers around the state. Goerch used his legislative connections to write "Around the Capitol," a column that included quotes, news, and comments from folks in state government. Writers such as W. O. Saunders, Bob Erwin, Mrs. Max Abernethy, Bill Sharpe (a future publisher), Frank Montgomery, and John Bragaw contributed stories to the magazine, along with Goerch's wife. Sibyl Goerch's column of conversation, recipes, and garden club happenings was published as "Merely a Woman's Opinion" by Carol Dare. Wives of two subsequent publishers also wrote the column under the same pen name.

But what defined the magazine more than any other type of story were his tidbits about human nature, such as the series "Just One Thing After Another" and "Funny Experiences." These short commentaries about Goerch's travels throughout the state often involved linguistic twists that might have gone unnoticed had Goerch not been a New Yorker writing about the North Carolina he loved. In the April 7, 1934 issue, he wrote:

"Mr. and Mrs. Sneed up in Murphy, have a little girl who is about four years old. A rather clever child. The other day she was playing around the kitchen, watching her mother getting ready to prepare dinner.

'Mother, what's that in that bucket on the table?'

'That's lard, darling.'

There was a moment's silence, during which some deep thinking was in progress. Finally—'Mother, is that the same kind of lard that our Sunday School teacher tells us about?'

'Why, what do you mean, sweetheart?'

'I don't know, but last Sunday she was praying and I heard her say: Good Lard, have mercy on us.'"

In addition to his good-natured stories, Goerch's business savvy and tireless networking made the *State* successful. The magazine's first advertisers were North Carolina's leading companies—Jefferson Standard, Wachovia Bank, Carolina Power and Light, Duke Power Company, Liggett and Myers, and American Tobacco. The enthusiastic promoter of his adopted state spoke to civic organizations and groups in nearly two hundred communities in North Carolina and in thirty-one other states—always gathering stories, support, and subscriptions.

In the early 1930s, weekly subscriptions numbered approximately 2,500 and circulation grew steadily to 20,000 by the time Goerch sold the magazine in 1951. By 2000, the circulation had grown to more than 70,000, and subscribers could recall stories their parents or grandparents told about encounters with the magazine's founder.

For those who knew Goerch, it seems his penchant for pranks nearly overshadowed other accomplishments. John Philips, business manager and ad salesman from 1964 until 1987, said that every morning he and Goerch approached each other with a silver dollar in their closed fists. Without ever saying a word, they opened their hands to reveal the coins—heads won, tails lost. Philips said they each won about half the time.

Although Philips estimated Goerch knew enough people to have been elected governor, not everyone who encountered Goerch was as amused by his antics. Loonis McGlohon, a Charlotte pianist and composer, said Goerch was driving slowly down Fayetteville Street in Raleigh when a motorist behind him began honking in hopes of making him speed up. Goerch stopped his vehicle, got out of the car, and walked back to the man in the car behind him.

"Is there something you need?" he asked the startled driver. The driver stammered that he just hoped to speed things up a bit.

With all the innocence Goerch could muster, it is said he responded, "And now look, I've just held you up a little longer."

Advocates for the construction of the Raleigh-Durham Airport must have been included in the list of Goerch's favorites. A member of the original planning committee for the airport, Goerch loved flying airplanes. Never one to miss an opportunity to promote his magazine, he offered those who would fly with him a free subscription.

Goerch's numerous adventures, stories, and radio talks were gathered into bound volumes that were published as *Down Home* (1943), *Carolina Chats* (1944), *Characters . . . Always Characters* (1945), *Pitchin' Tar* (1948), *Just for the Fun of It* (1954), and *Ocracoke* (1956).

Just as his columns and radio broadcasts served as chapters for his books, it appears that Goerch's synergistic relationships between all his interests sustained his multilayered career. In 1937 he began a man-on-the-street radio program that was broadcast every Saturday morning from the front of the Wake County Courthouse in Raleigh. Included in the show was a quiz, portions of which appeared in the *State* under the name "How Many Can You Answer?" Contestants answered questions for silver dollar prizes, often to the amusement of audience members, listeners, and eventually readers. One morning, a contestant matched wits with Goerch, and won. Asked to list three towns in North Carolina which include the names of body parts, a woman named "Morehead City and Scotland Neck." It appeared she was stumped and couldn't come up with a third when she asked if "Vass would be alright?" Passersby roared with laughter and Goerch handed over the prize money. But WPTF—whose motto was "We Protect the Family" —promptly ended the program and inserted a musical interlude.

Until the end of his life at the age of eighty-three, Goerch remained enthusiastic about life's foibles and fables without slipping into sentimentality. In a story that appeared in the *News and Observer* on June 26, 1966, Goerch said that he was watching a group of youngsters dance when a contemporary asked him if he wished to be young again. Goerch said, "No, sir. Not I. I wouldn't be as young as they are for anything in the world.

"Just think what that would mean: finding a job, getting married, going into debt for a house, automobile and many other things, educating and rearing children, having a deadline to meet every day—I've been over that road and I've enjoyed it, but once is enough."

Goerch seemed to be a man who lived without regrets. After he picked his successor Bill Sharpe to take over the *State* in 1951, he wrote that "quite a number of my friends shook their heads and said: 'You're the magazine and the magazine is you. Nobody else will be able to get out that kind of publication. And they were right. Nobody else could get out the kind of magazine I could get out—but they could get out a different kind of magazine which would be just as good and even better."

Amy Jo Wood is marketing director and contributing writer for Our State *magazine, the publication that Carl Goerch founded. The author of* Life Between Azalea Festivals, *she also contributed a chapter to* Greensboro: A Portrait in Progress.

For more information, see:

Atwater, Henry F. "What Ever Happened to Those Old Radios." *State* 53, no. 8 (January 1988).

"Carl Goerch Dies at Age 83." *News and Observer,* September 17, 1974.

Craven, Charles. "Carl Goerch: Bubbling With Energy at 74." *News and Observer,* June 27, 1965.

Goerch, Carl. "The Biography of the *State*." *State* 26, no. 5 (August 9, 1958).

———. "Grow (Don't Get) Old Gracefully." *News and Observer,* June 26, 1966.

———. "Just One Thing After Another." *State* 1, no. 45 (April 7, 1934).

———. "Solo Flight." *State* 38, no. 12 (November 15, 1970).

———. "There Ain't Nobody Had Any More Fun." *State* 37, no. 22 (April 15, 1970).

Lowery, Raymond. "Goings On." *News and Observer,* September 13, 1961.

Smith, Scott. "Remembering Carl Goerch." *State* 61, no. 1 (June, 1993).

HARRY L. GOLDEN

By Marion A. Ellis

BY SEVERAL QUIRKS of fate, writer Harry Golden became Charlotte's best-known celebrity during the late 1950s and early 1960s, primarily because of his humorous writings on American life and his liberal views on civil and human rights in the South. The publisher of a weekly newspaper called the *Carolina Israelite* in Charlotte, Golden wrote his first book in 1958 at the age of fifty-six. Surprisingly, *Only in America,* a collection of humorous observations and anecdotes about American life previously published in his monthly newspaper, became a national best-seller. As a result Golden became a popular speaker on college campuses and a frequent guest on the Jack Paar show and other national television talk shows. He became a friend to the famous, including Carl Sandburg, Eleanor Roosevelt, Adlai Stevenson Jr., Martin Luther King Jr., and Robert F. Kennedy. He went on to write a dozen other books before his death in 1981. Two more collections of his columns from *Carolina Israelite* —*For 2 cents Plain* (1959) and *Enjoy! Enjoy!* (1960)—also became best-sellers.

Golden's fame as a gentle spokesman for integration spread after the 1954 Supreme Court declared separate but equal schools unconstitutional. Golden's answer, and one that demonstrated his gift for satire, came in 1956, in testimony before the North Carolina Governor's Advisory Education Committee on the Pearsall Plan, a proposal to devise legal ways to avoid immediate integration of public schools. Golden argued that since whites and blacks could stand in the same checkout lines at supermarkets, banks, department stores, and other venues, then they surely could stand together in the same classroom. "I think my plan would not only comply with the Supreme Court decisions, but would maintain 'sitting-down' segregation," Golden said at hearings in Raleigh.

"Now here is the Golden Vertical Negro Plan. Instead of all those complicated proposals, all the next session [of the state legislature] needs to do is pass one small amendment which would provide only desks in all the public schools of our state—no seats." In addition to solving the racial mixing problem, Golden said his plan would save the state millions of dollars in seating purchases and speed up graduations, since students would not like to stand any longer than they had to. His tongue-in-cheek observation attracted national attention and he contributed articles to the *Na-*

Harry L. Golden (Courtesy of Charlotte Observer)

tion, Commentary, the *Democratic Digest,* and several other periodicals.

Golden was born Harry Lewis Goldhurst in 1903 on the Lower East Side in New York City and attended public schools there. He became a stockbroker and eventually became a partner in his own brokerage house. In 1929, he pleaded guilty to stock manipulation and was sentenced to five years in prison. In his autobiography, Golden explained that he had taken orders for stock purchases from customers, but not executed them immediately, betting that the stock price would fall the next day or later. He would execute them when the stock price fell and pocket the difference (a $100 share may have fallen to $97, for instance). But he was caught when the stock price in a big order went up instead of down and he had not executed the sale. This meant his customer was owed the difference. This miscalculation sent him into bankruptcy, and many other customers began to file complaints.

After serving three years, eight months, and twenty-two days, he was released in 1933, with time off for good behavior. Golden took a job as the manager of a hotel owned by his brother and stayed there five years. He then began writing and selling promotional advertising for New York newspapers and in 1940 took a job doing the same for a newspaper in Norfolk, Virginia. That was when he changed his name to Golden to avoid any potential problems. In late 1941, at the age of thirty-nine, he took a job selling ads for the *Labor Journal* in Charlotte, arriving there for the first time on the bus. When the owner died in 1942, Golden sold ads for the *Charlotte Observer* and in October of that same year started his monthly newspaper, the *Carolina Israelite*.

"Though the *Israelite* wasn't a Jewish paper as such, in the beginning I did include stories I got from the Jewish wire service," Golden wrote in his 1969 autobiography, *The Right Time*. "But calling my paper the *North Carolina Journal of Opinion* or *Golden's Report* was presumptuous."

Golden kept his newspaper going while he continued to work full-time for the *Observer* and later as advertising manager for Charlotte promoter I. D. Blumenthal's Midas Mineral Water. By 1947, he had built sales and subscriptions at the *Israelite* sufficiently to support himself. "Sometimes I lived in the office, the kitchen a desk drawer, the bed a battered couch under whose cushions I buried the sheets and blankets," Golden wrote. In 1950, he convinced a friend to buy a house at 1229 Elizabeth Avenue and let him rent it for his office and home. Later he purchased it.

Golden's first brush with fame began in 1954 when his newspaper attracted national attention for urging southerners to obey the Supreme Court decision to desegregate public schools. His friend Carl Sandburg, who lived in Flat Rock and often visited Golden in Charlotte, urged him to publish a book. His original title was *It Could Happen Only in America,* but friends convinced him to shorten it. He obliged and in 1958, *Only in America* became an instant hit. "I think there are certain reasons why *Only in America* became a popular success," Golden wrote. "There is humor in the book, much of it understated, and the publisher had the wisdom not to overstate its qualities. It was a success because it was a 'Jewish' book with a difference."

But as the book hit the best-seller list, Golden was exposed as a writer with a criminal past who had changed his name and moved south. On September 18, 1958, the New York *Herald-Tribune* received an anonymous letter detailing Golden's past and asked his publisher about the allegations. Golden admitted his past. "Twenty-five years of suspense, of 'constant fear of success,' ended yesterday for Harry L. Golden, au-

thor of the nation's top non-fiction best-seller, *Only in America,*" Judith Crist wrote in the newspaper's front-page story. "They ended with Mr. Golden's disclosure that twenty-five years ago he had served a Federal prison term for using the mails to defraud."

Golden and his family, which by then consisted of a wife and three boys, were devastated. He considered dropping out of sight and buying a small hotel in New York with his royalties. But Golden's friends rushed to his defense. "The story only ties me closer to him," Sandburg said. Adlai Stevenson told the *Associated Press* that Golden's story reminded him of another southern writer, O. Henry, who spent three years in prison before achieving fame for his short stories.

TV network personalities Jack Paar and Dave Garroway invited Golden to appear on their television programs. Edward R. Murrow came to Charlotte to broadcast an episode of his popular weekly show, *Person to Person.* Articles appeared in *Life, Time,* and the *Saturday Evening Post.* As a result, Golden received more than 40,000 new subscriptions to the *Carolina Israelite* to add to the 17,000 he had gathered in the previous fifteen years. Within the next ten years, he received a total of 500,000 letters from readers all over the world.

Golden wrote in his autobiography: "As a man with a prison past who wanted to keep it secret, I always knew there was one thing I could not do: run for elective office. *Only in America* taught me there's another thing an ex-convict cannot do if he wants to bury his past: He cannot write a best seller."

Only in America had been in print three months when playwrights Jerry Lawrence and Robert E. Lee, who had written *Inherit the Wind* and *Auntie Mame,* wrote a letter to Golden asking permission to make a play out of the book for Broadway. Director Herman Shumlin, whose best-known play was *The Little Foxes,* was chosen as the director and the play opened in the fall of 1959. It soon closed; New York drama critics savaged it.

But Golden was not discouraged. His lecture fee jumped from two hundred to a thousand dollars and he was being booked for thirty appearances per year. He used the money from his lectures and royalties to pay off debts he had built up over the years to keep the *Carolina Israelite* going, but other than that he noted no change in his lifestyle.

"I still have the same friends now I had before," he wrote. "I drink the same amount of bourbon, about three fifths a week: a healthy dollop in the morning, a drink or two before lunch, two in the afternoon, one before dinner, but never anything after sundown." He also continued to smoke the same brand of cigars.

As a result of his success, Golden hired his son Richard to help run the newspaper and started a syndicated column.

When the civil rights sit-ins started in Greensboro in 1960 and spread to Charlotte in 1961, Golden was asked to write an article about them for *Life* magazine. "The segregationist will stand himself before he lets the Negro sit," Golden wrote. "But the segregationist is dying. The current wave of sit-downs began in North Carolina. In this area—and apparently elsewhere in the South—the reaction of the white people has been significant. . . . Today's southern leaders would be extremely naïve if they failed to realize the serious nature of the newest demonstrations." Blacks had finally realized that they had a powerful weapon in their combined economic buying power, he wrote.

Golden seemed to be many places at once during his journalistic career. In the summer of 1960, he covered the Democratic National Convention in Los Angeles for the Bell-McClure Syndicate. Although he was an Adlai Stevenson backer for the presidential nomination, Golden promised John F. Kennedy he would work for his election if Kennedy won the nomination. After the convention, Golden traveled around the country giving speeches on Kennedy's behalf. "I was to give five speeches in Michigan and twenty in California, at meetings prearranged by the national campaign committee," Golden wrote. "I was to deliver lectures to Jewish and Negro audiences."

In California, he was joined by Sandburg. "When the audience was at a fever pitch, I would say, 'Folks, I have a bonus for you—Carl Sandburg.' Carl would shuffle from the wings onto the stage, shake hands with me, turn to the audience, and say in his measured tones, 'We are just a couple of North Carolina boys plugging for a Boston Irishman.'"

After Kennedy won the election in the fall of 1960, Golden continued to correspond with him about conditions in the South. After Kennedy proposed a new civil rights bill in June 1963 over national television and radio, Golden decided to write a book about Kennedy and his civil rights program called *Mr. Kennedy and the Negroes.*

Golden spent three weeks in Washington doing research on legal challenges by the Kennedy administration to voting rights problems in the South. He had three meetings with Kennedy during that time to discuss racial matters. Kennedy told him that he was fighting for civil rights legislation because blacks were continuing to be discriminated against because of their color. He said Kennedy told him: "This man, unlike the Irishman, cannot change his name to hide his origin. He cannot move away to achieve anonymity. No one will let him forget he is a black man. That is why he must have legislation every step of the way, and I mean to give it to him while I am in the White House." The book was published after Kennedy's assassination in November 1963, but Golden was convinced that it helped set the record straight on Kennedy's role in civil rights legislation.

As a Jew, Golden saw a direct correlation between members of his race and African Americans. In a June 3, 1962, commencement speech at North Carolina College (later North Carolina Central University) in Durham, he said, "The Negro is in the same position in 1962 that the Jews found themselves in at the beginning of the nineteenth century, when their poet Heine wrote, 'We must be twice as good to get half as much.'"

His paper remained in publication until 1968 when Golden, then sixty-five, put out the final issue. He died in 1981.

Marion A. Ellis is a Charlotte writer specializing in corporate histories and biographies. He is the coauthor with Howard E. Covington Jr. of Greensboro of Sages of Their Craft: The First Fifty Years of the American College of Trial Lawyers; Terry Sanford: Politics, Progress, and Outrageous Ambitions; *and* The Story of NationsBank: Changing the Face of American Banking.

For more information, see:

Golden, Harry. File. Robinson-Spangler Room, Public Library of Charlotte-Mecklenburg County.

Golden, Harry. *The Right Time: The Autobiography of Harry Golden.* G. P. Putnam's Sons, 1969.

J. MARSE GRANT

By Charles A. Clay

I f NORTH CAROLINA awarded battle stars and Purple Hearts for combat in the political and religious arenas, Marse Grant, the dean of Southern Baptist editors at the end of the twentieth century, would be one of the state's most decorated. But it was the values he learned as a youth in a High Point mill village that sustained him for years as editor of the *Biblical Recorder,* when he wielded editorial cudgels against liberal liquor laws and the fundamentalism of conservative Christians who seized control of the Baptist denomination.

Grant was born September 13, 1920, in High Point and reared in what he described as a cotton mill village where "everybody knew where the railroad tracks were." Looking back on those years, J. (for James) Marse Grant saw advantages and challenges in his childhood just prior to and during the Depression. "Good Christian homes, the church and sports made our village an outstanding community," he recalled in 2000. At the same time, his participation in and love of sports also shaped his life and taught valuable lessons. Late in life he pulled out an old photo of the cotton mill's baseball team and fondly remembered being a player and manager of a "hustling young ball club" that taught him about leadership. "Sports teaches you how to lose, and some people never learn this in life."

Grant worked a 3:30-to-midnight mill shift six days a week during the four years he attended High Point College (later High Point University), where he also was director of publicity for the college and editor of the college newspaper during his senior year. He graduated with honors and was awarded a medal for being the best all-around male in his 1941 class.

On June 16, 1942, a year after his graduation, Grant married the former Marian Gibbs of Greensboro and the two formed a hardworking Baptist team as well as a family. In 1949, while he was editor of the *Morganton News-Herald,* Grant was offered the editorship of *Charity and Children,* a Baptist newspaper published at the denomination's orphanage in Thomasville. This job offer was "the greatest opportunity I ever had," Grant said in a "Tar Heel of the Week" article in the Raleigh *News and Observer.* "It permitted me to combine a love for newspapering with religious work." It also allowed him to follow in what he called some big Baptist shoes, including those of John H. Mills,

J. Marse Grant (Courtesy of N.C. Office of Archives and History)

founder of the orphanage and the journal in 1887. And it paved the way for him to become the crusading editor of the weekly *Biblical Recorder,* the official publication of the Baptist State Convention.

A self-described "moderate in all things," Grant once said that "there are two philosophies" among Southern Baptists about the role a Baptist publication should play. "One is that it should be a house organ" primarily pushing promotional material. The other is that it should be a free publication . . . " with a responsibility to report and comment factually on Baptist issues.

At the helm of *Charity and Children,* the Grant team saw to it that the publication hewed to the latter category, and slowly but surely Tar Heel Baptists began to rely more and more upon the Grants' work for controversial as well as routine news and commentary. During those years, Grant said, "My wife [was] really my right arm in my work. She [wrote] a column for the paper and [was] quite adept at handling the camera when needed, which [was] often. She [was] an unpaid member of the staff, like a preacher's wife."

On January 1, 1960, Grant succeeded L. L. Carpenter as editor of the *Recorder*, which had been founded in 1833. Grant was the first non-preacher to hold the post since Josiah W. Bailey left the paper in 1907 to further his legal career and eventually enter politics and win election to the U.S. Senate. At the time, Grant said he hoped the *Recorder* would have "a strong editorial voice" under his leadership, and added, "We have had freedom at *Charity and Children*. We anticipate the same freedom" [at the *Recorder*].

To say that the Baptist journal had "a strong editorial voice" under Grant would be an understatement. During his tenure, it generated a virtual mountain of newspaper clippings about its reporting and editorial commentary on a wide range of issues, not just those pertaining to Baptists, but to all people. Those issues included the long-running competition between moderates and conservatives for control of the Baptist denomination in the South, racial segregation, and liberalization of the liquor laws.

Despite the extreme volatility of the issue of race relations at the time, Grant wasted no time in taking a stand that clearly was not pleasing to all Baptists. In February 1960, the second month of his editorship, he wrote: "God loves all people. To think that He prefers one over the other because of the color of skin is inconsistent with the teachings of the Bible." Grant said the editorial cost the journal "some sharp decreases in circulation" for a while, but by the time he ended his term on his sixty-second birthday in 1982, the *Recorder*'s circulation had almost doubled to 110,000, making it one of the most widely circulated publications in the state.

During the civil rights movement of the 1960s and 1970s, Grant worked to improve racial relations by advocating obedience to public school desegregation laws in North Carolina and the South to state and national organizations as well as in the *Recorder* and to his fellow Baptists. In 1963, Governor Terry Sanford appointed him to the Good Neighbor Council, the first state agency formed to deal in a hands-on way with racial problems. This groundbreaking organization later became the state's Human Relations Council. In 1970, President Richard Nixon named Grant to the Advisory Council on Education, a national group working for public school integration.

During these same decades, Grant fought against efforts to enact laws permitting by-the-drink liquor sales in North Carolina. Teaming with the Christian Action League, Grant helped defeat bills in battles that were bitterly fought, only to lose the war over the issue in 1978. In 1973, Grant and other "dry" leaders were jubilant in the wake of a lopsided victory over the "wets" in a statewide referendum on a local option mixed-drink bill. Drys won by "a margin of 70 to 30 percent, with 97 of 100 counties," Grant noted, and agreed with a wet leader that "the pulpit won." He called for greater participation by Christians and their churches in government and politics.

While acknowledging that it was "dangerous and risky to try to translate Christian concern into action" in the political arena, Grant wrote: "Let it be said without apology that our aim is for the voice of the church to be heard throughout the land, including the halls of government. If Christian people don't take the lead, who will?" In only a few years, however, the wets were back in the General Assembly with another local-option mixed-drink bill. This time its backers managed to push it through without a statewide referendum requirement. Fashioned by the 1977 legislative session, the law went into effect in early 1978, and for Grant it was a bitter pill.

His disappointment prompted him to resign from the chairmanship of the State Goals and Policies Board in June 1978. He wrote in the *Recorder* that he believed one of the reasons the drys lost was that he was not there to lobby against it. At the time of his resignation, Grant made it clear that he had not lost interest in helping the state deal with other problems.

Grant was more successful in the fight against drunken driving. He wrote a book in 1970 entitled *Whiskey at the Wheel: The Scandal of Driving and Drinking*. Published by the Boardman Press of Nashville, Tenn., the book sold nearly sixty thousand copies, but earned him "exactly a nickel in royalties," Grant said with a smile.

On the eve of the opening of the 1983 General Assembly, Governor Jim Hunt enlisted Grant's participation in the administration's successful effort to strengthen the state's laws against drunk driving. At Grant's suggestion and with his help, the Hunt administration's legislative package drew the support of several hundred religious leaders from across the state who were invited to the Governor's Mansion for strategy sessions. In February 1982, on the eve of Grant's planned retirement from the *Recorder,* Hunt and about four hundred others honored him and Marian at a retirement party. But if anyone thought they had heard the last of Grant, they were to be badly disappointed.

From his retirement in September 1982 until early

1993, Grant wrote a weekly column, mostly on Baptist affairs in the state and region, for the *Charlotte Observer*, the state's largest newspaper. A diabetic for fifty-seven years, Grant dropped the column after suffering a slight stroke in Copenhagen while he and his wife were on one of their many trips, some of them as tour guides. He continued, however, to write a column for his hometown paper, the *High Point Enterprise*.

Grant had warned against the conservative political takeover of the Southern Baptist Convention before it occurred in 1979 and 1980. He had suggested that former president Jimmy Carter, also a Southern Baptist, be elected president of the convention, but Carter declined. In 2000, Carter resigned from the convention, noting that leaders had adopted increasingly rigid creeds that violated the basic tenets of his faith. Grant, who attended fifty-two annual sessions of the Baptist State Convention, continued to keep a close eye on issues of interest to Baptists, who numbered about 1.1 million in the state and 15.5 million in the Southern Baptist Convention in 2000. As a result of the conservative Baptist movement's successes in North Carolina, the state convention took control of the Southeastern Baptist Theological Seminary at Wake Forest, eliminating theological moderates from its board of trustees and faculty.

But at the close of the first year of the new millennium, Grant saw a silver lining for moderates in their struggle with conservatives for control of the state convention. At the 2000 session in November at Winston-Salem, Grant said, "Two of the three vice presidents who were elected are moderates. . . ."

Grant never lacked for opposition among convention goers. During one session, a resolution was introduced attacking him for using the *Recorder* as "a biased tool . . . for degrading character." This followed a Grant editorial attack on the conservative Oklahoma preacher who was head of the Southern Baptist Convention for saying that "God doesn't answer the prayers of Jews." The state convention not only rejected the anti-Grant resolution, but passed one commending Grant and the *Recorder*, saying the publication had "maintained its commitment to the basic right of every Baptist to be fully informed concerning those matters which affect our denomination."

During one legislative battle over mixed-drink sales, anti-Grant legislators introduced a measure that would have stripped churches of their tax-exempt status if their activities included "carrying on propaganda or otherwise trying to influence legislation," or "publishing or distributing statements" aimed at legislation. The so-called "Marse Grant amendment" was promptly killed.

In the end, though, Grant, who received honorary doctoral degrees from Campbell University and High Point College, seemed to have the last word. At the start of a new millennium, the *Recorder* named its longtime editor as one of the twenty most important leaders in Baptist life in North Carolina in the last century.

Charles A. Clay is a Raleigh-based writer who was editor of the Fayetteville Observer *from 1965 to 1978. Prior to that he was a journalist in Durham and Raleigh before being named to the North Carolina Industrial Commission. He is the author of a biographical novel,* The Alien Corn.

For more information, see:

Baptist Historical Collection. Wake Forest University, Winston-Salem.

Charity and Children. Centennial Issue. Baptist Children's Homes of North Carolina, November 1987.

A Content Analysis of the Editorial Page of the Biblical Recorder, 1960–70. University of Georgia, 1971.

Ferguson, Ernest B. *Hard Right: The Rise of Jesse Helms*. W. W. Norton, 1986.

Grant, J. Marse. *Whiskey at the Wheel: The Scandal of Driving and Drinking*. Boardman Press, 1970.

"J. Marse Grant: Tar Heel of the Week." *News and Observer*, February 16, 1958.

THE JERVAY FAMILY

By J. Barlow Herget

THE PATRIARCH of North Carolina's Jervay Family of journalists lived an American success story life. No newspaper man himself, the Reverend William R. Jervay (1847–1910) nevertheless set a standard for leadership and learning for his children when such things were denied African Americans in the South of the late nineteenth century and early twentieth century.

Jervay was born a slave on a South Carolina plantation from which he fled to fight for the Union army in the Civil War. After the war, he returned to South Carolina, where he purchased and operated a large farm in St. Stephen Parish. He served as a member of the state's Constitutional Convention and then a member of the state house (1868–72) and state senate (1872–76). He learned the skills of a carpenter and prized education for his children. He sent his son, Robert Smith Jervay (1873–1941), to Charleston's Avery Institute and then Claffin University in Orangeburg, S.C. William spent the remainder of his years as a Methodist minister in Summerville, S.C.

His commitment to religion became a family trait. Indeed, churches were at the core of many African American communities in the segregated South, and those who rose to leadership positions often did so through church connections. Not surprisingly, one of the first printing assignments that helped launch the Jervay family into journalism was the publication of a church newspaper, the *Christian Star*.

It was William's son, Robert, who printed the church paper and founded the R. S. Jervay Printing Company and the *Cape Fear Journal*. Robert was born in Summerville, and following his education, he moved his family in 1892 to the Elbow Community in Columbus County. He worked as the bookkeeper and manager of the commissary for a lumber company, and it was from there that he printed church programs and newspapers. In 1898, he married schoolteacher Mary Alice McNeill of Wilmington and was named Elbow's postmaster. Three years later in 1901, he established the R. S. Jervay Printing Company.

Like his father, Robert wanted his children to receive a good education, and in 1911, he moved his family and his printing business to Wilmington. The children, eventually eight in all, attended the Gregory Normal Institute. The printing business was a family enterprise and mostly manual. The press was

T. C. Jervay (Courtesy of Wilmington Journal)

hand-fed and the type was set by hand. Mary Alice served as a typesetter and proofreader. Her sons—Henry, Paul, and Thomas—worked in various capacities. Thomas Clarence "T. C." Jervay recalled his job as an eight-year-old, delivering on his bicycle the printed minutes of fraternal civic organizations.

Robert Jervay saw that his children continued their education in college. It is not known where Henry, the oldest son, attended school, but Paul Reginald "P. R." Jervay and T. C. both attended Hampton Institute in Virginia. P. R. studied printing technology and then taught the subject at Hampton. T. C. concentrated on business and later transferred to Howard University in Washington, D.C., and then graduated with a B.S. degree from Virginia State University in Petersburg.

The 1920s were a tumultuous time for race relations in the South, and there were few outlets for African American opinion. Henry encouraged his father to begin a newspaper for blacks in the Wilmington area, and in 1927, the family began publication of the *Cape Fear Journal*, a four-page weekly tabloid that sold for a nickel. A year later, the Jervays had purchased a linotype machine and a flatbed press to print the paper. The dominant, white-owned newspaper, the *Wilmington Star,* praised the weekly in a 1929 editorial as "one of the most constructive Negro papers in the South." The Depression brought hard times for everyone, and the *Journal* struggled like other businesses. It suspended publication in 1930 for several months but was back on the streets by October of that year.

Copies of the early *Journal* were later destroyed in a bombing and fire in 1973, but its contents included typical police news of the community, religious commentary, and church news. Equally important, it also served as an advertising medium for black-owned businesses such as funeral homes that wanted to reach black audiences. The paper grew in size, as did the Wilmington area.

P. R. returned to Wilmington after teaching printing for eight years at Hampton Institute. He helped his father sell advertising and operate the typesetting machine. Henry, the paper's principal writer, died in the 1930s. At Hampton Institute, P. R. met and married Brenda Yancy of Atlanta, and after four years in Wilmington, they decided to search for work elsewhere. P. R. worked for the *Norfolk Journal and Guide* and the *Chicago Defender,* one of the best-known African American newspapers in the country. In 1938, they moved back to North Carolina, but to Raleigh, where P. R. worked for H. E. Fontillo-Nanton, who was associated with the *Carolina Times* in Durham and owner of *The Carolina Tribune* in Raleigh. P. R.'s wife taught home economics and later rose to department head at Shaw University in Raleigh.

In 1940, P. R. became owner, publisher, and editor of the *Tribune,* described as "an eight-page, seven-column newspaper with depressed circulation, scarce advertising and minimal good will." Jervay changed the name to the *Carolinian* and began to build the newspaper's circulation and upgrade its equipment. In the words of his son, Paul R. Jervay Jr., P. R. was a man "that believed in working!" He did "whatever was necessary—writing, setting type, selling advertising" to see that the paper was published. His mission was to "promote and push the *Carolinian*"; as he once told well-wishers who wanted to give him an award for his work, "You can recognize me by buying a copy of the *Carolinian.*"

In the beginning, he was concerned about the paper's appearance and gradually purchased better quality, secondhand equipment for his operation. During World War II, the paper continued to target the African American residents of the capital city with what Paul Jervay Jr. described as "church-centered, community-oriented" news. P. R.'s father-in-law, A. H. Yancy of Atlanta, helped finance the purchase of land and construction of a building for the newspaper in 1954–55, which was a turning point in the *Carolinian's* business life.

His younger brother, T. C. Jervay, returned to Wilmington in 1937 to help his father with the printing and newspaper business. When Robert died in 1941, T. C. assumed the leadership in the business, renaming the newspaper the *Wilmington Journal* in 1945. He became publisher and editor upon the death of his mother, Mary Alice, in 1948. Like his parents, T. C. and his wife Willie made the newspaper a family enterprise that would be handed down to their children.

Both newspapers became influential North Carolina journals during the second half of the century because of their outspoken positions in the civil rights movement and their unique expansion into other towns and cities. T. C. became a champion for civil rights for African Americans in Wilmington. In an August 1953 edition of the *Journal,* long before antidiscrimination laws and "affirmative action" hiring policies, T. C. called on the city of Wilmington to employ black firemen and policemen, and asked voters to elect blacks to the city council, board of education, and the city's housing authority. He also spoke out for more affordable housing for blacks and a black-owned drug store and supermarket.

However, in the years leading up to the civil rights movement of the 1960s, the newspapers primarily dealt with the events of everyday life of African Americans in Wilmington and Raleigh. Along with the local headlines were success stories and achievements of blacks on the state, national, and international scene. Paul R. Jervay Jr. noted that the *Carolinian* "covered everything that Dr. [Martin Luther] King [Jr.] did." The newspapers showed North Carolina African Americans, who were bounded by the laws of segregation and rules of Jim Crow custom, a larger world and one interested in their views, opinions, and patronage.

The civil rights era was a trying time for black businesses such as the *Wilmington Journal* and the *Carolinian.* White advertisers were sometimes reluctant to buy space, and a few vented their opinions through small indignities. For instance, one white merchant, reputedly a member of the Ku Klux Klan, would leave his weekly ad copy with his secretary so that he didn't have to personally hand it to the *Carolinian* salesperson. As protests and demonstrations became news-of-the-day, P. R. Jervay would report to his worried wife the threats of violence and vandalism out of the hearing of their children so that they were not frightened.

In Wilmington, T. C. Jervay did more than report about the societal changes roiling around him. He personally led the effort to integrate the public library and the city golf course. He was a local leader in the NAACP and motivated black business people to pay costs for the first African American to enter Wilmington College in 1962. The state's new human relations commission selected T. C. in 1963 to receive a community service award. He was president of the National [African American] Newspaper Publishers Association.

The influence of the *Journal,* however, can be determined in part by the fear it provoked in its enemies. One such enemy was a white supremacist named Lawrence Little, who, in 1973, used nine sticks of dynamite to blow up and set fire to the *Journal*'s building. Jervay and his family had once lived above the paper's office but luckily had moved. Little was caught and convicted, and Jervay attributed the bombing to his newspaper's tradition of defending the rights of black people. "They blasted my shop, but we never missed an issue," he said later.

The reach of the Jervays' journalism extended across North Carolina in the 1970s and 1980s through the use of "makeover" newspapers in other towns such as Rocky Mount, Wilson, Kinston, Greenville, Charlotte, Greensboro, and Winston-Salem. P. R. Jervay, for instance, would make minor changes to the copy of the *Carolinian* and then print the paper under a different nameplate, such as the *Rocky Mount/Wilson Dispatch*. Such "makeover" papers lasted only about seven years, but in some of the smaller cities, they introduced African American readers to a black press and prompted more coverage of the black community by other, established newspapers. Circulation for the newspapers in the 1980s was between nine thousand and ten thousand; the *Carolinian* became a twice-weekly paper in 1985.

P. R. and T. C. Jervay died in December 1993. Each had spent a lifetime in journalism and were enshrined in 1999 into the National Newspaper Publishers Association Black Press Archives at Howard University. The same year, T. C. was inducted posthumously into the North Carolina Journalism Hall of Fame at Chapel Hill. Their newspapers passed on to their heirs. Mrs. Willie Jervay, T. C.'s widow, became publisher of the *Wilmington Journal,* and daughter Mary Alice Jervay Thatch its editor. In 1997, Paul Jervay Jr. became publisher and editor of the *Carolinian*. With his wife, the Reverend Evelyn H. Jervay, he also published the *Carolina Call,* a bimonthly distributed in Warren, Halifax, Lenoir, Wilson, Nash, Edgecombe, and Wake counties.

At the end of the century, both newspapers continued to be the voice of their respective African American communities. Mrs. Thatch and her mother Willie Jervay held to the direction voiced by T. C.: "Our newspaper has succeeded and prospered because we have tried to be the servant for the human rights for all, especially blacks. I have worked hard for Wilmington, and Wilmington has been mighty good to me. My greatest aim and hope is to see blacks move forward politically and economically. This is the bottom line, and if this is not done, we are lost!"

In Raleigh, Paul Jervay Jr. and his wife reported in an October 26, 2000, 61st anniversary issue of the *Carolinian,* "It has always been our founder's desire that the paper remain independent and that it involve itself in the community beyond printing the news." They noted the family's support for the Nay-Kel Education & Training Center and the P. R. Jervay Living Learning Newspaper Foundation, both aimed at helping African American young people. And they proudly pointed to the paper's motto, "Dedicated to the Spirit of Jesus Christ," printed on each issue's front page. It was a mission that traced its roots to William R. Jervay.

J. Barlow Herget is a Raleigh writer, coauthor of The Insiders' Guide to the Triangle, *and served two terms on the Raleigh City Council. He received his master's degree in history from the University of Virginia and was a Neiman Fellow at Harvard University in 1970. A former editorial writer for the* News and Observer, *he was a special assistant in the N.C. Department of Commerce from 1977 to 1979 during Governor Hunt's first administration.*

For more information, see:
Jervay, Paul R., Jr. Interview by author, January 2001. Levine Museum of the New South, Charlotte.

"Footprints through Carolinian History." *The Carolinian,* October 26, 2000.
Marcroft, Bobbie. "Tom Jervay and *The Wilmington Journal*." *Scene Magazine,* November 1978.
Pratt, Bonnie. "T. C. Jervay, Dean of the Black Press." *Minorities and Women in Business,* September–October 1986.
Reaves, William M. *Strength through Struggle.* New Hanover County Public Library, Wilmington, 1998.

CHARLES B. KURALT

By Ralph Grizzle

BORN IN WILMINGTON in September 1934, with "rambling in [his] blood," Charles Bishop Kuralt grew up on his maternal grandparents' hundred-acre tobacco farm in Onslow County. Evenings, the young Kuralt delighted in curling up on the front porch next to his grandmother, Rena Bishop, as she read aloud the stories of O. Henry and the poems of Rudyard Kipling and Edgar Allan Poe.

Kuralt's dad, Wallace, eked out a living doing odd jobs before becoming a social worker for the county. It was a steady job—no small thing in the midst of the Depression—and Wallace excelled at it. His promotions through the social services ranks of the county, then later the state, kept the Kuralt family on the move. Still, they never ventured far from rural eastern North Carolina, and so Kuralt grew up, and remained till the end, a farm boy.

Bright, sensitive, and precocious, Kuralt loved words. "When Charles was six, he spoke like a twelve-year-old, and when he was twelve, he spoke like a high school graduate," remembered a cousin, Horace Gurganus. "He talked way over my head, and I was fourteen years older." Kuralt also knew he wanted to be a reporter; he'd pretend he was one when he'd wear his father's hat with a "press" card stuck in its band.

At the age of ten, he was already hawking his own mimeographed newspaper, the *Garden Gazette,* to neighbors for two cents a copy. As a reporter for the Alexander Graham Junior High School newspaper in Charlotte, where his family finally settled, Kuralt developed a reputation for coming back from an assignment with a story, no matter what. For example, when the celebrity he was to interview at a bus station never arrived, Kuralt returned with a story about the bus station.

Kuralt labored over the craft of writing, and his skill showed. In 1947, the sports desk of the *Charlotte News* agreed to pay him ten cents for each inch of published copy. He got his first byline when he covered a junior high school basketball championship in Charlotte. In 1948, fourteen-year-old Kuralt won the "I Speak for Democracy" contest at Charlotte's Central High School and gave his speech at a student assembly. Moreover, he was one of four national winners—out of 250,000 entrants—in the contest, sponsored by the National Association of Broadcasters. For his

Charles B. Kuralt with Loonis McGlohon (on his right at the piano) (Courtesy of Hugh Morton)

prize, he got to meet President Harry Truman at the White House.

The thirteen Emmy Awards he would later receive during his career at CBS would ultimately testify to Kuralt's greatness as a writer. Still, it was his sonorous voice—which would become his signature—that helped set him apart from his peers. Ed Yoder, his Chapel Hill chum, said Kuralt's voice was "as rich and resonant as the fine bourbon that none of us could afford to drink."

His voice opened many opportunities for him. He acted in high school plays, emceed assemblies, and was frequently asked to recite "Casey at the Bat," which he could do, complete with gestures and expressions. At age fourteen, he was one of the country's youngest radio announcers and doing color commentary for the Charlotte baseball team, the Hornets, on ABC-affiliate WAYS; the station also gave him his own weekly radio show, *Junior Sports Parade*.

Kuralt entered the University of North Carolina as a sixteen-year-old freshman in 1951. Unsurprisingly, he earned good grades, although, as an upperclassman, he would flunk or receive "Incompletes" for the required recreation courses. When WUNC hit the air in 1953, Kuralt was one of its first broadcasters, doing a half hour of radio drama. But he really made his name as editor of the *Daily Tar Heel*. He won the election for the job, which paid thirty dollars a week, in his junior year in 1954 on a pro-integration, anti-McCarthy platform. Upon winning, he proposed to his high school sweetheart, Sory Guthery, then a student at Woman's College in Greensboro. They were married that August. During their senior year, they lived in a cabin on the outskirts of Chapel Hill.

As editor of the daily newspaper, Kuralt was known for his "irrepressible enthusiasm," said associate editor Louis Kraar. "And that was infectious. He inspired us." Kuralt adopted racial integration as his crusade. Upon the landmark U.S. Supreme Court decision in 1954 striking down school segregation, he wrote an editorial that is still stirring for its eloquence. "We hold this one—like those other great truths declared in our Constitution—to be self-evident: It is time to stop postponing brotherhood," the editorial said. Kuralt made sure that North Carolina's all-white legislature got copies of the editorial, whereupon he was denounced on the floor as "a pawn of the communists."

During his college years, Kuralt worked summers for WBT Radio and WBTV, former CBS affiliates that were acquired by Jefferson Pilot Communications. Occasionally, he appeared in front of the camera to do commercials. Despite an offer to work for the radio station, Kuralt left UNC short of graduation and instead went to work for the *Charlotte News*. He did so on the advice of his hero, Edward R. Murrow, whom Kuralt had met once in Chapel Hill. The celebrated CBS broadcaster had counseled him to establish himself first as a print journalist before moving to broadcast news. Kuralt made fifty-five dollars a week.

After a year as a general assignment reporter, Kuralt was tapped to write human interest columns for the paper—clearly the forerunners to his *On the Road* segments at CBS. "He took people who would be considered nobodies by most people and made them somebodies," remarked Julian Scheer, a newspaper colleague. "It was like, 'You should know about this person because you passed him on the street and he has an interesting story to tell.'"

Kuralt's "People" columns attracted the attention of WCBS Radio, which hired him in March of 1957. It was the start of a thirty-seven-year career with the network known as "The Mighty Eye." Kuralt, Sory, and their first daughter, one-year-old Lisa, moved to New York and found an apartment in Brooklyn. Kuralt worked the midnight-to-8 A.M. shift, condensing reams of news wire copy into five-minute reports for the radio announcer to read. Network higher-ups quickly recognized his writing talent and promoted him to write for the *CBS Evening News with Douglas Edwards*. There he learned the most valuable advice of his career, from fellow staff writer Alice Weel. "Don't ever let your words fight the pictures," Weel told him. "Pictures are so strong that, in a fight, they always win." Arguably, Kuralt learned how to meld words and pictures better than any broadcaster in television history.

In 1959, CBS made Kuralt its youngest-ever news correspondent. He was twenty-four. The next year, he became anchor of a new weekly program called *Eyewitness to History*. The show was built around the week's major news event, with the anchorman trekking wherever in the world the news was happening. The new job thrilled Kuralt; he got to write, report, and have a say in the program's content. And Kuralt, always full of wanderlust, got to travel widely. It also paid him $30,000 a year. "This is it, something I've always wanted to do," he said in a 1960 interview.

Kuralt poured himself into the show, and it succeeded. His marriage, however, didn't. His travel kept him away from home and he became "dizzy with the import of it all," he wrote in his autobiography, *A Life on the Road*. Kuralt and Sory ended their five-year marriage over the phone. She moved back to North Carolina with Lisa and the couple's second daughter, Susan. Kuralt's career took a jolt, too. Jim Aubrey, the head of CBS Television, yanked him as *Eyewitness* anchor because of what Aubrey called Kuralt's overly "low-key" style, and replaced him with the anchor of the *CBS Evening News*, Walter Cronkite. Kuralt was exiled to Brazil, where he became CBS's only correspondent in South America.

Two years after his divorce, Kuralt remarried. The bride was Suzanna "Petie" Baird, Douglas Edwards's secretary. In 1963, CBS moved Kuralt back to the United States, to Los Angeles, where he became the network's chief West Coast correspondent. He didn't break many stories and, even worse, got scooped several times by rival reporters; CBS recalled him to

New York. There he began four years of work on documentaries, which again took him to far-flung places.

In 1967, Kuralt pitched the network on his idea of *On the Road*. The new president of CBS News, Dick Salant, gave him the green light for a three-month, low-budget project. Kuralt's agenda was to discover if the mood of Americans was really as unsettled as it so readily appeared on TV during the height of the 1960s social unrest. Kuralt and his small crew filed their first two-minute report from a leaf-strewn road in Vermont. It was a huge hit with the CBS brass.

The three-month experiment turned into a thirteen-year, 650-segment phenomenon. Kuralt filed reports from all fifty states; *Time* magazine in 1968 called them "two-minute cease-fires" sandwiched between the daily barrage of riots, grisly footage of the Vietnam War and its casualties, and student demonstrations televised on the nightly news. In 1969, *On the Road* won its first of twelve Emmies and first of three Peabody awards.

By 1980, the *On the Road* crew had worn out six campers. Kuralt, who had once admitted of "self-destructive" tendencies to an old girlfriend and was a lifelong chain smoker, also was showing signs of wear. He was arrested and pleaded no contest to a drunk-driving charge that year. The year before, he had started anchoring *Sunday Morning,* a leisurely ninety-minute show created around his poetic storytelling and curiosity. But anchoring meant he had to return to New York every weekend, and soon the romance of the road wore thin.

Kuralt's CBS colleagues loved him. Success didn't "pierce [Kuralt's] cloak of humility," said Cronkite. Margery Baker, an executive producer who worked with Kuralt on his last project with CBS, a program called "I Remember," said that people "glowed in his presence. He brought out the best in everyone."

But Kuralt's CBS colleagues also sensed that there was something essentially inscrutable about him. Speaking to Kuralt's inherent restlessness, Andy Rooney said, "No matter where he was, he wanted to go some place else. He loved North Carolina, but I've been in North Carolina with him, and whenever he was there, he wanted to leave." Baker added, "He was a very gentle and kind person, and in many ways delicate. . . . [You] knew that there were borders around him, and he had his private space. And you knew that there were certain places that you didn't step into." Terry Martin, another executive producer, recalled that postbroadcast dinners with Kuralt "would go on for hours, with Kuralt telling stories enthusiastically about everything." But Martin added, "I always had the feeling afterward, at the end of the dinners, that he was kind of sad to see them come to an end. . . . [I think] he was a very lonely man who really liked companionship but could only take so much of it." Following his death, the public learned of Kuralt's twenty-nine-year extramarital affair with Patricia Shannon.

Kuralt resigned from CBS in 1994. "It was a long, happy affair, and I was faithful," he wrote in his book, *Charles Kuralt's America.* "I loved CBS News ardently at first, as a boy loves a girl. . . . My passion tempered as the years went by, but inside the old flame burned. . . . Then I woke up one morning and realized I didn't love her anymore."

Kuralt yearned to get back to North Carolina, and especially Grandfather Mountain, where he had often found refuge over the years and where the mountain's owner, Hugh Morton, had given him a one-room cabin overlooking a scenic valley. He wanted to write "something that would live," Kuralt said in a 1996 interview. "It's getting a little late. I'd better get at it." The disease lupus, however, cut Kuralt's life short. He died at sixty-two of complications on July 4, 1997, in a New York City hospital and was buried in the Old Chapel Hill Cemetery on his beloved UNC campus.

Kuralt was a genuine American bard who simply permitted himself "to be detoured." Consequently, Kuralt, as a longtime colleague put it, discovered "what was best and most true about the rest of us."

Living in Asheville, Ralph Grizzle is a freelance writer and the author of Remembering Charles Kuralt.

For more information, see:

Kuralt, Charles B. Papers. Southern Historical Collection, University of North Carolina at Chapel Hill.

Grizzle, Ralph. *Remembering Charles Kuralt.* Kenilworth Media, 2000.

Kuralt, Charles. *Charles Kuralt's America.* G. P. Putnam's Sons, 1995.

———. *Dateline: America.* Harcourt Brace Jovanovich, 1979.

———. *A Life On The Road.* G. P. Putnam's Sons, 1990.

———. *North Carolina Is My Home.* Globe Pequot Press, 1986.

———. *On the Road With Charles Kuralt.* G. P. Putnam's Sons, 1985.

———. *Southerners: Portrait of a People.* Oxmoor House, 1986.

———. *To the Top of the World: The First Plaisted Polar Expedition.* Holt, Rinehart and Winston, 1968.

C. A. MCKNIGHT

By Jack Claiborne

THOUGH HIS FULL NAME was Colbert Augustus McKnight, only his mother called him that. He signed himself "C. A. McKnight," but everybody else, whether in high station or low, called him "Pete." At his birth, a neighbor said he looked "too puny" to carry a name as formal as Colbert, so he named him for Pistol Pete, a character in a newspaper comic strip. The name fit.

Pete McKnight grew up to be as open and personable as the name implied. He also was lean, fidgety, and alert to all that went on around him. He had thick, black, curly hair that bristled over his forehead and an angular, mischievous smile that lit up his whole face. He was talented in music, mathematics, languages, business, and diplomacy. He might have made a name for himself in any of a dozen fields. He chose journalism, and in the middle of the twentieth century as the editor of the *Charlotte News* and later of the *Charlotte Observer* was nationally recognized as one of the South's most effective newspaper editors.

McKnight was born in Shelby on August 19, 1916, when that cotton-farming, cotton-milling community was abuzz over the political potential of its leading families, the Webbs and the Gardners. They were busy forming "the Shelby Ring" that dominated North Carolina politics from the mid-1920s through the late 1940s. McKnight's father, John Samuel McKnight, was a wholesale grocer who introduced his three sons to hard work as laborers in his burlap-sack-lined storerooms and loading dock. His mother was Norva Proctor McKnight, a gifted teacher who taught her sons to read and appreciate literature and music. All were good students and all were college-educated. One became an *Associated Press* correspondent, principally in Latin America; another earned a Ph.D. in Spanish and taught at Davidson College.

As a boy Pete lost his right eye when a casing expelled from a .22 rifle tore through his eye, requiring him to wear thick glasses. That did not diminish his reading or his musicianship. He learned to play the piano and three brass instruments, specializing in the trombone. In 1933 he was valedictorian of his Shelby High School class and delivered a prescient address in behalf of racial justice. He intended to study Spanish and become a teacher, but postponed college for a year to learn Spanish in Havana, Cuba, where his

C. A. McKnight (Courtesy of Charlotte Observer)

brother was the *Associated Press* bureau chief. While there, he covered a hurricane that struck the island and wrote an eyewitness account of mob murders in a coup that toppled the government of President Geraldo Machado. After that Spanish took a backseat to journalism.

On his return home, he enrolled at Davidson College, where he waited tables and worked in the library. He spent summers on the *Cleveland Star,* an afternoon daily later renamed the *Shelby Star.* As the staff's fastest typist, he was assigned to take the daily *Associated Press* report, which came via telephone instead of telegraph. In 1938 he graduated from Davidson summa cum laude and Phi Beta Kappa, with a major in Spanish and a minor in economics.

He joined the *News,* then North Carolina's largest afternoon daily, as a reporter covering city, county, and federal offices. He also edited the book, radio, and music/drama pages. Throughout his life he maintained an interest in classical music, opera, and jazz. His index-card file of friends became the patrons list for the Charlotte Symphony Orchestra.

As a ham radio operator, he heard reports of the Japanese attack on Pearl Harbor before most of his colleagues and rushed to the *News* to help produce a Sunday afternoon extra that announced in big black headlines America's entry into World War II. In later years he often laughed at the memory of editing a wire service story that quoted a Hawaiian as saying, "I bet papers on the mainland exaggerate this."

In 1943 he left the *News* to become managing editor of the San Juan, Puerto Rico, *World-Journal,* an English-language newspaper circulated across the Caribbean, largely among U.S. military personnel. Within weeks he became the paper's executive editor and also served as correspondent for the *Associated Press,* the *Baltimore Sun,* and *Business Week* magazine. A year later, he returned to the *News* as news editor. In 1947 he was made managing editor and in 1949, at age thirty-three, was named editor.

It was a heady time to be on the *News,* then a crusading newspaper vigorously calling attention to social and environmental ills in Charlotte and North Carolina and urging both to plan carefully for post–World War II growth. Among McKnight's *News* colleagues were W. J. Cash, author of the celebrated *Mind of the South;* Burke Davis, who would write more than seventy-five books; Cameron Shipp and Marion Hargrove, both later Hollywood screen writers; and Harry Ashmore, one of McKnight's predecessors as editor who went on to win a Pulitzer Prize as editor of the *Arkansas Gazette* in Little Rock. In those years McKnight helped to establish two important Charlotte agencies, the City Planning Commission and later the Urban Redevelopment Commission. Both played pivotal roles in reshaping the postwar city.

As editor of the *News,* McKnight wrote editorials that crackled with energy and moral force. He relied more on facts and reason than on opinion. He was a leader in organizing the North Carolina Editorial Writers Conference that worked to strengthen newspaper editorial pages across the state. He also was a consistent winner of annual editorial-writing contests conducted by the North Carolina Press Association. One year his entries won first place, second place, and honorable mention.

His winning entry in 1951 was a long essay on the South's need to abandon separate-but-equal racial segregation. Entitled "Handwriting on the Wall," it analyzed three recent Supreme Court decisions striking down segregation at the University of Texas law school, the University of Oklahoma graduate school, and in railroad dining cars. The editorial warned that four similar lawsuits were pending against North Carolina institutions. "Let us not be lulled into thinking that our public school facilities for Negroes are equal to [those for] whites," it said. "The Education Commission report in 1948 gave convincing, well documented evidence that Negro school buildings and equipment are, in fact, woefully inferior to those for white students. No North Carolinian with any sense of justice can be happy about that." The editorial went on to say, "We have said it before. We say it again today. Segregation as an abstract moral principle cannot be defended by any intellectually or spiritually honest person."

McKnight used his perch as editor of the *News* to network with other editors across the country and especially in the South. Like other literate southerners, he had followed the rising dialogue among editors, educators, and social activists about the South's need to reform its social relations. He won the confidence of such editors as Virginius Dabney in Richmond, Ralph McGill in Atlanta, John Temple Graves in Birmingham, Mark Ethridge in Louisville, Jonathan Daniels in Raleigh, and Hodding Carter in Greenville, Miss. He read the studies of sociologists Howard Odum and Rupert Vance of the University of North Carolina at Chapel Hill, showing how segregation and racial oppression contributed to the South's ignorance and poverty. With other editors, he feared the storm that would break when the U.S. Supreme Court ruled on a series of southern and border state cases testing the constitutionality of segregated public schools.

In April 1954 he and other members of the American Society of Newspaper Editors appealed to the Ford Foundation's Fund for the Advancement of Education to help create an objective source of accurate information when the high court outlawed "separate but equal" schools. The Court ruled in May 1954, and in June McKnight took leave from the *News* to become executive director of the Southern Education Reporting Service (SERS) in Nashville. It was a clearinghouse for reliable information about southern schools and their response to federal court orders. The goal was to provide a calm voice that would prevent hysteria. McKnight recruited correspondents from the seventeen states where segregated schools existed and began publishing a monthly tabloid of facts and figures about schools, enrollments, costs, lawsuits, court orders, appeals, and desegregation proposals. The publication was distributed to thirty thousand government and school officials, federal agencies, news media, and interested citizens.

In February 1955, as he sought to build support for SERS among newspaper editors in the East and Midwest, McKnight called on Lee Hills, executive editor of the *Detroit Free Press* and chief talent hunter for John S. and James L. Knight, the brothers who six weeks earlier had purchased the *Charlotte Observer,* the Carolinas' largest newspaper. Hills asked McKnight what the Knights should do to improve the *Observer.* What McKnight recommended matched what Hills and the Knights thought. In late February, they offered him the opportunity to rebuild his erstwhile rival. McKnight accepted on condition he have six months in which to fulfill his obligations to SERS. In July McKnight took over as editor of the *Observer.*

From 1955 until 1976, Pete McKnight built the *Observer* into one of the best newspapers in the South. Just prior to the Knights' purchase of the paper, *Time* magazine had dismissed the *Observer* as "a newspapering nugget of gold that seldom glitters—a typographical mishmash—[with] the editorial voice [of] a whisper." Twenty-one years later, a few days before the sixty-year-old McKnight put down his editing duties, *Time* magazine praised the *Observer* as one of "Dixie's best dailies," along with the *Miami Herald,* the *St. Petersburg Times,* the Memphis *Commercial-Appeal,* and the Dallas *Times Herald.*

He had a rare ability to size up talent quickly and recruited dozens of bright young reporters and editors. He inspired them to produce a newspaper that was not only accurate but the conscience of its community and state. He taught with patience, humor, and trust, giving young men and women room to exercise the judgment but holding them accountable for errors. Their rewards were his smiles of approval.

Under McKnight's direction, the *Observer* leaped into covering local and Carolinas affairs, looking behind the headlines to expose conditions that gave rise to social and political inequities. The *Observer* stayed on top of the school desegregation story at every level and when the civil rights movement spread to other areas of community life, it covered those stories too. It exposed the leaders of White Citizens Councils and the Ku Klux Klan. It opened news bureaus around the Carolinas and in Washington, D.C., and reported on changing political attitudes about race and urban growth.

On its editorial pages, the *Observer* began interviewing and endorsing candidates for public office and championed a long list of causes, from court reform to reapportionment to slum clearance to urban redevelopment, to improved housing, public health, and mental health facilities. It began an aggressive coverage of business, of churches and religion, of the arts, and of higher education. As a result, the paper was a consistent winner of prizes in the annual North Carolina Press Association contests, and of national writing and reporting awards. It won at least four state press awards every year for ten years, including six in 1955, 1958, and 1963, and seven in 1964 and 1965. Nationally the paper won awards for coverage of religion, disturbed children, the Ku Klux Klan, and rural poverty. It also won a Pulitzer Prize for political cartooning.

In addition to building a powerful newspaper, McKnight exerted a leading voice in local and state affairs. He was a behind-the-scenes counsel to the Charlotte Chamber of Commerce in helping avoid the street demonstrations and violence that marked civil rights reforms in many southern cities. Having taught Spanish there, he was a leader in the movement that transformed the two-year Charlotte College into a fourth branch of the University of North Carolina, making public higher education accessible to thousands of students in the populous southern piedmont region of the state. He was a leader in the organization of the Charlotte Arts Council, in the establishment of the North Carolina Arts Council, and the North Carolina School of the Arts. He was the first president of the North Carolina Fund, an innovative program that became a model for President Lyndon Johnson's federal "War on Poverty."

He also was a leader within the newspaper profession, taking an active role in the American Society of Newspaper Editors (ASNE), editing its *Bulletin* publications, and serving as president in 1971. He directed a number of ASNE studies, including a massive 1977–81 survey to determine how newspapers could better serve the interests of their readers. He was rewarded with a life membership in the organization.

In the last ten years of his editorship, McKnight contracted glaucoma in his left eye and had difficulty reading. For months he had to have the newspaper read to him. In those periods, he grew morose and distant from the newsroom. By 1976, when he was almost blind, he relinquished the editor's chair and became associate publisher. In 1981 he retired and subsequently suffered a series of disabling strokes. He lived the last two years of his life in a nursing home, where he died in August 1986, three days before his seventieth birthday.

He was awarded honorary degrees by Colby College in 1965 and by Davidson College in 1977. He was among the first five members inducted into the North Carolina Journalism Hall of Fame at the University of North Carolina at Chapel Hill and the only non-alumnus. A six-hundred-seat lecture hall at the University of North Carolina at Charlotte is named for him, as is an endowed scholarship at UNC-Chapel Hill. He was married twice and was the father of four children.

For thirty-five years Jack Claiborne was a reporter, editor, and editorialist for the Charlotte Observer. *He was vice president and assistant to the chairman of Park Communications in Ithaca, N.Y., before becoming associate vice chancellor for university relations at the University of North Carolina at Charlotte in 1994. He is the author of five books, including a centennial history of the* Charlotte Observer, *and coeditor of an anthology entitled* Discovering North Carolina: A Tar Heel Reader.

For more information, see:

McKnight, Colbert Augustus. Papers. J. Murrey Atkins Library, University of North Carolina at Charlotte.

Claiborne, Jack. *The Charlotte Observer: Its Time and Place, 1869–1986.* University of North Carolina Press, 1986.
Gaillard, Frye. *A Dream Long Deferred.* University of North Carolina Press, 1988.
McKnight, C. A. "The Unique Experiment is Done." *Southern Education Report,* June 4, 1969.

JAMES H. SHUMAKER

By Jack Betts

FOR MORE THAN fifty years, James H. "Jim" Shumaker practiced a style of journalism founded on the simple belief that the media's job was to give the public the news without frills, fluff, or a coating to make the world go down more easily. He was an adherent of the thunder-and-lightning school of editorial writing whose style was developed from years as a reporter and editor, a job he left in the early 1970s to launch a new career as a teacher.

For the balance of the century he molded professional careers at the University of North Carolina at Chapel Hill, where an endowed teaching award was created in his honor at the School of Journalism and Mass Communication, and where he served as a one-man job referral service for hundreds of young journalists. Among his many protégés was Jeff MacNelly, the only editorial cartoonist to win three Pulitzer prizes.

Shumaker was born October 7, 1923, in Winston-Salem, but his early years were spent in Durham, where his father was a hotel manager and his mother worked in a department store. "I didn't pay much attention to them and they didn't pay much attention to me," he once quipped about his early years. As a youngster he delivered the *Durham Morning Herald,* often poring over the day's news before setting off on his rounds. He had no plans to be a newspaperman until he began writing a humor column for his high school paper. "I thought it was funny as hell but damned few other people did," he added.

He graduated from Durham High School in the spring of 1941 and, after a brief stint on a shipbuilding project at Newport News, Va., he joined the army air corps in 1942. He trained to be a pilot because "it seemed a glamorous way to go" but was busted out of flight training after he and a buddy swooped low over a passenger bus and ran it off the road near an air base in Texas as part of a victory flight. He was reassigned as a radio operator and gunner in a B-24 and shipped overseas with the 15th Air Force. Stationed in Italy, his unit was flying bombing runs over the Ploesti oil fields in Rumania when his plane was shot down over Albania. He parachuted safely—the lone survivor of his aircraft—and was captured immediately after he landed within a hundred yards of a German garrison. He spent the last year of the war as a prisoner of war—"starving but never mistreated"—

James H. Shumaker (Courtesy of North Carolina Collection)

in a stalag on the Baltic Sea that was liberated by Russian troops. A short story he later wrote about that experience—"The Remains"—won inclusion in *The Best American Short Stories* for 1953.

Upon returning to the states, he enrolled at the University of North Carolina at Chapel Hill in 1945 with hundreds of other veterans and began taking journalism courses. In his junior year he took a job at the *Durham Morning Herald* covering city hall. It paid twenty-four dollars a week and "I pretended to be going to college," he later said. He failed to graduate but not due to poor academic performance. Rather, a stubborn streak that would later shape his career in other ways kept him from his degree. He was due to pick up his diploma when he was informed by the university administration that he lacked a course in hygiene. He refused to return to fulfill the requirements and his degree was withheld until the require- ment was waived twenty years later by UNC Presi- dent William Friday, who qualified Shumaker by ask- ing him to identify a bar of soap.

Shumaker enrolled briefly at the Graduate School of Journalism at Columbia University in New York after leaving Chapel Hill but soon returned to Char- lotte, where he joined the *Associated Press* as night edi- tor for both Carolinas. "I stuck with it for three years and hated every minute of it," he groused years later. He returned to the *Morning Herald* as state editor in the early 1950s and became managing editor a few years later. He delighted in perfecting his gruff ex- terior and once asked a governor at a press confer- ence, "Governor, you wouldn't bull fertilizer us, would you?"

Shumaker once described himself as a "yellow-dog Democrat"—the sort who would vote for an old yel- low dog before voting for a Republican. His aversion to the GOP came from growing up during the De- pression, he said, when Franklin D. Roosevelt helped lead the country out of the economic morass.

In 1959 he became editor of the *Chapel Hill Weekly,* where Shumaker displayed editorial views that he called "pretty liberal," even though he shared the ed- itorial page with a young self-professed conservative named Jeff MacNelly. MacNelly had never drawn an editorial cartoon when he asked Shumaker for work. Over the next few years, he developed a distinctive detailed style of drawing and editorial perspective that won him a job at the Richmond newspapers, where his work eventually ended up in syndication and was seen around the world. During his career MacNelly won an unprecedented three Pulitzer prizes at the same time he was drawing a comic strip he called "Shoe" that was based in part on his old mentor from Chapel Hill. The strip's central character was "Purple Martin Shoemaker," a tennis-shoe-wearing, cigar- smoking columnist for the *Treetops Tattler Tribune.*

"We had a helluva operating procedure," Shumaker recalled of his time with MacNelly. "I'd draw these stick figures and say 'This is what I want a cartoon on.' He'd grin and go out and sit down at his drafting table and about fifteen minutes later he'd come back in with a finished cartoon system, sometimes a com- pleted idea. . . . Just absolutely incredible how fast he was."

Shumaker stayed at the *Weekly* for fifteen years— "constantly fighting with owner and publisher Orville Campbell"—before leaving in 1974. (For a few months in 1966 he left North Carolina to become editor of the *Boca Raton News,* but returned to the *Weekly* within weeks after deciding that the wealthy shores of south Florida were not to his liking.) He had begun teach- ing editorial writing in 1972 at the journalism school and added a second course after leaving the *Weekly.* In addition to teaching, he was host of the public af- fairs program called *North Carolina News Conference* on WUNC-TV, wrote a column for the *Charlotte Observer,* and contributed editorials for a succession of North Carolina newspapers, including the *Fayetteville Observer.* During a break from teaching in 1979 and 1980 he was editorial page editor of the *Wilmington Star-News,* but returned to Chapel Hill in 1980 as a full-time fac- ulty member.

During his career he won numerous journalism awards, including North Carolina Press Association prizes for spot news, features, community service, and editorials, National Newspaper Association awards for editorials, general excellence, typography, local news coverage, and freedom of information, and Golden Quill Awards for editorial writing. He also held a number of offices in professional organizations, such as the *Associated Press* Managing Editors Associa- tion, the North Carolina *AP* News Council, and the North Carolina Press Association.

Besides his distinctive personality and a tall (six- two), thin frame, Shumaker had other trademarks. His teaching uniform comprised wrinkled khaki pants and a white shirt that he often accompanied by tennis shoes and, when he was still smoking, a collection of cigars. Before health problems caught up with him, he was an enthusiastic smoker and drinker who once said that he began drinking when it got dark and didn't quit until bedtime—sometimes around 8 A.M.

His columns frequently reflected the rhythms of life at a certain filling station in Chatham County where the snack of choice was an RC Cola and a Moon Pie. He also wrote about the joys of living on the beach for a time in Brunswick County. Good old boys would talk about the world and the clay feet of their leaders. But his outlook on the news business remained fo- cused on the central mission of good journalism.

"The most important thing about journalism is to tell people what in the hell is going on," he preached to his students. While he had considerable experience in breaking news, Shumaker's favorite place to dis- play his work was on the editorial page, where he had more latitude. "I enjoyed that, and to a certain extent I enjoyed telling people what the hell to think," he added. "I also enjoyed all the hell you catch for it, too. . . . Good God Almighty, they'd come down to the paper and slam the damn paper down on the floor and stomp on it and shit like that. . . . Yeah, I loved that. They wouldn't have missed that paper for any- thing in the world."

He had no use for editorial pages without a point of view, a characteristic that became commonplace in later years of corporate journalism. Shumaker said, "A good editorial should provide some insight into a situation, and by all means, if you're going to be an editorial writer, come down on one side or another."

Editorial page editors "ought to be prepared to quit on any given day" when there is a matter of principle involved and they cannot agree with a publisher. When Shumaker was at the *Weekly,* Orville Campbell wanted to read his editorials before they were published, and Shoemaker refused. "And I said, 'read 'em like everybody else,'" when they appear in the paper.

Shumaker began his teaching career at a time when most of his students planned on careers in newspapers. Twenty-eight years later, a majority was interested in other areas of communications, such as advertising or public relations. Newspapers had lost their glamour, perhaps because salaries were not competitive. And students arrived on campus bright enough to operate a computer but unprepared for the rigor and discipline of deadline writing. "You tell them, 'Pronouns and antecedents should agree.' They don't know what the hell you are talking about," he laughed. "Most of our students come out of the North Carolina public schools. And what they are not teaching [about writing] in those schools is criminal."

Shumaker said he could not explain how he came to be regarded as an effective teacher, but he won several teaching awards on campus, including the Tanner Award for excellence in teaching undergraduate courses and another teaching excellence award from graduating seniors. "We have a lot of fun in my classes. I try to keep it light. The stuff I teach, editorial writing and news writing. The only way anybody learns editorial writing is by writing editorials. The way you learn news writing is by doing reporting. I go over their papers carefully, point out where I think they have made mistakes and what I think of their mistakes, and they learn that way. You don't teach editorial writing by standing up there and lecturing for an hour and a half. I work the hell out of them."

He also insisted on punctuality. Students who arrived late for his class found themselves locked out, at least for a while. "I don't give a damn about appearance" of students, he said, but he demanded that they arrive on time. He often let students "cool their heels" until he was ready to admit them to his classroom. When the journalism school moved to larger and nicer quarters in 1999, he complained that the classroom doors did not have locks.

A crusty curmudgeon, Shumaker, nonetheless, became a favorite of students and professional journalists, scores of whom benefited from his assistance to land their first jobs. In 1992, a group of his former students mounted a campaign to raise an endowment for the James H. Shumaker Term Professorship, a rotating award that provides a salary stipend for a designated teacher for demonstrated teaching excellence. The campaign to endow the professorship was publicized in the "Moon Pie Shulympics" in 1992, a send-up of an Olympics-style athletic competition featuring the use of Moon Pies supplied by the Chattanooga-based manufacturer of the southern snack.

Despite an array of health problems—two double bypass heart operations, one for prostate cancer, a hernia repair, and one operation to deal with a stroke—Shumaker remained in the classroom "I enjoy the young people. I love the students."

Would he still advise young people to go into journalism as a young Jim Shumaker did half a century earlier? "Oh, hell, yeah. I can't imagine any more enjoyable work. . . . What the hell, you can probably make more money selling insurance, but who wants to do that?" Newspapering, he said, was "a brand new adventure every day, and I always looked forward to it every damned day, even hung over."

After a long period of declining health while maintaining his schedule of two classes at UNC-Chapel Hill, Shumaker was admitted to UNC Hospitals in the fall of 2000, where doctors discovered that cancer had spread into his brain, shoulder blade, liver, lungs, and femur. He died on December 19, 2000, and was buried following a funeral service at Mount Hermon Baptist Church in Durham on December 22, 2000.

Jack Betts, an associate editor of the Charlotte Observer, *has written about North Carolina for more than thirty years. He has been a Washington and Raleigh correspondent for the* Greensboro Daily News, *editor of* North Carolina Insight *magazine, a publication of the North Carolina Center for Public Policy Research, and a columnist and editorial writer for the* Charlotte Observer *since 1992.*

For more information, see:
Betts, Jack. "R.I.P. SHU." *Charlotte Observer,* December 21, 2000.
Jenkins, Jim. "Shumaker's Legacy of and for Generations." *News and Observer,* December 28, 2000.
Norwood, Allen, and David Perlmutt. "Beloved Teacher, 77, Dies of Cancer." *Charlotte Observer,* December 20, 2000.
Perlmutt, David. "UNC's Shumaker Takes on Cancer Fight." *Charlotte Observer,* November 28, 2000.

CAPUS M. WAYNICK

By Owen Covington

CAPUS M. WAYNICK, who was called a "Tar Heel edition of a Renaissance man" by some, devoted more than fifty years of his life to public service as a newspaper editor, public official, financial planner, ambassador, and civil and labor rights troubleshooter for North Carolina governors from O. Max Gardner to Terry Sanford.

Waynick was born on December 23, 1889, one of eight children to James and Anna Waynick on the family farm in Rockingham County. When he was thirteen, his parents moved the family to Greensboro so their children could take advantage of the better schools. Capus graduated from Greensboro High School in 1907 and went on to the University of North Carolina in Chapel Hill. He left after his sophomore year, however, because, he later said, he became "disillusioned with higher education."

Waynick's thirty-year career in journalism began in 1911, when he took a job as a reporter for the *Greensboro Record.* What would be an off and on career had barely begun before he took a job peddling steel-bound toilets. In 1914, the same year he met his future wife, Elizabeth McBee, he joined the *Charlotte Observer* but left to try his hand at several newspapers in the Carolinas. In 1918, Waynick joined the army, serving as a second lieutenant until war's end, when he bought an interest in the *Greensboro Record,* where he was publisher for several years until selling his interest in 1922. The following year the Waynicks settled in High Point, a city they would adopt as their hometown and remain close to for the rest of their lives.

He got his first taste of political life when he was elected to the state house of representatives in 1931, one of many jobs he did not seek. Local Democrats put his name on the ballot after a High Point businessman running for the post committed suicide shortly before the election. Waynick made two speeches in two days and was elected. "These public jobs I've held, I've never held one that I asked for, or ever taken one without first refusing it, including an ambassadorship," Waynick said 1974. "Somehow I just sat around and they made me offers. I didn't seek any of them, didn't ask for any of them."

Waynick was elected to the state senate in 1933 and while there cast the deciding vote for a state sales tax, something he had argued against two years earlier when he was in the lower chamber. "There are some

Capus M. Waynick (Courtesy of High Point Enterprise)

who still regard me as a turncoat on the tax," Waynick said in a 1969 newspaper article. "But it was the only way I could see of raising needed funds to guarantee a six-month, state-supported public school system." Throughout his service in the General Assembly, Waynick maintained his job at the *High Point Enterprise,* but the appointment to various state posts in 1933 and 1934 and increasing involvement in public service would end his career at the paper for a short time.

Waynick was appointed to direct the National Reemployment Service for North Carolina in 1933, and helped find jobs for 300,000 Tar Heels during the worst years of the Depression. He resigned that job to return to the *Enterprise* in 1934, but was appointed chairman of the State Highway Commission. He also served as chairman of the State Planning Board and in 1937 was named director of the state's Purchase and Contract Division.

Waynick headed the paper until 1942 when he entered the field of public health. He was placed in charge of organizing and operating a program called the Venereal Disease Education Institute, a joint project of the United States Public Health Service and the Z. Smith Reynolds Foundation. The institute, which later became the Health Education Institute, produced and distributed thousands of health information materials to the armed services during World War II. Waynick left the Health Education Institute in 1948 only to find himself increasingly involved in North Carolina politics.

In 1948, W. Kerr Scott, a populist and reform-minded farmer from Alamance County, asked Waynick to manage his campaign for governor. "Scott came to me and asked me if I would take over his campaign. I told him I couldn't think of it," Waynick said later. "Finally Scott came to me and he said, 'I have a funny feeling that if you'll join me, I'll win and if you don't, I can't.'" Waynick took the position, and Scott won the Democratic Party nomination, defeating state treasurer Charles Johnson, the favorite of established party leaders.

As was the custom, Scott named Waynick to chair the state Democratic Party, which was burdened with the candidacy of President Harry Truman, whose civil rights record had made him a most unpopular figure in the South. Even Scott said he couldn't help Truman and claimed he had "his own furrow to plow." Members of the state's congressional delegation said their constituents were vehemently opposed to some of Truman's progressive views. "When I was made chairman of the party in 1948, our ticket was scared to death," Waynick later said. "I heard them all out, you know. I said, 'Gentlemen, I'm chairman of the party in this state and we are going to fight for the ticket from top to bottom.'" Waynick put all his efforts behind Truman, and North Carolina gave Truman one of the largest majorities of any state in the nation.

Truman sent a messenger to Waynick shortly after the election and asked him what he wanted in the government, to which Waynick replied, "'Nothing but four years of good government from you.' I told him I had a job." At Truman's insistence, Waynick finally agreed to become ambassador to Nicaragua in 1949. "I told my wife, 'Let's take this thing down in Nicaragua. It looks like the least of the four [positions offered], and try our Spanish on the natives and take a vacation at the expense of the American public,'" Waynick said later. "So that's how I became am-

bassador." He served for two years before moving to Colombia in 1951 to become ambassador there. During his time in both countries, he was awarded the countries' highest honors for his work. Among the programs he initiated while in South America were a vocational school in Nicaragua and an agricultural college in Colombia.

Waynick realized the importance of Latin American countries to the United States economy and pushed for closer economic and cultural relations with those countries. "The ties that endure between men and between nations are economic," Waynick told the High Point Kiwanis Club in 1954. "Our friendship and regard in which we are held by other nations is in direct proportion to our economic ties to those nations," he said. "Also, it is well to increase our cultural ties, particularly with relation to the education in this country of technicians from other countries."

This view was molded in part by Waynick's role in 1950 as the leader of President Truman's new Point Four Program. The program, which took its name from the fourth of four "major courses of action" proposed in Truman's 1949 inaugural address, offered technical aid in agriculture, health, education, and transportation to underdeveloped countries to help increase their economic standing. Waynick refused to take the job as permanent director of the program and returned to complete his assignment in Nicaragua. However, he did take many of the Point Four Program ideas back with him. He arranged to have a commission from the International Bank analyze the fiscal condition of Nicaragua and to make recommendations, which resulted in the improvement of the country's fiscal practices and credit.

When Waynick resigned his post in Colombia in 1953, North Carolina politicians speculated about his reentry into state politics. He dispelled those rumors, telling a reporter he intended to rest and "literally build some fences around my farm at High Point. We [he and his wife] wanted to be in North Carolina in the fall." The speculation was not completely without justification. In 1952, Waynick was visited in Colombia by Scott, and according to Waynick, the governor spent the entire day urging him to return to North Carolina and run as his successor. Waynick refused, saying he was very interested in what he was doing in Colombia and felt he had unfinished business there.

After a two-year hiatus from public life, Waynick accepted the offer of Governor Luther Hodges in 1955 to head the state's newly formed Small Industries Program. "When called upon to serve his state by developing a small industries plan, Mr. Waynick went to the work with great enthusiasm," Hodges wrote in his 1962 biography. "He grasped the problem quickly, did a far-reaching survey under the guidance of the governor's Small Industry Committee, and came in with the report." With this program, Waynick proposed and promoted the establishment of the North Carolina Business Development Corporation, which with $10 million in lending power helped advance small industries throughout the state.

In July 1957, Hodges appointed him state adjutant general following the resignation of John Hall Manning. As leader of the North Carolina National Guard, the post had most often been held by a man with a strong military background. Hodges tried to offset any uproar from the military by immediately defending his choice of Waynick, saying, "I am confident . . . that I will have a seasoned public servant whose previous work with our state government has convinced me he will aid greatly not only in the usual conventional military duties, but also in additional ones that I expect to give him."

Waynick left state government in 1961 for New York, where he was executive vice president of the Richardson Foundation, a job he held for three years when he returned to High Point and retirement. While he was with the Richardson Foundation, he helped push through grant proposals from Governor Terry Sanford. Among the grants the foundation approved was one for $125,000 to fund a state film board, which produced feature-length films about subjects related to the state.

When Waynick returned to North Carolina in 1963, he found a state wrestling with its segregationist past. North Carolina had been slow to integrate its school systems following the Supreme Court's 1954 decision that declared segregated schools were inherently unequal. Protests staged by the black community in High Point were becoming more frequent and intense in the spring of 1963 when Waynick returned. The day before one mass demonstration, Waynick voiced his opinion of the status of race relations in the city, the state, and the South in an article in the *Enterprise*. "Let all of us remember that the great problem of the South must be solved in such a way as to extend justice to all regardless of race or color," he said. "The great issue for us is not how to meet Negro demands grudgingly, but how far can we go to lift the stigma of 'second-class citizenship' from a large percentage of our people with a minimum impairment of education and other social problems," he said. "Let's remember that we cannot build a powerful and rich state without developing the potential of all our people."

Waynick called for a tolerant attitude toward the demonstrations, which centered around the desegregation of the city's movie theaters, restaurants, and hotels, and discouraged violent acts by counter-demonstrators. Waynick was soon appointed chairman of the High Point Biracial Committee, which had just been formed by Mayor Floyd Mehan to deal with race relations. As chairman, Waynick called on civic clubs, the Ministerial Alliance, businessmen, and other community leaders to take a "positive position" on the introduction of integration into High Point. "We would welcome stands in favor of integration which will relieve the Negro citizens of the feeling that they are not given a fair deal," he told the *Enterprise* in June 1963. "In order to accomplish anything important, influential citizens must act to create an atmosphere conducive to the relief of this situation."

The committee's work proved successful in heading off violent confrontations during the summer through public forums, almost daily meetings, and the preparation of a report recommending a course of action for peaceful integration in High Point. Waynick advised the city to deal with the issues. "These problems cannot be swept under a rug," Waynick said, according to newspaper accounts. "The things we have recommended are inevitable. There is no question of whether these things are going to be done, but the only question is the spirit in which it is done."

Waynick's negotiating of the civil rights issue was not the first time he had helped restore calm to his city. In 1932, Governor O. Max Gardner had depended on Waynick to bring an end to a bitter labor dispute that idled textile mills and furniture factories in High Point and Thomasville.

In 1963, another governor called. Terry Sanford was seeking a way to avoid further confrontation in the streets that threatened to become violent in cities across the state. Amid allegations from civil rights leaders that he was dragging his feet, the governor named Waynick to chair a new statewide biracial group called the Good Neighbor Council and serve as his chief counselor on civil rights issues. Waynick said early on he had "recognized the beginning of a new day and that the quicker we conformed to reasonable acceptance of changing circumstances and philosophy, the better it would be for everybody concerned." He once told a group of African American youth that if he were black he would be demonstrating too.

An article in the *Enterprise* that year described Waynick's "retirement" schedule, which included extended periods away from his High Point home, moving throughout the state talking with both civic and business leaders. "This is the greatest drama of the century," he told a youth group. "Do you want to be part of the problem or part of the cure?" He was later named to the Citizens Committee for Community Relations, an advisory committee to President Lyndon Johnson on racial matters throughout the country.

Waynick finally retired to his home on Fieldstone Farm in High Point in 1965 at the age of seventy-six. In 1971, he received the North Carolina Award, the highest honor bestowed by the state, and was named a "distinguished alumnus" by the University of North Carolina the following year.

Waynick died on September 7, 1986, at the age of ninety-six. Among those at his funeral was Sanford, who was campaigning for the U.S. Senate after his retirement as president of Duke University. Sanford gave a lot of the credit for the success of North Carolina's movement toward integration to Waynick, saying that Waynick's message was "We are not going to have confrontations. He did that in a superb way. Absolutely no state handled it better than North Carolina, and a tremendous part of the credit goes to Capus Waynick."

Another mourner, Mary Seymour, a former state legislator from Greensboro, said Waynick "gave himself so generously and so aggressively for the causes he believed in. There just aren't many leaders like that today."

Owen Covington began his newspaper career as a criminal justice reporter for the High Point Enterprise. *He is a 1996 graduate of Davidson College and a graduate student at UNC-Chapel Hill School of Journalism and Mass Communications.*

For more information, see:

Waynick, Capus. Interview with Bill Finger, February 4, 1974. Southern Oral History Program, Southern Historical Collection, University of North Carolina at Chapel Hill.

———. Papers. J. Y. Joyner Library, East Carolina University.

Hodges, Luther H. *Businessman in the Statehouse.* University of North Carolina Press, 1962.

McPherson, Holt. *High Pointers of High Point.* High Point Chamber of Commerce, 1972.

Waynick, Capus. *North Carolina Roads and Their Builders.* Superior Stone, 1952.

MEDICINE

WHEN NORTH CAROLINA'S young men reported for military service during World War II, the record they wrote at the receiving station was one that would reveal the deplorable condition of medical and health care in a state that took great pride in the quality of life. Forty percent of the white draftees and 60 percent of the black draftees were found to be unfit for military service. A closer look at the records also showed a state where a third of the counties did not have a single hospital bed and infant mortality was among the highest in the nation.

Numbers like these galvanized one of the most remarkable coalitions of public figures, who rallied behind the Good Health Campaign that popular song man and bandleader Kay Kyser chaired. The result was legislation that set the stage for construction of hospitals and clinics throughout the state and the expansion of the University of North Carolina medical school.

The conversion of the university's two-year medical program into a full four-year medical school was the responsibility of Dr. W. Reece Berryhill. He presided over an investment in health affairs education that began in the late 1940s and continued for twenty years. Among the programs Berryhill worked for was the state's comprehensive and unmatched Area Health Education Center system.

Before the war, local communities struggled the best they could and often depended on the dedication of caring physicians like Dr. Mary Sloop, who spent most of her adult life providing medical care and more to the people of the North Carolina mountains. She received national recognition when, at age seventy-eight, she was named the American Mother of the Year.

She followed in the footsteps of Dr. Annie Alexander of Charlotte, who was a pioneering doctor licensed to practice in an era when a woman doctor performing surgery in hospitals or practicing medicine in the South was unthinkable.

Dr. Watson S. Rankin was an early leader in the field of public health and personally shaped medical care in the Carolinas. He worked to eradicate hookworm, and had three distinguished careers that alone would make him one of North Carolina's leading twentieth-century physicians, but listing only those careers would ignore some of his most significant achievements. During his lifetime, he was the second dean of the Wake Forest College School of Medicine, the first full-time state health director, and founder of the hospitals and orphans section of the Duke Endowment, a major pillar of support for Carolinas hospitals for three-quarters of a century.

Rankin worked closely with Dr. Wilburt Cornell Davison, the first dean of the Duke University School of Medicine, who led the school from its formative years into the world of modern medicine. Davison's concern extended beyond the classroom. Even before the school enrolled its first class, he and Durham businessman George Watts Hill proposed the formation of a group health plan.

It was shelved during the early years of the Depression but was revived in 1933 as the Hospital Care Association.

Drs. Aaron Moore and Stanford Warren of Durham devoted their careers to the extension of medical care to African American citizens in Durham, where their work resulted in the building and growth of Lincoln Hospital, which at its peak was considered one of the finest hospitals devoted to serving African Americans in the South.

The hospital, begun with a gift from Washington Duke, who personally underwrote Warren's education and training, was accredited by the American Medical Association for internship training and approved as a class "A" hospital by the American College of Surgeons. The state of North Carolina rated the nurses training school a class "A" program.

Dr. James E. Davis, who died in 1997 at the age of seventy-nine, was one of the most outstanding physicians of his day. The only North Carolinian to be elected president of the American Medical Association, Davis repeatedly brought major change to medicine. He is considered the father of ambulatory surgery in North Carolina. He led the creation of a medical liability insurance company when the nation's principal malpractice insurer pulled out of North Carolina. He fostered a North Carolina Institute of Medicine modeled partly on the prestigious national Institute of Medicine. He conceived the City of Medicine, a concept that Durham—whose Watts Hospital was one of the finest in the South for fifty years—marketed successfully to attract numerous medically related companies and revitalize its economy.

Heart surgeons Paul Sanger and Francis Robiczek, both of Charlotte, also attracted national acclaim. Sanger developed the first artificial arteries in 1955 and supplied them to a number of noted heart surgeons, including Dr. Michael DeBakey of Houston. Robiczek left his native Hungary in 1956 and ended up in Charlotte, where he built a heart-lung machine and became one of the nation's best-known heart surgeons.

Dr. Eugene Stead was another outstanding physician/educator during the past century. A professor of internal medicine at Duke during the 1940s, 1950s, and 1960s, Stead trained many of the state's leading doctors. He was famous for Sunday rounds known as "Stead's Sunday School." His early interest in cardiovascular research led Duke to the excellence it enjoys today in that field of medicine.

Dr. Eloise Lewis was the founder and first dean of the School of Nursing at the University of North Carolina at Greensboro in 1966, where she served until her retirement in 1985. A native of Pageland, S.C., Lewis attended Winthrop College and then received her nursing degree at Vanderbilt University, her master's in education from the University of Pennsylvania, and her Ph.D. in education from Duke University. In 1945, she held the rank of first lieutenant and assistant director of the Cadet Nurse Corps in the U.S. Army Nurse Corps at Valley Forge General Hospital. She helped develop the School of Nursing at the University of North Carolina at Chapel Hill and served as a faculty member in the School of Nursing at the University of Pennsylvania.

ANNIE L. ALEXANDER

By Mary Kratt

S HE WAS a small woman with eyes the color of blue marbles, a pioneer doctor licensed to practice in an era when a woman doctor performing surgery in hospitals or practicing medicine in the South was unthinkable. Unfazed by the mindset, she quietly made the impossible a reality.

"Dr. Annie," as she was called in her home county, was born January 10, 1864, at her father's family homeplace about three miles northwest of Huntersville. Hers was a well-known Scotch-Irish clan of colonial-era settlers of the Carolina piedmont. Two were patriots during the American Revolution: the Reverend Alexander Craighead and the Reverend David Caldwell. Her mother was Ann Wall Lowrie. Her father, Dr. John Brevard Alexander, was a well-known physician and author who wrote two books: *The History of Mecklenburg County from 1740–1900* and *Reminiscences of the Last Sixty Years*.

Young Annie received her early education by tutor. Annie overheard her physician father tell his wife a tragic story one night after returning from a house call to one of his patients. The young woman had been too embarrassed to seek medical treatment from a man and had died. "Annie must be a doctor and help these people," she heard her father say. Her mother supposedly replied, "But think of the expense, and then she'll marry and that will be the end of it." Her father then said, "She must never marry. She will serve humanity."

Following this edict, the tutor and her father prepared Annie for entry to Woman's Medical College in Philadelphia. She was seventeen, fair-skinned with freckles, and sandy-colored natural curls. She remembered the hue and cry from some of her relatives when she left. Outraged by her radical departure from feminine propriety, they "asked her name not be mentioned in their presence." In letters to her father, young Annie wrote with awe and great enthusiasm about her experiences in surgery and treating patients.

In 1884, she declared: "I have performed seven operations. . . . I think I will make a surgeon. . . . I feel and imagine I look very professional sometimes, especially when I am operating. . . . I thought I would never be able to put a knife on human flesh." These were the days in medicine when surgery was a skill expected of any doctor.

Annie found the students at the prestigious Jeffer-

Annie L. Alexander (Courtesy of Robinson-Spangler Carolina Room, Public Library of Charlotte-Mecklenburg County)

son Medical College near her medical school expressed contempt for female medical students. The year she graduated, when she was twenty, three male medical students crossed the street to avoid her and one spat in her direction.

She interned a year at her medical school and became an assistant teacher of anatomy at the Woman's College of Baltimore, Md. When she obtained her license in 1885 from the Maryland Board of Medical Examiners, she had earned the distinction of being the only woman in the class of one hundred and she made the highest grade. Subsequently she did graduate work at New York Polyclinic. She considered practicing in other urban centers such as Atlanta, but returned to North Carolina in 1887 to become the first licensed female physician in the South.

In becoming a physician, she was one of the few women in America entering the traditionally male-dominated fields of medicine, law, dentistry, and phar-

337

macy. Even in 1900, less than 3 percent of North Carolina women workers were in these professions. Although Dr. Annie wrote of seven white women and one black woman practicing in the state in 1900, the census reports twenty-two, and by 1910, fifty-six, not noting, however, whether they were licensed.

In her writings and speeches later in her career, Dr. Annie commented on the lack of female physicians in a fictionalized account of a young woman physician and her experience in a piece entitled "Dr. Katherine":

"Study medicine! Be a doctor! Who ever heard of such a thing?"

"Are you in earnest or romancing?" asked Mary.

"Yes, I am going to be a doctor. It has been father's desire all my life, that I should be a physician."

"Your father must be a madman to allow such a thing or to consider it for a moment," said Nettie Bell.

"The idea of a daughter in a Southern family doing anything outside of home or the school room was unheard of. And to bring the idea closer home, for Katherine Caldwell, the petted daughter of Dr. and Mrs. Caldwell, to study medicine was shocking."

In May 1887 this notice appeared in a Charlotte newspaper: "A nice young female physician, Miss Annie Lowrie Alexander, has located in this city ready to practice among women and children and consult about female disorders generally. . . . She has been educated in the best Medical schools of the country. Her office is at Mrs. Lathan's nearly opposite the post office."

Dr. Annie boarded for a time, and in 1889 made a ten-dollar downpayment on a one-story house at 410 North Tryon Street, where she lived and kept office hours. She later added an upper story. Sometimes patients stayed over or the rooms were rented to boarders, who were usually secretaries or young single women. For a time, a newly widowed relative and her children moved into the house. In 1890, Annie's elderly parents moved from near Huntersville to live with her on North Tryon Street, where her father continued to work on his history of Mecklenburg County. Along with her address, her letterhead in the 1890s noted: "Office hours 9 A.M. to 12 P.M., 3–4:15 P.M."

Dr. Annie became a familiar sight in a carriage pulled by her horse, Conrad. Although her father approved of modern professional women, he did not approve of automobiles, so she delayed purchasing one until he died in 1911. Her Model T Ford was housed in the former stable behind her house where her nurse, Ona Pope, ran the office and doubled as housekeeper.

In an essay in the early 1900s, she wrote, "This pioneer woman in North Carolina was received with cold indifference by the professions and open curiosity by the laity." Her practice grew slowly and "it was more than two years before she was self-supportive." When one of the families she treated left a small orphan son named Robert Payne, she adopted him as her ward, and he became Bob Alexander. He recalled that she was very strict, but allowed him to have an adventurous childhood.

Young Bob often went with Dr. Annie on house calls. Occasionally he slept in the seat of her Model T until her mission was completed. Also accompanying her on calls was a young black man she had hired to crank the car. Her small stature and scars on her lungs from a bout with pneumonia and tuberculosis made her reluctant to aggravate her condition. So her aide cranked the car, rode with her to calls, stayed with her until she returned, and cranked the car again. This continued until she bought a self-starting car.

Her notebooks show that most of her patients were women and children, but Dr. Annie's endeavors reached far beyond medical treatment. She served on the staff of Presbyterian Hospital and St. Peter's Hospital, and for twenty-three years was physician for Charlotte's Presbyterian College for Women (later Queens College). During World War I when thousands of soldiers were in training at Camp Greene just west of Charlotte, she was appointed acting assistant surgeon, her primary duty being the inspection of thousands of public school children. Her inspections located cases of trachoma in one school and her prompt attention reportedly averted permanent eye damage for many.

Among the treasured memorabilia of Dr. Annie, owned by her relatives, was a long, narrow, foot-high wooden stool that Dr. J. B. Alexander made for his diminutive daughter to stand on when she operated on or examined patients. She is reported to have "treated everybody. She did not discriminate."

She served as president of the Mecklenburg Medical Society and a vice president of the Women's Physicians of the Southern Medical Association. In addition to her membership in the Daughters of the American Revolution, the Colonial Dames, the United Daughters of the Confederacy, and the Charlotte Woman's Club, she was an honorary member of the North Carolina Medical Society and the Southern Medical Society. She served as board member and longtime physician to the Florence Crittendon Home and was the examining physician for the physical education department of the YWCA, where for many years she was a member of the managing board. She fully funded the college education of several young people, including her nieces, and provided scholarships for the premedical studies of young Chinese women through the foreign mission organization of the Presbyterian Church U.S. One Charlottean recalled, "She used her money to help others. She was very religious."

When Dr. Annie died of pneumonia on October 16, 1929, at age sixty-five, members of the Mecklenburg Medical Association were honorary pallbearers at her funeral at First Presbyterian Church. Her obituary noted not only her extensive community and professional service, her prominent family connections and heritage, but also the great respect she had earned from other members of her profession, "despite the prejudice then current against women physicians."

In her father's history of the county, which chronicles prominent preachers, lawyers, and doctors, Dr. J. B. Alexander briefly noted his own medical tenure as surgeon for the Confederate army, his practice, and concluded with pride that his "second daughter was the first woman south of the Potomac that ever graduated in medicine—Dr. Annie L. Alexander. She is located in Charlotte, and has succeeded equal to expectations. . . . has been a successful practitioner . . . and has led the way in this new venture in all the Southern states where many have since followed, and are meeting with success in their new calling." As the Medical Society of the State of North Carolina noted in 1931 about Dr. Annie, "With her it was not an experiment. . . . She was recognized as a doctor of completed education at the outset of her professional career, establishing high rank, which was maintained to the end."

Mary Kratt of Charlotte is the author of numerous books of poetry, history, and biography. Twice winner of the Peace Prize–History Book Award from the N.C. Society of Historians, she received the 1999 Brockman/Campbell award for her poetry book, Small Potatoes, *and a 1996 N.C. Arts Council grant for a residency at the MacDowell Colony in New Hampshire. Her books about Charlotte include* Charlotte: Spirit of the New South *and* Remembering Charlotte: Postcards of a New South City.

For more information, see:
Blythe, LeGette. "Old Timers Recall Dr. Annie Alexander." *Charlotte Observer,* January 21, 1940.
Kratt, Mary. "The Lady Doctor." In *A Little Charlotte Scrapbook.* Briarpatch Press, 1990.
Pendleton, James D. "Dr. Annie, Mecklenburg's First Lady Doctor." *Charlotte Magazine,* July–August 1974.
Smith, Margaret Supplee, and Emily Herring Wilson. *North Carolina Women: Making History.* University of North Carolina Press, 1999.
Strong, Charles M. *History of Mecklenburg County Medicine.* 1902.

W. REECE BERRYHILL

By Robert Conn

TWO TOWERING ACHIEVEMENTS mark the life of Dr. Reece Berryhill: converting the University of North Carolina School of Medicine from two to four years while keeping it in Chapel Hill, and laying the groundwork for the state's comprehensive and unmatched Area Health Education Center (AHEC) system. Keeping the medical school *"in Chapel Hill"* was a signal achievement, according to several observers, amidst ambitions that led to some furious legislative battles to place the four-year school in Winston-Salem, Greensboro, or Charlotte. To win, Berryhill called on a network of friends from his undergraduate days at Chapel Hill.

And yet, just a few years later, he fostered a system of statewide hospital affiliations with UNC to expand training opportunities for doctors that included two of these competing cities. That led directly to the AHECs, a system that later reached all one hundred counties and included participation by the rival medical schools of Duke, Wake Forest, and East Carolina universities.

The two achievements are of such magnitude that his biographers had a hard time determining which is more important. William B. Blythe, M.D., said, "Over the short haul, the AHEC concept is probably more important, but I think that having a first class medical school is probably more important over the long haul." Meanwhile, Christopher C. Fordham III, M.D., both a former dean of the medical school and former UNC chancellor, declared, "Both are so important that it is hard to evaluate." After a pause, he added, "I would rate the number one contribution of Dr. Berryhill as getting the medical school on the university campus. Having an academic medical center on an elite state-owned campus was a moment of genius for Dr. Berryhill and his confreres across the state. It was a tough battle but they won it and I think his tenacity and intelligence were critical."

When Walter Reece Berryhill became dean of the school of medicine in 1941 (after serving a year as acting dean), he set the establishment of the four-year school as his primary objective. He first declined the post, then accepted only a five-year term, "a length of time he felt reasonable for determining the real interest of the university in expanding the school and its willingness to obtain the financial support necessary," Berryhill wrote in *Medical Education in North Caro-*

W. Reece Berryhill (Courtesy of Charlotte Observer)

lina: The First Hundred Years. "This decision was made only after he had received a firm commitment from the administration that a primary goal of the university was to expand the school when adequate financing became available and to seek such funds from the state and from private sources."

Though Berryhill conceded in the book's introduction that "the account of the years 1941–1964 is in a measure, and perhaps inevitably so, autobiographical," he always referred to himself in the third person, and others claimed the book deliberately downplayed Berryhill's role.

According to the book, the fight over location began under Berryhill's predecessor as dean, William D. MacNider, M.D., when the school received a quiet feeler from the Gray family about using funds from the Bowman Gray Foundation to relocate the medical school to Winston-Salem. "This was vigorously opposed by Dr. MacNider, who is quoted as saying that 'if the medical school was not located in Chapel Hill, it would be a failure and that he would rather for the state to have no medical school than to locate it outside Chapel Hill.'"

But Berryhill said that offer was never fully explored. "From the evidence available, it would appear that a very important decision was made in a very casual fashion without adequate data or careful thought. Even if a thorough study might have led eventually to the university's inability to accept the proposal, its position would have been much stronger after making a study."

As it turned out, Wake Forest did accept the offer, and the Bowman Gray School of Medicine graduated its first class in 1943. It was to be eleven more years before UNC produced its first physicians because with its limited two-year program, UNC had to send its students elsewhere to complete their M.D. degrees.

Throughout the 1940s, Berryhill continued to remind the university administration and the trustees of the need for a four-year school—in Chapel Hill. Ironically, the state's experience during World War II helped the cause. North Carolina experienced one of the nation's highest draft rejection rates. Poor nutrition was listed as one cause, but another important factor was access to good medical care. There simply were not enough doctors in the state.

Governor J. Melville Broughton created a study commission to examine the condition of health care in North Carolina, which prompted a statewide movement called the Good Health Campaign. With an aroused electorate calling Raleigh, the General Assembly passed enabling legislation and launched an unprecedented period of funding for health care and health education. A key component was a teaching hospital for a new four-year medical school at Chapel Hill.

According to the *North Carolina Medical Journal,* "The General Assembly of 1945 formally established the North Carolina Medical Care Commission and appropriated funds for loans to students in the medical schools of the state who would agree to practice in rural areas and authorized the trustees of the university to expand the medical school to four years." But an amendment called for a group of outside experts to determine the best location for the school before implementation of the authorization.

The Medical Care Commission appointed a national committee headed by Dr. William T. Sanger, president of the Medical College of Virginia in Richmond, to study the question. In 1946, the committee recommended that the UNC School of Medicine be expanded to four years and be located in Chapel Hill. It further recommended that the services of the medical school "be integrated effectively and continuously with a statewide network of hospitals and health centers insofar as these volunteer to cooperate."

There were doubters about the latter provision. John B. Graham, M.D., who had just joined the faculty, recalled in a *North Carolina Medical Journal* article, "I cynically assumed that the concept of a statewide hospital network was merely campaign oratory whose purpose was to assure the acquisition of the four-year medical school. Time has proved me wrong."

Though it was to take nearly another two decades, Berryhill took that recommendation very seriously. But first he had to push through the funding for the school and the teaching hospital in Chapel Hill, which was to become North Carolina Memorial Hospital (and now UNC Hospitals). According to Blythe, Berryhill called for help from his friends in the class of 1921. "If you look at that class, you'd find all the leadership of North Carolina there, and they were becoming leaders at about the time that Dr. Berryhill became dean here."

Despite a last-minute push by a Greensboro group that offered Moses Cone Hospital as the primary university hospital along with a substantial endowment, the General Assembly accepted the Sanger report and in 1947 approved expansion of the school and construction of the university hospital in Chapel Hill. N.C. Memorial Hospital opened in 1952 and the first four-year class graduated in 1954. "Graduation day marked the achievement of what Berryhill considered his major life goal," wrote Blythe.

Ten years later, when Berryhill retired as dean, he turned to fulfill the promise of the Sanger report for the statewide network. As director of the newly created Division of Education and Research in Community Medical Care, he set about building a network of hospitals and catalyzing the establishment of community-based centers of medical education. By 1969, the network included Charlotte Memorial Hospital, Moses Cone Hospital in Greensboro, Wake Memorial Hospital in Raleigh, New Hanover Memorial Hospital in Wilmington, and the Tarboro Clinic and Edgecombe County Hospital in Tarboro.

Fordham, by then the dean, said the affiliations that Berryhill developed laid the groundwork for the AHEC system. In 1971, the university applied for and got funds under a new federal program to formally create the system. "We got the largest contract in the history of the university, $8.5 million, to develop the AHEC program," Fordham said.

Berryhill noted that it was the only one of twenty-seven grants nationally that proposed covering an entire state. And very shortly, the system emerged that reaches all one hundred counties. Faculty and students and house staff from Chapel Hill fly to communities all over the state to provide clinics and educational experiences for doctors in practice and residents and students at community hospitals. The system includes a broad spectrum of the health care system.

Though Berryhill officially retired from active participation in activities of the division and AHEC in 1971, he stayed involved. And for his work in laying the foundation for the AHEC program, Berryhill was named a master of the American College of Physicians in 1977. He remained active in the affairs of the medical school until his death on January 1, 1979, and almost to the day he died, he was intimately involved in the planning for the centennial celebration of the school in February 1979.

So who was Reece Berryhill? Sarah Virginia Dunlap, his secretary, wrote in the *North Carolina Medical Journal:* "Two dominating facets of his personality, to me, were his integrity and his lack of ostentation. There was no small talk in Dr. Berryhill's conversation; all that he said had a point and it was not an isolated point. Matter-of-factness and evenness was in his voice and written style. He did not pause when he spoke. There were no hems and haws. He spoke as he wrote, always grammatically correct and coherent."

"He was an imposing and intimidating person and the most dreaded thing was to get called to his office," said William W. McLendon, M.D., emeritus professor of pathology and laboratory medicine. He once said, "One time, a student got called to his office and Dr. Berryhill made him sit there while he finished up some task. Finally Dr. Berryhill said, 'Do you like medical school?' and the student replied with great trepidation, 'Yes, sir, I do.' Dr. Berryhill said, 'Well that's good because you are in the top 10 percent of your class. Keep up the good work.'"

Recalled Blythe, "To students and to faculty, he was a stern person. But he was absolutely honest in his assessment. If he thought you were doing something wrong, he'd tell you in no uncertain terms. On the other hand, if he thought you were doing something right, he would congratulate and support you to the nth degree."

Blythe said his father, a classmate of Berryhill's, could not conceive of Berryhill as a stern person. Indeed, the 1921 student yearbook said he "could pass a pleasant and jovial smile, whose laugh was free, whose heart was ours and [one] of whose leadership we were proud."

Berryhill was born on October 14, 1900, in his fa-

ther's house in Steele Creek in Mecklenburg County, on land that later became a runway at Charlotte/ Douglas International Airport. He attended Dixie High School in Charlotte. He first planned to go to Davidson College, but after visiting UNC as a member of his high school debate team, he changed his mind, and enrolled there in 1917.

Blythe said that three Berryhill characteristics emerged during his undergraduate days: "his intelligence, his high quality as a leader and his ability to stimulate in others a sense of loyalty to him, the result of loyalty to his colleagues." He was elected to Phi Beta Kappa, won the Eben Alexander prize for the best English translation of a Greek passage, was president of the student council and of the senior class, and was an editor of the student newspaper, the *Tar Heel.*

Berryhill, who was descended from a long line of Scotch-Irish Presbyterians, started out to be a Presbyterian minister. But when he switched his goal to medicine, he had to repay the state for financial support. So after graduating in 1921, Berryhill taught school for two years in the Charlotte area. He returned to Chapel Hill for medical school in 1923, completed his basic sciences studies there, and then transferred to Harvard Medical School for his clinical years, graduating in 1927. After residency at Boston City Hospital, he entered private practice in Belmont, across the Catawba River from Mecklenburg. But after only six months, he was asked by Dr. Isaac Manning, then the dean and professor of physiology, to return to UNC to teach physiology. Berryhill protested that he didn't think he knew enough physiology to teach it. Manning reportedly responded, "Well, Reece, then this is a good way to learn some more!"

After his six-month stint substituting for Manning, Berryhill was invited to be chief resident in medicine at Western Reserve School of Medicine in Cleveland, after which he became an instructor at the school and attending physician at Lakeside Hospital. While there, he married Norma Connell of Warrenton, who he had met ten years earlier when she was a student at Peace College.

In 1933, UNC President Frank Graham wrote Berryhill asking that he return to Chapel Hill to become director of Student Health Services and physician-in-chief of the university infirmary. He accepted, and stayed the rest of his life. He also began teaching the second-year course in physical diagnosis. "He was a great teacher," Fordham said. "He understood the problems, he elaborated them beautifully and he tested fairly."

Though the medical school did not have its own

hospital, Berryhill was able to arrange clinical exposure for the students at Watts Hospital in Durham, and as a result, UNC students did well at the four-year schools where they finished, Fordham said.

In 1937, Berryhill became the sole assistant dean, with responsibility for admissions, guidance, and counseling of students. In 1941, when he became dean, he was just forty-one years old, the youngest man ever appointed to that position.

Fordham also recalled the gracious welcome that Reece and Norma Berryhill provided in their home for students, new house staff, and new faculty. "It gave a family atmosphere to the school." Sarah Dunlap said Norma Berryhill "assisted new faculty in finding housing [and] welcomed them on the first night in town with flowers and casseroles of hot nourishing food. . . ."

"We're so big now that it is hard to retain a family atmosphere," Fordham said. "He did establish the presence of civility and collegiality which persists. And that is what makes the institution almost unique."

Robert Conn has been science writer at Wake Forest University Baptist Medical Center in Winston-Salem since 1986. Before that he spent twenty-five years at the Charlotte Observer *as a writer and editor. Most of his writing experience was as medical reporter and editor, where he won a number of prizes, and he was part of a team that won the 1981 Pulitzer Prize Gold Medal for Public Service and the Robert F. Kennedy Grand Prize. He has continued to write about health issues outside Wake Forest on a freelance basis.*

For more information, see:

Berryhill, W. Reece, William B. Blythe, and Isaac H. Manning. *Medical Education at Chapel Hill: The First Hundred Years.* University of North Carolina Press, 1979.

Blythe, William B., M.D. "Walter Reece Berryhill: Physician, Medical Educator, and Innovator." *North Carolina Medical Journal,* October 1984.

Citron, David S., M.D. "Dr. Berryhill's Third Career, 1964–1978." *North Carolina Medical Journal,* October 1984.

Dunlap, Sarah Virginia. "Dr. Berryhill, My Boss: 1942–1964." *North Carolina Medical Journal,* October 1984.

Graham, John B., M.D. "Walter Reece Berryhill: Dean of Medicine, 1941–1965." *North Carolina Medical Journal,* October 1984.

Stinneford, Karen. "On the Occasion of the 100th Anniversary of His Birth, Walter Reece Berryhill MD Is Remembered for His Contributions to the School of Medicine." *Medical Alumni Bulletin,* October 1984.

JAMES E. DAVIS

By Robert Conn

WHEN Dr. James Davis of Durham became president of the American Medical Association (AMA) in 1988, he crusaded for doctors to participate in community service. "I ask every physician to tithe of your time for the benefit of the American people—just one-tenth of the normal work week, four hours a week serving the public in the way you think is most helpful," Davis said in his inaugural address in June 1988. He wasn't talking about the traditional charity care or donated time in a clinic, and thus almost single-handedly transformed the way doctors viewed community service.

"We also serve through involvement. For instance, you may choose to lead a church youth group, work with scouts, or give time in the school library. You may decide to coach a Little League team or drive the elderly to the grocery store . . . volunteer with Meals on Wheels or visit shut-ins," said Davis, the first and only North Carolinian to serve as AMA president during the twentieth century.

He returned to that theme throughout his presidency, and medicine changed. Before Davis, academic medical centers, the engines of scientific progress and teaching, had viewed their mission as a three-legged stool of education, research, and patient care. In the 1990s, most added a fourth leg: community service. The number of doctors holding public office mushroomed.

James E. Davis, M.D., who died October 27, 1997, at the age of seventy-nine, repeatedly brought major change to medicine. He is considered the father of ambulatory surgery in North Carolina. He led the creation of a medical liability insurance company when the nation's principal malpractice insurer pulled out of North Carolina. He fostered a North Carolina Institute of Medicine modeled partly on the prestigious national Institute of Medicine. He conceived the City of Medicine, a concept that Durham marketed successfully to attract numerous medically related companies and revitalize its economy.

During preparation of a 1989 magazine article on Davis, friends gave numerous examples of Jim Davis's extraordinary energy and ability to get things done. Take ambulatory surgery.

During a visit to New York, Davis watched patients being sent home from a hospital on the day of their operations. He was intrigued. After reading the

James E. Davis (Courtesy of Charlotte Observer)

handful of journal articles then published on ambulatory surgery, he was convinced the technique was worth a trial in North Carolina. He was chairman of the department of surgery at the old Watts Hospital in Durham, and in a 1988 interview he recalled saying to the hospital director, "We ought to try this." The director concurred and together they discussed the concept with officials at Blue Cross. After calculating that they would be paying the same fee to physicians but would save money on the hospital stay, Blue Cross agreed to pay for the time in the operating room and the recovery room, just as they would have paid for those on an inpatient basis.

"The three of us sat down and signed a contract that we would try this on a experimental basis," recalled Davis. And within days, surgeons at Watts were

344

operating on patients under general anesthesia in the morning and sending them home by nightfall. At year's end, the experiment was extended indefinitely.

Davis volunteered to promote the idea around North Carolina, and soon became one of the nation's leading advocates of ambulatory surgery—which has dramatically altered American medical care. In 1986, he wrote one of the definitive books, *Major Ambulatory Surgery*. Ambulatory surgery has continued to grow.

"It's cost effective and that's very important but the main reason behind its success is that the people like it. It does not interfere with their lifestyle as much as the alternative of going into the hospital," Davis wrote. Citing his own research, Davis added, "We certainly proved that it was safe. Patients did not undergo added jeopardy."

The experiment in ambulatory surgery is just one way that Davis made a difference in medicine. There were other examples. When the primary malpractice insurer abruptly pulled out of North Carolina, leaving physicians without protection, Davis led doctors in establishing a mutual insurance company that became a national model. Then president of the North Carolina Medical Society, he summoned an emergency session of the society's House of Delegates, and asked the state's doctors to put up their own money to provide the necessary capital. Davis served as chairman of Medical Mutual Insurance Company of North Carolina for twelve years until stepping down in 1988. Under his leadership, the company built a reputation for innovation, especially in helping doctors reduce their risk of malpractice suits.

North Carolina was the first state to develop an Institute of Medicine, to gather objective findings on options available on key health problems and make recommendations to the N.C. General Assembly. Davis was the first chairman of the institute, a coalition that includes business leaders, doctors, public officials, distinguished citizens, and representatives of the health care industry. The institute has evolved into an effective voice in health policy in the state.

When Durham, his adopted hometown, was foundering in the wake of the shuttering of numerous tobacco and textile facilities, but people were still employed, Davis suspected that medicine and health-related research had become the dominant industry. After detailed analysis confirmed his belief, Davis promoted the concept that Durham was the "City of Medicine." He raised money from doctors and others and pushed it through as a focus for economic development. The slogan later became the city's signature and was displayed on signs at the city limits, on all city vehicles, and at the airport. More importantly, it

worked. According to the *Durham Herald-Sun,* "With that new image has come more than 300 medical and health related companies that employ nearly one out of every three Durham residents and produce a combined annual payroll of more than $3 billion."

Davis was one of the few doctors anywhere to become president of a chamber of commerce. He headed the Durham chamber a few years after he developed the City of Medicine concept, and he promptly added a division to recognize the importance of medicine in its program of work. Chamber officials recalled that under Davis's leadership, the chamber launched a four-year accelerated economic development and image-building program. The program exceeded all of its goals.

The same activist pattern occurred repeatedly—when Davis was president of the N.C. Medical Society in 1975–76, president of the N.C. Board of Medical Examiners in 1966–67, chairman of the State Health Coordinating Council, North Carolina's official health planning agency, and as head of the general alumni association of the University of North Carolina. "Once he grabs something, he does it," recalled Eben Alexander Jr., M.D., of Winston-Salem, emeritus professor of neurology at Wake Forest University School of Medicine.

Davis originally became involved in organized medicine through his interest in parliamentary procedure. In North Carolina, he first served as speaker of the Medical Society's House of Delegates and then worked his way up to the presidency. At the national level, he ran for vice speaker of the American Medical Association House of Delegates in 1976—and lost. The next election, he was chosen as vice speaker, and subsequently became the speaker of the 420-member House of Delegates, which sets policy on hundreds of medical issues. He often had to rule on parliamentary matters, a matter on which he became an expert.

"Davis's good natured friendliness and well-articulated positions earned the respect of his medical colleagues," noted one observer. "He was known as the 'Tip O'Neill of the AMA', a tribute to his ability to win votes for legislation he considered essential." (O'Neill was longtime speaker of the U.S. House of Representatives.)

In 1992, he completed *Rules of Order: An Authoritative, Simplified Guide to Parliamentary Procedure*. Davis intended the book to be a reference manual on parliamentary procedure for presiding officers. "*Roberts's Rules of Order* is very bulky and highly technical," he told *American Medical News* in 1988, while he was still writing his book. "What I want is an accurate but brief reference that is quite usable on the spur of the moment. People can study it for background on parliamentary procedure, but they can also have it at their elbow while they're presiding over meetings."

After six years as speaker, Davis was chosen as president-elect, and automatically assumed the presidency in June 1988. But despite his election to the highest office in organized medicine, Davis told the *Durham Morning Herald,* "The acme of my career, the height, has been being allowed to practice surgery for 30 years and interact with patients. I've received tremendous pleasure and satisfaction out of working with patients, seeing them get well, seeing them relieved of pain, seeing their life extended. I just can't imagine anything more satisfying."

He was chairman of the department of surgery at Watts and its successor, Durham County General, for twenty-five years, and also served as hospital chief of staff. He stepped down as department chairman in 1983.

He said he loved teaching medical students. He simultaneously was professor of surgery at the University of North Carolina in Chapel Hill, associate clinical professor of surgery at Duke University, and a preceptor in the clinical clerkship program of what was then called Bowman Gray School of Medicine.

He won a host of awards, some of them unexpected accolades for a physician. For instance, he received Durham's Civic Honor Award, the kind of award usually given to patriarchs and heads of leading businesses, after he was selected by previous award recipients. They cited him for practicing what he preaches: "That a doctor's obligation to his profession and to society goes beyond caring for his patients: he must care for his community and the world community as well, and give freely of himself to them."

Davis was born in Goldsboro on March 2, 1918. His first try at leadership was as head of the stamp club in junior high school. As an undergraduate at the University of North Carolina, he was president of the student body and was so popular that he ran unopposed.

His determination also emerged. Davis had run track in high school, but short distances only. When the UNC coach asked him to run the mile, he responded that he had never run that distance. Told to work at it, Davis did. In 1939, he set a Southern Conference outdoor record for the mile of 4:14.2. The next year, he set the Southern Conference indoor record of 4:12.5. Both stood until the arrival of Charlotte's Jim Beatty in Chapel Hill. Beatty, who went on to become an internationally known track star, ran a 4:06.2 in 1957.

Davis's coaches wanted him to take a year off be-

fore medical school to try out for the Olympics. But Davis had other priorities and enrolled in the then two-year UNC School of Medicine at Chapel Hill before finishing at the University of Pennsylvania in 1943. On June 14, 1943, Davis married Margaret Best Royall of Goldsboro. Shortly thereafter, with World War II at its peak, he joined the navy.

After the war, he went to New York Hospital–Cornell University Medical Center for his residency, finishing in 1951. After a stint back in the military during the Korean War, Davis moved to Durham, established his practice, and quickly became known as a hard worker. By 1954, he was chairman of surgery at Watts.

Davis was outspoken throughout his career. He openly criticized the way doctors practiced, pointing to crowded waiting rooms as examples of arrogance and the unintentional starting point of many malpractice suits. By the time patients saw the doctor, they already were in a bad mood caused by the wait—a wait that could be avoided if doctors scheduled office patients thirty minutes later or started hospital rounds earlier.

"People don't like us," Davis said in 1988. "They're quick to criticize and they're fairly quick to sue. This is the point about keeping people waiting. It gives them a mind set that they are unhappy when they go in and then if things continue to go badly, they might very well cause trouble."

He talked from the perspective of a surgeon who kept his busy practice until the end. He died after collapsing on the fifth floor of Durham Regional Hospital, not long after consulting with Dr. Walter Loehr, a Durham surgeon who shared a practice with Davis for twenty-four years.

During his chairmanship of Medical Mutual Insurance Company of North Carolina, Davis championed practice evaluations. Though doctors voluntarily requested evaluations, the team came in unannounced. Davis said these visits documented the problem of routine delays. "Over 40 percent keep the patients waiting 30 minutes or longer," Davis said. Survey teams uncovered other problems as well. Doctors routinely were depending on their staffs to initially evaluate laboratory reports and tell them about abnormal ones, which he said was a dangerous practice. The teams found that more than 70 percent of informed consents were flawed. Sometimes, the patient didn't get enough information. Sometimes, the doctor didn't go through it with the patient.

"So we say to physicians: 'You may not be practicing as well as you think you are.'"

But he said some patients have unrealistic expectations. "Patient expectation is inflated so much that they're not able to understand why they don't get a perfect result. They read about the miracle of the week in the newspaper and in *Time* magazine. They expect everything that comes up to be miraculously cured. We can't do that.

"Medicine is an inexact science. It's based on pure science, but it's inexact in its practice. This is a judgmental professional work," Davis said. Good doctors, at the peak of their skills and knowledge, are more likely to attempt higher risk procedures. "Good doctors get sued more than bad doctors."

Though Davis crusaded for community service during his AMA presidency, it was his passion for improving quality of care that ran throughout his professional career. Indeed, in his valedictory as AMA president, he said: "Let's work together so quality health care will not only continue in America but will continue to improve."

Robert Conn has been science writer at Wake Forest University Baptist Medical Center in Winston-Salem since 1986. Before that he spent twenty-five years at the Charlotte Observer *as a writer and editor. Most of his writing experience was as a medical reporter and editor at the* Observer, *where he won a number of prizes, and was part of a team that won* the 1981 Pulitzer Prize Gold Medal for Public Service and the Robert F. Kennedy Grand Prize. He has continued to write about health issues outside Wake Forest on a freelance basis.

For more information, see:

Davis, James E., M.D. Address of the president. American Medical Association Archives, December 1988, 8–11.

———. Inaugural address. American Medical Association Archives, June 1988, 17–20.

———. "A Symphony of Service to American Medicine." American Medical Association Archives, June 1989, 9–12.

"James E. Davis, M.D.: Chronology." N.C. Medical Society Archives, n. d.

"James E. Davis, M.D.: A Distinguished Career, an Extraordinary Man." N.C. Medical Society Archives, n. d.

Conn, Robert H. "The Presiding M.D. on Dearborn Street." *Penn Medicine* (Spring 1989): 30–35.

Perrone, Janice. "Dr. Davis, Next AMA President, Sets His Sights on Stressing Service Ethic." *American Medical News* 31, no. 20 (May 27, 1988).

Zimmer, Jeff. *Durham Herald-Sun,* October 28, 1997.

WILBURT C. DAVISON

By Robert Conn

WILBURT CORNELL DAVISON was hired to be the first dean of the Duke University School of Medicine when the school was little more than an idea nurtured by William Preston Few, the president of the newly transformed Trinity College.

At the time, North Carolina had only two two-year "basic science" medical schools—at Wake Forest and Chapel Hill—and no four-year schools. Efforts in the early 1920s to develop a joint school with the University of North Carolina had failed when Few turned to James B. Duke, who had already directed $6 million of his vast wealth to turn Trinity into Duke University as a memorial to his father. In 1925, at his death, Duke made an additional bequest to the endowment and the university, including $4 million to establish a medical school, hospital, and nurses' home.

In 1926, with construction scheduled to begin on the medical school, Few began his search for a dean. According to James F. Gifford Jr., Few asked Dr. William H. Welch, a pathologist at Johns Hopkins University and "recognized dean of American medicine for help in locating 'the best man available. . . .'" Welch recommended Davison, a pediatrician who was also assistant dean at Hopkins. In March 1926, Few met with Davison and immediately became Few's first choice.

While the school and hospital were under construction, Davison busied himself assembling a faculty, acquiring the nucleus of a medical library, and conferring with architects on structural arrangements that worked for both students and patients at the new hospital.

By November, Davison began to organize the faculty, recruiting many from the Hopkins staff. "The success of this practice grew out of the uniquely high quality of scientific training given the men in residency and post-residency programs at that school," Gifford wrote. "Even those faculty chosen from positions at other institutions usually had trained or worked at The Hopkins. . . ."

Gifford also said, "The gamble on a young, relatively unknown faculty was born in part by necessity —the new school could not pay salaries large enough to attract full professors from established institutions. . . . What Davison's first faculty lacked in broad experience, it gained back in zeal, familiarity with a com-

Wilburt C. Davison (Courtesy of Duke University Archives)

mon pattern of operation and unity in the conviction that Duke's primary objective must be to provide a basic, practical education for its students, expressed first and foremost in the ability to make accurate clinical diagnoses."

According to another biographer, "The philosophy of medical education espoused by Davison called for the cultivated, intellectually disciplined physician who was civic minded and innovative. In the choice of faculty, including those requiring complex technical skills, he favored teachers with special interests; superiority was the common denominator."

Duke Hospital opened on July 21, 1930, and almost immediately began seeing more patients than had been anticipated. Thirty first-year and eighteen third-year students began their studies on October 2. The first degrees (for those who started at the third year) were awarded on June 8, 1932.

"Under Dr. Davison's guidance, the medical school grew into a community of scholars concerned with all phases of knowledge," said E. A. Stead Jr. "He concerned himself with the practice of medicine in the state, the South and the nation. He built an outstanding library. He operated a clinical center which has steadily grown until it has a worldwide reputation. He developed a system of private university clinics which bring a steady flow of visitors to Duke to study their operation." Stead added, "He recognized the vitalizing impact of research upon the corporate body of the medical school, but properly pointed to its inordinate demands."

Davison himself was also professor of pediatrics, serving as chairman of that department until 1954 and as James B. Duke Professor of Pediatrics until retirement. Davison was known to the faculty simply as "Dave," and was usually seen around the school coatless and tieless. "He believed that no rules should ever be written down if it were possible to avoid doing so. As with all good administrators, his word was his bond," said Stead. "He carried a little notebook attached to his wallet. Once he agreed to a course, it was noted in the book. The matter was then as good as accomplished." Dr. William Anlyan, writing in Duke's *Medical Alumni News,* concurred. "If you said something to him that got down in that notebook, 24 hours a day, you knew it would be done immediately. That was sort of an accessory brain that Dr. Davison used."

Davison got involved in many projects outside the university. He founded the North Carolina Pediatric Society. With the help of Dr. Watson S. Rankin, head of the hospitals and orphans section of the Duke Endowment, he made a detailed study of medical practice in the state's urban and rural communities, with particular attention to adverse conditions in a physician's practice.

Faced with the economic pressures on hospitals and physicians, Davison pioneered a solution in the form of medical care insurance, though it took several tries. His first attempt was the Durham Hospital Association in 1929. "Dues of 25 cents per week per family would entitle parents and children under 18, after payment of six-months dues, to the payment of all hospital bills up to $3 per day per person up to 21 days of care per person," wrote Gifford. (The cost of a ward bed was to be $3 per day at Duke.) The Durham Hospital Association was doomed before it could begin by the stock market crash.

He tried a second time with a proposed Duke University Medical Guild, a group coverage plan that called for pooling the medical bills and paying them, through payroll deductions, on the basis of equal shares per family enrolled. This plan failed, too, because some faculty objected, according to Gifford.

Finally, in 1933, he and George Watts Hill, a Durham banker and chair of the board of Durham's Watts Hospital, took a struggling voluntary care organization called the Hospital Care Association and formed the fourth nonprofit hospital plan to be incorporated in the United States and the first one successful to envision statewide operations. Shortly thereafter, the Hospital Savings Association was formed with help from the Duke Endowment

Though years of struggle followed, by 1940 the Hospital Care Association was in the black and repaying Duke and Watts hospitals the money each had advanced for underwriting the association. In the 1960s, Hospital Care and Hospital Savings merged into Blue Cross Blue Shield of North Carolina.

Davison headed the Committee on Veterans Medical Problems, a National Academy of Sciences (NAS) Committee initially established in 1946 under a contract with the Veterans Administration (VA). At about the same time, the Medical Follow-up Agency was established by the National Research Council of the NAS, and studies began on following clinical cases that were the direct result of World War II.

Davison took over as chair at about the time of the Korean War, when applying the lessons of World War II took on new urgency. The VA wanted to know whether the follow-up program was cost effective.

Davison reported for the committee, saying, "All of us expected concrete tangible and useful results from the VA follow-up projects, but none of us realized, until the meeting today, how excellent the progress has been and how important the reports are even in their preliminary stage." He went on to say that if the follow-up program continued, the military, the VA, and the taxpayers would "all profit enormously."

Davison was born in Grand Rapids, Mich., on April 28, 1892, the son of a Methodist minister, William L. Davison, and Mattie E. Cornell Davison. He spent his childhood on Long Island, N.Y., as his father moved from church to church. When Davison was injured playing football and had to stay out of school, the elder Davison hired a Harvard graduate to teach Wilburt Latin and Greek.

He entered Princeton in 1909 and graduated with honors in 1913, earning a Rhodes Scholarship for study at Oxford University. He chose to pursue a medical education. "Using a catalog from the Johns Hopkins University Medical School as his guide, he outlined for his first year a course of study covering the first two years of The Hopkins curriculum and obtained permission to follow this program from Sir William Osler, the Regius Professor of Medicine and dean of the medical school," wrote Gifford.

Notes Werner Wells, "Davison was one of the last students of this great medical humanist. During his Oxford years, he became an 'adopted' son to Sir William and Lady Grace and frequented their home at 19 Norham Gardens. . . . This intimate personal bond between a sensitive brilliant young man and his teacher strongly influenced Davison's later career as dean of the first four-year medical school in North Carolina."

When World War I began, Davison volunteered to serve with the French army, first as an orderly and then as an anesthetist. In January 1915, he went to Serbia to help fight an epidemic of typhus, a largely futile effort in which many patients died. After two months, Davison made his way back to England and resumed his medical studies. He earned a B.A. degree in 1915 and a B.S. degree in medicine in 1916.

Davison also did his first research project there, testing the efficacy of a new typhoid-paratyphoid vaccine. "The results of these experiments, which helped to justify the adoption of the vaccine by the British army, became the basis of Davison's first scholarly publication," said Gifford.

With Osler's recommendation, Davison was given credit for three years of medical school and entered the senior class at Johns Hopkins, where he earned his M.D. degree in 1917. Soon after graduation, he joined the U.S. Army, where he was assigned to Field Hospital 1.

After the war, he decided to become a pediatrician and completed his training at Hopkins. He subsequently joined the pediatrics faculty, rising to acting pediatrician in charge and assistant dean. That's when Few recruited him.

Davison retired on October 5, 1961, after nearly thirty-five years at the helm of Duke University School of Medicine and Duke Hospital. But he didn't stop working. He was a trustee and consultant for the Duke Endowment from 1961 to 1972, a member of the board of visitors of Davidson College from 1961 to 1972, and vice president of the board of the Doris Duke Charitable Foundation from 1938 to 1972. Over his career, he also was active in a broad range of national medical organizations, serving on the executive committee of the Association of American Medical Colleges, the editorial board of *Quarterly Review of Pediatrics,* vice chairman of the Division of Medical Sciences of the prestigious National Research Council, a colonel in the U.S. Army Medical Corps, a consultant to the army's surgeon general, and a member of the executive reserve of the office of the assistant secretary of defense (health and medicine), among numerous others.

"He was a key leader in the Veterans Administration," said Anlyan. "He persuaded the new leadership, post World War II, not to build veterans hospitals in political geographical areas of powerful congressmen, but to put them near academic medical centers where they could share in the intellectual resources. And thanks to Dr. Davison, we got one of those first VA hospitals in Durham."

He continued his foundation work, writing, and travel until shortly before he died of leukemia on June 26, 1972. "His ashes were placed behind a bronze tablet in the chapel of the medical school building that bears his name," wrote Wells.

"He was a man with deep compassion, a ready wit and a robust sense of humor," Wells said. "A world traveler, he had friends in many countries; foreign colleagues and students were frequent guests in his clinics and in the Davison home."

Over the course of his long career, Davison produced more than two hundred scientific and professional publications, as well as six editions of *The Compleat Pediatrician,* first published in 1934 and intended to be a shorthand compendium of pediatric practice for medical students. "In contrast to many pediatric books which too often resemble the old-fashioned hoop skirt in covering the subject without touching it, this book is like a G-string in touching the subject without any pretense of covering it," Davison said.

Not long after his retirement in 1961, Davison lent his support to the proposal for a one-thousand-dollar-a-year "Davison Club" when it was proposed by six faculty members. "Over a little bourbon, we persuaded him that it would be a good thing to start this $1,000 a year club," recalled Anlyan. "Of course, $1,000 a year in the 60s was a lot of money. But Dr. Davison concurred, and that's how we got started."

Davison himself wrote, "A medical school is only as good as its alumni. After all, they are its major product, and by their fruits, ye shall know them. Also the future support of any institution depends on its alumni. They are its living endowment, and if they know both the worth and the need of the university, they will help. It is the job of the administration, faculty and trustees to see that the worth of the institution is kept at a high level and that its needs are brought to the attention of the alumni."

Robert Conn has been science writer at Wake Forest University Baptist Medical Center in Winston-Salem since 1986. Before that he spent twenty-five years at the Charlotte Observer *as a writer and editor. Most of his writing experience* was as a medical reporter and editor at the Observer, where he won a number of prizes, and he was part of a team that won the 1981 Pulitzer Prize Gold Medal for Public Service and the Robert F. Kennedy Grand Prize. He has continued to write about health issues outside Wake Forest on a freelance basis.

For more information, see:

Anylan, Dr. William. "The Beginnings of the Davison Club." *Medical Alumni News,* Fall 1998.

Berkowitz, Edward D., and Mark J. Santangelo. *The Medical Follow-up Agency: The First Fifty Years, 1946–1996.* Institute of Medicine, National Academy of Sciences, 1999.

Davison of Duke: His Reminiscences. Ed. Dr. Jay M. Arena and Dr. John P. McGovern. Duke University Medical Center, 1980.

Gifford, James F., Jr. *The Evolution of a Medical Center: A History of Medicine at Duke University to 1941.* Duke University Press, 1972.

The First Twenty Years, A History of Duke University Schools of Medicine, Nursing, and Health Services and Duke Hospital, 1930–1950. Bulletin of Duke University, May 1952.

Stead, E. A., Jr. *What This Patient Needs Is a Doctor.* Ed. Galen S. Wagner, Bess Cebe, and Marvin P. Rozear. Carolina Academic Press, 1978.

Wells, Werner. In *Dictionary of North Carolina Biography.* University of North Carolina Press, 1996.

Aaron McDuffie Moore and Stanford Lee Warren

By P. Preston Reynolds

Drs. Aaron Moore and Stanford Warren of Durham devoted their lives to the extension of medical care to African American citizens in Durham —sometimes taking chickens and eggs in barter for their services—but their work resulted in the building and growth of Lincoln Hospital, which at its peak was considered one of the finest hospitals devoted to serving African Americans in the South.

The hospital, begun with a gift from Washington Duke, who was Warren's white father, was accredited by the American Medical Association for internship training and approved as a class "A" hospital by the American College of Surgeons. The state of North Carolina rated the nurses training school a class "A" program.

Aaron McDuffie Moore, born on September 6, 1863, in Elkton, was one of ten children—five girls and five boys—of Anna Eliza Spaulding and Israel Moore. Raised on a farm owned by Anna and Israel Moore in Columbus County, Aaron and his siblings were part of a large clan of three generations of free African Americans living and working as yeomen farmers well before the Civil War. The original Spauldings, Benjamin and his wife Edith Delphia Jacobs, first acquired land in Bladen County, from which Columbus County was formed.

According to J. H. Moore, a descendant of Benjamin and Edith Spaulding, the factor that most contributed to the family's early success was their mixed-race ancestry of Negro-Indian-Caucasian through intermarriage with Scotch, Irish, and Native Americans living in the area and thus, their easy identification as "mulatto." As mulattos, Moore's ancestors could legally own property, operate businesses, register and vote, and openly associate with whites before the Civil War. Benjamin, Edith, and their children attended the community church. With their continued increase in numbers, the local congregation encouraged Benjamin and his family to organize their own church and school. Located on two acres of land donated by Henry Spaulding, the log cabin served as a church year-round and as a school during the winter months.

Young Aaron and his brothers and sisters attended the local country school. He taught his siblings and cousins for three years before entering Whittin Normal School in Lumberton and a year later he entered the Normal School in Fayetteville. In 1885 Moore matriculated at Shaw University, aspiring to become a college professor. The leading educators at Shaw saw the brilliance of this young man and steered him into medicine. Moore completed the four-year curriculum in three years and in 1888, at the age of twenty-five, graduated from Shaw's Leonard Medical School. He ranked second in his group when examined by the North Carolina Medical Board for his license to practice medicine, and moved to Durham, becoming the town's first African American physician.

Dr. Moore, with the assistance of his cousin, treated patients surgically and medically on the back porch of his home or at their own residences, which often were just thin-walled shacks. As biographer L. D. Mitchell noted: "In the early years before the century, Dr. Moore assumed the fierce pace that is a natural inheritance of those who commit themselves to healing. He frantically answered calls from the destitute. He fed the hungry, delivered babies, comforted the bereaved and dashed about on horse and buggy in the black community to visit and bring relief to the miserable whom he learned to call 'the least of these, my children.' Dr. Moore worked arduously at his practice, trying to establish himself both as a physician in whom his patients could give their trust and as a civic leader. He often spoke of how poor his patients were—he would charge one dollar a visit, when and if he could collect—and casually complain that the populace often looked upon him as a witch doctor, as a man of magic, so ignorant they were. He vowed to do something about it, and set his life toward that purpose."

Dr. Stanford Lee Warren joined Moore in his effort to uplift the health of the African American community in Durham. Warren was born November 2, 1863, the son of Anne Warren, a fair-skinned "mulatto" woman, and Washington Duke, who with his sons later founded the Duke Tobacco Company. Stanford Warren spent the first two years of his life in Caswell County and at the close of the Civil War moved with

Aaron McDuffie Moore (courtesy of Duke University Special Collections Library) and Stanford Lee Warren (courtesy of Selena Wheeler)

his mother to Durham. Stanford Warren and three of his siblings were identified in the 1870 census as "mulatto," thus noting his mixed-race heritage. He attended private schools in Durham before entering Kittrell College. After graduating from college, Warren worked as a clerk in the Duke Tobacco Company and decided upon a career as a physician, most likely being influenced by the success of Dr. Moore. In 1891 Warren matriculated at Leonard Medical School and graduated four years later. He opened his general practice of medicine in Durham that same year.

Leonard Medical School of Shaw University had opened for classes November 1, 1881 (later recorded as 1882), with seven students enrolling in the four-year program. The first faculty consisted of two professors: James McKee, M.D., former superintendent of health for Wake County, who later became dean of the school, and I. A. Stafford, M.D., professor of anatomy and chemistry, later resident physician to the hospital. A twenty-five-bed hospital with three wards opened for patients on January 10, 1885, thus enhancing the curriculum with clinical instruction. During the same year, a dispensary was established "where students can have the opportunity of seeing

patients treated, and also of themselves learning to dispense medicine," and an ear and eye ward was added to the hospital. Within five years the faculty would expand to include six physicians, all leading practitioners from Raleigh.

The school year at Leonard started in 1882 with a five-month graded curriculum. The first year included courses in anatomy, physiology, and general chemistry. The second year focused on practical anatomy, medical chemistry, material medical, pathological anatomy, and the practice of medicine and surgery. The third year placed students into clinical activities, with course work in therapeutics, obstetrics, theory and practice, and surgery. The fourth year completed the curriculum, with instruction in ophthalmology, otology, dermatology, syphilis, laryngology, diseases of the nervous system, diseases of women, diseases of children, operative surgery, and forensic medicine.

Moore and Warren graduated from Leonard Medical School as well-trained professionals with a strong commitment to service. Warren was one of the last affluent African Americans in Durham to give up his horse and buggy for a Model T Ford. His practice centered on providing medical care to the poorest citizens, many of whom rarely could pay for his expertise except for the occasional chicken or basket of eggs. By modern standards he would be described as a general practitioner with a concentration in obstetrics. He was highly respected as a physician, a businessman, and a teacher. Every Wednesday afternoon he taught the student nurses the subject of obstetrics.

Moore had the vision of a hospital for African Americans in Durham. He was joined by Warren and John Merrick as founders of Lincoln Hospital in 1901. Washington Duke paid for the building construction at $8,551, and provided an additional $5,000 for an endowment to help defray the costs of its charity care. When the hospital opened its first fifty beds in August 1901, Moore was superintendent and Merrick was president of the board of trustees. As superintendent, Moore set the rules for the hospital and its medical and nursing staff. Every patient would be treated with the utmost respect—as if that patient were a family member and without regard to their financial resources.

The 1905 act incorporating the hospital gave the trustees the authority to "establish, conduct, and maintain a hospital in the county of Durham, for the reception and treatment of persons of the colored race, who may need medical or surgical attendance during temporary sickness or injury, and for the training of nurses under such rules and regulations as they may from time to time establish." Furthermore, they were directed to make all such rules, regulations, by-laws, and ordinances as necessary to manage the hospital. As a general hospital, the trustees also had to develop specific criteria for the selection, admission, treatment, and dismissal of patients. The trustees were entrusted to organize a nursing school.

Moore recruited Julia Latta as head nurse. In 1903 she enrolled the first students and in 1905 formally established the Lincoln Hospital School of Nursing as a two-year curriculum. Over the next fifteen years, students came to Lincoln from as far away as Michigan, New York, and the West Indies, reflecting the increasing importance of the hospital as a center of professional development. In 1910 the curriculum was lengthened to three years to conform to increasing standards for nursing licensure established by the North Carolina Board of Nursing.

The hospital's trustees reflected the medical, business, education, and political leadership of Durham. Warren succeeded Merrick in 1919 as president of the board, a role he served until his own death in 1940. Until 1921 the composition of the board of trustees was predominantly African American, whereas after completion of a successful fund-raising drive to build the second Lincoln Hospital, it changed to include representation from the Duke family, the white medical society, and Durham city and county governments. Moore knew a modern hospital would replace the original Lincoln Hospital when a fire nearly destroyed it in January 1922. He died in April 1923.

Moore was active as a physician, philanthropist, humanitarian, and business leader. He is best known as one of the founders of the North Carolina Mutual Life Insurance Company. Other institutions he started included the public library for African Americans, Mechanics and Farmers Bank, the Durham Drug Company, the Merrick-Moore-Spaulding Real Estate Company, and the Durham Textile Mill. As founder and medical director of the North Carolina Mutual, he helped establish the business on sound medical principles. At the time of his death, the Mutual was the largest African American–owned insurance company in the country.

He was the philosopher-physician and humanitarian-philanthropist whose intellect dominated emotions, but whose heart remained close to those he chose to serve. In his will, he bequeathed three houses adjacent to Lincoln Hospital to its board of trustees; the proceeds were to aid worthy girls who were enrolled in the school of nursing. The remainder was to be used for medicines and other purposes to aid the indigent sick, preferably those with tuberculosis, or widows and orphans.

Moore's successor as superintendent of Lincoln Hospital was Dr. Charles Shepard, a graduate of Leonard Medical School of Shaw University who worked closely with Warren to transform Lincoln into an institution recognized by regional and national hospital and residency accreditation authorities. The second Lincoln Hospital opened in January 1925, with the plant and equipment valued at $200,000 and an endowment of $8,100. The hospital incorporated modern architectural features and equipment for the laboratory and X-ray departments as well as for the minor and major surgery suites. In fact, the Duke Endowment, established by James B. Duke in 1925, regarded Lincoln as the best-equipped hospital for African Americans south of Washington, D.C.

Lincoln flourished under the administrative leadership of Drs. Warren and Shepard. Benjamin Duke in 1925 gave an additional $35,000 to build a home for the student nurses, later named the Angier B. Duke Nurses Home. By 1930 the number of graduate nurses had grown to five, with thirty-three student nurses. That year the city government contributed $6,000; the county, $3,250; and the Duke Endowment, $18,235. The hospital's property value had climbed to $213,045 and other assets totaled an additional $40,555. With a full complement of three interns, Shepard planned to hire a fourth.

Dr. Warren, like Dr. Moore, committed his intellect and financial resources to founding important institutions in the community. These included Mechanics and Farmers Bank, where he served as president of the board of directors for twenty years beginning in 1920, and the public library, where he served as president of the board of directors from 1923 until his death in 1940. Lincoln Hospital clearly remained his primary focus of civic responsibility. The year prior to his death, the hospital medical and surgical staff saw 5,636 patients in the outpatient clinic; provided 20,858 days of care to inpatients; conducted 21,502 laboratory tests and 1,796 X-ray examinations; and performed 236 major operations and 1,399 minor surgeries. Lincoln Hospital had grown into a vibrant center of professional education and patient care for African Americans in North Carolina. Beginning in 1935, Lincoln Hospital hosted an annual postgraduate day that over the years developed into a highly valued source of continuing education for physicians in North Carolina, South Carolina, and Virginia.

Moore married Cottie S. Dancy of Tarboro in 1889. They had two daughters, Martha and Mattie Louis. Warren married Julia McCauley of Washington, D.C., in 1904. Mrs. Warren for many years operated the only beauty salon in Durham catering to black and white women. Their daughter, Selena, served as head librarian of the Stanford Warren Library from 1932 until 1945. She was married to John Wheeler, who was later president of Mechanics and Farmers Bank and a senior trustee of Lincoln Hospital. Wheeler was the major architect of the merger of Lincoln Hospital with Durham County Hospital Corporation. He was instrumental in securing a future for the Lincoln Community Health Center when Lincoln Hospital closed in 1976.

Drs. Moore and Warren exemplified the values of community leadership and excellence in professional work. Respected by white and African American citizens, these two physicians created opportunities for biracial cooperation and racial tolerance unusual for their time. Both men effectively used their intellect, professional reputations, and personal connections to the wealthy establishment in Durham to build institutions of public worth and, in those enormous acts of service, created a lasting legacy.

P. Preston Reynolds received both her Ph.D. in history and her M.D. from Duke University. Her study of the history of Lincoln Hospital was published as Durham's Lincoln Hospital, *a photographic study, and as a full-length history,* At the Crossroads of Life: Lincoln Hospital and the Shaping of Health Care for African Americans in the New South.

For more information, see:

Anderson, Jean. *Durham County: A History of Durham County, North Carolina.* Duke University Press, 1990.

Andrews, R. McCant. *John Merrick: A Biographical Sketch.* Seeham Printery, 1920.

Ayanian, John Zaven. "Black Health in Segregated Durham, 1900–1940." Senior honors thesis, Duke University, 1982.

Mitchell, Louis D. "Aaron McDuffie Moore: He Led His Sheep." *Crisis* 87 (1980): 250.

Moore, J. H. *Noble Ancestry and Descendants.* Linprint Company, 1949.

Reynolds, P. Preston. "Watts Hospital: Paternalism and Race in the Evolution of a Southern Institution in Durham, NC, 1895–1976." Ph.D. diss., Duke University, 1986.

———. "Watts Hospital of Durham, NC: Keeping the Doors Open, 1895–1976." Fund for the Advancement of Science and Mathematics Education in North Carolina, 1992.

Weare, Walter. *Black Business in the New South: A Social History of the North Carolina Mutual Life Insurance Company.* University of Illinois Press, 1973.

WATSON S. RANKIN

By Robert Conn

WATSON S. RANKIN, had three distinguished careers, which alone would make him one of North Carolina's leading twentieth-century physicians, but listing only those careers would ignore some of his most significant achievements. During his lifetime, he was the second dean of the Wake Forest College School of Medicine, the first full-time state health director, and founder of the hospitals and orphans section of the Duke Endowment, a major pillar of support for Carolinas hospitals for three-quarters of a century.

But Rankin also was a pathologist whose work led to the virtual eradication of hookworm in the state, and indeed in the South. He also helped establish an early Blue Cross program of health and hospitalization in the Carolinas—one of the first promoters of hospital insurance in North Carolina—and served as one of twelve representatives on the hospital advisory board to the Committee on Economic Security, which President Franklin D. Roosevelt established in June 29, 1934, to write the Social Security Act.

He was such a towering figure in North Carolina medicine that buildings and prizes are named after him. When the new health department building opened in Charlotte in 1960, it was named the Watson S. Rankin Health Center and dedicated on Rankin's eighty-first birthday, January 18, 1960. The North Carolina Public Health Association's highest honor for career achievement in the field of public health is the Watson S. Rankin Award.

Rankin was born on a farm near Mooresville on January 8, 1879, the son of John Alexander and Minnie Isabella McCorkle Rankin, who had "at least" five sons and three daughters. Rankin attended schools in Mooresville and Statesville. He joined the fledgling Wake Forest College School of Medicine as professor of pathology in 1903, the year the school got its first students, at a salary of $1,250.

"He was young and enthusiastic," reported George Washington Paschal in his *History of Wake Forest College*. "He had already won a reputation in his practice at Morehead City by his investigation of the newly discovered hookworm." Dr. Coy C. Carpenter, in *The Story of Medicine at Wake Forest University,* said Rankin gave up his practice to take the low-paying faculty job, "convinced that this was a golden opportunity to make a significant contribution to his profession." He

Watson S. Rankin (Courtesy of Duke University Archives)

took over as dean on July 25, 1905, after Dr. Fred K. Cooke was forced by an ulcer to retire abruptly. "His ability, zeal and enthusiasm in his work had well indicated him for the place," said Paschal. "His own laboratories and office were models of cleanliness and order and he had been able to inspire his students with much of his own spirit."

One of Rankin's most significant accomplishments came in his fourth year as dean. The still-new school received high marks when it was evaluated as part of the national study by Abraham Flexner, a study that would force the closing of dozens of medical schools —including those in Mecklenburg County where Rankin had studied before getting his degree at the University of Maryland. The Flexner study was financed by the Carnegie Foundation for the Advancement of Teaching, and the president of the foundation said in a follow-up letter, "The admirable work of Wake Forest College in medicine has been a cheering thing to us in the wide desert of commercial institutions in the region. You have served a very admirable purpose in showing what can be done even in an isolated college with modest means under the right spirit and when the commercial basis is dropped. . . ."

Amusingly, Carpenter reported in his book that Dr. N. P. Colwell, the Flexner investigator, almost didn't get to see the school. "Dr. Rankin recalls that the distinguished visitor arrived on a Sunday and when he was taken to the Alumni Building [which housed the medical school], Dr. Rankin found that he did not have his key. An unlocked window afforded an unpretentious but effective entrance for Dr. Colwell." Carpenter wrote, "Rankin's philosophy of medical education was simple: There were too many unqualified doctors in the United States and the only basis for the existence of the Wake Forest medical school was to train good physicians."

Soon after Colwell's visit, Rankin resigned to become North Carolina's first full-time health officer. The state Board of Health had been authorized by the General Assembly in 1877, initially under the auspices of the state Medical Society. By 1909, when the General Assembly authorized a full-time health officer, a majority of the Board of Health were appointed by the governor. During Rankin's tenure, the powers of the position were constantly expanded. In 1913, the registrar of vital statistics was added to the job, with general supervision of a new central bureau of vital statistics to register all births and deaths.

Soon the state health officer was given the responsibility of carrying out sanitary measures, which turned out to encompass safe water, drainage and sewage, rural sanitation, and, by 1917, sanitary inspection of hotels and restaurants. Mattie U. Russell reported in the *Dictionary of North Carolina Biography* that "Rankin became widely known as the buggy-riding, top-hatted inspector of privies."

But she also noted that during Rankin's sixteen years as health director, "the state Board of Health became a model for other states." Rankin's interest in public health had begun much earlier, while he was professor of pathology at Wake Forest. After graduating from the University of Maryland, Rankin had done a year of postgraduate work at Johns Hopkins Medical School, followed by a residency in obstetrics at the hospital of the University of Maryland and a residency in pathology at the University Hospital in Baltimore.

His interest in hookworm began shortly before he arrived at Wake Forest. He realized that hookworm was endemic in North Carolina. One physician had sent him fifteen specimens, and, Rankin recalled in a 1965 interview, "all fifteen were heavily infected, so that made thirty-one for him. I proposed to him that he send me as many specimens as he could possibly find among his practice, whether they were patients or not. Get that stool and send them up there [to Wake Forest] and I'd diagnose them."

Rankin said the physician sent him close to 150 positive cases. Rankin then began screening the Wake Forest student body by county to see if they mirrored the incidence of hookworms. For example, he asked six students from Sampson County for stool specimens. Most of them were "lightly infected" with hookworms. However, there was one student who was heavily infected. "I didn't tell him that I thought he was saturated with hookworms, which as a matter of fact he was." He recalled eventually testing students from between twelve and fifteen counties, some from western North Carolina, some from the piedmont, and some from the east, and developing a distribution pattern. He made a report of what he had found to the North Carolina Medical Society in 1904 and published the results in *Medical News New York* in 1904 under the title, "Uncinariasis in North Carolina: Its Frequency, Etiology, Pathological Significance, Symptoms, and Treatment."

Dr. Manson Meads, in his book *The Miracle on Hawthorne Hill*, said, "His studies on the prevalence of hookworm in North Carolina are the first recorded research from the medical school. These studies led to the eventual eradication of the disease in the southern United States and brought national attention to the institution."

Russell said Rankin was interested in other infectious diseases, such as malaria. "In 1905, he went to Panama and learned Dr. Henry Carter's methods of mosquito control. The application of these methods causes a rapid decline in the incidence of malaria in North Carolina."

As health director, progress in the eradication of the hookworm was an annual feature of his state reports. But the importance of the office is revealed in his work fighting other diseases: pellagra, smallpox, tuberculosis, scarlet fever, malaria, typhoid, a diphtheria epidemic, polio, whooping cough, and the great influenza epidemic of 1918.

Rankin resigned as health director in 1925 to join the then new Duke Endowment as a trustee and director of the hospital and orphan section. "Dr. Rankin met James B. Duke through a mutual friendship with William P. Few, president of what was then Trinity College (later Duke University)," said David Roberson, director of communications for the Duke Endowment. He added that Rankin "was a vocal supporter of Few's goal of establishing a four-year medical school at Trinity." Rankin also believed that the serious shortage of doctors in rural areas and small towns in North Carolina could be alleviated by establishing a system of not-for-profit community hospitals. Rankin and Duke met in the early 1920s and Rankin's ideas about health care clearly influenced Duke, who was deeply involved by that time in planning the establishment of the Endowment. Until 1924, many of the hospitals in the Carolinas had been established and maintained by surgeons. "Rankin thought that the counties and the state as well as private philanthropy should contribute to their establishment and maintenance," Russell wrote.

One of the first actions of the twelve original trustees was to elect Rankin to the board and put him in charge of planning and beginning the work of the hospital and orphan section. Rankin initially outlined four areas of service the section would provide: support charity care by reimbursing every not-for-profit hospital a dollar a day for each day of free care the hospital provided patients (at the time the cost of an average day of hospital care was less than four dollars; the endowment still makes these annual grants); serve as a central repository for record-keeping regarding hospital costs and professional services in the Carolinas, and share this information with hospitals to help them improve their operating efficiency; help communities organize their own efforts to care for the sick; and help promote a close working relationship between a large hospital and medical school at Duke University and smaller community hospitals in the Carolinas.

Roberson said that by 1928 the endowment was also making grants to help construct new hospitals in the Carolinas, again largely through Rankin's influence. Rankin was also an early advocate of the new concept of group hospitalization or prepayment that emerged in the 1930s. Russell said that Rankin persuaded communities—with the help of the Duke Endowment—to buy private hospitals and maintain them as community responsibilities.

When he retired from directorship of the hospital and orphan section in 1950, his report for the previous year showed that 130 hospitals in North Carolina and 52 in South Carolina were receiving Duke Endowment funds for operations and for capital expenses.

He ended up helping Wake Forest when one of his successors as dean accepted the funds from the Bowman Gray Foundation to move the medical school to Winston-Salem. "He was very supportive of the initial expansion of North Carolina Baptist Hospital in 1940, which was critical to the success of the fledgling four-year medical school," reported Meads.

Rankin remained a trustee for another fifteen years. For thirty-one years, he served as chairman of the Duke Endowment trustees' committee on hospitals and child care. On February 23, 1965, at the age of eighty-six and after forty years as a trustee, he resigned. He was promptly elected trustee emeritus, continuing to serve until his death on September 8, 1970.

In a resolution after his death, the Duke Endowment trustees said, "His knowledge of health and child care problems, his executive ability and his talent in communicating to the public the importance of these two fields enabled him to design and administer a program which has touched the lives of countless Carolinians for over 45 years." Rankin continued to have an impact even in his retirement years. During the 1960s, he was one of the strongest advocates for establishing outpatient clinics and services at Carolinas hospitals.

Rankin's official positions included president of the American Public Health Association, chairman of the executive committee and the section on preventive medicine of the American Medical Association, president of the Conference of Secretaries of State and Provincial Boards of Health, vice president of the National Association for the Study and Prevention of Tuberculosis, vice president of the National Association for the Study and Prevention of Infant Mortality, field director of the Committee on Municipal Health Policies, and trustee of the American Hospital Association.

Davidson College, Duke University, Wake Forest University, and the University of North Carolina conferred the honorary Doctor of Science degree on Rankin. In 1956, the North Carolina Citizens Association named him its Citizen of the Year. He was also an honorary fellow of the American Association of Hospital Administrators, even though he was never a hospital administrator. The Alpha Chapter of the Delta Omega Society, the public health honor society, chose Rankin as an honorary member in 1924, a signal honor, for "raising public health administration standards and contributing to the solution of the problems of rural health and hospitalization."

Rankin was a Rotarian, a Democrat, and a Baptist. His funeral was held at Myers Park Baptist Church, of which he was a founder, and he was buried in Charlotte's Evergreen Cemetery. In an editorial the

Charlotte News called Rankin a "complete and broad-ranging man." The editorial continued, "Devoted to his region, but never provincial. Scholarly, inquisitive, delighting in discussion of theology and philosophy with learned men, and yet also a man who spent a lifetime motivating the plain citizens of North and South Carolina towns to work with him to build a better health system."

Robert Conn has been science writer at Wake Forest University Baptist Medical Center in Winston-Salem since 1986. Before that he spent twenty-five years at the Charlotte Observer *as a writer and editor. Most of his writing experience was as a medical reporter and editor at the* Observer, *where he won a number of prizes, and he was part of a team that won the 1981 Pulitzer Prize Gold Medal for Public Service and the Robert F. Kennedy Grand Prize. He has continued to write about health issues outside Wake Forest on a freelance basis.*

For more information, see:

Carpenter, Coy C., M.D. *The Story of Medicine at Wake Forest University*. University of North Carolina Press, 1970

Hardie, Beatrice R. *North Carolina State Board of Health*. North Carolina Division of Archives and History, February 28, 1957. Revised by Frances S. Ashford, March 13, 1961.

Meads, Manson, M.D., assisted by Katherine Davis. *The Miracle on Hawthorne Hill: A History of the Medical Center of the Bowman Gray School of Medicine of Wake Forest University and the North Carolina Baptist Hospital*. Wake Forest University, 1988.

Paschal, George Washington. *History of Wake Forest College*. Wake Forest College, 1935.

Russell, Mattie U. "Watson S. Rankin." In *Dictionary of North Carolina Biography*, ed. William S. Powell. University of North Carolina Press, 1996.

MARY MARTIN SLOOP

By Mary Kratt

CERTAINLY it was not unusual in a Presbyterian college town for visiting missionaries to regale their hosts at dinner with colorful stories of the hardships and splendors of far-away countries and strange people. Such guests and their tales marked the life of young Mary Martin of Davidson. Born in 1873, she was one of ten children of William Joseph Martin, a Davidson College chemistry and geology professor, and Letitia Costin Martin, an ardent early member of the Presbyterian Ladies Benevolent Society and the College Presbyterian Church.

When Mary was only five, she quietly determined she too would become a missionary. She didn't tell anyone, but practiced teaching village children in the yard, perhaps emulating Miss Lucy Jurney, who taught the one-teacher school Mary attended. Miss Jurney's School for Boys and Girls and the Davidson campus and village provided Mary's schooling until she was fifteen. Her father then insisted that she go to Statesville Female College for Women about twenty miles north of Davidson. She didn't want to go there because she preferred boys, having grown up in the company of young male students visiting in her home, but she graduated in 1891 at the age of eighteen.

Mary's mother had become an invalid, so for the next decade, Mary stayed home and nursed her. It was arranged that she could take some of the Davidson College classes during this period under her mother's watchful eye. "At first, Mother insisted that I take my lessons in Father's study where she could be the chaperone for the professor and me. Fortunately he was married and middle-aged, so she didn't have to come in often," Mary recalled. She did not tell her mother, but since she wanted to be a medical missionary in Africa, she took as many science courses as she could, and studied French, a more ladylike pursuit, to please her mother. She was Davidson's only coed.

At the time, students took their first two years of premed courses in a two-story building adjacent to the Davidson College infirmary owned by Dr. John Peter Munroe, the Davidson College physician. For their third and fourth years, students went to Charlotte's North Carolina Medical College on North Church Street. From her teens, Mary was surrounded by chemistry and medicine and those who taught and studied such matters.

When her mother died in 1901, Mary was free to

Mary Martin and Eustace Sloop (Courtesy of Charlotte Observer)

pursue her medical studies. She had not been allowed in the college anatomy classes, for it was thought improper to have a woman in the dissecting room with "all those naked cadavers . . . the neighbors would never have recovered from the shock," she said. In class she had become reacquainted with one of her father's former students, Eustace Sloop, who had returned to take premedical courses and also planned to be a medical missionary.

In response to a letter from Mary, the Presbyterian Mission Board had informed her that she was too old (at thirty-three) to be accepted as a candidate for the mission field. She was undeterred. In order to take anatomy and the other requirements for a medical degree, she continued her medical studies at the Woman's Medical College in Philadelphia and graduated in 1906.

Sloop completed Davidson and then attended

Jefferson Medical School in Philadelphia before beginning his own practice in the mountains of western North Carolina. He chose an isolated Avery County village named Plumtree in a mica mining area about twenty-five miles from Blowing Rock, an area in as much need of a medical missionary as any foreign country.

After her internship at the New England Hospital for Women and Children in Boston, Mary became the resident physician at Agnes Scott College, a Presbyterian women's college near Atlanta. In 1908, she and Dr. Sloop married in Blowing Rock, and afterward both bride and groom rode on horseback in the rain to the Eseeola Hotel in Linville, then again rode on horseback into the remote mountains where they set up their joint medical practice. The Plumtree location proved difficult for even mountain patients to reach, so after three years the couple were persuaded to relocate to Crossnore in the Linville valley, where they lived and worked as physicians for over fifty years.

The doctors' influence and efforts to assist mountain people were extraordinary. She had spent summers with her family in Linville since she was a child and he grew up on a farm not far from Davidson, so the two of them had many skills learned from rural life, such as knowledge of horses and horseback riding, familiarity with pumps, wells, motors, and tools; and experience coping with primitive conditions — skills as valuable to them as chemistry, anatomy, and surgery. They became medical missionaries in a rural region that at the time was inaccessible and untouched by medicine, autos, telephones, radio, electricity, newspapers, schools, or visitors, and as foreign to American urban life as the African career she had once imagined.

Mary Sloop saw immediately the dearth of educational opportunities that severely limited the children and led to teen marriages and early pregnancies. Diet, clothing, shoes, and books drew her attention as she assisted "Doctor," as she called him, in surgery in remote cabins or in the open air. "Doctor" almost lived in the saddle tending mountain families, Mary recalled. When "Doctor" was gone on calls for days at a time in hazardous weather, she staffed the clinic alone, performing appendectomies, mending broken bones, or attending whatever emergency case rode up the path. Often a patient was carried in on a makeshift stretcher or slung across a saddle, having been carried through gullies, streams, and over mountaintops in a roadless wilderness. The Sloops' patients were suspicious of both medicine and "larnin'." Their diet consisted mostly of pork, greens, and grease. The main industry was moonshining.

Mary Sloop began a forty-year push for better schools, for classrooms and dormitory rooms, and for clothes and books and funds. Within a year she and her husband had built a school. They called mass meetings and preached perfect attendance to students in order to have the numbers of students to qualify with the State Board of Education for additional teachers. The mountain people constructed the buildings, hauling in supplies by wagon and clearing the land with mules and dragpans. Their one-room school slowly grew to twenty buildings on 350 acres with college-trained teachers and a farm for feeding the children and staff, funded bit by bit through hundreds of letters of appeal to friends in Davidson, Charlotte, Philadelphia, and to Daughters of the American Revolution contacts, wherever Mary could find them.

The Crossnore School boarded orphans or mountain children who lived too far away to otherwise attend. Mary Sloop established vocational and manual training classes such as carpentry and hired a crafts teacher to revive the mountain art of weaving, teaching students to weave and then sell their own wares. This fostered a craft, a wage-earning trade, and pride in mountain heritage and folk skills. Essayist Emily Herring Wilson wrote that Mary Sloop became a "relentless fund-raiser and effective lobbyist for passage of a compulsory school law."

She went to Raleigh many times to lobby the legislators to raise the law to age sixteen and fund paved roads and agriculture assistance and training. She was known as a "steam engine in skirts." She was quite effective, and to the chagrin of some she worked for more effective law enforcement against moonshiners. Through her extensive network of church women, hundreds of boxes of secondhand clothing and books arrived for the children to wear or to be sold to benefit the school.

Her memoir includes a story about Hepsie, a bright young girl that Mary Sloop wanted to send on to the nearest high school, about thirty miles away in Banner Elk. Finishing the lower grades usually meant it was time to get married. Sloop had seen too often these "child wives" become old and worn out from childbearing by age thirty, so she set out to help Hepsie, but she needed clothes and money to pay for her board in the town. Mary Sloop wrote friends in Davidson and soon money and a box of clothes arrived. Unfortunately all the dresses in the box were black, not suitable for a schoolgirl. So Mary Sloop hung the dresses out on the front porch and sold them, using the money to buy more colorful dresses for Hepsie, who then went on to high school. The clothing sale became a regular event and garments from all over the Carolinas were recycled to aid the children and projects at Crossnore.

Sloop was determined to improve life for the people of Crossnore and to help them want a better life. Her husband helped them acquire electricity, but the lack of a dependable income-producing crop was a problem. She wrote officials in Raleigh about the problem and two men came, one an accomplished poultry farmer. "This country won't do for poultry raising," he said.

The other man asked what was the best crop being grown in the mountains. "Irish potatoes," Mary Sloop replied. After the expert from Raleigh learned that the elevation was more than three thousand feet, he smiled and said, "You've got a gold mine here! You ought to grow the best seed potatoes in the world."

Mary Sloop recalled, "How we did begin to listen to that man from the Department of Agriculture! He was speaking at a mass meeting, and everybody in our section of the mountains had turned out. . . . Potatoes were something we knew about. There was hope."

So they grew potatoes as a revenue crop, quite successfully, but it only emphasized the lack of good roads to get them to market because good potatoes often rotted before reaching their destination. So after further correspondence with Raleigh, Mary Sloop was invited to come to Raleigh for a meeting of the legislature and stay six weeks to work with the Good Roads Committee that was pushing for improved roads in the 1920s under Governor Cameron Morrison.

She went often. She pushed and wrote and persuaded. She attended any meeting that might influence roads being built in Avery County. The Blue Ridge mountains sliced through Avery and the one good road north of the mountains was inaccessible to the eastern side of the county. To the rebuttal, "but you have a road in Avery County, Miz Sloop," she insisted, "We have to have that road." They got it and it made a world of difference, not just for the income from revenue crops of potatoes, beans, and cabbages, but for the other benefits it brought to the county's residents. Referred to for years by mountain neighbors as "them Sloops," the couple gradually earned respect and admiration.

In 1951, Mary Sloop received national recognition when, at age seventy-eight, she was named the American Mother of the Year. In 1942, she received the Algernon Sydney Sullivan Award from the Southern Society of New York, an award given annually to a student and a citizen of Davidson who gave of themselves selflessly for the betterment of the college and community.

Her delightful and unassuming memoir entitled *Miracle in the Hills* was published in 1953. The account was told, almost as she spoke it, to Charlotte author LeGette Blythe. "Life was daring us," Mary Sloop wrote. "Life was dealing out the cards. I would pick up my hand and play it. And I'd have fun, too, doing it." She died in Crossnore in 1962, a year after the death of her husband.

Mary Kratt of Charlotte is the author of numerous books of poetry, history, and biography. Twice winner of the Peace Prize-History Book Award from the N.C. Society of Historians, she received the 1999 Brockman/Campbell award for her poetry book, Small Potatoes, *and a 1996 N.C. Arts Council grant for a residency at the MacDowell Colony in New Hampshire. Her books about Charlotte include* Charlotte: Spirit of the New South *and* Remembering Charlotte: Postcards of a New South City.

For more information, see:
Beaty, Mary D. *Davidson: A History of the Town from 1835–1937.* Briarpatch Press, 1979.
Sloop, Mary Martin, with LeGette Blythe. *Miracle in the Hills.* McGraw-Hill, 1953.
Smith, Margaret Supplee, and Emily Herring Wilson. *North Carolina Women: Making History.* University of North Carolina Press, 1999.
Strong, Charles M. *History of Mecklenburg County Medicine.* 1902.

PHILANTHROPY

P HILANTHROPY that originated from a personal sense of mission and responsibility built several North Carolina colleges and universities and paid for hospitals and churches across the state. By the end of the century private foundations had proliferated and were shaping the quality of life of the entire state.

The church had perhaps the greatest influence on the millionaires created by the state's tobacco wealth at the beginning of the twentieth century. The Dukes of Durham, especially Washington and his sons James B. and Benjamin N., were devoted Methodists and weathered the criticism of many in the religious community who considered their cigarettes the very embodiment of sin. Much of that had faded by the second decade of the century after James B. Duke had transformed his tobacco wealth into Duke Power Company, which became the engine that produced many of the millions in the Duke Endowment, one of the first and the largest of the state's private foundations.

With their money, the Dukes built a university in Durham, aided Methodist pastors, built countless churches, sponsored hospitals and orphanages, and even provided for annual stipends for "super-attenuated" preachers no longer able to mount the pulpit. Their generosity was followed by succeeding generations through the work of Benjamin Duke's granddaughter, Mrs. Mary D. B. T. Semans, and James B. Duke's daughter, Doris, who left a fortune that dwarfed even that produced by her father.

Like the Dukes, their partner George W. Watts was moved by his religious faith and training to turn his considerable wealth to the improvement of colleges. As a dedicated Presbyterian who superintended the Sunday school program at Durham's First Presbyterian Church for more than thirty years, Watts was a valuable underwriter of the denomination's seminary in Richmond, Va., and he paid for buildings on colleges in North Carolina and around the South that carried his name. One of his lasting legacies was Watts Hospital in Durham, an institution that set the standard for care and served for a time in the clinical training of medical students at the university at Chapel Hill. His son-in-law, John Sprunt Hill, and grandson, George Watts Hill, continued the family tradition with gifts to the university and the Research Triangle Park that came at critical points in their development.

The leaders of the University of North Carolina at Chapel Hill may have scraped for funds every two years from the General Assembly, but at mid-century University President Frank Graham and his chief administrator, W. D. Carmichael Jr., had a trio of competitive benefactors, each ready to outdo the other in his generosity. One well-known picture shows three classmates—John Sprunt Hill, William R. Kenan Jr., and John Motley Morehead—all of whom were worth millions, which they left to the university. Morehead's money paid for the Morehead Planetarium and the Patterson-Morehead Bell Tower, but his richest legacy was the creation of the Morehead Scholars program. Hill paid for buildings and was a lifelong subscriber to the university's library, especially the North Carolina Collection, which he had created with an initial gift in 1904.

The Kenan family wealth—founded largely on the vast estate left to William R. Kenan Jr.'s sister by her husband, Henry Flagler, early in the century—established the Kenan professorships, money used to supplement the salaries of outstanding faculty members, and later the Kenan Center, where Frank H. Kenan organized programs for the study of American business.

Greensboro's Joe Bryan generously enabled the university to open the first public television broadcasting facility in the state. He also provided richly for medical research at Duke University and left his estate, funded in part from his Jefferson Standard Life Insurance Company shares and personal investments, to a community foundation charged with improving his adopted hometown. Also in Greensboro, the Cone family built a hospital that became a regional medical center for the piedmont.

In Charlotte, two brothers, I. D. and Herman Blumenthal, helped create a cultural center in the center city. The Belk department store family also contributed heavily to Davidson College, the University of North Carolina at Charlotte, Presbyterian Hospital, and other civic and charitable institutions and causes.

Other fortunes in textiles and tobacco changed Winston-Salem. The wealth of the Hanes family enriched the cultural life of the city, as well as the state, and helped underwrite the opening of the N.C. School of the Arts. And heirs to R. J. Reynolds, as well as others from the tobacco company, built a medical school for Wake Forest and then relocated the college, now the university, to the Winston-Salem community.

It was Reynolds's son-in-law, William Babcock, a quiet, determined man of vision, who helped move philanthropy beyond bricks and mortar. Babcock showed the emerging foundation leaders of the 1960s how to be creative and innovative when the Mary Reynolds Babcock Foundation, which he headed, provided important seed money for Governor Terry Sanford's North Carolina Fund, a private-public partnership aimed at improving the life of individuals and communities.

I. D. AND HERMAN BLUMENTHAL

By M. S. Van Hecke

IT ALL BEGAN with a leaky car radiator.
From that quirky 1924 beginning came one of North Carolina's healthiest privately held businesses, and a long, distinguished record of philanthropy. The roles of the company, Radiator Specialty, and the two brothers—I. D. and Herman Blumenthal—who ran it were intertwined. Company profits provided the men with the wealth to share millions of dollars with their temples, their city, and their state.

The car with the radiator problem was a handsome Packard, the prized possession of I. D.—his given name was Isidore Dick but he was known to all as I. D.—who was a young salesman from Savannah, Ga. He pulled into a Charlotte garage, fearful that repairing the radiator would take the usual two to three days. The garage owner, however, suggested he try a locally made compound that stopped leaks after it was poured into the radiator.

To Blumenthal's surprise the leak vanished. Convinced that the compound, called Solder Seal, could be a hot item, he peddled a car full of samples of the product up and down the East Coast. He was so successful he eventually bought the Charlotte company that made it, Radiator Specialty.

In 1937, I. D.'s younger brother, Herman, was a freshman at the University of North Carolina at Chapel Hill. After thirteen years of running Radiator Specialty by himself, I. D. decided he needed help and summoned Herman to join him, so Herman studied during the week, but "on weekends, I sold Solder Seal."

When I. D. bought a rubber products company in California, Herman went west to operate it. The plant supplied products to virtually all the country's military aircraft in World War II, but by that time Herman was not there to oversee it. He volunteered for military service and spent four years as an army officer. After the war, he returned to Charlotte, bringing his bride, Anita, with him.

Reunited, the brothers ran the company together, although I. D. was the owner. Because of the twenty-one-year difference in their ages, Herman said the relationship was more father-son than brother-brother. "We never had a quarrel," he recalled. I. D. and Herman also shared a devotion to philanthropy. "Our parents taught us that you had to give back to the community," Herman said. He and I. D. were the sons

of Samuel and Fannie Blumenthal, Lithuanian immigrants who operated a profitable department store in Savannah. I. D. was born on September 2, 1894, in New York City and Herman was born August 3, 1915, in Savannah.

I. D.'s charity mostly was related to Jewish causes, including establishing the Blumenthal home for Jewish widows in Clemmons and the sponsorship of a circuit-riding rabbi who visited Jewish communities too small to support their own temple. A special gift was the result of an unusual purchase that I. D. made in 1936. At the urging of a real estate agent, he made a lowball offer of $6,500 to a bankruptcy court for a 1,400-acre tract of land that included two large buildings near Little Switzerland in the North Carolina mountains north of Morganton. I. D. deeply believed that what he considered divine intervention—a cloud —led to what was a successful bid.

A bankruptcy judge in Texas, who was overseeing the sale of the property, was dubious about the low bid on a property valued at close to $200,000 at the time, and he sent an appraiser to determine its real value. As I. D. told it, he drove the appraiser to the tract on a beautiful, sunshiny day, but as they turned onto the road into the property they were enveloped in a dense fog. As they inched their way along the eerie mountain road, the appraiser grew more and more fearful. When they finally reached the buildings, the fog was so thick that neither man could see more than a dim outline. The agitated appraiser demanded to be taken off the mountain so he could return to Texas. Not long afterward, I. D. was notified that the land was his at his offered price.

I. D. loved his mountain land, called Wild Acres. He told his biographer, LeGette Blythe, it was "by far the most profitable business I've ever had a hand in. The most satisfying, most genuinely rewarding venture I've taken part . . . even though it has cost me a lot of money over the years." He often told visitors that he was the junior partner in Wild Acres, with God as his senior partner.

In time, he established the property as an idyllic retreat center for nonprofit, artistic, educational, or intercultural groups. The Wild Acres retreat was in great demand from late spring to early fall for retreats and conferences by religious and cultural groups such as the Charlotte Choral Society. Wild Acres was oper-

365

I. D. Blumenthal and Herman Blumenthal (Courtesy of Blumenthal Foundation)

ated on a virtually break-even basis, with the Blumenthals chipping in periodically for unusual capital costs.

A program called Friday Scholars, named for former University of North Carolina President William C. Friday, was one of the undertakings at Wild Acres. Every two years the program brought twenty-five bright young leaders from across North Carolina to weekend gatherings devoted to a mingling of ideas and civic goals. In 1998 and 1999, the Blumenthal Foundation put $272,000 into the Friday Scholars program, plus another $145,000 for Wild Acres itself.

In the waning years of his life, which ended at age eighty-four in 1978, I. D. devoted more and more of his time and energy to charities, while Herman took on more of the responsibilities of operating the firm. He succeeded his brother as head of the company upon his brother's death.

The brothers were not much alike in personality, said Herman's son Alan, but they shared two ideals. Both insisted on high-quality products and sharing their wealth. "Uncle Dick," as Alan called him, was the outgoing supersalesman who enjoyed the spotlight, while his father was more reserved and soft-spoken. Herman modestly deflected questions about his obviously successful business career, quickly switching subjects.

I. D. sought guidance in adding new lines of mer-

chandise by taking advice from shop owners and workmen of all stripes that he called on for sales or just for ideas. One surprising request I. D. received was for a higher-quality float ball that controlled water flow in a toilet. The balls used widely at the time did not last, he was told. I. D. created a more durable product and it went into the catalog of Radiator Specialty. Herman continued the practice, constantly adding new rubber and chemical items through research and development of in-house products or by adding popular items made by others to the sales line.

An example Herman remembered was a high quality rubber hose for washing machines that Radiator Specialty first bought for resale. Then "the manufacturer came to us and said, 'Since you sell so many of my hoses, why don't you just buy the company?' So we did."

Among the best-known company products were Liquid Wrench, which is used to loosen rusty nuts and bolts, and Gunk, a product later modified for environmental reasons that was sprayed on dirty car engines. Eventually, one of three Liquid Wrench products could be found not only in auto repair shops, but in most homeowners' toolboxes.

One widely used but almost invisible product was an oval gummy device that formed a seal between a commode and the sewer line. Most homeowners were not even aware it was there except under the unhappy circumstance when it had to be replaced. Motorists became familiar with another Radiator Specialty product —the ubiquitous orange plastic traffic cones placed to direct vehicles around construction sites. The company also made the reflective vests worn by police officers and construction workers.

Alan Blumenthal, who became company chairman in August 2000, said Radiator Specialty manufactured just over half of the thousands of products it sold. An army of manufacturer's agents handled sales to repair shops, service stations, plumbing shops, hardware stores, home supply stores, convenience stores, and even groceries.

Radiator Specialty employed nearly six hundred workers at major facilities in two Charlotte locations and another in Union County's Indian Trail. Customers in California and Canada also found packaging printed in Spanish and French.

As Herman aged he reduced his work schedule, but even at age eighty-four he was still visiting his office two or three times a week. However, he never curtailed his community involvement. He and Anita attended a wide variety of musical, social, and educational events.

In 2000, the Blumenthal Foundation had assets of $25 million and was directed by Herman's son Philip, a leading environmentalist who also was in charge of Wild Acres. Herman's third son, Daniel, was a clinical psychologist but sat on the boards of both the company and the foundation. In 1999, the foundation gave away $2.5 million, twice the amount required of private foundations by federal regulators. However, the foundation's charities reflected only a portion of the Blumenthal gifts, which often came in multiyear grants. On occasion Herman made the entire gift, as when he donated Old Island off Beaufort, S.C., to the Nature Conservancy. On other occasions, the foundation acted alone. Often Herman personally gave at least a portion of the total for some cause, and the foundation provided the remainder.

A $3.5 million gift capped the public campaign that created the North Carolina Blumenthal Performing Arts Center, a glittering two-theater jewel in Charlotte's center city. Herman made the first several payments on a ten-year pledge, after which the foundation took over.

The foundation's published reports for 1998 and 1999 showed the trends in the Blumenthals' philanthropy, which Philip said were determined by the board, made up of his parents and the three sons. Multiyear gifts included $2.5 million to the Jewish Day School, $1.25 million for temple endowment funds,

$550,000 to the Jewish Federation of Greater Charlotte, and $500,000 for the Jewish Community Center's endowment.

Other nonsectarian grants included $850,000 to Charlotte's Arts and Science Council, $1 million to the Blumenthal Cancer Center at Carolinas Medical Center, $300,000 to Queens College for the Blumenthal Fellows M.B.A. program, $250,000 for the Blumenthal chair of Jewish Studies at the University of North Carolina at Charlotte, $500,000 for three projects at UNC-Chapel Hill, and $100,000 to the Sierra Club.

All this brought much honor to Herman Blumenthal. He won accolades from the Jewish community, the Charlotte World Trade Council (Radiator Specialty did business in eighty-three countries), and the National Council of Christians and Jews, among others.

"It would be impossible for me to really say how valuable Herman Blumenthal has been," said Hugh McColl Jr., former Bank of America chairman. "He is a great philanthropist, he has led by example, he has brought all of us an understanding of the value of not only the arts but education, compassion, leadership, everything."

"Herman is an angel," said Judith Allen, president of the North Carolina Blumenthal Performing Arts Center. "He is an extraordinary man with an extraordinary wife and extraordinary family who are committed to humanitarian and cultural causes. He is a warm human being, someone you want to be around and someone who wants to be around you."

"Herman sees things in a global perspective, through mankind," said Rolfe Neill, former *Charlotte Observer* publisher. "The geography is sort of irrelevant. In addition to helping his own religion, Judaism, he will help your religion—Presbyterian, Baptist, Hindu, Episcopalian, whatever. If it's global, if it's human kind, Herman is for it."

North Carolina Governor James B. Hunt, Jr. thanked Herman for his generosity and for "helping build relationships among the people of the state. You are just absolutely terrific, and we love you and admire you, and I'm glad to be your friend."

Herman Blumenthal died October 28, 2001.

M. S. Van Hecke of Waxhaw is a former editor and writer for the Charlotte Observer. *He wrote and produced* A Free and Independent People, *a video history of Charlotte and Mecklenburg County narrated by Charles Kuralt.*

For more information see:
Blumenthal Family. Special collections. Robinson-Spangler Room, Public Library of Charlotte-Mecklenburg County.

JOSEPH M. BRYAN

By Ned Cline

JOE BRYAN was walking casually along the streets of New York City on a crisp fall evening in 1947 when he noticed an excited group of people crowding around a large storefront window. Trouble, he thought, and he started to turn away. Then he realized no one else seemed frightened or was leaving. Rather, people in the crowd beckoned Bryan and anyone else within earshot to come and see for themselves.

Bryan walked to the window and for the first time witnessed something called television. He was mesmerized. So what if the picture looked like an out-of-focus snowstorm snapshot from a cheap camera and he had no idea what he was watching. If people in Manhattan could get that excited about a fuzzy talking picture inside a wooden box, Bryan instinctively knew he wanted to be a part of it. That was the start of what evolved into commercial television in North Carolina, followed shortly by the creation of public television. Bryan was a designing architect of both.

Joseph McKinley Bryan of Greensboro was a vice president of Jefferson Standard Life Insurance and in New York on business when he saw his first television broadcast. But from that moment on in his professional life, insurance took a back seat to broadcasting in general and television in particular. While Bryan got into broadcasting almost by accident, his success was anything but accidental. After convincing his father-in-law, Julian Price, who was then president of Jefferson, to spend $10,000 to save a bankrupt Greensboro radio station in 1934, Bryan set out to prove that determination and vision could bring success. He quickly began turning a profit at the station—whose call letters were WBIG (We Believe In Greensboro)—and recouped the purchase price during his first year.

That success led to Jefferson's 1945 purchase from CBS of Charlotte's WBT radio for a fraction over a competing bid of $1.5 million. WBT executive Charles Crutchfield had learned the *Charlotte Observer* was interested in buying the station and was planning to offer a bid of $1.5 million. Crutchfield, who knew of Jefferson's success with the Greensboro station, advised Bryan if he would add a mere $5,000 to the *Observer*'s bid, Jefferson could win the bid. That's exactly what happened and Bryan was handed the responsibility of running the station and given the title of Jefferson Broadcasting president.

While it was radio that got Bryan into broadcast-

Joseph M. Bryan (Courtesy of Joseph M. Bryan Foundation)

ing, it was television that moved him to the forefront of the industry. Within six months of his first glance at a television, Bryan set out to secure a license to launch North Carolina's first commercial station. "I was fascinated with television," Bryan said later. "I just said I want that [for Jefferson]. We've got to have that. It's the coming thing. So I came home and we put in an application for a license."

On July 15, 1949, less than two years after Bryan applied for a license, WBTV, under the leadership of Bryan and Crutchfield, made the first television broadcast in North Carolina. From that rapid-fire start, Bryan was on course to make WBTV a deserved and recognized leader among broadcasters in the South and across the country in the early days of commercial television. Under Bryan's leadership, Jefferson also started television stations in Virginia and South Carolina.

At the same time that Bryan was establishing the first commercial television station in Charlotte, officials of the University of North Carolina at Chapel Hill were putting together plans for a university-operated station under Federal Communications Commission plans to open channels for public television. UNC leaders wanted to be in the first wave, but progress came slowly. They got a big boost from Bryan.

In the early 1950s, Bryan was well along in his application for a second station, this one in the Durham-Chapel Hill area, which happened to be the same channel that UNC wanted for their station. Anxious about the competition, UNC administrators went to see Bryan. Not to worry, Bryan said, and he withdrew his application and worked to help get UNC's application approved. In addition, he turned over Jefferson's application team to the university and arranged for equipment from Jefferson to help get the UNC station on the air. "Joe just turned everything over to the university," Crutchfield later said. "He did it all for educational enhancement. That was one of the most meaningful things he ever did as a broadcast executive. It was his decision alone and he didn't hesitate at all."

At the time, Bryan's generosity cost his company thousands of dollars. Ultimately, the sacrifice amounted to millions, since Jefferson lost the potential of a profitable commercial station in one of the state's fastest growing markets.

Once UNC secured its television license and was ready to raise private money to supplement inadequate state funding and begin operation, Bryan was the first corporate leader to make a contribution. He later provided $1 million to help open the new UNC-TV studios in Research Triangle Park, which are named for Bryan and his wife, Kathleen, and in 1995 he left $1 million in his will for university television.

While Bryan was an important player in bringing both public and commercial broadcast excellence to North Carolina, that was just part of the positive impact he had on the state, particularly involving education and philanthropy. He was, however, an unlikely candidate for any of that.

Joseph McKinley Bryan was born February 11, 1896, in Elyria, Ohio, to a vagabond father unable to hold a steady job and a mother suffering from depression and incapable of caring for her six children born in less than eight years. The father deserted the family in 1902 when Bryan was still in elementary school, never to return or offer financial support. Thirty years later, his father did ask for forgiveness—by letter. Bryan's mother was placed in a mental institution for the hopelessly insane after her husband abandoned

his family, and the children were farmed out to relatives and strangers in boarding homes. One brother was literally given to a widowed acquaintance who said she had always wanted a little boy.

As an adult Bryan never publicly acknowledged the existence of either parent, possibly out of shame or embarrassment. When he was married in 1927, he said both his parents were deceased. (His father lived until 1939. His mother survived fifty-one years in New Jersey mental wards, dying in 1954. He did not attend the funerals of either parent.) Bryan discussed his early life with only a few close friends, and then only late in his life. The true story was found after Bryan's death in family records and papers Bryan donated to the University of North Carolina at Greensboro.

Bryan was named for his Irish-born paternal grandfather, Joseph, a Union soldier in the Civil War, and President William McKinley. The Bryan family was composed of staunch Republicans when Joe was born and, because Democrats had nominated William Jennings Bryan for president, the middle name McKinley was chosen as a way of showing disdain for Democrats and support for Republicans.

Bryan was bounced from school to school as his parents moved from town to town and he never earned a high school diploma. He was able to obtain one year of prep school, at Mount Hermon in Norfield, Mass., with a loan from an uncle who lived on Staten Island. He never attended college.

Bryan's closest friends said the trauma of his childhood drove him to succeed in business and investments to ensure that he could help others with basic needs. He started his business career in 1919 as a clerk for a brokerage company on Wall Street, following service in the medical corps in World War I in Europe. The clerkship job took him to Haiti for three years, where he brokered deals for cotton and other products. When he returned to the United States in 1923, he became the youngest member of the New York Cotton Exchange. Hard work and marriage to the right woman put Bryan on the road to financial security.

On November 19, 1927, Bryan married Kathleen Price of Greensboro, the daughter of the president of Jefferson Standard Life Insurance Company. After the marriage, the Bryans lived in New York for four years where daughters Kay and Nancy were born, until Kathleen's parents, Julian and Ethel Clay Price, decided it was time for their daughter to come home. To achieve that, Price offered his son-in-law a job at Jefferson, at a salary of sixty-five dollars a month in 1931. A son, Joe Jr., was born after the couple moved to Greensboro.

Bryan worked in insurance only a short time before launching the broadcast side of the company. He began investing in Jefferson stock in 1933, adding regularly to his portfolio, and retired in 1961 after serving in a series of corporate positions. Following his retirement, Bryan invested heavily in oil well drilling in the deep South and made millions more. His investments and his wife's inheritance made the Bryans wealthy.

His resources allowed him to socialize with the rich and famous in some of the most exclusive resorts in this country as well as England and Spain. While on frequent shooting trips to London, Bryan used a personal chauffeur-driven Rolls Royce. Among his friends were cowboy star Gene Autry and advice columnist Ann Landers. He was a longtime member of Augusta National Golf Club.

A man of strong will, Bryan was something of a paradox and at times a revolving contradiction. He could be magnanimous and gregarious one moment and unbending and intractable the next. The latter was especially true with his own family, where his relationships were seldom tranquil and often strained. Despite his staunch Republican upbringing, Bryan was a strong southern Democrat most of his adult life, supporting progressive North Carolina governors Kerr Scott, Terry Sanford, and Jim Hunt. But he switched to support Republican United States Senator D. McLauchlin Faircloth in 1992. Faircloth had once been married to his daughter, Nancy.

Bryan's North Carolina philanthropy was widespread, if not well known. He contributed millions to the school of business and other programs at the University of North Carolina at Greensboro. He contributed $4 million for a new student center at Duke University and donated more than $10.5 million for neurological research at Duke Medical Center, with emphasis on Alzheimer's research. Mrs. Bryan died of Alzheimer's in 1984 and Bryan willingly offered his financial resources in search of a cure.

Bryan was the first person to contribute to building the N.C. School of Science and Math in Durham. He paid for a dormitory at Guilford College and left half a million dollars in his will to colleges in Greensboro and Winston-Salem. His financial help was instrumental in developing and maintaining a massive public park and golf course in Greensboro.

Bryan and his wife created the Bryan Family Fund in 1955, but following her death he formed his own foundation with the stipulation that his assets be spent only in greater Greensboro. At his death in April 1995, eleven months before his one-hundredth birthday, Bryan's foundation had assets of some $80 million. At the beginning of 2000, after having given away millions, the foundation assets had grown to almost $160 million, most of it in Jefferson stock.

At his funeral, the minister said, "There are not many institutions around here that Joe Bryan hasn't started, saved or improved." Indeed, Bryan started, saved, and improved many things through his philanthropy. His goal, he said, was to add value to the lives he touched. He considered his generosity as an investment in people. In philanthropy and business, he expected high returns.

During Ned Cline's career as a journalist he was a reporter and editor with the Charlotte Observer *and the Greensboro* News and Record. *He is a graduate of Catawba College and was a Neiman Fellow at Harvard University, where he studied southern politics. His biography of Joe Bryan is titled* Adding Value: The Joseph M. Bryan Story from Poverty to Philanthropy.

For more information, see:

Bryan Family. Historic and business papers. Archives of the Special Collections Section, Jackson Library, University of North Carolina at Greensboro.

Cline, Ned. *Adding Value: The Joseph M. Bryan Story from Poverty to Philanthropy*. Down Home Press, 2000.

THE DUKE FAMILY

By Robert F. Durden

ORN to a hardscrabble yeoman farmer's life in what was then Orange County on December 20, 1820, Washington Duke plowed countless furrows in the years before the Civil War. When the penniless Confederate veteran returned from the war, however, he soon shifted into the business of the home manufacture of smoking tobacco. Then in the mid-1870s he and his family moved three miles from the homestead into the small but growing village of Durham. There in 1878, W. Duke Sons and Company was incorporated and joined the ranks of a number of small tobacco manufacturers, who were all overshadowed by the older and larger W. T. Blackwell and Company, owners of the world-famous "Bull Durham" brand of smoking tobacco.

In the mid-1880s the Duke company gambled on a new technology that proved to be the family's pathway to wealth. James Buchanan Duke, born on December 23, 1856, and Washington Duke's youngest child, proved to be the entrepreneurial genius of the family. He persuaded his father and the other partners in the company to take a chance on a new machine for making cigarettes that had been invented (but not perfected) by a young Virginian named James A. Bonsack. The well-established cigarette-producing companies in Richmond, Va., insisted that American smokers of the newfangled cigarette preferred the hand-rolled variety. "Buck" Duke, as his family and intimate friends called him, believed otherwise, and in exchange for an agreement to give the Bonsack machine an all-out trial, he gained a secret, advantageous rate for the rental of Bonsack's invention.

A self-trained "engineer" and tinkerer himself, young J. B. Duke also had the expert assistance of a young mechanic, William T. O'Brien, who accompanied the first Bonsack machines to Durham. O'Brien and Duke got the contraption to work smoothly, and within a few years W. Duke Sons & Company was the largest cigarette manufacturer in the nation. By 1890, after much complicated negotiation over several years, the Duke firm joined with four other major cigarette manufacturers to form the American Tobacco Company, a holding company that soon came to be popularly known as the "tobacco trust." The thirty-three-year-old James B. Duke, as the first president and prime organizer of the American Tobacco Company, was on his way to becoming "King of the Mountain"

in tobacco, and the Washington Duke family was growing rich, at first by strictly southern standards (for the South was by far the nation's poorest region) and then gradually even by national measurements.

The charitable gifts Washington Duke and his children made before that time are not known. What is known is that one of the earliest—and by far the most long-continuing—recipients of Duke philanthropy was Trinity College in Randolph County. Tracing its humble origins back to a one-room Methodist- and Quaker-sponsored school in 1838, the institution became affiliated with North Carolina Methodism in 1859 and took the name Trinity. It managed to graduate each year a small number of young men, most of whom became teachers and preachers.

In 1887, soon after Trinity had narrowly escaped closure, Benjamin Newton Duke, who was born April 27, 1855, and was J. B. Duke's older brother, gave Trinity a thousand dollars and agreed to become a trustee. In 1890 Trinity's new Pennsylvania-born and Yale-trained president, John F. Crowell, decided that Trinity would have to move from utterly bucolic surroundings in Randolph County (five miles from the nearest railroad) to one of the piedmont's up-and-coming industrial towns. Inviting bids from any and all North Carolina towns that might want to adopt a college, Trinity found Washington Duke's offer of $85,000 on behalf of Durham irresistible. Furthermore, another staunch Methodist of Durham, Julian S. Carr, offered some fifty acres of land on the city's western edge as a site for the college. Washington Duke's gift to Trinity was widely hailed as the largest single philanthropic gift of money up to that time in the state's history.

Crowell, ambitious for Trinity but also naive, thought Trinity would be well fixed once it occupied its new home in the fall of 1892. One could literally smell money in Durham at the time, where tobacco-related enterprises perfumed the air, and Crowell had grand—but totally unrealistic—ideas about a "Greater Trinity," even perhaps a university. The fact was, however, that Washington Duke and Julian Carr felt that they had done their share and that other Methodists in the state would have to step up and help. The "other Methodists," however, were, like most southerners at that time, in no shape to indulge in philanthropy. While the southern agricultural economy was never robust after the Civil War, the bottom truly fell

Left to right: James B. Duke and Benjamin N. Duke (courtesy of N.C. Office of Archives and History), Mary D. B. T. Semans (courtesy of the Duke Endowment)

out in 1893 when a massive depression—then called a "panic"—hit the entire nation.

Nevertheless, having played such a key role in bringing Trinity to Durham, Ben Duke, joined by his brother "Buck" and their only sister, Mary Duke Lyon (Mrs. Robert E. Lyon, who was born on November 17, 1853), decided to extend emergency support to the college of $7,500 a year for three years, while others beat the bushes to raise additional funds.

Meantime, friction with the trustees (for one thing, about the new game of football that Crowell had imported, along with many more purely academic ideas, from the North) led to Crowell's resignation in 1894. Fate then surely smiled upon Trinity, for as Crowell's successor the trustees named a spellbinding Methodist preacher from South Carolina named John C. Kilgo. Washington Duke heard Kilgo preach in the oldest Methodist church in Durham, Trinity, on his first Sunday morning in town and that evening at the church which the Dukes had originally begun in connection with their tobacco factory, Main Street Methodist Church (later Duke Memorial).

Soon Washington Duke was asserting to all who would listen that Kilgo was undoubtedly the greatest preacher since St. Paul. His enthusiasm about Trinity College rekindled, Duke in 1896 offered the college $100,000 for endowment if it would admit women students on an "equal footing" with men. Just why Duke wanted women students at Trinity is not known, for he did not say. Quite an independent thinker, he had earlier defied the white southern majority's orthodoxy by becoming in 1867 a staunch Republican, a "scalawag," when that party first appeared in North

Carolina. The sad death of his only daughter, Mary Duke Lyon, in April 1893 at age forty may have inspired Duke to make a silent tribute to her memory.

In 1898 Duke contributed another $100,000 to Trinity's endowment and the following year his son Ben gave the college $50,000 for various new buildings that Trinity needed. Ben, possibly aided by his father, persuaded his brother "Buck" in 1902 to foot the bill for a handsome new library building for Trinity, plus $10,000 for books. (The significance of the money that the Dukes gave to Trinity in the early years is pointed up by the fact that the state's appropriation to the University of North Carolina for 1899–1900 was $25,000. Moreover, the university's income from all sources for that time came to only $48,000.)

Although Trinity clearly had become the chief beneficiary of the Dukes' philanthropy, numerous other North Carolina colleges also received handsome contributions from the family. Washington Duke rescued the Methodist-sponsored Louisburg Female College in 1891, and later Ben Duke conveyed title to the property to the North Carolina Conference of the Methodist Church. When Methodist-sponsored Greensboro Female College faced a crisis in 1901, Ben Duke gave it $5,000 and another $10,000 a few years later for endowment.

Guilford College, the Quaker institution that had grown out of the New Garden School attended by the younger Dukes, had a special claim on the family's philanthropy. Accordingly, Ben and J. B. Duke gave the college $10,000 in 1897 for a new science building, and numerous other gifts to Guilford followed in later years.

Washington Duke had a friendly relationship with African American Tar Heels, and while the list of all of their schools and churches to which the Dukes contributed would require too much space, one institution, Kittrell College, may serve as a symbol. Washington Duke left it $5,000 in his will; and in the 1920s Ben Duke made much larger gifts to Kittrell as well as to a sizable number of other African American institutions.

While the Dukes obviously liked giving to colleges, especially but not exclusively those that were Methodist-related, higher education was by no means their only charitable concern. The Oxford Orphanage, sponsored by the North Carolina Masonic Order, to which Washington Duke belonged, became an early recipient of the family's attention. While J. B. Duke moved to New York City in the mid-1880s and never again lived in Durham, Ben Duke always kept a home there, even after he acquired a Fifth Avenue mansion in New York in the early 1900s. Accordingly, Washington and Ben Duke became deeply committed to supporting the orphanage, and spending the day at the orphanage to assess its needs.

When the Dukes' business partner, George W. Watts, gave Watts Hospital to the white people of Durham in the 1890s, the Dukes naturally also supported it. In 1901 Ben and J. B. Duke gave Lincoln Hospital to Durham's African American community and followed through with generous support for it in later years.

Another area in which the Dukes operated philanthropically, albeit unsystematically, concerned aging Methodist preachers and churches, especially the ones in the poorest rural areas. Circuit-riding preachers consoled and guided Washington Duke through various crises in his life—such as the untimely deaths of both his first and second wives. The church at the time made scant provision for elderly preachers, so Duke tried to do what he could to help those who appealed to him, as many did. Likewise, small, poverty-stricken Methodist congregations struggled to pay their preachers and maintain their buildings. Ben, acting as his father's agent, wrote countless letters, with checks enclosed.

The Dukes' motives for this philanthropy were undoubtedly mixed. In wanting to bring Trinity College to Durham, for example, they were obviously inspired partly by a desire to see their hometown acquire an adornment, a cultural asset. Like others in Durham, they much wanted the bustling city to be, and to be perceived as being, progressive and modern.

When all is said and done, however, the fountainhead of Duke philanthropy seems to have been in

Dr. Wilburt Davison, Doris Duke, and Dr. William Wannaker (Courtesy of Duke University Archives)

Washington Duke's profound, lifelong love and respect for the Methodist Church. Converted at an early age in Mount Bethel Methodist Church at a crossroads settlement known as Balltown (later Bahama) near his birthplace, he developed an absolutely unwavering devotion to the church and its teachings. Among those teachings was an ancient Christian idea about the stewardship of wealth. That is, those who were fortunate enough to possess wealth had a special responsibility both to use it wisely and to share it with those less fortunate. Not so much through words as through deeds, Washington Duke demonstrated his deep belief in that teaching of Methodism, and he raised his children to believe likewise.

After Washington Duke died in 1905 at age eighty-five, and especially after Kilgo left Trinity in 1910 to become a Methodist bishop, many people speculated that the Dukes would lose interest in the school. That was by no means the case, however, for William P. Few, the quiet English professor and dean who succeeded Kilgo as president, soon had Ben Duke more enthusiastic about, and generously inclined toward, the college than ever. In fact, by the time of World War I, Trinity had developed into one of the stronger liberal arts colleges in the South, thanks to a significant degree to the Dukes' generosity. With high academic standards and an able, ambitious faculty, Trinity had come far from its desperate situation in the 1880s.

Unfortunately, Ben Duke, who had long been the family's chief liaison with Trinity, became ill around 1915 and gradually slipped into semi-invalidism. J. B. Duke had long deferred to his older brother in the philanthropic area, as Ben Duke deferred to his younger brother in business. J. B. Duke then began, however, to take a more direct and larger interest in philanthropy. While totally divorced from the domestic tobacco industry after the Supreme Court ordered the dissolution of the American Tobacco Company in 1911, J. B. Duke continued to play a major role in the British-American Tobacco Company headquartered in London. Moreover, from 1905 onward he became increasingly involved in the building of a pioneering electric utility company headquartered in Charlotte. First known as the Southern Power Company, it became the Duke Power Company in 1924 and was destined, as J. B. Duke intended, to play a major role in the economic transformation of the Piedmont Carolinas.

Beginning around 1914, if not sooner, J. B. Duke, who always thought on a bigger and more elaborate scale than the other members of his family, began to revolve in his mind the notion of using a substantial portion of his equity in the power company as the basis for large-scale, perpetual philanthropy in his native region. World War I and other circumstances delayed the implementation of his plan, but in the interim Duke took some new philanthropic initiatives on his own. He and his brother had long been making substantial gifts to help with Trinity's annual budget, but in 1915 J. B. Duke not only assigned his own landscape architects to help with plans for Trinity's campus but also provided a special fund of $10,000 for the grounds. That was the one and only area of Trinity's operation where the Dukes became personally and directly involved, for they were model benefactors insofar as the academic side of the college was concerned—that is, they never interfered with or meddled in it.

Also starting in 1915, J. B. Duke began making an annual contribution of $10,000 to supplement the funds of the two Methodist conferences in North Carolina for retired preachers and the widows and orphans of deceased preachers. In addition, J. B. Duke began giving $25,000 annually for the building and current expenses of rural Methodist churches in North Carolina, with both funds being administered through Trinity College.

Around 1916 J. B. Duke intimated to President Few that at some time in the future he had "something big" in mind for the college. Finally, in 1919, J. B. Duke revealed something of his plan to use much of his stock in the power company as a basis for long-term support of both Trinity College and the Methodist causes. Naturally delighted, Few soon wrote J. B. Duke: "As I have thought of your plan, it grows in my mind. I think it really is a sounder idea than that around which any other large benevolence in this country with which I am familiar has been built." If Duke and his lawyers found that the charitable trust could not be administered under the charter of Trinity College, Few continued, then a separate foundation could be created and have as its trustees the seven members of the executive committee of Trinity's trustees.

As Few had painfully to learn, however, J. B. Duke was not ready to act, primarily because the power company's rates, as determined by North Carolina's regulatory body, were too low for the company's stock to pay adequate dividends. With Few and Trinity facing serious problems resulting from wartime inflation and a growing influx of both men and women students, however, Duke increased his gifts to the college.

Recuperating from an extended illness in 1921, Few had a brainstorm. Pulling together various ideas that had been circulating among Trinity's leaders since the 1890s and certain developments already under way, Few presented Duke with a memorandum outlining specific plans for the organization of a full-fledged university around Trinity. That is, Trinity would serve as the core or "heart" of a new institution that would include a divinity school, law school, several other schools, and, if sufficient funds were available, a medical school. To provide adequate facilities for women students, there would have to be a coordinate college for women.

Since there was already a Trinity University in San Antonio, Texas, and countless other colleges with that name throughout the English-speaking world, Few suggested that the new, expanded institution should have its own, distinctive name—Duke University. While Ben Duke had heartily endorsed Few's plan before its presentation to his brother, J. B. Duke was simply not ready to act, although he indicated his general approval of Few's projected university.

By 1924 J. B. Duke was ready to act on his plan for perpetual philanthropy in the Carolinas. From his home in Charlotte he announced early in December, 1924, that he was giving $40 million in prime securities (mostly, but not exclusively, stock in the Duke Power Company) to a charitable trust to be known as the Duke Endowment. It would have its own board of fifteen, self-perpetuating trustees and would distribute the annual income from the trust in the following manner: 32 percent was to go to Duke University; another 32 percent would go to assist communities in both Carolinas that wished to build non-profit hospitals and to help pay for the care of indigents in those hospitals — such assistance to be equally available to African American as well as white institutions; 12 percent to the above-mentioned Methodist causes in North Carolina; 10 percent for orphanages (later child care) for both whites and blacks in the Carolinas; and 14 percent to three additional educational institutions — 5 percent to Davidson College (Presbyterian), 5 percent to Furman University (Baptist), and 4 percent to Johnson C. Smith University (African American and Presbyterian).

As a result, Duke University was established in late December 1924. Few and Duke, in consultation with various others, had decided to redesign the old Trinity campus, add eleven red-brick Georgian buildings, and, when the buildings on the new campus a mile or so to the west of the old one were completed in the fall of 1930, turn the old or East Campus over to a coordinate Woman's College of Duke University. For the new or West Campus, where the undergraduate men and the professional schools would be located, Few, Duke, and others selected a Tudor Gothic style of architecture, with the colorful stone from a nearby quarry in Hillsborough. For these physical plants and a forested area of five thousand acres (later expanded to eight thousand) adjoining the West Campus, J. B. Duke provided around $19 million.

Just as construction had begun on the new buildings on the East Campus, however, death caught J. B. Duke by surprise in October 1925. He would have been sixty-nine in December, and by his will he added approximately $69 million to the original $40 million in the Duke Endowment. For a long period it would rank as the third largest foundation in the nation, but, as new and larger foundations multiplied in the closing decades of the twentieth century, its ranking fell.

Ben Duke, although a virtual invalid during the last several years of his life (he died early in 1929), acted as a one-man foundation during his last four years by giving away nearly $3 million to a wide variety of colleges and schools throughout the Southeast. Most of his wealth, which was not as great as J. B. Duke's, he divided among his wife, son Angier B. Duke, and daughter Mary.

Angier and Mary Duke, both Trinity graduates, carried on the family tradition by making large, annual gifts to the college and in 1922 by jointly contributing $25,000 toward a new gymnasium. Angier

Duke met an untimely death in a boating accident in 1923, but in his will he left $250,000 to Trinity College. The *Charlotte Observer,* in noting that gift, declared that the "descendants of the first great friend of that institution [Washington Duke] have developed a passion for education."

The subsequent gifts to Duke University of Ben Duke's daughter, Mary Duke Biddle (Mrs. Anthony J. Drexal Biddle III), continued throughout her life. Some of the more important ones were the Duke Homestead, which the university later gave to the state to become a historic site; the terraces in the Sarah P. Duke Gardens, as a memorial to her mother; the Durham home of the Ben Dukes, "Four Acres"; and, perhaps most importantly, a large and much-needed addition in 1949 to the original library on West Campus.

In 1956, four years before her death, Mrs. Biddle established the Mary Duke Biddle Foundation. Stipulating that at least half of the foundation's annual income should go to Duke University for various purposes selected by the foundation's trustees, she wished the remaining annual income to be used to further her lifelong interests in religious, educational, artistic, and charitable activities in the states of North Carolina and New York. At the end of 1998 the foundation had assets of over $18 million.

Although Mrs. Biddle's daughter, Mary Duke Biddle II, was born in New York on February 21, 1920, and spent her early years there, she developed stronger ties with North Carolina and Duke University than any other family member of her generation. Moreover, she virtually made a career of philanthropic and civic activity, which she carefully blended with the raising of her seven children.

Mary Duke Biddle II often visited Durham, especially with her grandmother, and because of her family's traditional ties to the institution she was inspired to attend Duke University, where she met her first husband, Dr. Josiah C. Trent. After marrying young, the couple had four daughters and built a home in Durham. A few years after Dr. Trent's untimely death, his widow married Dr. James H. Semans, and they had three children.

Becoming much involved in the affairs of both Duke University and Durham as well as North Carolina's civic and political life, Mary Semans became a trustee of the Duke Endowment in 1957, partly on the recommendation of another trustee, her great-aunt, Mrs. James B. Duke. In 1982 she became the first woman to chair the endowment's trustees, a position she still held in 2000. In addition to her work as a trustee and member of the executive committee of

Duke University, Mrs. Semans and her husband played leading roles in the establishment and support of the North Carolina School of the Arts in Winston-Salem and in other important state ventures.

In 1977 Mary Semans established the Josiah C. Trent Memorial Foundation in memory of her first husband. It provided start-up funds—seed money—to faculty and staff members of Duke University in certain specified areas. The family also established two other relatively small but highly creative philanthropies: the Duke-Semans Fine Arts Foundation and the Mary Duke Biddle Trent Semans Foundation. The former has "an overall purpose of reaching out to smaller communities and organizations to present the arts with the sole motive to raise the spirit, to stimulate and to inspire;" the latter foundation, with no geographical restrictions, disburses funds for innovative projects in the fields of community service, education, and the arts.

Unlike Mary Semans, her cousin Doris Duke, the only child of James B. Duke, never developed close ties with either North Carolina or Duke University. Although both her parents were born in the South (Mrs. James B. Duke was a native of Georgia), Doris Duke grew up and remained a cosmopolitan New Yorker and world traveler. If she did not inherit her father's distinctively southern sense of place and roots, she did, to a degree unknown during her lifetime, inherit the Duke family's penchant for philanthropy.

When Doris Duke (born November 22, 1912) died in October 1993 at almost eighty-one, many observers were astounded when her will revealed that she had left her fortune of over $1.2 billion to the Doris Duke Charitable Foundation. Making grants primarily in the areas of her special interests—the arts, the environment, and medical research—the foundation distributed in 1997–98, its first year of operation, around $55 million. That magnitude of philanthropy placed Doris Duke in the bracket with her father. What the public did not realize, however, was that she had been philanthropically inclined most of her adult life, but had studiously avoided publicity.

There was a story, possibly apocryphal but having the ring of truth to it, that she once remarked to her mother that she would like to attend college. Mrs. Duke, an unimaginative woman, is alleged to have replied, "Why should you attend college, Doris? You'll never have to teach school." So Doris Duke, to her lifelong regret, missed a college education.

As long as President Few lived, Doris Duke maintained a friendly relationship with both him and Duke University. She once visited the campus incognito, staying in a woman's dormitory, and returned to the campus on several ceremonial occasions at Few's request. After his death in 1940, however, she maintained a close relationship with only one person at the university, Dr. Wilburt C. Davison, the founding dean of the medical school. Acting anonymously, Doris Duke established Independent Aid in the 1930s, and one of its significant grants went toward the establishment of a much-needed social service department in Duke University Hospital. Such support, carefully hidden from the public, continued in later years, and she gave to many similar programs.

Only after her death, however, did her executors and the director of the Doris Duke Charitable Foundation gain access to records that will eventually allow a fuller knowledge of her philanthropy. That she founded and generously supported the Newport (Rhode Island) Restoration Foundation was widely known, but many of her other charitable activities went unpublicized. Her executors and the director of her foundation, having made a preliminary survey of records among Doris Duke's papers, estimate that during her lifetime she donated close to $400 million (in 2000 dollars). In short, while J. B. Duke's principal heir was indeed eccentric, especially toward the end of her life, there was a serious side to her that fit well with the family tradition of philanthropy.

When the Methodist church inspired Washington Duke to give generously of his material wealth, that set in train a long-lived family tradition of philanthropy, one that has clearly benefited the Carolinas most of all but one that has also enriched the nation.

Robert F. Durden is professor emeritus of history at Duke University.

For more information, see:

Duke, Benjamin N. Papers. Special Collections, Perkins Library, Duke University, Durham.

Durden, Robert F. *The Dukes of Durham, 1865–1929.* Duke University Press, 1975.
———. *Lasting Legacy to the Carolinas: The Duke Endowment, 1924–1994.* Duke University Press, 1998.
———. *The Launching of Duke University, 1924–1949.* Duke University Press, 1993.
Porter, Earl W. *Trinity and Duke, 1892–1924: Foundations of Duke University.* Duke University Press, 1964.

THE HILL FAMILY

By Howard E. Covington Jr.

By THE TIME John Sprunt Hill arrived in Durham in 1903, his fortune was much improved from when he had left Duplin County, where he was the youngest son of a large family. In the decade since his graduation from the University of North Carolina, he had accumulated a sizable bank account from his successful New York law practice and he had married Annie Louise Watts, the daughter of George W. Watts of Durham, easily one of the richest men in North Carolina. In the years to come, he would couple that wealth with his own vision, passion, and energy to create lasting contributions that would remain long after the aroma of tobacco had disappeared from Durham and the Hill name was no longer synonymous with banking.

The Hills—John Sprunt and his son, George Watts—were most generous to the University of North Carolina, where father, son, and a grandfather (Edward Hill) accounted for more than a century of service on the university's board of trustees, a tenure longer than any family in the state. But the generosity of the Hills, and George Watts, extended well beyond Chapel Hill to Presbyterian institutions and missions around the world, the city of Durham, and the Research Triangle Park.

John Sprunt Hill was born on March 17, 1869, into a family whose fortune was devastated by the Civil War. Hill's father had served in the legislature before the war and two of his brothers served in the years afterward. John—he was given the middle name of Sprunt in honor of a noted educator and minister in the district—finished all the schooling available in nearby Faison by the time he was twelve. He then clerked in a store in Faison for four years and continued his studies under his mother's instruction with books from his father's library. Professors at the university in Chapel Hill, where his father and brothers had graduated, were skeptical of his qualifications when he arrived to enroll, but by the end of the first term Hill had erased their doubts. He excelled in his studies and on graduation day in 1889—the centennial of the university's founding—he was second in his class, having missed top honors by a fraction of a point.

Hill returned to Faison to reopen a high school, where he not only repaired the building but recruited students from around Duplin County. Two years later he was back in Chapel Hill to enter law school. He finished one year and, in the wake of a disappointing love affair, left for New York with plans to join an older brother who was the American consul in Uruguay. When he got to New York, however, he landed a scholarship at the law school at Columbia University, where he finished, and entered private practice in the offices of a lawyer with connections to Chapel Hill.

Before Hill had left Chapel Hill, he had encouraged a revival of the school's alumni organization. He also had pledged an annual contribution to the university library in honor of the best historical essay produced by a student. Even in lean times he remained in close touch with his old professor, Kemp Plummer Battle, and faithful to his pledge to the library.

Hill adapted well to New York. His law practice flourished, in part because of his North Carolina connections and his forthright and efficient handling of an estate for a wealthy New York family. He moved easily among New York society and was well known among the city's southern émigrés, including tobacco millionaires like the Dukes and their partner, George Watts. The Dukes' new American Tobacco Company would soon control tobacco products in the United States and generate fabulous wealth for them all. Among those in Hill's social circle was Watts's daughter, Annie Louise, who was attending a finishing school in New York. In 1899, a year after Hill returned from service with the New York National Guard's Troop A, a cavalry unit that saw limited action against Spain in Puerto Rico, Hill and Annie Watts were married in Durham.

Before his marriage, Hill had begun to make a name for himself in Democratic Party politics. In 1900, he was a Tammany Hall candidate for Congress, and though he lost to the Republican candidate he polled more than the party's presidential candidate in his district. He was working on a national organization of young Democrats when, in 1903, he left New York for Durham. The Hills responded to the urgings of Annie Hill's parents and returned south with their first child, a son born October 27, 1901, whom they named George Watts.

Hill called himself a lawyer, but in Durham he

John Sprunt Hill and George Watts Hill (Courtesy of the Hill family)

would be known more for his business rather than his legal skills. Watts had told Hill he needed help in managing his business affairs, but Hill refused his father-in-law's payment of a thousand dollars a month, saying there wasn't enough work to warrant that kind of pay. Watts's affairs consisted mostly of following his many investments in tobacco, steel, and textile companies around the South. He also had substantial philanthropic interests, which included generous support of Durham's First Presbyterian Church; Union Theological Seminary, which he had helped relocate to Richmond and where he was president of the board; Presbyterian missions in Korea and Cuba; and a Lutheran mission in his father's name in India. Another major preoccupation was Watts Hospital, his gift to the citizens of Durham and considered one of the finest institutions in the South.

Hill and his father-in-law shared a love of golf. Watts belonged to golf clubs in New England and the two were seasonal regulars on courses at summer resorts in Maine and in Palm Beach in the winter. They also were among the first golfers at Pinehurst, and in time, Hill built an eighteen-hole course in Dur-

ham. (He later bought the Mid-Pines Resort in Pinehurst after it went into default during the Depression.) During his lifetime, Hill and his wife donated his Hillandale golf course to the city of Durham, along with the Durham Athletic Park, home of the Durham Bulls baseball team, and land for other public parks in white and black neighborhoods throughout the city.

Hill made his first mark in business in banking using his own money, along with investments from his father-in-law and the Dukes, to open the Home Savings Bank in Durham. Unlike his competitors, Hill vowed to fire any employee who charged a commission for loans, which was a common practice, and said he would pay interest on savings, which was considered another outrageous breach of financial etiquette. Other bankers said he would go bankrupt, but the bank survived and Hill opened a companion institution, the Durham Loan and Trust Company.

Hill put his bank in a new five-story office building on Durham's Main Street. Called the Trust Building, it was the city's first "skyscraper" and the elevator was a genuine novelty. A few years later, he supervised

George W. Watts (Courtesy of the Hill family)

the construction of new quarters for Watts Hospital and used leftover construction materials to erect a second downtown office building. In 1912, he finished construction of his large mansion on Duke Street, which was a project he followed to the smallest detail.

Throughout his life, Hill's focus was on Durham and North Carolina, but in 1913 he accepted an invitation to join a presidential commission organized to study aspects of rural life in Europe. On the trip over, Hill gravitated naturally to discussions about the crippling issue of financial credit for American farmers, who paid outrageous rates for money to plant and harvest their crops. The trip lasted nearly two months, and Hill became fascinated with the success of small credit union banks that were owned by and served farmers in Italy, Hungary, and elsewhere in Europe. The trip also took Hill to Paris, where he attended an international forestry conference, and he traveled to Ireland, where he had two friends lower him to kiss the Blarney Stone. (He claimed his March 17 birth date made him an honorary Irishman.)

Hill returned to Durham enthusiastic about the changes that credit unions could make in the lives of southern farmers, many of whom had little to show for their work after paying off crop liens. A true Jeffersonian, he saw nothing but virtue in the yeoman farmer, and he championed credit union legislation in Raleigh and Washington. The North Carolina law enacted in 1915 was considered one of the most progressive in the nation. North Carolina's first credit union was organized in December 1915 at Lowe's Grove, a rural community in Durham County, with Hill as one of the first investors.

Hill drew much of his supporting information on the condition of southern farmers from E. C. Branson, a rural sociologist on the faculty at the university in Chapel Hill. He helped pay for a biweekly newsletter sent to farmers around the state and at the same time he increased support for the library's North Carolina Collection, which had been created in 1904 with a gift from Hill. As a member of the trustees building committee, he personally supervised campus construction projects, and none of them claimed more of his attention than the building boom that followed the first major appropriations to the university in 1921.

Largely because of the interest of his father-in-law, Hill also attempted to unite the university and Trinity College (later Duke University) for the joint operation of a medical school that would use Watts Hospital for clinical training. Watts was ready to pledge several million dollars to the project when he died in 1921, just as the idea was gaining credibility. The proposal drew such opposition from those opposed to state and church schools working together that both Duke and the university pursued independent courses.

Unlike the Dukes, who made their money in North Carolina and then relocated to New York, Watts had remained in Durham, where his mansion, Harwood Hall, was filled with a collection of art and treasures gathered from his many trips abroad. He was a devoted churchman and directed the Sunday school at First Presbyterian Church for more than two generations. He was an early supporter of Union Theological Seminary, where Watts Hall was named in his honor after the school moved to Richmond. He also was generous in supporting other church-supported institutions, including Davidson College and the Barium Springs Orphanage in North Carolina. Watts had remarried after his wife died in 1916, and after his death in 1921, his widow married Governor Cameron Morrison and moved to Charlotte into an estate they called Morrocroft.

Nothing could shake Hill's allegiance to the university at Chapel Hill. As construction on new classrooms and dormitories got under way in the early 1920s, in the wake of renewed public support for the school, Hill made plans to build a hotel for Chapel Hill. Accommodations had long been lacking in the village before Hill's Carolina Inn opened in 1924 at a cost of more than $200,000. Twelve years later Hill gave it to the university. When the school's new library opened in 1931, the Hills donated more than $75,000 to pay for renovations of the old Carnegie Library. It was reopened as Hill Music Hall, complete with an auditorium and new organ, in honor of Annie Watts Hill. As the nation slipped into the Depression, Hill was one of the first to respond to University President Frank Porter Graham's call for help in building a scholarship fund to keep students on the campus.

At the same time Hill was reshaping the campus, he was helping to build a new road system for the state. Governor Cameron Morrison put him on his newly reorganized highway commission in 1921, and Hill all but handpicked the routes of major cross-state arteries in his district, which covered central North Carolina from Virginia to the South Carolina line. He remained on the commission until 1931 when he opposed Governor O. Max Gardner's highway reorganization plan and was not reappointed. Clearly unhappy about Gardner's program of changes to state government, Hill filed as a candidate for the state senate and won election in 1932.

While Hill was a courtly gentleman of the Old South, he had the fierce tenacity of a street fighter. The state senate gave him a soapbox on many issues, and there were few on which he felt unqualified to speak. At the end of his first session—during which he hired two personal assistants—a fellow legislator said that if all the time that Hill said he had devoted to his various careers as school-teacher, lawyer, farmer, banker, nurseryman, builder, and sportsman were added together, then he would be nearly three hundred years old.

The high point of Hill's battles came in the mid-1930s. He personally guaranteed every dollar in his Durham banks and easily survived bank runs when other financial institutions were closing their doors. He even took out newspaper ads promising to prosecute anyone who circulated rumors about a bank. He dragged out the consolidation of the University of North Carolina for a year with a protracted debate over the relocation of the engineering school from Chapel Hill to Raleigh. And in 1935, Hill led the effort to provide for sale of alcoholic beverages in the state.

The liquor bill found Hill in the middle of a firestorm, which he seemed to enjoy. Before it was over, some suggested he run for governor. The hypocrisy and corruption of prohibition irritated Hill, who had been a dues-paying member of the old Anti-Saloon League, which had been financed by his father-in-law. He advocated close state control that would allow men like himself to enjoy their spirits with civility. (He professed to be a teetotaler, but he liked honey in his bourbon.) His bill was defeated, but a loophole in the existing law was discovered that eventually led to state-owned stores.

In 1937, the Hills, father and son, completed their seventeen-story building in downtown Durham that became the home to their banks and the Home Security Life Insurance Company, which Hill had started in 1916, and various other enterprises. Watts Hill would have preferred to have been a doctor, but he followed his father into business after finishing law school at Chapel Hill. He became president of the bank and later the insurance company. Like his father, he also was a farmer. His herd of prize Guernseys on Quail Roost farm north of Durham at Rougemont was recognized as one of the best in the country.

Hill and his father organized one of the successful farmers' cooperatives in Durham that helped reduce the price of farm supplies and provide an outlet for the marketing of farm products. In 1933, Watts Hill revived a fledgling health care plan called Hospital Care Association and gave it his attention and financial support. Hospital Care and the Hospital Savings Association, formed a year later, eventually merged in 1968 to become Blue Cross Blue Shield of North Carolina.

Watts Hill was restless in the late 1930s and he became an energetic member of a group of southerners organized by Francis Pickens Miller, a Virginia state legislator and roving social activist. Hill's involvement with Miller's group, organized first to consider ways to improve economic conditions in the South, led to even more active participation with those alarmed at the rise of Adolf Hitler in Germany. Hill helped organize and paid the expenses of antifascist groups, and became a regular at the so-called Century Group, which orchestrated the lend-lease program and mounted a publicity campaign to aid the allies. At one point, Hill signed a petition circulated by Miller calling for a declaration of war on Germany in order to allow President Franklin Roosevelt to sell munitions to the English and French.

Hill missed military service in World War I because he was too young and almost missed World War II because he was too old. After hostilities opened with the Axis, he was able to secure a commission in the navy, but gave it up to become one of the early members of a super-secret organization that soon became known as the OSS. Hill spent the war in Washington as an army major, where he handled a variety of assignments, including outfitting agents for drops behind enemy lines.

After the war, Hill returned to Durham to assume responsibilities in the family business, and then turned much of his attention to the pressing needs of Watts Hospital, which was still dependent upon the family for its financial health. The demands of the war had demonstrated the shortcomings in health care all across North Carolina and the Hills—father, son, and daughter Dr. Frances Fox—helped finance the Good Health Campaign that produced a four-year medical school at Chapel Hill and led to local hospital building campaigns in communities across the state.

The Hills were among the early promoters of the Research Triangle Park. John Sprunt Hill provided the seed money for the Research Triangle Institute and Watts Hill helped raise the initial $1.5 million that took the park from a for-profit development into a nonprofit enterprise that became the economic engine for the entire region. Hill chaired the Research Triangle Institute's board for more than thirty years, during which time he contributed generously of both his time and money. His passion for the Research Triangle even eclipsed his interest in farming. In the 1960s he donated his home at Quail Roost to the University of North Carolina and it was used as a conference center until it was sold about fifteen years later. Hill earlier had given more than 1,300 acres of his Quail Roost farm to N.C. State University for use as the research farm of the school's forestry program.

The Home Savings Bank and Durham Bank and Trust Company (formerly Durham Loan and Trust Company) merged in 1951. A decade later, Durham Bank and Trust merged with the University National Bank of Chapel Hill and the name was changed to Central Carolina Bank. The merger came within weeks of the death of John Sprunt Hill on July 31. Among the beneficiaries of Hill's estate were the University of North Carolina (especially the North Carolina Collection), Durham's First Presbyterian Church, and the women's organizations of Durham, who were given his home on Duke Street as a permanent home for their community work.

Like his father, Watts Hill lived into his nineties; he died quietly at home in Chapel Hill on January 20, 1993. He did not live to see the opening of the $10 million Hill Alumni Center, the home of the university's alumni association to which he and his father had given a lifetime of support. Much of his wealth —estimated at more than $100 million—went into a foundation that Hill established to provide support for the university, the Research Triangle Foundation, and Durham Academy, where in his later years he had helped establish a special school for children with learning disabilities. His Chapel Hill home was given to the university and became the chancellor's residence.

Howard E. Covington Jr. of Greensboro is a writer and former journalist. He has written more than a dozen histories and biographies, including Terry Sanford: Politics, Progress, and Outrageous Ambitions *with Marion A. Ellis. He was commissioned by the University of North Carolina Foundation to write a biography of George W. Watts, John Sprunt Hill, and George Watts Hill.*

For more information, see:

Anderson, Jean Bradley. *Durham County: A History of Durham County, North Carolina*. Duke University Press, 1990.

Covington, Howard E., Jr. *The Hills of Durham: A North Carolina Family*. University of North Carolina Library, 2002.

Durden, Robert. *The Dukes of Durham, 1865–1929*. Duke University Press, 1975.

Wilson, Louis R. *Historical Sketches*. Moore Publishing Company, 1976.

———. *The University of North Carolina, 1900–1930: The Making of a Modern University*. University of North Carolina Press, 1957.

THE KENAN FAMILY

By Marion A. Ellis

JUST HOW members of the enterprising Kenan family of Duplin County came to direct some of the fortune of Standard Oil cofounder Henry Flagler to the University of North Carolina is a story filled with powerful high-finance, intrigue, and romance. It is also the story of a family's devotion to an institution that began at its founding in 1792.

James Kenan, who was among those who chose the site for the university campus in Chapel Hill, was the first of five family members who served as university trustees for fifty-one years before the consolidated university was created in 1931. In the years that followed, Kenans remained involved at the university, with James's descendant, Frank H. Kenan, eventually directing more than $85 million to the work of the modern Consolidated University.

North Carolina was little more than wilderness when the first members of the Kenan family emigrated from Scotland to Wilmington on the North Carolina coast in 1736. An enterprising lot, they developed vast expanses of land along the Cape Fear River in Duplin County, turning the pine forests into fields that produced cotton and other crops. They entered politics and held public office, and in 1818 Kenansville became the county seat.

During the Revolutionary War, Kenans led colonial forces and later, during the Civil War, their sons served as officers in the army of the Confederacy. Kenans tended to marry into other prominent families, and they branched out into various enterprises in addition to retaining their plantation interests near Kenansville, which by the end of the nineteenth century still amounted to little more than a sleepy agricultural center.

While William Rand Kenan married the great-granddaughter of Christopher Barbee, who donated the original 221 acres on the hill that became the university campus, it was industrial wealth and a fortuitous marriage in the twentieth century that provided the money that gave critical aid to the university at Chapel Hill.

William Rand Kenan Jr. and his sister Mary Lily Kenan Flagler were among the university's largest benefactors in the first quarter of the century. In answer to a call from alumni, William donated $275,000 for the construction of Kenan Memorial Stadium in honor of his parents, and set up the first athletic schol-

arships with another $25,000. He also helped underwrite the expenses of the new university press and provided the support for the library and the chemistry department from which he graduated in 1894. Before her death in 1917, his sister established the Kenan professorships with a bequest of $2 million. The Kenan Fund produced $75,000 each year for the endowed chairs that allowed first the university and later other institutions to enhance the salaries of selected faculty as incentive for their continued services.

William's road to fortune began in the university's chemistry department, where he was a student under Francis Venable—later a university president—who had been asked to analyze a mysterious gas for J. Turner Morehead of Spray, the son of former Governor John Motley Morehead, whose namesake was one of Kenan's classmates. Venable's analysis led to the discovery of calcium carbide and the resulting formation of the Union Carbide Corporation. William subsequently worked at Union Carbide until 1899 when he joined Henry Flagler, who with John D. Rockefeller had cofounded the Standard Oil Company.

Flagler asked Kenan to oversee many of his projects in Florida, where he was busy linking the state north to south with a railroad and a series of luxury hotels. Two years after joining Flagler, Kenan's sister Mary Lily, who was thirty-four years old, became the third wife of seventy-one-year-old Flagler in a ceremony at Liberty Hall on August 24, 1901. When Flagler died in 1913, he left her a fortune of $100 million, most of it in Standard Oil stock. At Mary's death, she left the bulk of her estate to her brother William and two sisters, Sarah and Jessie.

The Kenan professorships and the new stadium became the best known of the family's aid to the university. There were others. William donated $28,000 to build a field house at the stadium and in 1932, when the university was strapped for funds, Sarah Graham Kenan, William Jr.'s other sister, made a $25,000 gift that helped keep the university's doors open.

But it was Frank Hawkins Kenan, William Rand Kenan Jr.'s cousin, who a generation later brought the family into a modern era of philanthropy that went beyond bricks and mortar. Born August 3, 1912, in Atlanta, Frank Kenan and his brother James inherited a large portion of Mary Lily Kenan Flagler's estate, including the Breakers, one of the storied hotels at Palm Beach, Fla. After graduating from UNC in 1935, Kenan bought an oil distributorship in Durham and began building a chain of service stations called Tops Petroleum. He also organized Kenan Transport to carry oil from wholesale to retail outlets and also invested in real estate, including office buildings and shopping centers

William Kenan Jr. died in July 1965, leaving $95 million of his $161 million estate in the William R. Kenan, Jr. Charitable Trust to be used to advance education. When Frank Kenan became a key trustee at his cousin's behest in 1978, he set about to increase income from the trust. He took over as chairman and chief executive officer of the Flagler System, which included the Breakers Hotel, and along with his brother, James, from Atlanta, bought total interest in the Flagler System and began to develop real estate in Florida.

Kenan's ambition was to redirect the focus of his cousin's trust from established major universities like Harvard to lesser-known institutions. "Harvard already had hundreds of professors," Kenan once said. "What did one more professorship mean to them." Under Kenan's leadership, the trust began to distribute challenge grants ranging from $200,000 to $2 million to preparatory schools while continuing to give the $750,000 endowments for professorships at colleges and universities.

Kenan also noticed the widening gap between academia and business. At annual convocations of the Kenan professors in Chapel Hill, he observed "that few of them knew about business or the effect of business on education." That was when he decided the Kenan Trust should finance a special program to encourage the teaching of the needs and effects of private enterprise.

Under Kenan's leadership the trust committed $27 million to an independent William R. Kenan, Jr. Fund in 1983 to finance creation of the Institute for the Study of Private Enterprise within the UNC School of Business. In addition, Kenan arranged for the construction of the $8 million Kenan Center to be built adjacent to the business school at Chapel Hill, and relocated the headquarters of philanthropies there from New York City.

"I believe that all the freedoms that we enjoy are related to free enterprise," Kenan said at the time. "If we neglect that, we'll lose the others." In 1987, the directors of the Kenan Fund changed the name to the Frank Hawkins Kenan Institute of Private Enterprise. That same year, William C. Friday, who had recently retired as UNC president, was named executive director of the Kenan Trust. In time, six research centers were created to operate under the Kenan In-

William R. Kenan Jr. (Courtesy of North Carolina Collection)

stitute umbrella and its board of trustees read like a Who's Who in American business.

In 1990 the institute developed two new programs for international students with an initial focus on southeast Asia and central Europe. Also in 1990, the institute organized the MBA Enterprise Corps to provide management assistance for companies in countries changing from socialist to market economies in central Europe. Recent M.B.A. graduates from all over the nation were sent overseas for one to two years. The Kenan Trust and Kenan Fund financed many other programs, including one designed to eradicate illiteracy.

By 1992, the net worth of the Kenan Trust had

Frank H. Kenan (Courtesy of Kenan family)

climbed from $95 million at the time of William Kenan's death to $275 million and was creating about $13 million in annual income from its investments. But for the first time in the trust's history, it dipped into the principal instead of income when it created two new funds for the arts and sciences in North Carolina.

In March 1992, the trust announced a $20 million grant for the William R. Kenan, Jr. Fund for the Arts to finance the Institute for the Arts at the North Carolina School of the Arts in Winston-Salem. Another $20 million went to North Carolina State University to establish the William R. Kenan, Jr. Fund for Engineering, Technology, and Science.

"It will improve the quality of life for everybody—provide jobs and help the arts," Frank Kenan said. "We know that the three institutes for business, the arts and the sciences reflect William Rand Kenan Jr.'s strong interests. Whatever other directions the charitable trust may take in future years, we know he would be pleased to see these three areas protected and funded."

Frank Kenan had been responsible for more than $85 million committed to the UNC system. "He has discovered how effectively you can apply philanthropy," said William Friday.

Friday said Kenan was the embodiment of an enlightened philanthropist. "He has demonstrated that you can use the philanthropic dollar in a very creative way. You don't have to pick an area and stay with it the rest of your life. Another critical point he contributed is that he said, 'Let's make grants that are of such size that they will make a difference.' And he advanced the matching idea—you put $500,000 in to make somebody match it with a million dollars. That was a very, very unique thing."

By the end of the twentieth century, the trust had made philanthropic contributions totaling more than $300 million. Frank Kenan was proud of his stewardship. "We've done well by concentrating on a few special areas and by looking closely at the business side of programs—asking ourselves 'Where is the dollar going?' and 'What's our investment strategy?'"

Friends, family members, and business associates praised Kenan as a natural leader who had used the Kenan and Flagler fortunes for the betterment of higher education and other good causes. "I like to build things, bricks and stones and organizations," Kenan said. "I like to see success." He said he operated like a forester, planting business like trees, finding someone qualified to operate them, and then going on and planting new ones. "That's the thrill I have," he said.

Frank Kenan died on June 4, 1996, at the age of eighty-three. He was buried in the memorial garden at Durham's St. Stephen's Episcopal Church, which he had helped found in the 1950s.

His sons, Tom and Owen, from his first marriage to Harriet "Happy" DuBose, and his daughters, Liza and Ann, and stepson, Owen Gwyn, from his second marriage in 1966 to Betty Price Gwyn, carried on leadership of the family businesses and various foundations. Liberty Hall, the family home in Kenansville, was a historic site and museum.

Marion A. Ellis is a Charlotte-based writer specializing in corporate histories and biographies. He is the author of Frank Kenan's privately published biography and the coauthor (with Howard E. Covington Jr.) of Sages of Their Craft: The First Fifty Years of the American College of Trial Lawyers; Terry Sanford: Politics, Progress, and Outrageous Ambitions; *and* The Story of NationsBank: Changing the Face of American Banking.

For more information, see:

Kenan Family. Papers. Southern Historical Collection, University of North Carolina at Chapel Hill.

Campbell, Walter E. *Across Fortune's Tracks.* University of North Carolina Press, 1996.

THE MOREHEAD FAMILY

By Richard F. Knapp

John Motley Morehead III (left) and Frank Porter Graham (Courtesy of Hugh Morton)

IN THE MIDDLE of the 1800s, Governor John Motley Morehead prepared the way for North Carolina to enter the modern industrial world by his early interest in linking the regions of the state by roads, railroads, and canals, but it was his grandson who a century later used his considerable resources to provide the state and the nation with capable leaders of character. Both men chose as their vehicle for much societal advancement the University of North Carolina at Chapel Hill.

The governor's grandson—chemist, industrialist, and philanthropist John Motley Morehead III—left a sizable bequest in the John Motley Morehead Foundation in 1945, which created the prestigious Morehead Scholars program at the university his grandfather loved. The gift provided the state and nation with more than 2,300 talented leaders, including artists, bankers, entrepreneurs, journalists, judges, lawyers, missionaries, politicians, physicians, scientists, writers, and volunteers.

The governor, his philanthropic grandson, and other members of the family would have felt comfortable with such people and their abilities. Indeed, when John Motley Morehead III's cousin, John Lindsay Morehead II, died in 1964, eight Morehead Scholars were pallbearers at his funeral.

No other piedmont family, with wealth based not on tobacco but on textiles and transportation, had such a long-standing academic connection with and a comparable final impact upon the University of North Carolina at Chapel Hill. Eight male Morehead descendants of John and Obedience Morehead graduated from the university during its first two hundred years and became leaders and businessmen of some substance. At least two of them (both named John Motley Morehead) had a long-lasting influence on North Carolina.

The first John Motley Morehead, who lived from July 4, 1796 to August 27, 1866, entered the University of North Carolina as a junior. The "university," really a tiny college, had a faculty of about four, and less than one hundred male students, many of whom became an educated elite and state leaders. Graduating in 1817, Morehead briefly tutored at the institution, where he later was a trustee for thirty-eight years.

Morehead became a lawyer in Rockingham County and was elected to the legislature, where he allied himself with minority westerners who favored internal improvements and constitutional reform. Morehead favored public education, limited education for blacks although he was a slave owner, and treatment for the insane. After University of North Carolina President Joseph Caldwell proposed in 1827–28 building a railroad from Beaufort on the North Carolina coast to Tennessee, Morehead supported a defeated bill to survey a route. Meanwhile, the first American railroads opened in 1829 in Maryland and South Carolina.

Morehead won election as governor in 1840 in the first election in North Carolina in which gubernatorial candidates canvassed the state. By 1842 Morehead, echoing reformer Archibald D. Murphey, articulated a comprehensive plan for state internal improvements, with railroads (highlighted by an east-west line), turnpikes, a coastal ship canal, and studies for river improvements. After his second term, Morehead returned to business, and Greensboro, where he was an innovator in education and architecture. With five daughters to educate and the university accepting only men, he started the Edgeworth Female Seminary in Greensboro in 1840, just down the hill from his Tuscan-style mansion he called Blandwood.

The family's twentieth-century fortune grew from businesses run by his son, James Turner Morehead, who lived from August 5, 1840 to April 19, 1908. Following in his father's footsteps. he helped expand the family assets, which later would do so much for UNC, where he also graduated in 1861 with first honors. After the Civil War, Turner Morehead settled in Leaksville (in Rockingham County) to manage his father's various textile factories and businesses, which he inherited a year later. Like the governor, he became a local apostle of railroads and industrialism, and around 1872 he served two terms as state senator.

In 1891, seeking a way to use the water power at his factories to produce hydroelectricity to make aluminum, Turner Morehead hired a Canadian chemist, Thomas Willson. The corrosion-resistant metal aluminum did not rust and weighed only a third as much as steel, yet in alloy form it could be as strong as steel. World aluminum production expanded greatly after two cost-reducing key discoveries in the mid-1880s, but the process required enormous amounts of electricity.

In an effort to produce high temperatures to reduce aluminum from aluminum oxide, Willson installed at Spray near Leaksville one of the first electric arc furnaces in the country. Further experiments accidentally led to a new chemical compound, calcium carbide, and (as Morehead later said) "when we put it in water, it gave off clouds of smoke." Chemists at UNC analyzed a sample and identified acetylene gas, later recognized as a primary industrial gas used for cutting and welding metal (such as steel) and producing other chemical compounds.

The struggling aluminum company was increasingly unsuccessful, so Morehead and Willson in 1894 took fruit jars of carbide to New York, where they interested investors in forming the Electro-Gas Company to manufacture carbide and acetylene and sold all rights, except the chemical rights, to calcium carbide. Meanwhile back in Rockingham the duo's work yielded the first chromium alloy in the country and led to stronger armor plate and armor-piercing shells just in time for the Spanish-American War, assuring Morehead's financial security. He expanded into developing hydroelectric and industrial locations in Virginia and West Virginia. Years after his death, his patents for chemical processes and metal alloys and his industrial sites resulted in the founding of the Union Carbide Corporation.

James Turner Morehead's only son (of five children) was John Motley Morehead III, who was born November 3, 1870. After graduating Phi Beta Kappa in chemical engineering from UNC in 1891, he joined the aluminum company at Spray, where he and other employees used the electric arc furnace, and in 1892 he came upon one of the first large-scale means to obtain calcium carbide.

With the aluminum venture disintegrating, his father arranged a position for him in a New York bank, but the third John Motley soon joined Westinghouse Electric in Pittsburgh and in 1895 completed its highest advanced training. By 1897 he was building carbide and acetylene plants in various countries. In 1899 he designed a standard system for analyzing gases and in 1900 published *Analysis of Industrial Gases*.

In 1902 he moved to Chicago as chief chemist and testing engineer for People's Gas Light and Coke, which had taken over Electro-Gas and later would form Union Carbide. In World War I, although overage, he volunteered for the army and became chief of industrial gases in the War Industries Board. In the 1920s he moved to Rye, N.Y. (where he served three terms as mayor), to direct Union Carbide activities at nearby facilities. President Herbert Hoover appointed him ambassador to Sweden, and in 1931 he became the only foreigner to receive the gold medal of the Royal Swedish Academy of Sciences.

Morehead remained close to the university and in the mid-1920s, during a period of renovation and building on campus, he proposed to President Harry Chase that a bell tower be built on top of South Building, the university's main administration building. Chase was eager for Morehead's gift, but trustees and others objected to Morehead's choice of location and his request that South Building be renamed Morehead. Morehead suggested an alternate site, atop the new library, but the bell tower was incompatible with the dome planned for the library. Finally, Morehead and a cousin, Rufus L. Patterson, consented to a gift of $100,000 to build the Morehead-Patterson Bell Tower located between the library and Kenan Stadium, named in honor of the parents of Morehead's classmate, William R. Kenan Jr. Over the coming years, Morehead entered into an unspoken competition for gifts to the university between himself, Kenan, and a third companion from their college days, John Sprunt Hill of Durham.

When his wife of thirty years, Genevieve M. Birkhoff, died childless in 1945, he created the John Motley Morehead Foundation, beginning his major philanthropy to North Carolina. Morehead asked his younger cousin, John Lindsay Morehead II, the great-grandson of the governor, to be a chief officer of the foundation. The younger Morehead was the son of John Motley Morehead II (1866–1923, grandson of the governor), who was a UNC graduate, congressman, and president of the Leaksville Woolen Mills. John Lindsay Morehead attended UNC for a year but graduated from the University of Virginia in 1916. He became general superintendent of the woolen mills in 1917 and was president from 1929 until his death.

As leader of the multimillion-dollar Morehead Foundation beginning in the late 1940s, John Lindsay Morehead devised the elaborate selection process for the Morehead Scholars, a program modeled after the Rhodes Scholarships at Oxford University in Britain. The foundation spent its initial years building the Morehead Building and Planetarium at UNC. The state's first, and for many years only, planetarium provided vital training for American astronauts as well as thousands of school children. The building is also home to the Genevieve B. Morehead Art Gallery and the offices of the foundation.

The first Morehead scholarship was awarded in 1951. The program provides full four-year scholarships annually to about sixty men and (since 1974) women at UNC with tuition, all other normal expenses, and (also since 1974) a four-summer enrichment program. The awards are based on exceptional leadership capacity, scholastic ability, character, and physical vigor. Any secondary school in North Carolina, some eighty invited high and preparatory schools outside the state, and about thirty schools in Great Britain may nominate candidates for the merit awards.

Over the years, 75 percent of the recipients attained advanced degrees, chiefly in law and medicine. By 1995 the foundation was the ninth largest foundation in the state. In 1998 the agency gave away more than $3.8 million of its $119 million in assets.

In 1961 John Motley Morehead III gave the foundation fifty thousand shares of Union Carbide and that same year his second wife, Leila Duckworth Houghton, left a bequest of $500,000. Morehead died in 1965 after an accident in which he broke his hip while rushing from his office. He left most of his estate to the foundation. By that time Union Carbide had some 73,000 employees worldwide and manufactured six hundred products.

Morehead also gave Rockingham County a high school football stadium and chimes and significantly endowed a hospital, all later named for him. In 1964 he planned and gave a new city hall to Rye. For its long-lasting and widespread impact on North Carolina, the John Motley Morehead Foundation was the greatest of his gifts.

Richard F. Knapp is research curator for North Carolina Historic Sites. Among his recent publications are (with Charles W. Wadlington) Charlotte Hawkins Brown and Palmer Memorial Institute *and (with Brent D. Glass)* Gold Mining in North Carolina: A Bicentennial History. *He earned a doctorate at Duke University.*

For more information, see:

Connor, R. D. W. *Ante-bellum Builders of North Carolina*. North Carolina College for Women, 1914. Reprint 1971.

Edmunds, Mary. *Governor Morehead's Blandwood and the Family Who Lived There*. The author, 1976.

Morehead, John Motley III. *The Morehead Family of North Carolina and Virginia*. New York, 1921.

Web site of the John Motley Morehead Foundation is at www.moreheadfoundation.com. Blandwood, Governor Morehead's home in Greensboro, is operated as a house museum today. A Web site is at www.blandwood.org.

No LESS A POLITICIAN than former governor and senator Terry Sanford was often asked by those unfamiliar with North Carolina politics how it felt to have a comfortable Democratic Party majority. Sanford would then remind his questioner that this perception of North Carolina Democrats was incorrect. Republicans were always nipping at the party's heels, just 4 or 5 percent points away from a majority.

Sanford—who himself lost to a Republican in 1992—could recall 1928, when religion was stronger than politics and North Carolina Democrats turned their backs on presidential candidate Al Smith of New York, a Roman Catholic. That campaign signaled the beginning of the end for U.S. Senator Furnifold Simmons, the Democrat who had engineered the white supremacy campaign that elected Governor Charles B. Aycock at the turn of the century and gone on to control North Carolina politics for thirty years. Two years later, the party regained its footing under Governor O. Max Gardner of Shelby, whose influence would be felt for another two decades. The state really had three political parties—a divided Democratic Party (that would often elect wildcard candidates like Robert "Our Bob" Reynolds of Asheville to the U.S. Senate, a bombastic figure and isolationist, or farmer W. Kerr Scott as governor) and the Republicans.

A Lincolnton lawyer named Charles R. Jonas was the first Republican to put a dent in the Democrats' armor when he won election to Congress from the state's eighth district in 1952. Jonas's father had been a prominent Republican a generation before and one of the leaders in the GOP strongholds in the mountains and foothills of the state. Jonas was not a party builder, but as long as he kept defeating Democrats, something he did every two years for the next two decades, he offered hope.

The person most responsible for putting the modern Republican Party together was James E. Holshouser Jr., a quiet, studious young lawyer from the mountain town of Boone, who had been elected to the legislature before he turned thirty. Holshouser shouldered the heavy lifting of party building in the mid-1960s and put together a statewide organization that held fast to its traditional roots and expanded by appealing to newcomers—many of them Republicans—from bi-partisan states that were filling the suburbs of North Carolina cities, and to Democrats disaffected by the social programs of President Lyndon B. Johnson. The unbroken string of Democratic majorities crumbled with the reelection campaign of President Richard Nixon in 1972. Republicans and ticket-splitting Democrats elected Republican Jesse Helms to the U.S. Senate and Holshouser governor.

The Democratic Party's fractures had begun four years earlier, when Charlotte dentist and civil rights leader Reginald Hawkins became the first African

American to enter a statewide race since the nineteenth century. And they continued in 1972 when organized labor fielded its first candidate, state AFL-CIO President Wilbur Hobby.

Democrats regained position in the wake of the Watergate scandals that forced Nixon from office, but the shifting plates of political geography were only slowed and not stopped. Another Republican, former congressman James G. Martin, began two terms as governor in 1984 (between Governor James B. Hunt Jr.'s pair of dual terms) and by the 1990s the party seized majorities in the General Assembly, a condition unthinkable just a decade before.

Even without the Republicans, the state's legislature retained its conservative bent, yielding only to governors with favors to dispense, and unmindful of national trends such as adoption of the Equal Rights Amendment, a virtual lifelong crusade of women activists like Gladys Tillett of Charlotte, a founder of the state's League of Women Voters.

No North Carolina Republican—or politician from either party—was better known around the nation than Helms, who taught America's conservatives how to raise money and raise hell on the national stage. Like Jonas, Helms was not a party builder. His political organization was formidable and easily filled his campaign bank accounts with millions of dollars. He survived repeated challenges from Democrats, including two by former Charlotte Mayor Harvey Gantt, the first African American elected to office in the state's largest city.

But allegiance was not easily transferable, and most efforts at building a dynasty around the man himself were unsuccessful. One effort that did succeed was the election of Clinton businessman D. McLauchlin Faircloth to the U.S. Senate in 1992. Faircloth was perhaps typical of many late-twentieth-century Republicans. He had grown up a Democrat in eastern North Carolina and labored long in the fields, serving Democratic governors from Kerr Scott to Jim Hunt. Helms's chief advisor, Raleigh lawyer Tom Ellis, cultivated Faircloth's disaffection with the party and helped him win the Republican nomination in 1992. That fall, Faircloth defeated Sanford, who was sidelined by heart disease in the last weeks of the campaign. Sanford, who died in 1998, did not live to see Democrat John Edwards, a Raleigh lawyer and political newcomer, retire Faircloth after just one term. He had lived to see the margin between the parties narrow and shift to and fro across the middle.

CHARLES B. AYCOCK

By Christine Flood

ORN ON THE EVE of the Civil War in Nahunta (later known as Fremont) in eastern Wayne County, Charles Brantley Aycock was the youngest child in a farming family of ten dependent on cotton and livestock. Aycock's father, Benjamin, was a former slaveholder who served as clerk of court for eight years and as a member of the state senate for three years. As a boy during the war, Aycock witnessed the difficulties of the conflict and the bitterness of Reconstruction—his own father retired from politics rather than participate in "Yankee rule." As a schoolboy, Aycock walked miles from his farm with his six brothers to a subscription grammar school in Nahunta. For his secondary education, Aycock attended the Wilson Collegiate Institute, and then entered the University of North Carolina at Chapel Hill in 1877.

Aycock was a campus leader, excelled in Latin and English, and graduated in only three years in 1880. After graduation, Aycock began an apprenticeship in the Goldsboro law offices of A. K. Smedes and was admitted to the bar in January of 1881, the same year he married Varina Woodard of Wilson. Varina died after only eight years of marriage, leaving Charles a widower with two small children. In 1891, he married Varina's sister, Cora, and together they had five more children.

Aycock's first love was always Democratic Party politics. As early as 1882, he was active in county affairs as well as the campaigns in the state's third congressional district. Aycock was the quintessential party man of the late nineteenth century—he was an ardent advocate of the Democrats, win or lose, and worked for party unity in campaigns. During hot summer days in 1882, he canvassed Wayne County, speaking to farmers about the injustices of Republican national agriculture policy. Aycock's political enthusiasm led inevitably to journalism, and in 1885 he cofounded the Goldsboro *Daily Argus* with Joseph Robinson and William Clement Munroe. The *Daily Argus* did much to advance Democratic ideals in the Wayne County area, and helped to further the careers of local Democratic office holders, including Aycock.

In the presidential campaign of 1888, Aycock was a tireless campaigner for presidential candidate Grover Cleveland, giving speeches across the state in support of the reduction of the tariff and the abolition of internal taxes. Although disappointed by Cleveland's

Charles Brantley Aycock (Courtesy of North Carolina Collection)

loss in 1888, Aycock became a candidate himself in 1890 for the Democratic nomination for the third congressional district. Aycock's first venture into electoral politics coincided with the upsurge of the Farmer's Alliance, and he lost the congressional race to Benjamin Franklin Grady, an adamant Populist.

As Aycock was earning his experience and respect in Democratic politics, his views on public education were also becoming more defined. When he was only sixteen, Aycock had taught school in his hometown before attending UNC. He had seventy-five students, many of them older than him, and the schoolhouse was not much more than a crude, makeshift shack. Many believe that this brief teaching stint introduced Aycock to the inadequacies of public instruction and the need for more government involvement in education. Aycock believed that education was the key to a successful society and that the government must assume the responsibility for establishing a school system available free of charge to all children.

Aycock had good reason to advocate for universal education, for public education in the post-Reconstruction period was dismal at best. John Carter Scarborough, the state's superintendent of public instruction, wrote in his biennial report in 1882 that "the schools were poor beyond comparison. The school taxes were collected and spent and no adequate return of benefits was made. The school houses were in a state of decay and ruin. The incompetency of the public school teachers, with few exceptions, was proverbial. The system was a failure and a farce, and the people paid taxes unwillingly for its support."

The illiteracy statistics in North Carolina were alarmingly high. Among whites in 1880, illiteracy for males hovered at 23.4 percent and for females at 33.4 percent. For African Americans, the figures were worse: 76.4 percent for males and 84.8 percent for females. In response to this, the city of Goldsboro in 1881 had adopted a city tax and built two graded public schools, one for each race, and Aycock was chosen as the new superintendent of public instruction. The job was difficult. He worked with limited funds and this experience would lead Aycock to lobby more aggressively for state-supported education.

All the while, Aycock's beloved Democratic Party was falling on hard times. Having enjoyed a popular and electoral success since the end of Reconstruction, the forces of Populism were beginning to tear the party apart in the early 1890s. The Populists gained strength by waging a war based on agrarian class interests, and by joining forces with the Republicans to fuse their tickets against the Democratic Party. In 1896, Aycock campaigned for the party's presidential candidate, William Jennings Bryan, in good Democratic fashion, but despaired at the defeat of the party's ticket at home. The victorious gubernatorial candidate, Republican Daniel Lindsay Russell, received the fusion votes of many Populists that splintered the Democratic Party, as well as the votes of many African Americans.

As expected for a white man of his generation, Aycock was a firm believer in white supremacy. Populist/Republican fusionist politics brought about the election of local African Americans, which offended many Democratic whites, Aycock among them. Racial strife struck North Carolina repeatedly, culminating with a race riot in Wilmington in 1898. Aycock, and many others in the Democratic party, believed that the election campaigns of 1898 would arouse white voters by using the race issue, and they successfully returned the state legislature to white Democratic rule. Democrats authored a suffrage amendment to the state constitution that disfranchised blacks and secured white rule.

In 1900, Aycock campaigned not only for the amendment but for himself as governor. He anchored his campaign on the development of universal education, a progressive issue that also reassured illiterate whites they would not be left behind by the suffrage amendment. In his first campaign speech, delivered in Burlington on April 16, Aycock declared that "if you vote for me, I want you to do so with the complete understanding that I shall devote the four years of my official time to upbuilding the public schools of North Carolina." Aycock crossed the state several times, delivering speech after speech at country crossroads and county courthouses. Aycock's campaign relied solely on his strength as an orator and he carried seventy-four of the ninety-seven counties with a 60,000-vote margin over his competition. The suffrage amendment carried by a majority of 54,000.

Aycock's inaugural address in 1901 resounded the theme of his term as governor—improved education for all citizens. Aycock generalized that the biggest problem in North Carolina wasn't agricultural policy or the national tariff, but widespread ignorance and illiteracy. During his term he would go far in solving these problems. Aycock and the General Assembly revised the existing laws to provide for higher teaching standards and to encourage localities to tax for public schools. A textbook law provided that books would be chosen by the state board for all students, and the legislature doubled the appropriation for purchases. In the 1903 legislative session, Aycock received expanded funding for all of the state's colleges, expanded and improved facilities for the School for the Blind and the School for the Deaf and Dumb, as well as increased funding for the segregated African American schools throughout the state.

As Aycock's pro-education administration progressed, he gained national attention for his support of education for blacks and whites. The *New York Times* applauded Aycock as "a just-minded man of high ideals." He was often invited to other states, both north and south, to address legislatures and community groups on his theories of public education. He developed a speech that he commonly referred to as the "Universal Education Speech," in which he detailed his belief in mandatory public education supported by state and local taxes. Late in his life, Aycock would admit to his longtime assistant, Mrs. Frances Renfrow, that "I have never written out my

Universal Education speech, not even an outline of it, and yet I have been making it since I was a student at the University."

Aycock's four-year record was impressive. His concentration on consolidating small school districts, adopting local taxes, and building and improving schoolhouses produced results. While he was criticized for allocating state funds to educate African Americans, he was ultimately able to convince a broad range of southerners that universal education did not mean race equality, simply a more productive and intelligent class of African Americans in a white-ruled society.

Aycock left the governor's mansion in 1905, and found himself to be an "elder statesman" at the age of forty-five. He was touted as a vice presidential candidate in 1904, and was encouraged to run for the U.S. Senate in 1906. In 1911, after six years out of public life, Aycock announced that he would run for the Senate in 1912. In the midst of a tough Democratic primary campaign, he accepted the invitation of the governor of Alabama to present the Universal Education Speech in Birmingham. In this speech, Aycock boasted that "I am proud of the fact that we have built a schoolhouse in North Carolina every day since I was inaugurated as Governor," and that "I canvassed the State for four years on behalf of the education of the children of the State." At this point in his speech, Aycock collapsed on the stage in Alabama, suffering a fatal heart attack. He was fifty-two.

Aycock's legacy as governor, and a state and national leader, rested upon his support for public education. North Carolina's commitment to public education for both African Americans and whites began with his administration, not just with his legislative support for education, but his tireless work at promoting the revolutionary idea of universal education to a skeptical public.

In a fiftieth-anniversary address before the legislature to honor Aycock's inauguration, U.S. Senator Clyde R. Hoey called Aycock's administration a "turning point in the history and destiny of North Carolina." At the unveiling of Aycock's portrait in the state house, University of North Carolina President Frank Porter Graham chose to honor Aycock in his speech as "a flaming evangel sent from God for the education and redemption of all the children" and as "America's greatest educational governor."

Christine Flood is a graduate of the University of Maryland and earned a master's degree in history at the University of North Carolina at Greensboro, where her research was on the political role of border states in the secession crisis of 1860.

For more information, see:
Aycock, Charles Brantley. Papers. N.C. Office of Archives and History, Raleigh.

Connor, R. D. W., and Clarence Poe. *The Life and Speeches of Charles Brantley Aycock*. Doubleday, 1912.
Hamilton, J. G. de Roulhac. *North Carolina since 1860*. Lewis Publishing Company, 1919.
Harlan, Louis R. *Separate and Unequal: Public School Campaigns and Racism in the Southern Seaboard States, 1901–1915*. University of North Carolina Press, 1958.
Joint Sessions of House and Senate. *The Life and Services of Charles Brantley Aycock, Governor of North Carolina, 1901–1905*. General Assembly of 1951.
Orr, Oliver H., Jr. *Charles Brantley Aycock*. University of North Carolina Press, 1961.

HARVEY GANTT

By Marion A. Ellis

URING HARVEY GANTT's rise from growing up in public housing in Charleston, S.C., to an architectural career featuring award-winning commissions, he brought down racial barriers in public education and raised the hopes of African Americans in politics during two terms as mayor of North Carolina's largest city.

Gantt later gained national attention at the end of the century after he was selected to chair the National Capital Planning Commission and guide the creation of a monument to the veterans of World War II on the Mall in Washington, D.C.

The son of a shipyard worker in Charleston, Gantt was born there January 14, 1943. He spent his formative years in Charleston and was the quarterback on his high school football team before heading to college at Iowa State University in 1960. Deciding he wanted to study closer to home, he applied to Clemson University, a state-supported school where Jim Crow laws prohibited the enrollment of African Americans. Gantt said he did not choose Clemson to challenge the law, but because of his personal career interests. "There was no wish on my part to become a pioneer," Gantt recalled. "I just wanted to be a good architect . . . in the environment in which I was going to practice."

The school denied his application and Gantt filed a federal law suit in 1962 to gain admission. A lower court ruled against him, an appeals court ruled in his favor, and the U.S. Supreme Court upheld the decision.

When he arrived on the Clemson campus in January 1963, his entrance was marked by the presence of hundreds of highway patrolmen and law enforcement officers as authorities sought to prevent violence. Gantt recalled looking out on a crowd of more than four hundred as he gave his first and only press conference during his studies at Clemson. "There was some kid out at the end of the crowd that said, 'Leave this guy alone. He'll flunk out soon and this will all be over with,'" Gantt said. "I remember I started laughing about that."

After his classes began, Gantt sought to live life as quietly as possible. He usually studied and ate alone in an effort to relieve any tension among fellow students, but he did make a few white friends. His peaceful demeanor prompted notice from vocal critics of

Harvey Gantt (Courtesy of Charlotte Observer)

integration such as Jesse Helms, who was then a commentator for WRAL-TV in Raleigh. On one occasion, Helms editorialized: "If ever a man put his best foot forward, Harvey Gantt has done so. His conduct will not cause South Carolinians to relish court orders relating to integration, but he has done a great deal—probably more than he himself realizes—to establish respectful communications across sensitive barriers in human relations."

Gantt took the daily challenges in stride. "I learned to smile, really smile, at Clemson," he said. "I learned then that a couple of those incidents could throw me for a day, make me mess up a couple of exams. I couldn't afford this." Gantt's strategy paid off and the Clemson students accepted his presence. "I saw people going from being vocal about wanting to preserve segregation to a passive acceptance of social change," one of Gantt's fellow students, Hal Littleton of Asheville, recalled years later in an interview with the *Char-*

lotte Observer. "They saw Harvey didn't have two heads and the school wasn't going down the tubes."

Gantt graduated with a degree in architecture in 1965 and turned down three offers in Atlanta to join the Charlotte firm of Odell and Associates, where he was impressed with the influence of the firm's principal owner, A. G. Odell, who was an architect of national reputation and former president of the American Institute of Architecture. "I was struck by his ability to influence major city leaders on certain things he wanted to do," Gantt said. "I was motivated to say that architects could do more than just basically design a nice looking building."

After watching Odell and gaining experience, Gantt decided he needed more education to make a difference on the shape of the city. He entered Massachusetts Institute of Technology in Boston, where he received a degree in city planning in 1970, and then returned to Charlotte to open a practice in 1971 with Jeffrey Huberman. "I came out of MIT clearly understanding a lot more why cities look the way they look," Gantt said.

He also became involved in political affairs in Charlotte and worked on various issues with Charlotte City Councilman Fred Alexander, another African American. After Alexander was elected to the state senate and left the council in 1974, Gantt was appointed to fill the one year remaining in Alexander's term. In 1975, he ran for election to a full term and was elected as an at-large candidate. In 1979, he filed as a candidate for mayor, and narrowly lost to Eddie Knox, a former state legislator. In 1983, Gantt was elected mayor by an electorate that was overwhelmingly white. He was subsequently reelected to another two-year term in 1985 of the state's largest city of about 350,000.

During Gantt's time in office the city experienced exponential growth. It secured its first national sports franchise, the National Basketball Association's Charlotte Hornets; construction of a $47-million coliseum, which opened in 1988; completed a $68-million widening of Independence Boulevard; and started a $300-million headquarters for the state's largest bank, North Carolina National Bank (later the Bank of America).

As mayor, Gantt focused on revitalizing the center city and working to have the city adopt district representation on the city council. Also under his administration, Charlotte/Douglas International Airport completed a new ten-thousand-foot runway and the Afro-American Cultural Center was opened.

Gantt also helped organize mayors from other large cities in the state who were seeking alternatives to property tax as a way to pay for city services. "We talked about a payroll tax, land transfer taxes, things that dealt with the tenor of the economy, the growth aspects of the economy, rather than depending so heavily upon property taxes," Gantt said.

In 1990, Jesse Helms, the television commentator who had complimented Gantt on his campus demeanor, was finishing his third term in the U.S. Senate. First elected in 1972, Helms had become the national standard-bearer for the Republican Right during his eighteen years in the Senate. After defeating two previous Democratic efforts to unseat him, Helms was considered virtually unbeatable. As expected, Gantt's entry into the race created a flurry of attention. Gantt said his decision to run was simple. "I just couldn't let Helms win uncontested," he said.

Gantt said he did not consider himself a trailblazer in North Carolina statewide elections. "Howard Lee [of Chapel Hill] ran for lieutenant governor back in the Seventies," he said. "He lost a runoff race, but his candidacy opened up possibilities for African Americans who might want to extend beyond whatever local office they had run in. Most African Americans run from wards or districts where their population is likely to elect them. Fewer of us at that time in the Seventies and Eighties could run at-large campaigns and win a broader cross-section of people." Gantt said he thought he was able to attract white voters statewide because he had proved himself as mayor of the state's largest city.

Gantt led the field against white candidates in the first Democratic primary and subsequently beat Mike Easley, who later was elected governor, in a second primary. His nomination captured the attention of Democratic Party regulars and party special interest groups around the nation. Pledges of support poured into his campaign headquarters in Charlotte.

Throughout the race, Helms had portrayed Gantt as a typical "tax-and-spend liberal." Gantt responded by saying, "If a liberal means caring about education, caring about housing, caring about environment, if it means caring about people, then I'm a liberal." Helms also criticized Gantt for his role as a member of a group that received a license to own a new television station, only to sell it at a profit two and a half years later to a white-controlled corporation, Capitol Broadcasting Company of Raleigh, Helms's former employer.

Gantt, who characterized Helms as a slumlord who was hopelessly out of touch with modern America, mobilized a grassroots effort and campaigned vigorously. In the weeks prior to the election, some polls gave him the edge over Helms. The numbers turned less than two weeks before the election following the broadcast of a Helms campaign ad that many considered an obvious play on racial bias. The ad showed a white man crumpling a letter with a voiceover that intoned, "You needed that job. And you were the best qualified. But they had to give it to a minority because of a racial quota." The spot made it clear that Helms was on the side of the whites who may have felt that they had lost out to an African American because of affirmative action and other such programs.

Gantt accused Helms of race-baiting. "They [the Helms ads] are divisive," he said. "They are designed to scare people along the lines of race."

Gantt lost the 1990 election decisively: 46 percent to Helms's 54 percent.

Gantt ran against Helms again in 1996 and accused Helms of race-baiting in the campaign, but Helms retorted, "He claims everything he doesn't like is racist. He's going to have to grow up about that." Despite many offers, Helms refused to debate Gantt, saying, "I'm sure he has other folks who will help him raise a crowd. The only ones who call for a debate are the ones who are behind."

Gantt's second campaign coincided with the 1996 presidential campaign and he received national attention during an address to the Democratic National Convention at Chicago. In his four-minute speech he told his American success story from his rise from public housing to a successful career in architecture.

Gantt outspent Helms $7.9 million to $7.19 million, but again lost to Helms by a lopsided margin. Helms was gracious in his comments. "I wish him well," he said. "I assume he's a nice guy. I'm not going to kick him around."

"I still believe that in America anything is possible," Gantt told the *Charlotte Observer*. He said he would continue to try to find a way to serve the public, but despite many pleas he decided to forego more attempts to gain public office.

Some years after his political career ended, Gantt remained upbeat about the experience. "I think it [his candidacies] opened up all kinds of possibilities," Gantt said. "The clout of blacks in the Democratic Party was demonstrated in the primary wins that I had in 1990 and 1996, against strong candidates. People saw a wider opportunity for diversity in politics because while such candidacies were narrowly unsuccessful they clearly demonstrated that in a relatively short period of time, black candidates may be elected governor or senator one day."

At the beginning of the twenty-first century, Gantt Huberman Architects was a large Charlotte firm with forty-two architects and interior designers. It was chosen to design the Charlotte Transportation Center and the TransAmerica Center in Charlotte, and held contracts as far away as New York. The firm had won numerous awards for its buildings, including an American Institute of Architects (AIA) award for student housing at the University of North Carolina at Charlotte and a similar award from the Charlotte chapter of the AIA for the Charlotte Transportation Center.

"People always ask me if Harvey is still practicing architecture because of his high profile," Huberman said. "Harvey's first love has always been architecture. He practiced architecture even during his days as mayor and his two runs for the United States senate. People will tell you that even during meetings he was always drawing and sketching."

Huberman said Gantt's lasting legacy from his political service is his ability to act as consensus-builder. "He has always worked very hard to lead others with different ideas into a unified point of view or perspective," Huberman said. "He brought his background in architecture and planning with him. When he was mayor of Charlotte his foresight and knowledge gave him a view of what the city could be."

Gantt was recognized in 1987 as a fellow of the American Institute of Architects. He served on the North Carolina Board of Architecture, on the AIA National Minority Services Committee, as a juror on numerous design awards programs, and as a member of the accreditation committees at the schools of architecture at Howard University and Southern University. He was a lecturer and visiting critic at colleges and universities all across the nation, including Hampton, Yale, Cornell, University of North Carolina at Chapel Hill, Michigan, Tuskegee, North Carolina A & T State University, and Virginia Polytechnic Institute.

Marion A. Ellis is a Charlotte-based writer specializing in corporate histories and biographies. He is the coauthor with Howard E. Covington Jr. of Greensboro of Sages of Their Craft: The First Fifty Years of the American College of Trial Lawyers; Terry Sanford: Politics, Progress, and Outrageous Ambitions; *and* The Story of NationsBank: Changing the Face of American Banking.

For more information, see:
Gantt, Harvey. File. Robinson-Spangler Room, Public Library of Charlotte-Mecklenburg County.

REGINALD A. HAWKINS

By Darlene McGill-Holmes

BELIEVING HE WAS SHIELDED by "ten thousand angels on the end of his finger," Dr. Reginald Armistice Hawkins of Charlotte often encountered danger during his fight for civil and human rights. Indeed, the guardians guided him through turbulent times as he used his professional credentials as a dentist and ordained Presbyterian minister to further the cause to which he devoted much of his life and become the first African American candidate for statewide office in modern times.

Born in Beaufort on November 11, 1923, Hawkins knew little about segregation the first six years of his life. As a youngster he had contact with both races—whites and blacks—but he would never forget a childhood incident. "Sammy and I were like brothers," Hawkins recalled in an interview. "When we started school, I went to the so-called black school and he went to the so-called white school. But then he had a party and he didn't invite me. The professors asked me if I was going to Sammy's party and I didn't know anything about it. I asked my mother and she began to tell me about discrimination and segregation. I beat the living hell out of Sam, and that's been my attitude ever since."

His father worked for the United States Bureau of Fisheries and he provided the family with a decent living and a desire for learning. The Hawkins children heard daily from teachers and their parents that anyone could succeed. "There was no doubt that I was going to further my education, because my daddy said that's something they can't take away from you. That was his philosophy and he educated all of us and many other people in my community." That philosophy became part of Hawkins's legacy. All four of his own children graduated from college and pursued professional careers.

The Hawkins family was blessed with a tradition of ministers and professionals whose work included the World Council of the United Presbyterian Church, Livingstone College, and the AME Zion Church. Among his forebears was a great-great uncle who started the first black school in North Carolina. The first black Presbyterian and Congregational churches in Wilmington were believed to have been started by another uncle, Michael Jerkins, who was in the first class graduated from Howard University School of Religion in 1876.

Reginald A. Hawkins (Courtesy of Charlotte Observer)

Hawkins followed his father into science, but listened to the urgings of his Uncle Obeah, who gave him a Bible and told him not to forget the Lord. After high school, Hawkins entered Johnson C. Smith University and completed all the requirements for graduation in three years. "I was head of the student council at Johnson C. Smith University (JCSU) and active in the 1943 march on the post office for black postal workers and I got involved in civil rights, so I wanted something that would give me freedom to do what I wanted to do and yet maintain the medical profession." He was accepted into dental school at Howard University, but was drafted into the army, only to be declared unessential by the military and released to attend dental school. Though delayed, JCSU awarded him a bachelor of science degree in 1948, the same year he received his degree in dentistry.

He opened his dental practice in Charlotte and became the first dentist to perform oral surgery on blacks. He had married Catherine Elizabeth Richardson in 1945 and by 1951 the two had four children: Pauletta, Reginald Jr., Wayne, and Lorena. His practice was interrupted from 1951 to 1953, when he was commissioned a captain in the army's dental corps during the Korean War. After his military service, he returned to Howard for a graduate divinity degree.

Hawkins's professional career offered him insulation from the economic intimidation that faced many black civil rights activists, although it did not prevent him from becoming a target. He was visible on several fronts—education, health care, urban renewal, employment, and voter registration. He not only filed lawsuits, he organized demonstrations, sit-ins, and marches.

Hawkins used legislation and the courts to attack the system of segregation and discrimination. Over the years, he initiated seventeen legal challenges to what he called the "power structure" to remove barriers to black citizens. The one law suit of which he was particularly proud was *Swann v. Charlotte-Mecklenburg Board of Education,* the case heard by the United States Supreme Court that provided the legal foundation for use of massive busing to integrate schools.

"I'm the second name on that [*Swann*]," Hawkins said. "Matter of fact we started that case back in 1962 or 1963 at the old Harding High School and the judge threw it out, claimed that our lawyers hadn't filed it on time. That's how Julius Chambers got here [to Charlotte]. We brought him here to reinstitute the school suit. Swann was a very good friend of mine who was a missionary who had just come back from India to teach at Johnson C. Smith University. I got his application and because my name was on so many suits, I put his name first, but really I'm the one that instituted it and the one who caught hell for it. I am not a compromiser on rights. That's my upbringing, I compromise on some things if it's going to help, but I won't compromise if it's wrong."

Other challenges opened health facilities to all races and in 1962 Hawkins served as a consultant with the National Conference on Hospital Integration. As chairman of the full rights and privileges committee of the all-black Old North State Dental Society, which named him dentist of the year in 1961, Hawkins also challenged the North Carolina Dental Society, which precluded membership by African Americans. In this suit, one of the first brought against a professional society, Hawkins contended that since he was refused membership, he was denied privileges given to white dentists. For example, at the time, a dentist could not become a member of the American Dental Association without membership in the state organization.

Hawkins brought suit in 1960 after he inquired about membership and was told that the society had "no intention of admitting Negro dentists." Hawkins submitted his application anyway. The membership committee said it was incomplete, although Hawkins insisted the names of two persons endorsing him had been erased. A federal district court decision in favor of the society was overturned on appeal in 1966. The society's membership requirements were ruled unconstitutional and Hawkins became the first black member of the North Carolina Dental Society.

His challenge to the Charlotte schools took considerably longer. In September 1957, Hawkins had escorted three of the first four black students to attend integrated classes. "My clothes were torn off me and I was spit upon carrying Dorothy Counts," Hawkins said. Counts did not endure the badgering, but Gus Roberts stayed at Central and graduated. Hawkins also organized the successful 1961 boycott of Harding High School in Charlotte. Hawkins thought that boycotting the school system that treated blacks as second-class citizens would be a lesson in democracy for the younger generations.

"For our cause is right and we shall win in the end. Let us say to the world that Negroes in Charlotte can stand together and fight the common enemy of injustice instead of one another. Let us march on until freedom is won," he wrote in a letter to the Mecklenburg Organization on Political Affairs of the Parent-Teachers Association from West Charlotte High School.

Hawkins visibility in the civil rights movement put his life in jeopardy. Early one November morning in 1965, his home was bombed, along with the homes of Julius Chambers and civil rights leaders Kelly and Fred Alexander. Hawkins said the bombing was brought on by a suit the National Association for the Advancement of Colored People (NAACP) filed against the Shrine Bowl game, an annual event in Charlotte. When the officials failed to choose Jimmie Kirkpatrick, a star black running back, Hawkins and others sought to halt the game by filing suit against parks and recreation and the Shriners to prevent them from using Charlotte Memorial Stadium.

"That's when all hell broke loose," said Hawkins. Around 2 A.M., a bomb thrown at his house was deflected by the limb of a dogwood tree that stood by Hawkins's bedroom. The explosion shattered glass in the bedroom window and sprayed it across the room. Hawkins ran out of his house, shotgun in hand, and spotted the car as the bomb throwers sped off, but they were never found.

In 1968, Hawkins became the first African American to run for governor in the state's history. "My image as a political leader in this state is such that it could give hope to all the people, particularly the Negro, the poor white and the white liberal." Hawkins raised substantive issues about race, housing, and health care in the campaign against two well-known, prominent Democrats, Lieutenant Governor Robert W. Scott and Raleigh lawyer J. Melville Broughton Jr., the son of a former governor. Hawkins finished third with 130,000 out of 800,000 votes cast.

He announced his candidacy for governor again in 1972, and lost for a second time. He promoted himself as the "Candidate for Hope and Progress" in bumper stickers that featured red letters splashed against a black background. Hawkins said at a news conference during the campaign that "to promote the broad public interests, rather than the special interests that are now taken care of in North Carolina, fiscal and tax policies should be reorganized."

Following the 1972 campaign, Hawkins returned to Johnson C. Smith University, where he earned a master of divinity degree. He was ordained as a minister and held the pastorate of H. O. Graham Presbyterian Church in Charlotte from 1978 to 1985.

It could be said that a man who endured these perils had more than ten thousand angels on his finger and Hawkins believed that along with these spiritual beings he was also endowed with a sixth sense. "Filing these suits in civil rights came to me through experiences with God, and he gave me the guidance on how to manipulate them. People don't believe that I'm a mystic, but I talk with God every morning at four and get directions for the day. I know exactly when to struggle. When things look bad, I can go to God and it's just like déjà vu, everything is revealed."

Over the years Hawkins received many awards and recognition for his service. He was listed in several Who's Who categories—in America, in Health in America, in American Politics, in Religion, in the South and Southwest, in International Affairs, and in Personalities of the South. He was a Fellow of the Royal Society of Health and the Academy of General Dentistry, and was also a life member of the American Dental Association, the NAACP, and Kappa Alpha Psi Fraternity. He was state president of the Southern Christian Leadership Conference and was inducted into the Athletic Hall of Fame at Johnson C. Smith University in Charlotte in 1995.

He was a member of the board of trustees of North Carolina Central University at Durham, the board of the Charlotte-Mecklenburg Youth Council, and chairman of the Mecklenburg Organization on Political Affairs. In 2000, Hawkins said he saw his as a life fulfilled, but advised that blacks must get an education and they must make a difference. He believed the battle continued and emphasized that the church must become the focal point for the civil rights struggle.

Darleen McGill Homes is a graduate of Florida International University and a master's candidate at Queens College. She has worked on newspapers in Miami and Rock Hill, S.C.

For more information see:
Hawkins, Reginald A. Interview by author. Levine Museum of the New South, Charlotte.
———. Papers. Special Collections, J. Murrey Atkins Library, University of North Carolina at Charlotte.

Gaillard, Frye. *The Dream Long Deferred,* Chapel Hill: University of North Carolina Press, 1988.

JESSE HELMS

By David Mildenberg

FOR THE LAST THIRD of the twentieth century, the national and international image of North Carolina was intertwined with U.S. Senator Jesse Helms, whom the *Almanac of American Politics* once called the nation's most controversial politician. Such an identification was a source of pride to many North Carolinians, who, starting in 1972, elected Helms to five terms in Washington.

To those who helped Helms win with 52 percent to 55 percent of the vote in those races, he represented a principled advocate of limited government, American sovereignty, and free enterprise. But to his critics, Helms was an angry and divisive politician whose racially inflammatory campaigns and antagonistic public persona coarsened American politics.

Whatever one's opinion, however, Helms's political accomplishments were remarkable. He was the first Republican from North Carolina to be elected to the U.S. Senate after changing his affiliation from Democrat at age forty-eight in 1970. He was the only person to defeat James B. Hunt Jr., his opponent in 1984, who after seven statewide campaigns was arguably the most influential North Carolina politician of the last quarter century. He oversaw a campaign fund-raising machine unparalleled in American politics. And he chaired the Senate Agriculture Committee and, later, the Senate Foreign Relations Committee, where his personal views shaped American foreign policy.

And he achieved it all in a most unconventional manner.

Helms was born on October 18, 1921, in Monroe, twenty miles east of Charlotte, the son of Jesse and Ethyl Mae Helms, who were distant cousins. A farm community with an assortment of small textile mills, Monroe was "the finest hometown anybody could have," Helms once said. Though never overly prosperous, Monroe was in Helms's view an idyllic, wholesome place where people—blacks and whites—got along and cared for each other. His father, who had a fifth-grade education and served as both fire and police chief of Monroe, "was the smartest man I ever saw" because of his inherent understanding of people, Helms said during a biographical interview on WUNC-TV in 1999.

At an early age, Helms's greatest ambition was to become a newspaper reporter. He produced his first work in journalism while still in high school, writing

Jesse Helms (Courtesy of Hugh Morton)

sports and proofreading at the *Monroe Journal*. After one year at nearby Wingate College, he transferred to Wake Forest College, another Baptist-affiliated college then located fifteen miles northeast of Raleigh. His college days ended when he took a full-time job as a proofreader in the sports department of the *News and Observer,* one of the state's most prominent daily newspapers. He later became an assistant city editor at the smaller afternoon newspaper, the *Raleigh Times,* broadening his experience beyond sports.

Helms returned briefly to the *Raleigh Times* in 1945, but during his service in the navy he had grasped the potential impact of the radio industry on the news business. He left newspapering to run a news operation at a station in Roanoke Rapids, but was lured back to Raleigh a year later to join WRAL, a 250-watt

AM station owned by lawyer and businessman A. J. Fletcher, a pivotal move in Helms's career.

Helms was the one-man news staff at WRAL and aired stories throughout the day. One of the most exciting events he covered was the 1950 Senate race between Raleigh lawyer Willis Smith, a former president of the American Bar Association, and Frank Porter Graham, the liberal former president of the University of North Carolina whom Governor Kerr Scott named to succeed J. Melville Broughton, who had died in office the year before.

Graham led the field in the first primary, but did not win a majority. On the eve of the deadline for calling for a second primary, Smith was about to concede, but changed his mind. He was persuaded, in part, by a gathering of several hundred supporters who had been encouraged to convince Smith to stay in the race by radio ads produced and paid for by Helms and broadcast over WRAL. Smith subsequently defeated Graham in a race marked by racist leaflets and electioneering. Helms declined Smith's offer to go to Washington, but joined him a year later and worked with Smith until his death in 1953. Helms returned to Raleigh to become the executive director of the North Carolina Bankers Association.

While the job entailed basic trade association work of conventions, lobbying, and public relations, Helms added an unusual twist—lively, opinionated editorials and columns in the association's monthly magazine, the *Tarheel Banker*. While many columns included personal items and trivia, Helms's editorials reflected his views on controversial issues, including his opposition to the integration of public schools in the wake of the U.S. Supreme Court's *Brown* decision. In a 1957 editorial about the Court-ordered desegregation of the Little Rock, Ark., public schools, Helms wrote, "What is happening in America is exactly in tune with the forecasts of Karl Marx. . . . The cackles you hear have a Russian accent."

The magazine also featured Helms's first outspoken attacks on the Raleigh newspaper that had given him his start in the capital city. His columns "made the *News and Observer* mad as the dickens and that was good. I enjoyed that," he said in the 1999 interview. It also warmed the heart of his former employer, A. J. Fletcher, who had moved from radio to television in part to give eastern North Carolina an alternative political voice to the *News and Observer*.

Helms enjoyed his job with the bankers. He had an editorial outlet, good pay, and time to serve four years on the Raleigh city council, his first elected office. In his 1986 biography of Helms, *Hard Right: The Rise of Jesse Helms,* author Ernest Furgurson said that coun-

cilman Helms practiced a technique that he would perfect in the Senate: holding up appointments of city commission members until he got his own choices or extracted special promises from nominees.

Fletcher finally prevailed on Helms to join WRAL-TV in 1960 as news director and editorial voice of WRAL-TV's radio and television stations. Helms was thirty-nine years old when he mounted his powerful electronic soapbox with opinions that flattered Fletcher's own political conservatism. Over the next twelve years, Helms delivered 2,800 editorials that would send liberals and many moderates into political convulsions. He attacked institutions such as the United Nations and warned against "Red China," "socialized medicine," and the pitfalls to foreign aid to virtually any country, an issue that would raise his ire over the next thirty years.

Above all, Helms's editorials emphasized the benefits of free enterprise, the hallmark of Fletcher's own politics and the essence of what both men believed was the miracle of America. "And I think that is the reason I am in the Senate right now, because the people just deep down agree with that," Helms said in 1999.

Helms had already bolted the Democratic Party when he was recruited to run for the Senate by conservative Democrats. One of those who appealed to Fletcher to release Helms for the campaign was state Supreme Court Justice I. Beverly Lake, Fletcher's former law partner and a determined segregationist who was defeated in two attempts at the governorship. Helms joined the race and easily won the Republican nomination, despite his recent conversion. He headed into the fall campaign at the same time that southern Democrats were disaffected by U.S. Senator George McGovern's ill-fated presidential campaign. Political observers also agree that Helms benefited from the upset primary victory of Congressman Nick Galifianakis over the aging Senator B. Everett Jordan, who had been in Washington more than a dozen years.

Helms attacked Galifianakis as a McGovern clone and used a slogan, "Elect Jesse Helms—He's One of Us." Many Democrats interpreted the statement as a mean-spirited effort to raise questions about the Greek-American candidate, who was born in the United States and served in the Marine Corps. Helms's campaign was given an extra boost in the outer precincts, where weekly newspapers and local AM radio stations had been delivering his opinions for years.

Still, North Carolina had never elected a Republican to the Senate and it took a spirited effort for Helms to win the election with 54 percent of the vote. That same year, President Richard Nixon took

69.5 percent of the Tar Heel vote and Republican Jim Holshouser squeaked by a Democrat to win the governor's race.

Returned to the nation's capital, Helms quickly showed a willingness to speak out as boldly as he had on television. He refused to stay in the background like many freshmen and put himself on the record on virtually every issue. In his first year, he introduced ninety-six bills and twenty-one amendments and made 138 speeches on the Senate floor, while voting more consistently for President Nixon's agenda than any other member.

After Nixon's impeachment in 1974, Helms proved less loyal to President Gerald Ford, joining two other Republicans to vote against the nomination of former New York governor Nelson Rockefeller for vice president. The vote signaled Helms's willingness to split with less conservative members of his party.

By 1975 Helms was talking about the need for a conservative third party, charging that Republicans were drifting leftward. That summer, however, Helms's longtime friend and 1972 campaign manager, Raleigh lawyer Tom Ellis, invited Ronald Reagan to Charlotte for a fund-raiser in one of the first events held by the Congressional Club of North Carolina. More than two thousand people attended the dinner, emboldening Reagan as he started campaigning for the 1976 Republican nomination.

Helms became one of Reagan's key supporters in his 1976 presidential campaign and helped the California governor score an upset in the North Carolina presidential primary, thus reviving a campaign lagging behind Gerald Ford in earlier states. Though Ford later won his party's nomination, Reagan biographer Lou Cannon credits the North Carolina vote —and Helms's influence—as sustaining Reagan's influence, leading four years later to his 1980 presidential victory.

Meanwhile, the Congressional Club developed a direct-mail effort that in 1977 alone raised $2.3 million for Helms's upcoming reelection campaign the following year. In 1972, Helms's campaign had spent about $700,000 to earn his seat. The money proved too much for Democratic challenger John Ingram, a populist state insurance regulator who had pulled an upset in the primary over heavily favored Charlotte banker Luther Hodges Jr. After outspending Ingram by an astounding $8.1 million to $264,000, Helms won with 55 percent of the vote.

The election elevated Helms's stature in national Republican circles just as Reagan reemerged on the national political scene. At the Republican National Convention in Detroit in 1980, Helms thrilled conservatives by agreeing to be considered as a vice presidential candidate, only to withdraw when Reagan selected George Bush as his running mate. Still, Helms received fifty-four delegate votes and played a key role in rewriting the party platform to harden its position on abortion and eliminate the Republicans' previous endorsement of the Equal Rights Amendment.

As beloved as Helms was on the right, he had gained equal notoriety as a target for Democrats and liberal groups. Common Cause ran a full-page *New York Times* advertisement in 1982, seeking donations to repel Helms's bills to eliminate the authority of federal courts to rule on abortion, school prayer, and busing. The bills were easily defeated, but only after Helms incurred the wrath of many fellow senators, including famed Arizona conservative Barry Goldwater, for forcing them to vote on the politically volatile social issues.

Having polarized his opponents on the left and angered many in his own party, many political observers by 1983 were doubting Helms's staying power. Those doubts heightened as the state's popular two-term Democratic governor, Jim Hunt, geared up for the 1984 Senate campaign. Having barely topped Galifianakis and Ingram, Helms seemed vulnerable to Hunt, a master of centrist, unthreatening politics. Even Helms said: "I thought he probably would win. But I was determined that he was going to have to do it. We were not going to surrender."

The election gained national attention—and national money. In what was then a record for a Senate campaign nationally, Helms outspent Hunt $17.2 million to $11 million. Much of the money paid for Helms's television ads asking, "Where do you stand, Jim?" portraying Hunt as a flip-flopper with limited backbone. While Hunt benefited from record registration and strong support by African American voters, Helms's campaign worked with the Reverend Jerry Falwell and other religious leaders to register conservative Christians. By election day, Falwell's Moral Majority had a database of 45,000 supporters in North Carolina, up from 3,000 only three years earlier.

Helms won the election with 52 percent, 10 percentage points fewer than Reagan's margin that year in North Carolina. Like others, the senator credits the "Where do you stand, Jim?" ads. "That was where I stood," Helms said in the WUNC-TV interview. "And I wanted to know why he didn't stand where I did. That was a pretty interesting thing to do and it was effective."

Helms's next two election victories, in 1990 and 1996, both came against former Charlotte Mayor Harvey Gantt, an accomplished architect who was the first African American to attend Clemson University in South Carolina and whose admission to the school was noted by Helms when he was delivering editorials on WRAL-TV. Both times Helms received 53 percent of the vote in elections filled with ads attacking Gantt's support for "racial preferences in hiring."

While Helms's political campaigns focused on domestic issues, his Senate work largely centered on foreign affairs, culminating in his elevation to the chairmanship of the Foreign Relations Committee in 1995. His causes ranged from efforts to defeat the Panama Canal treaties in the 1970s to the Helms-Burton Act of 1996, which codified the U.S. trade embargo against Cuba. He was the State Department's worst nightmare, holding up confirmation of diplomatic appointments for months, and he spearheaded a plan in 1995 that cut $1.7 billion in agency spending over five years.

In language little different from his WRAL-TV editorials, Helms also was a consistent opponent of "Red China." In the mid-2000 debate over granting permanent normal trade relations to China, Helms displayed his hallmark independent streak by bucking his own party and the business community and opposing the treaty. In the midst of that debate, Helms met with top executives from one of North Carolina's largest and most influential companies who were promoting the bill. After finishing their presentations, the senator's chief of staff, Jimmy Broughton, said his boss looked at the men and said, "You fellows are very good and very convincing. But you haven't convinced me." Added Broughton, "Sen. Helms has often said that the thing he's most proud of is that he's never held his hand up in the wind and that he's never cast a political vote."

Helms's pace slowed in the later 1990s when he developed health problems. Knee surgery and assorted other ailments put him in a wheelchair. In late summer 2001 Helms announced he would not seek another term, a declaration that sent Republicans and Democrats scrambling to find a replacement.

David Mildenberg is associate editor of bizjournals.com, the Internet division of American City Business Journals. He previously was editor of the Business Journal *in Raleigh and worked for* Business North Carolina, *the* News and Record *of Greensboro, the* Charlotte Observer, *and* Charlotte News. *A Minnesota native, he earned a B.S. in journalism from Northwestern University and an M.B.A. from the University of North Carolina at Charlotte.*

For more information, see:
A collection of Helms's memorabilia and papers is open to the public at the Jesse Helms Center in Wingate, N.C., thirty-five miles east of Charlotte on U.S. 74. The center is open from 9 A.M. to 5 P.M. Monday–Friday. For information, call 704-233-1776.

Barone, Michael, and Grant Ujifusa. *The Almanac of American Politics 2000.* National Journal Group, 1999.
Furgurson, Ernest B. *Hard Right: The Rise of Jesse Helms.* W. W. Norton, 1986.
Helms, Jesse. *When Free Men Shall Stand.* Zondervan Books, 1976.
Snider, William. *Helms and Hunt: The North Carolina Senate Race in 1984.* University of North Carolina Press, 1985.

JAMES E. HOLSHOUSER JR.

By Rob Christensen

James E. Holshouser Jr. (Courtesy of Hugh Morton)

WHEN JIM HOLSHOUSER, a twenty-eight-year-old Republican lawyer from Boone, decided to run for the General Assembly in 1962, the state Republican Party had not mounted a successful statewide campaign since Herbert Hoover carried the state in 1928. No Republican had held the governor's office since 1900 and only one congressional district was considered safe for a Republican. The party's state legislators were powerless backbenchers.

But within ten years of James Ebert Holshouser Jr.'s arrival in Raleigh to serve in the legislature, North Carolina politics would undergo a seismic shift as the GOP was transformed from an also-ran into a powerful force. By 1972, the Republican Party had turned North Carolina into a bona fide two-party state. Republicans were electing congressmen, legislators,

county commissioners, and sheriffs. A Raleigh television commentator named Jesse Helms was on his way to the U.S. Senate. And Holshouser was soon inaugurated as the twentieth century's first Republican governor.

Few people played a greater role in turning North Carolina into a two-party state than Holshouser—as legislative leader, state party chairman, and then governor. At first glance, Holshouser appeared an unlikely political leader. A boyish-looking, mild-mannered man with chubby cheeks, and an "aw shucks" style about him, he seemed more like your next door neighbor. While prominent conservatives such as Helms and former congressman Jim Gardner of Rocky Mount—who came close to winning the governorship in 1968—thundered from the right, tapping into the white backlash against civil rights and the anti-Vietnam War demonstrations, particularly in eastern North Carolina, Holshouser represented a softer brand of conservatism linked to the party's established base in the mountains of western North Carolina. "He didn't threaten anybody," said Gene Anderson, his longtime political advisor. "Everybody who supported him thought he was on the same level. He was one of us."

Born in the Watauga County town of Boone in 1934, Holshouser grew up as part of the mountain Republican tradition. During the first two-thirds of the twentieth century, North Carolina—like the rest of the South—was a one-party state. The Democrats, as the party of white supremacy and segregation, had grabbed control of Tar Heel politics at the turn of the century. With only isolated pockets of Republican strength to worry about, winning Democrats who won the party's nomination in the spring primaries were virtually assured of victory in the fall general election.

But even during the years of Democratic domination, North Carolina had one of the strongest Republican minorities in the South. And most of the party's strength was concentrated in the mountains and foothills in the west—a holdover from the Civil War when many non-slave-holding mountaineers had remained loyal to the Union. One of those lifelong Republicans was Holshouser's father, J. E. "Peck" Holshouser, who was appointed United States attorney in the middle district during the administration of Dwight Eisenhower and who later was elected district court judge.

The younger Holshouser did not develop an interest in politics until he was in law school at the University of North Carolina at Chapel Hill. Intrigued by the legislative debate over court reform, he would frequently travel to Raleigh to watch the General Assembly. Two years out of law school in 1962, Holshouser was elected to the legislature.

Unlike the situation in the dominant Democratic Party, one could rapidly rise through the small but growing Republican Party in the sixties. In 1965, Holshouser was elected house majority leader, making him the highest-ranking Republican in state government. His new role enabled him to move across the state, speaking at party functions and making important contacts. In 1966, Holshouser, who was then only thirty-one, began a five-and-a-half-year tenure as state party chairman.

Holshouser's advancement was quickened by the 1964 Democratic landslide led by President Lyndon Johnson, which depleted the GOP's leadership ranks.

While the Johnson victory hurt the Republicans in the short term, it helped plant the seeds for a Republican revival across the South. Many conservative Democrats had crossed party lines for the first time to vote for Republican presidential candidate Barry Goldwater in 1964.

All across the South, the system of racial segregation was beginning to crumble and with it, the familiar patterns of life. There was a conservative backlash against the civil rights movement, against the rapid expansion in social programs as part of Johnson's Great Society programs, and against the civil unrest and counterculture that the Vietnam War spawned.

Holshouser credited the GOP's growth to the Vietnam War and downplayed the importance of opposition to the civil rights movement. "I don't view it as the [modern] Republican Party having been founded on the basis of race or have expanded in North Carolina on the basis of race," Holshouser said. "And yet clearly the sense of change drove some from the party of their ancestors. Vietnam was probably the most wrenching experience in the history of the country except for the Depression in the thirties and the Civil War," he said. "People who were not part of the younger generation, which was so unhappy with the Vietnam War, viewed with great dismay what seemed to be happening with the fabric of society at that time."

Holshouser was at the helm as Republicans scored major victories in the congressional and legislative races in 1966 and again in 1968. Prior to 1966, the party's victories in major races were limited to congressional races in the mountains and piedmont, where Charles R. Jonas had been elected to Congress in 1952. Jonas was joined just over a decade later by James T. Broyhill Jr., the son of another lifelong Republican, furniture manufacturer J. E. Broyhill of Lenoir. The party broke out of isolation in 1966 when Jim Gardner of Rocky Mount, a dynamic eastern North Carolina businessman, unseated the aging Fourth District Congressman Harold Cooley to become the first Republican congressman from eastern North Carolina in modern times. Gardner was the Republican's golden boy. The cofounder of the Hardee's hamburger food chain, Gardner was young, dynamic, and had a flair for winning headlines. Two years later, Gardner became the party's nominee for governor and came closer to victory than any candidate in years. Some said his courtship of voters favoring segregationist George Wallace alienated moderate Republicans in the piedmont, who turned their back on him and cost Gardner the election.

Holshouser remained in the trenches, pulling together victories as he could in local and legislative races and storing up credits with GOP leaders in every hamlet in the state. In the fall of 1971, Holshouser decided to cash in those chits and enter the governor's race. At the time, he did not anticipate a primary battle with Gardner, who emerged from his retreat to business and promotional ventures to enter the race.

The primary pitted the two competing factions of the Republican Party—the traditional party centered in the western part of the state and the business leaders in the piedmont and the more conservative erstwhile Goldwater wing, many of who were former Democrats from eastern North Carolina. Gardner led the first primary, but Holshouser had the momentum. Immediately after the primary, Gardner went on a two-week vacation while Holshouser was up the next morning shaking hands at a plant gate. In the runoff, Holshouser pulled off a stunning upset, winning the nomination by a 51-to-49 percent margin.

Holshouser won with a disciplined, driving work ethic and a broad knowledge of state government and politics. Underlying his soft-spoken style was an inner strength that some people failed to recognize, associates say. He also had a wealth of knowledge about the party and its workers that Gardner could never equal. "When somebody thinks of tough, it's somebody who you would go down an alley with," said Anderson, after he had left a life in politics. "But Holshouser is that kind of tough, day after day. He didn't always do the right thing, but he always did what he did for the right reasons. The whole deal was based on a Presbyterian belief in stewardship. It wasn't the driving competitive thing as much as he thought he was supposed to serve."

After a bruising primary battle, Holshouser faced a man considered one of the Democrats strongest candidates since Terry Sanford had won the governorship in 1960. Hargrove "Skipper" Bowles, a Greensboro businessman and a leading figure in Sanford's administration, had upset Lieutenant Governor H. Pat Taylor, who had been the favorite of the party organization. Bowles won with hard work and a lot of cash. The race left the Democrats badly splintered and Bowles did little to overcome the hard feelings of the spring campaign.

At the same time, a Republican tide was building in the state. President Richard Nixon had carried North Carolina in 1968—the first Republican to do so since Hoover—and he was clearly the favorite in 1972 with liberal Democrat Senator George McGovern as an opponent. On the Saturday before the vote, Nixon made a much-publicized campaign appearance with Holshouser and senatorial candidate Jesse Helms in Greensboro that may have swung the election.

On election day, Nixon swamped McGovern, and his coattails were long enough to give Helms a boost in the Senate race and pull Holshouser in by a slim margin over Bowles. No one was more surprised than Holshouser, who had done little to prepare an administration to run the state for four years. "I have told some people that probably the person who had more to do with my getting elected governor than anybody else was George McGovern," Holshouser said.

With his gentler style and his tinge of mountain populism, Holshouser had been able to reach many swing voters, particularly in the suburbs of the state's metropolitan areas, where Republican sentiment had been growing around newcomers to the state. He also ran well among women, young people, and even carried liberal Orange County—one of only two counties that voted for McGovern.

Although he faced a difficult task in manning his administration because of the scarcity of Republicans with state government experience, Holshouser brought many assets to the job. As a veteran lawmaker, he had a good relationship with the leadership of the Democratic-controlled legislature, a broad knowledge of state budgetary matters, and a willingness to share the political credit. Holshouser established a record as one of the South's moderate Republican governors, along with Linwood Holton of Virginia and Winfield Dunn of Tennessee.

"The Republican Party in North Carolina, Virginia and Tennessee marched to a little bit different drummer than the Deep South states," Holshouser said. He supported the creation of a statewide kindergarten system. He backed the Coastal Management Act, regarded as national landmark environmental legislation to protect the state's fragile seacoast. Holshouser helped start the rural health center program to provide more medical care in the countryside. He oversaw a major expansion of the state park system. He appointed African Americans and women to high visibility posts in state government. And he supported the creation of black-oriented enterprises such as Soul City, the new town project started in Warren County by civil rights leader Floyd McKissick of Durham.

Although viewed as a Republican moderate, Holshouser had always seen himself as a conservative, but not an antigovernment libertarian. "Both in the church and in politics, I find people on the left view me as a conservative and people on the right view me as a moderate or maybe moderate-conservative,"

Holshouser said. "I have never viewed myself left of center."

While the Republican Party had experienced breathtaking growth—GOP registration in North Carolina nearly doubled between 1966 and 1976—two events challenged the party's rise during Holshouser's administration. The Watergate scandal in Washington led not only to President Nixon's resignation. It had a catastrophic effect on North Carolina Republicans. During the 1974 elections, the GOP lost two congressional seats, forty state house seats, and fourteen of their fifteen state senate seats, leaving Holshouser with few legislative allies during his final two years in office. Democrat Robert Morgan easily retained the seat of retiring U.S. Senator Sam Ervin for his party.

To make matters worse, Holshouser was plagued by factional rifts between the party's traditional wing and the newer more conservative wing. The schism became open warfare in 1976, during the North Carolina presidential primary between President Gerald Ford and his challenger, former California governor Ronald Reagan. Holshouser and much of the party establishment backed Ford. Meanwhile, Senator Jesse Helms managed Reagan's North Carolina primary contest and pulled off a major upset over Ford. Reagan's victory in North Carolina gave his campaign a boost after his loss earlier in Florida and placed Helms and his followers solidly in control of the state party. Emotions ran so high at the state GOP convention, controlled by pro-Reagan forces, that Holshouser was openly booed and denied a place as a delegate to the national convention.

Unable to run for reelection, Holshouser moved to Southern Pines and opened a law practice. He was forty-two. Throughout his life, Holshouser had a private battle with kidney disease. Before running for governor, his doctor had warned him that the stress of the campaign and public office could shorten his life. His kidney problems worsened after he left the governor's office and eventually forced him to undergo a transplant operation.

He remained active the in Presbyterian Church and civic affairs, including service on the University of North Carolina Board of Governors. In an ironic twist, Holshouser served as legal counsel to his old adversary Jim Gardner, after Gardner's election in 1988 as the state's first Republican lieutenant governor of the century. In 1998, he joined former governor and senator Terry Sanford in a Raleigh law firm called the Sanford Holshouser Law Firm.

Looking back on his long career in politics, Holshouser said he had one overriding goal. "I felt like the first Republican governor was going to have to be somebody who could show the people of North Carolina that government would not fall apart under a Republican," he said. Even his critics agreed that Holshouser more than accomplished that goal, paving the way for future Republican growth.

Rob Christensen is the chief political writer and correspondent for the News and Observer *in Raleigh. He covered North Carolina state government and politics for more than twenty-five years.*

For more information, see:
Mitchell, Memory F., ed. *Addresses and Public Papers of James Ebert Holshouser Jr., Governor of North Carolina, 1973–1977.* N.C. Office of Archives and History, Raleigh, 1978.

JAMES B. HUNT JR.

By J. Barlow Herget

James B. Hunt Jr. (right), with President Jimmy Carter (Courtesy of Hugh Morton)

IT WAS IN THE COLD of winter in 1977. James Baxter Hunt Jr. had just taken office as North Carolina's sixty-ninth governor. The states of the Atlantic seaboard were in the grip of a paralyzing freeze right at the time of a national energy shortage. The state's one natural gas pipeline and supplier could not meet demand, and the thirty-nine-year-old governor had declared an energy crisis.

Hunt held daily meetings on the emergency in his southwest corner office in the historic Capitol. He pulled together an Energy Crisis Team from the state's Energy Division, the Utilities Commission, and the Department of Commerce to give him status reports on fuel supply, energy consumption, and compliance with his voluntary conservation rules. The initial meetings were daily, serious, and glum.

Toward the end of the second week, the famed Atlantic Coast Conference Basketball Tournament opened in Greensboro. Wake Forest University played in the first game on Thursday, March 3, and lost to an out-of-state team. The energy crisis group met later that afternoon and delivered its usual somber report. For a long moment, the governor stared at his desktop, lost in thought. Crisis team members exchanged glances, wondering if they had made the news sound overly grim. Hunt shook his head, looked up and sighed, "Poor old Wake Forest, they just don't have any luck, do they?"

Unlike the assembled bureaucrats, Hunt knew what was really on the minds of his constituents. The story illustrates Hunt's gift for understanding his state, its people, and the issues, political and cultural, that defined North Carolina in the final quarter of the twentieth century.

Hunt's page in North Carolina's history book is one of landmark achievements, especially in changing and empowering the office of governor. He established one of the most effective political organizations in the state's history and sparked the political careers of hundreds who served in his campaigns and administrations. He set the standard for gubernatorial salesmanship in promoting the state's economy, tirelessly pursuing new and high-tech industry to replace the once dominant textile, apparel, and furniture factories. He worked hardest, moreover, to improve the state's public schools and shepherd them through the academic and social challenges of racial desegregation. The title "education governor" is the one that followed his name.

Hunt's story read like an American classic. He was born in Greensboro on May 16, 1937, to middle-class parents. His father was a state soil conservation officer and his mother, Elsie Brame Hunt, was a high school English teacher. The family soon moved to the community of Rock Ridge in Wilson County, where Jim and his younger brother, Robert, grew up on a tobacco and dairy farm.

Hunt attended public schools and tested his political skills early when he was elected class president and state president of the Future Farmers of America. At North Carolina State University (NCSU) in Raleigh, he studied agriculture education but practiced politics, winning two terms as student body president. He collected friends and contacts during those years who came to be known in later years as the "Wolfpack Mafia" after the NCSU mascot. The group included a Supreme Court justice (A. P. "Phil" Carlton Jr. of Pinetops), a Charlotte mayor (Eddie Knox), a state representative (Tom Gilmore of Julian), a state cabinet officer (Norris Tolson), and former state senators Wendell Murphy and J. K. Sherron. They provided a core of support for his later campaigns for Young Democrats' leadership, lieutenant governor, governor, and the U.S. Senate, as well as constitutional amendment and bond referenda.

He graduated with a bachelor of science degree in 1959 and three years later received a master's degree in agricultural economics. He received his law degree from the University of North Carolina School of Law at Chapel Hill in 1964. Hunt left college with more than degrees. He had a wife and the first two of their four children.

Hunt met his future wife, Carolyn, an Iowa farm girl, at a national Grange meeting of high school seniors. Hunt knew she was the one. The romance flourished into Hunt's college years. During his sophomore year, for instance, he visited Carolyn during fall break, Christmas vacation, and spring break, which was no small feat for a poor college student with no car. He hitchhiked halfway across the country to be with her, a thirty-six-hour trip. "I had it down to a fine science. I would sleep in the car once I was satisfied the driver was safe. I got out a time or two." Carolyn moved to Raleigh to work and at the end of Hunt's junior year, they married.

After law school, he and his growing family traveled to Nepal, where he worked as an economic adviser paid by the Ford Foundation. They stayed there two years and returned to North Carolina, where Hunt opened a law practice in Wilson and immediately became involved in politics. In 1968, he won election as the president of the Young Democrats Club and two years later, in 1970, Governor Robert W. Scott appointed Hunt to chair a commission to review the state Democratic Party's rules. A series of hearings for the commission gave him exposure to party workers all across the state, and in 1971 he began preparing a race for lieutenant governor in 1972. When he announced his candidacy, he had the support of influential, wealthy, Democratic political veterans, including Winston-Salem oil dealer Bert Bennett, a former party chair and ally of former governor Terry Sanford.

Hunt won the 1972 election for lieutenant governor and overnight became the state's ranking Democrat with the election of James Holshouser as the first Republican governor since Reconstruction. At that time, the lieutenant governor presided over the senate but also commanded real power in his ability to appoint committee chairs. Hunt consolidated his base of support and supported a progressive legislative program. In 1976, he announced his campaign for governor and was elected in a strong Democratic tide that carried former Georgia governor Jimmy Carter to the White House.

Until Hunt, the North Carolina governor was the weakest in the nation. He had no veto and was limited to one four-year term. Successful governors such as O. Max Gardner and Terry Sanford led by force of personality and political persuasion. Hunt did likewise, but he also left a legacy of unprecedented political power to those who followed him. He filled the office like no politician before him simply by remaining there the longest: four terms for sixteen years total, 1977–85; 1993–2001. He led the 1977 campaign to amend the state constitution to allow a governor to serve more than one term and then put the amendment to the test by winning a second term in 1980.

He led the 1996 campaign to change the constitution to give North Carolina's governor the power of the veto. Interestingly, Hunt's famed ability to inspire supporters, arm-twist fence-sitters, and win over opponents meant that he never used the veto.

Hunt enhanced the office in other ways. He reorganized executive branches such as the commerce department and established new cabinet-level departments such as crime control and public safety. His initial act as governor in 1977 was to order high-level government appointees to sign a code of ethics that required, for the first time, financial disclosure.

As significant as any official achievement, however, was Hunt's personal energy on the job. He clearly loved his work and approached it much the way a zealous entrepreneur promotes his business. The first question a legislator would ask about a new bill during Hunt's administrations was, "Is this the Governor's bill?" If it was, the legislator knew what would follow: "When [Hunt] fixes you with those blue eyes and tells you how much the state's future depends on your vote, it's hard to say no," Hunt's press aide Gary Pearce once wrote about a legislator's reaction to the governor. Even in Hunt's final fourth term, the early observation by William D. Snider, editor of the *Greensboro Daily News,* continued to ring true. "As one who has seen Tar Heel governors in action for over three decades," wrote Snider, "I must confess that Governor Jim Hunt beats them all for sheer drive and enthusiasm."

Hunt presided over and helped hasten the decline of the old-fashioned party politics. Much of the change was cultural and technological, a national shift away from small-town, stump-speaking political gatherings and the influence of party officials. More and more voters, for example, received their political news from television rather than a political rally. Computerized direct-mail systems opened the mailboxes and pocketbooks of citizens for individual candidates, bypassing established party organizations.

Hunt's campaigns relied on his own organization of "political keys" who were personal friends and supporters loyal to him. Sometimes the keys were also local party officials, but often the local Democratic Party leaders were excluded from the actual Hunt campaign organization. Similarly, locally elected party officials did not have as much say over the spoils of office as did Hunt's own keys.

As the once-solid South of the Democratic Party broke apart, liberal and moderate white Democrats such as Hunt learned to form new coalitions with African Americans, women's rights advocates, and progressive businesspeople who were more interested in a strong economic climate than racial politics. Hunt never wavered in his commitment to equal rights. He said in 1999, "I became a strong advocate of equal opportunity and fair treatment, being treated right, which is what I think God expects us to do." He made history in naming African Americans and women to his respective administrations and, in his final term, by appointing the first African American, Henry Frye, to the position of chief justice of the state Supreme Court.

Race, however, was never far from the surface in North Carolina politics. It suffused the momentous U.S. Senate election in 1984, when Hunt challenged two-term Republican incumbent Jesse Helms. Each man represented the political poles of the state and each commanded passionate loyalists. Helms, a former television commentator, symbolized the movement of conservative, segregationist Democrats to the Republican Party. By 1984, he no longer argued the merits of segregation, but early in the campaign he attacked Hunt for supporting legislation to make Martin Luther King Jr.'s birthday a national holiday. Hunt's lead in the polls evaporated. Helms then attacked Hunt for increasing the state's gasoline tax. It was bloody trench warfare up to the election in November.

The campaign set a national spending record, over $25 million. Voters had seen nothing like it, and very few were undecided in their opinions of the candidates. The battle swelled with the weapons of a classic, late-twentieth-century political campaign: televised, thirty-second attack advertisements; negative direct mailings to millions of targeted voters; and emotional, divisive issues dredged out of focus group surveys and scientific polls. Helms won, with 52 percent of the vote, aided by President Reagan's swamp of Democrat Walter Mondale at the top of the North Carolina ballot, 59 to 41 percent.

Hunt entered private legal practice in Raleigh and retreated with his wife and family to his farm in Rock Ridge. He lost but was not beaten. Eight years later, he ran for an unprecedented third term for governor and triumphantly returned to his old office in 1993. In his fourth and final race for governor in 1996, his political campaign hummed like a flawless, oiled machine. He won with 56 percent of the vote.

When Hunt joined the old Raleigh firm of Poyner and Spruill after his Senate defeat, he spent much of his time doing what he had perfected as governor —recruiting new business to North Carolina and helping existing industry grow. Hunt's attention to the economy was a hallmark of each of his administrations, and his last two terms in office represented a "Golden Age" of prosperity and record low unemployment.

In part, economic development launched Hunt's gubernatorial career. The state's flagging new business growth became one of the biggest issues of his first gubernatorial race. He promised to renew the state's industrial recruiting and in his first year, he placed the economic development operation in a reconstituted commerce department and increased its budget. Hunt opened state economic development offices in Europe and Japan. He promoted a balanced budget constitutional amendment, and he quietly protected the state's anti-union, right-to-work law. The state soon ranked first in the nation as a place in which to locate a new business. More importantly, by the end of his second term, new industries had created over 250,000 jobs and spent $15 billion in capital investment.

Hunt focused on developing higher-paying jobs, especially those involving technology. The model for such growth was the 6,800-acre Research Triangle Park (RTP) that lay between the three research engines of Duke University in Durham, the University of North Carolina at Chapel Hill, and North Carolina State University in Raleigh. Hunt was a tireless salesman for RTP and saw it become a national center for computer, telecommunication, and pharmaceutical development. He also used government resources to complement and aid high-tech research. He established the Microelectronics Center at RTP and the North Carolina Super Computer Center. Later, he started the North Carolina Biotechnology Center, and he persuaded the legislature to appropriate money for his new state Technological Development Authority that invested public dollars in new private ventures.

He encouraged and helped Charlotte to develop its own, smaller version of RTP at University Park. His crowning economic achievement was his 1984 vision for his alma mater, NCSU, the eight-hundred-acre Centennial Campus. There, research and academia began to work together to develop new technology and its concomitant products. Hunt approved the transfer of land from the Dorothea Dix Mental Hospital to the university and became the project's highest-profile promoter. By 2000, six thousand people were working on the campus with twenty-five thousand total expected at completion.

The biggest single theme in Jim Hunt's biography was education. It was the public issue that was closest to his heart and that engaged him the most. He was the son of a teacher and when asked about his heroes in 1999, he listed first his parents, his high school's history teacher, English teacher, and agricul-

ture teacher. In the same interview, he described his epiphany on the issue: "When I started at N.C. State, I'd been valedictorian of my high school class. It had always come pretty easy, and I went to N.C. State and I found students there way ahead of me—particularly those who came from up north. Now, what it meant was that I had to work harder. . . . I realized how far ahead of us they were with their schools, and I didn't think that was right. I've always had a keen sense of justice. I think it came from my religion and my family. But it wasn't right for them to have a whole lot better schools than we had."

As lieutenant governor, he championed kindergarten for the public schools. In his first two terms as governor, he set up primary reading programs, reduced class size, and established the North Carolina School of Science and Mathematics. He also led by example. Every Monday morning, he and his wife would leave the Executive Mansion to volunteer in a local public school.

He moved onto the national stage as an education champion and became chairman of the Education Commission of the States in 1982. After leaving office in 1985, he continued to study and speak out on the subject. He established the National Board for Professional Teaching Standards and was an advocate for setting measurements for students and teachers alike. He served as chair of the panel appointed to monitor President George Bush's Goals 2000 plan for public education.

When Hunt was elected to his third term in 1992, he was more focused on what he wanted to do for education. He believed that children's ability to learn—and thus a chance at a better life—developed much earlier than kindergarten. He spoke in his inaugural of an idea called Smart Start. It depended on government, business, community, and church leaders to prepare children under the age of six for school with quality health care and childcare.

His commitment to Smart Start continued into his final term, when he told legislators in proposing the 1997 Excellent Schools Act, "Education is our future—it's everything. We must start with the basics for every child: quality early childhood education, safe schools, good teachers and the opportunity for higher education." The act raised teachers' salaries and standards and tied pay to performance.

In assessing his education achievements, he said, "One was Smart Start. You know, I said very clearly if I'm elected I want to see these children get a good start in life. That was in 1992. In 1996, I said, listen, we've got to have better schools and that means better teachers. We've got to get and keep good ones.

And if I'm elected, we're going to raise pay to the national average." Typically, in his final gubernatorial year in 2000, Hunt campaigned for a $3.1 billion bond referendum for the state's sixteen universities and fifty-eight community colleges. It was about education. (Voters approved it overwhelmingly.)

That commitment was reflected in what he asked to be chiseled on his headstone. "Tried to help the children of North Carolina." Jim Hunt, North Carolina governor.

J. Barlow Herget is a Raleigh writer, coauthor of The Insiders' Guide to the Triangle, *and served two terms on the Raleigh City Council. He received his master's degree in history from the University of Virginia and was a Neiman Fellow at Harvard University in 1970. A former editorial writer for the* News and Observer, *he was a special assistant in the N.C. Department of Commerce from 1977 to 1979 during Governor Hunt's first administration.*

For more information, see:

Addresses and Public Papers by James Baxter Hunt, Jr., Governor of North Carolina, 1977–81. N.C. Office of Archives and History, Raleigh, 1982.

Covington, Howard E., and Marion A. Ellis. *Terry Sanford: Politics, Progress, and Outrageous Ambitions.* Duke University Press, 1999.

Snider, William D. *Helms and Hunt: The North Carolina Senate Rate, 1984.* University of North Carolina Press, 1985.

HOWARD N. LEE

By Owen Covington

IN BECOMING THE FIRST African American mayor of a predominantly white southern town and the first viable African American candidate for state office in the twentieth century, Howard Nathan Lee's political career served as a model of how the politics of issues can triumph over the politics of race. He focused on issues to achieve social change and inspired others to a calling for public service, regardless of their race. "If I ever admit that I'm prevented from achieving anything because of race then why try?" Lee said in 2002. "If you allow race to become a factor, then you can't achieve anything."

Lee was born July 28, 1934, in Lithonia, Ga., a small rural community about six miles south of Stone Mountain, the symbolic home of the Ku Klux Klan. His father was a sharecropper and his family often had to do without. Lee once told a reporter about the feeling of hopelessness in his home one Christmas because of economic hardship. "I have to keep in mind that there's a difference between hopelessness and laziness," Lee said.

One of Lee's first encounters with a politician was a visit from a congressman who came through the area with a truckload of watermelons to give to his constituents. "Those people would stand there and eat those damn watermelons and spit seeds, and that was the only damn thing that man ever did for us," Lee said in 1972. "I think then I had some vague sense that there was something wrong with it, even though I ate the man's watermelons too."

Lee graduated from Fort Valley State College in 1959 with a bachelor's degree in sociology. An encounter in the mid-1960s with Frank Porter Graham while Lee was working as a juvenile probation officer in Savannah, Ga., eventually brought him to North Carolina. Lee met Graham through Frank Spencer, a retired shipping magnate in Savannah whom Lee had befriended. "Savannah was pretty segregated at that time," Lee recalled. "But Captain Frank had invited Dr. Graham and was holding a reception. He wanted me to come to the reception and this was basically unheard of at the time."

Before Graham began his lecture that evening, Lee said, an older woman began to protest the presence of Lee and his wife, Lillian, at the predominantly white gathering. After his talk, Graham and Spencer

Howard Lee (Courtesy of Charlotte Observer)

both apologized for the woman's behavior, and Lee told them their apologies were not necessary.

When Graham learned that Lee was applying to graduate schools to study social work, Graham told him if he were accepted to the School of Social Work at the University of North Carolina at Chapel Hill, he would help him secure financial aid for his studies. Lee was accepted, but denied funding, and Graham used his influence to help Lee obtain one of the largest fellowships the School of Social Work had ever given to a student. "I was so dumb, I didn't really know Dr. Graham," Lee later said with a laugh. "Had I known the stature of this individual, I'm not sure how comfortable I would have been around him."

Following the completion of his master's degree in 1966, Lee began work at Duke University as a member of the research faculty. The Lees made the decision to settle in Chapel Hill in part because they considered it to be a "very open and diverse community." But when the couple began looking for a home to purchase, Lee later said, they were shocked when they found that no realtor in town would consider selling them a house outside the town's traditional black neighborhoods. "We ran smack dab into absolute discrimination," Lee said. "It was months before we were able to find a house."

The Lees finally found a house in Colony Woods and became the first African American residents of this neighborhood. Their earlier experiences and the threats the couple received after buying the house prompted Lee to approach the Chapel Hill Board of Aldermen about passing an open housing ordinance. After the board twice refused to address the issue of integration of Chapel Hill's neighborhoods, Lee and a group of friends decided on another way to bring the matter to the public's attention. "We decided that there were enough issues in Chapel Hill and the only way to get them into a public forum for discussion involved one of us becoming a candidate for mayor," Lee later said. "And I ended up being the one."

Lee began campaigning for mayor in late 1968, and his formal announcement of his candidacy in March 1969 made him the first African American to seek the post. In announcing his candidacy, Lee said he was running to give voice to many in the town and at the university whose concerns were unheard. "I believe I can bring to the office of Mayor a fresh approach to town government, unencumbered by old obligations, or by old and inflexible approaches to today's community needs," Lee said in his announcement. "I do feel strongly . . . that our government should be more responsive to the ideas and needs of a broader spectrum of people."

Lee's opponent was Roland Giduz, a newspaperman and twelve-year veteran of the town's board of aldermen, who came from within what Lee referred to as Chapel Hill's "inner circle." To bolster his stand of more community involvement in the municipal decision-making process, Lee and his wife attended close to three hundred coffees and teas with citizens during the course of his campaign. The campaign was viewed by some in the local media as an integral part of what was being billed in a local newspaper as "the first real battle in recent history for the mayorship of Chapel Hill." An editorial in the *Chapel Hill Weekly* prior to the May election claimed "the mayor's race has turned out to be a black-versus-white contest. Howard Lee is going to be elected or defeated because he is black. Roland Giduz is going to win or lose because he is white."

Speaking of that campaign some years later, Lee said he didn't think race ultimately played an important part in the voters' decisions. Lee learned at a speaking engagement early in the campaign that the key to connecting with voters was to concentrate on the issues and not race. The engagement, a Junior Chamber of Commerce meeting, put Lee in front of an all-white audience composed primarily of Giduz supporters. "When I walked in there, I walked in knowing that Roland [Giduz] had 95 percent of the support in that room," Lee later said. "When I walked out of that room, it was totally reversed. I left there believing that I had successfully done what I've always wanted to do in my life, and that is to focus people away from the skin color and focus them on the ideas. From that point on, I made absolutely sure that no matter what setting I was in, the ideas were the focal point."

When Lee won the election with 55 percent of the vote, he became the first African American to be elected mayor of a predominantly white town in the South. Local newspapers reported that more than half of Chapel Hill's 8,400 residents had turned out for the election, nearly doubling the turnout of the previous mayoral election. Blacks, who made up 20 percent of the town's population, turned out in "unprecedented numbers," according to the Raleigh *News and Observer*.

Lee acknowledged following the campaign that he would feel unique pressures by being a black mayor in a white town. "Any black man elevated to this position is going to undergo more pressures than any white man," Lee told a reporter a few days after his victory. "He's going to be questioned by the militant blacks. He's going to be suspected by most blacks. They'll question whether he's sold out, whether he's become part of the establishment. He'll be accused of favoritism by white separatists. My mistakes will probably be more obvious to both. Like it or not, I'm on a tightrope between two extremes."

One of his first accomplishments was to fulfill a campaign promise to open a mayor's office in city hall. Having campaigned on the idea of giving residents more access to government, Lee bucked a recommendation by the city manager to place the newly established office away from the seat of the government. "I think people, as much as anything, appreciated the fact that they could know where they would find me," he later said. Lee also made good on his campaign promise of establishing a public transportation system, which began operating in 1974.

During his time in office, which lasted for two more terms, until 1975, Lee worked to challenge the town's existing relationship with the university. At the time, the mayor and city manager had to take the town's budget to the university for approval. "I took the position that the town was a partner, and not a child of the university," Lee said later. "The university had given birth to the town, had helped it grow up, but at that point it was time for us to stand on our own feet." Lee later recalled that that was the first step to creating a more symbiotic relationship with the university.

While mayor, Lee set his sights on Washington. In 1972 he mounted a campaign for Congress against incumbent Representative L. H. Fountain of Tarboro, a nineteen-year veteran of the House. During his bid for the Second District seat, Lee relied on his reputation in Chapel Hill and on turning out the black vote to win the election. Newspaper reports credited Lee volunteers with a district-wide voter registration drive that added seventeen thousand new black voters to the rolls.

Despite his appeal to black voters, Lee lost the Democratic primary to Fountain and attributed the loss to a low turnout of black voters. "I learned a lot from that election. I learned a lot about myself," Lee later said. "I learned I should not have gone away from my philosophy to make people focus on the issues. In this case, I had moved away from that and started to focus on race. . . . I have never abandoned that philosophy since."

The lessons that Lee learned in 1972 about running a more extensive campaign were put into practice four years later during his campaign for lieutenant governor. The Democratic primary pitted eight candidates against one another for the nomination, which almost assured there would have to be a runoff to determine the winner. "The polls showed I would come in last. My friends thought I would come in last," Lee said later. "And I led the ticket."

Running second in the primary was state House Speaker James Green, a conservative Democrat from Bladen County and seven-term legislator. Lee's support of tax reform and the Equal Rights Amendment, as well as his criticism of the death penalty, had earned him the progressive label and presented a contrast to Green's more conservative views.

Lee's success in the primary prompted him to address the race issue, but in a new way. Speaking to supporters after the primary results had been tallied, Lee said North Carolinians "have matured beyond the race issue" and are "going to elect people who care about this state." Lee felt confident throughout most of the campaigning before the runoff, but incidents close to the deciding election day upset what had been a fairly smooth campaign.

Dirty tricks marred the campaign. Just a week before the runoff, the State Bureau of Investigation began a probe into a letter concerning the campaign sent to newspapers. The letter, which was determined to be fake, was written on the letterhead of Democratic gubernatorial candidate James B. Hunt Jr. In the letter, Hunt was made to appear to endorse Lee, reminding readers that Lee was black and might be able to deliver the "black vote" for presidential candidate Jimmy Carter. Around the same time, Lee had to dispel rumors in the eastern part of the state that if both Lee and Hunt were elected, black militants would assassinate Hunt so Lee could take over the state's top post. "Of all the campaigns I have run, I have never been hit with having to respond to racism," Lee later said. His campaign did not have the money to adequately respond to the allegations, and the money stopped coming in, Lee said later, because people stopped believing he could win the election.

Lee ended up losing the mid-September runoff. But following his loss, Lee was upbeat about what he had been able to accomplish during the campaign. "This has been a great campaign," he told supporters after the results had come in. "We have crossed race, sex and economic barriers. We have given people hope. . . . We have lost this campaign, but we have won the battle."

Although the loss interrupted Lee's record in elected public office, he was named vice-chairman of the state Democratic Party shortly thereafter. Lee had previously served as the party's second vice-chairman and had been a Democratic National Committeeman. In 1972, he delivered a speech seconding the nomination of former North Carolina governor Terry Sanford for president at the Democratic National Convention in Miami. Lee's increased role within the state party was followed in 1977 with an appointment by newly elected Governor Jim Hunt to the post of secretary of the Department of Natural Resources and Community Development.

The appointment put Lee in a new environment and presented him with a new challenge. "It challenged me very much because it was very much a non-traditional area as far as people of color are concerned," Lee said. "I'm not sure Governor Hunt, or I, for that matter, was comfortable I could do it." He later recounted how a meeting with a group of commercial fishermen on the coast succeeded because of his ability to concentrate on the issues instead of race. Lee said he walked into the meeting dressed in a coat, button-down shirt, and tie only to be faced by white fishermen dressed in their work clothes. "I told them, 'I think I came here overdressed,'" Lee said. "But I rolled up my sleeves and told them, 'We're going to talk about where we go from here.' . . . I left with a standing ovation and never looked back."

When the issue of reappointment came about in 1981, Lee decided to take a break from politics and public life. "I was really kind of burned out in politics," he said. "I didn't realize what pressure was on me. . . . I had been cutting through for other people." Lee returned to the School of Social Work of UNC as a faculty member, where he taught for two years until he left academia for private business. After several business ventures, he established Lee Enterprises in 1985, a concessions company that he continued to head through the end of the century. Lee returned to politics in 1990 when he was appointed to fill a vacancy in the state senate. He won the seat in the regular fall election that year.

Lee equated his introduction to the senate with that of a transfer student at a new university—he was new to the school, but he knew what it was like to be a student. The connections he had made and the experiences he had had as Chapel Hill mayor, a candidate for statewide office, and then as a member of the state cabinet prepared him well to serve in the legislature. In 1992, when Senator Marc Basnight from Manteo made a bid for senate president pro tempore, he approached Lee for support and asked if he could use Lee's name to boost his campaign. Basnight went on to win, and the two became close colleagues in the senate.

Despite Lee's early success in the legislature, he received a shock in 1994 when he was defeated for reelection. "I still am not sure how I lost that election," he later said. Lee took the loss as a humbling experience and used the time to work on his business be-

fore campaigning for the seat again in 1996. When Lee was elected that fall, he became a member of the education committee, a role he used to be an advocate for the university, the community college system, and schoolchildren. "That is probably one of the most satisfying positions I have held in public life," Lee later said. "I certainly honestly believe the work we've done has set a new course for education in North Carolina." He later was appointed co-chair of the senate appropriations committee, one of the more powerful positions in the legislature.

Looking back on his career in public life, Lee viewed one of his major accomplishments as reshaping the Democratic Party in the state by opening it up to minorities and women. "I certainly think my being elected mayor gave rise to a new crop of political leaders," Lee said. "I hope I've been a model."

Owen Covington began his newspaper career as a criminal justice reporter for the High Point Enterprise. *He is a 1996 graduate of Davidson College and a graduate student at UNC-Chapel Hill School of Journalism and Mass Communications.*

For more information, see:
Donsky, Martin. "Green Has More Money; Lee Has More Contributors." *News and Observer,* September 4, 1976.
Dunn, J. A. C. "On the Road with Howard Lee." *Chapel Hill Weekly,* September 19, 1972.
"Lee, Green Make Sharp Contrast." *News and Observer,* September 8, 1976.
Scarborough, W. H. "Howard Lee: 'A Patient, Aggressive Man.'" *Chapel Hill Weekly,* May 11, 1969.

FURNIFOLD M. SIMMONS

By Kenneth Joel Zogry

FIVE-TERM United States senator and two-term state Democratic Party chairman Furnifold McLendel Simmons was perhaps the most influential North Carolina politician of the first half of the twentieth century. He was a major force behind both racial segregation and graded public education, and for the first three decades of the century exerted considerable political power through close association with a group of state officials and politicians who came to be known as the "Simmons machine."

Simmons was born on his family's plantation in Jones County on January 20, 1854. A child during the Civil War, he witnessed firsthand the wresting away of social, economic, and political power from families such as his own. Despite the war and its aftermath, the Simmonses managed to hold on to their property, though Simmons later described himself as "land poor." He attended Wake Forest College from 1868 to 1870, completed his degree at Trinity College in 1873, and was admitted to the state bar two years later. Simmons practiced law for a few years in Goldsboro, and then settled permanently in New Bern, not far from his home. In 1886 he was elected to the U.S. House of Representatives, but served only one term, losing his reelection bid to a Republican African American. This experience set the stage for the rest of his political career.

Simmons's 1886 defeat occurred within the context of the political realignment under way throughout the South during the 1880s and 1890s. During those two decades, African Americans, both those freed after the Civil War and those who had been free before the conflict, overwhelmingly supported the Republican Party—the party of Abraham Lincoln and abolition. The choice was not so clear-cut for white southerners, however, whose political loyalties divided along class lines. The former slaveocracy and the new industrialists were overwhelmingly Democrats. But yeoman white farmers became increasingly dissatisfied with the Democratic Party during this period, and several splinter groups formed, including the Farmer's Alliance and later the Populists. These groups soon realized that they would have to cooperate with one major party or the other to garner enough political clout to enact the reforms they supported. As a result the Populists (broadly termed) "fused" with the Repub-

Furnifold M. Simmons (Courtesy of North Carolina Collection)

licans, allowing the coalition to win elections throughout the South.

In North Carolina political fusion was particularly successful in the election of 1892, and their power grew with the election of Daniel Russell as governor in 1896. In the wake of the fusion victories, Populists and Republicans, including a number of African Americans, were elected or appointed to positions of authority at the local, county, and state levels.

Simmons, who had served as Democratic Party chairman between 1888 and 1890, was asked to step back into the position in 1898 to revive the party's diminishing power in the face of fusion control. He mounted a tough, no-holds-barred statewide campaign that portrayed black politicians as lazy and inept. Through editorials and cartoons in major newspapers, including the Raleigh *News and Observer* and the *Greensboro Daily News,* he also appealed to white voters by characterizing African American men as lascivious animals who lusted after the flower of white womanhood. In fact, Josephus Daniels, editor and publisher of the *News and Observer,* hired artist Richard Jenrett for the sole purpose of creating vicious cartoons to sully the reputations of specific prominent black North Carolinians (such as fellow newspaper editor James H. Young of Raleigh), as well as to denigrate African Americans in general.

The Democrats feared that words and cartoons alone would not restore them to power, and in some parts of the state party supporters resorted to violence. The most infamous incident occurred in Wilmington, where on November 9 and 10, 1898, a mob led by former congressman Alfred Moore Wadell attacked black businesses and elected Republican city aldermen, leaving more than a dozen people dead. The campaign succeeded; race triumphed over class as yeoman white farmers who previously supported the fusion ticket voted for the Democratic candidates. However, the "White Supremacy" campaign, as it was known, was not uniformly successful across the state. Counties in the east with large black populations and some western counties where the Republican Party was strong did not support the Democratic ticket.

Simmons now found himself at the head of a powerful Democratic Party that was determined not to lose control again. In 1899, the new Democratic-controlled legislature passed the first Jim Crow law — segregating blacks and whites on public transportation — and African American men began to be alarmed that the next step would be disfranchisement. As soon as the Democrats took office, Simmons began seeking information about how other southern states had effectively taken the vote away from African Americans, despite the provisions of the Fifteenth Amendment to the United States Constitution. Simmons sent Daniels to Louisiana on a fact-finding mission to see how that state had disfranchised men of color, and Daniels returned with a plan to add a suffrage amendment to the North Carolina constitution that would require that all eligible voters be literate. Soon known as the "literacy test," this plan gave polling officials (by this time almost all Democrats) the authority to refuse any man a ballot if he could not satisfactorily read and interpret the United States Constitution.

To quell the fears of uneducated white men who might be concerned that they too would be disfranchised, a so-called grandfather clause was added that allowed any man to vote whose father or grandfather had been entitled to vote before 1867 (when a limited franchise was first extended to freedmen). In addition, party leaders proposed dramatic expansion of the state's graded school system, which would provide basic education to every child. Thus, the rise of public education in North Carolina in the twentieth century was directly connected to the disfranchisement of men of color.

The suffrage amendment went on the statewide ballot in 1900, and Simmons and the party again mounted an all-out newspaper and stump-speech campaign for its passage and it passed by a margin of 59 to 41 percent. Simmons considered the adoption of the disfranchisement amendment "one of the greatest accomplishments of my life." "Until we were rid of the incubus of the Negro balance of power," he remarked in the 1930s, "there could be no progress in the state." Simmons was held personally responsible for the amendment, and his father's murder at the hands of an African American man in 1903 was thought by some to have been an act of vengeance.

Simmons himself was on the statewide ballot in 1900, running as the Democratic candidate for the Senate. He won easily, and began a senatorial career remembered more for its longevity than its accomplishments. However, for twenty-five years he was a member of the Commerce Committee, where he was able to steer funds to North Carolina to improve and maintain rivers and harbors. His most important contribution to the state was his involvement in the appropriations which led to the construction of the Intracoastal Waterway that ran from Boston to Wilmington. Simmons was most visible nationally through his chairmanship of the Finance Committee, particularly in his support for vital tax and revenue issues during the First World War. From Washington Simmons remained powerful enough to influence state politics. A so-called Simmons machine developed, led by friendly operatives such as A. D. Watts and Frank Hampton. Between 1900 and 1930, this organization was directly involved in the election of four governors.

He also remained involved in several issues about which he felt strongly, most notably the fight over prohibition. He was involved in the drafting of the 1903 Watts and 1905 Ward bills that permitted the sale of liquor only in large towns, and was involved in the successful passage of statewide prohibition in 1908.

By the late 1920s the national Democratic Party was changing, and Simmons found himself more and more at odds with the new direction. In 1928 he vehemently and very publicly opposed Alfred E. Smith, the party's presidential nominee. Smith, a Catholic, was an anathema to Simmons, supporting increased immigration, opposing prohibition, and being more tolerant on racial issues. His opposition to Smith was so strong that he did something he would have considered unthinkable three decades earlier — he formed an alliance with the state's small Republican Party and together they delivered North Carolina to Herbert Hoover. This was the first crack in the solid wall of support of the state's traditional Democrats for the national party.

Simmons was a man of his times, and his political life coincided closely with his natural life. He was beaten for reelection in the Democratic primary of 1930 by Josiah W. Bailey, winning only sixteen of the state's one hundred counties. His defeat was the result of a number of causes, including his opposition to privatizing the Wilson Dam at Muscle Shoals, which angered several different interest groups. He was also advancing in age and was less well known among the state's younger voters. Simmons himself stated that he felt "a sort of whispering campaign" was carried on against him, and that "a good many people who wished to vote for me were kept from doing so by inadequate or erroneous advice which led them to mark their ballots in a way that caused them to be thrown out." Simmons obviously missed the irony in this; he believed that he was defeated by the same type of voter fraud he had orchestrated against the Populists and Republicans in 1898 and 1900.

Simmons retired to New Bern, staying active in such local causes as supporting the plan to reconstruct Tryon Palace in that town. He died on April 30, 1940, at the age of eighty-three. In his memoirs, told to Duke Professor J. Fred Rippy a few years before his death, Simmons proudly stated that he had "little fear regarding the final judgment of posterity. . . . I believe that on the whole my policies have been sound and constructive. . . . I have little to regret and nothing to conceal. . . . I resign myself to the tribunal of history."

Kenneth Joel Zogry is executive director of the Pope House Museum Foundation in Raleigh and a doctoral candidate in American history at the University of North Carolina at Chapel Hill. He has published numerous journal and magazine articles, and two books: The University's Living Room: A History of the Carolina Inn *(1999); and* The Best the Country Affords: Vermont Furniture, 1765–1850 *(1995), which won the Charles F. Montgomery Award.*

For more information, see:

There is a small group of documents from the early 1930s entitled the "Furnifold M. Simmons Papers" in the Southern Historical Collection at the University of North Carolina at Chapel Hill. However, letters from him and documents about him can be found in thirty different collections in the Southern Historical Collection, including items in the papers of Julian Carr, Zebulon Vance, Daniel Tompkins, and the Morehead Family.

Edmonds, Helen G. *The Negro and Fusion Politics in North Carolina, 1894–1901.* University of North Carolina Press, 1951.

Escott, Paul. *Many Excellent People: Power and Privilege in North Carolina, 1850–1900.* University of North Carolina Press, 1985.

Leloudis, James. *Schooling the New South: Pedagogy, Self, and Society in North Carolina, 1880–1920.* University of North Carolina Press, 1996.

Rippy, J. Fred, ed. *F. M. Simmons, Statesman of the New South: Memoirs and Addresses.* Duke University Press, 1936.

GLADYS A. TILLETT

By Stan Brennan

LADYS TILLETT once observed that she would advise women who wanted to remain docile housewives to "live and let live. She can live her way and I can live mine. But I don't want to make washing dishes the crowning achievement of my life."

Washing dishes was not the crowning achievement of her life. It was the goals she achieved with a life-long passion for women's rights. To reach those goals, Mrs. Gladys Avery Tillett (she preferred Mrs. to the trendier Ms. of the time) followed the advice of her father, North Carolina Supreme Court Justice A. C. Avery, who told her: "Gladys, be pleasant, be patient, but be persistent."

For example, Charlotte women wanted improved garbage collection in the city. Tillett's husband, Charles, a lawyer and onetime president of the North Carolina State Bar Association, suggested that it might be wise to take along "a tall, big woman" since she was only five-feet-two herself. So Tillett recruited an older woman who stood well over six feet who also had an impressive social background. Accompanied by the woman, Tillett used sweet reason and quickly swept the city official off his feet. As the women were about to leave, the beleaguered man called Tillett aside. "Let me tell you, Mrs. Tillett," he said. "I want you to know that whatever you women want, you shall have it. And you just come down here quietly and tell me about it and you'll get it."

Gladys Avery Tillett was born in Morganton in 1892 (she closely guarded her actual birth date) and began her campaign for suffrage as a college student at Woman's College (later the University of North Carolina at Greensboro), where she marched in a suffrage parade. As president of the student body, she lobbied legislators who patronized her and her fellow students, saying, "As I look into your beautiful faces, I know you're not in favor of voting." They could not have been more wrong.

The suffrage campaign steeled her resolve, and thereafter, few causes escaped her attention. She fought against the "Scopes law" (banning the teaching of evolution in Tennessee) in the 1920s, stood for religious freedom in the 1928 presidential campaign when southern Democrats fled from their candidate Al Smith, a Roman Catholic, and she championed the New Deal, the labor movement, and civil rights. She was a founder of the Mecklenburg League of Women

Gladys A. Tillett (Courtesy of Charlotte Observer)

Voters—the state's first—in the 1920s and an early president of the state league. She was the first woman to serve as a member of the state Board of Elections.

When she developed an interest in Mecklenburg County politics, she called the county party chairman and asked where her precinct headquarters was located. She later confided to a friend that the chairman—a man—tried to discourage her from attending an upcoming precinct meeting. He told her, "Aw, Gladys, you don't want to go to a precinct meeting. There's just a lot of men drinking and cussin' there." She firmly replied: "Oh yes I do." When she got to the meeting she found an open Bible on the table and a respectful group of men in attendance.

Tillett was involved with the United Nations and Democratic Party politics on a national level for many years. In 1945 she was an observer at the UN's founding conference in San Francisco and later she was a keynote speaker for women at the Democratic National Convention. She was a vice chairman of the Democratic National Committee from 1940 to 1950 and a member of the National Democratic Advisory Political Committee from 1953 to 1959. In 1961 President John F. Kennedy appointed her United States delegate to the United States Commission on the Status of Women. President Lyndon Johnson reappointed her four years later.

Her initial appointment came as no surprise. "It is what I have been anticipating . . . something in which I have a deep interest and I just hope I can make some significant contribution in this [Status of Women] field," she said in an interview. "It's going to be a tremendous challenge. Mrs. [Eleanor] Roosevelt did so much in the area of human rights worldwide and this one pertaining to opportunities and responsibilities of women has had so little development."

In her UN post, Tillett's travels were many and varied. She was a consultant to the United Nations Educational, Scientific, and Cultural Organization (UNESCO) on the Development of Women's Programs, attending a conference in Paris, and a United States observer to the UN Regional Seminar on Participation of Women in Public Life in Ulan Bator, Mongolia, in 1965. She was a United States observer at the UN Regional Seminars on Women in Family Law in Tokyo in 1962, and a participant and vice-chair at the Western Hemisphere seminar in Bogota in 1963. In 1962, she traveled on a State Department grant to southeast Asia, conferring with government officials and leaders of women's voluntary organizations. Later that same year she was an official guest of the German Federal Republic for visits to Berlin and other cities in Germany. The next year she traveled under the auspices of the UN to fifteen Latin American countries.

In 1962, speaking to the opening session of the UN Commission on the Status of Women, she called on women to "move forward with confidence against age-old prejudices" against their sex. Noting that less than 150 years before there was not a female college graduate in the entire world and no woman could collect her own wages, she added that such prejudices "still withhold from many women the recognition of their essential human dignity."

Speaking in Charlotte at a UN workshop on "The Impact of the UN on Human Rights for Women," she said that the UN charter was the first international document for equal rights for men and women. The charter promised that women are entitled to fundamental equality in freedom and human dignity, freedom to choose among different life patterns, and freedom to choose among the alternatives of scope and dignity equal to those open to men.

"And once the choice has been made," she said, "freedom to participate as fully as men in the kind of life one chooses. Laws and mores and attitudes which interfere with the full potential of women as persons are contrary to the charter and to notions held in the 20th century of the inviolability of the human person."

Her experience as a political party worker in North Carolina and as vice-chairman of the Democratic National Committee from 1940 to 1950 was valuable in her United Nations work. "Much of my UN work is negotiation," she said. "And after all that's what political affairs are too."

The Commission on the Status of Women took the lead in working toward elimination of discrimination against women. Its Convention on Consent to Marriage, Minimum Age of Marriage, and Registration of Marriages had a considerable impact. "It has abolished polygamy in some places and has ended caste restrictions on women in Nepal, for example," Mrs. Tillett said. "I like to think we are working through the United Nations to open opportunities for women and not just spelling out women's rights."

Mrs. Tillett later turned her attention to pushing for ratification of the Equal Rights Amendment (ERA) by the North Carolina General Assembly. She made the comment about "washing dishes" at the initial meeting of the Mecklenburg Campaign for the Equal Rights Amendment where she was named chair. She soon led a massive writing, planning, and lobbying campaign for passage of the bill by the General Assembly in 1973. At the time, the amendment had been ratified by thirty-four states and needed thirty-eight for passage.

The subsequent campaign for ratification in North Carolina drew the celebrities. At one point, political novice and actress Jean Stapleton—Edith Bunker on television's *All in the Family*—and Liz Carpenter, former press secretary to former first lady Lady Bird Johnson, honored Tillett at an ERA rally in Charlotte. She delivered no speech but invited those interested in discussing the ERA to "come by my house and I'll talk long and as mean as you want. . . . Everybody running for the legislature should have a visit and a little conversation with us. A thoroughly polite one, of course."

Over an eighteen-month period, she traveled the state and gave an estimated seventy-five talks on why the amendment should be passed. She pointed out that at one time women could not own property. "We've come a long way, when you look back," she said. "Women had nothing when they started out." But the job would not be done until American men and women are granted equal rights under the Constitution, she said. "We need it in writing. 'All men are born equal' doesn't necessarily include women. It was written under the concept of British common law, which considers that husband and wife are one, and that one is he," Tillett told her audiences. "It never considered that men and women stand equal before the law."

She reminded listeners that Thomas Jefferson wrote: "Were our state a pure democracy, there would be excluded from our deliberations women, who, to prevent deprivation of morals and ambiguity of issues, should not mix promiscuously in gatherings of men." She said she hesitated to accept a Rotary Club invitation to speak on the Equal Rights Amendment "for fear that Jefferson might turn over in his grave."

Passage of the amendment by the General Assembly became a consuming desire. In 1976, she told a group of Central Piedmont Community College students in Charlotte: "No woman is free until all women are free." Later she walked slowly up Elizabeth Avenue to have lunch with some of her young friends. "I don't think the woman's movement is losing momentum," she said as she walked. "I think it's gaining, because women are becoming better informed."

When the women's movement began, she said, people tended to think it meant a contest between men and women. But there is no such contest, she added. "All my grandchildren are for it, and not because of me, but because the whole younger generation understands it perfectly."

Tillett and her husband, Charles, who died in 1952, had three children and ten grandchildren. She died in 1984 at age ninety-two. Her many honors included honorary degrees from the University of North Carolina at Chapel Hill and from Queens College.

At the time of her death, state representative Louise Brennan said, "A great, great lady has passed. It's like a pall has dropped when I realize Gladys is not alive. She really had a great influence on all of us. . . . She kept her sense of humor, and she knew how to deal with male politicians so they didn't get too mad at her. Always very delicate."

Tillett never lost her dream that the Equal Rights Amendment would be added to the Constitution, even though it was defeated twice by the North Carolina General Assembly. She continued to work with dedication, patience, and perseverance until her death. "We [women] have the vote, but that's not enough," she said. "Equality has been a long time in coming. It takes a lifetime for one day of winning. But as soon as our political leaders realize the value of women, as soon as men see that there are millions of women who work and still maintain a home and raise fine children, they'll realize there is nothing to their fears. . . . I know we'll win someday."

Stan Brennan retired after thirty-two years with the Charlotte Observer *as reporter and state and local news editor. Previously he had worked with newspapers in Durham, Greensboro, Birmingham, Ala. and Richmond, Va. He is a graduate of the University of North Carolina at Chapel Hill.*

For more information, see:

Tillett, Gladys Avery. Papers. Southern Historical Collection, University of North Carolina at Chapel Hill.

Department of State. *Gladys Tillett Headed U.S. Observer Delegation at Seminars on Participation of Women in Public Life.* Bulletin, January 27, 1966.
"Grandmotherly Suffragettes with a Spine of Steel." Tar Heel of the Week. *News and Observer,* February 2, 1975.

POPULAR CULTURE

Noᴿᴛʜ Cᴀʀᴏʟɪɴᴀ's performing artists—who would consider themselves just plain folks—carried the sounds of the mountains, the backwoods, and the mill villages to a broader audience during the twentieth century at the same time that Tar Heel performers created national and international names for themselves as singers, actors, and musicians.

From the late 1920s until he died in 1973, Bascom Lamar Lunsford, the self-styled "squire of South Turkey Creek," was known as "the minstrel of the Appalachians." He founded Asheville's Mountain Dance and Folk Festival in 1928 and directed it for more than forty years. Through the festival and his later contributions to the archives of Columbia University and the Library of Congress, he preserved a sound and culture that was fading with the modernization of the age.

While Lunsford took what he heard and saw around him in western North Carolina, hillbilly and bluegrass musicians were *making* music to be heard across the country on the radio and on records. Between 1925 and 1930, Charlie Poole of Randolph County was proclaimed the best-known banjo picker and singer in the Carolinas. He died when he was only thirty-nine. Poole inspired succeeding generations of bluegrass musicians, including Bill Monroe, Lester Flatt and Earl Scruggs, and Doc Watson. In that same era, Howard and Dorsey Dixon of Rockingham recorded for RCA Victor and others to add soulful duets, including the classic "Weave Room Blues," to the American repertoire.

Chatham County's Elizabeth Cotton's haunting "Freight Train, Freight Train," which became popular in the folk era, came from the sounds of the rails that ran near her home. Cleveland County produced Earl Scruggs, who later teamed with Lester Flat to create the Foggy Mountain Boys, perfected his three-finger style of picking by the time he was a teenager by listening to the music of older men in his community.

Avery County's Lulabelle Wiseman—who served a term in the General Assembly—and her husband, Scotty, were heard on WLS in Chicago from 1932 to 1958. Among Scotty's successful creations were "Have I Told You Lately That I Love You" and "That Good Old Mountain Dew," which he produced in collaboration with Lunsford.

Hollywood was populated with Tar Heels during the late years of the Depression, World War II, and postwar 1940s. One of the best-known personalities was bandleader Kay Kyser from Rocky Mount, whose career included radio and motion pictures. Before he retired to Chapel Hill, Kyser was the inspirational spark plug for the statewide Good Health Campaign in 1946, when he mobilized Hollywood on behalf of increasing awareness of health care in the state. A special edition of his popular radio show featured appearances by actresses Ava Gardner of Smithfield, Kathryn Grayson of Winston-Salem, and

Anne Jeffreys of Greensboro; band director John Scott Trotter of Charlotte; and actor Randolph Scott, also a Charlotte native.

Another Hollywood star of that era was Sydney Blackmer of Salisbury, who appeared with Shirley Temple in *The Little Colonel* and invigorated his career thirty years later with *Rosemary's Baby*.

Andy Griffith of Mount Airy began his acting career with the Carolina Playmakers, performed in Paul Green's *Lost Colony,* and then went on to Broadway. The long-running *Andy Griffith Show* in the 1960s assured his fame and convinced many viewers that there actually was a town in North Carolina called Mayberry and that it wasn't too far from Raleigh. In later years, Griffith was Matlock in a television show of the same name that was often produced in Wilmington, which by the 1980s had developed into an East Coast motion picture center.

Singer James Taylor, the son of a Chapel Hill physician, topped the pop charts for more than twenty years with a string of hits, and Wilmington's Charlie Daniels became one of the leading figures in southern rock music in the 1970s. Doc Watson of Deep Gap kept the mountain traditions alive with his recordings.

In 1974, George Hamilton IV was chosen by the U.S. State Department to become the first country singer to perform behind the Iron Curtain and became *Billboard* magazine's "International Ambassador of Country Music." Hamilton often sang at Grandfather Mountain's Singing on the Mountain, a favorite venue of Charlotte's Arthur Smith, whose "Dueling Banjos" was the driving theme of *Deliverance*.

Charlotte pianist and composer Loonis McGlohon not only accompanied such great singers as Judy Garland, but his songs were recorded by Frank Sinatra, Rosemary Clooney, Mabel Mercer, Eileen Farrell, Marlena Shaw, Marlene VerPlanck, George Shearing, Marian McPartland, and many others. McGlohon wrote songs for his children and friends, hymns and church music, and the theme music for CBS television's *On the Road* segments with his friend, Charles Kuralt.

In 1983, Governor James B. Hunt Jr. asked Kuralt and McGlohon to create something for the state's four hundredth birthday. They came up with the idea of making a recording with music by McGlohon and words by Kuralt, who didn't sing but whose distinctive voice was one of the glories of broadcasting. The result was "North Carolina Is My Home," a title song and a program of songs and stories about the state, some joyful, some hilarious, some simply beautiful.

DORSEY AND HOWARD DIXON

By Patrick Huber

The Dixon Brothers (Dorsey is on left, unidentified announcer in middle, Howard on right) (Courtesy of Southern Folklife Collection)

"THE DIXON BROTHERS, Dorsey and Howard, have been among the most popular groups heard on our Barn Dance Programs," explained a 1934 "Crazy Barn Dance" souvenir program. "They are now heard every day over WBT, Charlotte, with J. E. Mainer's Crazy Mountaineers, on the Crazy Water Crystals broadcasts. The Dixon Brothers compose most of the songs they sing, some of the most popular of which are 'The Weave Room Blues,' 'Don't Sales Tax the Gals' [*sic*], and 'Two Little Rose Buds.' We predict a big future for the Dixon Brothers in radio."

On the strength of such songs, the Dixon Brothers became one of the best-known hillbilly duets in the Carolina piedmont during the 1930s. Unfortunately, they earned few dollars for their radio and recording work. Yet whatever frustration the Dixons might have felt at their lack of financial gain was eased

somewhat by Dorsey's conviction that his compositions, especially his sacred numbers, were inspired by God and therefore intended not for personal profit but, as he often said, "to be a blessing to people."

For more than thirty-five years, Dorsey Dixon struggled to earn a living in textile mills, but by calling he was a guitarist, singer, and songwriter who believed that his special mission in life was to spread the gospel through music. A devout Free Will Baptist and regular churchgoer, Dixon transformed newspaper accounts of small-town tragedies and national disasters into songs about the wages of sin, the unknown hour of death, and the promise of eternal salvation. As jeremiads intended to generate spiritual renewal, Dixon's songs usually concluded with sober warnings to "get right with Jesus" and to lead righteous Christian lives. "When you think that you are wise,/Then you need not be surprised/If the hand of God should stop you on life's sea," the Dixon Brothers sang on "Down With the Old Canoe," a 1938 recording inspired by the sinking of the *Titanic*. "If you go on in your sin,/You will find out in the end/That you are just as foolish as can be."

Perhaps such dreadful incidents resonated with Dorsey Dixon in part because hardship and suffering deeply scarred his own life. But Dixon's music and his religion sustained him during his dark periods, including bouts with chronic depression, self-doubt, financial troubles, and serious health problems. "And friends," Dixon once wrote, "I know that the Great Power of God help[ed] me to win in every battle that I fought to stay in the world."

Dorsey Murdock Dixon was born into a white working-class family, the third of seven children, on October 14, 1897, in Darlington, S.C. His brother, Howard Britten Dixon, was born on June 19, 1903, in the nearby community of Kelley Town. Their father, William McQuiller Dixon, ran the steam engines at the Darlington Manufacturing Company, a local textile mill. Their mother, Mary Margaret (Braddock) Dixon, cared for her children and kept house. Dorsey was a tiny, oxygen-starved newborn who barely survived birth, and his devout parents interpreted his near-miraculous recovery as a sign that God had spared him for what they frequently referred to as "a great purpose."

Throughout most of Dorsey's life, though, doubts about his failure to carry out his divinely ordained mission plagued him. "I do not know if I have full filled [*sic*] the purpose that mother and father said I was left here for or not," he confessed in a memoir written when he was fifty years old. "But I do know that I have had a real tough time in life."

Like most other poor families in turn-of-the-century South Carolina, the Dixons scrambled to earn a living; their wanderings took them from sharecropper farms to industrial towns across northeastern South Carolina. In 1909, the Dixons returned to Darlington, where Dorsey dropped out of the fourth grade and began working in the Darlington Manufacturing Company, helping his older sister, Nancy, tend her spinning frames. By the age of thirteen, he was making bobbin bands in the mill's machine shop for fifty cents a day. The following year, Dorsey began taking violin lessons from a Darlington music teacher and then taught himself to play the guitar. Soon he was performing in the church orchestra at Sunday school and entertaining neighbors in Darlington's mill village.

Beginning in 1915, Dorsey and Howard worked as signalmen on the Atlantic Coast Line Railroad in the Darlington switchyard. But in 1920, Dorsey resumed work at the Darlington Manufacturing Company and learned how to be a weaver, one of the highest paid and most skilled factory jobs in the textile industry. Soon Howard followed him into the mill to work on a "floating gang," doing odd jobs in the factory. Between 1922 and 1924, Dorsey worked as a weaver in textile mills across the piedmont, including ones in Lancaster and Greenville, S.C. Meanwhile, Howard remained in Darlington and in 1920 married Mellie Barfield, with whom he eventually raised seven children.

In 1925, Dorsey settled in East Rockingham and went to work as a weaver at the Hannah Pickett Mill. Later that summer, Howard joined him there, taking a job in the cloth room. Upon his brother's arrival, Dorsey and Howard formed a fiddle-and-guitar combination to entertain at local house parties and church revivals, and, occasionally, they supplied the musical accompaniment to silent films at a local theater. In 1927, Dorsey married Beatrice Lucele Moody, a mill girl fourteen years his junior from Greenville, S.C., and together they raised four sons.

Dorsey always believed his parents' refrain that God had intended him to fulfill a great purpose, but it was not until the age of thirty-one that he discovered that this mission might be accomplished through songwriting. In 1929, he composed his first song, "Cleveland School House Fire," an elegy memorializing seventy-six people who had perished in a schoolhouse fire near Camden, S.C., six years earlier. By 1932, Dorsey was regularly composing topical songs and poems about national events such as natural disasters and high-profile crimes, and publishing them in his hometown newspaper, the *Rockingham Post-Dispatch*.

But what he did best was to craft verses commemorating the victims of local tragedies. In 1932, for example, when two girls drowned in a millpond, Dixon penned "Two Little Rose Buds" in their memory. Dixon's elegies, however, were more than merely descriptive narratives chronicling the unfortunate passing of East Rockingham residents. Rather, his songs transformed their deaths into religious exempla about divine judgment and redemption.

Several of Dixon's most popular compositions criticized what he saw as one of the profoundly disturbing trends of modern southern life: the erosion of bedrock Christian morals. Nowhere did Dixon make this point more clearly than in his best-known song, "Wreck on the Highway" [originally titled "I Didn't Hear Nobody Pray"], which was inspired by a deadly automobile accident near East Rockingham in 1938. As one music historian later noted, "what is even more horrifying [to Dixon] than the violence itself is the reaction of those who run out from their homes to witness the tragedy—namely, their failure to lift even a single voice in prayer for the souls of the dead and the dying." Thus, Dixon transformed a grisly scene on a small southern highway into a sweeping indictment of his increasingly secular and godless society. "Please give up the game and stop drinking," Dixon warned, "For Jesus is pleading with you./It cost Him a lot in redeeming,/Redeeming the promise for you./But it'll be too late if tomorrow/In a crash you should fall by the way,/With whiskey and blood all around you,/And you can't hear nobody pray."

A perceptive social observer of southern working-class life, Dorsey also composed songs about the hardships and frustrations of Depression-era textile work. One of his most famous textile songs, "Weave Room Blues," written in 1932, recounted both his difficulties operating his looms and his struggles raising a family on a weaver's wages. Eventually, he composed or arranged six more textile songs, more than any other hillbilly singer of his generation, including "Weaver's Life" and "Spinning Room Blues," all but one of which he recorded. Both "Weave Room Blues" and "Weaver's Life" emerged as emblematic protest songs among folk revivalists and trade unionists after World War II.

One particularly important and influential friendship that Dorsey struck up in the early 1930s was with Jimmie Tarlton, a fellow mill hand and accomplished steel guitarist who had recorded for Columbia with partner Tom Darby. In 1931, Dorsey and Howard went to hear Tarlton and, as Dorsey recalled, "we were both carried away with his style of playing." Until then, Dorsey had played guitar by simply "framming," or strumming chords, but he was impressed with how Tarlton plucked individual strings of his steel guitar with finger picks. Tarlton inspired Dorsey to develop his own distinctive guitar-picking style, using picks on all four fingers and thumb of his right hand. After weeks of practice, Dixon's playing resembled the delicate fingerpicking of many African American blues men of the region. Meanwhile, Howard bought himself a cheap steel guitar for three dollars and also began to teach himself to play in a style modeled on Tarlton's.

In 1932, Dorsey and Howard began performing together in East Rockingham as the Dixon Brothers, and they soon became one of the most sought-after musical groups in Richmond County. Two years later, their strident, gospel-inflected harmonies landed them a regular radio spot on the *Crazy Barn Dance,* a popular Saturday night jamboree broadcast over Charlotte's WBT and sponsored by the Crazy Water Crystals Company, the manufacturers of a best-selling laxative. The Dixon Brothers' radio broadcasts and stage shows earned them a large following in the Carolinas and helped launch their brief recording career. Between 1936 and 1938, they recorded a total of fifty-five sides for RCA Victor's budget-priced Bluebird label, many of them composed or arranged by Dorsey, including the now-classic songs "Weave Room Blues," "Intoxicated Rat," and "I Didn't Hear Nobody Pray." Although other recording artists later scored hits with Dorsey's original compositions, the Dixon Brothers themselves never achieved great commercial success. According to Dorsey, money-grubbing producers and recording artists took advantage of his trust, swindling him out of the copyrights and royalties to several of his most popular songs. Weary of juggling their musical careers with their regular textile jobs, and discouraged by their mistreatment by the music industry, the Dixon Brothers stopped performing together by World War II.

After the Dixon Brothers split up, they left East Rockingham. By 1941, Howard was playing steel guitar with Wade Mainer and the Sons of the Mountaineers, who had a regular radio spot on Asheville's WWNC. The following year, Howard returned to East Rockingham, where he worked at the Entwistle [later the Aleo] Mill and played with several local bands, including the Richmond County Ramblers and the Southern Hillbillies. Meanwhile, in 1941, Dorsey went to work at the Dunean Mill in Greenville, S.C., and occasionally performed on local radio station WFBC. In 1942, he discovered that the Grand Ole Opry's biggest headliner, Roy Acuff and his Smoky Mountain Boys, had recorded "I Didn't Hear Nobody Pray" under the title of "Wreck on the Highway." Over the next four years, Dixon wrote letter after letter to Acuff-Rose Publishing claiming authorship of "Wreck on the Highway," but he received no answer. Finally, in 1946, Dixon and Fred Rose, Acuff's music publishing partner, reached an out-of-court settlement. But much of Dixon's compensation went to pay legal fees and to buy out banjo player Wade Mainer, who in 1938 had hoodwinked the trusting songwriter into copyrighting the song in both of their names. Surprisingly, Dixon bore no hard feelings toward Acuff and Rose for pirating his song. "I'm certain the Lord worked through Acuff and Rose in my favor," he once wrote. "To my dieing day Acuff and Rose will have a warm place in my heart [*sic*]."

In 1947, with hopes of additional royalty settlements, Dorsey and his family moved to New York City. But he soon discovered that regaining control of his song copyrights would be difficult, if not impossible. The following year, Dixon and his family returned to East Rockingham. He worked at the Aleo Mill until 1951, when at the age of fifty-three his deteriorating eyesight forced him to retire. Later that year, he, his wife, and their youngest son moved to Baltimore, where, despite his poor vision, Dorsey worked in a munitions plant. In 1953, Beatrice Dixon left him after twenty-five years of troubled marriage. Devastated, Dorsey returned alone to East Rockingham in 1958.

Divorced and with most of his immediate family dead or scattered, Dorsey subsisted on meager Social Security disability payments and an occasional royalty check. Completely blind in one eye and in poor health, he sank into a deep depression and lost interest in music. But in 1960, a series of enthusiastic fan letters from John Edwards, a twenty-eight-year-old record collector and music historian from Sydney, Australia, inspired Dixon to revive the Dixon Brothers' musical career. But Howard was reluctant to leave his stable home life to return to music-making, and his sudden death from a massive heart attack on March 24, 1961, ended Dorsey's dreams of reuniting the act.

Nonetheless, Dorsey did launch a short-lived solo comeback during the American folk music revival. In 1962, with the assistance of hillbilly music historians and record collectors Archie Green and Eugene Earle, Dixon recorded the critically acclaimed album *Babies in the Mill,* which appeared on Testament Records. The title track, which Dixon had composed in 1945, remains the definitive musical portrayal of child labor in America.

Over the next eighteen months Dixon performed at the Newport Folk Festival and several folk music clubs in Washington, D.C. He also recorded thirty-eight numbers for the Library of Congress's Archive of American Folk Song (now the American Folklife Center), the premier repository for the nation's grass-roots music. But in October 1964, a heart attack derailed Dorsey Dixon's return to the folk music circuit. No longer able to care for himself, he moved to Florida to live with his oldest son and his family.

On April 18, 1968, at the age of seventy, Dorsey Dixon died of heart failure. His body was returned to his adopted hometown of East Rockingham and he was buried there in the Eastside Cemetery.

Patrick Huber received his Ph.D. from the University of North Carolina at Chapel Hill and is currently an assistant professor of history at the University of Missouri-Rolla, where he is working on a book entitled Hillbilly Music: The Modern Origins of an Old-Time Southern Sound.

For more information, see:
Dixon, Dorsey M. Correspondence and field recordings. American Folklife Center, Library of Congress, Washington, D.C.
———. Correspondence and autobiographical sketches. Southern Folklife Collection, University of North Carolina at Chapel Hill.
———. Interview by Archie Green and Ed Kahn, August 20, 1961. Southern Folklife Collection, University of North Carolina at Chapel Hill.
———. Interview by Eugene Earle and Archie Green, August 7–8, 1962. Southern Folklife Collection, University of North Carolina at Chapel Hill.

Huber, Patrick, and Kathleen Drowne. "'I Don't Want Nothin' 'Bout My Life Wrote Out, Because I Had It Too Rough in Life': Dorsey Dixon's Autobiographical Writings." *Southern Cultures* 6 (Summer 2000): 94–100.
Paris, Mike. "The Dixons of South Carolina." *Old Time Music* 10 (Autumn 1973): 13–16.

ANDY S. GRIFFITH

By Ryan Sumner

ANDY GRIFFITH took an acting career that began with Paul Green's outdoor drama *The Lost Colony,* and a hillbilly's hilarious interpretation of a college football game—"What It Was, Was Football"—and grew to international fame in movies, on television, and on Broadway with both comic and serious roles.

Most of his early roles were as lanky southerners, such as GI Will Stockdale in the Broadway hit *No Time for Sergeants,* and later in his career he interpreted his southern heritage in the life of a wily trial lawyer named Matlock in a popular television series of the same name. But he was perhaps best known as Andy Taylor, the sheriff of Mayberry, a town that bore a striking resemblance to Griffith's hometown of Mount Airy, which had a real Snappy Lunch, the home of a deliciously messy pork chop sandwich.

Andy Samuel Griffith was born on June 1, 1926, in Mount Airy, a small town in the northwestern foothills. Times were tough, and the only child of Carl Lee and Geneva Griffith was first cradled in a bureau drawer in the family home—a converted barn that was owned by Geneva's sister, Grace Moore, and her husband John.

Carl Griffith, whose education extended only into the fourth grade, was a skilled carpenter and craftsman of fine furniture. However, employment prospects were limited and Carl moved his family to Ohio, hoping to provide a better living for his family. The Griffiths returned to North Carolina three years later, this time to High Point, a major furniture-manufacturing center. When Andy was six, the family moved back to Mount Airy when Carl Griffith found work at the Mount Airy Chair Company, where his skill as a band saw operator and supervisor kept him employed throughout the Depression. "Growing up in Mount Airy, we were poor people," Andy Griffith said, "but we were not in poverty." The family eventually saved $435, which was used to purchase a new house on Haymore Street.

Carl and Geneva Griffith exercised a heavy influence on their young son. Andy's father was a great joker and a storyteller in the upland North Carolina tradition. According to a cousin, "There were never any dark moments with Carl Griffith." Andy's first wife commented that Carl was one of the funniest men she had ever known and that the source of Andy's hu-

Andy Griffith (Courtesy of Charlotte Observer)

mor was a subconscious desire to caricature his father. "I think my father had an enormous influence on me," the actor later expressed. "He was a Christian man, truly honorable and honest, a fine human being, and he had a magnificent sense of humor. He would have made a fine actor." Andy's mother imparted a love of music to her son. Geneva's family had always been musically inclined; she possessed a reputation as a fine singer and taught Andy his first simple chords on the guitar.

When Andy entered school, he found himself the object of ridicule and a victim of feelings of inadequacy. "I wasn't smart, my family wasn't wealthy, and I wasn't athletic. In a little town like Mount Airy, if you aren't wealthy or athletic, you aren't much." However, Andy did find acceptance with Edward Mickey, a Moravian minister and musician, who taught Andy to play the slide trombone. Andy became active in the Moravian Church, eventually leading the church band and singing in the choir. Because of Mickey's strong influence, Griffith wanted to become a clergyman, so in the fall of 1944, with thirty cents in his pocket, Griffith bid farewell to Mount Airy and enrolled at the University of North Carolina at Chapel Hill as a ministerial student.

He had great difficulty with his studies during his first year at Chapel Hill. His insecurities followed him and he was petrified of appearing uneducated. Sociology was particularly difficult and he walked out before the end of the term, taking an F. Despite spending long hours at study, Griffith retained little and failed classes in Latin and Greek and flunked political science on two occasions. He once remarked that failing political science twice was the only record he ever broke while at Chapel Hill. Believing that he was unsuited for the ministry, Griffith changed his major to music, playing trombone and sousaphone. When a childhood back injury returned and forced him into a steel and leather brace, he became eligible for tuition assistance for indigent students with disabilities.

With his financial and medical expenses taken care of, Griffith began to focus on university activities that interested him. He began singing in the campus glee club and became involved with the Carolina Playmakers, a group that produced an annual operetta. Griffith made his stage debut in Gilbert and Sullivan's *Gondoliers,* singing the role of Don Alhambra del Bolero, the Grand Inquisitor. Andy began acting every chance that he got, despite often becoming physically ill before appearing in front of an audience. Paul Young, the director of the university choral department, was impressed with his performances and began offering Griffith private lessons in return for his services as the music librarian. Griffith received the lessons for five years.

In 1946 Griffith met Barbara Bray Edwards in the Carolina Playmakers. The Troy native was the daughter of a North Carolina school superintendent and held a degree in music from Converse College for Women. The tall soprano had come to Chapel Hill to study drama, where she quickly became the star of the university campus. The two met during a spring production of Haydn's *The Seasons.* Reportedly, Griffith proposed three days after they met.

In the summer of 1946, Griffith joined the cast of Paul Green's outdoor drama *The Lost Colony,* staged on Roanoke Island in Manteo. For the next seven summers he was in the production, playing bit parts and supporting roles for two years and finally playing the lead of Sir Walter Raleigh. Barbara also joined the production, where she played Eleanor Dare. During his time with the production, Griffith developed a love for the Carolina coast and began performing comedy monologues on Saturday nights at the Beach Club in Nags Head. In 1949, after five years at the University of North Carolina, Griffith graduated with his degree in music and married Barbara Edwards in Nags Head.

When the play came to the end of its summer run, the newlyweds moved to Goldsboro. Barbara became the music director of the Methodist and Episcopal churches, while Andy taught music and glee club at Goldsboro High School. He once boosted his enrollment by addressing a freshmen assembly, where he said, "If you want to take a crip course, take music, take glee club. You can't fail. No tests. No catches." The twenty-three-year-old teacher had trouble disciplining his students, who regarded him more as a friend, but he remained at the school for three years.

During the time the Griffiths were in Goldsboro, Andy and Barbara put together a weekend act to entertain at various civic affairs. Andy delivered his comic monologues, played the guitar, and sang folk songs. Barbara also sang and did interpretive dancing. For seventy-five dollars per show, the duo performed at women's clubs, schools, and conventions all over North Carolina and other parts of the South.

While traveling between engagements on the "Rotary Club circuit," Griffith wrote a new monologue he called "What It Was, Was Football." It was delivered in the dialect of a backwoods preacher who was attempting to explain his first football game. The piece quickly became a staple of the act and was recorded at a Greensboro insurance convention in 1953. Andy sold the piece to Colonial Records, a Chapel Hill record label, for half the profits. Colonial pressed five hundred copies, with Griffith's country version of Romeo and Juliet on the other side. All of the copies sold in a single weekend after WRAL radio played the piece during a football game between UNC and Notre Dame. Capitol Records bought the recording, which sold more than 800,000 copies before 1960.

After touring through the South doing comedy engagements and performing as an opening act for Mae West, Griffith was cast in the role of Will Stockdale for the televised production of Mac Hyman's *No Time for Sergeants.* Griffith was perfect in the comedic role of a drafted hillbilly and was quickly given the same part in the Broadway production, which opened in October 1955 to sensational reviews. The Griffiths moved to New York, where Andy preformed in *Sergeants* for nearly the entire run.

In 1957, Griffith left Broadway when famed filmmaker Elia Kazan wanted him to star in his new feature film, *A Face in the Crowd,* a satiric drama about the power of television. Kazan placed Griffith in the lead, playing country music performer Lonesome Rhodes, who becomes crazed with power during his rise to fame. "Elia Kazan taught me all I know about formal acting," Griffith said, "He talked to me about the 'method,' which is nothing more than recall—remembering something from your past that relates to the scene being played." The director's coaching paid off, and Griffith's tour de force performance resulted in national attention and critical praise.

Griffith was busy after the success of *A Face in the Crowd.* He purchased the fifty-three-acre farm on Roanoke Island, which he still called home at the end of the century, and adopted his first child, Andy Jr. In late 1957, the actor began work on the movie version of *No Time for Sergeants,* which became one of the top five films of 1958. Griffith followed *Sergeants* with *Onionhead,* another military comedy, where he played a coast guard cook; unfortunately, the second film was a commercial failure. In 1959, Andy returned to Broadway in *Destry Rides Again,* while simultaneously performing comedy on numerous variety shows and starring in a weekday CBS radio show. In the fall of 1959, CBS producer Sheldon Leonard approached Griffith with a concept for a television series.

The *Andy Griffith Show* premiered on CBS on October 3, 1960, and introduced the nation to the fictional North Carolina town of Mayberry. The sitcom focused on Griffith's character, Andy Taylor, the town sheriff, justice of the peace, and father to Opie, who was played by Ron Howard. "We were working on something new," Griffith often said. "The central character [Sheriff Taylor] was a straight character and all of the others were comedians." The other characters, principally Don Knotts as Deputy Barney Fife, created the antic situations and comedic events, which provided the show's humor, while Taylor resolved the crises. The show ran for eight seasons, recording 249 episodes between 1960 and 1968. It captured six Emmys for the performances of Knotts and Francis Bavier [Aunt Bee]; it never placed lower than seventh in the A. C. Nielsen Ratings and finished first in its last year.

Griffith moved his family, which now included their adopted daughter Dixie Nann, to California and settled into eight years of hard work on the television series that bore his name. Every day Griffith awoke at 5 A.M. to read his script and start a sixteen-hour workday that consumed thirty-nine weeks of the year. Griffith, who owned a significant percentage of the show, arrived on the set half an hour early and was active in outlining the episodes and rewriting the script's dialog; Griffith's work on rewriting is often credited with giving the show its authentic feeling. In 1968, Griffith left the show to embark on a new motion picture career and the program was renamed *Mayberry RFD,* which Griffith produced until its cancellation in 1971.

Griffith's new movie career was short-lived. In 1969, after signing a five-year contract with Universal Pictures, Griffith starred in *Angel in my Pocket,* a G-rated story about an ex-marine who becomes a preacher. Though Griffith was proud of the picture, the film was a failure at the box office. "It died," the actor said, "just laid there and died." Griffith asked to get out of his contract when the studio suggested that he do his next picture with Don Knotts.

In the fall of 1970, Griffith returned to television in *The Headmaster,* a comedy-drama with him playing the head of an exclusive private school, where he was also the music teacher. The show attempted to address serious issues, like drug-abuse, but was ultimately rejected by audiences. The network canceled the show after fourteen episodes and replaced it in mid-season with *The New Andy Griffith Show;* this time, Andy was the mayor of Greenwood, N.C. This hollow revamp was not renewed at the end of the season.

In the 1970s Griffith began to change his image. He pursued gritty roles in made-for-television movies; he won critical acclaim for his role in *Go Ask Alice* and offered a chilling performance in *Pray for the Wildcats.* In 1972, Andy and Barbara Griffith divorced after twenty-three years of marriage and Andy later married Greek actress Solicia Caussuto in 1975, but divorced again in 1978.

Griffith married for love again, but illness cut the honeymoon short. The actor met Cindi Knight while she was working in *The Lost Colony.* They struck up a friendship, which built up over five years and culminated in their marriage of April 1983. However, six weeks after the wedding Griffith was struck with a "pain so encompassing that I could not feel my feet. I had no control over them, and fell to the floor in agony." A spinal tap revealed that he had Guillain-Barré syndrome, a rare form of nerve inflammation that causes intense pain and limited paralysis. With no drugs or surgery available, the actor embarked on six months of painful physical therapy to learn to walk again. It was a year before the pain subsided enough to let Griffith participate in everyday activities and the actor continued to experience a permanent pain in his feet.

Griffith's career entered a second renaissance beginning in the mid-1980s. In 1985 he was back in the primetime spotlight with the successful television series *Matlock*. Griffith was not only the star, but also the executive producer of the show about a Harvard-educated trial lawyer practicing in a fictional Georgia town. *Matlock* filmed primarily in Wilmington, which let Andy be closer to his Manteo home. Griffith enjoyed playing the attorney, who was frequently the comedy character and had numerous weaknesses. After *Matlock* finished its nine-year run, Griffith returned to his musical roots. He recorded two albums of gospel hymns, *I Love to Tell the Story* in 1996 and *Just as I Am* in 1997; the former won a Grammy.

Ryan Sumner is a graduate of the University of North Carolina at Charlotte, where he continued his studies for a master's degree in history and worked in the exhibit department of the Levine Museum of the New South in Charlotte.

For more information, see:
Griffith, Andy. Collection. Southern Historical Collection, University of North Carolina at Chapel Hill.
———. Interview by William Friday, December 1993. *North Carolina People.* University of North Carolina Center for Public Broadcasting.

Brower, Neal, *Mayberry 101: Behind the Scenes of a TV Classic.* John F. Blair Publisher, 1998.
Collins, Terry. *The Andy Griffith Story: An Illustrated Biography.* Explorer Press, 1995.
Edmonston, Russ. "Andy Griffith: He's Still the Sheriff." *Greensboro Daily News,* October 15, 1978.
Pfeiffer, Lee. *The Official Andy Griffith Show Scrapbook.* Citadel Press, 1994.
Rader, Dotson. "Why I Listened to My Father." *Parade,* February 4, 1990.
Vincent, Mal. "Andy Griffith Back Home—For a Spell," *Greensboro Daily News,* August 19, 1973.

GEORGE HAMILTON IV

By Frye Gaillard

IT WAS A COMMON SCENE in the Hamilton household, George IV packing frantically to catch a
flight overseas. In a career that began in the 1950s,
and continued unbroken through the early years of
the twenty-first century, he recorded more than ninety
albums, spanning a wide range of musical tastes. At
various times since he first stepped into a recording
studio in Chapel Hill in 1956, he was a teenage idol,
a country music superstar, and a fixture in the late
1960s folk music scene. He was a TV regular in half
a dozen countries, a forty-year-member of the Grand
Ole Opry, and later a musical headliner in the Billy
Graham crusades.

But his career also had its frustrations. Except at
the start, his fame was greater overseas than at home.
His last hit single in the United States came in 1971,
and there are those who say that with his three-piece
suits and aw-shucks demeanor, he was a little too
square for American fans. But Hamilton survived. In
the changing fortunes of the country music business,
he always managed to find his niche, and as more
than one music writer noted, he always did it on his
own terms.

Hamilton was born on July 19, 1937, in Winston-
Salem, a young man proud of his Scottish heritage
and his string of namesakes going back to the old
country. In 1956, he was a shy, skinny freshman at the
University of North Carolina at Chapel Hill, but he
could sing country songs and play the guitar, and his
buddies at the fraternity house were amused by his
talent. Those were the early days of Elvis Presley's
rock 'n' roll, and although Hamilton was impressed
by the energy and excitement, he was hooked nevertheless on the twang of country music. His ambition
was to perform on the Grand Ole Opry, and less than
four years later that's what he was doing.

In between, however, after he made a smash hit
about young love, he joined the ranks of the teenage
idols, crisscrossing the country with Chuck Berry,
Dion, Sam Cooke, and Buddy Holly. In the studios
of UNC's campus radio station, he had cut a teen ballad called "A Rose and a Baby Ruth." Hamilton didn't
even like the song, but he released it on a little Chapel
Hill label called Colonial Records. Fred Foster—then
a talent hunter for ABC Paramount Records—heard
it and bought the rights for ABC.

Foster's bosses were at first appalled. "They thought

*George Hamilton IV, right, with Orville Campbell in
Chapel Hill (Courtesy of Hugh Morton)*

it was terrible," he recalled years later. "But I had gotten this call from Buddy Deane who was a DJ at
WITH radio in Baltimore. Buddy said, 'I just played
this record by a kid from North Carolina, and the
phones went crazy.' So I went over and heard the song,
and I said, 'I don't know, man, I've heard better records.' And Deane said, 'I'm tellin' you, it's a hit.'

"Well, my immediate boss was named Larry Newton. He was a big, gruff guy who intimidated everybody, and I knew he would pick the record apart. So
I called Sam Clark, who was president of the label,
and I got his permission to buy it for ABC.

"When Newton finally heard it, he called me up
and said, 'You're a sick man, Foster, a sick man.' He
always said everything twice. He said, 'That's the worst
piece of crap I ever heard, the worst I ever heard.' So
I said, 'Look, Larry, if it doesn't go, you got my job,
but if it does go, I want a raise. . . . '"

It went, of course. The record sold more than a million copies, landing Hamilton on network television

—he later had his own show on ABC—and onto package tours with other teenage rock idols.

"We hit it off well," Hamilton said of his rockabilly buddies. "We were all in the same age group, and we were all scared as heck. But soon we began to notice some differences, some real cultural gaps in terms of who our heroes were. Some of the Northern kids—Fabian, Frankie Avalon, Paul Anka and some others—were all really into the Italian singers, like Sinatra or Tony Bennett. I tended to gravitate to the Southern kids—Buddy Holly, Gene Vincent, and especially the Everly Brothers—who were still hung up on Hank Williams.

"It was almost like the kids from the North were trying to rock Frank Sinatra, while the kids from the South were rocking Hank Williams. And then there were the black singers, which was really a revelation. I toured with Chuck Berry in Australia in 1959, and Chuck was an intellectual. He used to quote Shakespeare a lot. But he also had a little chip on his shoulder. He said, 'The difference between me and you, white boy, is that when you were there in Nashville diggin' the Grand Old Opry, you got to sit inside. I had to stand out in the alley.' Sam Cooke was different. He was a really gentle guy, very perceptive and decent, but like Chuck Berry he liked country music a lot.

"From all of that, you started to sense something about our common roots. We would tour together and start feeling like we were friends, like it didn't matter as much who was black and who was white. And then we would hit the South. The bus would drop the black stars off at some rundown little hotel on the black side of town, and that created some weird feelings. This was 1958, man, and I wasn't quite ready to say, 'Hey, drop me off at the black hotel.' But I knew it wasn't right."

Such memories dominated Hamilton's recounting of his teen idol days. He didn't talk particularly about the music he was making, for he saw it, even then, as far too syrupy and short on substance. So in 1959—while his rock 'n' roll career was still going strong—he decided to make a change. He headed for Nashville, and by 1960 he had sung his way into a spot on the Grand Ole Opry. He cut a string of country hits, peaking in 1963 with a folk ballad called "Abilene," which made its way into the country top five, then crossed to the pop charts and made the top twenty.

But after "Abilene" he seemed to grow restless once again in his musical inclinations. He found himself listening to the 1960s folk singers—people like Pete Seeger, Bob Dylan, and Joan Baez. They sang the old British folk songs that had been a part of Hamilton's family for several hundred years, mingling the ancient ballads with those of new vintage—protest songs about the problems of America.

Hamilton liked the mix, and he began recording songs by Dylan, Leonard Cohen, and especially Gordon Lightfoot. In 1967, he also cut Joni Mitchell's "Urge for Going," becoming the first artist in any field to have a top-ten hit with a Mitchell composition. But those were tumultuous times. America was caught in the Vietnam War and all the polarization that went along with it, and country music, with its legions of All-American fans, was clearly identified with the conservative side of the political spectrum.

Merle Haggard was going strong with "Okie from Muskogee" and "The Fightin' Side of Me," records extolling patriotism and denouncing the demonstrators who were tearing at the country. George Hamilton, meanwhile, was consorting with the folkies, the balladeers who were marching in the front ranks of protest.

It was about that time that Marty Robbins, a smooth country crooner with staunchly conservative inclinations, cornered Hamilton backstage at the Grand Ole Opry, and without a lot of subtlety, began to question his patriotism. Hamilton tried to respond in his own gentle way that music runs deeper, touches something more basic than political storms that come and go with the time. He knew that his answer had been poorly understood, but he felt driven somehow to do what he was doing. In 1968, he appeared at the Newport Folk Festival, sharing the stage with Pete Seeger, Joan Baez, and Janis Joplin.

The same year he did a benefit concert for Robert F. Kennedy's presidential campaign—responding to an emergency call from a Kennedy supporter. It was a bone-chilling night in the middle of March, and Kennedy was scheduled to speak in Nashville before 10,000 people at Vanderbilt University. But he was late. He had been delayed in Alabama, and it would be at least two hours before he arrived in Nashville. The sponsors were searching for somebody to entertain the crowd in the meantime. Plenty of country singers would have been willing to do it if the candidate had been George Wallace. But Kennedy, with his liberal affirmations of the rights of the poor, was another matter.

Hamilton, however, considered it an honor, and he entertained the waiting crowd for nearly two hours. It occurred to him then that in his own Mr.-Nice-Guy way, despite his three-piece suits and his amiable demeanor, he was an incurable nonconformist, who was perpetually caught up in a grass-is-greener restlessness about his career. When he was a rock 'n' roll star, he wanted to sing country music. When he made it in Nashville, he began to sing folk songs. And later he turned his attention to gospel.

Through it all, he made his share of music history. In 1974, he was chosen by the U.S. State Department to become the first country singer to perform behind the Iron Curtain. In Moscow, he gave a lecture-concert performance on the history of country music, and a short time later recorded an album in Czechoslovakia. Soon after his return, *Billboard* magazine named him the "International Ambassador of Country Music."

It was a title he continued to earn through the years. In the 1970s, he hosted his own television shows in Canada, Great Britain, New Zealand, and South Africa. In 1982, he set the record for the longest country music tour in the British Isles, a four-month run beginning in August. And in 1994, he became the first country artist to star in a musical in London's West End theater district.

In the 1980s, he recorded the first of two albums with his son, George Hamilton V, a Nashville songwriter who had become a frequent guest on the Grand Ole Opry, and about that time he had begun to turn his attention to gospel music. In addition to his appearances with Billy Graham, he recorded nineteen albums of spiritual songs, and won the Dove Award in 1989, the highest honor of the Gospel Music Association. But his greatest love was still country music. In the year 2000, he celebrated his fortieth year on the Grand Ole Opry, an event that took him back to graduation day in 1955, when his high school year-book was cheerfully inscribed: "Grand Ole Opry Here I Come."

In an interview early in the new millennium, Hamilton said it had been a long ride since the days of innocence, when he sang of the ache in a teenager's heart, a long way from there to his groundbreaking tour of the Soviet Union, or his appearances with Bobby Kennedy or Billy Graham. There were inevitable ups and downs, some frustrating lapses in success, but all in all, he wouldn't change a thing.

"I'm just a restless hillbilly," he said, "fortunate enough to make a living at my hobby. A lot of it has really been rocking chair stuff, something to tell your grandchildren about."

But in the middle of his fifth decade as a singer, Hamilton, who was living in Nashville, was not a performer content with his memories. He was still a member of the Grand Ole Opry, still recording, still touring overseas. He had adopted as his anthem a Bob Dylan song, wishing for his audiences the quality that he always wished for himself, and found through his music: "May you stay forever young. . . . "

Frye Gaillard is a North Carolina author who has written extensively about country music. He lives in Charlotte.

For more information, see:

Davis, Paul. *George Hamilton IV: Ambassador of Country Music*. HarperCollins, 2000.

Gaillard, Frye. *Watermelon Wine: The Spirit of Country Music*. St. Martin's Press, 1978.

Bascom Lamar Lunsford

By David Whisnant

From the late 1920s until he died in 1973, Bascom Lamar Lunsford was known far and wide as "the minstrel of the Appalachians," primarily for his work with Asheville's Mountain Dance and Folk Festival, which he founded in 1928 and directed for more than forty years. In the years after his death, the festival remained a central fixture on the cultural landscape of western North Carolina.

For most of his adult life, Lunsford lived just outside Asheville, styling himself "the squire of South Turkey Creek." But by any reasonable measure, he was a sophisticated and urbane man who worked all of his life to find a humane and manageable medium between the urban ways of tourist-oriented Asheville and the lives of ordinary working people in the outlying communities of Beaverdam and Candler, Soco Gap and Avery's Creek, Spook's Branch and Dunn's Rock. The Mountain Dance and Folk Festival opened every year "along about sundown" the first weekend in August, when a mountain fiddler stepped onto the stage and played "Grey Eagle." Especially during the early years, at a time when mountain people and their music were widely denigrated and stereotyped, the festivals projected a vital and dignified image of regional culture to a local, national, and international audience. Over the nearly half century that Lunsford directed it, the festival became an important transitional cultural venue between the old rural, traditional, community- and family-based culture, and the emerging urban, industrial, media-dominated mass culture that brought waves of change through the mountains from the 1880s onward.

Lunsford was born into the family of a self-taught but rather erudite schoolteacher in Mars Hill, in rural Madison County, just north of Asheville. His parents urged their children to memorize and recite poetry, and took a serious interest in their education. One of Bascom's fondest memories was of going with his father to hear fiddler Uncle Os Deaver; his mother—a fine singer herself—helped him make his first cigarbox fiddle. By the time Bascom was ten, he and his brother were playing at school entertainments. After getting as much education as he could at local public schools and a small private academy, and working intermittently at several jobs, Lunsford enrolled at Rutherford College, from which he graduated in 1909 (at the fairly late age of twenty-seven). After studying

Bascom Lamar Lunsford (Courtesy of North Carolina Collection)

law on his own and attending law school at Trinity College (later Duke University) for two years, he received his license to practice in 1913.

The jobs Lunsford held at various times in his life were many and for the most part brief: teacher at a local subscription school (1902–03), nursery and honey salesman (1903–06), solicitor of Burke County (1913–14), professor of English and history at Rutherford College (1914–16), small-town newspaper editor (1916–17, 1919), war bond salesman, auctioneer, reading clerk in the state legislature, agent for the U.S. Justice Department, and New Deal worker. His major passion was music, however, and he devoted all the time to it he could possibly spare while keeping his "day job" if possible, compromising it if it seemed to him necessary. Initially as a fruit-tree salesman, subsequently as western North Carolina field secretary for the (Methodist) Epworth League, and throughout his later life, Lunsford traveled widely in the southern mountains, collecting music from local people at every opportunity.

Lunsford's interest in presenting local culture emerged early in his life. In 1910, he had presented

Uncle Billy Hill as an entertainer at the Nebo school commencement. He himself also lectured on music and performed widely, and by at least 1925 had begun staging public entertainments at schoolhouses in which he gave a cash prize to the student who contributed the best ballad or story.

In 1925, Lunsford was able to move his family back to western North Carolina, onto land on South Turkey Creek that his wife Nellie Triplett inherited from her father. At that historical moment, Asheville was the major metropolitan center for more than a hundred miles in any direction. The railroad had arrived forty years before, snaking its way up the mountain from Old Fort and through the notorious Swannanoa tunnel that claimed many lives and that was immortalized in song ("Asheville junction, Swannanoa tunnel; All caved in, boys, all caved in. . . . "). George Vanderbilt arrived in 1889, bought 130,000 acres of mountain land, and spent five years building a 250-room French Renaissance chateau just outside town. St. Louis entrepreneur E. W. Grove (who made his money hawking Grove's Tasteless Chill Tonic) came in 1900, built the massive stone Grove Park Inn, decapitated Battery Park Hill to build a tourist hotel, and dumped the dirt into a ravine to create business property on what became Coxe Avenue. The population rose from only 2,600 in 1880 to 15,000 at the turn of the century. By 1925, Asheville was a major tourist center whose population was approaching 50,000. Taking its cues from burgeoning Miami, the Chamber of Commerce was sending "goodwill ambassadors" across the country to promote the "Land of the Sky." Real-estate speculation, overexpansion, and boosterism ruled the day. Four years later the wave broke amidst a Depression-era scandal that left city and county bonds on the ineligible list of the New York Stock Exchange for thirty years.

In 1925, however, the civic mood was buoyant, and Asheville's Rhododendron Festival presented a colorful extravaganza to tourists. In 1928, the Chamber of Commerce asked Lunsford to stage a presentation of traditional music in connection with the festival. Lunsford's event drew five thousand people to Asheville's central square; hundreds of spectators had to lean from the windows of nearby buildings to see and hear. By any measure, it was a spectacular success. The festival did not survive Asheville's fiscal crisis the following year, but Lunsford's Mountain Dance and Folk Festival became an annual event.

Lunsford's festival was a hybrid product of his experience as a hill-born lad, musician and dancer, public lecturer and performer, spectator and promoter of musical contests, newspaper writer and editor, and lawyer and college-educated sophisticate. Though it had substantial roots in the music and dance frolics associated with quiltings and bean stringings in the mountains for generations, in the long run it inevitably became the product of Lunsford's own consciousness, desires, and views of culture in the mountains of western North Carolina. He knew and loved the culture in which he had been raised, but he also viewed it within the wider intellectual frames of reference formed during his adulthood. Lunsford insisted that there was a connection between the cultural riches of the region and what he always called "the fine honor of our people." When he went into their homes, he treated mountain people as ladies and gentlemen. He refused to "talk country" in his public appearances (though he was frequently implored to do so by slick media promoters), and he prohibited on his stage the hillbilly garb routinely urged upon mountain musicians by commercial recording companies and radio advertisers.

It was this double insider-outsider perspective that gave Lunsford's work much of its particular form and quality. He placed himself actively at the center of the complex public conflict over the nature and meaning of traditional culture in the southern mountains. Such a role called upon him to walk a fine line, however, between projecting a dignified image of a self-respecting mountain man and merely self-interested self-promotion. Those both inside and outside the region who commented on his work sometimes had difficulty deciding which agenda was dominant. Nevertheless, over the course of his public life, Lunsford developed a remarkable functional understanding of what he himself could usefully contribute to the public debate over cultural styles and values. Making that contribution was, as he always called it, his main "work as a citizen."

Whatever Lunsford's view of culture in the mountains, or his role in developing and perpetuating the Mountain Dance and Folk Festival, there is no doubt that he presented year after year a stellar group of performers: banjoist and singer Aunt Samantha Bumgarner, scores of impressive square dance groups (preeminently the Soco Gap group led by "Dancin' Man" Sam Queen), the Madison County fiddle-banjo duo of Byard Ray and Obray Ramsey, ballad singer Cas Wallin, and countless others. They came from innumerable towns, small communities, and crossroads in western North Carolina (and a few from beyond): Leicester and Sandy Mush, Candler and Canton, Bear Wallow and South Turkey Creek, Old Fort and Marion, Marshall and Mars Hill, and Murphy and Bryson City. Lunsford chose them all according to his personal aesthetic, which he never articulated systematically. "In a festival you get as much good in as you can," he said vaguely, "and keep as much bad out as you can. We keep it as genuine as we can."

Critics of the festival pointed out that Lunsford excluded black performers, but their criticism was unavailing, even though for years he had collected songs from blacks. There were many black musicians in the mountains, and some of them lived within walking distance of Asheville's city auditorium where the festival took place, but none appeared upon the stage during Lunsford's lifetime. Religious music was not prominently represented, nor was there room for any even slightly bawdy or off-color songs, though the latter were well-documented and frequently encountered in mountain music. Lunsford also systematically excluded those mostly younger performers who linked their music to social issues that were salient during the 1960s and 1970s: racial equality, women's rights, environmentalism, and the Vietnam War.

Although Lunsford was known to most of the public primarily for founding and directing the Asheville festival, he also presented traditional music in a number of other venues. For several years in the early 1930s, he took performers to the National Folk Festival, directed by Sarah Gertrude Knott, who freely acknowledged Bascom's festival as her major inspiration. In 1935 he worked with the federal Rural Resettlement Administration community at Scottsboro, Ala., finding and presenting local musicians. Four years later he took a group of western North Carolina musicians and dancers to perform in the White House before England's King George VI and Queen Elizabeth. In 1946 he founded the Red Bud Festival, in connection with John Lair's Renfro Valley Gathering in Kentucky. During the late 1940s he established festivals at both the University of North Carolina and the North Carolina State Fair, and made less successful attempts to start others in several piedmont North and South Carolina cities.

From early in his career, Lunsford developed the ability to move easily from public festivals to the world of folklore scholars interested in documenting cultural traditions, and into the business of commercial recording. As early as 1922, folklorist Frank C. Brown recorded some of Lunsford's personal repertoire of ballads and songs, and fiddle and banjo tunes, and Robert W. Gordon recorded him again in 1925. In 1935 he contributed more than three hundred items from his personal repertoire to an archive at Columbia University, and he repeated approximately the same repertoire for the Archive of Folk Song at the Library of Congress in 1949. His commercial recording sessions began with Okeh in 1924–25 and continued with Brunswick in 1928 and Columbia in 1930. Folkways issued an album in 1952, and Riverside followed with another in 1956. Several years after Lunsford's death, Rounder issued *Music from South Turkey Creek: Bascom Lamar Lunsford, George Pegram, and Red Parham.*

Lunsford did not present to the public all that could have been presented; he did not say all that could have been said. The keeper of bees and of culture strained both honey and culture before offering them to the public. It is nonetheless to his great credit that in a period in which profit-oriented shysters and hucksters from Nashville to New York and Hollywood were buying and selling the mountains and their culture in every conceivable form—from gift shop knickknacks and phonograph records to movies and television shows, from ski slopes to gated second-home communities, Lunsford kept his integrity, his eye and ear for the authentic, his respect for both performer and audience, his sense of stewardship, and his precocious intuition that some of one's "work as a citizen" could—and indeed must—be carried on in the cultural arena. The passing of the years makes that seem an ever more impressive accomplishment.

David Whisnant, a native of western North Carolina, is the author of many books and articles on the Appalachian region, vernacular culture, and the politics of culture. He is retired from the faculty of the University of North Carolina and lives in Chapel Hill with his wife, Anne, and two sons, Evan and Derek.

For more information, see:
Lunsford, Bascom Lamar. Papers. Library, Mars Hill College, Mars Hill.

Becker, Jane S. *Selling Tradition: Appalachia and the Construction of an American Folk, 1930–1940.* University of North Carolina Press, 1998.
Jones, Loyal. *Minstrel of the Appalachians: The Story of Bascom Lamar Lunsford.* Appalachian Consortium Press, 1984.
Lunsford, Bascom Lamar. *Ballads, Banjo Tunes, and Sacred Songs of Western North Carolina.* Smithsonian Folkways, 1996.
Whisnant, David E. *All That Is Native and Fine: The Politics of Culture in an American Region.* University of North Carolina Press, 1983.
———. "Finding the Way Between the Old and the New: The Mountain Dance and Folk Festival and Bascom Lamar Lunsford's Work as a Citizen." *Appalachian Journal* 7 (Autumn–Winter 1979): 135–54.

LOONIS McGLOHON

By Jerry Shinn

Loonis McGlohon. The name rolls off the tongue as mellifluously as an old Scottish ballad. If he were not so unpretentious, people might suspect that he made it up. Stage names are, after all, a show business tradition. But McGlohon would never try to be someone other than himself, in name or otherwise. His parents were named McGlohon—his father was a mechanic who owned a garage, and his mother was a teacher and housewife—and Loonis was the name they gave him when he was born, in Ayden, in Pitt County, on September 29, 1921.

McGlohon was best known as a pianist and songwriter, but he was many other things as well. He surely could have had a successful career in New York or Los Angeles or one of the other culture capitals of the world. When he visited them to play piano with his jazz trio, or to accompany one of the many fine singers who would rather have had his accompaniment than anyone else's, he was always well received. But he and his wife, Nan, chose to live in Charlotte, because it was a good place to live and raise their three children, and it was home—meaning North Carolina.

Over the years WBT, the South's first radio station, and its affiliated station, WBTV, provided a home base and steady employment. McGlohon served as the radio station's music director as well as an on-air pianist for many years. As director of special projects at the television station, he directed its involvement in countless worthwhile community activities, including the establishment of the state's first Big Brother-Big Sister program. He created original television programs; some of them were musical or cultural and others focused on current events and contemporary issues. He also collaborated on two highly acclaimed series on great songs and great singers for National Public Radio. He won two prestigious Peabody awards, one in radio and one in television, and was inducted into the North Carolina Broadcasters Hall of Fame and the National Academy of Broadcasters Hall of Fame.

Meanwhile, he found time to jet around the nation and the world playing concerts in New York City, London, Rome, and the Far East, and recording albums with some of the finest singers of classic American popular music and jazz. With all that he was never too busy, or too impressed with himself, to perform

Loonis McGlohon (Courtesy of Loonis McGlohon)

at Charlotte wedding receptions, friends' parties, or local benefits. Wherever he went, he wanted to be back in town by Sunday if at all possible, because he also directed the choir at Carmel Presbyterian Church.

All that would have been more than sufficient for a distinguished career displaying an extraordinary array of talents. But he also wrote songs, hundreds of them, including some of the best songs anyone ever wrote, some both words and music, others in collaboration with other songwriters. Some of the better known in his oeuvre included "Songbird," "Blackberry Winter," "Nobody Home," "South to a Warmer Place," "The Wine of May," "Dinner on the Grounds," "Willow Creek," and "Grow Tall My Son."

McGlohon's songs were recorded by Frank Sinatra, Rosemary Clooney, Mabel Mercer, Eileen Farrell, Marlena Shaw, Marlene VerPlanck, Mike Campbell, Teddi King, Cleo Laine, Meredith D'Ambrosio, Anita Ellis, Julius LaRosa, Johnny Hartman, David Allyn, Barbara Lea, Mark Murphy, Dick Haymes, Daryle Rice, George Shearing, Keith Jarrett, Marian McPartland, and many others. Some of those names were famous, others were well known to the cognoscenti of that special genre of American popular music that preceded rock and roll. It was a genre that endured because of the genius and taste of its creators, its musical integrity and quality, and because the emotions it engenders are universal and its themes are timeless.

McGlohon also wrote songs for his children and friends, hymns and church music, and the theme music for a number of occasions and programs, including CBS television's *On the Road* segments with his friend Charles Kuralt.

To begin to understand Loonis McGlohon, it helps to know about some of the significant influences in his life and career—places, traditions, faith, and people. Most of all, people.

First is the place where he was born and reared—eastern North Carolina, where the pace of life was geared to the seasons and the weather, where what grew or failed to grow was important, where neighbors were loyal to one another, where churches weren't just for worship, but also were centers of social life. The area was far removed, in culture, ambience, and attitudes, from the entertainment capitals, the songwriting salons of Broadway and Hollywood and Tin Pan Alley in New York, and the urban venues where jazz flourished. But by the early twentieth century, radio and recordings and motion pictures were bringing the melodies and rhythms to every corner of the nation.

From those sources, young Loonis listened and learned. For the rest of his life, he would remember the first time he heard the Jimmy Lunceford band on the radio when he was about thirteen years old, and the jazz and swing music available on the 78-rpm recordings sold at "five and dime" stores on every small town main street. The music seemed to harmonize with his feelings, to speak of his youthful yearnings, as if its syncopated pulse were synchronized with the beating of his own heart. It wouldn't be enough just to listen to that music; he wanted to play it, to create it, to inhabit it.

He learned to play the piano by ear, and by the time he was a student at East Carolina Teachers College (later East Carolina University) and learned to read music, he already could play well enough to earn a spot in campus jazz and dance bands, and even, in summer, with touring bands. At East Carolina he met Nan Flournoy Lovelace, a fellow eastern North Carolinian whose charm, beauty, and personality made all the sweet sentiments in his favorite love songs suddenly seem very real and personal. And along with the charm were an abundance of common sense and competence, the kind of ballast a young musician needed in his life.

McGlohon spent much of World War II stationed in Florida as part of an air force dance band. After his discharge, he and Nan, by then his wife, visited Charlotte. He was planning to go to New York and then on the road with one of the popular big bands of the day, but Charlotte was a better fit for the kind of life he and Nan wanted. There he took a "day job," first in the local office of the Southern Railway, then with WBT and WBTV, and found a spot in a local band for after hours and weekend gigs.

One of McGlohon's local television productions led to his association with another of the major influences in his life. In the mid-1960s, he produced a show featuring local young people singing music by one of his favorite composers, Alec Wilder. A notoriously eccentric composer of both serious and popular music such as "I'll Be Around," "It's So Peaceful in the Country," and "While We're Young," Wilder also was something of a scholar in the field of American popular songs. He was revered by a small but influential body of singers, musicians, and critics. McGlohon had never met him, but he invited him to come to Charlotte to see and hear the show. Much to his surprise, Wilder accepted. And he agreed to stay at the McGlohon home, an open-ended invitation which he continued to accept in the future.

Wilder obviously recognized in McGlohon a fellow member of what Wilder called the "derriere-garde"—musicians and songwriters more interested in refining and contributing to the rich tradition of jazz and classic American popular songs, in relative obscurity, if necessary, than in chasing fame and fortune by trying to keep up with the latest musical fads. And in Wilder, McGlohon surely found an affirmation of the importance of what he himself had always been: a man with certain aesthetic and personal standards he refused to compromise at any price.

Otherwise, they were an unlikely pair: the gracious, gentle, good-humored southerner raising a family in a Charlotte suburb, and the acerbic, irascible New York bachelor who frequented the legendary Algonquin Hotel. But they immediately forged a deep friendship, and from then until Wilder's death in 1980 they collaborated on dozens of songs, including

"Blackberry Winter" and "South to a Warmer Place." And together they created the National Public Radio series, *American Popular Song,* a series of forty programs that featured Wilder's commentary, McGlohon's piano, and a parade of outstanding singers. Later, McGlohon and Eileen Farrell cohosted another National Public Radio series called *American Singers.*

If Wilder's influence stretched McGlohon's horizons, the influence of another close friend, Charles Kuralt, sent him back to his North Carolina roots for inspiration. McGlohon had known Kuralt since the 1950s when Kuralt, who was a high school student interested in jazz, came to see McGlohon rehearse one of his weekly television programs. Their friendship grew when Kuralt joined the WBT news department after graduating from the University of North Carolina at Chapel Hill and working as a reporter and columnist for the *Charlotte News.*

In 1983, Governor James B. Hunt Jr. asked each of them to create something for the state's four hundredth birthday, the anniversary of the first settlement on Roanoke Island. Kuralt called McGlohon to tell him of the governor's request and learned that McGlohon had received a similar one. They came up with the idea of a recording, music by McGlohon and words by Kuralt, who didn't sing but whose distinctive voice was one of the glories of broadcasting.

They wrote "North Carolina Is My Home," a title song and a program of songs and stories about the state, some joyful, some hilarious, some simply beautiful. It began as recorded words and music only, then was staged live at venues across the state with outstanding singers, choirs, and orchestras, then it was recorded on video, telecast on the state public television network a number of times, and published in a book illustrated with color photographs of some of North Carolina's finest scenery. It was a magnificent and enduring gift to the state from two of its most celebrated, loving, and beloved sons.

Another significant friend was Eileen Farrell, the opera diva. When she began performing popular music, McGlohon became her favorite accompanist. Together they appeared in several concerts and created a series of recordings that amount to a definitive collection of the greatest American songs by the greatest American songwriters.

When the First Baptist Church in downtown Charlotte was converted into an arts center and theater named Spirit Square, the old 720-seat sanctuary, with its fine acoustics, intimate ambience, and stained-glass windows, soon became one of McGlohon's favorite venues. With his help, Spirit Square began to draw some of the nation's top jazz musicians and singers to its stage, and McGlohon accompanied many of them in memorable performances there. It was originally called Performance Place, and later NCNB Performance Place, in recognition of a major grant from what became Bank of America. Eventually, it was renamed the McGlohon Theater, in honor of the man whose music and musical friends had made it such a special place over the years.

After he retired from the broadcasting business, McGlohon maintained a busy schedule of performances and recordings. He made dozens of records, some solo, some with his trio, but mostly with singers, including Julius LaRosa, Margaret Whiting, Dick Haymes, Marlene VerPlanck, Irene Kral, Mary Mayo, and many others. In 1998, New York City's Lincoln Center honored McGlohon with a concert of his compositions, performed by some of the nation's finest musicians and singers, and with an appearance by McGlohon himself.

It is difficult to say exactly what label best fit McGlohon. He surely would have said that husband, father, and friend are the roles that mattered most to him, and those who knew him would agree. He also was a great storyteller with a rich repertoire of funny and fascinating tales accumulated over a long life lived among interesting people. His friendship and generous encouragement were vital sources of support for countless musicians and singers. He was an effective champion of good causes. His work as a broadcaster was distinguished by creativity, taste, integrity, and conscience. And he was, of course, a very fine songwriter.

To call him a jazz pianist is to call him somewhat less than what he was. Certainly he was a pianist who could play jazz, but he had too little ego and too much respect for good songs to engage in the overly extended improvisations of some of the most acclaimed jazz soloists. He cared about the words as much as he cared about the music, and his playing often had more to do with honoring a good song than with a display of his virtuosity. That love of good songs and lyrics probably explains why knowledgeable critics considered him one of the two or three best accompanists of singers in the world.

Perhaps the best way to sum him up is to say simply that he was one of North Carolina's great natural resources. In one of McGlohon's songs, the lyrics say that the grass may be greener somewhere else, and there are bright lights not too far down the road, but the writer, or the singer, plans to stay put. The song is called "I Like It Here." Obviously, that's how widely traveled Loonis McGlohon always felt about North Carolina.

McGlohon died on January 26, 2002, after a nine-year battle with cancer.

Jerry Shinn is a Charlotte writer who graduated with honors and Phi Beta Kappa from the University of North Carolina at Chapel Hill in 1959. He has worked in advertising, public relations, and broadcasting, but most of his career has been spent at the Charlotte Observer, *where he began as a sports writer and later was a political reporter, editorial page editor, columnist, and associate editor, retiring in 1998.*

For more information, see:

McGlohon, Loonis. Interview with Jerry Shinn, n.d. Levine Museum of the New South, Charlotte.

Johnson, Charles. "He Writes for Old Blue Eyes." *Charlotte Observer,* January 8, 1982.
Smith, Dean. "It's a Busy Job Being Retired Musician." *Charlotte Observer,* January 11, 1991.
Stone, Desmond. *Alec Wilder in Spite of Himself.* Oxford University Press, 1996.

CHARLIE POOLE

By Patrick Huber

Charlie Poole with the N.C. Ramblers (Courtesy of Southern Folklife Collection)

C HARLIE POOLE," proclaimed a 1927 Columbia Phonograph Company catalog, "is unquestionably the best known banjo picker and singer in the Carolinas. A dance in North Carolina, Virginia, or Kentucky isn't a dance unless Charlie and the North Carolina Ramblers supply the pep. People everywhere dance all night long when these favorites supply the music."

Between 1925 and 1930, Poole and the North Carolina Ramblers recorded a total of more than eighty sides for Columbia, Paramount, and Brunswick, including such classics as "Don't Let Your Deal Go Down Blues," "White House Blues," and "If the River Was Whiskey." Their bluesy fiddle breakdowns and sentimental ballads, performed in a highly disciplined ragtime style, made them one of the most popular hillbilly string bands of the last half of the 1920s.

But even after they became one of Columbia's best-selling hillbilly-recording acts, Poole and the North Carolina Ramblers regularly spent weeks playing for house parties and country dances throughout southwestern Virginia and southern West Virginia. "The people always hated to see us leave," recalled fiddler Lonnie Austin, who often accompanied Poole on these musical excursions, "because they knew we took the music with us."

Charles Cleveland Poole was born into a white working-class family, one of thirteen children, on March 22, 1892, in Randolph County, probably in the textile village of Millboro. Both of his parents, John

443

Phillip Poole and Bettie Ellen (Johnson) Poole, worked in the local textile mills. Shortly after 1900, the family moved to Haw River, a few miles east of Greensboro, and there, at the age of twelve, Charlie began working as a doffer in the Granite Cotton Mill to help support his large family.

Little is known about Poole's early life, but he apparently became seriously interested in music while still a young boy. Both his father, who was the son of an Irish immigrant, and one of his older brothers played the five-string banjo, and they probably kindled Poole's desire to learn the instrument. By the age of nine, Poole was playing a miniature homemade banjo he had fashioned out of a dried gourd.

A few years later, with $1.50 of his hard-earned wages, he bought a factory-made banjo and set himself to mastering the instrument. By his mid-teens, Poole had gained a local reputation for being both a fine banjo picker and a neighborhood rowdy. He and his younger brother Henry sometimes drank heavily and got into fistfights in nearby Gibsonville, and on several occasions Poole was arrested for public drunkenness and disturbing the peace.

Poole married a seventeen-year-old textile worker named Maude Gibson on February 25, 1912, and tried to settle into the role of a responsible husband. But he soon began skipping work to pick his banjo on the streets of Haw River. He also began rambling on the open road for weeks on end, and on one occasion, he hopped freight as far west as Missoula, Montana. Poole was hoboing in Canada when his only child, James Clay Poole, was born on December 2, 1912. Soon afterward his wife divorced him.

Poole spent the next six years working sporadically in mills around Greensboro and rambling around Virginia, West Virginia, Maryland, and Pennsylvania, carousing and drinking. Here and there, he earned extra cash by picking his banjo and passing the hat among the street crowds who gathered to hear him play.

In 1918, during his wanderings, Poole met a crippled fiddler named Posey Rorer, who was then working in the coal mines at Sophia, W.Va., five miles southwest of Beckley. Poole and Rorer became close friends and soon were teaming together to entertain as a banjo-fiddle duet, first in the coal towns surrounding Beckley and then in the farming communities around Franklin County, Virginia, where Rorer had been born and raised.

In 1919, Poole moved to the textile town of Spray (later known as Eden), some ten miles south of the Virginia border, and found work as a speeder hand in the Leaksville Cotton Mill. Soon Rorer joined his for-

mer musical partner in Spray. Around this time, Poole began courting his friend's older sister, Lou Emma Rorer, who had been living in Spray for almost a decade. The couple was married in nearby Reidsville on December 11, 1920.

Earlier that year, Poole had formed the North Carolina Ramblers with Rorer and guitarist Will Woodlieff, another Spray mill hand, and soon the band attracted a large following in the surrounding textile towns and farming communities. On Saturday nights, the trio performed at local house parties, country dances, corn huskings, and other social gatherings. When Woodlieff dropped out of the band around 1922, his younger brother Norman Woodlieff, who also worked in the textile mills, replaced him as the regular guitarist in the North Carolina Ramblers. By 1924, the band was entertaining with their music at schoolhouses, theaters, and roadhouses throughout southwestern Virginia and southern West Virginia, and sometimes as far away as Kentucky, Tennessee, and Ohio.

By 1925, despite his alcoholism, Charlie Poole and the North Carolina Ramblers had established a considerable musical reputation for themselves in the north-central piedmont and southern Appalachia. Awakened now to the possibility of turning music into a full-time career, Poole struck upon the idea of making a few recordings of what was then called "hillbilly music." On July 27, 1925, Poole, Rorer, and Woodlieff auditioned in New York City for Frank Walker, who produced Columbia's hillbilly music series. Their music so impressed Walker that later that afternoon the band recorded their first four sides. The North Carolina Ramblers' debut release, "Don't Let Your Deal Go Down Blues"/"Can I Sleep in Your Barn Tonight Mister," was issued in September and sold an astonishing 102,000 copies at a time when hillbilly record sales of 20,000 constituted a certifiable hit. Their second release, issued a few weeks later, sold more than 65,000 copies. Altogether, Columbia made an estimated $40,000 on the North Carolina Ramblers' first two records, though the trio split a onetime payment of only $75.

With the spectacular sales of the band's first two releases, Walker wired Poole, inviting the North Carolina Ramblers to record some additional songs, but apparently Poole ignored him. Perhaps he felt that, in light of the tremendous record sales, Walker had swindled him and his band mates. In any case, it was not until September 1926 that Walker finally managed to entice Poole and the North Carolina Ramblers back into Columbia's studio by agreeing to pay them $150 per side plus royalties.

By then, Woodlieff, who suffered from tuberculosis, had left the band, and Poole had replaced him with Roy Harvey, a Beckley, W.Va., musician who would remain the band's regular guitarist for the next four years. Fourteen months after their debut session, Poole and Rorer, accompanied by Harvey, returned to New York City, where, over the course of five days, they recorded sixteen sides ranging from traditional fiddle tunes and blues ballads to vaudeville numbers and Tin Pan Alley hits. While there, Poole also signed a contract to record exclusively for Columbia, for which, he later claimed, he received several thousand dollars. With the increased earnings from his recordings, coupled with the ticket receipts from his musical tours, Poole finally achieved the financial freedom to abandon the textile work he so despised and earn his living as a professional musician.

Over the next four years, Poole and the North Carolina Ramblers maintained a heavy schedule of recording sessions, radio broadcasts, and stage shows that kept them away from home for weeks and sometimes months at a time. During this period the band underwent several personnel changes, most notably the departure of Posey Rorer. In 1928, after an argument with Poole over royalties, Rorer left the North Carolina Ramblers and embarked on a separate musical career with other piedmont string bands.

Tensions had arisen long before this incident. At least since 1926, Poole and Rorer had often disagreed about the band's evolving style of music. Poole increasingly favored a more polished uptown approach, while Rorer, who fiddled in a traditional short-bow style, steadfastly adhered to a more conventional string band sound. Poole recruited a gifted twenty-three-year-old fiddler from Spray named Lonnie Austin to replace his estranged brother-in-law at the band's recording sessions in July 1928 and May 1929. With the addition of Austin and later Odell Smith, both of whose ragtime fiddling featured smooth, long-bow strokes and fancy embellishments, the North Carolina Ramblers produced a more sophisticated, bluesy sound modeled in part on the contemporary popular music of the Jazz Age. Although both Poole and Rorer pursued independent recording careers after 1928, neither one of them ever approached the level of commercial success they had enjoyed during their musical partnership.

On their recordings, especially their later ones, Charlie Poole and the North Carolina Ramblers brought an unparalleled degree of elegance and sophistication to hillbilly music. Although he usually sang lead in a garbled, nasal baritone, Poole modeled his singing in part on Al Jolson's and Rudy Vallee's, sometimes even imitating their vocal phrasings and nuances. Poole's approach to the banjo, in turn, represented a dramatic departure from the more traditional claw hammer and double-thumbing styles of most other hillbilly banjoists. He picked the banjo with three, and sometimes four, fingers in a highly percussive, syncopated style that he adapted from newer classical banjo techniques popularized by Fred Van Eps and Vess L. Ossman. Especially on his experimental solos with piano, Poole elevated the banjo to a featured instrument in the North Carolina Ramblers, and as a consummate innovator, he pushed the instrument in exciting directions then unheard of in hillbilly music. Occasionally, he performed spectacular breakneck runs and instrumental solos on his recordings, both of which anticipated the development of modern bluegrass.

An avid fan of contemporary popular music, Poole also experimented with five-piece bands and recorded a series of classical banjo instrumentals with piano accompaniment inspired by Van Eps, Poole's idol and perhaps his single greatest musical influence. But his producer, Frank Walker, ever mindful of record sales, insisted that Poole and the North Carolina Ramblers imitate their previous successes rather than experiment with larger ensembles. Despite his frustrated attempts to break into the more lucrative popular music field, Poole and the North Carolina Ramblers remained immensely popular among hillbilly record buyers.

Clearly, much of Poole's success as a hillbilly musician can be attributed to his instrumental virtuosity, his selection of excellent sidemen, and his creative arrangements of popular songs, many of which he learned from Roy Harvey, who also clerked in a Beckley music store. On their recordings, the North Carolina Ramblers interpreted a wide range of American popular music, combining the fiddle tunes, minstrel songs, and ragtime numbers of Poole's youth with the more contemporary sounds of blues, vaudeville, and Tin Pan Alley.

Approximately half of the North Carolina Ramblers' recorded output consisted of popular songs of the 1890s and 1900s, especially maudlin ballads like "Goodbye Mary Dear" and "The Girl I Left in Sunny Tennessee," which were deeply informed by tragedy, loss, and separation from loved ones. But they also borrowed heavily from African American musical traditions. Several of the band's best-known numbers, among them "Don't Let Your Deal Go Down Blues," "If the River Was Whiskey," and "Ramblin' Blues," celebrated the rough masculine pleasures enjoyed by tramps and rounders who, like Poole himself, drank hard and refused to settle down to married life and steady work. Together, Poole and the North Carolina Ramblers crafted a signature sound of cleanly articulated, tightly knit dance music, which differed markedly from the loose, riotous sounds of Gid Tanner and the Skillet Lickers, the only other hillbilly string band to rival them in popularity during their heyday.

The Depression hit the hillbilly recording industry with a punishing force, but the North Carolina Ramblers, now accompanied by fiddler Odell Smith, continued to record for Columbia as late as September 1930. Although the band remained as popular as ever, the releases from their last sessions sold poorly, as hard times and unemployment prevented their largely rural and working-class fans from purchasing them. Shortly after the September session, Columbia canceled Poole's recording contract, sending him into a deep personal depression that he exacerbated by heavy drinking.

Within a couple months, however, Poole launched a comeback to try to save his floundering musical career. In the winter of 1930–31, he embarked on an extended theater-circuit tour across West Virginia and Ohio with a six-piece orchestra. But the tour flopped, and Poole reluctantly returned to shift work in a Spray textile mill.

Good news lifted his sagging spirits in the spring of 1931, when a Hollywood motion picture company hired him to bring his band to California to perform in a low-budget western. Poole celebrated his reversal of fortune by assembling a crew of his old drinking buddies and embarking on a marathon thirteen-week bender. On May 21, 1931, less than two weeks before he was to leave for California, Poole suffered a fatal heart attack at his sister's home in Spray. He was only thirty-nine years old. Sadly, like Hank Williams after him, Poole died at the height of his artistic powers, a victim, again like Williams, of his own hard traveling and self-destructive alcoholism.

After his untimely death, Poole and the North Carolina Ramblers' music were not forgotten. Their records inspired succeeding generations of American musicians, particularly bluegrass pioneers and folk revival artists, and dozens of musicians, including Bill Monroe and His Bluegrass Boys, Lester Flatt and Earl Scruggs, Doc Watson, and the New Lost City Ramblers, have covered at least one of the North Carolina Ramblers' songs.

But perhaps Poole's most enduring contribution to American popular music remains his distinctive three-finger banjo style, which profoundly influenced the instrumental styles of such legendary banjoists as DeWitt "Snuffy" Jenkins, Wade Mainer, and Earl Scruggs. Despite his far-reaching musical influence, Poole has yet to be inducted into Nashville's Country Music Hall of Fame. Nevertheless, he ranked as one of the most important figures in the history of early country music. Almost seventy years after his death, echoes of his innovative banjo picking could still be heard on modern bluegrass and country albums, enduring testimony to his musical innovations and artistic genius.

Patrick Huber received his Ph.D. from the University of North Carolina at Chapel Hill and is currently an assistant professor of history at the University of Missouri-Rolla where he is working on a book entitled Hillbilly Music: The Modern Origins of an Old-Time Southern Sound.

For more information, see:
Poole, Charlie, Jr. Interview by Eugene W. Earle and Archie Green. Southern Folklife Collection, University of North Carolina at Chapel Hill.

Poole, Charlie. *A Young Boy Left Home One Day.* Historical Records HLP 8005, 1975.
Poole, Charlie, and the North Carolina Ramblers. *Charlie Poole and the North Carolina Ramblers.* County Records 505, 1964.
———. *Charlie Poole and the North Carolina Ramblers,* vol. 2. County Records 509, 1966.
———. *Charlie Poole and the North Carolina Ramblers,* vol. 4. County Records 540, 1975.
———. *The Legend of Charlie Poole.* County Records 516, 1968.
———. *The North Carolina Ramblers, 1928–1930.* Biograph Records BLP 6005, 1972.
Rorrer, Clifford Kinney. *Charlie Poole and the North Carolina Ramblers.* Privately published, 1968.
———. *Rambling Blues: The Life and Songs of Charlie Poole.* McCain Printing, 1992.

ARTHUR SMITH

By Ralph Grizzle

THROUGHOUT THE 1940S, Charlotte area radio listeners frequently dialed in to WBT radio for the fifteen-minute morning broadcast of "Arthur Smith and the Crackerjacks." The Crackerjacks—the backup singers and players comprised of Arthur's brothers Ralph and Sonny, and a local boy, Roy Lear—derived their name by flipping through the dictionary. When they arrived at the word "crackerjack," which *Webster's Unabridged* defined as "a thing of highest excellence," they not only settled on a name but also a guiding principle that made theirs one of the most popular broadcasts in the history of North Carolina radio.

Cleanliness and Christianity were hallmarks of these and other broadcasts that Arthur Smith would be a part of for the next five decades. "We were the guys next door," Smith told the *Charlotte Observer* in 1995. "I reviewed the Sunday school lesson. We closed with a hymn. There was no vulgarity, no smut."

What made those early radio broadcasts particularly endearing was Arthur's guitar playing. He mesmerized listeners who had never heard anyone play quite so quickly. "My style of playing has always been fast and single-string," Smith says. "I never did the Chet Atkins style of playing. For country music, this was something new."

But it wasn't something new for Smith. Then in his twenties, he had been racing his fingers over the frets and strings since picking up his first guitar at age eight. Even before that, beginning at age six, he had played trumpet for Sunday afternoon concerts in a band sponsored by the Kershaw, S.C., textile mill where his father worked. "There were two things that textile companies did back in those days," Smith said. "They sponsored a semi-pro baseball team [for which Smith played] and a band. My dad taught people to play brass instruments for the band, but I liked string instruments, so I transferred what I could to the guitar." By doing so, Smith laid the foundation for a long career in the entertainment business.

Following in his father's footsteps, Smith went to work at the Spring Mills textile plant at age fourteen. On Saturdays, after the long workweek, he traveled (often driving, even though he was too young to have a driver's license) with his brothers to South Carolina radio stations in Florence, Columbia, and Charleston to perform. Executives at RCA Victor heard one of

Arthur Smith (Courtesy of Hugh Morton)

those broadcasts and sent word to the Smiths to ask if a field rep for the company might come out and record them. A year later, at age fifteen, Smith signed as a recording artist for RCA Victor.

Smith, who was gaining some notoriety as a musician, was also establishing himself as a radio personality. When he was twenty, he hosted shows on WSPA in Spartanburg. A couple of years later, WBT's station manager, Charles Crutchfield, called to ask Smith to come to work for the then-CBS affiliate. Smith packed his bags and moved to Charlotte, which he made his home. At WBT, Smith provided guitar and fiddle music for WBT's shows until 1943, when he was joined by his brothers Sonny and Ralph for the debut of his own show.

Carolina listeners quickly warmed to the voice and tunes of Arthur Smith. Then in 1948, his music spread beyond the borders of the Carolinas when Smith gained national notoriety for a song that he wrote and recorded called "Guitar Boogie." The fast-paced playing was something new for listeners. The recording challenged the music industry, because no one was quite sure what chart to put it in. This "Guitar Boogie" became the first instrumental to reach the top of the country charts and then cross over to reach the top of the pop charts. Smith's composition has sold more than four million copies. Impressive. But his biggest hit would come twenty-five years later.

With his career moving as fast as his fingers, Smith signed on with MGM—he and Bob Wills were the first country music artists to record for the entertainment giant. Then something extraordinary happened. In 1949, WBTV signed on to become the first television station in the Carolinas. Two years later, thirty-year-old Smith would stand in front of one of the station's new cameras each Thursday night to broadcast *The Arthur Smith Show*. It was WBTV's first live show to be syndicated nationally.

The show ran for thirty-two consecutive years, and it seemed that everyone in the Charlotte area was tuned in. In a 1995 interview with the *Charlotte Observer*, Smith said: "I have people ninety years old saying, 'Man, I've been watching you all my life.'" But the residents of Charlotte weren't the only ones listening. One of the show's biggest fans was golf great Arnold Palmer, who always tuned in to watch what he called his "favorite show." On Palmer's fiftieth birthday, Smith showed up on Palmer's doorstep in Latrobe, Pa. Winnie Palmer had arranged for the entertainer to perform for her husband and friends.

The list of guest appearances on *The Arthur Smith Show* reads like a Who's Who List of Entertainers. There were musical artists, including Loretta Lynn and Johnny Cash; celebrities such as Andy Griffith, who had applied for a job at WBT in 1941 but was turned down because he demanded $75 a week; and even politicians. Viewers never would have guessed that Richard Nixon, who appeared on the show in 1954, would later become the nation's president. The future leader of the United States tickled the ivories to play "Home on the Range." Smith recalled that performance as being "pretty good."

During the 1950s and 1960s, *The Arthur Smith Show* received about one thousand pieces of fan mail each week addressed to the fictitious TV station from which the show aired, WEE-TV in Happy Valley. Smith's show reportedly received more mail than WBT itself, and in 1962, *The Arthur Smith Show* boasted better ratings among Charlotte viewers than any other broadcast except for *Perry Mason*.

It was apparent that Smith's down-home style appealed to viewers. But one of the most unusual accounts of Smith's audience appeal came when he stood beside his friend Hugh Morton in the 1950s to wrestle the state and federal government. Morton, owner of Grandfather Mountain, discovered that the government was planning to condemn his property to acquire a new Blue Ridge Parkway right-of-way. The right-of-way would allow the government to cut a highway into and across Grandfather's rocky slopes. Morton claimed that such an act would be equal to "taking a switchblade to the Mona Lisa." Morton put up his fists.

He took his case to the State Highway Commission. The capital's WRAL-TV invited Morton to its studio to debate North Carolina's chief highway engineer. The station encouraged Morton to bring along an "expert." The commissioner brought a U.S. Army Corps of Engineers expert, who walked in with a cache of maps, charts, and graphs to show the audience. Morton brought Arthur Smith.

After the opposing side made their points and Morton had made his, Smith spoke up, directing his comments to the television audience. He told viewers that he was not a government expert and that he did not have charts or maps to prove his case but that he believed a man had a right to do what he wanted to do with his own property. Smith went on to say that in his opinion Morton was taking good care of Grandfather Mountain and that he did not see what right a bunch of Washington bureaucrats had to take it away from him. The switchboard lit up with calls from viewers who phoned in to express their support for Morton.

The debate arguably could have inspired Smith to write what would become his biggest hit, "Feuding Banjos." Smith, who had learned a thing or two about debating during the Morton episode, had to fight for something that the court later decided was rightfully his. Though he wrote the piece and recorded "Feuding Banjos" in 1955, it wasn't until 1973 that it became one of the all-time best-sellers. That year, Warner Brothers renamed and claimed the tune as a traditional adaptation for use as the theme in the motion picture *Deliverance*.

Wayne Haas, a friend of Smith's at a radio station, called to tell Smith: "I'm listening to Feuding Banjos, but they don't call it that, and it ain't got your name on it." Smith sued Warner Brothers and won a landmark copyright infringement case in federal court. "Dueling Banjos" became Broadcast Music Inc.'s (BMI) Song of the Year, selling more than eight million copies within six months of its release.

Smith owned more than five hundred copyrights. He recorded more than 100 albums—for ABC Paramount, CBS, Dot, MGM, Monument, Polydor, and RCA. He wrote more than one hundred inspirational and gospel music compositions recorded by such artists as George Beverly Shea, Johnny Cash, Barbara Mandrel, The Gatlin Brothers, The Statler Brothers, and Ricky Van Shelton. Smith's are some of the most recorded inspirational songs: "Acres of Diamonds," "Because Jesus Said It," "I Saw a Man," "I've Been with Jesus," "The Fourth Man," and "Not My Will." Smith also was the composer of twelve major motion picture soundtracks, including *Dark Sunday* and *Buckstone County Prison*.

Never one to sit still, Smith also produced, marketed, and syndicated national radio programs for twenty-five years hosted by Chet Atkins, Johnny Cash, Richard Petty, George Beverly Shea, and Amy Vanderbilt.

Smith's own syndicated radio show, *Top of the Morning,* ran for an unbroken span of thirty years for one sponsor, Bost Bread. On that show, Smith hawked bread and dispensed gospel teachings. "This is the day the Lord has made; rejoice and be glad of it," he twanged as the sun rose each morning. He and his wife, Dorothy, put music to those biblical words on the way to Myrtle Beach one day, Smith told the *Charlotte Observer.*

In 1957, Smith created the first recording studio in the two Carolinas. In addition to his own recordings, his studio productions included national artists: Johnny Cash, James Brown, Flatt and Scruggs, Pat Boone, Ronnie Milsap, George Beverly Shea, and The Statler Brothers, to mention a few. In the early years, the features for Billy Graham's *Hour of Decision* were produced at Smith's studios. The entrepreneur also operated Arthur Smith Family Inns, a hotel chain; The Meat Center, a grocery store chain; CMH Records, a specialty record company; and White Point, a seafood restaurant. Even his hobby, sportfishing, became something of a business. He founded the Arthur Smith Sportfishing Tournaments, which ran for almost twenty years at various sites on the Carolina coast, Florida, New York, and the Great Lakes. These were widely recognized as the world's largest sportfishing events.

Smith began the fishing tournaments out of concern for marine conservation. He even established a marine conservation endowment, which contributed to the construction of jetties, artificial reefs, and estuary enhancement in the site areas where the tournaments were conducted. His love of fishing led to the *Arthur Smith Sportfishing Series,* which aired on ESPN for twelve consecutive years. It was one of the original programs in the ESPN Outdoors block of programming.

One could argue that Arthur Smith accomplished all of this because he preferred string instruments to brass ones. His fame allowed him to do so much. But there's another explanation, one that is apparent to those who met Arthur Smith. And that is that he lived by the crackerjack principle, always aspiring to the highest level of excellence.

Awards presented over the years included the Broadcasters Hall of Fame presented by the North Carolina Association of Broadcasters; the 2001 North Carolina Award; State of North Carolina Order of the Long Leaf Pine; North Carolina Folk Heritage Award; American Advertising Federation Silver Medal Award; Broadcast Music Inc. (BMI) Special Citation of Achievement (over one million broadcast performances of original compositions); BMI Song of the Year Award 1973; Council on International Nontheatrical Events Golden Eagle Award; International Real Life Adventure Film Festival (First Place Award —Soundtrack); Doctorate of Human Letters, Steed College; Southeast Tourism Society Award 1985; American Legion Emphasis Award; Girl Scouts of America Emphasis Award; and Southern Baptist Layman of the Year Award 1969.

A journalism graduate of the University of North Carolina at Chapel Hill, Ralph Grizzle of Asheville is a contributing editor to Our State *magazine and author of* Remembering Charles Kuralt.

For more information, see:
Smith, Arthur. Recordings: *Jumpin' Guitar,* MGM; *Guitars Galore,* CBS/Monument; *Smith & Son,* CBS/Monument; *Battling Banjoes,* CBS/Monument; *Arthur Smith,* MGM; *Guitar Boogie,* MGM; *The Guitar of Arthur Smith,* Starday; *A Tribute to Jim Reeves,* Dot; *Great Country and Western Hits,* Dot; *Singing on the Mountain,* Starday; *The Arthur Smith Show,* Dot; *Down Home,* Starday; *Old Timers of the Grand Ole Opry,* MGM; *Original Guitar Boogie,* Starday; *Arthur Smith and Voices,* ABC Paramount; *Goes to Town,* Starday; *In Person,* Starday; *Arthur Smith and the Crossroads Quartet,* RCA; *Mister Guitar,* Starday; *Old Time Fiddle Tunes,* Starday; *Fingers on Fire,* MGM; *Specials,* Polydor; *Arthur Smith, Vol. 1,* Polydor; *The Original Dueling Banjoes,* CBS/Monument; *Plays Bach, Bacharach, Bluegrass & Boogie,* CBS/ Monument.

ARTHEL LANE "DOC" WATSON

By Ryan Sumner

OC WATSON, who rose to fame during the folk revival of the early 1960s, was one of the world's most accomplished flat-pickers who blended the traditional music of his Appalachian roots with blues, bluegrass, gospel, and rockabilly to create a decidedly individual style. A lifelong resident of North Carolina, he recorded on more than fifty albums, won five Grammy awards, was the recipient of the National Medal of Arts and the National Heritage Fellowship, and was credited with keeping the musical traditions of the Carolina mountains alive.

Doc was born Arthel Lane Watson on March 2, 1923, in the tiny mountain hamlet of Deep Gap in Watauga County, on a plot of land homesteaded by his great-great-grandfather. The Watsons lived in a three-room shack with no indoor plumbing. One of nine children, Doc shared a bed with two of his brothers. Doc remembered those years: "In real cold weather, you'd wake up in the morning with frost on your pillow. When hard blowin' snow came, you had to go up in the attic and sweep up the snow and put it through the shutter window. If you let it go until you got your big fire hot, it would melt and wet everything."

Like a younger sister, Watson lost his vision in infancy. The disability closed many avenues to young Arthel, who said, "If I could see like other people, I wouldn't have played music. It would have been a hobby. I would have been an electrician, carpenter, or maybe a mechanic." Watson's father saved his self-esteem by putting him to work at the end of a cross-cut saw: "If he hadn't done that, I'd still be sittin' in a corner somewhere."

The Watsons were a family steeped in musical tradition. Doc's mother Annie was an ardent Baptist, who sang on Sundays in the church choir and at home crooned old-time ballads, which were still alive in Watson's memory. "She'd sing around the house," Doc recalled, "while churning butter, or patching some of dad's overalls that he'd worn the life out of." General Watson, Doc's father, was a day laborer and farmer who led a church singing group and played the banjo. Each night, the family gathered to read a chapter of the Bible and sing hymns from *Christian Harmony,* a post–Civil War hymnal commonly found in the homes of mountain families. Because of his disability, Doc undoubtedly heard the music all the more clearly.

Doc Watson (Photo by Peter Figen)

His parents encouraged Doc's own musical growth. In his early years, musical training consisted of singing with the family, but when Doc was about six, his father began filling his Christmas stocking with a new harmonica every year. In the summer of 1934, General Watson crafted a banjo for his eleven-year-old son, and the cat belonging to Doc's grandmother provided the skin for the head. "She'd had that cat, I guess fourteen years," Doc explained, "and it got so old, decrepit, and blind, it couldn't eat and it was getting to where it couldn't even walk."

At the age of ten, Watson was enrolled at the Raleigh School for the Blind, where he spent four years becoming acclimated to his disability. This experience was terrible for Doc, and he refused to speak about it. He has said that to the disadvantaged students, who relied on state-supported tuition, "the teachers were tyrants back then. I went partway into the seventh grade and quit. I rebelled against their overlord stuff." His musical training did not completely stagnate; it was at the School for the Blind that he was exposed to classical music and received his first guitar lessons from a fellow student. After leaving Raleigh, Doc returned home to Deep Gap, where he continued his schooling with "talking books" from the Library of Congress Record Catalog.

Watson continued teaching himself guitar at home. At first, he began playing on a guitar left at the house by his first cousin. His early gains on this instrument so impressed his father that he agreed to buy his thirteen-year-old son a new guitar, if he were able to learn a complete song by the time he returned from work. He succeeded and that night played his first guitar song for his father, "When the Roses Bloom in Dixieland" by the Carter Family. True to his word, his father bought him a new twelve-dollar Stella guitar that Saturday.

Numerous influences shaped Watson's musical growth through his teenage years. In addition to playing with the musical members of his family, he learned from his mountain neighbors, fiddler and future father-in-law Gaither Carlton, and legendary banjoist Clarence "Tom" Ashley. Watson also learned a large amount of music from fifty or sixty records and a windup gramophone sold to the family by one of Doc's uncles: "There was everything from Jimmie Rogers to the Carter Family, Gid Tanner and the Skillet Lickers, and John Hurt. When I started to play guitar, I listened especially to the records of these people and others, including of course the Delmore Brothers, and later on, Merle Travis."

As a teen, Watson earned money by sawing wood and playing guitar for change in nearby towns. When he was eighteen, the young musician was featured in a radio show broadcast from a Lenoir furniture store. When the radio announcer complained that the "Arthel" was too long and stuffy for the radio, a young girl in the audience yelled out "Call him Doc." "I never found out who she was," Watson said, "The name Doc has come in very handy to me as a professional name because it's easy to remember."

In 1946 at age twenty-three, Watson met Rosa Lee Carlton, the daughter of fiddler Gaither Carlton. Shy and eight years younger, Rosa Lee was a third cousin who lived less than a mile away. Each night with walking stick in hand, the love-struck suitor walked to the Carlton's farm. "You might as well as hit me over the head with a bludgeon," Watson recalled. The couple married that same year and had two children, Merle in 1949 and Nancy in 1951.

After the birth of his daughter, Watson began to turn his musical ability into a career. He added to his state aid for the blind by tuning pianos and performing in a weekend dance band, led by Jack Williams, a local railroad worker who played piano. These were Doc's first paying gigs. "It was to get out there and earn a few bucks," he explained, "to help Rosa Lee raise the kids." Watson stayed with the band for seven years, during which time he played electric guitar; the absence of a fiddler in the troupe allowed Watson to develop his trademark "fiddle licks," lightning quick notes played on a guitar that were substituted in square dance numbers. The group toured throughout North Carolina and Tennessee, playing local dances. "We didn't do any hot records or hit TV shows, we played mostly for the enjoyment of it," Doc explained.

Watson's big break occurred in September 1960, when folklorist/folk music revivalist Ralph Rinzler "discovered" him. Rinzler journeyed from New York with a discographer to record Clarence "Tom" Ashley, who introduced Doc as a musician who "could play anything." Watson only had an electric guitar, which Rinzler thought was inappropriate for the recordings he intended to make. The next day Rinzler happened to be playing a banjo that someone had deposited in the back of a truck. According to Rinzler, Watson asked to see the banjo and "ripped off some of the best pure mountain picking imaginable." The folklorist was impressed and on the following day made recordings of Watson with his wife, children, and father-in-law, in Deep Gap.

One year later, Rinzler convinced Watson, Gaither, Ashley, and some other local musicians to journey to New York and perform in a Friends of Old-Time Music concert. The concert was a success and the group was soon invited to perform in college folk festivals and a two-week engagement at the Ash Grove in Los Angeles. By 1962, Watson was performing alone and gained national attention for his performances at Gerde's Folk City in Greenwich Village and the Newport Folk Festivals on Rhode Island, in 1963 with Bill Monroe and in 1964 with members of the Watson family.

At the Berkeley Folk Festival in 1964, Watson's career entered a new phase when his teenage son Merle joined him on stage. Merle played backup guitar and acted as Watson's road manager, guide, and friend. "If it hadn't been for all of the hard work he put into driving and getting to the shows, I don't know if I could have made it or not." Merle was an accomplished musician in his own right, playing banjo, acoustic, and slide guitar. Doc and Merle played together as a father and son team for two decades, often performing up to three hundred nights per year. "We got used to each other," Watson said, "He could feel what I was going to do; he could anticipate it. The same way with me." Tragically, Merle died on October 25, 1985, in a tractor accident on the family farm.

Watson felt the death of his son especially hard; he even stopped playing for a short while. The musician commemorated his son through his album dedications and in 1986, he founded MerleFest, a yearly musical festival held in Wilkesboro, which was broadcast over the Internet in 2000. Watson also slowed down after Merle's death and officially retired in 1990.

At the end of the century, the legendary folk singer still lived in Deep Gap in a ranch-style home, which Merle designed to accommodate his father's needs. Although retired, Watson had not stopped performing or recording and continued to tour; he claimed to work about one-tenth as much. Sadly, the aged crooner was one of the last keepers of Appalachia's musical heritage; according to Watson, "There is no old-time music in Deep Gap anymore, except me and a friend or two. All those people are gone now."

Ryan Sumner is a graduate of the University of North Carolina at Charlotte, where he continued his studies for a master's degree in history and worked in the exhibit department of the Levine Museum of the New South in Charlotte.

For more information, see:
Corbet, John. "The Doctor Is In." *Pulse!* July 1995.
"Doc Watson—American Folk Music Legend." Southern Folklife Collection, University of North Carolina at Chapel Hill. Web site at http://www.metalab.unc.edu/doug/DocWat/DocWat.html.
"Doc Watson Selected Discography." CBS Cable. Web site at http://www.country.com/gen/music/artist/doc-watson.html.
Watson, Arthel (Doc). *The Songs of Doc Watson.* Imprint. Oak Publications, 1971. J. Murrey Atkins Library, University of North Carolina at Charlotte.

PUBLIC SERVICE

Not long after the twentieth century began, University of North Carolina President Edward Kidder Graham put into practice a challenge from one of his trustees, John Sprunt Hill, to see that the university's borders were established well beyond the campus at Chapel Hill and were, in fact, coterminous with the boundaries of the state. The university was to serve the state, Graham and more than one of his successors argued, and likewise its graduates were obliged to become public servants as well.

That spirit thrived in a time when life moved at a slower pace and one's public life more easily blended with a career in business or the professions. For example, Thomas Pearsall of Rocky Mount managed a vast farming operation at the same time he became a leader in the state legislature, and later was a valued troubleshooter for more than one governor. A person's commitment was to something greater than a single community or private interest, it was to the state as a whole.

North Carolina also may have enjoyed a higher level of citizen participation in public affairs due to the diffusion of power in public office. For three-quarters of the century, leadership in the General Assembly, the most powerful legislative body in the nation and unchecked by gubernatorial veto, changed with the legislative seasons. In addition, the governor was limited to but one term.

The playing field was vast and individuals demonstrated commitment in a variety of venues, some in elective office, as appointees, or in government agencies. Gertrude Weil of Goldsboro, an indefatigable warrior for women's suffrage in the 1920, later ran what some called a "one-woman welfare department" to help those in need during the Depression. Harriett Morehead Berry of Chapel Hill never held elective office but she knew those who did and made sure that North Carolina roads got the attention they needed in the years before and after World War I. That done, she set out to develop the state's credit union movement. Former U.S. Representative Eva Clayton was a community organizer in eastern North Carolina before she went to Washington as the first black female member of the state's congressional delegation.

The Scotts of Haw River were exceptional, with four generations of family members holding the offices of governor, legislator, and commissioner of agriculture. The Page family of the Sandhills included Walter Hines, a journalist and ambassador to the Court of St. James, and his brother Frank Jr., who was responsible for the state's reputation as the good roads state in the 1920s. The Umsteads of Durham County included William B., who was a prosecutor, served in the U.S. House and Senate, and was the only governor to die in office. His brother, John W., was a tireless legislator whose efforts produced significant improvements for the quality of care of the mentally ill.

The Doughton brothers from the northwest mountains held as much sway as any family. At one point, Robert was in Washington, where he chaired the U.S. House Ways and Means Committee that wrote tax legislation for Franklin Roosevelt, while his brother, Rufus, a former lieutenant governor, was in the state legislature in Raleigh. A nod from Rufus determined the success or failure of a governor's legislative package. Their combined service amounted to more than eighty years.

The Royalls of Durham included Kenneth and his son, Kenneth Jr. The elder served as secretary of the army and during World War II was named to defend a group of German saboteurs before a controversial military tribunal. Kenneth Royall Jr. rose to prominence in the state legislature, where his calm demeanor and steady hand guided the state's budgetary process for two decades. The same pattern held for the Warrens of eastern North Carolina. Lindsay Sr. was a congressman and comptroller of the currency under Franklin Roosevelt. His son, Lindsay Jr. of Goldsboro, served in the state legislature and helped produce the compromise the created the Consolidated University in 1971.

From Greensboro came Hargrove "Skipper" Bowles, who served Governor Terry Sanford during his term as governor and was elected to the state legislature before launching his own unsuccessful bid for governor in 1972. "Retired" by the electorate, Bowles turned his energies to raising money for the university, where a center for alcohol studies and the Dean Smith Center stood in 2000 thanks to his work. Among his children in public service was his son Erskine, who headed the Small Business Administration in the first Clinton Administration and then moved to the White House as chief of staff in the second.

North Carolina enjoyed longtime service from a variety of persons who found their niche in state and local offices. David Coltrane of Raleigh had one of the most unusual careers. He remained on the job after one governor fired him and worked for nothing until the next governor took office. Stubborn, honest, and steady in his course, Coltrane was later used by Governor Terry Sanford to cobble together a coalition of local interracial committees in the 1960s to find answers in a state struggling with equal opportunities for all. Charlotte Mayor Ben E. Douglas was an leader in the postwar development of a city that started growing when he was in office and had not stopped by the end of the century.

As is most often the case, public service is equated to public office. The state enjoyed an array of elected leaders made exceptional by a clear understanding of responsibilities tested by the challenges of the day. Governor O. Max Gardner created modern North Carolina government by necessity: the state couldn't afford the old system. He inspired a young legislator from Laurinburg, Edwin Gill, to take a government job as paroles commissioner and he stayed in Raleigh for half a century, one-half of that time as state treasurer. Gill's service as state treasurer was surpassed only by another Council of State member, Secretary of State Thad Eure, whose fifty years in office qualified him for the name, "oldest Democratic rat in the barn."

Sam J. Ervin Jr. was a state legislator, served in Congress, and was on the state Supreme Court before he was asked to take an appointment to the U.S. Senate, which had seen the likes of Josiah Bailey and former governor Cameron Morrison in the North Carolina seats before him. Luther Hodges had ended a career in business and was in "retirement" when he was elected lieutenant governor, then governor, before he joined the cabinet of President John F. Kennedy as secretary of commerce. His job at the time of his death was as a "dollar-a-year" man for the Research Triangle Park, which had come to life during his term as governor.

Perhaps the most unique contribution came from Hugh Morton, a Wilmington native who was more closely associated with his Grandfather Mountain in Avery County. Throughout his life, he produced a photo archive that captured the life of North Carolina from the coast to the mountains during the second half of the century. At the same time, Morton preserved Grandfather Mountain for generations to come, spearheaded the movement to bring the battleship *North Carolina* to Wilmington, and was a steady foot soldier in a host of other campaigns.

JOSIAH W. BAILEY

By Jonathan Phillips

IN 1930 at the age of fifty-eight, Josiah William Bailey, a Baptist preacher's son, was elected to the U.S. Senate from North Carolina. He would serve until his death fifteen years later. During his tenure, he would establish himself as one of the leading Democratic conservatives in opposition to Franklin Roosevelt's New Deal—a significant contrast to the "progressive," at times radical, reputation he earned as a younger man involved in state and local politics.

Arguably the Senate's finest orator during his service, he was an aloof and proud man, uncomfortable with personal relationships. To many, he came across as pious and arrogant and straight-laced. His colleagues called him "Holy Joe," in reference to his deep religious beliefs. Yet his friends and family revered him. He had prepared most of his life for his role as senator and was considered imminently well-qualified. And, for three decades, he had been one of the most powerful and astute politicians in North Carolina. Yet until he took the oath of office in 1931, Bailey had never held an elected office.

Bailey was born September 14, 1873, in Warrenton, to Christopher and Annie Bailey. Three years later, the Bailey family moved to Raleigh when Christopher Bailey became editor of the *Biblical Recorder,* the newspaper of the North Carolina Baptist Convention. Josiah attended Raleigh-area schools until the age of fifteen, when he entered Wake Forest College where he studied classics and Greek. He demonstrated exceptional talent as a writer, which would serve him well early in his professional career. Bailey considered pursuing an academic career upon graduation in 1893, but his father's failing health persuaded him to return to Raleigh and take on the editorial duties at the *Recorder.* Two years later, after his father had died, the Baptist Convention elected him editor. He was not yet twenty years old and was now responsible for the periodical with the second-largest circulation in the Tar Heel State.

As editor, Bailey did not limit his writing to church issues. The April 10, 1895, edition of the *Recorder* gave a hint as to Bailey's plans for the paper. "Next to Baptist Churches," he averred, "the *Recorder* takes its peculiar aim to hasten the day when the State will be dotted with school houses, public schools, academies, boarding schools, and institutions of general learning." Hardly a new issue in the 1890s, prominent

Josiah W. Bailey (Courtesy of Southern Historical Collection)

North Carolinians such as Charles D. McIver, Edwin A. Alderman, and Charles B. Aycock had fought for better education for the past two decades. However, now the leading religious periodical in the state, long an advocate of parochial schools over public schools, supported state aid for improved secular education at the primary and secondary level.

Bailey devoted the next five years to issues concerning public schooling in North Carolina. As would become a familiar pattern throughout his career, many contemporaries (and even some scholars) suspected ulterior motives. One researcher noted that "it is perhaps fair to say that their [the Baptists] extensive arguments in behalf of public schools were largely smokescreens" for a larger plan to weaken state-supported colleges to the benefit of the Baptist College at Wake Forest. More money for primary and secondary education, so the argument went, resulted in a diminution of funding for the university. Bailey argued for the rest of his life that his motives had been both sincere and noble.

In 1895, Bailey accepted the appointment of Republican Governor Daniel Russell to the state Board of Agriculture. As a Democrat, Bailey took the minority seat on the board, but he would later come to regret his participation.

First, he would forever be vulnerable to claims that he had worked for the opposition party. In addition, Bailey worked with a black political appointee, the much-vilified James Young. Bailey resigned his position in 1897 and joined in with the notorious "white supremacy" campaign of the Democrats in 1898. As Bailey's biographer, John Robert Moore, noted, "Bailey reasoned that the Negro vote needed to be displaced before progress could resume." Some Democrats, such as Josephus Daniels, editor of the *News and Observer,* suspected that Bailey did not rejoin the Democrats without first securing an agreement that guaranteed the legislature would not vote for additional monies for public colleges. Once again, Bailey vehemently denied the claim.

In 1903, Bailey joined the temperance movement when he was elected chairman of the executive committee of the Anti-Saloon League. He used the *Recorder* as the voice of temperance and organized 174 local chapters throughout the state.

Bailey always supported local control of alcohol and argued against national regulation. "It should be a fixed rule of American politics," he asserted, "never to accept a responsibility which may be discharged to the electorate. . . . self-government does not proceed from the national head downward; it proceeds from the community upward." (Years later, Bailey would apply this philosophy to his duties in the Senate.) Bailey also opposed state-controlled prohibition, arguing that control of alcohol was only enforceable at the local level. However, the Anti-Saloon League advocated state-enforced prohibition and, therefore, Bailey resigned his post in 1907, although he continued to support the temperance movement.

While still deeply involved with prohibition, Bailey had undertaken the study of law. Eventually, he resigned his editorship with the *Recorder,* passed the state bar, and entered law practice with his brother-in-law. Why Bailey turned down an influential and successful career in journalism is a matter of conjecture. However, a decade later Bailey was considered one of the twenty best-paid lawyers in the state and earned a far greater and more consistent salary than he ever could have expected in journalism. In addition, serving as the editor of a denominational periodical restricted his political ambitions. Law provided greater opportunities in the political arena.

During the next several years, Bailey supported a variety of progressive causes: ballot reform, good government campaigns, improved education, and limits upon child labor. Bailey supported Woodrow Wilson for president in 1912 against the wishes of his mentor, U.S. Senator Furnifold Simmons. Nonetheless, Bailey, "as one of Simmons' right-hand men," guided Simmons's victorious Senate campaign at home while the candidate remained in Washington. In supporting the winning presidential and senatorial candidates, Bailey had put himself in contention for a political appointment. He was soon rewarded with the position of internal revenue collector for eastern North Carolina. Also in 1913, Governor Locke Craig appointed him to the N.C. Constitutional Commission, a group working on updating the state's constitution.

By 1914, Bailey had become firmly established as the leader of the liberal wing of the Democratic Party in North Carolina. He worked closely with Clarence Poe, editor of the *Progressive Farmer,* and H. Q. Alexander, president of the Farmers' Alliance, in promoting a progressive agenda for the state. In April 1914, Bailey convened a conference of progressives in Raleigh to consider his reform platform: a statewide primary, tax revision, judicial reform, public health and education, rural credit, freight and insurance rate controls, and child labor limits.

Bailey's efforts were stymied at every turn by the entrenched conservative wing of the Democratic Party. He did not give up. During the next fifteen years, he continued to advocate progressive reforms at the state level, and many of the agenda items from the 1914 reform effort were incorporated into the platform of his failed attempt to secure the governor's office in 1924, in a campaign he financed entirely out of his own pocket.

North Carolina Democrats were deeply divided in the presidential election of 1928. Simmons, the dean of the state party, refused once again to support his party's nominee, Governor Alfred Smith of New York, who was a Catholic and opposed prohibition. Bailey, although deeply concerned about Smith's stance on alcohol, remained loyal. In the general election Tar Heels voted for Herbert Hoover—the first time North Carolina supported a Republican presidential candidate in the twentieth century.

Bailey saw the party's lack of unity as an opportunity to oppose Simmons two years later. The resulting campaign was long and bitter. Bailey came to regret his independent streak as the young editor of the *Biblical Recorder.* The Simmons forces argued correctly that Bailey had accepted a political appointment from a Republican administration and had collaborated with an African American while serving in the appointed position. They also demonstrated that Bailey's support of prohibition was qualified and his support of Al Smith actually made him suspect. Bailey had also received campaign contributions from northerners opposed to Simmons.

However, Bailey's call for party unity, his progressive reputation, and the fact that many voters believed that Simmons had served long enough (thirty years) proved the winning combination for unseating the incumbent. In the November general election, he overwhelmed his Republican opponent, George M. Pritchard. At age fifty-eight, Bailey finally held elective office.

Of his intentions in Washington, Bailey stated, "I shall go to the Senate with no view to cultivating popularity." "I have gone uphill and upstream these thirty years. I shall continue in the same direction." However, as the Depression set in and the political tide changed, Senator Bailey found himself fighting upstream against a current of progressivism, and not the entrenched conservative wing of the Democratic Party.

Various publications predicted that Bailey would vote with the liberals in the Senate, but his reputation as a progressive reformer did not continue at the federal level. Bailey was committed to the supremacy of the individual over the state and local government over national government. He advocated self-help, a balanced budget, and efficient government—all tenets of southern progressives. A large, powerful, and intrusive federal bureaucracy did not fit with his notion of progress. Throughout the rest of his life, Bailey consistently worked against an ever-expanding federal government. Unlike many progressives of his day, such as his friend Clarence Poe, Bailey never realized that the national government was the last great hope for the southern economy.

Bailey was slow to grasp the seriousness of the Depression. He believed that the nation's economic system was sound. Though fearful of artificially propping up the economy, Bailey voted for many of Franklin Roosevelt's early New Deal programs. However, he guaranteed his reputation as a conservative by opposing both the Agricultural Adjustment Act (AAA) and the National Industrial Recovery Act (NIRA), one of the few Democrats to do so. In both cases, he feared the "transferral of power from Congress to the President." Like most southern Democrats, he opposed both attempts (1935 and 1938) to pass an anti-lynching law. In 1935, he argued that federal legisla-

tion was not needed to control this crime. In the second attempt, he commented that "the South would not tolerate a Democratic Party catering to the Negro vote." He stridently opposed Roosevelt's Court-packing scheme of 1937 for many of the same reasons that he voted against the AAA and NIRA. Roosevelt's plan for the Supreme Court generated a negative response from many Republicans and Democrats.

Bailey solidified his position as an opponent of the New Deal in 1937 when he prepared, with the assistance of several colleagues, what became known as the Conservative Manifesto. The document proposed a ten-point program for national recovery. Although the anti–New Deal label exaggerated the substance of the proposal, Bailey and his peers were harshly criticized for the underhandedness of the act. As John Robert Moore noted, the Conservative Manifesto did not create a bipartisan coalition opposed to the New Deal, but it did "reflect accurately the grounds upon which conservatives would attempt to restrain and later dismantle many New Deal programs."

Typical of many Americans, Bailey proved to be a "reluctant interventionist" during the late 1930s. And like many Americans, as the war came ever closer to American shores, he knew that U.S. involvement was inevitable. As he noted in the fall of 1941, "the question is not one of avoiding war—war will come to us. . . ." Mobilization severely challenged Bailey's economic assumptions. Eventually, Bailey would support substantial government control over the economy during wartime. After the defeat of Japan in August 1945, he quickly reverted to his previous belief that the federal government should have limited powers directed toward controlling the economy.

Illness greatly restrained Bailey's legislative efforts in the postwar period. On December 15, 1946, Bailey died of a cerebral hemorrhage. He was seventy-three. During his lengthy illness, he had decided not to run for reelection in 1948. He correctly assumed that he would not live that long.

In the last months of his life, Bailey prepared what has been aptly described as a "last will and testament on public questions" relating to his career and the nation's future. He supported unions and collective bargaining while, oddly, opposing the right to strike. He believed that labor unions should be held liable for damages incurred by their actions—such as striking. He greatly feared the Congress of Industrial Organization's "invasion" of the South, as he interpreted it. In foreign affairs, he proved more progressive. He supported the United Nations and was surprisingly tolerant of other political systems. "It is no concern of ours what sort of government Spain may have,"

Bailey argued, "or whether Russia is communistic or not, or whether France is communistic or not. Let them have such a government as they please." Had he lived longer, Bailey might well have amended this view. He believed the United States must keep its armed forces strong. He supported both the draft and universal military training. With the cessation of hostilities in 1945, he pressed for a substantial reduction in federal spending.

With the exception of the war years, Bailey's political philosophy remained essentially unchanged during his tenure in the Senate. He strongly adhered to the supremacy of the individual over the state. Although he knew that change was inevitable, he hoped change would reflect the best aspects of the past. He considered himself a statesman more than a politician. As his biographer noted, he did much in his Senate career to fulfill his role as a statesman, but he largely overlooked the importance of the federal government in supporting the "economic and social needs of citizens." Much of this came from his probusiness philosophy. He never understood that without the power of the federal government, the people were largely helpless in combating the power of big business. Like the philosopher Adam Smith, whom he greatly admired, Bailey relished capitalism in its purest state while fearing true democracy. As he observed soon after Roosevelt's election in 1936, "The trouble about it all is, when democracy gets free to do what it pleases, it usually does the wrong thing."

Jonathan Phillips's doctoral dissertation in history at the University of North Carolina at Chapel Hill examined the economic and cultural impact of the military presence in the Fayetteville and Sandhills region of North Carolina. In 2000–2001 he was a fellow at the Center of Military History.

For more information see:

Bailey, Josiah William. Papers. Manuscripts Department, Perkins Library, Duke University, Durham.

Abrams, Douglas Carl. *Conservative Constraints: North Carolina and the New Deal.* University of Mississippi Press, 1992.

Biblical Recorder. North Carolina Collection, University of North Carolina at Chapel Hill.

Moore, John Robert. *Senator Josiah William Bailey of North Carolina: A Political Biography.* Duke University Press, 1968.

Patteson, James T. *Congressional Conservatism and the New Deal: The Growth of the Conservative Coalition in Congress, 1933–1939.* For the OAH by the University Press of Kentucky, 1967.

Puryear, Elmer L. *Democratic Party Dissension in North Carolina, 1928–1936.* University of North Carolina Press, 1962.

Steelman, Joseph Flake. "The Progressive Era in North Carolina, 1884–1917." Ph.D. diss., University of North Carolina at Chapel Hill, 1955.

HARRIET M. BERRY

By Lydia Charles Hoffman

HARRIET MOREHEAD BERRY rarely left home without her hat and white gloves, the uniform of a North Carolina woman of "good breeding" in the early years of the twentieth century. Despite this demure image, the "mother of good roads" could hold her own in the rough and tumble of the General Assembly. Rising to the leadership of the N.C. Good Roads Association in 1919, while still unable to vote herself, Berry used her articulate tongue to lobby legislators to create a state-funded highway system with a commission granted authority to implement paved roads linking every county seat to its neighbor.

"If it hadn't been for that waspish woman I could have had my way," groused North Carolina's reputed "good roads" governor, Cameron Morrison, who had favored local funding to pay for half the cost of building and maintaining highways in their provinces. Berry argued that the state money should pay the entirety of the roads program as outlined in the Democratic Party platform of 1920—a platform she helped write. Good roads, Berry believed, were essential to uplifting the communities of the Old North State. Without them, poorer populations would not have access to the public services developing in the Progressive Era.

Berry was born in Hillsborough on July 22, 1877, the eldest of four children born to Dr. John and Mary Strayhorn Berry. The family had little money, as her mother's and her father's people "ha[d] been financial victims of the Civil War." She recalled later that her father's "energies [had been] sapped in his early years by four years in the war" and he was never quite the same. A small farm and fees from a few patients helped the Berrys make ends meet. Harriet's early years were spent at "Twin Chimneys," the Hillsborough home of her maternal grandparents. In 1882, five-year-old Harriet, already nicknamed "Little Lady," started her education at her mother's former school, the Nash and Kollok School. After one year, her mother taught Harriet, her brother, and two sisters, as well as two other neighbor children at home. At the age of twelve, after much persuasion from her mother, Harriet was allowed to join the classmates at Nash and Kollok she had left six years before. Her teachers did not believe that she would keep up with the others, but she graduated in four years.

In 1892, Berry entered the State Normal School

Harriet M. Berry (Courtesy of North Carolina Collection)

(later the University of North Carolina at Greensboro) with the intent of becoming a teacher. Her family's financial circumstances restricted her social activities, "which serve[d] to cast her more intensively into her school work." She failed sewing and drawing, which were required courses, and had a very difficult time with freshman Latin. With the assistance of her uncle "Tommie" Strayhorn, who lived with the family, and a well-worn copy of *Indirect Discourse,* she improved her standing and subsequently graduated with honors in 1897.

After graduation, Berry taught for two years at the Oxford Orphan Asylum to satisfy qualifications for a college scholarship. Looking for another career choice, she returned to her alma mater to work toward a degree in business. She taught herself shorthand and studied typewriting and bookkeeping, finishing in four months course requirements that usually took others two years.

Using her newly acquired degree, Berry began work as a stenographer for the North Carolina Geological and Economic Survey in 1901. The survey was a federally funded project charged with investigating mineral and other natural resources in North Carolina. Berry assisted the project director, geologist Joseph Austin Holmes, in assembling data relating to road construction and maintenance over the entire South. Another member of this small staff was mineralogist Joseph Hyde Pratt, a vocal proponent of land acquisition for roads. It was through her work with Pratt that Berry's long association with the N.C. Good Roads Association began.

The good roads movement in North Carolina began with grassroots activists who wanted to connect county seats for the betterment of rural districts. They advocated a centralized road system managed and paid for by the state. The Good Roads Association lobbied for short-distance, reliable roads connected to national railroad and waterway networks to help farmers transport their goods. It also pressured politicians to connect all county seats with at least macadam or soft-surfaced roads.

In 1904, the same year as her father's death, the survey promoted Berry to the position of acting secretary. She wrote articles and papers and made presentations on North Carolina minerals, roads, forestry, commercial fisheries, and other subjects "within the purview of the geological survey." With the increase in salary that came with the job, she was able to move her mother, brother, and sisters to live with her in Chapel Hill.

During her years with the survey, Berry belonged to many civic and professional associations, including the Southern Appalachian Association, the N.C. Drainage Association, and the N.C. Fisheries Association. In her hometown she was an active member of the Business Women's League, the Chapel Hill Community Club, and served as the vice president of the N.C. Equal Suffrage League. During World War I she assisted in the draft and chaired the Liberty Bond and Thrift Stamp drives in Orange County, was a member of the Committee on Women in Industry in North Carolina in the National Council of Defense, and served on the N.C. Legislative Council of Women.

In 1906, Pratt became the state geologist and secretary of the Good Roads Association. As his involvement in the association deepened, so did Berry's.

Her organizational and writing skills were an important asset to the burgeoning association. In 1915, she helped to draft the law establishing the first state highway commission. The proposal suggested that Pratt and his fellow engineers should begin laying out a state roads system. Construction costs would be financed locally, and proponents hoped the project would connect county seats and major cities.

Across the United States, good roads programs received a financial boost with the passage of the first federal highway act in 1916. The North Carolina legislature voted to match any funds the state might receive for its roads in 1917. In 1919, while Pratt served in World War I, Berry became the acting head of the survey. "For the first time," she believed, she "had a free hand" in implementing her ideas for a solid roads program. With Berry at the helm, a fire was lit under North Carolina's good roads movement.

Berry's first challenge was to mediate the debate between proponents of soft-surfaced and hard-surfaced roads. Firmer surfaces cost more money, but softer "dirt daubers," as they were called, could not withstand the growing number of modern automobiles and trucks. The other item on the agenda was to place financial responsibility for improving and maintaining roads with the state rather than the counties. Businessmen and politicians opposed this idea, arguing that state government should not take the business of road construction out of the private sector, nor should roads be paved with bond money that would require years to repay. In response to these concerns, Berry argued that "the proposed improvement determines our future history—by undertaking new projects with confidence and assurance, we stimulate business activity, put capital into circulation, create a demand for labor and materials and hasten generally the advent of an enlarged future for every citizen of the state."

Berry also told of the tremendous cost of maintaining bad roads. As one historian described her argument, "she showed that to haul a load on a hard surface road cost about a fourth as much as to haul a load on a pretty good road, and still less than to haul a load on sand or mud roads. The difference is so big that the ridiculously small cost of a good road is not worth considering alongside of the cost of hauling on any other kind of a road."

The 1919 Good Roads Association's bill did not pass, but Berry learned from the fight and began a statewide campaign to garner support for her next proposal. She planned to canvass the state, educating the public on the virtues of good roads and how they would benefit each and every citizen.

In 1920, the survey granted Berry a year-long sabbatical, enabling her to devote more time to the good roads program. During this period she assumed the position of executive secretary of the association. Berry wrote letters, prepared and distributed leaflets, composed news articles, and made speeches in support of good roads legislation. She hired field representatives to travel the state to explain the advantages of proposed legislation and to solicit members for the association. These efforts earned her much success in building grassroots support for the program, increasing membership in the association from 272 members in 1919 to 3,741 in 1920 and 5,500 members in 1921, with each contributing a five-dollar membership fee that built the association's treasury to $12,000. Moreover, the association's outreach in counties across the state resulted in better representation on this issue.

Between 1920 and 1922, Berry traveled to eighty-nine of the state's one hundred counties to speak about road improvement. She traveled by mule, wagon, bus, and automobile, and would infuse her speeches with anecdotes about how difficult it had been to reach each destination. She told audiences that every principal town should be connected to make the state whole, and that only through better roads could improving state educational and health programs be accessible to all. Moreover, with tobacco and cotton prices low and the state in the midst of a depression, improving roads meant jobs. "[T]housands of men . . . will be employed in the building of the roads, and the stimulus to industry that this work is going to give will revive the state," she was quoted as saying.

Berry's work paid off and the General Assembly passed a road bill in 1921 that assured state funding for construction and maintenance, the reorganization of a highway commission into district representation, and the establishment of a network of county seat-to-county seat roads. It helped that proponents argued that the main street of the hometown of virtually every legislator would be paved. The *News and Observer* credited her with "one of the most stupendous pieces of legislation in the history of the state. . . . It was her bill in the beginning, and it was her indefatigable work that held the general assembly in line until it had voted." Her success was all the more remarkable since she was a woman working in a virtually all-male world. Many of her male associates called her "Miss Hattie," which they considered a term of endearment, but she disliked it thoroughly and silently endured.

After her legislative victory, Berry joined an organization whose primary charge was to promote "the greatness" of North Carolina to its citizens and to seek out ways to garner the attention of potential capital investors and vacationers. "Knowing North Carolina" was to help the state overcome its "po' white" image. The group encouraged people to enjoy the new health resorts and sanatoriums in the mountains, to take advantage of the balmy beaches in the east, and to invest in the burgeoning textile industry in the piedmont. "Magnificent highways are being built into and through the heart of these mountain stretches, opening them to the thousands that are gradually beginning to learn of the greatness of North Carolina."

After nineteen years, Berry left the state Geological and Economic Survey in 1921. The following year she joined the *Greensboro Daily News* as the editor of the Department of Industries and Resources. She lived with her brother John, a Greensboro physician, and his family and their mother. The newspaper had hired Berry to give its readers "the opportunity of seeing North Carolina through a pair of eyes trained to perceive much that most of us overlook." In 1923, the paper suggested Berry as a gubernatorial candidate. Just as she had motivated North Carolinians to "pull themselves out of the mud," they wanted her to organize a well-equipped and centrally managed school system.

Berry's educational vision was similar to that which she had proposed for improving North Carolina roads. Producing better schools, modern textbooks, and better-qualified teachers were all part of her platform. To fund these improvements she favored "a statewide ad valorem tax sufficient to run all the schools of the state for six months. . . . counties to raise taxes for additional school terms." She would consolidate the separate county school administrations into one under the rule of the state, theoretically reducing overhead costs. "With improved transportation facilities, especially with a modern highway system, no region of North Carolina is so inaccessible as to make administration of its schools from central headquarters impossible," she said.

Berry took halfheartedly her employer's suggestion to run for the governor's office, but took seriously the importance of educating children. To any complaint registered against her proposed tax increase, she replied that the roads had cost money and the people paid for them with wonderful results. The same could be said about educating children: "[North Carolinians] will have to learn that in order to get things they must pay for them."

Berry worked for one year with the N.C. Credit Union Association after leaving the *Greensboro Daily News,* where she had become bored sitting behind a desk editing copy that was not her own. Joining the credit union movement, started by her good-roads ally, John Sprunt Hill of Durham, allowed her to work with farmers and families in rural areas. In 1924, she also represented North Carolina as a delegate at the Democratic National Convention.

The state agriculture department employed Berry as its secretary to oversee credit unions from 1925 until 1937. Working in Raleigh she used her political connections to bring the attention of legislators to the needs and concerns of North Carolina farmers and the farming industry. Following the lead of former governor Gardner's "Live-at-Home" program of 1929, she advocated a diversification of crops, lessening farmers' dependency on tobacco and cotton and thus on the credit-lien system that left farmers paying as much as 40 to 60 percent more for their farm supplies. She edited the department's *Market News* and held the office of director of publicity on behalf of credit unions, which were then under the supervision of the department.

Berry resigned from the Department of Agriculture in 1937 due to poor health. She had suffered from chronic conditions since the 1920s and died from heart complications on March 24, 1940. As earlier elegies had noted, "Miss Berry's name will forever be associated with development of the good roads movement in North Carolina. [She] is for progress. She is not grinding any axes. She is just helping along in woman fashion to make North Carolina the best possible place on earth to live."

Lydia Charles Hoffman is a former director of the Charlotte Hawkins Brown Historic Site. She received her B.A. in history from the University of California at Berkeley and her M.A. in history from the University of North Carolina at Chapel Hill. While completing doctoral work in cultural studies at George Mason University, she worked in the Smithsonian Institution's National Museum of American History affiliations program department.

For more information, see:
Berry, Harriet Morehead. Clipping Collection. North Carolina Collection, University of North Carolina at Chapel Hill.
———. Papers. Southern Historical Collection, University of North Carolina at Chapel Hill.

Berry, Harriet M. "Roads to Fulfillment." *Mountain Life and Work* 3, no. 4 (January 1928).
Crow, Jeffrey J. "Harriet M. Berry." *American Public Works (APWA) Reporter*, November 1977.

HARGROVE "SKIPPER" BOWLES JR.

By Alex Coffin

GREENSBORO'S Hargrove "Skipper" Bowles was a man of contrasts. He carried the label of being the first Democratic nominee of the twentieth century to lose a governor's race in North Carolina, but he set a standard of public service that became legendary and was carried on by his son, two daughters, and a daughter-in-law. After service in both houses of the state legislature, Bowles lost the gubernatorial contest to Republican James E. Holshouser Jr. in 1972, but not before he had introduced the state to modern political techniques that married continuous political polls with television commercials focused on an unwavering theme.

The political defeat was a crushing, life-shaping event. For a time he withdrew from public life, but before his death in 1986 from Lou Gehrig's disease, which also felled his daughter, Martha, he energized fund-raising for his alma mater, the University of North Carolina at Chapel Hill. His last project was a $40 million campaign that built the Dean Smith Student Activity Center—the so-called Dean Dome. He also raised funds for research on alcoholism and helped establish the Bowles Center for Alcohol Studies in Chapel Hill and served as chairman of the board of trustees of the Chapel Hill campus.

At the time of his death, his friend Tom Lambeth, executive director of the Z. Smith Reynolds Foundation in Winston-Salem, gave a moving eulogy. "To remember Skipper is to remember a man who sought to improve the world and to enjoy it. . . . In a time when some would insist on imposing hard-line ideological labels, his ideology was people. He saw issues in people terms. Jobs, education and housing were never statistics. They were always the hurts and needs and triumphs of individual people. In a period when his state came to grips with the travesty of a segregated society, he helped lead the way because his heart was too big to shut out others on the basis of their race or color or religion. . . . "

Bowles was born November 16, 1919, in Monroe, and grew up there, just a few blocks from Jesse Helms, who was successful in 1972 in his run as a Republican for the U.S. Senate. Bowles's father, Hargrove, was a banker who saw his bank fail during the Depression. When he came home to announce he was closing his bank, he was asked if he had taken his own money

Hargrove "Skipper" Bowles Jr. (Courtesy of Hugh Morton)

out first. "No, that wouldn't be fair," the elder Bowles replied. The family then moved to Greensboro, where Bowles became city treasurer.

Hargrove Jr. graduated from high school in Monroe, where he earned the nickname "Skipper" for his service as manager of the football team. He followed an older brother, John, to the University of North Carolina in Chapel Hill, where he first met Terry Sanford, who lived and worked with John in the basement of Swain Hall. Bowles was a popular man on campus. He had an easy smile, an infectious manner, and soon was leading a dance band. "I'm not sure how much music he knew, but he was a charming front man for the band," his friend Hugh Morton later recalled.

Bowles grew impatient with college life and dropped out before earning a degree in political science. Before his army service from 1943 to 1945, he married Jessamine Boyce of Greensboro and went to work with her father's wholesale food firm, the Thomas and Howard Company, which served a large chain of wholesale grocery concerns. He eventually took over management of the company and by the late 1950s was a successful businessman and a member of various corporate boards, including the First Union National Bank in Charlotte. He and Jessamine lived with their family—two sons, Hargrove III and Erskine, and two daughters, Martha and Holly—in a handsome residence overlooking a fairway at the Greensboro Country Club.

In 1959, Sanford prevailed on Bowles to lead the fund-raising for his campaign for governor. The two were not particularly close at the time, and when Sanford arrived at Bowles's home in Greensboro he suspected that the brother of his old college roommate might be a Republican (he was not). With no prior experience, but his characteristic enthusiasm for new adventures, Bowles joined the campaign and became one of the most loyal and steadfast members of the Sanford political family.

After Sanford's election in 1960, the new governor was eager to beat the industrial development record of his predecessor, Luther Hodges, and he brought Bowles in to lead the charge. As head of the state Department of Conservation and Development, Bowles organized industry-hunting tours in the first six months that continued the state's visibility as a welcome home for new industry.

During his service in Raleigh, Bowles retained his home in Greensboro and commuted to the capital with a chauffeur at the wheel of his Bentley, which he later exchanged for a less-expensive automobile. He frequently stopped in the governor's office before heading to his own and arrived one morning angry and frustrated. On his way to Raleigh, his African American driver had been refused service at a diner where the two had stopped for breakfast. The incident awakened Bowles to North Carolina's segregated way of life like nothing before. Within the next year, Bowles used his position to quietly and peacefully desegregate the state's park system—from restaurants to swimming pools—well before the 1964 Civil Rights Act required open public accommodations. By the end of Sanford's term, the governor's industrial development record surpassed Hodges's but Bowles's son Erskine said his father's most satisfying achievement was the change his father made in the park system.

Bowles returned to Greensboro after Sanford's term concluded in 1965 but he remained interested in politics. In 1966, he was elected to the North Caro-

lina House and in 1970 to the senate, where one of his signature bills was enabling legislation for personalized license plates. He worked to bring a school for the deaf to Greensboro and began laying the groundwork for a gubernatorial campaign of his own in 1972.

Before Bowles's 1972 bid for governor, North Carolina political campaigns had changed little from the days when opposing candidates delivered their campaign speeches from the courthouse steps. By the time Bowles was through, Tar Heel voters had learned about repeated issue polling, focus groups, and modern television production tailored to a consistent theme. In Bowles's case, it was education and preparing youngsters to compete in an industrial economy. Spending four times more than the favorite in the Democratic primary, Bowles beat Lieutenant Governor H. Pat Taylor Jr. and won the Democratic Party nomination. The campaign was largely a family affair. His son Erskine was his finance manager and his daughters worked in the campaign office located in downtown Raleigh at the Sir Walter Hotel.

North Carolina had been solidly Democratic until 1968, when Republican Richard Nixon had carried the state in the presidential race. In 1972, the state Democratic Party was more fractured than it had ever been with a presidential candidate, U.S. Senator George McGovern, who was unpopular in the South. Bowles campaigned hard in the fall and supplemented his daily schedule with a heavy barrage of television advertising. Ten days before the general election, the *Charlotte Observer* endorsed Bowles's Republican opponent, Jim Holshouser, saying he would "clear out some of the cobwebs" left by seventy years of Democratic rule in the state. Holshouser, who had served with Bowles in the General Assembly and was a former chair of the state Republican Party, had promised to lead the Republicans toward moderate progressivism. On election day, Nixon overwhelmed McGovern in a landslide and Holshouser inched by Bowles by 38,000 votes out of 1.4 million cast.

Bowles was stunned, but a few days after the election, he told an old friend, "The sad thing about this is that the people around me, my family especially, are depressed and down. It's over as far as I'm concerned. We did everything we could to win. Now, I am going out and do new things in my life, and undertake some new challenges."

Bowles returned to business with his brother, Kelly, and their ventures ranged far and wide, from oil exploration to hog farming. He devoted himself to the university at Chapel Hill, where he became chair of the trustees and raised money for alcoholism research and the Dean Smith Student Activities Center. The Hargrove "Skipper" Bowles Hall, a center for alumni gatherings, was named in his honor.

Erskine entered politics much the same as his father. He was a successful investment banker and married to Crandall Springs, who had known Hillary Clinton in college. When Hillary's husband, Arkansas Governor Bill Clinton, became a candidate for the Democratic presidential nomination in 1991, the couple went to work on the Clintons' behalf. After the campaign, Bowles helped organize President-elect Clinton's 1992 economic summit, and subsequently was called to Washington to work in his administration as head of the Small Business Administration (SBA). While at the SBA, Bowles, often described as a probusiness centrist, streamlined the agency, cut red tape, and made an additional $4 billion in loan money available. He ordered the size of an application for an SBA loan guarantee reduced to a single page.

His success so impressed Clinton's chief of staff, Leon Panetta, that he asked Bowles to join him at the White House as his deputy. One of Bowles's first tasks was to apply a time-management study to Clinton's calendar that resulted in freeing the president from a number of meetings. He also dramatically reduced the number of Clinton's public appearances to make sure the president had "think time." Bowles remained at the White House for over a year before returning to Charlotte to establish Carousel Capital, a merchant bank.

After Clinton was elected to a second term in 1996, he called on Bowles to become his chief of staff and Bowles agreed at a salary of a dollar per year. During his time in Washington he helped launch a presidential commission to study racism in America that was led by Duke historian Dr. John Hope Franklin. He also worked with Clinton to reverse President George Bush's ban on fetal-tissue research, which was being touted as leading to a cure for diabetes. (Both Crandall Bowles, and her son, Sam, are diabetics, and Bowles served as president of the international Juvenile Diabetes Foundation.) He also helped raise millions of dollars for causes, including research on Lou Gehrig's disease.

It was a tumultuous time during which Clinton once referred to Bowles as "my best friend in the White House." The president said Bowles had been a marvelous role model for White House workers. (It was Bowles who convinced Clinton's political adviser, Dick Morris, that it was time to go, after Morris was caught in an embarrassing episode with a call girl.)

When Bowles gave up his White House job to return to Charlotte, Clinton praised him at a November 25, 1998, news conference. "I want to say again how much I appreciate the indispensable role he has played in balancing the budget and developing sound economic policies, in improving our commitment to education in ways that will affect millions and millions of schoolchildren, and in his conviction that we were doing the right thing to pursue our race initiative. I will miss him very much. But most of all today I want to acknowledge his contributions to the people of the United States."

After Bowles returned to Charlotte, he considered a campaign for governor, but decided against it. He also was rumored to be a candidate for the chancellorship of the University of North Carolina at Chapel Hill and other powerful posts. He did accept Governor James B. Hunt Jr.'s request to chair the N.C. Commission on Rural Prosperity, which was charged with finding ways to bring prosperity to rural areas left out of the economic boom of the 1990s. In the fall of 2001, Bowles rejoined the political world as he began organizing a campaign to win the Democratic Party's nomination for the U.S. Senate.

Bowles's youngest sister, Martha, died in 1993 of Lou Gehrig's disease at the age of forty, but not before accumulating an impressive list of service to various causes, including Planned Parenthood and the Blumenthal North Carolina Performing Arts Center fund drive.

Another sister, Holly Bowles Blanton, a psychotherapist and clinical social worker in Raleigh, was a cofounder of the Wake County Child Abuse Prevention Services (later Interact) and a cofounder and first chair of the Wake County Parents Anonymous Chapter. She also worked to establish Oak Ranch, a Christian home for troubled children in Lee County, forty miles south of Raleigh. In addition, she helped establish Safechild and served on the boards of the Wake County Child Advocacy Council, the Wake County Child Abuse Prevention Service, and the Family Violence Prevention Center.

"We have been given a lot," Erskine said, "and once you have the tools, you have to take some time, as my daddy said, to add to the woodpile—to give back."

Alex Coffin worked at newspapers in Charlotte, Atlanta, and Vancouver, British Columbia, in addition to being a staff member for U.S. Representative Charles R. Jonas in Washington, D.C., and for Duke Power Company in Charlotte, before opening his own public relations firm in Charlotte in 1985.

For more information, see:

Ball, Karen. "Clinton's New White House Chief of Staff Is Known for His Tough, Blunt Approach." *New York Daily News,* December 14, 1996.

Barker, Robert, Richard S. Dunham, and Nicole Harris. "Just Which One Is the 'Other' Bowles?" *Business Week,* June 23, 1997.

Christensen, Kathryn. "Crandall Bowles: Family and Business Go Together." *Charlotte News,* June 16, 1979.

Claiborne, Jack. *The Charlotte Observer: Its Time and Place, 1896–1986.* University of North Carolina Press, 1986.

Covington, Howard E., Jr., and Marion A. Ellis. *Terry Sanford: Politics, Progress, and Outrageous Ambitions.* Duke University Press, 1999.

Gray, Tim. "Banker Bowles Over the SBA." *Business North Carolina,* May 1993.

————. "Lord of Discipline." *Business North Carolina,* January 1998.

Lambeth, Tom. "Skipper." *Golden Triad,* November–December 1986.

EVA MC. CLAYTON

By Charles Clay

U.S. REPRESENTATIVE Eva McPherson Clayton was the only African American woman sent to Congress from North Carolina during the twentieth century. She had been elected on a substantial record of helping the poor and disadvantaged, not only in her district in the eastern part of the state, but nationally.

According to a lengthy article in the *News and Observer* on October 13, 1998, her chances of winning reelection to Congress looked bleak. Clayton of Littleton was seeking her fourth term from the First Congressional District in the state's coastal plain, one of only two districts in the state with a majority of African Americans. The news article said "a successful legal attack on race-based congressional districts" had resulted in a loss of 165,000 core constituents for Clayton.

The article also noted that only Clayton, among Democrats in North Carolina's congressional delegation, was "facing an established officeholder with credible prospects." That candidate was a veteran Democratic state legislator who was diametrically opposed to nearly all the positions the unabashedly liberal Clayton had taken on issues ranging from abortion to minimum wage.

But when the votes were counted in 1998, Clayton had crushed her Democratic opponent by 67 to 33 percent and her Republican opponent in the general election by 66 percent to 33 percent. No doubt the makeup of the district played a significant role in Clayton's political success during the last decade of the twentieth century and into the initial years of the new century. Just as clearly, another critical reason had to be her widely acknowledged identification with and hard work on behalf of political issues of real benefit to a large majority of her constituents. Clayton, who was elected to a seat on the Warren County Board of Commissioners from 1982 to 1992 and chaired that board from 1982 until 1990, was approached during one of her congressional campaigns by a white man, who said: "You always get my vote because you're the only one up there who's looking after ordinary people."

Midway into her fifth two-year congressional term, Clayton surprised observers by announcing that she would not run again, although the consensus was that she would have no difficulty being reelected. The latest redistricting by the state legislature, based on

Eva Clayton (Courtesy of Eva Clayton)

the 2000 census, had made only minimal changes in her district. Clayton, who was then sixty-seven, said, "I want to write a new chapter in my life so I should move while I have good health and a high level of energy. You need to move at the top of your game." She said she was considering various options for her future, but had not chosen a specific route. Clayton said she would miss being in Washington. "You have a sense of loss just knowing you won't be there," she said. "It's a vibrant, high-pressure environment; you're going to miss it."

Clayton was born on September 16, 1934, in Savannah, Ga., the daughter of Thomas and Josephine McPherson. Her mother was a teacher who had been superintendent of the Methodist-supported Shiloh Orphanage in Augusta, Ga. Her father was an insurance salesman. The family was not poor and there was never any doubt that she would go to college because her mother and father emphasized the importance of education, even during the years of the Great Depression. So after graduating from Lucy C. Laney High School in 1951, Clayton enrolled in Johnson C. Smith University in Charlotte, where she met her future husband, Theaoseus T. Clayton Jr. "I was a freshman and I was smitten," Clayton said. They were married on Christmas Eve 1955, the same year she received her B.S. degree in biology from Johnson C. Smith.

Clayton received master's degrees in biology and general science in 1962 from North Carolina College for Negroes (later North Carolina Central University), where her husband earned his law degree. During the 1961–65 state administration of Governor Terry Sanford, she worked on community development in Warren County and northeastern North Carolina, assisting groups that took part in the North Carolina Fund, Sanford's pioneering antipoverty program. Later, Clayton was assistant secretary of administration for community development in 1977–81, during Governor James B. Hunt Jr.'s first term. And while a member and chairman of the Warren County Board of Commissioners, she founded a consulting firm, Technical Resources, in 1981 and served as its president until 1992.

In 1961, shortly after passing his bar exam, T. T. Clayton accepted an unusual job that brought the Claytons to Warren County. He said years later, "There was an attorney in Warrenton, a white attorney, looking for a law partner and he let it be known he didn't care if that partner was white or black, or 'colored' as we said at the time." The attorney was James D. Gilliland and he and Clayton practiced together until Gilliland's death in 1963. Clayton, who believed he was the "first black to integrate a law firm in the South," also was associated with Durham lawyer Floyd McKissick in the practice of law and in the failed effort in the 1970s to create a model black community called Soul City in Warren County.

Eva Clayton's first, and only close, election to Congress came in the May 5, 1992, Democratic primary. The First District seat came available with the retirement of veteran Representative Walter Jones, a conservative Democrat from Farmville in Pitt County. Jones died in September before the end of his term and his son, state Representative Walter Jones Jr., launched an effort to succeed him. Clayton and five other Democratic hopefuls also announced.

When the votes were counted, they showed that Jones ran first with 38.13 percent. Clayton was second with 31.15 percent and the other five accounted for the difference. Under state law, Clayton was entitled to call for a runoff because Jones had failed to get at least 40 percent. In the runoff, Clayton defeated Jones

55 percent to 45 percent and went on to win the general election against a Republican with 67 percent of the vote. Ironically, as some reports noted, that First District primary came in the wake of a crusade in the 1980s by civil rights leader Jesse Jackson to eliminate runoffs. In Clayton's case, it would have had a negative effect on creating brighter election prospects for minority candidates.

A national leadership role awaited Clayton in her early years in Congress. She was elected to chair her freshman class of Democrats in the House, then controlled by her party. And she soon became a leader in the chamber's Black Caucus, where she championed the cause of the poor.

After early winning reelection in 1994, Clayton found herself caught up in a House controlled by Speaker Newt Gingrich and other ultraconservative Republican leaders bent upon an antigovernment "revolution" aimed at federal social programs. Ironically, while Republicans were sweeping to victory that year in elections that wrested control of Congress from the Democrats, the country's voters also sharply increased the number of blacks in the House, from twenty-four in 1990 to forty in 1995. (In another political twist in the 1994 elections, Walter Jones Jr. switched to the Republican Party and was elected to Congress from the Third District.)

Clayton said Gingrich and the so-called Contract with America failed in the mid-nineties because House Republicans "worked themselves into a corner. They shut down the government twice, talking about morality. . . . "

The congresswoman also said she had "mixed emotions" during the long months of the unsuccessful Republican effort to remove President Bill Clinton from office through the impeachment process. "You wonder how such a smart person could do something like that," she said of Clinton. She noted that "the country should have been spared the trauma" of Clinton's impeachment in the House, which Clayton opposed, and his trial in the Senate, in which Clinton was acquitted.

Clayton was proud of her voting record, which was usually described as one of the chamber's most liberal. However, her record showed that she hardly fit the definition of what some pundits refer to as a "knee-jerk liberal." She could be counted on to vote for more public investment in programs that benefited the poor and needy, including welfare benefits, job training, food stamps, and affordable housing. She supported many of Clinton's initiatives, including those to protect the environment, expand Medicare and Medicaid, and provide more federal money for public schools and additional police officers. At the same time, she opposed Clinton's signing of the welfare reform program and voted with the labor movement against his administration's trade policies out of concern that they would adversely affect her constituents, including textile workers.

One of Clayton's most important legislative victories came in 1998 when she led the Congressional Black Caucus's successful effort to pave the way for black farmers to sue the federal government for racial discrimination in its farm subsidy program. She supported legislation that removed the statute of limitations on lawsuits against the U.S. Department of Agriculture's Farmers Home Administration in the award of farm credit. The government later settled a class-action suit in which the department agreed to pay over $600 million to 12,844 black farmers.

Clayton also was instrumental in reviving Congress's Rural Caucus. The enlistment of more than one hundred members breathed new life into the caucus. In the process, when members of the Black Caucus from urban areas of the nation sought her help on legislation, Clayton would ask, "Does it include rural areas?"

In December 2001, state Senator Frank W. Ballance Jr. of Littleton in Halifax County, a longtime friend and political colleague of Clayton's, announced his candidacy to succeed her. He had her strong support and endorsement. Ballance, a state legislator for almost two decades and the state senate's deputy president pro tem since 1997, said Clayton "will go down in history as one of the most outstanding leaders of North Carolina."

People "love and respect her primarily for her integrity and willingness to stand on principle," Balance added. "She brings people together. She can disagree with you without putting you down. She's the hardest working person in the county and she inspires other people to work hard."

Charles A. Clay is a Raleigh-based writer who was editor of the Fayetteville Observer *from 1965 to 1978. Prior to that he was a journalist in Durham and Raleigh. He also worked in Richardson Preyer's campaign for governor in 1964 and Jim Hunt's gubernatorial race in 1980. He served on the North Carolina Industrial Commission from 1980 to 1986. He also is the author of a biographical novel,* The Alien Corn.

For more information, see:
Clayton, Eva. File. *News and Observer,* Raleigh.

ELIZABETH H. DOLE

By Steve Bouser

Dr. John Robert Crawford, a Salisbury ophthalmologist, remembers a pretty girl named Elizabeth Hanford and a summer night in the 1950s. "We were sitting out at the river one night, looking at the moon," Crawford once told the *Salisbury Post*, "and I was trying to get Liddy to get serious about some courting. And she said, 'You know what?' And I said, 'What?' And she said, 'I want to be the first woman president of the United States.' "

He teased her about it for years after that, calling her or sending her little notes every time she took another step up the ladder toward national prominence. "Throughout the years since then," he recalled, "I'd say, 'Well, you're getting closer.' And when she married Bob [then Senator Robert Dole], I said, 'Well, you're getting up there.' "

In 1999, Elizabeth Hanford Dole came closer to achieving her goal of becoming president than any other woman in history. She resigned as head of the American Red Cross in January, announced an exploratory committee in March, and made her campaign official in July. She ran hard, attracting a core of warmly devoted supporters and finishing a close third in the Iowa GOP straw poll. But she never made much of a dent in George W. Bush's poll standings. And in October she announced that she was withdrawing from the race. She gave three reasons: "Money, money, money." Despite her heartiest efforts, she had been able to assemble only a tiny fraction of the $60 million mountain of campaign funds vacuumed up by Bush's political machine. Evangelist Billy Graham, a fellow North Carolinian and longtime admirer, sent her a letter the day after her withdrawal. He told her not to be discouraged. He said he believed the Lord had "something even more important" in mind for her.

In the summer of 2001, Dole announced her intentions to run for the Republican nomination for the U.S. Senate from North Carolina, the seat held by Jesse Helms, who was retiring at the end of his term in 2003.

Few who followed Dole's remarkable rise in all its increments over the years would rule out that possibility. There had always been awesome talent, drive, and ambition tucked away under her well-cultivated exterior of Southern charm and decorum. As Dole, then sixty-three, receded from the headlines with the

Elizabeth H. Dole (Courtesy of Charlotte Observer)

waning of the old millennium, those who knew her best and respected her most found it hard to believe that they had heard the last of her.

She was Elizabeth Hanford when she was born July 29, 1936, to Mary and John Van Hanford, a comfortably well-off couple who operated a family wholesale florist business in Salisbury. She was the second of two children, brother John being thirteen years older. "This is to certify," nurse Snowdie Safrit Beam wrote in her baby book, "that Elizabeth Alexander Hanford is the best little baby I have ever cared for, her habits from the beginning of life being near perfect."

It was an assessment that would be repeated with almost monotonous regularity over the years. The girl was always so bright, so accomplished, so pert, poised, and polite, that she seemed almost too good to be true. Her leadership qualities also came to the fore early. In the third grade, she mounted a successful campaign for the presidency of the Bird Club.

One thing she couldn't do well as a toddler was pronounce her own four-syllable given name.

"Elizabeth, where are you?" her concerned mother called out one day when her daughter was eighteen months old.

"Here Liddy," came the sweet reply.

And Liddy it was from that day forward—often to her chagrin. When she went away to college, she tried to ditch the nickname, but without success. Though most of her friends in Washington called her Elizabeth (as did her husband), she remained Liddy back home. The name issue caused something of a flap during her husband's 1996 presidential campaign against Bill Clinton. While interviewing her in a moving car, Leslie Stahl of *60 Minutes* inadvertently broke a promise not to use the "L" word, causing Dole to fall silent and stare icily out the window.

Young Elizabeth took piano lessons for ten years from a matron across Fulton Street. She won citizenship awards and essay contests. Every Sunday afternoon, she and some of her friends had cookies and lemonade in her grandmother's parlor while listening to her tell Bible stories. She impressed on Elizabeth that time was precious and should be put to good use. It was partly through her influence that Elizabeth became a self-described "compulsive organizer" and detail person—attributes that served her well.

In high school, she quickly moved to the top of the class of 1954, which became known for its unusual number of super-achievers who went on to various noteworthy accomplishments, mostly on the local scene. She kept busy with the drama club, the school paper, student government, the National Honor Society, float-building—and dates with John Robert Crawford. She readily confessed that she was more adept at conjugating verbs in Latin class than at sewing zippers in home economics.

Her father changed his political registration from Democrat to Republican when Dwight Eisenhower was president, but her mother remained staunchly Democratic. As a young adult, Elizabeth first registered as a Democrat, later changing to Independent, and ultimately to Republican.

After graduating from Boyden High School with high honors, she entered Duke University in 1954, where she also excelled. Though she lost an election to student government as a freshman, she was later elected president of the Women's Student Government Association, then the highest campus office available to a female. After receiving a bachelor's degree with honors in political science in 1958, she moved to Boston to work as secretary to the head librarian at the Harvard Law School Library, thus dashing forever her mother's hopes that she would major in home economics, marry, and move in next door.

Responding to a lifelong urge to use her time profitably and broaden her experiences, she spent the summers of 1959 and 1960 doing postgraduate work at Oxford University in England, visiting the Soviet Union, serving as a guide at the United Nations, and interning at the Peace Corps. Then she enrolled in Harvard under a joint-degree program that combined the study of government with the occupation of teaching. "The first was my emerging passion and the second was a vocational insurance policy," she wrote in her 1988 book, *Unlimited Partners*.

She needn't have bothered taking out that insurance, since finding a job would never be a problem. And each subsequent step would take her ever further away from education and toward a career in government service and politics. After graduating from Harvard with a master's degree, she landed a job in Washington with Senator B. Everett Jordan, a North Carolina Democrat. That led to a brief stint helping organize a campaign whistle-stop tour through the South for Democrat Lyndon B. Johnson, even though she was a registered Republican. During that time, she began dating young men with promising political futures. This led friends to kid her about her seeming determination to marry someone going to the White House—"or get there yourself"—though such a notion was still unimaginable to most people at the time.

She made the acquaintance of U.S. Senator Margaret Chase Smith of Maine, who offered one piece of advice: "Go to law school." So she did. When she told her parents in 1962 that she was enrolling in Harvard Law School, her mother became physically ill.

"Mother lost her dinner," she later told Rose Post of the *Salisbury Post*. "No doubt she thought she was losing her daughter."

Elizabeth Hanford received her law degree in 1965 and was admitted to the bar in Washington. She worked for a time as a staff assistant in the Department of Health, Education, and Welfare and practiced law privately before being named associate director of the White House Office on Consumer Affairs under Virginia Knauer. It was in this job, as well as in a subsequent position as deputy director of the Office of Consumer Affairs in the White House, that Hanford first began to attract serious attention. She was named Outstanding Young Woman of the Year in Washington. After President Nixon appointed her to the Federal Trade Commission (FTC) in 1973, *Time* magazine named her one of America's "200 Faces for the Future."

But perhaps more important to her future than any of those things was the day in 1972 when a chance meeting took place. The Republican Party needed a consumer plank for its platform. Once Knauer's office had prepared it, she sent Hanford to explain it to the GOP chairman, U.S. Senator Robert Dole of Kansas. She found him "awfully attractive." He wrote her name down on his desk blotter and years later could still remember exactly what she was wearing.

They married in 1975 and soon became known as one of Washington's power couples. They took up residence in an apartment in Washington's Watergate complex. Though they remained childless, they lavished attention on a schnauzer that she bought for Dole in the 1980s, naming it "Leader" for his role as Senate majority leader. She once asked the *Post* to print a retraction for incorrectly quoting her as saying the dog slept in the bed with them instead of on it.

"Bob had commented that our life together would never be dull," Dole wrote in *Unlimited Partners.* "But there was no way he or anyone else could have prepared me for the fall of 1976." She referred to the campaign that followed Gerald Ford's selection of Bob Dole as his running mate. The Secret Service, the travel, the fatigue, the confusion on the road, the loss of privacy—all these things would become all too familiar to her during the next twenty years. In 1979, she resigned from the FTC to help her husband campaign (unsuccessfully) for the Republican presidential nomination, as she did in 1987, when he tried again. Then in 1996, she was a candidate's wife again when her husband lost the presidential race to Bill Clinton.

In between election years, she continued to rise steadily through a succession of increasingly powerful Washington jobs. President Ronald Reagan named her as assistant to the president for the White House Office of Public Liaison, making her the highest-ranking woman in the Reagan White House.

In 1983, she joined the Reagan cabinet as secretary of transportation. In 1989, President George Bush appointed her secretary of labor—a position she resigned in 1990 to become president of the American Red Cross. She took a leave of absence from that job in 1995 to work in her husband's presidential campaign, returning in 1996. She left the Red Cross for good in 1999 to make her own run—but not before the Red Cross chapter in Salisbury had dedicated a splendid new Hanford-Dole Red Cross Center in her honor.

So many honors came her way over the years. *Harper's Bazaar* named her one of the country's ten most influential women in 1983. She was selected among the ten best-mannered Americans in 1986 and named as *Esquire*'s Woman of the Year—and its choice for vice president—in 1988. She was named one of the ten Most Fascinating People of the Year on a Barbara Walters television special, Most Inspiring Political Figure of the Year by MSNBC, a top Newsmaker of the Year by *Newsweek,* and Woman of the Year by *Glamour.* She received honorary degrees from thirty-three colleges and universities, including Johns Hopkins University, Smith and Dartmouth colleges, and the College of William and Mary.

Throughout her career, Elizabeth Dole always made it a point to pay frequent visits to Salisbury, where her mother meticulously kept an ever-growing collection of scrapbooks detailing her many accomplishments. Shelves holding the books covered most of a wall. In October 1999, after she announced that she was leaving the presidential race, she said the decision was not overly emotional. "I was at peace about it," she said. "It was the right decision, I felt. I think Bob felt some emotion at that point." She said she tried not to look back on her disappointing experience, adding: "I really don't think about what-ifs."

Editorialized her hometown paper: "Elizabeth Dole did it her way, and as always she has left herself in an attractive position. The question now is what choice assignment will she tackle next?"

Steve Bouser has been editor of the Pilot *of Southern Pines since August 1997. Before that he was editor of the* Salisbury Post *for eleven years and worked with the U.S. government aid programs of assistance to independent media in the former Soviet Union, living in Russia and Washington and traveling extensively in Russia and Eastern Europe.*

For more information, see:

Dole, Robert J., and Elizabeth Dole. *Unlimited Partners: Our American Story.* Norton Smith, 1988.

Kozar, Richard. *Elizabeth Dole (Women of Achievement).* Chelsea House, 2000.

Lucas, Eileen. *Elizabeth Dole: A Leader in Washington.* Gateway Biographies, 1998.

White, Jane, and Elizabeth Dole. *Few Good Women: Breaking the Barriers to Top Management.* Prentice Hall, 1992.

ROBERT AND RUFUS DOUGHTON

By Ralph Grizzle

I N 1908, friends prevailed upon Robert Lee Doughton to run for the state senate. A Democrat, Doughton knew that the district containing Alleghany, Ashe, and Watauga counties usually went Republican, so he agreed to humor his friends, figuring that when the incumbent beat him, he could return to his quiet work as a farmer and storekeeper.

But when Doughton discovered that his opponent had been present for only twenty-four of the 694 roll calls during the last legislative year, he became indignant. Doughton decided this was an election worth fighting for, and as he stumped the district with his opponent, as was the custom in those days, he would let the incumbent campaign, then would hold up a poster with the poor attendance record scrawled on it and say, "Look, where were you?"

That strategy won Doughton the legislative seat and established the beginning of his long career in politics. An astute campaigner, Doughton was consistently returned to office, even when much of his district was voting Republican. When he retired in 1953 he was undefeated after twenty-one consecutive terms in Congress under seven presidents. Together with his brother, Rufus, a political power in his own right in the first quarter of the century, the family wielded considerable influence over Democratic Party politics for nearly fifty years.

Robert Doughton was born in Laurel Springs on November 7, 1863, the son of Jonathan Horton and Rebecca Jones Doughton. A Confederate captain serving under Robert E. Lee, Doughton's father was away at the time of his son's birth. Doughton later said that while his father was gone off to war, scalawags robbed the homeplace of everything, including blankets off his baby bed. Named for the Confederate general that his father so admired, young Robert Lee quickly learned what it means to earn, and keep, a dollar.

The boy grew up a farmer. His big bony hands knew the feel of a hoe on hard ground. He rose early and worked until late in the evening. Later in life he joked that he considered himself to be on vacation any time he was not in the fields from sunup to sundown.

Robert attended Laurel Springs School two months out of the year. Later, his father and neighbors erected a mud-chinked building that they called Traphill Academy and hired a private tutor. Doughton later credited an itinerant teacher with opening his mind to the marvels of mathematics. Later in life, Doughton was awarded honorary degrees by the University of North Carolina and Catawba College.

After high school, he started a farm and stock-raising business. His hard work made the farm a success. Some of his achievements in that realm, in fact, were remarkable. In the early 1900s, Doughton, a few men, and a couple of well-trained dogs corralled "one of the largest droves of cattle [more than 500 head] ever driven" to Wilkesboro—from Doughton's farm in a beautiful stream-crossed valley on the western edge of Alleghany County. The hard-working Doughton eventually acquired five thousand acres, where he raised prize Herefords and Holsteins. His acumen in farming landed him on the state Board of Agriculture from 1903, the year that marked the beginning of his career in public life, to 1910.

From 1909 until 1910, the farmer was elected to the state senate and was on the state Prison Board from 1909 until 1911. That same year, Doughton acquired the majority stock in the Deposit Savings and Loan Bank in North Wilkesboro. He served as the bank president until 1936, when it merged with other banks in Sparta, Boone, and Spruce Pine to become the Northwestern Bank. After the merger, Doughton became chairman and director.

He demonstrated a knack for politicking. In 1910, during a Democratic primary for Congress, Doughton bought along a bag of hard apples, which turned out to be part of his campaign strategy. He knew his opponent would set up his main points by asking a leading question, then pause to allow a dramatic silence before delivering his punch line. During each pause, however, Doughton chomped down on an apple, breaking the silence and amusing the crowd. By the third pause, the crowd was roaring with laughter and his opponent was fully demoralized. From that day on, Doughton had only one primary opponent, in 1918.

At six-feet two-inches tall, the 215-pound Doughton was known as "Farmer Bob" or "Muley," the latter reportedly because of his stubbornness in Congress. "I don't like to change a decision, once made,"

Rufus Doughton (courtesy of N.C. Office of Archives and History) and Robert L. Doughton (courtesy of Asheville Citizen-Times)

he said. He wore a size 15 shoe, and when he gestured, wrote a reporter for the *News and Observer,* "he waves a hand half the size of a ham at you."

With the ascendancy of the Democrats under Franklin D. Roosevelt in 1933, Doughton became chairman of the House Ways and Means Committee, where all tax bills originated. The first farmer to serve that post, his was the job of digging deeper and deeper into taxpayers' pockets to fund economic recovery and the money needed for World War II and the postwar rehabilitation throughout the world.

He held the chairmanship longer than any other man in history (1933–47 and 1949–53), and on his retirement, he was credited with authoring more tax bills than any other member. But even though his job was to raise money for the government, he always tried to keep the taxpayer in mind. He was fond of admonishing his colleagues with the notion that "you can shear a sheep year after year, but you can take his hide only once."

Doughton drummed up money for Roosevelt's New Deal, national defense, and war. He did so gladly. But the North Carolina congressman was not afraid to lock horns with Roosevelt's treasury secretary, Henry Morgenthau Jr., when he requested in 1934 a $10.5 billion budget with $6.5 billion to come from added levies on personal income. Doughton's committee granted only $2 billion in additional revenue, with only $12 million of it from personal income tax. He commented to a reporter from the *Asheville Times:* "The taxpayer is up against about all he can take. . . . If you strangle business and profits with taxes, you don't get anymore taxes."

Doughton is credited with the formulation and passage of the Social Security Act in 1935, an act that he considered the hallmark of his career. He wrote to President Harry Truman in 1952, "I take more pride in my successful efforts on Social Security legislation than any other legislation I have ever been responsible for or actively supported."

Not particularly loquacious, Doughton could be unusually alert and diplomatic. During a hot Senate race in Raleigh between William B. Umstead and Governor J. Melville Broughton, a *News and Observer* editor asked Doughton what he made of the contest. "The man we got [Umstead] is doing a fine job, a fine job! Don't see that there's any need of turning him out," Doughton said, before discovering that Governor Broughton was standing at his elbow, at which point Doughton quickly added: "And I'd say the same thing for the other man if he already had the office."

Doughton went about his own work quietly, rising before daybreak to be the first congressman to get to work—at 6 A.M. He began the day with a hearty breakfast of cereal, bacon, eggs, fruit, and coffee, followed by a thirty-minute walk to his office. Even at age eighty, he maintained the same pace, claiming that he could walk fifteen miles if he had to, without tiring.

His work ethic knew few bounds. The *Asheville Times* joked in a headline that "Rep. Robert Doughton Will Celebrate 80th Birthday Not Working," but only because November 7 fell on a Sunday. A Baptist, "Farmer Bob" held the Sabbath holy. While he would work all night if needed, he would not attend any formal function that lasted as late as 10 P.M. Being up at that hour was all right for folks who could loaf in bed until 7 A.M. but Doughton had to get his work done. He did not know—nor did he care—how the rest of Washington lived.

One morning Doughton ran into a stenographer outside his office building who was just heading for bed after a night out. Not realizing the stenographer was on her way home, he said: "I wouldn't have asked you to come down so early, but now that you're here, we can go to the office and get a lot of work done before the others come in." A teetotaler, the strongest drink Doughton would touch was buttermilk.

He did not always expect others to work as hard as he did, but at times he could be demanding. When an *Asheville Times* reporter asked for an interview, Doughton gave strict orders for the reporter to show up at his Washington office at 8 A.M. sharp, otherwise no interview. A storm tied up traffic, so the reporter called to say he could not get transportation.

"Walk!" Doughton roared into the phone.

"Walk 10 miles? Are you kidding?" the reporter responded.

"That's only a stroll," Doughton replied. "Now get here. The day's half gone."

The reporter failed to say how he made it to Doughton's office, but when he arrived, Doughton set the parameters of the interview: "I have made it a practice to think that any reporter who says anything good about me is a great writer."

Despite his gruffness, Doughton could be a gentle man. He married twice: in 1893 to Belle Boyd Greer, who died in 1895; and in 1898 to Lillie Stricker Hix,

who died in 1946. He had two daughters and two sons.

In the late 1930s, friends and colleagues urged Doughton to run for governor. President Roosevelt, however, asked Doughton to stay in Congress. Doughton thanked the president and told him that he would seek reelection.

Doughton retired from public service in 1953 and returned to Laurel Springs to share a big nine-room house with his daughter, "Miss Reba," who had been with him twenty of his forty-two years in Washington.

At age ninety, he still started his day early. After breakfast, he walked to the post office and would stop to chat with the folks at the general store. He read the morning papers—all North Carolina dailies—then had a light lunch and a nap. Afterward, he might stroll the farm, still stocked with the Herefords and Holsteins. Dinner was at four in the afternoon. Before retiring, his daughter read at least one chapter of the Bible to him.

Three miles away from his farmhouse was the Blue Ridge Parkway. It occupied a warm spot in his heart. "There's nothing like it in the world," he told a reporter for the *Charlotte Observer*. Doughton had sponsored a bill providing for parkway construction through North Carolina and Virginia. The six-thousand-acre Doughton Park, on the parkway, was dedicated to him on October 10, 1953, an event that local papers called "the crowning honor accorded the beloved congressman." (Doughton also succeeded in his efforts to establish the Veterans Hospital in Salisbury after World War II.)

In the fall of 1954, he told a young reporter named Marse Grant that "retirement is the hardest job I've ever had." He died of a heart attack in his sleep three weeks later on October 3, 1954, a month shy of his ninety-first birthday. It was probably good genes that gave him long life. His brother, Rufus Alexander Doughton, lived to be eighty-eight.

Rufus served in seventeen different sessions of the state legislature and was the state's lieutenant governor from 1893 to 1897. By 1921, he was generally recognized as the most influential member of the House. In 1945, at his death, the *News and Observer* wrote that Rufus Doughton had "shaped" more legislation in North Carolina "than any man of his generation." One of his landmark achievements was cosponsoring the Highway Act in 1921, which committed the state to a $50 million highway construction program financed through the sale of state bonds.

The brothers were certainly doers. In a lengthy statement, Governor William B. Umstead said Robert Lee Doughton "probably sponsored and influenced the passage of more good legislation and helped to kill more bad legislation than any other man in the history of this nation. Children yet unborn will be benefited by legislation sponsored by him, such as the Social Security Act and the Unemployment Compensation Act."

Robert Doughton was buried at the cemetery of Laurel Springs Baptist Church, where he was a long-time member and deacon. His portrait hangs in the Ways and Means Committee office in Washington.

Ralph Grizzle is a freelance writer who lives in Asheville. He is the author of Remembering Charles Kuralt.

For more information, see:

"Doughton Honored at Parkway Event." *Asheville Citizen,* October 11, 1953.

"Doughton Will Celebrate His 82nd Birthday Today." *News and Observer,* November 7, 1945.

Grant, J. Marse. "A Stubborn Leader." *Winston-Salem Journal,* November 11, 2000.

Hayes, Johnson J. *The Land of Wilkes.* Wilkes County Historical Society, 1962.

"Retirement at 91 Hard Work, Says Energetic Bob Doughton." *Charlotte Observer,* September 17, 1954.

"R. L. Doughton, U.S. Lawmaker 42 Years, Dies." *Asheville-Citizen,* October 2, 1954.

SAMUEL J. ERVIN JR.

By Karl E. Campbell

O N THE FLOOR of the U.S. Senate, Sam Ervin appeared to be the quintessential southern politician. "To a casual visitor peering down from the gallery, he might look like some windbag Senator Claghorn, a walking Washington stereotype," wrote James K. Batten in the *Charlotte Observer*. "There, behind a desk piled high with law books, is Senator Samuel James Ervin, Jr., eyebrows rippling up and down, fulminating against the latest civil rights bill and regaling the Senate with the latest cracker-barrel humor from the mountains of North Carolina."

But, Batten observed, there was more to North Carolina's senior senator than met the eye. "If stereotypes are always misleading, they are downright laughable in the case of Sam Ervin. After thirteen years in the Senate, Ervin still regularly enrages first the liberals and then the conservatives. He defies all the easy generalizations of political journalism."

The North Carolina Democrat puzzled friend and foe alike during the twenty years—from 1954 through 1974—that he was in Washington. On one hand, Ervin earned a reputation as the Senate's leading constitutional authority and a champion of individual rights. He gained his greatest fame as the folksy ol' country lawyer who preserved the Constitution against Richard Nixon's abuses of presidential power during the Watergate crisis in 1973.

On the other hand, Ervin served as the principal legal adviser to the segregationist bloc in the Senate. He opposed virtually every civil rights bill proposed during his career, as well as every legislative effort to promote the rights of women or protect workers. Ervin explained his seemingly inconsistent political behavior by claiming to be just "preserving the Constitution." He argued that he would oppose any government action that threatened to interfere with an individual's constitutional rights, no matter if it was a liberal proposal to guarantee civil rights or a conservative program to protect national security. Ervin distrusted federal government power. As the senator often explained: "It is not the civil rights of some but the civil liberties of all on which I take my stand."

The senator's critics rejected such lofty philosophical explanations of his inconsistent record. Ervin, they argued, was a rational segregationist who misused the Constitution as a convenient cloak to hide his racist, sexist, and antilabor agenda. In spite of his

Sam J. Ervin Jr. (Courtesy of Hugh Morton)

reputation within the Senate, some legal experts dismissed Ervin as an overblown constitutional scholar who had stopped reading cases in 1936 and whose limited view of the Constitution did not go past the Tenth Amendment. Others agreed with liberal activist Joseph Rauh Jr., who concluded that Ervin was "a great man whose mind was in chains."

Many of the contradictions Ervin demonstrated during his tenure in the Senate had their roots in the history of his home state and reflected the worldview he accepted while coming of age in North Carolina. In many ways Ervin epitomized the Old North State's political culture and dominant ideals during the twentieth century. "Senator Ervin is the most North Carolinian of North Carolinians," a reporter explained. "This kind of man seems to be an ornament of Tar Heel History."

Like many southerners, Ervin's identity revolved around family and place. His Scotch-Irish ancestors emigrated from Ulster to the coast of South Carolina in 1732. The family maintained its Presbyterian religion and cultural heritage. Ervin once told the Senate, "I am the possessor of a great affliction — a Scotch-Irish conscience which will not permit me to follow after a great multitude to do what I perceive to be evil."

John Witherspoon Ervin, Senator Ervin's grandfather, moved his family to North Carolina in 1874. He escaped the poverty of the post–Civil War South by accepting an offer to teach in a small private school in Morganton, a sleepy little town in the foothills of the Appalachian mountains. The family's financial situation slowly improved but the trauma of the "Lost Cause" and Reconstruction cast a shadow over them for generations.

Samuel James Ervin, the senator's father, took a job as deputy postmaster when the family arrived in Morganton and studied law in his spare time. Admitted to the bar in 1879, he became one of the community's leading attorneys and was known throughout the state for his legal ability and distinguished appearance. "Little Sam," as the young Ervin was known as a child, grew up hanging around the Burke County Courthouse watching his father argue cases in old-fashioned Victorian cutaway tails.

Sam spent his boyhood in relative comfort and security during a period of rapid social transition. Born in 1896, the fifth of ten children, Ervin was known as an avid reader, a prankster, and the starting catcher for the local Sandy Flat baseball team. But during Ervin's happy childhood his hometown struggled through significant change. The new railroad brought industrialization to Morganton, and the Ervin family's prosperity depended on the growth of the New South. Race relations also went through a transition during Ervin's youth. A dedicated Democrat, the senator's father participated in the anti-Populist, anti-black political crusade of 1898 that firmly established Jim Crow segregation in North Carolina. During the senator's early years, race and class increasingly defined life in North Carolina.

Sam enrolled at the University of North Carolina in 1913, where he excelled academically, winning honors in history and literature. The class of 1917 elected him class historian, permanent class president, and "best egg." The outbreak of World War I in the spring of 1917 abruptly ended the idyllic life of Chapel Hill. A month before his graduation he volunteered for the armed forces and, after officer training in Georgia, spent eighteen months in Europe. Twice wounded in battle, he received the Purple Heart and the Distinguished Service Cross for heroism.

Ervin returned home shaken by the death and destruction he had encountered in the war. As would be the case throughout his life, he found solace in his studies. Ervin passed the bar exam after a brief refresher course at Chapel Hill, and then sought formal legal training at Harvard Law School. But there was a problem. He feared that in his absence the girl he was courting, Margaret Bell, might marry someone else. So, thinking he had better limit his time at Harvard, he took the third-year courses first. Finding Miss Margaret willing to wait a bit longer, he returned to Harvard and finished his degree before getting married. Ervin later claimed to be the only student to go through Harvard Law School backwards. Some of his critics joked that his constitutional philosophy was as backwards as his legal training.

In 1923 Ervin joined his father's law practice in Morganton and settled into the life of a small-town lawyer. He represented all manner of clients, from manufacturing interests to moonshining mountaineers. On one occasion a woman showed up at his office seeking legal advice. After an hour or so she rose abruptly to leave. Ervin politely asked her to pay a fee. "What for?" she asked. "For my legal advice," he replied. "Well, I ain't going to take it," she snapped, and walked out.

Ervin served the community in many capacities during the thirty years before he was appointed to the Senate in 1954. He was active in the National Guard, local business groups, the Masonic Order, the Presbyterian Church, and numerous other organizations. He served three terms in the North Carolina legislature, where he first demonstrated his ability to apply humor in the defense of civil liberties. In 1925 he helped defeat a bill outlawing the teaching of evolution in North Carolina's public schools with a speech in which he argued that it would gratify the monkeys to know that the state legislature wanted to absolve them from all responsibility for the conduct of the human race. In 1946 Ervin spent an unhappy year in the U.S. House of Representatives after agreeing to serve out the unexpired term of his brother, Joseph Ervin, who committed suicide on Christmas day, 1945, after a long illness. The following year Ervin refused renomination and returned to his law practice in Morganton.

Ervin accepted several judicial appointments during his career, including that as a judge in the Burke County criminal court (1935–37), the superior court (1937–43), and the Supreme Court (1948–54). While on the superior court, Ervin traveled around the state spending evenings swapping stories with his legal colleagues. He was highly respected and well-liked. Even after his two decades in the Senate, many of his old friends still referred to him as "Judge Ervin."

During his six years on the Supreme Court, Ervin established a reputation as a moderate conservative who wrote in clear but colorful legal prose. What others might describe as "obvious," Ervin suggested was "as clear as the noon-day sun in a cloudless sky."

On May 12, 1954, Senator Clyde Hoey died suddenly while sitting at his desk in the Senate Office Building. Just five days later the Supreme Court announced its ruling in *Brown v. Board of Education,* which struck down racial segregation in the public schools. In this racially charged environment, Governor William Umstead faced the daunting task of appointing Hoey's successor. After considerable deliberations, Umstead named Ervin, and on June 11, 1954, Ervin was officially sworn in by Vice President Richard Nixon.

Within a few months of his surprising appointment, Ervin found himself embroiled in two of the most significant episodes of recent American history—the McCarthy censure and the *Brown* ruling. The new senator was appointed to the committee exploring the excesses of Wisconsin Senator Joe McCarthy's crusade against communism. Ervin made a pivotal speech against McCarthy on the Senate floor in which he likened the Republican senator to Uncle Ephraim Swink, an arthritic mountaineer from down home in North Carolina. When Uncle Ephraim was asked at a revival meeting to say what the Lord had done for him, he struggled to his feet and declared, "Brother, he has might nigh ruint me." And that, Ervin argued, is what McCarthy had done to the Senate.

The senator's courageous stand against McCarthy revealed his civil libertarian leanings, but his simultaneous attack on the *Brown* ruling demonstrated the other side of Ervin's paradoxical philosophy. Ervin's criticism was polite, forceful, and based on legal and constitutional objections. As he would in all his many battles against civil rights, Ervin did not attack the ends of the decision—to ensure constitutional rights to African Americans—but the means: in the case of *Brown,* judicial activism. Ervin never relied upon racist rhetoric but on what reporters called a "soft Southern approach." The senator always found some constitutional reason to fight civil rights bills. One journalist summarized his strategy as "walk softly, but carry a law book," another concluded that Richard Russell was the South's "skilled generalissimo," and Sam Ervin was "his intellectual chief of staff."

By the mid-1960s Ervin had become an influential member of the Senate's inner circle and a leader in the southern bloc. Yet he never was one of the real power brokers in the Senate. In many ways Ervin was an apolitical politician, more comfortable with philosophical debate than behind-the-scenes deal-making. He served on the Armed Services and Government Operations committees (he was chair of the latter from 1972 to 1974), as well as several important select committees such as the McClellan Rackets Committee. It was in the Judiciary Committee and its subcommittees, however, that Ervin had his greatest impact.

The senator used his position as chair of the Constitutional Rights Subcommittee to launch his legislative agenda to protect civil liberties. Among his major accomplishments were the Criminal Justice Act of 1964, which provided legal counsel for indigent defendants, the Bail Reform Act of 1966, which expanded pre-trial release to indigent defendants, the District of Columbia Hospitalization of the Mentally Ill Act of 1974, which asserted a "bill of rights" for the mentally ill, and the Military Justice Act of 1968, which protected the rights of service men and women in military courts. In one of his greatest legislative victories, Ervin managed to add his "Indian Bill of Rights," guaranteeing constitutional protections to all Native Americans, to the Civil Rights Act of 1968, which he had opposed. During the floor debate he chided his suspicious liberal colleagues by asking how "anybody supporting a bill to secure constitutional rights to black people would be opposed to giving constitutional rights to red people?"

Ervin gained increasing respect from liberal civil libertarians during his frequent crusades to protect individual rights against big government. In 1966 he helped defeat the School Prayer Amendment, which would have established mandatory school prayer in the public schools, with an impassioned speech on the Senate floor in defense of the separation of church and state. Every year after 1966 he introduced legislation to protect the privacy of federal employees, and in 1971 he initiated a congressional investigation that revealed massive and illegal domestic intelligence gathering by the military.

Ervin's privacy agenda expanded greatly with the advent of the Nixon administration in 1968. Although he agreed with most of the president's conservative positions—such as his handling of the Vietnam War and opposition to school busing—Ervin considered Nixon's law and order proposals to be both draconian and unconstitutional. He also thought that the administration's repeated attacks on the press and antiwar protestors signaled a basic lack of respect for constitutional rights. Ervin emerged as the leader of the congressional counteroffensive against Nixon's rapid expansion of executive power. The senator held hearings on the administration's impoundment of funds, expansion of domestic surveillance, pocket vetoes, and increasing claims of executive privilege.

The height of Ervin's career came during Watergate when he chaired the Select Committee on Presidential Campaign Activities, which became known as the Watergate Committee. The same conservative understanding of the Constitution that had led the senator to oppose civil rights and defend civil liberties had put him on a collision course with Nixon.

During the televised hearings in the summer of 1973 Ervin became known as "Senator Sam." With his old-fashioned manners, natural Southern drawl, white hair, big jowls, and bushy eyebrows that swept up and down his face in uncontrolled excitement, the seventy-six-year-old Ervin served as the perfect contrast to the slick, young, media-savvy bureaucrats from the Nixon administration who testified before him. By the end of the hearings, Ervin had become a folk hero and Nixon was on the road to resignation.

The senator managed to push several significant bills into law during his last year in the Senate, including the Privacy Act, the Speedy Trial Act, and the Presidential Recordings and Materials Preservation Act. Ervin fought civil rights programs, especially busing and affirmative action, to the very end of his career. He declined to run for reelection in 1974 and returned to Morganton, where he spent the next decade reading history, giving speeches, and writing. Ervin authored three books, including *Humor of a Country Lawyer, The Whole Truth: The Watergate Conspiracy,* and his autobiography, *Preserving the Constitution.*

Ervin died April 23, 1985, at the age of eighty-eight. The senator's paradoxical career reflected both the strengths and weaknesses of the traditional constitutionalism that dominated the political culture of North Carolina and the South during the twentieth century. Ironically, Ervin's reputation as a foe of civil rights, a protector of civil liberties, and a defender of the Constitution led politicians from both the left and the right of the political spectrum to praise him "as the last of the founding fathers."

Karl E. Campbell is an assistant professor of history at Appalachian State University, where he specializes in North Carolina history. He is a graduate of Warren Wilson College and earned his master's and Ph.D. degrees from the University of North Carolina at Chapel Hill.

For more information, see:
Ervin, Sam J., Jr. Papers. Ervin Family Papers. Southern Historical Collection, University of North Carolina at Chapel Hill.
Senator Sam J. Ervin Jr. Library. Western Piedmont Community College, Morganton.

Campbell, Karl. "The Last of the Founding Fathers: Senator Sam Ervin and the Road to Watergate." Ph.D. diss. University of North Carolina at Chapel Hill, 1995.
Clancy, Paul. *Just a Country Lawyer: A Biography of Senator Sam Ervin.* Indiana University Press, 1974.

O. MAX GARDNER

By Kim Cumber Andersen

T o CALL THE NAME of Oliver Max Gardner," once wrote Edwin Gill, Gardner's faithful secretary and later state treasurer, "is to invoke memories of great movements, great undertakings, great crusades —to feel again a sense of excitement and adventure —to hear his voice speaking out in good times and in dark days of depression.

"He was a statesman in agriculture, in finance, in industry, in education, and, of course, in government. To measure the power and usefulness of his life, one has to but imagine a North Carolina that never knew him—a state that lacked his magnificent leadership."

Gardner's remarkable career included public offices as legislator, lieutenant governor, governor, and in his later years, maker of governors. He was a confidant to President Franklin D. Roosevelt and a counselor on Wall Street. As a youth he worked on a cattle boat and was the only man to ever quarterback the football teams at both the University of North Carolina in Chapel Hill and its rival in Raleigh. As governor he guided North Carolina through the darkest years of the Depression by encouraging North Carolinians to grow their way out of hard times with home gardens and purchases from local farmers. At the same time, he reshaped state government to fit a reduced budget. When he died of a heart attack, he was on his way to the Court of St. James as America's new ambassador.

Born on March 22, 1882, in Shelby, Max was the youngest of twelve children. His father, Dr. Oliver Perry Gardner, had lost most of his wealth during the Civil War, and he supported the family as a country doctor and farmer. Max attended public schools in Shelby, played football, and worked at various jobs on the farm and in local textile mills, and clerked at a store. He was an ambitious youth. At fourteen his sisters found him orating and walking the floor of their home, and he explained that he had to perfect his delivery for the day he would become governor. Too young to serve in the Spanish-American War, he signed on as a teamster with the Second Illinois Regiment in Camp Cuba Libre in Jacksonville, Fla.

In 1899, Gardner won a scholarship to the North Carolina College of Agriculture and Mechanic Arts (later North Carolina State University). He viewed this as a personal milepost and never underestimated the power of giving throughout his life. Gardner earned

O. Max Gardner (Courtesy of N.C. Office of Archives and History)

a degree in chemistry in three years while achieving many academic awards and accolades and playing football. He subsequently taught chemistry for two years at A & M and read law with Richard T. Battle in Raleigh before entering the law school at the University of North Carolina, passing the bar in 1906. In the fall of that year he worked as a football coach at Hampden-Sydney College in Virginia, then returned home to practice law with his sister Ollie's husband, J. A. Anthony.

Living in Shelby, Gardner focused on his law career, often defending poor blacks in criminal court who paid in commodities when short on cash. On November 6, 1907, Gardner married Fay Webb of Shelby, daughter of Judge James Webb and niece of Congressman E. Yates Webb. The marriage created a bond of political families that would later shape state politics. For his generosity and willingness to help when it was unpopular to do so, many black citizens of Shelby pooled their resources and purchased a beautiful rocking chair for Gardner as a wedding present.

In 1908 he became active politically, making a speech in Madison County in support of prohibition. The same year he spoke out against Furnifold Simmons's political organization, which dominated North Carolina politics. Viewed as a political misstep by some, Gardner used the break to establish his independence in the Democratic Party. He was elected to the state senate in 1910, reelected in 1914 on a platform that included support for a statewide primary, and in 1916, at the age of thirty-three, he was elected lieutenant governor.

In 1920, Gardner led the balloting in the first primary for the Democratic nomination for governor but lost to Simmons's candidate, Cameron Morrison, in a fiercely contested second primary. Gardner returned to his law practice in Shelby, built up the business of his Cleveland Cloth Mill and his farm, and concentrated on his growing family, a daughter and three sons. The Gardners lived at Webbley, 403 South Washington Street, two doors down from Miss Fay's childhood home. That would remain their home during all their years in politics. In Miss Fay, Gardner had found a soul mate and a phenomenal political asset. The very embodiment of southern charm and grace, she had a keen intellect and personal charisma. Their home exuded hospitality and warmth.

Gardner was a man of immense faith, and he organized a popular Shelby institution, the Men's Bible Class at the First Baptist Church of Shelby. He taught the class often when he was in town, and his personal magnetism as well as his physical presence (he stood six-feet-two and weighed 225 pounds) and oratory skills brought members from all over the community. He prayed aloud in the morning, as he told Miss Fay not long after their marriage, "when he and the world had been renewed."

In 1928, Gardner was unopposed for the Democratic nomination for governor and easily won the election. He was the first post–Civil War governor not to run on a platform related to Reconstruction. Once in office, he began working for the Australian ballot, workers' compensation, and increased funding for schools. Unfortunately, the nation's economy was crumbling, and within a year many of his plans had been put on hold as North Carolina descended into the throes of the Great Depression.

Because of the Depression and partially in spite of it, Gardner subsequently won legislative approval of a sweeping reorganization of state government, proposed at his request by the Brookings Institution, which included an overhaul of financing for roads

and schools. It took the longest legislative session in the state's history to do it. His bills abolished the county chain gang system and gave the state full responsibility for building and maintaining roads. This greatly relieved the financial burden of local government, then deep in debt. He took great pride in the consolidation of the University of North Carolina in Chapel Hill, North Carolina State College in Raleigh, and the Woman's College in Greensboro under one executive, one board of trustees, and a coordinated education program that streamlined overlapping curricula. State salaries were cut each year of his administration, and the governor started with his own salary. He was careful, however, to see that no cut devastated any one segment of society or business.

Gardner fought the declining economy of the Depression and worked to help North Carolinians face reality while fostering confidence that in time and with sacrifice and faith, they would prevail. Edwin Gill later said: "Gardner had a way of inspiring others to great achievement. After conferring with him, people had more confidence in themselves. By some strange alchemy, he was able to give courage to those who were dispirited, and to restore confidence to those who were losing hope." He was in a position personally to call upon some powerful friends in the business world on behalf of the state. In 1932, when some of the state's outstanding bonds came due and the state was short of funds, Gardner personally visited New York bankers to assure creditors that North Carolina would not default. Bonds were renewed. He so impressed one of these bankers, Albert H. Wiggin, board chairman of the Chase Manhattan Bank, that Wiggin later retained Gardner as an attorney on the basis of their one meeting.

Serving before federal recovery efforts, Gardner created his own programs for relief. Since agriculture played a significant role in the lives of most North Carolinians, Gardner created the "Live-at-Home" program that encouraged families to "grow it, can it, eat it, sew it, make it, wear it at home." This program succeeded because it worked functionally and was marketed to North Carolinians at every level of society. Miss Fay even practiced "Live-at-Home" at the mansion. Foreshadowing Franklin Roosevelt a few years later, Gardner gave "fireside chats" on the radio to bolster the morale of the suffering common man. Schoolchildren, white and black, competed in "Live-at-Home" essay contests. Newspapers covered these activities, and the movement was the salvation of thousands of small farmers in 1931 and 1932.

Economic strife not only touched the farming community but manufacturing interests as well. Gardner negotiated agreements between mill owners and striking workers embroiled in bitter battles. While he did not sympathize with communists, he expressly recognized their rights under the law. He also responded to mill owners who called for the National Guard to impose order, but he criticized them for imposing unfair long hours and paying low wages. His efforts to personally hammer out equitable solutions and avoid further violence drew the attention of *Time,* which published an article on the governor's arbitration.

When Gardner left office in 1933, Franklin D. Roosevelt was in the White House and federal relief efforts were just being initiated. As he prepared to leave the Executive Mansion, Gardner told a reporter that he would not take anything for the honor of having been governor, but that he would not give fifteen cents to hold the job another four years. Gardner went home to rest before beginning a speaking tour on governmental reform. He subsequently opened a law practice in Washington, D.C., and began representing various New York firms referred to him by his old friend, Wall Street banker John Hanes.

Gardner had met Roosevelt in July of 1929 at a governors' conference in New London, Conn., when both were leaders of their respective states. Each spoke at the conference and Gardner was immediately struck by Roosevelt's presence. After Gardner began his Washington law practice, Roosevelt called on him often for consultation and for advice. When the United States experienced difficulty in negotiating a contract with air mail carriers, Gardner, who represented the Sperry Corporation and Curtiss-Wright, stepped in with Roosevelt's blessing, and brought order to the situation. Gardner later recalled that "from that day [in 1934] on I had made it as a Washington lawyer."

Gardner established the law firm of Gardner, Morrison and Rogers in 1937. He had been practicing with Fred Morrison practically since his arrival in Washington, and in 1936, George Rogers, a tax specialist from the Bureau of Internal Revenue, joined them. Gardner achieved great success and was retained by, among others, Sperry, Coca-Cola, Pan American, the Pennsylvania Railroad, and the Cotton Textile Institute. Gardner spent a great deal of time representing the Cotton Textile Institute in labor disputes. He was asked to become its president in 1935 but declined.

Gardner moved freely in both liberal and conservative circles as an attorney and a political force and by 1940 he wielded as much power politically as any man in the capital. His influence also was felt at home. His choice for a successor as governor, J. C. B. Eh-

ringhaus, was elected in 1932, and in 1936, Gardner's brother-in-law, Clyde R. Hoey, succeeded Ehringhaus. Gardner's son, Ralph, was a member of the General Assembly, and other members of the family were on the bench. These close relationships, combined with those associated with his wife's politically influential family, created what came to be known in political circles as the "Shelby Dynasty," a controlling influence in North Carolina politics for more than twenty years.

The Gardners divided their year between Shelby and their Washington residence in an apartment at the Mayflower Hotel in the heart of the city. Gardner worked behind the scenes advising, organizing, and negotiating projects as diverse as the Revenue Act of 1939 and the third-term inauguration's governors' reception. Gardner possessed the rare ability to advise and to act in politics and in his personal life with the "long view" in mind. His approach allowed him to differ with his associates on small points but still remain focused on common larger issues. During the war, Gardner served officially as chairman of the advisory board to the Office of War Mobilization and Re-conversion.

When Roosevelt died in April of 1945, Gardner grieved deeply. Their lives had been inextricably associated for more than fifteen years. They were born in the same year and possessed similar personalities. Both exuded unlimited personal charm, had a keen delight in playing the political game, had a great capacity for lasting, true friendship, and were men of great vision. Gardner lost a very important part of his life at the passing of Franklin Roosevelt. Less than a year later, he lost his son Decker to suicide.

He continued his law practice until appointed undersecretary of the treasury in 1946 by President Harry Truman. After the war, J. P. Stevens and Company bought the Cleveland Cloth Mill for more than $3 million and agreed to donate $75,000 to Gardner-Webb College. Suddenly, Gardner, a man who had never been obsessed with money, was a millionaire. He had a copy made of the deposit slip for the proceeds of the sale to Stevens and joked to Republican Russell Leonard: "This is the first time I have ever had any real money, and being completely solvent, I am wondering what I am going to do with it. I think you can trust me to be very careful at this stage. I have been tight so long and poor for so many years, that I will never be able to recognize that I am really solvent. I ought to give it to the Franklin D. Roosevelt Memorial. If it had not been for him, you and I would still be hewing wood and drawing water."

On October 19, 1946, Gardner attended the North

Carolina-Navy football game in Maryland with friends. While climbing the stadium steps, he experienced chest pains. He stayed for the game, but was afterwards diagnosed as having had a heart attack. He rested over the weekend but returned to work the first of the week. Six weeks later, Truman appointed Gardner ambassador to the Court of St. James. He was a savvy choice since the Republicans had gained control of Congress. Gardner was a trusted Democrat but was also highly respected by and friendly with many Republicans.

The Gardners left Washington for New York on February 3, 1947, on the first leg of their trip to London. Upon their arrival they enjoyed a banquet and several private meals with friends, and a send-off party was planned for February 6. On the evening of February 5, he and Miss Fay dined quietly with Mr. and Mrs. Fred Morrison, Ralph Gardner, and Mae Alexander. They retired to their room, where Gardner made a call to his old friend, Edwin Gill, saying, "I won't be gone for long." At about three in the morning severe chest pains awakened Gardner. The hotel doctor and heart specialist diagnosed a coronary thrombosis. Gardner died that morning.

Thomas Jefferson said that great reforms could never come unless those in authority seized the opportunity afforded by some great crisis, when the people are broken up and in a state of flux, to put into effect new policies and advanced ideas. Gardner seized this opportunity for North Carolina, and the state emerged from his administration more efficient and organized. Gardner was a statesman in North Carolina and in Washington, and, as Edwin Gill put it, "he had a rare ability . . . of looking at both friend and foe with the eye of a scientist. It is well known that Gardner was a staunch and loyal partisan in pol-itics, and yet this did not prevent him from seeing clearly the virtues and the abilities of such outstanding Republicans as Arthur Vandenberg of Michigan and Robert Taft of Ohio. Gardner's greatest achievement may have been the development of his own personality. . . . Gardner is infinitely greater than any one act of his. His life was a work of art. He was a very great person."

Kim Cumber Anderson is an archivist with the N.C. State Archives, where she has focused on reference as the correspondence archivist researching requests received by mail and e-mail from patrons across the state, the country, and the world.

For more information, see:

Gardner family manuscripts can be found at Gardner-Webb College, the Southern Historical Collection at the University of North Carolina at Chapel Hill, and the N.C. Office of Archives and History in Raleigh.

Dedmond, Francis B. *Lengthened Shadows: A History of Gardner-Webb College, 1907–1956.* Gardner-Webb College, 1957.

Gardner, O. Max. *Public Papers and Letters of Oliver Max Gardner, Governor of North Carolina, 1929–1933.* Ed. David Leroy Corbitt. Introduction by Allen Jay Maxwell. Council of State, State of North Carolina, 1937.

Gill, Edwin. "Oliver Max Gardner—The Man." Speech. North Carolina State College, 1953.

Lockmiller, D. A. *The Consolidation of the University of North Carolina.* Edwards and Broughton, 1942.

Morrison, Joseph L. *Governor O. Max Gardner: A Power in North Carolina and New Deal Washington.* University of North Carolina Press, 1971.

EDWIN M. GILL

By Steve Bouser

ESSE QUAM VIDERI. To many people, North Carolina's motto may seem odd and uninspiring. What is "To Be Rather Than To Seem" supposed to mean? But Edwin M. Gill, who was a fixture in state government for nearly half a century, must have understood it perfectly. He could even have taken it proudly as his own personal watchword.

To the casual observer, Gill appeared colorless and boring. He walked with a stoop and seldom smiled at strangers. Though colleagues say his presence could quietly dominate a room, his dour and droopy visage, with his lower lip thrust out like a fleshy shelf on which the rest of his hollow-eyed face sat, was as homely as a mule's. Never married, he spent the most productive thirty years of his life living alone in a room in Raleigh's Sir Walter Hotel, whose lobby was once the hub of political activity, where he was one of the last residents to leave the hotel before it closed. Quiet and methodical, he could appear infuriatingly set in his ways.

But with a man, as with a state, what mattered was not what he seemed but what he was. And what Edwin Gill was, in the words of U.S. Senator Sam J. Ervin Jr., was "as fine a public servant as North Carolina has ever known."

Gill left an indelible mark in both finance and the arts. He was described by admirers as a conservative in the best sense of the word. He understood what made North Carolina great, and he wanted to help conserve it. He liked to compare his own caution to that of the Tar Heel State itself, which was the last to come into the Union after the Revolution and the last to leave it at the time of the Civil War. Honesty, prudence, and regard for tradition lay as deep inside him as his bones. It was these qualities that served him through five decades of public service, including twenty-three years as state treasurer.

"We keep our house in order," Gill told a reporter for the *News and Observer* of Raleigh in 1962. "We don't go in for rash experiments." While that attitude may have frustrated younger underlings eager to keep the office up to date, it also consistently earned North Carolina the very highest credit ratings possible and won the enduring respect of nine governors.

Edwin Maurice Gill was born in Laurinburg on July 20, 1899, in a house that was later given to the town as a historic site. His grandfather had been the

Edwin M. Gill (Courtesy of Southern Historical Collection)

town's first mayor. He learned about business from his banker father, Thomas Jeffries Gill, and inherited a love of art and music from his mother, Mamie North Gill. His favorite childhood activities included drawing pictures, acting with his sister, Leila May, on a stage his father built in the attic, and playing the piano.

After attending local schools, he considered a career in the arts, studying for a time at the New York School of Fine and Applied Arts. But he then turned to law, entering Trinity College—later Duke University—in 1922. He passed the bar examination in 1924.

Gill returned to Laurinburg to begin a law practice, but he was drawn to public life. He won election to the state house of representatives in 1928 and again in 1930. His two terms straddled the stock market crash of 1929, which for many marked the end of an era of prosperity, and the beginning of the Depression. Living through that pivotal crisis affected him strongly. "It was the most valuable experience I ever had," he told an interviewer, "because the two General Assemblies were exactly opposite. It was the peak of the boom in 1929. The crash didn't come until October of that year. In the 1931 session, we were sliding toward the bottom of the Depression. That session was the longest one we had had until that time. We had fiscal problems."

The economic crisis prompted a number of far-reaching legislative changes. The state adopted the Workmen's Compensation Act; took over the maintenance of state highways, thus relieving local government to pay for other needs; assumed oversight of the public schools and consolidated many state government agencies, including the University of North Carolina. Gill underwent a crash training course in state government and further developed the no-nonsense fiscal philosophy that would strongly influence him for the rest of his life.

The competent and serious-minded young legislator caught the eye of Governor O. Max Gardner, who invited Gill to become his private secretary at the end of Gill's second term in the legislature. He remained in that post until the close of Gardner's term in 1933, furthering his education in politics and government and making contacts that would serve him well in future jobs. He later compiled the governor's letters and papers for publication and remained a close friend until Gardner's death in 1949.

"It's difficult for me to be objective about him," Gill later said of Gardner. "I have never served under a man who had a finer brain. He understood government and he understood people. . . . Among other things, he led us as we preserved the state's credit. We didn't default."

Gardner's successor, J. C. B. Ehringhaus, needed an able administrator to organize and head the newly created state Parole Commission. He picked Gill. During eight years in that job, Gill laid the groundwork for the parole system as it is known today. He was credited with creating a model agency that received national attention and was widely copied by other states.

Former associates on the Parole Commission remembered a boss who was a stickler for ethical principle and who required them to avoid even the appearance of impropriety. Service on the commission offered temptations such as free haircuts, meals, and car washes within the prison walls. But Gill warned against such conflicts of interest. "He told us that if he heard of us abusing any of those things, he would call us in and give us an opportunity to hand him our

resignations," a former commission employee once recalled. "He has always been that way, all through his years in public service."

Next came eight years as commissioner of revenue under Governors J. Melville Broughton and Gregg Cherry. Then, in 1948, the normally astute Gill found himself on the wrong side in the Democratic gubernatorial primary when the Gardner wing of the party was tossed from office by state Agriculture Commissioner W. Kerr Scott, who defeated Gardner's candidate, Charles Johnson. Gill entered a four-year exile from state government and spent a year in Washington, D.C., working for Gardner's law firm. The atmosphere in Washington had little appeal, and he could not wait to return to his home state. U.S. Senator Frank Porter Graham obliged by prevailing on President Truman to appoint Gill revenue collector for North Carolina, a position he held until 1953, when Governor William B. Umstead set Gill's life's course by appointing him to fill an unexpired term as state treasurer.

Gill held that office—literally and politically— without interruption until choosing to retire in 1976, at which time he could rival Secretary of State Thad Eure's claim of being "the oldest rat in the Democratic barn." Until he was forced to vacate his office because of renovations of the capitol in the early 1970s, Gill occupied quarters in the southeast corner of the old building, just steps from the side entrance to the governor's office, which he used often except during the term of Terry Sanford. Gill's conservative approach never suited Sanford, who had once been Gill's paperboy in Laurinburg.

Gill had "serious" opposition in only two elections during nearly a quarter century in the office. On one occasion he won ninety-eight of the state's one hundred counties and a mere ninety-seven on another. He once harbored ambitions to run for governor, but support for his candidacy never developed.

He was not the typical politician. All who knew Gill agreed that he didn't win the office of treasurer by slapping backs, shaking hands, kissing babies, or hatching deals in smoke-filled rooms. Rather, he did it by bringing the same attributes that an individual expects in his personal accountant to the business of looking after the state's fiscal affairs: conservatism, careful attention, and a kind of bedrock, unquestioned honesty. In fact, people took to calling him Mr. Integrity.

"In North Carolina," Gill once remarked, "we have made a habit of good government." It was a typically nonflamboyant utterance, but it caught on. Slightly altered, it became an advertising slogan for the state during the 1960s: "Good government is a habit in North Carolina." As treasurer, Gill contributed greatly to good government by creating an atmosphere of old-fashioned stability, predictability, and risk aversion in the handling of public money.

"We have had a slight departure (in fiscal policy) here and there," he said in 1962, "but the amazing thing has been the stability in government. That stability, in my opinion, is what gives us our triple-A rating. With all our fighting and inter-party and intra-party battles, we have had a minimum of politics when it came to finance. . . . Businessmen looking for a place to locate are far more interested in the stability of government, the predictability of the future, than in things like taxes."

Gill's stubborn resistance to change extended to wider areas of state government than fiscal matters. He opposed allowing governors to run for reelection, preferring the tried and true one-term limit. He was against joining other states in giving the governor a veto. And, as a "double-dipped Democrat," he discounted the notion that North Carolina might benefit from a two-party system.

Once he had the treasurer's office in shape, Gill turned his attention to other subjects, including his love of art. He took up painting as a hobby. He also continued his interest in music and was considered a respectable pianist and organist. He was deeply involved with the N.C. Museum of Art, serving as an active board member and as a director of the State Art Society. He was a pivotal figure in helping the museum move into its new quarters. When Samuel Kress offered to donate $1 million, if matched, for works of art for the museum, Gill pressed the General Assembly successfully for the appropriation. At the time, it was said to be the largest appropriation that any state legislature had approved for the purchase of art.

Gill took a great personal interest in obtaining works of art for the museum, traveling far and wide as a prime mover in the selection committee and refusing to accept any state funds in reimbursement for his expenses. Without notes, he could expound at length on the origin and significance of many of the paintings acquired. The museum's collection today bears his mark in every department.

Among the documents Edwin Gill left behind was the manuscript of an unpublished book. Called "Conversations at Monticello—1824," it centered on a long evening of discussion among old friends Jefferson, Madison, Monroe, and Lafayette. Though much of the imagined discourse turns on politics, considerable time is devoted to art and its importance in pub-

lic life. The words Gill put in the mouths of these great men might be taken to reflect his own philosophy.

"It is my opinion," Gill has Jefferson saying, "that the more our people come to know and appreciate the beautiful in life, the freer they will be. Whenever I see a great painting or hear beautiful music or read a stately poem, the spirit of liberty rises within my heart and I rededicate myself to the welfare of the human race, which has demonstrated the capacity to produce sublime and unforgettable things."

An avid reader and book collector who often devoured as many as two books a day, Gill also donated numerous valuable volumes to libraries around the state. He also put his hand to writing a novel, which was set around life in a major hotel in a state capital city.

"Edwin Gill was North Carolina's first renaissance man of the latter part of the twentieth century," said William Friday, the former president of the University of North Carolina system. "His emphasis on art and its significance, his strong advocacy of the symphony, his unyielding concern for public education, all were the hallmarks of his remarkable career. Few people have had as much influence on the cultural growth of North Carolina. He was indeed a noble servant of the people. Because he had no family, he chose to live this kind of life as his way of making himself useful. He created a legacy we all enjoy."

A staunch Methodist, Gill attended the Edenton Street Methodist Church in Raleigh, where he taught Sunday school. He received honorary degrees from Duke University and Campbell University.

When he retired in 1976, he said he would be satisfied to go down in history simply as a prudent treasurer. "Whatever contributions I have made," he said, "my greatest achievement has been to uphold the standards of integrity that have so long been the cornerstones of our state government." He died July 16, 1978, and he was buried in Scotland County.

Gill wrote no autobiography. But some of the words he attributes to the aging and lonely Jefferson near the end of his manuscript "Conversations at Monticello" may bear echoes of the author's own musings:

"My life has been lived under the blessings of a benign providence. . . . I cannot recall ever lacking the common necessities. Adequate food and shelter have been available to me for every single day of my life. Here at Monticello, I have been privileged to enjoy the turning of the seasons—the tenderness of spring, the opulence of summer, the crisp glory of autumn and the clean white snows of winter.

"Here I have had the joy of my fiddle and the companionship of books. . . . I was permitted to drink the wine of antiquity, to hear great music played, to see the paintings of great Masters, to engage in discussions with philosophers. Yes, as I look back tonight over a full and happy life, I would be justified in saying, 'My cup runneth over.'"

Steve Bouser has been the editor of the Pilot *of Southern Pines since August 1997. Previously he was editor of the* Salisbury Post *for eleven years and worked with the U.S. govern-**ment aid programs of assistance to independent media in the former Soviet Union, living in Russia and Washington and traveling extensively in Russia and Eastern Europe.*

For more information, see:

Gill, Edwin M. Papers. Southern Historical Collection, University of North Carolina at Chapel Hill.

Morrison, Joseph L. *Governor O. Max Gardner: A Power in North Carolina and New Deal Washington.* University of North Carolina Press, 1971.

LUTHER H. HODGES

By Edwin L. Rankin Jr.

Luther H. Hodges (Courtesy of Hugh Morton)

IT WAS a quiet Sunday morning, a cool fall day, in Leaksville (later Eden) at the residence of Luther Hartwell Hodges, the lieutenant governor of North Carolina. He was reading a newspaper when the telephone rang. The message was unexpected and stunning. The governor of North Carolina, William Bradley Umstead, was dead. Luther Hodges, a tenant farmer's son who had retired from a successful business career at age fifty-two to enter public service, was the new chief executive of North Carolina.

The date was November 7, 1954. William Umstead was North Carolina's only twentieth-century governor to die while in office, and Hodges was the only lieutenant governor to become chief executive through succession. Reaching the governor's office was another step forward in the saga of a boy born poor in material things but rich in spirit, character, and courage, whose ability, intelligence, ambition, and hard work brought him great success in business and industry. He never forgot that his success was made possible by the freedom and opportunity offered by America's democratic way of life.

Hodges was a sturdy, alert, and friendly man noted for his vigor in everything—his daily life, family, relationships with friends and business associates, work, travel, hunting and fishing, physical fitness, and leadership in Rotary International. A world-class salesman and marketing executive, he viewed his work, whatever it might be, as a challenge and joy. Radiating confidence and action, Hodges looked like the successful businessman he was: highly shined shoes, smartly tailored suit, starched white shirt, ruddy, genial face, and neatly trimmed white hair, usually topped with a soft fedora.

He was the first businessman to become governor in nearly seventy years. There had been fourteen lawyers and two farmers since Thomas M. Holt, an Alamance County textile manufacturer, was chief executive in 1893. Hodges was well aware that he had served less than two years as lieutenant governor, his first elective office, and was considered a political novice by many leaders of his Democratic Party.

By contrast, Governor Umstead had served in the Congress, both as a senator and a member of the House, and as state party chairman; and his strong, statewide campaign organization had led to his victory totally independent of Hodges, who was left out of planning the details of his legislative programs. Their relations were polite, proper, and distant for reasons puzzling even to close Umstead supporters.

After the formality of taking his oath of office, Hodges entered the governor's office in the capitol for the first time on November 10, 1954. It was approximately two months before the convening of the 1955 General Assembly and he was confronted with supporting Umstead's legislative program and budget recommendations, plus new critical developments, such as the May 17, 1954, landmark decision by the U.S. Supreme Court ending desegregation of public schools.

Following the Court decision, and after many consultations with North Carolina's judicial, legal, and political leaders, Governor Umstead had announced in a statement, which he had first carefully written on a yellow legal pad, that "the decision presents complications and problems and difficulties of immeasurable extent" but that North Carolina would obey the decision. He named Thomas J. Pearsall of Rocky Mount as chairman of a statewide study committee to study the Court decision and the existing dual school system and to make recommendations to the governor on how to proceed. Pearsall was a respected lawyer, businessman, and farmer who had served as speaker of the state house of representatives.

Hodges shared Umstead's views on the Court decision, quickly grasped the value of Pearsall's leadership, and asked him to continue as committee chairman. This early decision, among others, marked Hodges's ability to deal with public and political issues and problems at the highest level. The Pearsall Plan, later adopted by the General Assembly and then passed by the voters as a constitutional amendment, proved over time to be a valuable "safety valve," as

described by historian H. G. Jones, in dealing with such a volatile public issue. While its provisions were never used, it allowed the public schools to be gradually integrated without the violence or disruption that closed public schools in other states.

Hodges was the son of John James and Lovicia Gammon Hodges and was born in Pittsylvania County, Va., on March 9, 1898. He graduate from the University of North Carolina at Chapel Hill in 1919 and went to work in a Marshall Field textile mill near Leaksville. His career was meteoric. In 1940, he was transferred to New York, where he became a vice president of the company. Following his retirement from Marshall Field in 1947, he spent more than a year as chief of the industry division of the Economic Cooperation Administration (the so-called Marshall Plan) in West Germany.

After his government service he returned to Leaksville, and began to talk with friends about some kind of public service. He was being urged to be a candidate for president of Rotary International (where years later he did serve). A close friend and state political leader, B. Everett Jordan, steered him toward running for lieutenant governor. Hodges began traveling around the state, talking with former business associates, fellow Rotarians, county political leaders, and others.

He had some business cards printed with his name, hometown, and the words "Candidate for Lieutenant Governor," and carried them in his coat pocket but did not give one to anyone. Why? Perhaps for the first time in his life, he was shy. Could he ask strangers, as a personal favor, to vote for Luther Hodges? As a very successful salesman, it was easy for him to sell his company's products or services. As a politician seeking public office, he was the product and it was different—an unsettling experience.

On an early trip, after spending the night in a local motel, Hodges had breakfast alone at a small-town cafe. He noticed that the cashier was a large woman who appeared friendly, so after paying his bill he quickly handed her his campaign card and said, "I'm Luther Hodges from Leaksville. I'm running for lieutenant governor and would appreciate your vote." The cashier read his card, looked up at him, and said, with a smile, "Mr. Hodges, nobody running for lieutenant governor has ever asked for my vote. So I'll vote for you. Good luck!" The candidate left with a new spring in his step.

After Governor Umstead and Lieutenant Governor Hodges were inaugurated on January 8, 1953, Hodges came prepared for his new task as presiding officer in the state senate, then the lieutenant governor's principal duty. Feeling somewhat an outsider in the new administration, and certainly a newcomer to the Raleigh political scene, Hodges made a simple statement on his first day at work. He stopped at a florist shop, bought a white carnation, and pinned it to his lapel. "I needed it for my spirit," he said.

He wore one each day, and it soon became his symbol—crisp, white, and jaunty. It was always fresh, except during a long trip to the Soviet Union with a group of other governors, when he had to substitute an artificial carnation. It was eight years—twenty-two months as lieutenant governor and six years and two months as governor—later that he took the white carnation off his lapel as he left the Executive Mansion.

It is often said that the governorship is a job for three persons: one to carry out the constitutional and legislative responsibilities (run state government, answer the mail, etc.); one to travel the state, accepting invitations to attend and speak to hundreds of important meetings or conferences each year; and one to work on economic development and other major projects and programs building for the future. When Hodges became governor, he plunged in headlong, quickly adjusting to all new challenges as best he could.

He quickly established an open and productive relationship with the news media, including regular weekly news conferences. During those early months in office, he asked a former business associate who was visiting to observe. The visitor was impressed with the rapid-fire exchange, for an hour, of questions, answers, and comments, the television lights, microphones, and tension. The room was crowded with reporters and other news professionals representing daily and weekly newspapers, wire services, radio, and television stations.

Later Hodges's guest asked the governor: "Luther, how can you handle so many questions? How do you remember what you say, or said last time on so many different subjects?" The governor grinned and replied, "Well, if you tell the truth, you don't have to remember, do you?" While he certainly had his share of press critics, Hodges earned and held their respect, even when opinions clashed. One editorial cartoonist, Hugh Haynie of the *Greensboro Daily News,* dubbed him "Luther the Lion Heart" and that one stuck throughout his six years in the governor's office.

Hodges brought a businesslike approach to operating the governor's office. He had learned long ago the necessity of being organized to achieve the best results with his time and efforts. A skilled professional manager, he knew how to select staff, delegate

responsibilities, and expect results. He did his homework and expected others to do the same. Punctuality ranked high with him, along with honesty and hard work. He considered tardiness a discourtesy.

In the office, his schedule consisted of primarily fifteen-minute appointments. No personal business was conducted in the office. He took no coffee break, had a light lunch, and then went back to the office for more of his fast-paced schedule. He detested red tape but was a prodigious reader of essential mail and other information, which followed him to the mansion each night in a large wooden box. Early the next morning the box returned with his dictation disks, cryptic notes, comments, and directions. Everything to and from him was dated (and with the hour, if important). The letters he wrote were as brief as possible and his telephone conversations the same.

As governor, Hodges's remarkable success in dealing with his first legislature in 1955 launched a history-making six-year term, when he completed the term of William Umstead and then was elected easily to his own four-year term in 1956. Early in his administration, Hodges was shocked to receive a report from the U.S. Department of Commerce that listed North Carolina as forty-fourth among the then forty-eight states in per capita income. Doubting the results of the study, he had it checked and verified by President Gordon Gray of the Consolidated University of North Carolina. North Carolina's rank had not been misstated. It was clearly apparent to Hodges that low per capita income was North Carolina's major problem —"a bread-and-butter problem that affected everyone in the state and every aspect of its future. Our low economic state was an unhappy fact, and I determined to do what I could to improve it."

A man of ideas and action, he traveled thousands of miles each year and made hundreds of speeches to develop a statewide spirit of enthusiasm and support for economic development and growth. He strengthened the State Board of Conservation, appointed top business and professional leaders, and, among many projects, led them and other North Carolinians on successful industry-hunting trips to major U.S. cities and western Europe.

A lifelong Rotarian, Hodges believed in the Rotary motto, "Service Above Self," and used its unselfish appeal to recruit highly qualified people for appointments and jobs in state government. His open, unabashed love for his state brought positive response from within and without North Carolina. He could be very convincing to a leading business executive with this appeal, "You have done well in North Carolina and you need to repay your debt to your state by helping my administration do something worthwhile for others less fortunate."

He provided such vigorous, constructive leadership that North Carolina responded with tremendous growth and new vitality. Before he left office the state was hailed as the southeast's industrial and agricultural leader. A *National Geographic* magazine article documented in considerable detail the state's program and described North Carolina as the "Dixie Dynamo."

A consummate salesman, Hodges loved to travel and work directly with people. In 1955, for example, he traveled 44,927 miles by automobile, airplane, train, helicopter, ship, and motor grader (the only transport available during a hurricane on the coast). A keen sense of humor was one of his greatest assets. He never forgot his humble beginnings and how he struggled to succeed, and realized the danger of taking himself too seriously. A natural showman, he was also a talented storyteller who used funny experiences, often his own, to illustrate his remarks or lighten the mood of the audience.

The North Carolina Trade and Industry Mission in 1959 told the state's story of economic opportunity to 1,600 European business, industrial, and political leaders. Hodges and sixty-eight business leaders, who paid their own expenses, covered ten major European cities in fourteen days in what may have been the first such intensive industrial trade mission by an American state. It was so successful that it became a model for later North Carolina missions that followed. (In the same year, Hodges was one of nine governors to make an unprecedented tour of the Soviet Union in the midst of the cold war.)

Under his dynamic leadership, the state's revitalized industrial development program resulted in more than $1 billion of new and expanded industry. From the start, Hodges sought only sound growth from reputable, diversified industries looking for economic opportunity. There were no state or local handouts. More than two hundred local industrial development organizations and many chambers of commerce worked enthusiastically and effectively to build better communities as part of the North Carolina program.

While the state industrial development program was successful, it had its share of problems in dealing with communities in one hundred counties. All wanted new industries, new jobs, and economic growth. At the dedication of a new highway bridge in eastern North Carolina, Hodges was introduced by the local mayor, who concluded with these words: "Governor, we are grateful for the new bridge but we want you to bring us a new industry."

Hodges was not amused. He thanked the mayor for his kind words, then turned and spoke directly to him: "Mr. Mayor, I can't bring your town a new industry. The state of North Carolina cannot bring your town a new industry. We are doing all we can to tell the North Carolina story of economic opportunity as widely as possible in the nation and the world. But when an industrial or business prospect shows an interest in our state, and indicates all its requirements for a new plant location, the point of sale is here in your town or elsewhere in North Carolina. Can you provide available land, skilled people, utility services, good schools, vocational training, health facilities, roads and streets, housing and all it takes to attract new residents and families? Your community must be prepared to close the sale."

Always receptive to new ideas, Hodges gave his leadership, support, and boundless enthusiasm to the Research Triangle Park when it was merely the germ of an idea. Without his early and determined support, this unique and complex North Carolina project, involving North Carolina State University, Duke University, and the University of North Carolina at Chapel Hill, may not have survived.

It was a far-reaching—some critics said completely impractical—idea that the scientific brains and research talents of the three universities, two state-owned and one private, could work together and with fiercely competitive private industries for the benefit of the state and nation. The governor said the Research Triangle was "a marriage of North Carolina's ideals of higher education and its hopes for material progress." Again, it was Hodges's ability to attract and convince state, national, and international leaders in business, industry, and government of the enormous potential and value of what has now become a world-renowned research park.

This tenant farmer's son and novice politician became best known as the "Businessman in the Statehouse." During his years in office, he won increased appropriations for public schools, higher education (especially faculty salaries), mental hospitals, schools for the mentally handicapped, and a revitalized program for juvenile delinquents. He created the Department of Administration in state government to coordinate and consolidate all fiscal and planning operations, as well as a Board of Higher Education to coordinate the growing ambitions of the state's colleges and universities. He helped develop a statewide system of vocational centers to train youths and adults in new industrial skills. The centers were so successful they proved to be the precursor of the state community college system that was established in 1963.

Hodges reorganized the state highway department by bringing the state highway fund directly under state budget control, replaced the full-time appointed chairman with an executive-administrator (a professional with experience in engineering, planning, and administration), and made a valiant effort to have construction and maintenance of all secondary roads based on an objective formula (traffic density, houses served, school bus routes, etc.) At his urging, the legislature also removed the prison system from under highway commission control, and created the state department of corrections. North Carolinians from all walks of life were inspired to contribute their time and money to many worthwhile public projects and programs, including the N.C. Museum of Art and various study commissions seeking answers to many vexing public and government problems.

While Luther Hodges was recognized for his many successes and achievements, six years as governor taught him some bitter lessons about public office. His decisions or courses of action did not always endear him to his critics. He had his share of enemies—in the political arena and the press—and they were quick to point out his failures, actual or perceived.

The Harriet-Henderson Textile Mills strike in 1958, when one thousand members of the Textile Workers Union of America walked out of two mills in Henderson, was one such lesson. Local law enforcement could not contain the violence, and Hodges and state government were soon involved in efforts to maintain the peace and attempt to mediate with management and union. From the beginning, Hodges, a former textile company executive, was suspect in the eyes of members and supporters of the union. As the strike and its problems escalated, it gained state and national attention.

Later, Hodges wrote, "I consider the Henderson strike and its aftermath the most tragic single matter to confront me during my administration as governor. The violence there was terrible and out of context for a developing industrial state like North Carolina. It cast a pall over practically the entire 1959 General Assembly and necessitated my sending in first the highway patrol and then the National Guard to preserve the peace. It was my responsibility as governor to maintain law and order and to have no fa-

vorites. That rule I followed during the Henderson strike and its aftermath."

When President-elect John F. Kennedy announced that Hodges was his choice for secretary of commerce, organized labor announced its opposition because of his involvement in the strike. He served successfully in the Kennedy administration, and following Kennedy's assassination, continued in President Lyndon Johnson's cabinet.

Hodges and his wife of forty-seven years, Martha, returned to North Carolina from Washington and bought a home in Chapel Hill. He took over the promotion of the Research Triangle Park as a "dollar-a-year" man. A tragic fire at their home caused Martha's death on June 25, 1969. Hodges suffered from smoke inhalation and minor injuries but survived. He died in Chapel Hill, on October 6, 1974, and was survived by his three children, grandchildren, and second wife, Louise Finlayson Hodges.

Hodges's son, Luther Jr., was one of the rising leaders of North Carolina National Bank (later Bank of America) when he resigned to run for the U.S. Senate in 1976. His campaign was unsuccessful and he subsequently left North Carolina to return to banking in Washington, D.C. He later retired to New Mexico.

Edward L. Rankin Jr. of Concord is a writer whose career in public relations and public affairs spanned fifty years and included senior appointive positions with governors William B. Umstead, Luther Hodges, and Dan K. Moore. He was inducted into the N.C. Public Relations Hall of Fame in 1989.

For more information, see:
Crabtree, Beth G. *North Carolina Governors.* N.C. Division of Archives and History, 1958.
Hodges, Luther H. *Businessman in the Statehouse.* University of North Carolina Press, 1962.
Morton, Hugh M., and Edward L. Rankin Jr. *Making A Difference in North Carolina.* Lightworks, 1988.
Patton, James W., ed. *Messages, Addresses, and Public Papers of Luther Hartwell Hodges.* N.C. Council of State, Raleigh.
Rankin, Edward L., Jr., ed. *A Governor Sees the Soviet: Letters from Governor Luther H. Hodges of North Carolina.* Privately published, 1959.

CAMERON MORRISON

By Lydia Charles Hoffman

"THE WHITES WILL RULE the Land or Die" read a banner carried by a Confederate veteran as he walked down the main street of Rockingham in 1898. Daniel M. Morrison, who organized the protest "in defense . . . not for aggression" against perceived "Negro domination," moved in step with the former soldier, along with dozens of other fellow veterans dressed in their customary red shirts. They marched in support of Daniel's son, Cameron, who was running for the state senate and had vowed to help reclaim the governmental body from the Populists and Republicans who were feared to be "taking over" the senate after the 1894 elections.

The elder Morrison was a recent convert to the Democratic Party. In fact, in 1890 he and his son had traveled to Raleigh, where "Cam" had served as a delegate to the state Republican convention. The Republican Party, the party of Abraham Lincoln, had supported political integration after the Civil War, but the Morrisons, like many small-time farmers and laborers in North Carolina, voted Republican, not in support of political equality between whites and blacks, but because they disliked the large landowners and oligarchs who dominated the Democratic Party in the postwar era. As fusion politics began to gain steam and blacks trickled into political offices and started to exercise their rights as citizens, many Republicans joined the white supremacy campaigns of the Democrats. The younger Morrison, at age twenty-two, denounced the Republican Party of his father "to follow where my honest convictions have for some time dictated. I will henceforth loyally support the Democratic Party." It is this Cameron Morrison who typified the evolution of politics in North Carolina and who led the state to become one of the more progressive southern states of the 1920s.

Cameron Morrison was born in Rockingham on October 5, 1869. His father was the son of Scottish immigrants who had settled in the western part of the state. His mother, Martha, was the daughter of John Worthy Cameron, an influential man in local and state politics who was elected to the General Assembly. Young Cameron attended the local rural school until his mother died when he was eight years old. To lessen the burden of raising four children under one roof, Daniel Morrison sent Cameron to Ellerbe Springs in Richmond County to attend a small school

Cameron Morrison (Courtesy of N.C. Office of Archives and History)

run by N. C. McCaskill. Cameron earned his board by working on a local farm because his father, an itinerant carpenter and contractor, could not support both his family and his son's private education.

Cameron returned to Rockingham in 1886 to help his father care for the family and to complete his studies. Although he dreamed of attending college, family finances made it impossible. After acquiring all the formal education local schools could offer, Cameron worked full-time in an assortment of jobs around Richmond County. He clerked at the register of deeds office, taught at a variety of free schools, and served as a postal clerk. After four years of switching occupations, Cameron decided to pursue a career in the law.

In 1890 Morrison moved to Greensboro to study under Judge Robert P. Dick. After two years of instruction, he passed the bar and began to practice law in North Carolina. In 1892, he returned to Rockingham, where he made his first campaign speech, and was elected mayor in 1893. He remained in his hometown until 1905, when, at age thirty-six, he moved to Charlotte, his home until his death in 1953.

In 1905 Morrison married Lottie May Tomlinson of Durham, an educated woman ten years his junior. Only one of their children, a daughter, Angelia, survived infancy. In Charlotte, Morrison practiced law and continued to be active in Democratic politics. He declined an appointment to the superior court, stating that he was "too fond of the stirring contests of life." He served one term in the state senate in 1900 and frequently functioned as platform chairman for state party conventions. In 1918, Morrison threw his hat into the ring for the governor's office.

It has been argued that the state had only one political party during this era, the Democratic Party, and Morrison proved to be an active member of one of the most stalwart Democratic "machines" in it. Although unified in name, the party was divided along ideological and economic lines: conservatives, led by U.S. Senator Furnifold M. Simmons, generally favored industrial interests (tobacco, textile, and railroad transportation), while liberals supported lowland farmers and piedmont workers.

Fusion politics had strengthened the conservatives' position as the state rallied to remove Populists and Republicans and to disfranchise blacks. Simmons, more than any other individual Democrat, organized the conservatives, with relentless attention to developing and molding young Democratic leaders. Moreover, his adroit application of the white supremacy issue earned him and those he endorsed success on election day. The Simmons organization helped elect Governor Charles B. Aycock in 1900 and his successor Robert Glenn. In 1912, not only was Simmons reelected to his seat in the Senate, but his brand of politics produced another conservative gubernatorial winner, Locke Craig. Thomas W. Bickett maintained the machine's hold on the state's executive branch in 1916, and Morrison hoped to be the next in line when he announced his candidacy in 1918.

However, in 1919 tragedy in the Morrison household placed Simmons's dominance of the governor's mansion in jeopardy. After a short illness, Lottie May Morrison died in November of that year. The grief-stricken candidate took to his bed for three months, worrying his supporters that Lieutenant Governor O. Max Gardner would run away with the nomination. Gardner's campaigning as a progressive leader of "young Democracy" had won him the praise of the *News and Observer* and the *Winston-Salem Journal,*

and though he did not have the support of Simmons, he seemed to be the decided choice as the next nominee. Gardner's efforts on behalf of William W. Kitchin's run for Simmons's seat in 1910 had placed him in bad standing with the machine. In order to block Gardner from winning the nomination in 1920, Simmons worked to bring Morrison out of seclusion.

Simmons and his associates played on Morrison's temperamental, impulsive, and emotional disposition. His debilitating depression after his wife's sudden death was evidence of a sensitive nature, a characteristic detractors would often use against him. To provoke Morrison to action, Simmons sent word of his intention to support Gardner unless Morrison reactivated his campaign. The gambit worked, and the fifty-year-old Morrison reapplied himself to winning the nomination for governor. He survived the first primary contest by fewer than a hundred votes but won the second primary by a wide margin.

Morrison's platform aligned nicely with the agenda of Simmons's conservative wing. As an outspoken participant in the Red Shirt campaign of 1898, Morrison had already proven his loyalty to the white supremacy movement. Now, by advocating restrictions on immigration, disfranchisement of Negroes, and opposition to women's suffrage, Morrison exploited the fears and won the support of rural and urban white North Carolinians. Simultaneously, he positioned himself as an "old-fashioned Southern Democrat" who would remain faithful to Governor Bickett's progressive program for improved educational and welfare systems, the building of "good roads," and the growth of industry. Unlike traditional progressives, who focused on obtaining political democracy, corporate regulation, and social justice, Morrison focused on building North Carolina's public services. As one historian has noted, this concern for "development rather than reform" typified a certain sort of 1920s Southern progressive.

Morrison's legacy to the state was the expansion of state support of public services. His inaugural speech denounced the piecemeal roads program of Bickett and called for a comprehensive road system that would replace well-worn dirt pathways with hard-surface roads. This program was funded by millions in highway bonds, to be repaid by a penny-a-gallon gasoline tax (raised to three cents per gallon in 1923), automobile license fees, and the federal government. Morrison reorganized the highway commission to oversee construction and maintenance of the new road system, placing Frank Page Jr. at the helm. Morrison delighted in showing off his new roads program to dignitaries from Australia, Italy, and Japan who came to North Carolina to study construction techniques. By the time he left office in 1925, 6,200 miles of North Carolina's roads had been repaired or vastly improved, with 1,480 miles resurfaced or under contract to be upgraded.

Financing the governor's plan for new school construction was more problematic. Under North Carolina's constitution, its construction fund could not be used to build new schools. Schools were supported by local property taxes, but these could not pay for new buildings, the extension of the school year to six months, or a teachers' pay raise, the latter two approved by the General Assembly in 1920. Although disturbed by this fiscal conflict, Morrison remained true to the state's obligation to teachers. The 1921 General Assembly passed an appropriations act of $7 million that helped the state Department of Public Instruction remain solvent and pay teachers, but it was the state Supreme Court's decision in *B. R. Lacy v. Fidelity Bank of Durham* that had Morrison literally sobbing with relief. Under this ruling, counties could incur debt for school construction without the consent of registered voters, thus loosening funds to improve the infrastructure of public education.

Morrison's vision to improve the educational system continued in the tradition of former governor Charles Aycock. Said Morrison, "I am trying to write the dreams of Aycock into action." Both believed that by providing a solid statewide educational program, North Carolinians would be better prepared to participate in the expanding industrialized economy.

During Morrison's term in office, total school expenditures and student per capita spending nearly doubled. Student enrollment rose from 619,000 to 810,000, and the number of teachers increased from 16,800 to 22,340. The University of North Carolina appropriations budget doubled, while that of the Woman's College (later the University of North Carolina at Greensboro) nearly tripled. Frank Porter Graham later recalled that the governor had once divulged to him that Morrison's "own inability to go to college. . . . later found compensation in his campaign to open wider the doors of the overcrowded university and colleges of North Carolina."

There were many who complained about the costs incurred by Morrison's development programs. Detractors criticized him for moving too fast, citing his attempt to complete in four years an eight-year plan to build new roads, expand the school system, and improve the quality of health services and penal institutions. When Morrison left office in 1925, North Carolinians owed $8.2 million in improvement costs, although an independent audit attributed $1.3 million

to Bickett's administration. However, this was a small sum compared to the benefits to North Carolinians: $65 million worth of new roads, $5 million spent on improving children's education, and $20 million spent to upgrade both penal and mental health facilities to a human standard.

Morrison's record on social issues was not as strong. Although he worked at improving the quality and quantity of schools, his conservative upbringing affected what was taught. As an ex officio chairman of the state Board of Education and an avid antievolutionist, he voted against the use of any biology texts that taught Darwin's theory of evolution, declaring that there is no room for "monkey business" in the public schools. He was indifferent to workers' compensation legislation and did not propose one significant bill or plan in favor of labor during his four years in office. Yet during a 1921 textile strike he said he believed that the workers had the right to picket, and he remained neutral during the confrontation.

Morrison maintained that the state would provide educational opportunities and other public services to African American citizens, but that all institutions should be segregated by race. During his administration, the Division of Negro Education within the Department of Public Instruction was established to hear the concerns and needs of African American schools. North Carolina College for Negroes (later North Carolina Central University) received a substantial budget increase in 1923. He told blacks in the state to "make yourselves so you need more schools and North Carolina will have them ready for you."

During his last year in office, Morrison suffered his first major legislative defeat as governor. He proposed the state build a state-owned shipping line and improve North Carolina's port terminals and commercial waterways in order to provide an alternative to rail transportation, but the plan did not find favor with his constituents. He argued that such an investment would allow the state to offer lower freight rates from New York, Philadelphia, and Baltimore and increase North Carolina's revenue. Port expansion could also stimulate growth of a "half dozen cities" on the eastern shore of the state and inland waterways. Although the General Assembly supported Morrison's proposal by approving a $2 million bond referendum, there were those who opposed the state's intrusion on privately owned shipping companies. There was also a geographical problem—only Wilmington, Southport, and Morehead City had deepwater harbors. In the end, North Carolinians voted down the proposal as too experimental and too costly.

At the end of his term, Morrison returned to Charlotte with a new wife. In 1924, he married Mrs. Sarah Watts, the wealthy widow of George Washington Watts of Durham. Along with the Dukes, Watts was one of the founders of the American Tobacco Company. The new Mrs. Morrison provided the means for her husband to live out his life as a gentleman farmer and reader of good literature—a favorite avocation. Their farm on the southern edge of Charlotte, purchased with "my wife's money, of course," was called Morrocroft and began as a 160-acre model dairy farm. By the 1940s the estate had expanded to include more than four thousand acres.

Morrison never really retired from politics. In 1930 Governor O. Max Gardner appointed him to complete the term of U.S. Senator Lee S. Overman, who died unexpectedly that year. Morrison was defeated for election to a full term in 1932 by Robert Reynolds of Asheville, who ridiculed Morrison's wealth and high-tone lifestyle. Twelve years later, at the age of seventy-three, Morrison was elected to Congress from the Tenth District but fell into disfavor with some of his conservative cronies for his support of President Roosevelt.

While vacationing with his grandson in Quebec in August 1953, the "Squire of Morrocroft" suffered a fatal heart attack in his hotel room. He was eulogized as the progressive "good roads" governor, although he preferred to be known for his contributions to education and institutional reform.

The land surrounding Morrison's beloved Morrocroft eventually became the site of some of Charlotte's finest neighborhoods and commercial locations. The property was developed by Morrison's son-in-law, James J. Harris, who carefully picked customers for the prize land. One of the first to build there was Celanese Corporation, which installed a research facility in the late 1960s where Morrison's black angus cattle once grazed. Later, Harris sold just over a hundred acres to Belk Brothers Company, which along with its downtown rival, Ivey's department stores, created the state's first regional shopping mall, South-Park, which opened in the early 1970s. The mall became the anchor for further development and by the end of the century, SouthPark had more than 400,000 shoppers visit each month.

Harris, who died in 1985 at the age of seventy-

eight, also created the James J. Harris and Company insurance agency. He served as chairman of numerous civic organizations and was always quietly active in civic, religious, and cultural organizations in Charlotte, including the YMCA, the expansion of Charlotte Memorial Hospital (later Carolinas Medical Center), and the Morrison Chapel at Covenant Presbyterian Church. He also provided support for numerous scholarships at the University of North Carolina at Charlotte and at Queens and Davidson colleges.

The James J. Harris and Angelia M. Harris Foundation charitable trust was established in 1984. The Harris children, Sara (Mrs. H. C. Bissell), Cameron, and John W., carried on the family tradition of community leadership and real estate sales and development, including Ballantyne, a two-thousand-acre office, residential, and resort community south of Charlotte.

Lydia Charles Hoffman is a former director of the Charlotte Hawkins Brown Historic Site. She received her B.A. in history from the University of California at Berkeley and her M.A. in history from the University of North Carolina at Chapel Hill. While completing doctoral work in cultural studies at George Mason University, she worked in the Smithsonian Institution's National Museum of American History affiliations program department.

For more information, see:

Morrison, Cameron. Clipping Collection. North Carolina Collection, University of North Carolina at Chapel Hill.

Abrams, Douglas Carl. "A Progressive-Conservative Duel: The 1920 Democratic Gubernatorial Primaries in North Carolina." *North Carolina Historical Review* 55, no. 4 (October 1978).

Graham, Frank Porter. *Cameron Morrison: An Address by. . . .* Privately printed, 1956.

Magruder, Nathaniel Fuqua. "The Administration of Governor Cameron Morrison of North Carolina, 1921–1925." Ph.D. diss., University of North Carolina at Chapel Hill, 1968.

Richardson, William H., and D. L. Corbitt, eds. *Public Papers and Letters of Cameron Morrison, Governor of North Carolina, 1921–1925.* Edwards and Broughton Company, 1927.

HUGH MC. MORTON

By Ralph Grizzle

Hugh Morton (Courtesy of Hugh Morton)

ONE BRIGHT JUNE DAY, Hugh Morton drove to the top of his Grandfather Mountain. As he gazed at the valley below and the distant mountains to the west, a pair of ravens rode the wind currents off the rocky precipice across the Mile High Swinging Bridge. Diving and rising without flapping a single beat, the two dark dots silently stroked the still blue sky with their gentle gliding.

It wasn't clear whether Morton was simply amused by the ravens' aerobatics or lulled into a sense of serenity by their peaceful flight, but he declared he could sit and watch them all day long. It was a nice thought, but an odd one, considering that it was coming from a man who seldom seemed to sit anywhere for long. Morton was, above all, a man on the move. Whether he was pitching in for a good cause, or promoting

the mountain and the state that he loved so dearly, Morton was always on the go. And as he neared his eightieth birthday, he showed no signs of slowing down. He continued to be driven by a lifelong mission: to make sure that all are able to gaze upon the glories of what he regarded as the true treasures of our state.

That explained, of course, why Morton traveled with a camera in tow for six decades, snapping photos of the state's treasures, why he fought to save the battleship *North Carolina* and the Cape Hatteras Lighthouse (though in its historic location), why he battled to keep the Blue Ridge Parkway from going over his mountain instead of around it, and why he fought to save the western North Carolina mountains from industrial polluters beyond the state's borders. (In 1948,

Morton also was among a group of business and civic leaders who conceived the original North Carolina Azalea Festival, which remained the largest annual event in the state. Morton quipped that he was "out of town" during one of the organization meetings and returned to find that he had been elected president.)

"Hugh Morton is North Carolina's greatest promoter," his good friend Charles Kuralt remarked when Morton was honored with the North Caroliniana Society Award for 1996. "Always, however, of things that ought to be celebrated."

Among the many public roles Morton played: He was chairman of the state advertising committee and president of the N.C. Travel Council. He received the Charles Parker Award, handed out only to those who have performed a great service for North Carolina tourism. In the 1950s, Morton was part of the team that elected Luther Hodges governor and thirty years later he performed yeoman service for former governor Terry Sanford when he ran successfully for the U.S. Senate in 1986. For years he was a delegate to the Democratic Party's national convention and he once tried a political campaign of his own. But after a few months on the trail asking folks to support his bid for governor in 1972, he called it off.

"John Harden, who was the private secretary for Governor Cherry, once told me that no matter who you are—a plumber, a carpenter or whoever—you owe something to the industry that you're part of and that you need to give something back," Morton says. So for the better part of his life now, Morton has been giving something back to the state he loves so much.

Hugh MacRae Morton was born in Wilmington on February 19, 1921, son of Julian Walker and Agnes MacRae Morton. The boy spent winters in Wilmington, where he attended Episcopal High School, and summers in Linville. "Every summer of my life, except the three when I was in Uncle Sam's Army, I've spent here in the mountains," Morton says. "When I was four months old, I was brought to Linville."

Between 1885 and 1892, Morton's maternal grandfather, Hugh MacRae, purchased sixteen thousand acres in the mountains. He founded Linville as a new mountain community and built eighteen miles of stagecoach road to connect it to Blowing Rock in 1891. (The state came along later, paved the road without straightening a single curve, and called it U.S. Highway 221.) The town never developed as he imagined, but Linville's hotel, the Eseeola Inn, became a popular mountain retreat for southerners.

At age thirteen, Morton attended Camp Yonahnoka and became the camp photographer. As a student at the University of North Carolina at Chapel Hill, he applied his newly acquired talent as a photographer for the *Daily Tar Heel,* the student-run newspaper, and *Yackety Yack,* the campus yearbook. In the years since, his pictures have graced the pages of *National Geographic, Life, Sports Illustrated, Time, Esquire,* the *Associated Press,* and many other publications. "What distinguished me as a photographer," Morton said, "was that I knew how to take my pictures to the mailbox."

In 1942, Morton left behind Chapel Hill to tour the South Pacific, courtesy of the U.S. government. A combat motion picture photographer for the Signal Corps, Tech Sergeant Morton earned a Purple Heart to go with his Bronze Star, when he and his company were injured at the mouth of a booby-trapped cave. The explosion destroyed his camera and sent rocks into his body, leaving a deep scar on his left arm and one on his chin.

Returning home, Morton went to work as a photographer for UNC Sports Information Director Jake Wade. At seventy-nine, Morton was still working as a sports photographer for Carolina basketball and could be found at the end of the court with his younger colleagues. "I'll continue to do it as long as I can," Morton said, noting that his knees occasionally gave him trouble after crouching for long periods.

During his six-decade career, Morton photographed such sports greats as Charlie "Choo Choo" Justice and Michael Jordan. Morton also captured on film a number of U.S. presidents, Thomas Wolfe's mother, Bob Hope, General Douglas MacArthur, Johnny Cash, Billy Graham, Sam Ervin Jr., Andy Griffith (when he played the *Lost Colony* role of Sir Walter Raleigh for six years before going on to greater fame), Queen Elizabeth, and, of course, Mildred the Bear.

Bears were dear to Morton's heart, especially Mildred, who came to Grandfather when she was two. "The trouble with Mildred was that she thought she was human," Morton said. Once, when another bear attacked an employee, Mildred came to the rescue, baring teeth and claws to scare the assailant. "There were no other people around," Morton said. "The fellow screamed for help, and Mildred came running. He swore until the day of his death that Mildred had saved his life."

In 1952, Morton inherited Grandfather Mountain when the family elected to divide the family property following his grandfather's death. Morton had spent much of his youth photographing landscapes and wildlife on Grandfather, so the family thought it right that the 4,500-acre tract around Grandfather Mountain be passed along to him. "They knew how much

I loved Grandfather Mountain, so I think the other members of the family wanted it to come to me," Morton said.

As the new owner, Morton extended the road to the crest of the mountain and built the Mile High Swinging Bridge, making the mountain one of North Carolina's top scenic attractions. "I was president of the family company, which was the Linville Company, and I had been urging them to go on up another mile and do what I eventually did, but they didn't want to spend the money," Morton said. "Grandfather Mountain wasn't making any money then. So when it came to me, I just did what I had been urging them to do all along."

From the start, Morton considered his role to be that of a steward of the land, working hard to preserve its natural beauty. Toward that end, Morton parceled out land, in the form of conservation easements, to the Nature Conservancy. Under the jurisdiction of this private, international conservation group, nearly three thousand of Grandfather Mountain's four thousand acres were protected from development, thus prohibiting the construction of roads and structures, ever. Fully 1,776 acres of the easements form what is known as an International Biosphere Reserve. Grandfather Mountain, one of the most biologically diverse spots in the nation, is the only private peak in the world to receive this designation.

In the early 1950s, Morton opened a long battle with the U.S. Park Service, which began when the service proposed a toll on the Blue Ridge Parkway. With twenty-five U.S. highways crossing the parkway and more than six hundred entry points, toll collection would have been inefficient. Moreover, cars would have had to stop so that the drivers could be identified as having paid. "Tourists would have been so mad at the state of North Carolina that they would never travel the parkway again," Morton said.

Governor Luther Hodges appointed Morton chair of a committee to build public opposition against the toll. "We did a good job," Morton said. "There wasn't any question. Everybody in the mountains was against it." The idea was sidelined; the Park Service disgruntled.

Following the parkway toll fight, the Park Service proposed a route across the top of Grandfather Mountain to complete a missing link of the parkway around the mountain. "I think they [the Park Service] really just wanted to get even with me," Morton says, "even though our family had already sold them eight miles of right-of-way, 1,000-feet wide, for a song, $25,000. It really was just a token payment."

Running a road over the top of Grandfather would be like "taking a switchblade to the Mona Lisa," he told the Park Service. "It would be conquering a mountain that didn't deserve to be conquered with cuts and fills of that nature." But the Park Service refused to use the right-of-way it had purchased along U.S. 221. "I said I would agree to a compromise route if they would stay down to a reasonable level," Morton said. "I told them I would donate the land for the so-called middle route, but I absolutely would not agree to the high route."

The battle continued for a dozen years, but Morton finally prevailed, arguing that Grandfather Mountain had already provided what the law required. His victory resulted in the Linn Cove Viaduct at Grandfather Mountain. The engineering marvel, modeled after structures in the French and Italian Alps, clings to the side of Grandfather Mountain and has won a dozen national awards for its aesthetic design.

Morton always had an aesthetic sensibility. That showed in the many photos he snapped over the years. In pursuit of his passion, in 1950 Morton became chairman of the Southern Short Course in News Photography. "North Carolina was at the absolute bottom of the scale at the time [with regard to photographic quality]," Morton said. "Soon after we started the course, our folks began to get jobs with *National Geographic* and *Life*. I like to think that these programs we've sponsored have done a lot to raise the standard of news photography in this part of the world." The program continued at various campuses across North Carolina and summers on Morton's mountain as the Grandfather Mountain Camera Clinic.

In 1989, Morton published four hundred of his own photographs in a book, *Making a Difference in North Carolina,* coauthored by Edward L. Rankin Jr. The inside flap on the dust jacket shed light on the difficulty of the selection process: "After several years of discussion and debate, the authors selected approximately 400 photographs . . . from Morton's vast collection, which he has made and kept since age thirteen." The large-format book weighed in just shy of seven pounds. One reviewer remarked that it was "the book of the year, for those with a very sturdy coffee table."

Morton's wife of fifty years, Julia, said one of her husband's greatest accomplishments was having provided a link between the private and public sectors of tourism in the state. In the mid-1970s, *Charlotte Observer* Publisher Rolfe Neill asked Julia to sum up her husband in just a few words. "I've thought about that many times since," she said, "and I think the best way to describe him is that he is a giant, larger than life." Morton received many awards in his life, including the North Carolina Award for Public Service, the state's highest, in 1983, and the William R. Davie Award from the University of North Carolina in 1991. He was presented the North Caroliniana Society Award in 1996.

Grandfather's guardian was indeed a giant, but one as gentle as Mildred the Bear and as graceful as the ravens that ride the currents of fresh June breezes on top of Grandfather Mountain.

A journalism graduate of the University of North Carolina at Chapel Hill, Ralph Grizzle of Asheville is a contributing editor to Our State *magazine and author of* Remembering Charles Kuralt.

For more information see:

Covington, Howard E., Jr. *Linville: A Mountain Home for 100 Years.* Linville Corporation, 1992.

Grizzle, Ralph. *Remembering Charles Kuralt.* Kenilworth Media, 2000.

Morton, Hugh M., and Edward L. Rankin, Jr. *Making a Difference in North Carolina.* Lightworks, 1988.

Sixty Years With a Camera. North Caroliniana Society, 1996.

WALTER HINES, FRANK JR., AND ROBERT N. PAGE

By Steven Niven

THE PATRIARCH of the Page family that figured prominently in the early half of the twentieth century set an example for his sons as a town builder and community leader. Allison Francis (Frank) Page was a broad, powerful man of great energy and uncompromising opinions who made a fortune in turpentine distilling, naval stores, and lumbering, but also fell deeply in debt on occasion. He established a community in Wake County, known locally as "Page's" or "Page's Station," but which Page insisted be named Cary, after a local prohibitionist of that name.

When his lumbering operations shifted south to Moore County, Page was also instrumental in establishing the town of Aberdeen and built several churches for both races and a hotel—with no saloon—in the area. All eight children of Frank Page and his wife, Catherine Frances Raboteau, contributed to the political, cultural, and economic life of North Carolina in the first quarter of the twentieth century. The eldest son, Walter Hines Page, born in Wake County in 1855, played by far the most significant role, not only in the state and in the region, but on the national and international stage as well.

Like his father before him, Walter Hines Page identified with the South of Thomas Jefferson, not of Jefferson Davis. Frank Page had been a staunch Whig who opposed the "foolhardy enterprise" of secession, and did not serve the Confederacy in either a military or a civilian capacity. His father's ambivalence about "the Cause" did not endear young Walter to many of his classmates at the Bingham Military Academy in Mebane, and, for a while, the boy gloried in the tales of derring-do of his mother's family, several of whom had been ardent Confederates. Yet by the time the rangy sixteen-year-old got to Trinity College (the precursor of Duke University) in 1871, he had come to embrace his father's Jeffersonian vision of a South free of "the aristocratic shackles" and courtly pretensions of the antebellum era.

Walter, an avid reader since boyhood, found Trinity—then in Randolph County—intellectually undemanding and stifling, and within a year, he transferred to Randolph-Macon College in Virginia. Page flourished as the campus's champion debater and enjoyed the relatively tolerant academic atmosphere.

Though Randolph-Macon, like Trinity, was a Methodist school, it did not require church attendance. That spirit of free inquiry would ultimately lead to a major family dispute. Much to his father's chagrin, Walter abandoned his earlier desire to join the ministry and contemplated a career as a writer or academic. Page even banged his fist on the table at one point and declared to his family that he was "damned if" he would "become a Methodist preacher."

Though Frank Page proved unable to punish his son by removing him from college—Walter graduated in 1875—he worked hard to keep his other sons from pursuing what he perceived as the "unmanly" calling of talking and writing. Only one of the boys, the youngest, Frank Jr., attended any college whatsoever—a semester at Chapel Hill—although a daughter, Emma, received a bachelor's degree. Walter, however, chose to pursue his academic calling as the youngest of the first fellows of the newly founded Johns Hopkins University, the nation's first college dedicated to graduate study. That experience, as well as a summer trip to Germany in 1877, convinced Page that the South could only be redeemed by education, hard work, and the practical application of knowledge. First as a teacher—at Chapel Hill—and then as a journalist in Missouri and New York, Walter Page began to articulate his ideas about the economic and social transformation then sweeping the North, and how such changes might transform his native region.

In 1883, Page returned to North Carolina to found a newspaper, the Raleigh *State Chronicle,* to further his goals. The *Chronicle*'s first edition highlighted several of Page's aims. It promised "plain speaking editorials about living subjects, advocating honest democratic politics, industrial education, material development, moneymaking and hearty living." The pragmatism of that manifesto persuaded several prominent Tar Heel businessmen to back Page's new venture. Not least of these was Frank Page Sr., whose support suggested that the father viewed journalism as a more manly and worthwhile profession.

With its frequent articles on the many new industries and businesses then developing in North Carolina, the *Chronicle* also fit nicely with the Page family's growing business interests, which, under the direc-

Left to right: Walter Hines Page (courtesy of North Carolina Collection), Frank Page Jr. and Robert N. Page (courtesy of Southern Historical Collection)

tion of Walter's younger brothers, Robert and Junius, had diversified from lumber into railroads and banking. Unlike other boosters of what came to be known as the "New South," however, Walter Page used the *Chronicle* to advance the cause of agriculture as well as of industry. True to the Jeffersonian ideal of the small independent producer, Walter Page also preferred the development of "many small independent shops and factories" to the growth of large industrial ventures and corporations.

In the era of James Buchanan Duke and R. J. Reynolds, such attitudes—and a belief that high wages, not cheap labor, would spur the southern economy— marked Page as an iconoclastic figure. The editor's attitude to blacks was even more out of step with his times. Though the paper supported the Democratic Party, which had recently redeemed the state from Republican rule, Page took the unprecedented step of capitalizing the word, "Negro," and of praising, in an editorial, "our brother in black." He also refused to follow the custom of addressing political candidates by their Confederate titles. After only two years at its helm, Page resigned from the *Chronicle,* in part for financial reasons—there simply were not enough readers in the state to sustain a weekly, relatively nonpartisan journal of ideas. But it was also because he believed that the leaders of North Carolina (whom he dismissed in an 1886 article as "mummies") were too unimaginative and preoccupied with the past to adapt to the new economic and social order of the United States.

The "Mummies" article and his departure from Raleigh signaled Page's growing frustration with his native state, but it did not reflect any lessening of his concern for southern improvement or his desire for a national reconciliation. Newspapers and magazines in Boston and New York readily accepted the scores of articles that Page drafted in his self-imposed exile, and he may well have been thinking of himself when he condemned the Mummies for driving "bright and promising men" out of North Carolina. The literary and publishing world of the Northeast provided Page a platform to fulfill that promise. By 1891 he became editor of an innovative monthly news magazine, the *Forum,* which not only reported current events, but pioneered a new style of investigative reporting of social problems and political corruption.

Forum's exposés of the failings of urban schools, municipal sanitation, and increasing corporate power foreshadowed the "muckraking school" of journalism that became such a feature of the early twentieth century's progressive era. Among those writing for Page's magazine were social work pioneer, Jane Addams, and two youthful political thinkers, Theodore Roosevelt and Woodrow Wilson, who in their later presidencies would institute many of the regulatory reforms of corporate power first advocated by the *Forum.* Yet again, Page's most passionate interest lay in the South, and he used the *Forum* to advance the cause of economic and industrial development and expanding education. He remained wary, however, of both the economic populism of southern and western farmers seeking agricultural reform and the racial populism of pro-lynching demagogues like South Carolina's "Pitchfork Ben" Tillman.

In 1899, after a period as a book editor at Houghton Mifflin and Company, and as editor of the venerable Boston monthly, the *Atlantic,* Page joined with New York publisher Frank Doubleday to found a major publishing house, Doubleday, Page and Company, which quickly emerged as one of the nation's most prestigious firms, publishing, among others, the muckraker Upton Sinclair and the social realist novelist Theodore Dreiser.

In keeping with Page's self-appointed role as the South's ambassador to the literary North, Doubleday published many prominent southern writers, including fellow Tar Heel Thomas W. Dixon, Ellen Glasgow, and Booker T. Washington. One year later, Page also founded the *World's Work,* a news magazine that, like the *Forum,* addressed current affairs and social problems, but that foreshadowed later titles such as *Life, Look,* and *Time* in its use of photography. Yet again, he used the journal as a vehicle for his views on the centrality of education to the social problems of the South. More than any other national magazine, *World's Work* focused attention on developments in the African American world, and again, Page served as a fierce partisan of Booker T. Washington's philosophy of black enterprise and racial uplift.

Though book and magazine publishing consumed much of Page's time, he even found time in 1909 to write (under a pseudonym) a novel, a thinly disguised autobiography called *The Southerner.* The book, serialized in the *Atlantic,* is narrated by a central character who was born during the Civil War, attended military school, then college in the North, and comes to work in the cause of southern progressive reform. The novel also provides a rare example of a southern white author writing a sympathetic account of a consensual interracial love affair, particularly at a time when even rumors of black-white sexual relations could precipitate a lynching.

Several southern newspapers—including the Raleigh *News and Observer*—condemned *The Southerner* as anti-southern, anti-Confederate, and "holier than thou" Yankee propaganda. The bottom line, however, was that Page's literary skills were better served in his short articles and in his flair for innovative publishing. As a novelist, he found few admirers, North or South, and *The Southerner* proved to be one of Doubleday, Page's least successful publications.

Increasingly, Page came to use his emerging national prestige to aid southern efforts to tackle the problems caused by rapid industrialization. Beginning in 1896, he served on boards to promote public education for blacks as well as whites, and for women as well as men, and to increase awareness of public health —particularly the problem of hookworm. In both of these campaigns, Page used the *World's Work* to highlight the changes that groups such as the Southern Education Board and the Hookworm Commission had begun to achieve in his native region.

He noted the successes of progressive-minded governors such as Charles B. Aycock of North Carolina, and the Virginia-born president of Princeton and later governor of New Jersey, Woodrow Wilson. Though most of his southern allies were Democrats, Page enjoyed the patronage of Republican President Theodore Roosevelt, who appointed him to the Country Life Commission, a seven-member panel charged with addressing rural and environmental problems. After 1908, he also urged southern whites to embrace the Republican Party of William Howard Taft as they had once embraced the Whig Party in his father's time. At the same time he persuaded Taft to allay white southerners' fear that Republicans would interfere in matters of "social equality."

In 1912, Page viewed the Democratic nominee for president, Woodrow Wilson, as a kindred spirit: a southern expatriate seeking national reconciliation, a man of letters, and an advocate of moderate social reform and corporate regulation. Page worked vigorously, both through his connections in the South and through the *World's Work,* to promote Wilson's achievements and candidacy. True to his deep-seated Whiggish sympathies, Page was less supportive of Wilson's party. Page's less than solid support for the party of the Solid South probably cost him a seat in Wilson's first cabinet.

The new president did call on Page to serve, but not, as the Carolinian had expected, as secretary of agriculture. Instead, he received an appointment as the U.S. ambassador to Great Britain, arguably the most prestigious diplomatic post at that time. Though he had no diplomatic training whatsoever, Page's strong links to the literary and cultural world of New York and Boston served him well, at least in peacetime. He enjoyed a favorable press, in part, perhaps, because London's newspapermen and magazine writers saw him as one of their own. Page also established an early and firm friendship with the British foreign secretary, Sir Edward Grey.

Page's unconventional approach to his post—he preferred plain-speaking, informal discussion to the more arcane arts of diplomacy—helped ease tensions between Britain and the United States over conflicting interests in Central America. Page's unfamiliarity with European affairs left him remarkably unprepared for the outbreak of hostilities on that continent in the late summer of 1914. In July, Page had decamped—with a full retinue of servants—from the embassy to a country retreat outside of London. In one of his many letters home, he looked forward to a "very happy, quiet time for three months . . . to enjoy the roses and geraniums . . . and sweet peas . . . and hundreds of other flowers."

In only a matter of weeks, however, Page—like all diplomats in Europe—was swept up in last minute efforts to prevent war. The American ambassador looked on in astonishment as the leaders of the world's greatest powers appeared, literally, to go mad. As diplomacy failed, Page observed, in quick succession: the German ambassador appears to be a "crazy man" in his pajamas; Sir Edward Grey weeps on telling of Britain's ultimatum to Germany; and King George V throws his hands in the air and declares, "My God, Mr. Page, what else can we do?" Page confided in his diary that "Nero in Hades must blush for shame that his achievements were so tame. The Goths and Huns were mere novices and played for mere penny stakes."

To his credit, the ambassador showed a remarkable degree of calmness, particularly in the first months of war when thousands of Americans sought evacuation from Europe to Britain and passage back to the United States. As the ambassador of a neutral nation, Page also had to assume the responsibility for the many German and Austrian citizens still resident in Britain at the time of war, and for prisoners of war thereafter. Despite Page's clear pro-British sympathies, the German authorities declared that he performed his task "in an exemplary manner."

Page's strong pro-British sympathies soon came in conflict with the views of most Americans, notably President Wilson, who believed their nation should adopt a neutral attitude to the war. Wilson was wary of antagonizing the Democratic Party's many supporters of German and Irish descent, particularly on the eve of his reelection bid in 1916. Increasingly, Page's relations with the British people and diplomatic corps became more harmonious than his dealings with his own government. Indeed, Walter's empathy with the allied cause differed sharply from the views of his own brother, Congressman Robert Page, who refused to seek election because he feared the Wilson administration was not neutral enough. Though Wilson came close to removing his friend from the Court of St. James, he found it more problematic to find a replacement, particularly after the United States finally entered the war in 1917.

Page barely saw the end of the conflict, however.

As he explained to President Wilson, "The war, five London winters, the monotony of English food and the unceasing labor which is now the common lot" took their toll. Page did not mention that he had also been a heavy smoker for more than forty years, and was averaging fifty large, strong cigars a week shortly before he entered the famed Duff House sanatorium in Banff, Scotland. The doctors there found that he was suffering from hardening of the arteries and hypertension and recommended that he retire and return to his native North Carolina. He died at the Page family home in Pinehurst on December 21, 1918, and was buried in Aberdeen three days later, on Christmas Eve.

Page received many posthumous honors. Randolph-Macon College named its library and Johns Hopkins University named its School of International Relations in his honor. The outpouring of sympathy in Britain was even greater. The former British Foreign Secretary, Edward Grey, unveiled a marble tablet which eulogized Page as "The Friend of Britain in Her Sorest Need" in a service at Westminster Abbey. To this day, he is one of only three Americans—James Russell Lowell and Henry W. Longfellow are the others—to be so commemorated at the Abbey. Ironically, Page's renown was arguably greater after his death than in his lifetime, following the publication of three volumes of his letters and reminiscences. *The Life and Letters of Walter Hines Page* became an instant best-seller, in part because they provided one of the first inside accounts of the Great War, but mainly—as Woodrow Wilson attested—because Page's letters were so beautifully crafted.

Walter's brother, Robert Newton, the second-born son, followed his footsteps in attending Cary Academy and the Bingham Military School, but thereafter their paths diverged markedly. In contrast to Walter, Robert enjoyed a life and career spent almost entirely within North Carolina. Perhaps because of the family tensions caused by Walter's spell at Randolph-Macon and Johns Hopkins, Robert did not attend college but devoted himself to the Page business empire. He served as the general manager of the Page Lumber Company and as an executive of the Aberdeen and Asheboro Railway.

Increasingly, however, he devoted his time to politics, representing Montgomery County in the N.C. General Assembly for one term from 1901 to 1903. In 1903, he began the first of seven terms as congressman from North Carolina's Seventh District. Though he was loyal to President Wilson's domestic agenda—notably in regulating the power of trusts and corporations—he opposed the administration's decision to increase military spending in preparedness for entry into World War I.

The South, as a region, was conspicuously more pro-intervention than the rest of the nation. Nevertheless, in 1916 Robert Page announced that he could not seek reelection as a member of Wilson's party "without violating his self-respect and intellectual integrity." His brother, Walter, reacted with considerable venom to his brother's actions. He wrote another brother, Henry Allison, that Robert had "too kindly a feeling for and lived too close to, certain yellow dogs in Washington—the most ignorant men of any race or nation or time in the history of the entire human race."

Although he had opposed entry, Robert Page supported Wilson's policies once the United States entered the war in 1917. Governor Thomas W. Bickett appointed him as a member of the N.C. Council of Defense, a body concerned with assisting the war effort on the home front. Page was not finished with politics, however, and made a major effort to secure his party's nomination for governor of North Carolina in 1920. In that campaign he embodied many of the domestic Wilsonian policies he had championed in Congress, notably improvements in the state's public highways, public schools, and public health. However, Page failed to build an effective statewide organization behind his candidacy and was defeated by both of his more charismatic opponents, O. Max Gardner, and the eventual winner, Cameron Morrison. After the election, Page returned to the family business and to Moore County, serving primarily as the president of the Page Trust Company, and, in 1931–32, as the president of the N.C. Bankers Association. Robert died in October 1933.

The youngest of the Page brothers, Frank Jr., was born in 1875, two decades after the eldest son, Walter. Like his brothers he attended a military academy, but unlike all but Walter, he also attended college, studying at the University of North Carolina for two years before joining his father and brothers in the lumbering, banking, and railroad businesses in Aberdeen. In World War I, he served as a major in the Army Corps of Engineers, and spent some of that time in road construction. That experience proved invaluable when he returned home to North Carolina in 1918 and Governor Bickett appointed him as the first chairman of the State Highway Commission. Page became a powerful advocate for better roads, and especially for a state-driven program of construction and maintenance. As he told a meeting of the N.C. Good Roads Association in Asheville in 1920, the roads program should be "independent of any county or other

political subdivision and without their participation or financial aid."

Indeed, Page had an almost messianic zeal for the cause of better roads. The building of new and better highways, he believed, would have a "socializing influence upon our people. Most of the strife and conflict, most of the prejudiced and undesirable things of life, are born of human ignorance. Nothing will do more to banish ignorance and to encourage that spirit of charity that makes the world kin than a system of highways providing easy transportation, banishing distance and isolation, and enabling the whole people of the State to enjoy fellowship with their neighbors as well as brethren from afar."

After 1920, under Governor Morrison, North Carolina executed the type of ambitious road-building program that Page envisioned. The state authorized bonds of more than $20 million, levied a one-cent gasoline tax, and dramatically increased motor vehicle license fees. In 1921, Morrison established a permanent, politically powerful State Highway Commission, and nominated Frank Page as its chairman. By the end of Page's tenure in 1929, North Carolina had authorized bonds for $115 million and established a reputation as the "Good Roads State."

Frank Page's success in transforming North Carolina's roads resulted in his appointment to several national and international highway boards. In the mid-1920s, President Calvin Coolidge nominated Page to the Pan American Road Congress in South America, and Coolidge's successor, Herbert Hoover, appointed him as chairman of the National Highway Safety Council. Page also served as president of the American Road Builders Association and the American Association of State Highway Officials. In recognition of his contribution to the state, the University of North Carolina awarded Frank Page an honorary doctorate of laws in 1923. In the final five years of his life, Frank turned his attention to banking, serving as a vice president of Wachovia Bank and Trust Company. He died in 1934 and was buried in the Page family plot in Aberdeen.

The accomplishments of the remaining Page siblings are also noteworthy. Brothers Junius and Henry Allison worked in the family banking and railroad businesses and promoted civic affairs in Aberdeen. Henry helped build the railroad line between Aberdeen and High Point, and worked with Herbert Hoover in directing the U.S. Food Administration during World War I. Another brother, Jesse, was a physician, while a sister, Mary Esther, was involved in philanthropic efforts.

Although Walter turned away from the church, his

brother Jesse became a Methodist minister and a sister, Emma Catherine, taught Bible studies at the Woman's College in Greensboro. Indeed, the collective contributions of the Page family were matched by few others in late-nineteenth- and early-twentieth-century North Carolina. The Pages may have served the state in different ways, and with differing degrees of significance, but they were united by a common faith, instilled by their parents, of public service and the public good.

Steven Niven received his M.A. from Edinburgh University and was a student and researcher at the University of Pennsylvania in the early 1990s. As a doctoral candidate in UNC Chapel Hill's history department, his dissertation, "Shades of Whiteness," examined the complexities of the white response to the civil rights movement in North Carolina. He has written for the North Carolina Literary Review *and* Southern Cultures.

For more information, see:

The major depositories of Walter Hines Page's Papers are the Houghton Library, Harvard University, Cambridge, Mass., and the Walter Hines Page Library at Randolph-Macon College in Ashland, Va.

Page, Robert Newton. Letters. Southern Historical Collection, University of North Carolina at Chapel Hill.
———. Papers. Special Collections, Duke University, Durham.
Page, Thaddeus Shaw. Papers. Southern Historical Collection, University of North Carolina at Chapel Hill.

Arnett, Alex M. *Claude Kitchen and the Wilson War Policies*. Boston, 1937.
Cooper, John Milton. *Walter Hines Page: The Southerner as American*. University of North Carolina Press, 1977.
Gregory, Ross. *Walter Hines Page: Ambassador to the Court of St. James*. University Press of Kentucky, 1970.
Hedrick, Burton J. *The Life and Letters of Walter Hines Page*. 3 vols. Doubleday, Page and Company, 1922–25.
Link, William A. *The Rebuilding of Old Commonwealths, and Other Documents of Social Reform in the Progressive Era South*. Bedford Books, 1996.
Waynick, Capus. *North Carolina Roads and Their Builders*. Superior Stone Company, 1952.

THOMAS J. PEARSALL

By Steven Niven

THOMAS JENKINS PEARSALL was an attorney, farmer, businessman, speaker of the North Carolina General Assembly, and a key mover in the expansion of higher education in his state in the 1960s. But it was his participation in developing the state's response to the U.S. Supreme Court's *Brown v. Board of Education* decision desegregating public schools that put his name forever in North Carolina history.

The so-called Pearsall Plan provoked clear differences among North Carolinians. At the time, many African Americans criticized it as an effort to circumvent the *Brown* ruling, while the vast majority of white North Carolinians approved it in a lopsided referendum that won a majority in all hundred counties. In later years, former governor Terry Sanford applauded Pearsall's "vision, compassion, concern, and, above all, courage" and said he "[opened up] opportunities for blacks in the early 1960s."

Pearsall spent most of his life in Rocky Mount, the two-county town where he and his two siblings were born. Although born on February 11, 1903, on the Edgecombe County side of town, he later moved to the Nash side. He once explained to a reporter: "If you're born in a good country, it's just as well to stay there. There's no use looking for greener grass somewhere else." His father, Leon, worked for fifty years as a locomotive engineer on the Atlantic Coast Line, and Thomas showed a similar dedication to his labor of love: public education. He attended Rocky Mount public schools through the tenth grade, but transferred to the Georgia Military Academy in College Park, Ga., because "Daddy thought I needed a little discipline." On graduation in 1923, Pearsall entered the University of North Carolina, and UNC's law school two years later. An athlete in both high school and college, Pearsall played on the Carolina basketball, football, and baseball teams. He also established a longtime friendship with his fraternity brother, Gordon Gray, who later became president of the Consolidated University. Pearsall did not receive a college degree, however. "Money was a problem, and I had to go out and get to work," he recalled. Armed with his law license, Pearsall returned to Rocky Mount to practice law.

Pearsall began his long association with politics at the age of twenty-five when he was elected solicitor of the Rocky Mount Recorder's Court, a post he held

Thomas J. Pearsall (Courtesy of Southern Historical Collection)

for five years. In 1940, local Democrats appointed him to complete the state legislative term of William Fenner, who died two days after winning the election. Pearsall ran unopposed for the next three legislative sessions, and chaired the house agriculture committee in 1943 and the house appropriations committee in 1945. In 1947 his fellow legislators elected him as speaker, a post that he insisted satisfied all of his personal political ambitions.

In 1948, he managed Charles M. Johnson's unsuccessful gubernatorial race against Kerr Scott. Many of his colleagues urged him to run for state office on his own accord in subsequent elections, but in spite of his strong support in the east and among Democratic Party leaders, Pearsall preferred to focus on his varied business interests.

Those interests were considerable, particularly his management of the M. C. Braswell Company and its twenty-two thousand acres of farmland in Nash, Edgecombe, Halifax, and Martin Counties. Pearsall's wife, Elizabeth, had inherited the company on the death of her father, Mack Braswell, in 1935. In the 1950s, Pearsall employed more than nine hundred people to farm Braswell's peanuts, cotton, corn, and tobacco, and another seventy people to administer its operations. Although he viewed himself as a businessman rather than a farmer, Pearsall had a deep love of his native land. He said that his acres around Battleboro were "like the Garden of Eden," and told a reporter that "down here we live a little better than most folks because we live close to the soil, and have time to enjoy other things."

From the outset, Pearsall dedicated his company to a distinct philosophy of conserving both its land and forests and its human resources. In addition to improving the fertility of its soil, the Braswell company encouraged and gave financial assistance to its tenants, most of them black, to buy their own land. It also wired all 130 tenant houses for electricity in the late 1940s and offered health care. As a result of such policies, tenant turnover declined from a yearly high of 25 percent to less than 5 percent by the early 1950s. By that time, the Braswell empire had also expanded to include a cannery.

In addition to his farming interests, Pearsall maintained a busy law practice and a wide range of civic and business affairs. He was president of Rocky Mount's Citizens' Savings and Loan, owned an oil and fuel distributing company, and served on the board of directors of the Planters National Bank. An active Episcopalian, Pearsall was a member of the vestry and senior warden at the Church of the Good Shepherd in Rocky Mount. Even after he left the legislature, Pearsall remained active in local and statewide Democratic politics. He also served on the executive committee of the board of trustees of the University of North Carolina. In the mid-1950s, Pearsall looked forward to the day when he would have more time for the "F's: family, fishing, and fooling around," but the Supreme Court's school desegregation decision thrust Pearsall back into the public arena again.

In May 1954, the Supreme Court ruled that racially separate schools were inherently unequal and in violation of the constitutional provision of equal protection before the law. Shortly thereafter, Governor William B. Umstead called on Pearsall to chair a committee to study the impact of the ruling on North Carolina schools. *Brown* inflamed white Tar Heel passions. U.S. Senator Sam Ervin declared the decision "a tragedy, an invasion of states' rights and an attempt by the court to amend the constitution." Attorney General Harry McMullan, his assistant, I. Beverly Lake, and every member of the North Carolina Supreme Court urged Umstead to refuse to comply with the Court's request that southern states submit a brief outline of how they would comply with the ruling. In their view, the Court's request for an amicus brief was a "diabolical scheme to trap the State of North Carolina" into integrating immediately. In the advisory committee and in his discussions with the governor, Pearsall argued strongly that North Carolina could not simply ignore *Brown,* or flagrantly circumvent it by privatizing the schools, as Lake would later propose.

Nor did Pearsall advocate speedy compliance. In late December 1954, his committee—consisting of sixteen whites and three blacks—submitted its report to Governor Luther Hodges. (Umstead had died a month earlier.) That report concluded that the "mixing of the races *forthwith* in the public schools" would threaten the maintenance of the peace throughout the state and "should not be attempted." Reflecting the growing support within the state for privatizing the schools, the committee left open the possibility of "abandoning or materially altering" public education in the future. For the present, though, it urged Tar Heels to work within the public school system, and to let local communities determine the pace of any change. To do so, Pearsall recommended transferring authority over school enrollment and assignment from the state Board of Education to local school boards.

That change made it more difficult for blacks to gain admission to white schools. Pearsall wanted to "avoid a situation where one lawsuit against the state could wipe out the entire state school system." Rather than filing suit against a single state system, litigants would have to file in 167 separate county and city systems. Blacks seeking to enter white schools would also have to petition local boards on an individual basis. Such petitions could be denied on the basis of a variety of "local conditions" other than race, such as proximity of the school, previous school attended, or "the best interest of all students." The final arbiters of pupil assignment would be the local boards; except in a few big cities, segregationist whites dominated these boards. In the spring of 1955, the General Assembly unanimously passed a pupil assignment that incorporated Pearsall's recommendations.

Later that year, Governor Hodges convened a second Advisory Committee on Education and again tapped Pearsall as its chair. This new committee was much smaller than its predecessor—seven members rather than nineteen—and did not include black members. Pearsall recalled that "we didn't think we could get an objective feeling from blacks. They wanted integration at any cost and we wanted to save the schools at any cost." The second committee developed two proposed amendments to the state constitution. The first would provide tuition grants for private schooling and would give parents the right to transfer their children from schools integrated by a federal court order. The second, much more controversial amendment, would enable local communities to hold elections to close their schools if Court-ordered integration led to "an intolerable situation." The Pearsall committee contended that these amendments offered a much-needed "safety-valve" that would ease racial tensions and prevent the abandonment (by whites) of "all public schools."

In September 1956, North Carolinians went to the polls to decide whether to accept the so-called Pearsall Plan's proposed constitutional amendments. A vocal body of opinion opposed it. Most African Americans viewed tuition grants and local option to close the schools as a flagrant evasion of *Brown.* Several prominent newspapers, most notably the *News and Observer,* and a few liberal-minded white churchmen and lawyers agreed. Support for the Pearsall Plan was more widespread, however. In the weeks leading up to the referendum, Governor Hodges built a broad supporting coalition that ranged from the segregationist Patriots of North Carolina to Terry Sanford, Kerr Scott, and others on the liberal wing of the Democratic Party. On election day, 82 percent of the electorate endorsed the amendments. Only in Winston-Salem and Durham, cities with a strong black vote, was the margin even close.

Pearsall and Hodges believed that the Pearsall Plan provided a psychological outlet for the white majority. "They had to know that if things got really terrible"—namely, if schools integrated too quickly—"they could close the schools." An advisor to the committee later recalled that the "force of national opinion" and the Supreme Court's authority made integration inevitable, just as the force of state opinion was "determined to keep [the schools] segregated." To declare openly the inevitability of integration, however, would have played into the hands of more hard-line politicians, such as Beverly Lake, who urged closing or privatizing the schools rather than allow any change at all. The Pearsall Plan for North Carolina would therefore be one of "resisting [integra-

tion] at every point as far as you could legally and decently, but always keeping open the road down which you could get to [the] eventual landing place" of integration.

In 1957, school boards in three piedmont cities, Winston-Salem, Charlotte, and Greensboro, began the integration process. Pearsall later conceded that "it was token integration," but argued that "it gave whites time to adjust and to let blacks know that we were trying." At the time, however, many blacks might not have been so sanguine. After three years, a mere 0.026 percent of black students attended schools with whites. That figure was even lower than in states such as Virginia and Arkansas that had pursued a more defiant path of "massive resistance," where schools were ultimately desegregated by court order. In 1966, federal courts declared the Pearsall Plan to be unconstitutional, but the crisis had passed. Its provisions to close schools or provide tuition grants were never used.

In the 1960s, Pearsall again played a major role in North Carolina education. In 1963 Governor Terry Sanford asked him to a chair a committee on the consolidation of the University of North Carolina system and the expansion of the state's community colleges.

In the summer of 1963, Pearsall considered a campaign for governor. He had the support of certain conservative elements within the Democratic Party who were eager to regain control of the governor's office. Some feared an extreme reaction to four years of the relatively liberal and activist Sanford administration might lead to the election of segregationist I. Beverly Lake. Pearsall appeared to be a moderate candidate who could appeal to eastern North Carolina and be acceptable to moderate-to-liberal voters elsewhere in the state. Pearsall and Dan K. Moore, a former superior court judge from western North Carolina, emerged as likely candidates and even met together in Chapel Hill to discuss who should run. When Pearsall hesitated in the days that followed, Moore announced his candidacy and subsequently won the Democratic nomination by defeating Richardson Preyer, Sanford's choice as a successor. Indeed, Lake did run, but he did not survive the first primary.

In his final decade and a half, Pearsall maintained a busy schedule. He helped establish North Carolina Wesleyan College on land provided by his wife Elizabeth and her sisters, and served on numerous state boards, among them North Carolina Wesleyan and North Carolina A & T, a historically black college. He also was chairman of the board of the Roanoke

Island Historical Association and a member of the board of governors of the Research Triangle Institute.

He died in 1981 in Rocky Mount. UNC President William Friday hailed Pearsall's accomplishments in university consolidation and praised him as a "powerful force, a constructive influence . . . and just a thoroughly decent human being. Former governor Sanford went further. "In my opinion, North Carolina has had no greater citizen in my lifetime."

Steven Niven received his M.A. from Edinburgh University, and was a student and researcher at the University of Pennsylvania in the early 1990s. As a doctoral candidate in UNC-Chapel Hill's history department, his dissertation, "Shades of Whiteness," examined the complexities of the white response to the civil rights movement in North Carolina. He has written for the North Carolina Literary Review *and* Southern Cultures.

For more information, see:

Pearsall, Thomas Jenkins. Papers. Southern Historical Collection, University of North Carolina at Chapel Hill.

———. Southern Oral History Program, Southern Historical Collection, University of North Carolina at Chapel Hill.

Batchelor, John E. "Rule of Law: North Carolina School Desegregation from *Brown* to *Swain,* 1954–1974." Ph.D. diss., North Carolina State University, 1992.

Chafe, William. *Civilities and Civil Rights: Greensboro, North Carolina, and the Black Struggle for Freedom.* Oxford University Press, 1981.

Covington, Howard E., Jr., and Marion A. Ellis. *Terry Sanford: Politics, Progress, and Outrageous Ambitions.* Duke University Press, 1999.

Dunn, Charles. "An Exercise of Choice: North Carolina's Approach to the Segregation-Integration Crisis in Public Education." Master's thesis, University of North Carolina at Chapel Hill, 1959.

Niven, Steven J. "Shades of Whiteness: Southern Whites Confront the Second Reconstruction, Durham, NC, 1945–1971." Ph.D. diss., University of North Carolina at Chapel Hill, 2000.

O' Keefe, Herbert. "Tar Heel of the Week." *News and Observer,* August 10, 1952.

Rogers, Dennis. "Pearsall Recalls Buying Time for Integration." *News and Observer,* November 7, 1976.

TERRY SANFORD

By Howard E. Covington Jr.

H E WAS A LAWYER, a soldier, a legislator, a governor, a university president, and finally a
U.S. senator, but for Terry Sanford the title that
meant the most was the one he held as governor from
1961 to 1965. That was the job he really liked. As governor he could have an idea at breakfast and someone
would be working on it by noon. It was the job where
he could demonstrate that government could be a
force for good and raise the quality of life for his fellow citizens in North Carolina.

He was indefatigable in his efforts to show the best
of his fellow man and of the American dream of democracy. In the weeks before his death from cancer
in 1998, Sanford compiled a list of things to do when
he got well. It was an agenda that would have bent
the back of one half his age. Among the items was
the creation of a $100-million performing arts center
in the Research Triangle.

Sanford was such a figure in the state Democratic
Party that although constrained by the constitutional
limitation of one term as governor, he reshaped the
politics of North Carolina so profoundly that his followers carried his label forty years after he left office.
His legacy was a battalion of protégés who occupied
public office all across the state long after he was gone.

He was born James Terry Sanford on August 20,
1917, in Laurinburg, but only the army used his first
name. His mother, Betsy Martin, was a Virginian
teaching school in Laurinburg when she met his father, Cecil Sanford, whose family owned a hardware
store. Laurinburg was mostly a farming community
and the Sanford family—which included Terry's
brother and two sisters—lived on the edge of town,
within sight and sound of the textile mills that spun
into yarn the cotton grown on the fields of surrounding Scotland County.

The Depression fell hard on towns like Laurinburg. Cecil Sanford lost his business and for a time
depended on government jobs for a subsistence income. Betsy Sanford returned to the classroom, where
she would teach more than three generations of students before retirement (she lived to her one hundredth year). She made sure her own children were
well educated, and continued their instruction in a
home where books, music, and conversation were an
everyday part of life. Terry also thrived on being close
to nature and when his school principal formed a

Terry Sanford (Courtesy of Hugh Morton)

Boy Scout troop, he was one of the first to join. He
earned scouting's highest rank, Eagle, in two years.

Terry Sanford began his college education at Presbyterian Junior College, where he washed windows
and did other odd jobs to cover tuition. After only
one full semester he decided to attend the University
of North Carolina at Chapel Hill, where he was a
productive, but not outstanding, student. On graduation he wanted to be a Boy Scout executive or go to
South America with a large oil company, but no one
was hiring. When a freak storm washed out a boys'
camp that figured in his career plans, he returned to
Chapel Hill and entered law school.

Law school and a job at the new Institute of Government quickened his interest in politics. He was
elected student body president—using a campaign organization he later adapted to his race for governor
—and was in his second year of law school when the
Japanese attacked Pearl Harbor. He had been turned
down for a commission in the navy and marines be-

cause he did not have perfect eyesight, so when J. Edgar Hoover accepted his application for the Federal Bureau of Investigation (FBI) he jumped at the chance. Six months later, however, bored with stateside FBI duty, he volunteered to become one of the army's early paratroopers. In the late spring of 1944, Second Lieutenant Terry Sanford shipped out to become part of the Allied invasion of Europe.

Sanford jumped into southern France and his unit fought its way north to Belgium. After three months of combat, he was bivouacked in Belgium when the German army launched a breakthrough in the Ardennes. Sanford's unit was rushed to the front and remained in action through the Battle of the Bulge and the surrender of Germany in 1945. He was on his way to join the fighting in the Pacific when Japan surrendered.

The war had a profound impact on Sanford and others of his generation. He returned to finish law school with an allegiance to his studies he had not shown before. He found himself among many whose lives had been put on hold by war and who were determined to make their home a better place to live. Sanford got his law degree in 1947 and remained in Chapel Hill on the staff of the Institute of Government before setting off to Fayetteville to open a law practice.

Sanford moved to Fayetteville a virtual stranger with the intention of using the town as a base for a campaign for governor. He helped organize the new National Guard outfit there, became president of the Jaycees, and in 1949 was elected state president of the Young Democrats Club. In 1952, he opened his first campaign for public office and was elected to the state senate. Two years later he was the campaign chairman of former governor W. Kerr Scott's successful campaign for the United States Senate. Sanford seriously considered running for governor in 1956 and had his filing fee in his pocket when he decided not to oppose Governor Luther Hodges, who was running for his first full term after succeeding the late Governor William Umstead.

Before Sanford, most North Carolina governors had come from the senior ranks of the Democratic Party. He upset the pecking order by blending the old Scott campaign organization based in the rural areas of the state with a new generation of leaders shaped by the lessons of public service taught by UNC President Frank Porter Graham. Sanford promised "a new day" in his announcement speech from the Old Market in Fayetteville in February 1960 and he faithfully campaigned in all of the state's one hundred counties. The returns of the party primary in late

May gave Sanford the lead, but segregationist candidate I. Beverly Lake had sufficient support to call for a runoff election. It proved to be the most trying political contest of Sanford's career.

North Carolina was unmarked by the violence and hatred that had accompanied the desegregation of public schools in the rest of the South. Lake, however, became the standard bearer for those in North Carolina who—like Lake—refused to honor the U.S. Supreme Court's 1954 school decision. Sanford denied Lake's claims that he was an "integrationist" but he campaigned on the premise that the Court's decision was the law of the land and he would not stand in its way. Sanford skillfully turned the school issue into one about improving education while casting Lake as the threat to the future of public schools in the state. Sanford finished well ahead of Lake.

Sanford was virtually assured of election in the fall —Republicans had not elected a governor since 1896 —and he risked his own commanding lead to support the presidential nomination of John F. Kennedy, a war veteran like himself who had campaigned as a new kind of leader. Sanford underestimated the religious bias of North Carolina voters, however, and many recoiled at his endorsement of a Roman Catholic. Sanford's risk-taking secured for him and the state a favored spot in the new Democratic administration in Washington, which included former governor Luther Hodges, whom Kennedy named secretary of commerce on Sanford's recommendation.

The new governor took office with an eye on the calendar. He knew he only had four years and an impressive agenda of programs, most of them aimed at improving public schools. With the state short on cash to pay for his education package, Sanford asked the legislature to extend the sales tax to cover food. His proposal caused an uproar, but when the legislature adjourned in early summer, Sanford had succeeded with his education program and had the money to pay for it. The extra money gave a boost to public education, and particularly education professionals, who enjoyed their first serious pay raise in more than a decade. While voters would never forget Sanford and the food tax, he showed he was serious about improving the quality of life in North Carolina.

By the end of Sanford's first year in office he had accomplished much of what he had in mind on inauguration day. Rather than coast for the balance of his term, Sanford sought out creative thinkers like writer John Ehle and asked for ideas. Ehle, a novelist and faculty member on the campus at Chapel Hill, worked from an upper story in the capitol and funneled ideas to the governor that led to the creation of the North

Carolina School of the Arts, a special school for underachievers in the public schools, and the creation of the North Carolina Fund, the first statewide anti-poverty program in the nation. Other Ehle-inspired ideas—creation of a state zoo and the North Carolina School of Science and Math—came to fruition under later administrations. Sanford would later advise every governor to put a novelist on their staff.

Terry and his wife, Margaret Rose, brought a young family to the governor's mansion. Their daughter, Betsee, became a teenager there and her younger brother, Terry Jr., learned how to play blues guitar from mansion workers, who were convicted felons. The governor's vigor and vitality extended out the door. He visited public schools all across the state and on occasion took over the classroom from admiring teachers to give a lesson in government. He also led vigorous forays into the nation's industrial heartland to attract new industry to the state.

Nothing set the tone of the administration more than Sanford's creation in 1963 of the Good Neighbor Council, an interracial commission he charged with eliminating discrimination in jobs and other areas for African Americans. Sanford's action came as the race relations in the state were reaching a crisis point. Yet at no time during his term did he use the National Guard or overwhelming armed force in the face of demonstrations.

The governor was still creating programs as he was on his way out the door. During his final year he established the first state commission on the status of women and launched a major effort on behalf of highway safety. The General Assembly approved the creation of new community colleges that extended post–high school education to another entire level of the society.

After leaving office, Sanford returned to the practice of law and management of a special study of American states funded by the Carnegie Corporation and Ford Foundation of New York. Sanford worked from Duke University on the study, which had two goals. The first was to establish an interstate compact of states to help states further their efforts in primary and secondary schools. The second was a study of the capacity of the American states to manage their affairs in the rapidly changing environment of the twentieth century. The study resulted in publication of *Storm Over the States,* which described the strengths and weaknesses of state governments. He also wrote *But What About the People?,* a book about his own four years in office.

Sanford's name was put on the short list of nominees to head the prestigious Ford Foundation and he also considered several opportunities in the corporate world. In 1968 he came close to a campaign for the U.S. Senate. Rather than become a candidate himself that year, he managed the citizens' campaign for Democrat Hubert Humphrey's unsuccessful presidential bid. The taste of national politics convinced Sanford that he could run for president and he was intrigued by the opportunity to be the candidate of a new southern politics.

He had roughed out a campaign for president in 1976 before the trustees of Duke University offered him the presidency of the university late in 1969. Sanford accepted in the last of 1969 and he and Margaret Rose shifted their allegiance from the University of North Carolina to Duke, the school Terry's father had wanted him to attend had the family had the money. When asked about faculty concerns that he did not hold an earned doctorate, Sanford quipped that he wouldn't begrudge them since they didn't have a law degree.

Sanford had been hired to raise the level of Duke beyond its status as a good regional university. His plans for a transformation that would astound even his sharpest critics were put on hold during his first few months in office in 1970, however. Students at Duke and campuses across the land were aroused over the continuing war in Vietnam in the spring of 1970. When National Guardsmen called in to clear the campus at Kent State University fired on and killed students, Duke was one of hundreds of schools where students rose in protest and threatened to bring operations to a standstill. Students demanded that Sanford close the campus in protest over the war, but he refused and waded into crowds on campus to talk directly about the war. He inspired students to channel their energy into more effective political action and won the respect of students, faculty, and the trustees that would stay with him throughout his tenure.

Students took Sanford at his word and in 1972 urged him to run for president of the United States. He wavered and then accepted the challenge in a political campaign that was unplanned, unorganized, and unbelievable to many who knew him. Sanford hoped to defeat segregationist George Wallace in the new North Carolina presidential primary and arrive at the national convention as a new kind of southern Democrat acceptable to labor, women, young voters, and liberals elsewhere in the nation. Wallace easily outpaced Sanford and the result was a stunning personal defeat. Sanford prepared another presidential campaign four years later, but had to withdraw because of health concerns. In 1976, former Georgia governor Jimmy Carter became the new kind of southerner sent to Washington.

Duke University flourished under Sanford. Rather than the four to five years that he had planned to stay, Sanford remained as president until 1985. During his tenure, he saw the institution become one of the top universities in the nation. Its medical school gained worldwide recognition and Sanford successfully raised money for a business school, a school of forestry, a new student union, and a host of other changes. In his farewell to the faculty, he urged them to seek "outrageous ambitions," which could easily have been his own watch phrase.

North Carolina Democratic Party politics was in disarray in 1986 as the party sought a candidate for the United States Senate. Sanford, just retired from Duke, had never had the fire to be a senator as he had to be a governor, but throughout the fall he talked seriously about becoming a candidate. Another potential contender was his old friend, Lauch Faircloth of Clinton. Finally, Sanford jumped into the race in a manner that infuriated Faircloth, who was about to declare himself when he learned of Sanford's decision.

Sanford faced a popular Republican, former congressman James T. Broyhill, who had been appointed to fill the unexpired term of U.S. Senator John East, who had died in office. Sanford brought a host of young workers into his campaign and trusted them with tasks normally given seasoned veterans. He successfully countered Broyhill's reminder to voters that Sanford had asked for the sales tax on food a quarter century earlier by citing the importance of the community college system that had been built with money raised by the sales tax he endorsed as governor. Sanford loped through the campaign with a strong sense of humor and once told a friend he couldn't think of anything more ridiculous than two old warhorses like him and Broyhill, with whom he was friendly, racing across the state campaigning for the Senate. Sanford won in the fall and began preparations for a new career.

The Senate was not a place where Sanford could work most effectively. He liked the freedom of an executive office like governor, and was impatient with the internecine quicksand of the Senate. He had promised to do something about the continuing war in Central America during the campaign, so when he set to work on it, he went around the bureaucracy and the politics of Washington, and rounded up foundation support for his work. The result was a recovery plan for the region that would help rebuild the institutions and confidence of a people torn by war.

Sanford's Senate career was mostly unremarkable.

He suffered a couple of political blunders that tended to suggest he was inept and out of his league. He chafed under the constant struggle to raise money for the past campaign and prepare for the next one. The turgid pace of the legislative process left him cold.

There were highlights that gave him a sense of pride and accomplishment. He voted against President George Bush's nomination of Robert Bork to the Supreme Court and he challenged the president on the Gulf War. Sanford and Senator Bob Kerrey, two of only a handful of decorated war veterans in the chamber, stood against the president's call for expanded war powers in a controversial vote in January 1990. Bush prevailed and the successful lightning war against Iraq for the liberation of Kuwait left Sanford politically vulnerable.

Sanford struggled with running for a second term, but finally decided his party needed him to stay in Washington. His opponent this time was Faircloth, who had changed his party registration after a lifetime as a Democrat. Sanford was ahead in the fall of 1992 when he was hospitalized with heart problems and forced to withdraw from the campaign temporarily. He had always taken pride in running his own campaigns and with the erstwhile campaign director laid up in Duke Hospital, Sanford's reelection bid came to a standstill. Sanford left the hospital early, but his schedule was limited. The damage had been done and Faircloth was elected.

Part of the Sanford family tradition begun long before Terry was governor had been education. The former governor, university president, and senator easily slipped into a place as president emeritus at Duke. He taught a class on state government and helped young people who had come of age hearing politicians complain about government learn how it could work for the public good. He continued to write and published a book on health and old age. A novel that he had begun some time earlier received fresh attention.

Sanford opened a new legal practice, first with former South Carolina governor Robert McNair and later with former North Carolina governor James E. Holshouser Jr. He handled assorted chores for Duke University and became a very real and everyday presence among students at Duke's new Terry Sanford Institute of Public Policy. Young Democrats paid him visits and Sanford continued his efforts to strengthen the party, now wearied and worn by internal conflict and successive losses to Republicans.

In December 1997, Sanford learned he had throat cancer and his prognosis was grim. He entered Duke Hospital, where he told doctors that he had confidence in their work. Joking, he reminded them that they had told him his cancer was inoperable, but they didn't say it was incurable. His condition declined steadily, however, and he died April 18, 1998.

Volunteers from the 82nd Airborne Division carried his casket into Duke Chapel for services. The huge cathedral was packed with dignitaries and public officials from the state and the nation's capital. But there among the powerful and the important were many who had known him as just Terry, someone who liked to fish and hunt and talk and just share life with his friends. None of those there that day knew him as well as Dickson Phillips, a boyhood friend and former law partner, who was a judge on the Fourth Circuit Court of Appeals.

Phillips was one of a chosen few asked to offer a eulogy. Speaking softly and reverently, he said, "And looking back, it all seems very simple to me: why he was what he was, and did what he did, and persevered to the end. He took an oath when he was twelve years old and kept it. It started out, 'On my honor, I will do my best to do my duty to God and my country,' and included such things as 'help other people at all times.' He believed it; he was the eternal Boy Scout. It is just that simple."

Howard E. Covington Jr. of Greensboro is a former newspaper reporter and editor. He is the author of fifteen histories and biographies, including Terry Sanford: Politics, Progress, and Outrageous Ambitions, *which he co-authored with Marion A. Ellis.*

For more information, see:

Terry Sanford's papers are located in three archives. Papers related to his term as governor can be found at the N.C. Office of Archives and History in Raleigh. Duke University Archives has papers related to his presidency as well as other personal papers. Additional papers, especially those related to Sanford's early political campaigns, are in the Southern Historical Collection at the University of North Carolina at Chapel Hill.

Covington, Howard E., Jr., and Marion A. Ellis. *Terry Sanford: Politics, Progress, and Outrageous Ambitions*. Duke University Press, 1999.

Dresher, John. *Triumph of Good Will*. University of Mississippi Press, 2000.

Ragan, Sam, ed. *The New Day*. Record Publishing Company, 1964.

Sanford, Terry. *But What About the People?* Harper and Row, 1966.

———. *A Danger of Democracy*. Westview Press, 1981.

———. *Outlive Your Enemies: Grow Old Gracefully*. Nova Science Publishers, 1996.

———. *Storm Over the States*. McGraw-Hill Book Company, 1967.

THE SCOTTS OF HAW RIVER

By William D. Snider

FEW TWENTIETH-CENTURY FAMILIES epitomize the rough-hewn, unpretentious, and independent spirit of North Carolina better than the Scotts of Hawfields, who in one century produced a legislator and prominent leader in the Farmers' Alliance, two governors (one of whom went on to the U.S. Senate), a legislator of impressive influence, and a modern commissioner of agriculture with a law degree to her credit.

All rose from one remarkable family who first arrived among the adventurous Scotch-Irish immigrants who trudged the great "Wagon Road" from Pennsylvania in the early 1700s and carved out their small family farms among the rolling foothills of the piedmont just west of Hillsborough and south of Danville.

Their staple crops were small grains, flax, cotton, and tobacco. Not associated with the eastern plantation society, they easily became a typical part of the pioneer culture labeled by the Old North State's haughty neighbors in Virginia and South Carolina as a "vale of humility between two mountains of conceit."

The Scott family joined the leadership of North Carolina in the twentieth century. The first Robert Walter Scott was born during the Civil War on July 21, 1861, and was educated at the Hughes Academy, the Bingham School, and the University of North Carolina. He left college to take over the management of the family's war-wrecked farm and bought out his brothers and sisters. Scott was intent on studying and utilizing new farming methods and visited prosperous farms in Pennsylvania and New York to bring new inventions, like the wheat thresher, to Hawfields.

On July 17, 1883, the enterprising twenty-two-year-old married Elizabeth Hughes, the daughter of the principal of his old preparatory school. Soon afterwards, he became busy improving the tobacco factory started by his father, Henderson Scott, and extending sales to Ohio, Indiana, and Tennessee. He became known as "Farmer Bob" and a leader in the Farmers' Alliance, which had been organized in the South in 1874 to encourage better farm practices. The organization spread widely across North Carolina, where farms lay in wrack and ruin after the war. As the Alliance became a powerful political organization in the poverty-stricken economy, Scott, then twenty-seven, recognized its potential. In 1888, he became a candidate for the state house of representatives, thus beginning a long career that included five terms representing Alamance County.

Scott took a leading role in the farming renaissance as well as the "Young Turks" political movement in the early 1900s. Scott ran for the state senate from Alamance and won by a large majority and was on hand when Governor Charles B. Aycock began to turn North Carolina's gaze to the future and away from the war and Reconstruction, with his crusade for public education. He backed Aycock's education program, campaigned for tax support of the Hawfields Public School, and joined the leadership that established what later became North Carolina State University, where he was named a trustee.

The new governor appointed him to the state Board of Agriculture—a job that he held under six succeeding governors—and the Scott farm became a showplace for new agricultural ideas. He built herds of purebred Jersey cows, Shropshire sheep, and Berkshire hogs. He supported the beginning of the farm demonstration work in Alamance County as well as crop rotation and soil improvements. All ran counter to the prevailing practices of most farmers, who had so little livestock that some had to purchase milk for their own table and who depended on crops of cotton and tobacco planted year after year on land soon depleted from misuse.

His influence in the state was enhanced by the continued growth of the Farmers' Alliance. In the years just before World War I, its annual meetings in Raleigh drew thousands to sessions that focused attention on new ideas and resolutions to old problems, such as burdensome farm credit. The Raleigh-based *Progressive Farmer* was a virtual house organ for the Alliance, and Scott's wife, Lizzie, a savvy businesswoman who managed the farm in the absence of her husband, was a regular contributor before her death in 1914.

The power of the Alliance declined in the years following the war, but Scott remained active. In 1928, he was elected again to the state senate after a hiatus of nearly thirty years. Against the protests of his friends, he resigned from the state Board of Agriculture, saying it was not proper to serve in two public offices at the same time. No successor was appointed and as soon as the General Assembly adjourned,

Robert W. Scott (left) and W. Kerr Scott (above) with Charlotte Mayor Ben Douglas (Courtesy of Hugh Morton)

Governor O. Max Gardner reappointed Scott to the board, a position he held until his death at the age of sixty-eight on May 16, 1929.

Scott and his wife produced a family of fourteen children and established a dynasty destined to influence North Carolina for the rest of the century. One son, Samuel Floyd, became a beloved family physician in Alamance County, delivering more than six thousand babies in his fifty-year career. A daughter, Elizabeth Scott Carrington, was a nurse and chair of a committee that founded the School of Nursing at the University of North Carolina in Chapel Hill. Another son, Ralph Henderson, organized Melville Dairy and was an influential member of the state senate whose service spanned three decades. During his legislative career he created the state Milk Commission, supported legislation for education, agriculture, and social service, and was a counselor to governors, including Terry Sanford, whose programs he championed.

The dominant figure of this generation was William Kerr Scott, a brush-browed, tobacco-chewing, hefty bull of a man who came suddenly on the post–World War II scene and changed the shape of North Carolina politics.

Kerr, as he was known, was born April 17, 1896, and educated at N.C. State College (later North Carolina State University). He founded Melville Dairy with his brother and was an outspoken figure in the farm movement. He was elected state commissioner of agriculture in 1936, unseating William A. Graham. Once in office, Scott roamed the back roads of the state and aggressively worked for farmers struggling against

foreclosure during the Depression. He was reelected in 1940 and 1944 and announced as a surprise candidate for governor in 1948, largely because he could not get the road to his family farm paved.

Scott challenged the ruling political establishment of Governor O. Max Gardner, whose pick for governor was state treasurer Charles Johnson. He claimed he only wanted to "let a little fresh air" into the public life of North Carolina and with the mud of Haw River on his shoes edged into second place in the Democratic primary. He captured the Democratic nomination in a runoff enlivened by leaflets Scott workers left at country stores that showed the money state banks made from non-interest-bearing state accounts.

Scott wrought something of a Tar Heel political revolution. He spoke of his victory as "the bottom layer overturning the top." But Scott brought with him far more than the stereotyped redneck, wool-hat tradition of the Deep South. His family, in the best sense, represented the state's traditional independent ruralism. It was chitlins and cornbread, but also light and enlightenment.

Scott immediately set about proclaiming the need for a $200-million bond issue to get North Carolina's "branch-head boys" out of the dust and mud of rural back roads. When the major oil companies launched a publicity campaign against the bonds, Scott's principal adviser, Capus Waynick of High Point, suggested the bond issue be cut in half. Scott plowed on and his bond package passed both the legislature and a referendum in 1949. Coming well before the rise of post–World War II inflation, the bond funds allowed many of the state's residents to remain in their rural residences, but use farm-to-market and farm-to-factory roads for employment and commerce.

Scott used his four-year term to focus attention on farmers, children in double-shift classrooms, and rural homes without electricity and phones. He was characteristically blunt and outspoken. At a dedication ceremony for a new power plant, he challenged the utilities to justify their franchise by extending service to rural areas. (There was little love lost between Scott, a champion of rural cooperatives, and the privately owned utilities like Carolina Power and Light, whose president, Louis V. Sutton, Scott privately referred to as "Low-Voltage Sutton.") At an august dinner meeting of the state's business leaders, the governor told them the name of their magazine, *We The People,* should be changed to *We The People Against The People.*

But while establishment politicians feared Scott's radicalism, they soon found it surprisingly progressive and profitable. Scott's roads improved farm markets and moved rural workers closer to the growing number of factory jobs.

He also moved to fuse ruralism with intellectualism. Following the death of another Gardner establishment veteran, newly elected U.S. Senator J. Melville Broughton, the governor ended a speech in Chapel Hill with the unexpected announcement that he was appointing UNC President Frank Graham as his replacement. The appointment led to a fiery political campaign in 1950 and Scott could not keep his rural followers and the intellectuals in line. In a contest marked with bitter racial demagoguery and bombast, Graham went down to defeat at the hands of the establishment's Willis Smith. Two years later, Scott's handpicked successor, Hubert Olive, was defeated by William Umstead. When Scott left office he summed up his fours years in office by saying the most satisfying achievement was rural roads and the access they had provided for members of country churches.

The Scott family had long been an important part of the Hawfields Presbyterian Church. The governor's father had served as a deacon and elder, was superintendent of the Sunday school, and taught a class there. He took a leading role in raising endowment funds for a cemetery and championed the Sunday school building fund. In 1927, he was elected to represent Orange Presbytery at the meeting of the General Assembly of the Southern Presbyterian Church. Scott continued to attend the church throughout his term, walking to services with his brother, Ralph, while they talked politics.

Scott left Raleigh for his farm in Alamance County with a police escort that lasted only to the Wake County line. There he stopped along the side of the road for a picnic lunch with his wife prepared by the staff at the Executive Mansion. When he got home he pulled on his brogans and went rabbit hunting. Two years later, he was back in a political fight that his followers called "the third primary," a reference to Graham's loss in 1950, as he campaigned for the United States Senate.

Scott conducted a campaign that *New York Times* writer Tom Wicker later used as a model for his novel, *Facing The Lions.* It was homespun and freewheeling, but a bit more controlled than earlier outings under the direction of his young manager, Terry Sanford. After Scott easily defeated Senator Alton Lennon, the man Umstead had named to replace Senator Clyde R. Hoey, who had died at his desk, he headed to Washington.

In the Senate, Scott again confounded his critics. Many had expected a continuation of his feisty behavior, but he proved to be a quiet freshman, listening and learning. He sported a red rose in his lapel and led prayer breakfasts. His chief interests were in agriculture and development of water resources and on these issues he formed abiding alliances with many western colleagues. It was no surprise, however, that he avoided the demagoguery of race that had become synonymous with Southern politics after the 1954 *Brown* decision. As governor, he had appointed the first African American to the state Board of Education. His service was cut short by a heart attack and death on April 16, 1958. He was sixty-two.

On July 2, 1919, Kerr Scott had married Mary Elizabeth White, who had attended the State Normal School (later the University of North Carolina at Greensboro), and they raised three children, a daughter and two sons. The youngest boy was named for his grandfather and became Robert Walter Scott II. Born June 13, 1929, he would follow his father to the governor's mansion and become the only son of a governor to hold that office since Richard Dobbs Speight Jr. in 1835.

Bob had set out to study medicine at Duke University but later transferred to North Carolina State College, where he received a degree in animal husbandry in 1952. In the family tradition, he returned to Alamance County, where he worked at church and agricultural affairs as owner and manager of Melville Farm and was named Young Farmer of the Year. He married Jessie Rae Osborne in 1951 and steered clear of politics until the early 1960s.

Scott and many of his father's followers helped

Terry Sanford win the governorship in 1960 and one old warhorse, Ben Roney of Rocky Mount, suggested that young Bob should try in 1964. That was not to be, but Roney did convince him to run for lieutenant governor. Scott edged out two seasoned legislators in the spring primary and four years later, in 1968, he used the office as a stepping stone to the governorship.

The youthful governor had many of the strikingly independent qualities of his father, but they were put together in a different way. Scott, the son, represented a smoother, updated version of the rough-hewn Scott, the father. Like the younger generation of Longs of Louisiana and Talmadges of Georgia, he reflected the gray flannel suit, post–World War II generation. Tom Bost, longtime Raleigh correspondent of the *Greensboro Daily News,* once wrote that if Kerr Scott ever thought he had any tact, he'd take something to get rid of it. Although Bob Scott could be bullheaded and make tough decisions, he had a more genial and gentle demeanor.

During the racial unrest of the late 1960s, Governor Scott intervened in the food service strike by the Black Student Movement at the Chapel Hill campus of the university. Scott refused to follow the advice of President William Friday and Chancellor Carlyle Sitterson, who had recommended further negotiations. The governor, deciding a show of force was necessary, released a twelve-point statement listing procedures if attempts were made to occupy state-owned buildings. He ordered four National Guard units assembled in Durham as a "precautionary measure" and sent five squads of State Highway Patrolmen to the campus with orders to reopen the dining hall.

The governor's firmness worked. Black activists were cleared from the building. A few days later, the governor's uncle, Senator Ralph Scott, introduced a bill for an immediate 10 percent raise for nonacademic employees. The food service director was assigned to another post after auditors found cases of unpaid overtime wages.

Scott's most controversial public action during his four-year term involved his call for the state's first tax on tobacco and a soft drink levy that he said were needed to alleviate a budget crisis. The governor also backed a two-cent increase in the gasoline tax, pushing the state tax to the highest in the nation. Following his father's example, Scott was action-prone. He prevailed over opponents who tried to portray him as an irresponsible spendthrift, a farmer-governor who knew nothing about good business management.

During the last two years in office, he presided over the most comprehensive reorganization of state government since the 1930s and a merger of the state's sixteen institutions of higher learning, then engaged in destructive competition and infighting. The state's distinguished consolidated universities—the nationally known research institutions at Chapel Hill, Raleigh, and Greensboro—had encountered a head-on clash with former community and teachers' colleges across the state. As these campuses flourished, their influence grew in the General Assembly, which, in the words of the critics, established a plethora of "instant" universities eagerly seeking money to expand.

Until Scott's initiative, no effective way had been found to apportion functions and powers to all institutions. They needed overall supervision in budgets to curb swarms of lobbyists who flocked to the legislature from the campuses.

After a long and bitter fight with both old-line supporters of the Consolidated University—a powerful educational establishment—and new college leaders from outside, Scott succeeded in forcing a compromise. Amazingly, it maintained the quality and reputation of the mainline schools and at the same time provided room for new ones to grow and prosper. Because of the skilled management of UNC system President William Friday, who unanimously won support for supervising the reshuffled infrastructure, the compromise worked.

Scott recognized that he should use Friday's skill and experience to, in his own words, "get sufficient power in the center to insure effective control and coordination." Scott, in a talk at St. Louis, also recognized his own need for enlightenment when he declared, "I have entitled my talk 'The Reorganization of Higher Education in North Carolina' but I could just as easily have called it 'The Higher Education of Bob Scott.'"

Scott's education achievement won even the begrudging respect of the *Chapel Hill Weekly,* a strong adversary of the governor during the reorganization fight. In an editorial entitled "Say a Word for Old Bob," it declared, "[Scott] was heavy-handed, abrasive and abusive" and he "dangled political plunder more openly and more cynically than any other governor in recent history." But the newspaper went on to say, " . . . you have to concede that he took on the University of North Carolina and its thousands of loyal alumni in a deadly struggle—something no other governor dared do—and virtually staked his place in history on the outcome. The boldness of his plan was stunning. The changes it will bring about will be profound. The reward it will bring to higher education will be a long time coming. . . . Chances are good that [his achievement] will stand as deep and tall as his daddy's in taking the farmer out of the mud and kerosene lamplight, and as O. Max Gardner's in putting together the original Greater University."

After leaving office, Scott led the state's agribusiness lobby and was named director of the Appalachian Regional Commission by President Jimmy Carter. He later was named president of the state community college system.

In 2000, the Scott family made history again when a member of the fourth generation was elected to statewide office. Bob Scott's daughter, Meg Scott Phipps, was sworn in as commissioner of agriculture in 2001 after winning a close race against a Republican opponent in the 2000 general election.

When people occasionally questioned Kerr Scott about complex foreign policy questions in various parts of the world, he often, with a twinkle in his eye, would reply, "Now, that's a long way from Haw River." Clearly the Scotts of Hawfields had moved a "long way from Haw River" and contributed vastly to the uplift of North Carolina.

William D. Snider is the retired editor of the Greensboro News and Record *and the author of* Helms and Hunt, *a study of the 1982 senatorial contest between Senator Jesse Helms and Governor Jim Hunt, and* A Light on the Hill, *a history of the University of North Carolina.*

For more information see:

Roberts, Bruce, and Nancy Roberts. *The Governor.* Heritage Printers, 1972.

Scott, Robert W. *Official Papers of Governor Robert W. Scott.* N.C. Council of State, Raleigh, 1973.

Scott, W. Kerr. *Official Papers of Governor W. Kerr Scott.* N.C. Council of State, Raleigh, 1953.

Speck, Jean. *The Gentleman from Haw River.* Privately published, 1990.

Turner, Dr. Herbert S. *The Scott Family of Hawfields.* Privately published, 1971.

GERTRUDE WEIL

By Steven Niven

Few Tar Heels matched Gertrude Weil's zeal or contribution to the cause of women's rights during the twentieth century. Weil was a founder of both the North Carolina Federation of Women's Clubs and the state's Equal Suffrage League, and also served as the first president of the North Carolina chapter of the League of Women's Voters. In the 1920s, a time when state and local provision for the poor was minimal, she came to be known as the "one-woman welfare department" in her native Wayne County.

With the onset of the New Deal, she also worked with state and federal authorities to ensure that the government extended a basic standard of welfare provisions for Tar Heels of all races. Like many liberal whites in the mid-century South, Gertrude Weil worked to improve interracial cooperation but did not directly challenge segregation. Nonetheless, once African Americans began to challenge the color line, she proved to be a supportive and consistent white ally.

Gertrude Weil was born in 1879 in Goldsboro to Henry Weil, a German-Jewish immigrant, and Mina Rosenthal Weil, the daughter of German-Jewish immigrants. Henry Weil, a Confederate veteran, and his brothers Hermann and Solomon had established a general store in Goldsboro at the end of the Civil War, and had rapidly expanded the family business holdings to include, among other interests, the Pioneer Tobacco Company, the Goldsboro Savings Bank, and the Goldsboro Oil Company. By 1900, the Weil family business ranked among the most successful in the state, and earned more than a million dollars in sales.

The family also played a prominent role in civic affairs in Wayne County. In the 1880s, two decades before Governor Charles B. Aycock's expansion of the state public school system, the Weil brothers helped found a graded public school in Goldsboro, modeled on the German system. In fact, the graded school that Gertrude attended as a young girl was arguably the most advanced in the state, and certainly one of the few that enabled young girls to gain an education and to compete on a level playing field with young boys. Gertrude was thus born into a world of relative privilege, but also, an admirer noted, into a "home that was a school for citizenship." That background helped to nurture an early commitment to public service. One of Gertrude's earliest memories was of helping her mother at a Goldsboro charity bazaar for the victims of the Charleston earthquake of 1886.

At thirteen, Gertrude moved to New York to study at the Horace Mann School, a preparatory college affiliated with Columbia University. One of her teachers there, Margaret Stanton Lawrence, was the daughter of Elizabeth Cady Stanton, arguably the preeminent American feminist of the nineteenth century. On graduation from Horace Mann, Gertrude attended Smith College in Massachusetts, and, in 1901, was the first North Carolinian to earn a degree from the exclusive women's college.

At both Horace Mann and Smith, Weil enthusiastically challenged the Victorian ideal of "true womanhood." She enjoyed physical exercise, especially basketball and long bike rides, and, much against the convention of the time, refused to wear restraining corsets. Weil maintained her love of strenuous activity, particularly horse riding, swimming, and diving, well into her seventies. She also expressed an interest in traditionally male academic subjects such as mechanical drawing and political economy, and, at Smith, began a lifelong interest in the then new discipline of sociology. Intrigued by the structural and social bases of poverty and economic equality, she immersed herself in Marx, Engels, and other radical social thinkers, but was increasingly drawn to the work of feminist activist and theorist Charlotte Perkins Gilman. In 1899, Gilman, author of *Women and Economics,* made a rare trip to the South, to Goldsboro, to address the Ladies Benevolent Society at the request of Gertrude's Aunt Sarah.

Weil graduated from Smith College in 1901, ready to take on the many exciting opportunities that the new century offered to a young woman of her qualifications and background. Yet if Gertrude wanted to take on the world—and she traveled widely in Europe in the next few years—the demands of home and family drew her inexorably back to Goldsboro, at first to look after an ailing aunt. Marriage might have provided something of an escape from family concerns, but, as she later recalled, "nobody wanted me."

In fact, several suitors pursued Gertrude, but the ranks of eligible Jewish bachelors in eastern North Carolina were slim, and she found none with whom

Gertrude Weil (Courtesy of N.C. Office of Archives and History)

she could tolerate "sharing three meals a day;" only her brother and a close female friend ever fulfilled that requirement. Yet the choice of spinsterhood was not at all atypical for women of her class and educational background. More than two-thirds of the graduates of Seven Sisters colleges at the turn of the century remained single, and like many of these women, Gertrude preferred the social and intellectual company of her own gender. In Goldsboro, that brought Weil increasingly into the world of the Women's Club movement that her mother, aunts, and the philosophy of Charlotte Perkins Gilman had helped to launch.

In 1902, Sallie Southall Cotton established a state-wide body, the North Carolina Federation of Women's Clubs (NCFWC), and encouraged the twenty-three-year-old Weil to take a prominent leadership role. Weil supported the broad goals of the club movement—increased participation by women in community affairs, improved working and social conditions for women and children, and better welfare provision—but she increasingly concentrated her energies on one issue that the NCFWC ignored: women's suffrage.

Weil believed that women's right to vote was self-evident, since "women breathe the same air, [and] get the same education." It was "ridiculous," she thought, for women to have to spend "so much energy and elocution on something so rightfully theirs."

Most Tar Heel men and many Tar Heel women remained unconvinced of that argument at a time when only a few western states granted both sexes the vote, but Weil worked hard to persuade them. In 1912, she mounted a successful crusade to allow women to sit on local school boards, even though the state legislature still prohibited women from *voting* for the boards. Such gradualist tactics eventually won the support of many more conservative women and men, who were uncertain about the expansion of the "male" franchise, but believed that women had a special role in influencing education.

With that principle accepted, however, a growing number of women and men began to come around to Weil's view that women needed the vote to exercise such feminine influence. Younger women, in particular, were attracted to the N.C. Equal Suffrage League (NCESL) that she helped establish in 1914. For the next six years, Weil traveled the length and breadth of the state and worked with national suffrage leaders like Carrie Chapman Catt to win passage of a constitutional amendment to grant women the vote. In 1919 and 1920, with Weil as president, the NCESL lobbied the state legislature vigorously to adopt the nineteenth amendment. Yet as was the case half a century later with the Equal Rights Amendment, the conservative forces in Raleigh prevailed. In 1920, however, Tennessee succeeded where North Carolina failed, and ensured the two-thirds of the states majority required to give all women the vote.

Almost immediately, Weil helped found and lead the North Carolina League of Women Voters (NCLWV) to ensure that women in her state would understand and exercise that new-won right. She was also determined to expose political corruption wherever she saw it, and to ensure that all voters, male or female, had a fair electoral choice. In 1922, in one of the first elections in the state in which women could vote, Weil entered the Goldsboro courthouse and was outraged when an election official handed her a ballot marked with approved candidates. She promptly tore up the sample ballot and proceeded to destroy hundreds of others stacked on a nearby table.

With political—or at least electoral—equality won, Weil turned her attention to matters of economic equality and social justice. In particular, she focused on the issues of child labor, women's working conditions, and the right to unionize. Her early training in sociology, and her understanding of feminist thinkers like Charlotte Perkins Gilman, convinced Weil that the vote was not an end in itself, but a means for women to fight for greater social justice.

As she looked at conditions in North Carolina's mills and factories, Weil saw much injustice. On the issue of child labor, she succeeded in bringing the League of Women Voters and at least some of the state's more progressive minds along with her. In the 1920s, North Carolina, like other southern states, began to place restrictions on the number of hours that children under fourteen could work. Weil's support of organized labor proved much more controversial. When it came to striking textile workers in Marion, and later in Gastonia, in the 1920s, the predominantly well-to-do women of the NCLWV chose solidarity with their anti-union husbands and families rather than with the many women members of the United Textile Workers. Not for the first time, Weil's social and economic philosophy was simply too radical for most of her friends in North Carolina's close-knit, broadly conservative elite.

In 1927, as president of the Goldsboro Bureau of Social Service, Weil offered a concise statement of that philosophy. "It is not enough," she wrote, "to eliminate one case of poverty after another, but to eliminate poverty itself. We must look beyond the immediate problem of the special case to the underlying physical and social conditions that lead to dependence and maladjustment."

Such views found few backers in the laissez-faire era of President Calvin Coolidge and North Carolina's "businessman governor," Angus MacLean. They even went beyond the relief policies introduced six years later by President Franklin Roosevelt to deal with the Depression. As a pragmatist, Weil welcomed FDR's New Deal and served as Goldsboro's director of public relief, but, again, her belief in attacking the structural basis of inequality stood outside the consensus shared by North Carolinians—or at least by most state politicians and shapers of public opinion in the 1930s. Indeed, as Lyndon Johnson and Governor Terry Sanford found in their efforts to wage a war on poverty thirty years later, most Americans would continue to view poverty as a matter of individual failings and not, as Weil insisted, as a matter of social structure.

Weil's experiences during the Depression convinced her that North Carolinians would not only need to address economic and gender inequality, but the consequences of racial inequality as well. In 1932, at the request of Governor O. Max Gardner, she joined the North Carolina Commission on Interracial Cooperation (NCCIC). The NCCIC was a moderate organization, but it offered a rare forum in which blacks and whites could at least debate matters such as job training and economic opportunity for blacks. Its white members supported segregation, and most blacks in the NCCIC in the 1930s who opposed Jim Crow did not use the organization as a platform for such views. In the late 1940s, when the NCCIC and its regional parent, the Southern Regional Council, did begin to call for integration, many of its most prominent white members left the NCCIC. Weil, significantly, did not.

Weil stuck resolutely by her faith in interracial cooperation, even as the state became more polarized in the wake of the Supreme Court's 1954 *Brown* decision. She supported the NCCIC's successor, the N.C. Council on Human Relations (NCCHR), which tried to ease white fears that school desegregation would lead to "race mixing." As in the case of women's suffrage, however, Weil and the NCCHR found it "very difficult to convince people of something they don't already believe in." Weil was in her eighties when the National Association for the Advancement of Colored People (NAACP) and later the sit-in protestors began to challenge the myth of separate and equal facilities, and her first response reflected, perhaps, a touch of progressive era pragmatism and noblesse oblige. When whites in Wayne County denied blacks access to "their" swimming pool and other recreation facilities, she donated land that she owned in a black Goldsboro neighborhood to help build a swimming pool and a park. But Weil also recognized that separate and equal solutions could only be temporary.

In the early 1960s, as civil rights demonstrations shifted from the urban piedmont to the east, she offered her home as a meeting place for interracial gatherings, and helped found the Goldsboro Bi-racial Council. For her efforts in promoting racial tolerance, the Council on Human Relations awarded her its Howard Odum Award in 1965.

Weil's own membership in a minority group may have been a factor in her support for civil rights. Certainly, her Jewish faith never wavered. She rarely missed services at her local synagogue, taught classes at Goldsboro's Oheb Sholom Temple for many years, and was prominent in the regional leadership of Hadassah and Sisterhood. Like her mother and aunts before her, she took a leadership role in the North Carolina Association of Jewish Women, serving as president of that organization three times. During World War II—as in World War I—Weil was active in the Red Cross, but she also played a major role in welcoming, entertaining, and educating the unprecedented number of Jewish GIs who had come to North Carolina's military bases, notably to Goldsboro's Seymour Johnson Air Force Base.

Unlike her father, and, indeed, unlike many southern Jews of the Reform tradition, Weil was also a committed Zionist. Her father, Henry Weil, had traveled to the Holy Land in 1910 and declared it "criminal" to "settle poor Jews in Palestine on barren soil." The far greater crimes of the Nazi regime and the Holocaust persuaded his daughter to take a quite different view, however.

In the 1930s, Weil had worked to rescue Jewish families from persecution, and after the war, she became a passionate advocate for a separate Jewish state. In 1951, she traveled to the new state of Israel to take part in its third anniversary celebrations. She argued that there could be "no Judaism without Israel," vigorously supported closer American ties to Israel, and supported the expansion of faith-based Jewish education within America.

Throughout her career, Weil maintained the respect of Tar Heel movers and shakers, even though many—probably most—of North Carolina's leading citizens strongly disagreed with her views. Even as the race- and red-baiting intensity of the 1950s raged around the state, she still gloried in the label of "socialist." She also refused to join many of her fellow clubwomen in the United Daughters of the Confederacy. She was immensely proud of her southern roots, and claimed that it was easier to be Jewish in the South because fundamentalist Protestants respected Jews' commitment to their faith, but she dismissed the war her father fought in as "something that should be forgotten."

Her political incorrectness (for those times) appears not to have been a bar to winning a host of accolades, however. In 1951, the Chi Omega Sorority named her Outstanding Women of the Year, and North Carolina Woman's College (later the University of North Carolina at Greensboro) presented her with an honorary doctorate of laws the following year. For the range of her contributions to civic and interfaith affairs, her hometown of Goldsboro named Weil "Woman of the Year" in 1953, and the North Carolina B'nai B'rith honored her with its distinguished service award in three years later.

In 1965, her alma mater named Weil as one of the first five recipients of the Smith Medal, in recognition of a "lifetime of service to the cultural, charitable, religious, and political welfare of [her] State." To a greater degree than her previous awards, the Smith Medal citation recognized not only Weil's humility and commitment to public service, but also her essential radicalism. "The Women's Suffrage Council of half a century ago and today's bi-racial council," the citation noted, "shared a common concern for equal rights and human freedom."

Weil died at age ninety-one in 1971, in the same Goldsboro home in which she had been born. In that same year, albeit fifty years later than she had hoped, the North Carolina legislature finally passed the nineteenth amendment.

Steven Niven received his M.A. from Edinburgh University, and was a student and researcher at the University of Pennsylvania in the early 1990s. As a doctoral candidate in UNC-Chapel Hill's history department, his dissertation, "Shades of Whiteness," examined the complexities of the white response to the civil rights movement in North Carolina. He has written for the North Carolina Literary Review *and* Southern Cultures.

For more information, see:

Weil, Gertrude. Clipping File. North Carolina Collection, University of North Carolina at Chapel Hill.

————. Papers. Private Manuscript Collections, N.C. Office of Archives and History, Raleigh.

Evans, Eli N. *The Provincials: A Personal History of Jews in the South.* Atheneum, 1973.

Rountree, Moses. *Strangers in the Land: The Story of Jacob Weil's Tribe.* Dorrance and Company, 1969.

Smith, Margaret Supplee, and Emily Herring Wilson. "Gertrude Weil." In *North Carolina Women Making History.* University of North Carolina Press, 1999.

Wilkerson-Freeman, Sarah. "The Emerging Political Consciousness of Gertrude Weil, Education, and Women's Clubs, 1879–1914." Masters thesis, University of North Carolina at Chapel Hill, 1986.

ELLEN B. WINSTON

By Lydia Charles Hoffman

ELLEN BLACK WINSTON contended that she did not have a southern accent. However, traces of her North Carolina roots were present in the smoothed edges of her speech. She laughed when she spoke of her mother's suggestion to attend college in South Carolina, where she hoped her eldest daughter's dialect would become more pronounced. As her mother wished, Winston's educational career did begin on a Spartanburg campus, and from there she continued to Chicago and came back to Raleigh. But it was in Washington, D.C., that this Tar Heel reformer's demand for professionalism and quality service in the area of social welfare earned her national repute.

Ellen Engelmann Black was born on August 15, 1903, in Bryson City, the oldest of four children born to Marianna Fisher and Stanley Warren Black. Ellen's father practiced law until becoming president at the local bank. He also served for three years as the chairman of the county school board while his children attended its public schools. Her mother was trained as a teacher and taught briefly in Illinois prior to her marriage. In Bryson City she organized the Woman's Club, the PTA, and the town's first library. The library was first located in the grand jury room —operated two afternoons each week—and was personally attended by Mrs. Black.

Ellen later stated that she and her siblings were "expected to be concerned about the less fortunate." Acting as an example for her children, Mrs. Black worked to raise funds for the county's black schools to insure that they had "play equipment and books." And on occasion she brought apples to the school to reward students who applied themselves and continued their studies. After her death, the Works Progress Administration (WPA) built a small library in Bryson City and named it the Marianna Black Library.

Ellen's brothers, Stanley W. Black Jr. and Fischer Black, both chose to remain in their home state after graduating from college. Stanley Jr. became secretary and vice president of the American Trust Company in Charlotte. Fischer, an electrical engineer, served as editor of *Electrical Age*. Ellen's sister Louise graduated from her elder sister's alma mater in South Carolina. She went on to study design at the Katherine Gibbs School in New York City. It was in New York that she met and married Oscar Cox. The newlyweds set up house in Washington, D.C., where Oscar joined

Ellen B. Winston (Courtesy of North Carolina Collection)

President Franklin D. Roosevelt's Administration as assistant general counsel and coauthored the Lend-Lease bill.

After graduating from Swain County High School in Bryson City, Ellen attended Converse College in Spartanburg, S.C., where she majored in English with a minor in French. "I don't think that there was ever any question that [I] would become a teacher," she said in a 1974 interview. Her mother had taught, and as a "traditional southern girl" it was one of the few respectable professions for a young educated woman. She began in the mathematics department, but found the material unchallenging once the "basic formulas were mastered." She changed her focus to education but "thought [the courses in that area] were rather stupid . . . the only thing that I ever felt

I learned from those courses, was somebody's statement, 'Let knowledge come from a smiling face,'" a phrase she said "stood me in good stead" in her future dealings with the North Carolina state legislature and federal agencies.

After graduating from Converse at the top of her class in 1924, Ellen returned to North Carolina to teach in Raleigh public schools. She taught English while continuing her own education by taking afternoon classes at North Carolina State College in Raleigh and the University of North Carolina in Chapel Hill. It was during these personal academic endeavors that she developed her interest in sociology—and where she met her future husband, Sanford R. Winston, a sociology professor at N.C. State. After much counsel from her parents and Sanford, Ellen turned down her acceptance in the master's program in sociology at UNC and began graduate studies at the University of Chicago in 1926.

During her first year in Illinois, her mother's home state, Ellen lived in the city with an aunt and uncle. Her second year found her in the upperclasswomen's dormitory, Green Hall. It was there that she found a community of intelligent young women whose mealtime conversations concerned "women's rights and pushing back the horizons" on national and local social and political issues. "This residence hall was a very good thing for someone coming up from the South, who hadn't had too much experience," Winston said. Dinners were served family style, with one female faculty member at the head of each table. Ellen found the atmosphere stimulating and challenging. There was a diversity of field interests in the residence hall: "home economics, biology, chemistry," and of course, sociology, were all represented. Listening to cultural events and topics filtered through the various disciplines informed Miss Black's educational formation. "We had a great mixture. . . . it really was great fun."

Soon after earning her master's degree in 1928, Ellen married Sanford. While she worked on her dissertation, she and her husband maintained two households. They shared a small apartment in Chicago, and Sanford commuted to Raleigh, where he still had teaching responsibilities. In 1930, Ellen completed her doctoral training, submitting "A Statistical Study of Mental Disease" as her thesis. She returned to the Tar Heel state to teach English and social science at Raleigh High School, while also serving as the campus director of guidance and dean of girls. From 1934 to 1939 she added to her workload, editing technical publications in the field of public relief for the Works Progress Administration Division of Research.

In addition to her publishing duties, Ellen super-

vised WPA training in the state. Fourteen years prior to *Brown v. Board of Education,* she desegregated WPA training sessions, arguing that "separate meetings . . . and informational sessions on the basis of race [was] too time-consuming, inefficient, wasteful."

In 1940, Winston joined the faculty at Meredith College and chaired the sociology department until her departure four years later. During her tenure she published numerous articles on the status of social welfare and assistance programs in North Carolina and throughout the United States. She also coauthored four well-received books: *Seven Lean Years* (1939), *The Plantation South 1934–1937* (1940), *Foundations of American Population Policy* (1940), and *The Negro's Share* (1943). The books documented her lifelong commitment to considering the "human elements" when addressing reform policies, as, in her words, "It is not what is done alone, but how it is done so that welfare services truly promote human dignity, independence and self-respect."

To better implement her philosophy of social reform, Winston left her position at Meredith in 1944 to become commissioner of North Carolina's Public Welfare Department. The training of not only her staff, but also of assistance recipients, was paramount to the program she envisioned. She asserted that North Carolinians should not have the "limited" idea of social work as mere financial assistance to the needy "[a belief] which is held by many people." Rather, the agency should emphasize "helping families to help themselves." Relief programs were set up to help undergird families so that the cycle of poverty did not continue: "If we deprive children of the essentials for healthy growth and development, we shall reap another generation who must be cared for by society because they lack the necessary education and job training."

North Carolina's welfare department was responsible for inspecting and setting the standards for jails, "child caring institutions," and other domestic service organizations. During Winston's tenure, more than five hundred private homes for the aged were licensed by the agency, the number of foster homes grew from 87 to 1,500, and the state's adoption program more than doubled.

Raising the standards within the department itself was also one of the new commissioner's edicts. The "professionalization" of welfare reform, changing from a volunteer-based to an academically prepared staff program, slowly gained momentum after the Depression years. Winston's insistence to hire only those who met particular experiential and academic "qualifications" mirrored this shift. Under her leadership, compensation and classification of welfare professionals were reevaluated and improved based on employee credentials, thereby raising the standards and respect for a traditionally female career domain.

Prior to taking her job as welfare commissioner, Winston served as the president of the North Carolina Legislative Council, chairman for the North Carolina Federation of Women's Clubs, and the international relations chairman for the North Carolina division of the American Association of University Women. In 1946, she was appointed to the National Commission on Children and Youth for "her experience in the field of public welfare administration," and continued her advocacy of social initiatives and professional development as chair of the North Carolina Governor's Coordinating Committee on Aging (1956–63) and president of the American Public Welfare Association (1957–59).

Winston's commitment to public service and human welfare captured the attention of President John F. Kennedy, and after eighteen years of service to her state, she joined Kennedy's administration as the first U.S. commissioner of public welfare in 1962. But before leaving for Washington, D.C., she worked to install a "data processing unit" to put "all State welfare cases on punch cards" to help keep track of those receiving assistance. Located under the umbrella of Health, Education, and Welfare Services, Winston's new department headed the Bureau of Family Services, the Children's Bureau, the Office of Juvenile Delinquency and Youth Development, and the Cuban refugee program.

From 1962 until her retirement as commissioner in 1967, Winston worked on national policies concerning research on and reporting of child welfare issues, the functions and relationships between federal and state agencies concerning maternal and child heath, as well as assistance for the elderly, medical assistance to the impoverished and underemployed, and aid to families with dependent children as well as the disabled. She contributed to the Johnson administration's "War on Poverty" initiatives, including Medicare and Medicaid, and spoke of building a "floor of hope" beneath the nation's poor. She understood the financial costs attached to such programs, but asserted that "you are going to continue to have poor people, continue to have sick people, and continue to have people of all ages who need help. . . . and in a civilized country, you are going to have to help them."

At the age of sixty-three, Winston resigned as commissioner of public welfare. After "twenty years

of progressively greater administrative responsibilities," she wanted to "be free to carry out varied projects close to [her] heart in the broad field of social welfare policy." Her husband, Sanford, had died the year before, so Ellen wanted to slow down a bit and return to North Carolina. Although she remained active in areas of child and family welfare, Winston focused her energies on aging in the United States during her "retirement." She was either chair or cochair of the North Carolina Committee for the 1961, 1971, and 1981 White House Conferences on Aging. She also served as chairman for the National Voluntary Organizations for Independent Living for the Aging (1971–75), N.C. Committee on the Aging (1972–73), and the N.C. Governor's Advisory Council on Aging (1977–84). She was elected president of the National Council on the Aging in 1980 and served until 1982.

Two years prior to her death, Winston explained her lifelong interest in social welfare. "The values you have, you get in your childhood. I was raised with the belief that we should help others." She was very disappointed with the congressional reductions in welfare funds during the early 1980s. "I see us going backward in so many areas that affect the daily lives of the people who are poor," she said. "But while I am deeply concerned about the effects reduced funds will have on older people, I'm more worried about the coming children. If we have a child who does not have adequate food and an adequate learning environment, he inevitab[ly] will grow up unable to compete in [an] urbanized society." Having no children of her own, Ellen Black Winston strove for the rights and welfare of others. She died in her home in Raleigh at the age of eighty.

Lydia Charles Hoffman is a former director of the Charlotte Hawkins Brown Historic Site. She received her B.A. in history from the University of California at Berkeley and her M.A. in history from the University of North Carolina at Chapel Hill. While completing doctoral work in cultural studies at George Mason University, she worked in the Smithsonian Institution's National Museum of American History affiliations program department.

For more information see:
Winston, Ellen Black. Papers. Special Collections, North Carolina State University.
———. Papers. Southern Historical Collection, University of North Carolina at Chapel Hill.
———. Papers. Special Collections, University of North Carolina at Greensboro.

RELIGION

Ｎorth Carolina has produced its share of fundamentalist preachers, tub-thumping prohibitionists, and even the world's best-known evangelist, Billy Graham, but also from the ranks of organized religion have come those who established the principles of academic freedom at a critical hour and spoke for the open exploration of ideas and social change, no matter how controversial.

No man of the cloth was better known—or more controversial—in the first two decades of the century than Mordecai Ham, an anti-Semitic revivalist whose career rose with the Anti-Saloon League and was at its peak in 1927 during a failed attempt to have the North Carolina General Assembly enact legislation to prohibit the teaching of evolution.

The organized church and religion held a strong grip on the life of the state. Towns went dry long before national Prohibition due to campaigns led by religious leaders; many Sunday activities—most certainly retail sales—were outlawed until into the 1970s. But nowhere in the early years was religion more influential than in higher education.

A quarter of the century had passed before the state funding for publicly owned institutions approached the level of what the Presbyterians, Methodists, and Baptists devoted to their schools. Ironically, from these campuses came men like Trinity College (Methodist) President John C. Kilgo and Wake Forest College (Baptist) President William L. Poteat to defend academic freedom.

It was Kilgo's presence in the pulpit that first attracted the attention of Washington Duke, who with his sons would endow Trinity and create Duke University. But it was Kilgo's defense of Trinity professor John Spencer Bassett against the editorial brickbats of Josephus Daniels and the *News and Observer* that established the right for free expression for Trinity, and even for other southern institutions. Likewise, Poteat stood against the imposition of legislative will on what should be taught—breaking with a majority of his Baptist brethren to help defeat the so-called monkey bill under debate in the legislative session of 1927.

Ham was on the wane in 1934 when a Charlotte teenager named Billy Graham answered one of his altar calls. Graham entered religious study and set a course for a career as an evangelist. Fifteen years later, in 1949, during a crusade in Los Angeles, his words caught the attention of newspaper publisher William Randolph Hearst, whose attentions helped create a national reputation. For more than twenty years, a string of presidents from Harry Truman to Richard Nixon recognized the benefits of cordiality with Graham, and the evangelist, for his part, returned their affection.

The Graham phenomenon at mid-century was matched in the black community by the rise of Charles Manuel Grace—or Bishop Sweet Daddy Grace, as he was known—who founded the United House of Prayer for All People and established one of his twelve churches on the East Coast in Charlotte. In his later years, Grace came under attack for a lifestyle of opulence that later brought down Jim Bakker of Charlotte with his PTL (Praise The Lord) Club, an electronic church that attracted millions of dollars in contributions before Bakker's indiscretions and a federal conviction toppled his kingdom.

More prevalent were those religious leaders and thinkers who moved more simply through life. Willis D. Weatherford was the Young Men's Christian Association for many in the South, particularly after he founded the YMCA's Blue Ridge Assembly grounds near Black Mountain. A generation later came a Baptist named William Finlator, the longtime pastor of Raleigh's Pullen Memorial Church, who during the turbulence spawned by social issues in the 1960s and 1970s used his pulpit to preach that the Sermon on the Mount made sound social doctrine.

Likewise, Charlotte's Carlyle Marney was considered one of the nation's leading theologians in the 1960s, and from his pulpit at Charlotte Myers Park Baptist Church he pricked the conscience of many of that city's business and political elite. Later, he founded Interpreters' House, an interdenominational midlife training program for ministers at Lake Junaluska.

Durham produced not only the center of black capitalism in America but a church at White Rock Baptist to offer spiritual support. For more than thirty years, the Reverend Miles Mark Fisher was a spokesman for human rights from his pulpit in Durham's White Rock Baptist Church.

North Carolina also produced Shirley Caesar, one of the nation's best-known gospel singers, who turned her fame, and the fortune it produced, back to the community for service in Durham.

SHIRLEY CAESAR

By Marsha Cook Vick

WITH THEIR BROTHER Solomon holding a Bible and wiping his face with a handkerchief as he waved his arms and "preached" in the backyard, twelve-year-old Shirley Caesar and her sister Anne followed his instructions to "Jump up and shout 'Jesus' three times." The young Caesar children often "played church," but this time was different. Before she hit the ground after jumping for the third time, Shirley felt the presence of the Lord and the power of the Holy Ghost within her. "From that day forward," she later said, "I have known that Jesus is Lord, and I have tried to reflect this reality in my life and music." Her commitment to God manifested itself in her ministries as an evangelist and a church pastor and in her outreach ministry of providing for the needs of the underprivileged and unemployed in her hometown of Durham. In her gospel music ministry Shirley Caesar captivated audiences for more than forty years and prevailed as the nation's best-known gospel singer.

Shirley Caesar was born in Durham on October 13, 1938, the tenth of twelve children to Hallie Martin Caesar and James S. Caesar. Shirley inherited a passion for gospel music from her father, who was a tobacco factory worker, a minister, and the leader of a dynamic gospel quartet. She absorbed essential musical techniques and refined her musical gifts both at church, where she "sang out" with her powerful voice in the children's choir, and at home, where she and her sister Anne sang at an open window as they washed dishes, attracting a following in the neighborhood and in the greater community.

After Jim Caesar's death in 1945, the large family remained together through the strong will of their mother, a homemaker and semi-invalid. With the Christian faith as the foundation of their lives and their home, the Caesar family was able to survive intense poverty, largely because of the earnings of young Shirley. As a ten-year-old, Shirley was singing at school and in local churches with the Caesar Sisters, a quartet that included her sisters Anne and Joyce and a cousin, Esther, and also with a gospel quartet led by her brother LeRoy. During her teenage years she sang in churches and in concerts throughout North Carolina and the South with Leroy Johnson, who featured her as "Baby Shirley Caesar"; with The Charity Singers; and with the popular group Thelma Bumpass and the Royalettes. She often re-

Shirley Caesar (Courtesy of Charlotte Observer)

turned to Durham exhausted and with just enough time to change clothes and rush to school. She graduated from Hillside High School and in 1958 completed her freshman year at North Carolina College for Negroes (later North Carolina Central University) in Durham.

At the age of nineteen, Shirley Caesar got her big break in gospel music when the Caravans, a renowned gospel group, was touring in North Carolina. At their Raleigh concert, Shirley was determined to fill the position of the missing fourth singer in the group and tried to get a message to the Caravans' lead singer, Albertina Walker, but she failed, so she followed the Caravans to their next concert in Kinston. Sitting near the front of the auditorium, Shirley sent the mistress of ceremonies a note saying, "Please call on Shirley Caesar to sing a solo." As she heard her name called, Shirley jumped up, ran to the stage, and sang "The Lord Will Make a Way Somehow." Albertina Walker immediately asked her to join the Caravans.

Even though she was self-assured about her singing, Shirley was uneasy about leaving her mother in Durham and moving to Chicago, the home base of the Caravans. But after the Reverend C. L. Franklin, father of popular singer Aretha Franklin, called Mrs. Caesar and reassured her that the Caravans would take care of her daughter, Shirley sold a college textbook to raise the money for bus fare and joined the Caravans in Washington, D.C., in August 1958. She began performing the following night, bringing to the group high energy and a God-given ability to bring audiences to a near-fever pitch, causing them to shout, sway, sing, and dance in the aisles of churches and concert halls. Her powerful performances, marked by a fast tempo, improvisation, shouts for Jesus, and sermonettes, added a distinctive style and spontaneity to the abundant talent of the other members of the Caravans and helped to establish their standing as the nation's most popular gospel singers.

Shortly before leaving Durham, Caesar had received God's call to preach, through a voice she heard initially in a college typing class and subsequently while lying across a bed that same day at her mother's home. The message, she said, came from the Lord, "Behold, I have called you from your mother's womb, and I have anointed your lips to preach the gospel." In the fall of 1958, she preached her first sermon, entitled "See the Signs of the Time," in a storefront church in Chicago. She took her call seriously and preached at revival services and crusades whenever the Caravans were not performing. The conflict between her commitments to the Caravans and to her calling as an evangelist, along with an offer from Hob Records to record as a solo artist, precipitated her leaving the group members whom she loved and who had taught her so much about music and about life, especially life on the road.

In August 1966, after eight years with the Caravans, Caesar embarked on her ministry as a singing evangelist. Her sermonette-song technique, a rhythmic discourse that blended the preaching of a Christian message with singing and dramatic enactment, was a style that came naturally to her and quickly became her trademark. She moved to Durham, happy to live near her family and to be able to take care of her mother. Though she continued to travel and to interact with and excite her audiences, she was lonely on the road and was not as professionally proficient because of having to rely on last-minute arrangements with local instrumentalists and singers, if they were available at all, wherever she sang. In 1968 she established her own backup group—the Shirley Caesar Singers—that included her sister Anne, who had left her career as a nightclub singer to accompany Shirley on the road. Traveling in a custom-made bus, decorated with announcements of "The Electrifying Evangelist" and the "Shirley Caesar Singers," the group traveled eight months a year and generally covered more than 250,000 miles.

As Shirley Caesar was preparing to eat Thanksgiving dinner in 1970, she was watching a television documentary on world hunger and received another message from God: "Shirley, feed My sheep." At first she did not take the message literally, but as she kept receiving the same message, she discerned the meaning to refer to actual food rather than spiritual food. Within weeks she established in her hometown Shirley Caesar Outreach Ministries, an organization funded primarily by Caesar's own income to serve those in need by providing counseling, food, clothes, shelter, and emergency funds.

In 1971, Shirley Caesar won her first Grammy, the music industry's most prestigious award, from the National Academy of Recording Arts and Sciences. Her album *Put Your Hand in the Hand of the Man from Galilee* won in the category of Best Soul Gospel Performance. Shortly thereafter, gospel music enthusiasts began referring to Caesar as the "First Lady of Gospel," a title that she deservedly retained.

In the 1970s, Shirley Caesar's success grew phenomenally: she had her first national recording hit and certified gold record for the sermonette-song "No Charge," she signed a million-dollar contract with Roadshow Records, she released her thirtieth gospel album, she was elected to *Ebony* magazine's Music Hall of Fame, and she was the Top Female Gospel Singer in the 1977 *Ebony* Music Poll.

Although her switch from Hob Records to Roadshow Records promised a wider audience for her recordings, Caesar was not happy because the executives at Roadshow steered her into a gentler, contemporary style of gospel music and away from the traditional gospel style where she could ad-lib, inserting words and dialogue, and shout and clap for joy. Realizing that she had little say in which tracks would be selected for her albums, she recorded those required and included as many of her original songs as she could. Her change in style did not bring the expected sales of her albums. When neither her fans nor new listeners related well to her new sound, she knew that her discontent was justified. She continued to perform on radio and in gospel concerts and to hold revivals and crusades. She also sang in Germany for soldiers in the armed forces and at the White House for President and Mrs. Jimmy Carter in 1979.

In 1980, Shirley signed with Word Records and recorded the album *Rejoice,* for which she won her second Grammy Award and her first Dove Award—the Christian music equivalent of the Grammy Awards. Caesar added a new dimension to her career when she performed three songs in *Gospel* (1984), a commercial movie that depicted the experience of attending a gospel concert. That same year, her album *Sailin'* won two Grammy Awards and a Dove Award. Her later albums, however, remained in a contemporary vein that made Caesar uncomfortable. She explained at the time that the words of traditional gospel songs "say" more than contemporary gospel, in that they convey more of the meaning of depending on Jesus.

When Hallie Caesar told her daughter, "I want my old Shirley back, the way she used to sing. . . . Sing the songs that bless the people," Shirley promised her mother that she would make a change. Because Word Records had already planned another contemporary album, *Celebration* (1985), she was obligated to record it. Not long afterward, Hallie Caesar had a mild stroke, and Shirley, remembering her vow to her mother, became more determined than ever to go back to her musical roots. She convinced Word Records to allow her to record live with a choir; "Let me minister," she said, "let me be me." The result was her gospel album *Shirley Caesar, Live in Chicago with the Thompson Community Singers* (1988), which stayed at the top of *Billboard*'s gospel chart for fifty weeks, sold an average of twenty-five thousand copies a week during that time, and earned Caesar her eighth Grammy Award.

The 1980s brought several events that altered Caesar's life in other ways. On June 26, 1983, she married Bishop Harold Ivory Williams, the senior bishop of the Mount Calvary Holy Churches of America. The couple had a wedding that Caesar describes as "incredible," with a wedding party of 106 people and more than three thousand guests and fans, many of whom had to stand outside during the ceremony in the Durham High School Auditorium. Traveling by horse and carriage to the reception at the Durham Civic Center, the newlyweds greeted their family, friends, and well-wishers, and served them from a wedding cake that was more than five feet tall. After a honeymoon to Hawaii and London, the couple returned to their home in Durham. Shirley Caesar re-

sumed her studies in business management and religion at Shaw University in Raleigh, where she graduated magna cum laude in 1984. She also became co-pastor with her husband at Mount Calvary Holy Church in Winston-Salem.

In 1986, Hallie Caesar died, causing Shirley to fall into depression and to doubt the Lord for not answering her prayers for the healing of her mother. Her husband helped her to overcome her grief and doubts by taking long walks and quoting victory passages of scripture with her. In 1987, Shirley Caesar added another attribute to her already multifaceted career when she won election as a member of the Durham City Council. Wanting to give even more back to the community that had supported her for so long, she diligently worked in the political arena for such issues as affordable housing, programs for the poor and elderly, and preservation of the environment. Her fellow council members expressed public appreciation for Caesar's role as a "moral guide" for this political body during her tenure. She served her four-year term and declined to run for reelection because of the many demands of her several ministries.

In 1990, Caesar accepted the pastorate of the Mount Calvary Word of Faith Church in Raleigh. At the time, the church had seventeen members. In a decade of growth under her spiritual leadership, the congregation grew to 600, and built a new sanctuary to hold 1,500 congregants. As she expanded the scope of her work for the Lord, Shirley Caesar became a national and international celebrity during the last decade of the twentieth century. While serving in her church pastorate, she continued to be an active evangelist in crusades, to perform singing engagements, and to provide hands-on leadership at her Outreach Ministries. She performed in three Broadway gospel musicals, sang at the White House for Presidents George Bush and Bill Clinton, sang on motion picture soundtracks, and continued to record gospel albums. In a tremendous undertaking, Caesar wrote an autobiography, *Shirley Caesar—The Lady, the Melody, and the Word: The Inspirational Story of the First Lady of Gospel,* which was published in 1998. At the turn of the century, she added her tenth Grammy Award and induction into the Gospel Music Hall of Fame to her large collection of commendations from the recording industry and many other organizations.

Even after more than four decades of performing, Caesar continued to deeply touch and inspire audiences and congregations worldwide with her distinctive voice, style, energetic delivery, and genuine sense of urgency in conveying the Christian message. For Shirley Caesar—the Queen of Gospel, the evangelist, the pastor, the civic leader, and the humanitarian—there was no time to rest on past accomplishments; there was still much to do.

In the fall of 2000, Caesar embarked on a tour that took her music ministry to sixty cities in the United States; in 2001, she toured Australia. Continuing to soar in new directions, she was once again a student, with plans to complete her master's degree in divinity at the Duke University Divinity School. "I believe in shooting for the moon," Caesar said, "so if I fall somewhere, I'm still on higher ground."

Marsha Cook Vick is the author of Black Subjectivity in Performance: A Century of African American Drama on Broadway. *She was a speechwriter and research assistant for U.S. Senator Terry Sanford and taught in the Afro-American Studies Curriculum at the University of North Carolina at Chapel Hill.*

For more information, see:

Caesar, Shirley. Interview by Catherine Louise Peck. Southern Folklife Collection, University of North Carolina at Chapel Hill.

Broughton, Viv. *Black Gospel: An Illustrated History of the Gospel Sound*. Sterling Publishing Company, 1985.

Burnim, Mellonee Victoria. "The Black Gospel Music Tradition: Symbol of Ethnicity." Master's thesis, Indiana University, 1980.

Caesar, Shirley. *Shirley Caesar—The Lady, the Melody, and the Word: The Inspirational Story of the First Lady of Gospel*. Thomas Nelson Publishers, 1998.

"'First Lady' of Gospel: Shirley Caesar." *Ebony*, September 1977.

Heilbut, Anthony. *The Gospel Sound: Good News and Bad Times*. Limelight Editions, 1985.

Hine, Darlene Clark, ed. *Black Women in America: An Historical Encyclopedia*. Carlson Publishing, 1993.

Hubbard, Kim. "Shirley Caesar Belts the Gospel According to God and Grammy." *People Weekly*, November 9, 1987.

Jones, Dr. Bobby, and Lesley Sussman. *Touched by God: Black Gospel Greats Share Their Stories of Finding God*. Pocket Books, 1998.

"Putting the Gospel Truth into Politics." *Ebony*, December 1988.

"Shirley Caesar: The Queen of Gospel." *American Gospel Magazine*, March–April 1992.

Smith, Jessie Carney, Ed. *Notable Black American Women*. Gale Research, 1992.

CHARLES M. GRACE

By M. S. Van Hecke

CHARLOTTE IS KNOWN for its preachers, from the esteemed Billy Graham to the infamous Jim Bakker, but Sweet Daddy Grace, as he was called, was in a category of his own. Bishop Charles Manuel Grace founded the United House of Prayer for All People, Church of the Rock of the Apostolic Faith. At the peak of his success, he claimed three million followers in congregations from Los Angeles to Washington. His followers were almost entirely African Americans, most with few economic opportunities.

His members loved him, adored him, came close to worshipping him. Despite their lack of funds, they poured their crumpled dollar bills into the washtubs he sometimes used for collection plates. "He was the sweetest person," recalled devoted follower Nancy Harrison of Charlotte. "He was a good man, who done for the people. And a preacher, my lord what a preacher." Mrs. Harrison's late husband, James, often served as Bishop Grace's chauffeur during his Charlotte stays.

Critics said that Sweet Daddy—aside from his role as the church's spiritual leader—responded to his members' gifts with a lavish lifestyle that he felt let them share vicariously in the better things in life. A respected minister of another denomination told *Charlotte Observer* columnist Kays Gary: "Grace took a rock no other builder would use and made it the cornerstone of his church. He gave those people there a new self-identity. He gave them hope and something to be happy about." The minister told Gary that Grace knew what would appeal most to those who would be drawn to his church and "there was member pride in his Cadillac, diamonds, mansions and vast property holdings, all in the name of his church."

Mrs. Harrison and her daughter, Elizabeth Evans, said that the talk of great riches and a mansion was much overstated. Mrs. Evans was a singer who performed at various Houses of Prayer for many years. She said Grace's "eighty-five room mansion," which reputable reference works said he owned in Los Angeles, was in fact a hotel occupied by followers, adding, "I know. I went there several times." She said Bishop Grace's quarters consisted only of a bedroom and a reception room. As for his lavish wardrobe, followers said Grace bought nice clothes but wore them until they were ragged, and his black shoes often had holes in the soles.

Charles M. Grace (Courtesy of Charlotte Observer)

Like his house a few blocks up the street, the church in Charlotte also fell victim to a massive urban renewal program that turned the area into Mecklenburg County's new government center. The replacement church, a magnificent gold-topped building on Beatties Ford Road, became the largest of the ten Houses of Prayer for All People in Charlotte. It also was red, white, and blue in places but not with the dramatic flair of the former church on McDowell Street.

Grace's aims were set forth in the original constitution and bylaws of the church: "The purpose of the organization is to establish, maintain and perpetuate the doctrine of Christianity and the Apostolic Faith throughout the world among all people; to erect and maintain houses of prayer and worship where all people may gather for prayer and to worship the Almighty God in Spirit and in Truth, irrespective of denomination or creed and to maintain the Apostolic Faith of the Lord and Savior, Jesus Christ."

The *Encyclopedia of African American Religious Bodies* states: "As early as 1926 Daddy Grace conducted integrated services in congregations in numerous Southern cities. His innovative ecumenical spirit served as an early forerunner in ecumenical trends that were to follow and served as a model for the increased emphasis by later religious leaders on equality and the brotherhood of man.

"The United House of Prayer for All People has always upheld this principle. However, it was the African American population of the United States that fully accepted Daddy Grace's message. Indeed, the faith is based on the Apostolic Creed—One Lord, One Faith and One Baptism, and One Leader to teach the same."

Even after moving his church headquarters from Charlotte to Washington, D.C., Grace returned often to Charlotte, where his spectacular street parades and mass baptisms created a public sensation. Thousands of onlookers, black and white, would watch brass bands, white-gowned women, or "angels" as Grace called them, and Grace himself, seated on a throne in a dazzling white automobile. Supporters would rush from the sidewalk to thrust paper money between his fingers with their three-inch fingernails always painted red, white, and blue.

A Daddy Grace parade was something to see, particularly for those from less spontaneous denominations. Some Charlotte ministers complained that the parades and Grace's spirited services drew members away from their churches. A coalition of preachers even attempted unsuccessfully to persuade Charlotte authorities to arrest him on a variety of minor pretexts.

Grace was born in 1881 in either Portugal or that country's Cape Verde Islands. The son of a stone mason, his name was Marcelino Manoel de Graca. The *African American Encyclopedia* gives his ancestry as Portuguese and African, "but he preferred to pass as white when possible." He migrated to the United States about 1900, settling initially in a Portuguese enclave in New Bedford, Mass. Grace worked as a cranberry picker, salesman, grocer, and then a cook on the Southern Railroad. He began to attend services at Pentecostal and Holiness revivals and soon felt a call to preach. After a visit to the Holy Land in 1921, he became an active evangelist, opening several missions in Massachusetts and preaching up and down the East Coast.

Like Father Divine, a competing religious organizer of the day, Grace stressed his personal abilities to solve problems. However, unlike Father Divine, he did not claim divine status, at least not exactly. He may have been making a religious pun when he claimed that "only through Grace could there be salvation," but the *African American Encyclopedia* insisted "he assured his followers that God was on vacation and that he would care for humanity in God's absence."

The *Directory of African American Religious Bodies* reports these similar comments: "Salvation is by Grace only. Grace has given God a vacation and since He is on vacation don't worry about him. If you sin against God, Grace can save you but if you sin against Grace, God cannot save you." In another instance, he was quoted as saying: "I never said I was God, but you cannot prove to me I'm not."

There were two ways of looking at a statement that "God is on vacation." One was the obvious implication that Grace was to be accepted as a substitute for the missing God. The other was that his followers should not look to God for the blessings He showered down on His white churches. If God was off somewhere looking after his white congregations, poor black followers should follow Bishop Grace in his stead.

Dressed in his usual white suit and white hat, Grace was a striking figure with his shoulder-length hair and Salvador Dali-like thin moustache. A charismatic, flamboyant leader, Grace would don white robes for mass baptisms in church pools. For one group in a pool-less Virginia church, Grace used a water hose to douse the new initiates. Grace demanded unquestioned loyalty and set a high moral standard for his flock, urging them to reject welfare, to find steady employment, and to spurn alcohol and promiscuous behavior.

The *African American Encyclopedia* gives this account of Grace in action: "Worship services were raucous affairs involving Bible readings, boisterous services and even brass bands and the alleged possession of followers by the Holy Spirit on some occasions. Members of the church were forbidden from smoking, drinking, dancing or attending public entertainment.

"Personal testimonials by followers tended to emphasize healing as the main reason for their conversion to his ministry."

"I had always wanted to see a miracle," one follower said. "One night an ambulance brought to services a woman who had been in her bed for fifteen years." Her stretcher was placed just off the speaker's platform, and during his sermon Bishop Grace called out to her, "You must have faith." The woman got up and walked in front of the congregation, the follower said. "It was a sight to see."

Folklorist Susan Levitas was quoted in a National

Endowment for the Arts' article as saying: Grace's church had "an emphasis on the direct, physical experience of the spirit. Music and 'shouting'—a form of ecstatic worship in which the congregants 'catch' the spirit and then shake, run or jump in place, spin and speak in tongues—were central to worship services. All forms of musical instruments were used, as Daddy Grace interpreted Psalm 150 literally: 'Praise ye the Lord, praise Him with the sound of the trumpet. Praise Him with psaltry and harp. Praise Him with the timbrel and dance. Praise Him with stringed instruments and organ. Praise ye the Lord.'"

Bill McNamara, writing in the *New Bedford Standard-Times,* said, "In Daddy's day, members were expected to attend services seven days (or evenings) a week. They would spend the first twenty minutes on their knees, then an hour or more 'coming to the mountain'—singing, clapping, speaking in tongues, sometimes writhing on the always spotless floor." All of that was true, his followers said. Even in the earliest days under a tent, washtubs, tambourines, and guitars would be used to make music and the "shout" would go on for hours.

"He told us how to do and how to live," one follower said. "He would pray for you to have the faith or you wouldn't get to heaven. He took drunkards and robbers and taught them how to serve the Lord. He did so many things to keep young people out of trouble. You couldn't help but humble yourself before him."

Grace commissioned and sold an array of personal care products, including toothpaste, soap, cold cream, talcum powder, hair dressing, cookies, and stationery. Some adherents believed Daddy Grace products had healing properties, which were "blessed" by their leader. Rivals criticized Grace's enterprise, but he defended it, saying he was only giving employment to needy followers. Bishop Grace was not above chastising his congregants when they went astray. One follower recalled an occasion when Grace spanked her for having her hair cut short.

Perhaps the thing that brought the greatest criticism of Daddy Grace was his fondness for property. By the end of his long career, he had accumulated real estate in Cuba, Los Angeles, and Washington, D.C., and homes in most of the cities where he had a House of Prayer. The federal government sued Grace for $6 million in back taxes, but Grace claimed that the church owned the property and the case was settled for $2 million.

Death came to Sweet Daddy Grace in 1960 at the age of seventy-nine in Los Angeles. His body was brought across the country and rested in state in his Charlotte church for twenty-four hours.

"All night long the people went 'round and 'round that body," a follower recalled. "The funeral home bought a new hearse just to bring the body to the church. It was so sad. That was a night, that was a night."

The body was taken to Washington for similar rites and then to New Bedford for burial. As he had in many other matters, Bishop Grace had the last word. He delivered his own funeral oration—on tape he had prepared for the end.

M. S. Van Hecke is a former editor-writer for the Charlotte Observer *now living in Waxhaw. He wrote and produced* A Free and Independent People, *a video history of Charlotte and Mecklenburg County narrated by Charles Kuralt.*

For more information, see:
African American Encyclopedia, vol. 3. Marshall Cavendish, 1993.
Babb, Edward. "Who Started Shout? Daddy Grace and the House of Prayer for All People." National Endowment for the Arts, National Heritage Awards, 1997.
Directory of African American Religious Bodies. Howard University School of Divinity, 1995.
Encyclopedia of African American Religions. Garland Publishing Company, 1993.

BILLY GRAHAM

By Frye Gaillard

I T WAS AN IMAGE that became familiar through the years: the great evangelist Billy Graham gazing out across a crowd, as the stadium filled with the sound of his voice, rich and honey-toned and gently pleading. His thoughts and phrases were mostly unremarkable, but the urgency of the message was always there —streams of certainty about the power of the faith, the disaster that looms at the end of other paths.

"You come forward now, men and women, black or white; you come, hundreds of you. It'll only take a moment to come. Mothers, fathers, young people too. The ushers will show you. You may be an elder or a deacon in a church, but you come. . . . "

And they always came, moving forward quietly in numbers that were startling—some weeping softly, others holding hands, or singing with the choir, but coming, streaming down the aisles from throughout the arena, and above it all the same hypnotic voice: "You come now. . . . It's important that you come. There's something about coming forward that helps settle it in your mind."

When you saw Billy Graham in that kind of setting, when he stood before the crowds with his sun-tanned face and his pale blue-eyed stare, there was an air about him of absolute sincerity. He was, indisputably, a good steward of his calling, resisting the temptations of money and sex that became the undoing of many of his colleagues. It was an accomplishment rooted not only in his faith, but in the simple decency at the heart of who he was.

"From the very first moment I met him," said one of his biographers, Marshall Frady, "I thought this was as good a man, basically, as I had been in the presence of."

But there have been some critics, including Frady, who have questioned the depth of Billy Graham's message, and Graham himself, in later years, sometimes judged his accomplishments harshly. The dimensions of his fame were beyond all dispute. In the course of his work spreading the gospel of Christianity, he had spoken live—been personally beheld—by more human beings than almost any other person on the face of the planet. And yet, there were those who continued to say that he should have been more outspoken on the issues, the social and moral implications of his faith.

To understand that critique, it helps to look back

Billy Graham (Courtesy of Charlotte Observer)

at the evolution of his ministry. It began, you could argue, when he was a handsome, thoroughly ordinary teenager, given to occasional transgressions regarding girls and fast cars. He lived on a farm on the outskirts of Charlotte, where he was born November 7, 1918. One night when he was sixteen, he and a friend decided to take in a revival. They winced at the ferocity of the presiding evangelist, an itinerant fundamentalist named Mordecai Ham, but they moved forward tremulously at the altar call.

Graham said later that he nearly didn't go. But at the last possible moment, with an ill-defined guilt surging violently inside him, he walked up the aisle and asked Jesus to forgive him.

The experience left him with an exalted sense of propriety, a tendency to scold friends for the most minor misbehavior, and before long you could find him on Charlotte street corners, raging and preaching to anyone who would listen. A year and a half later, in 1936, he graduated from high school and went away to college—first to the ultrafundamentalist Bob Jones University, where he was miserable, and then to the Florida Bible Institute. There in the Gulf Coast suburbs of Tampa, his thinking and his style took on the first hint of polish. His faith seemed to deepen. His fire and brimstone understanding of sin became at least a little tempered by his sunny disposition and his gathering optimism about the effectiveness of the faith.

After graduation, as his evangelizing gained momentum in the 1940s, the crowds seemed caught in his rush of good will. He still lunged about the pulpit and lashed the air with his pointed forefinger, still warned his listeners of the ravages of hell. But there was an undeniable humility about him when he stood before the people at the altar call, and told them softly: "I have no power to save anybody, to forgive anybody, to heal anybody. . . . I'm praying right now while I'm talking to you, 'Lord, help me say the right thing to that person before me. . . .'"

In those early days, there was one more component in Graham's appeal, and it caught the attention of some powerful people and thrust him suddenly into national prominence. Bill Graham was a patriot. He saw America as God's great hope, a righteous instrument to evangelize the world.

During a Los Angeles crusade in 1949, he proclaimed that the planet "is divided into two camps. On the one side we see communism. On the other, we see so-called Western Culture, with its fruit and its foundation in the Bible, the word of God. . . . communism, on the other hand, has declared war against God, against Christ, against the Bible. . . . " Such words fell pleasantly on the ears of William Randolph Hearst, the irascible West Coast newspaper magnate. "And that was when," explained Grady Wilson, Graham's associate for more than thirty years, "Mr. Hearst gave the order to 'puff Graham.'"

What Hearst ordered, his reporters did, and suddenly Graham's face was splattered across the pages of the nation's biggest papers, prompting *Time-Life*'s Henry Luce to get into the act. As Wilson remembered it, "Mr. Luce ran a three-page color spread and story. . . . "

Graham was stunned by the sudden and unrelenting gales of attention, which quickly spread to the realm of politics. For more than twenty years beginning in the 1950s, a string of presidents from Harry Truman to Richard Nixon recognized the benefits of cordiality with Graham, and the evangelist, for his part, returned their affection.

As the Vietnam War gained momentum in the 1960s, Graham clearly picked the side of the presidents against their growing numbers of critics. American soldiers, he said, "know why they are fighting in Vietnam, and they believe what they are doing is right." And when Martin Luther King Jr. denounced the war, Graham called it "an affront to the thousands of loyal Negro troops who are in Vietnam."

But then something happened that brought him up short. Richard Nixon resigned in the throes of scandal, and Graham—who had supported Nixon with more ardor and affection than he had ever felt for a political figure—found himself reeling in pain and disbelief. He listened carefully to the Watergate tapes, with all their vulgarities and sinister plottings, and two years later he told Marshall Frady: "I just couldn't understand it. I still can't. I thought he was a man of integrity. I looked upon him as the possibility of leading this country to its greatest and best days. And all those people around him, they seemed so clean, family men, so clean-living. Sometimes when I look back on it now, it has the aspects of a nightmare. . . . "

He brooded about it in his spacious log house in the Blue Ridge mountains, staring out across the hills, often in the company of Ruth, his wife, an accomplished writer and poet who was fiercely devoted to her husband and his career. It was a moment of disillusionment and grief, but Billy Graham emerged in the 1980s as a more reflective person, and there seemed to be some subtle changes in his message. He spoke out about issues like hunger and peace, and called for an end to the nuclear arms race. "Let us call the nations and leaders of our world to repentance," he declared in Moscow in 1982. "We need to repent as nations over our past failures—the failure to accept each other, the failure to be concerned about the needs of the poor and the starving of the world, the failure to place top priority on peace instead of war. . . . "

Throughout that speech and the interviews that followed, Graham insisted that our nationalistic ways of thinking had failed us—that they were attached to a technology where one miscalculation or a single excess of cynicism could lead to Armageddon. And for millions of Third World people, he added, Armageddon is here—for they exist day to day on the edge of starvation, while the world's greatest nations, those with the resources to make a dent in the suffering, squander billions instead on weapons of destruction.

"Have we gone mad?" he demanded. "Are we seeking the genocide of the whole human race?"

For those kinds of statements, he won the praise of people who had criticized him in the past. Will Campbell, for example, a Baptist minister, writer, and civil rights activist, had once written an open letter to Graham taking issue with his public friendship with Nixon and his support of the war in Vietnam. But after seeing a text of Graham's speeches in Moscow, Campbell was moved by the power of the words and the depth of Graham's understanding of the faith. "I once accused him of being the court prophet to Richard Nixon," Campbell declared. "I have to say, he's God's prophet now."

But if Graham made new friends on his mission to Moscow, he also found new critics as well. Conservative columnist George Will called him "America's most embarrassing export," and there were others whose words were equally as strong. In the years that followed, Graham's instinct for caution seemed to take control of his ministry once again. "The gift of an evangelist," he told one reporter, "is a very narrow gift."

So he set out to do what he had done in the past. He stood before the crowds in the great arenas of the world, and he called people forward, speaking in a voice that was gentle and sure: "You come now. . . . It's important that you come. . . . "

He kept working at it as his health began to fail, and he prepared to turn over the leadership of his ministry to his son, Franklin Graham, also an evangelist of international renown. In 1996 he came home to Charlotte, preaching what he said was certain to be his last crusade in his hometown. He was seventy-eight, and he looked so frail as he entered the stadium, hunched forward slightly on the seat of a golf cart. At the edge of the podium, two men had to help him up the steps, each at an elbow providing support. It was a shock to those who remembered better days when he looked so tanned and vigorous and strong. But it was, in a way, one more testament to the strength of his call.

Ever since his conversion at the age of sixteen, he had been a man who believed in the love of Jesus Christ and set out to proclaim that message to the world. If he had his critics off and on along the way, there were few, if any, who doubted his sincerity, or questioned the integrity and grace of his commitment.

"You come now. . . . It's important that you come."

For Billy Graham, the most famous evangelist the world has ever known, that particular invitation was a mission and a calling that consumed him completely.

Frye Gaillard, former religion writer at the Charlotte Observer, *is a North Carolina author who has written extensively about Billy Graham.*

For more information, see:

Frady, Marshall. *Billy Graham: A Parable of American Righteousness.* Little, Brown, 1979.

Gaillard, Frye. *The Heart of Dixie: Southern Rebels, Renegades, and Heroes.* Down Home Press, 1996.

Martin, William. *A Prophet With Honor: The Billy Graham Story.* William Morrow, 1991.

CARLYLE MARNEY

By Marion A. Ellis

As PASTOR OF CHARLOTTE's Myers Park Baptist Church and later the founder of Interpreters' House, an interdenominational midlife training program for ministers at Lake Junaluska, Dr. Carlyle Marney was a widely popular speaker, an early advocate for equal rights for African Americans, and a prolific writer on theological themes. The recipient of several honorary degrees, including one from Glasgow University, he was named by *Time* magazine as one of the nation's leading theologians in the 1960s. He was the author of several books, lectured at Princeton, Duke, and other leading seminaries, and appeared on national television as a Bill Moyers subject and on CBS's Christmas Eve program in 1965.

During the civil rights movement of the 1960s, Marney formed a committee of seven ministers to meet with Charlotte Mayor Stan Brookshire and other community leaders to defuse potential problems. Marney, Brookshire, *Charlotte Observer* editor C. A. McKnight, and others spearheaded a movement to take African American guests to lunch at several of the city's most prominent restaurants.

By the early 1960s, outbreaks of racial violence had begun to crop up throughout the South as Birmingham, Selma, and Jackson exploded. Charlotte had managed to avoid the violence that was seen across the South as the civil rights movement gathered strength, and local leadership seemed determined to keep the city's reputation unblemished.

Against this backdrop, Charlotte's leadership was bracing for trouble and looking for a way out. Then on May 20, 1963, Charlotte dentist and civil rights leader Dr. Reginald Hawkins led a march of about sixty-five blacks, mostly students from Johnson C. Smith University, through downtown, sparking fears of reprisals by the Ku Klux Klan and other white supremacist groups. "We shall not be pacified with gradualism; we shall not be satisfied with tokenism. We want freedom and we want it now," Hawkins told the marchers and onlookers, according to the *Charlotte Observer.*

Charlotte leaders reacted on May 23 when the board of directors of the Chamber of Commerce approved a resolution urging all businesses to serve customers without regard to race, creed, or color. After the chamber board presented its resolution to the public, members of the executive committee met in a closed

Carlyle Marney (Courtesy of Charlotte Observer)

session with representatives of Charlotte hotels, motels, theaters, and restaurants.

Marney was a member of the chamber's community relations committee. "I was amazed at the ethical awareness of some of the business leaders," he said. "But I read through their ethical language to see that what they were seeing was that, economically, this is a thing we had better do. But I didn't chide them for that. I was willing for it to happen for whatever reason. What's the advantage of having 150,000 citizens buying grits and fatback instead of top-notch supplies? The real issue in Charlotte never was race. It was economics, money, banking, interest rates, loan policies, employment."

Marney deplored the fact that the organized church was not on the cutting edge of social change. "The conscience of the South has never been the institutional church," he told the *Observer.* "We've always gone along as we were hired to do."

Marney was a big man—more than six feet tall—with the wide shoulders of a football player, although he stood slightly stooped. He smoked a pipe and on occasion the smoke would swirl above his head like a halo. He called himself Marney and wanted others to call him that, correcting them if they tried to refer to him with institutional titles such as Doctor or Reverend.

He spoke in a booming, resonant, deep voice that penetrated foggy minds and rose above all others. He disliked traveling in airplanes, so he drove himself to most of his frequent speaking appearances. His vehicle, usually a station wagon, nearly always had a saddle in the back and he was accompanied by Copper, his Irish setter, whenever possible.

When he mounted the raised pulpit at Myers Park Baptist Church on Sunday mornings, especially when he wore the resplendent red and black robe denoting his honorary doctorate from Glasgow, he presented an awesome figure. And when he spoke, his rich voice often put the fear of God in more than one repentant sinner who had been out too late the night before.

He read widely and had impressive recall. Once, his entire sermon consisted of reading T. S. Eliot's poem "The Love Song of J. Alfred Prufrock." His ability to mix religion, history, sociology, philosophy, psychology, poetry, drama, dreams, personal experience, and the mundane into his sermons made him a popular figure at home and on the campuses of Duke, Princeton, Yale, Chicago, Furman, Colgate, and Rochester.

On May 24 and 31, 1964, Marney and Archie Carroll, a layman in the church, appeared on CBS television's "Look Up and Live" program, along with Dr. Rubin Youngdahl, the pastor, and Dr. Arnie Rydland, a layman, from the Mt. Olivet Lutheran Church in Minneapolis.

Born July 8, 1916, in Harriman, Tenn., Marney grew up in Baptist churches because his parents were of that denomination, but his grandparents were Methodists and he had relatives who were Presbyterian, Episcopalian, Unitarian, and even Catholic. He often said he was a Baptist because it was the only denomination that would let him do what he wanted.

As a boy in the hills of east Tennessee, Marney had vivid recollections of the famous "monkey trial" being played out in the dusty crossroads town of Dayton in the summer of 1925, just sixty-three miles south of Harriman. Every Sunday his father and mother, grandparents, and other relatives would gather to discuss the progress of the famous trial based on what they had read in the *Knoxville Sentinel* and the *Cincinnati Post.* "The debate [between his relatives] was whether Jesus and William Jennings Bryan would win over Satan and Clarence Darrow at the Scopes trial," Marney recalled.

In his book *Faith in Conflict,* published in 1957, Marney credited this 1925 clash with the beginnings of his quest for religious truth. The opening sentence read: "For even as a boy you know of the conflict [between scientific evidence and faith]." The discussions at his grandfather's house made a profound impression and by the time he was nineteen he had forsaken a career in forestry for the ministry. He attended nearby Carson-Newman College, where he played football and trombone, and then went on to Southern Baptist Seminary at Louisville for his master's and doctorate in theology.

"I think the difference between me and many of my classmates was that I took my teachers more seriously than they did," Marney said. "And those teachers were in touch with the classics. A man can get a fairly classic education south of God. He doesn't have to go to New England, really."

At the age of twenty-four, Marney became a chaplain at Fort Knox, Ky., while he was still a seminary student. He preached five times on Sundays and held the post four years. His first pastorate was at Immanuel Baptist Church in Paducah, Ky., where he stayed for four years.

Marney was called to become senior minister of First Baptist in Austin, Texas, when he was thirty-two years old. It was a prestigious, intellectual church with five thousand members—many of them influential members of the state legislature and other government officials—and had a staff of twenty-five.

Only fourteen months after he had arrived in Austin, Marney became embroiled in the most painful controversy of his career. He found himself continually at odds with a staff member he had inherited and the staff member took his case to the chairman of the board of deacons. The chairman, who was a professor at the university, sided with the staff member and insisted upon Marney's resignation. Marney took it to the congregation.

"The vote was 696 to sixteen, and I stayed nine more years," Marney said. The chairman of the deacons resigned and left the church, taking other members with him, and they started another Baptist church in Austin.

While in Texas, Marney became active politically—then U.S. Senator Lyndon Johnson and a young minister named Bill Moyers became his friends, and he worked in the Texas legislature with a liberal coalition to successfully defeat thirteen different bills advocating racism in one form or another. Marney called in his friend Brooks Hays, a former congressman from Arkansas, to help lobby for the defeats. Years later, with Moyers as his press secretary, President Johnson invited Marney to be one of one hundred people at a White House session in 1965 on what could be done to handle race relations in the South.

On Christmas Eve of 1965, Myers Park Baptist's worship service was featured on CBS television and Marney got a chance to talk to a national audience. His sermon created controversy because it emphasized man, not God, on the day traditionally given over to worshipping the Lord. The *Observer* wrote: "In a Christmas Eve sermon beamed throughout the nation by CBS television, Dr. Carlyle Marney of Myers Park Baptist Church said that peace in the world was possible only through the emergence of a new kind of man. 'He must be a man as Christ was a man,' Marney said, 'a man able to transcend the bounds of race and region and nationality and see himself as part of the whole of humanity, part of a community of love. Only when men's lives are lived on this basis will peace come,' he said."

The sermon prompted more than five hundred letters and telegrams from all over the nation. Most of the comments were favorable, even laudatory. Meanwhile, Marney continued to speak out against racism and segregation, especially after unknown terrorists exploded bombs on the night of November 22, 1965, at the homes of three prominent Charlotte African Americans—state NAACP President Kelly Alexander, his brother Fred, and civil rights attorney Julius Chambers.

In 1966, Marney decided the time had come for Myers Park Baptist—whose membership included the social and business elite of the city—to declare itself open to membership from all races. "When it came time to integrate that church, instead of starting a campaign by voice vote, I chose the former chairs of the board, who were presidents of banks and power people in the community, and asked them to write the document and help me persuade the people to accept it," Marney recalled. "I helped them compose the document that would integrate that church. At first they weren't willing to do that. We twisted each other's tails for three months. Then at the City Club, of all places, one of them, a fourth-generation manufacturer of power and wealth, sat there and cried like a little boy and said, 'By God, I hate it, but it's right, and I'll help write it and I'll sign it.' The president of the biggest bank had already expressed himself as being open.

"Why start with folks who were already for it?

Why not start with the opposition and where the power really is? This is why our Lord said you have to be wise as a serpent if you're going to be harmless as a dove. If you are going to play power, you had better use power." On March 14, 1966, the Myers Park Baptist congregation approved a resolution stating that the church's membership was open to all and closed to none.

Marney loved horses and dogs. For relaxation he rode his favorite quarter horse, Buck, and took a leisurely trail ride through the mountains near his summer retreat on Wolf Pen Mountain near Waynesville. Copper usually was by his side.

Marney's prodigious workload, his proclivity for long, late-night discussions, his constant smoking, and his habit of rising at four o'clock every morning to study and write eventually began to take a toll on his health. On Sunday, September 4, 1966, after he had completed the 8:30 A.M. worship service and was preparing for one at eleven o'clock, Marney became nauseated, had chest pains, and was rushed to Charlotte Memorial Hospital. Doctors said he had had a heart attack. He was fifty years old.

After weeks in the hospital, Marney retreated to Wolf Pen Mountain for rest. He and his wife Elizabeth lived in a small tenant house they had remodeled on this apple farm on the side of a mountain, and they had turned the apple storage barn on the property into a study. On December 5, 1966, he underwent surgery in Charlotte for the removal of a small nonmalignant growth from the lower lobe of a lung.

Finally, Marney made his decision to resign and wrote to the congregation from Wolf Pen Mountain on Good Friday in 1967. He said he had decided to take his own advice and follow a new light by establishing Interpreters' House, a center for the regeneration of clergy and laity at Lake Junaluska, just a few miles from his Wolf Pen Mountain lair.

So Marney embarked on a new career he had been thinking about for years—ministering to ministers. He patched together a series of grants from individuals and institutions, rented space at the Lambuth Inn at Lake Junaluska, the Methodist assembly grounds, gathered a staff, and in the fall of 1967 threw open the doors to ministers and laypeople of all faiths struggling to find some new answers or just needing three weeks of respite from unreasonable demands. His staff included Dr. Dan Zeluff, a Presbyterian; Dr. Richard Beauchamp, a Methodist; Dr. Harold Bixler, a psychologist; and Sam Buchlender, a Jew from Poland who had studied at the London School of Economics.

Marney's work at Interpreters' House attracted international attention, and he was featured in dozens of newspaper and magazine articles as well as on the Public Broadcasting System television show, *Bill Moyers Reports.*

"I'm not a refugee from a church that wasn't happening," Marney told Moyers during the program. "I'm a burnt-out hulk from one that was happening faster than I could keep up with it."

Marney operated Interpreters' House for nearly eleven years before his death on July 3, 1978, from another heart attack, this one at Interpreters' House. He was sixty-one years old.

Marion A. Ellis is a Charlotte-based writer specializing in corporate histories and biographies. He is the coauthor with Howard E. Covington Jr. of Greensboro of Sages of Their Craft: The First Fifty Years of the American College of Trial Lawyers; Terry Sanford: Politics, Progress, and Outrageous Ambitions; *and* The Story of NationsBank: Changing the Face of American Banking.

For more information, see:

Ellis, Marion A. *By a Dream Possessed.* Myers Park Baptist Church, 1997.

Finger, Bill. "Preaching the Gospel South of God." *Christian Century,* October 4, 1978.

Kratt, Mary. *Marney.* Myers Park Baptist Church, 1979.

Marney, Carlyle. *Beggars In Velvet,* Abingdon, 1960.

————. *The Carpenter's Son.* Abingdon, 1967.

————. *The Coming Faith.* Abingdon, 1970.

————. *The Crucible of Redemption.* Abingdon, 1968.

————. *Dangerous Fathers, Problem Mothers, and Terrible Teens.* Abingdon, 1958.

————. *Faith in Conflict.* Abingdon, 1957.

————. *He Became Like Us.* Abingdon, 1964.

————. *Priests to Each Other.* Judson Press, 1974.

————. *The Recovery of the Person.* Abingdon, 1963.

————. *Structures of Prejudice.* Abingdon, 1961.

————. *The Suffering Servant.* Abingdon, 1965.

————. *These Things Remain.* Abingdon, 1953.

Willimon, William. "A Prophet Leaves Us: Carlyle Marney." *Christian Century,* July 19, 1978.

WILLIS D. WEATHERFORD

By Karl Rohr

ON TURKEY RIDGE high above the town of Black Mountain even the hottest days of summer are cool. The wind rushes across the top of the ridge and whistles around the log walls of a house that has one of the finest views in the southern Appalachians. Willis Duke Weatherford built the house from surrounding poplar and fallen chestnut trees and made the deck high enough that he could easily see the Black Mountains across the valley.

That view nearly killed him in 1961. He had stepped out onto the deck and locked himself out of the house. Instead of forcing a window to let himself back in, the eighty-six-year-old Weatherford, who was alone at the time, leaped off the fifteen-foot-high deck. He only suffered two cracked ribs and a scolding from his doctor. It was typical Weatherford; think, then act immediately. Even today, his spirit seems to overlook his handiwork from the log home he fondly called Far Horizons. His massive white-columned Young Men's Christian Association (YMCA) Blue Ridge Assembly on the slope below his house stands as a reminder that his vision was clear, focused, grand, and epic.

Weatherford hated pessimism, poverty, laziness, ignorance, and immorality, and fought them for ninety-four years. Tall, ramrod-straight, fiercely driven, and never without his Phi Beta Kappa key, he combined intense religious zeal, a schoolmaster's sternness, the vision of a pioneer, and public relations savvy as he relentlessly pursued his goal of uplifting his native South. One of Weatherford's coworkers, Appalachian scholar Loyal Jones, fondly remembered Weatherford as "quite a character. He was from another century in a way." Simply defining Weatherford as an evangelist or educator does not do him justice. He developed his own brand of reform that drew equally upon religious and intellectual principles. He defined sin as the "destruction of personal relationships." This definition epitomizes the philosophy of a man who worked tirelessly to help young people find successful paths in life.

Weatherford's work in the southern mountains might label him as a social reformer, but his daughter-in-law, Anne Weatherford, said that description was too limiting. "I don't think you can say any one thing was his main interest." She remembered him as a natural-born teacher, a powerful speaker, and a

Willis D. Weatherford (Courtesy of Weatherford family)

man motivated by the Christian idea that any human being is of worth.

In 1912 he established a permanent YMCA conference center at Black Mountain called the Blue Ridge Assembly, followed by the YMCA Graduate School in Tennessee. He headed the Department of Religion and Philosophy at Fisk University in Nashville from 1936 to 1946 and served on the board of directors of Berea College in Kentucky for most of his life. He launched an important socioeconomic study of the Appalachian region in 1957 that would serve as a reference for national policies on poverty and education. He wrote or edited nineteen books, including influential studies of race in the South.

In all of his endeavors, he maintained an unshakable belief that the improvement of the educational environment of young people would reform society at large. In an era that saw the growth of strict religious fundamentalism that criticized the combination of religion and intellectual pursuits, Weatherford advocated a Christianity that saw intellectual achievement as the fulfillment of God's plan. Weatherford looked to large, established denominations as the key to progressive social reform. Benevolence and moral improvement of his fellow man through education and fund-raising became Weatherford's Christian duty. He wrote extensively on his religious beliefs and emphasized how a person could develop a personal relationship with God that would bring personal rewards. He believed that people did not possess truths until they had the power to act on them. Weatherford argued that "sin robs you of that power of action."

He was not a native of Appalachia. He was born on December 1, 1875, on a small farm in Weatherford, Texas, where family members had migrated from North Carolina and Tennessee. His parents raised cotton, corn, sweet potatoes, and seven children on the Texas farm. When he was ten, Weatherford asked his father to let him have a plot of land so he could start saving money. He absorbed the religious influence of his grandfather, a hellfire-and-damnation Baptist preacher. Weatherford also attended the local Methodist revival meetings and announced his intention to join the church when he was eight years old. When Weatherford was thirteen, his father moved the family to town.

Weatherford lived at home while he attended Weatherford College, where he graduated as valedictorian. After graduation he worked as an elementary school teacher and principal until typhoid fever struck him in the spring of 1897. He recovered enough to enter Vanderbilt University in the fall and graduated with a B.A. in literature in 1894. Weatherford decided to stay at Vanderbilt for graduate school, earning his M.A. and Ph.D. in classical studies and theology. While still a graduate student, he coached Vanderbilt's first basketball team, although he knew little about the game. He worked tirelessly to financially support himself and became leader of several student organizations. Most important, he became the first graduate student to be elected president of the local YMCA.

Weatherford's involvement with the YMCA had begun at Weatherford College. In 1902, shortly before his graduation from Vanderbilt, he received a telegram from John Mott, the head of the international YMCA and the eventual recipient of the 1946 Nobel Peace Prize. Mott offered Weatherford the job of international YMCA student secretary for colleges in the South and Southwest. He accepted the job for three years and set off on marathon recruiting tours of every major college and all state universities in the two regions. Weatherford began his talks at each university with scripture and acquired a reputation as an entertaining public speaker. He became a master of public relations and self-promotion. At one college where Weatherford encountered apathy from students and administration, he challenged the school's best athletes to an exercise workout. The showdown attracted attention and Weatherford packed the auditorium for his speech that night.

Weatherford's life took a fateful turn after his first year with the YMCA. He married Lula Belle Trawick, whom he had met at Vanderbilt. In 1904 he and his wife moved to western North Carolina and lived for a season on the North Fork of the Swannanoa River. That formative summer also led to Weatherford's idea of a permanent YMCA conference center in the region. He began looking for a site and eventually chose a mountainside near Black Mountain. Weatherford and A. L. Phillips of the Presbyterian Sunday School Board launched a fund-raising mission with a goal of $50,000. Weatherford increased the goal to $500,000 because the loftier price tag would sound like a more serious project. The gamble worked. He eventually received enough donations to purchase 1,585 acres of land.

Weatherford received other joyous news during the fund-raising efforts. His wife was expecting the couple's first child. But in June 1907, his wife died during childbirth. Weatherford's cherished dreams of a family retreat in the mountains were suddenly destroyed, but he continued to work on the YMCA conference center. His dream came true in 1912 when the Blue Ridge Assembly opened for its first summer of classes and conferences. Among the students who came to the center was Julia McCrory, a student from Winthrop College who was also a YWCA secretary. They fell in love and were married in 1914.

The success of Blue Ridge Assembly led to thousands of applications each year for the limited number of openings. Weatherford created an open forum for discussion at the center and hosted leading theologians and business leaders as guest speakers. But in a controversial decision, Weatherford provided a location for open discussions on race relations. Black speakers who visited included scientist George Washington Carver, poet James Weldon Johnson, and Tuskegee Institute President Robert Russa Moton. These discussions were dangerous in a Jim Crow South. Weatherford received anonymous threats because of his invitations to black speakers.

Weatherford's success at Blue Ridge brought him other opportunities in higher education. In 1919 he founded the YMCA Graduate School in Nashville, Tenn. Weatherford became its president and developed a curriculum that included classes at Vanderbilt.

The YMCA Graduate School was perhaps most significant for becoming the first in the United States to require a course on race relations. Weatherford juggled duties between Nashville and Blue Ridge until the graduate school closed in 1936. The number of potential donors had dwindled during the Depression, and Vanderbilt, which held a mortgage on the graduate school's land, foreclosed on the property.

Weatherford enjoyed better success with a kindred institution that would forever remain close to his heart. W. G. Frost, president of Berea College in Kentucky, visited the center in 1915 and noticed the similarity between the work and study program at Berea. He saw Weatherford's love of Appalachia and invited him to join the Berea board of trustees. Weatherford accepted and maintained a lifelong connection with Berea. He refused an offer to become president of Berea, but in 1946, at the age of seventy, he became an active fund-raiser and student recruiter for the college.

In 1944 Weatherford severed official ties with the Blue Ridge Assembly to devote himself to other projects, including heading the Fisk University Department of Religion and Philosophy. Weatherford had joined the Fisk faculty in 1936 and had found the perfect opportunity to explore race relations. He devoted so much of his writing to the topic of race that it is easy to conclude he was deeply troubled by it.

Weatherford was a product of his time, but it was an extraordinary feat that he transcended the racism of his era and tried to articulate a way of life based on mutual understanding between races. Weatherford did not reach his conclusions easily. His first book on race, *Negro Life in the South,* appeared in 1910 and became a college textbook on race relations. It was an indictment of white ignorance and race-baiting demagogues as well as a criticism of "radical" blacks who demanded immediate justice. Weatherford considered them as detrimental to black progress.

Weatherford wrote in a paternalistic vein that described whites as the protectors of blacks; he argued that slavery had been an uplifting institution because it brought blacks into Christianity and positive contact with whites. But he also understood the debilitating effects of racism upon the South and called for an end to racial injustice. John Egerton concluded in a 1994 study of the pre-civil rights generation that Weatherford's ideas seemed advanced in his younger days but "lagged ever further off the pace of change as the decades passed." Egerton argued that Weatherford's inability to move beyond a paternalistic acceptance of segregation showed the difficulty of change in a tightly controlled society. But Egerton pointed out that Weatherford challenged the injustices of the

white South earlier than almost any other whites of his time.

Weatherford coauthored *Race Relations* in 1934 with Charles Johnson, a respected Fisk sociologist. Johnson argued that social definitions of racial difference were recent developments and not products of scientific evidence. Weatherford, however, emphasized differences between whites and blacks and defended the separate but equal concept. He resigned from the Fisk faculty in 1946 and said that his age was a factor. He also explained the commitment he had made to Berea College. But he did not mention the changes taking place at Fisk, including the selection of Johnson as the school's first black president. Weatherford never wrote extensively on race again. Instead, he focused on Appalachia.

Loyal Jones called Weatherford's *The Southern Appalachian Region: A Survey* "enormously influential." When it appeared in 1962, nothing like it had ever been seen before in the region. Fueled by a $250,000 grant from the Ford Foundation, Weatherford and researchers from eleven universities compiled social, religious, and economic statistics and survey results from the mountain regions of seven states. The study's goal was "to give the people in America at large a fuller knowledge and appreciation of the mountain people and their problems." The results showed a changing culture and migratory people who left the mountains better educated than the ones who stayed but worse educated than their new neighbors. It identified leading health problems and found that one-fifth of the adult population had less than 5 years of schooling and that children attended school an average of 7.2 years, 2 years below the national average.

A distinctive Weatherford imprint appeared in the conclusions about mountain religion. He found that 43 percent of Appalachian ministers had only a twelfth-grade education or less. Weatherford concluded that too many small, struggling, substandard churches populated Appalachia. Weatherford argued that the major denominations should join in Christian work and spiritual progress. Despite the personal interpretations, the study's data made an impact. The Appalachian Regional Commission formulated a resolution in 1965 recognizing Weatherford's study and pointing out the influence it had on bringing national attention to the people of Appalachia.

Weatherford worked on the Appalachian project under severe emotional and physical stress. Julia had taken a series of anti-rabies shots in 1933 that had left her an invalid. Weatherford devoted much time and money to improve her condition but nothing could be done. Julia died in 1957 and Weatherford never remarried. He suffered a stroke in 1960 as he was completing his study.

Loyal Jones remembered Weatherford's last years as productive ones at Berea. "He was pushy," he said. "He wanted people to move." But death finally came in Berea Hospital on February 21, 1970. His *New York Times* obituary identified him as a longtime trustee of Berea College and called his Appalachian study "the definitive work on the area." It also mentioned his work to improve race relations, the YMCA Graduate School, and Fisk University.

North Carolina and the Blue Ridge Assembly were not mentioned. But the epitaphs on two graves on the Blue Ridge grounds tell a fuller story. Weatherford and Julia's graves are marked by plaques embedded into a large, natural rock. Julia's marker calls her "a great sufferer but a radiant soul." Weatherford's epitaph calls him a "man of God and servant of men. Life-long student, lover of youth and friend of all races. Man of social passion and faith in God who taught the sacredness of persons and the dignity of creative labor." Weatherford would most certainly have approved.

Karl Rohr is a Ph.D. candidate in history at the University of Mississippi and visiting lecturer in history at Western Carolina University, where he earned his undergraduate degree. He specialized in southern culture and environmental history.

For more information, see:

Weatherford, Willis Duke. Papers and manuscripts. Southern Historical Collection, University of North Carolina at Chapel Hill.

———. Papers related to *The Southern Appalachian Region: A Survey*. Hutchins Library, Berea College, Ky.

Dykeman, Wilma. *Prophet of Plenty*. University of Tennessee Press, 1966.

Egerton, John. *Speak Now Against the Day*. Alfred Knopf, 1994.

Johnson, Charles. Correspondence. Fisk University Archives, Nashville, Tenn.

Weatherford, Willis D. *American Churches and the Negro*. Christopher Publishing House, 1957.

———. *Christian Life: A Normal Experience*. Association Press, 1916.

———. *Educational Opportunities in the Appalachian Mountains*. Berea College, 1955.

———. *Introducing Men to Christ*. Publishing House of the M. E. Church South, 1916.

———. *James Dunwoody Brownson DeBow*. The Historical Publishing Company, 1935.

———. *Life and Religion in Southern Appalachia*. Friendship Press, 1962.

———. *Studies in Christian Experience*. Association Press, 1910.

———, with Charles Johnson. *Race Relations: Adjustment of Whites and Negroes in the United States*. Negro Universities Press, 1934.

———, ed. *Religion in the Appalachian Mountains*. Berea College, 1955.

SOCIAL MOVEMENTS

NORTH CAROLINA ENJOYED a reputation as a racially moderate state largely through the prominence of liberal leaders like Frank Porter Graham and Governor W. Kerr Scott, but by mid-century that image was seriously challenged as African American men and women fought for the equal treatment that had been denied them as in the rest of the South. Those challenges produced the first successful sit-in demonstrations, but it was through the courts that final redress was achieved.

In late 1938, Pauli Murray's application for admission to the graduate school at the University of North Carolina put the state's best-known liberal, Frank Porter Graham, in a most difficult spot. Raised in Durham, and a graduate of New York's Hunter College, Murray was unquestionably qualified. But she was an African American and Graham was not ready to challenge state-mandated segregation. Murray's application was denied.

Murray would earn her law degree from the University of California at Berkeley before North Carolina would even fund graduate programs at segregated black campuses. And it would take nearly two decades before Graham's beloved university would admit its first African American. Such was the paradox of North Carolina on race, the most important social issue of the twentieth century. The university, a southern liberal beacon, closed its doors to a woman who would later earn degrees from Yale, cofound the National Organization for Women, and become the first female ordained in the Episcopal Church.

North Carolina's racially moderate image meant little to African Americans at mid-century, some of whom had fought for freedom abroad and returned home to the same Jim Crow laws that had regulated life for their grandfathers. Change would come, and largely because of men like the Alexander brothers of Charlotte. Kelly Alexander began building the National Association for the Advancement of Colored People (NAACP) in the 1940s and before he was through the state's membership would be one of the largest in the nation. His brother, Fred, entered politics, was elected to the Charlotte City Council, and later became the first African American to sit in the state senate since Reconstruction.

The NAACP found its strength in leaders like Greensboro's George Simkins, a dentist who challenged the status quo. His legal challenge to segregated hospitals is said to have done for health care what *Brown v. Board of Education* did for public schools. Raleigh's NAACP leader was Ralph Campbell, a postal worker whose son was the first to attend integrated schools. That son, his namesake, would later be elected mayor of Atlanta, and his brother, Bill, would win a statewide election as state auditor. In Durham, lawyer Floyd McKissick combined his leadership of the NAACP with his organizing for CORE, the more aggressive Congress for Racial Equality, to bring down barriers in public accommodations, housing, and education.

None proved more steady and resolute than four students from the North Carolina A & T State College campus in Greensboro, who, on the first of February 1960, quietly took seats at the lunch counter in Woolworth's and asked to be served a cup of coffee. In a matter of days, this unannounced demonstration inspired a generation of young black people, and the sit-ins spread across the South, reviving the civil rights movement. Ella Baker from Littleton shaped that movement by her work with the NAACP, Martin Luther King Jr.'s Southern Christian Leadership Conference (SCLC), and the Student Non-Violent Coordinating Committee, which she helped form on the campus of Raleigh's Shaw University in the weeks following the Greensboro sit-ins.

The sit-ins and steady push for change aroused white segregationists in ways not seen since the Red Shirt days of the late nineteenth century. Many saw in the face of the young marchers the defiance of Monroe's Robert Williams, a militant NAACP leader who fled in 1961 first to Cuba and later to China to escape criminal charges arising out of an armed confrontation with police. A Granite Quarry salesman named Bob Jones capitalized on white fears and prejudices to revive the Ku Klux Klan and raised the North Carolina organization into one of the largest in the South. Before Jones came along in the early 1960s, the Klan had stumbled into dormancy after being run out of an eastern North Carolina county by angry Lumbee Indians. Jones later spent a year in jail for contempt of Congress after refusing to relinquish his membership lists.

The Klan collapsed upon itself while the civil rights movement, led by men like Golden Frinks, the SCLC's leader in eastern North Carolina, continued on. South Carolina-born Jesse Jackson, whose leadership skills were kindled while a student at A & T, became a national movement leader and eventually a candidate for president of the United States. The Reverend Ben Chavis Jr., imprisoned after a flawed trial in Wilmington following racial unrest there, became the national president of the NAACP before resigning under pressure. He later converted to Islam and joined the Nation of Islam as Benjamin F. Muhammad.

The sixties produced a revival of the state's labor movement under Wilbur Hobby of Durham, a beefy tobacco worker who gave organized labor its strongest voice since the late 1920s and 1930s, when violence marked strikes at textile mills. In Gastonia, the frail image of Ella May Wiggins, who was killed in a shooting incident with police, appeared on labor posters. Fifty years after the textile strikes, Hobby was a familiar figure at the legislature, worked in Democratic politics, and even mounted a campaign for the party's nomination for governor in 1972.

The specter of communist influence in the labor movement and later in the civil rights movement fed popular thought that only outsiders could provoke the working class, black and white, to rise up against the established order. But Junius Scales of Chapel Hill certainly did not fit that profile; he was the son of an Old South family of money and position. In the years after World War II he actively pursued the communist cause and finally, in 1961, after his own disillusionment with communism, he became the only southerner convicted in a southern court of anything having to do with communism. His sentence of six years in prison was commuted after one year served. Twenty years later, a rally led by Greensboro social activist Nelson Johnson and the Communist Workers

Party would end with death and violence following an armed confrontation with a group of armed Ku Klux Klansmen.

Howard Odum had established the Institute for Research in Social Science (IRSS) in Chapel Hill before the Depression to track the changes of the region. His successor at the end of the century was John Shelton Reed, who chronicled a southern culture and lifestyle that included newer concerns such as the quality of life in North Carolina's mountains and coastline. There was no more outspoken advocate for regulation of development on the coasts of North Carolina —indeed throughout the East Coast—than Duke Professor Orrin Pilkey, whose very presence on a sand dune would send developers calling for their lawyers.

Change also reached into the dark coves of western North Carolina, the home of the Cherokees who had resisted relocation more than 150 years before. Near the end of the century, teacher and educator Joyce Dugan was elected the first chief of the Cherokee nation.

FREDERICK D. AND KELLY M. ALEXANDER

By Darlene McGill-Holmes

RIVING ON DARKENED ROADS, with the constant fear of being stopped by bigoted police officers, was not unusual for many African Americans during the 1940s and 1950s. What was unusual was the steadfast position Kelly Alexander took when it happened to him. Although frightened by the prospect of a beating or worse, Alexander, a proud and responsible proponent of his rights and the rights of other human beings, would not be deterred. "Don't look back. Don't let them know you're watching," was only one bit of advice that sons Alfred and Kelly Alexander Jr. learned from a father who made the civil rights movement his life's mission.

"I would travel with him on occasion to his speeches all over the state," Alfred said. "I guess that's why now when I travel I go first to a gas station (to fill the tank) because back in those days we didn't know how we'd have to leave that city—nine times out of ten we would have to leave in a hurry."

Kelly Alexander forged a vital path throughout the city of Charlotte and North Carolina and molded the footsteps of his sons and others with a legacy of leadership with the National Association for the Advancement of Colored People (NAACP). During this same period, his brother Fred, who was five years older, served on the Charlotte City Council from 1965 to 1974, when he became the first black member elected to the North Carolina Senate since Reconstruction.

Born in Charlotte on February 21, 1910, Frederick Douglas Alexander grew up in a segregated society. After graduating from Lincoln University in Pennsylvania in 1931, he returned to Charlotte to work in his father's funeral home. In 1962, he became the first African American member of the Charlotte Chamber of Commerce and a year later became a member of the Mecklenburg County Board of Public Welfare. He also was a charter member of the Charlotte-Mecklenburg Council on Human Relations. Although he retained his interest in the family funeral home business throughout his life, Fred also was an agent and a member of the board of directors of the Southern Fidelity Mutual Insurance Company and manager of the Double Oaks Apartments in Charlotte.

Kelly Miller Alexander was born in Charlotte on August 18, 1915, the youngest of five children born to Zechariah and Louise B. McCullough Alexander. At a young age it was apparent that Kelly would become a prolific speaker. He would wrap up in a bathrobe and position himself in front of a mirror or on the front porch, where he would practice delivering speeches. "He could give a speech on anything," said his wife, Margaret. "He would just stand up and start talking and you'd find yourself listening." She spoke admiringly of the man she married in 1946. A gracious and delicate woman, she was as soft-spoken as her husband was vocal. "He was very persuasive," she said.

His speaking talent enabled Alexander to revive the dormant Charlotte branch of the NAACP in 1940. From that time on, he made civil rights his major community interest. Elected president of the North Carolina NAACP State Conference in 1948, he held that office until he retired in October 1984. He not only led the revival of the organization to one of the largest state memberships in the nation, but guided it through the difficult years of the end of legal segregation in the 1950s and 1960s. He was named to the board of directors of the national NAACP in 1950, became a life member in 1954, and was elected vice chairman in 1976 and chairman of the national board in 1984.

Although he twice lost races for the Charlotte City Council in the 1950s, he served on many national boards and committees and contributed to NAACP policies and procedures on the national, regional, state, and local levels. In 1984 Governor Jim Hunt proclaimed the week of August 18 Kelly Miller Alexander Sr. Week in North Carolina. He also received awards from the house of representatives of South Carolina and from Mecklenburg County, N.C. Belmont Abbey College awarded him an honorary degree in 1984. That same year, the North Carolina Conference of the NAACP presented him with its first Kelly Miller Alexander Sr. Humanities Award for outstanding, loyal, and dedicated service from 1942 to 1984.

Of the leading civil rights organizations active in his lifetime, Alexander said he chose the NAACP because it was "a legal organization, and it was a non-violent organization, and it was a Christian organization—the type of organization that will actually combat the evils I detest."

Educated in the public schools of Charlotte, he graduated from Second Ward High School. He con-

Frederick D. Alexander and Kelly M. Alexander (Courtesy of Charlotte Observer)

tinued his training at Tuskegee Institute in Alabama and at the Renouard College of Embalming in New York City.

In the 1930s, before Kelly took over the family funeral home business, he was hired by a Jewish merchant from New York to sell jewelry boxes. Traveling throughout the South, he experienced the stings of racism and discrimination. On occasion, he was threatened by police officers and told to leave town. He and his Jewish employer were often refused restaurant and hotel services.

Alexander used these experiences to shape his life's mission. He turned to the NAACP to improve the lot of minorities through litigation, legislation, and education. It was in this atmosphere that voter registration, a nonpartisan political action, was first encouraged, and plans were laid for desegregation of schools, hospitals, golf courses, swimming pools, and other public facilities. Alexander also successfully directed a campaign for the admission of black patients to tax-supported Charlotte Memorial Hospital.

Although Charlotte did not experience the violence of some other southern cities, it was not immune from confrontation and racial tension. During the 1950s, Alexander publicly complained that the public school policy of assigning blacks and whites to separate schools was unconstitutional. The school board replied that if black students wanted to attend traditionally white schools they would have to apply for a transfer. Alexander and others submitted their children's names. Five of forty were accepted, prompting a local segregationist group to declare that they had been "sacrificed . . . to the evils of mixed schools."

Kelly and Fred inherited the spirit of justice from their father. Zechariah Alexander was born a dozen years after the end of the Civil War and died in 1954, the year the United States Supreme Court overturned the legal concept of separate but equal. The elder Alexander was a graduate of Biddle University (later Johnson C. Smith University). He served in the Spanish-American War as a regimental sergeant major of the North Carolina Volunteers. In 1902, he became

Charlotte district manager of the North Carolina Mutual Life Insurance Company, at the time the largest black-owned business in the country. He ran and lost a race for Charlotte City Council in 1937.

In an interview in mid-2000, his grandson, Kelly Alexander Jr., said, "This thing [striving for justice] has a foundation, and as near as I'm able to determine that foundation gets laid in my grandfather's generation. By 1896 you had the *Plessy v. Ferguson* decision, and it looked like black folk were going all the way back to slavery, and I think you have to understand the backdrop to understand the courage it took for an individual to take the positions he took.

"One of the most radical actions that my grandfather got involved in, and my father ultimately crawled up on, was his attempt to organize an NAACP chapter here [Charlotte] very early. At the time he did it the NAACP was considered a radical organization and would be akin to organizing a chapter of the Communist Party in 1952 at the beginning of the cold war."

At one time Zechariah worked in the building trade. This and serving as district director of North Carolina Mutual soon linked Zechariah with selling insurance to the funeral home business. He bought an interest in the W. L. Coles Undertakers business after Coles died in 1914. Over the ensuing years, he bought all the interest in the business that was eventually taken over by his sons.

"The point about all this is he had a mindset about independence and not wanting to be dependent upon white people for his economic sustenance because at that period of time to be independent meant not to be subservient," Alexander said. "He imbued his kids with this same kind of notion of being independent, being self-reliant, all the great, good American traits. What the family has done in the area of civil rights is an extension of that basic philosophy."

Alexander cited his grandfather's involvement in the renovation of the old Myers Street school as another example. During the time of separate but equal, the school, a two-story wooden structure, was designated for blacks only. To get it upgraded to a brick building like those used by white students, Zechariah Alexander challenged local authorities to live up to this standard, and a new school was built.

Since the Alexanders did not rely on the white community for their livelihood, family members took a more active role in advocating civil rights. As Charlotte author Harry Golden wrote of Zechariah in his autobiography, *The Right Time,* "He and his two sons [Kelly and Fred] could agitate and speak out for Ne-

gro rights. It was hard for whites to discipline them."

"I think my father, and my grandfather especially, took the self-reliant notion seriously," according to his grandson. "If you have talents, if you've got advantages, you owe something back to the race. To some extent I think their emphasis on humanitarianism limited their focus on economics. So the degree of self-sufficiency really revolved around the fact that we were in a business that was a segregated business and that has remained segregated pretty much. That independence was important. If you didn't have people who could do that, you wouldn't have the progress that we have experienced."

These battles were not fought without risk. On the night of November 22, 1965, Kelly Alexander, his wife, and sons were asleep in their home when a bomb was exploded under the front porch. That night, bombs also exploded at the homes of his brother, Fred, Dr. Reginald Hawkins, and civil rights attorney Julius Chambers. The *Charlotte Observer* and Mayor Stan Brookshire established a fund to repair the damage. No arrests were ever made for the assault.

"I'll never forget that date and, of course, we could have folded up our tents and said, 'Let's forget this,'" Alexander said. "After all that's your life on the line. But nobody that evening sat in that room and said, 'Let's stop this.' We all said let's move forward and continue to help people."

After his father's retirement, his son Kelly became president of the state NAACP and served until 1996. He also was twice president of the Charlotte branch, from 1982 to 1986 and from 1990 to 1996. He was a member of the national board, while his brother, Alfred, served as chairman of the Charlotte NAACP political action committee.

Kelly Jr. was educated in Charlotte public schools and graduated from the University of North Carolina at Chapel Hill with a degree in political science and a master's in public administration. After finishing his education, he entered the family business, Alexander Funeral Home, in Charlotte. He continued to work at increasing black voter registration and other projects into the twenty-first century.

When Fred Alexander died in April 1980 at the age of seventy, the *Observer* noted that he had "set a standard for dignity and responsibility that helped both blacks and whites adjust to a new era in human and political relations." Two years later, a docudrama based on his life entitled *Fred: A Man Who Made the Difference* was released.

On April 2, 1985, Kelly Alexander, the man who had devoted so much of his life to improving civil rights for others, died at home on his own terms—sitting up, instead of lying down.

Darleen McGill Homes is a graduate of Florida International University and a master's candidate at Queens College. She has worked on newspapers in Miami and Rock Hill, S.C.

For more information, see:

Alexander, Kelly, Jr. Interview by Darleen McGill-Holmes. Levine Museum of the New South, Charlotte.

Gaillard, Frye. *The Dream Long Deferred*. University of North Carolina Press, 1988.
A Gift of Heritage: Black Civil Rights Leaders. vol. 4. Empak Black History Publication Series, 1990.
Jackson, Jesse, and Elaine Landau. *Black in America: A Fight for Freedom*. Julian Messner, 1973.
Taylor, Kimberly Hayes. *Black Civil Rights Champions*. The Oliver Press, 1995.

ELLA J. BAKER

By Steven Niven

Ella Josephine Baker was one of the quiet giants of the civil rights movement. "You didn't see me on television, you didn't see news stories about me," she recalled shortly before her death. "The kind of role that I tried to play was to pick up pieces or put together pieces out of which I hoped organization might come. My theory is, strong people don't need strong leaders."

In terms of longevity and influence, no other woman matched her contribution to the movement. If Rosa Parks, the seamstress who sparked the 1956 Montgomery bus boycott, was the defiant face of that struggle, Baker—who recruited Parks—was its organizational heart and its inspirational soul. Moreover, few activists of either gender played such a pivotal role in the three major civil rights organizations, the National Association for the Advancement of Colored People (NAACP), the Southern Christian Leadership Conference (SCLC), and the Student Non-Violent Coordinating Committee (SNCC).

Baker was born in Norfolk, Va., on December 13, 1903, but she had roots deep in Tar Heel soil. After Emancipation, her paternal grandfather, Mitchell Ross, purchased 250 acres of the Warren County land on which he had toiled during slavery. He also served as the first pastor of the Roanoke Chapel Baptist Church.

By the end of Reconstruction, Mitchell and his wife, the patriotically named Betsy Ross, had established themselves as one of the most prominent black families in the county. In 1895, their daughter, Georgianna, married Blake Baker and set up home with him in Norfolk. In addition to Ella, the Bakers had two children who lived past infancy, and five children who did not. Blake Baker's job as a waiter on the Norfolk-to-Washington ferry required that he spend considerable time away from home, but the family remained close-knit. Young Ella spent her summers in Littleton, and the family moved there permanently in 1910. According to Georgianna Baker, North Carolina was more "cultured" than Virginia. Small town Littleton also offered the bronchial Georgianna and Ella a healthier climate than bustling, smoky Norfolk.

In 1918, Ella was sent to Shaw boarding school in Raleigh. On graduation she moved up to Shaw University proper, graduating with a bachelor of arts degree in 1927. She was class valedictorian at both graduations. Despite academic success, Baker displayed what came to be a characteristic restrained rebelliousness at Shaw. Indeed, only the intervention of sympathetic faculty members prevented her expulsion in her senior year. Among other protests, Baker had demanded that men and women be allowed to walk together across campus, and that young women who "had good legs" be allowed to wear silk stockings if they so wished. She also refused to perform—or in her view, "be shown off"—in a gospel recital for visiting white benefactors.

Ella Baker (Courtesy of Schomburg Center for Research in Black Culture and New York Public Library)

After graduation in 1927, Baker headed for New York. The Harlem Renaissance, an unprecedented blossoming of African American culture and consciousness, was then in full swing, and Baker immersed herself in the city's vibrant intellectual scene. She worked as a journalist for the *National Negro News* and other black publications, and came to know activists and intellectuals, notably George Schuyler, then the most widely read columnist in black America. Even after Schuyler's later shift to the anticommunist right, and Baker's migration to the radical left, the two remained firm friends. When the Great Depression struck in the 1930s, Baker adopted a more activist role, promoting tenants' and consumers' rights, at first in Harlem, and by 1931, nationally, as secretary of the Young Negroes Cooperative League (YNCL), an organization founded by Schuyler. Modeled on the British cooperative movement, the YNCL hoped to promote a locally based collectivist alternative to competitive capitalism. The YNCL failed to make much of an impression outside of Harlem, but in many ways it shaped many of the ideas that Baker came to cultivate in the 1960s civil rights movement. First, the cooperative movement encouraged participation by women and young people. Secondly, it favored grassroots democracy over hierarchical leadership. Finally, the YNCL tried to maintain a coherent, practical organizational structure while promoting a clear ideological vision. Though she did not waver from that vision, Baker accepted that politics was the art of the possible. After 1933 she endorsed President Roosevelt's New Deal relief policies and worked for a time as a consumer advocate for the Works Progress Administration (WPA).

In 1940, again at Schuyler's behest, Baker began what would be a volatile but ultimately rewarding relationship with the NAACP. For many black Americans, World War II became a battle on two fronts: victory over the forces of tyranny and racial supremacy both abroad and at home. As an NAACP field secretary from 1941 to 1943 and, after 1943, as its national director of branches, Ella Baker brought this "double-V" campaign to her native South. Traveling for as much as half of the year—no easy feat given Jim Crow restrictions on public accommodations and travel for African Americans—she embraced an inclusive vision for the NAACP. A typical week might have found her addressing the insurance executives of Durham's Mutual one day, and the less well-heeled cosmeticians of the Apex School of Beauty the next. Indeed, Baker felt more at home in the beauty shops and bootblack parlors of the small-town South than in the boardrooms of the citified black bourgeoisie. That philosophy helped build strong local NAACP branches focused on single issues most relevant to a particular community, such as voting rights, improved job opportunities, or equalizing teacher salaries.

Baker may have been effective—NAACP membership increased from 50,000 to 500,000 during the war—but she was not without her critics. Her willingness to seek confrontations sometimes provoked tensions with black leaders fearful of straining "good relations" with whites. Her emphasis on grassroots

democracy also set her at odds with the top-down leadership style of the NAACP's executive secretary, Walter White. By the end of the war, it was clear that White's determination to keep a tight bureaucratic ship was incompatible with Baker's desire for a locally based mass movement. Baker resigned from the national leadership of the NAACP in 1946.

In the decade that followed, Baker maintained close links with the hundreds of black southern activists she had nurtured during the war, but shifted her focus to New York. There she was active as a fund-raiser for the National Urban League and also served as president of the New York City branch of the NAACP. Baker ran for elective office for the first and last time in 1953, as a Liberal Party candidate for New York City Council; but the incumbent, endorsed by both the Republicans and the Democrats, won handily. Two developments in the 1950s would shape Baker's later return to the South. First, she established a close friendship with activist Bayard Rustin, a homosexual, a draft resister, and (briefly) a communist, who shared her commitment to local democracy and mass action. Secondly, Baker devoted an increasing amount of time to the issue of school desegregation, first in New York, and then, following the Supreme Court's landmark 1954 ruling of *Brown v. Board of Education,* in the South as well.

By 1956, Baker and Rustin's organization, In Friendship, had emerged as one of the most prominent financial and strategic northern backers of southern campaigns to desegregate the schools. In Friendship also raised funds for the Montgomery bus boycott of segregated buses that began in 1956. Baker saw the spontaneous but well-orchestrated efforts of the Montgomery Improvement Association (MIA) as a model for the dynamic grassroots protest she believed essential in a broad-based civil rights movement. Indeed, the MIA was in many ways a legacy of Baker's wartime organizing for the NAACP. Rosa Parks, the seamstress whose refusal to give up her seat had sparked the boycott, had attended one of Baker's leadership training sessions in 1946 and the two had remained close friends ever since.

Yet Baker did not enjoy as harmonious a relationship with the Reverend Martin Luther King Jr., the young minister who served as president of the MIA and who emerged as the charismatic leader of its successor, the Southern Christian Leadership Conference. In Baker's view, King's domination of the SCLC obscured the role of Rustin and herself in using Montgomery as a springboard to create a mass, nonviolent, southern-based movement. Despite reservations, she moved to Atlanta in 1958 to serve as SCLC's executive secretary and as head of its voter registration campaign. Baker found the experience frustrating. First, she faced considerable resistance from southern NAACP branches distrustful of cooperation with the new rival. More significantly, she felt restricted by the boys'-club atmosphere of SCLC's ministerial leadership and by what she saw as a "cult of personality" that had developed around King. "Martin did not make the movement," she later reflected, "the movement made him." For his part, King had little time for women activists in SCLC, even though women had traditionally formed the backbone of the southern black churches. King's insistence that Baker take time away from voter registration to answer his personal mail or promote his autobiography merely confirmed her fear that SCLC had become a "leader-centered group" rather than a "group-based leadership" for the mass of southern blacks.

The final straw for Baker, however, was SCLC's lack of organization. Baker believed that King's inspirational sermons, trips to India, and forceful personality helped deliver a powerful message, but she felt that a movement also needed mimeograph machines, office stationery, telephones, a network of volunteers, and, above all, a strategy to defeat segregation. In a memo to fellow board members in 1959, Baker outlined the three key elements of such a strategy for SCLC. First, it should "facilitate *coordinated* action by local groups." Second, "while serving existing leadership," SCLC should also *develop potential leaders*." Finally, and most importantly, a "corps of persons" would be needed to develop a "vital movement of non-violent direct mass action against racial discrimination."

The student sit-in protests in Greensboro in February 1960 suggested to Baker that the energy, leadership, and vitality of southern black students offered a better vehicle for such a mass movement than the SCLC. All that was needed was organization: Baker was determined to provide it. In April of that year, Baker planned a conference for the young sit-in leaders at Shaw University in Raleigh. That Easter weekend conference helped resurrect the dynamic, grassroots crusade that had begun in Montgomery, but that Baker believed had been stifled by SCLC. Her primary goal at the conference (addressed by both King and herself) was to prevent the SCLC from taking over the student movement. After winning that battle of wills, with the establishment of a separate organization, the Student Non-Violent Coordinating Committee, Baker resigned from SCLC in July 1960.

From its founding, SNCC's youthful and often precocious leaders identified far more closely with the fifty-six-year-old Baker than with the much younger King. SNCC leader and later U.S. Representative John Lewis recalled that "in terms of ideas and philosophy and commitment she was one of the youngest persons in the movement." For her part, Baker remembered that she "had no difficulty relating to the young people [and] spoke their language." She also served as a cool arbitrator between the two factions that had quickly developed in the fledgling organization: one group urged a focus on voter registration while the other sought a continuation and escalation of the "direct action" tactics used at the first lunch-counter demonstrations. Baker negotiated a compromise that enabled SNCC to develop both strategies. Always, she urged students both to focus on the practical matters at hand and to see beyond the immediate protests. Just as she had told the Shaw conference that the sit-ins were about "more than a hamburger," Baker reminded SNCC activists in Hattiesburg, Miss., in 1963 that securing the vote and ending segregation were only steps toward an ultimate goal. "Remember we are not fighting for the freedom of the Negro alone, but for the freedom of the human spirit, a larger freedom that encompasses all mankind."

As Baker had predicted, legislative successes were not enough in themselves. The 1964 Civil Rights Act may have ended segregation in public accommodations, but "freedom" was still a long way off. In 1964, Baker played a major role in establishing the Mississippi Freedom Democratic Party (MFDP) as a protest of the segregationist regular Democratic Party of Mississippi. The MFDP argued that since its overwhelmingly black membership supported the National Democratic Party platform (and President Lyndon Johnson's pro–civil rights agenda), it should be seated as the official delegation at the party's national convention in Atlantic City. Johnson, fearful of losing white support in the South, maneuvered to prevent the MFDP from being seated. Despite that defeat, the MFDP experiment exemplified the grassroots community organizing that Baker had long advocated. The MFDP's Freedom Schools brought thousands of ordinary blacks into the political process, enabling them to select and elect their own political leaders for the first time since Reconstruction. That movement in turn helped fuel a shift among black activists toward the concept of black power.

Baker was sympathetic to that sentiment. As late as 1963, she had argued that "whites coming into the movement should forget that they are white" and that "we should forget that we're Negro." By the mid-1960s, however, she came to agree with militants like Stokely Carmichael who hoped to build on the MFDP's experiment in black self-reliance. Many whites—and some black SNCC activists like John Lewis and Marion Barry—were wary of the connection between "black power" and black violence, but Baker had a more complex understanding of the term. On the one hand, the experience of five decades in the segregated South convinced her of the need for self-defense. A favorite painting in her New York apartment depicted a black woman with a gun at her feet. More prosaically, Baker saw the black power movement of the late 1960s as a way for African Americans to not only make their own decisions, but "make their own mistakes" too. Yet as her work with the interracial Southern Conference Education Fund showed, Ella Baker remained committed to the ultimate goal of integration.

Despite failing health, Baker remained a prodigious activist well into the 1970s. She supported the feminist movement, the cause of radical activists such as Angela Davis, liberation struggles in the Third World, and Puerto Rican nationalism. She also received many awards for her efforts to further human rights, including an honorary doctorate of letters from the City College of New York in 1985.

By the 1980s, however, Alzheimer's disease had begun to take its toll. On December 13, 1986, her birthday, Baker died. She and Thomas J. Roberts, whom she married in 1940, had no children, but they both helped raise Baker's niece, Jacqueline Baker, from the age of nine. In a broader sense, however, her children included the thousands of young people in SNCC and other civil rights groups who were empowered by Baker's practical commitment to organization and emboldened by her vision of a truly free society.

Steven Niven is a native of Scotland who received his M.A. from Edinburgh University. A doctoral candidate in the University of North Carolina at Chapel Hill's history department, his dissertation, "Shades of Whiteness," examined the complexities of the white response to the civil rights movement in North Carolina. He has written for the North Carolina Literary Review, Southern Cultures, *and the* Independent.

For more information, see:

Baker, Ella. Interview by Eugene Walker, 1974. Southern Oral History Program, Southern Historical Collection, University of North Carolina at Chapel Hill.

———. Papers. Schomburg Center for Research in Black Culture, New York City.

Carson, Clayborne. *In Struggle: SNCC and the Black Awakening of the 1960s*. Harvard University Press, 1981.

Garrow, David J. *Bearing the Cross: Martin Luther King, Jr., and the Southern Christian Leadership Conference, 1955–1968*. Vintage, 1988.

Grant, Joanne. *Ella Baker: Freedom Bound*. Wiley, 1998.

———. "Fundi: The Story of Ella Baker." Fundi Productions, New Day Films, 1981.

Zinn, Howard, *SNCC: The New Abolitionists*. Beacon, 1965.

JOYCE DUGAN

By William Anderson

JOYCE CONSEEN DUGAN, principal chief of the Eastern Band of Cherokee Indians, educational leader, and advocate for cultural preservation, was born August 25, 1948. Her mother was Lucy Ann Conseen Queen, the only child of James Conseen and Stacy Teesateskie of Snowbird Community, an area that contains the highest percentage of Eastern Band full-bloods. Although her father was white, her mother was a full-blood of the Bird Clan, a matrilineal lineage that Cherokees traditionally follow and one proudly inherited by Joyce Dugan.

Dugan grew up in a single-parent family. She once described herself as a "tow-headed child until about the third grade, when it wasn't good to be a 'white Indian.'" But, Dugan said, "I never saw myself as half-white; I just saw myself as Indian." During her elementary years she was timid and did not believe herself to be very smart, although she was promoted from the first to the third grade. For many years, Dugan believed that she had bypassed a grade because the second grade was overcrowded. She attributed her insecurity in part to being a "white Indian" and partly to the federal Bureau of Indian Affairs school system, whose teachers were not always nurturing and encouraging.

"Being a white Indian means you don't take your Indian heritage for granted and causes you to be in constant search for your identity in a community that is in large part different from you. I think it causes you to appreciate that cultural heritage more than those whose physical traits are more distinctive to their people." Her cultural pride and the desire for fellow tribal members to share that pride would give her direction in later years.

Dugan lived on the Cherokee reservation in western North Carolina and was strongly influenced by her mother and "grandfather" Joe Bigwitch, a Cherokee who was of no relation. A stabilizing force, Bigwitch instilled in Dugan a deep appreciation of her Indian heritage and patiently taught her about the natural world as they explored the mountains around his home on the reservation. Bigwitch took her mother into his home when her daughter left for boarding school in the twelfth grade, because the mother had nowhere to go.

From her mother, Dugan learned independence and a strong work ethic. Although a victim of diabetes

Joyce Dugan (Courtesy of Joyce Dugan)

that resulted in the loss of both her legs, Lucy Dugan remained strongly independent. Once the wind blew the laundry from the porch rail where it had been placed to dry. Rather than call on friends or relatives for help, Lucy retrieved it from the yard by using a fishing pole and hooked line.

Along with her family, the Methodist church also had a strong influence on Dugan. A pastor's wife encouraged Dugan to attend Vashti School, a Methodist boarding school for girls in Thomasville, Ga., where she graduated as valedictorian in 1965. Attending the school changed her life. For the first time, she realized she was capable of much better performance. Daily, teachers expressed their high expectations of her and she, in turn, placed high expectations on herself and aspired to go to college.

Dugan first attended Bacone Junior College, an Indian school established in 1880 in Muskogee, Okla. After one year of study she became a teacher's assistant at the Cherokee Central School in Cherokee, where she began a twenty-year career in education. Dugan worked as a teacher's assistant for five years before she left in 1972 to resume her education at Western Carolina University. She graduated magna cum laude in 1974 with a bachelor of science degree in education and began teaching in the Cherokee middle and high schools. While teaching full-time, Dugan also earned a master's degree in education from Western Carolina.

In 1985 Dugan was appointed director of federal programs for the Cherokee Central Schools. In this capacity she was responsible for the supervision and administration of special education and Chapter I (Title I) programs. Her duties also included supervising approximately ninety teachers, teacher's assistants, and support staff. She also served on the National Advisory Committee for Exceptional Education for the Bureau of Indian Affairs (BIA).

In 1990 Dugan was made director and superintendent of education for the entire Cherokee school system, at the same time that the Eastern Band of Cherokees assumed local control of the school system from the BIA. The Cherokees had controlled their own schools since before much of the tribe had been forcibly removed from the North Carolina mountains to Oklahoma in 1838.

"This was a very exciting time for us," Dugan later recalled. "We had the autonomy to develop as we believed we should, not how others believed. We were able to keep what worked under the BIA system, what we liked of the state system and incorporate [that] into one local policy, [while] maintaining accreditation. Although the federal system had been stifling of creativity we had to be careful that we didn't move too quickly and with haphazard planning."

After three years of local control, Dugan proposed a strategic planning process that was adopted by the school board and designed to prepare a five-year plan for continuous improvement. This plan was developed by staff, parents, and community leaders, and stressed academic needs along with cultural emphasis to ensure that Cherokee culture was integrated throughout the curriculum in all grades. While serving as director of education, Dugan was awarded North Carolina's Most Distinguished Woman in Education Award and was a finalist for Citizen of the Year, an award granted annually by the Asheville *Citizen-Times*.

In 1995, after ten years of administration in the Cherokee schools, Dugan became a candidate for principal chief. During the campaign the "theme of sovereignty was apparent in almost every issue," she said. Dugan told a *Citizen-Times* correspondent: "We are supposed to be a sovereign nation, and I don't feel we are a sovereign people until we are totally in control of our future, and that only comes through education. It's natural that I'd run on education. We will not attain true sovereignty until we have Indian

people running every phase of our government, and that will require education and easier access to funding for college."

After the field of ten candidates was reduced to two in preliminary voting, Dugan defeated incumbent Chief Jonathan Taylor and became the first woman to serve as chief for the Eastern Band of Cherokees. Dugan believed she won because the tribe was at a crossroads in its history with the newfound wealth that was to come from the tribal casino operations, and that she was needed to bring the necessary structure and organization protecting those assets. Her election was a personal honor and a reminder that traditionally, Cherokee women were an important part of government, having an equal voice in all issues before the tribe.

Dugan's term as chief was full of challenges and she found that her work in education prepared her for the new role, especially in planning. She established a cabinet-like organization and assigned each tribal program to a division headed by a director. She was particularly pleased with one of the new divisions assigned to cultural resources. Within this division evolved the expanded Kituwah Language Preservation Project (which was initiated in the Cherokee Central School System), headed by Robert Bushyhead and his daughter Jean Bushyhead. The other important initiative was the development of a Cherokee immersion language program within the preschool Headstart program.

The cultural resources division was also given the responsibility for preserving the integrity of gravesites. When the $80 million Harrah's Casino was about to be built, the proposed site had to be changed because of the discovery of human remains at the site. Harrah's not only brought new jobs to the unemployed, but helped push wages up throughout the area. Employers outside Cherokee lands found that they had to increase wages or lose employees to higher-paying jobs on the reservation.

The casino brought many new opportunities to the tribe, including per capita payments to each tribal member, as well as savings, investments, and funds for new tribal programs and initiatives, including the construction of a dialysis center. With one in four Cherokees affected by diabetes, the opening of the Seven Clans Dialysis Center in 1999 was a major step toward addressing health needs with local resources rather than relying on the federal government.

Dugan's greatest obstacle during her term was politics. "I have always done things because I thought they were right and this is what I brought to the office," she said. "But in the world of politics that is not often how things are done." She considered herself a novice in politics and felt that her actions were not politically motivated but inspired by what was right for the tribe.

Dugan's greatest personal triumph as chief was establishment of a new standard in tribal government characterized by policies and procedures, many of which were written into law. Even her opponents agreed that she taught the Cherokees the importance of internal controls. "Without them you can do things any way, right or wrong. But following established policies and procedures keeps your feet to the fire and makes you accountable, not only to the people but to yourself as well.

"The administrative issues aside, I feel my greatest legacy will be in the area of cultural acknowledgment by the government and my advocacy of cultural integrity and preservation throughout the Cherokee community and beyond it." She said that she arrived at this place of acknowledgment after witnessing the struggle of all Cherokees, especially the youth, to live in two worlds—the white man's world and the Indian world. She emphasized her belief that "in order to survive, the white man's world cannot be ignored, yet to survive as a people the Cherokee world cannot be ignored, and in fact must be strengthened through greater acknowledgment."

Another important part of her legacy was the purchase of three hundred acres in Swain County, known to most non-Cherokees as the Ferguson farm. But to the Cherokees it is Kituwah, the site of perhaps the most ancient and sacred town of the Cherokee Nation. Some Cherokees opposed the purchase and indeed, Dugan admitted it may have been the most controversial thing she did while in office. Many opposed it because they believed that too much money was spent on it while they had other, more pressing needs. For Dugan and many other Cherokees, however, the land was priceless for its cultural importance, not only to the Eastern Band but also to their brothers and sisters of the Cherokee Nation and the Kituwah Band of Oklahoma.

Dugan lost a bid for reelection in the fall of 1999 to Leon D. Jones, who had formerly served as a council member and magistrate.

William Anderson is professor of history at Western Carolina University, where he is the director of the Cherokee studies program and editor of Journal of Cherokee Studies. *He has coauthored or edited four books, including* Guide to Cherokee Documents in Foreign Archives *and* Cherokee Removal: Before and After.

For more information, see:

"Cherokee Chief: 'The Methodist Church Saved My Life.'" United Methodist News Service, April 27, 1999.

Comer, Susan. "The Politics of Being Cherokee." *Our State,* November 1999.

"War Woman." *Native Peoples,* Winter 1999.

THE GREENSBORO FOUR: FRANKLIN McCAIN, JOE McNEILL, DAVID RICHMOND, EZELL BLAIR

By Frye Gaillard

David Richmond, Franklin McCain, Ezell Blair, and Joe McNeill (Courtesy of the News & Record)

FOR ALL OF THE SURVIVORS, there are moments when the memory of it comes rushing back—the feeling that they had when they took their place at the counter on the padded swivel stools beneath the laminated signs promoting lemon pie. They had given little thought to the history they were making. They were barely eighteen, and they didn't really care. All they knew was that the world was not what they thought it should be. Everywhere they turned there were White Only signs and a way of life in the South rooted in the common affront of segregation.

Franklin McCain, one leader of the group, which soon became known as the Greensboro Four, said the day finally came when he had had enough. With his three closest friends on the dormitory hall, Joe McNeill, David Richmond, and Ezell Blair, he made a decision one cold winter's night that he simply was not going to take it anymore. As far as McCain and the others were concerned, the laws of segregation no longer applied.

And so it was that on February 1, 1960, they made their way to the Woolworth's lunch counter, a popular gathering place in Greensboro, and took their seats on the white people's stools. Many years later, it was clear what it meant. It was the first sit-in of the 1960s, the moment when the movement finally came of age. Until then, it had sputtered. There had been a victory or two here and there—the Montgomery, Ala., bus boycott, for example, which had ended in 1956 and made a hero out of Dr. Martin Luther King Jr.

But in the intervening years, King had struggled over what to do next. He had preached in pulpits all over the country, flashing his oratory and his passion, hoping somehow for a critical mass. But so far, he had failed. The crowds most often would roar their approval, but the movement itself—the great awakening that King had proclaimed—was nothing but a caricature of his dreams.

Then came Greensboro and Woolworth's. News of the protest spread through the South, and within a matter of days there were similar demonstrations in fifty-four cities, including Charlotte, Durham, Winston-Salem, Montgomery, and Nashville, Tenn., as black Americans, many of them young, issued their elemental claim to respect. It was a turning point in the history of the country, which was not what the Greensboro Four had in mind. Not at first, anyway. McCain said he and the others were merely trying to make a statement for themselves.

For their whole first semester at N.C. A & T State College, they had gathered in Blair and McNeill's dorm room, a cluttered sanctuary where *Atlantic Monthly* magazines were scattered on the floor amid the philosophy texts and the most recent issues of *Physics Today*. On the night of January 31, 1960, they were talking once again about the curse of segregation, which night after night had become their obsession. They had pored through the writings of Frederick Douglass and W. E. B. Du Bois, and they had railed against the members of their parents' generation who had lived with humiliation and oppression, and had failed to find any way to resist.

All four of them came from middle-class families. Born, like the others, in 1941, McCain was raised in Washington, D.C., the son of a homebuilder, Warner McCain, who was a good provider and expected his children to get an education. "College," said Franklin, "was simply the 13th grade. It was expected." McNeill came from Wilmington, where his father ran a janitorial contracting business. Richmond grew up in Greensboro, where his father installed water meters for the city and his mother worked as a teacher's aide in a school for children with cerebral palsy. And then there was Blair, who, more than the others, came from a family of civil rights activists. His father, Ezell Sr., was a Greensboro teacher who had long been active in the National Association for the Advancement of Colored People (NAACP), and his mother, Corene, supported the organization as well. But for four young

freshmen at North Carolina A & T, the NAACP seemed to be too patient. It was typical, in a way, of their parents' generation, which seemed to have made a grudging kind of peace with the oppressive racial order of the South.

But on the night of January 31, it occurred to Mc-Cain and his three friends that they were also guilty. All they had done was complain to each other about the things that were wrong, and the more they talked about their own acquiescence the worse they felt. Finally Joe McNeill could not stand it any longer. "Let's do something," he said, and in the silence that followed that simple suggestion, all of them knew that a corner had been turned. McNeill was serious. He began to talk about public accommodations—how the nearby stores like Walgreen's and Woolworth's would accept their money for merchandise, but refused to allow them to eat at their lunch counters.

Sometime around dawn on February 1, they decided they would go that day, no need to put it off, to the lunch counter down at Woolworth's, and demand to be served. A shiver of fear quickly went through the group, as they asked themselves if they really had the nerve. Blair was the most uncertain, remembering when he had boasted to friends as a nine-year-old that he would one day drink from the white people's water fountains and eat at their segregated lunch counters. But now that it was time to make good on his boast, he was not sure he was ready for the challenge.

Many years later, he remembered tossing and turning that night, then calling his parents to ask their advice. His mother told him simply to do what he must and to carry himself with dignity and grace. After that, there was nothing more to say. As Joe McNeill pointed out, they were all afraid. Under the circumstances, it was normal. The question was how they managed that fear—whether they would let it cripple their resolve or whether they would be able to push it aside.

For McCain, the answer was easy. They might go to jail. They might even be killed. But in a segregated world, they had to be prepared to pay such a price. "We had nothing to lose," he said looking back. His anger quite simply was stronger than his fear, and before it was over the others felt the same. The moment of their personal liberation was at hand.

The following afternoon, they set out together on the twelve-minute walk from the campus to the store. They did not say much, and when they got through the door they split into pairs—McCain and McNeill, Richmond and Blair. They bought school supplies and kept the receipts. Then McCain and McNeill, who happened to be the closest, decided it was time to move toward the lunch counter. As McCain remembered it, they hesitated for maybe a minute, maybe even five, then took their seats to the general astonishment of people all around.

For McCain, it was a moment unique in his life, and he felt a sense of exhilaration and relief. "I can't even describe it," he said years later. "Never have I experienced such an incredible emotion, such an uplift. As a journalist friend of mine once put it, 'My soul was rested.'"

But soon the scene became tense. McNeill said a policeman arrived and began to pace back and forth at the counter, tapping his nightstick firmly in his hand.

"Joe," said Franklin. "I think this is it."

"Yeah," said McNeill. "I think so."

The policeman's gesture, however, was merely a threat, and when the two young men at the counter did not flinch, he suddenly seemed to be confused. So did everybody else in authority, as Richmond and Blair made their way toward the stools, and the waitress tried to explain once again that they would have to leave.

"We don't serve Negroes here," she said.

But McCain replied with manicured politeness, referring to the school supplies they had bought: "I beg to disagree. You do serve us and you have."

And McNeill added stubbornly, "We have the receipts to prove it."

The standoff continued until just before five, when C. L. Harris, the manager of the store, decided to close the counter. As stiffly polite as they had been from the start, the four left and headed back to campus, reveling together in their moment of deliverance, but knowing already that this was a mission much bigger than themselves.

They called a meeting of the campus leadership and asked for volunteers, and by the following afternoon there were two dozen students sitting at the counter. The protests grew for the rest of the week, and by Saturday morning, February 7, the city was tense. Demonstrators assembled by the thousands downtown, but the streets were teeming with white people too. There were bomb scares and a lot of young white toughs parading through the streets, screaming epithets and throwing water balloons from the fifteenth floor of a hotel.

After a while it became a defining character of the movement—the dignity of the black students massing at the counters and the ugly obscenity of the whites who opposed them. Even the segregationists began to notice. As one southern columnist put it at the time, "Here were the colored students, in coats,

white shirts, ties, and one of them was reading Goethe and one was taking notes from a biology text. And here, on the sidewalk outside, was a gang of white boys come to heckle, a ragtag rabble, slack-jawed, black-jacketed, grinning fit to kill. . . . It gives one pause."

As the protests spread through the rest of the South, some officials grew weary of the bad publicity and quietly set out to negotiate a settlement. In Greensboro, only five months after the sit-ins began, restaurant owners agreed to serve blacks on an equal basis with whites. Charlotte and Nashville soon followed suit. But in other cities, from St. Augustine, Fla., to Birmingham, the Ku Klux Klan and other white supremacists launched their assaults on peaceful demonstrators, as local officials stood by and let it happen—and sometimes even directed the attacks.

In Birmingham, for example, Police Commissioner Bull Connor's officers turned fire hoses and German shepherds on protesters even younger than the Greensboro Four. But the civil rights movement simply grew more intense, more determined than ever, and eventually overturned the laws of segregation and those that kept black people from the polls.

As other leaders emerged in the Greensboro movement, including a young orator named Jesse Jackson, the original four continued to support the push for integration. But they also began to move on with their lives.

Ezell Blair was elected president of the student body at A & T, and after graduation entered law school at Howard University. He eventually dropped out because of health problems and moved to Boston, where he converted to the Muslim faith, changed his name to Jibreel Khazan, and began working as an employment counselor in the inner city.

Joseph McNeill began a distinguished career in the military. He accepted a commission in the air force, flew combat missions in Vietnam, and eventually was promoted to general.

Franklin McCain got his master's degree in chemistry and took a promising job with the Celanese Corporation in Charlotte. Over time, he became an important civic leader, heading an antidrug campaign called Fighting Back and chairing a citizens' group called the Committee of 25, which led a push for integration and racial equity in the schools. David Richmond, meanwhile, faced a difficult road. He married while he was at A & T and began to juggle the demands of family, schoolwork, and the civil rights movement. He began to fall behind in his classes and never got his degree, moving frequently from one job to the next. Soon, he developed an alcohol problem, which began to take its toll on his health. In 1993, he died.

Blair noted sadly at the time that Richmond's struggles were not uncommon among veterans of the movement, who were not unlike the veterans of combat. They were battered by the fear and the emotional strain that were simply an inevitable part of their commitment. But even Richmond believed it was worth it. Whatever the cost, they were part of a watershed moment in the history of the country. They were leaders in a generation that knew that the time had finally come to take a stand.

Frye Gaillard, former Southern Editor at the Charlotte Observer, *has written extensively about southern race relations, religion, politics, and culture. He is a graduate of Vanderbilt University and the author of seventeen books,* *including* The Dream Long Deferred; Watermelon Wine: The Spirit of Country Music; *and* If I Were a Carpenter: Twenty Years of Habitat for Humanity. *He lives in Indian Trail.*

For more information, see:

Branch, Taylor. *Parting the Waters.* Simon and Schuster, 1988.

Chafe, William. *Civilities and Civil Rights.* Oxford University Press, 1980.

Gaillard, Frye. *The Greensboro Four: Civil Rights Pioneers.* Main Street Rag Publishing, 2001.

Goldfield, David. *Black, White, and Southern.* Louisiana State University Press, 1990.

Newfield, Jack. *A Prophetic Minority,* New American Library, 1966.

WILBUR HOBBY

By Steven Niven

Wilbur Hobby (Courtesy of Hugh Morton)

IN 1975, Wilbur Hobby, then president of the AFL-CIO in North Carolina (American Federation of Labor-Congress of Industrial Organizations), looked back on his long career in the labor movement and "remember[ed] rather vividly" his first encounter with the unions. The front porch of his house looked out on "The Lawn," the only recreation area for the children of Edgemont, East Durham's hardscrabble mill town and home to the Durham Hosiery Mill and the Golden Belt Manufacturing Company. As an eight-year-old in the summer of 1934, he watched as his playground became a tent city for hundreds of striking textile workers who pitched their tents and set up soup kitchens.

Hobby recalled, "I didn't know what the strike was about or anything, it was just a lot of fun to me out there eating with them, walking and singing with them. I played all over The Lawn during that strike, never realizing what the strike was all about or what was happening."

What was happening, Hobby later realized, involved the largest industrial dispute in the United States up to that point. In September 1934, an estimated 400,000 textile workers walked off the job, demanding union recognition, an end to ever-increasing workloads (the "stretchout"), and a twelve-dollar minimum wage for a thirty-hour week. The dispute lasted less than a month, ending in what one historian has called a "catastrophic defeat that cast its shadow over future organizing attempts." The strikers' union had provided no more than token assistance, and the Roosevelt administration had proved unwilling or unable to offer support or protection from company-sponsored intimidation, violence, and victimization. Legislation that might have aided the workers, the Wagner Act that guaranteed the right to organize, would not pass Congress until the following year. The mill workers' folk memory of the Great Textile Strike of 1934—that despite union promises of food, "the food never came"—hampered further union progress in the state for the rest of the twentieth century. Indeed, North Carolina and South Carolina have consistently placed last in the nation in terms of union membership. Throughout his career as a union organizer and Democratic Party activist, Wilbur Hobby fought hard to reverse the Carolinians' antipathy to the labor movement that he loved.

Ultimately, he failed in that goal. The determination of North Carolina businesses to resist union drives and a weakening of labor efforts nationally ensured that "Tar Heel unionism" remained an oxymoron at the end of Hobby's tenure as state AFL-CIO president. He also fared poorly in a race for the Democratic gubernatorial nomination in 1972, and ended his career in a federal prison, having been found guilty of fraud and conspiracy to misuse federal job training funds.

Yet Hobby's career was not without significant accomplishment. In terms of his support for the civil rights movement in the 1950s and 1960s, he had few peers among whites—within or outside the labor movement. He also showed a rare sensitivity to the needs and aspirations of low-paid female workers and served as a mentor to young activists of both races who rose to greater prominence than Hobby himself ever achieved.

The year of North Carolina's Great Textile Strike, 1934, had a further significance for eight-year-old Wilbur Hobby, who was born November 8, 1925. His father was a bricklayer who was soon separated from Wilbur's mother, Carrie Holsclaw. Wilbur remembered his father as a "kind of rough and tumble guy . . . [always] looking to make a million dollars the easy way," by running bootleg joints. Hobby added, more in sorrow than in anger, that "he could have done it if he had just stuck to laying brick." In her husband's absence, Carrie Hobby struggled to raise five sons on intermittent wages from cleaning chickens and work in a Works Progress Administration (WPA) sewing room. Often Wilbur had to take a day off from school to get the groceries that were handed out to the city's poorest families during the Depres-

sion. He remembered "pulling home [a wagon] with bags of grits and cabbage, half of which was rotted . . . and sweet potatoes . . . and occasionally, some canned meat." Hobby "knew that we were poor," and assumed that "everybody was poor."

But even in Edgemont, most mill workers had the security of company-owned houses. The Hobbys always rented and moved more than twenty-five times in two decades, usually because of their inability to pay rent. From an early age, Wilbur did what he could to augment the family income, working in the store where his mother cleaned chickens, shining shoes, and, on leaving school in the ninth grade, becoming the first uniformed batboy for the Durham Bulls. "Zero" Hobby as he was affectionately named—perhaps because of the number on his jersey, perhaps because of his already rounded girth—moved briefly to Ohio as an assistant trainer of the Dayton Ducks minor league baseball team. He returned to Durham in 1942, enlisted in the navy, and served in the South Pacific until 1946.

On returning to Durham, Hobby found a job at the night shift of the American Tobacco Company, oiling cigarette machines for seventy-five cents an hour. Shortly afterwards he met and married his first wife, who also worked for American. Within a few months, Hobby joined Local 183 of the Tobacco Workers International Union; weeks later he had been elected president of Local 183's three hundred night-shift members.

By the late 1940s, he began to play a major role in Voters for Better Government (VBG), a Durham political action group that sought to increase the political clout of the city's fifteen thousand union members. Soon, VBG began to work closely with the Durham Committee on Negro Affairs (DCNA), the city's largest black organization, to elect progressive candidates to office. This alliance achieved some dramatic early successes. In 1949 it helped elect Dan Edwards, a liberal-minded young attorney and war hero, as Durham's mayor. Before the war, Hobby had shined Edwards's shoes; after the war, they worked together in the Democratic Party and in Durham's American Veterans Committee. By 1950, VBG, led by Hobby, and black voters, led by Dan Martin of the DCNA, had captured the Durham County Democratic Party, a remarkable development in a South where most whites remained hostile to both blacks and unions.

Hobby had grown up sharing the basic racial prejudices of most southern whites—a high school friend, C. P. Ellis, later headed the Durham Klan. Yet Hobby had also worked closely with blacks as a bricklayer's assistant for his father, who had taught his son to treat people equally, regardless of race. The Durham labor movement of the late 1940s also encouraged close cooperation between black and white unionists, even though they belonged to racially separate locals. North Carolina's 1950 Senate race between Frank Porter Graham, a liberal on both race and the unions, and conservative Willis Smith, was a turning point for Hobby, however. Sickened by the race baiting of that campaign, he reenlisted in the navy, which was now integrated. There, on a ship leaving from New Orleans, he forced himself to dine—for the first time ever—next to two black men sitting on their own. He had expected to feel great physical pain, and was relieved, indeed liberated, when he did not.

Hobby returned to Durham and to American Tobacco in 1951, having spent "17 months, 5 days, 3 hours and 20 minutes" aboard an aircraft carrier. He returned to active unionism and politics immediately, again working on the night shift, and also enrolled as a full-time day student at Duke University. When Hobby added another task to that list in 1955—editor of the *Durham Labor Journal*—something had to give and he dropped out of Duke.

Hobby tried to use the paper to keep the unionized members of both races united. That was no easy task in the wake of the Supreme Court's 1954 *Brown v. Board of Education* ruling, which declared segregated schools unconstitutional. On the whole, southern whites of all classes resented the ruling, but working-class whites were particularly hostile. Unlike wealthier whites, they did not have the option of sending their children to private schools. In Durham, white unionists, many of them tobacco workers, flocked to various pro-segregationist organizations. One of these, the Durham United Political Education Committee (DUPEC), allied with conservative businessmen to oust Hobby and other liberals from their control of the Democratic Party. After what Hobby recalled as a "knock-down, drag-out battle" in 1956, the segregationists succeeded.

In that year's Democratic Party primary, DUPEC also campaigned vigorously to split the black-labor alliance. Conservative activists drove a "Bloc Vote-Blockbuster"—a flatbed truck with a thirty-four-foot trailer—through Durham County's narrow city streets and country lanes, their loudspeakers denouncing Hobby and other "integration believers" for "selling [white workers] jobs to the NAACP."

By 1960, according to one union organizer, racial tensions in Durham had destroyed "the best labor organization in the state." Looking at the even deeper racial divisions in southern labor as a whole at this time, however, historians have delivered a far more positive assessment. At a time when some union halls doubled as klaverns, Durham was "the one bright spot on an otherwise bleak landscape" of the post-*Brown* southern labor movement. If so, that was largely because of the efforts of Hobby, who used the *Durham Labor Journal* as a bully pulpit for racial tolerance. If the unions focused instead on "the bread and butter facts of . . . unemployment compensation, workman's compensation, the minimum wage, the loan shark problem, taxes, [and] child labor laws," Hobby told his readers, the segregationists' "frenzy" would eventually fade away.

Despite Hobby's efforts that frenzy did not abate in the 1960s. White unionists in Durham and the rest of the state flocked to the segregationist banner of gubernatorial candidate I. Beverly Lake in 1960 and 1964 and presidential candidate George Wallace in 1968. In that decade, Hobby served as southeast regional director for the AFL-CIO's Committee on Political Education (COPE), working to secure the election of progressive candidates such as Senator Albert Gore in Tennessee and Congressman Claude Pepper in Florida.

Because of animosity against Hobby and his like-minded brothers in North Carolina, however, his permit did not include North Carolina. That did not stop Hobby from supporting the sit-in demonstrations of 1960. Nor did it stop him from lobbying for the integration of the Asheville hotel where North Carolina unionists gathered for their annual conference. That was the first time that a hotel in that city had broken the color barrier, and only the fourth to do so in the South. In 1964, Hobby urged southern workers to support the Civil Rights Bill, legislation opposed by even liberal southern whites like the elder Senator Albert Gore of Tennessee. Hobby argued that "civil rights are not [just] Negro rights. Civil rights are the human rights of every American citizen."

In 1969, at his fourth attempt, Hobby finally became head of the North Carolina AFL-CIO. Three years later he ran for the Democratic gubernatorial nomination, the first time that a union official had done so. He ran a populist campaign, fighting for the little man (and woman) against the "Big Boys" of North Carolina. Despite some feisty campaign speeches and a relatively sympathetic reception from the state's major newspapers, Hobby finished last among four candidates. He won only one municipality in the state, liberal Chapel Hill. As an opponent of the Vietnam War, an ardent supporter of George McGovern, and a passionate white defender of civil rights opposed in the primary by two moderate whites and a liberal African American, Hobby knew in his heart that he could not win. He believed, however, that the publicity would at least place issues like the minimum wage, women's rights, and occupational safety on the public agenda.

Hobby also viewed James B. Hunt's election as governor in 1976 as a potential boost to the Tar Heel labor movement. The two had been friends and active in the Kerr Scott-Terry Sanford wing of the Democratic Party in the 1960s and Hobby secured from Hunt support for a program to provide training for women workers. He also set up a nonprofit company, the Carolina Skill Advancement Center, to help train low-income women in traditionally male crafts like painting, welding, and bricklaying. Believing that computer skills would be essential in the workforce of the late twentieth century, Hobby secured $1 million in state and federal grants to help provide basic data entry skills to women and to assist them in training for the more traditional manual trades. Ten thousand dollars of the aid was spent on buying a bulldozer for training women. A significant portion of the federal monies was allocated to Precision Graphics, a company headed by Hobby.

In 1980, the state auditor began an investigation of irregularities in Precision Graphics' bookkeeping procedures. Soon the FBI began its own inquiries; in 1981 a federal grand jury indicted Hobby on the grounds of defrauding the U.S. government.

In September 1981, the growing scandal persuaded the state's AFL-CIO members to oust Hobby from its presidency. Three months later, a federal court found Hobby and his partner, Mort Levi, guilty of fraud and conspiracy. Despite appeals to the U.S. Supreme Court—Hobby's lawyers argued that he had not received a fair trial since blacks had been systematically excluded as foremen of the grand jury that indicted him—Hobby was fined $40,000 and served a year in federal prison in Lexington, Ky. On release from prison, Wilbur Hobby returned to work at American Tobacco on the same cigarette-stamping machine where he had begun forty years earlier.

He died on May 9, 1992, at the Durham Veterans Administration Hospital after a long illness. A diabetic, he suffered from a weak heart and lungs and obesity. His legacy, the *Charlotte Observer* noted in 1997, lay less in his own accomplishments than in the lives he touched. James Andrews, recruited to the AFL-CIO during Hobby's tenure as president, became that organization's first black president in 1997. Charles Jeffress, Hobby's Chapel Hill campaign manager in 1972, played a leading role in cleaning up North Carolina's Labor Department after the Hamlet chicken-processing plant fire in 1991 exposed the tragic consequences of a state paying too little heed to workers' rights and workplace safety. In 1997, President Bill Clinton nominated Jeffress as head of the U.S. Occupational Safety and Health Administration.

On losing the presidency of the North Carolina AFL-CIO in 1981, Hobby had offered a characteristically humorous, but deeply felt farewell. Talking about his funeral plans, he told his fellow unionists, "If there is a headstone . . . I want it to read, 'He did his Damnedest.'"

Steven Niven is a native of Scotland who received his M.A. from Edinburgh University. A doctoral candidate in the University of North Carolina at Chapel Hill's history department, his dissertation, "Shades of Whiteness," examined the complexities of the white response to the civil rights movement in North Carolina. He has written for the North Carolina Literary Review, Southern Cultures, *and the* Independent.

For more information, see:

Hobby, Wilbur. Clipping Files. North Carolina Collection, University of North Carolina at Chapel Hill.
————. Papers. Special Collections, Perkins Library, Duke University, Durham.

Draper, Alan. *Conflict of Interests: Organized Labor and the Civil Rights Movement in the South, 1954–1968*. ILR Press, 1994.
Hall, Jacquelyn Dowd, et al. *Like a Family: The Making of a Southern Cotton Mill World*. W. W. Norton, 1987.
Minchin, Timothy J. *"What Do We Need a Union For?": The TWUA in the South, 1945–55*. University of North Carolina Press, 1997.
Smith, William M. "Labor's 'Big Boy' Works 15 Hour Days." Durham *Morning Herald*, August 29, 1976.
Williamson, E. R. "Voters for Better Government: What, and Who Is It?" *Durham Labor Journal*, May 17, 1951.

J. ROBERT JONES

By Ned Cline

BOB JONES, the man who led the resurgence of the Ku Klux Klan in the 1960s, was born under the astrological sign of Leo the Lion. And he loved to roar. He also loved money and power. In truth, however, he never had much of either, although chances are he had somewhat more of the former than he ever admitted and significantly less of the latter than he frequently boasted.

Like thousands of other poor whites and blacks across the South who grew up on hard times shortly after the Great Depression, Jones struggled to do the best he could within his limitations of low skills and lack of education. Unlike a lot of others, however, Jones had a great gift of gab and a knack for political opportunism that he saw as his way out of poverty. For a while, it worked. But a case of greed and distrust and the heavy hand of an aggressive federal government came together to bring him down. He wound up essentially where he started, little noted nor long remembered outside his family and home community.

But for a few fleeting years, Bob Jones was considered the godfather of white supremacy in North Carolina, feared by a few, revered by some, but ignored by most. For that, however, he earned a place in the state's record of race relations in the years of the civil rights movement.

Jones was the self-proclaimed exalted head of the United Knights of the Ku Klux Klan (KKK) in North Carolina for most of the 1960s. His rise was meteoric and his fall just as rapid, but in his prime he was a troublesome presence and one that could not be ignored as the state worked its way through the difficult days of desegregation. During his reign, the KKK was in its modern heyday in North Carolina, reaching its largest membership since its birth after the end of the Civil War. At its zenith the KKK had approximately six thousand dues-paying members across the state, according to the FBI, which kept close tabs on Klan happenings through successful infiltration of the organization. But there were undoubtedly sizable numbers of nonmember sympathizers who didn't attend Klan rallies, respond to his race-baiting speeches, or spend good money for Klan paraphernalia.

He was both an evangelist of religious and racial purity and a marketer of consummate skill. The more members who responded as he played on their prejudice and fears, the more dues he collected. The more

J. Robert Jones (Courtesy of Salisbury Post)

who showed up for the rallies, the more robes he sold for forty dollars each. With one style for men and another for their spouses, he could double the profits. With an estimated weekly income of $300 for Jones and his wife, it was at least as much as many of his members earned from their full-time jobs.

Jones quit his day job as a lightning rod salesman when he realized the potential for Klan rhetoric and profits. He savored both. He used Klan income to build a cinder-block home on Gold Knob Road in eastern Rowan County. It was hardly a palatial domicile but it was the first one he could ever call his own.

As Jones's influence within the KKK expanded during the turbulent days of the 1960s, so did the interest of the federal government. The Klan was able to do little that the FBI and other law enforcement agencies, working through paid informants, didn't know about, often before Jones did. There was even some evidence that federal authorities promoted certain nonviolent Klan activities in an effort to publicly expose and embarrass the organization and hopefully snag participants in illegal acts.

But it wasn't just federal agents who were watching Jones. After a time, some of his once-faithful followers began to question his leadership, some not liking what they perceived as a treasury Jones was building and others wanting a piece of that treasury for themselves. The internal dissension played into the hands of federal authorities. As Jones focused more on money, the government put its agents' attention in the same place. Federal lawyers later contended that Jones was hiding income from both his colleagues and the Internal Revenue Service.

Following publication of a series of stories in North Carolina newspapers and some national media on KKK finances, a congressional committee ordered Jones and Klan leaders in other southern states to turn over their bank accounts. Most complied but Jones refused even in the face of a threat of federal prison. That was the beginning of the end for Jones as a Klan leader and, in effect, for the Klan in North Carolina as it then existed. Jones was convicted in January 1969 of contempt of Congress for refusing to make public his financial records and was sentenced to one year in federal prison and ordered to pay a $1,000 fine. The federal judge who sentenced Jones was John Sirica, later a judge in the Watergate case. Jones served ten months in the federal prison in Danbury, Conn.

Jones was never particularly bitter about his prison time. In fact, he seemed to relish it as a badge of honor just as he did his entire Klan leadership role. He never missed an opportunity to condemn the government's handling of his case. Federal authorities, he said, wanted to shame him as much as they wanted him in prison. On the eve of his federal trial, Jones said a justice department lawyer offered him a deal: a suspended sentence in exchange for a public repudiation of the Klan. "I told the bureaucratic son-of-a-bitch to get himself and his briefcase off my property," he later said.

While Jones was standing on what he said was principle for the Klan and went to prison, some of his buddies back home saw an opportunity. Several different Klan members attempted to move into the vacuum—and the money trough—in his absence. They were unsuccessful. Upon his return from prison, Jones sought to pick up where he left off. He held a homecoming party, charging $3 a person. But the division among the membership was too wide and the internal bickering too intense for success to last. Gradually, the Klan as a viable organization slipped into oblivion. Splinter groups continued to come and go, including a few prone to violence. By the time a small group of Klansmen took up arms in 1979 and confronted anti-Klan demonstrators in Greensboro, killing five of them, Jones was a decade removed from his glory days as the leader of the hooded order.

The Klan under Jones thrived mostly on rhetoric and cow-pasture pep rallies that always concluded with a ritualistic cross burning. Mostly, members used the rallies to strut what they perceived as their power or prestige over racial or religious minorities. Unlike other Klan leaders, Jones never advocated violence (although he did routinely carry a .38 Smith & Wesson under his coat after he said he received death threats), and North Carolina never witnessed the deadly terrorism that the Klan promoted elsewhere. During Jones's reign, Klansmen issued verbal threats and burned crosses to intimidate civil rights workers, African Americans, and others advocating desegregation. In 1964, a cross was burned on the lawn of the governor's mansion in Raleigh. In 1968, twelve Klansmen were tried in federal court in Rowan County for a series of criminal acts that included attempted arson and shootings into houses, but all were acquitted. Klan participation carried no stigma. In the late 1960s, two Klan members were elected to public office in Rowan County as Republicans, one as sheriff and the other as register of deeds.

In one sense, James Robert Jones was raised into the Klan. One of eight children, he was born in Salisbury July 26, 1929. His father, Payton, was a railroad man in Rowan County who joined the Klan during a national resurgence in the 1920s. His mother, Pearl, was a member of the Klan Ladies Auxiliary. Hard times and bad luck dogged the family. A stray bullet killed one daughter. One son suffered a severe head injury when hit accidentally with a baseball bat. Jones was left with a permanent limp from injuries in an auto accident. Jones never sought pity from his hardships. "Everybody had hard times in those days," he said.

Jones attended public school in Salisbury, once a major railroad town along the banks of the Yadkin River some forty miles east of Charlotte, but never graduated. Upon leaving school, he joined the navy during the Korean War. While in service, he married in San Diego but the marriage turned into the first of his many legal battles. He was charged with perjury for falsifying the date of that marriage when he sought a divorce in order to marry his second wife, Sybil

Bryan, who was his faithful mate in life and in the Klan until his death on April 16, 1989. Sybil died in 1991.

Without a hint of apology or regret, Jones would say he was raised on antipathy for racial minorities. He grew up, he said, hearing both his parents scorn blacks as shiftless and mean, no better than what was called "white trash." Throughout his adult life, before and after his Klan leadership role, Jones spoke long and often about what he called "sorry" whites and blacks. His daughter Sheila Baker, once the Klan mascot, insisted her father was not a racist, merely a segregationist. "He didn't hate black people," she said. "He just was in favor of segregation and didn't believe in putting the races together."

He once said he was not opposed to blacks, Jews, and Catholics moving up in the world, so long as they did it apart from him. "They want to get in with us, and I'm opposed to that," he said. "The Klan is the only organization working for white American Protestants," Jones said in 1973. "The Catholics have the Knights of Columbus, the Jews have the B'nai B'rith, the niggers got the NAACP. Who have we got?"

Jones was once an active church member and an usher at Haven Lutheran Church in Salisbury. He left that church after he declared that if a black worshipper came, he would refuse to seat him and ask the person to go to a black church.

"He was a wonderful father," Sheila Baker said. "He was a good man. There was no one else like him and never will be. He was Leo and he did love to roar, but he was not the two-headed monster that many people thought or wanted him to be. But I had an interesting upbringing, the daughter of a grand dragon. He enjoyed that job."

Some law enforcement agents contend enjoy was the right word to use. His pleasure, they say, was more than his passion.

"I always thought he saw the Klan as an opportunity for some easy money," said former Rowan County Sheriff R. G. (Bob) Martin, who was an Alcohol, Tax, and Firearms agent during the days of Jones's Klan activity. "I think he had some feelings for the Klan, but those feelings were not as strong as some might have thought. The FBI targeted him as a major civil rights violator, but I never felt he was that. I think the Klan to him was sort of a big joke. He thrived on the publicity."

An experienced FBI agent, who spoke only with a promise of anonymity because of bureau restrictions, agreed with Martin. "Jones was in the Klan for the revenue it could bring him," the agent said. "He needed the Klan money. It took money to do what he did and that was his only source. I don't know that he was

ever a threat to anyone, but he liked for people to think he had power and prestige as the grand dragon."

It also seems clear that Jones saw integration as an economic impairment for some white people, especially those of limited skills and educational standing who made up most of the Klan membership. Jones didn't hide his fear that if black workers succeeded in the white-dominated business environment, it would be at the expense of white workers, likely starting with his Klan followers.

Whether Jones's Klan beliefs were primarily philosophical or financial is debatable, but he was something of a contradiction on that point. Throughout his Klan activity, Jones maintained contact with some African Americans, so long as they didn't attempt to take away the jobs of his Klan members, move into white neighborhoods, or attend schools with white students. After his prison sentence, Jones regularly provided transportation to a black coworker who didn't own a car.

"People get uncomfortable when I use the word nigger," Jones said in 1973. "They think when I use that word I mean all black people. Well, I don't. There are black people or colored people who work hard and are just as fine as anyone. To me, a nigger is like white trash. Trouble is not black people. Trouble is the radicals and niggers."

Jones worked as a truck salesman following his prison term and twice unsuccessfully sought election to the state house as a Republican.

Jones was a Klan loyalist to the end even though he was no longer a member and the organization was dormant. For his obituary, Jones insisted that his biographical background include the fact that he was a Klan grand dragon. His KKK leadership, he often said, was the highlight of his life.

Jones and the 1960s Klan in North Carolina seemed to fit each other. Both he and his followers thrived on fear, distrust, and attempted intimidation. They were continuously fighting their perceived demons. The existence of the Klan is not a pretty part of North Carolina history, but it's a part that should not be ignored.

During Ned Cline's career as a journalist, he was a reporter and editor with the Charlotte Observer *and the Greensboro* News and Record. *He is a graduate of Catawba College and was a Nieman Fellow at Harvard University, where he studied southern politics.*

For more information, see:
Jones, J. Robert. *Race Relations Reporter,* November 1973.

FLOYD BIXLER MCKISSICK

By Steven Niven

THE LIFE AND CAREER of Floyd Bixler McKissick exemplified the complex and at times seemingly contrary goals of the twentieth-century civil rights movement. He was an integrationist pioneer who helped break the color line at the University of North Carolina, but held a deep and enduring faith in black power. A lifelong Democrat, he endorsed the Republican Party in 1972, just as Richard Nixon launched a "southern strategy" designed to contest George Wallace's appeal to conservative whites. McKissick, however, viewed his political beliefs as remarkably consistent. "What I'm doing right now is the same thing I [have been] doing since I was twelve years old," he told an interviewer in the 1970s.

McKissick was the grandson of preachers—his paternal grandfather was a Baptist; his maternal grandfather a Methodist—and was born March 3, 1900, in Asheville and raised in the A.M.E. Zion faith. His parents, who had both graduated from Livingstone College in Salisbury, had four children: Floyd, and three girls. Floyd's mother, Marjorie Esther Thompson, worked as a seamstress; his father, Ernest Boyce McKissick, had two jobs, as an insurance agent for the Durham-based North Carolina Mutual, the world's largest black-owned insurance company, and as the head bellman at the Langren and Vanderbilt resort hotels in Asheville. Throughout his life, Floyd McKissick drew on both worlds: his memories of traveling with his father as he sought clients for the Mutual helped instill a faith in black capitalism, while waiting outside the white-only Langren Hotel taught an early lesson of inequality in a white-dominated society.

Indeed, McKissick met with the harsh realities of the Jim Crow South at an early age. At four, an Asheville streetcar conductor warned his aunt that he was "headed for trouble unless someone taught him his place"; young Floyd did not then know that that place was at the back of the streetcar. A more dramatic confrontation with the color line came ten years later when McKissick had been assigned by his scoutmaster to patrol his Boy Scout troop of youthful black ice skaters. Floyd's duty was to prevent his fellow scouts from straying beyond a boundary roped off for the skaters. When some boys went beyond the rope, McKissick tried to rein them in. For his pains, a white police officer demanded that he get his "black ass across that rope." When Floyd responded that he was

Floyd B. McKissick (Courtesy of Charlotte Observer)

merely following orders, the policeman slapped him twice with a thick glove, drawing blood. McKissick retaliated by swinging an ice skate at the policeman. The intercession of Ernest McKissick and other prominent black Ashevillians kept Floyd from spending a night in the cells, but did not prevent him from appearing in court two weeks later. The judge decided that a "good thrashing" by his father would be punishment enough, however, and dismissed the case.

That first taste of the inequity of Jim Crow transformed McKissick's life. Up to that point, he had hoped to follow in his grandfathers' footsteps and become a minister. Seeing that he would have had no black representation in court had his case gone to trial, he became determined to train as a lawyer and joined the National Association for the Advancement of Colored People (NAACP). On graduation in 1939 McKissick attended Morehouse College in Atlanta, primarily because that school offered pre-law courses. Unable to pay full tuition, he served as a waiter in the university dining hall and later became the personal waiter to W. E. B. Du Bois, the noted black intellectual.

World War II interrupted McKissick's studies. In 1942, he enlisted in the army and also married Evelyn Williams, a family friend since childhood. After a brief stint at Fort Benning in Georgia, McKissick spent most of his army career in his native state, at Fort Bragg, where he taught recruits basic mathematics and rudimentary literacy skills. He quickly earned the rank of sergeant but failed to win entrance to Officers Training School. In McKissick's view, white unease at the growing assertiveness of blacks such as himself had denied him that opportunity. In 1944, McKissick finally departed for Europe as part of the 13th Engineer Brigade in General George Patton's Third Army. McKissick returned from Europe with five Battle Stars and a Purple Heart, but also with a determination that blacks' service in the war abroad demanded first-class citizenship at home. He also believed that the United States–led restructuring of Western Europe could serve as a model for the economic restructuring of black America. The idea for the federally funded Soul City, he later recalled, had its genesis in the Marshall Plan.

After the war, McKissick applied to the law school of the University of North Carolina, but the segregated university failed even to acknowledge his application. When the university formally rejected his second application, Thurgood Marshall, lead counsel of the NAACP, filed suit to secure his entrance. In the meantime McKissick transferred from Morehouse to the North Carolina College for Negroes in Durham. In 1951, just after he had graduated from N.C. College, the NAACP won McKissick's case and won his admission to the state's flagship law school. One year later, McKissick passed the bar examination and started his own law firm with another black lawyer, Moses Burt, in 1955. The firm quickly earned a reputation for supporting and sometimes winning civil rights cases. Their clients included the first black undergraduates to attend Chapel Hill in 1955, the first of North Carolina's sit-in protestors—at Durham's Royal Ice Cream parlor in 1957—and the black families of Durham who successfully integrated that city's school system in 1959. In the latter case, the lead plaintiffs were McKissick's daughter, Jocelyn, then fourteen years old, and her mother, Evelyn.

When the sit-in movement broke out in the North Carolina piedmont in 1960, McKissick took an early and aggressive role. By then, he had already established a friendship with the Reverend Douglas E. Moore, a Methodist minister who had led the failed ice cream parlor sit-in in 1957. Indeed, McKissick found Moore, who was a classmate of Martin Luther King Jr.'s at Boston University, to be a far more kindred spirit than the talented but cautious businessmen of North Carolina Mutual who dominated black Durham's political and economic life. McKissick and Moore encouraged black students to take part in the sit-ins and other demonstrations, including a boycott of downtown Durham merchants who refused to hire black workers.

McKissick was no stranger to such direct action. Indeed, in 1947 he had briefly joined the Journey of Reconciliation, an effort by the Congress of Racial Equality (CORE) to test the color line on southern bus lines. In the early sixties, McKissick worked closely with CORE to teach nonviolent workshops and provide legal assistance for arrested demonstrators. McKissick remained committed to CORE's nonviolent principles, but recognized the growing militancy of young blacks. His choice of a name for the NAACP youth chapter that he led, the Commandos, reflected that more assertive mood. So too did his decision in 1963 to invite the Black Muslim leader, Malcolm X, to Durham for a debate on the "Future of the Negro in America." McKissick denied Malcolm X's charge that whites were beyond redemption, but his willingness to even approach the Nation of Islam —very much a pariah organization at the time— signaled his growing sympathy for a more radical, black-centered approach to civil rights.

McKissick saw no conflict in his friendship with Malcolm or in his activism in both CORE and the NAACP. Indeed, CORE's emphasis on direct action and the NAACP's legal approach neatly complemented each other. Others saw the matter differently. Kelly Alexander, president of the state NAACP, charged that CORE was poaching from the NAACP's youth members. That charge contained an element of truth. Many young blacks had switched allegiance to CORE, particularly after McKissick and James Farmer launched a "Freedom Highways" campaign in 1961 to desegregate prominent highway motels and restaurants. By the late summer of 1962 nearly half of the state's Howard Johnson's had integrated. Led by McKissick, the Durham CORE-NAACP emerged as one of the most vigorous youth movements in the South.

In May 1963, CORE achieved its most dramatic successes in North Carolina. For several days, CORE staged mass demonstrations and sit-ins in Durham, Greensboro, and High Point, forcing local authorities to arrest thousands of demonstrators. By June, McKissick had helped to establish biracial commissions in these cities, and the Durham committee achieved an almost complete integration of public facilities by that summer. Nonetheless, the state NAACP continued to chafe at McKissick's continued affiliation with CORE, and the Durham lawyer resigned from the former organization in 1963. Shortly thereafter he began to take a more prominent role in CORE's national leadership.

In 1964, the passage of the Civil Rights Act finally removed most of the legal barriers preventing integration. By that time, CORE had begun to shift from its original integrationist and pacifist origins toward a black power philosophy that borrowed heavily from Malcolm X, among others. McKissick's election in 1963 as national chairman of CORE had already signaled the organization's desire for a more dynamic and blacker image. Some critics—and some supporters—of his election argued that McKissick had won because the unmistakably southern cadences of the Asheville native "sounded black."

Yet regardless of how he said it, it became increasingly clear that what McKissick said as a CORE spokesman struck a chord with many blacks throughout the nation. In 1966, he was elected national director of CORE and served as one of three national civil rights leaders who led a March Against Fear in Mississippi in June. That march symbolized the growing antagonisms between the nonviolent strategy of Martin Luther King Jr. and the more aggressive call for "black power" that had begun to emerge from the Student Non-Violent Coordinating Committee (SNCC). Increasingly, McKissick's pronouncements during the march conformed more closely to SNCC's Stokely Carmichael than to King. At the end of the march McKissick declared that "1966 shall be remembered as the year we left our imposed status of Negroes and became Black Men. . . . 1966 is the year of Black Power. The year when black men realized their full worth in society—their dignity and beauty—and their power—the greatest power on earth—the power of *right.*"

Yet despite that clear shift in ideology and rhetoric, McKissick's leadership of CORE was troubled. The biggest problem was money. With the shift to black power, white funding declined precipitously, particularly among Jewish benefactors uneasy at the pro-Islam or anti-Semitic pronouncements of some CORE members (though never McKissick.) Black power by its very nature meant that African Americans themselves would provide the financial backing for the movement, but McKissick recognized that that would not be easy. In the short term CORE still needed to solicit funds from major foundations, most of which were run by whites. By the fall of 1968, a

separatist and anticapitalist black power faction urged the national chairman's ouster. For McKissick, black power had always been a matter of racial pride and self-determination, not separatism. He also remained passionately devoted to the idea of black capitalism. In order to pursue that goal, McKissick resigned from CORE in September 1968 to establish a consulting firm to help black businesses.

In the final two decades of his life, Floyd McKissick dedicated his life to building Soul City, a new town that would be open to all races, but that would encourage black-owned and black-controlled businesses to flourish. McKissick planned to build the community in Warren County, one of the poorest counties in North Carolina, sixty miles north of his Durham home. He realized that major financial investments and infrastructure development would be necessary to realize his goal of a city of more than forty thousand residents. Only the federal government could provide such assistance, and McKissick courted the Nixon administration assiduously. Prior to the summer of 1972, McKissick Enterprises had received only $250,000 in federal money; in late June of that year, the Nixon administration's Department of Housing and Urban Development (HUD) promised $14 million to help finance Soul City. Critics—most notably the *News and Observer* of Raleigh—charged that McKissick's surprising endorsement of Nixon only three weeks earlier had influenced HUD's decision. McKissick denied any quid pro quo, claiming that blacks would be ill-advised to put all their eggs in the Democratic Party basket. African Americans would have much more leverage, he argued, if both political parties were vying for their votes. That argument had much validity, but the appearance, in the era of Watergate, of any suspicious dealings with the Nixon administration brought with it intense scrutiny. Subsequent investigations found that the Nixon reelection campaign had been hoping to recruit a "black superstar," and McKissick fit that bill. It did not help that the HUD official who recommended the Soul City grant also played a leading role in the campaign's efforts to woo blacks.

Valid or not, the early criticisms of Soul City plagued McKissick's efforts. Despite the support of some North Carolina Republicans, notably Governor Jim Holshouser, others remained hostile to Soul City. The most vocal opponent was U.S. Senator Jesse Helms, who like McKissick was a recent convert from the Democrats. He lambasted the new town as "an expanse of bare land that has been . . . tarnished by the most massive wasteful boondoggle anyone in the area can remember." In part because of Helms's dogged opposition, but also because of Soul City's inability to attract more than 130 residents, HUD finally cut off all aid in 1979.

McKissick remained a resident of Soul City until his death in 1991. In his final years, he established a law firm with his son, Floyd Jr., and was appointed by Governor Jim Martin, a Republican, to a district court judgeship in June 1990. He died ten months later, on March 28, 1991, of lung cancer, and was survived by his wife, Evelyn, his son, and three daughters, Jocelyn, Andree, and Charmain. In the final analysis, McKissick told a reporter in the 1970s, "I was always an integrationist, still am, always will be. That's what it was all about. That's what Soul City is about. The black man has got to be part of the system. We've never been in it, so we don't know if it will work. I say, 'Get in and see.'"

Steven Niven is a native of Scotland and received his M.A. from Edinburgh University. A doctoral candidate in the University of North Carolina at Chapel Hill's history department, his dissertation, "Shades of Whiteness," examined the complex-ities of the white response to the civil rights movement in North Carolina. He has written for the North Carolina Literary Review, Southern Cultures, *and the* Independent.

For more information, see:

McKissick, Floyd. Interview by Jack Bass and Walter DeVries. Southern Historical Collection, University of North Carolina at Chapel Hill.

————. Interview by William A. Link. Southern Oral History Program, Southern Historical Collection, University of North Carolina at Chapel Hill.

————. Papers. Southern Historical Collection, University of North Carolina at Chapel Hill.

Davidson, Osha Gray. *The Best of Enemies: Race and Redemption in the New South*. Scribner's, 1996.

McKissick, Floyd B. *Three-fifths of a Man*. Macmillan, 1969.

Meier, August, and Elliott Rudwick. *CORE : A Study in the Civil Rights Movement, 1942–1968*. Oxford University Press, 1973.

BENJAMIN F. MUHAMMAD
(FORMERLY BENJAMIN F. CHAVIS JR.)

By Ryan Sumner

LONG BEFORE BEN CHAVIS converted to Islam and changed his name to Benjamin F. Muhammad, he was a key figure in one of the most controversial trials in North Carolina that grew out of a civil rights disturbance in Wilmington. Chavis was convicted, and while serving a portion of his sentence, he continued his studies in the divinity school at Duke University. Upon his early release he returned to the movement and gained national attention as president of the National Association for the Advancement of Colored People (NAACP), a post he had to relinquish in the wake of personal problems in the 1990s.

Chavis, who was born on January 22, 1948, in Oxford, North Carolina, came from a family with a long history of involvement in civil rights. Many of the men in his family had been ministers, including his great-great-grandfather, John Chavis. He was the first black graduate of Princeton University and an outspoken abolitionist who was killed for teaching children of color to read and write. W. E. B. Du Bois praised Chavis's English and manners as "impressive" and said his explanations were "clear and precise." Additionally, historian John Hope Franklin called Chavis "the most important free Negro in North Carolina." No doubt, his accomplishments were celebrated in the Chavis family and constantly reinforced with young Benjamin.

Ben Chavis's lifelong involvement in civil rights began in his youth. He joined the NAACP at the age of twelve, and when he was just fifteen, he began leading protests that resulted in the desegregation of the Oxford public library and a movie house. That same year, he participated in the 1963 March on Washington with his NAACP youth council. Dr. Martin Luther King Jr.'s "I Have a Dream" speech inspired Chavis to return to North Carolina and "change everything and make it better."

After graduating from Mary Potter High School in 1965, Chavis enrolled at St. Augustine's College, a small, historically black college in Raleigh and the alma mater of his father, who died shortly after the beginning of the fall term. Ben threw himself into his books, made the dean's list, and was elected class president. However, depressed over his father's death,

Benjamin F. Muhammad (Benjamin F. Chavis Jr.)
(Courtesy of Charlotte Observer)

he left school over Christmas break and moved to Charlotte to live with his sister June. He planned to enter the University of North Carolina at Charlotte, which was welcoming its first class as the fourth campus of the university.

In the fall of 1966, Chavis and seven other African American students became the first students of color to attend the university. It was his first experience of sharing a classroom with white students. Initially he felt isolated and became very withdrawn. However, he became progressively more involved and outspoken. Within a year, Chavis became head of Students for Action, a campus antiwar organization, and was elected president of the UNC-C Student Union. Chavis also became involved in campus chapters of the

NAACP, the Congress on Racial Equality (CORE), and the Southern Christian Leadership Conference (SCLC). He led demonstrations to establish the Black Student Union and a "black studies" department, to hire additional African American faculty, and to establish recruitment programs to bring more black students to the school. Sometimes Chavis's tactics got him into trouble. He was suspended during his senior year for defacing school property after he placed protest signs on the administration building and replaced the school's American flag with the Black Liberation flag at half-mast.

Off campus, Chavis became involved in Charlotte's African American community, along with local activists T. J. Reddy, Charles Parker, Walter David, Theodore Hood, and James Grant. This group formed the Black Cultural Association in 1968 and attracted the attention of the Charlotte police and federal agents, who suspected the group in several Charlotte-area bombing incidents. The group disbanded in 1969, and Chavis joined Charlotte's Black Panther organization. He became the party chairperson and established programs such as free breakfasts for African American children. With the backing of the Panthers and the Black Political Organization, Chavis ran unsuccessfully for Charlotte City Council in 1969. He also became a labor organizer with the AFL-CIO and helped organize and lead marches in support of striking city garbage workers, as well as organizing two major marches with SCLC.

After graduating from UNC-C with a degree in chemistry, Chavis returned to Oxford, where he planned to become a teacher. Instead, he took temporary assignments as a substitute teacher and became a community organizer. In May 1970, a few months after his arrival, Chavis organized a three-day march from Oxford to Raleigh in protest of police behavior in the investigation of the murder of an African American youth.

In the fall of 1970, Chavis began working in Henderson as a field organizer with Leon White of the Commission of Racial Justice of the United Church of Christ. Chavis organized protests, marches, and boycotts over school disputes. Violence again accompanied his efforts. In Henderson, riots following one of his marches left two people dead and a tobacco warehouse in flames. Racial violence also escalated following Chavis-led boycotts in Warrenton in Warren County; Elizabethtown, near Wilmington; and East Arcadia in Davidson County.

In February 1971, White sent him to Wilmington to aid in the protest surrounding the closing of the all-black Williston High School. Rather than unite the African American community in Wilmington, Chavis's speeches and revolutionary rhetoric appealed to the Williston students, who believed "that revolution meant 'black retaliation.'" Tension escalated over several days and violence erupted. Mike's Grocery, a white-owned store in an African American neighborhood, was firebombed. The troubles escalated and before it was over, two people were dead, six were injured, and $500,000 worth of property had been damaged. A year later, Chavis was arrested along with eight high school students and a white female civil rights worker. The group, later dubbed the "Wilmington 10" by the press, was convicted on charges of arson and conspiracy to shoot firefighters and policemen.

Chavis was sentenced to thirty-seven years in prison and began serving his sentence in 1972 in Raleigh's Central Prison. He later said he found "more humanity among the prisoners at Central Prison than I do now. . . . old inmates taught me to survive in prisons. It was a code of honor not violence." However, the experience was not without its horrors. In 1972, a fellow inmate was burned to death, and threats against Chavis followed. He remembered, "he was an inmate a couple of cells down from me. . . . [someone] threw a five-gallon can of paint thinner in his cell and lit a broom."

While in prison, Chavis used a state-sponsored study-release program to earn a master's degree in divinity at Duke University, attending the school escorted in leg irons and handcuffs. He avoided Central Prison's 10:00 P.M. "lights-out" rule by studying in the prison bathroom. While in prison, he wrote two books: *An American Political Prisoner: Appeals for Human Rights* and *Psalms from Prison*.

In 1978, the Wilmington 10 case attracted the attention of Amnesty International, which declared Chavis and his nine fellow plaintiffs to be political prisoners in the United States. The discovery that a prosecution witness's testimony had been coerced by police prompted Governor James B. Hunt Jr. to reduce Chavis's sentence by a third. Chavis was paroled in 1979 and a federal appellate court overturned his conviction a year later.

After obtaining a doctorate of divinity from Howard University in 1981, Chavis rejoined the United Church of Christ's Commission for Racial Justice in 1983, this time as deputy director, and became executive director two years later. While at the helm of the organization, Chavis concentrated on issues such as gang violence, drug use, and high school dropout rates. On the national stage, he lobbied against United States aid to assist the rebellion against the Marxist regime in Angola, and served as clergy coordinator to Jesse Jackson's 1984 presidential campaign.

During his tenure at the Commission for Racial Justice, Chavis became closely associated with what he called "environmental racism." Chavis's involvement began in 1983 with a protest against the dumping of contaminated soil in Warren County, where the population was 75 percent African American and mostly poor. Chavis issued a report entitled *Toxic Wastes and Race in the United States* that showed that three of the nation's five largest toxic waste landfills were in minority neighborhoods. "We must not only point to overt forms of racism, but also institutionalized racism," Chavis explained. He saw the issue as analogous to school desegregation—"separate and unequal quality of environmental protection." In 1992, Chavis served as an adviser to the Clinton-Gore transition team, studying the Departments of Energy, Interior, and Agriculture, as well as the Environmental Protection Agency. He also was involved in writing the Environmental Justice Act in 1993.

Chavis was elected president of the NAACP in 1993. Eager to reinvigorate and redirect the organization, Chavis sought to raise membership among African American youth, to expand the organization to include the interests of Hispanics and Asians, and to establish NAACP chapters in Africa and the Caribbean. Issues on his agenda included poverty, gang violence, and environmental racism. However, Chavis's tenure as president lasted only sixteen months: problems arose shortly after his election. He ruffled the feathers of the NAACP's old guard by endorsing President Bill Clinton's lifting of the ban on gays in the military and by appointing two controversial figures as his top assistants. Soon the NAACP board began to question Chavis's integrity and financial responsibility, pointing to a number of misrepresentations regarding increases of membership and the apparent spending of $1.9 million more than his budget allowed.

The most serious incident arose in June 1994, when Mary Stansel, Chavis's administrative assistant, sued him and the NAACP for sexual discrimination and harassment. Without consulting the NAACP board,

Chavis secretly offered Stansel $332,400 to drop the suit, creating the appearance that Chavis was using the organization's funds to pay hush money for personal misconduct. The NAACP board voted overwhelmingly to relieve Chavis of his job.

In February 1994, Chavis announced his religious conversion to the Nation of Islam (NOI) and changed his name to Benjamin Muhammad, becoming a minister in the organization. In 1995 Louis Farrakhan, leader of the religious group, appointed Minister Muhammad to organize the group's successful 1995 Million Man March. For this success, Farrakhan appointed Muhammad to head Harlem's Mosque Number 7, a position once held by Malcolm X, and to become NOI's sole representative in New York. In September 2000, the *Village Voice* published a report about financial mismanagement at the mosque and allegations that the minister sexually harassed and attacked a young Muslim woman whom he had been counseling for marriage problems. Amid the scandal, Minister Muhammad was transferred to another position in the NOI, outside of New York.

Ryan Sumner is a graduate of the University of North Carolina at Charlotte where he continued his studies for a master's degree in history and works as the assistant curator at the Levine Museum of the New South in Charlotte.

For more information, see:

Black Student Union History, University of North Carolina at Chapel Hill. Web site at www.uncc.edu/bsu/bus_history.html.

Chavis, Ben (Benjamin F. Muhammad). *An American Political Prisoner: Appeals for Human Rights*. UCC Commission on Racial Justice, 1979.

———. File. *Charlotte Observer*. Web site at www.charlotte.com.

———. *Psalms from Prison*. Pilgrim Press, 1983.

"Dr. Benjamin Chavis Jr." Paper. NAACP Library, Baltimore, Md.

Thomas, Larry. "The True Story Behind the Wilmington 10." U.B. & U.S. Communications Systems, 1993.

HOWARD W. ODUM

by Stephanie Adams

I N THE EARLY PART of the twentieth century, North Carolina, like the rest of the southern states, was struggling to repair a ruined economy and a devastated sense of regional identity. The bitter years of Reconstruction were fresh memories, and North Carolinians were eager to focus on developing industries, promise of a secure financial future and a renewed pride in their historical heritage. Religious fundamentalism enjoyed new growth as well. Against this complex background of religious and fiscal conservatism and ambition, the University of North Carolina sought to establish itself as a nationally competitive institution of higher learning. The administration wanted to hire the best faculty possible to make the university an educational leader in the South. One of these professors was sociologist Howard Washington Odum.

Odum was dean of the School of Liberal Arts at Emory University in 1920 when his friend Harry W. Chase, the president of UNC, invited him to come to Chapel Hill and establish a program in the nascent discipline of sociology. Odum was already developing ambitious plans for the study of social issues in the South and had been frustrated by the lack of support he received at Emory. With an enthusiastic affirmative to Chase, Odum immediately began to correspond with his new colleague E. C. Branson to discuss his arrival at UNC. "There are really so many things to talk over and so many aspects of this work that we shall need all the informal time possible to discuss them adequately," Odum wrote Branson in March 1920 as they arranged to meet on the New Orleans-Atlanta train line.

Without delay he set about creating a sociology program with an impressive range of topics of study. One historian wrote that "in addition to standard courses in social theory, community health, family case work, educational sociology, child welfare, recreation, and statistics, students could choose from offerings in social pathology, juvenile delinquency, labor problems, Negro problems, and 'Problems of the Small Town and Mill Village'—courses that started out assuming some conspicuous defect in southern society. It was a bill of fare unavailable anywhere else in the South at that time."

Within a few years of his arrival Odum was well on his way to making the University of North Carolina

Howard W. Odum (Courtesy of Southern Historical Collection)

the center for the study of social science in the South. He founded the Institute for Research in Social Science (IRSS) in 1924, the first of its kind in the nation, to provide funding for promising students to conduct research on social issues in the South. Notable scholars who benefited from its support were Rupert B. Vance, Arthur F. Raper, Guy B. Johnson, and George S. Mitchell. Just prior to the establishment of the institute, in 1922, Odum began the *Journal of Social Forces* (now known as *Social Forces*), which quickly became recognized as an important publication in the discipline of social science. It was highly regarded in both the North and the South, winning the praise of even the acid-tongued Henry L. Mencken, who delighted in mocking the South's backward ways in his *American Mercury*.

From the beginning Odum and his educational

initiatives faced resistance from outside the university. "Sociology" was widely confused by people with the hated "socialism," a misconception that was strengthened by Odum's interest in labor relations and the textile industry. Public welfare, a topic for which Odum would create a stand-alone department, was viewed with equal suspicion. But what the public most disliked was Odum's belief that there were social ills in the South that stood in the way of its progress. He was optimistic about education's role in curing these ills, but the state's constituency flinched at his unromantic views of the condition of Southern affairs and his equally blunt statements about them. Odum's belief in the ability of the South to claim its place in the modern world was tempered with an understanding of the region's own culpability in creating its current situation.

In "A Southern Promise," Odum wrote, "We are tired, eternally tired, of limitations. Tired of wrong impressions, tired of defense complex and mechanism, tired of unending ridicule, tired of taking second and third and fourth rate places in achievement, tired of undeveloped potential, tired of lack of opportunity, tired of complacency, ignorance, poverty, and all the paradoxes that now flower out of a soil which can produce better."

During the twenties Odum's tenure at UNC was marked with friction between the institution and the citizens of North Carolina. It came to a head in 1925, a year that opened with explosive debate in the legislature over the teaching of the theory of evolution in public schools. The issue was the subject of hostile debate across the United States, culminating in the courtroom with Tennessee's Scopes trial. University President Chase became embroiled with the problem, and his friend Odum lent him vocal support in defeating the proposed Poole antievolution bill. Odum was breezy with some correspondents about the affair, but with others he could not hide his dismay at the situation. In a letter to the Reverend M. T. Plyler on February 12, 1925, Odum remarked: "But I can't understand why leaders of the Church can stand up and see their principles of American democracy and the very essence of Christianity violated, and how Methodists, for instance, would follow Baptist Ku Kluxers in making assault on all hope for religious freedom and real Christianity. Many of our dominant Ku Klux and Ministers would, without any doubt in my judgement, lynch Christ Himself in the name of religion and anti-evolution."

In the midst of the evolution furor, Odum's *Journal* published two excerpted chapters about religion by a pair of northern scholars, one of which was a scientific discussion of religion. Bombastic in tone, it was a dismissive treatment of the topic, and when word of it reached the populace of North Carolina, it ignited a firestorm of protest on the part of the fundamentalists. A typical response appeared in a letter to Odum from Johnston Avery of the *Hickory Daily Record* on March 2, 1925. He stated, "Without going into the right and wrong of their articles, I deny you the right under the constitution of North Carolina as a state paid teacher to spread teachings, be it original or contributed, which would tend to destroy the faith of young men and women in things held sacred by the fathers." Odum had been aware of the risk he took in printing these articles, but did not anticipate how vicious and how personal the attacks would be. Groups of ministers in Charlotte and Gastonia banded together to demand that the *Journal* and Odum be ousted from the university, and the resulting unpleasantness amounted, as he said in a letter, "pretty nearly to persecution."

The intolerance was especially frustrating to Odum since he attributed many of the South's problems to demagoguery. Writing to H. L. Mencken in September 1923, he noted that "in my own native Georgia, I consider that there are two dominant personalities in the last two decades, one a political demagogue, and the other an ecclesiastical demagogue, who in my judgment have thrown the state more out of its order than all the other forces combined." The squabbling threatened to set back the progress being made toward bringing the state into step with modernism. In his letter to Frank W. Hankins at the beginning of the ministerial assault in 1925, Odum commented, "If we can ever get the South (and for that matter a great many of our 100 per cent fundamentalists all over the country) to a place where they will stop wanting to kill somebody for differences of opinion, we will have gone a long way towards progress." The battle raged for many months, and although Odum and the university prevailed, it was a clear indication that progress would come at a cost.

Even within the university community, Odum's views came up against old, engrained attitudes, particularly on the subject of race. He and a number of his research associates had a strong and sympathetic interest in African American culture. Some of the important work of the IRSS focused on collecting folk stories and studying black folk cultures and history. In doing so, their more enlightened stance sometimes shocked people on campus. Guy and Guion Johnson, in their history of the IRSS, note that when they first began to correspond with black leaders in the state they "sometimes had to reassure a secretary at the Institute that it was quite all right to address such people as 'Mr.' or 'Mrs.' when typing letters and envelopes." Odum himself had a more painful experience when the Institute of Human Relations invited poet James Weldon Johnson to speak at the university in 1927. The Johnsons wrote that "when [Odum] addressed him as 'Mr. Johnson,' he was mortified to see a member of the Institute's Board of Governors get up and stalk out of Memorial Hall."

Odum recognized the role race played in the southern culture. His advocacy for change showed both in his scholarly interests and his involvement with organizations such as the Hampton and Tuskegee Institutes and the Commission on Interracial Cooperation, of which he was chairman in 1937. His attitudes had evolved over the years. His earliest writing expressed conventional conclusions about the appropriateness of racial separation. But by 1936, his beliefs had changed so much that he said of his early work, "I hope I have come a long way since that was written."

It is ironic that the Odum pilloried by the "common folk" was one of their own, a man who identified deeply with their concerns and values. Born in 1884 on a small farm near Bethlehem, Georgia, he knew firsthand the problems plaguing the rural South, and his background and experience are reflected in his work. Educated first at Emory University, like many other promising scholars he went to the North to attain his doctoral degrees. He returned to the South to teach at the University of Georgia before assuming his position as dean at Emory in 1919. By the time he came to the University of North Carolina, he was already demonstrating the phenomenal drive and talent that would define his career.

His colleague, university librarian Louis Round Wilson, said of Odum that "he was an agent of social change, and at times the area around him seemed charged with ozone." Even as he was establishing groundbreaking institutions and courses of research, Odum published prolifically, producing more than twenty books and two hundred articles about his many interests. His works ranged from scholarly texts and articles about sociological concerns and regionalism to books about African American folklore. As an agent for social reform, he was concerned with race relations and education along with social science issues. As busy as he kept himself professionally, Odum found time for a hobby—raising prize-winning Jersey cows. Interspersed in his correspondence with his scholarly peers are enthusiastic letters about the cattle business.

Odum's dynamic personality and tremendous energy fueled his ambitious career. He was uniquely equipped to help North Carolina, and the South, overcome the social, political, economic, and racial problems that were keeping the region from realizing its potential. His death on November 8, 1954, marked the end of an era of extraordinary service to education, scholarship, and the people of the South.

Stephanie Adams is the processing archivist for the Special Collections unit of the Clemson University Library. She is also engaged on a Howard Odum project for the Institute for Research in Social Science at the University of North Carolina at Chapel Hill. Adams received her bachelor's degree in fine arts from the Evergreen State College in Olympia, Wash., and her master's in liberal studies from UNC-Chapel Hill.

For more information, see:

Odum, Howard Washington. Papers. Southern Historical Collection, University of North Carolina at Chapel Hill.

Brazil, Wayne D. *Howard W. Odum: The Building Years, 1884–1930*. Garland, 1988.
Dorman, Robert L. *Revolt of the Provinces: The Regionalist Movement in America, 1920–1945*. University of North Carolina Press, 1993.
Egerton, John. *Speak Now Against the Day: The Generation Before the Civil Rights Movement in the South*. Alfred A. Knopf, 1994.
Johnson, Guy B. *Research in Service to Society: The First Fifty Years of the Institute for Research in Social Science*. University of North Carolina Press. 1980.
Singal, Daniel Joseph. *The War Within: From Victorian to Modernist Thought in The South*. University of North Carolina Press, 1982.

ORRIN H. PILKEY JR.

By Stan Swofford

ORRIN H. PILKEY JR.'s impish build—he stood but five-feet four-inches tall—along with his ruddy, weather-beaten face, full salt-and-pepper beard, ample belly, and twinkling eyes were evidence of good times and good humor, not angry confrontations. Yet Pilkey was thrown off private property, and asked to leave public property, in just about every beach town in the Carolinas. His name was anathema to developers and property owners, who could recognize him from a hundred yards down the beach. Coastal newspapers called him a plague on the land. Beach-town politicians welcomed him like the red tide.

But he was a hero to thousands, because Pilkey, who retired in 1999 as the James B. Duke Professor of Geology at Duke University, had more impact on beach policy along the East Coast, and especially North Carolina, than anyone in the last half of the twentieth century. A prolific researcher and writer, Pilkey documented the fragility and migration of the barrier islands. With bulldog tenacity and missionary zeal seldom seen in scientific circles, Pilkey showed how development of the shoreline—and the structures, devices, and practices used to protect that development—ultimately destroy the islands' beaches, just as they destroyed most of the once-beautiful shoreline of New Jersey.

"New Jerseyization," he would say with a shudder, would turn the state's barrier islands into a coastal wasteland if the state's policy was aimed at protecting property for a privileged few rather than protecting the beaches for use by all. Pilkey's determination to stop that from happening earned him the enmity of coastal property owners, politicians, and the U.S. Army Corps of Engineers, the agency that builds seawalls and other shoreline protective devices.

People may retire from jobs, but they don't retire from a cause. And for Pilkey, that's what North Carolina's three-hundred-mile-long necklace of barrier island pearls were. It was a precious, living, breathing cause he shouldered in the 1970s, one he vowed to carry until the islands' fragile shorelines were safe from development. After he retired from teaching, he continued to campaign against shoreline development as director of Duke's Program for the Study of Developed Shorelines, which he founded. He also continued his practice of taking students to the beach to see firsthand what he told thousands in classrooms

Orrin H. Pilkey Jr. (Courtesy of Charlotte Observer)

at Duke and other schools. That's news beach politicians and developers didn't want to hear. "If it was up to Orrin Pilkey, nobody would be at the beach," Topsail Beach Mayor Bill Stamper once said. "I think he'd like to make a bird sanctuary out of the islands and not let anybody on them."

That's close, Pilkey said. "These beaches belong to our children and our children's children," he said. "What a tragedy, what an atrocity, if we kill them." Pilkey hammered out his message in twenty-two books, dozens of newspaper editorials and magazine articles, and countless appearances before civic, community, and school groups, and state and federal legislative committees. Along the way, he and his wife Sharlene raised five children in their rambling old farmhouse on thirteen wooded acres near Hillsborough. There, hundreds of Pilkey's former students, many of them later coastal geologists, partied several times a year. They drank good wine, maybe ate a turkey or two, and talked about the latest in Pilkey's war on development at the beach.

Pilkey taught them not to be bashful with their science. "Orrin believes if you've got it and you know it's right and important, you ought to put it out there for the public," said David Bush, a geology professor at the University of West Georgia and one of Pilkey's former students. Bush said that, unlike most scientists, Pilkey never believed in publishing his research in arcane professional journals. Coastal geologists called it "Pilkey science," Bush said. "Get good data, good ideas, then publish. And do it as fast as you can."

Pilkey possessed impeccable scientific credentials long before he began studying shoreline development. His research into deep-sea sedimentology, the movement of sediments along the ocean floor, earned him acclaim from his peers and about every award in the field. That acclaim helped him immensely when he immersed himself in what he calls his "radical" science of barrier island behavior, and became a vocal —some said strident—advocate for strict curbs on the development of barrier island shorelines.

"Most of academia looks askance on advocates," said Rob Young, a professor of geology at Western Carolina University and one of Pilkey's former students. "But Orrin's detractors couldn't just pass him off as another personality." Pilkey's writings and testimony spearheaded the drive that prompted the N.C. General Assembly in 1985 to outlaw most seawalls, an action based on conclusions by Pilkey and his colleagues that seawalls hasten the destruction of a beach. Other states, including South Carolina, Maine, and Massachusetts, also limited the use of seawalls and other hard-structure barriers, largely as a result of Pilkey's research. But Pilkey wanted much more than a ban on seawalls, and that's why beachfront property owners and coastal politicians could get so furious as to officially condemn him, as the Folly Beach, S.C., town council did when it called his views "insulting, uninformed and radical."

Pilkey believed that, to save the beaches, people would have to retreat from them. Retreat in an orderly fashion before the inevitable storms, rising sea levels, and migration of the islands ensured a chaotic flight. When the ocean threatened a building, move it or lose it, Pilkey said. In addition, new beachfront development should be prohibited. If the ocean took a house, don't let the owner rebuild. And don't encourage rebuilding with federal guarantees of low insurance rates. Renourish sparingly, if at all. "Beach renourishment," as the Corps of Engineers called it, was the building of artificial beaches and dunes with sand dredged from the ocean, sounds, or coastal rivers. The answer was to retreat and allow the ocean and the islands to have their way, Pilkey believed. Because, ultimately, they will have their way, he warned. "To think otherwise is ludicrous," Pilkey said. "Ludicrous."

To Pilkey, a barrier island was far more than a lifeless spit of sand. "These islands are virtually alive," Pilkey said one day while examining a handful of beach sand at Topsail Island on the coast north of Wilmington. He let the sand slip slowly, reverently, through his fingers, sniffed the salty air, and walked down the beach, his short, powerful legs propelling him rapidly on the way. He didn't like what he saw. For him, the island was a textbook example of what developers and government should not do to a barrier island. Houses crowded the shoreline, even though debris from past hurricanes remained piled beside damaged homes. A house was under construction in the middle of a dry inlet, an opening that the ocean would almost certainly plow through during the next storm. "Madness, sheer madness," Pilkey said, over and over again. "There's a truth developers and politicians can't seem to grasp. Beaches will always exist, but not in the same place. Beach erosion is not a problem unless a building is there."

Pilkey dug a little sand with his foot and picked up an oyster shell about eight inches long. "They don't make them that big any more," he said. It was a fossil, perhaps ten thousand years old: proof, he said, that the island was migrating. Oysters are found in the sound, not the ocean. Finding ancient shells on the beach—and the Topsail Island shore was littered with them—could only mean that the island had migrated to where the sound used to be, he said. Peat or black mud from the marsh was often found on the beach, another sign, he said, of island migration.

Barrier islands are "dynamic, living things," Pilkey said. "Every time I come here I'm awed." Pilkey, however, scoffed at the idea of vacationing on a barrier island. Instead, he traveled far inland, back to his roots, to the wilds of Washington, the Dakotas, Montana. It was as if it would be an insult to the islands if their protector vacationed on them.

And Pilkey firmly believed he was destined to be their protector. Born in New York City in 1934, he grew up in Richland, Wash., where his father, a civil engineer, worked in a plutonium plant. He quickly developed a love for the outdoors. He hunted, fished, hiked, and searched for rocks and minerals, developing a passion for geology. He got a job with the United States Forest Service at sixteen and became a smoke jumper, sometimes parachuting in alone to fight fires in Washington, Oregon, and Montana.

At Washington State University, the young geology major met his future wife. "It was a blind date, and Pilkey had his logging boots on," she said. "He stepped on my foot and broke it, but I married him anyway. Even then, he was different from anybody I had ever known. It's been crazy ever since."

After their wedding, she and Pilkey packed their old station wagon and headed down the Baja Peninsula searching for sand dollars. Pilkey had decided to write his master's thesis on the chemistry of sand dollars. He developed his love for coastal geology while bouncing along the remote Baja's dusty, unpaved road, knocking on farmers' doors to beg for gasoline and sleeping in the station wagon. "It was wonderful," Pilkey said. "We could smell the ocean all the time."

Pilkey said he became "a real seaman" in the early 1960s on Sapelo Island off the Georgia coast, when he was researching the evolution of the continental shelf. He began to shift toward his "radical" science as he did sedimentology research on the Duke research vessel *Eastward* off the North Carolina coast. He could see the shoreline becoming packed with houses and high-rises, and he could see how the beaches were disappearing.

It took Hurricane Camille, however, to push Pilkey firmly into the ranks of advocacy science. Camille, one of the most powerful and destructive hurricanes ever to hit the United States, smashed into Waveland, Miss., where Pilkey's father and mother lived, in 1969. Their home was three blocks from the beach, but it was damaged beyond repair. The catastrophe made Pilkey think long and hard about the negative impact that development along the shorelines and the use of structures such as seawalls can have on beaches.

In 1975, Pilkey, along with his father, Orrin, and brother, Walter—both of them engineers—cowrote *How to Live with an Island*. The book discussed scientifically, but in language the average person can understand, the vulnerability of barrier island beaches to ever-increasing development. Pilkey said he was amazed at the book's reception. "Holy cow! The phone didn't stop ringing. I got calls to be on radio, on television. There were newspaper stories every day. It was unbelievable." The response was not all positive, however. Beach-town politicians, developers, and engineers were defensive, and often downright hostile.

Love him or hate him, Pilkey became something of a legend as he wrote his name in the shifting, shimmering sands of North Carolina's barrier islands. One of his five children, Kerry Pilkey, had to deal with that legend often. Like millions of other people, but unlike his father, Kerry Pilkey and his family liked to vacation at the beach. But he discovered long ago that if he hoped to get a decent room, or any room, he'd better not use his name when seeking a reservation. He used his wife's name. And then held his breath when it was time to sign the bill.

Stan Swofford worked for the News and Record *of Greensboro for thirty years. He spent most of those years as a general assignment, enterprise, and investigative reporter and won numerous state and national awards for his reporting and writing.*

For more information, see:
Bush D. M., O. H. Pilkey, and W. J. Neal. *Living by the Rules of the Sea*. Duke University Press, 1996.
Kaufman, W., and O. H. Pilkey. *The Beaches Are Moving: The Drowning of the American Shoreline*. Anchor-Doubleday, 1979.
Pilkey, O. H., W. J. Neal, and O. H. Pilkey Sr. *From Currituck to Calabash*. N.C. Science and Technology Research Center, 1978.
Pilkey, O. H., W. J. Neal, S. R. Riggs, C. A. Webb, D. M. Bush, J. Bullock, and B. Cowan. *The North Carolina Shore and Its Barrier Islands*. Duke University Press, 1998.
Pilkey, O. H., O. H. Pilkey Sr., and Pilkey, Walter. *How to Live with an Island*. N.C. Department of Natural and Economic Resources, 1975.

SPORTS

On July 4, 1984, race car driver Richard Petty, of a North Carolina hamlet called Level Cross, won the Firecracker 400 stock car race in Daytona Beach after Ronald Reagan, the first sitting president of the United States to witness a NASCAR (National Association for Stock Car Auto Racing) event, had given the drivers the order to start their engines by radio from Air Force One. But Petty produced such a thrilling finish that race fans remembered Petty, not Reagan, when the race was done.

Such a scene would have been inconceivable to Petty's father, Lee, who led his family into auto racing in the late 1940s, when the sport was considered barely legal and haunted by a heritage of the hot cars bootleggers built to outrun revenue agents. But the Pettys—particularly the one called "King Richard"—turned stock car racing from outlaw contests on the North Carolina back roads to a sport of international prominence.

Stock car racing produced the stuff of legends, as did the storied careers of other North Carolina men and women with amazing achievements in more traditional sport on the gridiron, on the court, on the mound, on the track, and on the greens. In addition, over the century sport moved from amateurs competing for engraved trophies and silver trays to big business, both for the sponsors and for the athletes. None had the impact of superstar Michael Jordan—a corporation unto himself—whose basketball career began in Wilmington, flourished at the University of North Carolina, and expanded beyond all imagination with the Chicago Bulls. Another Wilmington ball player, Meadowlark Lemon, played around the world as the Harlem Globetrotters' "Clown Prince of Basketball."

The rise of basketball as the unofficial state sport was the product of a succession of coaches at North Carolina colleges and universities who produced national champions over a span of fifty years. Everett Case started the reputation of "Tobacco Road" in basketball at North Carolina State University in the late 1940s and 1950s. He was followed by Dean Smith at the University of North Carolina at Chapel Hill, who became the winningest coach in Division I basketball; Mike Krzyzewski at Duke, whose teams won back-to-back NCAA (National Collegiate Athletic Association) men's championships in 1991 and 1992 (and again in 2001, ending twenty seasons at Duke with a 533–164 record); and the fiery Jim Valvano at N.C. State, who also captured national titles in 1974 and 1983. Down the road was Clarence "Big House" Gaines at Winston-Salem State University, whose own record of victories in Division II were just short of what Smith and Kentucky's Adoph Rupp had done in Division I.

Football produced storied greats, among them the legendary Wallace Wade, the football coach at Duke University who developed national champions and had the distinction of competing in a Rose Bowl played in Durham. (World

War II had just erupted with the attack on Pearl Harbor and the 1942 contest was moved east to avoid the threat of another aerial attack. Duke lost to Oregon State, 20 to 16.) At the end of the war, there was no more popular player on the gridiron than UNC's Charles "Choo-Choo" Justice, some of whose records on the field went unsurpassed for more than fifty years.

Dr. Leroy Walker produced Olympic champions on his track in Durham at North Carolina College for Negroes (later North Carolina Central University) and then helped organize the 1996 Olympic games in Atlanta. Charlotte's Floyd "Chunk" Simmons won two consecutive bronze medals in the Olympics of 1952 and 1956. In the early 1960s, a young Charlotte athlete named Jim Beatty claimed seven American track records while at UNC, including the first mile run indoors under four minutes and a world record for two miles.

Professional golf was only beginning to come of age when North Carolina golfers—men and women—claimed titles on the courses at Pinehurst, the home of the World Golf Hall of Fame. Two women, Marjorie Jane "Marge" Burns of Greensboro and Estelle Lawson Page of Chapel Hill, were among the first women professionals and helped found the Ladies Professional Golf Association. Page beat Patty Berg for the 1937 U.S. Amateur title, lost in the finals to Berg a year later, and won numerous regional championships, as did Burns. Arnold Palmer was a son of Pennsylvania but he sharpened his early golf skill while a student at Wake Forest University. Ray Floyd, another leading professional golfer, came from Wilmington.

MARJORIE JANE "MARGE" BURNS

By Irwin Smallwood

MARJORIE JANE "MARGE" BURNS, perhaps North Carolina's most accomplished female athlete of the twentieth century, had to make the decision of her life at the age of twenty-four. Should she gamble her considerable golf talent on the fledgling Ladies Professional Golf Association (LPGA) tour or play it safe and pursue an amateur career and a more secure lifestyle? She opted for the safety of a good business opportunity and never looked back, even though it may well have cost her the fame and fortune associated with success in the sports world today. "Maybe I was born twenty years too soon," she said shortly after celebrating her seventy-fifth birthday, "but I have no regrets."

Regrets? How does one with a truckload of silverware signifying unprecedented dominance of golf in her home state have regrets? Marge Burns won the North Carolina Amateur championship a record ten times. She won the Carolinas Amateur six times. Five times she won the Teague Award, given annually for many years to the number one male and female athletes in the Carolinas. No one else won the Teague Award more than twice. But her remarkable career did not end with the victories and the trophies and the well-earned recognition she earned as one of the premier players on the East Coast.

When an injury all but ended her competitive career in 1970, she turned to teaching professionally, and six years later she was named the LPGA's national Teacher of the Year. At the LPGA's fiftieth-anniversary celebration in Palm Beach, Fla., in 1999, Marge Burns was one of a half-dozen teachers recognized by the LPGA among its top fifty people. In the end, she was better known nationally as a teacher than as a player.

So how did she make that life-altering decision back in 1950? Lack of money played a major role. She didn't have any and the LPGA Tour didn't have much. Besides, she said in retrospect, "I would have been playing against established players like Patty Berg, Babe Zaharias, Betty Jameson, Louise Suggs, Kathy Whitworth, and Mickey Wright, and I didn't want to be playing for $100 at the end of the line."

But that wasn't all of it. Her father had just become one of the thirteen original distributors of Tupperware kitchen containers, and he invited her to work for him and play as much amateur golf as she

Marjorie J. "Marge" Burns (Courtesy of Marjorie J. Burns)

wanted. It was an offer she couldn't refuse, and the association lasted for twenty years—the heart of her winning years. "As I look back, I'm glad I did it that way," she said, "because I learned a lot about business from my father and enjoyed being in business with him."

The only nag she really felt in regard to the LPGA Tour had nothing to do with fame or fortune. "I was a competitor," she said. "I didn't like to lose." Also, she had grown up in Greensboro when the idea of a women's professional organization was being hatched there, and as a starstruck teenager she naturally had notions of becoming a great professional player herself one day.

But, she insisted, "My business experience probably served me better in the long run. And I did well in amateur golf. I didn't win the National Amateur or anything like that, but I won my share of tournaments." That *share* of tournaments, by her rough estimate, was about fifty out of nearly five hundred she played between 1950 and 1970. She won the prestigious Harder Hall in Florida five times, the Mid-Atlantic Amateur twice, and the Eastern Amateur in 1961. She was a Curtis Cup alternate in 1962 and twice (1959 and 1961) was named one of the top ten women amateurs in the nation by *Golf Digest*. All of which was sufficient to land her in the North Carolina Sports Hall of Fame and the Carolinas Golf Hall of Fame in 1984.

Burns was born in Orlando, Fla., on July 13, 1925, and moved to Greensboro with her family when she was six. She knew competitive golf was her game when she was just thirteen years old. George Corcoran was her pro and teacher at Starmount Country Club and had played a major role in founding the Greater Greensboro Open the year before. He had learned the value of promotion from his brother, Fred, who was manager of the still-young Professional Golfers' Association (PGA) Tour, and he wanted to showcase the talents of his tall, skinny pupil. So he brought in a young pro named Patty Berg, who had won the U.S. Amateur the year before, to play an exhibition match with Marge, and that did it. She was so smitten by the experience that she never again had another doubt about what she wanted to do with her life.

Before that time, she said, "I didn't have any sense that this [golf] would become a major part of my life. As a kid I had an old tennis racquet and I hit balls up against the garage door. I played dodge ball and kick ball in elementary school. I was always doing something athletic. In junior high I was a good basketball player. I threw a mean hook shot."

But about that time her dad bought her a set of Patty Berg golf clubs, and she took a half-dozen lessons from Corcoran, when she was ten or eleven, and other sports suddenly were not so important. She broke 100 by the time she was about twelve, aggravating some of her elders with her talent. "Allie Belle Neese (a Starmount member and avid golfer) took me to Mt. Airy to play in a Piedmont Women's Golf Association tournament," she said, "and I shot a 93. I won what must have been the first flight and those women said I couldn't play any more."

A year or so later, in 1940, she won the first Carolinas Junior Girls championship at Starmount, beating, among others, Agnes Morton Woodruff (sister of Grandfather Mountain's Hugh Morton) and Mary Clay O'Connor of Durham. "We were the three best players, and I think I shot an 88 and an 84 to win the first one. Aggie was second and then won it in 1941. Mary Clay won in 1942 and then we all went off to college."

Her father had sold the business and her decision to go into teaching as a professional was firmly made when Marge hit forty-five, but she still had a competitive itch to scratch. By then she was a member of the LPGA, and "I wanted at least to try to get my card (to play the tour)," she recalled. "You had to beat the bottom third of the field in three out of four tournaments to do it, and I had done that twice, in the first two tournaments I played in. I was waiting to go to Texas for the third one when I hit a shot one day and I just felt everything pop in my elbow. That was the end of that. I wound up having three surgeries on my elbow and was pretty much out of competition altogether for close to two years."

The day Marge and Aggie Morton faced off in the finals of the Carolinas championship at Cape Fear Country Club in Wilmington was a classic. The two had graduated from high school the same year, then from Woman's College (later the University of North Carolina at Greensboro) the same year, and "were kind of *the* rivals in North Carolina in the early 1950s." Aggie had beaten Marge a year or so earlier in the Linville Invitational, and "I think the whole city of Wilmington [Aggie's hometown] turned out to see the match," Burns said. It turned out to be one of Marge's six Carolinas titles.

Burns's record ten victories in the North Carolina Amateur came in a fifteen-year stretch from 1953 to 1968. It might have reached eleven except for Sandy Barnhill. Burns remembered her as "a girl from down east who had announced with great determination that she was going to have my neck one year and I said, 'Come on.'" Barnhill finally succeeded in the last one Marge played. "The only thing I can say is that I had torn up my ankle stepping in a hole and was playing practically on one leg," Marge still protested years later about that unceremonious defeat in 1969.

If Burns had a genuine nemesis in her pursuit of golf championships in the Carolinas, it was Estelle Lawson Page of Chapel Hill, who beat Patty Berg for the 1937 U.S. Amateur title, lost in the finals to Berg a year later, and won a career load of regional championships in her heyday. Page had the reputation as a player who could get inside the heads of her opponents, and Burns, who failed in three tries to beat her, did not deny that she may have been somewhat intimidated by Page. Still, she had nothing but the greatest admiration for her. "She was tough and one of the most competitive people I've ever known," Burns said, "She would talk to me, but she would never show me that little shot she had from off the edge of the green with that great old big-headed Kroydon 8-iron she used."

Their best match was in the North and South Amateur at Pinehurst in the early 1950s, when Burns was close to the top of her game. "I had qualified pretty well," Burns said, "but I looked up and sure enough I had drawn Estelle in the first round. On the first hole I have it on the edge of the green and she is in the bunker over there to the right. She holes it. Birdie. One down. To make a long story short, she beat me 5 and 4 and she was absolutely even fours for fifteen holes on No. 2 in Pinehurst. Afterwards, Estelle told me she had heard I was playing pretty well in Florida and 'I knew I had to get on my horse. I was determined to beat you as bad as I could.'"

The rivalry was short-lived, however. "Estelle was not well, and after she lost to Barbara McIntire in the first round of the U.S. Amateur at Myers Park [country club] in Charlotte in 1955, she never played in competition again," according to Burns.

College days during the mid-1940s were lost golf years for Burns. There was no golf program, though Ellen Griffin, who later would become one of the nation's top golf instructors, tried to teach the game to the physical education majors with what little equipment they had. The frustration vanished when she graduated and went to work as a physical education teacher, first at Danville High School in Virginia, then at Pfeiffer Junior College. Her first time back in competition she ran into her old friend Aggie Morton again and lost in the semifinals of the Carolinas Amateur at Sedgefield Country Club in Greensboro. "Aggie went on to the finals but had to play Estelle and, of course, lost," she recalled. It took Burns four long years after college to save enough money to launch what would be her salad days in competition in 1950.

An amateur named Hope Seignious, who had moved to Greensboro with her cotton broker father in the early 1940s, was one of the leaders of a group that had the urge to form some type of women's professional organization. According to Burns's recollections, "Betty Hicks, a nationally known player who was writing a book on group golf instruction with Ellen Griffin [of UNC-G], came to Greensboro to meet with Hope and Kathryn Hemphill [a well-known amateur from South Carolina] to talk about it. Babe Zaharias was in on it, too, and so was Patty Berg."

The upshot was that the Women's Professional Golf Association (WPGA) was formed, a women's golf magazine was started (financed by Seignious's father and published in Greensboro), and a measure of organization was finally brought to women's golf at the professional level. The new WPGA played a National Women's Open in Spokane, Wash., in 1946 at match play, and Patty Berg won it. And then they moved to Greensboro to play what would be the first Women's Open contested at stroke play. Thus, Burns got to play, at age twenty-two, in a historic event right at home.

"I played with Louise Suggs in the first round, and on the first tee we both drove it just past the 200-yard marker," she says, "and I hit my second shot and didn't quite reach the green. Suggs stood up there and cold topped it. She didn't hit it fifteen yards. She never changed her expression one bit, just took that same club and took a big old swing at it and it flew the green. That little bitty lady could really hit it.

"It was the first time I had seen Betty Jameson play. That was a gorgeous golf swing. Two amateurs, Polly Riley and Sally Sessions, led that thing for a while, but Jameson played the last round in 74 or 75 and became the first woman to break 300 for 72 holes, finishing at 295. Riley and Sessions tied for second at 301."

(The WPGA staged the Women's Open again in 1948, in Atlantic City, N.J., and then became the LPGA, which sponsored it for four years. The United States Golf Association began conducting the championship in 1949).

Like most athletes in their later years, Burns occasionally wondered what might have been. A lot of speculation about her possible lost potential centers around the fact that she was never very strong. It would have helped if she had been blessed with the physical strength of most of the great ones of her day, but, she would tell you in all candor, "I also believe that if there had been more stroke play tournaments, my amateur record would have been better."

At the end of the twentieth century, she was a national evaluator in the LPGA Teaching Division, playing in occasional benefit golf outings, and teaching on the practice tee.

She was breaking eighty occasionally before she suffered two strokes in 1999. Afterward, she said, "I'm probably at 84 to 86. I lost about 20 yards a club. I'm trying to keep it going simply because I enjoy it."

Irwin Smallwood, a Greensboro News and Record *writer and editor for forty-two years, observed golf up close since the late 1940s. In the 1960s he won the* American Golf Writers Association *news division competition for three consecutive years. He is a member of the North Carolina Journalism Hall of Fame, the Carolinas Golf Hall of Fame, and the North Carolina Sports Hall of Fame.*

EVERETT N. CASE

By Charles A. Westmoreland Jr.

Long before North Carolina became known as a hotbed for college basketball, one man led the way for such growth. An outsider, Everett Norris Case invaded North Carolina during the 1940s and his coaching tenure at North Carolina State College (later North Carolina State University) resulted in an unprecedented expansion of basketball's popularity. To comprehend how such legendary coaches as Duke University's Mike Krzyzewski, University of North Carolina's Dean Smith, N.C. State's Jim Valvano, and Wake Forest University's Bones McKinney had such an alluring impact on North Carolina, an understanding of Everett Case, the "Old Gray Fox," is paramount.

Case was born in Anderson, Ind., on June 21, 1900. From the time he was old enough to shoot a basketball, he had a love of the game. While an avid fan, Case's lack of size (he was smaller than average) prohibited him from playing for his high school team. In fact, he never played a game of organized basketball in his life, but Case had an affinity for learning the nuances of basketball. He coached a Methodist youth basketball team and immediately knew that he wanted to teach and coach the game for a living. Growing up in the Hoosier State, Case could not escape the love his state had for basketball. Called by writer Phillip House "the hottest basketball town on earth," Anderson was the ideal place for young Everett Case.

Case worked on his college degree while holding an assistant coaching position at Connersville High School. Earning summer school credits from various colleges, Case finally finished his undergraduate degree at Central Normal College in Indiana and he eventually obtained his master's degree from the University of Southern California (USC). To no one's surprise, Case's master's thesis dealt with basketball. He focused his project on various styles of free throw shooting. In "An Analysis of the Effects of Various Factors on Accuracy of Shooting Free Throws," Case argued that an underhand method led to greater accuracy than the standard overhand style. As evidence that Case had done his research well, Rick Barry became one of professional basketball's greatest free throw shooters by using the underhand method.

At the age of twenty, Case became the head coach at Columbus High School, where his team had a solid

Everett N. Case (Courtesy of Hugh Morton)

20–10 record. Case left Columbus after one year to take a head-coaching job at Smithville High. A 32–6 record in 1922 showed that Case could carry success anywhere. To further prove that point, Case left Smithville after the 1922 season for Frankfort High School, where he took the Frankfort High Hot Dogs to the apex of Indiana high school basketball. In only his third year at Frankfort, Case directed a victory over Kokomo High in the state championship. The 1924–25 title was Case's first of four as the king of Indiana basketball.

Case's success bred contempt from his rivals. Accusations of rule-breaking clouded his days at Frankfort as critics denounced Case for trying to lure players from other high schools. During the 1928–29 season, these violations resulted in the forfeiture of several games, and allegations of illegal recruitment haunted Case throughout his high school coaching career.

In 1931, Anderson High School attracted Case back to his hometown, but the reunion was short-lived. The 1932–33 Anderson team went on probation for using an ineligible player and other vague rule violations. Case left Anderson in 1933 to finish his degree at USC. He returned to Indiana in 1934 and regained his position at Frankfort. By 1939, while still young but a coaching veteran, Case became the first coach to win four Indiana state titles. His last chance to win a fifth title came in 1942. However, Washington High knocked out Frankfort in the state semifinals. During his twenty-plus years as an Indiana high school coach, Case compiled a record of 467–124–1, including an unprecedented four state titles.

In 1942, Case enlisted in the navy, but basketball remained at the core of Case's life. "The navy knew what to do with Everett Case," noted historian Jim Sumner. He was assigned to coach several naval training station teams, resulting in a total record of 56–5. Case's naval service ended in 1946, but he chose not to return to Indiana.

Case took his act south in 1946. In his book on N.C. State athletics, *The Wolfpack,* Bill Beezley wrote, "Before 1946 the tale is almost exclusively about football—the college game." When Everett Case arrived, things changed dramatically.

"State College alumni probably got more thrills from crossword puzzles than basketball before 1946," said Beezley. N.C. State was seen as a "Cow College" for its history as a land-grant school and perceived academic and athletic inferiority. After 1946, however, basketball reigned on the Raleigh campus. Case wasted little time in transferring his recipe for success to the college game. He brought a fast-paced style to N.C. State, relying on full-court presses and higher scoring games. Case's first season was nothing short of a success.

The Wolfpack, or "Red Terrors" as many called them, finished the 1946–47 campaign 26–5 and won the Southern Conference championship with a 50–48 tournament victory over arch-rival UNC. The Wolfpack's season ended in the National Invitation Tournament (NIT) with a 60–42 loss to Adolph Rupp's Kentucky Wildcats. This meeting was the first of many on- and off-court contests between Case and Rupp. The Wolfpack then defeated West Virginia 64–52 in the consolation game.

The 1946–47 season saw State win its first conference title since 1929, and campus interest soared. Raleigh's 3,500-seat Memorial Auditorium could not hold the excitement generated by State basketball. Most games featured standing-room-only crowds, climaxing in an odd, yet symbolic development during a regular season game with UNC. The crowd for the UNC contest was so large that local fire marshals would not allow the game to take place. Furious N.C. State students carried their frustration across the entire campus, setting off numerous fire alarms.

An insatiable enthusiasm for basketball was not the only thing Case brought from Indiana. He recruited heavily in his home state. Wolfpack stars Dick Dickey and Sammy Ranzino were just two of several Indiana natives who followed Case south. Also, future N.C. State coach Norm Sloan, a Case recruit, hailed from the Hoosier state. These "Hoosier Hotshots" gave Case the firepower necessary to dominate the Southern Conference for a solid decade.

The late 1940s and early 1950s were the pinnacle of Case's success. State won six conference titles in Case's first six seasons for a combined record of 161 wins and 39 losses. Unfortunately for Wolfpack fans, State played in the National Collegiate Athletic Association (NCAA) tournament only three times. The tournament's selection committee almost always chose Rupp's Kentucky team as the representative from the South and the competition spawned a feud between the "Old Gray Fox" and "The Baron of Bluegrass."

State overtook rival UNC in Case's first twelve games against the Tar Heels. It was not until the 1952–53 season that North Carolina finally beat the Wolfpack under Case. That year, the Tar Heels won the first meeting, 70–69. The Wolfpack got revenge by winning the rematch 87–66 and a first-round conference tournament game, 52–51.

N.C. State christened Reynolds Coliseum in 1949. The twelve-thousand-seat complex hosted all Wolfpack home games and officials hoped it would avoid any future fire code violations. Reynolds Coliseum quickly became the mecca of southern college basketball. In addition to being the home of Case's Wolfpack, the arena played host to the annual Dixie Classic, the Southern Conference tournament, and later the Atlantic Coast Conference (ACC) tournament. The Dixie Classic became the staple event at the coliseum during the 1950s.

The inaugural Dixie Classic took place in December 1949. This holiday tournament featured eight teams playing over three days between Christmas and New Year's Day. The Big Four of North Carolina hoops—Duke, UNC, N.C. State, and Wake Forest—were the tournament's permanent fixtures. These schools hosted four other schools from all across the U.S. Normally, the non-North Carolina teams were national powerhouses. From the tournament's inception until 1953, N.C. State dominated. In 1949, the Wolfpack defeated Penn State to claim the first Dixie Classic championship. Then, State overwhelmed Colgate in 1950, Cornell in 1951, and Brigham Young in 1952, to assume Dixie Classic superiority. In the process, the Wolfpack regularly beat the other North Carolina schools, as they did during the conference regular season.

Case and the Wolfpack did not relinquish their superior status when the ACC was formed in 1953. State won the first ACC tournament title in 1954, defeating North Carolina, Duke, and Wake Forest by a combined seven points. The next few years were a repeat of Case's earlier success. N.C. State defeated Duke 87–77 to win the 1955 league title. Case's group made it three ACC titles in three years with a 86–64 thrashing of Wake Forest.

Case's first decade at N.C. State was one of dominance with a combined record of 267 wins and 60 losses. A decade of success, however, gave way to nine years of turmoil and decline. Recruiting violations and Duke's, UNC's, and Wake Forest's ability to catch N.C. State in talent sent the Wolfpack and their coach into a downward spiral.

Similar to what he faced in Indiana, Case was targeted as a rule-breaker. The NCAA placed State on a one-year probation during the 1954–55 season and Case violated the NCAA's no-tryout clause with the recruitment of Ronnie Shavlik, a scoring star from Colorado. Then, after a surprise loss to tiny Canisius College in the 1956 NCAA tournament, Case's program went on a downslide.

In the 1956–57 term, State received four years on probation, one of the stiffest penalties ever delivered by the NCAA. This ruling prohibited the Wolfpack from playing in the NCAA tournament and all Wolfpack teams were placed on probation. Scandal—which haunted all of college basketball in the 1950s—put Wolfpack basketball on a path of trouble.

But the other state schools' marked improvement equally hurt Case. In 1953, North Carolina hired Frank McGuire to challenge Case. By 1957, the Tar Heels did something Case could never accomplish—win an NCAA title. McGuire's squad, known to many as the "Noo Yawk" Tar Heels for their contingent of New York City players, defeated the Wilt Chamberlain-led Kansas Jayhawks in the 1957 NCAA championship. Also, in 1959, Duke hired former Case protégé Vic Bubas to rejuvenate the Blue Devil program. Wake Forest improved its program as well, reaching the 1962 NCAA Final Four under coach Bones McKinney.

Case coached only two games during the 1964–65 season, retiring abruptly after a loss to Wake Forest. Following the game, he was weak and dizzy from a condition diagnosed as myeloma, a type of bone marrow cancer. When he left, his record at N.C. State was 377 wins and 134 losses.

Case died on April 30, 1966. He was honored as a member of the Naismith Memorial Basketball Hall of Fame, the North Carolina Sports Hall of Fame, and the Indiana Basketball Hall of Fame. At Frankfort High in Indiana, teams play in Case Arena and the ACC tournament's most valuable player receives the Everett Case Award.

Case once said that he would not be successful until "he saw a basketball hoop nailed to every barn and tree in North Carolina." Of course, these expectations were unrealistic. But to not call Everett Case a success would be a serious oversight. "Tobacco Road" was never the same once Everett Case came to town.

Charles A. Westmoreland Jr. is a University of Tennessee doctoral candidate in history with emphasis on the post-Reconstruction South. A native of Southside Virginia, he received his B.S. degree in history from Ferrum College and his M.A. in history from the University of North Carolina at Charlotte, where his thesis was entitled "Strong Legs Running: The Integration of the North Carolina-South Carolina Shrine Bowl."

For more information, see:
Beezley, Bill. *The Wolfpack: Intercollegiate Athletics at North Carolina State University*. North Carolina State University, 1976.
Menzer, Joe. *Four Corners: How UNC, N.C. State, Duke, and Wake Forest Made North Carolina the Center of the Basketball Universe*. Simon and Schuster, 1998.
Sumner, Jim. *A History of Sports in North Carolina*. N.C. Office of Archives and History, 1990.
Williams, Bob. *Hoosier Hysteria: Indiana High School Basketball*. Icarus Press, 1982.

CLARENCE E. "BIGHOUSE" GAINES

By Charles A. Westmoreland Jr.

W HEN YOUNG CLARENCE GAINES stepped on the Morgan State University campus in 1941, someone told him, "Boy, I never seen anything bigger than you but a house." Gaines, a three-sport athlete at the historically black school, carried the nickname "Bighouse" for the rest of his life. His coaching achievements were certainly "big" in the annals of college basketball. While at Winston-Salem State University, Gaines put together one of the most impressive records of all time. At the end of the century, only Dean Smith of the University of North Carolina and the University of Kentucky's Adolph Rupp had more wins.

Coaching at a small Division II school could have made it virtually impossible for a coach to gain national recognition. Gaines, however, surpassed all expectations and was recognized in the last two decades of the century as a pioneer in college basketball coaching. Gaines's exploits were not limited to teaching and coaching basketball. He was active in various civic and community organizations, particularly in the Winston-Salem area.

Upon his retirement in 1993, the *News and Observer* noted, "And don't let anybody ever tell you Coach Gaines isn't as vast in all of his many good qualities as he is in physical stature." Standing at roughly six-foot-three and weighing nearly 290 pounds, Gaines was large in more ways than one. By the time of his retirement, avid basketball fans across the country knew of "Bighouse" and his success at Winston-Salem State University.

Clarence Edward Gaines was born May 21, 1923, in Paducah, Ky. His parents, Lester and Olivia Bolen Gaines, emphasized achievement in diverse areas. They wanted young Clarence to take school and extracurricular activities seriously. He heeded their advice and performed well in the classroom, earning salutatorian honors from Paducah's Lincoln High School. Gaines also excelled in athletics, with football and basketball being his two main sports. Although he would be known many years later for his basketball mind, playing football may have been his strongest suit. His size definitely gave him an advantage on the gridiron. Gaines earned All-State honors as a Lincoln High football player. Illustrative of his well-rounded youth, Gaines also played trumpet in the school band. By the time of his graduation in 1941,

Clarence E. "Bighouse" Gaines (Courtesy of Charlotte Observer)

Gaines seemed well on his way to success in whatever field he chose.

Segregation dampened Gaines's chances of attending any major universities. He met virtually every major school's academic requirements, but the racial climate of the time prevented him from going to more prominent academic and athletic institutions, especially in the South. Instead, Gaines took the advice of a family physician to attend Morgan State University. Known for its strong football program, the all-black Baltimore school offered Gaines many opportunities.

Led by coaching great Eddie Hurt, Morgan State was attractive in many respects. Gaines's studies never faltered, and he graduated in 1945 with a degree in chemistry and plans to attend dental school. Athletically, Gaines expanded his interests to track and field. Yet he continued to excel at basketball and football, where he was an All-American lineman.

After graduation Gaines put his plans for dental

school on hold and became an assistant coach to Brutus Wilson at Winston-Salem State Teachers College (later Winston-Salem State University). For Gaines, this move changed his plans altogether. A year later, in 1946, Wilson left the school for Shaw University in Raleigh and Gaines succeeded him. Almost a one-man athletic department, Gaines became the school's athletic director, head football coach, head basketball coach, trainer, and ticket manager, in addition to his duties as a teacher of physical education. From 1946 to 1949, Gaines coached the football squad. His 1948 team posted an 8–1 record, thereby earning Gaines the Central Intercollegiate Athletic Association (CIAA) Coach of the Year award. Beginning in 1949, Gaines put all his energies toward basketball and the duties of athletic director. In the process, he met Clara Berry, a teacher in the Forsyth County school system. They married in 1950 and had two children, Lisa and Clarence Jr. Amidst these changes, Gaines completed his master's degree in education from Columbia University.

Gaines quickly showed that he could lead the Rams' basketball program to respectability. In 1947, his first basketball team went 15–7, followed by a 17–10 campaign in 1948. During his first six years on the job, Gaines led his team to an 80–55 overall record (.615 winning percentage). Until 1953, though, the teams had never won a CIAA title. Gaines called his first CIAA title in 1953 his "biggest thrill" on the basketball court. "Because of primacy, remembering the first things foremost, I might say our CIAA title in 1953 was my biggest thrill. We were a teachers college, 85 percent female, and we weren't known for athletics." His 1953 team compiled a 23–5 record, the first of eighteen twenty-win seasons that added up to an astounding 116–32 record from 1953 to 1957. After three somewhat subpar years (a 49–31 record) by Gaines's 1950s and 1960s standards, Winston-Salem State's basketball program went on a dominating seven-year run. From 1961 to 1967, the Rams won 172 games and only lost 35 (an .831 winning percentage). In that span, Gaines won CIAA Tournament Outstanding Coach awards in 1961, 1963, and 1966. He won the overall CIAA Coach of the Year honor twice during that stretch, in 1961 and 1963. Ironically, Gaines did not win either award in 1967, the year he fielded his greatest team ever.

The year 1967 was magical for Gaines, his team, and the entire Winston-Salem State campus. Three years earlier, Gaines signed the school's most heralded athlete, Earl "The Pearl" Monroe, Philadelphia basketball star. Gaines somehow managed to lure the future National Basketball Association (NBA) All-Star to Winston-Salem. When asked how he accomplished this recruiting feat, Gaines replied jokingly, "Because of grits, gravy, and me." In reality, Gaines set Monroe straight early on in his career. After his freshmen year, Monroe went to Gaines and expressed dissatisfaction with his lack of playing time and said he was considering leaving.

Gaines asked Monroe why he came to Winston-Salem State. Monroe answered, "to play ball." Gaines disliked the response and told the young player that if he came to the college to just play ball, then "We've got a problem. Let's call your mother." After Gaines talked with Monroe's mother, Rose, Monroe returned for his sophomore year. Monroe later said that "Coach Gaines prepared me to handle what I would encounter in the NBA. He set the basis for how I would proceed in life."

Going into the 1967 CIAA basketball tournament, Winston-Salem State was undefeated. The team's 25–0 record made the Rams the favorites to overcome all CIAA competition en route to the National Collegiate Athletic Association (NCAA) Division II tournament. Monroe led the team and the country in scoring that year, averaging over forty points per game. He was also named to the Associated Press Little All-America team (which included NBA great Walt Frazier from Southern Illinois and future Chicago Bulls and Los Angeles Lakers coach Phil Jackson of North Dakota).

In the CIAA semifinals, though, the N.C. A & T State University Aggies did the seemingly impossible: they kept Monroe in check and pounded the Rams by over twenty points. N.C. A & T defeated Winston-Salem State 105–82, ending the Rams' twenty-five-game winning streak. Monroe had a lackluster performance. "The Pearl" scored only twenty points, well under his season average. N.C. A & T ended up winning the CIAA tournament title over Howard University, while Winston-Salem captured third place by beating Johnson C. Smith in the consolation game. The season was not over, however. The Rams made the NCAA Division II tournament and had a perfect chance to redeem themselves. Gaines, Monroe, and the squad did exactly that. Despite not being honored by the CIAA in 1967, Gaines became the first African American to win the Division II Coach of the Year award when he was honored that year. For Gaines, no single season could ever match 1967.

After the national championship and Monroe's graduation, Gaines suffered his first losing season in 1968. Nonetheless, Gaines and the Winston-Salem State basketball program rebounded quickly. The Rams were 20–8 in 1970, which led to another streak of eleven consecutive winning seasons. During the 1980s, Gaines still managed to put winning teams on the floor, but they were not the national contenders that they were during the 1960s and 1970s. Gaines won his last CIAA Tournament Outstanding Coach award in 1977 and his last CIAA Coach of the Year honor in 1980.

In 1982, Gaines received one of the greatest honors bestowed upon those involved in professional and amateur basketball when he was inducted into the Naismith Basketball Hall of Fame. In addition to this honor, Gaines had been inducted into the CIAA Hall of Fame in 1975, the North Carolina Sports Hall of Fame in 1978, and earned the Paul Robeson Award in 1980. Gaines's success on the court had slipped somewhat, but the 1980s were a decade of recognition for his years of hard work at Winston-Salem State.

During forty-seven years of coaching, Gaines had only six losing seasons. On February 18, 1993, Gaines announced his retirement from coaching. He told reporters at a news conference that "my pressure to resign came at 11 o'clock at night and at 6:30 in the morning from my wife, Clara. In coaching, the wife sometimes catches more flak than the coach. When somebody in the stands says, 'Old man, get on,' I might just tell them, 'Go jump in the lake,' but that kind of thing hurts my wife and family."

Gaines began duties as professor emeritus on January 1, 1994, and also assumed fund-raising responsibilities for the school. At the press conference, Gaines said that he would not miss coaching. "It's time to give someone younger a chance. If I had three seven-footers I might feel different, but there's no joy in losing."

Winston-Salem State Chancellor Cleon Thompson said, "Today marks the end of an era. Bighouse Gaines has been Winston-Salem State athletics. I know I speak for the entire university family. We have been privileged to have known and worked with such a great influence—athletically and academically. He had the two-dimensional approach."

In all, Gaines amassed a 828–440 career record. He won eleven CIAA titles, the first coming in 1953 and the last in 1977. He became a member of the Basket-ball Hall of Fame. He was president of the National Association of Basketball Coaches, founder of the Winston-Salem State University National Youth Sports Program, administrator for the Naismith Basketball Hall of Fame Board of Trustees, and an active participant in various other civic organizations.

Earl Monroe was Gaines's greatest player, but Gaines also helped Cleo Hill become the first player from a historically black college to be drafted first by the NBA. In 1961, the St. Louis Hawks took Hill, the former Winston-Salem State star, with their first pick. Hill and Monroe were just two of the many players that Gaines helped shape.

Gaines said his greatest achievements came in molding his athletes into productive men. "My greatest thrill is not the wins and losses I've had. If you've got the horses, you're supposed to win. I've turned out some good citizens—an associate mayor here in town. I'll never be hungry, broke or have to worry about a place to sleep. The kids liked me, and I loved them," he said.

While legendary Carolina coach Dean Smith called Gaines "the type of person this profession needs," the casual fan probably knew little, if anything, about him. His work transcended basketball, though, and had redeeming value for fans and non-fans of college basketball. Above all the wins, trophies, and coaching honors, Gaines was an educator who always pushed his students and players to reach their fullest potential.

Charles A. Westmoreland Jr. is a University of Tennessee doctoral candidate in history with emphasis on the post-Reconstruction South. A native of Southside Virginia, he received a degree in history from Ferrum College and his M.A. in history from the University of North Carolina at Charlotte, where his thesis was entitled "Strong Legs Running: The Integration of the North Carolina-South Carolina Shrine Bowl."

For more information, see:
Gaines. Clarence E. Papers. C. G. O'Kelly Library, Winston-Salem State University.

MICHAEL J. JORDAN

By Donald W. Patterson

As they used to say on the playgrounds, Michael Jordan had game. So much game, in fact, that he could play basketball better than anyone who ever laced up a pair of Nikes. And he had the pictures to prove it.

One, taken on March 29, 1982, at the end of his freshman year at the University of North Carolina, showed him hitting the basket that gave the Tar Heels a 63–62 NCAA (National Collegiate Athletic Association) championship win over Georgetown.

The other, taken on June 14, 1998, captured Jordan's last shot—the basket that gave the Chicago Bulls, his NBA (National Basketball Association) team, its third straight title and the sixth of Jordan's career.

Between those two photos, between those two shots, between those two championships, Jordan became the most-recognized, most-accomplished, most-popular athlete of the last century. Want proof? In 1999, ESPN, the cable sports network, selected Jordan as the athlete of the century, ahead of the likes of Babe Ruth and Muhammad Ali. Jordan, not Ali or Ruth or Thorpe, had become the greatest.

And we saw and heard and read it all.

For more than fifteen years, Jordan dominated the headlines and the airwaves unlike any athlete in history. His exploits became required viewing on countless sports highlight shows. His name appeared in an average of one hundred newspaper and magazine stories a day. He became the subject of more than seventy-five books. Right before our eyes, "a goony looking . . . snotty-nosed kid from Wilmington"—that's his own description—had become a hero of almost mythic proportions. A basketball player for the ages. A role model for the world.

How famous was Jordan? Well, a woman in Gary, Ind., once stretched out in front of his car, hoping to be run over by it. A midget signed up for his basketball camp. And a kid in Yugoslavia sent him a card addressed Michael Jordan, USA, and he got it. Now that's famous. "There is a once-in-a-lifetime thing going on here," Bob Greene, a columnist for the *Chicago Tribune,* once said of Jordan's popularity. "He has to be a combination of Babe Ruth, Santa Claus and Elvis."

Jordan's father realized his son's special gifts early on. James Jordan once said that on February 17, 1963, God wanted to do something special, so he created

Michael J. Jordan (Courtesy of Hugh Morton)

Michael. "Until someone comes up with something better," James Jordan said, "I'd just as soon believe that."

In 1962, James and Deloris Jordan had left their home in Wallace, in eastern North Carolina, and moved to Brooklyn, N.Y. Michael Jeffrey, the third of the Jordans' five children, was born there, not in North Carolina, as most Tar Heels think. When Mike was five, his parents returned to North Carolina, settling in Wilmington. They moved into a middle-class neighborhood on Gordon Road north of town, not far from what later became Interstate 40.

Jordan's was a loving, hardworking, churchgoing family. "This kid came from a stable home, unlike so many black athletes," said Kenneth E. McLaurin, the former principal at Laney High School, Jordan's alma mater. "His support system was well entrenched."

Like his older brothers, Jordan took an early interest in sports. Friends remember that at about age five, Michael would hoist a basketball behind his head and heave it two-handed toward the basket. But basketball wasn't his first love. It was baseball. By age twelve, he starred on Little League teams, playing first base, shortstop, and the outfield. He also pitched, hurling several no-hitters.

Whatever the sport, Jordan liked to compete against older players. When it came to basketball, his main source of competition was his brother, Larry, a year older and much more accomplished. Their backyard games often ended in fights. "Every competitor needs a driving force," Jordan said. "He was [mine] ever since I was a kid. I couldn't beat him, but I kept trying until I was able to, and then I looked to something else. And that is when I got cut. That was my next point to prove."

The making of the Michael Jordan legend dates to his sophomore year at Laney High, when he failed to make the varsity team. Instead of playing with the big boys, Jordan got relegated to the junior varsity, where he became a star, averaging more than twenty points a game.

It was about this time that two important changes occurred in Jordan's life. First, he began to grow, much to the surprise of his parents, neither more than 5-feet-10. In the ninth grade, Jordan measured only 5-feet-9, but by the eleventh grade he'd grown to about 6-feet-4. "Mom," Jordan would ask, teasingly. "How tall was the milkman?"

Second, Jordan began to focus on basketball. Friends noticed that during baseball practice, Jordan would take his place in the outfield and then disappear. "We'd find him in the gym shooting baskets," said David Bridgers, a friend from Wilmington. "From his junior year on, basketball was his love." From that point on, said Larry Jordan, "he's been at the right place at the right time." Jordan subsequently became a high school all-star and enrolled at the University of North Carolina at Chapel Hill, one of the most respected and highly publicized basketball programs in the country. Playing for the legendary Dean Smith, he started his first game as a freshman.

The legend continued to grow when Jordan hit the game-winning basket against Georgetown in the 1982 NCAA Finals. Still growing, he became an All-American in his sophomore year, averaging twenty points a game. After winning the national player of the year honor as a junior, Jordan turned pro at Smith's urging. But he eventually returned to Carolina to get his undergraduate degree, majoring in geography.

In 1984, he starred on the gold-medal-winning U.S. Olympic team, further enhancing an already squeaky-clean image. Later that year, the Chicago Bulls, one of the NBA's worst teams, made him the third pick in the league draft. But being drafted by the Bulls gave Jordan the opportunity to play in one of the best sports towns in America and one of its leading media centers. He also signed with a then-struggling shoe company called Nike, which in turn created a stir with its Air Jordan basketball shoes.

Jordan created a stir wherever he went, especially on the court. In 1985, Jordan won Rookie of the Year honors, averaging 28.2 points, 6.5 rebounds, 5.9 assists, and 2.4 steals a game.

His was a charmed life. As he once told NBC's Maria Shriver, "Even my mistakes have been perfect." Even physical setbacks worked to enhance his image. Three games into his second season, he broke his foot. The injury pitted Jordan against the Bulls' management in a highly publicized dispute. Late in the season, Jordan felt he had recovered and wanted to play. But the Bulls wanted him to sit out the rest of the season. Although not publicly stated, their reasoning seemed obvious.

If Jordan didn't play, the Bulls probably wouldn't make the playoffs, thereby assuring them the opportunity to draft one of the nation's best college players. But Bulls' officials relented, and America saw that Jordan played because he loved the game. And did he ever play. In a playoff game against the Boston Celtics that year, he scored sixty-three points, a performance that caused Celtic star Larry Bird to say: "He was God disguised as Michael Jordan."

Jordan had become a superstar. But it wasn't until 1991, after seven years of struggle and disappointment, that he finally led the Bulls to an NBA championship. By that time he had put his stamp on the game. Kids and grown-ups wanted to "be like Mike," the commercial catch phrase made popular by Gatorade, one of more than fifteen products or companies that Jordan endorsed at the time.

Youngsters started wearing number 23 on their jerseys, like Jordan did. Players began sporting baggy shorts, like Jordan did. Men began to shave their heads, like Jordan did. Jordan did it to hide the fact that he was going bald. Everybody else did it to be cool.

Mr. Jordan had evolved into Mr. Right. "If you were going to invent the prototype for the athlete for the nineties," said David Falk, Jordan's agent, "you would create an athlete who is articulate, clean-cut but not too square, with just enough spice to be fun, who is in touch with the community, who cuts across demographic boundaries, who has diverse skills, who is genuine and overall is fun to watch play. When you got finished, you'd have Michael."

One thing set Jordan apart from the rest. He had "the total package." That's how Adolph Shiver described his friend's rare combination of gifts. Off the court, he possessed good looks, charm, and style, the traits any advertiser would want in a pitchman. His handsome face and shaved head were on ads for everything from hot dogs to batteries to Jordan's own brand of cologne.

On the court, he displayed speed, jumping ability, and grace. At 6-foot-6 and 198 pounds, Michael Jordan represented one mean basketball machine.

From his size-13 feet to his 34-inch waist to his balding head, his body looked as sleek as a missile and as hard as a backboard. He had the spindly yet muscular legs of a long-distance runner, the huge hands of a seven-footer, the broad and powerful shoulders of a football player. "He was blessed by God," said John Bach, a former Bulls' assistant coach.

His repertoire of shots was longer than the waiting list for season tickets to Bulls' games. The spins, the reverses, the fall-aways, the double-pumps, the leaping leaners, the glides. Then there were the dunks: the cradle jam, the rock-a-baby, the tomahawk, and the leaner. That was the one where Jordan turned his body sideways and seemed to look down in the basket. He executed them all with his tongue hanging out, a habit he picked up from his father.

But Jordan's success on the court went beyond his athletic ability. He had a will to win and competitive desire that always led the league. Witness his performance in game five of the 1997 NBA finals against the Utah Jazz. Playing on the road and suffering from a flu that had him vomiting until just before tip-off, Jordan scored thirty-eight points. His three-pointer with twenty-five seconds left led the Bulls to a 90–88 victory and a 3–2 lead in the series.

During one time-out late in the game, Jordan had to be helped off the court. Several times he looked as if he might faint. In addition to all his points, he also had seven rebounds, five assists, three steals, and a block. "We wanted it real bad," Jordan said after the game.

No matter what the challenge, Jordan felt he could deliver. And usually he did. "He's thrown in more tremendous, ungodly shots than anybody," Tim Hallam, the Bulls' director of media services, once said of Jordan. "He comes up with the big shot when he needs it."

But not all of Jordan's heroics occurred on the court. Jordan took a great interest in kids, especially sick ones. Bob Greene, the Chicago columnist, recounted a chilly winter night when Jordan was leaving Chicago Stadium. As he walked toward his car,

Jordan spotted a youngster in a wheelchair at the edge of the waiting crowd. When Jordan walked over and spoke, the child struggled to get out of the chair. While Jordan calmed the youngster, the father asked if he could take a photo. Sure, Jordan said. But the camera wouldn't work. Take your time, Jordan said. Once the picture had been snapped, Jordan went on his way. The child's eyes glistened with tears.

"You can't be taught that," Greene said. "That made that kid's life."

But not all of Jordan's actions had such happy endings. In fact, some of Jordan's actions left parents wondering if they wanted their children to "be like Mike" after all. Jordan's first child was born out of wedlock, he owed gambling debts to a convicted drug dealer named Slim Bouler, and a former golfing buddy named Richard Esquinas accused him of being a gambling addict. Esquinas said Jordan lost $1.2 million on a golfing binge in September of 1991. Jordan denied he had a gambling problem.

Not everyone liked how Jordan lived his life. Some criticized him for endorsing the Illinois State Lottery; some rebuked him because teens killed other teens for their Air Jordan shoes; some didn't approve because his shoes cost more than $125; and some took him to task for not endorsing Harvey Gantt, the former mayor of Charlotte and a black man, in his two bids to unseat North Carolina's Republican Senator Jesse Helms. (One magazine reported that Jordan told a friend he didn't get involved in the race because "Republicans buy shoes, too.")

In 1991, former baseball star Hank Aaron and ex-football great Jim Brown, among others, charged that Jordan had sold out to corporate white America, adding that he had failed to speak out on issues concerning blacks and that he wasn't doing enough for black children.

Stung by the criticism, Jordan shot back. "Though I am a black individual, most people try to see me as a person," he said. "You can't expect me to be a role model and then tell me I can only be a role model for blacks. That's not fair. And that's racist in itself."

Jordan pointed out that he did much of his charitable work through the Michael Jordan Foundation, started in 1989 by the player and his mother. Among other charities, the foundation aided the United Negro College Fund, the Special Olympics, and the Make-a-Wish Foundation.

Jordan let it be known that the basketball court provided an escape for his problems. On the hardwood, he continued to find success. Jordan and the Bulls won two more championships a "three-peat," as everyone called it in 1992 and 1993.

Then tragedy struck. In August 1993, Jordan's father, James, was shot to death while he was parked by a busy highway in Lumberton. His body was dumped in a creek in South Carolina. When columnists speculated that the senior Jordan's death might be related to his son's gambling problems, Jordan rebuked them. "I was outraged . . . ," he said. "These unsubstantiated reports reflect a complete lack of sensitivity to basic human decency."

Then, less than two months later, Jordan did the unthinkable: he retired. He made it clear that his decision wasn't directly related to his father's murder in what turned out to be a carjacking. Rather, he said, he had lost the desire he needed to perform up to his own standards. He wanted to quit while he was on top. At the age of thirty, he left the game behind.

But he also left the door open to a possible comeback. Then in February 1994, Jordan did the unexpected again. He announced a return to his first love: baseball. That year, he batted .202 for the Birmingham Barons, the Class AA affiliate of the Chicago White Sox.

In March of 1995, Jordan retired again. This time he gave up baseball for basketball. "I'm back," he said by way of announcement. Jordan rejoined the Bulls in March, deep in the season, and played in seventeen games. Looking at times rusty and out of shape, Jordan couldn't regain the magic of past seasons. He and the Bulls got ousted in the second round of the playoffs by the Orlando Magic.

Jordan blamed himself and vowed it would never happen again. And it didn't. At the age of thirty-two, Jordan retooled his game. After his seventeen-month retirement, he depended less on drives to the basket and more on fall-away jumpers, arguably the most difficult shot in the game. In the process, he led the Bulls to another three-peat championships in 1996, 1997, and 1998. And then he retired again.

"Mentally, I'm exhausted," he told reporters on January 13, 1999. "I don't feel I have a challenge. . . . This is the perfect time for me to walk away from the game." He took with him an impressive résumé: six NBA championships, six finals Most Valuable Player awards, five regular-season MVP awards, ten scoring titles, nine defensive first-team selections, eleven All-Star game appearances, a Rookie of the Year Award, 29,277 points (third highest in league history, a 31.5 regular-season scoring average (the highest ever), a 33.4 post-season scoring average (the highest ever), and too many other achievements to count.

Jordan made major headlines again in January of 2000 when he joined the lowly Washington Wizards as part-owner and president of basketball operations. But everyone knew that no matter how successful the Wizards became under his leadership, Jordan would never excel in the front office the way he did on the court. Administrators don't have game. Players do. And no one ever had it like Jordan.

"The best ever," *Newsweek* magazine called him. "Period."

Jordan again reentered the professional basketball ranks in the fall of 2001 as a player and part-owner for the Wizards.

Donald W. Patterson is a feature writer for the News and Record *in Greensboro and has written numerous stories about Michael Jordan: the person, the player, and the public idol.*

For more information, see:

Greene, Bob. *Hang Time: Days and Dreams with Michael Jordan.* Doubleday, 1992.

———. *Rebound: The Odyssey of Michael Jordan.* Viking, 1995.

Halberstam, David. *Playing For Keeps: Michael Jordan and the World He Made.* Random House, 1999.

Naughton, Jim. *Taking to the Air: The Rise of Michael Jordan.* Warner Books, 1992.

Smith, Sam. *The Jordan Rules: The Inside Story of a Turbulent Season with Michael Jordan and the Chicago Bulls.* Simon and Schuster, 1994.

———. *Second Coming: The Strange Odyssey of Michael Jordan from Courtside to Home Plate and Back Again.* Harper Collins, 1995.

CHARLES "CHOO CHOO" JUSTICE

By Jerry Shinn

EVERY COLLEGE FOOTBALL STAR is a legend in his time. Charlie "Choo Choo" Justice became a legend for all time.

New seasons bring new heroes who rewrite the record books, obscuring the memories and once-famous names like layers of paint. Since the 1949 season, when Charlie Justice last played for the University of North Carolina at Chapel Hill, the average college football player has grown progressively larger, stronger, faster, and quicker, and has been better trained and better coached from an earlier age. As a result, records for running, passing, and kicking, for yards gained and points scored, rarely stand more than a few years. But more than fifty years after what UNC fans knew forever as the Justice Era, ten of the many school records Justice established remained unbroken.

As of 2000, no one UNC player had accounted for as many touchdowns running and passing in a career. No one had exceeded his record for most touchdowns running and passing in a season, although quarterback Chris Keldorf tied it in 1996. No one had compiled as high a rushing average for a season as the 7.2 yards per carry Justice posted in 1946, his freshman year. His record of scoring a touchdown in nine consecutive games remained untouched. His punt return and kickoff return records for average yardage, most yardage, and most touchdowns were still unmatched.

As college football offenses became more proficient and more productive over the years, Justice's UNC career total offense record of 4,883 yards was unequaled for forty-five years. Quarterback Jason Stanicek finally surpassed it in 1994 with 5,497 yards.

The statistics are sufficient to sustain the legend, but they are only part of the explanation for the Justice phenomenon. Timing was a major factor. World War II was over when he arrived on campus. An era of relative peace and unprecedented prosperity was on the horizon, and Americans were ready to celebrate a return to such peacetime pursuits as college football. The military victory had confirmed for many Americans the inherent virtue of their country and their way of life. It was a time of innocence and optimism.

Charlie Justice was the ideal hero for such a moment. About five-feet ten-inches, and weighing 165

Charles "Choo Choo" Justice (Courtesy of Hugh Morton)

pounds, he was hardly a physical superman. But he was square-jawed and photogenic, with a boyish grin that dimpled his cheeks. And he was unfailingly polite and modest, seizing every opportunity to give the credit for his spectacular play to his teammates, particularly his blockers. He was a gentleman on the field as well. He was visibly enthusiastic, always cheering on his teammates, but it would have been unimaginable for Justice to trash-talk or taunt an opponent or perform any sort of celebratory dance in the end zone after one of his many touchdowns.

Good looks and good manners wouldn't have mattered, of course, if there had not been the extraordinary talent—or, more accurately, talents. He was first of all a fine natural athlete who could have been a good college baseball player or excelled at some other sport if he had not chosen football. He was the best punter of his time and one of the best ever. He was a better-than-average passer and a reliable pass receiver. He was an excellent blocker and could hold his own as a defensive back.

But what made him perhaps the best college back

in the nation during the four years he played—only Doak Walker of Southern Methodist University could challenge him for that distinction—was his ability to avoid being tackled. It wasn't a matter of speed or power. He wasn't exceptionally fast, and a lot of ball carriers, including teammate fullback Hosea Rodgers, were better at running over people. But Justice could stop in a step and start again at full speed, changing directions without slowing down. He seemed to possess a special kind of vision and instinct that allowed him to find and maneuver through openings in a field crowded with larger men determined to bring him down. Time and again he left them grabbing air.

Part of the legend is that he honed his skills scampering through the crowded halls of his high school and running along the sidewalks of downtown Asheville, dodging and weaving his way through the shoppers.

Given his combination of talents, Justice was fortunate to play for a coach, Carl Snavely, who still believed in the single-wing offense. Justice was one of the last of the "triple-threat" backs—runner, passer, punter. By the early 1950s almost every team had abandoned the single-wing for the more versatile and deceptive T-formation or one of its variations, in which the quarterback was the primary passer and a halfback or tailback was the primary ball-carrier. As a single-wing tailback, Justice was both primary passer and primary ball-carrier, which is one reason his total offense statistics were so impressive.

From that position he also could quick-kick—something that a few years later had disappeared from the playbooks, but which was once a popular strategy for surprising the other team, sacrificing possession in return for an advantage in field position. For instance, a Justice quick-kick against Duke in 1948 traveled sixty-eight yards and rolled dead at the one-yard line, putting the Blue Devils in a deep hole and helping the Tar Heels gain a 21–20 victory.

So the time was right, and Justice had the looks, personality, and talents. He was not only a coach's dream, he was the son every parent would love to have. And if all that weren't enough, there was his nickname. No one ever had one more irresistible to the media or more easily etched into the fans' imagination.

According to legend, Justice acquired the nickname when he was part of a navy team at Bainbridge, Md., in 1943 when he was just nineteen years old. "That Justice kid runs just like a choo-choo train," an onlooker remarked. A sportswriter overheard the remark and used the nickname in his story. It quickly spread, along with reports of Justice's dazzling runs

and booming punts. But the Justice legend began even before his years in the navy. His achievements as a high school player also were extraordinary.

He was born in Asheville on May 18, 1924, one of seven children of Nell Foster and Parley Wittington Justice, who worked for the railroad. At Lee Edwards High School in Asheville, Justice was the star of a team that was itself legendary, unbeaten in regular season play in 1941 and 1942. In 1941, his junior year, Justice scored nineteen touchdowns. The following year it was twenty-seven. Against Hickory that year, he scored on runs of 21, 85, 22, and 92 yards as Asheville won, 94–0.

At the end of his senior season he was invited to Charlotte to play in the Shrine Bowl, an annual charity game that matched high school senior all-stars from North Carolina against those from South Carolina. North Carolina won that year, 33–0, with Justice scoring three touchdowns to tie the Shrine Bowl scoring record set four years earlier by his brother Bill.

After such a spectacular high school career and three outstanding years with naval base teams, which helped spread his reputation, Justice was perhaps the most highly recruited football player of his time—recruited not only by college teams but by several professional ones. Of course, one of the schools recruiting him was the University of North Carolina. But Justice returned from a visit to Chapel Hill with the impression that the stern-faced, taciturn Coach Snavely wasn't very interested in him. He was leaning toward going to the University of South Carolina until his older brother, Jack, insisted that because he was a North Carolinian he should go to UNC.

So North Carolina it was. It may have helped that the university arranged to let his wife, Sarah, his high school sweetheart he had married while in the navy, attend on scholarship while the GI Bill paid Charlie's way. Apparently such an arrangement was within the rules at the time. For the next four years "Choo-Choo" and an outstanding cast led the Tar Heels into the upper echelons of intercollegiate football. They ranked consistently in the top ten in the nation and for a while were number one during the 1948 season.

In the first year they won eight games, lost one, and tied one during the regular season and became the first team in the school's history to go to a bowl game, although they lost 20–10 to Georgia in the Sugar Bowl at New Orleans. The next season they again won eight games and lost two. After winning nine with one tie in 1948, again they went to the Sugar Bowl, losing this time to Oklahoma, 14–6.

In his senior season Justice was hampered by injuries and the Tar Heels slipped to seven wins and four losses, including a 27–13 defeat by Rice University in the Cotton Bowl at Dallas. That was also the season of Justice's two greatest personal disappointments. He was too ill to play in the national spotlight when the Heels lost to Notre Dame, 42–6, in Yankee Stadium, and he was runner-up in the voting for the Heisman Trophy for a second consecutive year. Notre Dame's Leon Hart edged him out in 1949 and SMU's Doak Walker won it in 1948.

But there was plenty of compensation. He was featured on the cover of *Life* magazine and in the pages of numerous other publications. The bands of the great clarinetist Benny Goodman and Johnny Long, who was a Duke graduate, recorded "All the Way Choo-Choo," a bouncy paean to Justice written by Orville Campbell of Chapel Hill, who helped launch actor Andy Griffith's career a few years earlier. More important, he was named All-American and Southern Conference Player of the Year in 1948 and 1949, and in 1948 he won the Walker Camp Memorial Trophy and was named national Player of the Year by the Washington Touchdown Club. Later he would be inducted into the College Football Hall of Fame.

And he was named Most Valuable Player in the 1950 College All-Star game in Chicago, where he and quarterback Eddie LeBaron of the College of the Pacific led the collegians to a 17–7 victory over the Philadelphia Eagles, defending champions of professional football.

At first Justice resisted offers from professional teams, fearing he was too small. Washington Redskins owner George Preston Marshall kept the pressure on. His team was the closest thing to a southern franchise in the pros and Marshall knew Justice would draw fans from the South, especially Virginia and the Carolinas. Instead of joining the pro ranks, Justice took a job with UNC's Medical Foundation in Chapel Hill, but quickly decided he wasn't cut out for that kind of work.

Snavely offered him a position as assistant coach beginning in January 1951, but with nothing to do until then, Justice decided to give pro football a try at $1,000 per game. He joined the Redskins in midseason and was the team's leading rusher in the remaining five games.

After the season he returned to Chapel Hill to join Snavely's staff, still not sure he had a future in pro football. But Marshall's offer of $12,000 for the coming season and $10,000 for each of the next two was too tempting. By late summer of 1952 he was back in a Redskins uniform.

In the opening game on the night of August 21, 1952, against the Los Angeles Rams, before a Coliseum crowd of 87,582, Justice broke away for runs of 49, 53, and 63 yards, gaining a total of 199 yards on 11 carries. It was one of the most spectacular performances in pro football history. But in the final quarter he broke his wrist, which put him out of action for much of the rest of the season. Despite Marshall's protestations, Justice decided to retire. He went home to Asheville and eventually settled in the insurance business.

There is one more piece to the Justice legend, and it has to do with a rare kind of integrity. Another distinguished North Carolinian, Hugh Morton, watched Justice through a camera lens from the sidelines and up close as a friend, for more than half a century. He once pointed out that even in Justice's time a superstar had plenty of opportunities to sell his name and fame for big money, but that Justice wouldn't do it. Being Charlie "Choo Choo" Justice wasn't exactly a handicap in selling insurance, but other than that, Morton said, Justice refused to cash in on his reputation—as if to sell it would be to tarnish it, and all that it meant to his school and his fans.

Instead, he chose a modest, small-town North Carolina kind of life, graciously consenting to interviews and accepting the greetings of admirers during football weekends in Chapel Hill. Over the years he lent his name and presence to worthy causes. And he never did anything that would reflect badly on his university, or set a bad example for youngsters, or disappoint his fans.

By mid-2000, Justice had retired to the small town of Cherryville with his wife Sarah, his activities limited by failing health.

Jerry Shinn graduated with honors and Phi Beta Kappa from the University of North Carolina at Chapel Hill in 1959. He worked in advertising, public relations, and broadcasting, but most of his career was at the Charlotte Observer, *where he began as a sports writer and later was a political reporter, editorial page editor, columnist, and associate editor, retiring in 1998.*

For more information, see:

Morton, Hugh M., and Edward L. Rankin Jr. *Making a Difference in North Carolina.* Lightworks, 1988.

Quincy, Bob, and Julian Scheer. "Choo-Choo: The Charlie Justice Story." 2000 Football Media Guide, University of North Carolina at Chapel Hill.

"Tar Heel Legends." *Daily Tar Heel,* November 29, 1999.

HORACE A. "BONES" MCKINNEY

By Wilt Browning

Horace A. "Bones" McKinney, left, with N.C. State University coach Jim Valvano (Courtesy of Hugh Morton)

THE SPORTS WORLD is eternally looking for the next legend. The next Mantle. The next Jordan. The next Palmer. The next Petty. Yet, no one has ever been called the next Bones McKinney, nor ever will be, and for good reason. Horace Albert "Bones" McKinney was one of a kind. An honest-to-goodness original. A basketball disciple unlike any other.

What can be said is that McKinney spent a lifetime loving his game as a player, coach, and television analyst and if one knew nothing more about the lanky North Carolinian, McKinney's abilities in each of those areas set him apart. As a player, McKinney was a star at Durham High School on perhaps the greatest prep team in the state's history. He was an all-Southern Conference player at North Carolina State College (later North Carolina State University) and finished his collegiate career with one postwar season at North Carolina as a key member of a Final Four team. He twice was a member of the all-NBA (National Bas-

ketball Association) team as a star for the Washington Caps and the Boston Celtics.

By most standards, his collegiate coaching career was modest in terms of longevity. Seventeen coaches in Atlantic Coast Conference (ACC) history recorded more victories than McKinney, some of them exceeding his 122 triumphs (he lost but 94) several times over. He coached at Wake Forest for only eight seasons, but won two ACC championships, took the Deacons to the Final Four for the first time, and twice was named coach of the year in the league. McKinney burned out with an 8–2 record against college basketball's winningest coach in the twentieth century, Dean Smith, which alone would set him apart.

As a player, McKinney saw two of his jerseys retired, the number 5 he wore during World War II at Fort Bragg, and the number 17 he wore with the Celtics, though that one was in honor of John Havlicek and not McKinney.

What is better remembered than any of the standard biographical information are the red socks and flashy bow ties he wore when he coached the Wake Forest basketball team, his running dialogue with basketball referees, his unpredictability, and most of all his humor.

McKinney's sense of humor set him apart in the eyes of the public. He said that it was no accident that he was born with the initials HAM in the down-east hamlet of Lowland, where Goose Creek empties into Pamlico Sound. In his formative years, McKinney discovered that his was a poor family. "I didn't know how poor we were until I went over to a friend's house and opened the refrigerator door—and the damn light came on," he once said. "But we did have running water. We'd run out into the yard and get the water and run back in."

He grew up less than two blocks from the Duke campus, played at both State and Carolina, coached at Wake Forest, and was a favorite throughout the ACC. *Sport* magazine once featured McKinney, calling him the "Magnificent Screwball."

Even his nickname, Bones, came with an unexpected twist. Though it perfectly fit an Ichabod Crane man who at 6-feet-6 frequently towered over fellow coaches and even many of his own players, McKinney was stuck with the moniker when he was cast as "Beau Brummel Bones" in a high school version of *A Midsummer Night's Dream*. McKinney never acted again, and he never lost the nickname.

An ordained Baptist minister, McKinney nevertheless confessed to a handful of vices. "I plead guilty to driving through life at about 80 miles an hour, drinking 60,000 Pepsi-Colas, smoking some 2 million cigarettes and threatening the lives of several hundred referees." He also said he worried about losing his job at Wake Forest. "I had a lifetime contract at Wake Forest," he said of his agreement with President Harold Tribble. "Then Dr. Tribble called me one day, pronounced me dead and fired me."

Like so many things in McKinney's life, that was an exaggeration. Truth is, McKinney wound up as the Wake Forest University coach, and eventually the coach of the American Basketball Association (ABA) Carolina Cougars, almost by accident. He accepted a job as an assistant to Wake coach Murray Greason to help ease the financial strain of attending seminary in preparation for what he thought was a career in the pulpit. Indeed, in his final year before ordination, McKinney accepted an invitation to fill in for an ailing pastor at a small church. After a year, the thirty faithful members had grown to about 250 and more than thirty awaited baptism.

"Now, that's preaching," McKinney bragged. "I should have rented a bus and taken all thirty of those folks to Lowland and baptized them in Goose Creek. If you ain't been put under in Goose Creek, you ain't been thoroughly baptized."

McKinney's aversion to referees and his fear of flying were almost as well known as his preaching. And the two came together when he and golf pro Mack Briggs boarded a plane during McKinney's stint at Wake Forest. "If anything happens to us now," McKinney said solemnly as the plane taxied for takeoff, "me and you are going to different places. When you get to where you're going, tell any referees you see what I think of 'em."

It was McKinney's relationship with referees, it was said, that drove him to his one-of-a-kind conduct along the sidelines, where it was not unusual for him to toss his sports jacket and occasionally his shoes into the crowd in his animated work with his players along the sidelines. One of his shoes wound up on the playing floor near the top of the circle during one game and when McKinney, hoping to retrieve the shoe while the action was at the other end of the floor, reached for the large footwear, a fountain pen fell from his pocket. With both shoe and pen in his hands once again, McKinney looked up to see the teams coming at him on a fast break.

"I just tried to play good defense," he deadpanned.

It wasn't the only time the coach became directly involved in the action. Retrieving a ball that once rolled into the Wake Forest bench area, McKinney absentmindedly threw it back to his star shooting guard, Billy Packer. Packer took the coach's pass, dribbled to the top of the circle, and hit a jump shot. Game referees never knew about the assist.

So active was McKinney on the Wake Forest bench that ACC Commissioner Jim Weaver once sent him a stern letter warning McKinney that further outbursts against referees would be dealt with in the most serious manner. McKinney announced that he would respond to the Weaver warning by wearing a seat belt on the Deacon bench. At the start of the January 20, 1964, game against Maryland, McKinney buckled himself to the bench. It worked until the Deacons lost a twelve-point, first-half lead. He unbuckled to try to rally his team and never wore the device again.

If McKinney had a counterpart among the game's referees, it was the colorful Lou Bello, who frequently worked Wake Forest games. In one of those games, Bello stopped before the Wake Forest bench and bent low, speaking directly to the coach.

"Bonesy," Bello said, "everybody in here thinks I'm chewing your ass out."

Seldom at a loss, McKinney balled up his fist and, nose to nose with Bello, replied, "And now they think I'm going to knock the hell out of you." Despite his protracted battle with referees, McKinney confessed years later that "I never lost a game because of officiating."

McKinney's own team was not immune to his barbs. After a game in which his team shot dismally, McKinney told writers in his post-game press conference, "This team is so bad on offense that when we took the backboards down to be painted they didn't even miss them."

When referee Charlie Eckman came down with the flu midway through one of Wake Forest's games at N.C. State and could not continue, McKinney apologized to the press. "I knew we were playing poor ball," the coach said, "but I didn't know it was bad enough to make the official sick."

To remember the man only for his humor would be a disservice. There was a depth to the preacher/player/coach that never drew the sort of attention that his humor brought to him. One of his former players, Jerry Steele, a longtime college coach himself, once said that most people are lucky to have one good father. "But I had two," Steele said. "My own dad and Bones."

And in his own quiet way, McKinney played a significant, if unheralded, role in the integration of the National Basketball Association. In 1952, Earl Lloyd, the first African American to play in the NBA, made history by joining the Washington Caps, where he became a teammate of McKinney's. As had been the case with baseball's Jackie Robinson before him, Lloyd faced what was still predominately a white pro sports world.

In a Black History Month panel discussion held in February 2000, Lloyd remembered those days and his first trip to Fort Wayne, Ind., and to the hotel into which the Caps were booked. "They allowed me to sleep there, but they did not allow me to eat there," Lloyd said. "I guess they didn't want folks to see me downstairs eating. But fortunately, I had a guy, a guy that played for Red (Auerbach, then the team's coach). His name was Bones McKinney, an outstanding individual. I'd heard the term 'red necks,' and I didn't know what it meant but I know his neck was really red. But I didn't know his red neck was his attitude.

"He found out that I was in my room—you don't forget things like this—and Bones took it upon himself to knock on my door and come in and sit down and have dinner with me.

"All he was telling me was, 'You are an integral part of this basketball team. I can't change this but we're going to share it together.' He didn't have to do that."

Neither his love of basketball nor his humor ever deserted the man. In the mid-1990s, McKinney was the guest speaker at a banquet honoring Jerry Steele, who had been an assistant coach to McKinney with the ABA Cougars. Steele in the season then just ended had recorded his five hundredth coaching victory in a long career that included work at both Guilford College and High Point University. "You know you're getting old when one of your players has 500 coaching victories," McKinney told the dinner crowd. "But I've known for some time that old age was creeping up on me. Most of you don't know it and probably can't see it from where you're sitting, but I wear a hearing aid now. They're so small now and so soft that they fit down into your ear and almost nobody knows they're there.

"I get up early and the other morning I was feeling around on the nightstand trying to find my hearing aid without turning on the light and waking Edna [his wife of more than half a century]. Then I tried to put the hearing aid in my ear and Edna woke up. She asked me what I was doing.

"'Trying to put this hearing aid in my ear,' I told her. Edna asked if she could help. 'I wish you would,' I told her and I handed it to her. She fiddled with it a minute, then she said, 'Bones, this ain't your hearing aid. It's a suppository.'"

"I said, well, I guess I know where my hearing aid is."

McKinney died at the age of seventy-eight on May 16, 1997, at the Wake Medical Rehab Center in Raleigh of complications from a stroke he suffered on May 2. In a column marking McKinney's death, *Charlotte Observer* sportswriter Ron Green Sr. paid McKinney the ultimate tribute when he wrote, "He helped us to see life doesn't have to be a missed free throw."

Wilt Browning was sports editor and columnist for newspapers in Atlanta, Ga.; Charlotte and Greensboro; Greenville, S.C.; and Topeka, Kan. He also was public relations director for the Atlanta Falcons and then the Baltimore Colts.

For more information, see:
McKinney, Horace A. Clipping Files. Sports Information Office, Athletic Department, Wake Forest University, Winston-Salem.

RICHARD PETTY

By Tom Higgins

T HE TWO CARS THUNDERED off the fourth turn side by side at Daytona International Speedway, scrubbing sheet metal hard enough to generate sparks and smoke. On the inside lane was Richard Petty, NASCAR's (National Association for Stock Car Auto Racing) immensely popular, all-time victory leader and seven-time champion. On the outside was tough, fiercely determined Cale Yarborough. A few feet before reaching the flag that would decide the winner of the Pepsi Firecracker 400 on July 4, 1984, Petty surged slightly ahead in his red, white, and blue number 43 Pontiac. A local politician back home in little Level Cross, Petty triumphed by inches.

The stirring victory was the two hundredth of Petty's storied stock car racing career, and it triggered a roar among thousands of spectators that some guessed sounded like a volcano erupting. Among those watching—and cheering the awesome action—was Ronald Reagan, the only sitting president ever to attend a NASCAR race.

"Me and Cale beating and banging at almost 200 miles an hour blowed the president's mind," said a grinning Petty after briefly meeting with Reagan.

The president was to have been the star that day after flying into Daytona Beach, Fla., aboard Air Force One, from which he had given the 400's drivers the order to start engines via radio. However, that warm, sunny Independence Day belonged to Petty, who had observed his forty-seventh birthday just two days earlier. For the only time in American history, a county commissioner upstaged the president of the United States. It was the grandest moment in a great motor-sports career.

Wowing a president was far-fetched beyond belief when Richard Petty's father, Lee, almost inadvertently led his family into auto racing in the late 1940s. Many of NASCAR's pioneer drivers trace their racing roots to hauling moonshine out of the North Carolina mountains under the cover of darkness. Their "racing" rivals were federal agents, often called revenuers, assigned to catching the transporters with loads of non-tax paid whiskey.

Lee Petty sped through the night in defiance of the law quite often in this era, too. However, Petty's car wasn't carrying illegal corn liquor from stills deep in the Blue Ridge Mountains. Petty's violation was using the highways and back roads around Randolph

Richard Petty (Courtesy of Charlotte Observer)

County for prearranged races on which relatively substantial amounts of money were bet.

"As long as I can remember, the Petty family always has had a fast car, or at least a car with a big motor in it," recalled Richard Petty, eldest of Lee's two sons. "Right after World War II, when I was ten or eleven, Daddy and his brother Julie had a car they raced on the highways.

"I'm not trying to rationalize that was right. But there wasn't much traffic back then, especially on rural roads. The racing was done in the dead of night when hardly anyone was out, so the only people the road racers were endangering were themselves.

"Fellers came to Level Cross from as far away as Atlanta to try and outrun Daddy and take his money. When they left, he usually had their money.

"In 1949 my Daddy heard that a man named Big Bill France had formed an organization called NASCAR and planned to run a 150-mile race in Charlotte on a three-quarter mile dirt track just west of town. Daddy borrowed a Buick Roadmaster for that race—it was on June 19, 1949—and filed an entry. About the halfway point, Daddy crashed and tore that car all to pieces. He had a lot of explaining to do to the owner. . . . ”

"Despite wrecking at Charlotte, Daddy was enthused about NASCAR. He saw it was pretty well organized and that the promoter, Bill France, wasn't going to be running off with the money like some others had. Daddy saw he could make a living in NASCAR and joined up.

"In just his fifth oval track race Daddy was the winner. It was a 100-mile race on a dirt track near Pittsburgh. Daddy won $1,500, a lot of money in those days, and that pretty well assured the Pettys were in NASCAR to stay.”

A third of the way into the 2000 season, drivers with the surname of Petty had accounted for 262 victories at NASCAR's top level, far more than any other family in what is a clannish sport. "Poppa" Lee Petty won fifty-four races and three points championships before an accident in 1961 at the Daytona track left him with injuries that ended his driving career. Richard retired at the end of the 1992 season with a runaway record of those two hundred triumphs, never winning again after his storied show before President Reagan in 1984. Third-generation driver Kyle, Richard's son, who was still active as a driver at the end of the century, listed eight victories.

There were lows along the way for the Pettys that sadly tempered the highs of Victory Lane. Lee Petty's life-threatening injuries in the 1961 crash at Daytona left him with a limp for the rest of his life, which ended on April 5, 2000, of a stomach aneurysm at age eighty-four. Randy Owens, twenty, brother of Richard's wife, Lynda, lost his life on May 4, 1975, in a pit road accident during the Winston 500 at Talladega, Ala. Another harsh, stunning blow came on May 12, 2000, when Adam Petty, Kyle's son and Richard's grandson, was killed in a crash while practicing for a NASCAR Busch Grand National Series race at New Hampshire International Speedway. Just a month earlier Adam, nineteen, had become the first, and only, fourth-generation driver to qualify for a Winston Cup Series race.

After quitting the cockpit in 1992, Richard Petty has continued in stock car racing as a team owner, posting two victories with Bobby Hamilton as driver and one with John Andretti at the wheel. These triumphs pushed the total for Petty Enterprises to 271 wins, easily a record for NASCAR team owners.

During his colorful thirty-five-year career as a driver, Richard Petty became an American sports icon, among the most popular and respected athletes in the country. He was also one of the most recognizable, thanks to a big Stetson hat, wraparound sunglasses with an STP logo, and a seemingly ever-present smile. "There was never any doubt in my mind that I was going to follow Daddy as a race driver," said the lanky Tar Heel who came to be known as "King Richard." "It was simply accepted that when Daddy decided the time had come and I was ready, I'd move up from helping in the shop and working on the pit crew to join him as a driver."

Richard "warmed up" by entering a few races in a NASCAR "Convertible Division" in 1957. "I thought it would be easy, a piece of cake," he recalled. "But the physical demands were way beyond what I expected and it was tough mentally, too. I saw that I had a whole lot to learn." Richard dedicated himself to the task, aided by younger brother Maurice and cousin Dale Inman, two associates who would be in the Petty pits for many, many years.

In midsummer of 1958, Lee Petty decided that Richard was ready for NASCAR's top tour. His first start came on July 18 in a race at Toronto, Canada. "I qualified pretty good, seventh in a '57 Olds," recalled Richard. "But I hit the fence after about 50 laps or so and finished 17th. I won $115. It wasn't much of a start for me, but Daddy won the race and that sort of made up for it.”

Richard achieved his first top ten finish later in 1958, taking ninth at a track in New Jersey. He ran twenty-one races in 1959, scoring several top fives, but failing to win.

"This disappointed me. . . . I felt it was time," said Richard. "But I can't complain too much about that season, 'cause Daddy won the first running of the Daytona 500.

"One of the most vivid memories of my life is going to Daytona International Speedway for the first time in February of '59. Of course, none of us had ever run on a track so big, 2.5 miles. I remember walking out to pit road and looking toward the first turn. It seemed so far away that it looked like it went over the horizon.

"I couldn't wait to get on the track. NASCAR officials warned us to take it easy the first few laps of practice, to stay on the apron and get an idea of the layout and size of the place. I couldn't help myself! The second lap I gunned the throttle and shot up onto the banking to go around there fast!

"The NASCAR people weren't amused by that and let me know it. They had me black-flagged off the track. So the story is true. I was black-flagged and sent to the garage to be chewed out the first time I ever ran at Daytona."

Petty sheepishly took the tongue-lashing, having no idea that he eventually would win the Daytona 500 a record seven times, including a triumph in perhaps the most memorable race in NASCAR history, a victory that set stock car racing on a roll toward immense popularity.

Richard Petty scored the first of his many victories on February 28, 1960, at the Southern States Fairgrounds in Charlotte. "I remember pretty much everything about that first race I won, like Daddy being on the pole and the fairgrounds track being on the verge of shutting down," he said. "To me, being able to recollect this race and others in that time span is a strange sort of deal. I can recall what happened in them pretty well. But the races later on? They all sort of run in together. I guess the earlier races made more of a lasting impression because I was younger and new to it and awfully excited."

Some of the accomplishments, incidents, and events he did recall in detail are listed chronologically:

• Soaring out of the Daytona track during a preliminary to the 500 in 1961, sustaining only minor injuries. But as Richard left the infield infirmary, he learned that his father, incredibly, also had flown over the railing in an accident during a following event, sustaining career-ending internal injuries.

• Winning both the Daytona 500 and the series championship for the first time in 1964.

• The fabulous 1967 season, in which he won twenty-seven of forty-eight races overall and ten in a row, both NASCAR records that are very unlikely to be broken. "We even won the Southern 500 at Darlington, [S.C.], a race that had eluded Petty Enterprises for eighteen years," marveled Petty, who was given the "King Richard" nickname during this sensational season.

• The 1976 Daytona 500, in which he and archrival David Pearson collided and crashed two hundred yards or so short of the finish line while battling for the lead. Both spun into the grass between the track and pit road. Pearson somehow got going again and took the checkered flag at about five miles per hour while Richard remained stalled in the grass.

• The storied 1979 Daytona 500, the first NASCAR race televised live nationally flag-to-flag. Yarborough and Donnie Allison locked in a two-car aerodynamic draft to pull away by about a third of a lap. With the checkers awaiting during the final lap, the two tangled while battling for the lead going into turn three, crashing hard. From far back, Petty sped by the smok-

ing cars and held off Darrell Waltrip and A. J. Foyt to win. As Petty took the flag, Yarborough fought with brothers Donnie and Bobby Allison on the apron in the third turn. A blizzard blanketed much of the nation that Sunday in February, creating what amounted to a captive audience for CBS-TV. Many observers credit that wild, dramatic finish for the NASCAR boom that led to a mind-boggling $2.8 billion television contract with NBC and the Fox Network beginning in 2001.

• Coming from behind in the point standings during the season finale at Ontario (Calif.) Motor Speedway to win his seventh title in 1979 by eleven points over Waltrip, the closest-ever chase for the championship at the time.

• Making a gamble on taking a splash of gas only, no new tires, during a final pit stop pay off in a seventh Daytona 500 triumph in 1981, beating the far-faster car of Bobby Allison.

And perhaps the warmest memory of all, the Sunday he made his one thousandth start on Father's Day in June of 1986 in the Miller 400 at Michigan International Speedway. Track officials had arranged for Richard and Lynda Petty's daughters—Sharon, Lisa, and Rebecca—to give the command to start the engines.

"They didn't say, 'Gentlemen, start your engines,' at least not right away," recalled Richard. "They said, 'Daddy, start your engine!' I flipped the switch. After only my engine ran for about a minute, the girls then said for the other guys to start their engines. It was a pretty emotional thing and the crowd got swept into it. I could hear the cheering over the roar of my engine."

At the end of a touching "Farewell Tour" in 1992, Richard Petty retired with 1,184 starts, 200 victories, and 126 pole positions, all records. He ran 307,836 laps and led 52,194 of them, both also records. He was at front at some point in 599 of his races, still a record eight years after his retirement. He earned $8,541,218 in an era before NASCAR purses became so huge.

Along the way Petty became by far the best ambassador of good will in his sport's history, like Arnold Palmer in golf and Babe Ruth in baseball. Immediately following many races, he sat on pit walls until darkness fell, signing autographs for adoring fans. Petty also was known for "playing hurt," or driving while injured or ill. During one stretch he grittily ran several races with a broken bone in his neck, keeping the injury secret for fear that NASCAR officials would sideline him.

Petty's charitable and civic works—accomplished mostly behind the scenes—led to many honors, including North Carolina's Order of the Long Leaf Pine and an honorary doctor of humanities degree from Pfeiffer University in 1992.

He even became involved in local and state politics. He was elected to the Board of County Commissioners of Randolph County and in 1992 was the Republican candidate for North Carolina secretary of state. He lost that race after an embarrassing incident. A motorist claimed Petty bumped his car at high speed to indicate his impatience. It was a tactic he used often on the track. It did not play on the public highways, however.

Perhaps Petty's race-driving peer, Buddy Baker, best assessed what King Richard the driver and man meant to the sport of stock car racing. Said Baker: "NASCAR getting to where it is without Richard Petty would have been like trying to have a Wild West Show a century ago without Buffalo Bill."

Tom Higgins reported on NASCAR racing over a span of five decades for newspapers in Asheville, Winston-Salem, Durham, and Charlotte, where he retired in 1997 after twenty-nine years. He received the North Carolina Press Association first-place honor for his story on the death of driver Tim Richmond and the NASCAR Award of Excellence for lifetime achievement in New York.

For more information, see:
Burchard, M., and S. Burchard. *Sports Hero: Richard Petty*. Putnam, 1974.
Higgins, Tom, et al. *Richard Petty's Official Guide to 50 Years of NASCAR*. Corporate Sports Marketing Group, 1999.
Neely, William. *King Richard I*. MacMillan, 1986.
Vehorn, Frank. *A Farewell to the King*. Down Home Press, 1992.

DEAN SMITH

By John Kilgo

BEFORE HIS FIFTH BIRTHDAY, Dean Smith knew exactly what he wanted to do with his life. While many five-year-olds think they know what they want to be when they grow up, Smith knew. Positively.

His dream was to teach math and coach high school football and basketball. Smith was reminded of this ambition almost on a daily basis, when as a young boy he followed his father to the athletic fields and courts of Emporia High School in Kansas to play catch or shoot baskets or retrieve foul balls as his father coached the school's football, basketball, baseball, and track teams. He also traveled with the Emporia teams on many of their road trips, and when a player would call out a number, Smith would quickly—and correctly—identify the Emporia athlete who wore that number on his uniform. Even at this early age, Dean Smith was as much a student of the games as he was a fan. His appetite for learning was insatiable and he would greet his father in the evenings with a list of strategic questions.

Smith was born in Emporia on February 28, 1931, the second of two children. His father, Alfred Smith, had a full load teaching hygiene and physical education in addition to his coaching duties, while his mother, Vesta Edwards Smith, taught at all levels, from elementary school reading to college-bound psychology courses. She also served as school superintendent in Lyon County, Kan., for eighteen months, finishing the unexpired term of an elected superintendent. Dean inherited his mother's punctuality, but otherwise took more after his father, who was not very concerned with money.

Profanity was not tolerated in the Smith home. Alfred Smith even refused to allow Dean to caddy at the local country club, fearing he might pick up the salty language from frustrated golfers. The Smiths were members of the First Baptist Church in Emporia, where Alfred Smith was a deacon and his wife was the church organist. Their children attended Sunday school, the 11 A.M. worship service, and returned that night for youth fellowship and more preaching. During the week, the family conducted daily devotions before dinner.

Alfred Smith introduced his son to sports, competition, strategy, sportsmanship, and the joy of participating in games, while Dean's mother enforced the

Dean Smith (Courtesy of Hugh Morton)

rules of the house. She insisted that he read a book each week and he was not available for any games if his schoolwork suffered. He mopped floors at Emporia State University for twenty-five cents an hour beginning at age twelve, and later he spent summers digging ditches for seventy-five cents an hour. Meanwhile, his parents taught him to "value each human being." They taught that each person, regardless of race, background, or occupation, stood equal in the eyes of God.

The Smiths practiced what they preached. In 1934, Alfred Smith integrated the basketball team at Emporia High. He included on his roster a young black man named Paul Terry, who was the son of a janitor at the local bank. Many state sports organizations, as well as many opposing teams, criticized the coach, but he was steadfast in his decision. That Emporia team of 1934, often going up against bigger and seemingly more powerful teams from Wichita and Topeka, pulled a major upset by winning the Kansas state championship.

Dean became a quarterback on the football team, a guard on the basketball team, and a catcher in baseball. In 1947, the family moved to Topeka, where Alfred took a job with the Veterans Administration.

Dean was apprehensive about the move to a much larger school, but he made the adjustment and starred on the athletic teams as well as in the classroom.

Upon graduation from high school, Dean was offered athletic scholarships to Emporia State University and Ottawa, a nearby American Baptist school. But he wanted something bigger. He was offered academic scholarships to both the University of Kansas and Kansas State, with the opportunity to sell football programs on game days and work at other jobs in order to earn spending money.

Smith chose Kansas, where he played football, basketball, and baseball as a freshman. But believing that his best sports were basketball and baseball, he gave up football after his freshman season. He played basketball at Kansas for the legendary coach Dr. Forrest "Phog" Allen, a spellbinding speaker who had a knack for inspiring his athletes. Allen's assistant was Dick Harp, a man well-schooled in basketball strategy and fundamentals. Smith asked Harp questions constantly, and the two remained close friends until Harp's death in 2000. With Smith on the team, Kansas won the national championship in 1952 by defeating St. John's, 80–63, and its nationally prominent Frank McGuire. In Smith's senior year at Kansas, the Jayhawks made it back to the national championship game, but lost to Indiana, 69–68.

After graduating from Kansas, Smith married a fellow Kansas student, Ann Cleavinger, in 1954. He entered the air force, which sent him to Germany. Most of his time there was spent on the basketball court, playing on and later coaching the base team at Furstenfeldbruck Air Force Base near Munich. His team, comprised mostly of military policemen, finished the season 11–1, and the players presented him with a Rolex watch that he wore proudly for more than forty years.

While in Germany, Smith met an air force pilot named Bob Spear, a decorated airman who had flown a B-54 in the Berlin airlift. He was also a brilliant basketball coach who had served as an assistant to coach Ben Carnevale at the U.S. Naval Academy. When Spear was named head basketball coach of the new U.S. Air Force Academy in Colorado, he persuaded Smith to join him as his assistant.

What he learned at the Air Force Academy would prove invaluable for the rest of his career. Since the academy was new, the air force team was made up of first- and second-year players. No player was taller than six-four, since pilots had to be able to fit into the cockpits of fighter planes. Going against bigger, faster, more experienced, and generally more talented players, Spear and Smith had to find ways to overcome those disadvantages with innovative coaching. They came up with an offense that featured much cutting and movement without the ball, which not only chewed up time but was extremely difficult to defend. And on defense, Smith refined a zone that coach Clair Bee had used at Long Island University and turned it into air force's point zone, which proved to be highly effective.

The Spear-Smith combination guided the Air Force Academy team to a surprising 11–10 record in its first year. The second season ended 17–6, an accomplishment that captured the attention of basketball coaches around the nation. Among those was Frank McGuire, who had left St. John's to coach at the University of North Carolina. McGuire and Spear were friends, and McGuire received Spear's blessing to hire Smith as his assistant in August 1958 at an annual salary of $7,500.

McGuire, whose Tar Heel team had just won the national collegiate championship in 1957, gave Smith much responsibility in drawing up plans and coaching during practice, with McGuire often observing from the stands with a megaphone in his hands. The two men, who became close friends, produced records of 20–5, 18–6, and 19–4 in the three years they coached together at Chapel Hill. But storm clouds were gathering in late 1960. The National Collegiate Athletic Association (NCAA) cited McGuire's program for "excessive recruiting expenditures," an allegation that McGuire and the university denied. Even after UNC won an appeal to have the penalties reduced, the university's program was placed on probation for one year. The penalty kept North Carolina's 1960–61 team, one of the nation's best, out of the NCAA championship tournament.

UNC Chancellor William Aycock wrote McGuire a stern letter, warning him that his contract would not be renewed if there were any more NCAA violations. He also criticized the coach for lax team discipline, because fights had broken out between players and fans at Wake Forest and Duke. Facing these and other problems, McGuire resigned to become head coach of the professional Philadelphia Warriors basketball team. While many Tar Heel boosters pressured Aycock to hire a nationally known replacement for McGuire, the chancellor turned to the young Smith and paid him $9,200 a year.

"You give the university a basketball program it can be proud of," Aycock told Smith, "and you'll have a job here as long as I am chancellor." Smith also received a call that day from his pastor, the Reverend Bob Seymour of Binkley Baptist Church in Chapel Hill, urging him to put a black player on his team. A year before, Smith had accompanied Seymour and a black student to a Chapel Hill restaurant to help break down color barriers in the town.

After Smith's first year resulted in an 8–9 season, Tar Heel boosters called for his head, but Aycock stuck with his young coach. It turned out to be the only losing season in Smith's long tenure at UNC.

Smith fielded better teams in the next few years, but he still had not won over the fans in his fourth year. After a 85–107 loss to Wake Forest, he was burned in effigy on campus in January 1965. "I knew it was a dummy of me because of the long nose," Smith was able to quip. Three days later, the Tar Heels upset a ranked Duke team 65–62 and a crowd of students urged him to speak. Smith smiled and refused, saying, "There's something tight around my neck that keeps me from speaking."

Smith's program was gaining national attention, and one of the most important prospects was Charlie Scott, an African American who had played at Laurinburg Institute, a black prep school in Laurinburg. Smith had already had one black member on his 1964–65 squad, William Cooper, but he had quit after his freshman year to concentrate on academics. Scott signed with Carolina in 1966, becoming one of the first black athletes in the South.

In 1976, Carolina won the Atlantic Coach Conference (ACC) championship and finished in the top ten in the nation, and Smith was named head coach of the USA Olympic Basketball Team. It was a controversial assignment because the USA team had lost in 1972 and expectations were high for a rematch. Smith's team went unbeaten and honor was restored. "I never talked to my North Carolina teams about winning," Smith said. "But it was the only thing I talked to our Olympic team about, because it was what was important." While the players stood on the podium receiving their gold medals, Smith stood to one side with tears streaming down his face as the national anthem was played.

In his thirty-six years at Carolina, Smith's teams won or shared a record seventeen ACC championships, won thirteen ACC tournaments, won national championships in 1982 and 1993, and never was cited for an NCAA infraction. A full 97 percent of Smith's

players at Carolina received degrees and nearly half of those went on to further study. In 1982, Smith was inducted into the Basketball Hall of Fame at Springfield, Mass..

The Dean E. Smith Center opened on January 18, 1986, with the Carolina team trading up from Carmichael Auditorium with a seating capacity of 8,800 to a hall that could seat nearly 22,000. The "Dean Dome," as it was dubbed, was built with private funds after a subscription campaign led by Hargove "Skipper" Bowles. On the day of its dedication, Smith's Tar Heels defeated Duke 95–92 in a game broadcast on national television.

Smith's 1997 team was his last at Carolina. It started with three straight ACC losses and then rallied to win sixteen games in a row, the ACC championship, and an NCAA Final Four berth. Included was a win over Colorado in the NCAA tournament that gave Smith 877 victories, breaking the national record held by Adolph Rupp of Kentucky. The capacity crowd chanted Smith's name, but he modestly sprinted to the locker room, where he was greeted by many former players.

One was Joe Brown, who had played for Carolina in 1967–69. "There's something about the man that makes us work hard not to disappoint him," Brown said. "It was that way when I played for him, and it's still that way now that I'm fifty years old and well into my career." Smith ended his career with two more victories for a record of 879. He retired in October 1997.

Columnist and broadcaster John Kilgo of Davidson reported on Dean Smith's basketball teams for thirty-five years. He is the author of A Coach's Life, *the memoirs of Dean Smith, and coauthor of* Season of Dreams *and* Racing Lifestyles.

For more information, see:
Chansky, Art. *Dean's Domain: The Inside Story of Dean Smith and His College Basketball Empire*. Longstreet Press, 1999.
Smith, Dean, and John Kilgo, et al. *A Coach's Life: My Forty Years in Basketball*. Random House, 1999.
Sports information office, Athletic Department, University of North Carolina at Chapel Hill.

WALLACE WADE

By Charles R. Westmoreland Jr.

Wallace Wade (Courtesy of Hugh Morton)

ON SEPTEMBER 29, 1967, when Duke University named its football stadium in honor of former head football coach Wallace Wade, sports information director Glenn Mann declared: "So when historians of the future check into the records of all the outstanding football coaches of all time, they just may come up with what in our opinion is the truth. That truth is that Wallace Wade is the greatest football coach in all our American history."

Many would have disagreed with Mann's assessment. Names like Knute Rockne, George Halas, Paul "Bear" Bryant, and Vince Lombardi usually were listed before Wade's. However, Wade should be remembered for his role in the emergence of southern college football and why Duke honored him by naming its stadium in his honor.

Wade was born on June 15, 1892, to Robert Bruce and Sarah Ann Wade in Trenton, Tenn. He graduated from Peabody High School before attending Morgan Park Academy, a preparatory school in Chicago. After a year at Morgan Park, Wade entered Brown University, where he was a standout guard for the football team. Tall, slender, and strong, Wade helped guide Brown to a national championship game in 1916 against Washington State University in the Rose Bowl. Although Washington State defeated Brown, Wade would make many more trips to Pasadena, Calif.

Following his days at Brown, Wade enlisted in the army in World War I and was sent to Fort Still, Okla., where he was promoted to captain. He was prepared to ship out for France when the war ended. Wade accepted a coaching job at Fitzgerald-Clarke Preparatory School in Tullahoma, Tenn., where he compiled an impressive 16–3 record in two years.

In 1921, Wade took an assistant coaching position at Vanderbilt University. While in Nashville, Wade helped the Commodores to a 16–0 overall record. Like his stint with Fitzgerald-Clarke, Wade stayed at Vanderbilt for only two years. In 1923, the thirty-one-year-old Wade began an eight-year stint at the University of Alabama, where his first team finished with a 7–2–1 record. The following year, Alabama won the Southern Conference championship. It would be the first of ten such honors in Wade's career.

In spite of its dominance across the South, Alabama had difficulty earning national respect. When the Tide was preparing to face the University of Washington Huskies in the 1926 Rose Bowl, one official scoffed, "I've never heard of Alabama as a football team and I can't take a chance on mixing a lemon with a rose." Nonetheless, the Rose Bowl committee chose Alabama, although most prognosticators gave Alabama virtually no chance of winning. New York sportswriter Lawrence Perry wrote, "A crushing defeat of Alabama is indicated."

Wade ignored the opinions of so-called experts. A stern disciplinarian, Wade wanted his players to stay focused on their mission. "In order to get in the right mental attitude," he declared, "no more entertainment [particularly California sightseeing] will be indulged in."

Wade and his young players had made the experts look ridiculous. A two-to-one underdog at game time, Alabama pulled off one of the most surprising wins —20 to 19—in Rose Bowl history. But this game meant more than newfound success for Alabama's football program. As historian Andrew Doyle suggested, this Rose Bowl win was somewhat redemptive for the South's history of poverty, defeat, and humiliation in the national spotlight. "Alabama's performance instantly transcended the realm of sports and became a symbolic indication of Southern honor," Doyle wrote. "Whites throughout the Deep South reveled in the victory." With his victory at Pasadena, Wade became a college football icon.

Wade's team followed the 1926 Rose Bowl win with a 9-0-1 record the following year. This effort earned Alabama a share of the national championship and a third consecutive Southern Conference title. The only imperfection on Alabama's record was a 7-7 tie with Stanford in the 1927 Rose Bowl. After eight years in Tuscaloosa, Wade had won sixty-one, lost thirteen, and tied three games. Along with four Southern Conference titles and three national championships, Wade had established himself as a hot commodity.

After several visits with Duke officials in March 1930, Wade made a commitment to leave Alabama following the 1930 season for the burgeoning new university in North Carolina. The 1931 Rose Bowl was Wade's last game at the University of Alabama, but his success would not end in Pasadena. Durham would be the site of many future victories and triumphs.

Duke's football program had struggled mightily in the 1920s. Although Coach James Dehart put together a 8-1-2 season in 1930, his previous four had been mediocre. Wade turned the Blue Devils into winners. In 1931 and 1932, the Devils finished a combined 12-6-2. From 1933 until 1941, Duke dominated the Southern Conference. The 1933 Duke team won nine games, losing only one. Wade's first Southern Conference championship team at Duke, led by Fred Crawford and Corky Cornelius, paved the way for what many called "The Golden Years of Duke Football."

Wade engineered the Blue Devils to a 31-7-1 standard over the next four years. Along the way, Duke won two more conference championships, bringing Wade's overall total to seven. This success spilled over into 1938 with the astonishing "Iron Dukes" team, probably the most memorable team the school has ever produced. Dan "Tiger" Hill and Eric Tipton were named All-Americans. Future All-Americans George McAfee, Tony Ruffa, and Allen Johnson helped Hill and Tipton as Duke tallied a perfect 9-0 regular season. Altogether, this team outscored its regular season opponents 114-0, an accomplishment never repeated in the regular season. The Blue Devils closed the season with two 7-0 wins over in-state rival North Carolina State College and the University of Pittsburgh. Again, Wade took a team to the Rose Bowl. This time, the opponent was the University of Southern California (USC) Trojans.

The Duke-USC clash took place on January 1, 1939. As Duke had shown all year, scoring on the vaunted Iron Dukes would take a near miracle. Duke took a 3-0 lead in the early stages of the fourth quarter behind Tony "Old True Toe" Ruffa's field goal.

With two minutes left in the game, USC coach Howard Jones inserted fourth-string quarterback Doyle Nave to spark the stagnant Trojan offense. Jones's move worked as Nave threw a 16-yard touchdown pass to Al Krueger. This score gave the Trojans a 7-3 victory. Following the game, Wade said, "I hated to see the boys lose it when they played such a great game. We did well as long as they used only two teams, but when they put in those third and fourth teams, they were too much for us." A mere seven points—the only points to be registered all year against the Iron Dukes—kept Wade from his fourth national title.

A one-point loss to Pittsburgh kept Duke from another undefeated season in 1939. In 1940, Duke slipped a little, winning seven games and losing two. Nevertheless, after a decade at the helm of Duke's football program, Wade had elevated the Blue Devils from obscurity to national prominence. His 76-17-3 record certified his status as an elite coach.

For the second time in four years, Duke went through its 1941 season unscathed and secured another spot in the Rose Bowl. This time, the Oregon State College Beavers were to meet Duke in the Rose Bowl when war broke out following the Japanese attack at Pearl Harbor. Rose Bowl officials worried such a large gathering would become a likely target for the Japanese, and on December 13, Lieutenant General John Lesene Dewitt canceled the game, which had been scheduled for New Year's Day, 1942. Meanwhile, Duke officials devised a plan to bring the Rose Bowl to Durham. After several days of deliberation, Rose Bowl officials agreed and Oregon State headed for North Carolina. Duke lost the game, 20-16, but Durham's hospitality was remarkable in itself. A plaque was installed at the stadium to commemorate the unique event.

Immediately after the Rose Bowl, the army commissioned Wade a lieutenant colonel and assigned him to the European theater. He participated in the Battle of the Bulge and the crossing of the Rhine River as the Ninth Army advanced through Germany in the war's waning days. He was awarded a Bronze Star and a military service award from the French government. After the war, Wade returned to Durham as head football coach, but he would never regain the winning edge.

Wade ended his coaching career in 1950 with a 7-0 win over arch-rival University of North Carolina and spent time as Duke's athletic director and later Southern Conference commissioner. In his sixteen years at Duke, his teams compiled a record of 110 wins, 36 losses, and 7 ties and won seven conference titles. As a coach at Alabama and Duke, Wade's record was an imposing 171–49–10. He also had produced over thirty All-Americans.

Georgia Tech coach Bobby Dodd once said of Wade: "If we must lose to anyone, I'd choose to lose to Wallace Wade. When we have beaten him, Mr. Wade has always come over and congratulated us in a way that made us know he meant what he said. He has never blamed the weather or the field, the officials or hard luck. He has never complained that he lacked material or that his players fell down on him. You cannot grudge a victory to such a man."

Wade died on September 23, 1986, and was later enshrined in the National Football Hall of Fame.

Charles A. Westmoreland Jr. is a University of Tennessee doctoral candidate in history with emphasis on the post-Reconstruction South. A native of Southside Virginia, he received a degree in history from Ferrum College and his M.A. in history from University of North Carolina at Charlotte, where his thesis was entitled "Strong Legs Run-

ning: The Integration of the North Carolina–South Carolina Shrine Bowl."

For more information, see:

Cromartie, Bill. *Battle of the Blues*. Gridiron Publishers, 1992.

Doyle, Andrew. "Turning the Tide: College Football and Southern Progressivism." *Southern Cultures* 11 (Fall 1997): 28–51.

Mann, Glenn. *A Story of Glory: Duke University Football*. Doorway Publishers, 1985.

———. "A Tribute of Gratitude and Affection to Wallace Wade on the Occasion of the Wallace Wade Recognition Dinner," September 29, 1967. Duke University.

Sumner, Jim. "The Rose Bowl Comes to North Carolina." *Carolina Comments* 39 (November 1991): 186–95.

———. "A History of Sports in North Carolina." N.C. Office of Archives and History, 1990.

LeRoy T. Walker

By Charles A. Westmoreland Jr.

Growing up in Jim Crow Atlanta, few could have expected that LeRoy Tashreau Walker would one day become the highest-ranking official on the United States Olympic Committee (USOC). Even fewer people could have anticipated that this grandson of slaves would help bring the world's most renowned athletic competition to the once-torched and devastated South. Paralleling the history of his own region, Walker emerged from a past marked by racism and inequality to lead an influential life. Walker represented the faith, perseverance, and discipline of a South rising from the ashes of Jim Crow and poverty and moving toward a region filled with promise and hope.

Although Walker became well-known internationally for his expertise in track and field and his work in attracting the Olympics to Atlanta, the foundation for his success can be found in his stint beginning in 1945 at all-black North Carolina College for Negroes (later North Carolina Central University). While in Durham, Walker paved the way for years of success in athletics and administration. Before then, however, his journey took many different twists and turns.

On June 14, 1918, Mary Walker gave birth to her thirteenth child, a young boy named LeRoy Tashreau. The family lived in southwest Atlanta, where virtually all of the city's African Americans resided. In addition, inequality in the workforce meant that blacks occupied the most menial, labor-intensive jobs. Willie, LeRoy's father and the family patriarch, loaded coal onto locomotives. LeRoy's brothers and sisters took a variety of domestic service jobs. Despite these humble circumstances, the family valued a strong religious faith and an unquestioned discipline. Known for using the "leather belt" to discipline his children, Willie was always evenhanded, said LeRoy Walker. As biographer Charles Gaddy wrote, "His father was fair and before administering the corporal punishment would go over in great detail what the issue was all about." Along with his Christian faith, a stern disciplinarian in his father, and an industrious work ethic, Walker acquired a love for sports at an early age. This affinity guided young LeRoy Walker throughout the rest of his life.

Boyhood contests on Parsons Street in Atlanta eventually gave way to high school athletic stardom in Harlem. After his father died in 1926, LeRoy moved

LeRoy T. Walker (Courtesy of Charlotte Observer)

to New York to live with his brother Joe, a watchful big brother, who understood that his younger brother loved sports. But Joe made certain that LeRoy did not neglect other areas like music, drama, and, most importantly, his schooling.

LeRoy was a star for Harlem's Haaren High basketball team, foreshadowing his future athletic triumphs. Although he was small, Walker was a gifted athlete with passion and confidence. His on-field success did not lead to classroom deterioration. At Haaren and Booker T. Washington High, where Walker transferred after returning to Atlanta for his senior year, he was a diligent student. He went back to Harlem for a year before enrolling at Benedict College in South Carolina, where he continued to succeed in the classroom and on the athletic field.

Walker lettered in basketball and was a promising young sprinter. Yet his most surprising achievements came on the football field. His speed and intelligence compensated for his lack of size. Not gifted in height or bulk, Walker noted that "in shorts, I weighed in at 155." Walker moved into the starting lineup as a junior, when an injury ended the starting quarterback's season, and led Benedict to a conference championship.

Educational and athletic preoccupation did not prevent LeRoy from meeting Katherine McDowell, his future wife. The couple would have two children, LeRoy Jr. and Carolyn. After marrying Katherine, Walker obtained his master's degree in physical education and health sciences from Columbia University, where he was an honors student. In 1957, Walker earned his Ph.D. in exercise physiology and biomechanics from New York University.

It could have been easy for Walker to have gotten lost in the shadows of coaching greats John McLendon and Herman Riddick. McLendon, N.C. Central's innovative basketball coach, and Herman Riddick, the school's winningest football coach, developed a solid athletic reputation for the college. Walker capitalized on this image and even strengthened it. He relied on simple, yet important, coaching methods.

Conditioning was paramount. For Walker, athletes could not be effective unless they were in peak physical condition. Resulting from this philosophy, Walker's practices were filled with drills to improve physical stamina and strength. Secondly, Walker insisted that, following the development of good conditioning, specific skills must be mastered. Whether one participated in the shot put, 100-meter dash, the hurdles, or the long jump, understanding the rudimentary techniques associated with a certain event was critical. In this regard, Walker allowed for more flexibility, noting that individual athletes must find a routine that was compatible with their own tastes.

This approach merged with a broader coaching philosophy. He called it the "four Fs": "I am firm, fair, and friendly. If that doesn't work, then it's farewell." The first three Fs undoubtedly overshadowed the final F. Walker's system bred numerous track champions from N.C. Central. Even more importantly, Walker took pride in the fact that he helped many young athletes develop into productive citizens. His first main track champion led the way for future victories.

Lee Calhoun, a track star from Indiana, first met Coach Walker at the 1952 Indiana High School Championship. After a day of futility, Calhoun wept beside the track. Walker approached the young man and consoled him, beginning the recruitment of his most highly regarded athlete. Even though Calhoun did not perform up to standards, Walker saw something special in the kid. His "God-given gifts of height and spirit" convinced Walker that he could develop Calhoun into a great track competitor.

Calhoun enrolled at N.C. Central in the fall of 1952 and began a journey that would result in a gold medal at the 1956 Summer Olympics in Melbourne, Australia. Walker's guidance and Calhoun's ability in the 110-meter hurdles had finally paid off. Calhoun outlasted the University of Southern California's outspoken hurdler Jack Davis in Melbourne. This was more than a personal achievement for Calhoun. His victory elevated Walker into the national and international spotlight as a fine track coach.

From 1945 to 1983, Walker produced 111 All-Americans, 40 national champions, 12 U.S. Olympians, 8 U.S. and world record holders, and at least 1 N.C. Central track representative in 7 consecutive Summer Olympics. Showing his versatility as an educator, Walker even served as N.C. Central chancellor from 1983 to 1986. His reputation as a coach and teacher would grow and eventually extend from Durham to the Middle East to Africa and back to his hometown of Atlanta.

From the beginning of his tenure in Durham, Walker and the N.C. Central track program established close, friendly contact with Duke University's track team. Walker formed a lifelong friendship, first with Duke track coach Bob Chambers, then his successor Al Buehler. Durham was part of the segregated South, with racial separation clearly marking the city's demographics. This division, though, did not prohibit Walker and Buehler from becoming close partners and friends. As a sign of their closeness, N.C. Central often held practices at Duke University's training complex.

Ultimately, the Buehler-Walker alliance spearheaded numerous integrated meets at Duke University. Walker's squads proved quite capable against Buehler's squads and many others. Their most memorable triumph together came during the 1971 Pan Africa-USA Games in Durham. The two coaches worked well together in organizing this monumental track competition. More than fifty thousand fans from both the United States and Africa packed Duke's Wallace Wade Stadium.

In 1959, Walker began a tour of the Middle East and Africa. The U.S. State Department, in conjunction with the National Association of Sport and Physical Education, called upon Walker to travel to Syria, Ethiopia, and Israel. While away from home,

Walker taught classes and coached track in various high schools and universities, including Wingate University near Tel Aviv, known for its physical education studies. His ambassadorial work prompted Walker to be named the head track coach for the 1960 Israeli and Ethiopian Olympic teams.

Walker shared his expertise with many African runners, who then used his guidance to became the world's greatest distance runners. By 1965, Walker was responsible for track and field programming and training throughout the entire African continent, except for South Africa. Walker's travels had opened his eyes to new pools of athletic talent and willing learners. During the 1970s, Walker would finally be recognized as the United States' top track coach.

Although several recruiting mishaps placed the N.C. Central track program on probation during the early 1970s, Walker's reputation as a great coach and leader did not suffer. He served as a volunteer with athletes from across the globe in the 1970s, helping organize various track meets. This renown earned him the head coaching position of the 1976 U.S. Olympic track team.

Walker led the U.S. team to a fine performance. Decathlete Bruce Jenner and hurdler Edwin Moses were the team's two main stars. Moses told NBC's Tom Brokaw, "I thought at first Dr. Walker was trying to kill me [in preparation and workouts]! I was confused and it was Dr. Walker who said this is what you have to do. He is modest, but those of us who know him think he is a genius." Moses concluded, "Dr. LeRoy Walker gets credit for my success." Moses was one of many gold medalists who would work with the track "genius" throughout the years.

In 1976, Walker was inducted into the North Carolina Sports Hall of Fame and received the O. Max Gardner Award, one of the highest honors awarded by the University of North Carolina system.

Atlanta businessman Billy Payne, Mayor Andrew Young, and Walker spearheaded the effort to bring the 1996 Olympic Games to Atlanta. Payne and Young had organized a formidable campaign, but both knew that Walker had the nuts-and-bolts Olympic experience. The three saw their dreams come true in September 1990, when Atlanta was chosen.

Following the Atlanta Olympics, Walker stepped down as USOC president, a job he had held since 1992. His farewell address expressed pride and concern for the Olympic movement. This "labor of love . . . made me keenly aware of the value of time, the obligation of duty, the dignity of simplicity, the worth of character, the power of kindness, the virtue of patience, the joy of originating, and the influence of example," Walker attested. Walker valued all these characteristics throughout his life.

In turn, Andrew Young paid Walker a high compliment: "Circumstances and the times create great men and people somehow think of these great men as accidents, sort of springing full-blown out of the head of Zeus, but they are all a part of a process. The world ends up knowing Martin Luther King and Nelson Mandela, but there are probably 100 other people who have labored virtually in anonymity . . . but who have been just as effective in their fields and in terms of peace-making around the world, who never get any attention. LeRoy Walker is one of those."

Walker committed his life to improving the lives of America's youth. This devotion was shown when he served as the president of the 1999 Special Olympics World Summer Games, which were held in the Raleigh-Durham-Chapel Hill area. Another example of Walker's dedication to coaching America's young athletes can be found in the L. T. Walker International Human Performance Center. Located at East Carolina University in Greenville, the Walker Center serves as a "very cost-effective school and training facility for athletes, coaches, trainers, and administrators." Walker's efforts revealed a continued commitment to athletics and education, even as he entered his eighties.

Charles A. Westmoreland Jr. is a University of Tennessee doctoral candidate in history with emphasis on the post-Reconstruction South. A native of Southside, Virginia, he received a degree in history from Ferrum College and his M.A. in history from the University of North Carolina at Charlotte, where his thesis was entitled "Strong Legs Running: The Integration of the North Carolina-South Carolina Shrine Bowl."

For more information, see:
Gaddy, Charles. *An Olympic Journey, The Saga of an American Hero: LeRoy T. Walker.* Griffin Publishing Group, 1998.
L. T. Walker International Human Performance Center. Web site at www.walkercenter.com.
Sumner, Jim. *A History of Sports in North Carolina.* N.C. Office of Archives and History, 1990.
Walker, LeRoy. *Championship Techniques in Track and Field.* Parker Publishing, 1969.
———. *Track and Field for Boys and Girls.* Athletic Institute, 1983.

Caesar, Shirley, 532; *profile of,* 533–536

Caldwell, J. P., 51

Caledonia prison, 37

Calhoun, John C., 56

Calhoun, Lee, 621

Cambridge, Mass., 157, 206

Camden, S.C., 426

Camel cigarettes, 4, 184

Camel City Flying Service, 141

Cameron, C. C., *profile of,* 160–162

Cameron-Brown Company, 160

Camp Battle, 7

Camp Butner, 7

Camp Davis, 7

Camp Lejeune, 7, 187

Camp Sutton, 7

Camp Yonahnoka, 500

Campbell College, 262; Lundy-Fetterman School of Business, 264; Norman A. Wiggins School of Law, 264

Campbell Starling (investment brokerage), 214

Campbell, Howell, 84

Campbell, J. A., 263

Campbell, John C., 210

Campbell, Leslie H., 262

Campbell, Olive Dame, *profile of,* 210–213

Campbell, Orville, 329, 330, 606; *pictured with George Hamilton IV,* 433

Campbell, Ralph, 551

Campbell, Ralph, Jr., 551

Campbell, Sandy, 45

Campbell, Will, 542

Campbell, William "Bill," 551

Canaday, Pernell, 231

Can a Man Be a Christian Today? (Poteat), 258

Cannon Foundation, xii, 128

Cannon Manufacturing Company, 126

Cannon Mills Company, 115, 127, 154

Cannon, Charles A., 4; *profile of,* 126–128

Cannon, Charles A., Jr., 127

Cannon, David, 126

Cannon, Hugh, 78, 280

Cannon, James G., 54

Cannon, James William, 126

Cannon, Mariam, 127

Cannon, Ruth, 127

Cannon, William C., 127

Canton, 67

Cape Fear Country Club, 25

Cape Fear Journal, 318

Cape Fear River, 80

Cape Hatteras Lighthouse, 499

Capitol Broadcasting Company, 308

Capitol Records, 430

Capitol Theater Orchestra, 104

Caravans, the, 533–534

Carbonton, 25

Carlton, Gaither, 451

Carlton, A. P., Jr., 267, 409

Carlyle Commission, 234, 270

Carlyle, Irving E., 233, 267; *profile of,* 269–271

Carmel Presbyterian Church, 439

Carmichael and Carson, 214

Carmichael, Margaret McCaull, 214

Carmichael, Stokely, 561, 578

Carmichael, W. D. "Billy," Jr., 43, 204, 214, 232, 238, 280, 363; *profile of,* 214–216

Carnegie Corporation, 77, 515

Carnegie Foundation for the Advancement of Teaching, 356

Carolina Call, 320

Carolina Chats (radio program), 309

Carolina Freight Carriers, 118

Carolina Israelite, 312–313

Carolina Magazine, 71, 80

Carolina Opera School, 307

Carolina Panthers, 173

Carolina Playmakers, 81, 111

Carolina Power and Light Company (CP&L), xii, 191, 520

Carolina Skill Advancement Center, 572

Carolina Times (Durham), 298, 319

Carolina Tribune, The (Raleigh), 319

Carolina Trucking Company, 24

Carolinian (Raleigh), 298, 319–320

Carpenter, L. L., 316

Carr, Julian S., 260, 303, 371

Carson, Rachel, 17

Carson-Newman College, 221

Carter, Hodding, 325

Carter, Jimmy, 12, 274, 409, 516, 522, 535; *pictured with James B. Hunt Jr.,* 408

Carver, George Washington, 548

Cary, 8, 116, 143

Cary Academy, 145

Casbah club, 74

Case, Everett, 233, 589; *profile of,* 594–596

Case, Phyllis, 45

Cash, W. J., 325; *profile of,* 299–301

Castle Hayne, 15, 24–25

Caswell County, 353

Catawba College: Ralph W. Ketner Hall of, 155; Ketner School of Business of, 156, 181

Catawba River, 37

Cato Corporation, 115

Cato, Edgar, 115

Cato, Wayland, Jr., 115

Catt, Carrie Chapman, 278

CBS, 297; orchestra, 108; *Wings Over Jordan* (program), 208, 322; *CBS Evening News,* 322; *Eyewitness to History* (program), 322; *On the Road* (program), 323

Cecil, William A. V., 116; *profile of,* 129–132

Cecil, William A. V., Jr., 132

Cedar Lodge plantation, 39

Celanese Corporation, 44, 498, 567

Celebration (Caesar), 535

Centennial Exposition of 1876, 194

Center for American Studies, 72

Central Carolina Bank, 381

Central Intercollegiate Athletic Association (CIAA), 598–599

Central Michigan Normal School, 87

Central Piedmont Community College, 421

C. Grier Beam Truck Museum, 118

Chagall, Marc, 67

Chambers, Bob, 621

Chambers, Julius, 268, 398, 545; *profile of,* 272–275

Chanute Field, Ill., 84

Chapel Hill, 10, 12, 54, 59, 85–86, 97, 100, 104, 164, 188, 221, 297, 424, 453, 461; and election of Howard Lee, 414; and Business Women's League, 461

Chapel Hill Weekly, 521–522; under James H. Shumaker, 329–330; and election of Howard Lee, 414

Chappell, Anne Maye Davis, 67

Chappell, Fred, 12–13, 59; *profile of,* 67–69, 95

Chappell, James Taylor, 67

Charity and Children (magazine), 315

Charles H. Tompkins Company, 52

Charles Kuralt's America (Kuralt), 323

Charleston, S.C., 47, 97

Charleston, W. Va., 183

Charlotte, 13, 39, 44, 48, 50, 187, 204, 297, 424, 496, 540, 554; as largest city in North Carolina, 1910–2000, 1; as leading banking center, 3; as site of United States Mint, headquarters of North Carolina National Bank and First Union National Bank, 8; as Queen City, 8; as scene of court-ordered busing to achieve racial balance in schools, 10; as scene of first NASCAR-sanctioned stock car race, 12; Spirit Square, 44; Fourth Ward of, 50; Alexander Graham Junior High School of, 50, 53; Second Ward School of, 53; Double Oaks School of, 54; Wilson Junior High School of, 54; Public Library of, xiii, 54, 63; Charlotte Coliseum and Auditorium of, 54; Elmwood Cemetery of, 58, 61; Committee to Restore and Preserve Third Ward, 173; Arts and Sciences

Hanes, John W., 127
Hanes, John W., Jr., 150
Hanes, Lucy, 150
Hanes, Philip, 149
Hanes, Pleasant Henderson, 149
Hanes, R. Phillip, 149
Hanes, Robert M., 116, 137–138, 149
Hannah Pickett Mill, 426
Hanson, Howard, 107–108
Hard Circus Road: The Odyssey of the North Carolina Symphony (Swalin), 103
Hard Right: The Rise of Jesse Helms (Furgurson), 401
Harden, John, 500
Hargrove, Marion, 325
Harkins, Thomas F., xiii
Harper and Brothers (publishers), 112
Harper, Walter, 43, 45
Harper's Ferry, W. Va., 276
Harrah's Casino, 563
Harriet-Henderson Mills, strike of, 9, 494
Harriman, Tenn., 544
Harris, C. L., 567
Harris, James J., 498
Harris, Ken, 219
Harris, Lucille, 92
Harris, Rosemary, 79
Harrison & Fouilhoux architects, 53
Harrison, Nancy, 537
Harrison, Wallace K., 53
Harry, Arthur, 120
Harry, D. R., 120
Harry, Sam, 120
Harry-Belk Brothers, 120
Hartsell, William, 53
Harvard College, 157
Harvard Law School, 472, 479
Harvard School of Business: Spangler Center of, 187, 189–190
Harvard University, 11, 44, 111; Board of Overseers, 190, 225, 228
Havre, Mont., 88
Hawfields Presbyterian Church, 520
Hawkins, Caroline Frances, 205
Hawkins, Catherine E. (Richardson), 398
Hawkins, Mingo, 205
Hawkins, Reginald A., 389, 543, 556; *profile of,* 397–399
Haw River, 33, 518–520
Hayden, Glen, 104
Hayes, Robin, 128
Haynie, Hugh, 492
Hays, Brooks, 545
Heading West (Betts), 65
Headmaster, The, 431
Heald, Henry, 200
Health care: in early part of century, 337–338, 357; during World War II,

341; and attitude of doctors, 346; in the South, 356; in rural areas, 361
Heath, B. D., 120
Helms and Mulliss (law firm), 287
Helms, Jesse, 2, 391–392, 410, 471, 578; challenged for U.S. Senate seat by Harvey Gantt, 10; challenged for U.S. Senate seat by Jim Hunt, 11, 12, 82, 239, 298; as A. J. Fletcher protégé, 306–307; editorials of, 394; and election of 1972, 395; *profile of,* 400–403
Helwig, Jane, 143
Henderson, 205
Henderson, Archibald, 204
Herald-Tribune (N.Y.), 313
Herndon, Alonzo P., 199
Herring, Dallas, 203; *profile of,* 240–243
He Who Gets Slapped (Pantaloon) (opera, Ward), 108
Hickory, 4, 87
Hickory Daily Record, 584
High Point, 4, 315
High Point College, 315
High Point Enterprise, 261, 331
Highland Park mill, 39
Hight, Edmund H., 205
Hill family, 280
Hill, Dan "Tiger," 618
Hill, George Watts, 335, 363; and Hospital Care Association, 349; *profile of,* 379–381
Hill, John Sprunt, 3, 60, 196, 363, 453, 463; *profile of,* 377–379
Hills Beyond, The (Wolfe), 113
Hills, Lee, 326
Hillsborough, 97, 460, 586–587
Hilton Head Island, S.C., 305
Hindman Settlement School, 211
Hinshaw, Davie, xiii
History of Cabarrus County in the Wars, A, 128
History of the Several Regiments and Battalions from North Carolina, in the Great War 1861–1865 (Clark, ed.), 277
Hitchings, George, 38
H. L. Coble company, 44
Hobby, Wilbur, 390, 552; *profile of,* 569–572
Hodges, Brandon, 44–45
Hodges, Louise (Finlayson), 494
Hodges, Luther, 8–9, 38, 44, 138, 151, 191, 240, 242, 245, 454, 465, 514; and Capus Waynick, 332–333; and Hugh Morton, 500, 501; and Pearsall Plan, 510–511; *profile of,* 490–494
Hodges, Luther, Jr., 402, 494
Hodges, Martha, 494
Hoey, Clyde R., 2, 5, 29, 270, 393, 479, 484, 520

Hogan, Ben, 196
Holding family, 116
Holland, Spessard, 238
Hollanders, 24
Holley, Augustus L., 57
Hollins College, 97, 100
Holly Farms, 16
Holly Springs College, Tenn., 221
Hollywood, 81, 83
Holman, Bill, 32
Holmes, Joseph Austin, 461
Holshouser, James E., Jr., 2, 12, 389, 409, 464, 465, 516, 578; *profile of,* 404–407
Holt, Thomas, 491
Holton, Linwood, 406
Home Savings Bank, 378
Home Security Life Insurance Company, 380
Hood, Theodore, 581
Hook, Charles, 54
Hook, Walter, 54
Hooper, Mary Jane, 50
Hoover, Herbert, 41, 267, 301
Hope, C. C., Jr., 162
Hope, John, 199
Hope, Lugenia, 199
Hopkins Review, 98
Horton, Lester, 75
Hospital Care Association, 336; creation of, 349, 380. *See also* Blue Cross Blue Shield of North Carolina
Hospitals, development of, 358
Hospital Savings Association, 349, 380. *See also* Blue Cross Blue Shield of North Carolina
House of Connelly, The (Green), 81
House, Robert Burton, 232
Hovis, George, 68
Howard University, 74, 208, 229
How to Live with an Island (Pilkey), 588
Howard, Bill, 142
Hoyt, Bill, 148
Huberman, Jeffrey, 395
Hudson brothers, 120
Hudson River Valley, 76
Huffstetler, Palmer, 118
Hughes, Langston, 62, 237
Human Betterment League of North Carolina, 149
Humphrey, Hubert, 515
Humphreys, Josephine, 94
Hunt, Carolyn, 409
Hunt, James B., 2, 49, 77, 188, 243, 255, 268, 284, 316, 367, 390, 424, 441, 466, 469, 572; and Senate campaign of 1984, 11, 12, 402; *profile of,* 408–412
Hunt, Richard Morris, 131
Hunt, Satie, 124

Madison County, 436, 437, 483

Majestic, Va., 101

Making a Difference in North Carolina (Morton and Rankin), 501

Malcolm X, 577, 582

Mammy: An Appeal to the Heart of the South (Brown), 207

Manhattan Project, 50

Manley, Hendren and Womble law firm, 269

Mann, Horace, 221

Mann, Glenn, 617

Manning, Isaac, 342

Manpower Development Corporation (MDC), 77

Manteo, 12, 430; Elizabethan Gardens of, 128

Manufacturers Record, 57

Marion, 117

Marlette, Doug, 298

Marney, Carlyle, 532; *profile of,* 543–546

Mars Hill, 436

Marshall Field (company), 491

Marshall Plan, 491

Marshall, George Preston, 196, 238, 606

Marshall, Margaret, 84

Marshall, Thurgood, 229, 273, 577

Martha's Vineyard, 195

Martin, James G., 1, 12, 31, 389

Martin, Joe, xii

Martin, Mary, 48

Martin, Thomas T., 258

Mary Duke Biddle Foundation, xii, 375

Mary Reynolds Babcock Foundation, 364

Massachusetts Institute of Technology, 24–25, 44

Massengill, Steve, xiii

Matlock (television program), 432

Matthews (department stores), 120

Matthews, Jim, 218

Mauney Transfer, 118

Mayberry, 14, 424, 431

Mayfarm, 40

Mayhew, Ken, 118

Mayo, Jim, 309

Mays, J. H., 40

Maysville, 40

Mays' Worth, 40

Maysworth, 40

McAfee, George, 618

M.C. Braswell Company, 509

McCain, Franklin (Greensboro Four), *profile of,* 565–568

McCall, Adeline, 105

McCarthy, Beta, 280

McCarthy, Joseph, 33, 480

McClatchy Group, 305

McColl, Hugh L., Jr., 8, 188, 367; *profile of,* 171–173

McCorkle, Jill, 59, 97–99

McCraw, Carl, *profile of,* 160–162

McDonalds, 287

McGee, William G., 140

McGill, Ralph, 325

McGlohon, Loonis, 424; *profile of,* 439–442

McGovern, 401, 406, 465

McGuire, Frank, 596, 615

McGuire, Thomas, 308

McIver, Charles D., 207, 248, 302, 456

McKenzie, Thorpe, 179

McKimmon, Charles, 27

McKimmon, Jane S., 15; *profile of,* 27–29

McKinley, William, 369

McKinney, Horace Albert "Bones," 594; *profile of,* 607–609

McKissick Enterprises, 578

McKissick, Floyd B., 10, 199, 406, 469, 551; *profile of,* 576–579

McKnight, C. A. "Pete," 543; *profile of,* 324–327

McLaurin, Kenneth E., 600

McLean, Angus, 3, 525

McLean, Malcolm, 115

McLendon, John, 621

McLendon, William W., 342

McLohon, Loonis, 310; *profile of,* 439–442

McMahon, Alex, 280

McMahon, Martha Maxine, 104

McMillan, Hamilton, 252

McMillan, James B., 10; *profile of,* 286–289

McMullan, Harry, 510

McNair, Robert, 516

McNeill, Joe (Greensboro Four), *profile of,* 565–568

Meads, Manson, 357

Mebane, 4

Mechanics and Farmers Bank, 5, 166, 198, 354

Mecklenburg County, 61; Board of Public Welfare, 554

Mecklenburg League of Women Voters, 420

Mecklenburg Medical Association, 338

Medgar Evers College, 75

Media General, 148

Medical education, 353, 379

Medical Mutual Insurance Company of North Carolina, 345

Medlin, John G., 137

Mehan, Floyd, 333

Melberg, Jerald, 63

Melville Dairy, 519

Mencken, H. L., 71, 300

Menlo Park, N. J., 191–192

Mentally Ill Act of 1974, 480

Mercer, Lucy, 305

Merck and Company, 44

Meredith College, 78, 192, 528

Merlefest, 452

Merrick, John, 5, 354; *profile of,* 163–167

Merrick-Moore-Spaulding Real Estate Company, 166

Messick, John, 245

Methodist church, 371, 372, 488

Miami Herald, 326

Michael Jordan Foundation, 602

Midas Mineral Water, 313

Mid-Pines resort, 196

Midquest (Chappell), 68

Mildred the Bear, 500, 502

Military Justice Act of 1968, 480

Millboro, 443

Miller, Arthur, 108

Millis, Ed, 280

Mind of the South, The (Cash), 299, 325

Minneapolis Symphony, 103

Mint Museum of Art (Charlotte), 60, 63, 92

Miracle in the Hills, 362

Miracle on Hawthorne Hill, The, 357

Mississippi Freedom Democratic Party (MFDP), 560

Mississippi Power and Light Company, 192

Mississippi Quarterly, 68

Mississippi State University, 16, 37

Mitchell County, 88

Mitchell, George S., 583

Mitchell, Judy, xiii

Modern Language Association, 98

Monk, Thelonious, 13

Monroe, 400, 464, 552

Monroe, Bill, 423

Monroe, Earl "The Pearl," 598

Monroe Journal, 400

Montreat, 56–57

Moore County, 45, 91

Moore, Aaron McDuffie, 5, 163–167, 336; *profile of,* 352–355

Moore, Cottie (Dancy), 355

Moore, Dan K., 219, 246, 511

Moore, Douglas E., 577

Moore, W. L., *profile of,* 252–255

Mooresville, 117, 356

Moral Majority, 402

Moravian Church, 91, 137

Morehead City, 247, 497

Morehead Planetarium, 364

Morehead, J. Turner, 382

Morehead, John Lindsey, II, 387

Morehead, John Motley, 215, 385

Morehead, John Motley, II, 387

Morehead, John Motley, III, 363; *profile of,* 385–387